INTERNATIONAL MONETARY COLLABORATION

by

Richard W. Edwards, Jr.

TN TRANSNATIONAL PUBLISHERS, INC.
Dobbs Ferry, New York

Richard W. Edwards, Jr. is professor of law at the University of Toledo

Library of Congress Cataloging in Publication Data

Edwards, Richard W., 1935–
  International monetary collaboration.

  Includes index.
  1. International finance. 2. Financial institutions,
International. I. Title.
HG3881.E33 1984   332'.042   84-248
ISBN 0-941320-05-7

Manufactured in the United States of America

TO
SIR JOSEPH GOLD

Summary of Contents

III. THE CODE OF GOOD CONDUCT

APPENDICES

Table of Contents

II. BALANCE-OF-PAYMENTS FINANCING

Chapter 9: The Transferable Ruble and the Settlement and Credit Operations of the International Bank for Economic Cooperation

APPENDICES

Preface

The Articles of Agreement of the International Monetary Fund state in Article I that the Fund is to provide "the machinery for consultation and collaboration on international monetary problems." The word "collaboration" is also used in other provisions of the Articles of Agreement that define obligations concerning exchange rate arrangements, monetary reserve asset policies, and the functioning of the system of special drawing rights. The concept is also embodied in instruments of other international organizations that have responsibilities in the monetary sphere. This book, through an examination of institutions, rules, and policies, explores what collaboration means in practice in its many facets in a plurality of organizations.

This book is intended primarily for persons whose professional careers, whether as economists, bankers, lawyers, or academics, involve the formulation, application, or appraisal of international monetary policies. A secondary audience includes graduate students who are preparing for careers in the international financial field and teachers and scholars with general interests in international law and international organizations. It is my hope that this book will for all readers contribute to a deeper understanding of the organizational structure of international monetary relations. An appendix provides general background for those readers who may not have formally studied international economics or money and banking.[1]

Although this book is long, the text is meant to be read from cover to cover in the order in which the chapters are presented. The reader should gain the most from the book if it is approached in this manner. If the footnotes are disregarded, it is about a 450-page book. If necessary, Chapters 7, 8, and 9 can be omitted in the first reading. The footnotes provide support for statements in the text and guidance for further research. The book is also designed to serve as a reference tool.

The book is divided into three parts. The first two chapters contain an in-

---

[1] See Appendix A at page 663.

troduction to the International Monetary Fund and other multilateral organizations in the monetary sphere. The second part, consisting of Chapters 3–9, examines the institutions, rules, and policies relating to balance-of-payments financing. The third part, entitled "The Code of Good Conduct," deals with international restraints on the use of exchange controls, the legal regimes applicable to exchange rate arrangements, and pervasive features of the systems of consultation and collaboration on monetary problems. We shall see that, in a strict sense, the international monetary system is not a "system." It is a network of formal and informal agreements, arrangements, procedures, and customs which over time have evolved, or been purposefully developed, and which interrelate with each other.

Money has historically played a critical role in the production, control, and distribution of economic wealth. The monetary instrument, broadly conceived, is a powerful tool. One must, nevertheless, keep in mind when reading this book that international monetary relations compose only a part of international economic relations, and those relations in turn form only a part of the larger world order in which individuals, firms, and organized political entities interact.

The institutions, rules, and policies studied in this book embody economic assumptions. It is obvious that those who designed the rules and organizations intended them to carry out favored economic policies or at least to be compatible with the favored policies. A description and critique must expose the economic assumptions, and I have tried to do that. I have, however, left it to others to probe the economic merits of particular policies. I have focused on the law and institutions seen as a framework in which policies are agreed to and carried out. Existing institutions can be adapted to future policy changes to a greater extent than may be generally realized. Inevitably a book also reflects the bias of the author. I am by nature an optimist. I tend to look for the positive opportunities in multilateral endeavors. When I make criticisms, I intend them to be constructive.

The work presented here is a distillation of study and writing over a period of a dozen years. The manuscript of this book was completed in September 1983 and typesetting began shortly thereafter. It was possible to make some changes in the proofs. The book is basically up to date through January 1984. The final date for acceptance of the revised quotas in the IMF's Eighth Quota Review, March 15, 1984, had passed when the proofs were returned to the publisher.

Many persons, generous with their time, read and commented on portions of drafts of the manuscript. I wish to thank especially Raj Aggarwal, Professor of Finance, University of Toledo; A. Bascoul, Assistant Secretary General, Committee of Governors of the Central Banks of the European Economic Community; William E. Butler, Professor of Comparative Law, University of London, and Director, Centre for the Study of Socialist Legal Systems, University College London; Kenneth W. Dam, Deputy Secretary of State, and formerly Provost, University of Chicago; Arghyrios A. Fatouros, Ambassador of Greece to the Organisation for Economic Co-operation and Development; Henri Guisan, formerly The Legal Adviser, Bank for International Settlements; Ivan Iskroff, Special Assistant, Foreign Exchange Department, Federal Reserve Bank of New York; F. E. Klein, The Legal Adviser, Bank for International Settlements; Roger M. Kubarych, Senior Vice President and Deputy Director of Research, Federal Reserve Bank of New York; Andreas F. Lowenfeld, Professor of Law, New York University; John B. McLenaghan, Assistant Director, Bureau of Statistics, International Monetary Fund; Jean-Jacques Rey, Head of the Foreign Department, Banque Nationale de Belgique, and Faculty, Institut d'Etudes Européenes, Université Libre de Bruxelles; Stephen A. Silard, Assistant General Counsel, Legal Department, International Monetary Fund; Ralph W. Smith, Jr., Assistant Director, Division of International Finance, Board of Governors of the Federal Reserve System; Jozef Swidrowski, formerly Senior Economist, Exchange and Trade Relations Department, International Monetary Fund; Jozef M. van Brabant, Officer-in-Charge, Centrally Planned Economies Section, United Nations Secretariat; and James K. Weekly, Professor of Marketing, University of Toledo. John V. Surr, Senior Counsellor in the Legal Department of the International Monetary Fund, deserves my very special thanks. He read most of the chapters through several successive drafts. A caveat, however, must be stated. The persons who read portions of the manuscript gave me suggestions but did not dictate what I would say. Nor did they always see the final version. Errors are entirely my responsibility. All expressions of opinion and judgment are also my responsibility.

I wish to thank William E. Butler for translating the documents that appear in Appendix D. These include the Agreement on Multilateral Payments in Transferable Rubles and on the Organization of the International Bank for Economic Cooperation, and the Charter of the Bank.

Karl Krastin, Francis X. Beytagh, and John W. Stoepler, successive deans of the University of Toledo College of Law, provided support and encouragement to me throughout the project. The University of Toledo granted a sabbatical leave in 1979. A number of students, most of whom have now graduated and are well along in careers of their own, provided research assistance. I wish to thank especially James P. Hermance, David W. Content, Peter R. Weisz, Fred C. Pedersen, Howard V. Malovany, James F. Allen, James H. Searles, Philip J. Daunt, Katherine J. Wieczorek, Tracy V. Drake, Hugh P. Callahan, Phillip D. Wurster, Ralph M. Reisinger, Bruce A. Jenkins, Matthew J. Mitten, Patrick J. O'Mara, and Gary J. Rosati.

My secretary, Rae Grabowski, typed virtually all of the manuscript through many drafts. She has been exceptionally careful, and always cheerful as well. My wife, Alice, typed much of the manuscript as it moved from the penultimate draft to the final version. Alice's dedication, assistance, and support have known no bounds. She and our children, Evelyn and Kenneth, assisted in the repeated processes of proofreading. They sacrificed family pleasures so that I would have time to work on the book.

I am deeply grateful to Heike Fenton of Transnational Publishers. The production of this book would tax the patience and resources of any publisher. She has been both understanding and helpful. Marjorie Moore of Transnational Publishers worked closely with me as the manuscript was edited into its final version. No author could ask for a better editor.

This book is dedicated to Sir Joseph Gold. Sir Joseph, who was knighted in 1980, has had a most distinguished career in international monetary affairs. He joined the Legal Department of the International Monetary Fund in 1946 and was General Counsel of the Fund from 1960 until his retirement in 1979. He has subsequently served the Fund as Senior Consultant. He has played a central role in the development of the International Monetary Fund, its law, and its policies. His life exemplifies international civil service at its very finest.

I formed a friendship with Mr. Gold, as he then was, during a conference of legal advisers of international organizations held in Bellagio, Italy, in 1965.[2] That friendship has continued and grown closer through the years. This book could not have been written without the benefit of his publications which are cited throughout this work.[3] Even more important to me have been Sir Joseph's advice, his kindness when making criticisms (there are a number of points on which he differs with me), and his personal encouragement. It is with great pleasure that I dedicate this book to a scholar, public servant, and friend, Sir Joseph Gold.

Richard W. Edwards, Jr.
Toledo, Ohio
May 1984

---

[2] A summary of the discussions at the conference was published in H.C.L. Merillat, *Legal Advisers and International Organizations* (Dobbs Ferry: Oceana Publications, 1966).

[3] A biographical sketch of Sir Joseph Gold appears in Joseph Gold, "Developments in the International Monetary System, the International Monetary Fund, and International Monetary Law Since 1971," in Hague Academy of International Law, *Recueil des Cours*, vol. 174 (1982-I), p. 107 at p. 114. A bibliography of Sir Joseph's principal published works through 1982 appears *idem*, pp. 115–20.

I
International Organizations

Introduction to Chapters 1 and 2

An understanding of multilateral organizations concerned with monetary policy is essential to the study of international monetary law. Creations of the twentieth century, the organizations reflect the reality of an ever-shrinking world and the necessity of collaboration among states in the monetary sphere.

Of all the organizations, the International Monetary Fund (IMF) is clearly the most important. The decision to regulate the international monetary system through a comprehensive treaty with a powerful central organ has been called "the key international monetary policy decision of the century."[1] In Chapter 1 the International Monetary Fund is described and its activities surveyed. Other international organizations that play significant roles in monetary matters are treated in Chapter 2.

The two chapters are intended to provide essential institutional background for discussions in later chapters of legal aspects of financing payments deficits, liberalization of exchange controls, management of currency exchange rates, surveillance of national decision-making, and other matters.

---

[1] Kenneth W. Dam, *The Rules of the Game: Reform and Evolution in the International Monetary System* (Chicago: University of Chicago Press, 1982), p. 71.

Chapter 1: International Monetary Fund

History

The International Monetary Fund was created at Bretton Woods, New Hampshire, in 1944, near the close of World War II. Creation of the Fund was not a hasty act; it was preceded by five years of intensive planning within the governments of the United States and the United Kingdom. The experience of the 1920s and 1930s affected this planning.[1] United States officials saw the practices of the 1930s that disrupted trade patterns—such as competitive currency devaluations, the use of multiple currency practices whereby a currency would be exchanged at one rate for one purpose and at a different rate for another, the wide use of exchange controls and import licensing, and bilateral trade deals—as causes of unemployment in export industries, the world-wide depression, and even World War II. One of the "inescapable problems" of the postwar period as seen by the United States was "to prevent the disruption of foreign exchanges and the collapse of monetary and credit systems."[2]

The overriding objective of the United States was the reconstruction of a genuinely multilateral system of world trade. This contemplated that countries would agree to cooperate to reduce barriers to trade and barriers to payments. Barriers would be reduced to moderate levels and made nondiscriminatory in application. Currencies would become convertible. In particular, exporters receiving a foreign currency in exchange for goods or services would be able to convert that currency and use its proceeds in other countries.[3]

---

[1] See Ragnar Nurkse, *International Currency Experience: Lessons of the Inter-War Period* (Geneva: League of Nations; Princeton: Princeton University Press, 1944); and Kenneth W. Dam, *The Rules of the Game: Reform and Evolution in the International Monetary System* (Chicago: University of Chicago Press, 1982), pp. 41–70. See also Alfred E. Eckes, Jr., *A Search for Solvency* (Austin: University of Texas Press, 1975), pp. 1–31; and Frank A. Southard, Jr., "International Financial Policy, 1920–44," *Finance and Development*, vol. 2, no. 3 (September 1965), p. 135.

[2] Statement of Harry Dexter White in the introduction to his Preliminary Draft Proposal for a United Nations Stabilization Fund and a Bank for Reconstruction and Development of the United and Associated Nations (April 1942), in J. Keith Horsefield and Margaret Garritsen de Vries, *The International Monetary Fund, 1945-1965: Twenty Years of International Monetary Cooperation* (3 vols.; Washington: IMF, 1969), vol. 3, p. 37. (This publication is hereinafter cited *IMF History 1945-65*.)

[3] See Richard N. Gardner, *Sterling-Dollar Diplomacy* (rev. ed.; New York: McGraw-Hill Book Co., 1969), chapter 1.

The British perspective on postwar monetary institutions was set forth by the Chancellor of the Exchequer on the floor of the House of Commons in early 1943:

We want an orderly and agreed method of determining the value of national currency units, to eliminate unilateral action and the danger which it involves that each nation will seek to restore its competitive position by exchange depreciation. Above all, we want to free the international monetary system from those arbitrary, unpredictable and undesirable influences which have operated in the past as a result of large-scale speculative movements of capital. We want to secure an economic policy agreed between the nations and an international monetary system which will be the instrument of that policy. This means that if any one Government were tempted to move too far either in an inflationary or a deflationary direction, it would be subject to the check of consultations with the other Governments, and it would be part of the agreed policy to take measures for correcting tendencies to dis-equilibrium in the balance of payments of each separate country. Our long-term policy must ensure that countries which conduct their affairs with prudence need not be afraid that they will be prevented from meeting their international liabilities by causes outside their own control.[4]

The United Kingdom and the United States played the dominant roles in the postwar economic negotiations. The United Kingdom's economy was dependent upon trade, and London had been the center of international finance. The United States would emerge from the war with both political influence and economic strength. Although there was an interest in involving the Union of Soviet Socialist Republics in postwar economic negotiations, that country played a minor role. Its primary attention was given to rebuilding its internal economy and consolidating its political position in Eastern Europe. It was to play a much larger role at the San Francisco Conference on the United Nations in 1945 than at Bretton Woods in 1944. While recognizing the importance of Anglo-American cooperation, the United States took a multilateral approach to monetary problems with a goal of currency stability throughout the world.

During this war-time period, economic organization in the postwar era was seen as involving three elements: currency stability and a system of international payments, economic reconstruction of war-ravaged economies, and a regime for trade and foreign investment. While the elements were interrelated, governmental planners assumed that there would be a separate international in-

---

[4] House of Commons, *Parliamentary Debates (Hansard)*, 5th Series, vol. 386, column 826 (February 2, 1943), quoted in Gardner, *supra* note 3, p. 78.

stitution concerned with each aspect: an international monetary fund, an international bank for reconstruction and development, and an international trade organization. These three economic organizations would be related to a United Nations organization responsible for maintaining the peace.[5]

As it turned out, the United Nations was formed in 1945 with near universal membership but with uneasy relations between the Western Powers and the Union of Soviet Socialist Republics. The three economic organizations were formed without Soviet membership. The International Bank for Reconstruction and Development, formed at Bretton Woods in July 1944, was designed as the vehicle to provide capital to the war-torn economies of Europe and for the economic advancement of the less-developed countries.[6]

After difficult negotiations a charter was concluded at Havana in March 1948 for an International Trade Organization concerned with the regulation of international trade and investment. The charter died in the United States Senate. However, the General Agreement on Tariffs and Trade survived. The GATT agreement, signed October 30, 1947, entered into force in January 1948. It had originally been conceived as a body of internationally agreed rules within the broader institutional context of the projected ITO.[7]

Plans for an international monetary organization had been drafted within the United States and British governments. Harry Dexter White, Assistant to the U.S. Secretary of the Treasury, produced one plan; and Lord John Maynard Keynes, a special consultant to the British Treasury, produced the other principal plan.[8] Both plans accepted the need for a new international institution and both contemplated that it be staffed by professional economists who would be international civil servants. Both plans started from the premise of relatively stable exchange rates as compared to floating rates. Changes in currency exchange values should be reserved for serious and fundamental imbalance. Devaluations would be subject to a measure of international control, would be orderly, and should not spark competitive devaluations. Both plans assumed that

---

[5] See Preliminary Draft Proposal for a United Nations Stabilization Fund and a Bank for Reconstruction and Development of the United and Associated Nations (April 1942), *supra* note 2. See also Resolution VII on "International Economic Problems" adopted at the Bretton Woods Conference, *Proceedings and Documents of the United Nations Monetary and Financial Conference, Bretton Woods, New Hampshire, July 1-22, 1944* (2 vols.; Washington: U.S. Department of State, 1948), vol. 1, p. 941.

[6] The Articles of Agreement of the International Bank for Reconstruction and Development entered into force December 27, 1945. The bank is described in Chapter 2, *infra*, pages 44–48.

[7] The General Agreement on Tariffs and Trade is described in Chapter 2, *infra*, pages 63–68.

[8] The comparison of the White and Keynes plans presented here draws upon Abram Chayes, Thomas Ehrlich, and Andreas F. Lowenfeld, *International Legal Process* (Boston: Little, Brown & Co., 1969), vol. 2, pp. 719–22. The texts of the two plans are set forth in *IMF History 1945–65, supra* note 2, vol. 3, pp. 3–36 and 37–96, respectively, and other proposals appear at pp. 97–135. Documents, papers, and correspondence concerning the development of the plans are collected in Donald Moggridge (ed.), *The Collected Writings of John Maynard Keynes* (Cambridge: Macmillan and Cambridge University Press), vols. 25 and 26 (1980). For further background see *IMF History 1945–65,* vol. 1, pp. 3–88; Gardner, *supra* note 3, pp. 71–99 and 110–43; Dam, *supra* note 1, pp. 71–114; Eckes, *supra* note 1, pp. 33–80; and Armand Van Dormael, *Bretton Woods: Birth of a Monetary System* (London: Macmillan, 1978), pp. 5–139.

countries must adopt policies that achieve balance-of-payments equilibrium over the long term. And, both assumed that international codes of good conduct—in the monetary arrangements themselves or in other instruments like the proposed trade charter—would ban many of the restrictive and retaliatory practices of the inter-war years.

The most serious differences between the two plans related to the manner in which resources would be provided to countries facing balance-of-payments deficits and the magnitude of the resources to be provided. Lord Keynes, representing a prospective deficit nation, wanted a substantial volume of credit available at the request of a member. In his plan, entitled "Proposals for an International Currency (or Clearing) Union," the international institution would provide this credit by creating a new form of international money, called "bancor." The Currency Union was conceived as a central bank for government central banks. The Union would extend overdraft rights to deficit countries and would credit surplus countries with an equivalent amount in bancor. Then, when a surplus country went into deficit, it could use its bancor balance to offset this deficit. The aggregate total of overdraft rights to be authorized under Lord Keynes' plan was estimated at U.S. $26 billion.[9] Since in practice the only major country likely to run a significant surplus in the immediate postwar period was the United States, the plan was, in effect, a prescription for a $26 billion long-term line of credit from the United States to the rest of the world.

For the United States, as the prime potential creditor, the idea of a $26 billion line of credit was unacceptable. It feared that an overdraft approach, even with safeguards, might cause the United States to lose control over the size of its obligations. The United States wanted to limit the magnitude of its liability to finance the adjustment processes of other countries. And, it wanted authority in the international institution to require deficit countries to adopt policies that would restore their international accounts to balance. The limited liability would be protected by deficit states obtaining the currencies they needed to settle international accounts, not simply by means of credits from other members monitored by an international institution, but instead from a finite fund owned and managed by the international institution itself and composed of gold and national currencies. Each member of the organization, which Mr. White called a "Stabilization Fund," would contribute an agreed amount of its own currency and gold. These resources would form a pool on which a deficit country could draw if it were prepared to comply with the conditions imposed by the international authority. The total amount of the fund would be at least U.S. $5 billion. The contributions of the member countries would be determined by a formula related to an appraisal of their general economic strength, with the obligation of the United States being less than $3.5 billion.

---

[9] Lord Keynes did not use a specific figure in his proposals. This figure was calculated by Joan Robinson, "The International Currency Proposals," *Economic Journal,* vol. 53 (1943), p. 161.

The differences between the plans were debated in the period 1942–1944 by representatives of the two countries, often Lord Keynes and Mr. White themselves. During this period the U.S. Federal Reserve Board suggested modifications in the White plan. Proposals were also put forth by France and Canada. A "key-currency plan" of John H. Williams, which stressed the importance of the economic policies of the major industrial powers, also received attention.[10] Finally the differences were resolved at the conference at Bretton Woods, New Hampshire, in July 1944, attended by 44 nations. Germany and Japan, against which the war was being fought, were, of course, not in attendance. The Soviet Union did take part. The conference drew up Articles of Agreement for both the International Monetary Fund and the International Bank for Reconstruction and Development.[11] In moving acceptance of the Final Act of the conference, Lord Keynes paid a special tribute to the lawyers and added: "[T]hey have turned our jargon into prose and our prose into poetry. And only too often they have had to do our thinking for us."[12]

The text of the Fund Agreement most closely resembled the White plan. However, the special drawing rights system, created by the First Amendment to the Agreement in 1969 (some 25 years later), adopted many of the features of Keynes' "bancor" proposal. In the year following Bretton Woods, there was a spirited struggle to gain acceptance by the United States Congress of U.S. membership in the Fund.[13]

The IMF Agreement in a Nutshell

Note on the Text of the Articles

The original Articles of Agreement of the International Monetary Fund (adopted at Bretton Woods July 22, 1944) entered into force December 27, 1945.[14] The Articles were first amended effective July 28, 1969, at the time the provisions respecting special drawing rights were introduced.[15]

---

[10] See *IMF History 1945–65, supra* note 2, vol. 1, pp. 26–88, and vol. 3, pp. 83–135; and Eckes, *supra* note 1, pp. 81–133.

[11] See *IMF History 1945–65, supra* note 2, vol. 1, pp. 89–118, and vol. 3, pp. 128–214; Eckes, *supra* note 1, pp. 135–64; and Van Dormael, *supra* note 8, pp. 139–239. The debates, committee reports, and other documents of the Bretton Woods Conference are printed in *Proceedings and Documents of the United Nations Monetary and Financial Conference, supra* note 5. British documents, papers, and notes, and some documents originating in other delegations, are assembled in *The Collected Writings of John Maynard Keynes, supra* note 8, vols. 25 and 26.

[12] *Proceedings and Documents of the United Nations Monetary and Financial Conference, supra* note 5, vol. 1, pp. 1109–10; also in *The Collected Writings of John Maynard Keynes, supra* note 8, vol. 26, pp. 101–03.

[13] See Eckes, *supra* note 1, pp. 165–209; and Van Dormael, *supra* note 8, pp. 240–303.

[14] The original text appears in *IMF History 1945–65, supra* note 2, vol. 3, p. 185; *United Nations Treaty Series*, vol. 2, p. 39; *United States Statutes at Large*, vol. 60, p. 1401. This text is identified by the word *"original"* throughout this book.

[15] The full text of the Articles of Agreement as amended effective July 28, 1969, appears in Margaret Garritsen de Vries, *The International Monetary Fund, 1966–1971: The System Under Stress* (2 vols.; Wash-

A second amendment to the IMF's Articles entered into force on April 1, 1978. While many provisions of the Articles were not significantly changed, the amendment was sufficiently comprehensive that it took the form of the substitution of a complete new text of articles and schedules in place of the former text. This book describes and comments on the monetary system following the Second Amendment.[16] The steps leading up to its adoption should be noted as background.

Negotiations leading to the Second Amendment formally began in July 1972 when the Board of Governors of the IMF established the Committee on Reform of the International Monetary System and Related Issues, informally called the "Committee of Twenty."[17] The Governing Board's action followed a series of turbulent events in 1971 and 1972 that made it apparent that the exchange rate provisions of IMF Article IV, *original* and *first,* required reconsideration. As recounted in Chapter 11,[18] the exchange rates of many currencies were realigned in December 1971 and early 1972. The first devaluation of the U.S. dollar since the IMF was formed was announced in December 1971 and was formally effected in May 1972. Other provisions of the Articles, particularly those that interrelated with the exchange rate provisions and the provisions regarding gold, would also be reviewed by the Committee of Twenty.

The Committee of Twenty submitted its final report, intended to guide the reform process, in June 1974. The report included an "Outline of Reform," various annexes, and technical papers.[19] The Committee of Twenty was then

ington: IMF, 1976) [hereinafter cited *IMF History 1966–71*], vol. 2, p. 97. This text is identified by the word *"first"* throughout this book.

The 1969 amendment by itself, together with a report of the Executive Directors, appears in *IMF History 1945–65, supra* note 2, vol. 3, p. 497; and in *IMF History 1966–71, supra,* vol. 2, p. 52. The amendment alone also appears in *United Nations Treaty Series,* vol. 726, p. 266; *United States Treaties and Other International Agreements,* vol. 20, p. 2775. The negotiations leading to the First Amendment are treated in Chapter 5, *infra,* pages 167–173. See also Joseph Gold, "Legal Technique in Creation of a New International Reserve Asset: SDRs and Amendment of the Fund's Articles," in Joseph Gold, *Legal and Institutional Aspects of the International Monetary System: Selected Essays* (Washington: IMF, 1979) [hereinafter *Selected Essays*], p. 128; and Joseph Gold, *The Reform of the Fund* (IMF Pamphlet Series no. 12; Washington; 1969).

[16] The Articles of Agreement are variously cited in this book as "IMF Agreement," "Fund Agreement," or "the Articles." Unless otherwise indicated, references to the articles and schedules refer to the text of the Second Amendment. Occasionally, where there might otherwise be confusion, the word *"second"* is used to refer to the current text.

The complete text of the Articles of Agreement and Schedules is printed in Appendix B of this book at page 694. For commentary, see *Proposed Second Amendment to the Articles of Agreement of the International Monetary Fund: A Report by the Executive Directors to the Board of Governors* (April 1976), reprinted as IMF, *Summary Proceedings of the 31st Annual Meeting of the Board of Governors, 1976—Supplement* [hereinafter cited *Report on Second Amendment*].

[17] Board of Governors Resolution No. 27–10, effective July 26, 1972, in IMF, *Summary Proceedings of the 27th Annual Meeting of the Board of Governors, 1972* [hereinafter cited *Summary Proceedings, 19—*], p. 353. See John V. Surr, "The Committee of Twenty: Its Origins, Evolution, and Procedures," *Finance and Development,* vol. 11, no. 2 (June 1974), p. 24.

[18] At pages 494–507, *infra.*

[19] IMF, *International Monetary Reform: Documents of the Committee of Twenty* (Washington: IMF, 1974). See Joseph Gold, "Law and Reform of the International Monetary System," *Selected Essays, supra*

dissolved, and the Board of Governors established the Interim Committee of the Board of Governors on the International Monetary System.[20] The Interim Committee was originally charged to negotiate unresolved issues and guide the Executive Directors as they considered drafts of amendments to the Articles of Agreement. The Interim Committee continues to this day to play an important role in the Fund.[21]

The Interim Committee completed its work on the amendment at a meeting in Kingston, Jamaica, in January 1976.[22] Thereafter the proposed Second Amendment was submitted to the Board of Governors, which adopted a resolution approving submission of the amendment to the member countries for their acceptance.[23] The amendment could be accepted only in its entirety.[24]

The internal procedures by which a member is authorized to accept amendments to the IMF Articles of Agreement vary from country to country. In many countries the legislative branch must give its approval.[25] The Executive Branch in the United States has not treated the original Articles of Agreement or amendments to them as treaties that required the advice and consent of the Senate but, instead, as executive agreements that required congressional collaborative efforts through legislation.[26] The Bretton Woods Agreements Act provides that the President of the United States is not to accept any amendment of the IMF's Articles unless Congress authorizes that action.[27] The Bretton Woods Agreements Act was amended in 1976 to authorize U.S. acceptance of the Second Amendment and to make conforming changes in U.S. national legislation.[28]

In accordance with Article XVII(a) of the Articles of Agreement then in effect, *original* and *first,* the Second Amendment was accepted by the required three-fifths of the members, having four-fifths of the total weighted voting

note 15, p. 75 at pp. 97–113; and Robert Solomon, *The International Monetary System, 1945–1981* (New York: Harper & Row, 1982), chapter 14.

[20] Board of Governors Resolution No. 29–8, adopted October 2, 1974, in IMF, *Summary Proceedings, 1974*, p. 364, and in *Selected Decisions of the International Monetary Fund and Selected Documents* (10th issue; Washington: IMF, 1983) [hereinafter cited *Selected Decisions*], p. 343.

[21] See page 26, *infra*.

[22] See Solomon, *supra* note 19, chapter 15; and Joseph Gold, "The Fund's Interim Committee—An Assessment," *Finance and Development*, vol. 16, no. 3 (September 1979), p. 32.

[23] Board of Governors Resolution No. 31–4, effective April 30, 1976; IMF, *Summary Proceedings, 1976*, p. 300.

[24] *Report on Second Amendment, supra* note 16, part 3, section 3.

[25] For an examination of the internal procedures followed in member countries in connection with the acceptance of the First Amendment, see John V. Surr, "Special Drawing Rights: A Legislative View," *Finance and Development*, vol. 8, no. 3 (September 1971), p. 40.

[26] See Joint Department of State–Treasury Department memorandum, "Constitutionality of the Bretton Woods Agreements Act," in *Bretton Woods Agreements Act: Hearings on H.R. 3314 before the Senate Committee on Banking and Currency,* 79th Congress, 1st Session (1945), p. 529.

[27] Bretton Woods Agreements Act, section 5; *United States Code,* title 22, sections 286 et seq. at section 286c.

[28] Public Law 94–564, approved October 19, 1976; *United States Statutes at Large,* vol. 90, p. 2660.

power. (Future amendments will require a different majority.[29]) The Second Amendment entered into force April 1, 1978.[30] France and about 35 other countries had not accepted the Second Amendment when it entered into force, but, by remaining in the organization, became bound by the amendment.[31]

Purposes of the IMF

The purposes of the International Monetary Fund are set forth in Article I of the Articles of Agreement. Each word is pregnant. The text follows:

> The purposes of the International Monetary Fund are:
>
> (i)   To promote international monetary cooperation through a permanent institution which provides the machinery for consultation and collaboration on international monetary problems.
>
> (ii) To facilitate the expansion and balanced growth of international trade, and to contribute thereby to the promotion and maintenance of high levels of employment and real income and to the development of the productive resources of all members as primary objectives of economic policy.
>
> (iii) To promote exchange stability, to maintain orderly exchange arrangements among members, and to avoid competitive exchange depreciation.
>
> (iv) To assist in the establishment of a multilateral system of payments in respect of current transactions between members and in the elimination of foreign exchange restrictions which hamper the growth of world trade.
>
> (v)   To give confidence to members by making the general resources of the Fund temporarily available to them under adequate safeguards, thus providing them with opportunity to correct maladjustments in their balance of payments without resorting to measures destructive of national or international prosperity.
>
> (vi) In accordance with the above, to shorten the duration and lessen the degree of disequilibrium in the international balances of payments of members.

---

[29] Future amendments will require acceptance by three-fifths of the members having 85 percent of the total weighted voting power. Article XXVIII, *second.*

[30] See *IMF Survey,* April 3, 1978, p. 97.

[31] See decision of the Conseil Constitutionnel of France of April 29, 1978, applying IMF Article XVII(b), *original* and *first; Journal Officiel,* April 30, 1978, p. 1942. For comments on that decision, see Joseph Gold, *The Fund Agreement in the Courts* (Washington: IMF; vol. 1, 1962; vol. 2, 1982), vol. 2, pp. 284–94, and articles there cited.

The Fund shall be guided in *all* its policies and decisions by the purposes set forth in this Article. [emphasis added]

The "recognizing" clause at the beginning of present Article IV also states purposes served by the Fund:

Recognizing that the essential purpose of the international monetary system is to provide a framework that facilitates the exchange of goods, services, and capital among countries, and that sustains sound economic growth, and that a principal objective is the continuing development of the orderly underlying conditions that are necessary for financial and economic stability, each member undertakes. . . .

The Fund has a range of functions that flow from these purposes, the three most significant being: (1) administration of a large pool of monetary assets to which members have access to finance balance-of-payments deficits; (2) administration of a system of "special drawing rights," and (3) administration of the "rules of good conduct" embodied in the Articles, relating to exchange rate arrangements, currency controls, and other matters, and the system of consultations on domestic and international policies affecting economic growth, employment, and monetary and financial stability.

Drawing Rights in the General Resources Account

The International Monetary Fund administers a pool of monetary assets upon which members can draw to meet balance-of-payments needs. The General Resources Account of the Fund consists of national currencies, special drawing rights, and gold. The contribution of each of the original member countries to this pool was determined broadly in accordance with a formula designed generally to reflect the importance of the member's currency in the world economy.[32] This fund was originally set at U.S. $8.8 billion, with the United States' quota at $2.75 billion and the United Kingdom's at $1.3 billion.[33] The Fund undertakes a general review of quotas at least every five years and as a result of that review can increase or decrease quotas. The Fund can consider at any time the adjustment of a particular quota at the request of the member concerned.[34]

The member's quota determines the size of its subscription to the Fund, drawing rights in the General Resources Account, share in allocations of special drawing rights (SDRs), and voting power.

Quotas were generally increased in 1958–59, in 1965–66, in 1970–71, in 1978, in 1980, and in 1983–84. There have also been some changes in the inter-

---

[32] Original Article III, section 1; and Schedule A.

[33] Schedule A. The quota for the Union of Soviet Socialist Republics was set at U.S. $1.20 billion; the U.S.S.R., however, did not accept the Agreement and never became a member.

[34] Article III, section 2. See also Rules D-2 and D-3, *By-Laws, Rules and Regulations* (40th issue, 1983).

vening years for particular countries. Total quotas following implementation of the Eighth General Quota Review effective November 30, 1983,[35] amount to about SDR 89 billion.[36] Quota allocations among countries that were set at Bretton Woods essentially followed a formula, although there were behind-the-scenes negotiations with respect to some of the quotas. The quota increases in 1958–59 and 1965–66 were essentially consistent with the Bretton Woods formula.[37] The magnitude and distribution of increases effective in 1970–71 and 1978 were very much "bargained out."[38] The increase effective in 1980 was essentially an across-the-board increase of 50 percent with some further upward adjustments for Middle East oil exporting states and a few other countries.[39] The quota increase in 1983–84 was in part an across-the-board increase and in part upward adjustments intended to reflect the relative position of members in the world economy.[40] Criteria to be taken into account in increasing or decreasing quotas are discussed in Chapter 12.[41]

Quotas under the present Articles are expressed in terms of the special drawing right (SDR) which is the IMF's unit of account.[42] Prior to the Second Amendment, most members paid 25 percent of their initial quota subscriptions, and 25 percent of their quota increases, in reserve assets (SDRs, currencies of other members specified by the Fund, or gold) and paid the 75 percent balance in their own currencies.[43] Those members that prior to the Second Amendment

---

[35] Board of Governors Resolution No. 38–1, adopted March 31, 1983, effective November 30, 1983; IMF, *Annual Report, 1983*, p. 139; *Selected Decisions* (10th issue, 1983), p. 381.

[36] The Fund extended the date for acceptance of the new quotas to March 15, 1984, for those members that had not yet accepted them. *IMF Survey*, December 5, 1983, pp. 373 and 383–84; February 6, 1984, p. 40; and March 26, 1984, p. 85.

[37] See *IMF History 1966–71, supra* note 15, vol. 1, p. 291 (note 5); and Van Dormael, *supra* note 8, pp. 176–83.

[38] See *IMF History 1966–71, supra* note 15, vol. 1, chapter 16; and Solomon, *supra* note 19, pp. 282–84. See also the report of the Executive Directors to the Board of Governors on the Sixth Quota Review; IMF, *Annual Report, 1976*, p. 103.

[39] See Board of Governors Resolution No. 34–2, adopted effective December 11, 1978; IMF, *Summary Proceedings, 1979*, p. 330; *Selected Decisions* (10th issue, 1983), p. 371. See also the Executive Board's report to the Board of Governors; IMF, *Annual Report, 1979*, p. 118; *Selected Decisions*, p. 365.

[40] See report of the Executive Directors to the Board of Governors on the Eighth Quota Review; IMF, *Annual Report*, 1983, p. 137; *Selected Decisions* (10th issue, 1983), p. 376.

[41] At pages 642–644. Any change in quotas requires an 85 percent majority of the total weighted voting power and the decision must be taken by the Board of Governors. Any change in a member's quota, in addition, requires its consent. Article III, sections 2 and 3.

[42] Article III, section 1. Rule J of the *By-Laws, Rules and Regulations* (40th issue, 1983) prescribes the IMF's accounting procedures. The SDR is presently valued in relation to an index of national currencies and its value in relation to any one currency can fluctuate from day to day. On December 31, 1983, the SDR was equivalent to U.S. $1.04695. See generally Chapter 5, *infra*, page 176 et seq.

Under the original Articles quotas were expressed in terms of the U.S. dollar of the gold weight and fineness in effect in 1944 (U.S. $1 = 0.888671 gram of fine gold). From March 20, 1972, through March 31, 1978, quotas were expressed in terms of the SDR which then carried a gold value of 0.888671 gram of fine gold. Since April 1, 1978, the SDR does not have a stated gold value.

[43] Under the Articles prior to the Second Amendment, unless monetary reserves were low, 25 percent of the quota subscription was to be paid in gold. See former Article III, sections 3 and 4, and former Article IV, section 1, *original* and *first*.

paid less than 25 percent of their quota subscriptions or quota increases in reserve assets were required before April 1, 1982, to make the necessary payments or enter into other transactions to put themselves and the Fund in essentially the same position as if 25 percent of their subscriptions and increases had been paid in reserve assets.[44]

When quotas are increased in the future a member is to pay 25 percent of the increase in SDRs or (if it is not a participant in the Special Drawing Rights Department explained below) in the currencies of other members specified by the Fund.[45] The Fund has the authority, should it choose to exercise it, to permit or direct that the 25 percent portion that is normally to be paid in SDRs be paid instead in specified currencies (presumably currencies the Fund particularly needs) or to permit or direct that it be paid in the member's own currency.[46] This authority was exercised in the case of the quota increase that became effective in 1978.[47] The portion of a new member's quota to be paid in reserve assets will be stated in the membership resolution, but one can expect it to normally be in the range of 20–25 percent. The balance of any quota increase of an IMF member or the balance of the initial quota of a new member (usually 75–80 percent) is to be paid by the member in its own currency.[48]

Each member has an obligation to assure that balances of its currency held by the General Resources Account when drawn by another member can be exchanged for a freely usable currency if the country's own currency has not been designated by the Fund as a "freely usable currency."[49]

The Fund can augment its resources through borrowings. It can borrow from the treasuries and central banks of members and nonmembers. With the concurrence of a member, the Fund has authority to borrow currency issued by that country from official or private sources within or outside that country's territory.[50]

Article V states the conditions for the use of the pool of resources held in

---

[44] See Schedule B, paragraphs 2–5.

[45] Article III, section 3(a). See also E.B. Decision No. 5702 -(78/39)G/S (March 22, 1978; effective April 1, 1978), as amended; *Selected Decisions* (10th issue, 1983), p. 110.

[46] Article III, section 3(a).

[47] Each member was permitted to pay its entire quota increase effective in 1978 in its own currency. Alternatively, a member could choose to pay 25 percent of its quota increase in SDRs or in currencies of other members specified by the Fund. Board of Governors Resolution No. 31-2, effective March 22, 1976; IMF, *Summary Proceedings, 1976*, p. 295.

The Board of Governors specified that 25 percent of each member's quota increase in 1983–84 be paid in SDRs or in currencies of other members specified by the Fund or a combination of the two. Board of Governors Resolution No. 38-1, *supra* note 35. See also Chapter 5, *infra*, p. 212 (note 204).

[48] Article III, section 3(a). See also Rule E, *By-Laws, Rules and Regulations* (40th issue, 1983).

The IMF Articles contain special rules for dealing with the reduction of quotas, should reduction ever be made. Article III, section 2(c). For other special rules, see Chapter 6, *infra*, pages 294–298.

[49] Article V, section 3(e); and Article XXX(f). The concept of "freely usable currency" is explained in Chapter 5, *infra*, pages 197–200.

[50] See Article VII, section 1. Borrowings by the IMF to supplement its resources are discussed in Chapter 6, *infra*, page 283 et seq.

the IMF's General Resources Account. The Fund deals only with governments or monetary authorities. Under conditions specified in the article, a member may purchase special drawing rights and currencies from the Fund in exchange for its own currency. The transaction is cast in the form of a purchase and sale. But, there is a "repurchase" obligation, and charges must be paid by a member in accordance with the Fund's rules. Thus, a purchase, or "drawing" as it is generally called, is not a loan but has some of a loan's characteristics.[51] The Fund pays remuneration to the countries whose currencies are drawn from the General Resources Account once they are drawn down below a threshold level.[52]

Currencies and SDRs drawn from the Fund are available for general balance-of-payments support and the Fund does not specify the uses to be made of them. They may be used to redeem balances of the country's currency held by foreign central banks and treasuries. They may be added to the national treasury to restore a depletion of reserves. They may be sold on the exchange markets to stabilize exchange rates. They may be provided to the commercial banks for sale to their customers for payments abroad.

A portion of the Fund's resources is available automatically—the member's "reserve tranche." Drawings beyond the reserve tranche require justification.[53] A member may obtain a "stand-by arrangement" or "extended arrangement" from the Fund to assure that the country will be able to draw on the Fund's resources up to a specified amount during the period of the arrangement, usually one to three years. The member requesting a stand-by or extended arrangement describes the economic and financial policies it intends to pursue and the Fund, if satisfied with these policies, approves the request.[54]

In addition to "regular" drawing rights in the General Resources Account, the Fund has also established a number of "facilities" within that account to make foreign currencies and SDRs available to members for specific purposes. The Fund operates an "extended facility" which permits drawings over a period of up to three years of large amounts in relation to quota and which allows a longer repurchase period than the three-to-five year norm applicable to most drawings in the General Resources Account, the facility being intended primarily for use by developing countries while they make structural adjustments in their economies. There is also a facility to assist in dealing with

---

[51] The concept of a "drawing" is explained further in Chapter 6, *infra*, page 223 et seq.

[52] Charges and remuneration are explained in Chapter 6, *infra*, pages 229–230.

The Fund's net income resulting from transactions and operations in the General Resources Account is assigned to a general or special reserve. Article XII, section 6, contains provisions respecting the investment, use, and distribution of these assets. All or a portion of the reserve may be transferred to the Investment Account to earn interest by investment in marketable obligations of international financial institutions (such as World Bank bonds) or in marketable obligations of the member whose currency is used for the investment. See also Article V, section 12(f) and (g), relating to the investment of profits from the sales of gold.

[53] These matters are explained in Chapter 6.

[54] Stand-by and extended arrangements are studied in Chapter 6, *infra*, beginning at page 248.

problems caused by certain export and import fluctuations and another to deal with the financing of commodity buffer stocks. A "policy on enlarged access" enables the IMF to provide assistance to members in amounts larger than it might otherwise be able to finance.[55] Developing countries, in addition to making drawings in the General Resources Account to finance temporary balance-of-payments deficits, may also receive financial assistance from special trust funds and, possibly in the future, the Special Disbursement Account.[56]

Special Drawing Rights Department

Pursuant to Articles XV and XVIII, the Fund creates and allocates "special drawing rights" to members that have chosen to be "participants" in the Special Drawing Rights Department.[57] The special drawing right (SDR) is a monetary reserve asset of which the Fund is the issuer. This is a form of fiat money usable only by monetary authorities and other official agencies. Participants in the Special Drawing Rights Department have agreed, under the rules stated in Articles XV–XXV, to exchange SDRs for a freely usable national currency.

The SDR represents a right to obtain an equivalent amount of a "freely usable currency."[58] The Articles of Agreement and decisions of the Fund specify the situations in which the right may be exercised and also delineate the circumstances under which a participant may be required to provide a freely usable currency to another participant and accept in return special drawing rights from it. The Special Drawing Rights Department of the IMF maintains the account books that record allocations, operations, and transactions in special drawing rights.

Periodically, the Board of Governors reviews the operations of the Special Drawing Rights Department and may take decisions to create additional special drawing rights or to contract the total volume of SDRs. It acts on the basis of proposals of the Managing Director that are concurred in by the Executive Board. Each participant's quota in the General Resources Account is used as a yardstick to determine what proportion of the total of any new allocation of SDRs it will receive. At the present time over 21 billion SDRs are in existence.[59]

In a typical transaction in special drawing rights, a holder of SDRs will notify the Fund that it wishes to exchange SDRs for one of several national currencies recognized by the Fund as "freely usable."[60] These are currencies that are

---

[55] These facilities and policies are described in Chapter 6, *infra*, beginning at page 277.

[56] Trust funds and the Special Disbursement Account are treated in Chapter 6, *infra*, at pages 294–298.

[57] See Article XVII. At the present time all IMF members are participants in the Special Drawing Rights Department.

[58] Article XIX, sections 2(a) and 4. The concept of "freely usable currency," defined in Article XXX(f), is explained in Chapter 5, *infra*, pages 197–200.

[59] See Chapter 5, *infra*, page 214. See also IMF, *Annual Report, 1983*, pp. 128–31.

[60] This transaction is only one example of many types of transactions and operations in special drawing rights explained in Chapter 5.

widely used for making payments for international transactions and are widely traded in the principal exchange markets. The Fund will then designate a participant to accept the SDRs and to provide a freely usable currency in exchange. In this transaction the value of the SDR is currently determined by an index of national currencies or "standard basket." The exchange rate between the SDR and the currency provided by the designee is based on the market exchange rate between the "basket" of currencies and the particular currency provided.

The present practice of defining the SDR's exchange value in terms of an index composed of small amounts of five national currencies is not required by the Articles. A change in this "principle" of valuation can be made by decision of an 85 percent majority of the total weighted voting power of all members together with an 85 percent majority of the total weighted voting power of participants in the SDR Department. A change in the "method" of valuation requires 70 percent majorities of the total weighted voting power both of members and of participants.[61]

The Fund Agreement and decisions also provide that some transactions in special drawing rights can take place voluntarily by participants without designation by the Fund. SDRs may also be used in a variety of transactions between a member and the Fund's General Resources Account, such as payment of charges on drawings in that account.

The SDR is used by the IMF as the unit of account in all of its transactions and in its reports. A member's quota in the General Resources Account is stated in terms of SDRs, and all transactions in that account use the SDR as the measure of value.[62]

The matters summarized here are explained in detail in Chapter 5, which is devoted entirely to the special drawing right.

Code of Good Conduct

Each member of the International Monetary Fund undertakes "to carry out all of its obligations under this Agreement."[63] By subscribing to the Articles a member has agreed by treaty to conform its national actions to specified practices which have come to be called the "code of good conduct." We shall survey these rules at this point. Joseph Gold, writing in 1965, characterized the adoption of the rules of good conduct in the monetary sphere as "a remarkable development in international relations because it represents massive agreement on the introduction of the rule of law into an area in which previously the discretion of states to act as they wished was almost wholly unlimited."[64]

---

[61] These matters are explained further in Chapter 5, *infra*, beginning at page 176.

[62] Article III, section 1; Article V, sections 10 and 11; and Article XIX, section 7(a). See also note 42, *supra*.

[63] Article XXXI, section 2(a).

[64] Joseph Gold, *The International Monetary Fund and International Law: An Introduction* (IMF Pamphlet Series no. 4; Washington, 1965), pp. 10–11.

Exchange Rate Arrangements. Article IV, *second,* entitled "Obligations Regarding Exchange Arrangements," and Schedule C, *second,* were intended by their drafters as a complete agreement on the international legal regime applicable to the methods and rates at which currencies are exchanged.[65] Under Section 1 of Article IV all members undertake to collaborate with the Fund and other members to assure orderly exchange arrangements and to promote a stable system of exchange rates. There is a general obligation to pursue policies that (a) foster orderly economic growth with reasonable price stability taking into account the circumstances of the country, and (b) foster orderly economic and financial conditions and a stable monetary system. This general obligation is directed to both domestic policies and international policies. In addition members have an obligation to follow exchange policies that are compatible with these obligations and, in particular, to avoid manipulating exchange rates or the international monetary system in a manner that prevents effective balance-of-payments adjustment or that creates an unfair competitive advantage over other members.

Under Section 2 each IMF member, so long as it fulfills the obligations of Section 1, is given freedom to choose the arrangements under which its currency is exchanged for other currencies and the rates at which exchanges take place. Most IMF members have chosen to maintain stable rates for their currencies in terms of a widely used foreign currency or in terms of a composite of several currencies (such as valuing the currency in relation to the SDR). Some countries issuing currencies that are widely used in international transactions have chosen to use floating rates—that is, exchange rates are set by market forces with governments intervening to maintain orderly markets but not necessarily to maintain any particular fixed rate. In early 1984, currencies floating independently included the U.S. dollar, Canadian dollar, U.K. pound sterling, and Japanese yen. The authorities issuing these currencies have maintained some control over rate movements, the firmness of that control varying from case to case. The members of the European Economic Community that participate in the European Monetary System's exchange rate arrangement have allowed their currencies to float in a managed manner against the U.S. dollar, while stable rates are maintained within the currency group.[66]

The Fund under Section 3 of Article IV is given broad powers of surveillance, powers to call for consultations, and authority to articulate principles to

---

[65] The exchange rate regime of IMF Article IV receives full treatment in Chapter 11. The reason for postponing an in-depth discussion to that point is that the discussion of exchange rates will have greater meaning when the reader understands well the techniques of financing balance-of-payments deficits, the uses of special drawing rights, and exchange controls.

[66] Various types of exchange rate arrangements are described in Chapter 11.

If a wide measure of agreement is achieved (85 percent of the total weighted voting power) the Fund can under section 2 of Article IV provide for general exchange arrangements. By the same majority, the Fund has the power under section 4, should it choose to exercise it, to institute a par value system. These matters are also treated in Chapter 11.

guide members in fulfilling their exchange obligations. The Fund holds broad-ranging formal consultations with each member, in principle annually, under Article IV. These consultations encompass all aspects of domestic and international economic policy. Consultations may be held with some members more frequently, especially countries whose currencies are widely used in international transactions or actively traded in the exchange markets. Formal consultations may be supplemented by informal contacts.[67]

Convertibility. Under Section 2(a) of Article VIII a member undertakes that, unless it is availing itself of the transitional arrangements of Article XIV or unless the Fund approves, it will not impose restrictions on the making of payments or transfers in respect of current international transactions.[68] This means that it must refrain from impeding—whether by limiting, unduly delaying, or prohibiting—the making of financial settlements for current international transactions. Accordingly, the member must allow its residents—private citizens and companies as well as governmental bodies—to use the national currency or to acquire foreign currencies that are required for making those settlements.[69]

Section 2(a) of Article VIII has a further effect: A nonresident payee that has received the payor's currency (of a country accepting Article VIII) in settlement for a current international transaction has the right to use or transfer it. Under Section 2(a) of Article VIII the issuing country cannot (unless it relies on Article XIV or the Fund approves) prevent the nonresident from transferring the currency to someone else in a current transaction. That is, if a foreigner (F_1) received a bank deposit in a bank of country B in payment for goods or services, B cannot order the bank to refuse to recognize a transfer of that deposit by F_1 to another foreigner (F_2) or to a national of B in settlement of a current transaction.

Section 4 of Article VIII places an obligation upon the issuer of a currency to convert balances of its currency held by central banks or government treasuries of other members if presented for conversion. If member A is holding balances of member B's currency, and these balances are the proceeds of current transactions, or conversion of the balances is needed for making payments for current transactions, A may present these balances to B and B must convert them. B has a choice of providing to A the currency of A or special drawing rights. This obligation of B is subject to a number of conditions which are set forth in Section 4.[70]

Section 3 of Article VIII bars "discriminatory currency arrangements" in

---

[67] Fund consultations with members under Article IV are treated at a number of places in Chapters 11 and 12, especially at pages 558–568 and 571–580.

[68] Only a brief summary of convertibility is presented here. The subject is treated thoroughly in Chapter 10.

[69] E.B. Decision No. 1034 -(60/27) (June 1, 1960); *IMF History 1945-65, supra* note 2, vol. 3, p. 260; *Selected Decisions* (10th issue, 1983), p. 241.

[70] Conversions of currencies actively traded in the principal exchange markets take place through those markets.

connection with payments and transfers for current transactions. Any such arrangement between one member and another is prohibited, and any favorable arrangement between one member and a nonmember which is not generalized to all members is also barred. Section 3 also prohibits "multiple currency practices." Thus countries under the Article VIII regime cannot use different exchange rates for different transactions. The Fund has authority to approve practices that are otherwise prohibited by Sections 2 or 3.

The prohibition of multiple currency practices in Section 3 of Article VIII probably should be understood to apply to capital movements as well as current transactions, although that has not been definitively established.[71] The other provisions of Sections 2(a) and 3 of Article VIII described above deal only with restrictions relating to current transactions. Section 3 of Article VI allows controls on capital movements, provided that they do not restrict or unduly delay payments or transfers respecting current transactions.[72] The classification of a transaction as "capital" or "current" has important consequences, and the Fund's Articles give "payments for current transactions" a broad expansive definition.[73]

Taken together Sections 2, 3, and 4 of Article VIII carry forward a Fund purpose, stated in Article I, "to assist in the establishment of a multilateral system of payments in respect of current transactions between members." When a country complies with Article VIII, its currency is said to be "convertible" for current account purposes. Individuals, companies, and governments contemplating export sales to countries that comply with Article VIII and have no approved restrictions can make their decisions on whether and with whom to enter into transactions without having their freedom of decision narrowed by an inability to use or convert the proceeds obtained. Likewise, a potential importer in a country that complies with Article VIII and has no approved restrictions knows that it can obtain foreign currency with which to make payment or that its own currency, being convertible, will be acceptable to the foreign seller.

The regime of IMF Article VIII is only imperfectly in place in the world today. About three-fifths of the IMF's members do not yet accept all the obligations of Article VIII and, instead, use the "transitional" arrangements permitted by Article XIV.[74] In many of these countries exchange restrictions may deny residents the right to obtain foreign currencies to make payments abroad. Payments of the local currency to nonresidents may also be restricted. Nonresidents holding the country's currency may find they cannot exchange the currency and may thus be forced to use the currency for purchases of goods or services in the issuing state and, in some cases, may find even this use to be

---

[71] This issue is discussed in Chapter 11, *infra,* pages 551–554.

[72] Capital controls are treated in Chapter 10 at page 449 et seq.

[73] Article XXX(d).

[74] Only 59 out of 146 member countries of the IMF accepted the obligations of Article VIII, sections 2, 3, and 4, as of January 1, 1984.

blocked. While time may pass before countries availing themselves of Article XIV withdraw existing restrictions, they cannot, unless Fund approval is obtained, impose new restrictions without offending Article VIII.

About two-fifths of the IMF's members have accepted Article VIII, Sections 2, 3, and 4.[75] Many of these countries have liberalized currency controls to a greater degree than Article VIII requires. The IMF has designated several currencies as "freely usable currencies" as that concept applies to drawings in the General Resources Account and operations and transactions in SDRs.[76] The issuer of each of the currencies that have been designated by the Fund as "freely usable" (currently the U.S. dollar, Deutsche mark, French franc, Japanese yen, and U.K. pound sterling)[77] has accepted the obligations of Article VIII and also permits its currency to be used in many capital transactions, the precise range of capital transactions not requiring official approval varying among the five countries. The U.S. dollar, Deutsche mark, and U.K. pound sterling are the most free of controls.

Provision of Information. The Fund acts as a center for the collection and exchange of information on monetary and financial problems, and members are obligated to furnish detailed information on their economic and balance-of-payments situations, exchange rate arrangements, currency controls, and the like. The information that must be supplied is listed in Section 5 of Article VIII. (See also Section 3 of Article IV.) As a result of its information-gathering activities, the staff of the Fund has published useful and comprehensive documents such as the periodically issued *Annual Report on Exchange Arrangements and Exchange Restrictions,*[78] *International Financial Statistics, Government Finance Statistics Yearbook, Direction of Trade Statistics,* and *Balance of Payments Statistics.* The *Annual Report of the Executive Board* reports on developments in the world economy as well as on the Fund's own activities.[79] Articles by staff members are published in *International Monetary Fund Staff Papers.* Books, papers, and special studies are distributed from time to time. The biweekly newsletter *IMF Survey* contains useful information on developments in member countries and on the Fund's activities. Information gathered by the Fund is used in the annual review of members' economies and is discussed in consultations with members. It is used in making decisions of both general and individual application.[80]

---

[75] *Idem.*

[76] See pages 14 and 16, *supra.* The concept of "freely usable currency" is explained in Chapter 5, *infra,* pages 197–200.

[77] See Chapter 5, *infra,* page 199.

[78] The title of this publication prior to 1979 was *Annual Report on Exchange Restrictions.*

[79] The Fund's fiscal year ends April 30 and the report is issued in September. Throughout this book it is cited simply *Annual Report.*

[80] The disclosure requirements of Article VIII, section 5, may have figured in the decision of the Union of Soviet Socialist Republics, which had attended the Bretton Woods Conference, not to ratify the Fund Agree-

Consultation and Collaboration. Obligations to consult and to collaborate with the Fund and with other members form the heart of the "code of good conduct." We have already seen that IMF members have undertaken to collaborate with the Fund and with other members to promote a stable system of exchange rates. We have noted that the Fund holds broad-ranging consultations with its members under Article IV.[81] Members maintaining exchange restrictions that are inconsistent with Article VIII must regularly consult with the Fund about their continued retention of the restrictions whether or not they have accepted Article VIII, Sections 2, 3, and 4, or avail themselves of Article XIV.[82] Countries that use the Fund's general resources under stand-by or extended arrangements and other Fund policies implementing Article V commit themselves to consult with the Fund about the correction of their problems.[83] Consultations under Articles IV, V, VIII, and XIV bring within their scope domestic as well as international policies as they bear upon a country's international position. Member-participants in the Special Drawing Rights Department are required to collaborate with the Fund and with other countries to facilitate the effective operation of the Department and the proper use of SDRs.[84] All IMF members are committed to collaborate with the Fund and other members to ensure that their reserve asset policies conform with the objectives of promoting better surveillance of international liquidity and making the SDR the principal reserve asset of the international monetary system.[85] And, finally, the first-listed purpose of the International Monetary Fund is "To promote international monetary cooperation through a permanent institution which provides the machinery for consultation and collaboration on international monetary problems."[86]

By the time the reader comes to the end of this volume, he or she will have encountered the words "consultation" and "collaboration" many times. The words will be given additional meaning in their concrete applications. The key thing to remember is that the obligation to consult and to collaborate is the fundamental obligation of international monetary law.

---

ment. The Soviet Union in conversations with a U.S. Interdepartmental Committee in early 1944 took the position that a member should be obliged to furnish the Fund only such information as it and the Fund would mutually decide. However, the Soviet Union did not formally object to section 5 of Article VIII at Bretton Woods. See note 103, *infra.*

The application of section 5 was a factor in the compulsory withdrawal of Czechoslovakia at the end of 1954 (note 189, *infra*) and the voluntary withdrawal of Cuba in 1964 (Chapter 10, page 410, note 87).

[81] Article IV, sections 1 and 3, discussed at pages 18–19, *supra.* See also Chapters 11 and 12, *infra,* pages 558–568 and 571–580.

[82] Article XIV, section 3, and Fund policies on the exercise of its approval jurisdiction under Article VIII, sections 2 and 3. See Chapter 10 *infra,* page 401 et seq., and Chapter 12, page 571 et seq.

[83] See, e.g., the policies on stand-by and extended arrangements, Chapter 6, *infra,* pages 248–276.

[84] Article XXII. See Chapter 5 generally.

[85] Article VIII, section 7; and Article XXII. See Chapter 12, *infra,* pages 630–642.

[86] Article I(i).

Technical Assistance

The Fund provides technical assistance to its members at its offices in Washington and in the field. The Bureau of Statistics and the Fiscal Affairs Department help members establish or improve systems of governmental accounting, budgetary systems, tax policy, and tax and customs administration. The Exchange and Trade Relations Department occasionally provides assistance in exchange control matters. The Central Banking Service helps members draft central banking, general banking, and deposit insurance legislation. The IMF Institute conducts training programs. Consultants are provided, sometimes for extended periods, to advise on open market operations, interest rates, foreign exchange management, organizational structure, and the like.[87]

The IMF as an International Organization

The International Monetary Fund, an international organization created by treaty, possesses juridical personality including the power to contract, to acquire and dispose of property, and to institute legal proceedings.[88] It is a Specialized Agency of the United Nations under Article 57 of the UN Charter and has concluded a relationship agreement with the United Nations, under Article 63 of the Charter, which recognizes the Fund as an independent international organization and defines its relationship with the UN.[89]

Membership

The International Monetary Fund had a membership of 146 countries in January 1984. Only "countries" can be members of the organization.[90] The obliga-

---

[87] See IMF, *Technical Assistance Services of the International Monetary Fund* (IMF Pamphlet Series no. 30; Washington, 1979). See also *IMF History 1966–71, supra* note 15, vol. 1, pp. 578–90.

[88] In addition to the powers granted to it in Article IX, the IMF has inherent powers as an international organization. It has concluded international agreements with nonmember states as well as with members. See, e.g., agreements with Switzerland and the Swiss National Bank cited in Chapter 6, *infra,* pages 283–284 and 289–290 (notes 236 and 270–273). See generally Henry G. Schermers, *International Institutional Law* (Alphen aan den Rijn: Sijthoff & Noordhoff, 1980), chapters 11 and 12; and Finn Seyersted, "International Personality of Intergovernmental Organizations," *Indian Journal of International Law,* vol. 4 (1964), pp. 1–74 and 233–68. See also the memorandum of the Legal Department of the IMF on borrowing agreements between the IMF and its members, which appears as Annex D to the attachment to E.B. Decision No. 6843 -(81/75); *Annual Report, 1981,* p. 172 at p. 187; *Selected Decisions* (10th issue, 1983), p. 173 at p. 199.

[89] Agreement between the United Nations and the International Monetary Fund, entered into force November 15, 1947; *United Nations Treaty Series,* vol. 16, pp. 325 and 328; *IMF History 1945–65, supra* note 2, vol. 3, p. 215; *Selected Decisions* (10th issue, 1983), p. 403. See Chapter 2, *infra,* pages 48–50.

The United Nations Convention on the Privileges and Immunities of the Specialized Agencies applies to the International Monetary Fund, subject to certain provisions set forth in Annex V of the Convention. Article IX, section 32, providing for reference of disputes to the International Court of Justice, is limited to disputes about privileges and immunities derived from that Convention only. The Convention and Annex V became effective for the Fund on May 9, 1949. *United Nations Treaty Series,* vol. 33, p. 261; *Selected Decisions,* p. 411.

[90] Article II of the IMF Agreement. Lord Keynes in his plan, *supra* note 8, used the term "member State;" White's plan, *supra* note 8, used "country." The word "country" in the constitutional instruments of the

tions of the Articles penetrate to all levels of the member countries including all governmental organs, monetary and fiscal agencies, and central banks.[91] Each member, before signing the Agreement or accepting any amendment to it, is required to deposit an instrument setting forth that all of the obligations of the Agreement can be carried out under its domestic law.[92] Later, we shall trace the procedures followed in admitting a new member. Let it simply be said here that, before admitting a country to membership, the Fund satisfies itself that the country conducts its own international affairs and that the obligations of the Articles can be performed. It is not a condition of admission to membership in the Fund that a country must belong to the United Nations.[93]

In the practice of the Fund, each country is a separate member, even where two or more countries are associated in an economic or financial coalition or where they share a common currency. Members that belong to customs unions or share particular interests do, of course, coordinate the policies they pursue in the IMF and may agree on common spokesmen. This is, indeed, necessary when an executive director represents several members. The Fund, however, treats its legal relationship with each member separate from the others and does not deal with blocs.[94]

The People's Republic of China,[95] Hungary,[96] Romania,[97] Vietnam,[98] Yugoslavia,[99] and a number of other socialist states in Asia, Africa, and Latin

---

IMF and IBRD appears in practice to be given approximately the same application as the word "state" in the charters of other international organizations. See Joseph Gold, *Membership and Nonmembership in the International Monetary Fund* (Washington: IMF, 1974), pp. 41–89 and 468–71.

[91] Article V, section 1 (relating to agencies authorized to deal with the Fund) and Article VIII (relating to exchange restrictions), as examples, indicate an intent that government ministries, central banks, domestic courts, and all other official organs are bound by the Agreement.

[92] Articles XXVIII and XXXI.

[93] No one member of the IMF by its vote alone can prevent admission of a new member to the IMF or the recognition of a successor government. The unified Socialist Republic of Vietnam was formally recognized as the representative of Vietnam in the IMF (succeeding the Republic of Vietnam) by an Executive Board decision of September 15, 1976. See Joseph Gold, *A Second Report on Some Recent Legal Developments in the International Monetary Fund* (Washington: World Association of Lawyers, 1977), pp. 50–52. While unable to prevent the IMF's actions, the United States on November 15, 1976, by casting a veto in the Security Council, prevented the admission of unified Vietnam to the United Nations at that time.

[94] See Gold, *Membership and Nonmembership, supra* note 90, pp. 90–124 and 149–56. The election of executive directors is explained at pages 28–30, *infra*. See also pages 33–34, *infra*.

[95] The People's Republic of China was recognized as the representative of China in the IMF on April 17, 1980. See IMF, *Summary Proceedings, 1980*, pp. 99–103 and 315–16. See also documents on the recognition of the People's Republic as the representative of China in the World Bank. *International Legal Materials*, vol. 20 (1981), pp. 777–81. See also note 123, *infra*.

[96] Hungary became a member of the IMF on May 6, 1982. See IMF, *Summary Proceedings, 1982*, pp. 285–88; and *IMF Survey*, November 9, 1981, p. 349, and May 10, 1982, p. 129.

[97] Romania became a member of the IMF on December 15, 1972. See IMF, *Summary Proceedings, 1973*, pp. 281–85 and 373–76.

[98] See note 93, *supra*.

[99] Yugoslavia is one of the original members of the IMF.

America are IMF members. Czechoslovakia,[100] Poland,[101] and Cuba,[102] are not presently members of the IMF, although they were members at an earlier time. The Union of Soviet Socialist Republics and a number of other socialist states in Eastern Europe and Asia have never joined the Fund.[103] Switzerland, also, has not joined the organization.[104]

Structure of the Organization

The Fund has a Board of Governors, an Executive Board, a Managing Director, and a staff. The Board of Governors has authority to establish a Council as an additional permanent organ.[105]

Board of Governors.   The senior organ of the Fund is the Board of Governors. All powers of the Fund not directly conferred on the Executive Board or Managing Director (or the Council if established) are vested in the Board.[106] It consists of one Governor and one Alternate appointed by each member. Generally, a member appoints either its finance minister or central bank president as its governor. Although not required to meet regularly, the Board of Governors usually meets in September each year, together with the Board of Governors of the International Bank for Reconstruction and Development, to review the activities of the Fund and the World Bank Group. The Board may meet at other times and has from time to time acted by mail ballot between meetings, for example to admit a new member, approve an increase in quotas or allocation of

---

[100] See note 189, *infra,* on the compulsory withdrawal of Czechoslovakia.

[101] Poland withdrew from the IMF and the World Bank in 1950, after being denied a loan by the Bank. It claimed the two organizations had become submissive to U.S. policy. See Edward S. Mason and Robert E. Asher, *The World Bank Since Bretton Woods* (Washington: Brookings Institution 1973), pp. 170–71; and *IMF History 1945–65, supra* note 2, vol. 1, p. 258.

Poland formally submitted an application to rejoin the IMF on November 10, 1981. Martial law was declared in the country before the IMF was ready to act on the request. See *IMF Survey,* November 23, 1981, p. 365; and *The Hindu* (Madras), November 12, 1981, p. 9.

[102] See Chapter 10, *infra,* page 401 (note 87), on the withdrawal of Cuba.

[103] Although the U.S.S.R. took part in the 1944 Bretton Woods Conference, it has not become an IMF member. It appears to have been concerned about the role the Fund might play in respect to the exchange rate of the ruble and the obligation to ultimately make the ruble convertible. The Soviet Union also objected at Bretton Woods to provisions relating to the transfer of gold to the Fund. See *IMF History 1945–65, supra* note 2, vol. 1, pp. 77–78 and 117; Eckes, *supra* note 1, pp. 141–45, 205–08, and 309; Gold, *Membership and Nonmembership, supra* note 90, pp. 135–36; Raymond F. Mikesell, "Negotiating at Bretton Woods," in Raymond Dennett and Joseph E. Johnson (ed.), *Negotiating with the Russians* (Boston: World Peace Foundation, 1951), pp. 101–16; and *Foreign Relations of the United States,* 1946, vol. 1 (1972), pp. 1387–88. The formal objections to the Articles stated at Bretton Woods by the Soviet delegation are set forth at *Proceedings and Documents of the United Nations Monetary and Financial Conference, supra* note 5, vol. 1, pp. 1090–91. See note 80, *supra,* concerning the Soviet Union's attitude toward information disclosure.

[104] Switzerland concluded agreements with the IMF associating that country with the General Arrangements to Borrow. The Swiss National Bank has concluded agreements with the IMF to loan currency to the Fund. See Chapter 6, *infra,* pages 283–284 and 289–290 (notes 236 and 270–273).

[105] Article XII, section 1.

[106] Article XII, section 2(a); and Schedule D, paragraph 6.

SDRs, or approve amendments of the Articles for submission to governments.[107] The Board of Governors may delegate to the Executive Board, or to the Council if it is created, authority to exercise any powers not directly conferred on the Board of Governors or another named organ by the Articles of Agreement.[108] However, only the Board of Governors can approve proposed amendments of the Articles, admit a new member, expel a member, change a quota (which determines a member's drawing rights and voting power), allocate (create) special drawing rights, or take action on a number of other matters.[109]

Council and Interim Committee.   The Board of Governors, acting by an 85 percent majority of the total voting power, has authority to apply Schedule D and thus establish a Council.[110] This organ described in Schedule D would be placed between the full Board of Governors and the Executive Board.[111] The Council would bear primary responsibility for certain matters that are politically sensitive. The Council, if created, will "supervise the management and adaptation of the international monetary system, including the continuing operation of the adjustment process and developments in global liquidity. . . ." It will also review developments in the transfer of resources to developing countries. The Council will consider proposed amendments to the Articles. In addition it will exercise other powers conferred upon it by the Board of Governors.[112]

There are to be the same number of councillors as there are executive directors. Persons appointed councillors are to be governors of the Fund, ministers in their governments, or persons of comparable rank in their governments. The idea is that these persons will be in a position to commit their governments to joint courses of action and to assure that Council decisions requiring action by governments will be carried out. Members of the Council will usually be politically senior to executive directors, but they may not be as knowledgeable about the operations of the Fund. Schedule D provides that executive directors attend meetings of the Council without vote. In addition, each councillor may potentially have as many as seven associates.

---

[107] By-Laws, section 13; *By-Laws, Rules and Regulations* (40th issue, 1983). See Frank A. Southard, Jr., *The Evolution of the International Monetary Fund* (Essays in International Finance no. 135; Princeton: Princeton University International Finance Section, 1979), p. 3.

[108] Article XII, section 2; and Schedule D, paragraph 3(a).

[109] For a summary of the nondelegable powers of the Board of Governors and the voting majorities required for their exercise, see *Report on Second Amendment, supra* note 16, part 2, chapters M, O, and P, and annex to part 2.

[110] Article XII, section 1. Voting power is explained at pages 32–35, *infra*.

[111] Schedule D, paragraph 3(c), provides: "The Council shall not take any action pursuant to powers delegated by the Board of Governors that is inconsistent with any action taken by the Board of Governors and the Executive Board shall not take any action pursuant to powers delegated by the Board of Governors that is inconsistent with any action taken by either the Board of Governors or the Council."

[112] Schedule D, paragraphs 2 and 3(a).

Those who proposed the creation of a Council viewed its creation as necessary to reestablish the Fund as the central organization concerned with balance-of-payments adjustment, monetary expansion and contraction both within domestic economies and at the international level, and other policies affecting trade, payments, and capital movements. In the period since 1955 organizations outside the IMF had assumed increasing responsibility for coordination of national policies bearing upon the achievement of balance-of-payments equilibrium. Among these forums were: Working Party No. 3 (concerned with short-term balance-of-payments forecasting and exchange policy) of the Economic Policy Committee of the Organisation for Economic Co-operation and Development (OECD), the "Group of Ten" industrial states that have agreed to provide their currencies upon call to the IMF to supplement the Fund's currency holdings, and the "Basle Club" of central bank governors meeting under the auspices of the Bank for International Settlements.[113] As early as 1969, a study panel of the American Society of International Law, reflecting on activities in these other forums and on the importance of the IMF, began discussion of a proposal for a high-level council within the Fund to oversee the adjustment process.[114]

While it may be desirable to involve persons with political "clout" in their own countries more actively in the work of the Fund, this poses a danger that the Fund's activities will be affected to a greater extent than in the past by political factors. Lord Keynes, while favoring the involvement of high national officials in Fund decision-making, was concerned that politicalization be avoided. In his closing speech to the first meeting of the Board of Governors in 1946, he wondered if some malicious fairy would curse the Fund and World Bank: "You two brats," he feared her saying, "shall grow up politicians; your every thought and act shall have an *arrière-pensée;* everything you determine shall not be for its own sake or on its own merits but because of something else."[115] A Council is not necessary. The Executive Board, whose members are less prominent in national political arenas, can perform most of the functions that

---

[113] The OECD and the Group of Ten are described at pages 68–74. The Bank for International Settlements is described at pages 52–63.

These organizations assumed importance in the 1960s in part because of the economic growth of Western European states and their desire that decisions be made in forums in which their positions would dominate. The level of representation was also a factor. Representation at the monthly meetings of the Bank for International Settlements is by the heads of government central banks. The heads of delegations at meetings of OECD Working Party No. 3 have often ranked higher in their governments than IMF executive directors. These officials travel to these meetings at a frequency of every four to eight weeks for the express purpose of contact with their counterparts. *Long-Term International Monetary Reform: A Proposal for an Improved International Adjustment Process* (Washington: American Society of International Law, 1972), pp. 14–22.

[114] See *Long-Term International Monetary Reform, idem.*

[115] The full speech is printed in *The Collected Writings of John Maynard Keynes, supra* note 8, vol. 26, pp. 215–17; and in Roy F. Harrod, *The Life of John Maynard Keynes* (London: Macmillan, 1951; New York: St. Martin's Press, 1963), pp. 631–32.

would be assumed by the Council. If the Council is established, it cannot later be abolished except by a new amendment of the Articles.[116]

At the present time, in place of a Council the Fund has a body called the "Interim Committee of the Board of Governors on the International Monetary System."[117] This committee might better be described as a ministerial committee, as the members must be governors of the IMF or hold the rank of minister in their governments. The Committee, unlike a Council if established, has an advisory role only and lacks the power to adopt binding decisions. The Committee's composition, however, is the same as provided for the Council and in fact the Committee has had considerable influence on decisions taken by the Board of Governors and the Executive Board. It is a *de facto* Council without decision-making authority.

The Interim Committee normally meets two or more times a year. The Committee engages in discussions of the world economic outlook and its implications for members and for the Fund. Major initiatives of the Executive Board, such as significant changes in rules concerning the special drawing right (SDR), are usually vented in the Committee. The Committee has ironed out difficulties that the Executive Board has been unable to resolve, such as problems that arose in the Sixth and Seventh Quota Reviews and other problems that have required political compromise or involved significant new governmental commitments. The meetings are normally carefully prepared and relatively brief. Because observers from other organizations (such as the OECD, Bank for International Settlements, World Bank, and other bodies) have been allowed to attend formal sessions, discussions do not in fact have the same degree of confidentiality as IMF Executive Board deliberations. A press communiqué is usually issued after each meeting.[118]

Executive Board.   The Executive Board is in practice the most important organ of the Fund. Until a Council is created, the Board of Governors can be expected to continue to follow its past practice of delegating to the Executive Board all the powers that the Board of Governors can delegate to it.[119] The Executive Board may well continue to be the most important organ even if a Council is created. It is responsible for the general operations of the Fund. The Board

[116] See Gold, *Voting Majorities in the Fund, infra* note 143, p. 12. See generally Joseph Gold, " 'Political Bodies' in the Fund," *Selected Essays, supra* note 15, p. 238.

[117] The Interim Committee was created by Board of Governors Resolution No. 29-8, *supra* note 20. The Committee was originally formed to bring to conclusion negotiations for the Second Amendment to the Articles. Following completion of that task, the Interim Committee has devoted its attention to the matters to which a Council would give attention, i.e., those listed in paragraph 2 of Schedule D. See generally Gold, "Fund's Interim Committee," *supra* note 22.

[118] The language of Interim Committee communiqués often lacks precision. There typically is more haggling over language than when other IMF organs make decisions. See Gold, "Fund's Interim Committee," *supra* note 22, p. 34. See generally F. Lisle Widman, *Making International Monetary Policy* (Washington: Georgetown University International Law Institute, 1982), pp. 66–68 and 97–98.

[119] See By-Laws, section 15; *By-Laws, Rules and Regulations* (40th issue, 1983).

is in continuous session and this prevents directors from having regular responsibilities in countries that appoint or elect them.[120]

At the present time the Executive Board consists of twenty-two executive directors plus the Managing Director as chairman. Five executive directors are appointed by the members having the largest quotas,[121] currently the United States, United Kingdom, Federal Republic of Germany, France, and Japan. The Board of Governors has decided that there shall be sixteen elected executive directors.[122] The directors are elected at two-year intervals (in the even-numbered years) by a complicated allocation system in which a number of members join together to elect one director to represent the group.[123]

Each of the two members whose currencies have been drawn from the General Resources Account in the largest absolute amounts in the two years before an election of executive directors is permitted to appoint an executive director if it does not already have the right to do so. The purpose of this provision is to ensure that the members whose currencies have been heavily used by the Fund have a clear voice in the day-to-day affairs of the Fund.[124] Saudi Arabia appointed an executive director pursuant to this provision in 1978, 1980, and 1982.[125]

The Executive Board following the 1980 and 1982 elections consisted of five appointed executive directors, the Saudi Arabian executive director, and sixteen elected executive directors, plus the Managing Director. Each executive director appoints an alternate who has full power to act in the absence of the executive director. Each *Annual Report* of the IMF lists the names of executive directors and their alternates, the countries they represent, and the voting power of those countries.

[120] Article XII, section 3. See also By-Laws, section 14(d), (g), and (h); *By-Laws, Rules and Regulations* (40th issue, 1983). See generally Southard, *supra* note 107, pp. 4–11. For background on early views on the proper role of the Executive Board, see Dam, *supra* note 1, pp. 110–14.

[121] Article XII, section 3(b)(i).

[122] Article XII, section 3(b)(ii), provides for fifteen elected executive directors with the Board of Governors being authorized to change the number. The Board of Governors changed the number of elected directors to sixteen in 1980 and reaffirmed that decision for the 1982 election. See A.W. Hooke, *The International Monetary Fund: Its Evolution, Organization and Activities* (IMF Pamphlet Series no. 37; Washington, 1982), p. 12. See also note 123, *infra;* and IMF, *Summary Proceedings, 1981,* pp. 386–87.

[123] The procedures for the appointment and election of executive directors are spelled out in Article XII, section 3, and in Schedule E. When the Board of Governors increased the number of elected directors from fifteen to sixteen in 1980, there was a gentlemen's understanding that the People's Republic of China could elect an executive director representing only that country. See Hooke, *supra* note 122, p. 12; and *IMF Survey,* October 13, 1980, p. 324. See also note 95, *supra.*

[124] Article XII, section 3(c). The present provision is permissive while the former provision was mandatory. See *Report on Second Amendment, supra* note 16, part 2, chapter O, section 2(a)–(d). See also IMF By-Laws, section 18, *By-Laws, Rules, and Regulations* (40th issue, 1983).

[125] When a member appoints a director pursuant to Article XII, section 3(c), that uses up one of the elected director "slots," unless the Board of Governors decides, as it did in the Saudi Arabian case, that it shall not have that effect.

Canada appointed an executive director in 1958 and Italy appointed an executive director in 1968 pursuant to former Article XII, section 3(b)(ii) and (c), *original* and *first.*

Each executive director and the members of the constituency he represents are free to determine the frequency of his contacts with the members of the constituency, the depth of those contacts, and the way in which the executive director obtains guidance or instructions.

The Executive Board functions in continuous session at the Fund's office in Washington and meets as often as the business of the Fund requires. It regularly meets two or three times a week. In addition, there are frequent, less formal meetings of executive directors. The Executive Board, because it is "in house" and meets frequently, exercises closer day-to-day control over staff activities than policy-making bodies in most other international organizations. The deliberations of the Executive Board are confidential. Throughout this book there will be references to decisions taken by the Executive Board.[126]

Managing Director and Staff.   The Executive Board selects the Managing Director. The Managing Director is the chairman of the Executive Board and has no vote except a casting vote in the remote event of ties. He participates in meetings of the Board of Governors—regularly giving a major address—but without a vote.[127]

The Managing Director heads the staff of the Fund and directs its work. He is responsible, subject to the general control of the Executive Board, for the organization, appointment, and dismissal of the staff. The Managing Director and the staff are international civil servants.[128] The staff presently numbers about 1,500. The bulk of the staff is organized into several functional departments (Administration, Secretary, Treasurer, Exchange and Trade Relations, Fiscal Affairs, Legal, Central Banking, External Affairs, Research, and Training Institute), and five area departments (African, Asian, European, Middle Eastern, and Western Hemisphere). The staff also serves offices in Paris and Geneva and performs special services (e.g., Statistics, Computing Services, and Language Services).[129]

Procedures in Admitting a New Member

The generalizations previously made about the organization may take on more meaning as we trace the procedures in the admission of a new member. Article II, Section 2, of the Fund Agreement provides that new members may be admitted to the organization "at such times and in accordance with such terms as may be prescribed by the Board of Governors." While under the former articles the Board of Governors admitted some new members under terms significantly dif-

---

[126] See page 36, *infra*.
[127] Article XII, section 4.
[128] Article XII, section 4(b)–(d). See generally Southard, *supra* note 107, pp. 6–11.
[129] See organization chart in Hooke, *supra* note 122, p. 16.

ferent from those applied to original members,[130] a new sentence in Section 2 states that the terms of admission of new members, including the terms of subscriptions, "shall be based on principles consistent with those applied to other countries that are already members."[131]

After receipt of an application for membership from a country, the Executive Board considers the application and proceeds to work out proposed terms and conditions of membership. Matters to be considered, among others, are the proposed quota and subscription for the country. The exchange rate arrangements of the country, and currency restrictions in effect in the country, are studied, but special provisions relating to them are normally not included in membership resolutions. The quota is determined on the basis of the country's holdings of foreign currencies and other reserve assets (its reserve position), its national income and volume of trade, and other economic considerations. The prospective member can be expected to bargain for a large quota, since quota size is a basis for future substantial drawings if needed and determines the allocation of special drawing rights and the country's voting power in the Fund.[132] The amount of the quota to be paid in reserve assets will normally be calculated so that the ratio of the new member's quota to the amount paid in reserve assets will be the same as that of other members.[133]

When, after negotiations between the Executive Board and the representative of the applicant, agreement is reached on membership terms and conditions, a proposed resolution will be submitted to the Governors for a vote, usually by mail.[134] The date ending the vote is the day the resolution takes effect, if passed. The applicant then has a period of time, usually six months, to accept membership.[135]

Before the end of this period, the country will transmit to the Fund a memorandum indicating that it has adopted legislation enabling it to comply with its obligations in the Fund. In addition, before its representative signs the Articles of Agreement, a prospective member must deposit with the Fund an "Instrument of Acceptance" stating that it accepts in accordance with its laws the Articles of Agreement and all the terms and conditions prescribed in the resolution of the Board of Governors respecting its membership.[136] Its representative then

[130] See, e.g., the resolution admitting Bangladesh, under which it paid 98.4 percent of its quota subscription in its own currency and only 1.6 percent in reserve assets. Board of Governors Resolution No. 27-6, adopted effective June 13, 1972; IMF, *Summary Proceedings, 1972,* p. 345.

[131] Through the transitional provisions of Schedule B, all members belonging to the Fund on April 1, 1978, were required to effectively pay 25 percent of their total quota subscription in reserve assets, if they had not previously done so. See note 44, *supra,* and accompanying text.

[132] See "Multiformula Method Adds Flexibility in the Calculation of Members' Quotas," *IMF Survey,* June 5, 1978, p. 166.

[133] See E.B. Decision No. 6266—(79/156)(September 10, 1979); IMF, *Annual Report, 1980,* p. 140; *Selected Decisions* (10th issue, 1983), p. 4.

[134] See, e.g., Board of Governors' resolutions admitting Zimbabwe in 1980, Vanuatu and Bhutan in 1981, and Hungary in 1982. IMF, *Summary Proceedings, 1980,* p. 312; *1981,* pp. 387 and 390; and *1982,* p. 285.

[135] See By-Laws, section 21, and Rule D-1; *By-Laws, Rules and Regulations* (40th issue, 1983).

[136] See Article XXXI, section 2(a).

signs the Articles of Agreement and the country officially becomes a member of the Fund that day. Once a member, a country may become a participant in the Special Drawing Rights Department by depositing an appropriate instrument with the Fund.

The portion of the General Resources Account quota paid in the state's own currency will be calculated in terms of the representative exchange rate between the new member's currency and the special drawing right.[137] This currency portion of the quota (normally 70–75 percent) may be paid entirely by crediting the IMF's demand deposit account maintained with the country's central bank or monetary authority or it may be paid partly in this way and partly by issuing to the Fund a non-negotiable, non-interest-bearing security denominated in the country's currency and payable at face value on demand.[138] Membership resolutions normally provide that the remainder of the quota subscription—the reserve asset portion—will be paid in SDRs or national currencies of other members specified by the Fund.[139] Unless an exception is granted, the General Resources Account quota subscription must be paid in full to the Fund before that country can make drawings in the General Resources Account.

Voting

A system of weighted voting is used in the International Monetary Fund. The votes of members are based on their quotas. As a result, voting power differs considerably among members. Each member has 250 votes plus one additional vote for each part of its quota equivalent to SDR 100,000.[140]

The basic rule in the Articles, unless a special majority is specified, is that decisions are made by a majority of the weighted votes cast.[141] However, there are many situations in which special majorities are required. Some decisions relating to matters that are not routine but are of an operational character require a 70 percent majority of the total voting power (not simply 70 percent of the votes cast). Decisions of particular importance and sensitivity require 85 percent of the total voting power. A few decisions such as expulsion of a member require other special majorities.[142] Thus, members that can muster over 15 percent of

---

[137] Article V, sections 10(b) and 11(a); Article XIX, section 7(a); and rules and decisions adopted thereunder.

[138] Article III, section 4. See also Rules E-1 and E-2; *By-Laws, Rules and Regulations* (40th issue, 1983).

[139] See Article II, section 2; and *Report on Second Amendment, supra* note 16, part 2, chapter B, section 1. See membership resolutions cited in note 134, *supra.*

[140] Article XII, section 5(a). The *Annual Report* lists the current weighted vote of each member country. For background see Joseph Gold, "The Origins of Weighted Voting Power in the Fund," *Finance and Development,* vol. 18, no. 1 (March 1981), p. 25.

[141] Article XII, section 5(c). Votes not cast are excluded from the calculation and are not treated as negative votes except with respect to qualified majorities. *Report on Second Amendment, supra* note 16, part 2, chapter N, section 1.

[142] A table listing situations in which special majorities are required is printed in *Report on Second Amendment, idem,* part 2, annex.

the total voting power can block the adoption of decisions to adjust quotas, to establish a Council, to provide for general exchange arrangements, to institute a par value system, and a number of other matters.[143] Each member is given a veto over certain matters directly affecting it, including an increase or decrease in the size of its quota and an increase in its allocation of special drawing rights.[144]

Decisions relating exclusively to special drawing rights are taken only by votes of members that are participants in the Special Drawing Rights Department. The number of votes held by a participant is based upon the member's quota in the General Resources Account, not on net allocations of SDRs nor on actual number of SDRs held by it.[145]

In two types of decisions respecting the General Resources Account, the weighted voting power is adjusted in accordance with the net use made by the Fund of a member's currency or the net use that a member is making of the Fund's resources: (1) decisions to waive conditions on the use of the Fund's General Resources Account and (2) certain decisions to declare a member ineligible to use the General Resources Account or to limit its use of that account.[146] Voting power for decisions affecting the Special Drawing Rights Department is not adjusted on the basis of use made of special drawing rights.

In votes taken by the Board of Governors, each governor casts the votes of the member appointing him.[147] In the Council, if established, each councillor will cast the votes of the membership constituency that appointed him and can split his votes to reflect divergent views within the constituency he represents.[148] In votes taken in the Executive Board, each director casts the votes of the members that appointed or elected him. An executive director (unlike a councillor) cannot split his votes to reflect the attitudes of the several countries that elected him if they differ on an issue.[149] However, if the Executive Board or Council is considering a request made by, or a matter particularly affecting, a member that is not entitled to appoint an executive director or councillor, the member may send a representative to speak for it at a meeting of the Executive Board or Council, but that representative cannot vote. The executive director

---

[143] See generally Joseph Gold, *Voting Majorities in the Fund: Effects of Second Amendment of the Articles* (IMF Pamphlet Series no. 20; Washington, 1977), which describes voting rules following the Second Amendment. These rules differ significantly from those in the former Articles, described in Joseph Gold, *Voting and Decisions in the International Monetary Fund* (Washington: IMF, 1972), pp. 117–70; and Gold, "Weighted Voting Power in the Fund: Some Limits and Some Problems," *Selected Essays, supra* note 15, p. 292.

[144] Article III, section 2(d); and Article XVIII, section 2(e).

[145] Article XXI; and Schedule D, paragraph 5(b).

[146] Article XII, section 5(b). See Gold, *Voting Majorities in the Fund, supra* note 143, at p. 3.

[147] Article XII, section 2(e).

[148] Schedule D, paragraph 3(b).

[149] Article XII, section 3(i).

will cast the votes of the entire group. Thus, it is possible for the member's votes to be cast against its own cause.[150]

Despite the elaborate voting procedures, or in fact because of them, Fund organs rarely resort to formal votes except when required by the Articles and then most of these votes are unanimous or nearly so. Joseph Gold has commented:

> In practice, a maximum effort is made to reach an agreement which all can accept or at worst not oppose. This is not confined to minor matters. In fact, the more important the issue, the more strenuous and sustained is the effort that is made to reach a decision in which all can concur.[151]

Only a small number of decisions of the Executive Board requiring a simple majority of the weighted votes cast have been adopted by a formal vote in the last twenty-five years. The normal practice, even when special majorities are required, is to adopt decisions on the basis of the "sense of the meeting."[152] The practice finds expression in Rule C-10:

> The Chairman shall ordinarily ascertain the sense of the meeting in lieu of a formal vote. Any Executive Director may require a formal vote to be taken with votes cast as prescribed in Article XII, Section 3(i), or Article XXI(a)(ii).[153]

Voting strength becomes very important when special majorities are required. And, even when only simple majorities are required, voting strength is not irrelevant even if formal voting is avoided. A position must be supported by executive directors having sufficient votes to carry the question in order for the chairman to declare a decision by consensus. The Executive Board, desiring broad-based support for decisions, has traditionally tried to avoid taking actions that are supported by only a minority in number of executive directors even if those directors have the necessary majority of the voting power.

In addition to formal meetings of the Executive Board, directors may also meet in informal sessions. An executive director may at an "informal session," which is nevertheless a meeting of the Board, express his own views on a matter without implying that the position stated is that taken by the constituency the

---

[150] Article XII, section 3(j); and By-Laws, section 19, *By-Laws, Rules and Regulations* (40th issue, 1983).

[151] Gold, *The International Monetary Fund and International Law, supra* note 64, p. 10.

[152] See Southard, *supra* note 107, pp. 5–6; and Gold, *Voting and Decisions, supra* note 143, pp. 196–97.

[153] Rule C-10. See also By-Laws, section 11, relating to meetings of the Board of Governors; *By-Laws, Rules and Regulations* (40th issue, 1983). See the detailed report of the confidential IMF Executive Board meeting of November 3, 1982, when a stand-by arrangement for South Africa was approved. Jonathan Kwitny, "Going Along: How IMF Overcame Political Issues to Vote a Loan to South Africa," *Wall Street Journal*, May 5, 1983, p. 1 at p. 26.

director represents. A lengthy account in the form of minutes, but not a verbal record, is made of formal meetings. Although "minutes" are not kept of "informal" sessions, a record in the form of a journal is made.

Papers for Executive Board consideration are prepared by the staff. A subject for study or future decision by the Board may be raised in the course of Board discussions or raised within the staff. A small group of senior staff members may first explore a problem and then a Fund department or interdepartmental working group will be assigned to give the matter intensive study.[154] The Committee on Reform of the International Monetary System and Related Issues (Committee of Twenty) and the Interim Committee of the Board of Governors that developed the revised IMF regime embodied in the Second Amendment to the Articles were also given much staff support. Both committees were formed by decisions of the Board of Governors.

It is too early to say what precise procedures will be used in the Council, if it is created, respecting preparation of materials and agendas for Council meetings, the use of committees, and the extent to which formal votes will be taken. It is expected that the Fund's staff and Executive Board will play major roles in preparing materials for Council deliberations and decisions.

The Fund's Corpus Juris

The main elements in the Fund's *corpus juris* are:

(a) *The Articles of Agreement.* This is the Fund's basic charter. It appears in Appendix B.[155]

(b) *By-Laws, Rules and Regulations.* The Articles provide that the Board of Governors, and the Executive Board to the extent authorized, "may adopt such rules and regulations as may be necessary or appropriate to conduct the business of the Fund."[156] The By-Laws have been adopted, and are amended from time to time, by the Board of Governors. The Rules and Regulations are adopted and amended by the Executive Board, subject to review by the Board of Governors.

The Fund's by-laws, rules, and regulations, some of its decisions, and a number of its procedures have been amended or changed since the

---

[154] The possibilities of compensatory financing of export fluctuations were investigated by the staff for two years prior to the Board's decision. *IMF History 1945–65, supra* note 2, vol. 2, pp. 16–17. The facility is described in Chapter 6, *infra,* pages 277–281.

[155] At pages 694–761 of this book. See also pages 8–11, *supra.*

[156] Article XII, section 2(g). The Council's authority to adopt regulations is stated in Schedule D, paragraph 4.

Second Amendment entered into force. Those in effect April 1, 1978, that have not been changed remain in effect until changed.[157]

(c) *Resolutions of the Board of Governors.* Decisions of the Board of Governors usually take the form of resolutions which may be adopted at a meeting of the Governors or by mail or by cable ballot.[158] They relate, *inter alia,* to interpretations of the Articles, the terms for admission of a new member, compulsory withdrawal from membership, general or special adjustments in members' quotas, allocations of SDRs, rules for the election of and the terms of service of executive directors, determinations with respect to the use of the Fund's net income, review of the Fund's financial statements, formal agreements with other international organizations, and approval of amendments to the Articles to be submitted to member governments. The Board of Governors also embodies in resolutions any special requests it makes to the Executive Board (or to the Council if created) for studies or for the development of policy. Resolutions of the Board of Governors, including those adopted during the year by mail ballot, are printed in the *Summary Proceedings* of the Annual Meetings of the Board of Governors.[159]

(d) *Decisions of the Executive Board.* Much of the Fund's law is to be found in the decisions of the Executive Board. They may be of a general nature relating to the rights and obligations of members; they may establish policies and procedures of the Fund; or they may deal with a request or problem of a particular member. Those decisions of general interest, or of a law-making nature, are selected and published in the *Annual Report of the Executive Board.*[160] From time to time the decisions are collected in *Selected Decisions of the International Monetary Fund and Selected Documents.*[161] The reader should be advised that most decisions of the Executive Directors, such as those relating to the problems of individual countries, are not published.

[157] Schedule B, paragraph 6. In case of conflict between the amended Articles and a prior decision, the amended Articles will of course control. See *Report on Second Amendment, supra* note 16, part 2, chapter S, section 3.

Unless otherwise indicated, the references in this volume to by-laws of the Fund or to rules of the Fund refer to the by-laws and rules as compiled in IMF, *By-Laws, Rules and Regulations* (40th issue, August 1, 1983).

[158] By-Laws, section 13, as amended June 13, 1978; *By-Laws, Rules and Regulations* (40th issue, 1983). Section 13 of the By-Laws was interpreted by a specially appointed Joint Committee of the Boards of Governors of the IMF and the World Bank. The committee's report, issued in 1981, is cited in note 162, *infra.*

[159] See, e.g., note 17, *supra.*

[160] Throughout this book the *Annual Report of the Executive Board* is cited *Annual Report.*

[161] Unless otherwise indicated, the references in this volume to *Selected Decisions* are to the tenth issue dated April 30, 1983.

The Fund's Power of Interpretation

The Articles grant the Fund the power to adopt interpretations of its own charter. Article XXIX provides that any question of interpretation of the provisions of the Articles arising between any member and the Fund, or arising between members of the Fund, must be submitted to the Executive Board for its decision. The Board formally acts on a basis of a simple majority of the weighted votes cast. Any member may require that the interpretation given by the Executive Board be referred to the Board of Governors, whose decision is final.[162] There is a qualification to the rules stated in Article XXIX: Only a participant in the Special Drawing Rights Department can request a formal interpretation under Article XXIX of a provision of the Agreement pertaining only to that department.[163]

In the IMF system interpretative decisions are made by officials who are familiar with the working of the IMF Agreement as a whole and who have a stake in the outcome. Interpretation has, nevertheless, been approached as a legal task and memoranda prepared by the Legal Department have been given great weight in the interpretative process.[164] The weight of authority holds that interpretative decisions of the IMF taken under Article XXIX are binding on national courts as well as executive and other organs of the member countries.[165] The authority of the IMF under Article XXIX has been said, however,

---

[162] The procedure in the Board of Governors is as follows. The question is considered by a "Committee on Interpretation" of the Governors in which each committee member has one vote (rather than a weighted vote). (The membership, procedures, and voting majorities of the Committee are determined by the Board of Governors.) The Committee's decision is the Board's decision unless the Board by an 85 percent vote of the total weighted voting power decides otherwise. See generally Gold, "Weighted Voting Power," *supra* note 143, pp. 302–06.

A Board of Governors Committee on Interpretation has been constituted only once, but that committee was not the committee referred to in Article XXIX. This occurred in 1980 when a Joint Committee of the Boards of Governors of the IMF and the World Bank was appointed to interpret not the Articles of Agreement but section 5(b) of the By-Laws of the Fund (and corresponding provisions applicable to the World Bank), relating to the authority of the Chairman of the Board of Governors to invite observers to attend the annual meeting, and section 13 of the By-Laws relating to voting by the Board of Governors without meeting. For the committee's report, dated January 23, 1981, see IMF, *Summary Proceedings, 1981*, pp. 298–384. See also note 169, *infra*.

[163] Article XXI(c).

[164] See generally the following writings by Joseph Gold: Gold, *The Rule of Law in the International Monetary Fund* (IMF Pamphlet Series no. 32; Washington, 1980), pp. 43–51; Gold, *Interpretation by the Fund* (IMF Pamphlet Series no. 11; Washington, 1968); Gold, "Interpretation by the International Monetary Fund of its Articles of Agreement—II," *International and Comparative Law Quarterly*, vol. 16 (1967), p. 289; *IMF History 1945–65, supra* note 2, vol. 2, pp. 567–73 (section by Joseph Gold); and Gold, "Weighted Voting Power," *supra* note 143, pp. 302–06.

[165] See U.S. Federal Communications Commission opinion in *International Bank for Reconstruction and Development and International Monetary Fund v. All America Cables & Radio, Inc.*, decided in 1953; *Federal Communications Commission Reports*, vol. 17 (1953), p. 450; *International Law Reports*, vol. 22 (1958), p. 705; discussed in Gold, *Fund Agreement in the Courts, supra* note 31, vol. 1, pp. 20–27 and 55–59. Compare the reasoning of the decision of the Conseil Constitutionnel of France of April 29, 1978, cited in note 31, *supra*. The reasoning but not conclusion of that decision is criticized in Gold, *Fund Agreement in the Courts, supra*, vol. 2, pp. 284–94; and in Dominique Carreau, "L'Augmentation de la Quote-

not to extend to the interpretation of borrowing agreements made by the Fund to replenish its currency holdings.[166]

In the Fund's history only a few of the many Executive Board decisions have been characterized by the Board as formal interpretations of the Articles. In each case there was a special reason why it was thought desirable to characterize the decision as a formal binding interpretation not easily subject to later change or amendment.[167] Commenting on the small number of formal interpretations, the General Counsel of the Fund has said:

> The fact that the Fund can adopt authoritative interpretations has made it possible for the Fund to adopt numerous interpretations without giving them the solemnity of adoption under Article XVIII [the predecessor of present Article XXIX]. Nevertheless, these interpretative decisions have been supported by the same legal analysis as is devoted to interpretations under Article XVIII and are regarded by the Fund and members as elements of the Fund's *corpus juris*.[168]

The IMF–United Nations relationship agreement authorizes the IMF to seek advisory opinions from the International Court of Justice in certain cases, but that has never been done.[169] It is difficult to conceive of a question to be submitted to the Court by the IMF that would not in some aspect require the

part de la France au Fonds Monétaire International: La Décision du Conseil Constitutionnel du 29 Avril 1978," *Revue Générale de Droit International Public,* vol. 83 (Paris, 1979), p. 209.

F. A. Mann has argued that an interpretation by the Fund, even under the formal interpretative procedures of the Articles, is entitled only to great weight and is not binding upon a court or arbitral tribunal. See F. A. Mann, "The 'Interpretation' of the Constitutions of International Financial Organizations," *British Year Book of International Law,* vol. 43 (1968–69), p. 1, reprinted in F. A. Mann, *Studies in International Law* (London: Oxford University Press, 1973), p. 591.

[166] See memorandum of the Legal Department of the IMF, annexed to E.B. Decision No. 6843, *supra* note 88.

[167] The difficulty of changing or amending a formal interpretation is illustrated by the Executive Board decision in 1961 that the Fund's general resources could be used to finance certain capital transfers notwithstanding an earlier formal interpretation that had been previously understood to the contrary. See Chapter 6, *infra,* page 242 (note 97).

[168] Statement of Joseph Gold in H.C.L. Merillat (ed.), *Legal Advisers and International Organizations* (Dobbs Ferry: Oceana Publications, 1966), p. 100.

[169] Article VIII of the Agreement Between the United Nations and the International Monetary Fund, entered into force November 15, 1947, *supra* note 89.

On October 2, 1981, by Resolution No. 36-12, the Board of Governors requested the Executive Board to consider recommending to the Board of Governors that it request an advisory opinion from the International Court of Justice on the validity of Board of Governors Resolution No. 35-9 that denied the request of the Palestine Liberation Organization for observer status at the 1980 annual meeting. The Executive Board, following consideration, did not recommend that action to the Governing Board. See IMF, *Summary Proceedings, 1981,* pp. 394–95. For background, see the committee report of January 23, 1981, cited in note 162, *supra.*

Court to pass on questions that under IMF Article XXIX are to be decided definitively by the Fund itself.[170]

The IMF has adopted rules for dealing with complaints of one member against another.[171] Iran invoked the procedures in 1979 to challenge United States actions, during the period of the hostages' seizure, that blocked Iranian funds with official and commercial banks in the United States and with branches of U.S. commercial banks in other countries.[172]

Assuring Compliance with Decisions

The Fund has a variety of techniques available to it to assure that members comply with their obligations under the IMF Agreement and decisions of the Fund. We shall examine the Fund's practice in specific cases in later chapters. A few generalizations may be helpful to the reader at this time.[173]

We should first note rules and procedures that minimize the likelihood of formal violations. On some matters about which members may be sensitive, such as exchange rate arrangements, the Articles are not particularly restrictive and Fund decisions may state guidelines rather than legislated obligations.[174] A country's statement of economic policy intentions in a letter of intent supporting a stand-by or extended arrangement is not a legal commitment, and failure to achieve the results stated has important consequences but the failure is not a breach of a legal obligation.[175] When the Fund adopts a decision legally binding the conduct of members, an effort is made, as with all decisions, to assure broad support for the decision before it is adopted. The Fund has authority in many cases to grant waivers or suspend provisions of the Articles. The Fund in some cases has authority to approve justified actions that, without Fund approval, would be violations of the Articles.[176]

---

[170] See James E.S. Fawcett, "The Place of Law in an International Organization," *British Yearbook of International Law,* vol. 36 (1960), p. 321 at p. 328. Mr. Fawcett was General Counsel of the IMF 1955–1960.

[171] See, e.g., Rules H-2 and H-3 relating to exchange controls, discriminatory currency arrangements, and multiple currency practices. *By-Laws, Rules and Regulations* (40th issue, 1983).

[172] See Gold, *Fund Agreement in the Courts, supra* note 31, vol. 2, pp. 367–68.

[173] See generally Gold, *The Rule of Law in the International Monetary Fund, supra* note 164, pp. 26–59; Gold, " 'Sanctions' of the Fund," *Selected Essays, supra* note 15, p. 148; Gold, " 'Pressures' and Reform of the International Monetary System," *Selected Essays, idem,* p. 182; and Gold, *Voting Majorities in the Fund, supra* note 143, pp. 24–26. See generally Merillat, *supra* note 168; Stephen M. Schwebel (ed.), *The Effectiveness of International Decisions* (Dobbs Ferry: Oceana Publications; Leyden: A.W. Sijthoff, 1971); and Roger Fisher, *Improving Compliance with International Law* (Charlottesville: University Press of Virginia, 1981).

[174] See Chapter 11, *infra,* pages 519–521.

[175] See Chapter 6, *infra,* pages 267–269.

[176] See Article V, section 4 (waiver of conditions on drawings in the General Resources Account); Article VII, section 3(b) (scarce currencies); Article VIII, sections 2 and 3 (Fund approval of exchange restrictions); Article XIV, section 2 (exchange restrictions during "transitional period"); Article XXIII, section 1 (suspension of operation of provisions relating to special drawing rights); and Article XXVII (emergencies and unforeseen circumstances). Some of these provisions are more flexible than in the former Articles. See *Re-*

The Fund relies heavily on consultation procedures. Each year the Fund reviews the economic situation and monetary policies of its members. The reviews on a country-by-country basis provide an opportunity for the Fund to comment on a member's policies.[177] The Fund is explicitly given the right under the Articles to communicate its views informally to a member at any time on any matter arising under the Agreement.[178] In some situations the Fund has the power to make "representations."[179] The Fund is also permitted to publish a report that censures a member's monetary policies, but this has never been done.[180]

Drawings in the IMF's General Resources Account may be conditioned upon compliance with particular Fund decisions or policies as well as compliance with the country's own previously stated policy objectives. The ability of the Fund to withhold its resources is an incentive to compliance. Alexandre Kafka, an Executive Director of the Fund (Brazil), has made the blunt assessment:

> Despite the availability of other "sanctions," the Fund's only practical one has proved to be denial of access to its resources in individual cases. This means of pressure has been bolstered where other major creditors have taken their cue from the Fund.[181]

The Fund may, in certain circumstances, formally declare a member ineligible to use the General Resources Account.[182] This has been done only once (Czechoslovakia 1953).[183] In a second case (France 1948) ineligibility followed automatically under the Articles in their form at that time.[184] In 1978 Kampuchea's right to use the general resources of the Fund was suspended, but this was short of ineligibility.[185] A member-participant's right to use special

---

port on Second Amendment, supra note 16, part 2, chapter R. For comments on the practice under the previous provisions, see Joseph Gold, " 'Dispensing' and 'Suspending' Powers of International Organizations," *Selected Essays, supra* note 15, p. 352; and Gold, "Weighted Voting Power," *supra* note 143, pp. 294–300.

[177] The review of member economies and policies receives extended treatment in Chapters 6, 11, and 12.

[178] Article XII, section 8.

[179] See, e.g., Article V, section 7(b); Article XIV, section 3, and Article XIX, sections 2(d) and 3(b). See also Article VII, sections 2 and 3.

[180] Article XII, section 8. See Gold, *Voting Majorities in the Fund, supra* note 143, pp. 7 and 24.

[181] Alexandre Kafka, "The International Monetary Fund in Transition," *Virginia Journal of International Law,* vol. 13 (1972–73), pp. 135–57 and 539–52 at p. 149.

[182] Article V, section 5; Article VI, section 1; and Article XXVI, section 2. See also Rules K-1-K-5; *By-Laws, Rules and Regulations* (40th issue, 1983).

[183] See note 189, *infra.* Cuba voluntarily withdrew from the Fund in 1964 when a declaration of ineligibility was being considered. See Chapter 10, *infra,* page 401 (note 87).

[184] France became automatically ineligible to use the Fund's general resources when it adopted a new unauthorized par value in January 1948; it was again declared eligible in October 1954. See *IMF History 1945-65, supra* note 2, vol. 1, pp. 200–06 and 412.

[185] The provisions on ineligibility are more flexible under the present Articles than they were previously. Article XXVI, *second,* grants the Fund powers to declare a member ineligible to use the general resources and

drawing rights is suspended if it violates Article XIX, Section 4, relating to the obligation to provide a freely usable currency when designated by the Fund to accept SDRs. A participant's right to use SDRs acquired in the future can be suspended for violation of other obligations.[186] Exercising its authority, the Fund in 1978 adopted a decision that suspended Kampuchea's right to use SDRs acquired thereafter.[187]

"Compulsory withdrawal," expulsion from the organization, is the final remedy.[188] This has been done only once (Czechoslovakia 1954).[189]

There have been cases when members departed from their obligations under the Articles and the Fund neither imposed sanctions nor formally suspended applicable provisions. At various times and often for extended periods after May 1971 countries issuing widely used currencies floated their currencies in the exchange markets. These acts were in violation of former Article IV. Not until June 1974 did the Executive Board formally (at least publicly) act to deal with those practices.[190] During the period before the June 1974 decision, the Fund, when informed of a float, would publicly take note of it but avoid using language that approved or disapproved. The impression left was that the Fund would not take action against the "offending" country, but would engage in consultations with it. While some might describe the Fund's lack of action as self-restraint, the result can also be described as "waiver" through tolerance of a violation. The reason for this "non-action" was that the directors understood the reasons why members were floating their currencies and, indeed, ques-

---

powers to compel withdrawal, but the *exercise* of these powers is permissive and lesser measures are authorized. See also Article V, section 5; and Schedule C, paragraph 7. The IMF exercised its powers under present Articles V and XXVI when, in December 1978, it suspended Kampuchea's access to the Fund's general resources. The action was taken because Kampuchea had failed to observe its repurchase obligations in the General Resources Account. See IMF, *Annual Report, 1979*, pp. 160–61.

[186] Article XXIII, section 2. See also Rules S-1-S-8; *By-Laws, Rules and Regulations* (40th issue, 1983).

[187] The IMF, in December 1978, exercised its powers under Article XXIII, section 2, and suspended Kampuchea's right to use subsequently acquired SDRs because Kampuchea had failed to meet its reconstitution obligations and had failed to pay charges and assessments applicable to its use of SDRs. Thus, when Kampuchea received new allocations of SDRs on January 1, 1979, and thereafter, it was not permitted to use them. The suspension can be terminated 180 days after the end of the first calendar quarter in which it complies with its obligations. See IMF, *Annual Report, 1979*, p. 165. See generally Chapter 5, *infra*, pages 210–212.

[188] Article XXVI, section 2. See also By-Laws, section 22; *By-Laws, Rules and Regulations* (40th issue, 1983).

[189] In 1953 the Executive Board declared Czechoslovakia to be ineligible to use the Fund's resources. A year later, the Board of Governors in September 1954 decided to require Czechoslovakia to withdraw from the Fund unless it supplied certain information before the end of the year. When the information was not supplied, the country was informed that its membership had lapsed. See IMF. *Summary Proceedings, 1954,*. pp. 97–101 and 143, and Resolution 9-8 at p. 113; Gold, *Membership and Nonmembership, supra* note 90, pp. 345–72; *IMF History 1945–65, supra* note 2, vol. 1, pp. 359–64; and Southard, *supra* note 107, pp. 14–15.

[190] E.B. Decision No. 4232 -(74/67)(June 13, 1974) and annexed guidelines; IMF, *Annual Report, 1974*, p. 112.

tioned the wisdom of Article IV as it then was. At the same time they recognized the need for the IMF to maintain some discipline over exchange arrangements, without knowing exactly how, pending amendment of the Articles.[191]

As a result of this and other experiences, the provisions permitting temporary suspension of some of the Articles were made more flexible. The Executive Board by an 85 percent majority of the total voting power can suspend certain provisions for up to one year, and the Board of Governors by the same majority can extend the suspension for up to two additional years.[192] Further, many substantive provisions are less rigid. Much greater use is made in the present Articles of enabling clauses permitting action by Fund organs (sometimes by special majorities) often accompanied by express or implied authority to modify or rescind the actions taken.

Innovations of the IMF

In its early years, many knowledgeable persons were concerned about the limited role the Fund was playing on the international plane. Harry Dexter White, the principal author of the Bretton Woods institutions, in the spring of 1948 made the comment: "A candid appraisal of the contributions which both institutions have so far made toward the stated objectives would force us to the conclusion that achievement has been much less than anticipated."[193]

In succeeding years the Fund has demonstrated its ability to play the role its founders intended. Dramatic progress was made in the late 1950s in eliminating currency restrictions by the industrialized member states and in the 1960s and 70s progress was made by other members, although much remains to be done. The development of stand-by arrangements, which assure members that foreign currencies will be available to them, involved novel conceptions about the nature of legal obligations. The Fund's agreements with member

---

[191] As early as 1954 the Fund adopted a decision on rates of exchange in the General Account involving "fluctuating currencies." E.B. Decision No. 321 -(54/32)(June 15, 1954)(subsequently superseded); *IMF History 1945–65, supra* note 2, vol. 3, p. 222. There was concern at the time the decision was adopted that it might encourage violations of the Articles.

The problem of floating currencies became acute in May 1971 when the monetary authorities of the Federal Republic of Germany and the Netherlands decided to float their currencies and pressures developed for devaluation of the U.S. dollar. See Chapter 11, *infra,* pages 495–498. The contemporary personal views of the General Counsel of the Fund on legal aspects of violations of the Articles when the par value system was under stress in 1971 are set forth in Joseph Gold, "Unauthorized Changes of Par Value and Fluctuating Exchange Rates," *American Journal of International Law,* vol. 65 (1971), p. 113; and Gold, " 'Dispensing' and 'Suspending' Powers of International Organizations," written in 1972, *supra* note 176, pp. 366–69 and 384–86.

Present Article IV, studied in Chapter 11, permits each IMF member to choose its own exchange arrangements which may include floating exchange rates.

[192] Article XXIII, section 1; and Article XXVII, section 1. See note 176, *supra,* and accompanying text.

[193] Quoted in Gardner, *supra* note 3, p. 305. See Eckes, *supra* note 1, pp. 211–36.

states and a nonmember (Switzerland) to borrow currencies from them—the General Arrangements to Borrow—were important innovations.

The First Amendment to the Fund Agreement effective in 1969 and the Second Amendment effective in 1978 embodied far-reaching changes. The First Amendment created the Special Drawing Account (now Special Drawing Rights Department) and introduced a new reserve asset to be used by monetary authorities. The Second Amendment changed a number of articles in fundamental ways and made the provisions of others more workable.

The original system of stable exchange rates based on par values stated in terms of gold ultimately failed. It has been replaced by a more flexible exchange rate regime in the present Articles. The extent to which the Fund can maintain surveillance over, and influence, national decision-making is still a sensitive issue. The tools available to the Fund in its surveillance role, and the wisdom with which they are exercised both with respect to exchange rates and other economic policies, will in large part determine the effect that the Fund will have on the quality of life in the member states.

One other subject that will require more attention than it has received in the past is the relationship of the Fund to the socialist countries associated politically and economically with the Soviet Union. At the present time the only members of the Council for Mutual Economic Assistance, headquartered in Moscow,[194] that are members of the IMF are Hungary, Romania, and Vietnam. Czechoslovakia, Poland, and Cuba withdrew from the Fund during the cold war period.

The reader should at this point have an understanding of the International Monetary Fund adequate for the discussions that follow in later chapters.

---

[194] See Chapter 2, *infra*, page 87. See also pages 24–25, *supra*.

Chapter 2: Other International Organizations

Note

Chapter 2 is devoted to international organizations other than the International Monetary Fund that are involved in significant ways with monetary policy and international payments. Some international organizations, such as the Bank for International Settlements, give their primary attention to monetary subjects, while others, like the United Nations Conference on Trade and Development and the Organisation for Economic Co-operation and Development, deal with monetary matters as only one segment of a range of economic concerns. The World Bank Group and the General Agreement on Tariffs and Trade primarily focus on financing of development or on trade, and are involved with monetary policies as they impinge on those concerns. Some organizations draw their members from throughout the world, while membership in others is limited to states in a specific geographic region. Some are limited to members sharing a particular social or political orientation.

Global Organizations

World Bank Group

The International Bank for Reconstruction and Development (IBRD) was created at the 1944 Bretton Woods Conference as a sister organization to the International Monetary Fund.[1] The IBRD or World Bank, as it is often called, pro-

---

[1] The Articles of Agreement of the International Bank for Reconstruction and Development, effective December 27, 1945, as amended effective December 17, 1965. The original text appears in *United Nations Treaty Series,* vol. 2, p. 134; *United States Statutes at Large,* vol. 60, p. 1440. The 1965 amendment appears in *United Nations Treaty Series,* vol. 606, p. 294; *United States Treaties and Other International Agreements,* vol. 16, p. 1942. For historical accounts of the work of the World Bank Group, see Edward S. Mason and Robert E. Asher, *The World Bank Since Bretton Woods* (Washington: Brookings Institution, 1973); and Robert W. Oliver, *International Economic Co-operation and the World Bank* (London: Macmillan, 1975). For legal overviews, see Aron Broches, "The World Bank," in Robert S. Rendell (ed.), *International Financial Law: Lending, Capital Transfers and Institutions* (London: Euromoney Publications, 1980), p. 251; and

vides development loans to its member countries. A requirement for membership in the Bank is that the country be a member of the IMF.[2] IMF members, however, are not required to belong to the Bank. The Boards of Governors of the IMF and the World Bank traditionally hold their annual meetings jointly.

The organizational structure of the IBRD is comparable to that of the IMF. It has a Board of Governors and an Executive Board with a system of weighted voting. The responsibilities of the President of the World Bank are comparable to those of the Managing Director of the IMF but, given the differences in the purposes of the two organizations, are not as wide-ranging. The World Bank has a large and expert staff. Its headquarters is adjacent to that of the IMF in Washington.

The IBRD and its affiliate, the International Development Association (IDA),[3] have since April 1, 1978, used the special drawing right (SDR), as valued from time to time by the International Monetary Fund, as their unit of account for financial statements, and translate the SDR amounts into current U.S. dollars at the rate published by the Fund for the final day of the fiscal year. This practice, however, has been challenged by one member (the United States).[4]

While quota subscriptions provide the main source of the funds administered by the IMF, and borrowings by the IMF provide a secondary source, quotas in the IBRD serve principally as a base upon which the Bank floats bonds or otherwise borrows large sums in the international capital markets. These funds

Lester Nurick, "The International Bank for Reconstruction and Development and the International Development Association," in Walter Sterling Surrey and Don Wallace, Jr. (ed.), *A Lawyer's Guide to International Business Transactions* (2d ed.; Philadelphia: American Law Institute, 1979), part 2, p. 49.

[2] Articles of Agreement of the IBRD, Article II, section 1. Purposes served by this requirement are discussed in Joseph Gold, "The Relationship Between the International Monetary Fund and the World Bank," *Creighton Law Review*, vol. 15 (1981–82), p. 499 at pp. 506–09.

[3] Articles of Agreement of the International Development Association, effective September 24, 1960; *United Nations Treaty Series*, vol. 439, p. 249; *United States Treaties and Other International Agreements*, vol. 11, p. 2284.

[4] The IBRD Articles, Article II, section 2(a), value capital stock subscriptions in terms of "United States dollars of the [gold] weight and fineness in effect on July 1, 1944," and the IDA Articles, Article II, section 2(b), value initial subscriptions in the same manner with the reference being to U.S. dollars of the gold value of January 1, 1960 (which is the same). The General Counsel of the IBRD and IDA rendered an opinion that the references in the cited sections should be read to mean the SDR subsequent to the entry into force on April 1, 1978, of the Second Amendment of the IMF's Articles, given that the IMF treats the SDR as maintaining continuity of value with the 1944 U.S. dollar.

The United States has claimed that the U.S. dollar adjusted for the devaluations of 1972 and 1973 (U.S. $1.20635) is the proper measure of value. It has argued that to substitute the SDR would create new obligations respecting maintenance of value of capital subscriptions, and that such a change should be effected only by an amendment of the Articles of the IBRD and IDA. The matter has not been finally resolved. The International Finance Corporation is not involved since its Articles refer to U.S. dollars without any reference to gold value. See World Bank, *Annual Report, 1978*, p. 149 (note to financial statements of IBRD) and p. 167 (note to financial statements of IDA); World Bank, *Annual Report, 1983*, p. 167 (note to financial statements of IBRD) and p. 204 (note to financial statements of IDA); and Stephen A. Silard, "The General Standard of International Value in Public International Law," in American Society of International Law, *Proceedings of the 73d Annual Meeting* (Washington, 1979), p. 15 at pp. 21–22.

are then re-loaned under loan agreements to member governments or with governmental guarantees of repayment. IBRD loans are usually at medium- or long-term, to be repaid typically in 20 years, and carry interest at, or approximately at, market rates.

The International Development Association obtains most of its funds through periodic "replenishments" (which are like voluntary contributions) from its member countries. It, in turn, makes these funds available to the poorest of developing countries. IDA loans (called "credits") do not have to be fully repaid for 50 years. They carry an administrative charge but no interest charge. Sometimes the resources of the IBRD and IDA are blended when a particular project or program is supported.

The International Finance Corporation (IFC),[5] also an affiliate of the IBRD, may make equity investments in governmental or private enterprises, and governmental guarantee of repayment is not required. The IFC obtains funds through borrowings and also sales of participations in its investments.

The Articles of Agreement of the International Bank for Reconstruction and Development state that loans made or guaranteed by the Bank shall "except in special circumstances, be for the purpose of specific projects of reconstruction or development."[6] The Articles further provide: "The Bank shall make arrangements to ensure that the proceeds of any loan are used only for the purposes for which the loan was granted. . . ."[7] The Articles of Agreement of the International Development Association provide that financing provided by the Association, "except in special circumstances, shall be for specific projects."[8] An early formal interpretation of the Bank's Articles established that the "special circumstances" clause could be read broadly to authorize the Bank to make long-term stabilization loans.[9] An expansive reading of the term "specific projects" was also decided upon early in the Bank's history.[10]

Both the Bank and IDA have made loans and credits primarily for projects such as the construction of a hydro-electric power plant. However, in recent

---

[5] Articles of Agreement of the International Finance Corporation, effective July 20, 1956, as amended effective September 21, 1961, and September 1, 1965; *United Nations Treaty Series*, vol. 264, p. 117; vol. 439, p. 318; and vol. 563, p. 362; *United States Treaties and Other International Agreements*, vol. 7, p. 2197; vol. 12, p. 2945; and vol. 24, p. 1760. See generally R.B.J. Richards, "International Finance Corporation," in Surrey and Wallace, *supra* note 1, part 2, p. 97.

[6] Articles of Agreement of the IBRD, Article III, section 4(vii). See also section 1.

[7] Article III, section 5(b).

[8] Articles of Agreement of the IDA, Article V, section 1(b).

[9] Interpretation of the IBRD Executive Directors of September 20, 1946; in IBRD, *First Annual Meeting of the Board of Governors: Proceedings and Related Documents* (Washington, 1946), pp. 40–45. See also Bretton Woods Agreements Act, section 12. *United States Statutes at Large*, vol. 59, p. 512 at p. 516.

[10] In 1950 the IBRD Executive Directors described the "specific project" requirement as follows: "The objective of this provision is simply to assure that Bank loans will be used for productive purposes. In effect, the only requirement which it imposes is that, before a loan is granted, there shall be a clear agreement both as to the types of goods and services for which the proceeds of the loan are to be expended and the uses to which these goods and services are to be put." IBRD, *Annual Report, 1950*, p. 7. See generally John Syz, *International Development Banks* (Dobbs Ferry: Oceana Publications, 1974), pp. 171–74.

years, drawing on the early interpretation of the "special circumstances" clause and a broad reading of the term "specific projects," the two organizations have made loans and credits for such purposes as the financing of agricultural credit institutions in developing countries that in turn make loans to farmers and farm cooperatives for purchase of seed, fertilizer, and equipment. They have also engaged in "program lending" to support development of sectors of a country's economy such as energy or education.[11]

The Bank and IDA have also in recent years understood their Articles to authorize loans in support of structural adjustment by countries—that is adjustment of industry, agriculture, and labor to changes in the international economy. "Structural adjustment loans" have only been made since 1980. They finance imports that are important to development of particular sectors of the economy or the economy as a whole.[12] These loans, although supporting defined programs, are so broad in scope that they are very much like generalized support of the balance of payments. In the result accomplished (if not in form and legal structure), they are similar to IMF extended arrangements.[13] IMF and IBRD staff members now are assigned to missions of the sister institution when medium-term assistance is contemplated, in order to assure a measure of coordination.[14]

The World Bank, as a lender, is concerned with the general creditworthiness of the governments in countries where it makes loans.[15] While prior to 1979 the World Bank would insist upon borrowers making changes in policies bearing directly on projects financed, it tended to use only persuasion respecting macroeconomic policies. Now the Bank, as well as the IMF, may make it clear that changes in macroeconomic policies (such as domestic credit policies and government budget policies) may be required to obtain assistance, at least for structural adjustment loans.[16] The World Bank and the Fund, although they

---

[11] See Bettina S. Hürni, *The Lending Policy of the World Bank in the 1970s: Analysis and Evaluation* (Boulder, Colorado: Westview Press, 1980), pp. 7–98.

[12] See Ernest Stern, "World Bank Financing of Structural Adjustment," in John Williamson (ed.), *IMF Conditionality* (Washington: Institute for International Economics, 1983), p. 87; Pierre M. Landell-Mills, "Structural Adjustment Lending: Early Experience," *Finance and Development*, vol. 18, no. 4 (December 1981), p. 17; and E. Peter Wright, "World Bank Lending for Structural Adjustment," *Finance and Development*, vol. 17, no. 3 (September 1980), p. 20. The first structural adjustment loan was made to Turkey in 1980. Structural adjustment loans may be made by the Bank or by IDA and, in some cases, the resources are blended.

[13] IMF extended arrangements are examined in Chapter 6, *infra*, page 248 et seq.

[14] It appears that the Bank and Fund have deliberately not defined their cooperative arrangements in formal agreements. They have prepared parallel memoranda on their respective responsibilities for the guidance of their staffs. See Gold, "Relationship," *supra* note 2, pp. 511–21.

[15] Articles of Agreement of the IBRD, Article III, section 4(v).

All IBRD loans are made to governments or with government guarantees of repayment. *Idem*, Article III, section 4(i). The IDA is not required to obtain a government guarantee for loans to entities other than member governments nor is the IFC required to obtain government guarantees for its investments. See Articles of Agreement of IDA, Article V, section 2(d).

[16] See statement of Stanley Please, Senior Economic Adviser of the IBRD, as quoted in *The Hindu* (Madras), December 7, 1981, p. 8.

cooperate, apply their own criteria in appraising requests for assistance. On occasion the World Bank has indicated its desire that a prospective borrowing country accept the self-imposed discipline associated with an IMF stand-by or extended arrangement. On other occasions, without requiring an IMF arrangement, the World Bank has borrowed the Fund's technique of requiring a letter of intent stating economic policies from the country's finance minister.[17]

Because of the limited resources available from the World Bank Group, members of the IMF (particularly developing countries) have sought to fashion Fund policies that make assistance available to them in larger amounts for their special needs. IMF extended arrangements, previously mentioned, are designed to provide IMF resources in larger amounts in relation to quota over a longer time period than the normal stand-by arrangement.[18]

The Board of Governors of the IMF and the IBRD in 1974 established a Joint Ministerial Committee on "the transfer of real resources to developing countries."[19] This Committee (also called the Development Committee) makes recommendations on the coordination of the work of the two organizations.[20]

United Nations

The San Francisco Conference that adopted the Charter of the United Nations took place in 1945, a year after the Bretton Woods Conference that created the IMF and the IBRD.[21] In the hierarchy of international agreements, the UN Charter occupies a unique place. Article 103 of the Charter provides: "In the event of conflict between the obligations of the Members of the United Nations under the present Charter and their obligations under any other international agreement, their obligations under the present Charter shall prevail." An agreement between the United Nations and the International Monetary Fund defines the legal relationship of the two organizations.[22] By that agreement the United Nations recognizes that the IMF is an "independent international organiza-

---

[17] See Stern, *supra* note 12, p. 99. The use of letters of intent in IMF stand-by and extended arrangements is explained in Chapter 6, *infra*, page 250 et seq.

[18] See Chapter 6, *infra*, pages 248–250 and 291–292.

[19] IMF Board of Governors Resolution No. 29-9 and IBRD Board of Governors Resolution No. 294, approved October 2, 1974; in IMF, *Summary Proceedings, 1974*, p. 367; and IBRD, *Summary Proceedings, 1974*, p. 179.

[20] Reports of the Committee are published in the *Summary Proceedings* of the IMF's annual meeting.

[21] Charter of the United Nations, signed at San Francisco June 26, 1945, entered into force October 24, 1945, amended effective August 31, 1965, June 12, 1968, and September 24, 1973. For the amended text see *Yearbook of the United Nations*, vol. 34 (1980), p. 1349.

[22] Agreement between the United Nations and the International Monetary Fund, entered into force November 15, 1947. *United Nations Treaty Series*, vol. 16, pp. 325 and 328; *Selected Decisions of the International Monetary Fund and Selected Documents* (10th issue; Washington: IMF, 1983), [hereinafter *Selected Decisions*], p. 403.

tion'' with ''wide international responsibilities . . . in economic and related fields. . . .''[23]

When the UN Security Council acts under Articles 41 and 42 of Chapter VII of the Charter to deal with threats to the peace, breaches of the peace, or acts of aggression, it has authority to adopt decisions that are binding on UN member states. Article 48 obligates UN members to carry out Security Council decisions under Chapter VII ''directly and through their action in the appropriate international agencies of which they are members.'' The IMF for its part in the UN–IMF relationship agreement ''takes note'' of Charter Article 48, and states that in the conduct of its activities it will ''have due regard for decisions of the Security Council under Articles 41 and 42 of the United Nations Charter.''[24] The language was deliberately chosen so as not to imply that Security Council decisions are binding on the IMF as an organization.

The relationship agreement provides for representatives of the UN to attend, without vote, meetings of the IMF's Board of Governors and for IMF representatives to attend meetings of the UN General Assembly, Economic and Social Council, and Trusteeship Council. In preparing the agenda for meetings of its Board of Governors, the IMF is to give due consideration to the inclusion of items proposed by the UN; and the UN Economic and Social Council and its commissions and the Trusteeship Council are to do the same with respect to proposals of the IMF for inclusion of items on their agendas.[25] However, there is a specific provision for maintenance of independence: ''Neither organization, nor any of their subsidiary bodies, will present any formal recommendations to the other without reasonable *prior* consultation with regard thereto.'' [emphasis added][26] Both parties under another provision agree to consult together and exchange views on matters of mutual interest. Formal recommendations made after consultations are to be considered by the appropriate organ as soon as possible.[27] These provisions for consultation and procedures for handling formal recommendations apply to resolutions of the UN General Assembly, resolutions of the Security Council other than decisions under Articles 41 and 42, and resolutions of other UN bodies such as the Economic and Social Council and the United Nations Conference on Trade and Development as well

[23] *Idem*, Article I(2).

[24] *Idem*, Article VI. The IMF approved restrictions by its members on transactions with Rhodesia that were imposed pursuant to Security Council decisions under Chapter VII of the UN Charter. See Chapter 10, *infra*, page 416.

In 1951 the IMF's Board of Governors adopted a resolution stating that the Fund would have ''due regard'' for recommendations of the UN General Assembly for the maintenance or restoration of international peace and security, when the Assembly's recommendations are adopted pursuant to the ''Uniting for Peace'' resolution. Board of Governors Resolution No. 6-8, adopted September 13, 1951. IMF, *Summary Proceedings, 1951*, p. 56; *Selected Decisions* (10th issue, 1983), p. 338.

[25] UN–IMF Agreement, *supra* note 22, Article III.

[26] *Idem*, Article IV.

[27] *Idem*, Articles IV and V.

as recommendations of the IMF to the UN.[28] The recommendations of the UN to the IMF and of the IMF to the UN are not legally binding on the organization addressed. For example, the IMF in November 1982, in the lawful exercise of its authority, approved a stand-by arrangement for South Africa, notwithstanding a General Assembly resolution calling upon it not to do so.[29]

One of the functions of the UN Economic and Social Council (ECOSOC) is to "co-ordinate the activities of the specialized agencies through consultation with and recommendations to such agencies and through recommendations to the General Assembly and to the Members of the United Nations."[30] The ECOSOC normally meets twice a year, once during the winter in New York and once during the summer in Geneva. The Managing Director of the IMF usually addresses the meetings in New York. During the ECOSOC's sessions, its work is guided by a Sessional Coordinating Committee. Between sessions an inter-sessional Committee on Programs and Coordination meets. The ECOSOC's work comprehends an extraordinarily wide range of economic and social concerns. Among the many commissions of the ECOSOC, the regional economic commissions deserve special mention: Economic Commission for Europe (ECE), Economic Commission for Latin America (ECLA), Economic Commission for Africa (ECA), Economic and Social Commission for Asia and the Pacific (ESCAP), and Economic Commission for Western Asia (ECWA). These commissions have studied monetary matters and have been involved in the formation of regional monetary institutions such as the Asian Clearing Union and the clearing system of the Latin American Integration Association. The ECE has served as a forum for discussion of international monetary matters, as well as other economic matters, by representatives of the industrial democracies of Western Europe and the socialist states of Eastern Europe.

On the recommendation of the ECOSOC, the General Assembly convened a United Nations Conference on Trade and Development (UNCTAD) in Geneva in March 1964. Out of this conference and succeeding conferences has evolved an organization that is ultimately responsible to the General Assembly but has in fact assumed a degree of autonomy. Under General Assembly Resolution 1995 (XIX), adopted in 1964, the UNCTAD is to "review and facilitate the co-ordination of activities of other institutions within the United Nations system in the field of international trade and related problems of economic de-

---

[28] *Idem.*

[29] See Jonathan Kwitny, "Going Along: How IMF Overcame Political Issues to Vote a Loan to South Africa," *Wall Street Journal,* May 5, 1983, p. 1. See also *IMF Survey,* November 15, 1982, p. 362; UN General Assembly Resolution No. 37/2, Session XXXVII, adopted October 21, 1982; United Nations documents nos. A/37/474 and corr. 1 (October 4 and 29, 1982); UN Weekly Press Summary no. WS/1100 (November 5, 1982), pp. 3-4; and *Wall Street Journal,* November 4, 1982, p. 5. For documents on an earlier affair involving the World Bank, see *International Legal Materials,* vol. 6 (1967), pp. 150–87. See generally Joseph Gold, "Political Considerations are Prohibited by Articles of Agreement When the Fund Considers Requests for Use of Resources," *IMF Survey,* May 23, 1983, p. 146.

[30] UN Charter, Article 63.

velopment.''[31] The developing countries, called the ''Group of 77''[32] but now much expanded in number, have determined the agenda of the UNCTAD. This agenda, which has been given the name ''New International Economic Order,'' comprehends: (1) increasing financial assistance on concessional terms to developing countries, (2) rescheduling and forgiveness of external debts, (3) commodity agreements and their financing, (4) trade preferences for developing countries, and (5) control by developing countries of the development and use of their natural resources.[33]

Every United Nations member state participates in the UNCTAD and some other states do so as well. Each state has one vote. Decisions on substantive matters require a two-thirds majority; other decisions are made by a simple majority. A consensus procedure is used before controversial decisions are taken in an effort to reconcile the views of the participating states.[34] Between conferences, the UNCTAD functions through its Trade and Development Board. It also has specialized committees and working groups. The UNCTAD has a Secretary-General and a Secretariat headquartered in Geneva.

In the monetary field a subgroup of the Group of 77, called the ''Intergovernmental Group of 24 on International Monetary Affairs,'' has acted as a spokesman for developing countries in the IMF and in other forums. The Group of 24 is independent of the UN and of the UNCTAD but receives secretariat services from the UNCTAD Secretariat in formulating and supporting its positions.[35]

In May 1974 the United Nations General Assembly adopted a Declaration on the Establishment of a New International Economic Order[36] and a Programme of Action on the Establishment of a New International Economic Order.[37] The statements in the two resolutions were not agreed principles, but

[31] Paragraph 3(d) of UN General Assembly Resolution 1995, Session XIX, adopted December 30, 1964.

[32] The name ''Group of 77'' is derived from the fact that 77 countries, self-styled ''developing countries,'' issued a joint declaration at the conclusion of the 1964 UNCTAD Conference. See *Yearbook of the United Nations, 1964*, pp. 205–06. Subsequently other countries have joined the group. See also UNCTAD, *The Declaration and Principles of the Action Programme of Lima* (UN document no. TD/143; November 12, 1971); and Karl P. Sauvant, *The Group of 77: Evolution, Structure, Organization* (Dobbs Ferry: Oceana Publications, 1981).

[33] See page 75, *infra.* On UNCTAD see generally Ernst-Ulrich Petersmann, ''International Governmental Trade Organizations—GATT and UNCTAD,'' in *International Encyclopedia of Comparative Law* (Tubingen: J.C.B. Mohr [Paul Siebeck]; Alphen aan den Rijn: Sijthoff & Noordhoff, 1981), vol. 17, chapter 25; and Autar Krishan Koul, *The Legal Framework of UNCTAD in International Trade* (Leyden: A. W. Sijthoff; Bombay: N. M. Tripathi, 1977). See also the articles collected in the symposium, ''The New International Economic Order: Development or Dependence?'' *St. Louis University Public Law Forum*, vol. 3A (1984).

[34] See UN General Assembly Resolution 1995 (XIX), *supra* note 31, paragraph 25. See also Koul, *supra* note 33, pp. 49–62.

[35] See pages 74–76, *infra.*

[36] UN General Assembly Resolution No. 3201, Special Session VI, adopted May 1, 1974.

[37] UN General Assembly Resolution No. 3202, Special Session VI, adopted May 1, 1974. See also General Assembly Resolution No. 3281, Session XXIX, adopted December 12, 1974, entitled ''Charter of Economic Rights and Duties of States''; General Assembly Resolution No. 3362, Special Session VII, adopted September 16, 1975, entitled ''Development and International Economic Co-operation''; and General As-

rather demands of those UN members that had styled themselves "developing countries"[38] The principal demands stated in the two resolutions that bear on international monetary matters are noted later in this chapter.[39]

The principal representatives of member states in UN bodies, including the UNCTAD, usually come from foreign ministries. This contrasts with the membership of the Board of Governors, Interim Committee, and Executive Board of the IMF, which is drawn primarily from finance ministries and, to a lesser extent, central banks. While generalizations are always subject to qualification, a difference in outlook can be detected. Finance ministry and central bank officials tend to prefer practical actions that deal with economic problems for which they have direct responsibility. Representatives of foreign ministries, lacking operational responsibilities, tend to be somewhat more concerned with public image and political relationships.

The United Nations and its subordinate bodies such as the ECOSOC and the UNCTAD are mentioned only rarely in this book. In the monetary field UN bodies have influenced decisions in other organizations but have seldom assumed operational responsibilities. Where they have had an especially significant influence, such as in the development of the IMF's Facility for Compensatory Financing of Export Fluctuations, this is noted.[40] UN bodies have by and large respected the primacy of jurisdiction of the IMF in international monetary matters.

Bank for International Settlements

Historical Background. The Bank for International Settlements (BIS) was established in Basle, Switzerland, in 1930 as an institution "to promote the co-operation of central banks and to provide additional facilities for international financial operations; and to act as trustee or agent in regard to international financial settlements entrusted to it under agreements with the parties con-

---

sembly Resolution No. A/RES/35/56, Session XXXV, adopted December 5, 1980, entitled "International Development Strategy for the Third United Nations Development Decade."

[38] See statements made in the General Assembly on May 1, 1974, collected in *International Legal Materials*, vol. 13 (1974), pp. 744–66, especially the statement of the U.S. Permanent Representative at p. 745. See also the study prepared by Wil D. Verwey for the United Nations Institute for Training and Research, *Progressive Development of the Principles and Norms of International Law Relating to the New International Economic Order: Analytical Papers and Analysis of Texts of Relevant Instruments* (United Nations document no. UNITAR/DS/5; August 15, 1982).

The principal criterion of whether a country is a "developing country" for purposes of membership in the Group of 77 is whether it claims that status. A number of members of the group have very high per-capita incomes.

[39] At pages 74–76, *infra*. See generally Richard W. Edwards, Jr., "Responses of the International Monetary Fund and the World Bank to the Call for a 'New International Economic Order': Separating Substance from Rhetoric," *St. Louis University Public Law Forum*, vol. 3A (1984), p. 89.

[40] See Chapter 6, *infra*, page 278.

cerned.''[41] The BIS is a unique institution. Many of its operations are of types normally performed by a commercial bank, but it is owned principally by central banks, is managed by central banks, and its principal customers are central banks. The constitutional documents of the Bank consist of:

(1) Convention Concerning the Bank for International Settlements between Switzerland and Belgium, France, Germany, Italy, Japan, and the United Kingdom, signed at the Hague, January 20, 1930, entered into force February 26, 1930.[42]

(2) Constituent Charter of the Bank for International Settlements, annexed to the Convention above, as amended.[43]

(3) Statutes of the Bank for International Settlements, annexed to the Constituent Charter above, as amended.[44]

While at the 1944 Bretton Woods Conference it was thought that the BIS could be dissolved after the International Monetary Fund was formed,[45] it was

---

[41] Statutes of the Bank for International Settlements, *infra* note 44, Article 3.

The organization and work of the Bank for International Settlements are surveyed in *The Bank for International Settlements and the Basle Meetings* (Basle: BIS, 1980) [hereinafter *BIS 1930–80*]; and Robert Pierot, *La Banque des Règlements Internationaux* (Paris: La Documentation Française, 1973). Other general treatments include Henry H. Schloss, ''The Bank for International Settlements,'' in New York University Graduate School of Business Administration, Institute of Finance, *The Bulletin,* nos. 65–66 (September 1970), p.l; Henry H. Schloss, *The Bank for International Settlements* (Amsterdam: North-Holland Publishing Co., 1958); and Roger Auboin, *The Bank for International Settlements, 1930–1955* (Essays in International Finance no. 22; Princeton: Princeton University International Finance Section, 1955). The essay by Mr. Auboin is reprinted as an appendix to Bank for International Settlements, *25th Annual Report—1st April 1954—31st March 1955* (Basle, 1955)[hereinafter BIS, *25th Annual Report 1954/55*]. See also BIS, *The Bank for International Settlements: A Profile of an International Institution* (Basle, September 1980).

[42] The Convention is reproduced in Appendix C of this book at page 762. It also appears in *League of Nations Treaty Series*, vol. 104, p. 441; reprinted with notes in Manley O. Hudson (ed.), *International Legislation* (9 vols.; Washington: Carnegie Endowment for International Peace, 1931–50), vol. 5, p. 307. The Government of Switzerland on December 26, 1952, announced that Japan had renounced all rights, titles, and interests acquired under the Convention.

[43] The Constituent Charter is reproduced in Appendix C of this book at page 763. The original text appears in *League of Nations Treaty Series,* vol. 104, p. 444; Hudson, *supra* note 42, vol. 5, p. 310. References in the Constituent Charter to the Statutes were amended December 10, 1969, to take into account the renumbering of the articles of the Statutes, but no other changes have been made. The text in Appendix C includes the amendments.

[44] The Statutes are reproduced in Appendix C of this book at page 765. The original text of the Statutes appears in *League of Nations Treaty Series,* vol. 104, p. 448; Hudson, *supra* note 42, vol. 5, p. 314. The Statutes have been amended on six occasions, most recently July 8, 1975. The text in Appendix C includes the amendments.

[45] Resolution V of the Bretton Woods Conference recommended that the BIS be dissolved. *Proceedings and Documents of the United Nations Monetary and Financial Conference, Bretton Woods, New Hampshire, July 1–22, 1944* (2 vols.; Washington: U.S. Government Printing Office, 1948), vol. 1, p. 939. The resolution was based on an assumption that the Bank had been subservient to the interests of Germany during World War II. It was also thought that the clearing of claims among central banks would take place through the International Monetary Fund. See Armand Van Dormael, *Bretton Woods: Birth of a Monetary System* (London:

not dissolved and today is a major institution of international monetary collaboration. In 1977 it occupied a new headquarters building in Basle and currently has a staff of about 300 persons. Given the volume and range of the Bank's activities, its staff has always been small.[46]

Structure and Functions. The Bank uses a unique unit of account—the "gold franc"—in its financial statements.[47] The accounting for national currencies in this unit is explained in a footnote.[48]

The authorized capital of the BIS is 1,500 million "gold francs."[49] Approximately 85 percent of the shares that have been issued are held by central banks and 15 percent of the shares are in private hands. Private holders have no voting rights, all voting rights being vested in the central bank or other designated financial institution of each country in which shares have been issued.[50] The central banks of 28 countries are shareholders in the Bank. These include all of the members of the Group of Ten (except the United States), a number of Eastern European countries, and a number of other countries.[51] While representatives of the U. S. Federal Reserve System participate in meetings and committees under the auspices of the BIS, the Federal Reserve is not a shareholder. The shares of the American issue were not subscribed by the Federal

Macmillan, 1978), pp. 203–06; and Erin E. Jacobsson, *A Life for Sound Money: Per Jacobsson, His Biography* (Oxford: Oxford University Press, 1979), pp. 186–92.

[46] See Richard F. Janssen, "Thriving on Trouble, Settlements Bank Sees Its Influence Growing," *Wall Street Journal,* October 10, 1980, p. 1.

[47] Statutes, Article 4.

[48] The original version of the Statutes referred to the "Swiss gold franc" at a time when the Swiss national currency was valued at 0.29032250 gram of fine gold. The gold value of the BIS unit was retained when the Swiss franc's gold value was suspended in 1936. After a new valuation of the Swiss franc by the Swiss monetary authorities in 1953, the BIS dropped the "Swiss" designation and simply referred to its unit of account, which continued to have the same gold value as previously, as the "gold franc."

In June 1979 the BIS decided that after June 30, 1979, assets and liabilities in currencies would be converted into the Bank's gold franc unit of account at the rate of 1 gold franc equals U.S. $1.94149. (This conversion rate, which has been used in subsequent financial statements, was based on the average market price of gold [U.S. $208 an ounce] during the Bank's 1978–79 financial year.) Other currencies are valued in terms of gold francs on the basis of market rates of the currencies against the U.S. dollar. Assets and liabilities directly involving physical amounts of gold are valued in gold francs on the basis of physical weight at 1 gold franc equals 0.29032258 gram. It should be emphasized, however, that the BIS employs the gold franc solely for balance-sheet purposes. It does not use it in the course of its day-to-day business. See *BIS 1930–80, supra* note 41, pp. 41–43; and BIS, *50th Annual Report 1979/80,* p. 159. See also Henri Guisan, "La Banque des Règlements Internationaux et les Unités de Compte," in Jean-Louis Guglielmi and Marie Lavigne (ed.), *Unités et Monnaies de Compte* (Paris: Economica, 1978), p. 13; and Henri Guisan, "Nature et Objet de l'Unité de Compte de la Banque des Règlements Internationaux," *Revue Internationale d'Histoire de la Banque,* vol. 20–21 (1980), p. 136.

[49] Statutes, Article 4.

[50] Statutes, Article 14.

[51] Central banks of the following countries hold shares in the BIS and send representatives to the Bank's annual meeting: Australia, Austria, Belgium, Bulgaria, Canada, Czechoslovakia, Denmark, Finland, France, Federal Republic of Germany, Greece, Hungary, Iceland, Ireland, Italy, Japan, Netherlands, Norway, Poland, Portugal, Romania, South Africa, Spain, Sweden, Switzerland, Turkey, United Kingdom, and Yugoslavia.

Reserve but, instead, by an American banking group that offered them on the market.[52] The central banks of Belgium, France, Federal Republic of Germany, Italy, and the United Kingdom hold over 50 percent of the votes.[53]

In June of each year, representatives of the shareholder central banks and other financial institutions entitled to vote meet in what is known as the General Meeting. Certain powers are reserved to the General Meeting. These powers include the approval of the annual report, approval of the auditor's report, election of the auditor for the ensuing year, appropriations to the reserve and special funds, declaration of dividends, fixing the remuneration and allowances for members of the Board of Directors, discharge of the Board from personal responsibility, and extraordinary matters including amendment of the Statutes, increase or decrease in the capital of the Bank, and liquidation of the Bank.[54]

With the exception of the powers reserved to the General Meeting, the policies of the Bank are determined by the Board of Directors. The Board also oversees the Bank's operations. It normally meets at least ten times a year.[55] For many years the Board of Directors has been composed of thirteen members. The governors of the central banks of Belgium, France, Federal Republic of Germany, Italy, and the United Kingdom serve as directors *ex officio*. The central bank of a sixth country—the United States—is entitled to have its governor serve *ex officio* but has chosen not to be represented on the Board. Each of the *ex officio* directors (currently five) appoints an additional director of his nationality who represents finance, industry, or commerce. The Board has authority to elect up to nine additional directors from among governors of central banks of countries in which BIS shares have been subscribed, and has for many years in fact elected the governors of the central banks of the Netherlands, Sweden, and Switzerland.[56]

The functions of the Chairman of the Board of Directors and the President of the Bank have for many years been performed by the same person. The President, elected by the Board, is responsible for carrying out the policies decided upon by the Board and controls the administration of the Bank. The General

---

[52] The Federal Reserve System of the United States has chosen not to be a shareholder in the BIS and not to exercise the voting rights of shares issued in the American market. Citibank of New York has been designated by the Board of the BIS to exercise the voting rights of these shares pursuant to Article 12 of the Statutes. Transfers of all BIS shares are subject to restrictions.

[53] Statutes, Articles 4–16. Article 8 of the Statutes provides that if the authorized capital of the BIS is increased, the central banks of Belgium, England, France, Germany, Italy, and the United States (or some other financial institution of the United States acceptable to these central banks) shall be entitled to subscribe in equal proportions to at least 55 percent of the additional shares. Shares are otherwise to be distributed with a view to associating with the BIS the largest possible number of central banks that make substantial contributions to international monetary cooperation and to the Bank's activities.

[54] Statutes, Articles 44–47.

[55] Statutes, Articles 26–43. See *BIS 1930–80, supra* note 41, pp. 106–07; and Pierot, *supra* note 41, pp. 18–19.

[56] Article 27 of the Statutes sets forth the rules for composition of the Board of Directors. The names of directors are listed in each *Annual Report*.

Manager, appointed by the Board, is normally the senior executive of the BIS resident in Basle. He is responsible to the President and is the chief of the operating staff. The Assistant General Manager, the Heads of Departments, and Managers are also appointed by the Board.[57] While competence and capacity are the first concerns, nationality is given some weight in making these elections and appointments.

The BIS is fundamentally a bank for central banks and performs banking functions for them. Shareholder central banks and other banks hold current and time deposits with the BIS and clear claims against other central banks through the BIS. The Bank makes advances to central banks. It purchases and sells gold, foreign exchange, and negotiable securities, and, in general, engages in a wide range of banking transactions and operations for its own account or as agent or correspondent of central banks.[58] While the Bank regularly makes a profit, the profit motive is secondary to serving the collective interest of the shareholder central banks.

Most central bank currency deposits with the BIS are placed with it at sight or with very-short-term maturities, rarely over twelve months. Deposits are primarily in U.S. dollars, although the Bank also receives substantial deposits in Deutsche mark, Swiss francs, and other currencies. The advantages for central banks in placing deposits with the BIS include the flexibility of the facilities, the high credit-standing of the Bank, and the maintenance of anonymity when the Bank is used as intermediary in making deposits and withdrawals with commercial banks, many of the transactions being in the Eurocurrency markets. It is not unusual for central bank deposits with the BIS to amount to ten percent of world currency reserves. The BIS also accepts deposits from non-shareholder central banks, commercial banks, and international institutions.[59]

The BIS engages in currency exchange operations for central banks that wish to rely on the Bank's expertise. It frequently acts as agent for central banks that plan to intervene in the exchange markets while maintaining anonymity or to intervene at times outside their own business hours. The Bank also participates in currency exchange operations on its own behalf. It is an active participant in Eurocurrency markets and gold markets.[60]

The Bank is forbidden to open current accounts in the name of "governments" or to make advances to "governments" as distinguished from central banks.[61] Most of the operations the BIS is authorized to carry out with central banks it can, with the agreement of the central bank involved, carry out with

---

[57] Statutes, Articles 38 and 40. The organization of the staff of the BIS is described in *BIS 1930–80, supra* note 41, pp. 106–09.

[58] The powers of the BIS are set forth in Articles 19–25 of the Statutes. A summary of the operations of the Banking Department appears in each *Annual Report* together with a balance sheet showing the assets and liabilities of the bank.

[59] *BIS 1930–80, supra* note 41, pp. 34–35.

[60] *BIS 1930–80, supra* note 41, pp. 36–37.

[61] Statutes, Article 24.

other official entities, commercial banks, and private entities in a country.[62] The BIS is forbidden to issue notes payable at sight to bearer—e.g., a paper currency such as a central bank can issue. There are certain other activities that are forbidden to it.[63] By decision of the International Monetary Fund, the BIS is permitted to hold and use IMF special drawing rights.[64]

The Bank may enter into special agreements with central banks to facilitate the settlement of international transactions between them.[65] It was the trustee for bonds issued by the governments of Germany and Austria in 1930 on several markets.[66] It managed technical features of the European Payments Union in operation during the 1950s.[67] It assumed responsibilities under central bank arrangements in 1968 and 1977 concerning sterling balances.[68] It is the depositary for pledged collateral backing bonds issued between 1954 and 1961 by the European Coal and Steel Community.[69]

The Bank acts as agent for the European Monetary Cooperation Fund (FECOM), an organ of the European Economic Community, and maintains the accounts for the FECOM including the FECOM's accounts relating to short-term financing of interventions in the European Monetary System.[70] The Bank also acts as agent for the FECOM in the administration of borrowing and lending operations of the European Economic Community pursuant to decisions of the Council of the European Communities.[71]

The Bank has on several occasions granted, with the support of a number of central banks, large-scale short-term support in favor of central banks of countries in serious balance-of-payments difficulties. Financial resources may be provided while the countries work out stand-by or extended arrangements with the International Monetary Fund. The beneficiary central banks may or

---

[62] Statutes, Article 22.

[63] Statutes, Article 24.

[64] IMF E.B. Decision No. 6484 -(80/77)S (April 18, 1980); *Selected Decisions* (10th issue, 1983), p. 274. See also IMF, Board of Governors Resolution No. 29-1, effective January 21, 1974; IMF *Summary Proceedings, 1974*, p. 355; *Selected Decisions*, p. 339. See generally Chapter 5, *infra*, page 175.

[65] Statutes, Article 23.

[66] See, e.g., Articles III and IX of the Agreement in Regard to the German Government International 5-½% Loan 1930 (Young Loan), signed at Paris June 10, 1930; *League of Nations Treaty Series*, vol. 112, p. 237; Hudson, *supra* note 42, vol. 5, p. 569. For background see *BIS 1930–80, supra* note 41, pp. 82–85.

Issues concerning currency valuations under the Young Loan were arbitrated. See award of May 16, 1980, in the case of *Belgium, France, Switzerland, U.K., and U.S. v. Federal Republic of Germany; International Legal Materials*, vol. 19 (1980), p. 1357; *International Law Reports*, vol. 59, p. 494. The bonds were redeemed later in 1980. BIS, *50th Annual Report 1979/80*, pp. 168–70.

[67] See Chapter 7, *infra*, pages 300–302.

[68] See Chapter 3, *infra*, pages 104–108.

[69] Act of Pledge dated November 28, 1954; *United Nations Treaty Series*, vol. 238, p. 340 at p. 348. Only the 15th series maturing in 1986 remains to be redeemed. See *BIS, 1930–80, supra* note 41, pp. 71–72; and BIS, *52d Annual Report 1981/82*, p. 179.

[70] The European Monetary Cooperation Fund is introduced at page 84, *infra*. The financing facilities operated by the FECOM are treated in Chapter 8. The Bank's roles are described in the *Annual Reports* of the BIS.

[71] See Chapter 8, *infra*, pages 339–341.

may not be shareholders in the BIS. These so-called "bridge loans" can be arranged with great speed. The support is usually for six months or less and is normally not accompanied by economic policy conditions.[72]

The BIS, under an agreement with the International Monetary Fund, in 1981 opened a facility for the benefit of the IMF. The IMF may borrow on the facility to supplement its resources.[73]

The Statutes of the BIS require that financial operations of the Bank for its own account "shall only be carried out in currencies which in the opinion of the Board satisfy the practical requirements of the gold or gold exchange standard."[74] This provision, as it is understood in current practice, does not require that the currency be convertible into gold at a fixed price, it being sufficient that the currency is readily convertible into other currencies. The Bank in its operations attempts to minimize exchange risks. The Statutes of the Bank state that the Bank "shall be administered with particular regard to maintaining its liquidity, and for this purpose shall retain assets appropriate to the maturity and character of its liabilities" and further provide that "the proportion of the Bank's assets held in any given currency shall be determined by the Board with due regard to the liabilities of the Bank."[75]

The Statutes of the BIS draw a sharp distinction between central banks and governments. Central banks are shareholders of the BIS and hold accounts with it. The Bank, as noted earlier, is forbidden by its Statutes from making advances to "governments" or opening current accounts in the name of "governments."[76] A finance minister or other government official, unless also a central bank governor, is prohibited from serving on the Board of Directors.[77]

The Bank in all of its operations is required to act in conformity with the monetary policies of the central banks of the countries concerned. The Bank's

---

[72] In the financial year ended March 1983 alone, the following arrangements were made under the auspices of the BIS for assistance to the central banks of countries that encountered difficulties: $925 million arrangement for Mexico, $1.45 billion for Brazil, $500 million for Argentina, $510 million for Hungary, and $500 million for Yugoslavia. See BIS, *53d Annual Report 1982/83*, pp. 126–29 and 164–66. See also *Wall Street Journal*, December 13, 1982, p. 3; December 15, 1982, p. 35; December 20, 1982, p. 6; and December 24, 1982, p. 2.

BIS financial arrangements can take the form of loans or swaps. In a swap arrangement, the BIS sells a needed currency to the central bank of the country in difficulty in exchange for the country's own currency, gold, or other financial assets, with the arrangement calling for the parties to reverse the transaction at an agreed maturity. See generally Chapter 4, *infra*, page 135 et seq. especially pages 157 and 164–166.

[73] The agreement entered into force June 1, 1981. Drawings by the IMF on the facility are denominated in SDRs with U.S. dollars at the Federal Reserve Bank of New York being the currency to be provided by the BIS unless the IMF and BIS agree on another currency. The text of the agreement appears as the annex to IMF E.B. Decision No. 6863 -(81/81)(May 13, 1981), as amended; *Selected Decisions* (10th issue, 1983), p. 204. Borrowing agreements of the IMF, used to replenish its resources, are explained in Chapter 6, *infra*, page 283 et seq.

[74] Statutes, Article 20.

[75] Statutes, Article 25.

[76] Statutes, Article 24. The Bank may, however, place funds in treasury bills or other marketable short-term government securities. Article 21(e).

[77] Statutes, Article 30.

normal practice is to give a central bank an opportunity to object to a proposed operation in its currency or on markets in its country. The Bank can assume that an operation requested by a central bank is in accordance with that bank's monetary policy. If the Board approves a proposed operation and a governor of a central bank is present and does not vote against the operation, the operation is deemed to be consistent with that central bank's policy.[78] The Bank's financial operations are conducted on a confidential basis that protects Bank–client relationships. Details of transactions, whether they are conducted for the BIS's own account or as agent or correspondent for central banks, are usually not reported.[79] The *Annual Report* of the BIS provides only the most general information on the Bank's own operations.

In addition to performing financial operations, the BIS engages in research, both general research on monetary matters and research requested by central bank clients. The Bank's *Annual Report,* usually issued in June, is widely read for the information and insights it provides. The report, which expresses the views of management (not the Board of Directors), includes comments on economic developments in various countries, international trade and payments, and the international credit and capital markets. It also includes world-wide estimates of Eurocurrency deposits. The BIS prepares special studies for its member central banks and for other bodies such as the OECD.

The Bank is a very important forum for multilateral consultations on monetary matters. The meeting of the Board of Directors (ten times a year) is used as an occasion for consultations among the governors of the central banks of the Group of Ten plus Switzerland. Representatives of the central banks of the United States, Canada, and Japan (and sometimes other countries) come to Basle at that time and join the governors (or their deputies) of the eight central banks represented on the BIS Board for wide-ranging confidential discussions of monetary developments. These meetings, their subject matter, and the deceptively informal procedures by which they are conducted are treated in the concluding chapter of this book.[80] In addition to these "tour d'horizon" discussions, bilateral, small group, and committee meetings may be held in Basle. Some of these meetings deal with operations of the BIS and others with matters with which the BIS is not directly involved. For example, national authorities responsible for supervision of commercial banks meet under the Bank's auspices to consider issues in the supervision of banks engaged in the Eurocurrency markets.[81]

Representatives of the BIS regularly attend all meetings of the Group of Ten and participate in meetings of Working Party No. 3 of the OECD's Eco-

---

[78] See Statutes, Article 19.

[79] A central bank can draw on the BIS without the transaction's being publicly disclosed by the BIS. By contrast, the IMF publishes information on each member country's use of IMF resources.

[80] At pages 585–589, *infra.*

[81] See Chapter 12, *infra,* pages 620–624.

nomic Policy Committee.[82] The General Manager and Economic Counsellor of the BIS attend meetings of the IMF's Interim Committee on the International Monetary System.[83] The BIS provides staff support for meetings of the Committee of Governors of the Central Banks of the EEC member states and for the meetings of the Board of Governors of the European Monetary Cooperation Fund (FECOM).[84]

Legal Personality. The nature of the legal personality of the BIS in national and international law was commented upon in legal journals at the time the Bank was formed.[85] The Bank is a complex institution that performs activities of the types engaged in by international organizations, central banks, and commercial banks. The Constituent Charter and Statutes of the Bank were drafted at an international conference, and Switzerland's acts in granting and sanctioning them were carried out at the direction of an international Convention. That Convention, clearly governed by public international law, was concluded between Switzerland and Belgium, France, Italy, Japan, and the United Kingdom and entered into force at the same time as the Statutes of the BIS in 1930.[86] Switzerland's authority over the Bank is severely limited. The Convention obligates Switzerland not to abrogate or amend the Constituent Charter or to sanction amendment of the Statutes of the BIS except in accordance with their terms unless this is done in agreement with the other signatory governments. While some amendments to the Statutes require governmental approval, other amendments can be made without the agreement of Switzerland.[87]

The Bank enjoys in Switzerland most of the privileges and immunities accorded to public international organizations. The salaries of non-Swiss personnel are exempt from taxation in Switzerland.[88] The Bank's assets, reserves, and profits are exempt from taxation in Switzerland.[89] The assets of the Bank and all deposits and funds entrusted to it are immune at all times from expropriation and seizure.[90] Gold exports and imports and currency transfers by the Bank are not to be restricted even in time of war.[91] Further, the Constituent Charter states that the Statutes of the BIS and any amendments made to them in accordance

---

[82] See pages 71 and 582–585.

[83] See Chapter 1, *supra*, pages 126–128. The General Manager and Economic Counsellor also attended meetings of the IMF's Committee of Twenty during the period of its work. See pages 9–10.

[84] See pages 83–86, *infra*.

[85] See Sir John Fisher Williams, "The Legal Character of the Bank for International Settlements," *American Journal of International Law*, vol. 24 (1930), p. 665; and Louis Trotabas, "La Banque des Règlements Internationaux," *Revue de Droit International et de Legislation Comparée*, vol. 12 (1931), p. 61. For recent analyses, see *BIS 1930–80, supra* note 41, pp. 94–104; and Pierot, *supra* note 41, pp. 21–24.

[86] Convention, *supra* note 42. See also Williams, *supra* note 84, pp. 670–72.

[87] Convention, Article 1; and Constituent Charter, preamble and paragraphs 3–5.

[88] Constituent Charter, paragraphs 6(e) and 8.

[89] Constituent Charter, paragraphs 6–9.

[90] Constituent Charter, paragraph 10.

[91] Constituent Charter, paragraph 10.

with the Constituent Charter "shall be valid and operative notwithstanding any inconsistency therewith in the provisions of any present or future Swiss law."[92] Thus, the Bank in performing the activities authorized in its Statutes is not required to conform to Swiss laws and regulations applicable to commercial banks governing nonresident accounts, reserves, discount rates, and other matters.[93] Other countries have also accorded the Bank immunities similar to those enjoyed by other international financial organizations.[94]

The BIS has the capacity to conclude agreements that are governed by public international law. A number of agreements to which the BIS is a party (not merely an entity mentioned in a treaty) have been published in treaty series.[95] We previously noted that actions of the Bank authorized by its Statutes (and the Statutes grant a wide range of powers) are immune from challenge on the basis that they violate Swiss law. While the matter may potentially be subject to some dispute, the better view appears to be that when the BIS assumes the role of depositary or agent under an agreement with central banks, international law rather than national law should be presumed to measure the nature and extent of the Bank's rights and obligations.[96]

---

[92] Constituent Charter, paragraph 5.

[93] The Swiss Banking Law of 1934 is not applicable to the BIS. See *BIS 1930–80, supra* note 41, p. 102; and Pierot, *supra* note 41, p. 22. However, operations in Swiss francs are conducted with the concurrence of the Swiss National Bank just as BIS operations in any currency of a shareholder bank must be done with the concurrence of the issuer. See text accompanying note 78, *supra*.

[94] See Article 10 of the Agreement Concerning the Complete and Final Settlement of the Question of Reparations [implementing Young Plan], signed by Germany, Belgium, France, Great Britain, Italy, and Japan at the Hague January 20, 1930, entered into force May 17, 1930; *League of Nations Treaty Series*, vol. 104, p. 243; Hudson, *supra* note 42, vol. 5, p. 135. See also Protocol Concerning the Immunities of the Bank for International Settlements, opened for signature July 30, 1936; *League of Nations Treaty Series*, vol. 197, p. 31; Hudson, *supra*, vol. 7, p. 404; and comment of Manley O. Hudson, "Immunities of the Bank for International Settlements," *American Journal of International Law*, vol. 32 (1938), p. 128.

During the period prior to August 15, 1971, when the United States sold gold to foreign monetary authorities at prices based on $35 an ounce, gold was sold to the BIS for its own account on the same terms as to national monetary authorities.

[95] Agreements concluded since World War II to which the BIS is a party that clearly are governed by public international law include:

Agreement between the BIS and France, the United Kingdom, and the United States on the return of gold looted by Germany during World War II, signed May 13, 1948; *United States Statutes at Large*, vol. 62, p. 2672; *United Nations Treaty Series*, vol. 140, p. 187.

Separate agreement between the BIS and the Federal Republic of Germany, signed January 9, 1953, which is sub-annex A to Annex I of the Agreement on German External Debts, signed at London February 27, 1953; *United States Treaties and Other International Agreements*, vol. 4, p. 443 at p. 530; *United Nations Treaty Series*, vol. 333, p. 3 at p. 114.

Agreement between the BIS and the Federal Republic of Germany on settlement of financial questions concerning the 1930 Young Plan, signed November 29, 1965, ratified by German Federal Parliament April 1966, entered into force May 14, 1966; *Bundesanzeiger*, 1966, no. 209.

Agreement between the BIS and the International Monetary Fund entered into force June 1, 1981, *supra* note 73.

[96] A case decided by the Swiss Federal Tribunal in 1936 used Swiss law to determine the scope of the Bank's duties as trustee under the Young Loan. *Aktiebolaget Obligationinteressenter v. Bank for International Settlements* in *Arrêts du Tribunal Fédéral Suisse*, vol. 62, part 2 (1936), p. 140. The case might well be decided differently today given the subsequent history of the Bank's operations and responsibilities. The

The capacity to conclude agreements governed by public international law does not prevent the Bank from making agreements in contemplation of a national legal system. When the Bank engages in currency transactions in the market with commercial banks and other private entities, it accepts the same obligations and market conventions as others who participate in the market with respect to timely delivery of currency balances and other similar matters. This is not peculiar to the BIS. The same is true with respect to financial operations in the market engaged in by, for example, the International Bank for Reconstruction and Development.[97] Currency swap agreements between the BIS and central banks (and gold swap agreements) would appear to be governed by the same legal principles applicable to swap agreements between central banks, a subject treated later in this volume.[98] The legal character of understandings reached among central bankers in Basle consultations is also treated later.[99] The BIS, like many institutions that operate in the international arena, usually does not specify the governing law in agreements it concludes. Thus, whether a particular arrangement is governed by public international law or by a national rule is potentially open to dispute. Legal disputes between central banks are, however, rare as the continuous working relationships among central banks and the importance of maintaining mutual confidence provide strong incentives to settle differences on an amicable basis.

The Statutes of the BIS provide for the use of a special autonomous tribunal should disputes arise between the Bank, on the one side, and any central bank, financial institution, or other bank referred to in the Statutes, on the other side, or between the Bank and its shareholders, with regard to the interpretation or application of the Statutes of the Bank.[100] Other disputes can be heard by national courts or other tribunals.[101] In order to give confidence to creditors, the assets of the Bank are subject to measures of compulsory execution for enforcement of monetary claims. However, all deposits entrusted to the Bank, all claims against the Bank, and shares issued by the Bank are, without the prior agreement of the Bank, immune from seizure, sequestration, attachment, or compulsory execution within the meaning of Swiss law.[102] The BIS has worked

---

practical import of the 1936 precedent has been minimal, because the Bank since World War II has not used the word "trustee" in agreements it has concluded. It has instead used the words "depositary" or "agent" and used them in contexts that indicated that Swiss law was not being referenced to determine their meaning. It is submitted that the agency relationship between the BIS and the European Monetary Cooperation Fund is governed by international law rather than any national legal system.

[97] See generally Georges R. Delaume, *Transnational Contracts: Applicable Law and Settlement of Disputes* (5 vols.; Dobbs Ferry: Oceana Publications, binder service, 1983 ed.), vol. 1, sections 1.10–1.13 and 5.06.

[98] See Chapter 4, *infra,* pages 157–164.

[99] See Chapter 12, *infra,* pages 588–589.

[100] Statutes, Article 54. The Bank has never been a party to such an arbitral proceeding. There was an arbitration proceeding involving the Young Loan of which the BIS was trustee. See note 66, *supra.*

[101] Statutes, Article 55.

[102] Statutes, Article 55.

in both the public and private realms for over fifty years, and disputes have been few.

Comments. The Bank for International Settlements is mentioned from time to time throughout this book. It plays a very important role in international monetary affairs. It can carry out quickly and efficiently, and without publicity, operations for its central bank clients. It can act as a principal or agent in central bank transactions and in operations in the exchange markets. The Bank, further, is in a position to assist monetary cooperation between East and West. All of the central banks of Eastern European countries (except those of the Soviet Union, Albania, and the German Democratic Republic) are both shareholders in and active clients of the Bank. Representatives of central banks of Eastern Europe attend the annual General Meeting. Officers of the BIS regularly visit Eastern European central banks in the course of Bank business.

General Agreement on Tariffs and Trade

Overview. The General Agreement on Tariffs and Trade (GATT) regulates trade practices among some 90 countries.[103] It is an international agreement which combines a code of conduct on trade policies with a series of schedules regarding customs treatment which signatory states have agreed to accord designated products from other contracting parties. The GATT Agreement establishes procedures for negotiating reductions in trade barriers and for dealing with conflicting interests and adverse actions of contracting parties in the trade sphere. There are periodic comprehensive negotiations to reduce tariffs and other barriers to trade.[104]

---

[103] The General Agreement on Tariffs and Trade entered into force January 1, 1948, and is applied in accordance with the Protocol of Provisional Application and subsequent protocols by which other parties have acceded to the Agreement. The text of the GATT Agreement consists of a group of general articles and many volumes of detailed tariff schedules. The general articles were last amended effective June 27, 1966, although the schedules have been amended many times subsequently. The text of the general articles as amended appears in GATT, *Basic Instruments and Selected Documents* (Geneva: GATT), vol. IV (1969); reprinted in John H. Jackson, *World Trade and the Law of GATT* (Indianapolis: Bobbs-Merrill Co., 1969), p. 799. The text is accompanied by official interpretative notes.

Comprehensive book-length studies of the GATT from a legal perspective include Jackson, *idem;* Kenneth W. Dam, *The GATT: Law and International Economic Organization* (Chicago: University of Chicago Press, 1970); and Thiébaut Flory, *Le GATT: Droit International et Commerce Mondial* (Paris: Librairie Général de Droit et de Jurisprudence, R. Pichon & R. Durand-Auzias, 1968). Comprehensive articles include Petersmann, *supra* note 33; John H. Jackson, "The General Agreement on Tariffs and Trade," in Surrey and Wallace, *supra* note 1, part 1, p. 37; and Jock A. Finlayson and Mark W. Zacher, "The GATT and the Regulation of Trade Barriers: Regime Dynamics and Functions," *International Organization*, vol. 35 (1981), p. 561.

[104] Jan Kolasa, *Law-Making and Law-Enforcing for International Trade: Some Reflections on the GATT Experience* (Princeton: Princeton University Center of International Studies, 1976), pp. 1-19, provides a legal perspective on the negotiation of tariff concessions.

A basic principle of nondiscrimination finds expression in the General Agreement. With certain exceptions (applicable to developing countries, customs unions, and special situations), a tariff reduction on a product that is negotiated with one party is "bound" (cannot subsequently be raised unilaterally) and is generalized to all other parties pursuant to the most-favored-nation provisions stated in Articles I and II. Other provisions of the Agreement reinforce the commitment not to raise tariffs that have been bound and not to discriminate among GATT members. Specifically, they are designed to prevent the evasion of tariff obligations by the use of non-tariff barriers. Rules prescribe limits on the use of quotas,[105] subsidies,[106] and state trading enterprises.[107] Internal taxation and regulatory measures must be applied to imports in a manner that is at least as favorable as that applied to domestically produced goods.[108] Other provisions deal with customs administration including customs valuation, marks of origin, fees and formalities, and publication of regulations.[109]

Four instruments relating to the framework of international trade were adopted by consensus by the CONTRACTING PARTIES in November 1979. The instruments were adopted in the form of a "declaration," an "understanding," and "decisions" in order that all parties to the GATT would participate in them and so that parties would not have to submit them to national parliamentary bodies for review.[110] The four instruments are authoritative statements of shared understandings of the way in which the contracting parties intend to apply the General Agreement.[111]

---

[105] Articles XI–XIV.
[106] Article XVI.
[107] Article XVII.
[108] Article III.
[109] Articles VII–X.
[110] The following instruments were adopted November 28, 1979, effective that date:

Declaration on Trade Measures taken for Balance-of-Payments Purposes;

Understanding Regarding Notification, Consultation, Dispute Settlement and Surveillance;

Decision on Differential and More Favourable Treatment—Reciprocity and Fuller Participation of Developing Countries; and

Decision on Safeguard Action for Development Purposes.

For the texts, see GATT, *Basic Instruments and Selected Documents*, 26th supplement (1980), pp. 203–18.
[111] See Article 31, paragraph 3(b), of the Vienna Convention on the Law of Treaties relating to the interpretation of international agreements. The Vienna Convention is in force for those countries that have ratified or acceded to it. Many of the Convention's articles codify rules of general international law that bind states whether or not they are parties to the Convention. The text appears in *United Nations Conference on the Law of Treaties, First and Second Sessions, Vienna, 26 March–24 May 1968 and 9 April–22 May 1969: Official Records, Documents of the Conference* (United Nations document no. A/Conf. 39/11/add. 2; sales no. E.70.V.5; 1971), p. 287. See generally Ian Sinclair, *The Vienna Convention on the Law of Treaties* (2d ed.; Manchester, England: Manchester University Press, 1984).

Some instruments that modify obligations under the General Agreement have been concluded as separate agreements binding only the parties that have consented to them. A number of such agreements negotiated in the "Tokyo Round" of trade negotiations entered into force in 1980 and 1981.[112]

One of the effects of the GATT Agreement and related agreements and declarations is that a country that liberalizes its exchange controls at the urging of the IMF cannot easily substitute trade controls in their place if it is a member of the GATT, nor can it frustrate trade liberalization achieved through reduction of tariffs and quotas by substituting currency restrictions in their place.[113] Article XV of the GATT Agreement calls for coordination between the CONTRACTING PARTIES (the GATT organization) and the Fund and *inter alia* makes clear that the CONTRACTING PARTIES "shall seek cooperation with the International Monetary Fund to the end that the CONTRACTING PARTIES and the Fund may pursue a co-ordinated policy with regard to exchange questions within the jurisdiction of the Fund and questions of quantitative restrictions and other trade measures within the jurisdiction of the CONTRACTING PARTIES."[114] For members of the GATT that belong to the IMF, the IMF is the body that regulates currency exchange restrictions. At the present time Cuba, Czechoslovakia, Poland, and Switzerland belong to the GATT but not to the IMF. The GATT has jurisdiction over currency restrictions of these states to the extent that they frustrate the trade objectives of the GATT.[115]

The general obligations of the GATT Agreement in the field of trade are subject to an assortment of exceptions and escape clauses.[116] Among these are provisions that permit the imposition of quantitative restrictions on imports by countries facing balance-of-payments problems.[117] The practice of the GATT is to seek and to accept the IMF's judgment on the validity of the balance-of-payments reasons advanced by a country to support the imposition or maintenance of trade restrictions. The relationship between IMF and GATT bodies, the working of the detailed provisions of the GATT Agreement which bear on quantitative restrictions for payments purposes, and the GATT Declaration on

---

[112] The agreements, opened for signature at Geneva, April 12, 1979, and now in force, are collected in GATT, *Basic Instruments and Selected Documents*, 26th supplement (1980), pp. 3–188. For background see GATT, *The Tokyo Round of Multilateral Trade Negotiations* (Geneva: GATT, 1979); John H. Jackson, *MTN and the Legal Institutions of International Trade, Report for Subcommittee on International Trade, Committee on Finance, United States Senate*, 96th Congress, 1st Session (1979)(Committee Print No. 96-14); and note, "GATT: A Legal Guide to the Tokyo Round," *Journal of World Trade Law*, vol. 13 (1979), p. 436.

[113] GATT Article XV. From an economic point of view, trade controls and exchange controls are interchangeable instruments. See Chapter 10, *infra*, pages 428–429.

[114] Article XV, paragraph 1.

[115] See Chapter 10, *infra*, pages 439–440.

[116] See, e.g., Articles VI, XVIII–XXI, XXIV, XXVIII, and XXXVI–XXXVIII.

[117] GATT Articles XII–XV and section B of Article XVIII.

Trade Measures taken for Balance-of-Payments Purposes[118] are examined in Chapter 10 of this book.[119]

In addition to specific exceptions and safeguards, the GATT Agreement includes an all-encompassing waiver provision. The CONTRACTING PARTIES (capital letters indicating the signatory parties acting jointly) can waive any GATT obligation, in exceptional circumstances not otherwise provided for, by a decision taken by two-thirds of the votes cast with a majority exceeding one-half of the contracting parties (each member having one vote).[120] The use of the waiver authority where trade measures otherwise prohibited are taken to protect the balance of payments is treated later in this book. GATT's practice with respect to import deposit requirements and customs surcharges is also examined at that time.[121] The GATT's concern with trade restrictions (whether in the form of tariffs, quotas, or other barriers) that are maintained for reasons other than balance-of-payments protection is beyond the scope of this book.

Organizational Structure.   The GATT Agreement was not drafted as a constitution of an international organization. Indeed, because of objections to the creation of an International Trade Organization expressed by U.S. congressmen and senators, the GATT Agreement was presented in 1947 as a body of rules to be administered by the contracting parties themselves or which could be adapted to administration by an organization if later separately created. The expedient was chosen of vesting in the CONTRACTING PARTIES (capital letters indicating the signatory parties acting jointly) those powers that would normally be granted to an organization.[122] The contracting parties normally meet as the CONTRACTING PARTIES—the senior organ of the GATT—once a year and can meet more frequently. Each party has one vote. Unless otherwise provided, decisions are taken by a majority of the votes cast.[123]

Other bodies that together with the CONTRACTING PARTIES today compose the GATT organization find their origins in decisions of the CONTRACTING PARTIES and practice under those decisions and not in the text of the GATT Agreement itself. The Council of the GATT consists of representatives of all GATT members wishing to appoint representatives. It can be convened on three-days' notice. In fact, it meets about once a month. It has broad powers, but actions require a vote equal to that required for decisions taken by

---

[118] See note 110, *supra.*

[119] At page 428 et seq.

[120] Article XXV, paragraph 5. See John H. Jackson, *Legal Problems of International Economic Relations: Cases, Materials and Text on the National and International Regulation of Transnational Economic Policies* (St. Paul: West Publishing Co., 1977), pp. 412–18.

[121] See Chapter 10, *infra,* pages 432–439.

[122] See *International Trade Organization: Hearings before the Committee on Finance,* U.S. Senate, 80th Congress, 1st Session (1947), part 2, pp. 1380–1402 especially pp. 1383 and 1399–1400.

[123] Article XXV.

the CONTRACTING PARTIES. Further, a member adversely affected by a Council decision can appeal to the CONTRACTING PARTIES and during the period of the appeal can require that the Council decision not be applied.[124]

Separate from the Council, in which all members can participate, is a Consultative Group composed of high-level officials of eighteen countries representative of the membership. The Consultative Group of Eighteen, which meets about every three months, reviews international trade developments, facilitates negotiations on important and controversial matters, and lays the groundwork for decisions by the Council or CONTRACTING PARTIES.[125] One of the tasks of the Consultative Group is to review trade aspects of the international adjustment process and assist the coordination of the GATT and the IMF.[126] There are a number of GATT committees, including a Committee on Balance-of-Payments Restrictions.[127] The CONTRACTING PARTIES, Council, Consultative Group, and committees are assisted by a Secretariat in Geneva headed by the Director-General.[128] In addition, special committees and other bodies operate under agreements, separate from the General Agreement, that have been concluded under the auspices of the GATT relating to non-tariff barriers and other matters.[129]

Comments. Unlike the IMF Agreement,[130] the GATT Agreement contains no provision granting any organ power to make interpretations that are binding on all members. Nevertheless, the CONTRACTING PARTIES have in fact made interpretations of the GATT Agreement which have been understood as entitled to great weight.[131]

The GATT Agreement and related agreements contain elaborate provisions for avoiding or resolving disputes. John H. Jackson has identified nineteen clauses in the General Agreement which obligate parties to consult in specific instances.[132] In addition, Article XXII entitled "Consultation" can be

---

[124] See the decision of the CONTRACTING PARTIES of June 4, 1960, that established the Council. GATT, *Basic Instruments and Selected Documents,* 9th supplement (1961), p. 8.

[125] The Consultative Group was established by a decision of the Council of July 11, 1975. GATT, *Basic Instruments and Selected Documents,* 22d supplement (1976), p. 15. The Consultative Group was given a permanent mandate by the decision of the CONTRACTING PARTIES of November 22, 1979. GATT, *Basic Instruments and Selected Documents,* 26th supplement (1980), p. 289. Reports of the Consultative Group are printed in *Basic Instruments and Selected Documents.*

[126] Decision of November 22, 1979, *idem.*

[127] See Jackson, *World Trade and the Law of GATT, supra* note 103, pp. 158–59.

[128] See Jackson, *idem,* chapter 6. The Secretariat issues an annual report for the organization entitled *"GATT Activities in [year]."* It also publishes the supplements to *Basic Instruments and Selected Documents.*

[129] See, e.g., the agreements cited in note 112, *supra,* and the discussion of their institutional features in Jackson, *MTN and the Legal Institutions of International Trade, supra* note 112.

[130] See Chapter 1, *supra,* pages 37–39.

[131] See Jackson, *Legal Problems of International Economic Relations, supra* note 120, pp. 411–12.

[132] Jackson, *Legal Problems of International Economic Relations, idem,* pp. 422–23. See also Jackson, *MTN and the Legal Institutions of International Trade, supra* note 112.

invoked by a member with respect to "any matter" concerning the operation of the General Agreement. A number of provisions permit the compensatory modification of concessions. Some compensatory actions can be taken unilaterally without any action by the CONTRACTING PARTIES or other organs. While Kenneth W. Dam has said that "treaty enforcement is not regarded in GATT circles as an important function,"[133] it is clear that the remedy provisions are intended to assure a balanced system of rights and obligations.

If a member considers that a benefit accruing to it under the Agreement is being nullified or impaired or that an objective of the Agreement is being impeded, and the matter cannot be resolved through consultation, the member can under Article XXIII request the CONTRACTING PARTIES to investigate the matter and make appropriate recommendations and rulings. This is seen as a last resort procedure when other remedial clauses of the Agreement cannot be effectively used. Normally the CONTRACTING PARTIES establish an expert panel or a working party to investigate the problem and prepare a report and recommendations for adoption by the CONTRACTING PARTIES.[134] Delays have been encountered in the use of Article XXIII and political considerations can affect the results.[135]

With respect to balance-of-payments matters, as subsequent discussions will show, GATT substantive rules are few and the heart of the law is the consultation procedures.[136] The aim is not so much to apply substantive rules as to clarify interests and to adjust national actions to maintain a cooperative order.

Organisation for Economic Co-operation and Development

The Organisation for European Economic Co-operation (OEEC) was formed in 1948 to make arrangements for distribution of aid to the nations of Europe under the European Recovery Program (Marshall Plan) and to coordinate recovery efforts.[137] When that task was completed and after the currencies of the

---

[133] Dam, *The GATT, supra* note 103, p. 355.

[134] The Understanding Regarding Notification, Consultation, Dispute Settlement and Surveillance, adopted November 28, 1979, *supra* note 110, clarifies the GATT's dispute settlement procedures and includes an annex containing an agreed description of customary dispute settlement practice in the GATT.

[135] Regarding dispute settlement in the GATT, see Dam, *The GATT, supra* note 103, chapters 1 and 20; John H. Jackson, "Governmental Disputes in International Trade Relations: A Proposal in the Context of GATT," *Journal of World Trade Law,* vol. 13 (1979), p. 1; Jackson, *World Trade and the Law of GATT, supra* note 103, chapters 8 and 29; Robert E. Hudec, *The GATT Legal System and World Trade Diplomacy* (New York: Praeger Publishers, 1975); Kolasa, *supra* note 104, pp. 19–37; and Gerard and Victoria Curzon, "The Management of Trade Relations in the GATT," in Andrew Schonfield (ed.), *International Economic Relations of the Western World 1959–1971* (2 vols.; London: Oxford University Press for Royal Institute of International Affairs, 1976), vol. 1, p. 141 at pp. 204–83.

[136] See Chapter 10, *infra,* pages 429–440.

[137] The Convention for European Economic Co-operation which established the OEEC, done in Paris, April 16, 1948, appears in *United Nations Treaty Series,* vol. 888, p. 141. See generally Alexander Elkin, "The Organisation for European Economic Co-operation: Its Structure and Powers," *European Yearbook,*

major Western European countries were made convertible, a successor organization, the Organisation for Economic Co-operation and Development (OECD), was formed in 1961.[138] Twenty-four countries are presently members of the OECD, and among these are the principal industrialized countries with market-oriented economies.[139] While the OECD membership is geographically diverse, the organization does not aspire to universality. Each of the countries (the Group of Ten) participating in the General Arrangements to Borrow, by which the IMF has borrowed currencies to supplement the holdings of its General Resources Account, is a member of the OECD.[140]

The Convention on the OECD is a relatively short document. The aims of the organization, stated in Article 1, are to promote policies designed:

> a) to achieve the highest sustainable economic growth and employment and a rising standard of living in Member countries, while maintaining financial stability, and thus to contribute to the development of the world economy;
>
> b) to contribute to sound economic expansion in Member as well as non-member countries in the process of economic development; and
>
> c) to contribute to the expansion of world trade on a multilateral, non-discriminatory basis in accordance with international obligations.

The OECD is essentially a consultative organization. It undertakes research and affords a forum for high-level discussion of economic problems. The Council, which includes all members, is the senior organ of the OECD. It

vol. 4 (1956), p. 96; Hugo J. Hahn and Albrecht Weber, *Die OECD: Organisation für Wirtschaftliche Zusammenarbeit und Entwicklung* (Baden-Baden: Nomos Verlagsgesellschaft, 1976), pp. 27–53; A. H. Robertson, *European Institutions: Co-operation, Integration, Unification* (3rd ed.; London: Stevens & Sons; New York: Matthew Bender, 1973), pp. 72–78; Marjorie M. Whiteman, *Digest of International Law* (Washington: U.S. Department of State), vol. 14 (1970), pp. 1094–1102; and *Foreign Relations of the United States,* 1947, vol. 3 (1972), pp. 197–484, and 1948, vol. 3 (1974), pp. 352–501.

[138] The Convention on the OECD, done in Paris, December 14, 1960, entered into force September 30, 1961, appears in *United States Treaties and Other International Agreements,* vol. 12, p. 1728; *United Nations Treaty Series,* vol. 888, p. 179. The work of the organization is described in Hahn and Weber, *supra* note 137; Miriam Camps, *"First World" Relationships: The Role of the OECD* (Paris: Atlantic Institute for International Affairs; New York: Council on Foreign Relations, 1975); Henry G. Aubrey, *Atlantic Economic Cooperation: The Case of the OECD* (New York: Frederick A. Praeger, 1967); Gilbert Guillaume, "L'Organisation de Coopération et de Développement Économiques et l'Évolution Récente de ses Moyens d'Action," *Annuaire Français de Droit International,* vol. 25 (1979), p. 75; and the annual reports of the Secretary-General issued under the title *Activities of OECD in [year].*

[139] The members of the OECD are: Australia, Austria, Belgium, Canada, Denmark, Finland, France, Federal Republic of Germany, Greece, Iceland, Ireland, Italy, Japan, Luxembourg, Netherlands, New Zealand, Norway, Portugal, Spain, Sweden, Switzerland, Turkey, United Kingdom, and United States. Yugoslavia, although not a member, participates in the OECD's work in certain fields.

[140] The Group of Ten is described at page 72.

may meet in sessions either at the level of governmental ministers or at the level of permanent representatives. The Council annually chooses a chairman to preside over ministerial sessions. When the Council meets in sessions composed of permanent representatives, the Secretary-General presides.[141]

Decisions are normally adopted by mutual agreement and are binding on members only to the extent that they accept them.[142] This rule applies both to decisions adopted by the Council and decisions adopted by committees and working parties.[143]

The Executive Committee, composed of fourteen members, prepares the Council's work. There is also an Executive Committee in Special Session (a separate organ in which all OECD members participate). The latter committee has considered such subjects as "North–South" and "East–West" relations. Most of the work of the OECD is done through a multitude of committees and specialized organizations that span the full range of governmental concerns, including energy, agriculture, industry, transport, environment, education, scientific research, labor, development assistance, and economic policy. The OECD has a permanent staff at the headquarters in Paris that prepares reports, often influential, on these subjects and assists the Council and the various committees.[144]

---

[141] Convention on the OECD, *supra* note 138, Articles 7–10.

[142] Articles 5 and 6 of the Convention on the OECD, *idem,* provide:

Article 5

In order to achieve its aims, the Organisation may:
a) take decisions which, except as otherwise provided, shall be binding on all the Members;
b) make recommendations to Members; and
c) enter into agreements with Members, non-member States and international organizations.

Article 6

1. Unless the Organisation otherwise agrees unanimously for special cases, decisions shall be taken and recommendations shall be made by mutual agreement of all the Members.
2. Each Member shall have one vote. If a Member abstains from voting on a decision or recommendation, such abstention shall not invalidate the decision or recommendation, which shall be applicable to the other Members but not to the abstaining Member.
3. No decision shall be binding on any Member until it has complied with the requirements of its own constitutional procedures. The other Members may agree that such a decision shall apply provisionally to them.

For an analysis of these articles, see opinions of the Legal Adviser of the U.S. Department of State in *Senate Executive Report 1* [on Senate Executive Document E], 87th Congress, 1st Session (1961), Appendix 4, pp. 18–20; and Appendix 5, pp. 20–21; reprinted in *American Journal of International Law,* vol. 55 (1961), pp. 699–701. See also Hahn and Weber, *supra* note 137, pp. 95–99 and 307–52.

[143] OECD Rules of Procedure 17, 18, and 19.

[144] See Hahn and Weber, *supra* note 137, pp. 77–92, 211–306, and 353–75. Examples of influential OECD reports on economic matters are *The Balance of Payments Adjustment Process* (1966); *Trade Measures and Adjustment of the Balance of Payments* (1971); *Towards Full Employment and Price Stability* (1977); and *Positive Adjustment Policies-Managing Structural Change* (1983).

The OECD's principal role is as a forum for multilateral consultations and policy coordination. With respect to coordination of economic policies, the organization's Economic Policy Committee is the main forum. It brings together top-level national officials several times a year. The committee, in addition to its own meetings, currently has several working parties concerned with interlocking aspects of economic policy:

Working Party No. 1—Macroeconomic and Structural Policy Analysis.[145]
Working Party No. 3—Policies for the Promotion of Better International
                Payments Equilibrium.
Working Group—Short-term Economic Prospects.

Working Party No. 3 is restricted to the ten OECD members that compose the Group of Ten plus Switzerland. Within this working party the monetary and balance-of-payments problems and policies of the countries are examined, compared, and debated by finance ministry and central bank officials.

The economic position and prospects of each OECD member are subjected to an annual multilateral review within the OECD's Economic and Development Review Committee which is different from the Economic Policy Committee. The Development Assistance Committee is a forum for coordinating economic aid flowing from developed to developing countries. The Trade Committee examines the international trade policies and practices of OECD member countries. There is also a Committee on International Investment and Multinational Enterprises.

Some of the OECD's activities in the economic sphere have gone beyond consultation and have resulted in formal instruments. The original OEEC gave much attention to liberalization of trade and payments, and the successor OECD continues this work. The OECD administers a Code of Liberalisation of Capital Movements and a Code of Liberalisation of Current Invisible Operations. The OECD's Committee on Capital Movements and Invisible Transactions is charged with overseeing the operation of these codes.[146] During the oil-import financing crisis in the early 1970s an agreement was concluded within the OECD to establish a facility to assist members in financing petroleum imports, but the agreement has not entered into force.[147] The members of the

---

[145] This committee was formed in 1980 through combining former Working Party No. 2 (Problems Concerning Economic Growth and the Allocation of Natural Resources) and former Working Party No. 4 (Costs of Production and Prices), both of which have now been abolished. See *Activities of OECD in 1980*, p. 16.

[146] The Invisibles Code is discussed at page 443 and the Capital Code at page 460 of Chapter 10.

Five members of the OECD have not yet accepted the currency convertibility obligations of Article VIII, sections 2, 3, and 4, of the IMF Agreement: Greece, Iceland, Portugal, Spain, and Turkey. Switzerland is not a member of the International Monetary Fund.

The European Payments Union operated by the OEEC in the period 1950–1958 is described in Chapter 7, *infra*, pages 300–302.

[147] The facility is mentioned in Chapters 6, *infra*, pages 293–294.

OECD have also adopted declarations on trade policy[148] and on international investment.[149]

Because virtually no economic topic is viewed as beyond the range of concern of the OECD, and because its procedures center on consultation rather than formal decision-making, the organization is used by industrialized nations as a principal forum for coordinating their economic policies. For example, officials from treasuries and central banks of the Group of Ten may meet under the auspices of the OECD, with the organization providing staff support, to deal with monetary crises and to coordinate policies that they pursue in the International Monetary Fund. Domestic economic policies that have external effects are subjected to searching examination within the OECD. Usually high-level officials with important responsibilities in their own governments participate in these policy reviews which are given further attention in the last chapter of this book.[150]

On the twentieth anniversary of the OECD, M. Valery Giscard d'Estaing commented: "The OECD is . . . the natural place for the industrialized countries to come together when they seek to engage in joint reflection or action."[151] The perceptive comment in the quotation is the reference to reflection. In many organizations the emphasis is on putting forth national positions, negotiating, and taking action. OECD's processes encourage multilateral thinking and reflection on actions already taken or which may be undertaken.

Group of Ten

In 1961 the Group of Ten was created. It consists of Belgium, Canada, France, Federal Republic of Germany, Italy, Japan, Netherlands, Sweden, United Kingdom, and United States. The impetus for the formation of the Group of Ten was the desire of these industrial countries to assure that the IMF would have currency resources adequate to meet the market-intervention needs of the members of the group following a liberalization of controls over capital movements. The financial arrangements were formalized in the General Arrangements to Borrow (GAB) which provide a line of credit to the IMF for the very substantial amounts it may need to give assistance to these ten countries and, since an amendment made in 1983 took effect, to other countries as well. The Group of Ten was established to consult on the implementation of calls for re-

---

[148] See Declaration on Trade Policy adopted June 4, 1980; *Activities of OECD in 1980*, p. 93; *European Yearbook*, vol. 28 (1980), p. 225. This permanent declaration replaces a declaration adopted in 1974 and renewed thereafter from year to year and amended in 1978. For the original text, see *Activities of OECD in 1974*, p. 79; *European Yearbook*, vol. 22 (1974), p. 269; *International Legal Materials*, vol. 13 (1974), p. 995.

[149] See Chapter 10, *infra*, page 465.

[150] At pages 580–585.

[151] Statement on December 15, 1980, quoted in *Activities of OECD in 1980*, p. 11.

sources by the Fund under the GAB.[152] Once the pattern of meeting together was established, the Group of Ten did not limit itself to issues concerning the IMF's General Arrangements to Borrow. Consultations on the balance-of-payments adjustment process, international liquidity, coordination of domestic and international monetary policies, and formulation of proposals for new or modified international monetary arrangements have taken place within the Group of Ten.

Meetings of the Ministers and Governors of the Group of Ten are usually attended by the finance ministers and central bank governors of the participants in the GAB, with their counterparts from Switzerland, the Managing Director of the International Monetary Fund, the General Manager of the Bank for International Settlements, and Secretary-General of the Organisation for Economic Co-operation and Development as nonvoting participants. The deputies of all these officials meet as the "Deputies of the Group of Ten" to prepare proposals and crystallize unresolved issues for decision by the Ministers and Governors of the Group of Ten. The Group of Ten relies for staff support upon the finance ministries and central banks of the member countries and the staffs of the IMF, BIS, and OECD. Meetings may be held in Washington, Frankfurt, Paris, or other cities.[153]

Representatives of the same ten countries and Switzerland meet many times a year in other forums restricted to the eleven countries, with representatives of the IMF, BIS, and OECD being invited guests. These meetings are less formal than the meetings of "ministers and governors" or even of the "deputies." The central bank governors meet about ten times a year in Basle at the time of meetings of the Board of Directors of the Bank for International Settlements.[154] Finance ministry and central bank officials meet several times a year within Working Party No. 3 of the OECD's Economic Policy Committee.[155]

Together the members in the Group of Ten command votes in excess of a majority of the total voting power of the IMF, which means that their agreed positions on many issues are very likely to be followed by the Fund. This influence was recognized in 1966 and 1967 when the IMF Executive Directors held informal joint meetings with the Deputies of the Group of Ten to discuss proposals that led to the first amendment of the IMF Articles of Agreement to authorize the creation of special drawing rights (SDRs).[156]

On several occasions when the Deputies or the Ministers and Governors of the Group of Ten took an agreed position on matters other than the GAB, offi-

---

[152] The IMF's General Arrangements to Borrow are described more fully in Chapter 6, *infra*, pages 283–291. See generally Jacobsson, *supra* note 45, pp. 358–85.

Although Switzerland is not a member of the IMF, the Swiss National Bank has become a participating institution in the GAB following a 1983 amendment to the GAB decision.

[153] Communiqués following meetings at the ministerial level are usually published in *IMF Survey*.

[154] See pages 585–589.

[155] See pages 582–585.

[156] See Chapter 5, *infra*, pages 169–171.

cials from some members of the IMF that had not participated expressed dissatisfaction at having been excluded from participation at a crucial stage of the decision-making process. Some of this dissatisfaction built up in the 1960s during the drafting of the amendment to provide for special drawing rights.[157] Some dissatisfaction was also evident following the Smithsonian Agreement of December 18, 1971, at which the Group of Ten agreed upon a realignment of the exchange rates of their currencies. The realignment affected the trade and financial relations of other countries and necessitated a re-examination of their exchange rate practices.[158] The Group of Ten also met separately in December 1975 to review the French-U.S. draft of the new Article IV of the IMF Agreement before it was formally presented to the IMF's Executive Board.[159] The Group of Ten at meetings in December 1982 and February 1983, decided to substantially expand the resources available to the IMF under the General Arrangements to Borrow and to make the direct benefits of the IMF borrowings available to other IMF members in addition to the ten.[160]

Group of Twenty-Four

In November 1971 a group of developing countries known as the "Group of 77,"[161] meeting in Lima, Peru, decided to establish a subgroup of finance ministers and central bank governors who would meet in order to coordinate the policies of developing countries on financial questions important to them. This latter group, called the "Intergovernmental Group of 24 on International Monetary Affairs,"[162] normally meets at the finance minister or deputy finance minister level two or three times a year. Meetings are normally held at the time of meetings of the IMF's Interim Committee of the Board of Governors, at the time of the joint annual meeting of the International Monetary Fund and the World Bank, and at the time of meetings of the joint Fund-Bank Development Committee. Communiqués of the Group of 24 normally deal with the world economy and current situation of developing countries, matters requiring immediate attention of the IMF and the IBRD, policy issues for the Fund and the Bank in the immediate future, and issues to be addressed over the longer term.

---

[157] Idem.

[158] See Chapter 11, infra, pages 498–499. See also Margaret Garritsen de Vries, The International Monetary Fund, 1966–1971: The System Under Stress (2 vols.; Washington: IMF, 1976), vol. 1, chapter 26.

[159] See Chapter 11, infra, page 506.

[160] See Chapter 6, infra, pages 287–291. The Group of Ten, at meetings in December 1982 and February 1983, also worked out a common position on an increase in IMF quotas in the Eighth Quota Review. See Chapter 1, supra, page 13.

[161] See note 32, supra, and accompanying text.

[162] See Declaration and Principles of the Action Programme of Lima, supra note 32, attachment, pp. 13–14; and Sauvant, supra note 32, pp. 59–69. The Intergovernmental Group of 24 on International Monetary Affairs currently consists of Algeria, Argentina, Brazil, Colombia, Egypt, Ethiopia, Gabon, Ghana, Guatemala, India, Iran, Ivory Coast, Lebanon, Mexico, Nigeria, Pakistan, Peru, Philippines, Sri Lanka, Syria, Trinidad and Tobago, Venezuela, Yugoslavia, and Zaire.

Unlike the Group of Ten, which developed countries use both as a forum to coordinate policy vis-à-vis the rest of the world and as a forum for internal policy coordination, the Group of 24 is primarily a body through which the Group of 77 confronts the developed world. It has to date not been a vehicle for internal policy coordination. The principal demands of the Group of 24 are embodied in the Programme of Action on the Establishment of a New International Economic Order adopted by the United Nations General Assembly in May 1974.[163] They are developed in a 1979 Group of 24 document entitled "Outline for a Program of Action on International Monetary Reform"[164] and in subsequent G-24 communiqués. These demands have been:

(1) The demand for greater participation by developing countries in the decision-making of international financial organizations.[165]

(2) The demand for the provision of financial resources in larger amounts, under milder conditions, with easier repayment terms.[166]

(3) The demand for establishment of a "link" between development finance and allocations of special drawing rights (SDRs) by the IMF.[167]

(4) The demand for recognition of special needs of developing countries when benefits and burdens are assigned.[168]

The Group of 24 is independent of the IMF, IBRD, UN, and UNCTAD.[169] It receives secretariat support from the UNCTAD Secretariat[170]

---

[163] See note 37, *supra,* and accompanying text.

[164] The text appears in IMF, *Summary Proceedings, 1979,* p. 312.

[165] Programme of Action, *supra* note 37, part 2, section 1(d) and (g) and section 2(c); and Communiqué of the Group of 24 of September 3, 1982, in *IMF Survey,* September 20, 1982, p. 290, paragraph 10. See Edwards, "Responses," *supra* note 39, pp. 94–100. Developing countries at the present time hold about 37 percent of the weighted votes in the IMF. At the present time eleven executive directors of the IMF represent developing countries exclusively and four executive directors represent constituencies that include developing and developed countries. See Chapter 1, *supra,* pages 32–35.

[166] Programme of Action, *supra* note 37, part 2, section 1(h) and (i) and section 2(a), (b), (h), and (i); and Communiqué of the Group of 24, *supra* note 165, paragraphs 8, 9, and 13–26. See Edwards, "Responses," *supra* note 39, pp. 100–09.

[167] Programme of Action, *supra* note 37, part 2, section 1(f), and operative paragraph 8(b); and Communiqué of the Group of 24, *supra* note 165, paragraph 11. The "link" proposal is discussed in Chapter 5, *infra,* pages 216–217. See also Edwards, "Responses," *supra* note 39, pp. 109–12.

[168] Programme of Action, *supra* note 37, part 2, sections 1(i) and 2(h). See Edwards, "Responses," *supra* note 39, pp. 112–14.

[169] Representatives of these organizations usually, however, attend meetings of the Group of 24.

[170] See, e.g., *Money, Finance and Development: Papers on International Monetary Reform* (United Nations document no. TD/B/479; sales no. E.74.II.D.15; 1974).

and from the IMF. Communiqués issued following meetings of the Group of 24 are normally published in *IMF Survey.*

Regional Organizations
European Economic Community

Scope of Community Activities. The member states of the European Economic Community (EEC)[171] have mutually undertaken obligations in the economic sphere that are more comprehensive and penetrating than those they have assumed in larger organizations of more diverse membership. The broad goals of the Community are stated in Article 2 of the Treaty Establishing the European Economic Community (also called the Treaty of Rome):

> The Community shall have as its task, by establishing a common market and progressively approximating the economic policies of Member States, to promote throughout the Community a harmonious development of economic activities, a continuous and balanced expansion, an increase in stability, an accelerated raising of the standard of living and closer relations between the States belonging to it.

A common market among the EEC members has been established through the elimination of tariff barriers on internal trade and the establishment of a common external tariff. Non-tariff barriers to economic transactions have also been systematically reduced including monetary and other restrictions respecting trade, invisible, and capital transactions. The importance of coordinating the economic policies of the member states and remedying disequilibria in the

---

[171] Belgium, France, Federal Republic of Germany, Italy, Luxembourg, and the Netherlands were original signatories of the Treaty Establishing the European Economic Community [hereinafter "Treaty of Rome" or "EEC Treaty"], signed at Rome March 25, 1957, entered into force January 1, 1958. Denmark, Ireland, and the United Kingdom became members of the EEC on January 1, 1973, and Greece became a member on January 1, 1981. Other states may later join the EEC.

Relevant treaties of a constitutional character are the Treaty of Rome, *supra;* Treaty Establishing a Single Council and a Single Commission of the European Communities effective July 1, 1967; Act of Accession of Denmark, Ireland, and the United Kingdom effective January 1, 1973; and the Act of Accession of Greece effective January 1, 1981. Official English texts of each of these instruments, except the Act of Accession of Greece, appear in *Treaties Establishing the European Communities* (Brussels: European Communities, 1978). Documents concerning the accession of Greece appear in *Official Journal of the European Communities* [hereinafter *Official Journal*], no. L-291, November 19, 1979.

Two comprehensive commentaries are Commerce Clearing House, *Common Market Reports* (Chicago: CCH) [hereinafter *CCH Common Market Reports*], which is a looseleaf service kept up to date through biweekly reports; and Hans Smit and Peter E. Herzog (ed.), *The Law of the European Economic Community: A Commentary on the EEC Treaty* (6 vols.; New York: Matthew Bender, binder service, 1983 ed.), which is also supplemented from time to time.

balance of payments is recognized in Article 3(g) of the EEC Treaty and a separate chapter of the treaty (Articles 103–109) is devoted to this topic.

Of all the Community's work, only that in the monetary field receives attention in this book. The reader should note this limited focus, for the Community is also active in the fields of customs and commercial policy, finance and taxation, establishment of businesses, competition policy, freedom of movement of persons, labor policy, agricultural policy, transportation policy, and energy policy, all of which can intersect with monetary policy.

The member states of the EEC in 1971 stated a long-term intention to establish a monetary union, and that goal was reaffirmed in 1978 and subsequently.[172] While the goal is far from achieved, a number of steps have been taken toward the objective. At this point it may be useful to review in broad outline relevant EEC Treaty provisions and Community actions.

Consultation on economic policy is required by the Treaty of Rome. Article 103 requires member states to treat their conjunctural (business cycle) policies as a matter of common concern. It obligates them to enter into consultations with each other and with the Commission of the Community. The Council of Ministers has authority to adopt decisions in some situations. Article 104 provides: "Each Member State shall pursue the economic policy needed to ensure the equilibrium of its overall balance of payments and to maintain confidence in its currency, while taking care to ensure a high level of employment and a stable level of prices." Article 105 requires collaboration among the competent authorities of the member states, including the central banks, to obtain coordination of their economic policies in pursuit of these goals. The Economic Policy Committee, Monetary Committee, and Committee of Central Bank Governors, described below, as well as the Council, serve as forums for consultation. The procedures for coordination of economic policies are examined in the final chapter of this book.[173]

The members of the European Economic Community are very conscious of the impact of exchange rates upon trade flows, service transactions, and capital movements among their countries and thus upon the achievement of economic integration. Each member is obligated by Article 107 of the EEC Treaty to treat its policy with regard to exchange rates as a matter of common concern. While the Treaty of Rome contains no provision giving Community organs authority to require a member to adopt a particular rate of exchange, the Commission can authorize members to take safeguard measures under Article 107, paragraph 2, if one of their number alters an exchange rate in a manner which is inconsistent with the objectives stated in Article 104 of the treaty.

A primary purpose of the Community's European Monetary System (EMS), which entered into force on March 13, 1979, is to foster stability in ex-

---

[172] The decisions are detailed in Chapter 12, *infra,* page 591 et seq.
[173] At page 589 et seq.

change rates. All of the member states of the European Economic Community except the United Kingdom and Greece are participants in the EMS exchange rate system, and the United Kingdom and Greece have indicated that they may join at a later time. The EMS involves a coordinated system of exchange rates among the participating national currencies, arrangements for financing market interventions for purposes of maintaining exchange rates within agreed limits, the pooling of a portion of national monetary reserves to undergird the financing arrangements, the use of a unique currency unit called the European Currency Unit (ECU), and efforts to improve coordination of monetary and other economic policies. The EMS replaced the European narrow margins arrangement, informally called "the snake," which previously linked several of the currencies of EEC members. The EMS is more comprehensive, and somewhat more complex, than the snake, which was never more than an exchange rate arrangement with a related financing mechanism. The legal features of the European Currency Unit (ECU) and the financing mechanism of the EMS are treated in Chapter 8, the details of the exchange rate arrangements in Chapter 11, and some broader issues in Chapter 12.[174]

The importance to the common market of eliminating national barriers to the movement of goods, supply of services, and transfer of capital is recognized in the Treaty of Rome and implementing decisions. The liberalization of restrictions on trade, invisible, and capital transactions, including those that take the form of controls on currency payments and transfers, are addressed in Articles 67–73, 106, and 108–09. These articles reinforce commitments undertaken in the International Monetary Fund[175] and the Organisation for Economic Co-operation and Development.[176] The provisions respecting capital movements, which go beyond the obligations undertaken in either the IMF or the OECD, receive special attention in Chapter 10.[177]

The Treaty of Rome contains special provisions outlining measures countries can take when facing balance-of-payments problems. Derogations from Community obligations are permitted where necessary to deal with balance-of-payments problems if the authorization of appropriate Community institutions is obtained or if the measures are taken to meet a sudden crisis.[178] A variety of financial procedures have been developed to provide assistance from Community institutions or directly from other members to those member states that find themselves in balance-of-payments difficulty. Financial assistance may be con-

---

[174] At pages 315, 536, and 589, *infra.*

[175] All ten current members of the EEC belong to the IMF and all except Greece have accepted the currency convertibility obligations of IMF Article VIII, sections 2, 3, and 4. See Chapter 1, *supra,* page 20.

[176] All ten current members of the EEC belong to the OECD and have subscribed to its Codes of Liberalisation of Current Invisible Operations and of Capital Movements. The OECD codes are discussed in Chapter 10, *infra,* beginning at pages 443 and 460.

[177] At page 465, *infra.*

[178] See EEC Treaty, Articles 108 and 109. The application of these articles is examined in Chapter 10, *infra,* at pages 473–477.

ditioned on the adoption of policies to correct the underlying problems and at the same time avoid damage to the common market and legitimate interests of other member states.[179]

Organs of the EEC. The principal organs of the European Communities are the Council of Ministers, Commission, Parliament, and Court of Justice. In this book references to these organs sometimes are preceded by "EC." These organs serve the European Economic Community (EEC), the European Coal and Steel Community (ECSC), and the European Atomic Energy Community (EURATOM), collectively referred to as the European Communities. In addition to the four principal organs, there are subsidiary bodies.

Council of Ministers and "European Council." The Council of Ministers is composed of representatives of member states, each member being entitled to one representative. These persons normally hold ministerial or deputy ministerial rank in their governments. The particular representatives in the Council change in accordance with the topic on the Council's agenda. If the issue to be addressed is transportation policy, national ministers of transportation are the representatives; agricultural policy, ministers of agriculture. When monetary issues are addressed, the representatives to the Council are national ministers of finance or their deputies.[180]

Governments maintain supporting staffs for their representatives in Brussels, the seat of the Council and Commission. The Treaty specifies the voting majority required for the Council to take action on different matters. For some decisions a simple majority of the votes cast is sufficient, for others a special qualified majority vote system is used, and some decisions require unanimity. An effort is normally made to achieve unanimity on important matters before proceeding to a vote.[181]

Many provisions of the Treaty of Rome grant power to the Council. Sup-

---

[179] Various financial assistance arrangements (including short-term financing and support through the European Monetary Cooperation Fund, medium-term assistance under EEC Treaty Article 108, and Community loans for balance-of-payments support) are described in Chapter 8.

[180] See generally Hans-Joachim Glaesner, "Some Reflections on the Council," *International Business Lawyer*, vol. 11 (1983), p. 173.

[181] For voting rules, see generally EEC Treaty, Articles 148 and 149. Many treaty provisions specify the voting requirement.

A gentlemen's agreement called the "Luxembourg compromise" of January 1966 provided that the Council when acting on a proposal of the Commission, which under the Treaty of Rome the Council could only amend by unanimous decision but could adopt by a qualified majority vote, would continue discussion until unanimity was achieved. The Luxembourg compromise was partially superseded by an understanding of the heads of governments in December 1974 renouncing the practice of making agreement on all questions conditional on unanimous agreement of the member states. On May 17 and 18, 1982, the Council adopted, in accordance with the EEC Treaty's voting procedure, a large number of regulations dealing with agricultural matters despite the opposition of the United Kingdom. See Smit and Herzog, *supra* note 171, part 5, pp. 120–23 (section 148.09); and *Bulletin of the European Communities*, 1982, no. 5, point 2.1.73, and no. 6, point 2.4.2.

plementing other provisions, Article 235 grants a broad residual enabling power:

> If action by the Community should prove necessary to attain, in the course of the operation of the common market, one of the objectives of the Community and this Treaty has not provided the necessary powers, the Council shall, acting unanimously on a proposal from the Commission and after consulting the Assembly, take the appropriate measures.

When heads of state or government of the member states of the European Communities meet, their actions and communiqués are normally identified as adopted by the "European Council." There is no organ recognized by that name in any of the treaties of the European Communities. The resolutions and communiqués of the European Council normally state intentions rather than legal obligations. While heads of state or government, as representatives of states, have authority under general international law to assume binding legal obligations if that is their intention, that intention should not be lightly presumed. Perplexing questions may be raised about the legal status of some of the European Council's actions.

For example, the precise legal effect of the European Council Resolution of December 5, 1978, on the establishment of the European Monetary System (EMS), mentioned earlier in this section, is far from clear. The preamble of the resolution is short and does not refer to any articles of the EEC Treaty. The resolution throughout uses the word "will" rather than "shall," which implies intention rather than legal obligation. The resolution was not published in the *Official Journal* as a legal instrument. It was published in the informational periodical, *Bulletin of the European Communities*.[182] The coup de grace was a decision of the Conseil Constitutionnel of France that held that the resolution was a political document and not an international agreement which would require parliamentary approval under the French constitution.[183]

---

[182] *Bulletin of the European Communities*, 1978, no. 12, p. 10; reprinted in European Communities Monetary Committee, *Compendium of Community Monetary Texts* (Brussels-Luxembourg, 1979), p. 40.

[183] Conseil Constitutionnel of France decision of December 29, 1978. *Journal du Droit International*, vol. 106 (Paris, 1979), p. 79 (with note by David Ruzié).

For the views of legal scholars on the status of the resolution, sample Dominique Carreau, "Vers une Zone de Stabilité Monétaire: La Création du Système Monétaire Européen au sein de la C.E.E.," *Revue du Marché Commun*, no. 229 (September 1979), p. 399 at pp. 403–04; Jean-Victor Louis, "Het Europees Monetair Stelsel," *Sociaal-Economische Wetgeving* (S.E.W.), vol. 27 (1979), p. 441 at pp. 451–56; Luca Radicati di Bròzolo, "Some Legal Aspects of the European Monetary System" *Rivista di Diritto Internazionale*, vol. 63 (1980), p. 330 at pp. 339–45; and Jean-Jacques Rey, "The European Monetary System," *Common Market Law Review*, vol. 17 (1980), p. 7 at pp. 10–12. For historical background, see Peter Ludlow, *The Making of the European Monetary System* (London: Butterworths, 1982). For general background on the European Council, see Anthony Parry and James Dinnage, *Parry & Hardy: EEC Law* (2d ed.; London: Sweet & Maxwell, 1981), pp. 53–56; and Christopher Bo Bramsen, "Le Conseil Européen: Son

But, to disregard the resolution because of questions about its formal legal status would be like studying the specifications for construction of components of a building and disregarding the architect's master plan. No other document provides a comparable comprehensive design of the European Monetary System at its present stage of development. The acts of the Council of Ministers, the acts of the European Monetary Cooperation Fund, and the agreements of central bank governors implementing the EMS, which clearly have legal force, cannot be understood, and certainly not interpreted, without reference to the European Council resolution. Thus, without shame or apology, that resolution will be cited frequently in later chapters when the EMS is discussed. Bear in mind, however, that the legal obligations arise primarily from the implementing instruments, and the resolution is cited for purposes of interpretation.

The regulations, directives, and decisions of the Council of Ministers implementing the European Monetary System are authorized by specific provisions of the EEC Treaty or the residual authority of Article 235 quoted above. It is possible that some actions of the Council of Ministers in the future may require new international agreements. Regulations and decisions of the Council of Ministers and agreements of the participating central banks are the sources of legal authority for implementing actions of the European Monetary Cooperation Fund.[184]

Commission. The Commission is the administrative organ of the Communities. It currently is composed of fourteen members who are selected, within certain prescriptions, on the basis of general competence. Although nationality is taken into account in their selection, they are not representatives of member states. The Commission has the power of initiative to put proposals for new regulations or directives to the Council. Those proposals range from detailed and technical regulations to general programs of basic economic and political significance. In some cases the Commission is given direct authority to act by the Treaty of Rome. For example, under Article 108 it is given direct authority to approve derogations from Treaty obligations for countries in balance-of-payments difficulty. Council decisions often delegate responsibilities to the Com-

---

Fonctionnement et ses Résultats, de 1975 à 1981,'' *Revue du Marché Commun,* no. 262 (1982), p. 624. The Solemn Declaration on European Union, signed by heads of state and government at Stuttgart on June 19, 1983, states: "When the European Council acts in matters within the scope of the European Communities, it does so in its capacity as the Council within the meaning of the Treaties." Paragraph 2.1.3 of the Declaration; *Bulletin of the European Communities,* 1983, no. 6, point 1.6.1.

[184] The Agreement between the Central Banks of the Member States of the European Economic Community, dated March 13, 1979, laying down the operating procedures for the European Monetary System, and Decisions Nos. 12/79 and 13/79 of the European Monetary Cooperation Fund adopted the same day are key instruments implementing the EMS. The legal authority for the central bank agreement is discussed in Chapter 8, *infra,* page 321. The text of the agreement appears in *Compendium of Community Monetary Texts* (1979), *supra* note 182, p. 55, and in *European Economy* (published by the Commission of the European Communities), no. 3 (July 1979), p. 102. Decisions Nos. 12/79 and 13/79 appear in *European Economy, idem,* pp. 109 and 111.

mission. The Commission plays an important role in assuring compliance with Community law. The Commission is supported by a large staff composed of approximately 10,000 persons.

Parliament. The Parliament, sometimes referred to as the Assembly, publicly debates issues before the Communities and puts questions to members of the Commission and Council. Some provisions of the Treaty of Rome provide that the Parliament is to be consulted before the Council takes action. Representatives are elected in direct elections held throughout the ten-country area. While the Parliament is a consultative rather than a legislative body, its relative political importance in relation to other organs is beginning to increase.

Court of Justice. The Court of Justice has exclusive final jurisdiction to interpret EEC law. The legality of acts of the Council and the Commission, other than recommendations or opinions, is subject to judicial review by the Court on the initiative of any member state, the Council, or the Commission. Any natural or legal person may institute proceedings against a decision or regulation of direct and individual concern to that person. There is a procedure whereby the Commission can obtain Court review of a member state's failure to comply with its obligations under the EEC Treaty. The Court also provides interpretations of Community law in cases referred to it by national courts. Its judgments are legally binding throughout the member states.

Economic Policy Committee. In the monetary sphere several subsidiary bodies assume importance. The Economic Policy Committee consists of four representatives of each member state plus four representatives of the Commission. Two of the four representatives of each state are usually the same persons who serve on the Monetary Committee to be described below. The Committee provides a forum for policy coordination among representatives of the member states. It also provides advice to the Council and Commission. It assists in coordinating general economic policies, makes a comparative examination of budgetary policies and their implementation, prepares preliminary drafts used by the Commission in drafting the short-term and the medium-term economic policy programs for the member states which are submitted to the Council, reviews the economic policies of the member states, and analyzes developments to determine the reasons for any departures from the programs.[185] The work of this Committee is examined in Chapter 12.[186]

---

[185] See EC Council Decision No. 74/122 of February 18, 1974, setting up an Economic Policy Committee. *Official Journal,* no. L-63, March 5, 1974, p. 21; reprinted in *Compendium of Community Monetary Texts* (1979), *supra* note 182, p. 18. When the Economic Policy Committee was established in 1974, three committees established some years earlier were abolished—the Conjunctural Policy Committee (also called Short-Term Economic Policy Committee), the Medium-Term Economic Policy Committee, and the Budgetary Policy Committee. The Provisional Rules of Procedure of the Economic Policy Committee, adopted June 7, 1974, appear in *Compendium of Community Monetary Texts* (1979), p. 20.

[186] At page 589, *infra.*

Monetary Committee. Pursuant to Article 105 of the Treaty of Rome a Monetary Committee has been formed to keep under review the monetary and financial situation in the member states and in the Community as a whole and the system of currency payments of the states.[187] Each member state appoints two members plus two alternates. The Commission also appoints two members and two alternates. The Monetary Committee, which receives secretariat support from the Commission staff, regularly reports to the Council and to the Commission and makes recommendations, in the form of "opinions," to the Council and Commission. The opinion of the Monetary Committee is required for implementation of some Council acts relating to capital movements and to balance-of-payments issues. The Committee issues an annual report on its activities which is usually published in the *Official Journal of the European Communities.*

Committee of Governors of Central Banks. There is a Committee of Governors of Central Banks.[188] In practice anything falling within the sphere of central bank responsibility is within the Committee's scope of concern. It has developed into an organ of permanent consultation and cooperation of the member states' central banks and even deals with matters outside the scope of the EEC Treaty. Its discussions are often highly confidential. It is composed of the central bank governors.[189] A representative of the Commission also regularly attends the meetings. While the Monetary Committee relies upon the EC Commission for secretariat services, the Central Bank Governors Committee has a secretariat that is responsible directly to the Governors Committee and not to the EC Commission or Council. The Committee's secretariat services are provided by staff of the Bank for International Settlements in Basle.[190] In addition

---

[187] EEC Council Decision of March 18, 1958, drawing up rules governing the Monetary Committee, as amended by EEC Council Decision of April 2, 1962, the Act of Accession effective January 1, 1973, EC Council Decision No. 72/377 of October 30, 1972, and EC Council Decision No. 76/332 of March 25, 1976. *Official Journal,* no. 17, October 6, 1958, p. 390 (*Official Journal-Special [English] Edition,* 1952–1958, p. 60); no. 32, April 30, 1962, p. 1064 (*Special Edition,* 1959–1962, p. 131); no. L-257, November 15, 1972, p. 20 (*Special Edition,* 1972 [November], p. 44); no. L-84, March 31, 1976, p. 56; and Act of Accession of Denmark, Ireland, and U.K., Annex I, point VII (1). The consolidated text of the rules appears in *Compendium of Community Monetary Texts* (1979), *supra* note 182, p. 9. The rules were amended to accommodate Greek representatives by the Act of Accession of Greece, Annex I, point VII(5). *Official Journal,* no. L-291, November 19, 1979, p. 17 at p. 96.

[188] EEC Council Decision No. 64/300 of May 8, 1964, on cooperation between central banks. *Official Journal,* no. 77, May 21, 1964, p. 1206; *Official Journal-Special [English] Edition,* 1963–1964, p. 141; *Compendium of Community Monetary Texts* (1979), *supra* note 182, p. 13. The Rules of Procedure of the Committee of Governors of the Central Banks adopted by the Committee of Governors, October 12, 1964, appear in *Compendium of Community Monetary Texts* (1979), p. 15.

[189] A representative of the Luxembourg monetary authorities is invited to attend meetings of the Committee of Governors but does not take part in decisions. Luxembourg's interests are represented by the Banque Nationale de Belgique for the two states of the Belgium–Luxembourg Economic Union.

[190] See Rules of Procedure of the Committee of Governors of the Central Banks, *supra* note 188, Article 7.

to BIS staff directly serving the Committee, the Economic Adviser of the BIS usually attends meetings of the Committee.[191]

Although not vested with any decision-making power by the EEC Treaty, the Governors Committee is involved in the preparation of decisions and resolutions of the Council concerning monetary policy and the functioning of the currency exchange system. Acting parallel with the Monetary Committee, it is involved in surveying the economic conditions in the member states.

The governors of the central banks possess substantial powers under their national laws. These powers were exercised when the governors as heads of their respective central banks, and not as members of a committee, concluded in March 1979 the key agreement implementing the European Monetary System's exchange rate arrangement.[192]

European Monetary Cooperation Fund and Proposed European Monetary Fund. The European Monetary Cooperation Fund was established by the Council of Ministers in 1973 and has separate legal personality. It is sometimes referred to by its English initials EMCF but more frequently by the French acronym FECOM. The Fund is the issuer of the European currency unit (ECU), which serves as the FECOM's unit of account and as a means of settlement among EEC central banks and between EEC central banks and the FECOM as well as performing other functions[193]

The FECOM is managed by a Board of Governors consisting of the same persons who serve on the Committee of Central Bank Governors plus a representative of the Luxembourg monetary authorities. A member of the Commission has a right to take part in the proceedings and regularly attends meetings.[194] Decisions are taken on the basis of unanimity.[195] While the FECOM has its formal location in Luxembourg, its operations are handled from Basle

---

[191] See generally *BIS 1930–80, supra* note 41, pp. 72–75.

[192] See note 184, *supra.* The exchange rate features of the agreement are examined in Chapter 11 at page 536 et seq. The financing features are examined in Chapter 8 at pages 320–326 and 326–332.

[193] Statutes of the FECOM appear as an Annex to EC Council Regulation No. 907/73 of April 3, 1973; *Official Journal,* no. L-89, April 5, 1973, p. 2; *Compendium of Community Monetary Texts* (1979), *supra* note 182, p. 44. EC Council Regulation No. 3180/78 of December 18, 1978, effective January 1, 1979, established the ECU (explained in Chapter 8 at page 315) as the FECOM's unit of account; *Official Journal,* no. L-379, December 30, 1978, p. 1; *Compendium of Community Monetary Texts* (1979), p. 133. Previously the unit of account was stated in terms of monetary gold. In creating the FECOM the EC Council used its broad powers under Article 235 of the EEC Treaty.

The Provisional Rules of Procedure of the FECOM, adopted by its Board of Governors and approved by the EC Council on June 28, 1973, appear in *Compendium of Community Monetary Texts* (1979), p. 48. See generally Francesco Masera, "European Fund for Monetary Cooperation: Objectives and Operating Guidelines," in Banca Nazionale del Lavoro (Italy), *Quarterly Review,* no. 106 (September 1973), p. 269, which proposed a more ambitious role for the FECOM than it initially assumed.

[194] FECOM Statutes, *supra* note 193, Article 1. The representative of the Luxembourg monetary authorities takes part in decisions whenever the rights and obligations of Luxembourg are not exercised by the Banque Nationale de Belgique on behalf of the two states of the Belgium-Luxembourg Economic Union.

[195] FECOM Rules of Procedure, *supra* note 193, Article 2.

and the meetings of its Board of Governors usually take place there. The Bank for International Settlements provides the secretariat of the FECOM[196] and has been designated as the FECOM's agent for the execution of technical aspects of the Fund's operations.[197]

The European Monetary Cooperation Fund is a center for cooperation and coordination of certain operations carried out by EEC central banks. As already noted, it is the issuer of the European currency unit (ECU). The FECOM is involved in some matters relating to reserve asset policies of EEC members.[198] The FECOM also plays a role in "the concerted action necessary for the proper functioning of the Community exchange system."[199] It administers short-term central bank credit facilities described in Chapter 8.[200] Through these financing facilities, the FECOM exercises its responsibility for "the multilateralization of positions resulting from interventions by central banks in Community currencies and the multilateralization of intra-Community settlements."[201] It also acts as agent for certain Community loans.[202] The FECOM submits semiannual reports to the EC Council and Commission, but they are not published.

The member states of the European Economic Community are presently considering the establishment of a "European Monetary Fund." The EMF, when established, will probably be managed at its highest policy levels by finance ministry rather than central bank officials. The EC Council has expressed its intention to merge the FECOM into the new Fund. The Council's original timetable called for the EMF to begin operation by early 1981, but the date was postponed. The new Fund's organizational structure, decision-making procedures, initial capital, and scope of operations have not yet been defined.[203]

In studies by the Commission and Monetary Committee, four models have

---

[196] FECOM's secretariat is provided by officials of the BIS pursuant to FECOM Rules of Procedure, *supra* note 193, Article 8. See *BIS 1930–80, supra* note 41, pp. 72–75.

[197] The BIS has served as Agent of the FECOM since June 1, 1973. See FECOM Rules of Procedure, *idem*, Article 9. The Bank's activities with respect to FECOM are summarized briefly each year in the *Annual Report* of the BIS. See also *BIS 1930–80, supra* note 41, pp. 75–76.

It has been suggested that the agency relationship between the FECOM and the BIS is governed by public international law. Radicati di Bròzolo, *supra* note 183, pp. 343–44 (note 52). This appears to be the correct view. As explained earlier (pages 60–63 *supra*), the BIS has the capacity to conclude agreements governed by public international law. It should be presumed to have done so in this case. The BIS is based outside the European Economic Community and should not be treated as having subjected its relationship to the FECOM to Community law without specific acts demonstrating that intention. And, it would be absurd to treat the relationship, concerning high-level governmental policies, as governed by the municipal law of Switzerland or Luxembourg.

[198] See Chapter 8, *infra*, pages 323–325.

[199] EC Council Regulation No. 907/73, *supra* note 193, Article 3. See also EC Council Regulation No. 3181/78 of December 18, 1978; *Official Journal*, no. L-379, December 30, 1978, p. 2; *Compendium of Community Monetary Texts* (1979), *supra* note 182, p. 53.

[200] At page 326 et seq.

[201] EC Council Regulation No. 907/73, *supra* note 193, Article 3.

[202] See Chapter 8, *infra*, page 339 et seq.

[203] See paragraph 1.4 of European Council Resolution of December 5, 1978, *supra* note 182; and the preamble to EC Council Regulation No. 3181/78 *supra* note 199.

been considered: (a) an "accounting agent" fund along lines of present operations of the FECOM, (b) a "central bank" type fund, (c) a "regional IMF" type fund, and (d) a *sui generis* fund that would have economic as well as monetary powers.[204] If the new European Monetary Fund is to be vested with only minimal powers, the Council may be able to establish it using the authority of Article 235 of the Treaty of Rome.[205] A treaty will probably be necessary if the powers to be possessed by the new Fund are substantial and if its activities are to displace some activities now performed by national treasuries and central banks.

Comments.   An integrated system of economic law is emerging through the application of the EEC Treaty and related treaties and the work of the institutions of the European Communities. This legal system is supranational in character and penetrates to the level of individuals and firms as well as states. The Court of Justice of the European Communities in the landmark case of *Costa v. ENEL* stated: "By contrast with ordinary international treaties, the EEC Treaty has created its own legal system which, on the entry into force of the Treaty, became an integral part of the legal systems of the Member States. . . ."[206]

The reader should be aware that some provisions of the Treaty of Rome apply directly in the member states and others require implementation through regulations, directives, or decisions by the Council or Commission.[207] A "regulation" has general application and is binding and directly applicable in the member states without the need for implementing national legislation. A "directive" is binding as to the result to be achieved upon each member state to which it is addressed but leaves to the national authorities the choice of form and methods for implementation. A "decision" is binding on those to whom it is addressed. Recommendations and opinions lack binding force.[208] Treaties and agreements concluded by the member states and other commitments made

[204] See study papers collected in Directorate-General for Economic and Financial Affairs, "The European Monetary System," *European Economy,* no. 12 (July 1982), p. 7 at pp. 48–64 and 88–128. See also Tom de Vries, *On the Meaning and Future of the European Monetary System* (Essays in International Finance no. 138; Princeton: Princeton University International Finance Section, 1980), pp. 25–39.

[205] Article 235 is set out at page 80, *supra.*

[206] Case No. 6/64, decided July 15, 1964. Court of Justice of the European Communities, *Reports of Cases Before the Court* [hereinafter *European Court Reports*], 1964, p. 585 at p. 593.

[207] Direct applicability of EEC Treaty Article 67(1), relating to liberalization of capital movements, was considered and rejected in the case, *In Re Guerrino Casati.* See Chapter 10, *infra,* page 467.

[208] EEC Treaty, Article 189. See also Articles 190 and 191. In the economic and monetary policy sphere, Council actions often take the form of directives. As noted in the text, the member state has flexibility in the method used to achieve the directed result. If a member should take the position that the directed goal is unnecessary, the directive can be reviewed by the Court of Justice. For a case interpreting the effect of a directive, see the opinion of the Court of Justice of the European Communities in *SACE v. Italian Ministry for Finance,* Case No. 33/70, decided December 17, 1970. *European Court Reports,* 1970, part 2, p. 1213; *CCH Common Market Reports, supra* note 171, paragraph 8117. For further background on Article 189, see *CCH Common Market Reports,* paragraph 4902; and Smit and Herzog, *supra* note 171, part 5, pp. 572–622.3.

by representatives of member states in their capacity as representatives of their states rather than simply members of the Council may supplement provisions of the EEC Treaty.[209]

Before concluding this section, it is important to note the relationship of the EEC to the International Monetary Fund. The countries of the EEC together hold in excess of 25 percent of the quotas of the IMF. Thus, acting together they can block actions in the IMF that require an 85 percent majority of the total voting power. France, the Federal Republic of Germany, and the United Kingdom each have large quotas and individually appoint executive directors. The other EEC states, up to the present time, have usually split up and joined with non-EEC countries that share their interests when electing directors who will represent them and cast their votes rather than banding together in the election of directors. Notwithstanding separate representation in the IMF, the member states of the EEC coordinate the policies they pursue in the IMF through the EC Monetary Committee and by less formal means.

EEC countries have used Community organs to coordinate positions pursued in the Interim Committee of the Board of Governors of the IMF.[210] In some cases the EEC has authorized derogations from the Treaty of Rome for a country in balance-of-payments difficulty and the representatives of EEC countries have then articulated a common position in the IMF Executive Board when the country's acts required IMF approval.[211]

Council for Mutual Economic Assistance and Related Monetary Institutions

The Council for Mutual Economic Assistance (CMEA) was founded in 1949 to foster economic cooperation among socialist states.[212] At the present time

---

[209] See, e.g., the treaties cited in note 171, the central bank agreement cited and discussed in note 184, and the European Council resolution cited and discussed in notes 182 and 183.

[210] EEC Council Decision No. 64/301 of May 8, 1964, on cooperation in the field of international monetary relations, states that the EC Monetary Committee is to be consulted on any decision or position of the member states concerning the general functioning of the international monetary system, recourse to financial resources within the IMF or under other international agreements, and participation in arrangements to provide monetary support to third countries. *Official Journal*, no. 77, May 21, 1964, p. 1207; *Official Journal–Special [English] Edition*, 1963–1964, p. 143; *Compendium of Community Monetary Texts* (1979), *supra* note 182, p. 12. The more important common positions taken by EEC states in the IMF are described each year in the annual report of the Monetary Committee which is usually published in the *Official Journal*.

[211] See, e.g., discussions in Chapter 10, at pages 405–409 and 473–477, of the coordinated actions respecting French exchange restrictions in 1968 and Italian restrictions in 1976.

[212] The Russian name of the CMEA is Soviet Ekonomicheskoi Vzaimopomoshchi. Some writers in the West use the acronym "COMECON."

For eleven years the CMEA existed on the basis of a communiqué without a formal constituent instrument. The communiqué appears in *Pravda*, January 25, 1949, p. 2, trans. in William E: Butler, *A Source Book on Socialist International Organizations* (Alphen aan den Rijn: Sijthoff & Noordhoff, 1978), p. 123.

The Charter of the CMEA, signed at Sofia December 14, 1959, entered into force April 13, 1960, was amended in June 1962, December 1962, June 1974, and June 1979. The Russian text as amended June 28,

CMEA members include Bulgaria, Cuba, Czechoslovakia, German Democratic Republic, Hungary, Mongolian People's Republic, Poland, Romania, Union of Soviet Socialist Republics, and Vietnam.[213] Of these countries, only Hungary, Romania, and Vietnam are currently members of the International Monetary Fund.[214] A number of socialist states belong to the IMF and not to the CMEA, including the People's Republic of China, Democratic Kampuchea, Lao People's Democratic Republic, People's Democratic Republic of Yemen, and several other states. Yugoslavia, although not a member of the CMEA, participates in some CMEA activities.[215] Czechoslovakia, Hungary, Poland, and Romania joined the Bank for International Settlements in Basle before World War II and continue their memberships in that organization.

The purpose clause of the CMEA Charter in many respects is not dissimilar from those of such organizations as the OECD and the European Economic Community. The first paragraph of Article I in its present form reads:

> The Council of Mutual Economic Assistance shall have as its purpose to promote through uniting and coordinating the efforts of the member countries of the Council the further deepening and improvement of cooperation and the development of socialist economic integration, the planned development of the national economy and the acceleration of the economic and technical progress in these countries, the raising of the level of industrialization of the countries with a less-developed industry, an uninterrupted growth of labor productivity, the gradual coming together and equalizing of the levels of economic

1979, appears in P. A. Tokareva (ed.), *Mnogostoronnee Ekonomicheskoe Sotrudnichestvo Sotsialisticheskikh Gosudarstv: Dokumenty [Multilateral Economic Cooperation of the Socialist Countries: Documents]* (Moscow: Iuridicheskaia Literatura, 1967, 1972, 1976, 1981), 1981 ed., p. 13; trans. in William E. Butler, *Materials on Socialist International Organisations* (2d ed.; London: University of London, 1981), part 2, p. 2. See related documents in Butler, *Source Book, supra,* pp. 1–147. The editions of Tokareva, *supra,* constitute a series, each edition including documents concluded in the period immediately preceding its publication.

For background on the CMEA, see Jozef M. van Brabant, *East European Cooperation: The Role of Money and Finance* (New York: Praeger Publishers, 1977), pp. 1–65; Jozef M. van Brabant, *Socialist Economic Integration* (Cambridge: Cambridge University Press, 1980), p. 1–54 and 172–244; and Giuseppe Schiavone, *The Institutions of COMECON* (New York: Holmes & Meier, 1981), pp. 1–218.

[213] Albania joined the CMEA in 1949, but has not been active since 1961. See Schiavone, *idem,* pp. 85–87.

[214] See Chapter 1, *supra,* pages 21–22 and 40–41.

[215] Agreement between the CMEA and Yugoslavia Concerning Participation of Yugoslavia in the Work of CMEA Organs, signed September 17, 1964, entered into force April 24, 1965. Russian text in Tokareva, *supra* note 212, 1972 ed., p. 213; trans. in Butler, *Source Book, supra* note 212, p. 277. See also Agreement on Cooperation between the CMEA and Finland, signed May 16, 1973, entered into force July 14, 1973, and Statute of the Commission for Cooperation of the CMEA and Finland. *United Nations Treaty Series,* vol. 894, p. 59; Tokareva, *supra,* 1976 ed., pp. 153 and 156; trans. in Butler, *supra,* pp. 270 and 273. Mexico and Iraq also maintain cooperation agreements with the CMEA.

development, and a steady increase in the well-being of the peoples of the member countries of the Council.[216]

The Council for Mutual Economic Assistance is designed on the theory that state sovereignty shall be preserved at the same time that a more rational "internationalization of productive forces" is pursued.[217] The CMEA has five principal organs: the Session of the Council which meets at least once each year, the Executive Committee, committees of the Council, permanent commissions of the Council, and a Secretariat. The Session of the Council is the highest organ with representation typically at the deputy head of government level or higher.[218]

Decision-making in the Council is based on equality of members. All member states have equal representation on the Council. All actions require the unanimity of all members affected by the action unless the members have declared their disinterest or non-participation.[219] Actions addressed to member states are cast in the form of "recommendations." They are adopted by consensus among the representatives of the states affected by the proposed recommendation. Members not directly affected by a recommendation or that do not wish to participate declare their disinterest or non-participation. Recommendations, following adoption by a Session of the Council or other authorized organ, become legally binding on interested members only after acceptance by them.[220]

The 1979 amendments to the CMEA Charter introduced a new class of actions called "arrangements." Arrangements are used where it is desired that CMEA organs participate in the implementation of measures that member states have agreed upon. Only those states that wish to participate take part in adopting arrangements. Arrangements were seen by the drafters of the amendments as a way of multilateralizing and involving CMEA organs in consultations and integration measures that would otherwise be agreed strictly bilaterally.[221] The CMEA Charter also uses the term "decision," but the Charter

---

[216] CMEA Charter, *supra* note 212. The translation is from Butler, *Materials, supra* note 212, part 2, p. 2.

[217] See generally William E. Butler, "Legal Configurations of Integration in Eastern Europe," *International Affairs* (London), vol. 51 (1975), p. 518.

[218] CMEA Charter, Articles V–X. For the statutes and rules of the various organs, commissions, and other bodies, see Butler, *Source Book, supra* note 212, pp. 149–281. See generally Schiavone, *supra* note 212, pp. 44–128.

[219] CMEA Charter, Article III, section 2, and Article IV.

[220] CMEA Charter, Article IV, sections 1 and 3. The Comprehensive Program for Integration, *infra* note 224, following its adoption by the Session on July 29, 1971, was subsequently formally approved by joint decrees of the central committee of the ruling party and the state council in each country.

The legal character of CMEA "recommendations" upon national acceptance is discussed by Butler, "Legal Configurations," *supra* note 217, pp. 525–28; and by Endre Ustor, "Decision-Making in the Council for Mutual Economic Assistance," in Hague Academy of International Law, *Recueil des Cours*, vol. 134 (1971-III), p. 163. Both papers consider the question whether particular recommendations upon acceptance become binding international commitments as well as national legislative acts.

[221] See amended Article III, section 1(b) and (e); Article IV, section 3; Article VII, section 4(a); and Article X, section 2(a), (d), and (e). See also Petr Hanzal, "Changes in CMEA Charter," *Rude Pravo* (Prague),

applies this term only to actions relating to CMEA organizational and procedural questions.[222]

The CMEA serves as a forum for coordinating plans for trade among CMEA countries and coordinating economic and financial policies.[223] In July 1971 the twenty-fifth Session of the Council of the CMEA adopted the Comprehensive Program for the Intensification and Improvement of Cooperation and the Development of Socialist Economic Integration of CMEA Member Countries.[224] The program has been described as "perhaps the most important single document to emanate from a socialist international organization."[225] The lengthy document outlines a program for economic collaboration in the socialist sphere in some respects comparable to collaboration achieved in the West through the combined efforts of the IMF, the GATT, the European Community, and the OECD. The program is intended to institute a process that entails:

> The international socialist division of labor, the coming together of their economies, and the formation of a modern, highly effective structure of their national economies; the gradual coming together and equalizing of the levels of their economic development; the formation of deep and lasting ties in the principal branches of the economy, sciences, and technology; the expansion and strengthening of the international market of these countries; and the improvement of commodity-monetary relations.[226]

The program does not contemplate transforming the CMEA into a supranational organization. Economic integration is to be achieved through closer cooperation. A section of Chapter I of the Comprehensive Program calls for the approximation and equalization of the levels of economic development of the member countries. Chapter II deals with consultations on basic problems of economic policy including improvement of financial and monetary relations.

International Bank for Economic Cooperation.   The International Bank for Economic Cooperation (IBEC) began operations in 1964 under CMEA auspices to handle the clearing of accounts for CMEA members on a

---

August 16, 1979, p. 3; trans. in Joint Publications Research Service, *East Europe Report: Economic and Industrial Affairs (no. 1932)*, J.P.R.S. no. 74160 (September 11, 1979), p. 11.

[222] CMEA Charter, Article IV, sections 2 and 3.

[223] See generally Brabant, *Socialist Economic Integration, supra* note 212, pp. 99–171.

[224] The Russian text appears in *Ekonomicheskaia Gazeta* (Moscow), August 1971, no. 33, p. 2; Tokareva, *supra* note 212, 1972 ed., p. 29; and the Russian text and translations appear in *United Nations General Assembly Official Records*, 26th Session, 2d Committee; UN document no. A/C.2/272/attachment (November 17, 1971). A translation also appears in Butler, *Source Book, supra* note 212, p. 33. The latter translation is used with permission in this book.

[225] Butler, "Legal Configurations," *supra* note 217, p. 526.

[226] Comprehensive Program, *supra* note 224, chapter I, section 1, subsection 2. The translation is from Butler, *Source Book, supra* note 212, p. 37.

multilateral basis. [227] Although the IBEC has the same membership as the CMEA, it is an independent organization, has authority to conclude international agreements in its own name, and possesses its own juridical personality.[228] It is affiliated with the CMEA and has a relationship agreement with that organization.[229] It has its headquarters in Moscow.[230]

The establishment of the IBEC has made it possible for socialist organizations to buy and sell goods in intra-CMEA trade for a financial instrument, called the "transferable ruble," that has uses on a multilateral basis. This instrument, however, cannot be used as freely as a Western convertible currency. The transferable ruble is issued by the IBEC and is not to be confused with the ruble of the Soviet Union. Its valuation and use are explained in Chapter 9.

The original nominal capital of the International Bank for Economic Cooperation was set at 300 million transferable rubles. It may be increased by consent of the member countries of the Bank and is also increased when new mem-

---

[227] The Russian name of the IBEC is *Mezhdunarodnyi Bank Ekonomicheskogo Sotrudnichestva*. The two principal documents on the IBEC are the Agreement on Multilateral Payments in Transferable Rubles and on the Organization of the International Bank for Economic Cooperation, signed in Moscow October 22, 1963, and the Charter of the International Bank for Economic Cooperation of the same date. The Agreement on Multilateral Payments and the Charter were amended December 18, 1970, and November 23, 1977. Translations of the amended texts appear in Appendix D of this book at pages 776 and 782. The amended texts in Russian appear in Tokareva, *supra* note 212, 1981 ed., pp. 128 and 135.

The Russian texts and translations of the Agreement and Charter in their original form prior to the 1970 amendments appear in *United Nations Treaty Series,* vol. 506, pp. 197 and 216. The Russian texts as amended in 1970 appear in Tokareva, *supra,* 1972 ed., pp. 237 and 244; trans. in Butler, *Source Book, supra* note 212, pp. 286 and 294. The IBEC issues an *Annual Report* in English. It also publishes an *Economic Bulletin.*

For general background on the IBEC, see Adam Zwass, *Monetary Cooperation Between East and West* (trans. by Michel Vale; White Plains, N.Y.: International Arts and Sciences Press, 1975), pp. 97–233; Brabant, *East European Cooperation, supra* note 212, pp. 66–196 and 343–54; and Henryk Francuz, "The International Bank for Economic Cooperation," *IMF Staff Papers,* vol. 16 (1969), p. 489. See the following works in Russian: M. S. Liubskii, L. Kh. Suliaeva, and V. M. Shastitko, *Valiutnye i Kreditnye Otonosheniia Stran SEV [Currency and Credit Relations of the CMEA Countries]* (Moscow: Nauka, 1978), chapter 2; V. P. Komissarov, *Mezhdunarodnye Valiutno-Kreditnye Otnosheniia SSSR i Drugikh Sotsialisticheskikh Stran [International Currency and Credit Relations of the U.S.S.R. and Other Socialist Countries]* (Moscow: Mezhdunarodnye Otonosheniia, 1976), chapters 8–10; and Iurii A. Konstantinov, *Den'gi v Sisteme Mezhdunarodnykh Ekonomicheskikh Otonoshenii Stran SEV [Money in the System of International Economic Relations of the CMEA Countries]* (Moscow: Finansy, 1978), chapters 4 and 5.

[228] Agreement on Multilateral Payments, *supra* note 227, Article XI; and IBEC Statutes, *supra* note 227, Article 2.

The British Foreign and Commonwealth Office in correspondence with the Bank of England in 1978 expressed the Office's opinion that the IBEC possesses legal personality under the Agreement on Multilateral Payments and the Charter, and can sue and be sued in English courts with respect to borrowing agreements concluded by it with British commercial banks. See Thomas L. Shillinglaw, "Recent Developments in the Council for Mutual Economic Assistance," *International Lawyer,* vol. 13 (1979), p. 523 at pp. 529–30.

[229] Protocol on the Character and Forms of Cooperation between the CMEA and the IBEC, signed July 20, 1970. The Russian text appears in Tokareva, *supra* note 212, 1972 ed., p. 227; trans. in Butler, *Source Book, supra* note 212, p. 307.

[230] Headquarters Agreement between the IBEC and the U.S.S.R., signed December 23, 1977. Russian text in Tokareva, *supra* note 212, 1981 ed., p. 146; trans. in Butler, *Source Book, supra* note 212, p. 313.

bers join the Bank.[231] During the first year of the Bank's operation (1964), each member contributed 20 percent of its capital subscription in transferable rubles. Since only the IBEC is the issuer of this currency, the capital appears to have been "paid in" by each IBEC member assigning to the IBEC a claim for payment for delivery of goods from that country denominated in transferable rubles in the appropriate amount.[232] In 1966 and 1971–72, IBEC members paid in a total of an additional 20 percent of the nominal capital, with the payments being made in Western convertible currencies; and in 1983 they agreed to pay in a further 22 percent (part in transferable rubles and part in convertible currencies).[233] The convertible currency contributions were seen as providing a capital base for the Bank that was acceptable in the West as it proceeded to borrow convertible currencies in Western markets (primarily at short-term) and to relend those currencies (i.e., extend Eurocurrency credit) to its member banks engaged in East-West trade.[234]

The IBEC is authorized to extend credit, make guarantees, and conduct a wide range of other operations in transferable rubles.[235] The Bank is also authorized to extend credit, accept deposits, handle payments, make guarantees, and conduct other operations in freely convertible national currencies, other currencies, and gold.[236] The IBEC presently maintains correspondent relationships with over 300 central banks and commercial banks around the world.

The highest organ of the International Bank for Economic Cooperation is the Council consisting of representatives from each of the member countries. Each member country has one vote irrespective of its share in the capital of the Bank. The Council takes actions on the basis of unanimity in the same manner as the Council for Mutual Economic Assistance.[237] It determines the general lines of the Bank's activity; approves the credit plans submitted by the Bank's Executive Board; approves the Bank's rules on clearing, credit, and other financial operations; establishes interest rates; and appoints the chairman and members of the Executive Board of the Bank and the members of the Audit Commis-

---

[231] Agreement on Multilateral Payments, Article III; and IBEC Charter, Article 5. The nominal capital was increased when Cuba joined the Bank in 1974 and when Vietnam joined in 1977. It now totals 305,262,000 transferable rubles. The size of a member's total exports to other members was the initial basis for allocating capital subscriptions.

[232] Agreement on Multilateral Payments, Article III, paragraphs 2 and 3. See Zwass, *Monetary Cooperation, supra* note 227, pp. 128–30; and Brabant, *East European Cooperation, supra* note 212, pp. 127–38.

[233] Agreement on Multilateral Payments, Article III, paragraph 3; IBEC, *Annual Report, 1970;* and *Foreign Trade* (Moscow), 1983, no. 8, p. 52. See Zwass, *Monetary Cooperation, supra* note 227, p. 130; and Brabant, *East European Cooperation, supra* note 212, pp. 138–40.

[234] Under the Charter, Article 5, paragraph 7, as amended in 1977, in the event of liquidation, the subscriptions and other holdings of the Bank are to be refunded to the member countries only after the claims of creditors have been paid.

[235] Agreement on Multilateral Payments, Articles II and V–IX; and IBEC Charter, Articles 9–24.

[236] Agreement on Multilateral Payments, Articles II and VIII; and IBEC Charter, Articles 11, 15, and 24. The IBEC's convertible currency operations have been mainly in U.S. dollars, Deutsche mark (Federal Republic of Germany), and Swiss francs.

[237] IBEC Charter, Articles 25–27. See notes 217–222, *supra*, and accompanying text.

sion.[238] The Executive Board is responsible for current operations.[239] There are four principal departments (administrations). The Transferable Ruble Department handles planning of credit operations in transferable rubles. The Convertible Currency Department handles deposits and exchange transactions in foreign currencies including spot, forward, and swap transactions. The department also handles short- and medium-term credit operations in convertible currencies, rediscount of bills, and correspondent relations with other banks. The Operations Department operates the mechanism of IBEC clearing and credit operations in both transferable rubles and convertible currencies. There is also an Economic Information and Research Department.[240]

The transferable ruble and the settlement and credit operations of the IBEC are examined in further detail in Chapter 9.

International Investment Bank. The Agreement on the Formation of the International Investment Bank and the Charter of the International Investment Bank were concluded July 10, 1970.[241] All active members of the CMEA are members of the International Investment Bank (IIB). It is a separate institution from the IBEC, and has relationship agreements with that institution[242] and with the CMEA.[243] It has its headquarters in Moscow.[244] The principal task of the Bank is to grant medium-term credits (up to five years) and long-term credits (up to fifteen years) for industrial projects, such as projects to develop raw material and fuel resources, likely to benefit the CMEA territory as a whole. Projects jointly pursued by two or more CMEA members are favored. The Bank also administers a Special Fund for assistance to developing countries.[245]

---

[238] IBEC Charter, Article 28.

[239] IBEC Charter, Articles 29–32.

[240] See annual reports issued by the IBEC.

[241] The Russian name of the International Investment Bank (IIB) is Mezhdunarodnyi Investitsionnyi Bank. The Agreement on the Formation of the Bank entered into force on February 5, 1971, and the Bank commenced operations that year. The Russian texts of the Agreement and Charter appear in *United Nations Treaty Series,* vol. 801, pp. 319 and 330; and in Tokareva, *supra* note 212, 1972 ed., pp. 255 and 263. Translations of the two documents appear in *UNTS,* vol. 801, pp. 342 and 364; and in Butler, *Source Book, supra* note 212, pp. 320 and 330. The IIB issues an *Annual Report* in English.

For background on the IIB, see generally Brabant, *East European Cooperation, supra* note 212, pp. 197–244; Alois Baran, "Origin and Development of the International Investment Bank," *Finance a Úvěr,* 1978, no. 12, trans. in *Soviet and Eastern European Foreign Trade,* vol. 15, no. 4 (winter 1979–80), p. 79; Albert Belichenko, "International Investment Bank: An Important Instrument Assisting Socialist Economic Integration," *Foreign Trade* (Moscow), 1981, no. 11, p. 10; and Lawrence J. Brainard, "CEMA Financial System and Integration," in Paul Marer and John Michael Montias (ed.), *Eastern European Integration and East-West Trade* (Bloomington: Indiana University Press, 1980), p. 121 at pp. 127–29. See in Russian Liubskii et al., *supra* note 227, chapter 3; and Komissarov, *supra* note 227, chapters 11–12.

[242] Agreement on Cooperation between the IIB and the IBEC, signed July 26, 1971. Russian text in Tokareva, *supra,* note 212, 1976 ed., p. 179; trans. in Butler, *Source Book, supra* note 212, p. 310.

[243] Protocol on the Character and Forms of Cooperation between the CMEA and the IIB, signed December 21, 1979. Russian text in Tokareva, *supra* note 212, 1981 ed., p. 109.

[244] Headquarters Agreement between the IIB and the U.S.S.R., signed December 23, 1977. Russian text in Tokareva, *supra* note 212, 1981 ed., p. 150.

[245] See Chapter 9, *infra,* page 369 (note 80).

The capital of the Bank and member quota subscriptions are defined in transferable rubles, the CMEA collective currency issued by the IBEC. The Bank is authorized to accept deposits in transferable rubles, in national currencies of CMEA countries, and in Western convertible currencies, and is authorized to pay interest on those deposits. It is also authorized to float bonds in Eastern and Western markets. Credit can be extended to banks, business organizations, and enterprises of member countries and also to international organizations formed by CMEA countries. Credit under procedures established by the IIB Council can also be extended to banks and economic organizations of other countries. Credit can be extended in transferable rubles to be used to pay for goods deliveries from socialist states or can be extended in convertible currencies for purchases in the West or in socialist states.

The International Bank for Economic Cooperation (IBEC) maintains accounts for the IIB in transferable rubles and effects settlements concerning IIB-granted credits. The IBEC has authority to credit the IIB with transferable rubles which it in turn uses to extend credits.

Related Bodies. The CMEA Permanent Commission on Financial and Monetary Questions studies and recommends policies in its sphere of responsibility.[246] The International Institute of Economic Problems of the World Socialist System is a research and planning institution for the CMEA countries.[247] Both the IBEC and the IIB maintain relationships with the Institute.

Note. Chapter 9 is devoted to the transferable ruble and the clearing and credit operations of the International Bank for Economic Cooperation. The organization of the economies of CMEA countries, the role of price systems, and currency convertibility issues are treated at that time. Due to the relative isolation of CMEA monetary institutions from other institutions studied in this book, CMEA practices will not otherwise be treated integrally with the practices of other organizations in later chapters of this book that focus on specific problems.

Other Regional Arrangements

A number of regional organizations not discussed in this chapter provide balance-of-payments financing to their members. These regional systems are examined in Chapter 7.

---

[246] The Russian text of the Statute on the Permanent Commission on Financial and Monetary Questions, confirmed April 25, 1963, amended April 24, 1975, appears in Tokareva, *supra* note 212, 1976 ed., p. 45; trans. in Butler, *Source Book, supra* note 212, p. 228.

[247] The Russian text of the Statute on the International Institute of Economic Problems of the World Socialist System, confirmed July 24, 1970, appears in Tokareva, *supra* note 212, 1972 ed., p. 194; trans. in Butler, *Source Book, supra* note 212, p. 264.

Chapter Conclusion

In this and the previous chapter, we surveyed the principal multilateral institutions concerned with monetary policy. The chapters that follow focus on particular issues: the financing of balance-of-payments deficits, currency convertibility and payments restrictions, the management of exchange rates, international surveillance of national decision-making, and the coordination of national and international policies. Decisions, as we shall see, are often made in an institutional context in which the International Monetary Fund and other organizations may figure prominently.

II
Balance-of-Payments Financing

Introduction to Chapters 3–9

This part of the book is devoted to the resources and facilities available to monetary authorities for the financing of balance-of-payments transactions. Before proceeding, the reader may wish to review the material in Appendix A on balance-of-payments accounting and the use of foreign currencies and other monetary assets by national authorities.

Chapter 3 considers the composition of monetary reserves and the features, particularly legal features, of the various monetary instruments that are considered reserve assets. Chapter 4 examines techniques of financing that do not require the involvement of international organizations.

Chapters 5–9 consider multilateral institutions that provide financing for balance-of-payments support. The legal features of the IMF special drawing right (SDR) are studied in Chapter 5. Drawing rights in the General Resources Account of the International Monetary Fund and related accounts of the IMF are treated in Chapter 6. Multilateral institutions and arrangements outside the IMF that provide balance-of-payments financing receive attention in Chapters 7–9.

The reader should be advised that the financing facilities discussed in this part of the book cannot be considered in isolation from issues treated in the final part of this work. Exchange controls, examined in Chapter 10, may be used to conserve monetary reserves and channel funds to preferred uses. Exchange rate policies and other economic and monetary policies, discussed in Chapters 11 and 12, bear upon the underlying conditions that may give rise to balance-of-payments financing needs.

Chapter 3: Monetary Reserve Assets

Note

This is the first chapter in a group of chapters on the sources available to official monetary authorities (national treasuries, central banks, and exchange stabilization funds) for obtaining resources for the financing of international transactions. It is assumed that the reader already understands the situations in which national authorities may wish, or find it necessary, to use foreign currencies, special drawing rights (SDRs), or other monetary assets to directly make payments abroad, to supply their residents for payments abroad, to intervene in exchange markets, or for other purposes.[1]

Our task in this chapter is to identify monetary instruments that are classified as "assets" and that, as such, are held by monetary authorities as "reserves." We shall also consider some of the features possessed by the several types of monetary reserve assets. These assets are understood to be stores of purchasing power that can be readily used to finance, or obtain financing for, international transactions. It is essential that they be usable on demand without any conditions respecting the country's policies and without any need for negotiations.

Chapters 4–9 consider methods by which the monetary reserve assets identified in this chapter can be obtained. Finally, in the last chapter of this book, we shall appraise the multiple reserve system of the present time, consider proposals for the harmonization of reserve asset policies and for giving the IMF special drawing right an enhanced role, review proposals for "substitution accounts" in which one reserve asset (say SDRs) is to be substituted for another which is to some degree to be immobilized (say gold or U.S. dollars), and reflect on issues relating to the measurement and control of international liquidity.[2]

---

[1] The reader may wish to review Appendix A of this book, especially pages 672–682.
[2] Chapter 12, *infra*, pages 630–644.

Composition of Monetary Reserves

The present international system is a multiple reserve system. There is no single asset used exclusively in dealings in which national monetary authorities take part. Rather, there are a number of different monetary instruments, possessing different features as well as names, that are held and used by monetary authorities. In most cases one type of instrument can be used to acquire another type, and thus for some purposes they are interchangeable.

Most economists treat the following items when held by the central bank or national treasury of a country as international monetary reserve assets:

(a) Holdings of foreign currencies (at least those currencies that qualify as "reserve currencies").

(b) Holdings of special drawing rights (SDRs) allocated by the International Monetary Fund (and holdings of European currency units (ECUs) issued by the European Monetary Cooperation Fund).

(c) Reserve tranche drawing rights in the International Monetary Fund (and similar rights exercisable on demand without conditions in other organizations).

(d) Indebtedness of the International Monetary Fund to the country under loan agreements, repayment of which can be immediately demanded by the country in event of need.

(e) Holdings of gold.

The International Monetary Fund in its monthly publication, *International Financial Statistics,* reports each member country's official holdings of these items. While foreign currencies and gold are capable of being held by commercial banks, firms, and individuals, only holdings by monetary authorities are treated as reserve assets of the state. The term "monetary authorities" is taken to include central banks, national treasuries, currency boards, and exchange stabilization funds.

Each of the five major components of monetary reserves is described further below. In order to be a monetary reserve asset, a monetary instrument must serve as a medium of exchange in international transactions, serve as a medium of exchange in transactions at least among central banks or national treasuries, or be readily exchangeable into such media without loss in value. Its use must not be subject to significant conditions. The word "reserve" suggests that the asset must be a store of purchasing power.

In the past, the larger the magnitude of monetary reserve assets under the exclusive control of its national treasury or central bank, the greater the freedom enjoyed by a country in managing its international transactions and domestic economy. This continues to be true today, although some restraints have been imposed in the interest of a cooperative world monetary order.[3] Reserve assets can be used at any time to make needed purchases abroad, to finance chronic or crisis balance-of-payments deficits, or to intervene in exchange markets to maintain the exchange value of a national currency. Ideally, they should provide an unconditional store of financial purchasing power for a "rainy day." The existence of substantial reserve assets may permit a country to ride through times of economic stress without undue pressure on its monetary and fiscal policies.

The classification of a particular monetary instrument as a reserve asset may also have domestic monetary implications. If the particular item is treated as a reserve under the domestic law of the holder, it may in some countries serve as a basis for expanding the domestic money supply.[4]

Official Holdings of Foreign Currencies

Overview

One component of a country's monetary reserves, and often the largest, is the monetary authorities' holdings of foreign currencies. These officially owned foreign currency reserves may be held with commercial banks as well as with the central banks of issue, and may also be held in Eurocurrency deposits (directly or through the Bank for International Settlements).[5] They may be held in the form of demand deposits, time deposits, treasury bills, short-term or marketable longer-term government securities, or other monetary instruments.

The Articles of Agreement of the International Monetary Fund at one time included an agreed definition of the foreign currency component of monetary reserves. Under that definition only "convertible currencies" and other currencies specified by the Fund were included in reserves. "Convertible currencies" were defined to include (a) currencies issued by IMF members that accepted the obligations of Article VIII (i.e., did not avail themselves of Article XIV, Section 2); (b) currencies issued by IMF members availing themselves of Article XIV, Section 2, if the Fund deemed the particular currencies to be convertible;

---

[3] At a number of points in this book the special obligations of countries with strong balance-of-payments and reserve positions are pointed out. See, e.g., pages 224–225 (currencies provided by IMF General Resources Account), 210–211 (designation of countries to accept special drawing rights), 517–519 (exchange rate policies), and 611–619 (economic policy generally).

[4] See Appendix A, *infra,* pages 668–671.

[5] For an explanation of Eurocurency deposits, see Appendix A at pages 679–682. The role of the Bank for International Settlements as a bank for central banks is mentioned in Chapter 2, *supra,* pages 52–63.

and (c) currencies issued by nonmembers if the Fund determined them to be convertible.[6]

Definitions of monetary reserves and of the currency component of reserves no longer appear in the IMF Articles. While the present Articles at a number of places use the terms "reserve assets" and "balance of payments and reserve position," these terms are not defined in the Articles. The present text, by omitting a definition, recognizes that the determination of a country's reserve position involves an element of judgment in appraising the usefulness of a country's foreign currency holdings in relation to the country's needs for foreign exchange. A particular foreign currency that is not readily exchangeable into others may have utility for one holder but not for another. A currency that is convertible within the terms of Article VIII may lawfully, for example, be subject to restrictions when used in capital transactions or even, with the IMF's approval, for some current transactions.[7]

The particular foreign currencies in which central banks and other monetary authorities *in fact* choose to hold substantial parts of the currency portion of their reserves are called "reserve currencies." This is not a term that has a legal definition. While the criteria for use of the term by officials, bankers, and economists lack precision, it is possible at any point in time to identify at least a few currencies to which the term clearly applies.

Members of the IMF making drawings in the General Resources Account or using special drawing rights are entitled to obtain a "freely usable currency." Unlike "reserve currency," the term "freely usable currency" is a term with a legal definition. The IMF Articles of Agreement define a "freely usable currency" as a "member's currency that the Fund determines (i) is, in fact, widely used to make payments for international transactions, and (ii) is widely traded in the principal exchange markets."[8] The Fund determines which currencies are freely usable currencies and can add a currency to or delete it from its list. At the present time the U.S. dollar, Deutsche mark, U.K. pound sterling, French franc, and Japanese yen are designated as freely usable currencies.[9] Freely usable currencies are in practice likely to be currencies that central banks would be willing to hold in substantial quantities. Thus, of all the national currencies, a "freely usable currency" would appear to qualify as a reserve asset by almost any definition. It must be recognized, however, that the IMF's decision to add a currency to or delete it from its list of "freely usable

---

[6] See Article XIX(a)–(e) and (g), *original* and *first* (which differ). A precise definition of "monetary reserves" was necessary under the Articles before the Second Amendment, effective April 1, 1978, because repurchase obligations in the IMF's General Account were based upon formulas that required calculations of the exact size of reserves. Article V, section 7, *original* and *first*.

[7] The obligations of IMF Article VIII are summarized in Chapter 1, *supra*, pages 19–21, and are treated more fully in Chapter 10.

[8] Article XXX(f).

[9] See Chapter 5, *infra*, pages 197–199.

currencies" may be affected by political as well as economic considerations, notwithstanding the apparent objective criteria the Fund is to apply.

Judgments of monetary authorities on the inclusion of a currency in reserves are influenced by a range of economic and political as well as legal considerations. Economic and legal factors include usability in international payments, exchangeability, freedom from current and capital controls, strength of the economy of the issuing country, interest rates, and the expected purchasing power of a unit of the currency at a future time when it may be used.[10] The United States dollar is more widely used than any other currency to make international payments and is readily exchangeable into other currencies on the exchange markets. Its use in current and capital transactions is subject to few restrictions. Further, the range of goods and services produced by the United States economy is large and diverse. The U.S. dollar is presently held in monetary reserves in larger quantities than all other national currencies combined.

Officially held claims against nonresidents that are denominated in the holder's own currency were at an earlier time not included in monetary reserves, but now are included in IMF tables showing reserves.[11] Some claims against international organizations that are payable on demand without conditions may also be included in the foreign exchange component of reserves.[12]

Foreign currencies enter official reserves in a variety of ways. They are acquired in exchange for the national currency by monetary authorities pursuant to currency surrender requirements that are maintained by many countries.[13] A central bank can purchase foreign currencies in exchange for the national currency in transactions with commercial banks or foreign monetary agencies either directly or through open market operations. Monetary authorities can also obtain foreign exchange by use of many other credit and exchange techniques which are discussed in later chapters.

Exchange Value Guarantees to Holders of a Currency

A state holding a foreign currency in its reserves bears the risk that the currency will depreciate in value. On occasion, authorities issuing a currency have made guarantees to a foreign central bank or treasury holding that currency that the exchange value will be maintained. Usually, the *quid pro quo* is that the hold-

---

[10] See discussion of the reserve currency roles played by the U.S. dollar, Deutsche mark, Japanese yen, Swiss franc, and U.K. pound sterling in Robert V. Roosa et al., *Reserve Currencies in Transition* (New York: Group of Thirty, 1982). See also "The Deutsche Mark as an International Investment Currency," *Monthly Report of the Deutsche Bundesbank*, November 1979, p. 26.

[11] The IMF did not regularly begin to obtain and publish this data until 1970.

[12] See notes 38 and 40, *infra*, and accompanying text. See generally the introduction to each issue of *International Financial Statistics* published by the International Monetary Fund.

[13] A surrender requirement compels residents to sell foreign currencies they obtain to authorized banks in exchange for the local currency. Commercial banks may in turn be required to sell the foreign currencies to the central bank. Surrender requirements receive attention in Chapter 10, *infra*, pages 385–386 and 392.

ing state agrees to maintain a certain portion of its total reserves in that currency or to delay converting its holdings. The United Kingdom's sterling guarantees in the period 1968–1974 provide an example. In 1968 the United Kingdom entered into a series of bilateral agreements with countries in the "sterling area" in which the United Kingdom guaranteed the value, in terms of the U.S. dollar, of a defined part of the officially held sterling balances of its treaty partners.[14] In the agreements, each of the countries promised to maintain a "minimum sterling proportion" within its total official monetary reserves. The precise proportion was arrived at through negotiation in each case.[15] The United Kingdom's value guarantee was typically expressed in the following language:

> The Government of the United Kingdom undertake to maintain the sterling value in terms of the United States dollar of the balances eligible for guarantee, provided that the Minimum Sterling Proportion referred to below has been maintained by [name of country] up to and including the date of implementation of the guarantee. The circumstances in which the guarantee would be implemented and the terms of implementation shall be defined in consultation between the two Governments.

The idea was that if the U.K. pound sterling was formally devalued or if it depreciated in the exchange markets in relation to the U.S. dollar, the United Kingdom would make a payment in sterling to the country in an amount that would restore the dollar value of the guaranteed portion of that country's sterling balance.[16] The purpose of the agreements from the United Kingdom's

[14] Bilateral agreements were concluded with over 30 countries. When the agreements expired in September 1971, most of them were extended until September 1973. The minimum proportions of reserves to be held in sterling were modified in some of the extension agreements. The agreements were allowed to expire on September 24, 1973. See generally *The Basle Facility and the Sterling Area* (U.K. Command Paper 3787; London: Her Majesty's Stationery Office, October 1968); M. R. Shuster, *The Public International Law of Money* (London: Oxford University Press, 1973), pp. 236-40; and Christopher W. McMahon, "The United Kingdom's Experience in Winding Down the Reserve Role of Sterling," in Roosa et al, *supra* note 10, p. 42 at pp. 42–47. The texts of the various agreements appear in *United Nations Treaty Series*, vol. 655, pp. 43–51; vol. 686, pp. 349–407; vol. 687, pp. 3–199; vol. 705, pp. 189–97; vol. 713, pp. 101–07; vol. 745, pp. 259–65; and vol. 820, pp. 459–99; and in U.K., *Treaty Series*, 1968, No. 118 (Cmnd. 3834); 1969, No. 110 (Cmnd. 4176); 1969, No. 124 (Cmnd. 4224); 1970, No. 38 (Cmnd. 4415); 1971, No. 85 (Cmnd. 4847); 1972, No. 10 (Cmnd. 4884); and 1973, No. 69 (Cmnd. 5325); and also Cmnd. 3835 (1968).

[15] The IMF judged the United Kingdom's requirement that "sterling area" countries receiving the exchange guarantee maintain a "minimum sterling proportion" to be a limitation on the use and convertibility of sterling which required Fund approval under Article VIII, section 2(a). Approval was given November 18, 1968. Margaret Garritsen de Vries, *The International Monetary Fund, 1966–1971: The System Under Stress* (2 vols.; Washington: IMF, 1976) [hereinafter *IMF History 1966–71*], vol. 1, pp. 441–42.

[16] The guarantee was to be implemented if the middle exchange rate between the pound and the dollar should fall and remain for 30 consecutive days more than 1 percent below $2.40 which was the parity at the time the agreements were concluded. The amount to be paid would make good the difference between 2.40 dollars and the closing middle sterling–dollar rate in London on the last working day of the 30-day period. Written answer of the Chancellor of the Exchequer to a question in Parliament. House of Commons, *Parliamentary Debates (Hansard)*, 5th series, vol. 845, column 242 (Written Answers) (November 9, 1972).

point of view was to make it easier for that country to maintain the value of sterling during what turned out to be a difficult period in international finance. The arrangements assured that large sterling holdings in the hands of other governments were not presented to the United Kingdom for conversion or sold on the exchange markets.[17] During the period the agreements were in force, the United Kingdom in November 1972 paid £ 59 million to implement the guarantee. The payments were required by the depreciation of sterling in the exchange markets following the U.K. decision in June 1972 to allow the pound to float.[18]

Instead of negotiating new bilateral agreements when the agreements expired in September 1973, the United Kingdom on September 6 that year made a unilateral declaration guaranteeing the value of sterling balances in relation to the U.S. dollar for the period September 25, 1973, to March 31, 1974.[19] Compensation totaling approximately £ 80 million was subsequently paid as a result of a fall in the exchange rate for sterling in relation to the U.S. dollar.[20] The unilateral guarantee was renewed for the nine-month period April 1, 1974, to December 31, 1974. This last declaration changed the basis of the arrangement from the exchange rate of sterling against the U.S. dollar to the exchange rate of sterling in relation to a group of currencies. The unilateral guarantees expired on December 31, 1974, with no compensation due. They were not renewed.[21]

Eighteen central banks of countries belonging to the Organisation for Economic Co-operation and Development (but not the central banks of the United States, Canada, and Japan) concluded an Agreement Concerning an Exchange Guarantee that entered into force on January 1, 1973. Its purpose was to provide an exchange guarantee to cover amounts held as working balances by a

---

[17] To reduce the need of "sterling area" countries to draw upon their sterling reserves, the Bank for International Settlements agreed, if it became necessary, to provide credits to finance payments deficits of these countries. Further, the central banks of twelve industrial countries agreed to provide the Bank of England with a $2 billion stand-by credit through the Bank for International Settlements to finance the conversion of sterling balances that might be withdrawn. Private as well as official balances were covered. See *The Basle Facility and the Sterling Area, supra* note 14; BIS, *39th Annual Report 1968/69,* p. 117; and Benjamin J. Cohen, *The Reform of Sterling* (Essays in International Finance no. 77; Princeton: Princeton University International Finance Section, 1969).

[18] Her Majesty's Treasury Press Release, September 6, 1973. See Chapter 11, page 499 (note 41), respecting the U.K. decision in June 1972 to float the pound sterling.

[19] Treasury Press Release, September 6, 1973, *supra* note 18. The guarantee was set at $2.4213, which was the average of the exchange rates at noon on the three days preceding the announcement. The guarantee was to be implemented if the average of the daily rates for the entire six-month period should be below the guarantee rate. The sterling balances eligible for the guarantee were defined somewhat differently than in the previous bilateral agreements.

[20] Her Majesty's Treasury Press Release, November 12, 1974. The average rate for sterling during the period was $2.3335 compared to the guarantee rate of $2.4213.

The United Kingdom had an obligation in international law to honor its unilateral declaration which had been relied upon by other states that had maintained their reserves in sterling. See decision of the Permanent Court of International Justice in *Legal Status of Eastern Greenland (Denmark v. Norway).* Permanent Court of International Justice, *Judgments, Orders and Advisory Opinions,* Series A/B, Case No. 53 (1933).

[21] Her Majesty's Treasury Press Releases, March 15, 1974, and November 12, 1974.

participating central bank with another participating central bank in the latter's currency. The agreement was for an initial period of three years and the Bank for International Settlements acted as agent. The agreement entered into force at a time when it appeared that, with the exception of the floating pound sterling, a system of stable exchange rates was functioning.[22] Compensation was paid on only one occasion. That was following rate changes announced in February 1973. No compensation was paid for changes resulting from fluctuating rates in the period after March 1973.[23] In a general review of the agreement in 1975, it was decided that the agreement had little practical value under the floating rate system of the time. The agreement was nevertheless renewed for an additional three years, but in a suspended form in which no new claim would arise. The agreement terminated December 31, 1978. The participating central banks agreed that any outstanding balances covered by the agreement at that time were to be settled without compensation.[24]

Under the reciprocal currency arrangements between the U.S. Federal Reserve System and foreign central banks, discussed in the next chapter, the exchange risk normally falls on the country drawing on the arrangement. In the past, however, some of the arrangements have included features for the sharing of profits and losses from exchange rate changes.[25]

Issuing-State Concerns About Foreign Holdings of its Currency

The state of issue of a currency held in large amounts in the monetary reserves of other states may find that it must take into account the attitudes of the foreign holders of its currency when it considers changes in domestic policies. That is, domestic actions, such as changes in interest rates, may precipitate movements into or out of its currency. These movements may require the issuing state to pursue stabilization actions in the exchange markets.

Rather than encourage countries to hold large quantities of sterling in their official reserves as it did in the period 1968–1974, the United Kingdom's policy (in part taken at the urging of its partners in the European Economic Community) in later years was the opposite; that is, it encouraged monetary authorities in other countries to draw down their sterling balances in an orderly manner. The reasons for the policy were to reduce the reserve currency role of sterling and avoid monetary disturbances such as those that had occurred in the past as a result of fluctuations in official sterling balances. Arrangements for an orderly

---

[22] See Chapter 11, *infra*, pages 498–499.

[23] See Chapter 11, *infra*, pages 499–501.

[24] See decisions of the Council of the OECD of December 13, 1972, and November 7, 1975, in *European Yearbook*, vol. 20 (1972), p. 267, and vol. 23 (1975), p. 439; and comment in BIS, *49th Annual Report 1978/79*, pp. 174–75.

[25] See pages 145–151, *infra*.

reduction of balances were worked out in Basle in January 1977. Foreign official holders were requested to draw down their sterling balances over a two-year period to working-balance levels. These official holders of sterling were offered the opportunity to exchange any part of their sterling holdings (which typically had been invested in U.K. treasury bills) for negotiable bonds with maturities of five to ten years denominated in currencies other than sterling, the bonds being issued by the U.K. Treasury on market-related terms.[26]

As indicated in the sterling case discussed above, a country can request foreign authorities not to accumulate the country's currency above working balances and, if they have done so (even with earlier encouragement of the issuer), to reduce their holdings to working-balance levels. The sterling case above, the practice of central banks in reducing holdings of Swiss francs when requested to do so by the Swiss National Bank,[27] and the practices of the EEC central banks in controlling the growth of their reserve holdings of member currencies[28] indicate that a customary rule of international law may be emerging that calls for honoring an issuer's request to reduce reserve holdings of its currency, at least where reduction of the balances can be accomplished without loss of value.

Proposals to Reduce the Currency Component of Reserves

The International Monetary Fund's Committee on Reform in the early 1970s considered ways to reduce, world-wide, the currency component of official reserves. While the Committee was not able to reach agreement on how to control the currency component of reserves, the Outline of Reform in its final report in June 1974 stated:

> Countries will cooperate in the management of their currency reserves so as to avoid disequilibrating movements of official funds.

---

[26] To support the Bank of England's program, the Bank for International Settlements extended a stand-by credit facility, amounting to U.S. $3 billion, to the Bank of England for a period of two years with an optional third year. The Bank of England was entitled to draw on the credit facility, subject to certain conditions, to finance the exchange of sterling for foreign currencies where foreign authorities chose to make a direct currency exchange when they drew down their sterling balances rather than accept the U.K. bonds denominated in foreign currencies. See *Bank of England Quarterly Bulletin*, vol. 17, no. 1 (March 1977), pp. 8–9; Board of Governors of the Federal Reserve System, *64th Annual Report, 1977*, pp. 172–74; BIS, *47th Annual Report 1976/77*, p. 144; and McMahon, *supra* note 14, pp. 47–49. The central banks of eleven countries, including the U.S. Federal Reserve System, agreed to extend credit to the BIS, should that be necessary, to back its extension of credit to the Bank of England. See also Chapter 6, *infra*, page 273 (note 203). The special sterling arrangement terminated in accordance with its terms in February 1979. IMF, *Annual Report, 1979*, p. 89.

[27] The Swiss National Bank has made such requests when it has believed foreign central banks were accumulating Swiss francs above working-balance needs. See, e.g., *Minutes of Federal Open Market Committee*, 1972, pp. 480–82. See also *idem*, 1975, p. 808. For information on FOMC Minutes, see Chapter 4, *infra*, page 137 (note 31).

[28] An understanding among EEC countries is mentioned in Chapters 8 and 11, *infra*, pages 328 and 549.

Among the possible provisions for achieving this objective, the following have been suggested but are not agreed:

(a) Countries should respect any request from a country whose currency is held in official reserves to limit or convert into other reserve assets further increases in their holdings of its currency.

(b) Countries should periodically choose the composition of their currency reserves and should undertake not to change it without prior consultation with the Fund.

(c) Countries should not add to their currency reserve placements outside the territory of the country of issue [Eurocurrency holdings] except within limits to be agreed with the Fund.[29]

These three proposals did not have the full support of the Committee and were not reported as agreed recommendations. Note the proposed role of the country of issue: It could request states holding its currency in official reserves not to increase the holdings, and this request was entitled to "respect." Note the role of the Fund: Members would increase holdings of Eurocurrencies (that is currency holdings in banks outside the state of issue) only if they obtained the agreement of the Fund.[30] Also members would not shift the currency component of their official reserves from one currency to another except after consultation with the Fund. These proposals were not incorporated into the amended Articles. However, a clause was added at the end of Article VIII under which each member agrees to collaborate with the Fund and with other members to ensure that its reserve assets policies are consistent with the objective of making the special drawing right the principal reserve asset in the international monetary system.[31]

[29] IMF Committee on Reform of the International Monetary System and Related Issues (Committee of Twenty), *International Monetary Reform: Documents of the Committee of Twenty* (Washington: IMF, 1974), p. 7 at p. 15 (Outline of Reform, June 14, 1974, paragraph 23). See also Annexes 5, 6, and 7, at pp. 37–42; and the Report of the Technical Group on Global Liquidity and Consolidation to the Committee on Reform at pp. 162–82.

[30] The central banks of the Group of Ten at Basle on June 12, 1971, made an agreement not to place additional official reserves in Eurocurrency deposits and, as it became prudent to do so, to reduce Eurocurrency holdings. The agreement was for a three-month period. At a meeting in Basle on September 12, 1971, the conclusion was reached to discontinue a formal "commitment" but generally to continue the same "attitudes" against official Eurocurrency placements. Within agreed procedures, central banks were to continue to provide the BIS with data on central bank holdings in the Eurocurrency market and commercial bank assets and liabilities in Eurocurrencies. See *Minutes of Federal Open Market Committee, supra* note 27, 1971, pp. 427, 612–15, 720–22, and 924–26. The attitudes to limit placements of official reserves in the Eurocurrency market and the agreement to continue to provide the BIS with data were reaffirmed in December 1978. BIS, *The Bank for International Settlements and the Basle Meetings* (Basle, 1980), pp. 55–56. Some countries outside the Group of Ten hold large portions of their official reserves in Eurocurrency deposits with commercial banks.

[31] Article VIII, section 7, *second.* See text accompanying notes 89 and 90, *infra,* for alternative wordings considered by the Interim Committee of the Board of Governors and the language finally chosen.

The Committee on Reform also recommended that the IMF establish a "substitution account." The idea was that members would transfer foreign currency balances to the Fund and in exchange receive a monetary instrument valued in terms of the special drawing right. The effect would be to transfer claims against particular countries into claims against the system as a whole.[32]

The substitution account idea was given only a very limited authorization in the amended Articles. Under Article V, Section 6(b), a member of the IMF that participates in the Special Drawing Rights Department may, with the agreement of the Fund, sell its holdings of currencies issued by other members to the IMF's General Resources Account and receive SDRs in exchange. However, the Fund is prohibited from purchasing currencies above the level at which the issuing country would be subject to charges.[33] A number of proposals looking toward the establishment of a special substitution account have been studied.[34]

Foreign Currency Holdings—A Concluding Thought

The purchasing power and usefulness of a foreign currency—even one called a "reserve currency" or a "freely usable currency"—is dependent upon the economic and monetary policies and the state of the economy of the issuing state. The actions and policies of the issuing state may be guided by its obligations as a member of the IMF and other commitments it has undertaken. Important as those commitments are, the value of the currency ultimately rests upon the issuing country's policies and economy and the expectations that participants in world finance have about the value of the currency. It should not be surprising that central bankers prefer to hold some currencies as compared to others and that, indeed, central bankers prefer holding some currencies, in which they have firm confidence, in larger amounts than they hold special drawing rights (SDRs).

Holdings of Special Drawing Rights

As previously explained,[35] the special drawing right (SDR) is a monetary reserve asset created by deliberate action of the International Monetary Fund. Its

---

[32] See *International Monetary Reform, supra* note 29, pp. 14–15 (Outline of Reform, para. 22), 41–42 (Annex 7), 130–33, and 166–76. In the Committee's technical group discussions there was a wide divergence of views on the necessity and wisdom of sharply reducing the currency component of reserves. Some experts favored a substantial reduction, possibly leading to the elimination of all but working balances; others believed that the extent of the reduction should be left to the individual decisions of countries. *Idem* at p. 166.

[33] See Chapter 5, *infra,* pages 207–209.

[34] See Chapter 12, *infra,* pages 638–642.

[35] At pages 16–17, *supra.*

role as a medium of exchange is circumscribed by legal rules respecting its use. SDRs are transferable among monetary authorities of IMF members that have agreed to be participants in the Special Drawing Rights Department and in transactions with other official entities (such as the Bank for International Settlements) prescribed by the IMF as holders of SDRs. SDRs can be exchanged almost as freely as convertible currencies among official monetary authorities but cannot enter the private market.[36]

Chapter 5 is devoted to the special drawing right. Legal rules surrounding its valuation, allocation, and use are examined at that time. We shall not anticipate that discussion here.

The effective role of the special drawing right as a reserve asset is dependent upon judgments about the long-term usefulness of the SDR and the maintenance of its purchasing power. An assessment entails addressing a number of questions that are not easy to answer. These include:

(a) How can a proper balance be struck between incentives to use the asset and incentives to hold it?

(b) What criteria should determine the selection of the interest rate and charges applicable to SDR holdings?

(c) At the present time the SDR's exchange value is determined by a composite of national currencies. What influence can and should the Fund exercise over the economic policies of the countries that issue currencies included in the composite as those policies in turn affect the purchasing power of the SDR in relation to goods and services?

(d) What criteria should the Fund use in considering changes in the make-up of the composite of national currencies in terms of which the exchange value of the SDR is calculated?

(e) What criteria should the Fund use in considering changes in the principle of the SDR's valuation, such as, for example, substituting a commodity index in place of a composite of currencies?

These are only a few questions that bear upon the SDR as a reserve asset. They are addressed in Chapters 5 and 12.[37]

The European currency unit (ECU), discussed in Chapter 8, shares some of the features of the special drawing right. It is also valued in terms of a com-

---

[36] The various transactions and operations in which SDRs can be used are surveyed in Chapter 5, *infra*, pages 194–209.

[37] At pages 176–194, 210–221, and 635–642 *infra*.

posite consisting of portions of national currencies. Likewise, it can be held only by official entities. It is, like the special drawing right, treated as a monetary reserve asset.[38]

Reserve Tranche Drawing Rights in the IMF

A country's right to make a drawing in its "reserve tranche" in the General Resources Account of the IMF is not subject to challenge. Since exercise of the right to make a reserve tranche drawing is automatic, the amount that can be drawn is normally included as a component of a country's monetary reserves.[39] The right to make drawings in the General Resources Account beyond the reserve tranche is *not* treated as a reserve asset. That right is of great value nevertheless to a state facing balance-of-payments difficulties, but it is subject to conditions.

One sometimes sees references to a country's "reserve position" in the IMF. This is the total of the country's reserve tranche drawing rights plus any readily repayable indebtedness of the Fund to that country as explained in the section which follows.

A country may have a right to make a drawing of foreign exchange on demand without conditions or review in organizations besides the IMF. The right to an "automatic loan" in the Arab Monetary Fund is an example. This right may be treated as a reserve asset.[40]

Readily Repayable Indebtedness of the IMF to a Country

The International Monetary Fund has on occasion borrowed currencies to supplement its resources in order to provide balance-of-payments assistance in a magnitude that it might otherwise have been unable to finance.[41] The indebtedness, if any, of the IMF that is readily repayable under a borrowing agreement is normally treated as a reserve asset by the country to which the indebtedness is owed. The IMF's General Arrangements to Borrow (GAB) and borrowings in connection with the policy on enlarged access, the supplementary financing facility, and the oil facility are the principal examples.[42] The arrangements typically provide for repayment to the lending country within a stated time (often

---

[38] See Chapter 8, *infra*, pages 315–326 and 342–345, especially pages 324–325. The International Monetary Fund for statistical purposes classifies ECU holdings with foreign exchange assets in *International Financial Statistics*.

[39] The calculation of the size of a country's reserve tranche rights and the procedure for making a reserve tranche drawing are explained in Chapter 6, *infra*, pages 235–238.

[40] See the introduction to each issue of the IMF's publication *International Financial Statistics*. The Arab Monetary Fund is treated in Chapter 7, *infra*, pages 311–313.

[41] Article VII, section 1(i), authorizes the IMF to borrow currencies to replenish its holdings.

[42] Legal aspects of Fund borrowings are treated in Chapter 6, *infra*, pages 283–287.

five or seven years) and include an acceleration clause. That clause guarantees that the lender will promptly receive from the Fund the currencies it needs should it be overtaken by balance-of-payments difficulties in the meantime. In the case of the GAB, it reads:

> Before the date prescribed . . . [usually five years; more or less in some circumstances] a participant [lender of currency to the Fund] may give notice representing that there is a balance of payments need for repayment of part or all of the Fund's indebtedness and requesting such repayment. The Fund shall give the overwhelming benefit of any doubt to the participant's representation.[43]

The IMF's borrowings to fund the enlarged access policy, supplementary financing facility, and oil facility in some cases have had long maturities (up to seven years). The borrowing agreements, as in the case of borrowings under the GAB, include an acceleration clause. In the case of borrowing agreements with central banks for the enlarged access policy, it states:

> The lender may obtain repayment of a claim on the Fund before maturity if: (i) the lender is a member, the central bank, or another agency of a member; (ii) the lender represents that its balance of payments and reserve position, or that of the member's if the lender is a central bank or another agency of a member, justifies early repayment; and (iii) the Fund, having given the lender's representation the overwhelming benefit of any doubt, determines that there is such a need for early repayment.[44]

The Fund's borrowing agreements under the supplementary financing facility and oil facility contain similar clauses.[45]

---

[43] Paragraph 11(e) of the General Arrangements to Borrow (GAB), annexed to E.B. Decision No. 1289 -(62/1) (January 5, 1962), as amended and extended. IMF, *Selected Decisions of the International Monetary Fund and Selected Documents* (10th issue; Washington, 1983) [hereinafter *Selected Decisions*], pp. 117–31 and 131–47. This provision is unchanged by a recent amendment to the GAB. E.B. Decision No. 7337 -(83/37)(adopted February 24, 1983, effective December 26, 1983); IMF, *Annual Report*, 1983 p. 145; *Selected Decisions*, pp. 131–45.

Where the Fund makes early repayment in accordance with the clause quoted, the Fund (after consulting the participant) is to make the repayments in the currencies of other members that are "actually convertible" or in special drawing rights as the Fund determines. When repayments are made in accordance with the normal maturity schedule, they are to be made in the lender's currency "whenever feasible" or in SDRs. Other currencies that are actually convertible can be used in scheduled repayments only after consultation by the Fund with the participant. GAB, paragraph 11(a) and (e).

[44] Paragraph 7(a) of E.B. Decision No. 6864 -(81/81)(May 13, 1981); IMF, *Annual Report, 1981*, p. 191; *Selected Decisions* (10th issue, 1983), p. 207. For the language in the agreement with the Saudi Arabian Monetary Agency, see paragraph 10 of attachment to E.B. Decision No. 6843 -(81/75)(May 6, 1981); IMF, *Annual Report, 1981*, p. 172; *Selected Decisions*, p. 173.

[45] For the supplementary financing facility, see paragraph 5(c) of annex to E.B. Decision No.

A claim to repayment under the GAB is transferable "with the prior consent of the Fund and on such terms and conditions as the Fund may approve."[46] A Fund decision prescribed circumstances under which a lender to the oil facility could transfer its repayment claim without the need for further Fund approval.[47] The borrowing agreements for the supplementary facility and the enlarged access policy define a broad transferability right not dependent upon Fund approval.[48] It should also be noted that the Fund's repayment obligations under borrowing agreements, made under the authority of the GAB and under decisions respecting the enlarged access policy, supplementary facility, and the oil facility, are backed by all of the assets of the General Resources Account.

The acceleration clause, the transferability right, and the Fund's financial strength are the bases upon which countries rely when they count Fund indebtedness to them in their monetary reserves.[49]

5509 -(77/127) (August 29, 1977); IMF, *Annual Report, 1978,* p. 115; *Selected Decisions* (10th issue, 1983), p. 162. For the oil facility, see paragraph 5(c) of annex to E.B. Decision No. 4242 -(74/67) (June 13, 1974); IMF, *Annual Report, 1974,* p. 124; *Selected Decisions,* p. 219.

[46] Paragraph 13 of the GAB, *supra* note 43. The terms and conditions are spelled out in E.B. Decisions Nos. 7628 and 7629 -(84/25)(February 15, 1984, effective April 10, 1984); IMF, *Annual Report, 1984,* pp. 139–41. For background see *IMF History 1966–71, supra* note 15, vol. 1, pp. 374–76; and Robert Solomon, *The International Monetary System, 1945–1981* (New York: Harper & Row, 1982), pp. 153–54 and 164.

[47] E.B. Decision No. 5974 -(78/190)(December 4, 1978); IMF, *Annual Report, 1979,* p. 135; *Selected Decisions* (10th issue, 1983), p. 229.

[48] The transferability clause in borrowing agreements under the enlarged access policy states:

> The lender shall have the right to transfer at any time all or part of its claim on the Fund, which results from drawings outstanding under its commitment that have not less than three months to maturity from the requested transfer, to any member, the central bank or another agency of any member, or any official entity that has been prescribed as a holder of Special Drawing Rights. . . .

Paragraph 8 of E.B. Decision No. 6864, *supra* note 44. For the similar clause in the borrowing agreement with the Saudi Arabian Monetary Agency, see paragraph 14(a) of attachment to E.B. Decision No. 6843, *supra* note 44. For the comparable clause in borrowing agreements for the supplementary financing facility, see paragraph 8(a) of annex to E.B. Decision No. 5509, *supra* note 45.

If certain conditions are met at the time of transfer (including the transferee being in a "net creditor position in the Fund"), the transferee will be able to subsequently assert its own balance-of-payments need for early repayment. See E.B. Decisions Nos. 7628 and 7629, *supra* note 46 (GAB); paragraphs 7 and 8 of E.B. Decision No. 6864, *supra,* and paragraphs 10 and 14 (c) of attachment to E.B. Decision No. 6843, *supra* (enlarged access policy); paragraphs 5(c) and 8 of annex to E.B. Decision No. 5509, *supra* (supplementary financing facility); and paragraph 2(a)(iv) of E.B. Decision No. 5974, *supra* note 47 (oil facility). "Net creditor position in the Fund " is defined in E.B. Decision No. 6008 -(79/3)(January 5, 1979); IMF, *Annual Report, 1979,* p. 136; *Selected Decisions* (10th issue, 1983), p. 170.

[49] The Fund's borrowing agreements have additional interesting features which are treated in Chapter 6, *infra,* pages 283–287.

Official Holdings of Gold

Historical Role of Gold

Gold has been the model of a commodity–currency.[50] As a metal it has industrial and decorative applications. For centuries gold has also been used as a money. Because gold is a scarce commodity and expensive to mine, the world supply increases at a relatively slow rate. Some persons who favor tight controls on the expansion of the supply of money have seen a system based upon gold or the convertibility of currencies into gold at fixed rates as a means of maintaining limits on monetary expansion. The historical experience has been that during wars and economic crises, when national monies often depreciated, gold retained its purchasing power better than paper currencies. Further, it could be used in periods of diplomatic tension and even during major wars.

The present Articles of Agreement of the International Monetary Fund contemplate that gold will play at most only a minor role as a reserve asset in the international monetary system in the future. Governments have been unwilling to allow economic development, employment, and trade relations to be determined or even significantly affected by the economics of the gold-mining industry. That industry is concentrated in a few countries of the world (South Africa, Soviet Union, Canada, and the United States) and is a small industry in relation to the economy of all of those countries but South Africa.

International Monetary Role of Gold Prior to the Second Amendment of the IMF's Articles of Agreement

In order to understand the present place of gold in monetary reserves it is necessary to review the history of this asset in the period since World War II.[51] Under the original Articles of Agreement of the International Monetary Fund, gold was the numeraire (common denominator) of the par value system upon which exchange rates were based.[52] Gold was the standard in terms of which rights and obligations vis-à-vis the Fund were valued.[53] A portion of each country's quota subscription was paid in gold, unless special provision was made.[54] When the IMF Articles were amended in 1969 to provide for the creation of

---

[50] See Appendix A at pages 663–667.

[51] The operation of the classic international gold standard in the period 1879–1914 and the role of gold in international monetary affairs in the period between World War I and World War II are brilliantly examined, from a legal perspective, in Kenneth W. Dam, *The Rules of the Game: Reform and Evolution in the International Monetary System* (Chicago: University of Chicago Press, 1982), pp. 14–70. The role of gold in the period 1944–1971 is reviewed, *idem,* pp. 95–98 and 133–42.

[52] Old Article IV, section 1(a), *original* and *first.* See also Chapter 11, *infra,* pages 491–501.

[53] Old Article IV, sections 1 and 8, *original* and *first.*

[54] Old Article III, section 3, *original* and *first.*

special drawing rights, gold was used as the standard for valuing the SDR.[55] By 1976 gold had in fact ceased to perform these functions. The present Articles remove gold from all these roles.

Each member of the IMF under the original Articles of Agreement was obligated to state a par value for its currency in terms of gold as a common denominator or in terms of the U.S. dollar of the gold weight and fineness in effect on July 1, 1944.[56] This obligation was the foundation of the par value system of stable exchange rates, colloquially called the "Bretton Woods system of exchange rates."[57] Each member had a further obligation not to buy gold at a price for gold above par value plus a margin prescribed by the IMF, or to sell gold at a price below par value minus a margin prescribed by the Fund.[58] This had the consequence that gold transactions between monetary authorities of Fund members had to be within the prescribed margins. Further, a member wishing to acquire a currency issued by another member by selling gold was required to sell the gold to the Fund for the currency desired if the member could "do so with equal advantage."[59] There was a qualification to this obligation to sell gold to the Fund if gold was to be sold for foreign currencies: "Nothing in this Section shall be deemed to preclude any member from selling in any market gold newly produced from mines located within its territories."[60]

At the time the IMF was formed in 1944, the United States expressed its readiness to buy and sell gold in transactions with monetary authorities at their demand at prices based on U.S. $35 per ounce.[61] This policy made it possible

---

[55] Old Article XXI, section 2, *first*.

[56] Old Article IV, section 1(a), *original* and *first*.

[57] The Bretton Woods par-value exchange-rate system is explained in Chapter 11, *infra*, pages 491–499.

[58] Old Article IV, section 2, *original* and *first*. Under decisions of the Fund the margin, on each side of the par value, could either be one-fourth of 1 percent of par plus certain handling and transportation charges or 1 percent including those charges. Rule F-4 adopted June 10, 1947, amended October 15, 1954, extended November 5, 1954, terminated April 1, 1978. The rule appears in J. Keith Horsefield and Margaret Garritsen de Vries, *The International Monetary Fund, 1945–1965: Twenty Years of International Monetary Cooperation* (3 vols.; Washington: IMF, 1969) [hereinafter *IMF History 1945–65*], vol. 3, p. 292.

[59] Old Article V, section 6, *original* and *first*.

[60] Old Article V, section 6(b), *original* and *first*. The "this Section" reference was to section 6 of Article V, which stated the qualified obligation to sell gold to the Fund, not to section 2 of Article IV that prohibited sales of gold at prices below the defined margin from par value.

[61] See letter of John W. Snyder, U.S. Secretary of the Treasury, to Camille Gutt, Managing Director of the IMF, May 20, 1949, in *The Balance of Payments Mess: Hearings before the Subcommittee on International Exchange and Payments of the Joint Economic Committee*, 92d Congress, 1st Session (June 1971), p. 417. The historical context in which the letter was sent is explained in *IMF History 1945–65, supra* note 58, vol. 1, pp. 251–56, and vol. 2, pp. 181–88. See also Joseph Gold, "Developments in the International Monetary System, the International Monetary Fund, and International Monetary Law Since 1971," in Hague Academy of International Law, *Recueil des Cours*, vol. 174 (1982-I), p. 107 at pp. 180–85. Other countries besides the United States, if they chose, could have adopted a similar policy, but none did so. Joseph Gold, *Use, Conversion, and Exchange of Currencies Under the Second Amendment of the Fund's Articles* (IMF Pamphlet Series no. 23; Washington; 1978), pp. 39–40. See also Joseph Gold, "Legal Structure of Par Value System Before Second Amendment," in Joseph Gold, *Legal and Institutional Aspects of the International Monetary System: Selected Essays* (Washington: IMF, 1979), p. 520 at pp. 547–49. The United States rescinded its commitment on August 15, 1971. See Chapter 11, *infra*, pages 495–499.

for the U.S. dollar and currencies convertible into the dollar to be substituted for gold in international transactions. The volume of gold actually exchanged was small. As the volume of currencies held in monetary reserves expanded, gold holdings in fact expanded at a much lower rate. This eventually raised doubt about the ability of the United States to honor its policy commitment to provide gold, should large quantities of dollars be presented to U.S. authorities for conversion into gold.

After the price of gold on the London gold market moved to a premium in 1960, newly mined gold from South Africa and the Soviet Union went to the London market rather than to the U.S. Treasury. The London premium also tempted foreign monetary authorities wishing to exchange gold from their reserves for U.S. dollars to make the exchange through the London gold market rather than with U.S. authorities. With the market situation depriving the United States of reliable sources of gold to replenish reserve holdings, U.S. authorities developed a number of techniques to avoid or delay redeeming dollar balances with gold.[62] The United States continued, however, to affirm its commitment to sell gold to foreign monetary authorities at prices based on $35 an ounce. Throughout the 1960s gold was delivered from time to time to countries, such as France, that tested the U.S. willingness to exchange gold for dollar balances presented for conversion.[63]

Some countries (such as France, Switzerland, and the Netherlands) had traditionally held a larger portion of their reserves in gold than most other countries. In the mid-1960s the Group of Ten, recognizing the instability that would be caused by the conversion in large amounts of dollar balances into gold, considered a proposal for harmonization of the ratios of gold holdings to other reserves among the ten countries. The proposal, however, did not receive general acceptance.[64]

"Prices based on $35 an ounce" is the technically precise phrase because the obligation undertaken by the United States, pursuant to Article IV, section 4(b), *original* and *first,* was to buy and sell gold within Fund-prescribed margins of the par value. See note 58, *supra.*

[62] See generally Charles A. Coombs, *The Arena of International Finance* (New York: John Wiley & Sons, 1976), chapters 1–5. The U.S. Federal Reserve System's reciprocal currency (swap) arrangements described in Chapter 4, *infra,* beginning at page 135, were developed initially to reduce the incentive of countries to present dollar balances for conversion into gold. Bonds denominated in foreign currencies were also issued by the U.S. Treasury for this purpose. See page 133, *infra.*

[63] France in early 1965 decided to convert into gold some $300 million of its dollar holdings and thereafter step up its monthly purchases of gold from the United States. President Charles de Gaulle at the time indicated a desire to see the "gold exchange standard" terminated and to restore the "gold standard." Solomon, *supra* note 46, p. 55.

[64] Report of the Deputies of the Ministers and Governors of the Group of Ten, July 8, 1966, in Group of Ten, *Communiqué of Ministers and Governors and Report of Deputies* (Frankfurt: Bundesbank, August 25, 1966), p. 5. The report is discussed in Joseph Gold, "The Composition of a Country's Reserves in International Law," *Journal of World Trade Law,* vol. 5 (1971), p. 477 at p. 482.

In 1970 the Japanese Executive Director of the IMF, Hideo Suzuki, suggested that the IMF sell gold to its members under procedures that would lead to a harmonization of the ratios of gold holdings to other reserve assets among the IMF's members. The proposal was not accepted. *IMF History 1966–71, supra* note 15, vol. 1, pp. 417–18.

From the fall of 1961 until early 1968 a London Gold Pool was operated under a gentlemen's agreement among the U.S. Federal Reserve System, the Bank of England, and a number of European central banks. The pool bought and sold gold, like a buffer stock in a commodity agreement, to hold prices close to U.S. \$35 an ounce. Under the agreement the United States contributed half of the pool's gold requirements (59 percent after June 1967) and the other participants supplied the balance in fixed proportions. In fact, until the 1967 devaluation of the U.K. pound sterling, the pool was overall a net buyer of gold.[65] When it became clear in early 1968 that officials could not hold the London price from rising without massive sales, the governors of the central banks of the United States, the United Kingdom, the Republic of Germany, Italy, the Netherlands, Belgium, and Switzerland in a March 1968 announcement stated that they would no longer supply gold to the London market. Prices in that market would be allowed to find their own level based on supply and demand. But, the monetary authorities would continue to deal in gold among themselves at prices based on U.S. \$35 an ounce.[66]

This arrangement was deliberately designed to prevent a rise in the price of gold in private market dealings from causing a devaluation of national currencies. Central bankers would pretend in transactions among themselves that gold did not have any value except the value monetary authorities agreed to give to it. It should also be noted that the rapid rise in the market price of gold after early 1968 and the wide fluctuations in that price, largely as a result of speculator activity, deprived gold of a role as an effective standard setter.[67] It must also be remembered that proposals for the creation of a new monetary reserve asset, the special drawing right, were being considered within the IMF at this time.

On August 15, 1971, the United States announced the suspension of the convertibility of the dollar into gold. No other country offered to assume the

---

[65] The mechanics of the London Gold Pool are described in "The London Gold Market," *Bank of England Quarterly Bulletin*, vol. 4 (1964), p. 16. Its history is recounted in Federal Reserve Bank of New York, *54th Annual Report, for the Year 1968*, pp. 32–35; and Dam, *supra* note 51, pp. 137–42. See also Susan Strange, "International Monetary Relations," in Andrew Schonfield (ed.), *International Economic Relations of the Western World 1959–1971* (London: Oxford University Press for Royal Institute of International Affairs, 1976), vol. 2, chapter 3.

[66] See generally Peter E. Pront, "Termination of Two-Tier Gold," *Law and Policy in International Business*, vol. 7 (1975), p. 273; Andreas F. Lowenfeld, *The International Monetary System* (New York: Matthew Bender, 1977), pp. 93–101; Coombs, *supra* note 62, chapters 4 and 9; Solomon, *supra* note 46, chapter 7; *IMF History 1966–71*, *supra* note 15, vol. 1, pp. 403–09; and Strange, *supra* note 65, pp. 278–95. Arrangements were made in December 1969 for South Africa, the world's largest gold producer, to sell a portion of its production to the IMF at U.S. \$35 while it retained the freedom to also sell on the market at market prices. E.B. Decision No. 2914 -(69/127)(December 30, 1969); *IMF History 1966–71*, vol. 2, pp. 203–06. The negotiations with South Africa are described in *IMF History 1966–71*, vol. 1, pp. 409–16; Solomon, *supra*, pp. 124–27; and Strange, *supra*, chapter 10. See also Dam, *supra* note 51, pp. 139–42.

The seven central banks that participated in the two-tier system terminated it in November 1973. South Africa's arrangements for gold sales to the IMF were terminated in December 1973.

[67] See David Williams, "The Gold Markets 1968–72," *Finance and Development*, vol. 9, no. 4 (December 1972), p. 9.

role the United States previously played and freely buy and sell gold for its own currency in transactions with other monetary authorities at prices based on par values.[68] In 1972 the IMF began to use the SDR as its unit of account.[69] Notwithstanding the provision of old Article XXI, Section 2, *first,* that defined the value of the SDR in terms of gold, subsequent to June 1974 the SDR was valued in terms of a composite of portions of national currencies. Gold's relation, if any, to that composite was essentially fictitious.[70] Finally, the IMF permitted new members to join the Fund under procedures that did not require an actual gold contribution to the quota subscription.[71]

International Monetary Role of Gold Following the Second Amendment of the IMF's Articles of Agreement

The experience, summarized above, led to the following conclusions that are embodied in the IMF's Articles of Agreement following the Second Amendment effective April 1, 1978:

(a) Gold cannot be used by members as a denominator for exchange rates nor can it be used as the numeraire of a par value system of exchange arrangements should one be established.[72]

(b) The principle and method of valuing the SDR is for the Fund by special majorities to decide.[73]

(c) The SDR is the standard of value for all operational rights and obligations vis-à-vis the Fund.[74]

(d) Gold can continue to be held in national monetary reserves as a subsidiary reserve asset; the special drawing right is to become the principal reserve asset of the international monetary system.[75]

---

[68] See Chapter 11, *infra,* pages 496–499.

[69] Board of Governors Resolution No. 27-3, adopted effective March 20, 1972; IMF, *Summary Proceedings, 1972,* p. 339.

[70] See Chapter 5, *infra,* page 177.

[71] See, e.g., the 1973 resolution admitting the Bahamas to membership. Board of Governors Resolution No. 28-3, adopted effective July 3, 1973; IMF, *Summary Proceedings, 1973,* p. 377. The procedures used at an earlier time for countries to acquire gold for transfer to the Fund when they became members or when their quotas were increased are described in *IMF History 1966–71, supra* note 15, vol. 1, pp. 416–23.

[72] Article IV, section 2(b); and Schedule C, paragraph 1.

[73] Article XV, section 2. The former provision (Article XXI, section 2, *first),* that stated the value of the SDR in terms of gold, has been eliminated.

[74] Article V, sections 10 and 11.

[75] Article VIII, section 7.

(e) A member is no longer required to pay a portion of its quota subscription in gold.[76]

William E. Simon, former U.S. Secretary of the Treasury, has said the Second Amendment (the present Articles) has placed gold "on a one-way path out of the system."[77] The Articles provide authority for the Fund to dispose of its gold holdings, and, indeed, required that it dispose of a part of them.[78] The sale of 50 million ounces (representing about one-third of the IMF's holdings) was required by Schedule B, paragraph 7. Twenty-five million ounces were to be offered for sale at the carrying value (SDR = 0.888671 gram) to all IMF members that were members on August 31, 1975, in proportion to their quotas on that date.[79] Twenty-five million ounces were to be sold in a manner chosen by the Executive Board, with part of the amount received above the carrying value transferred directly to members identified as "developing countries" and the balance credited to a special Trust Fund or the Special Disbursement Account.[80] These sales have taken place.

Article V, Section 12, provides authority for the Fund to sell its General Resources Account gold holdings held on April 1, 1978, above the 50 million ounces whose disposition has already taken place in accordance with Schedule B. Either of two methods is permitted: (1) sales to members that were members on August 31, 1975, in proportion to their quotas at that time at the price equivalent to the carrying value of the gold;[81] or (2) sales "on the basis of prices in the market" in exchange for currencies specified by the Fund—with currencies obtained equivalent to the carrying value of the gold sold (0.888671 gram

[76] The General Resources Account quota subscription is to be paid in special drawing rights and currencies. Article III, section 3.

[77] Statement in *To Provide for the Amendment of the Bretton Woods Agreements Act: Hearings on H.R. 13955 before the Subcommittee on International Trade, Investment and Monetary Policy of the Committee on Banking, Currency and Housing,* U.S. House of Representatives, 94th Congress, 2d Session (June 1976), at p. 37. See also the statement of Edwin H. Yeo, III, Under Secretary of the Treasury for Monetary Affairs, in *International Monetary Fund Amendments: Hearings on S.3454 before the Committee on Foreign Relations,* U.S. Senate, 94th Congress, 2d Session (1976), p. 4 at pp. 18–20.

[78] The provisions described in the text resulted from complex negotiations that sought to compromise ideological and political differences. The negotiations are summarized in Solomon, *supra* note 46, pp. 274–80. See also *The IMF Gold Agreement: Hearing before the Subcommittee on International Economics of the Joint Economic Committee,* U.S. Congress, 94th Congress, 1st Session (1975).

[79] The Fund began sales to members of portions of this 25 million ounces before the new Articles entered into force. The action was taken on the basis of old Article VII, *original* and *first.* The first restitution to members at the carrying value took place in January and February 1977 and the last of the 25 million ounces were sold to members in December 1979 and January and February 1980. See IMF, *Annual Report, 1977,* pp. 58 and 60–61; and *Annual Report, 1980,* pp. 84–89. See also E.B. Decision No. 5274 -(76/163)(December 7, 1976) and No. 5314 -(77/6)(January 10, 1977); IMF, *Annual Report, 1977,* pp. 104–05.

[80] The Fund sold portions of its gold holdings by public auction in the period June 1976–May 1980. The auctions were held at intervals of four to six weeks. The procedures followed in the sales and the use of the proceeds are explained in Chapter 6, *infra,* pages 294–298, where the Trust Fund and Special Disbursement Account are discussed.

[81] Article V, section 12(e).

equals 1 SDR) being credited to the General Resources Account and the balance applied to the Investment Account or to the Special Disbursement Account.[82] Subject to certain conditions respecting the currencies that can be acquired, the General Resources Account can sell gold acquired after April 1, 1978, but only "on the basis of prices in the market."[83]

Decisions to sell gold pursuant to the authority of Section 12 require an 85 percent majority of the total voting power.[84] The Fund also has authority to buy gold from a member in any operation or transaction authorized by the Articles. Exercise of this authority requires decisions of 85 percent of the total voting power and the prices must be based on "prices in the market."[85]

The Fund's actions in buying and selling gold are to be guided by the objectives of making the special drawing right the principal reserve asset in the international monetary system, promoting better surveillance of international liquidity, avoiding the establishment of a fixed price for gold in the market, and avoiding the management of the market price of gold.[86] This means that the Fund in buying or selling gold is not to make judgments whether the market price is "too high" or "too low." The concept is that the Fund is obligated to allow the price of gold to float in the market. It is inappropriate for the Fund to manage the price of a metal that has commodity as well as monetary uses. The market should simply be allowed to react and accommodate itself to any actions the Fund takes. The Fund has assumed it could fulfill its obligations by sales at public auction of specified amounts of gold at regular intervals with advance publicity.[87] The Fund at present holds about 103 million ounces of gold and is likely to continue to hold a substantial amount of this gold in the future.[88]

What are the obligations of IMF members with respect to the purchase and sale of gold? They can, of course, buy and sell gold in transactions with the Fund that are authorized by Article V, Section 12, or Schedule B, paragraph 7, which we have discussed. Members have an obligation under Article VIII, Section 7:

> Each member undertakes to collaborate with the Fund and with other members in order to ensure that the policies of the member with respect to reserve assets shall be consistent with the objectives of promoting better international surveillance of international liquidity and

---

[82] Article V, section 12(c), (e), (f), and (g).

[83] Article V, section 12(c). The manner of determining the carrying value for accounting purposes of gold acquired after April 1, 1978, is to be decided by the Executive Board. Rule J-1 as amended April 1, 1978; *By-Laws, Rules and Regulations* (40th issue, 1983).

[84] Article V, section 12(b). See also *United States Code*, title 22, section 286c.

[85] Article V, section 12(b) and (d).

[86] Article V, section 12(a); and Article VIII, section 7.

[87] See *IMF Survey*, May 17, 1976, pp. 150–54; and IMF, *Annual Report, 1978*, pp. 70–71.

[88] See Günter Wittich, "Gold in the Fund Today," *Finance and Development*, vol. 19, no. 3 (September 1982), p. 36.

making the special drawing right the principal reserve asset in the international monetary system.[89]

The IMF's Interim Committee in 1975 considered wording the section: "Each member undertakes to collaborate with the Fund and with other members to promote the establishment of the special drawing right as the principal reserve asset and the reduction of the role of gold . . . in the international monetary system." Some European states indicated they would accept this text only if it also mentioned reducing the role of reserve currencies. The language finally chosen finessed the difference of view.[90]

The IMF Articles do not forbid a member to hold gold in its monetary reserves. A member can buy gold at an IMF auction or in transactions with private or official entities. The Fund may take actions in the future to call upon members pursuant to the collaboration obligation of Section 7, quoted above, to reduce the gold portion of their reserves in order that the special drawing right may have a more prominent place, but until that is done (and some might argue even then) there is no explicit obligation on IMF members to reduce their gold holdings.[91]

IMF Article IV, Section 2(b), forbids a member to use an exchange rate arrangement under which it maintains the value of its currency in terms of gold.[92] If the Fund should apply a par value system of exchange arrangements, gold cannot be the numeraire of that system.[93] However, it would appear that a country is permitted to issue gold coins for numismatic purposes.[94] A country

---

[89] See also Article XXII.

[90] See *17th Report on the Activities of the Monetary Committee [of the EEC], Official Journal of the European Communities*, no. C-132, June 14, 1976, p. 1 at pp. 2 and 12 (paragraph 11 and Annex II, paragraph 6).

[91] The members of the Group of Ten and Switzerland at one time agreed that the total stock of gold in the hands of the Fund and the monetary authorities of these eleven countries would not be increased. These arrangements entered into effect on February 1, 1976, and were allowed to lapse January 31, 1978. The agreement was embodied in the communiqué of the IMF's Interim Committee, dated August 31, 1975. IMF, *Summary Proceedings, 1975*, p. 299 at p. 302; IMF, *Annual Report, 1976*, p. 119 at p. 121. See IMF, *Annual Report, 1976*, p. 54; *IMF Survey*, September 15, 1975, p. 265, and February 6, 1978, p. 34; and *Wall Street Journal*, January 24, 1978, p. 18. See also Solomon, *supra* note 46, pp. 278–80.

[92] The provision prohibiting the use of gold as a denominator of the value of a currency in Article IV, section 2(b), is prefaced by the words "Under an international monetary system of the kind prevailing on January 1, 1976." Sir Joseph Gold, who was the IMF's General Counsel at the time the present Article IV was negotiated, has stated: "The words were not intended to suggest that gold might be used as a denominator in new conditions. The permanence of the prohibition is illustrated by the provision [in Schedule C, paragraph 1] that would prevent the Fund from choosing gold as a common denominator of a par value system." Joseph Gold, "Gold in International Monetary Law: Change, Uncertainty, and Ambiguity," *Journal of International Law and Economics*, vol. 15 (1981), p. 323 at p. 353.

[93] Schedule C, paragraph 1.

[94] At the time the Second Amendment was negotiated, a number of IMF members issued gold coins for numismatic purposes; no country retained a domestic gold standard. For example, South Africa issues the Krugerrand, a gold coin valued at the market value and legal tender in South Africa. The South African rand, the primary currency, is not valued in terms of gold.

may also be able to value its currency in terms of gold for limited internal purposes so long as this valuation does not in fact affect the exchange rate.[95]

Mobilization of Gold Reserves

Under the IMF's Articles of Agreement, in their present form, a country is not required to buy or sell gold in transactions with monetary authorities of other countries nor is it required to participate in the gold market. Its actions can be based on its judgment of whether the market price is attractive or unattractive at the time. Gold can be bought and sold by monetary authorities and used as collateral in dealings among them. If the valuation of gold in these transactions is based on prices in the market, the monetary authorities would appear to be in compliance with their obligations under IMF Article IV, Section 2(b), not to maintain the value of their currencies in terms of gold.

The central banks of the member states of the European Economic Community contribute a portion of their gold and U.S. dollar reserves to the European Monetary Cooperation Fund (FECOM) and in return receive an equivalent amount of European currency units (ECUs) issued by the FECOM. Gold is valued for this purpose under a formula related to the price of gold in the market. The particular formula chosen, explained in Chapter 8, appears to be consistent with the countries' obligations under the IMF Articles respecting transactions in gold.[96]

The arrangement under which Italy's central bank in 1974 pledged a portion of its gold reserves as collateral to secure a loan from the central bank of the Federal Republic of Germany, if entered into today, would also appear to be consistent with Article IV, Section 2(b). Under that arrangement, concluded in August 1974, Banca d'Italia pledged approximately 20 percent of Italy's gold reserves as collateral for credit extended to it by the Deutsche Bundesbank equivalent to U.S. $2 billion. Under the agreement if Banca failed to make repayments on their maturity, the German authorities could sell the pledged gold on the free market and liquidate the debt at $120 an ounce. If the market price was below $120, the Bundesbank could, but was not required to, postpone the sale. If the price realized was above $120 an ounce, Banca was to receive the difference. At the time the agreement was made, the $120 figure was about 20 percent less than the average price of gold on the London market during the

---

[95] See Joseph Gold, *The Fund Agreement in the Courts* (Washington: IMF), vol. 2 (1982), pp. 250–51; and U.S. Gold Reserve Act of 1934, section 14(c), as amended October 19, 1976; *United States Statutes at Large,* vol. 90, p. 2660 at p. 2661; *United States Code,* title 31, section 405b.

Possible changes in the United States law and practice that would give an enhanced role to gold in U.S. economic policy were considered in *Report to the Congress of the Commission on the Role of Gold in the Domestic and International Monetary Systems* (2 vols.; 98th Congress, 2d Session, 1982). The report was prepared pursuant to an amendment to the Bretton Woods Agreements Act of October 7, 1980. Public Law 96-389, approved October 7, 1980; *United States Statutes at Large,* vol. 94, p. 1551 at p. 1555.

[96] See pages 320–325, *infra,* especially page 322.

previous eight weeks. An arrangement of this type would probably be consistent with present IMF Article IV, Section 2(b), because the degree of adjustment from market prices is reasonable for protection of the creditor.[97]

In September 1982 the Philippines sold 130,000 ounces of gold under a swap arrangement (an arrangement providing for subsequent repurchase). Argentina, Chile, and Uruguay were reported to have engaged in, or to have considered, such transactions during 1982. It was rumored in late 1982 that Brazilian authorities obtained about U.S. $75 million under an arrangement in which seven tons of gold were pledged as collateral or placed under a swap arrangement. The amount of gold involved, assuming the rumor to be true, was a little less than 10 percent of Brazil's official reserves. It was later reported, in July 1983, that Brazil had sold, pledged, or swapped virtually all of its gold reserves.[98]

The arrangements whereby monetary authorities pledge or swap gold may be entered into with monetary authorities of other countries, with the Bank for International Settlements, or with commercial banks. Typically, gold in these transactions is valued at a discount of about 20–25 percent from the market price for a six-month swap arrangement. The maturity of the swaps is usually limited to six months or twelve months, because as stated by a gold analyst, "Further out than six months is risky, the price fluctuates too much."[99] When a swap matures, a new swap arrangement may be entered into based on a new gold valuation. Private participants in the gold market have predicted that swap transactions will in some cases lead to outright sales of gold by countries that need to acquire large amounts of foreign currencies to service debt obligations.[100]

In some countries the monetary authorities buy all of the gold mined in the country and then market all or a portion of it. The formulas under which the authorities purchase the gold are normally related to current international market prices. The currencies provided by the authorities to the mining companies are not valued in terms of gold weight. The actions appear consistent with Article IV, Section 2(b).[101]

Members of the IMF, unlike the Fund itself, are permitted to manage the price of gold so long as they do not maintain the value of their currencies in

---

[97] For background on the loan and collateral arrangements, see *Report of the Deutsche Bundesbank for the Year 1974*, p. 52; *Keesing's Contemporary Archives,* September 16–23, 1974, p. 26,719; *New York Times,* September 1, 1974, pp. 1 and 6; and *The Economist* (London), September 7, 1974, p. 63.

[98] Peter Truell, "Countries Try Swapping Gold Holdings for Cash to Fill Short-Term Credit Needs," *Wall Street Journal,* December 1, 1982, p. 31; and "Brazil Runs Out of Gold to Repay its Massive Debt," *Wall Street Journal,* July 14, 1983, p. 30.

[99] Truell, *supra* note 98.

[100] *Idem.*

[101] See, e.g., the laws of Colombia, Philippines, and South Africa summarized in IMF, *Annual Report on Exchange Arrangements and Exchange Restrictions, 1983,* pp. 148, 383, and 419. See discussion of these laws in Joseph Gold, *SDRs, Currencies, and Gold: Fourth Survey of New Legal Developments* (IMF Pamphlet Series no. 33; Washington, 1980), p. 90.

terms of gold and they fulfill their Article VIII collaboration obligation noted above. Monetary authorities are not prohibited from coordinating their actions in buying and selling gold in the market and also coordinating decisions to refrain from intervention in the market.[102] Given gold's industrial uses and the psychological impact of gold price movements on economic expectations, it is as appropriate for countries to attempt to stabilize the price of this commodity as to stabilize the prices of tin, copper, or other commodities,[103] but it should normally not be the monetary authorities that assume this responsibility. If a country's market actions have the effect of fixing the price of gold in terms of its own currency and maintaining that price at a set level, those actions would be inconsistent with the country's obligations under Article VIII, Section 7, quoted earlier, and would in effect establish a value for its currency in terms of gold in violation of Article IV, Section 2(b). The Fund also has authority under these provisions to object if members attempt to fix the price of gold in transactions among themselves.[104]

The monetary authorities of the Group of Ten and Switzerland made an agreement in August 1975 not to "peg" the price of gold. This agreement was made before the text of the Second Amendment to the IMF's Articles had been fully negotiated, and was allowed to lapse in early 1978.[105] It is submitted that the Second Amendment, through Article VIII, Section 7, and Article IV, Section 2(b), places an obligation on all IMF members to refrain from pegging the price of gold. Separate agreements, like the former one among the Group of Ten, are no longer necessary.

One can expect that countries will in the future continue to hold a portion of their monetary reserves in gold, particularly given the large amount of gold presently held in reserves. Persons bearing monetary responsibilities will not easily forget that gold has maintained its purchasing power better than most national currencies during times of war and crisis. Under the present IMF Articles the purchasing power of gold, as we have seen, is to reflect the market price of gold rather than a value imputed to that metal by monetary authorities. Gold is

---

[102] In January 1980, when gold was selling above U.S. $750 an ounce, finance ministry officials of the United States, Federal Republic of Germany, France, Japan, and the United Kingdom met in Washington to consider possible actions and, following those consultations, decided not to intervene in the gold market at that time. Central bank officials met in Basle and also decided to do nothing at the time. See *Wall Street Journal,* January 17, 1980, p. 2, and January 18, 1980, p. 2.

[103] South Africa, as a principal gold miner and refiner, can be expected to attempt to stabilize prices. The Soviet Union, also a major gold miner and not a member of the Fund, can also be expected to do so.

[104] Although the Fund's authority is available in the provisions cited, the Fund's General Counsel has commented that it is stated "with less clarity and force than would have been apparent had other proposed drafts been accepted." The IMF's Interim Committee during 1975 considered a clause that said, "Transactions in gold will not be undertaken with the objective of *de facto* establishing a fixed price of gold." See Joseph Gold, "Law and Change in International Monetary Relations," *The Record* [of the Association of the Bar of the City of New York], vol. 31 (1976), p. 223 at p. 234; and *17th Report of the Monetary Committee* [of the EEC], *supra* note 90, at p. 12 (Annex II, paragraph 5, and Appendix I to that annex).

[105] The agreement, cited in note 91, *supra,* was allowed to lapse January 31, 1978.

no longer an official standard of value. So long as gold is readily accepted by monetary authorities it can be used as a medium of exchange, but in fact it is not performing this monetary function at the present time.

Sophisticated economists will no doubt measure the purchasing power over time of national currencies and of gold in terms of prices and cost-of-living indices. Gold will simply be one convenient, but imperfect, form of holding purchasing power. Even if gold should be "demonitized" and no longer held in monetary reserves, it could still be stock-piled like any other mineral for future need. Indeed, any commodity can serve as a store of purchasing power if it will be in demand over time. In the words of an often quoted comment, "Gold may have no official status in the monetary system. But it is not unloved."[106]

Volume and Distribution of Reserve Assets

The IMF's *Annual Report* each year provides information on the levels and composition of reserves, a breakdown of official holdings of foreign exchange by type of claim, and information on the distribution of reserve holdings among groups of countries, as well as commentary on the contemporary situation as seen by the Executive Board of the IMF. Discussions of this information take place in the IMF and in other forums under the general heading of "international liquidity." The information is relevant to decisions to allocate special drawing rights, increase quotas in the General Resources Account of the IMF, or take other actions that affect the size of monetary reserves, their composition and distribution, and the amounts and terms of credit facilities that are available to supplement reserves. To the extent that legal issues are posed, the questions are addressed in the final chapter of this book.[107] One can predict that a deliberate effort may be made over a period of years to increase the combined size of SDR holdings in the hands of national authorities and reserve tranche positions in the IMF in relation to the size of total reserves.[108]

There has been a tendency in the past to assess reserve adequacy solely

---

[106] Statement of René Larre, when General Manager of the Bank for International Settlements, quoted in David Marsh, "Gold Suppliers Get Wise to a Surge in Demand," *Financial Times* (London), July 7, 1980, p. 12.

[107] At pages 630–647.

[108] For future comparison, data on the situation at the end of May 1978, shortly after the Second Amendment of the IMF Articles became effective, may prove of interest. At that time reserve positions in the IMF totaled SDR 17 billion, and SDRs in the hands of national authorities totaled 8 billion—the two combined amounting to less than 6 percent of the aggregate reserves of all IMF members. Foreign exchange was the largest component of official reserves, amounting to SDR 207 billion. Gold holdings totaled 1 billion ounces with a value of SDR 187 billion at the London market price at the time. Data with respect to foreign exchange claims indicated that slightly over 50 percent were claims on the United States, another 30 percent were claims in Eurodollars, and the balance consisted of claims against other countries, Eurocurrency claims denominated in currencies other than the dollar, and miscellaneous foreign exchange claims. IMF, *Annual Report, 1978*, pp. 44 and 53.

with reference to official reserve holdings. Private holdings of international liquid assets should also be considered when appraising the adequacy of reserves. These assets can be used to finance private trade and investment transactions as well as other transactions. The staff of the IMF has attempted to estimate the size of private international liquidity, which consists primarily of privately held short-term foreign exchange claims, but has encountered difficulties in getting reliable and complete data.[109] The Bank for International Settlements in its *Annual Report* includes data on external liabilities and assets of banks in selected countries.

Reserve Assets and National Wealth

Monetary reserve assets, with the possible exception of gold, are readily acceptable in payment for international transactions or, alternatively, can promptly, with no loss in value, be exchanged for national currencies required for settlement of accounts. Obviously the conventions described in this chapter that are used to define monetary reserves cannot describe accurately all of the assets that can be marshalled readily in the case of need. A state may have other assets which, while not immediately acceptable to settle payments obligations, can be converted into money. Financial instruments that are not classified as "money" fit this category; for example, government bonds maturing in more than one year are normally not classified as "money" yet can readily be converted into money perhaps with some loss in the liquidation.

A country may have access to credit sources that, if required conditions are met, can supply needed currencies. Oil is a form of wealth which is in demand and can be sold for money. Other natural resources can play similar roles. And, manufacturing plants and a productive labor force that make and sell needed goods and services also contribute to national wealth and are a means for obtaining claims on foreign governments. The point that deserves emphasis is: The size of monetary reserve assets is not a complete measure of national wealth. Reserve assets are economic instruments seen within a universe of the world monetary system and this system, in turn, is only part of a much larger world economic universe.

---

[109] In 1974 the IMF's *Annual Report* included a table at p. 44 showing "estimated private international liquidity," but subsequent annual reports did not include such a table. However, in 1984 the IMF's *International Financial Statistics* introduced world tables that include private international liquidity.

Chapter 4: Financing Methods that Do Not Require Use of Multilateral Arrangements

Introduction

Many methods are used by central banks, national treasuries, and other monetary authorities to obtain foreign currencies in order to augment reserve holdings, make payments abroad for government agencies or other "customers," supply commercial banks of the country requiring foreign exchange, or conduct exchange market operations to maintain orderly trading conditions or influence rates. The focus of this chapter is on techniques that do not require recourse to the International Monetary Fund or other multilateral arrangements. The first part of the chapter considers financing methods that do not even require the active participation of monetary authorities in a second country. Most of the chapter is devoted to an examination of bilateral reciprocal currency (swap) arrangements between the U.S. Federal Reserve System and other central banks and between other monetary authorities. These arrangements have unique features and large volumes of currencies are involved.

Unilateral and Bilateral Methods

Purchases and Sales of Currencies in the Market

Monetary authorities can purchase foreign currency balances from commercial banks in their own country or abroad in exchange for their own currency. Since in many countries a foreign currency balance is a reserve on the basis of which a bank can extend credit, a central bank acquiring foreign currency is entitled under its own law, without further cost, to credit the seller with domestic currency (i.e., the bank creates domestic money on the basis of the foreign currency it obtains and places in its reserves).[1]

---

[1] See Appendix A, *infra,* pages 668–671.

In countries with currency surrender requirements, commercial banks and firms may be required to sell foreign balances received to the central bank in exchange for the national currency.[2] In countries without surrender requirements, these transactions may take place by mutual consent. If the foreign currency desired by the central bank is traded in an open market, the bank can buy the currency on that market in exchange for its own currency or another currency that it holds.

Where exchange rates are allowed to adjust to supply and demand for currencies in an open market, the purchases and sales of currencies by monetary authorities in the market can affect exchange rates. Central banks, therefore, often find it necessary to have sources of foreign currencies upon which they can draw without affecting the market. For example, if a central bank at a particular point in time decides to stabilize exchange rates by selling a foreign currency and buying its own in the open market, it must either find a source of the needed foreign currency outside the market or else draw down foreign currency balances it has held in its reserves.

Official Borrowing from Commercial Banks for Balance-of-Payments Support

Unlike the exchange of one currency for another, a loan normally involves the extension of credit in a particular currency in exchange for a promissory note obligating the debtor to pay interest and, in accordance with a maturity schedule, to repay the principal of the loan in the same currency. Loans providing foreign exchange may be made by commercial banks, governments, or international organizations.

As noted earlier, loans from the International Bank for Reconstruction and Development finance projects and programs and are not normally intended for undifferentiated balance-of-payments support.[3] Government-to-government "loans" for balance-of-payments support often take the form of reciprocal currency arrangements, discussed in the next part of this chapter.[4]

Commercial banks have traditionally provided financing for export and import transactions. They have provided funds to firms for investment projects, financing of inventory, and the like. The banks have also made loans to governments, usually for specific projects or to bridge payments and receipts. Commercial bank lending to foreign governments for general balance-of-payments support, on the massive scale of recent years, is a relatively new phenomenon.

---

[2] Surrender requirements are explained further in Chapter 10, *infra*, pages 385–386.

[3] Structural adjustment loans may provide balance-of-payments support while a country makes changes to improve the competitiveness of its economy. See generally Chapter 2, *supra*, pages 47–48.

[4] Beginning at page 135.

This large scale lending developed out of the roles played by commercial banks as financial intermediaries during the period of dramatic increases in petroleum prices in 1973 and the following years. The banks accepted deposits from oil exporting states and, on the basis of those deposits, extended credit to countries requiring financing for the increased prices of oil imports and other needs. The banks have also made loans for general balance-of-payments support to countries embarking on ambitious development plans. The loans have typically been provided in the form of deposit credit with the banks denominated in the currency of the country where the bank is chartered or in Eurocurrencies.[5]

While developing countries have borrowed particularly heavily from commercial banks in recent years, they have not been the only countries in the market. The French Government, for example, in the fall of 1982, entered into an agreement with a syndicate of private commercial banks (including nationalized French banks and commercial banks based in other countries) to borrow up to the equivalent of U.S. $4 billion for use in exchange market interventions, and subsequently the full amount was drawn.[6]

The world-wide severe recession in the late 1970s and early 1980s placed added strains on the ability of some countries to finance the external payments associated with the heavy debt loads they were carrying. In the winter of 1982–83 serious payments arrears occurred or were threatened in a number of countries with large foreign currency obligations to commercial banks, including Poland, Romania, and Yugoslavia in Eastern Europe and Argentina, Brazil, and Mexico in Latin America. Governments delayed payments on their external obligations. Firms in the countries were unable to obtain foreign exchange to meet their obligations.[7] The problems, while not unforeseen,[8] properly provoked great concern.[9]

---

[5] It has been estimated that in 1974–1976 almost one-half of the financing requirements of the non-oil-producing countries was provided by the commercial banking system. See "Coping with the Imbalance in International Payments," in Morgan Guaranty Trust Company of New York, *World Financial Markets,* January 1977, p. 1 at p. 4.

It is difficult to obtain reliable estimates of the external indebtedness of the public and private sectors of countries with market economies, particularly data broken down by maturities. Available data on developing countries are examined in Bahram Nowzad, Richard C. Williams, et al., *External Indebtedness of Developing Countries* (IMF Occasional Paper no. 3; Washington, 1981), pp. 8–11 and 30–40; G. G. Johnson with Richard K. Abrams, *Aspects of the International Banking Safety Net* (IMF Occasional Paper no. 17; Washington, 1983), pp. 6–9; and *International Debt: Hearings on Proposals for Legislation to Increase the Resources of the International Monetary Fund before the Subcommittee on International Finance and Monetary Policy of the Committee on Banking, Housing, and Urban Affairs,* U.S. Senate, 98th Congress, 1st Session (1983).

[6] See *Wall Street Journal,* September 16, 1982, p. 34; October 22, 1982, p. 28; and January 24, 1983, p. 26.

[7] See, e.g., *Wall Street Journal,* July 28, 1982, pp. 1 and 14 (Romania); January 19, 1983, p. 34 (Yugoslavia); and January 12, 1983, p. 33 (Mexico).

[8] See *International Debt: Hearings before the Subcommittee on International Finance of the Committee on Banking, Housing, and Urban Affairs,* U.S. Senate, 95th Congress, 1st Session (1977); *International Banking Operations: Hearings before the Subcommittee on Financial Institutions Supervision, Regulation and Insurance of the Committee on Banking, Finance and Urban Affairs,* U.S. House of Representatives, 95th Congress, 1st Session (1977); Jonathan Eaton and Mark Gersovitz, *Poor-Country Borrowing in Private Financial Markets and the Repudiation Issue* (Princeton Studies in International Finance no. 47; Princeton:

National governments and their central banks and the International Monetary Fund stepped in to provide large-scale temporary financing to avoid a potential international financial crisis. For example, the U.S. Treasury, the Federal Reserve, and the central banks of other countries through reciprocal currency arrangements provided assistance to Mexico. The U.S. Treasury through currency swap arrangements provided assistance to Brazil, which was followed later by assistance from central banks through the Bank for International Settlements.[10] The International Monetary Fund approved stand-by or extended arrangements for Argentina, Brazil, and Mexico, as well as other countries.[11] A decision was made to increase the General Arrangements to Borrow under which the IMF may supplement its resources.[12] The Managing Director of the IMF personally mounted efforts to persuade commercial banks to reschedule payments due by governments rather than to formally declare default or withdraw from further lending.[13]

There is a growing legal literature on commercial bank lending to governments. Much of the literature focuses on private law issues, including choice of the national law governing loan agreements, sovereign immunity claims, conditions precedent and borrower representations, legal aspects of negative pledges, use of *pari passu* clauses, and coordination of creditor actions in dealing with problems of arrears and default. These issues, primarily relating to application of national law and conflict of laws rules, are outside the scope of this book.[14]

Princeton University International Finance Section, 1981); Lawrence G. Franko and Marilyn J. Seiber (ed.), *Developing Country Debt* (New York: Pergamon Press, 1979); and panel, "Third World Debt and Related Financial Arrangements," in American Society of International Law, *Proceedings of the 72d Annual Meeting, 1978*, p. 56.

[9] See *International Debt: Hearings [1983], supra* note 5; Geoffrey L. Bell, John G. Heimann, et al., *Risks in International Bank Lending* (New York: Group of Thirty, 1982); William J. Gasser and David L. Roberts, "Bank Lending to Developing Countries: Problems and Prospects," in Federal Reserve Bank of New York, *Quarterly Review*, vol. 7, no. 3 (Autumn 1982), p. 18; and Chandra Hardy, *Rescheduling Developing-Country Debts, 1956–1981: Lessons and Recommendations* (Washington: Overseas Development Council, 1982).

[10] See pages 155–156, *infra*, regarding assistance provided by the U.S. Treasury. See Chapter 2, *supra*, page 58 (note 72), regarding assistance provided through the Bank for International Settlements.

[11] See *IMF Survey*, January 10, 1983, p. 1 (Mexico); February 7, 1983, p. 38 (Argentina); and March 7, 1983, p. 65 (Brazil). See also *New York Times*, January 22, 1983, pp. 35 and 42.

[12] See Chapter 6, *infra*, pages 290–291.

[13] See *Wall Street Journal*, January 25, 1983, p. 37. See also *idem*, November 24, 1982, p. 30; and January 21, 1983, p. 2. In the words of a Mexican official, "You can argue that we should never have borrowed $20 billion. But banks simply can't lend that much to a country one year and try to cut it to zero the next." *Wall Street Journal*, October 22, 1982, p. 28.

It was estimated that over $90 billion of payments originally due commercial banks in 1982 and 1983 would be rescheduled. See M. S. Mendelsohn, *Central Banks and the Restructuring of Cross-Border Debt* (New York: Group of Thirty, 1983).

[14] See Philip Wood, *Law and Practice of International Finance* (New York: Clark Boardman, binder service, 1984 ed.); Robert S. Rendell (ed.), *International Financial Law: Lending, Capital Transfers and Institutions* (London: Euromoney Publications, 1980); F. John Mathis (ed.), *Offshore Lending by U.S. Commer-*

Sometimes banks encounter difficulties in obtaining reliable information on a country's economic situation and the extent of the indebtedness it has already assumed. In an effort to deal with this problem, a group of commercial and investment banks from around the world in 1983 established the Institute of International Finance, Inc. as a non-profit corporation based in Washington, D.C. Membership in the Institute is limited to banks that make loans for the purpose of profit. The purposes of the Institute are:

> to promote a better understanding of international lending transactions generally; to collect, analyze and disseminate information regarding the economic and financial position of particular countries which are substantial borrowers in the international markets so as to provide the Members with a better factual basis on which each member independently may analyze extensions of credit to borrowers in such countries; and to engage in other appropriate activities to facilitate, and preserve the integrity of, international lending transactions. This includes promoting the collection and dissemination of information concerning the financial situation, development plans, economic policies and existing and proposed foreign exchange obligations of sovereign and other borrowers so as to improve the ability of Members independently to analyze the risk of international exposure to such borrowers.[15]

Peri N. Nash, one of the lawyers involved in the organization of the Institute, has commented:

> Membership is open to all lending institutions which have or propose to have in the immediate future international exposure as a result of holding international loans in their portfolios at their own risk and for profit.
> The major activities of the Institute will be to:
> —Gather information on the economic, political, and financial outlook of major borrower countries;
> —Furnish members of the Institute with analytical country reports based on the information gathered;
> —Serve as a focal point for dialogue between the international commercial banking community and multilateral institutions, central banks, and supervisory authorities in the developed countries;

---

cial Banks (2d ed.; Washington: Bankers Association for Foreign Trade; Philadelphia: Robert Morris Associates, 1981); and articles in the symposium, "Default by Foreign Government Debtors," *University of Illinois Law Review*, vol. 1 (1982), pp. 1–384.

[15] Articles of Incorporation, Article 3. The text of the Articles of Incorporation is printed in *International Legal Materials*, vol. 22 (1983), p. 569.

—Discuss with borrower countries on a strictly voluntary basis their economic plans, assumptions, and financing needs.

Once fully operational, the Institute will have a permanent independent professional staff which will direct these activities. The Institute will not be involved in setting credit criteria nor in establishing ratings for credit-worthiness, nor will it constitute a vehicle for deciding what credits should be provided or the terms of such credits. Neither will it serve as vehicle for the exchange of information among its members regarding lending practices. The information disseminated by the Institute will be designed to enhance the ability of each member individually to make decisions regarding its international loan portfolio.[16]

Commercial banks are almost never in a position to negotiate comprehensive national programs of economic and monetary stabilization with their borrowers. We shall come to appreciate the value to commercial banks, and to governments, of knowledge that countries are, or are not, in fact successfully pursuing stabilization programs negotiated with the International Monetary Fund and supported by IMF stand-by or extended arrangements. Conditions precedent to disbursements under commercial bank loan agreements that are keyed to stabilization programs negotiated with the IMF are treated later in this book.[17]

Issues concerning official supervision of commercial bank practices in international lending are addressed in the final chapter, along with questions concerning the role of national monetary authorities and the International Monetary Fund in providing liquidity at times of financial crisis.[18]

Sale of Government Bonds

A bond is simply a specialized form of promissory note given 4o a creditor making a loan. A country's national treasury can sell a bond in exchange for foreign currency balances. A bond may be provided to a particular creditor or be sold in a public offering. The purchaser of the bond will normally carry the risk that the purchasing power of the currency in which the bond is denominated may depreciate between the time of the loan and the date of its repayment. Value maintenance clauses can be used to adjust the repayment obligation in the light of changes in currency exchange rates.

Another approach, possibly making a bond more attractive to its purchaser, is for the national treasury issuing the bond to denominate it in a cur-

---

[16] *International Legal Materials*, vol. 22 (1983), pp. 569–70. See also Chapter 12, *infra*, page 624 (note 251) and 627–628, regarding collection and dissemination of information to commercial banks.

[17] See discussion in Chapter 6, *infra*, pages 272–275.

[18] See Chapter 12, *infra*, page 619 et seq.

rency other than its own. That is, the bond entails an obligation to deliver a specified amount of a foreign currency at a specified future date. The foreign currency proceeds from the sale of such bonds can be used to settle accounts resulting from the importation of goods or services, to finance capital transactions, or to intervene to stabilize exchange markets. A bond denominated in a foreign currency may also be issued by a country's treasury in exchange for balances of its own currency held by foreign governments or their central banks.

The United States Treasury in the period 1962–1971, for example, sold bonds that were denominated in Deutsche mark and in Swiss francs to the Deutsche Bundesbank (central bank of the Federal Republic of Germany), the Swiss National Bank, and the Bank for International Settlements.[19]

In 1978 and 1979 the United States Treasury, with the consent of authorities in the Federal Republic of Germany and Switzerland, from time to time sold notes, backed by the full faith and credit of the United States, on the public markets of the two countries, with purchasers restricted to residents of the countries. The notes denominated and payable in Deutsche mark were sold through the Deutsche Bundesbank as agent, and the Swiss franc issues were sold through the Swiss National Bank. The Deutsche mark and Swiss francs acquired by the U.S. Treasury were used to liquidate obligations to the central banks and to augment reserves available for use in a period of active exchange market operations.[20]

The United Kingdom Treasury in 1977 offered bearer bonds to official holders of sterling. The bonds were offered in Deutsche mark, Japanese yen, Swiss francs, and U.S. dollars at varying maturities and interest rates. This was part of a program to reduce sterling balances. A number of banks and security

---

[19] See Gerald A. Pollack, "Perspectives on the United States International Financial Position," in *The United States Balance of Payments—Perspectives and Policies: Staff Materials and Other Submissions Prepared for the Use of the Joint Economic Committee*, U.S. Congress, 88th Congress, 1st Session (1963), p. 1 at p. 51; Daniel L. Kohn, "Foreign Official Institution Holdings of U.S. Government Securities," in Federal Reserve Bank of Kansas City, *Monthly Review*, September–October 1974, p. 11; John H. Makin, "Swaps and Roosa Bonds as an Index of Cooperation in the Crisis Zone," *Quarterly Journal of Economics*, vol. 85 (May 1971), p. 349; and Charles A. Coombs, "Treasury and Federal Reserve Foreign Exchange Operations," in Federal Reserve Bank of New York, *Monthly Review*, October 1971, p. 214. See also *To Amend the Par Value Modification Act of 1972*, infra note 37, pp. 351–52; and Coombs, *Arena of International Finance*, infra note 26, pp. 37–41 and 88–89.

[20] The different issues of U.S. notes varied in maturity from 2½ to 4 years. The notes were issued under the authority of the Second Liberty Bond Act, approved September 24, 1917, as amended; *United States Code, Title 31*, section 766. The Swiss franc notes contained a choice of law clause which stated that the notes "shall be governed by and construed in accordance with the laws of the United States of America." The Deutsche mark notes did not contain a choice of law clause. The terms under which the notes were issued were stated in the invitation for subscriptions for each issue. See *Authorization for Treasury's International Affairs Functions; Hearing [on S. 976] before the Subcommittee on International Finance of the Committee on Banking, Housing, and Urban Affairs*, U.S. Senate, 96th Congress, 1st Session (1979), p. 13. For background on United States exchange market policy at the time, see Chapter 11, infra, pages 533–534.

houses agreed to assist holders in selling their bonds to others, including private buyers, if they wished to do so.[21]

Many governments have issued bonds denominated in U.S. dollars and other currencies on markets outside their territories. The Republic of Finland, for example, in November 1981 made a public offering of notes denominated in U.S. dollars.[22] Innumerable examples could be cited.[23]

Bilateral Payments Arrangements

Bilateral payments arrangements came into widespread use during the 1930s and 40s. A number of socialist countries that are not members of the International Monetary Fund, and some IMF members with stringent currency restrictions, continue to make use of bilateral arrangements. Under these arrangements, exchange restrictions in each country channel payments for goods and services, between that country and its partner, through the central banks. Payments are settled by means of special accounts maintained by each central bank with its partner.

Bilateral payments agreements between the Soviet Union and Iran, and between Romania and Ghana, Guinea, and the United Arab Republic, are discussed in Chapter 9. Legal features of bilateral systems, and procedures used in their operation, are discussed at that time.[24] As explained in Chapter 10, bilateral payments arrangements commonly involve discriminatory currency practices that, for members of the International Monetary Fund, are inconsistent with obligations under the IMF's Articles of Agreement.[25]

Reciprocal Currency (Swap) Arrangements

Arrangements Between the U.S. Federal Reserve System and Other Central Banks

General Background. Since 1962 the Federal Reserve Bank of New York has been authorized to buy and sell foreign currencies on the open market for the purpose of countering disorderly market conditions between the United

---

[21] See Chapter 3, *supra*, page 108. See also *Exchange Stabilization Fund: Hearing [on S. 2093] before the Subcommittee on International Finance of the Committee on Banking, Housing, and Urban Affairs*, U.S. Senate, 95th Congress, 1st Session (1977), p. 127.

[22] *Wall Street Journal*, November 13, 1981, p. 44.

[23] See, e.g., Chapter 8, *infra*, page 340 (notes 125, 126, and 131), respecting notes issued by the European Economic Community to finance balance-of-payments assistance provided to France, Ireland and Italy.

[24] Chapter 9, *infra*, pages 358–360. See also Chapter 7, page 300 (note 2).

[25] This subject is discussed at page 400, *infra*.

States dollar and foreign currencies.[26] In these operations the bank acts as agent for the United States Treasury and the Federal Reserve System. The New York Bank conducts these transactions pursuant to general directives of the Federal Reserve System's Open Market Committee and in consultation with the Treasury. The manager of the System's Open Market Account, a senior officer of the Federal Reserve Bank of New York, is given two responsibilities: (1) to operate in the spot and forward exchange markets for the dollar and authorized foreign currencies and (2) to operate a network of arrangements for reciprocal currency exchange with foreign central banks.[27] At the present time open market operations are authorized in Austrian schillings, Belgian francs, Canadian dollars, Danish kroner, French francs, Deutsche (German) mark, Italian lire, Japanese yen, Mexican pesos, Netherlands guilders, Norwegian kroner, Swedish kronor, Swiss francs, and United Kingdom pounds sterling.[28] Central banks of

---

[26] Some open market transactions took place on behalf of the U.S. Treasury in 1961. Regular procedures for Federal Reserve operations were established in 1962. The historical context in which these operations were begun is described in Charles A. Coombs, *The Arena of International Finance,* (New York: John Wiley & Sons, 1976), pp. 1–82.

[27] The two principal operational documents are the Federal Open Market Committee (FOMC)'s Authorization for Foreign Currency Operations and the FOMC's Foreign Currency Directive. The directive in effect at the time this book went to press provides:

1. [Federal Reserve] System operations in foreign currencies shall generally be directed at countering disorderly market conditions, provided that market exchange rates for the U.S. dollar reflect actions and behavior consistent with the IMF Article IV, Section 1.
2. To achieve this end the System shall:
   A. Undertake spot and forward purchases and sales of foreign exchange.
   B. Maintain reciprocal currency ("swap") arrangements with selected foreign central banks and with the Bank for International Settlements.
   C. Cooperate in other respects with central banks of other countries and with international monetary institutions.
3. Transactions may also be undertaken:
   A. To adjust System balances in light of probable future needs for currencies.
   B. To provide means for meeting System and Treasury commitments in particular currencies, and to facilitate operations of the [Treasury's] Exchange Stabilization Fund.
   C. For such other purposes as may be expressly authorized by the Committee.
4. System foreign currency operations shall be conducted:
   A. In close and continuous consultation and cooperation with the United States Treasury;
   B. In cooperation, as appropriate, with foreign monetary authorities; and
   C. In a manner consistent with the obligations of the United States in the International Monetary Fund regarding exchange arrangements under the IMF Article IV.

The text of the authorization and the directive are published each year in the *Annual Report* of the Board of Governors of the Federal Reserve System. Amendments in the course of the year are published in the *Federal Reserve Bulletin.* The above text of the directive is from the Board of Governors of the Federal Reserve System, *69th Annual Report, 1982,* p. 84.

The Federal Reserve's authority derives from *United States Code,* title 12, sections 248, 263, 348a, 358, and 632. See *Code of Federal Regulations,* title 12, part 214 (Relations with Foreign Banks and Bankers—Regulation N), and title 12, part 270 (Open Market Operations of Federal Reserve Banks).

[28] FOMC Authorization for Foreign Currency Operations, paragraph 1.A. The text of the authorization and amendment of August 28, 1982, appear in Board of Governors of the Federal Reserve System, *69th Annual Report, 1982,* pp. 82–84 and 120–21.

other countries also use the U.S. dollar and other currencies to intervene in exchange markets to maintain orderly trading conditions and to influence rates, or to make payments abroad for their residents, or to supply to commercial banks for this purpose. The Federal Reserve Bank of New York may also act as an agent for a foreign central bank in buying or selling that country's currency in the New York foreign exchange market.

Bilateral swap agreements for the direct exchange of currencies are maintained by the Federal Reserve with the fourteen central banks that issue the currencies listed above and with the Bank for International Settlements (BIS).[29] These agreements provide sources of funds for market interventions and for other purposes.[30] The agreements, the operation of which are explained below, are normally treated as confidential and are not published. Reports on market operations and on use of the currency agreements are regularly published under the title ''Treasury and Federal Reserve Foreign Exchange Operations'' in the *Federal Reserve Bulletin* and in the *Quarterly Review* of the Federal Reserve Bank of New York.[31]

History and Basic Concepts.   It was recognized in the early 1960s that when the principal Western European countries accepted IMF Article VIII, Sections 2, 3, and 4,[32] and further liberalized controls on capital movements,[33] trading in the exchange markets would become much more active. Authorities of these countries would need access to substantial amounts of funds, primarily U.S. dollars because the dollar was the principal intervention currency, for official exchange market interventions to maintain rates within the prescribed margins of parity relationships as required by the provisions of the IMF Agreement in effect at the time.[34]

While the United States would satisfy its maintenance-of-parity obliga-

---

[29] The U.S. Federal Reserve System presently has two arrangements with the BIS: one is an arrangement for drawing Swiss francs and the other is an arrangement for drawing other currencies. These arrangements supplement the bilateral arrangements maintained with the fourteen foreign central banks. Many BIS drawings are simply overnight drawings on the Federal Reserve by the BIS in dollars against European currencies for the BIS's account to be used in bridging payments and receipts in accounts that the BIS maintains for its member central banks. See table on page 155, *infra*.

[30] See FOMC Foreign Currency Directive in note 27, *supra*. See also discussions of exchange market interventions in Chapter 11, *infra*, pages 521-526, 531-535, and 546-548.

[31] The *Minutes of Federal Open Market Committee*, available for public examination at the U.S. National Archives and the Federal Reserve Banks, record in detail deliberations in the FOMC on foreign exchange operations and on discussions of central bankers in Basle during the period 1961-1975. Minutes respecting these operations and discussions have, however, not been kept subsequent to March 1976. Coombs, *Arena of International Finance, supra* note 26, comments on the operations and personalities involved in the period 1961-1975. Policy actions of the FOMC are regularly reported in the *Annual Report* of the Board of Governors of the Federal Reserve System and in the *Federal Reserve Bulletin*. The deliberations are summarized in very general terms.

[32] See Chapter 10, *infra*, page 403 (note 94).

[33] See Chapter 10, *infra*, page 460 et seq.

[34] IMF Article IV, sections 3 and 4, *original*. See Chapter 11, *infra*, page 492 (note 6).

tions by buying and selling gold on the demand of foreign monetary authorities,[35] it was seen that stability would be fostered, and the necessity of gold sales reduced, if U.S. authorities were to intervene in the New York market in the interest of maintaining exchange rate order. U.S. authorities would, however, need access to foreign currencies they would wish to sell, potentially in large amounts.[36] U.S. authorities wanted to avoid having to sell gold to acquire the needed currencies. They also needed a way to provide an exchange guarantee to foreign central banks on the portion of their dollar holdings that, in the absence of protection, they would present for conversion into gold.

The first reciprocal currency agreement was that between the Banque de France and the Federal Reserve Bank of New York, effective March 1, 1962.[37] It established the basic concept: Each of the two central banks that are parties to a reciprocal currency arrangement agrees to exchange its own currency for that of the other party up to a prearranged maximum amount during a specified period of time. A purchase of a foreign currency in exchange for the bank's own currency under the agreement is called a "drawing." A central bank making a drawing under a swap arrangement incurs an obligation to sell back the currency drawn at the same exchange rate within three months unless the period is extended. This obligation to make a future exchange to liquidate the drawing is called a "forward exchange" commitment. Thus, the financial concept of a "swap" is the simultaneous purchase and sale of a currency for different maturities. The overall arrangement usually has a one-year duration and is renewed by mutual agreement.

Following the agreement with the Banque de France, reciprocal currency agreements were concluded by the Federal Reserve Bank of New York, as agent for the Federal Reserve System, with the central banks issuing the other thirteen currencies listed in the previous section and with the Bank for International Settlements. Some refinements in technical features of the agreements were made during the 1960s.[38]

---

[35] See Chapter 3, *supra,* pages 115–119, and Chapter 11, *infra,* page 492.

[36] Drawing rights in the International Monetary Fund were not judged sufficient for the potentially large operations contemplated. See Chapter 6, *infra,* page 287.

[37] The text of the agreement appears in Coombs, *Arena of International Finance, supra* note 26, pp. 75–76.

Legal memoranda prepared in 1962 by the General Counsel of the Federal Open Market Committee and by the General Counsel of the U.S. Treasury on the authority of the Federal Reserve to engage in open market operations in foreign currencies and to enter into reciprocal currency arrangements with foreign central banks appear in *To Amend the Par Value Modification Act of 1972: Hearings [on H.R. 4546] before the Subcommittee on International Finance of the Committee on Banking and Currency,* U.S. House of Representatives, 93d Congress, 1st Session (1973), pp. 352–71. The concept of the swap arrangements when they were first established is described in Board of Governors of the Federal Reserve System, *49th Annual Report, 1962,* pp. 54–63.

[38] The agreement between the Federal Reserve System and Danmarks Nationalbank (the central bank of Denmark), for the year December 1, 1971, to December 1, 1972, which is typical of agreements in use in the latter years of the Bretton Woods par value system, appears in *Gold and the Central Bank Swap Network:*

Following dramatic monetary events of the period 1971–1973, which are described in Chapter 11, the authorities of countries issuing widely traded currencies decided in March 1973 to allow the exchange rates of their currencies to float against the U.S. dollar. By mid-1973 market conditions had become very disorderly.[39] Central bankers in a meeting in Basle, Switzerland, in July 1973 agreed on procedures for restoring order in the exchange markets. The essential terms of the swap agreements in use until December 1980 were worked out at that time.[40]

In December 1980 a new pattern was established for reciprocal currency (swap) agreements. The terms of present agreements will be considered later.[41] The agreements in use in the period 1973–1980 are of interest because they were heavily used by both the Federal Reserve and by foreign central banks. The Federal Reserve intervened actively in the markets during much of this period, while the Federal Reserve's interventions subsequent to early 1981 have been infrequent and modest. The agreements also contained some unique legal features not reflected in current arrangements.

Currency Swap Agreements (1973–1980)—Bank of England Arrangement. Set forth below is the agreement between the Federal Reserve System and the Bank of England of December 2, 1977, for the year to December 4, 1978:

Reciprocal Currency Agreement Between the U.S. Federal Reserve System and the Bank of England[42]

To: Bank of England, London
From: Federal Reserve Bank of New York
Date: December 2, 1977
No.: 1398

FOR SANGSTER FROM HOLMES
REFERENCE OUR NO. 1189 AND YOUR NO. 1198 BOTH OF 1976.

I.   FEDERAL RESERVE SUGGESTS RENEWAL AT MATURITY
     FOR ONE YEAR TO DECEMBER 4, 1978 OF OUR $3,000,000,000

Hearings before the Subcommittee on International Exchange and Payments of the Joint Economic Committee, U.S. Congress, 92d Congress, 2d Session (1972), pp. 171–72.

[39] See Chapter 11, *infra,* pages 499–500.

[40] See *Minutes of Federal Open Market Committee, supra* note 31, 1973, pp. 708–23.

[41] At page 151.

[42] Reprinted from the text provided by the Federal Reserve System in response to a request by the author under the U.S. Freedom of Information Act. This agreement for the year to December 4, 1978, was confirmed by the Bank of England.

U.S. DOLLAR/STERLING RECIPROCAL SWAP ARRANGE-
MENT, SUBJECT TO USE BY EITHER PARTY ON TWO BUSI-
NESS DAYS' NOTICE. THIS ARRANGEMENT MAY BE EX-
TENDED BY MUTUAL AGREEMENT.

II.   DRAWINGS UNDER THE ARRANGEMENT MAY BE USED IN
EXECUTION OF SPOT OR FORWARD TRANSACTIONS CON-
CLUDED IN CONSULTATION WITH THE OTHER PARTY. EACH
DRAWING WILL HAVE AN INITIAL MATURITY OF THREE
MONTHS, SUBJECT TO RENEWAL UPON MUTUAL AGREE-
MENT. THE SAME RATE OF EXCHANGE SHALL BE APPLIED
TO THE DRAWING AND ITS LIQUIDATION. THIS RATE SHALL
BE BASED UPON THE SPOT RATE RULING IN THE MARKET AS
AGREED BETWEEN THE TWO PARTIES AT THE TIME THE
DRAWING IS ARRANGED.

III.   PROCEEDS OF DRAWINGS WILL BE EMPLOYED AS FOL-
LOWS:
   (A) THE UNITED STATES DOLLARS ARE TO BE CREDITED TO
       YOUR CURRENT ACCOUNT "G" UNDER CABLE ADVICE.
       TO THE EXTENT THAT THESE FUNDS ARE NOT RE-
       QUIRED IMMEDIATELY FOR PAYMENTS, YOU WILL AU-
       THORIZE US TO DEBIT YOUR CURRENT ACCOUNT "G"
       AND PLACE THE AMOUNT OF UNITED STATES DOLLARS
       IN QUESTION IN A NONTRANSFERABLE U.S. TREASURY
       CERTIFICATE OF INDEBTEDNESS WHICH THE SECRE-
       TARY OF THE TREASURY IS PREPARED TO ISSUE TO YOU
       AT PAR, TO MATURE THREE MONTHS AFTER DATE OF
       ISSUE. SUCH CERTIFICATE WILL BE REDEEMABLE AT
       PAR UPON TWO BUSINESS DAYS' NOTICE AND WILL
       BEAR INTEREST AT A RATE BASED UPON THE AVERAGE
       RATE OF DISCOUNT AT THE AUCTION OF THE LAST IS-
       SUE OF THREE-MONTH U.S. TREASURY BILLS PRECED-
       ING THE DATE OF ISSUE OF THE CERTIFICATE IN TWO
       DECIMAL PLACES AND IF SUCH DECIMAL IS NOT A
       MULTIPLE OF .05, IT WILL BE ADJUSTED TO THE NEXT
       HIGHER MULTIPLE OF .05. THE CERTIFICATE WILL BE
       ISSUED AND REDEEMED AT THE FEDERAL RESERVE
       BANK OF NEW YORK, AS FISCAL AGENT OF THE UNITED
       STATES, AND WILL BE HELD IN YOUR U.S. TREASURY
       CERTIFICATE OF INDEBTEDNESS ACCOUNT.

   (B) THE STERLING IS TO BE CREDITED TO OUR ACCOUNT
       "A" UNDER CABLE ADVICE. TO THE EXTENT THAT

THESE FUNDS ARE NOT REQUIRED IMMEDIATELY FOR
PAYMENTS, WE WILL AUTHORIZE YOU TO DEBIT OUR
ACCOUNT "A" AND PLACE THE FULL AMOUNT OF
STERLING IN QUESTION IN OUR ACCOUNT "A"—SUB
ACCOUNT MONEY EMPLOYED. STERLING IN SUCH AC-
COUNT WILL EARN A RETURN WHICH IS EQUAL TO A
RATE OF INTEREST BASED UPON THE AVERAGE RATE
OF DISCOUNT AT THE AUCTION OF THE LAST ISSUE OF
THREE-MONTH U.S. TREASURY BILLS, AS CALCULATED
ABOVE. SUCH BALANCES MAY BE WITHDRAWN BY US
ON TWO BUSINESS DAYS' NOTICE.

IV.   IF YOU AGREE, PLEASE CONFIRM.

FEDERAL RESERVE BANK OF NEW YORK

In the period July 1973–December 1980, the Federal Reserve's currency
swap arrangements with the central banks of Austria, Canada, Denmark, Italy,
Japan, Mexico, Norway, and Sweden followed the above pattern. The arrangement was designed for a regime of managed floating of exchange rates and
could also be applied to currencies whose rates were pegged to the dollar.

While under the Federal Reserve–Bank of England agreement either party
had the legal right to make a drawing, the parties in fact expected that the Bank
of England would be the party doing so. The drawing of funds took place as
follows: The Bank of England held a large part of its monetary reserves in the
form of U.S. Treasury securities, dollar deposits with the Federal Reserve Bank
of New York, and dollar deposits with commercial banks, the total of these
holdings being measured in billions of dollars. When the Bank of England
bought sterling in the exchange market to counter disorderly conditions in the
market or to support sterling's rate, it normally fulfilled these exchange contracts by transferring relatively small portions of these large dollar balances.
However, its interventions in the market or contingency plans for interventions
in the market might result, or be anticipated to result, in drawing down its dollar
balances to a level below that which the Bank of England wished to maintain.

The Bank of England, through a drawing on the currency swap arrangement
with the Federal Reserve, could augment its reserves. The swap agreement was
like an unconfirmed credit line. The procedure for and terms of a drawing were
stated in advance in the cable agreement set forth above. Drawings under the
agreement, however, require consultation: "Drawings under the arrangement may
be used in execution of spot or forward transactions concluded in consultation with
the other party." Consultations would cover the purpose of the drawing and the
amount to be drawn. Where large drawings were contemplated, consultations
might cover the policies the Bank of England intended to pursue to correct the conditions that had caused a decline in its reserves. Consultations might take place by

telephone or in person-to-person meetings. The Bank of England usually requested drawings of $100 million or more at a time.

Let us assume that the consultations resulted in the U.S. Federal Reserve concurring with the Bank of England's request for a drawing of $200 million. The Bank of England would then proceed to make the drawing under the reciprocal currency arrangement. It would send a cable to the Federal Reserve Bank of New York. The cable would reference the swap agreement set forth above and would state the amount of the drawing. Two business days later[43] the New York Bank would credit the dollars to Current Account "G" in the agreed amount. At that point the United Kingdom's gross monetary reserves increased. The funds would be used to purchase a non-transferable U.S. Treasury certificate of indebtedness unless the Bank of England instructed that the funds be used in another manner.[44] That certificate could be redeemed with two days' notice if the Bank of England wished to increase its working balances or to use the dollars for making payments.[45]

Two business days after the Bank of England sent the cable mentioned in the previous paragraph, that bank reciprocally credited the New York Bank with sterling.[46] The exchange rate for this transaction was based upon the spot rate in the market as agreed between the two banks at the time the drawing was arranged.[47] The sterling credited to the Federal Reserve would earn interest.[48]

The reciprocal crediting is the essential feature of a central bank reciprocal currency transaction. The actions of the two banks created money augmenting the monetary reserves of the partners without either bank's having to dispose of other monetary assets. Under U.S. law the credit received by the Federal Reserve in sterling is itself a reserve on the basis of which the New York Bank could credit the Bank of England in dollars. The Bank of England, which entered a credit in sterling in favor of the New York Bank, received a credit in dollars that augmented its reserves. One can see that reciprocal crediting is a simple bilateral procedure for expanding international liquidity. Liquidity would be contracted when the swap was liquidated.[49]

On or before the three-month maturity date, unless a longer period was

---

[43] Two business days is the conventional period for effecting spot exchange transactions. See Appendix A, *infra,* page 678.

[44] The Bank of England could, for example, request that the dollars be transferred to the credit of a commercial bank or official institution to which it had sold dollars.

[45] See paragraph III(A) of the reciprocal currency agreement.

[46] See paragraph III(B) of the agreement.

[47] See paragraph II of the agreement.

[48] See paragraph III(B) of the agreement.

[49] The effects of swap drawings and repayments upon domestic monetary aggregates have routinely been neutralized in the United States. See Roger M. Kubarych, "Monetary Effects of Federal Reserve Swaps," in Federal Reserve Bank of New York, *Quarterly Review,* vol. 2, no. 4 (Winter 1977–78), p. 19. On the merits of sterilized versus unsterilized intervention, see Philippe Jurgensen et al., *Report of the Working Group on Exchange Market Intervention* (Washington: U.S. Department of the Treasury, March 1983). The report was commissioned by the June 1982 Versailles Summit Conference.

agreed,[50] the parties were required to fulfill what can be described as the "forward" part of the contract. The Bank of England would transfer 200 million dollars (the amount of the original drawing) to the Federal Reserve and the Federal Reserve would transfer sterling to the Bank of England. The exchange rate for this transaction was the same rate used when the Bank of England made the original drawing.[51] The Bank of England had to acquire the dollars that it would use in this transaction at its own cost and risk. It might take them from its reserves, it might acquire them in the market by selling sterling, it might draw dollars from the IMF, or it might obtain them from other sources. If sterling had depreciated from the originally booked rate, the Bank of England would suffer a loss; if sterling had appreciated, the Bank of England would make a profit.[52]

Following the liquidation of the swap, the New York Bank would still hold a residual amount of sterling representing the interest earned on the sterling balance that had been reciprocally credited to it while the Bank of England's drawing was outstanding.[53] The New York Bank would normally sell this residual sterling balance in the market.

Currency Swap Agreements (1973–1980)—Deutsche Bundesbank Arrangement.

Set forth below is the agreement between the Federal Reserve System and the Deutsche Bundesbank (the central bank of the Federal Republic of Germany) of December 7, 1977, for the year to December 29, 1978:

Reciprocal Currency Agreement Between the U.S. Federal Reserve System and the Deutsche Bundesbank[54]

To: Deutsche Bundesbank, Frankfurt/Main
From: Federal Reserve Bank of New York
Date: December 7, 1977
No.: 770

---

[50] When the Bank of England made arrangements to draw up to $1 billion on the swap facility with the Federal Reserve in June 1976, it was agreed at that time that drawings would be repaid within six months. See note 120, *infra*. The author understands that, with the exception of Swiss franc drawings under a special agreement of October 1976 (*infra* page 163), nearly all swap drawings made in the period July 1973–December 1980 were liquidated in six months or less.

The U.S. Federal Open Market Committee's Authorization for Foreign Currency Operations, *supra* notes 27 and 28, paragraph 1.C, requires that drawings by either party be fully liquidated within twelve months unless the FOMC specially authorizes a delay.

[51] See paragraph II of the agreement.

[52] The swap agreements in use prior to July 1973 included a clause to protect a country against the upward revaluation of its partner's currency. See text accompanying note 104, *infra*.

[53] While the Federal Reserve had the legal right to draw down the sterling balance reciprocally credited to it by the Bank of England during the period the British bank's drawing was outstanding, the actual practice of the Federal Reserve was simply to allow the balance to earn interest. When the Federal Reserve needed sterling, it normally purchased it in the market.

[54] Reprinted from the text provided by the Federal Reserve System in response to a request by the author under the U.S. Freedom of Information Act. Although identified as a draft, the text was accepted without change by the Bundesbank and was confirmed as the final agreement.

FOR SCHOLL FROM PARDEE
DRAFT FOR YOUR CONSIDERATION AS PER OUR TELEPHONE
CONVERSATION OF TODAY. REFERENCE OUR NO. 730 AND
YOUR NO. 889 BOTH OF 1976.

I.   FEDERAL RESERVE SUGGESTS RENEWAL AT MATURITY
     FOR ONE YEAR TO DECEMBER 29, 1978 OF OUR
     $2,000,000,000[55] U.S. DOLLAR/DEUTSCHE MARK RECIPRO-
     CAL SWAP ARRANGEMENT, SUBJECT TO USE BY EITHER
     PARTY ON TWO BUSINESS DAYS' NOTICE AND IN CIRCUM-
     STANCES TO BE MUTUALLY AGREED UPON. THIS ARRANGE-
     MENT MAY BE RENEWED UPON MUTUAL AGREEMENT.

II. DRAWINGS UNDER THE ARRANGEMENT MAY BE USED IN
     EXECUTION OF SPOT OR FORWARD TRANSACTIONS CON-
     CLUDED IN CONSULTATION WITH THE OTHER PARTY. IN
     THIS CONNECTION, IT IS UNDERSTOOD THAT INTERVEN-
     TIONS IN DEUTSCHE MARKS AGAINST DOLLARS WILL TAKE
     PLACE UNDER CLOSE COOPERATION AND PRIOR CONSUL-
     TATION WITH THE BUNDESBANK. EACH DRAWING WILL
     HAVE AN INITIAL MATURITY OF THREE MONTHS, SUBJECT
     TO RENEWAL UPON MUTUAL AGREEMENT. EVERY EFFORT
     WILL BE MADE BY BOTH PARTIES TO FACILITATE THE
     EARLY LIQUIDATION OF ANY FEDERAL RESERVE DRAW-
     INGS UNDER THIS ARRANGEMENT. IN ANY CASE, UNLESS IT
     IS MUTUALLY AGREED AT THE TIME THAT FURTHER RE-
     NEWALS ARE APPROPRIATE, EACH DRAWING WILL BE RE-
     PAID NO LATER THAN SIX MONTHS AFTER ITS INCEPTION.
     THE DEUTSCHE MARKS REQUIRED BY THE FEDERAL RE-
     SERVE TO EFFECT SUCH REPAYMENTS WILL BE ACQUIRED
     IN THE MARKET UNLESS IT IS MUTUALLY AGREED THAT DI-
     RECT TRANSACTIONS BETWEEN THE FEDERAL RESERVE
     AND THE BUNDESBANK WOULD BE DESIRABLE. THE SAME
     RATE OF EXCHANGE SHALL BE APPLIED TO THE DRAWING
     AND ITS LIQUIDATION. THIS RATE SHALL BE BASED UPON
     THE SPOT RATE RULING IN THE MARKET AS AGREED UPON
     BETWEEN THE TWO PARTIES AT THE TIME THE DRAWING IS
     ARRANGED.

III. PROCEEDS OF DRAWINGS WILL BE EMPLOYED AS FOL-
     LOWS:

---

[55] The amount of the arrangement was increased to $4 billion on March 11, 1978, and was further in-
creased to $6 billion on November 1, 1978. Board of Governors of the Federal Reserve System, *65th Annual
Report, 1978,* pp. 140–42 and 239–41.

(A) THE UNITED STATES DOLLARS ARE TO BE CREDITED TO YOUR SPECIAL ACCOUNT UNDER CABLE ADVICE. TO THE EXTENT THAT THESE FUNDS ARE NOT REQUIRED IMMEDIATELY FOR PAYMENTS, IT IS UNDERSTOOD THAT YOU WILL PLACE THE DOLLAR BALANCES CREDITED TO YOUR SPECIAL ACCOUNT IN NONTRANSFERABLE U.S. TREASURY CERTIFICATES OF INDEBTEDNESS WHICH THE SECRETARY OF THE TREASURY IS PREPARED TO ISSUE TO YOU AT PAR, TO MATURE THREE MONTHS AFTER DATE OF ISSUE. SUCH CERTIFICATES WILL BE REDEEMABLE UPON TWO BUSINESS DAYS' NOTICE AND WILL BEAR INTEREST AT A RATE BASED UPON THE AVERAGE RATE OF DISCOUNT AT THE AUCTION OF THE LAST ISSUE OF THREE-MONTH U.S. TREASURY BILLS PRECEDING THE DATE OF ISSUE OF THE CERTIFICATE IN TWO DECIMAL PLACES AND IF SUCH DECIMAL IS NOT A MULTIPLE OF .05, IT WILL BE ADJUSTED TO THE NEXT HIGHER MULTIPLE OF .05. THE CERTIFICATES WILL BE ISSUED AND REDEEMED AT THE FEDERAL RESERVE BANK OF NEW YORK, AS FISCAL AGENT OF THE UNITED STATES, AND WILL BE HELD IN YOUR SECURITY CUSTODY ACCOUNT.

(B) THE GERMAN MARKS ARE TO BE CREDITED TO OUR ACCOUNT "A" UNDER CABLE ADVICE. IT IS UNDERSTOOD THAT BALANCES IN THIS ACCOUNT WILL EARN A RETURN WHICH IS EQUAL TO A RATE OF INTEREST BASED UPON THE AVERAGE RATE OF DISCOUNT AT THE AUCTION OF THE LAST ISSUE OF U.S. TREASURY BILLS, AS NOTED ABOVE. SUCH RETURN WILL BE EXPRESSED AS THE DIFFERENCE BETWEEN THE SPOT AND FORWARD EXCHANGE RATES WHICH ARE APPLIED TO THE TRANSACTION.

IV.   TAKING INTO ACCOUNT THE PRESENT EXCHANGE REGIME, WE AGREE THAT PROFITS AND LOSSES TO THE FEDERAL RESERVE AS A RESULT OF RATE MOVEMENTS IN THE MARKET WILL BE SHARED EQUALLY WITH THE DEUTSCHE BUNDESBANK. THE EXCHANGE RATES FOR SWAP REPAYMENTS WILL BE ADJUSTED WHERE NECESSARY TO ACHIEVE THIS EQUAL DIVISION OF PROFITS OR LOSSES.

V.   IF YOU AGREE, PLEASE CONFIRM.

FEDERAL RESERVE BANK OF NEW YORK

While under the Bank of England agreement discussed previously the central bank making a drawing carried the full profit or loss risk in its liquidation, the Bundesbank agreement provided for the equal sharing between the Federal Reserve and the Bundesbank of gains and losses when the Federal Reserve made drawings of mark under the agreement.[56] This clause figured in Federal Reserve–Bundesbank agreements in use from July 1973 through December 1980. Provisions for equal sharing by the Federal Reserve of its gains and losses from market interventions in its partner's currency, along the lines of the Bundesbank agreement, were included in the agreements with the central banks of Belgium, France, Netherlands, and Switzerland. The Federal Reserve was offered the clause as an inducement for it to undertake more active intervention in the exchange markets to counter disorderly conditions such as those that had developed in the early summer of 1973.[57]

Note that the clause was asymmetrical. It did not apply to drawings of dollars that might be made by the Bundesbank under the agreement. When the clause was negotiated at Basle in July 1973, foreign central banks requested that the Federal Reserve agree, as a complementary measure, to share the profits and losses applicable to dollar balances acquired by foreign authorities in their market interventions in which their currencies were sold for dollars. The U.S. authorities said such an arrangement was not acceptable.[58]

The profit and loss sharing provisions were terminated in all of the Federal Reserve's reciprocal currency agreements in which they appeared in December 1980.[59] A few months after this change and the inauguration of President Ronald Reagan, U.S. Treasury and Federal Reserve officials announced a shift in U.S. market intervention policy that resulted in less frequent interventions.[60] The change in U.S. intervention policy was not, however, caused by the changes in the reciprocal currency agreements.

The Federal Reserve–Bundesbank reciprocal currency agreement was a collaborative arrangement in the full sense of the word between the issuers of two pivotal currencies. It is one of the most important agreements from both legal and economic points of view treated anywhere in this book. The manner in which the agreement was implemented and the continuous process of consultation that was involved deserve elaboration.

As is the case today, there was in the middle and late 1970s daily communication between the New York Federal Reserve Bank and the central banks issuing actively traded currencies. Information was exchanged on supply and demand factors in their respective foreign currency markets and about the direction in which the exchange rates were moving. They shared information on

---

[56] See paragraph IV of the Bundesbank agreement.

[57] For background on the original negotiation of profit and loss sharing clauses respecting Federal Reserve market interventions in foreign currencies drawn on the swap lines, see *Minutes of Federal Open Market Committee, supra* note 31, 1973, pp. 710–13 and 719–23. See also Chapter 11, *infra*, page 500 (note 46).

[58] See *Minutes of Federal Open Market Committee, supra* note 31, 1973, p. 712.

[59] See page 151, *infra*.

[60] See Chapter 11, *infra*, page 534.

large transactions they understood might take place in the market. They indicated in general terms their own plans with respect to official actions that were contemplated to counter disorderly market conditions, to smooth out rate dislocations that might be caused by large transactions, or to influence exchange rate movements.[61] In periods of unsettled market conditions, such communications might take place several times during a day. In addition to providing information, the consultations helped minimize conflicts in the implementation of exchange rate policies. At times consultations led to coordinated forceful market intervention. Consultations took place most frequently by telephone among officers with day-to-day operating responsibilities. They might be raised to higher levels when important policy decisions had to be made and in times of crisis. Consultation between the Federal Reserve and the Bundesbank was particularly close.[62]

While both the Federal Reserve–Bank of England and the Federal Reserve–Bundesbank agreements stated that drawings might be used in execution of spot and forward transactions "concluded in consultation with the other party,"[63] the consultation provision in the Bundesbank agreement in addition stated that "it is understood that interventions [in the market] in Deutsche marks against dollars will take place under close cooperation and prior consultation with the Bundesbank."[64] While the profit and loss sharing provision provided a special reason for this consultation clause, the primary reasons for the clause were the concerns of the Bundesbank about the effects of interventions on exchange rates and on the liquidity of German banks and non-bank financial institutions.[65] The consultation clause was understood to permit the Bundesbank to object to the Federal Reserve's sale of mark at times when it believed it

---

[61] During the period July 1973–January 1981, the general policy of the United States, articulated by both Treasury and Federal Reserve officials, was to intervene in the markets to counter disorderly conditions but not to seek any particular rate. Some central banks attempted to maintain stable rates with the dollar or other currencies. Even among countries that limited intervention to the purpose of countering disorderly conditions, there might be differences in the "quickness on the trigger." Differences in exchange-rate management policies among countries are explored in Chapter 11, *infra*, at page 521 et seq.

[62] Charles A. Coombs has described an hour meeting in London in February 1975 of top level officers of the U.S. Federal Reserve, the Deutsche Bundesbank, and the Swiss National Bank which resulted in coordinated intervention at that time that had the effect of halting the decline in the dollar's rate. See Coombs, *Arena of International Finance, supra* note 26, pp. 236–37; and *Minutes of Federal Open Market Committee, supra* note 31, 1975, pp. 245–49. In December 1977 the Secretary of the U.S. Treasury took a direct part in consultations with Bundesbank officials that resulted in a policy statement on intervention and the conclusion of a Treasury-Bundesbank reciprocal currency agreement. See note 87, *infra*. Consultations between U.S. authorities and the Deutsche Bundesbank, Bank of Japan, and Swiss National Bank preceded the U.S. announcement in November 1978 of a package of measures to counter the decline in the dollar's rate in the exchange markets. See Chapter 11, *infra*, page 533 (note 156). These are only three of what could be many examples.

[63] Paragraph II of the Bank of England agreement, page 140, and paragraph II of the Bundesbank agreement, at page 144.

[64] Paragraph II of the Bundesbank agreement, *idem*. The consultation clause is asymmetrical. It did not apply to interventions by the Bundesbank in dollars against mark. See also page 151, *infra*.

[65] There has been less flexibility in Germany than in the United States to offset the effects on liquidity through open market purchases and sales of government securities.

inappropriate for officials to offer mark to the market. Because of the importance of the mark–dollar exchange rate, as well as the quoted consultation provision, consultations between the Federal Reserve and the Bundesbank in the middle and late 1970s were more continuous and intense than with other central banks.

How the Federal Reserve Drew on the Bundesbank Arrangement.
The practice of the United States has been to hold its monetary reserves primarily in IMF special drawing rights, reserve position in the IMF, and gold. Since most countries have held a substantial portion of their reserves in dollars and have been prepared to use and accept dollars to settle international payments, neither the Treasury nor the Federal Reserve has found it necessary to hold large balances of foreign currencies.[66] Dollars could be used to make payments. While the Federal Reserve was sometimes able during the 1970s to finance modest interventions by the use of foreign-currency working balances, the Federal Reserve's normal practice at that time was to finance any substantial market interventions in foreign currencies by making drawings under swap agreements to settle the particular commitments rather than use working balances, because its foreign-currency working balances were usually too small. Its way of using a swap line was thus different from that of the Bank of England. The following is an example of the Federal Reserve's procedure.

Suppose that on a particular day there was heavy selling of dollars for mark in Frankfurt and the dollar's rate was falling sharply. Officers of the Foreign Department of the Federal Reserve Bank of New York and their counterparts at the Bundesbank in Frankfurt in telephone conversations in the early morning would discuss market conditions. They would attempt to identify factors leading to the decline of the dollar and review the Bundesbank's operations in Frankfurt. Suppose they anticipated that the heavy selling of dollars for mark would spread to New York when that market opened and that bid and asked prices for mark might widen sharply, reflecting disorder in the market. The officers of the two banks would develop contingency plans for the day. They might agree in their telephone conversation–negotiation that the Federal Reserve would sell mark that day in New York to counter disorderly conditions that appeared in the market. The magnitude of the contemplated intervention would be agreed. They would also agree that the intervention would be financed by drawings under the swap agreement. Early in the day it might not be possible to be precise about the exact amount to be used. The amount of mark that had to be sold to counter disorder would depend on rate movements, the volume of transactions in the market, and the volatility of the market. In a big

---

[66] In 1979 and 1980 the Federal Reserve System and the U.S. Treasury's Exchange Stabilization Fund did accumulate large foreign currency balances as a result of sales of dollars in the markets. See Chapter 11, *infra*, page 534 (note 161).

operation officers of the two central banks might be in touch with each other several times during the day.

The actual market operation by the New York Bank could proceed before drawings were actually made on the swap line with the Bundesbank. The New York Bank would, usually through the agency of a commercial bank in New York, offer to exchange mark for dollars at a particular rate. The commercial bank would offer the mark in the market (i.e., to other banks and brokers) the same as it would offer mark for sale for its own account or for any customer without disclosing the customer's identity (in this case without disclosing that it was acting for the New York Bank). Exchange contracts were made with those who accepted the offers. The contracts might be for spot or forward delivery.[67] Alternatively, the Federal Reserve Bank of New York might make direct offers of mark to several commercial banks.[68] And, it might make bids and offers simultaneously.

Let us suppose that during the course of a day the Federal Reserve Bank of New York, using Chase Manhattan Bank as its agent, sold 40 million mark in exchange for dollars under contracts for spot delivery. In accordance with previous consultations, the New York bank intended to draw on the swap facility with the Bundesbank to settle its obligations. The Federal Reserve Bank of New York would at the close of the day send a telex message to the Deutsche Bundesbank. The message would reference the swap agreement set out previously and the telephone conversations earlier in the day about the specific drawing. The message would in substance state that two business days later:

(1) The New York Bank would credit the Bundesbank's account at the New York Bank with, say $18.8 million (the same dollar amount the New York Bank was to receive for the mark sold earlier in the day) and would, in accordance with the swap agreement, invest this amount for the Bundesbank in an interest-bearing U.S. Treasury non-marketable security.[69]

(2) The Bundesbank was requested to reciprocally credit the Federal Reserve's special account with 40 million mark (the amount of mark sold earlier in the day). (This completed the drawing.)

(3) The Bundesbank was instructed to debit the New York Bank's

---

[67] The mechanics of currency exchange transactions are explained in Appendix A, *infra*, pages 672–679. See also Anatol B. Balbach, "The Mechanics of Intervention in Exchange Markets," in Federal Reserve Bank of St. Louis, *Review*, February 1978, p. 2.

[68] The commercial bank the Federal Reserve Bank of New York would select for the particular operation or, if it followed the alternate course, the banks to which it would make direct offers would be among the commercial banks with which the New York Bank had established approved foreign-currency-dealing relationships.

[69] Paragraph III(A) of the reciprocal currency agreement, pages 144–145, instructed the Federal Reserve Bank of New York to invest the dollars in a non-marketable U.S. Treasury obligation redeemable on two-days' notice, yielding a rate of interest defined in that paragraph. The Bundesbank could at any time, on two-days' notice, demand redemption of the Treasury obligation.

account by 40 million mark and credit the account of, say, Chase Manhattan–Frankfurt for the credit of Chase–New York (the agent bank that sold the mark for the Federal Reserve).[70]

At the same time that this cable was sent, the New York Federal Reserve Bank would record on its books the forward exchange commitment, provided for in the reciprocal swap agreement,[71] to sell 40 million mark to the Bundesbank in exchange for dollars in three months at the same exchange rate at which the Federal Reserve sold mark earlier in the day. (This exchange rate would be adjusted, as explained later, when the forward transaction was effected.)

Within the three-month period, unless the maturity was rolled over another three months, the drawing was liquidated. The Bundesbank agreement, like the Bank of England agreement, provided that each drawing had an initial maturity of three months "subject to renewal upon mutual agreement." The Bundesbank agreement followed this with two additional sentences not in the Bank of England agreement: "Every effort will be made by both parties to facilitate the early liquidation of any Federal Reserve drawings under this arrangement. In any case, unless it is mutually agreed at the time that further renewals are appropriate, each drawing will be repaid no later than six months after its inception."[72] These provisions were understood to impose a more stringent obligation than the Bank of England agreement. Recall the concerns of the Bundesbank about the increased liquidity of German banks while the drawings were outstanding as well as the profit and loss sharing arrangement between the two central banks.

The Federal Reserve usually performed its repayment (forward) obligation by acquiring mark in the market (again, in consultation with the Bundesbank) and then exchanging those mark for dollars with the Bundesbank to liquidate the original drawing. The exchange rate for this repayment transaction in which the Federal Reserve in our example would sell 40 million mark to the Bundesbank was to be midway between the booked rate at which the New York Bank sold the original mark (say $ 0.470) and the rate at which the New York Bank bought mark in the market to be used in the repayment (say $ 0.460). Thus, the original rate of the forward commitment of $ 0.470 was adjusted to $ 0.465 in accordance with the reciprocal swap agreement,[73] which resulted in the two central banks sharing equally in the profit relating to the drawing.[74] U.S. Treasury securities held by the Bundesbank were, in accordance with its

---

[70] Chase–Frankfurt on instructions of the Chase Manhattan Bank of New York would deliver mark to the banks to which Chase–New York sold the mark.

[71] See paragraph II of the agreement.

[72] See paragraph II of the agreement.

[73] See paragraph IV of the agreement.

[74] Had the Federal Reserve acquired mark for repayment at $ 0.480, the rate for the repayment transaction would have been $ 0.475, each bank sharing equally in the loss.

instructions, redeemed ($18.8 million) and $18.6 million of the proceeds were transferred to the Federal Reserve to satisfy the Bundesbank's reciprocal commitment respecting the liquidation of the Federal Reserve's drawing. In our example the Federal Reserve's drawing was liquidated at a profit of $ 0.2 million to each bank.

As we can see, although a drawing on the swap line and the market interventions were in the name of the Federal Reserve, they were in reality a joint venture of the two banks given the consultations that took place and the risk sharing. Profits and losses were shared equally.[75] In addition, of course, the Bundesbank earned interest on the investment of its reciprocal dollar balances in non-transferable U.S. Treasury certificates of indebtedness during the period the swaps were outstanding (this interest was paid by the Treasury for its use of the dollars during the period).

The provision requiring close cooperation and prior consultations on interventions in mark against dollars and the risk sharing provisions were asymmetrical. That is they did not apply to Bundesbank market interventions in dollars against mark nor did they apply to Bundesbank drawings of dollars under the agreement should it choose to draw on it. The agreement permitted the Bundesbank to draw dollars from the Federal Reserve but at its full risk of profit or loss. The parties, however, when they worked out the agreement, assumed that only the Federal Reserve would make drawings under the agreement. As noted earlier, the profit and loss sharing provisions were deleted in December 1980.

Currency Swap Agreements—Current Terms. In December 1980 changes were made in certain provisions of reciprocal currency agreements used by the Federal Reserve System. The profit and loss sharing provisions in the agreement with the Deutsche Bundesbank and in similar agreements with other banks, previously discussed,[76] were terminated.[77] All of the Federal Reserve's agreements currently follow, with some variations, the same standard form set forth below:

---

[75] A table displaying profits and losses year to year from 1961 through 1977 on U.S. Treasury and Federal Reserve foreign exchange operations appears in Alan R. Holmes and Scott E. Pardee, "Treasury and Federal Reserve Foreign Exchange Operations," in Federal Reserve Bank of New York, *Quarterly Review*, vol. 3, no. 2 (Summer 1978), p. 51, at p. 54. Reports under the same title in later issues of the *Quarterly Review* provide information for subsequent years.

[76] See discussion at pages 145–151, *supra*.

[77] Scott E. Pardee, "Treasury and Federal Reserve Foreign Exchange Operations," in Federal Reserve Bank of New York, *Quarterly Review*, vol. 6, no. 1 (Spring 1981), p. 54 at p. 56.

Current Model of Reciprocal Currency Agreements of the U.S. Federal Reserve System Sample Telex Message[78]

I. FEDERAL RESERVE SUGGESTS RENEWAL AT MATURITY FOR ONE YEAR TO [month, day, year] OF OUR $[amount] U.S. DOLLAR/[foreign currency] RECIPROCAL SWAP ARRANGEMENT, SUBJECT TO USE BY EITHER PARTY ON TWO BUSINESS DAYS' NOTICE. THIS ARRANGEMENT MAY BE EXTENDED BY MUTUAL AGREEMENT.

II. DRAWINGS UNDER THE ARRANGEMENT MAY BE USED IN EXECUTION OF SPOT OR FORWARD TRANSACTIONS CONCLUDED IN CONSULTATION WITH THE OTHER PARTY. EACH DRAWING WILL HAVE AN INITIAL MATURITY OF THREE MONTHS, SUBJECT TO RENEWAL UPON MUTUAL AGREEMENT.

III. IN SWAP DRAWINGS INITIATED BY THE FEDERAL RESERVE:

(A) THE SPOT TRANSACTION OF THE SWAP WILL BE EXECUTED AT THE PREVAILING MARKET SPOT EXCHANGE RATE AND THE FORWARD TRANSACTION OF THE SWAP WILL BE EXECUTED AT A FORWARD RATE BASED ON THE INTEREST RATE DIFFERENTIAL BETWEEN THE RATE ON THREE-MONTH U.S. TREASURY BILLS, AS DEFINED IN III(B) BELOW, AND THE CORRESPONDING RATE ON [foreign government securities], AS DEFINED IN III(C) BELOW, AS AGREED BETWEEN THE TWO PARTIES AT THE TIME THE DRAWING IS ARRANGED OR, IN THE CASE OF RENEWALS, TWO BUSINESS DAYS BEFORE MATURITY. IN THE CASE OF PREPAYMENTS, THE FORWARD RATE WOULD BE ADJUSTED ACCORDINGLY.

(B) THE UNITED STATES DOLLAR PROCEEDS OF DRAWINGS ARE TO BE CREDITED TO YOUR CURRENT ACCOUNT "X" UNDER CABLE ADVICE. TO THE EXTENT THAT THESE FUNDS ARE NOT REQUIRED IMMEDIATELY FOR PAYMENTS, YOU WILL AUTHORIZE US TO DEBIT YOUR CURRENT ACCOUNT "X" AND PLACE THE AMOUNT OF UNITED STATES DOLLARS IN QUESTION IN A NONTRANSFERABLE U.S. TREASURY CERTIFICATE OF INDEBTEDNESS WHICH THE SECRETARY OF THE TREASURY IS PREPARED TO ISSUE TO YOU AT PAR, TO MATURE THREE MONTHS AFTER DATE OF ISSUE. SUCH

---

[78] Reprinted from the model text provided by the Federal Reserve System to the author on January 31, 1983, in response to a request under the U.S. Freedom of Information Act.

CERTIFICATE WILL BE REDEEMABLE AT PAR UPON TWO BUSINESS DAYS' NOTICE AND WILL BEAR INTEREST AT A RATE BASED UPON THE AVERAGE RATE OF DISCOUNT AT THE AUCTION OF THE LAST ISSUE OF THREE-MONTH U.S. TREASURY BILLS PRECEDING THE DATE OF ISSUE OF THE CERTIFICATE IN TWO DECIMAL PLACES AND IF SUCH DECIMAL IS NOT A MULTIPLE OF .05, IT WILL BE ADJUSTED TO THE NEXT HIGHER MULTIPLE OF .05. THE CERTIFICATE WILL BE ISSUED AND REDEEMED AT THE FEDERAL RESERVE BANK OF NEW YORK, AS FISCAL AGENT OF THE UNITED STATES, AND WILL BE HELD IN YOUR U.S. TREASURY CERTIFICATE OF INDEBTEDNESS ACCOUNT. THE [foreign currency] PROCEEDS ARE TO BE CREDITED TO OUR ACCOUNT "Y" UNDER CABLE ADVICE.

(C) THE CORRESPONDING RATE ON [foreign government securities] SHALL BE BASED UPON THE LAST ISSUE OF [foreign government securities] PRECEDING THE DATE OF THE SWAP DRAWING. SUCH RATE WILL BE EXPRESSED IN TWO DECIMAL PLACES AND IF SUCH DECIMAL IS NOT A MULTIPLE OF .05, IT WILL BE ADJUSTED TO THE NEXT HIGHER MULTIPLE OF .05.

IV.   IN SWAP DRAWINGS INITIATED BY THE [foreign central bank]:

(A) THE SAME RATE OF EXCHANGE WILL BE APPLIED TO BOTH THE SPOT AND FORWARD TRANSACTIONS OF THE SWAP. THIS RATE WILL BE BASED UPON THE PREVAILING MARKET SPOT EXCHANGE RATE, AS AGREED BETWEEN THE TWO PARTIES AT THE TIME THE ORIGINAL DRAWING IS ARRANGED OR, IN THE CASE OF RENEWALS, TWO BUSINESS DAYS BEFORE MATURITY.

(B) THE [foreign currency] IS TO BE CREDITED TO OUR ACCOUNT "Y" UNDER CABLE ADVICE. TO THE EXTENT THAT THESE FUNDS ARE NOT REQUIRED IMMEDIATELY FOR PAYMENTS, WE WILL AUTHORIZE YOU TO DEBIT OUR ACCOUNT "Y" AND PLACE THE FULL AMOUNT OF [foreign currency] IN QUESTION IN OUR MONEY-EMPLOYED ACCOUNT "YY". [Foreign currency] IN SUCH ACCOUNT "YY" WILL EARN A RETURN WHICH IS EQUAL TO A RATE OF INTEREST BASED UPON THE AVERAGE RATE OF DISCOUNT AT THE AUCTION OF THE LAST ISSUE OF THREE-MONTH U.S. TREASURY BILLS, AS CALCULATED ABOVE. SUCH BALANCES MAY BE WITHDRAWN BY US ON TWO BUSINESS DAYS' NOTICE. THE U.S. DOLLARS ARE TO BE CREDITED TO YOUR CURRENT ACCOUNT "X" UNDER CABLE ADVICE.

V.   IF YOU AGREE, PLEASE CONFIRM.

The reader will recognize the similarity between the model above and the Federal Reserve–Bank of England agreement discussed earlier.[79] The main difference is that no matter which party draws on the arrangement, that party pays interest at the creditor country's treasury bill rate or the nearest equivalent rate.[80] This is accomplished, where the drawing is initiated by the foreign bank, by the provision that the foreign currency reciprocally credited to the Federal Reserve is to earn interest at the U.S. Treasury bill rate.[81] Where the drawing is initiated by the Federal Reserve, the same result is accomplished by the foreign bank earning interest on the dollars reciprocally credited to it by investing them in a U.S. Treasury security[82] with the forward exchange rate on the swap being adjusted to take into account the interest rate differential between the U.S. Treasury bill rate and the foreign country's comparable interest rate on its currency which was drawn by the Federal Reserve.[83]

The recent size of each of the bilateral swap facilities between the U.S. Federal Reserve System and central banks of other countries is set forth below:

Federal Reserve Reciprocal Currency Arrangements[84]
Amount of Facility—December 1982
(million U.S. dollar equivalents)

Austrian National Bank	250
National Bank of Belgium	1,000
Bank of Canada	2,000
National Bank of Denmark	250
Bank of England	3,000
Bank of France	2,000
German Federal Bank (Deutsche Bundesbank)	6,000
Bank of Italy	3,000
Bank of Japan	5,000

[79] At page 139 et seq.
[80] See Pardee (Spring 1981), *supra* note 77, p. 56.
[81] See paragraph IV(B) of the agreement.
[82] See paragraph III(B) of the agreement.
[83] See paragraph III(A) of the agreement.
From the inception of the swap agreements in 1962 until the changes in December 1980, the interest rates paid on any drawings, either by the Federal Reserve or by the foreign central banks, were based on the current rates for U.S. Treasury bills. Pardee (Spring 1981), *supra* note 77, p. 56.
[84] FOMC Authorization for Foreign Currency Operations, *supra* note 28, paragraph 2, as amended August 28, 1982. The special temporary arrangement with the Bank of Mexico terminated in August 1983.
Alan R. Holmes and Scott E. Pardee, "Treasury and Federal Reserve Foreign Exchange Operations," in Federal Reserve Bank of New York, *Quarterly Review*, vol. 1 (Winter 1976), p. 40 at p. 43 (table I), provide data on the size of each facility when originally instituted and changes in overall amounts available from year to year through 1976. Data on subsequent changes are provided in reports under the same title in later issues of the *Quarterly Review*.

Bank of Mexico	
Regular	700
Special (temporary arrangement)	325
Netherlands Bank	500
Bank of Norway	250
Bank of Sweden	300
Swiss National Bank	4,000
Bank for International Settlements	
Dollars against Swiss francs	600
Dollars against authorized European	
currencies other than Swiss francs	1,250
Total	30,425

Tables that summarize, quarter by quarter, drawings and repayments by the Federal Reserve under reciprocal currency arrangements, and drawings and repayments by other central banks and the Bank for International Settlements under the swap arrangements with the Federal Reserve, are published and periodically brought up to date in the *Quarterly Review* of the Federal Reserve Bank of New York and in the *Federal Reserve Bulletin*.[85]

Reciprocal Currency Agreements Between the U.S. Treasury's Exchange Stabilization Fund and Foreign Monetary Authorities

The United States Treasury, through its Exchange Stabilization Fund,[86] has entered into reciprocal currency (swap) agreements with central banks of other countries. For example, the United States Treasury and the Deutsche Bundesbank concluded such an agreement on January 4, 1978.[87] The Treasury may also conclude currency swap agreements with monetary authorities in some countries with which the Federal Reserve has not maintained reciprocal currency arrangements. For example, the Treasury concluded three such ar-

---

[85] See text accompanying note 31, *supra*. Detailed tables for the entire period 1962–1976 appear in Holmes and Pardee (Winter 1976), *supra* note 84, pp. 44–47 (tables II and III).

[86] The *United States Code*, title 31, section 822(a), provides authority for the United States Treasury to operate the Exchange Stabilization Fund. Reports on the operation of the Exchange Stabilization Fund are submitted annually to the U.S. Congress and are published in the *Annual Report of the Secretary of the Treasury on the State of the Finances*. See *Authorization for Treasury's International Affairs Functions, supra* note 20, pp. 15–33. See also *Wall Street Journal,* December 7, 1982, p. 36.

[87] See U.S. Treasury and Federal Reserve System press releases of January 4, 1978, quoted in Alan R. Holmes and Scott E. Pardee, "Treasury and Federal Reserve Foreign Exchange Operations," in Federal Reserve Bank of New York, *Quarterly Review,* vol. 3, no. 1 (Spring 1978), p. 54 at p. 59.

rangements with Brazilian authorities for a total of $1.23 billion in the fall of 1982.[88]

Although the language may differ in some respects, the basic terms of the Treasury agreements have been similar to those of the Federal Reserve. The Treasury's 1978 agreement with the Deutsche Bundesbank contained profit and loss sharing provisions similar to those in the Federal Reserve's agreement in effect at the same time, discussed earlier.[89] When the profit and loss sharing provisions were deleted from Federal Reserve agreements, they were also deleted from Treasury agreements,[90] so that such provisions no longer appear in any Treasury agreements. At the present time, Treasury agreements, like those of the Federal Reserve, provide that interest on drawings is paid at rates prevailing for Treasury bills issued by the creditor country or the nearest equivalent rate.[91]

While some of the Treasury's arrangements, like most of the Federal Reserve's arrangements, are continued from year to year, the Treasury's arrangements are often *ad hoc* agreements for temporary periods. The Treasury, for example, opened a swap arrangement with the Banco de Mexico in mid-August 1982, which was replaced by another temporary facility at the end of that month. The three facilities opened by the Treasury for the benefit of Brazil in the fall of 1982 were each of a temporary character.[92]

Where U.S. authorities make drawings on a Treasury swap agreement (for example, with the Deutsche Bundesbank) to finance exchange market interventions, the day-to-day operations under the Treasury agreement are usually entrusted to the same persons responsible for operations under the Federal Reserve's agreement with the foreign authorities. The difference is that the accounts are handled for the profit and loss of the Treasury's Exchange Stabilization Fund rather than the Federal Reserve System. Often the two agreements have been used in parallel.[93]

---

[88] Sam Y. Cross, "Treasury and Federal Reserve Foreign Exchange Operations," in Federal Reserve Bank of New York, *Quarterly Review*, vol. 7, no. 4 (Winter 1982–83), p. 52 at pp. 53 and 55–56; and *idem,* vol. 8, no. 1 (Spring 1983), p. 55 at pp. 59–60.

[89] See discussion at pages 145–151, *supra.*

[90] Pardee (Spring 1981), *supra* note 77, p. 56. See page 151, *supra.*

[91] *Idem.*

[92] See sources cited in note 88, *supra.* See also text accompanying notes 115–117, *infra.*

[93] The Federal Reserve System has a "warehousing" agreement with the Treasury. Where the Exchange Stabilization Fund holds foreign currency that is not immediately needed, the Federal Reserve buys the currency from the Treasury in exchange for U.S. dollars and agrees to sell the currency back to the Treasury at a later date at the same exchange rate. The Federal Reserve then places the foreign currency in an interest-earning investment with the foreign central bank issuing the currency. See Board of Governors of the Federal Reserve System, *64th Annual Report, 1977,* pp. 174–75; *65th Annual Report, 1978,* pp. 252–53; *67th Annual Report, 1980,* p. 113; *68th Annual Report, 1981,* p. 107; and *69th Annual Report, 1982,* pp. 98–99.

Wide Use of Currency Swap Technique

While our discussion has centered primarily on reciprocal currency arrangements to which U.S. monetary authorities are parties, the technique is also used in other bilateral agreements. For example, the Bank of Japan in April 1980 concluded a swap agreement with the Swiss National Bank in the amount of yen 200 billion (or the equivalent in Swiss francs). In May 1980 the Bank of Japan and the Deutsche Bundesbank put into effect a swap agreement in the amount of DM 2.5 billion (or the equivalent in Japanese yen).[94] The central banks of Denmark, Finland, Iceland, Norway, and Sweden are parties to an Agreement on Short-Term Foreign-Exchange Assistance that uses the swap technique.[95]

The central banks participating in the European Monetary System swap gold and U.S. dollars for European currency units (ECUs) issued by the European Monetary Cooperation Fund.[96] The swap technique is also used in some other regional balance-of-payments financing facilities.[97]

Law Governing Reciprocal Currency Agreements

Are reciprocal currency agreements, such as those between the Federal Reserve System and other central banks, governed by private commercial law or by public international law? In ordinary times an answer to the question is not critical. The agreements are performed, and disputes do not arise. The agreements, however, are also intended to operate when exchange markets are in crisis.

The question whether the agreements are governed by private commercial law or public international law is not trivial. Suppose that after a central bank has made a large drawing on a swap facility, its government enacts legislation that prohibits the bank from fulfilling its repayment obligation. Or suppose that the creditor central bank's use of the reciprocal deposit is blocked. If the agreement is governed by private commercial law, the debtor may assert a defense of *force majeure.* On the other hand, if the agreement is seen as made by organs of the states responsible for their countries' monetary policies and as governed by public international law, then the subsequently enacted law is not a valid defense at the international level. The basic concept is that a state cannot avoid its treaty obligations to other states through its own acts. Article 27 of the Vienna Convention on the Law of Treaties, which codifies a long-standing principle of customary international law, states: "A party may not invoke the provisions of

---

[94] Unpublished comments of Kumiharu Shigehara at Seminar on European Monetary Integration, Copenhagen, March 13–14, 1981.

[95] The agreement, effective February 1, 1976, appears in Danmarks Nationalbank, *Report and Accounts for the Year 1975,* p. 95; and in Norges Bank, *Economic Bulletin,* vol. 47, no. 1 (March 1976), p. 33.

[96] See Chapter 8, *infra,* pages 320–325.

[97] See Chapter 7, *infra,* pages 308–309.

its internal law as justification for its failure to perform a Treaty.''[98] Lest the reader be scared by the word "treaty," it should be pointed out that the Vienna Convention applies that term to all written agreements between states that are governed by international law.[99]

James E.S. Fawcett, former General Counsel of the International Monetary Fund, has argued that swap agreements between monetary authorities are governed by international law. He based his conclusion on an examination of the capacity of the parties and the subject matter of the agreements:

> The central banks are creatures of municipal law. They may be public corporations or private companies, and their degree of autonomy may greatly vary both in law and practice. But there appears to be no reason why a central bank may not in certain cases act, not in its own right, but as agent for and on behalf of the State and, in that capacity, enter into agreements governed by international law. Such a case would, it is suggested, be an agreement for purpose of currency management, as part of the monetary policy of the State, this being a State function *par excellence.*[100]

Expanding on this solidly reasoned point of view, it should also be noted that, in addition to dealing with financing (in amounts that for the United States rival the resources available to it in the International Monetary Fund), the agreements provide for consultation in the conduct of official exchange market intervention policies and, as we have seen, in some agreements the sharing of risks in official market interventions to counter disorder in the exchange markets. The agreements, thus, when seen in context are more than simply exchange contracts of the type concluded between commercial banks. It is appro-

---

[98] Vienna Convention on the Law of Treaties, Article 27. A special exception stated in Article 46 relates to some situations where consent to be bound by an agreement was expressed in violation of domestic law. Many of the Convention's articles, including Articles 27 and 46, codify rules of general international law that bind states whether or not they are parties to the Convention. For citation to the Vienna Convention, see Chapter 2, *supra*, page 64 (note 111).

[99] Vienna Convention on the Law of Treaties, Article 2.

[100] James E.S. Fawcett, "Trade and Finance in International Law," in Hague Academy of International Law, *Recueil des Cours,* vol. 123 (1968-I), pp. 215 at p. 235. See generally *idem,* pp. 232–37. See also M.R. Shuster, *The Public International Law of Money* (Oxford: Oxford University Press, 1973), pp. 308–10; and Luca Radicati di Bròzolo, "Some Legal Aspects of the European Monetary System," *Rivista di Diritto Internazionale,* vol. 63 (1980), p. 330 at p. 340.

It is generally recognized that when central banks perform central bank functions and not simply functions of commercial banks, their acts should not be subject to review in terms of the national law of other countries. Ernest T. Patrikis has pointed out: "No other activities of a sovereign are more inherently characteristic of sovereignty than the custody and management of a country's financial reserves." Patrikis, "Foreign Central Bank Property: Immunity from Attachment in the United States," *University of Illinois Law Review,* vol. 1 (1982), p. 265 at p. 286. See also legislation and court decisions indexed under the heading "central banks" in *Materials on Jurisdictional Immunities of States and Their Property* (United Nations Legislative Series; New York: United Nations, 1982).

priate that the parties have the protections of public international law. It should also be pointed out that the application of public international law does not preclude reference by that law to principles of private commercial law and to other rules of domestic law, where appropriate, to define the agreed scope of obligations and the procedures to be followed with respect to various issues that may arise in the operation of the agreements.[101]

The valuation of reciprocal credits related to drawings made by the Federal Reserve in Belgian francs and Swiss francs prior to August 15, 1971, was a subject of dispute following the collapse of the Bretton Woods system of stable exchange rates. This is the only legal dispute worthy of comment, of which the author is aware, that has arisen in connection with central bank reciprocal currency agreements. It involved very large sums. An agreed solution was achieved in 1975 and 1976. The pre-August 15, 1971, Belgian franc and Swiss franc drawings were liquidated by the end of the latter year. Although the revaluation clause that figured in the dispute has been omitted in agreements concluded since 1973, the case merits comment.[102]

The swap agreements in use prior to August 15, 1971, were designed for operation within the framework of the Bretton Woods system of stable exchange rates. Exchange rates among currencies were then maintained on the basis of par values expressed in terms of gold or the U.S. dollar of the gold weight and fineness in effect in 1944.[103] A revaluation clause in the swap agreements protected the debtor country against exchange losses that would result from the creditor country's revaluing its currency by increasing its gold value. If the relationship between the two currencies was altered through a devaluation of the currency of the debtor country (by changing the gold value of its currency), the debtor country alone assumed the foreign exchange risk. The text of the clause typically read as follows:

> To protect each party against the remote risk of a revaluation of the other's currency we suggest the following procedure: We [Federal Reserve] place with you a standing order to be executed when necessary for that purpose to purchase for our account kroner [the foreign currency] against dollars in an amount sufficient to replenish any

[101] See Georges R. Delaume, *Transnational Contracts: Applicable Law and Settlement of Disputes* (5 vols.; Dobbs Ferry: Oceana Publications, binder service, 1983 ed.), section 1.10; and Delaume, *Legal Aspects of International Lending and Economic Development Financing* (Dobbs Ferry: Oceana Publications, 1967), chapter 3.

[102] Much of the factual information in the discussion that follows was obtained in interviews and correspondence. Some information is provided by Charles A. Coombs, "Treasury and Federal Reserve Foreign Exchange Operations," in Federal Reserve Bank of New York, *Monthly Review*, vol. 53 (October 1971), p. 214 at pp. 224–26, 227, and 229; Board of Governors of the Federal Reserve System, *62d Annual Report, 1975*, pp. 251–52; *63d Annual Report, 1976*, pp. 279–80 and 311–12; and *Minutes of Federal Open Market Committee*, *supra* note 31, 1971, pp. 525–26 and 835–38; *idem*, 1974, pp. 1011–15; *idem*, 1975, pp. 44–45, 726–32, 905–09, 1093–95, 1202–03, 1307–08, and 1324–27; and *idem*, 1976, pp. 3 and 14–20.

[103] See Chapter 11, *infra*, pages 491–495.

earlier drafts upon our krone balance created by the swap. We shall accept from you a similar standing order to be executed when necessary for that purpose to purchase U.S. dollars against kroner in order to replenish any earlier drafts upon your dollar balance created by the swap.[104]

The revaluation clause used a "standing order" concept because few central banks had legal authority to make exchange rate guarantees. Charles A. Coombs, who invented the idea, records the following exchange with William Braun, one of the lawyers at the Federal Reserve Bank of New York:

I said: "Well, what do you think of it?"
He said: "It isn't worth the paper it's written on."
I said: "I don't give a damn whether it will stand up in court. In this business, no central bank is going to sue another one. What I want to know is whether acceptance of such a standing order is a binding moral commitment."
He said: "Assuming your foreign central bank friends have a sense of morality, they might find it hard to get off the hook."
I said: "That's all we need."[105]

The operation of the revaluation clause as the Federal Reserve intended it to work is illustrated by the Netherlands Bank's action in 1971. At the beginning of May that year the Federal Reserve had $250 million in drawings outstanding under the swap line with the Netherlands Bank. Just before the move to a floating rate for the guilder on May 5,[106] the Netherlands Bank executed the standing order contained in the revaluation clause. The Federal Reserve subsequently settled its guilder obligation by transferring SDRs equivalent to $150 million to the Netherlands Bank and by the U.S. Treasury purchasing guilders equivalent to $100 million from the International Monetary Fund which were transferred to the Netherlands Bank. It should be noted, however, that in the Netherlands case there had been a prior understanding that made it clear that the standing order clause was to be applied if the Netherlands guilder moved to a floating rate.[107]

When Belgium in May 1971 took steps that permitted the free market rate for the franc (applicable to a range of capital transactions and some current transactions) to move above the official rate, the Federal Reserve had Belgian franc drawings outstanding. The Banque Nationale de Belgique did not, however, execute the standing order because the bank apparently did not consider it

---

[104] Paragraph (d) of the Federal Reserve System–Danmarks Nationalbank agreement, cited in note 38, *supra*. The clauses in the agreements with other central banks were similar.

[105] Coombs, *Arena of International Finance, supra* note 26, p. 40.

[106] See Chapter 11, *infra*, page 495.

[107] See *Minutes of Federal Open Market Committee, supra* note 31, 1971, pp. 524–25 and 607.

applicable to the situation. Later, in July and early August the Federal Reserve drew additional Belgian francs under swap arrangements.

When Switzerland revalued its currency in relation to gold (and the U.S. dollar), effective May 10, 1971, there were no outstanding Federal Reserve drawings in Swiss francs. However, by the end of the second week of August the Federal Reserve had drawn the full amount available under the arrangement with the Swiss National Bank and had also drawn Swiss francs from the Bank for International Settlements.

The Federal Reserve had drawn the Belgian francs and Swiss francs to avoid the necessity of converting into gold the dollar balances acquired by foreign authorities in market interventions, as well as to finance its own interventions. The Belgian and Swiss francs drawn were, for the most part, used to redeem dollar balances held by the foreign authorities. The foreign authorities were left with fresh dollar balances (the countervalue of the francs drawn), but the Federal Reserve's swap obligation to buy them back in effect gave them a guarantee against a devaluation of the dollar. Large Belgian franc and Swiss franc drawings were outstanding when the United States on August 15, 1971, announced that it was suspending the convertibility of the dollar into gold. After that announcement the market rates sharply diverged from the rates based on parity relationships.

When it appeared that the Federal Reserve would buy in the market Belgian francs and Swiss francs needed to repay the swap drawings, the Belgian and Swiss authorities, concerned that Federal Reserve purchases of their currencies would put additional upward pressure on their rates, asked the Federal Reserve not to purchase their currencies in the market. They extended the time limits for the Federal Reserve to repay the outstanding drawings.[108]

A series of events added additional complexity. The United States devalued the dollar, in accordance with announcements in December 1971 and February 1973, each time declaring a new legal gold value of the dollar. Belgium in December 1971 established a central rate for its currency that represented a modest revaluation, but never formalized a new par value in terms of gold. Switzerland, having revalued its franc by 7.07 percent in May 1971 before the Federal Reserve's drawings in question, did not make any further changes in its par value. In December 1971 Switzerland declared a central rate against the U.S. dollar that in effect represented a small devaluation of its franc in relation to the dollar's gold value at the time the drawings were made.[109] Following decisions made in January and March 1973, the Swiss franc and Belgian franc floated against the U.S. dollar.[110] How were the obligations with respect

---

[108] See *Minutes of Federal Open Market Committee, idem*, 1971, pp. 525–26, 607–08, 731–32, 835–38, 950, 1026–30, and 1099–1101.
[109] See generally Chapter 11, *infra*, pages 495–499.
[110] See Chapter 11, *infra*, page 499–501.

to the repayment of the pre-August 15, 1971, drawings by the Federal Reserve to be valued? Should the Federal Reserve bear the full risk?

In December 1975 the contractual exchange rates of the Federal Reserve's commitments in Swiss francs and Belgian francs were adjusted to take account of the two dollar devaluations and the Belgian franc revaluation (resulting from establishment of official central rate). These adjustments resulted in a reduction of the Belgian franc swap commitments measured in terms of Belgian francs and an increase in the dollar countervalue of these commitments. The amount of Swiss franc commitments measured in terms of Swiss francs remained unchanged, because the Swiss franc had not been raised in value; and the dollar countervalue was increased to take into account the two dollar devaluations. These adjustments in the contractual exchange rates of the swaps resulted in losses, when measured in each party's own currency, to the Federal Reserve and to Belgium's central bank but not to the Swiss National Bank or to the Bank for International Settlements. (In connection with these rate adjustments, a portion of the Federal Reserve's Swiss franc commitments to the BIS was transferred to the Swiss National Bank in December 1975. The remainder was transferred from the BIS to the Swiss National Bank in February 1976.)

The adjustments to the contractual exchange rates agreed in December 1975 took account only of formal value changes. No adjustments were made for the consequences of floating rates prevailing after early 1973. Thus, the adjusted contractual rates on the swap commitments remained below the market exchange rates for Belgian francs and for Swiss francs. In a system of floating exchange rates it was not possible to determine whether the appreciations of the Swiss and Belgian francs vis-à-vis the dollar constituted revaluations of those currencies or a devaluation of the dollar. How the revaluation clause in the swap agreements should be applied, if at all, to floating rates remained in dispute.

With the Belgian franc market exchange rate only slightly above the adjusted contractual rate of the Federal Reserve's Belgian franc swap debt, the Federal Reserve acquired the necessary francs (12.6 billion Belgian francs) for repayment of its debt in the market (and from correspondents) at prevailing exchange rates. By the time the outstanding swap drawings were fully liquidated in November 1976, the Federal Reserve had incurred modest losses, since repayments of the swap drawings were made at the adjusted contractual exchange rates (not at market rates). The Federal Reserve absorbed these losses.

In the case of the Swiss franc drawings, the losses to be incurred by the Federal Reserve loomed to be large. Federal Reserve officials argued that Switzerland should share some part of the losses since, unlike Belgium, it had not revalued its franc subsequent to the Federal Reserve's drawings in the summer of 1971. On the Swiss side it could be argued that Switzerland had already done its ''share'' when it revalued its franc in May 1971, shortly before the Federal Reserve's drawings were made. The Federal Reserve and the Swiss National Bank sought, and reached, a negotiated solution. In October 1976 the two banks concluded an agreement on an orderly procedure for repaying the Swiss franc drawings outstanding since before August 15, 1971.

On October 29, 1976, the entire amount of outstanding pre-August 15, 1971, drawings (about 3.9 billion Swiss francs) was repaid and the reciprocal credits liquidated at the adjusted contractual rates calculated in December 1975. The Swiss francs for this single massive repayment were acquired by the Federal Reserve through drawing on a newly established medium-term swap facility with the Swiss National Bank. The rate at which the Federal Reserve drew francs under the new facility was the same rate as the adjusted contractual rate on the pre-August 15, 1971 drawings. The effect was to postpone the date when the loss caused by floating rates would be accepted.

The agreement on the new facility provided that the October 29, 1976, drawing be liquidated over a three-year period, in accordance with a set schedule, with Swiss francs acquired by the Federal Reserve in the market, from correspondents, or directly from the Swiss National Bank. Since the cost to the Federal Reserve in dollars for the francs acquired under the new facility was substantially below what the francs would have cost in the market at the time, there was little doubt that the Federal Reserve would incur losses in acquiring francs to make the scheduled repayments. In this connection, the Swiss National Bank agreed to a formula under which it partially shared with the Federal Reserve the losses arising from the repayment of the swap debt with francs purchased at rates above the swap contract rate.

The U.S. Treasury, which had obligations denominated in Swiss francs amounting to 5.4 billion Swiss francs outstanding since before August 15, 1971, also reached an agreement with the Swiss National Bank on an orderly repayment procedure. The terms of the Treasury agreement were similar to those of the Federal Reserve settlement described above. All the Swiss francs drawn under the special facility for the Federal Reserve and all the francs drawn under the facility for the U.S. Treasury have now been repaid. The Swiss National Bank partially shared the losses incurred.

As we review the case, we see that the central banks, by choosing to allow their currencies to float, had the potential to radically transform their own and their partners' positions under the reciprocal currency agreements with respect to outstanding drawings. The "standing order" provision[111] did not by its terms anticipate the precise problem that arose and, even if it had, its enforceability under domestic laws of the countries was uncertain. Despite the difficulties, an attempt to give application to the "standing order" clause in terms of the expectations of the parties appears to have guided negotiation of the settlements. While it is always difficult to draw conclusions from negotiated settlements, it seems clear the parties recognized that their official roles in managing their countries' currencies made the case very different from the resolu-

---

[111] The language of the provision appears in the text accompanying note 104, *supra*.

tion of a private contract dispute and that the case would have been inappropriate for national courts. Reciprocal currency agreements between central banks are properly understood as agreements governed by public international law. The case discussed illustrates the necessity of that view.

Concluding Comments

An attractive feature of reciprocal currency arrangements is that they provide access to large volumes of foreign currency balances for short-term use, without prolonged negotiations on the terms at the time drawings are to be made. Drawings are, however, subject to a consultation obligation and are normally not automatic.[112] Consultations preceding and following drawings may take place by telephone or in person-to-person contacts.

Central banks have on occasion sought to obtain commitments in advance that their partners would not object to future drawings for particular purposes. They have also requested agreements in advance that the period for repaying drawings be, say, six months instead of three. The Banca d'Italia, for example, in February 1976 made arrangements with several central banks to obtain currencies upon call—the arrangements giving support to Italy's policies aimed at halting a decline in the lira's exchange rate. The Federal Reserve agreed that, out of the $3 billion total amount of the Reserve–Banca d'Italia reciprocal currency agreement, $500 million in addition to $250 million already drawn would be available on call to Banca d'Italia.[113]

As explained in Chapter 6, stand-by and extended arrangements for access to the higher credit tranches of the International Monetary Fund's General Resources Account are approved by the Fund only after a searching review of the country's policies, and drawings under the arrangements are conditioned upon progress by the country in correcting its problems.[114] The procedures for use of central bank reciprocal currency agreements are less formal and the policy conditions have not been stated with the same rigor as in IMF stand-by or extended arrangements. Where a country faces a severe problem, the prompt provision of currency under a short-term swap facility can give breathing space while negotiations proceed with the IMF on the terms of its assistance.

The Banco de Mexico, for example, in 1982 made heavy use of currency swap arrangements to meet immediate needs while Mexican officials negotiated a stabilization program with the IMF. Mexico's bank made large overnight drawings on its arrangement with the Federal Reserve on several occasions and

---

[112] See paragraph II of the Bank of England agreement (page 140), paragraphs I and II of the Deutsche Bundesbank agreement (page 144), and paragraph II of the model current agreement (page 152). Recall discussions at pages 141–142 and 146–148 *supra*.

[113] See Alan R. Holmes and Scott E. Pardee, "Treasury and Federal Reserve Foreign Exchange Operations," in Federal Reserve Bank of New York, *Monthly Review*, vol. 58 (September 1976), p. 218 at p. 230.

[114] See page 248 et seq.

then in early August drew the full $700 million for an initial period of three months.[115] In mid-August the Banco de Mexico entered into a $1 billion swap arrangement with the U.S. Treasury's Exchange Stabilization Fund. Later that month the Banco de Mexico negotiated additional financial arrangements with the central banks of the Group of Ten countries, Switzerland, and Spain, under the aegis of the Bank for International Settlements, totaling $1.85 billion. The United States agreed to provide half of this amount—$325 million under a special one-year swap agreement of the Federal Reserve and $600 million under an agreement of the Treasury's Exchange Stabilization Fund. The financing program provided that drawings by the Banco de Mexico would be contingent on Mexico's progress in negotiating with the IMF an adjustment program that the IMF would support with an extended arrangement.[116] Drawings were made on the facilities.[117] In December 1982 the IMF approved an SDR 3.6 billion extended arrangement for Mexico.[118]

Countries are not always successful in negotiating financial arrangements with the IMF. As mentioned above, the Banca d'Italia in February 1976 obtained an advance commitment from the Federal Reserve to draw up to $500 million on its swap agreement. During the same period Italian negotiations with the IMF for a $530 million stand-by arrangement were broken off.[119]

Sometimes by using a central bank currency swap arrangement, a country has been able to postpone or avoid taking economic policy actions that would have been expected by the IMF. Other times, by postponing corrective measures, the country's situation has grown worse. For example, United Kingdom authorities, although taking steps to restrain wage inflation, delayed taking strong measures to control government budget deficits when the Bank of England was able to obtain assurances in June 1976 that it could draw up to $1 billion under its $3 billion reciprocal currency arrangement with the Federal Reserve, another $1 billion under an arrangement with the U.S. Treasury, and $3.3 billion from central banks of other countries and the Bank for International Settlements over a six-month period to replenish its reserves as it intervened in the exchange markets. In the fall of 1976, in a deteriorating economic situation and with the December date for swap repayments approaching, British authori-

---

[115] See Sam Y. Cross, "Treasury and Federal Reserve Foreign Exchange Operations," in Federal Reserve Bank of New York, *Quarterly Review*, vol. 7, no. 3 (Autumn 1982), p. 53 at pp. 58 and 78–80; and Cross (Winter 1982–83), *supra* note 88, pp. 53 and 55.

[116] See "Record of Policy Actions of the Federal Open Market Committee Meeting Held on August 24, 1982," *Federal Reserve Bulletin*, vol. 68 (1982), p. 631 at pp. 635–36. See also appendix I of the statement of Paul A. Volcker, Chairman of the Board of Governors of the Federal Reserve System, in *International Debt: Hearings [1983]*, *supra* note 5, pp. 320–22; and Bank for International Settlements, *53d Annual Report 1982/83*, pp. 128 and 165.

[117] See Cross (Winter 1982–83), *supra* note 88, pp. 53 and 55; and Cross (Spring 1983), *supra* note 88, pp. 58–59 and 75–78.

[118] *IMF Survey*, January 10, 1983, p. 1.

[119] See Chapter 6, *infra*, page 270 (note 191).

ties had to adopt a tougher budget-deficit control program, to obtain an IMF stand-by, than if they had "taken the medicine" earlier.[120]

The large amounts of funds potentially available and the speed with which they can be marshalled make reciprocal currency arrangements extremely important instruments in international monetary collaboration. In our discussion of the Federal Reserve–Bundesbank arrangement, we saw how the Federal Reserve was able to obtain and sell Deutsche mark within minutes without having to draw down its total foreign currency balances or use other United States reserve assets.[121] Reciprocal currency arrangements, operating as they do independently from the regular exchange markets, made available to U.S. authorities in 1978 and 1979 large quantities of the foreign currencies the United States needed most (Deutsche mark, Japanese yen, and Swiss francs) for a program of active exchange market intervention in support of the U.S. dollar.[122]

The use of reciprocal currency agreements, like other international monetary policy actions, is subject to the surveillance and consultation procedures under Article IV of the IMF Agreement.[123]

---

[120] The swap drawings were repaid when they matured in December 1976 by the Bank of England using currencies held in monetary reserves. A stand-by arrangement in the amount of SDR 3,360 million, approved by the IMF on January 3, 1977, permitted the United Kingdom to draw currencies and SDRs from the Fund to replenish its holdings. For background see F. Lisle Widman, *Making International Monetary Policy* (Washington: Georgetown University International Law Institute, 1982), pp. 166–70; *IMF Survey,* January 10, 1977, p. 1; Holmes and Pardee (September 1976), *supra* note 113, p. 225; Holmes and Pardee, "Treasury and Federal Reserve Foreign Exchange Operations," in Federal Reserve Bank of New York, *Quarterly Review,* vol. 1 (Winter 1976), p. 40 at p. 41; and *idem,* vol. 2, no. 1 (Spring 1977), p. 50 at p. 51.

[121] See pages 148–150, *supra.*

[122] See Chapter 11, *infra,* page 533 (note 156).

[123] See Chapter 11, *infra,* page 558 et seq., especially pages 558–560, and Chapter 12, page 571 et seq.

Chapter 5: The Special Drawing Right

Introduction

The special drawing right (SDR) is a monetary reserve asset created and sustained through multilateral collaboration within the International Monetary Fund. The holder of an SDR has the right to obtain an equivalent amount of a "freely usable" national currency in exchange for the SDR. The SDR is "special" because it is surrounded by a unique set of rules.[1] Only member countries of the International Monetary Fund that have agreed to be participants in the Special Drawing Rights Department, the Fund itself, and other countries and official institutions designated by the Fund can hold special drawing rights.[2] Private individuals, firms, commercial banks, and other institutions are not permitted to hold SDRs, but may hold and use instruments valued in terms of the special drawing right.[3]

Overview
Economic Rationale

The roles of money as a standard of value, a medium of exchange, and a store of purchasing power are explained in Appendix A.[4] Economists are interested in the relationship between the volume of money in an economy and the volume of economic transactions. There are two aspects: (1) For a given volume of economic transactions, what is the volume/velocity of money that is necessary to handle the associated payments; that is, to perform the medium of exchange

---

[1] See earlier discussion of special drawing rights in this book in Chapter 1, pages 16–17, and Chapter 3, pages 110–112. Joseph Gold, "Special Drawing Rights: Renaming the Infant Asset," *IMF Staff Papers*, vol. 23 (1976), p. 295, provides amusing comments on the name. IMF Rule B-6, adopted July 26, 1983, provides that the term "SDR" (or "SDRs" as appropriate) shall be standard usage in Fund documents where a reference to special drawing rights is intended. *By-Laws, Rules and Regulations* (40th issue, 1983).

[2] See pages 175–176, *infra.*

[3] See note 42, *infra*, and Chapter 12, pages 636–637.

[4] At page 663.

function?[5] (2) How do changes in the quantity of money affect economic activity and what is the desirable level of monetary expansion for the particular economy?[6]

A number of economists in the early and mid-1960s addressed these questions as they pertained to the international economy. The discussion took place under the rubric "international liquidity." The questions were: What total volume of money (reserves) with what distribution among the countries of the world would best facilitate the growth of world trade and investment without excessive inflation?[7] If agreement could be reached that reserves of central banks should be increased, but there was disagreement about the desired total amount of reserves or the way in which they should be distributed, then could an institution be designed within which those decisions would be made? A premise of the influential writings of Robert Triffin was that the expansion and contraction of national treasury and central bank reserves should be subject to centralized control. The particular concern at the time was to design a mechanism for the planned and controlled expansion of world-wide reserves.[8]

The judgment of many economists was that a higher volume of reserves was desirable to support a higher volume of international transactions rather than depend on increased money velocity.[9] These additional reserves could be

---

[5] The term "volume/velocity" is used because a small amount of money can accomplish the medium of exchange function in an economy with a large number of transactions if there is rapid turnover in the use of money—if the ownership of bank deposits is transferred frequently.

[6] In the aggregate, interest rates, the price structure, and the production of goods and services are affected by the quantity of money in the particular economy. Decisions of individuals, firms, and governments to undertake economic transactions are greatly influenced by the amount of money readily available to them as well as by their economic needs and their expectations for the economy.

[7] For general background see chapters 1 and 2 of volume 1 of Margaret Garritsen de Vries, *The International Monetary Fund, 1966-1971: The System Under Stress* (2 vols.; Washington: IMF, 1976) [hereinafter cited *IMF History 1966-71*]; and chapter 4 of Robert Solomon, *The International Monetary System, 1945-1981* (New York: Harper & Row, 1982). An early IMF study was *International Reserves and Liquidity* (1958), in J. Keith Horsefield and Margaret Garritsen de Vries, *The International Monetary Fund, 1945-1965: Twenty Years of International Monetary Cooperation* (3 vols.; Washington: IMF, 1969) [hereinafter cited *IMF History 1945-65*], vol. 3, at p. 349.

[8] See Robert Triffin, *Gold and the Dollar Crisis: The Future of Convertibility* (1st ed.; New Haven: Yale University Press, 1960); and Robert Triffin, *The World Money Maze: National Currencies in International Payments* (New Haven: Yale University Press, 1966). See also *IMF History 1966-71, supra* note 7, vol. 1, pp. 17-24; Solomon, *supra* note 7, pp. 70-71; Herbert G. Grubel (ed.), *World Monetary Reform: Plans and Issues* (Stanford: Stanford University Press, 1963); Fritz Machlup, *Plans for Reform of the International Monetary System* (Special Papers in International Economics no. 3; Princeton: Princeton University International Finance Section, 1962, revised 1964); Fritz Machlup and Burton G. Malkiel (ed.), *International Monetary Arrangements—The Problem of Choice: Report on the Deliberations of an International Study Group of 32 Economists* (Princeton: Princeton University International Finance Section, 1964); and papers of Edward Bernstein printed in *Guidelines for International Monetary Reform: Hearings before the Subcommittee on International Exchange and Payments of the Joint Economic Committee, U.S. Congress, 89th Congress, 1st Session* (1965), part 2, pp. 230-81.

[9] At the time plans for creation of the special drawing right were being considered, 1963-1969, there had been no recent significant increase in monetary gold holdings, and the increase of foreign currency holdings in the hands of national treasuries and central banks had been modest. In 1958, world monetary reserves stood

created in two ways: States could acquire additional reserves (1) by assuming debt either to other states or to an international organization;[10] or (2) through money creation without incurring debt. The special drawing right represents the selection of the latter method.

Concept of the SDR

Robert Triffin, Edward Bernstein, and other economists proposed during the early 1960s that the international community create a new monetary reserve asset—similar to the "bancors" proposed by John Maynard Keynes in the 1940s—usable only by central banks and treasuries.[11] The Group of Ten countries participating in the General Arrangements to Borrow with the IMF decided in 1963 to undertake a "thorough examination" of the international monetary system. Subsequently, a study group was appointed by the Group of Ten to look specifically at proposals for the creation of new reserve assets. The Study Group, chaired by Rinaldo Ossola (Italy), submitted its report in 1965. That 119-page report outlined the concept of a "collective reserve unit" which was later to be given the name "special drawing right."[12]

Negotiations proceeded in two forums, the Deputies of the Group of Ten and the IMF's Executive Board.[13] This caused considerable awkwardness, for

at about 57 percent of the value of imports; by 1967 the proportion had declined to 36 percent. See Chart 11 in IMF, *Annual Report, 1975*, p. 40. See also Joseph Gold, *Special Drawing Rights: Character and Use* (2d ed.; IMF Pamphlet Series no. 13; Washington, 1970), p. 7. Few economists anticipated the dramatic increase in foreign-currency holdings of central banks that took place after 1970. See *IMF History 1966–71, supra* note 7, vol. 1, pp. 220–21.

[10] It has been said by some writers that for world-wide holdings of a particular national currency (say, the French franc) to expand, the issuer of that currency (France) must run a balance-of-payments deficit. Such statements are misleading and, in some respects, inaccurate. The writers are thinking of world-wide holdings of French francs increasing because France runs a balance-of-payments deficit (for example, imports more than it exports) and pays for its imports in francs. One should bear in mind that world-wide holdings of French francs can also be increased by foreigners' going into debt to French residents while France runs a surplus in its trade account. The Netherlands treasury can, for example, obtain francs from the French government and issue a note to the French government in return.

[11] See note 8, *supra*. Lord Keynes' bancor concept is outlined in Chapter 1, *supra*, page 7.

[12] Group of Ten [countries participating in the General Arrangements to Borrow], *Report of the Study Group on the Creation of Reserve Assets: Report to the Deputies of the Group of Ten* (transmitted by R. Ossola) (Rome: Bank of Italy; May 31, 1965). The report is reprinted in *Balance of Payments—1965: Hearings before a Subcommittee of the Committee on Banking and Currency, U.S. Senate*, 89th Congress, 1st Session (1965), part 2, p. 1103. Discussions among the Deputies of the Group of Ten and within the Ossola Group are summarized in Solomon, *supra* note 7, pp. 63–79.

The IMF staff prepared studies for the Ossola Group and J. Marcus Fleming, Deputy Director of the IMF's Research and Statistics Department, represented the Managing Director at its meetings. See generally *IMF History 1966–71, supra* note 7, vol. 1, pp. 36–37, 52, and 58–61. See also Communiqué of the Ministers and Governors of the Group of Ten issued September 28, 1965, in IMF, *Summary Proceedings, 1965*, p. 279.

[13] The negotiations during the period of 1964–67 are described in *IMF History 1966–71, supra* note 7, vol. 1, chapters 3–6; Solomon, *supra* note 7, pp. 74–85 and 128–43; and Susan Strange,."International Monetary Relations," in Andrew Shonfield (ed.), *International Economic Relations of the Western World 1959–1971* (2 vols.; London: Oxford University Press for Royal Institute of International Affairs, 1976), vol. 2, chapters 7 and 8.

example, when IMF staff, who attended G–10 meetings as personal representatives of the Managing Director, briefed members of the IMF's Executive Board who were not permitted to attend.[14] A major early question was whether the new financial instrument would be available to all IMF members or only to members of the Group of Ten. The issue was resolved in favor of universality coupled with special majorities for important decisions.[15] Joint meetings of the Deputies of the Group of Ten and the IMF's Executive Directors were held in 1966 and 1967.[16]

In the summer of 1967, after sustained negotiations, agreement was reached in the IMF Executive Board and the Group of Ten on an "Outline of a Facility Based on Special Drawing Rights."[17] During the preceding months there had been much debate about the verbal characterization of the new monetary instrument and about the technical procedures surrounding its use. Some officials, notably French representatives, wished to perceive the emerging monetary instrument in credit terms, while others saw it as a reserve asset. The Outline contemplated endowing the special drawing right (SDR) with features that would enable it to be a reserve asset while the name chosen deferred to the French preference. Throughout the Outline, language was carefully chosen and shows the hand of Joseph Gold, the Fund's General Counsel. Professor Fritz Machlup praised the mediators:

> The conflict was resolved . . . applying the recipe of avoiding all the words which the nations had written on their banners and for which they were valiantly battling. The words "credit," "credit facility," "reserve asset," "reserve units," "borrowed reserves," "owned reserves," "loans," "repayments"—all of them were, with great circumspection, avoided in the Outline drafted. Words not burdened with a history of controversy, not associated with recognizable ideologies, and not widely used in monetary theories, words, therefore, with still neutral and not always fixed connotations were put in place of the old, battle-scarred and now banished words.[18]

Margaret Garritsen de Vries, the Fund's historian, has written:

> The choice of this terminology was quite deliberate. Its use was instrumental in reconciling opposing positions. Words were selected

---

[14] See, e.g., *IMF History 1966–71, supra* note 7, vol. 1, pp. 35–36, 66–69, 76–77, 89–91, and 102–08. The composition of the Group of Ten and its relationships with the IMF and the OECD are noted in Chapter 2, *supra,* pages 72–74.

[15] See *IMF History 1966–71, idem,* vol. 1, pp. 41–42, 45–46, 68–69, and 77–100.

[16] See *IMF History 1966–71, idem,* vol. 1, pp. 76–77, 102–08, 134–37, 141–43, 150–58, and 162–65.

[17] The negotiations in 1966–67 are recounted in *IMF History 1966–71, idem,* vol. 1, chapter 4 (beginning at p. 86) and chapters 5 and 6. Papers prepared by the IMF staff are collected, *idem,* vol. 2, pp. 3–44. See also Solomon, *supra* note 7, chapter 8.

[18] Fritz Machlup, *Remaking the International Monetary System: The Rio Agreement and Beyond* (Committee for Economic Development, Supplementary Paper no. 24; Baltimore: Johns Hopkins University Press, 1968), p. 9, quoted in *IMF History 1966–71, supra* note 7, vol. 1, pp. 154–55.

that were not only innocuous but in some ways ambiguous, so as to make agreement possible. In the words of the General Counsel, it "enabled the proponents of divergent views to insist that their opinions had prevailed."[19]

At the Annual Meeting in September 1967, the creation by the IMF of a Special Drawing Account was formally approved in principle by the Board of Governors, with instructions to the Executive Directors to draft the necessary amendment to the Fund's Articles of Agreement.[20] As the amendment to the IMF Articles was put into concrete language, a number of the ambiguities in the Outline were resolved. The amendment was transmitted to the Governors in April 1968 for a mail vote and was then submitted to governments for their acceptance. The amendment took effect July 28, 1969.[21] The first allocation of SDRs was made on January 1, 1970. Following the most recent allocation, completed in January 1981, over 21 billion SDRs are now in existence.[22]

The reader of the Fund's official history will be impressed with the range of alternatives that were considered in the negotiations that led to the definition of the special drawing right and its characteristics. The creation of this instrument was not preordained.[23] Some significant changes in the features of the SDR were made in the Second Amendment to the IMF's Articles of Agreement.[24] This chapter describes the amended SDR system.

---

[19] *IMF History 1966–71, idem,* vol. 1, p. 154. The quoted words can be found in Joseph Gold, *Special Drawing Rights: The Role of Language* (IMF Pamphlet Series no. 15; Washington, 1971), p. 2.

[20] The "Outline of a Facility Based on Special Drawing Rights," approved in principle by Board of Governors Resolution No. 22-8 (September 29, 1967), appears in *IMF History 1966–71, supra* note 7, vol. 2, pp. 47–51 and 54–55; and in IMF, *Summary Proceedings, 1967,* pp. 271–79. For commentary see Joseph Gold, "The Next Stage in the Development of International Monetary Law: The Deliberate Control of Liquidity," *American Journal of International Law,* vol. 62 (1968), p. 365; and Joseph Gold, "Legal Technique in Creation of a New International Reserve Asset: SDRs and Amendment of the Fund's Articles," in Joseph Gold, *Legal and Institutional Aspects of the International Monetary System: Selected Essays* (Washington: IMF, 1979), p. 128.

[21] See generally *IMF History 1966–71, supra* note 7, vol. 1, chapters 7 and 8. The instrument of amendment appears in *United Nations Treaty Series,* vol. 726, p. 266; and *United States Treaties and Other International Agreements,* vol. 20, p. 2775. The text together with the report of the Executive Directors, under the title *Establishment of a Facility Based on Special Drawing Rights in the International Monetary Fund and Modifications in the Rules and Practices of the Fund: A Report of the Executive Directors to the Board of Governors Proposing Amendment of the Articles of Agreement* (1968), appears in *IMF History 1945–65, supra* note 7, vol. 3, p. 497; and in *IMF History 1966–71,* vol. 2, p. 52. The internal legislative acts adopted in member countries to implement the amendment are surveyed in John V. Surr, "Special Drawing Rights: A Legislative View," *Finance and Development,* vol. 8, no. 3 (September 1971), p. 40. See also Chapter 1, *supra,* pages 8–11.

[22] Details on the number of SDRs allocated are set forth in notes 30 and 207, *infra.*

[23] See *IMF History 1966–71, supra* note 7, vol. 1, chapters 1–12, and vol. 2, pp. 3–94. See also chapters 4 and 8 of Solomon, *supra* note 7, which gives the perspective of a U.S. official on the negotiations which spanned several years.

[24] The gold value of the SDR was terminated and a procedure for changing the principle and method of valuing the SDR was adopted. The variety of transactions and operations in which the SDR can be used was liberalized. A number of other changes were made. See generally IMF, *Proposed Second Amendment to the Articles of Agreement of the International Monetary Fund: A Report by the Executive Directors to the Board*

The international community within the IMF created a new monetary reserve asset when it established the Special Drawing Account (now Special Drawing Rights Department). While French authorities were initially hesitant to describe the SDR as a reserve asset, by 1969 they too were using that term.[25] The Second Amendment explicitly describes the special drawing right as a "reserve asset" and members undertake to collaborate to make it the *principal* reserve asset in the international monetary system.[26] The drafters of the Second Amendment considered renaming the SDR but decided that "special drawing right" and "SDR" had become so much a part of the financial vocabulary that a change in name would not be appropriate.[27]

The world-wide volume of this monetary asset can be expanded or contracted by deliberate multilateral decision of the Fund's members. Member-country "participants" are allocated special drawing rights by the IMF simply for "playing the game"—that is, by agreeing to abide by the rules for their allocation and use. It is not necessary to export, not necessary to accept foreign investment, nor is it necessary to go into debt to receive this asset. The SDR is a form of fiat money, allocated by the IMF, which has no backing except the promises of the member countries that participate in the Special Drawing Rights Department that they will accept SDRs under the rules set in the IMF Articles and Fund decisions. The SDR is a unique asset that is not readily comparable to any other monetary instrument.[28]

Countries participating in the Special Drawing Rights Department periodically receive, in accordance with allocation decisions, a predetermined amount of new SDRs which can be used to obtain freely usable currencies. This has been likened to players in the game of Monopoly,[29] who receive a fixed amount of the money used in that game each time they pass "Go." Unlike Monopoly, however, the participants in the Special Drawing Rights Department do not actually receive any paper money. The Fund simply credits the member on the

---

of Governors (April 1976), reprinted in IMF, *Summary Proceedings, 1976—Supplement* [hereinafter *Report on Second Amendment*], especially part 2, chapters B, D, I, and Q.

[25] The French representatives early pointed to the reconstitution requirement attending the use of the SDR (explained at pages 210–212, *infra*) as precluding the instrument's being a reserve asset. Compare the statement of Michel Debré, French Minister of Economy and Finance, at the 1967 IMF Annual Meeting, with that of his successor, Giscard d'Estaing, at the 1969 meeting. IMF, *Summary Proceedings, 1967*, p. 66; and *1969*, p. 58.

U.S. officials saw the creation of the special drawing right as a step toward the demonetization of gold. See Solomon, *supra* note 7, p. 147.

[26] Article VIII, section 7; and Article XXII. Article XV, section 1, *second*, retains the original language of Article XXI, *first*, and speaks of SDRs being allocated as a "supplement to existing reserve assets"—the language used in the deliberately ambiguous 1967 Outline. Article XVIII, section 1, *second*, also retains the ambiguous language of Article XXIV, *first*.

[27] See Gold, "Special Drawing Rights: Renaming the Infant Asset," *supra* note 1.

[28] The various items that are generally accepted as international monetary reserve assets are described in Chapter 3.

[29] Monopoly is a popular board game in the United States that involves the simulated purchase, sale, and rental of real estate.

books of the Special Drawing Rights Department. Whenever new reserves are created, each participant is credited with an appropriate amount of SDRs, based on its quota in the Fund.[30]

A substantial portion of inter-governmental transactions now involve SDRs. As illustrative of an SDR transaction, consider a country with a balance-of-payments deficit. The deficit country transfers SDRs to a country "designated" by the Fund. The designee, required to accept the SDRs, provides a "freely usable currency" in exchange. The deficit country then uses this currency, or provides it to its residents, to make payments to nonresidents. The designee can in turn transfer the SDRs and obtain a freely usable currency when it has balance-of-payments need. This example and others will be developed in more detail later in the chapter.

Order of Presentation of the Remainder of the Chapter

A guide to the remainder of the chapter may be helpful to the reader. First, a summary of the features of the special drawing right will be listed. These features will then be explored and elaborated. The rules respecting ownership and use of special drawing rights will be identified. Legal aspects of the valuation of the special drawing right will be examined. Typical transactions among government treasuries and central banks that involve special drawing rights will then be set forth. This will lead into the basic concept that a country can use SDRs to obtain a "freely usable currency" in an amount "equivalent" in value to the SDRs transferred. Attention will then turn to a variety of transactions and operations in which the Fund itself receives or transfers SDRs.

Discussion then shifts to a more general level. The legal framework within which decisions are made to create and allocate special drawing rights will be explored. Attention will be given to particular features designed to keep the Special Drawing Rights Department working, such as the rules on "designation" and "reconstitution" and the payment of interest and assessment of charges. Finally, the chapter concludes with a general appraisal of the special drawing right.

---

[30] The first allocation of special drawing rights was effected on January 1, 1970, to 104 countries which had agreed to be "participants" in the Special Drawing Acaount. Thereafter, additional SDRs were allocated in January 1971 and 1972. See Walter Habermeier, *Operations and Transactions in SDRs: The First Basic Period* (IMF Pamphlet Series no. 17; Washington, 1973). A second series of allocations began January 1, 1979, and was completed on January 1, 1981. See note 207, *infra*.

Features of the SDR

Some of the features of the SDR,[31] later to be probed in depth, are:

(1) An SDR is a right to obtain a "freely usable currency."
(2) The Fund by special majorities of the total voting power determines the principle and method of valuing the SDR. (The exchange value of the SDR is presently computed in terms of a composite consisting of portions of five national currencies.)
(3) SDRs are deliberately created reserve assets. Whether to create and how much to create are determined by the IMF Board of Governors in accordance with procedures spelled out in Article XVIII of the IMF Agreement.
(4) Allocations of SDRs among participating countries are proportionate to the countries' quotas in the IMF General Resources Account.
(5) Only member governments of the IMF, the IMF itself, and other countries and official institutions designated by the IMF can hold SDRs. Commercial banks and private individuals or organizations are not permitted to hold SDRs.
(6) A participant in the SDR Department agrees to accept SDRs from any other participant upon designation by the IMF and to provide to that member an equivalent amount of a freely usable currency (which may be its own currency or the currency of another member if deemed by the Fund to be freely usable). There are, however, limits on the amount of SDRs that a country may be required to accept.
(7) Unlike drawing rights in the IMF's General Resources Account beyond the reserve tranche, the use of SDRs is not conditioned on the pursuit of policies to correct balance-of-payments problems.
(8) The Fund can require each participant to maintain average daily holdings of SDRs above a stated percentage of its net cumulative allocation, which can be changed by Fund decision. (Currently there is no requirement to maintain minimum average daily holdings.)
(9) The Special Drawing Rights Department of the IMF is the record keeper for transactions and operations in SDRs. All transactions and operations involving SDRs are required to be conducted through that Department.[32]

---

[31] For a discussion of the legal rights and obligations of participants in the Special Drawing Account prior to the Second Amendment, see Gold, *Special Drawing Rights: Character and Use, supra* note 9.

[32] Article XVI. Transactions and operations denominated in SDRs as a unit of account that do not involve actual transfers of SDRs are not conducted through the Special Drawing Rights Department.

Participants and Holders

Only members of the IMF can be "participants" in the Special Drawing Rights Department. However, a member of the IMF is not required to be a participant.[33] To become a participant, an IMF member must file an instrument of participation under Article XVII, Section 1:

> Each member of the Fund that deposits with the Fund an instrument setting forth that it undertakes all the obligations of a participant in the Special Drawing Rights Department in accordance with its law and that it has taken all steps necessary to enable it to carry out all of these obligations shall become a participant in the Special Drawing Rights Department. . . .

Any participant can terminate its participation in the Special Drawing Rights Department without withdrawing from the Fund. Any participant which withdraws from the Fund is treated as simultaneously terminating its participation in the Special Drawing Rights Department. At the time of withdrawal the Fund is required to redeem any SDRs the withdrawing participant then holds, and the withdrawing participant is required to pay to the Fund freely usable currencies equal to its net cumulative SDR allocation. The effect is to put the member in the position it would be in had it not joined the SDR system originally.[34]

The General Resources Account of the IMF is authorized to hold and engage in transactions and operations in SDRs.[35]

The IMF has authority to permit members that are not participants in the SDR Department, nonmembers, institutions that perform functions of a central bank for more than one member, and other official entities to become "other holders" of special drawing rights.[36] The IMF has "prescribed" a number of such official institutions as "other holders."[37] They are permitted to hold and

---

[33] Article XVII, section 1. Currently all IMF members are participants in the Special Drawing Rights Department. Prior to January 1, 1979, the following IMF members were not participants in the Special Drawing Rights Department: Kuwait, Lebanon, Libyan Arab Republic, Saudi Arabia, Singapore, and United Arab Emirates. All but Kuwait chose to become participants effective January 1, 1979, and Kuwait became a participant in April 1980.

[34] Article XXIV. See pages 217–219, *infra*.

[35] Article XVII, section 2. See pages 205–209, *infra*.

[36] Article XVII, section 3; and Rule Q-1, *By-Laws, Rules and Regulations* (40th issue, 1983).

[37] The Bank for International Settlements was the first institution to be "prescribed" (permitted) to hold SDRs. Other institutions subsequently prescribed to be "other holders" include: Andean Reserve Fund, Arab Monetary Fund, Asian Development Bank, Bank of Central African States, Central Bank of West African States, East African Development Bank, East Caribbean Central Bank, International Bank for Reconstruction and Development, International Development Association, International Fund for Agricultural Development, Islamic Development Bank, Nordic Investment Bank, and Swiss National Bank. Abu Dhabi is also an "other holder." Decisions prescribing individual institutions as other holders are collected in *Selected Decisions of the International Monetary Fund and Selected Documents* (10th issue; Washington: IMF, 1983) [hereinafter *Selected Decisions*], pp. 274–76 and 339–42.

use SDRs only under the terms stated in Fund decisions. These terms may be stated in general Fund decisions and in decisions concerning particular institutions. The terms may be changed from time to time.[38]

Under the presently operative general decision,[39] official entities prescribed as "other holders" of SDRs can acquire and use SDRs voluntarily in transactions and operations by agreement with any other holder and with any participant. They have the same freedom as participants to buy and sell SDRs both spot and forward; to borrow, lend, or pledge SDRs; to use SDRs in swaps; or to grant or receive SDRs in donations.[40]

The general decision on "other holders" provides for consultation between the Fund and other holders. It also includes a general undertaking by other holders to collaborate with the Fund, participants, and other holders. The Fund may terminate the prescription of an "other holder" at any time and the holder is then required to dispose of its SDR holdings as expeditiously as possible.[41]

Commercial banks and private individuals or organizations cannot become "other holders" and are not permitted to hold SDRs.[42] They may, however, hold and use instruments denominated in SDRs as the unit of account.[43]

Valuation and Interest Rate

Historical Survey

The IMF Articles of Agreement, as presently in force, do not state a value for the SDR. No value is prescribed in relation to national currencies, gold, other monetary instruments, commodities, or indices. Article XV, Section 2, gives the Fund unlimited authority to change at any time the principle and method of

---

[38] See generally Joseph Gold, *SDRs, Currencies, and Gold: Fifth Survey of New Legal Developments* (IMF Pamphlet Series no. 36; Washington, 1981), pp. 21–26.

[39] E.B. Decision No. 6467 -(80/71)S(April 14, 1980); IMF, *Annual Report, 1980*, p. 143; *Selected Decisions* (10th issue, 1983), p. 271.

[40] "Other holders," not being participants, do not receive allocations of SDRs, nor do they have either the rights or obligations that arise for participants from their receipt of allocations. They are not required to pay assessments or charges (interest) because these obligations apply only to participants that have received allocations of SDRs. As holders, they do earn interest on SDRs they hold which is periodically credited to them by the Special Drawing Rights Department. Article XX; and Rules T-1 and T-2, *By-Laws, Rules and Regulations* (40th issue, 1983). See pages 193–194, *infra.*

"Other holders" are not subject to IMF designation to provide currency and receive SDRs in exchange. They do not have recourse to the designation mechanism if they wish to exchange SDRs for currency; rather, they must arrange a transaction or operation by agreement with another holder or a participant. IMF, *User's Guide to the SDR: A Manual of Transactions and Operations in Special Drawing Rights* (Washington: IMF Treasurer's Department, 1982), p. 5. See generally pages 194–205, *infra.*

[41] E.B. Decision No. 6467, *supra* note 39.

[42] Article XVII, section 3.

[43] See Chapter 12, *infra*, pages 635–636.

valuing the SDR provided that decisions are taken by the required majorities as explained below.

At the time of the initial creation of the Special Drawing Account in 1969, the value of the SDR was established as equivalent to 0.888671 gram of fine gold.[44] After the suspension of the convertibility of national currencies into gold on the basis of par values, the Fund found it necessary to adopt a new principle for valuing the SDR.[45] Effective July 1, 1974, the IMF calculated the value of the SDR in terms of a composite consisting of small amounts of sixteen national currencies, selected and weighted taking into account the issuing countries' shares of world exports and other considerations.[46] The IMF's General Counsel reconciled the new principle with the gold value stated in Article XXI, Section 2, *first,* by characterizing the new approach as embodying a "fictitious valuation of gold" adopted by the Fund "acting on the principle of effectiveness."[47] Article XV, Section 2, *second* (replacing Article XXI, Section 2, *first*) eliminates any reference to gold, national currencies, or anything else. Instead, it simply provides:

The method of valuation of the special drawing right shall be determined by the Fund by a seventy percent majority of the total voting

[44] Former Article XXI, section 2, *first.* In 1969 the U.S. dollar also had a par value of 0.888671 gram of fine gold and the U.S. Treasury expressed its readiness to freely buy and sell gold at prices based on par values in transactions with official monetary authorities. The SDR thus had a value of U.S. $1.00. In transactions among countries that involved the exchange of SDRs for currencies other than the U.S. dollar, representative exchange rates based on market exchange rates between the U.S. dollar and those currencies determined the amount of the currencies to be exchanged. Original Rules O-3 through O-5, adopted September 18, 1969, in *IMF History 1966–71, supra* note 7, vol. 2, p. 187. See generally *IMF History 1966–71,* vol. 1, pp. 168–70 and 186–87.

[45] On August 15, 1971, the United States announced that it was suspending the convertibility of the dollar into gold or other reserve assets. In the period following that announcement, transactions in SDRs came to a halt, because of uncertainty about the amount of currency that could in the future be received in exchange for the SDR. See *IMF History 1966–71, idem,* vol. 1, p. 244. Later in 1971 the United States announced that the dollar would be devalued in relation to gold (and the SDR). In 1973 the United States announced a second devaluation. See Chapter 11, *infra,* pages 491–499. After these two U.S. devaluations the exchange value of the SDR (which continued to have a gold value of 0.888671 gram) was U.S. $1.20635. However, the exchange values of the currencies of other countries in relation to the SDR fluctuated from day to day depending on the rates in the exchange markets between those currencies and the dollar.

After the introduction of floating exchange rates for widely used currencies in March 1973 (see Chapter 11, *infra,* pages 499–501) and when it became clear that U.S. authorities did not intend to re-establish the convertibility of the dollar into gold, new bases for valuing the SDR began to be explored that would break the direct tie between the exchange value of the SDR and the exchange value of the U.S. dollar. See IMF Committee on Reform of the International Monetary System and Related Issues (Committee of Twenty), *International Monetary Reform: Documents of the Committee of Twenty* (Washington: IMF, 1974), pp. 15–16 and 21 (Outline of Reform, June 14, 1974, paragraphs 26 and 38) and pp. 43–45 (Annex 9). See also J. J. Polak, *Valuation and Rate of Interest of the SDR* (IMF Pamphlet Series no. 18; Washington, 1974).

[46] For the composition of the composite in the period July 1, 1974, through June 30, 1978, see Table 2 that accompanies note 55, *infra.*

[47] Joseph Gold, "Law and Change in International Monetary Relations," *The Record* [of the Association of the Bar of the City of New York], vol. 31 (1976), p. 223 at p. 236. See also Joseph Gold, *Floating Currencies, Gold and SDRs* (IMF Pamphlet Series no. 19; Washington, 1976), pp. 1–15 and table on p. 16.

power, provided, however, that an eighty-five percent majority of the total voting power shall be required for a change in the principle of valuation or a fundamental change in the application of the principle in effect.[48]

When the Second Amendment to the Articles went into effect on April 1, 1978, the 1974 system of valuing the SDR was continued in effect.[49] Effective July 1, 1978, changes were made both in the sixteen currencies in the composite and the relative weights of the currencies. These changes primarily reflected adjustments for countries' shares of world trade.[50] Effective January 1, 1981, the number of currencies in the composite was reduced from sixteen to five. At the time of the change these currencies were issued by the five members of the IMF with the largest exports of goods and services in the period 1975–1979.[51] It also happens that the five currencies possess certain qualities that were not universally shared by all the other eleven currencies in the previous composite. They are actively traded in exchange markets and forward rates are also quoted in the markets. In addition, they had previously been designated as "freely usable currencies" and thus enjoyed a special status under the IMF's Articles.[52]

Present System

At the present time the exchange value of the SDR is set against a composite (sometimes called a "market basket") consisting of small amounts of five national currencies listed in the first column of Table 1 below. These amounts were fixed effective January 1, 1981, and are not expected to be changed until January 1, 1986.[53] These amounts were calculated on the basis of relative weights originally assigned each currency in the composite. Those initial relative weights, which are shown in the right column, were based on the size of the issuing countries' exports of goods and services and the size of official holdings of the currencies in the monetary reserves of IMF members. Exchange market fluctuations subsequent to January 1, 1981, change the relative weights of the currencies from day to day, so that the relative weights in the right column primarily have historical interest.

---

[48] The distinction between "principle" and "method" is discussed *infra* at pages 189–192.
[49] Schedule B, paragraph 6.
[50] The terms of the change were stated in E.B. Decision No. 5718 -(78/46) G/S, adopted March 31, 1978, before the Second Amendment entered into force, and became effective in accordance with those terms and Schedule B, paragraph 6, of the Second Amendment on July 1, 1978. See note 56, *infra.*
[51] See pages 185–187, *infra.*
[52] See pages 197–200, *infra.*
[53] See page 188, *infra.*

TABLE 1

SDR Valuation as from January 1, 1981[54]

One SDR is equal in value to the sum of the values of the five currencies below		Percentage weight of each currency in the composite at time composite established in 1981
U.S. dollar	0.54	42
Deutsche mark	0.46	19
French franc	0.74	13
Japanese yen	34.	13
U.K. pound sterling	0.071	13
		——
		100

During the period July 1, 1974, through June 30, 1978, the value of the SDR was the sum of small amounts of sixteen currencies, as shown in the first column of Table 2. During the period July 1, 1978, through December 31, 1980, the value of the SDR was determined by a composite of sixteen currencies with a different composition. See the first column of Table 3. The relative weightings of the currencies at the time each of the two valuation formulas was adopted, primarily of historical interest, are shown in the right-hand columns of the tables.

[54] The Executive Board decision fixing the SDR with these components is E.B. Decision No. 6708 -(80/189)S(December 19, 1980), amending Rule O-1 effective January 1, 1981, and implementing E.B. Decision No. 6631 -(80/145)G/S (September 17, 1980); IMF, *Annual Report, 1981,* pp. 142–43. See also explanations in the IMF, *Annual Report, 1981,* pp. 95–96; and *IMF Survey,* October 13, 1980, pp. 297 and 325–27, January 12, 1981, pp. 1 and 6–7, and January 26, 1981, pp. 18–24.

TABLE 2

SDR Valuation July 1, 1974 - June 30, 1978[55]

One SDR is equal in value to the sum of the values of the 16 currencies below		Percentage weight of each currency in the composite at time composite established in 1974
U.S. dollar	0.40	33.
Deutsche mark	0.38	12.5
U.K. pound sterling	0.045	9.
French franc	0.44	7.5
Japanese yen	26.	7.5
Canadian dollar	0.071	6.
Italian lira	47.	6.
Netherlands guilder	0.14	4.5
Belgian franc	1.60	3.5
Swedish krona	0.13	2.5
Australian dollar	0.012	1.5
Spanish peseta	1.10	1.5
Norwegian krone	0.099	1.5
Danish krone	0.11	1.5
Austrian schilling	0.22	1.
South African rand	0.0082	1.
		100.0

[55] The SDR valuation system introduced July 1, 1974, was established by E.B. Decision No. 4233 -(74/67)S (June 13, 1974), as amended by Decision No. 4261 -(74/78)S (July 1, 1974); IMF, *Annual Report, 1974*, pp. 116–17. See also *IMF Survey*, June 17, 1974, pp. 177 and 185; and July 8, 1974, pp. 209 and 213–14.

The currencies in this first SDR ''basket'' were those of the sixteen IMF members that had a share in world exports of goods and services in excess of one percent on average over the 5-year period 1968–1972. The relative weights for these currencies (within the composite at the time it was established) were set broadly proportionate to the shares of the issuing countries in international transactions, using as a guide average exports of goods and services. The 33 percent weight for the U.S. dollar was somewhat arbitrary, the thought being that exports of goods and services were not an accurate measure of the dollar's weight in the world economy. IMF, *Annual Report, 1974*, pp. 51–52. See also Polak, *Valuation and Rate of Interest of the SDR, supra* note 45, pp. 1–2 and 23–24.

TABLE 3

SDR Valuation July 1, 1978 - December 31, 1980[56]

One SDR is equal in value to the sum of the values of the 16 currencies below		Percentage weight of each currency in the composite at time composite established in 1978
U.S. dollar	0.40	33.
Deutsche mark	0.32	12.5
Japanese yen	21.	7.5
French franc	0.42	7.5
U.K. pound sterling	0.050	7.5
Italian lira	52.	5.
Netherlands guilder	0.14	5.
Canadian dollar	0.070	5.
Belgian franc	1.60	4.
Saudi Arabian riyal	0.13	3.
Swedish krona	0.11	2.
Iranian rial	1.70	2.
Australian dollar	0.017	1.5
Spanish peseta	1.50	1.5
Norwegian krone	0.10	1.5
Austrian schilling	0.28	1.5
		——
		100.0

Each time the method of valuing the SDR has been changed, the amounts in the new composite have been set so that their sum on the last day of the old composite equalled the value of the old composite. This has been done to maintain continuity of value as the former composite is superseded by the new one.

Let us now turn to the way in which the amount of U.S. currency yielded by one SDR is calculated under the present valuation system. The amount is *not* calculated by multiplying 0.54 by 100/42 as Table 1 might at first blush sug-

---

[56] The Executive Board decision fixing the SDR composite with these components is E.B. Decision No. 5847 -(78/100)G/S(June 30, 1978) amending Rule O-1 effective July 1, 1978, and implementing E.B. Decision No. 5718 -(78/46)G/S(March 31, 1978); IMF, *Annual Report, 1978,* pp. 129–31. See also pp. 56–57 of the 1978 *Annual Report.*

Trade data for the five-year period 1972–1976 were used in the revision of the SDR valuation composite put in effect July 1, 1978. A decision was made to continue to use exactly sixteen currencies. Data on exports of goods and services were used to determine relative weights, except that the U.S. dollar was given a weight of 33 percent of the total to reflect "both its commercial and financial importance." IMF, *Annual Report, 1978,* pp. 56–57.

gest. Such a technique would ignore the realities of changes in exchange rates in the exchange markets. Rather, the amount of U.S. currency equivalent to one SDR is calculated daily, in accordance with Rule O-2(a), by converting each of the currency components in the composite into U.S. dollar equivalents at market rates and then adding them up.[57] The way these calculations were made for April 30, 1981, to determine the amount of U.S. dollars equivalent to one SDR on that date is set forth in Table 4 below.

TABLE 4

SDR Valuation, April 30, 1981[58]
(Calculated in Accordance with Rule O-2(a))

Currency (1)	Currency Amount Under Rule O-1 (2)	Exchange Rate (3)	U.S. Dollar Equivalent (4)
U.S. dollar	0.54	1.0000	0.540000
Deutsche mark	0.46	2.2145	0.207722
French franc	0.74	5.2540	0.140845
Japanese yen	34.	215.13	0.158044
U.K. pound sterling	0.071	2.1404	0.151968
			_____
			1.198579

SDR value of US$1   =   0.834321
U.S. dollar value of SDR   =   1.19858

Such a table is prepared for each business day by the IMF staff. The currency amounts in column 2 are fixed by Rule O-1.[59] The exchange rates in column 3 are established in accordance with procedures decided from time to time by the Fund. The present procedure is as follows:

Collection of Exchange Rates for Calculation of Value of SDR
   (1) For the purpose of determining the value of the United States dollar in terms of the special drawing right pursuant to Rule O-2(a),

---

[57] Rule O-2(a) provides:

> The value of the United States dollar in terms of the SDR shall be equal to the reciprocal of the sum of the equivalents in United States dollars of the amounts of the currencies specified in Rule O-1, calculated on the basis of exchange rates established in accordance with procedures decided from time to time by the Fund. (*By-Laws, Rules and Regulations* (40th issue, 1983))

[58] Reproduced from IMF, *Annual Report, 1981*, p. 95.
[59] See Table 1 and note 54, *supra*.

the equivalents in United States dollars of the amounts of currencies specified in Rule O-1 shall be based on spot exchange rates against the United States dollar. For each currency the exchange rate shall be the middle rate between the buying and selling rates at noon in the London exchange market as determined by the Bank of England.

(2) If the exchange rate for any currency cannot be obtained from the London exchange market, the rate shall be the middle rate at noon in the New York exchange market determined by the Fund on the basis of the buying and selling rates communicated by the Federal Reserve Bank of New York or, if not available there, the middle rate determined by the Fund on the basis of the buying and selling rates at the fixing in the Frankfurt exchange market communicated by the Deutsche Bundesbank. If the rate for any currency against the United States dollar cannot be obtained directly in any of these markets, the rate shall be calculated indirectly by use of a cross rate against another currency specified in Rule O-1.

(3) If on any day the exchange rate for a currency cannot be obtained in accordance with (1) or (2) above, the rate for that day shall be the latest rate determined in accordance with (1) or (2) above, provided that after the second business day the Fund shall determine the rate.[60]

At the present time each of the five currencies is traded in a unified exchange market. If a currency is traded in a dual market with a different rate for some capital transactions compared to current transactions, the IMF's practice is to use the rate applicable to current transactions.[61]

The exchange rates shown in column 3 of Table 4 are the middle rates between the spot buying and selling rates at noon in London as determined by the Bank of England. In accordance with the practice of the market, the rates are expressed in currency units per U.S. dollar except for the U.K. pound sterling, which is expressed in U.S. dollars per pound sterling. Column 4 shows the U.S. dollar equivalents of the currency amounts in column 2 at the exchange

---

[60] Paragraph (d) of E.B. Decision No. 6709 -(80/189)S(December 19, 1980); IMF, *Annual Report, 1981*, p. 144; *Selected Decisions* (10th issue, 1983), p. 270.

Note that the London rate is "determined by the Bank of England;" New York and Frankfurt rates are "determined by the Fund" on the basis of buying and selling rates "communicated" by the Federal Reserve Bank of New York or the Deutsche Bundesbank. The reason for the difference appears to be to give the Fund the ability to adjust for time variations or unusual events in the market if that is judged necessary.

The procedures presently in use differ in some respects from practices at earlier times. For example, in the period 1974 through 1980 the preferred rate for the Japanese yen was the rate reported from Tokyo. E.B. Decision No. 4234 -(74/67)S(June 13, 1974); IMF, *Annual Report, 1974*, p. 117. See Joseph Gold, *SDRs, Currencies, and Gold: Fifth Survey, supra* note 38, p. 12.

[61] The precedent was established when the Belgian franc was included in the composite (1974–1980) and when the U.K. pound sterling was traded in a regular and in an "investment currency" market (1974–1979). Dual exchange markets are explained in Chapter 11, *infra*, pages 551–554.

rates in column 3; that is, column 2 divided by column 3, *except* for the pound sterling, for which the figures in columns 2 and 3 are multiplied. On April 1, 1981, the SDR was equal to U.S.$1.19858.

Since all of the currencies in the composite are convertible into the U.S. dollar, separate sets of calculations like that above for the U.S. dollar need not be made each day for each currency. Rather, for convenience, the Executive Board has decided that the U.S. dollar equivalent of the SDR shall be calculated each day as in Table 4, and then the U.K. sterling equivalent, as an example, of one SDR is determined by applying the spot exchange rate between the dollar and sterling to the dollar equivalent of the SDR that was already calculated. Rule O-2(b) provides:

> The value of a currency other than the United States dollar in terms of the SDR shall be determined on the basis of the value of the United States dollar in terms of the SDR in accordance with (a) above [Rule O-2(a), note 57] and an exchange rate for that other currency determined as follows:
>
> (i)   for the currency of a member having an exchange market in which the Fund finds that a representative spot rate for the United States dollar can be readily ascertained, that representative rate;
>
> (ii)   for the currency of a member having an exchange market in which the Fund finds that a representative spot rate for the United States dollar cannot be readily ascertained but in which a representative spot rate can be readily ascertained for a currency as described in (i), the rate calculated by reference to the representative spot rate for that currency and the rate ascertained pursuant to (i) above for the United States dollar in terms of that currency;
>
> (iii) for the currency of any other member, a rate determined by the Fund.[62]

Rule O-2(c) provides that procedures to establish "representative rates" under Rule O-2(b), quoted above, shall be determined by the Fund in consultation with members.[63] In those consultations to date, members have insisted that the representative rates be taken from markets in their countries. A consequence is that, while the U.S. dollar–Deutsche mark rate used under Rule O-2(a) is normally taken from the London market, the dollar–mark rate used to determine the SDR–mark rate under Rule O-2(b) is taken from the Frankfurt market.

---

[62] Rule O-2(b) as amended April 1, 1978. *By-Laws, Rules and Regulations* (40th issue, 1983).
[63] Rule O-2(c) as amended April 1, 1978. *By-Laws, Rules and Regulations* (40th issue, 1983).

While the dollar–French franc rate used under Rule O-2(a) is normally taken from the London market, the dollar–franc rate used to determine the SDR–franc rate under Rule O-2(b) is taken from the Paris market. While the dollar–yen rate used under Rule O-2(a) is normally taken from the London market, the dollar–yen rate used to determine the SDR–yen rate under Rule O-2(b) is taken from the Tokyo market with a very significant time difference.[64] Remember that the SDR rate determined for a currency will be operative for the day notwithstanding changes in the market.

The IMF should be urged to modify its practices under Rule O-2(b). The same Deutsche mark–dollar, French franc–dollar, Japanese yen–dollar, and U.K. sterling–dollar rates used under Rule O-2(a) to determine the SDR–dollar rate should also be used to calculate SDR rates against the four other currencies. This would avoid a consequence of the present practice of using different rates gathered at different times, which has meant that SDR transactions when translated into national currencies have not always been valued "equally," at least as a banker or economist would understand the word.[65]

One can understand the reluctance of members to have the Fund use rates in markets outside their territories to determine the value of the SDR in relation to their currencies. But, at least, the issuers of the five currencies used to value the SDR should be willing to tolerate this under Rule O-2(b) as well as Rule O-2(a) in the interest of the principle of equal value as well as simplicity.

The SDR rates for more than 40 currencies are made available to the public by the Fund each day. These rates are carried by several wire services on a daily basis and are published twice monthly in *IMF Survey.*

Rationale for the Present Principle/Method

The change to the present five-currency composite for valuing the special drawing right and the decision to use the same composite to determine the interest rate of the SDR was endorsed by the IMF's Interim Committee in April 1980.[66] The Executive Board's decisions to adopt the five-currency composite for

---

[64] For example, the Deutsche mark–dollar rate in London on January 2, 1981, used under Rule O-2(a) was 1.97400 while that in Frankfurt used under Rule O-2(b) was 1.9768. Because of time differences between London and Tokyo, the yen–dollar rates under Rule O-2(a) and Rule O-2(b) for the same day can differ significantly. On April 30, 1981, the date of Table 4, the yen–dollar rate in London used under Rule O-2(a) was 215.13 while the Tokyo rate used under Rule O-2(b) was 215.00.

Not only are the rates under Rules O-2(a) and O-2(b) taken from different markets and often at different times, the methods of ascertaining the rates vary from country to country. For some countries the Fund has agreed that the representative rate under Rule O-2(b) is the middle rate between buying and selling rates at a particular point in time during the day, in others the middle rate between the high and the low for the day as a whole, in others the last transaction before the close, and in others some other criterion. Normally the rate is ascertained by the central bank of the country and transmitted by it to the Fund.

[65] See Article XIX, section 7, which states the principle of "same value" which the Fund is to apply.

[66] Paragraph 7 of the Press Communiqué of the Interim Committee, April 25, 1980. IMF, *Annual Report, 1980,* p. 154 at p. 157.

valuing the SDR and to use that composite to determine the interest rate were made in September 1980, and became effective January 1, 1981.[67]

The change in the method of valuing the SDR effective January 1, 1981, reduced the number of currencies in the composite from sixteen to five—the currencies issued by the five IMF members having the largest exports of goods and services during the five-year period 1975–1979.[68] Because the five currencies in the present composite are widely traded in the financial markets (and all the rates for calculating the SDR's value, at least in relation to the dollar and sterling, can normally be obtained in the London market) the present valuation method has made it possible for commercial banks and other public and private participants in the financial markets to replicate the SDR in the exchange markets. The same five-currency composite is used by the IMF to determine the interest rate on the SDR. This simplification has some importance. The principle/method of valuing the SDR and the interest rate together determine the effective yield of the SDR from an economic perspective.

It was believed that the new, simpler method of valuing the SDR and unifying the method of valuation and method of interest calculation would enhance the attractiveness of the SDR as an international reserve asset. The new method of valuation was expected to encourage the use of the SDR as a unit of account in which obligations could be expressed by both public institutions and private firms. This has proved to be the case,[69] in part because it is now possible, as noted, for commercial banks, by packaging the five currencies in the same proportions stated in Rule O-1 and holding them in the same interest-bearing form as stated in Rule T-1, to replicate the market performance of the SDR even though they cannot hold SDRs directly.

It was also believed that by eliminating eleven currencies from the basket, most of which IMF members would not wish to hold in their monetary reserves, the newly valued SDR would more closely replicate most countries' desired composition of reserves than the former valuation. Thus, countries would find it more attractive than previously to substitute SDRs or SDR-denominated obligations for national currencies in their reserve holdings.

Some additional benefits have flowed from the present method of valuing the SDR. The five currencies are those that the Fund has determined to be "freely usable currencies"—currencies that have a special role under the Articles; and presently no other currencies enjoy this status.[70] Active forward exchange markets exist in each of the five currencies, which was not true for many of the other eleven currencies in the former composites. This makes it possible

---

[67] E.B. Decision No. 6631, *supra* note 54; and E.B. Decision No. 6632, *infra* note 104.

[68] IMF Press Release No. 80/66 issued September 18, 1980; *IMF Survey*, October 13, 1980, p. 297. In accordance with the principle of continuity of value, the new composite was fixed to exactly equal the former one on December 31, 1980. E.B. Decision No. 6631, *supra* note 54, paragraph 4.

[69] See Chapter 12, *infra*, pages 635–636.

[70] See pages 197–200, *infra*.

to calculate a forward value for the SDR. There is, however, no requirement in the September 1980 SDR-valuation decision that the currencies in the composite be "freely usable" or that forward markets exist for them. The stated criterion is simply that the composite be composed of five currencies issued by the five members having the largest share of exports of goods and services.[71]

The press release accompanying the September 1980 decision states that the relative weights of the five currencies in the composite were intended to "broadly reflect the relative importance of these currencies in international trade and finance, based on the value of the exports of goods and services of the members issuing these currencies and the amounts of their currency officially held by members of the Fund over the five years 1975–1979."[72] The agreed initial weights were converted into units of each of the five currencies, using London noon exchange rates averaged over a three-month period ended December 31, 1980.[73]

The September 1980 decision provides that the amount of each currency (not the percentage weighting) shown in Table 1 shall remain fixed until January 1, 1986.[74] The decision provides for the composite to be revised at that time.[75]

By providing for an adjustment to be made effective January 1, 1986, the Fund has not limited its authority to change the principle and/or method of valuing the SDR in the meantime in accordance with Article XV.[76] There is, however, a value to providing a measure of predictability about future changes and adjustments.

Legal Considerations Respecting Future Changes

The IMF Agreement in Article XV, Section 2, states:

> The method of valuation of the special drawing right shall be determined by the Fund by a seventy percent majority of the total voting power, provided, however, that an eighty-five percent majority of the total voting power shall be required for a change in the principle of

---

[71] IMF Press Release No. 80/66, *supra* note 68.

[72] IMF Press Release No. 80/66, *supra* note 68, p. 326. The phrase "broadly reflect" recognized that the weighting might not be exact. See Gold, *SDRs, Currencies, and Gold: Fifth Survey, supra* note 38, pp. 6–10.

[73] E.B. Decision No. 6631 and Decision No. 6708, *supra* note 54. See also *IMF Survey*, January 12, 1981, pp. 1 and 6.

[74] E.B. Decision No. 6631, *supra* note 54, paragraph 3.

[75] See further discussion at page 188, *infra*.

[76] Decision No. 5718 of March 1978, *supra* note 56, paragraphs 3 and 4, provided for an adjustment in that sixteen-currency composite, retaining a composite of sixteen currencies, to be made effective July 1, 1983. That decision did not prevent the Fund from subsequently superseding that decision by changing to a five-currency composite pursuant to E.B. Decision No. 6631 of September 1980, *supra* note 54.

valuation or a fundamental change in the application of the principle in effect.

Decision No. 6631 of September 1980 provides for the composite in terms of which the SDR is valued to be revised effective January 1, 1986, and on the first day of each subsequent five-year period.[77]

Under the present system, during the period a particular SDR valuation composite is in effect, no adjustment is made in the amounts of any of the currency components for currency devaluations or revaluations or for depreciations or appreciations of currencies in the exchange markets. If the market value of one currency in relation to the others in the "basket" declines, the market value of other currencies relative to the depreciated currency will increase. The normal effect of a depreciation will be to lower the number of SDRs that a unit of the depreciated currency will purchase and to raise slightly the number of SDRs that a unit of each of the other currencies in the basket will purchase. Suppose the value of one of the currencies appreciates. This will normally result in a slight decline in the market exchange rate between each of the other currencies and the SDR. That is, a unit of each of these other currencies will be

---

[77] E.B. Decision No. 6631, *supra* note 54, paragraph 3. The decision states the following "principles" to be applied in making the revisions:

3. The list of the currencies that determine the value of the special drawing right, and the amounts of these currencies, shall be revised with effect on January 1, 1986 and on the first day of each subsequent period of five years in accordance with the following principles, unless the Fund decides otherwise in connection with a revision:

(a) The currencies determining the value of the special drawing right shall be the currencies of the five members whose exports of goods and services during the five-year period ending 12 months before the effective date of the revision had the largest value, provided that a currency shall not replace another currency included in the list at the time of the determination unless the value of the exports of goods and services of the issuer of the former currency during the relevant period exceeds that of the issuer of the latter currency by at least one per cent.

(b) The amounts of the five currencies referred to in (a) above shall be determined on the last working day preceding the effective date of the relevant revision in a manner that will ensure that, at the average exchange rates for the three-month period ending on that date, the shares of these currencies in the value of the special drawing right correspond to percentage weights for these currencies, which shall be established for each currency in accordance with (c) below.

(c) The percentage weights shall reflect the value of the balances of that currency held at the end of each year by the monetary authorities of other members and the value of the exports of goods and services of the issuer of the currency over the relevant five-year period referred to in (a) above, in a manner that would maintain broadly the relative significance of the factors that underlie the percentage weights in paragraph (2) above. The percentage weights shall be rounded to the nearest 1 per cent or as may be convenient.

4. The determination of the amounts of the currencies in accordance with . . . (3) above shall be made in a manner that will ensure that the value of the special drawing right in terms of currencies on the last working day preceding the five-year period for which the determination is made will be the same under the valuation in effect before and after revision.

equivalent to slightly less SDRs. No change is made in the quantity of any of the currencies in the basket.[78] A consequence is that over time it is possible for a strong currency to become dominant in the basket. Note that the amount of Deutsche mark in the basket was reduced from 0.38 to 0.32 effective July 1978 while the relative initial weightings in 1974 and 1978 remained the same. The amount of sterling had to be increased in 1978 even though its relative weighting was to be less than in 1974 at the outset of the former basket.[79]

As noted at the beginning of this section, Article XV, Section 2, gives the Fund unlimited authority to change the principle and method of valuing the SDR provided that decisions are taken by the required special majorities. Any future change in the "principle" of valuing the SDR, or any fundamental change in the application of the principle then in effect, requires a decision by an 85 percent majority of the total voting power of the members of the Fund (whether or not members of the SDR Department) and an 85 percent majority of the total voting power of participants in the SDR Department.[80]

A change in valuation that does not involve a change in the principle of valuation of the SDR nor a fundamental change in the application of the principle then in effect, but only involves a change in the "method" of valuation, is determined by a double 70 percent majority of the total voting power of all IMF members and of SDR Department participants.[81] These high majorities were judged necessary because of the importance these decisions can have. The value determines the basis upon which the SDR can be exchanged for a currency. Further, the SDR is the basic unit of account for all transactions and operations of the International Monetary Fund.[82] Finally, the Articles of Agreement contemplate that the SDR shall become the principal reserve asset in the international monetary system.[83]

The Articles of Agreement themselves and the *Report on the Second*

---

[78] The Committee of Twenty in 1973 and 1974 considered and rejected methods for adjusting the "basket" for currency depreciations, such as increasing the number of units of a depreciated currency in the basket or decreasing the number of units in the basket of a currency that appreciates. The Committee also rejected a proposal designed to connect the value of the currency components and gold. A method of augmenting the purchasing power of the SDR was also rejected by the Committee. This would have involved introducing regular, small, and uniform increases in the amount of each currency in the basket. Thus over time the SDR would buy more currencies. Thus the purchasing power in goods and services of the SDR could be maintained in a situation where the countries whose currencies make up the basket experience domestic price inflation. The effect of the resulting appreciation in the capital value of the SDR on its total yield could be offset by a corresponding reduction in the interest rate that the SDR would carry. These alternatives to the use of fixed amounts of currencies are discussed in *International Monetary Reform: Documents of the Committee of Twenty, supra* note 45, pp. 15–16 and 21 (Outline of Reform, paragraphs 26 and 38) and pp. 43–45 (Annex 9). See also Polak, *Valuation and Rate of Interest of the SDR, supra* 45.

[79] Compare Tables 2 and 3, *supra*.

[80] Article XV, section 2; and Article XXI(a)(iii). See Chapter 1, *supra,* pages 32–35, respecting voting generally.

[81] Article XV, section 2.

[82] Article III, section 1; and Article V, sections 10 and 11.

[83] Article VIII, section 7; and Article XXII.

Amendment do not provide guidance for differentiating between "principle" and "method." Where there is a consensus on the classification of the proposed change, a decision on which majority is required can probably be taken by a simple majority of the weighted votes cast.[84] The interpretative procedures of Article XXIX are available should there be disagreement concerning the meaning of the words used in Article XV, Section 2.

It is submitted that a proposed change should be judged in relation to the system from which a change is being made. The change in the composition of the composite of currencies used to value the SDR, that became effective July 1, 1978, realigned the weights in accordance with export data while continuing to use shares of world exports as primary criteria for selection of currencies and their weighting. The number of currencies remained the same. It is submitted that this change involved a change in the "method" of valuation when seen in relation to the prior system in effect from July 1974. The matter is not free from doubt because the 1978 decision introduced data on amounts of currencies held in reserves of other countries as an additional criterion which might arguably be seen as involving a change that was one of principle. The Fund's *Annual Report* used the word "method" to characterize the change.[85]

A more difficult case to judge was the change approved in September 1980 which established the present five–currency composite in use since January 1, 1981.[86] The memorandum prepared by the Legal Department to aid the Executive Board in determining, prior to the vote, whether the change was one of "principle" or "method" has not been released. However, Sir Joseph Gold, retired General Counsel who served as a consultant to the Fund at the time of the change, has discussed the issue. He has argued that the change was one in method and not principle and has given the following reasons:

> The smaller of the two special majorities was sufficient for the [1980] decision on the second revised basket and on the criteria for future changes in the valuation basket, notwithstanding the reduction in number of currencies from 16 to 5 and in the representativeness of the basket. No change in principle was involved because valuation continues to be based on a basket of specified amounts of specified cur-

[84] See *Report on Second Amendment, supra* note 24, part 2, chapter Q, section 1; and Joseph Gold, *Voting Majorities in the Fund: Effects of Second Amendment of the Articles* (IMF Pamphlet Series no. 20; Washington, 1977), p. 31.

[85] IMF, *Annual Report, 1978,* p. 56. On March 31, 1978, the Executive Board adopted decision No. 5718, *supra* note 56, which provided for the change in the SDR valuation composite that became effective July 1, 1978. The decision was adopted the day before the Second Amendment entered into force. Because this action was taken under the old Articles it did not require a special majority. It was, thus, not necessary to decide whether the decision made a change in the "method" of valuing the SDR that today would require a double 70 percent majority of the total voting power of IMF members and SDR Department participants or a change in the "principle" of valuation that would require an 85 percent majority.

[86] E.B. Decision No. 6631, *supra* note 54.

rencies. The same criteria were applied for the weighting of currencies in the basket. . . . The value of the SDR in terms of currencies
in general was unlikely to be sharply different as a result of the
change.

For the smaller special majority to apply, it was necessary to
find not only that there was no change in the principle of valuation but
also that there was no fundamental change in the application of the
principle in effect [since July 1, 1978]. The considerations that had
led to the principle in effect were respected in the second revision,
which meant that a finding could be made that no fundamental change
was being made in the application of that principle.[87]

Sir Joseph has made the issue look a little too simple. While Decision No.
6631[88] and the press release that accompanied it[89] indicated that the five currencies were chosen only because the issuing countries had the largest exports of
goods and services during the period 1975–1979 and were the currencies in the
basket already used to determine the interest rate on the SDR, there appear to
have been additional reasons for the selection of the five currencies. An important consideration was that active forward exchange markets as well as spot
markets exist for the currencies.[90] While it has been said that the fact that the
five currencies were "freely usable" currencies under Article XXX(f), and
thus enjoyed a special status under the Articles, was "not a consideration" in
setting the number of currencies in the revised basket at five,[91] this was probably too strong a statement. Certainly there appears to be no doubt that the Executive Board (especially executive directors representing industrialized countries) wanted to prune out of the basket currencies that were not widely used to
make payments for international transactions and widely traded in the principal
financial markets—the very criteria the Fund applies in designating freely usable currencies.

If the primary purpose for setting the number at five and selecting the particular five currencies was to assure identity of the SDR valuation basket and
the SDR interest-rate basket, to assure that the currencies were widely used for
making payments in international transactions, and to assure that the currencies
were actively traded in the principal financial markets both spot and forward,
then the use of trade data as the sole official basis for selection may have been
simply a happy coincidence that gave the appearance of continuity to the 1980
decision compared to the 1978 one. Thus, on a narrow technical view the
change was one of "method" and not "principle." But a consequence is that

---

[87] Gold, *SDRs, Currencies, and Gold: Fifth Survey, supra* note 38, p. 11.
[88] Note 54, *supra.*
[89] Note 68, *supra.*
[90] Gold, *SDRs, Currencies, and Gold: Fifth Survey, supra* note 38, p. 3.
[91] *Idem,* at p. 7.

the criteria stated in the 1980 decision to determine the revision in the basket effective January 1, 1986,[92] are not the only, nor even the most important, criteria that in fact determined the 1980 decision. It is desirable that the official rationale advanced for a decision as important as the 1980 decision on the valuation of the SDR match the true underlying, and here completely legitimate, reasons. The change which resulted from the 1980 decision probably should have been characterized as one of principle. In any event, the change effective January 1, 1981, was a worthwhile one.

A future change that would value the SDR in relation to a commodity, group of commodities, price index, a single currency, or a composite of currencies selected on a basis other than the shares of the issuing countries in world trade would, it is submitted, be a change from the ''principle'' now said to be in use.

Another question is whether implementation of the provisions in the 1980 decision relating to changes to be made effective January 1, 1986,[93] will require a 70 percent special majority, as a change in ''method'' of valuing the SDR, or only a simple majority, as a mere implementation of the 1980 decision. The language ''in a manner that would maintain broadly the relative significance of the factors that underlie the percentage weights''[94] would suggest that a measure of discretion is to be applied.

The interest rate applicable to the SDR and the principle/method of valuation together determine the effective yield of the SDR from an economic perspective. Interest rates are discussed in the next section.

Because the principle and method of valuing the SDR can be changed by decisions of the Fund taken by special majorities, public and private parties to agreements and contracts which make reference to the SDR need to recognize the possibility of changes. Techniques by which parties to agreements and contracts can deal with this matter, while important, are beyond the scope of this book.[95]

Notwithstanding the IMF's authority, if the majorities specified in Article XV are obtained to change the principle and/or method of valuing the special drawing right, modifications in the value of the SDR should be approached by the Fund with caution. Those who hold and use SDRs and SDR-denominated obligations should be allowed to anticipate a measure of predictability and continuity in the valuation.

---

[92] See note 77, *supra.*
[93] Provisions of E.B. Decision No. 6631 quoted in note 77, *supra.*
[94] *Idem,* at paragraph 3(c).
[95] See, however, Chapter 12, *infra,* pages 635–636. Some guidance is provided in Gold, *SDRs, Currencies, and Gold: Fifth Survey, supra* note 38, pp. 26–59; and Gold, *Floating Currencies, Gold and SDRs, supra* note 47.

Interest, Charges, and Assessments

Charges (like interest) are periodically paid to the Special Drawing Rights Department on net cumulative allocations of SDRs.[96] "Net cumulative allocation" means the total of all special drawing rights allocated to a participant by the Fund minus the participant's share of any special drawing rights cancelled by the Fund under a decision, should such a decision ever be taken, to reduce the volume of outstanding SDRs.[97]

Interest is paid by the Special Drawing Rights Department on holdings of SDRs. The rates of charges–debits and interest–credits are equal.[98]

Because SDR allocations are made only to participants, only participants pay charges. Because interest is credited on holdings, interest is periodically credited to participants, other holders,[99] and the IMF's General Department[100] based on their holdings. Thus, for a participant with holdings that match net cumulative allocations there is no net interest debit or credit. Participants with SDR holdings above net cumulative allocations receive a net interest credit, while participants with holdings below net cumulative allocations have a net interest (charges) debit. Interest is credited and charges are debited in SDRs.[101]

The rate of interest on the SDR is determined by decisions taken by a 70 percent majority of the total voting power.[102] It would appear that the interest rate on the SDR is considered together with remuneration on creditor positions in the General Resources Account, so that the resulting decision is a matter that pertains both to the Special Drawing Rights Department and to the General Department, thus requiring a 70 percent majority of the total voting power of participants and a 70 percent majority of the total voting power of all IMF members.[103]

The interest rate is intended to compensate a country or institution for holding SDRs as compared to earning interest on a foreign-currency holding which it could obtain in exchange for SDRs. The interest rate is a sensitive matter that can affect the attitude of countries toward holding and using SDRs. The effective yield on the SDR must be high enough to make it attractive to acquire and hold, but not so high as to make countries reluctant to use SDRs when in deficit.[104]

---

[96] Article XX, sections 2, 3, and 5.

[97] Article XXX(e). "Net cumulative allocation" does not include SDRs transferred to a participant nor interest credited to a participant—only SDRs *allocated* to it.

[98] Article XX, sections 1, 3, and 5.

[99] See pages 175–176, *supra.*

[100] See pages 205–209, *infra,* regarding the General Resources Account as a holder of SDRs.

[101] See generally Article XX; and Rules T-1 and T-2, *By-Laws, Rules and Regulations* (40th issue, 1983).

[102] Article XX, section 3.

[103] See Article XXI(a). The remuneration rate in the General Resources Account (Chapter 6, page 229) is related to the SDR interest rate. The interest rate affects the economic value of the SDR which is the Fund's unit of account.

[104] Polak, *Valuation and Rate of Interest of the SDR, supra* note 45, analyzes issues surrounding the choice of an interest rate. Solomon, *supra* note 7, at pp. 246 and 254–55, comments on discussions in the Committee of Twenty about the SDR's interest rate.

Since January 1975, the interest rate has been adjusted on the basis of formulas, changed from time to time,

There are also assessments for the operation of the SDR Department itself. The General Department handles the administration of the SDR Department. The Fund from time to time levies assessments on participants to reimburse its expenses. These expenses are levied in SDRs and are based upon each participant's net cumulative allocation.[105]

Transactions and Operations
Transfer of SDRs Using IMF Designation Procedure

From a legal perspective the basic transaction in the Special Drawing Rights Department is the transfer of SDRs from one participant to another in exchange for a freely usable currency. A participant wishing to exchange SDRs that it holds for a national currency has the right, under Section 2(a) of Article XIX, to request the Fund to arrange the transfer. The notice to the Fund by the participant (hereinafter "transferor" of SDRs) is typically in the following form:

1. PLEASE ARRANGE TO CREDIT ACCOUNT OF [OFFICIAL AGENCY] WITH [NAME AND LOCATION OF BANK WHERE ACCOUNT MAINTAINED] WITH [NAME OF FREELY USABLE CURRENCY DESIRED][106] EQUIVALENT TO SDR [AMOUNT].

2. WE STATE THAT THIS INTENDED USE OF SDRS IS IN ACCORDANCE WITH ARTICLE XIX, SECTIONS 2(A) and 3(A).

[TEST NUMBER]
[FISCAL AGENCY][107]

The purpose of the reference in paragraph 2 of the cable to Article XIX, Section 2(a), is to indicate that the transferor is invoking its legal right under

related to short-term interest rates of the five currencies in terms of which the SDR is now valued. In September 1980 the Executive Board decided that effective January 1, 1981, the formula for determining the interest rate of the SDR would be designed to replicate the short-term interest to be earned on holding the five currencies in the relative portions of their weights in the "basket." E.B. Decision No. 6632 -(80/145)S(September 17, 1980); IMF, *Annual Report, 1981*, p. 143. Since May 1, 1981, the rate of interest has been set at 100 percent of the market rate calculated for the basket. Rule T-1 as amended effective May 1, 1981. *By-Laws, Rules and Regulations* (40th issue, 1983). For background see Gold, *SDRs, Currencies, and Gold: Fifth Survey, supra* note 38, pp. 14–20.

[105] Article XVI, section 2; Article XX, sections 4 and 5; and Rule T-2, *By-Laws, Rules and Regulations* (40th issue, 1983).

[106] A transferor is entitled to receive a "freely usable currency," as explained in the next section, but not a particular freely usable currency. However, knowledge of the currency desired may affect the Fund's decision on the participant(s) to be designated to accept the SDRs and provide a freely usable currency.

[107] This standard form of cable is set forth in IMF, *User's Guide to the SDR, supra* note 40, p. 30. This cable form is in accordance with Rule P-1(a), *By-Laws, Rules and Regulations* (40th issue, 1983).

that section to exchange SDRs for a freely usable currency and is not simply requesting the Fund to use its good offices to try to arrange a transfer.[108]

The statement in paragraph 2 of the transferor's cable that the intended use of SDRs is in accordance with Article XIX, Section 3(a), is required by a rule of the Fund.[109] Section 3(a) states that a transferor of SDRs in a transaction by designation is "expected" to use SDRs "only if it has a need because of its balance of payments or its reserve position or developments in its reserves." The section further states that a transferor is "expected," except in special cases, not to use SDRs for the "sole purpose of changing the composition of its reserves."[110]

The definition of "need" is the same as in Article V, Section 3(b)(ii), relating to drawings in the General Resources Account.[111] However, unlike drawings in the credit tranches of the General Resources Account, the Articles do not require that a transferor of SDRs make a "representation" of need that is subject to prior review.[112] The Fund is required to designate a transferee and allow the SDR transaction to proceed even if the transferor is not fulfilling "expectations."[113] A transferor can draw its holdings of SDRs down to zero.[114]

Upon receipt of the proper notice (as set forth above) from the transferor,

---

[108] If a participant is not entitled to make a request under Article XIX, section 2(a), because for example it does not have "need" as explained later in the text or because it desires a particular currency other than one designated freely usable, it may request the Fund to assist it in arranging a transaction by agreement, as explained at pages 201–203, *infra*.

[109] Rule P-4, *By-Laws, Rules and Regulations* (40th issue, 1983). Alternatively, the transferor may state that it is relying on a waiver under Article XIX, section 3(c).

[110] Article XIX, section 3(a). See waiver provision in Article XIX, section 3(c).

[111] The concept of need is discussed in detail in Chapter 6, *infra*, pages 239–241.

[112] See Chapter 6, *infra*, pages 232–235, 239–240, and 243–247.

[113] Article XIX, section 3(b). Whether the use of SDRs would be conditioned by a "representation" of balance-of-payments need was much discussed in 1967 by those who negotiated the original provisions respecting special drawing rights. See *IMF History 1966–71, supra* note 7, vol. 1, pp. 149, 160, 182–84, and 242–43.

The Fund's practice is to examine recent developments in a transferor's balance-of-payments and reserve position immediately after the SDR transaction has been completed to ascertain that the expectation of need has been met. The Fund may make a representation to the transferor if in the Fund's judgment the transaction was not justified by need. Precedents were established in 1971. Israel and Turkey in that year used SDRs to obtain currencies and it turned out that they did not have balance-of-payments need to use the SDRs in the light of developments in their gross reserves at the time. Their judgment errors were not intentional. With the approval of the Executive Board, they reversed the transactions by acquiring special drawing rights from the General Account (now General Resources Account). In subsequent similar cases participants have, alternatively, been placed at the top of designation lists to be transferees of SDRs. IMF, *Annual Report, 1971*, p. 39; *IMF History 1966–71*, vol. 1, p. 243; IMF, *User's Guide to the SDR, supra* note 40, pp. 18–19. A transferor that persists in using SDRs for the sole purpose of altering the composition of its reserves may be suspended from using SDRs it acquires in the future. Article XXIII, section 2(b).

[114] A participant can use all of its special drawing rights. There is no obligation to hold back any percentage. Indeed, on April 30, 1974, South Africa held only 465,000 SDRs out of a total net allocation of 88,920,000. This was 0.5 percent of the cumulative net allocation. IMF, *Annual Report, 1974*, p. 85. As of January 31, 1977, Sudan had reduced its holdings to zero. IMF, *Financial Statement of the Special Drawing Account*, for quarter ended January 31, 1977. However, there may be (but presently is not) a reconstitution obligation. The IMF has authority to require participants to maintain at least a certain average proportion over time. See pages 210–212, *infra*.

the Fund is obligated to designate another participant in the SDR Department (hereinafter "transferee-designee") to accept the SDRs and provide an equivalent amount of a freely usable currency.[115] The obligation of the transferee-designee is to accept the SDRs from the transferor and to provide the transferor with a freely usable currency in an amount equivalent to the exchange value of the SDRs it receives.[116]

The form of the Fund's cable to the transferee-designee, assuming U.S. dollars have been requested by the transferor and the Fund knows that the participant it intends to designate as transferee normally provides dollars as the freely usable currency in response to designation, is as follows:

1. UNDER CURRENT SDR DESIGNATION PLAN [PARTICIPANT] IS HEREBY DESIGNATED IN AMOUNT OF SDR [AMOUNT].

2. AT RATE OF SDR [RATE] PER U.S. DOLLAR ON [DATE], THIS AMOUNT IS EQUIVALENT TO U.S. DOLLARS [AMOUNT]. PLEASE PLACE THIS AMOUNT OF U.S. DOLLARS AT THE FUND'S DISPOSAL AT FEDERAL RESERVE BANK OF NEW YORK, NEW YORK,[117] VALUE [DATE] UNDER CABLE ADVICE TO THE FUND.

3. THE SDR ACCOUNT OF [PARTICIPANT] WILL BE CREDITED WITH SDR [AMOUNT] ON DATE CURRENCY IS PROVIDED.

[TEST NUMBER]
TREASURER'S DEPARTMENT
INTERFUND[118]

Article XIX, Section 5, Schedule F to the Articles, and plans adopted by the Executive Board pursuant to Rule P-5 provide guidelines to the Fund in deciding which of all the participants shall be designated to accept the SDRs in the particular case. These guidelines will be reviewed later in this chapter.[119] For the moment, let us simply assume that the Fund has designated a participant to accept the SDRs (the "transferee"). It should be noted that a transferee-designee cannot refuse that designation, unless its holding of SDRs following

---

[115] Article XIX, sections 3(b) and 5(a). See also Rules P-1(b) and P-2 *By-Laws, Rules and Regulations* (40th issue, 1983).

[116] Article XIX, section 4. See also Rules P-2 and P-3, *By-Laws, Rules and Regulations, idem.*

[117] The currency is to be provided at an official agency of the issuer of the currency. Rule P-2, *By-Laws, Rules and Regulations, idem.*

[118] This standard form of the Fund's cable is set forth in IMF, *User's Guide to the SDR, supra* note 40, p. 31.

[119] At pages 210–211, *infra.*

the transaction would be in excess of 300 percent of its net cumulative allocation.[120]

The obligation of the transferee-designee, as stated above, is to accept the SDRs from the transferor and to provide to the transferor a "freely usable currency" in an amount "equivalent" to the exchange value of the SDRs it receives. Section 4 of Article XIX specifies that the currency shall be "freely usable" and Article XXX(f) defines that concept; Section 2 of Article XIX states that the amount provided shall be "equivalent"; and Section 7 of that article is the authority for the use of market exchange rates. We shall explore each of these aspects in turn.

Tables showing the use and receipt of SDRs in transactions with designation for each participant during the fiscal year are published annually in the IMF's *Annual Report*. The report also includes commentary.[121] Quarterly data are published in *Financial Statements* issued by the Fund.

Obligation to Provide a "Freely Usable Currency"

A participant transferring SDRs to a transferee designated by the Fund is entitled to obtain a "freely usable currency." The designee is under a duty to provide such a currency.[122] "Freely usable currency" is not a general description. It is a term specially defined in Article XXX(f) of the IMF Agreement to mean "a member's currency that *the Fund determines* (i) is, in fact, widely used to make payments for international transactions, and (ii) is widely traded in the principal exchange markets." [emphasis added] The 1976 Executive Board report on the Second Amendment to the IMF Articles stated:

> The Fund will apply this definition [of "freely usable currency" stated in Article XXX(f)] and establish which currencies are to be deemed freely usable for the purposes of the Articles. The Fund would be able to add to or subtract from the list should changing circumstances make these modifications necessary. It can be expected

---

[120] Article XIX, section 4. See the text accompanying note 97, *supra*, for the definition of "net cumulative allocation."

If a participant believes it should not have been designated by the Fund as transferee, the procedure is for it nevertheless to provide the currency and accept the SDRs. It then requests the Executive Board to review the matter. This problem will, however, normally not arise, because the participant will have previously requested the Executive Board to review its inclusion in the current designation plan. See Rule P-5, *By-Laws, Rules and Regulations* (40th issue, 1983).

A participant, although not required to accept designation to receive SDRs above 300 percent of net cumulative allocation, may voluntarily agree to do so. If the participant makes such an agreement in advance, the acceptance is obligatory up to the agreed amount. There is no defined upper limit in the Articles on the amount of SDRs a participant may choose to hold. Internal legislation in some countries places restraints or prohibitions on the acquisition of SDRs above 300 percent of net cumulative allocations. See Surr, *supra* note 21, at p. 45.

[121] IMF, *Annual Report, 1980*, at p. 92, presents a ten-year summary table for 1970–80.

[122] Article XIX, section 4(a).

that the Fund would consult a member before placing its currency on the list or removing it, but the final decision would rest with the Fund.[123]

The IMF's General Counsel has said that the criterion of "wide use" means actual use in trade, service, and capital transactions by transacting parties other than the issuer. Data on the member's share of total world exports, the volume of its currency in the monetary reserves of other countries, and the number of members holding the currency in their reserves may permit, but not compel, an inference that a currency is widely or not widely used. The criterion of "wide trading" in the principal exchange markets does not require trading in all the principal exchange markets. A requirement that the currency be traded in all the principal markets was proposed and rejected when the provision was negotiated.[124]

The definition of "freely usable currency" places primary emphasis on the Fund's determination. The criteria the Fund is directed to apply have factual references—wide use in payments for international transactions and wide trading in the principal financial markets. The definition makes no reference to formal aspects of convertibility or freedom from exchange restrictions.[125] These matters do affect wide use and wide trading and, thus, presumably can be taken into account when the Fund makes a determination that a particular national currency is a "freely usable currency." Also, just as the Fund can determine that a currency is a "freely usable currency," it can also determine that it has ceased to be so.

At the time the provision was negotiated, in the mid-1970s, there was no doubt that, at least, the United States dollar would be placed on the list of freely

---

[123] *Report on Second Amendment, supra* note 24, part 2, chapter D, section 14. See also Rule O-3; *By-Laws, Rules and Regulations* (40th issue, 1983).

[124] Joseph Gold, *Use, Conversion, and Exchange of Currency Under the Second Amendment of the Fund's Articles* (IMF Pamphlet Series no. 23; Washington, 1978), p. 62.

[125] Prior to the Second Amendment of the IMF Articles, a transferor of SDRs to a transferee designated by the Fund was entitled to receive what was then called "currency convertible in fact." Old Article XXV, section 4, *first.* Article XXXII(b), *first,* defined that term by reference to procedures for converting the currency and the currency's freedom from restrictions. The Fund determined that the U.S. dollar, U.K. pound sterling, and French franc were each convertible in fact. These were the primary convertible-in-fact currencies because the three issuing countries, in addition to accepting the convertibility obligations of Article VIII, sections 2, 3, and 4, had consented for the currencies to be so named and had established procedures whereby balances of each of these three currencies obtained in transactions involving SDRs could be exchanged for either of the other two currencies at representative exchange rates under old Article XXV, section 8, *first.* The Fund determined that the Belgian franc, Deutsche mark, Italian lira, Mexican peso, and Netherlands guilder were currencies convertible in fact, within a second definitional category, since the issuing countries accepted the obligations of Article VIII and balances of each of the currencies were convertible into at least one of the first category currencies (U.S. dollar, U.K. pound sterling, or French franc) at representative exchange rates under old Article XXV, section 8, *first.* Apparently no other countries requested the Fund to recognize their currencies as convertible-in-fact under old Article XXXII(b), *first.* See Gold, *Use, Conversion, and Exchange of Currency, supra* note 124, pp. 45–55 and 63–68; and *IMF History 1966–71, supra* note 7, vol. 1, pp. 168–70 and 223–26, and the Executive Board decisions there cited which appear in vol. 2, pp. 220–23. See also old Rules O-1 and O-2 adopted September 18, 1969, *idem.,* vol. 2, pp. 186–87.

usable currencies. The Fund has determined, in accordance with Article XXX(f), that the following currencies are freely usable: United States dollar, Deutsche mark, French franc, Japanese yen, and United Kingdom pound sterling.[126] The Fund has authority to add currencies to or delete them from the list. The IMF's General Counsel has argued the merits of a short list:

> [A] narrow definition and a short list of freely usable currencies would increase the likelihood that a purchaser receiving a freely usable currency in a purchase from the Fund would be able to use the currency for its purposes without the need for exchanging it, and that, if an exchange were required, it could be made in a broad market in which there was the reasonable assurance that even a large transaction would not have an adverse effect on the rate of exchange. The interests of members could be safeguarded by basing the conclusion that such an assurance existed in relation to a currency on factors that included the volume of trading in the currency, the extent to which it was held in the working balances of foreign commercial banks, the existence of forward markets for the currency, the availability of daily spot quotations, and the narrowness of the spread between buying and selling rates.[127]

It happens that the five currencies presently designated as freely usable are the same five currencies presently in the composite used to value the special drawing right, but there is no legal requirement that this be the case.[128]

If the transferor of SDRs desires a specific currency, it will indicate that in its request to the Fund, but the transferee designated by the Fund to accept the SDRs is not required to satisfy the request even if the currency requested is of its own issue. The transferee-designee's obligation is to deliver a "freely usable currency"—which can be any currency (or combination of currencies) of its choosing that the Fund has determined meets the test. If the transferor and transferee agree, however, a currency that is not designated as freely usable may be provided in exchange for the SDRs.[129] If the transferor obtains one freely usable currency and needs another currency, it is submitted that the issuer of the currency obtained by the transferor and the issuer of the currency desired have collaboration obligations to do what reasonably can be expected of them to assist the transferor to obtain the currency desired.[130]

---

[126] E.B. Decision No. 5719 -(78/46) (March 31, 1978); IMF, *Annual Report, 1978*, p. 127; *Selected Decisions* (10th issue, 1983), p. 301.

[127] Gold, *Use, Conversion, and Exchange of Currency, supra* note 124, p. 60.

[128] See pages 190–192, *supra*.

[129] See discussion of transfers by agreement at pages 201–203, *infra*.

[130] Article XXII. See pages 200–201 and note 134, *infra*. If the Fund knows the currency desired by the transferor of SDRs, it may take that into account in selecting the transferee-designee. See notes 106 and 108, *supra*. See generally IMF, *User's Guide to the SDR, supra* note 40, pp. 19–20 and 30–32.

Normally the currency will be delivered in the form of bank balances. The Fund has required that currency balances be provided through an official agency of the country that is the issuer of the currency.[131] A participant, say Brazil, designated to be a transferee of SDRs cannot simply deliver to the transferor of SDRs ownership of a Eurodollar deposit with a London bank or even a dollar deposit with a New York commercial bank. Brazilian authorities must first move their dollar deposits to a U.S. Federal Reserve Bank. Brazilian authorities then place the dollar deposit with the Federal Reserve at the disposal of the Fund for transfer to the transferor of the SDRs.

A transferee that fails to fulfill its obligations to provide a freely usable currency will find that its use of SDRs will be suspended pursuant to Article XXIII, Section 2, unless the Fund otherwise decides.

Currency "Equivalent" in Amount

In SDR transactions by designation under Section 2(a) of Article XIX the transferor of SDRs is to receive "an equivalent amount" of currency. Section 7 of that article directs the Fund to adopt regulations to assure that a transferor using SDRs "shall receive the same value whatever currencies might be provided and whichever participants provide those currencies. . . ." This is called the "equal value" rule. The Fund has adopted regulations that use "representative" rates derived from actual exchange rates to measure equivalency of amount of a currency and the SDR.[132] SDR transactions between a participant and the IMF's General Resources Account also take place on the basis of representative rates whether the participant is the transferor or transferee.[133] The Fund regularly publishes the representative rates of the SDR against more than 40 currencies for each business day.

In an SDR transaction by designation, the transferee delivers a freely usable currency of its choice at the representative rate published by the Fund. If the freely usable currency received by the transferor of SDRs is not a currency it desires, it bears the burden of arranging at its own cost and risk for exchange of the currency for one it does desire. Although not required to do so, the Fund has provided assistance to participants in arranging an exchange if they have encountered difficulty in doing so.

Commenting on this matter, the Executive Board stated:

> It is hoped that participants in the Special Drawing Rights Department will collaborate regarding the exchange of freely usable curren-

---

[131] Rule P-2; *By-Laws, Rules and Regulations* (40th issue, 1983).

[132] See Rules O-2(a) and O-2(b) set forth and discussed at pages 181–185, *supra*. See also Rule P-2, *By-Laws, Rules and Regulations, idem.*

[133] Article V, sections 3(e), 3(f), 7(i), and 7(j). See also Chapter 6, *infra*, pages 225–227.

cies provided in transactions with designation, as would be normal practice pursuant to Article XXII.[134]

Normally, on the same day the Fund receives the transferor's request, the Fund's instructions go out to the transferee-designee. The critical date for applying the representative exchange rate is the date of dispatch of the Fund's designation instructions.[135] The value date (date of the actual exchange of SDRs for the currency) is the third business day after the date of dispatch of the Fund's instructions or as close thereto as is practicable.[136] The Fund records the transaction on the books of the Special Drawing Rights Department as of the date the currency is provided.[137] Section 3 of Article XVI provides that changes in holdings of SDRs take effect only when recorded by the Fund in the Special Drawing Rights Department.[138]

The transferee of SDRs is entitled to no special assistance in obtaining a freely usable currency to provide to the transferor. It must obtain the currency at its own cost and risk. It may provide a freely usable currency held in its reserves, it may make a drawing under a currency swap agreement, it may buy the currency in the market, or it may use some other technique. If the necessary conditions are met, it may draw the needed currency from the IMF's General Resources Account as explained in Chapter 6.

Transactions by Mutual Agreement

Participants in the Special Drawing Rights Department[139] may by mutual agreement make spot exchanges of special drawing rights for currency without the transferor's requesting the Fund to designate a transferee. The situations in which such voluntary transactions may take place have been greatly liberalized by the Second Amendment to the IMF Articles.[140]

---

[134] *Report on Second Amendment, supra* note 24, part 2, chapter Q, section 2(xi). If the exchange of the currency received for the currency desired can be made in the market, probably nothing further is required of the issuer of either currency. If the issuer of a currency to be exchanged requests that the exchange be made through its central bank, that request is to be respected and the bank for its part is required to make the exchange at the "same value" exchange rate as explained in the text. The United Kingdom, for example, has made a request that exchanges involving the pound sterling be made through the Bank of England. The current procedures among the issuers of the five currencies presently designated as freely usable respecting exchanges involving their currencies are summarized in IMF, *User's Guide to the SDR, supra* note 40, p. 92. See generally Gold, *Use, Conversion, and Exchange of Currency, supra* note 124, pp. 84–86.

[135] Rule O-6(b), *By-Laws, Rules and Regulations* (40th issue, 1983).

[136] Rule O-6(c), *By-Laws, Rules and Regulations, idem.*

[137] Rule P-9, *By-Laws, Rules and Regulations, idem.*

[138] The importance attached to this provision is noted in *IMF History, 1966–71, supra* note 7, vol. 1, p. 147.

[139] "Other holders" of SDRs may also engage in transactions by agreement. See pages 175–176, *supra.*

[140] Under old Article XXV, section 2(b), *first,* a participant could enter into a voluntary transaction in special drawing rights with another participant, without Fund designation, only if the transferor of SDRs was exchanging them for its own currency held by the transferee or if the Fund authorized the transaction.

In the original negotiations in the 1960s leading to the establishment of the SDR system there was much

Under Section 2(b) of present Article XIX, participants can enter into agreements to exchange SDRs for an equivalent amount of a currency without the necessity of Fund authorization and free of some requirements applicable to SDR transactions by designation. A participant using SDRs in a transaction by agreement with another participant is not subject to the expectation that it has balance-of-payments or reserve position "need" for currency which applies to transactions where the transferor requests the Fund to designate the transferee. A country can enter the transaction for the sole purpose of changing the composition of its reserves so long as the action is consistent with its general obligations under Article XXII.[141] This considerably enhances the freedom of participants to engage in SDR transactions. The transferee in a transaction by agreement is not required to provide a freely usable currency. It can provide any currency mutually agreeable. Section 2(b) transactions are particularly useful to a country wishing to redeem its own currency or to acquire a specific other currency.[142] Participants in transactions by agreement are, however, required to observe the rule that an "equivalent amount" of currency be provided, unless the Fund authorizes the parties to agree on a different exchange rate.[143] Joseph Gold has commented that the cautious attitude toward permitting departures from equal value even in consensual transactions "is inspired by concern that a market in SDRs in which their value would fluctuate might undermine the standing of the asset."[144]

There is an obligation on both parties to an SDR transaction by agreement to notify the Fund of the Section 2(b) transaction so that the Fund is informed of it and can record it in the books of the Special Drawing Rights Department. The Fund may require the participants to furnish it with such other information as it deems necessary.[145]

---

discussion of the degree of freedom to be allowed in the transfer of SDRs by mutual agreement versus guided transfers through IMF designation procedures. See *IMF History, 1966–71, supra* note 7, vol. 1, pp. 115–16, 129, 148, 160, and 184–85.

[141] See *Report on Second Amendment, supra* note 24, part 2, chapter Q, section 2 (viii). Section 3 of Article XIX applies only to section 2(a) transactions—i.e., transactions where the transferee is designated by the Fund. See page 195, *supra.*

[142] Transactions by agreement may be arranged directly by participants and other holders of SDRs with other participants and/or other holders, or the Fund's assistance may be requested in making the arrangements. See IMF, *User's Guide to the SDR, supra* note 40, pp. 7–8, 20–21, and 31–33.

[143] Article XIX, section 2(b). The Fund is empowered by section 7(b) of Article XIX to adopt policies by an 85 percent majority of the total voting power under which, in exceptional circumstances, it can permit transactions by agreement at other exchange rates. The application of such a policy requires a decision by a 70 percent majority of the total voting power. See also Gold, *Use, Conversion, and Exchange of Currency, supra* note 124, pp. 43–45 and 83–86.

[144] Gold, *Use, Conversion, and Exchange of Currency, idem,* p. 84.

[145] Article XVI, section 3. In all cases, the transferor of SDRs must inform the Fund immediately upon receipt of currency closing the transaction. The form of the cable notice is set forth in IMF, *User's Guide to the SDR, supra* note 40, p. 32.

The Fund records SDR transactions by agreement in the books of the Special Drawing Rights Department as of the date the currency is provided, the same as in transactions with designation. Rules P-8 and P-9, *By-*

If the Fund is of the view that any transaction by agreement prejudices the designation process (i.e., Section 2(a) transactions and the selection by the Fund of designees under Section 5), it may make a representation to the member or members. The Fund may also make a representation if it believes any transaction is inconsistent with a member's Article XXII duty to "collaborate" to facilitate the effective functioning of the SDR Department, the "proper use" of SDRs, and the aim of making the SDR the principal reserve asset of the international monetary system.[146]

Tables showing use and receipt of SDRs in transactions by agreement for each participant during the fiscal year are published annually in the IMF's *Annual Report*. The report also includes commentary.[147] Quarterly data are published in *Financial Statements* issued by the Fund.

Operations by Mutual Agreement

Under the Fund's Articles, "transactions" in SDRs means spot exchanges of SDRs for other monetary assets. Other uses of SDRs are described as "operations."[148] The Fund, by a 70 percent majority of the total voting power of participants, can, acting under Section 2(c) of Article XIX, authorize "operations" in SDRs that are undertaken by agreement between participants. Participants entering into operations by agreement must observe any terms or conditions that the Fund sets when it "prescribes" (authorizes) the operations.[149] Drawing on its combined authority under Article XVII, Section 3, and Article XIX, Section 2(c), the Fund can authorize "other holders" to engage in SDR operations.[150]

Under decisions adopted by the Fund, SDRs can now be used for virtually

---

Laws, Rules and Regulations (40th issue, 1983). Changes in holdings of SDRs take effect only when recorded by the Fund in the Special Drawing Rights Department. Article XVI, section 3.

The critical dates for exchange rates are stated in Rule P-6(a):

> Currency shall be provided in a transaction by agreement between participants at an exchange rate determined under Rule O-2 for the third business day preceding the value date [date of actual exchange of currency for SDRs], or for the second business day preceding the value date if agreed between the participants, unless the transaction is carried out at another exchange rate pursuant to authorization by the Fund under Article XIX, Section 7(b). (*By-Laws, Rules and Regulations* (40th issue, 1983))

[146] Article XIX, section 2(d); and Article XXIII, section 2(b). A member that persists in entering into such transactions may have its right to use subsequently acquired SDRs suspended. See Rules S-1 - S-8, *By-Laws, Rules and Regulations* (40th issue, 1983).

[147] IMF, *Annual Report, 1980*, at p. 92, presents a ten-year summary table for 1970-80.

[148] Article XXX(i).

[149] Article XIX, section 2(c).

[150] See pages 175-176, *supra*.

any recognized financial operation between participants, between other holders, and between participants and other holders (other than the Fund's General Resources Account) by mutual agreement. There are restrictions on the use of gold and there are requirements designed to prevent the equal value concept[151] from being prejudiced. Fund decisions now permit participants and other holders, by agreement with other participants or other holders, to use SDRs in the following operations:

(1) Swap arrangements, in which SDRs are exchanged at the equal-value rule for a currency or another monetary asset, other than gold, with an agreement to reverse the exchange at a specified future date at an exchange rate agreed between the parties;[152]

(2) Forward operations, in which SDRs may be bought or sold for delivery at a future date, against currency or another monetary asset, other than gold, at an exchange rate agreed between the parties;[153]

(3) Loans in which the interest rate and maturity may be agreed between the parties and repayment of the loans and payment of interest may be made in SDRs;[154]

(4) Settlement of financial obligations;[155]

(5) Security for the performance of financial obligations;[156]

---

[151] See pages 200–201, *supra.*

[152] E.B. Decision No. 6336 -(79/178)S (November 28, 1979); IMF, *Annual Report, 1980,* p. 141; *Selected Decisions* (10th issue, 1983), p. 285.

Currency swap arrangements are discussed in Chapter 4. Parties entering into swap arrangements are permitted to exchange SDRs for any currency or other monetary asset (including units of account such as the European currency unit—ECU) except gold. The initial transfer of SDRs under a swap arrangement is exactly like a transaction by agreement under Article XIX, section 2(b). Therefore, the equal value exchange rate for spot transactions applies in all cases to the initial transfer of SDRs in a swap. The parties are allowed to set, by agreement among themselves, the maturity date and exchange rate for the reversal of the transfer of SDRs. As a practical matter, central banks in some circumstances may prefer an SDR–currency swap to a currency–currency swap because it can be used to distribute the exchange risk. See generally IMF, *User's Guide to the SDR, supra* note 40, pp. 9–12 and 36–38, and Joseph Gold, *SDRs, Currencies, and Gold: Fourth Survey of New Legal Developments* (IMF Pamphlet Series no. 33; Washington, 1980), pp. 10–11.

[153] E.B. Decision No. 6337 -(79/178) S (November 28, 1979); IMF, *Annual Report, 1980,* p. 142; *Selected Decisions* (10th issue, 1983), p. 287. See IMF, *User's Guide to the SDR, supra* note 40, pp. 12–15 and 38–39, and Gold, *SDRs, Currencies, and Gold: Fourth Survey, supra* note 152, p. 11.

[154] E.B. Decision No. 6001 -(79/1)S (December 28, 1978); IMF, *Annual Report, 1979,* p. 131; *Selected Decisions* (10th issue, 1983), p. 279. See IMF, *User's Guide to the SDR, supra* note 40, pp. 15 and 34, and Gold, *SDRs, Currencies, and Gold: Fourth Survey, supra* note 152, p. 7.

Under the borrowing agreements between the IMF and institutions providing currencies to be used in the IMF's Supplementary Financing Facility, or under the Policy on Enlarged Access, the lending institutions are authorized to transfer their claims for repayment by the Fund (which are denominated in SDRs) at a premium or discount in relation from equal value. See Chapter 3, *supra,* page 114.

[155] E.B. Decision No. 6000 -(79/1)S (December 28, 1978), as amended by E.B. Decision No. 6438 -(80/37)S (March 5, 1980); *Selected Decisions* (10th issue, 1983), p. 278. See IMF, *User's Guide to the SDR, supra* note 40, pp. 15–16 and 33–34; and Gold, *SDRs, Currencies, and Gold: Fourth Survey, supra* note 152, pp. 5–7.

[156] SDRs may be used as security for the performance of financial obligations in two ways:

(1) A transfer-retransfer agreement, under which SDRs are transferred as security for the performance

(6) Donations.[157]

The amounts of SDRs used in any of the permitted operations above are left to the parties to agree upon. The exchange rate to be used for a loan or settlement of a financial obligation not denominated in SDRs must accord with the principle of equal value as determined by the Fund.[158]

As in the case of transactions by agreement, the parties are required to inform the Fund of the operation and the Fund decision under Section 2(c) that authorizes it. Fund rules and decisions prescribing operations specify information that is to be provided to the Fund relating to value dates, maturity dates, exchange rates, currencies or other assets involved, and the like. A change in the holdings of SDRs takes effect only when recorded by the Fund.[159] As in the case of transactions by agreement, the Fund may make a representation to any participant respecting any operation that the Fund believes prejudices the designation process or is inconsistent with Article XXII.[160]

Use of the IMF's General Resources Account

The SDR transactions and operations discussed so far in this chapter have involved the transfer of SDRs from one member-participant to another. The IMF through its General Resources Account is authorized to participate in SDR transactions and operations. Article XVII, Section 2, of the IMF Agreement provides:

> The Fund may hold special drawing rights in the General Resources Account and may accept and use them in operations and transactions

---

of an obligation and are to be returned to the original transferor when its obligation under the agreement has been fulfilled. E.B. Decision No. 6054 -(79/34)S (February 26, 1979), as amended by E.B. Decision No. 6438 -(80/37)S (March 5, 1980); *Selected Decisions* (10th issue, 1983), p. 283. See IMF, *User's Guide to the SDR, supra* note 40, pp. 17 and 35-36.

(2) A pledge, with the SDRs being earmarked for the duration of the pledge in a special register kept by the Fund. E.B. Decision No. 6053 -(79/34)S (February 26, 1979), as amended by E.B. Decision No. 6438 -(80/37)S (March 5, 1980); *Selected Decisions, supra,* p. 281. See IMF, *User's Guide to the SDR, supra* note 40, pp. 16 and 34-35; and Gold, *SDRs, Currencies, and Gold: Fourth Survey, supra* note 152, pp. 7-10.

[157] E.B. Decision No. 6437 -(80/37) S (March 5, 1980); IMF, *Annual Report, 1980,* p. 143; *Selected Decisions* (10th issue, 1983), p. 288. SDRs may be freely given or received by agreement. The recipient, like all holders, receives interest from the Special Drawing Rights Department on the SDRs. As with all other SDR transactions and operations, the transfers have no effect on participants' net cumulative allocations. Participants pay charges (like interest) and assessments on net cumulative allocations, including SDRs that they have donated. See pages 193-194, *supra.* See also IMF, *User's Guide to the SDR, supra* note 40, pp. 16 and 39; and Gold, *SDRs, Currencies, and Gold: Fourth Survey, supra* note 152, p. 12.

[158] E.B. Decision No. 6001, *supra* note 154; and E.B. Decision No. 6000, as amended, *supra* note 155. See generally pages 200-201 and 202, *supra.*

[159] Article XVI, section 3; and Rules P-7 and P-9, *By-Laws, Rules and Regulations* (40th issue, 1983).

[160] See note 146, *supra.*

conducted through the General Resources Account with participants in accordance with the provisions of this Agreement. . . .

The Fund acquires special drawing rights in these ways:

(a) Normally a member pays 25 percent of any increase in its General Resources Account quota subscription in special drawing rights.[161]

(b) The Fund must accept SDRs transferred to the General Resources Account by a country that chooses to use SDRs to repurchase its own currency pursuant to Article V, Section 7(i).[162]

(c) The General Resources Account receives SDRs in payment of charges levied pursuant to Article V, Section 8(e).[163]

(d) The Fund from time to time assesses participants in the Special Drawing Rights Department for reimbursement of the expenses of the General Department in managing the Special Drawing Rights Department. These assessments are levied in SDRs and are calculated on the basis of net cumulative allocations.[164]

(e) The General Resources Account may, pursuant to Section 6(a) of Article V, obtain SDRs in transactions in which members transfer SDRs to that account in exchange for national currencies held in that account.

The last category is of particular interest. Article V, Section 6(a), transactions may be attractive to a member desiring a particular currency that it needs but could not necessarily expect to obtain in a transaction by designation under Article XIX, Section 2(a).[165] The Fund's authority to enter into a Section 6(a) transaction is subject to two conditions:

(i) The currency provided by the Fund must be one that it would provide to a country making a drawing in the General Resources Account.[166]

(ii) The country issuing the currency to be provided by the Fund must concur in the sale of its currency by the Fund.[167]

---

[161] Article III, section 3(a). See Chapter 1, *supra*, pages 13–14.

[162] See Chapter 6, *infra*, pages 227–229. For historical background see *IMF History 1966–71, supra* note 7, vol. 1, pp. 173, 229–30, and 234–37. See also E.B. Decision No. 5703 -(78/39)(March 22, 1978), as amended by E.B. Decision No. 6862 -(81/81) (May 13, 1981); *Selected Decisions* (10th issue, 1983), p. 105.

[163] See Chapter 6, *infra*, pages 229–230.

[164] Article XVI, section 2; and Article XX, section 4.

[165] The designee in an Article XIX, section 2(a), transaction is permitted to supply any freely usable currency and is not required to supply the particular currency desired by the transferor of the SDRs. See pages 197–200, *supra*.

[166] Article V, sections 3(d) and 6(c). See Chapter 6, *infra*, pages 224–225.

[167] The issuer has no such veto in the normal purchase transaction where the country making the drawing transfers its own currency rather than SDRs to the General Resources Account.

A country transferring SDRs in a Section 6(a) transaction is not required by the Articles to have balance-of-payments or reserve position need for currency, although the Fund could adopt a policy requiring need.[168] The Fund is not required to enter into Section 6(a) transactions, and it can adopt policies for Section 6(a) transactions which set conditions additional to those required by that section.

The General Resources Account is authorized to use SDRs in the following ways:

(a) If a country's quota is decreased, the Fund may pay the member a portion of the decrease in SDRs.[169]

(b) The Fund normally pays remuneration to members in special drawing rights.[170]

(c) The Fund may make distributions of net income or of the general reserve in SDRs.[171]

(d) The Fund may pay interest or principal in SDRs on borrowings that it makes.[172]

(e) The Fund can require a member country (if it is a participant in the SDR Department) to sell its currency to the Fund in exchange for SDRs held in the General Resources Account so that the Fund can replenish its holdings of that currency.[173]

(f) When a country makes a drawing in the General Resources Account the Fund may agree to provide special drawing rights rather than national currencies. Article V, Section 3(f), requires the Fund to adopt policies and procedures for these transactions. The Fund has authority to grant broad approvals for purchases of SDRs under general policies or to limit its agreement to specific cases.[174]

---

[168] Article V, section 6(a); and *Report on Second Amendment, supra* note 24, part 2, chapter D, section 17. Compare regular drawings in the reserve and credit tranches. See Chapter 6, *infra,* pages 235–247.

[169] Article III, section 3(c).

[170] Article V, section 9(d). Remuneration is explained in Chapter 6, *infra,* pages 229–230. The Fund or the member concerned may decide that remuneration will instead be paid in that country's currency.

[171] Article XII, section 6(e).

[172] See Chapter 6, *infra,* pages 283–287.

[173] Article VII, section 1(ii). There is no requirement that the Fund first canvass other means of replenishment. *Report on Second Amendment, supra* note 24, part 2, chapter Q, section 3(e). However, the country can decline to enter into the transaction with the Fund if it would raise that country's holdings of SDRs above 300 percent of net cumulative allocation or higher agreed limit. See pages 196–197, *supra.* Normally the Fund does not require a country to sell its currency to the Fund for SDRs unless that country-participant is subject to "designation" to accept SDRs. See pages 210–212, *infra.*

[174] See *Report on Second Amendment, supra* note 24, part 2, chapter D, section 16.

One of the early cases in which a country made a portion of a "regular" drawing in SDRs was the purchase by the United Kingdom in July 1972 of 292 million SDRs in exchange for sterling. The United Kingdom then immediately transferred the SDRs to Belgium, France, Federal Republic of Germany, the Netherlands, and

(g) Under Article V, Section 6(b), the Fund may provide a member-country participant in the SDR Department with SDRs held in the General Resources Account in exchange for the currencies of other members.

Transactions in the last category above provide a means for a member to dispose of holdings of foreign currencies which it judges excessive to its needs without selling them on the exchange markets or presenting them to the issuing country for exchange. Such transactions also open up the possibility for a country to try to make SDRs the primary form in which it holds its monetary reserve assets. The use of Section 6(b) is subject to three important conditions:

(i) As a result of the transaction the General Resources Account's holdings of the currencies acquired by it must not be increased above the level at which the issuer would be subject to periodic charges.[175]

(ii) The currencies to be purchased by the Fund must be currencies that would be acceptable to the Fund in repurchase transactions.[176]

(iii) The country issuing the currency being sold to the Fund must concur in the sale of its currency to the Fund.[177]

The Fund is not required to enter into Section 6(b) transactions. The section simply provides authorization. The Fund is expected to adopt policies for Section 6(b) transactions. Since these transactions should tend to promote the objective of countries holding their monetary reserves primarily in SDRs,[178] the Fund can be expected to adopt policies that facilitate or perhaps even encourage Section 6(b) transactions. To date, however, the Fund has been cautious in authorizing Section 6(b) transactions. During the period a reconstitution obligation was in effect, the Fund decided that Section 6(b) transactions could be used by countries to "reconstitute" their SDR holdings.[179] Section 6(b) transactions were authorized in connection with the Seventh General Review of Quotas so that members needing SDRs for quota subscription payments could acquire

---

Norway to redeem balances of sterling that had been acquired by those countries in supporting sterling in the exchange markets. IMF, *Annual Report, 1973,* pp. 49–50 and 81–82.

The IMF today regularly includes SDRs in its operational budget that specifies which assets held in the General Resources Account will be sold to a member making a drawing in that account. Availability of SDRs depends on the SDR holdings of the General Resources Account and the current policy on sales of SDRs by that account. E.B. Decision No. 6275 -(79/158) G/S (September 14, 1979); IMF, *Annual Report, 1980,* p. 136; *Selected Decisions* (10th issue, 1983), p. 91; and E.B. Decision No. 7397 -(83/70) S (May 16, 1983); IMF, *Annual Report, 1983,* p. 145. See IMF, *User's Guide to the SDR, supra* note 40, pp. 27–28. See also Chapter 6, *infra,* pages 224–225.

[175] Article V, section 6(b).

[176] Article V, section 6(c). See also Article V, section 7(i), and discussion in Chapter 6, *infra,* at pages 227–229.

[177] Article V, section 6(c).

[178] See Article XXII.

[179] E.B. Decision No. 5699 -(78/38) G/S (March 22, 1978, effective April 1, 1978); IMF, *Annual Report, 1978,* p. 123. Reconstitution is explained at pages 210–212, *infra.*

them from the General Resources Account.[180] Section 6(b) transactions are authorized where participants need SDRs to pay charges in the General Resources Account or charges or assessments in the Special Drawing Rights Department.[181]

The Committee on Reform of the International Monetary System and Related Issues (Committee of Twenty) recommended the establishment of a ''substitution account.'' Members would transfer foreign currencies to this account and receive SDRs in exchange.[182] In one illustrative scheme in the Committee's report, members could sell foreign currencies to the account for SDRs but could not acquire currency balances for SDRs from the substitution account. The Committee's proposal was designed to reduce not only the holdings of foreign currencies in national monetary reserves but also the role played by national currencies in the settlement of international transactions.[183] Section 6(b) is not as far-reaching.

As explained above, Section 6(a) and (b) of Article V provide broad authority for the Fund to exchange SDRs for national currencies in transactions with members. It is not possible to predict with precision how the provisions will be applied in the future. Because transactions under these provisions can further the Fund's policy favoring the use of SDRs as the principal form in which national authorities hold international reserves, the Fund should consider the adoption of policies that in general facilitate Section 6(a) and (b) transactions.

Tables showing receipts and transfers of SDRs by the General Resources Account during the fiscal year are published annually in the IMF's *Annual Report*. The report also includes commentary.[184] Quarterly data are published in *Financial Statements* issued by the Fund.

---

[180] E.B. Decision No. 6663 -(80/160)S (October 31, 1980); IMF, *Annual Report, 1981*, p. 145; *Selected Decisions* (10th issue, 1983), p. 100.

[181] E.B. Decision No. 5702 -(78/39) G/S (March 22, 1978), as amended by E.B. Decision No. 7096 -(82/57)G/S (April 23, 1982); *Selected Decisions* (10th issue, 1983), p. 110.

[182] See *International Monetary Reform: Documents of the Committee of Twenty*, supra note 45, pp. 14–15 (Outline of Reform, paragraph 22), pp. 41–42 and pp. 169–76.

[183] *Idem*, at p. 41. See discussion of substitution account proposals in Chapter 12, *infra*, pages 638–642.

One of the unsettled issues in proposals during the early 1970s for a separate substitution account was: What obligations would the issuer of a currency sold to the account in exchange for SDRs have respecting maintenance of value of the currency and payment of interest and respecting amortization of excess currency balances held in the account? Section 6(b), by using the mechanism of the IMF's General Resources Account, places upon the issuer those obligations that attach to currency held in that account. The requirement that currency acquired by the General Resources Account under section 6(b) not increase holdings above the level at which the user is subject to periodic charges places significant limits on the quantity of currency that can be sold to the Fund.

[184] IMF, *Annual Report, 1980*, at p. 92, presents a ten-year summary table for 1970–80.

System Maintenance Rules

Principles of Designation and Obligations of Reconstitution

Serious problems in keeping the Special Drawing Rights Department work-ing might arise if a large number of participants were only transferors of SDRs. To assure that a participant does not simply spend its SDRs after their allocation and then press for the creation of more, "rules of the game" have been established to assure that a participant is sometimes a transferor and at other times a transferee. These rules relate to the "designation" of transfer-ees and to the obligations of participants to reconstitute their SDR holdings (to maintain average minimum daily balances). The rules are logically inde-pendent of each other.

Let us consider the principles used by the Fund in determining which par-ticipants shall be designated transferees in SDR transactions initiated by partici-pants that, acting under Article XIX, Section 2(a), request the Fund to desig-nate transferees to provide freely usable currency in exchange for SDRs. A participant is subject to designation as a transferee of SDRs if (i) the country's balance-of-payments and gross reserve position is sufficiently strong,[185] or if (ii) it is under an obligation to reconstitute, has a negative SDR balance, or has pre-viously failed to fulfill the expectation of need in transferring SDRs in a Section 2(a) transaction.[186] Countries falling in category (ii) are to be placed at the top of the list for designation.[187] In general, the Fund's designation practice should promote over time a "balanced distribution" of SDRs.[188]

The Fund prepares designation plans quarterly, listing participants and the number of SDRs they may be designated to accept. Up to the present time the Fund has, in preparing designation plans, sought to promote equality among participants in the ratios between SDR holdings in excess of net cumulative al-locations[189] and holdings of other reserve assets. The implementation of this principle has tended to lead to a concentration of designation on participants whose SDR holdings were below their allocations. It has been the practice, when the balance-of-payments and reserve positions of such countries have be-

---

[185] Article XIX, section 5(a)(i), uses the phrase "sufficiently strong." A country with a strong reserve po-sition may be in a sufficiently strong position for designation as a transferee even though it has a moderate balance-of-payments deficit. For criteria in the assessment of the strength of balance-of-payments and reserve positions for SDR designation, see E.B. Decision No. 6273 -(79/158) G/S (September 14, 1979); IMF, *An-nual Report, 1980*, p. 134; *Selected Decisions* (10th issue, 1983), p. 88. The decision is discussed in Chapter 6, *infra*, pages 224–225.

[186] See pages 194–195, *supra*.

[187] Article XIX, section 5. It has been the Fund's normal practice to arrange consensual transactions be-tween a participant and the General Resources Account or to encourage the participant to enter transactions by agreement with other participants before it becomes necessary for the Fund to assign the participant a priority status in a designation plan because it is in category (ii).

[188] Article XIX, section 5.

[189] See page 193, *supra*, for the definition of "net cumulative allocation."

come sufficiently strong to enable them to be designated, to aim at the reversal of their previous use of SDRs over a period of several quarters, providing that their balance-of-payments and reserve positions continue to justify designation.[190]

As explained earlier, a participant designated by the Fund to accept SDRs must accept them and provide a freely usable currency.[191] Failure to perform this role immediately suspends the right to use SDRs held by the participant unless the Fund decides otherwise.[192] However, the participant cannot be prevented from immediately, after accepting the SDRs, turning around and transferring them.[193] But, it can later be designated to again accept SDRs. A transferor that persists in using SDRs for the sole purpose of altering the composition of its reserves may be suspended from using SDRs it acquires in the future.[194]

Prior to April 30, 1981, participants in the Special Drawing Rights Department were required to observe a "reconstitution" obligation. From the time SDRs were first allocated in January 1970 through December 1978, a participant's net use of its special drawing rights had to be such that the average of its daily SDR holdings over five-year periods ending on the final day of successive calendar quarters were not less than 30 percent of the average of its daily net cumulative allocation of SDRs over the same period.[195] A participant with average daily holdings below the specified percent of net cumulative allocation was said to have an obligation to "reconstitute" its SDR holdings.

Effective January 1, 1979, the reconstitution obligation was reduced to 15 percent,[196] and on April 30, 1981, the specific rules of reconstitution were abrogated.[197] The rationale for abrogating the rules was that the rules operated as a restraint on the use of the SDR and that there was no similar restraint on the use of national currencies held in monetary reserves. It was believed that abro-

---

[190] At the time this book went to press the rules in Schedule F continued in effect. The Fund at any time can, by a simple majority of the weighted votes cast, adopt rules different from those in Schedule F. Article XIX, section 5(c).

Conclusions reached in a review of designation practice in 1979 are stated in E.B. Decision No. 6209 -(79/124)S(July 24, 1979). IMF, *Annual Report, 1980,* p. 132; *Selected Decisions* (10th issue, 1983), p. 289. Current procedures and practice in the preparation of designation plans are described in IMF, *User's Guide to the SDR, supra* note 40, pp. 21–25 and 51–55.

[191] See pages 194–197, *supra.*

[192] Article XXIII, section 2.

[193] See page 195, *supra.*

[194] Article XIX, section 3(b); and Article XXIII, section 2(b).

[195] Old Article XXV, section 6, *first,* and Schedule G, *first;* and present Article XIX, section 6, *second,* and Schedule G, *second.* See Gold, *Special Drawing Rights: Character and Use, supra* note 9, pp. 67–70.

[196] E.B. Decision No. 5936 -(78/168)S (October 25, 1978); IMF, *Annual Report, 1979,* p. 129. The Interim Committee of the Board of Governors endorsed the change. See paragraph 5 of its communiqué of September 24, 1978; IMF, *Annual Report, 1979,* p. 140 at p. 142. See also Gold, *SDRs, Currencies, and Gold: Fourth Survey, supra* note 152, pp. 13–14.

[197] E.B. Decision No. 6832 -(81/65)S (April 22, 1981); IMF, *Annual Report, 1981,* p. 145; *Selected Decisions* (10th issue, 1983), p. 293.

gation of the specific rules of reconstitution would tend to promote the SDR's becoming the principal reserve asset in the international monetary system.[198] Also, effective May 1, 1981, the interest rate on the SDR has been set at a full 100 percent of the rate of the currency composite in terms of which it is measured.[199] Using the market rate of interest, it was said, would supply an incentive to maintain SDR balances to avoid charges on their use.[200]

The Fund is empowered to reintroduce a reconstitution requirement. A 70 percent majority of the total voting power is required to adopt, modify, or abrogate rules of reconstitution.[201] Notwithstanding the abrogation of reconstitution rules, paragraph 1(b) of Schedule G remains in force:

> Participants shall also pay due regard to the desirability of pursuing over time a balanced relationship between their holdings of special drawing rights and their other reserves.[202]

The definition of a reconstitution obligation figured prominently in the negotiations in the 1960s that led to the original creation of the special drawing right.[203] The author tends to believe that the abrogation of all specific reconstitution rules since April 30, 1981, was unwise. It is doubtful if the SDR Department can continue to function effectively if it should ever happen that a substantial number of participants spend their SDR balances essentially down to zero and leave them there and if SDR holdings become concentrated in the possession of the Fund and a few participants and other holders. The designation rules and the interest charges may not be enough to prevent this from occurring some time in the future. Reconstitution rules were prudent rules of the game and should again be adopted.[204]

---

[198] See *Special Drawing Account—The Rules of Reconstitution: Report of the Executive Directors to the Board of Governors* (November 15, 1972) in IMF, *Annual Report, 1973*, p. 95 at p. 96. See also Gold, *SDRs, Currencies, and Gold: Fifth Survey, supra* note 38, pp. 20–21.

[199] Rule T-1 as amended effective May 1, 1981. *By-Laws, Rules and Regulations* (40th issue, 1983). See pages 193–194, *supra*.

[200] See IMF, *Annual Report, 1981*, pp. 96–97.

[201] Article XIX, section 6.

[202] See Gold, *SDRs, Currencies, and Gold: Fifth Survey, supra* note 38, p. 105 (note 25).

[203] See Solomon, *supra* note 7, pp. 137–43; and *IMF History 1966–71, supra* note 7, vol. 1, pp. 113–14, 151, 156–58, 160–61, and 186.

[204] Almost a third of participants have taken advantage of the abolition of the reconstitution requirement to reduce holdings to virtually zero. On October 31, 1982, for example, 47 countries had SDR holdings below 3 percent of net cumulative allocations. IMF, *Financial Statement of the Special Drawing Rights Department*, for the quarter ended October 31, 1982.

When the Eighth General Quota Review was implemented in late 1983 and early 1984, many IMF members lacked the SDRs needed to pay the reserve asset portions of their quota increases. They borrowed the needed SDRs from other members, paid them into the General Resources Account, simultaneously made reserve tranche drawings receiving SDRs, and used the drawn SDRs to repay their borrowings. As one person put it, "It was all done with mirrors."

Allocations of SDRs

The basic authority to allocate SDRs is set forth in Article XV, Section 1:

> To meet the need, as and when it arises, for a supplement to existing reserve assets, the Fund is authorized to allocate special drawing rights to members that are participants in the Special Drawing Rights Department.

We noted at the outset of this chapter that the SDR was created at a time when it was believed there was a need to inject more money into the international economy. Each new allocation of SDRs increases the official monetary reserves of the participating countries. When participants that are transferees in SDR transactions issue their own currencies in exchange for SDRs, the gross total of world monetary reserves further expands. The total international monetary reserves of the transferor of SDRs show no change as it replaces an SDR holding with a foreign currency holding. The transferee of the SDRs, however, increases its international monetary reserves by the amount of SDRs received for which it provides its own currency and increases its liabilities to foreigners in the amount of its own currency that it issues. Transactions in SDRs lead to a contraction of world-wide monetary reserve holdings when a country uses SDRs to redeem balances of its own currency held by foreign authorities. World-wide international monetary reserves would, of course, be contracted as a result of a decision of the IMF, should it ever be taken, to cancel SDRs previously allocated. While the IMF can by allocations and cancellations control the total quantity of SDRs in the system, it has less control over whether SDRs are used at any particular time to redeem outstanding currency balances or to create new currency liabilities. Further, the IMF does not at the present time control the velocity with which SDRs are exchanged among participants in the system. Interest rates applicable to SDR holdings may have some influence on these matters, but there are no special rules that participants must follow. The point is that decisions taken in the IMF to allocate or cancel SDRs can have far-reaching implications. However, the precise consequences cannot be easily predicted and are not subject to any finely tuned controls exercised by the IMF.

The procedures for allocating SDRs and the criteria to be applied are spelled out in Article XVIII. The Fund in allocating (or cancelling)[205] SDRs is required to consider the long-term global need for this reserve asset and is to avoid allocating so few as to lead to economic stagnation and deflation and to avoid allocating so many as to cause excess demand and inflation. The focus is the long-term world need for reserves and not the problems of

---

[205] See notes 227 and 228, *infra,* and accompanying text.

particular countries in financing balance-of-payments deficits.[206] Consequently, the Fund is not expected to make short-term decisions on the desired volume of reserves. Decisions to allocate SDRs are to be made for "basic" periods of five years or some other suitable length. The actual allocations take place in installments (e.g., annually) during the basic periods. The phased allocations are intended to result in a steady expansion of SDRs in accordance with long-term world reserve needs. The Fund may change the rates or intervals of allocations at any time in response to "unexpected major developments."[207]

The By-Laws of the IMF require the Executive Board to include in the *Annual Report* a review of the "adequacy" of global reserves. This is often one of the most difficult to write parts of the report.[208] There are no mechanical tests stated in the Articles or in IMF decisions for determining global reserve needs. Much attention has been given by officials and scholars to how statistical information can be used in the assessment.[209] However, there is no statistically precise concept of reserve adequacy that commands widespread acceptance. There can be considerable disagreement about the magnitude of immediate reserve needs and, inevitably, there is greater uncertainty when reserve needs are projected into the future. The Managing Director's proposal for the SDR allocations in 1979–81 included this comment:

---

[206] Article XVIII, section 1. See Gold, *Special Drawing Rights: Character and Use, supra* note 9, p. 16.

[207] Article XVIII, section 3. The first basic period began in January 1970 and ran three years. Phased allocations were authorized of 3.5 billion SDRs on January 1, 1970; 3.0 billion more on January 1, 1971; and 3.0 billion more on January 1, 1972. These allocations were at the rate of 17.5 percent of quota for the 1970 allocation and 15 percent for the 1971 and 1972 allocations. See Board of Governors Resolution No. 24-12 (October 3, 1969), in IMF, *Summary Proceedings, 1969*, p. 326; and *IMF History 1966–71, supra* note 7, vol. 2, p. 262. The Managing Director's proposal appears in vol. 2 at p. 251. For background on discussions at the time, see *IMF History 1966–71*, vol. 1, chapters 10 and 11; Solomon, *supra* note 7, pp. 148–50; and *Minutes of Federal Open Market Committee* (described in Chapter 4, page 137, note 31), 1969, pp. 475–78 and 837–38. See also note 9, *supra*. Some members chose not to participate, and actual allocations were slightly above 9.3 billion.

Because of a dramatic increase in foreign currency holdings in the period after 1970 and uncertainty about future exchange arrangements, the Managing Director did not submit a proposal for a new allocation of SDRs for the second basic period. The second period of five years came to a close on December 31, 1977.

The third basic period began without any new allocation. See the report of the Managing Director of June 29, 1977, in IMF, *Annual Report, 1977*, p. 110. Later, phased allocations of slightly over 12 billion SDRs were approved by the Board of Governors on the proposal of the Managing Director. The Fund allocated a little over 4.0 billion on January 1, 1979, 4.0 billion more on January 1, 1980, and a final 4.05 billion on January 1, 1981. The third basic period was adjusted to four years in length and ended on December 31, 1981. See Board of Governors Resolution No. 34-3 (December 11, 1978), in IMF, *Summary Proceedings, 1979*, p. 334. For the Managing Director's proposal and the communiqué of the Interim Committee of the Board of Governors that recommended the SDR allocations, see IMF, *Annual Report, 1979*, pp. 123–28 and 140–43.

The fourth basic period began January 1, 1982, without any new allocations.

[208] By-Laws, section 10, *By-Laws, Rules and Regulations* (40th issue, 1983).

[209] See, e.g., *International Monetary Reform: Documents of the Committee of Twenty, supra* note 45, pp. 176–79; and IMF, *International Reserves: Needs and Availability* (Washington: IMF, 1970). The paper entitled "The Need for Reserves: An Exploratory Paper" in the appendix to the latter book at p. 369 was considered a path-breaking study when it was circulated in 1966.

With greater exchange rate flexibility, countries might have been expected to make do with much smaller reserves. Moreover, important changes have taken place in world financial markets in the last decade, and most countries can obtain reserves by making use of international money and capital markets.

Experience shows, however, that countries want to increase their reserves as the level of their international transactions rises, and such increases can be expected to continue in the coming years. While it is true that most countries have a means for satisfying their need for reserves when international capital markets are as free as they are today, the decision to allocate special drawing rights does not depend on a finding that the long-term global need cannot be met except by allocation. A characteristic of a system in which countries add to their gross reserves as their international indebtedness increases is that they are faced with the need for periodic refinancing. This difficulty does not arise when additions to net reserves are made through allocation of special drawing rights.

Another consideration is the objective of making the special drawing right the principal reserve asset of the international monetary system, as set out in Article VIII, Section 7 and Article XXII. Exclusive reliance on the accumulation of reserve currencies to provide the needed reserve increases would hardly be compatible with that objective.[210]

Because criteria for determining the need to allocate SDRs lack precision, the procedure for reaching allocation decisions takes on great importance. The procedure of Article XVIII, Section 4, is intended to assure that allocation decisions are technically well conceived and that they have wide acceptance by governments. The procedure should minimize recriminations for allocations that in retrospect may be seen as either too large or two small.

The procedure is that the Managing Director, after consultation with members, submits an allocation proposal concurred in by the Executive Board to the Board of Governors for the latter's decision. The adoption of an allocation decision requires an 85 percent majority of the total voting power of participants in the SDR Department.[211] The high majority obviously assures that decisions to create additional SDRs, or to cancel a portion of previously issued SDRs, have wide support. The high majority is also intended to act as a brake

---

[210] IMF, *Annual Report, 1979*, p. 123 at pp. 124–25; *Selected Decisions* (10th issue, 1983), p. 388 at p. 390. Compare the report of the Managing Director of June 9, 1981, in which he indicated he would not propose that an allocation of SDRs be made at the outset of the fourth basic period that began January 1, 1982. IMF, *Annual Report, 1982*, p. 134; *Selected Decisions*, p. 398.

[211] Article XVIII, section 4; and Article XXI. Voting in the IMF is treated generally in Chapter 1, *supra,* pages 32–35.

on excessive allocations. The United States alone has the votes to block an allocation or cancellation. The European Community acting as a group possesses blocking votes. The requirement that the decision be ultimately taken by the Board of Governors is intended to assure that the question receives the attention and acceptance of senior governmental officials. The Managing Director's role is of central importance. He commands a respected professional staff that has or can obtain needed information and is in a position to formulate tentative plans. He can engage in confidential discussions with member-participants about the world reserve situation, can solicit comments on tentative plans, can adjust a proposal to meet objections, and may engage in behind-the-scenes efforts to persuade reluctant countries to join in support.[212]

Allocations are expressed as percentages of quotas in the General Resources Account.[213] Thus, the larger the quota the larger is the entitlement to SDRs. Some scholars and officials have suggested that SDRs be allocated on a basis other than quota size. The use of SDRs to transfer "real" resources would be achieved by making augmented allocations of SDRs to developing countries.[214] These countries would in turn transfer, with no intention to reconstitute, some portion of the SDRs allocated to them in order to permanently finance a portion of their balance-of-payments deficits. However, a consequence could be the acquisition of bookkeeping assets (SDRs), probably in excess of their needs, by developed countries in exchange for their parting with "real" resources. This might place strains on the usability and purchasing power of this monetary instrument. While much study has been given to linking SDR allocations to needs of developing countries, the amended Articles deliberately provide no authority for allocating SDRs on any other basis than relative quota size.

However, the establishment of quotas in the General Resources Account, while primarily based on trade volumes, has taken into account problems of developing countries. Quotas in recent years have been established in a bargained-out process without close adherence to any economic formulas. When, for example, it was decided in 1976 to increase quotas, oil-producing states received the largest increases, but non-oil-producing developing countries received larger proportionate increases than more highly developed countries even though the share of these developing countries in world trade had not in-

---

[212] The discussions that preceded the adoption of the first allocation plan (*supra* note 207) are recounted in *IMF History 1966–71, supra* note 7, vol. 1, chapter 10; and Solomon, *supra* note 7, pp. 148–50.

[213] Article XVIII, section 2(b).

[214] Various proposals to "link" SDR allocations to development needs, together with arguments pro and con, are summarized in the report of the Technical Group on the SDR/Aid Link of the IMF's Committee of Twenty. See *International Monetary Reform: Documents of the Committee of Twenty, supra* note 45, pp. 95–111. For historical background see *IMF History 1966–71, supra* note 7, vol. 1, pp. 110–11, 219–20, and 245–46; and Solomon, *supra* note 7, pp. 250, 255, and 263. See also William R. Cline, *International Monetary Reform and the Developing Countries* (Washington: Brookings Institution, 1976), pp. 48–95.

creased.[215] Since quota subscriptions are normally paid in SDRs and a country's own currency, and SDRs are allocated in amounts larger than needed for quota subscriptions, there is little incentive for a country anticipating balance-of-payments deficits to seek a small quota.

Participants can opt out from allocations to themselves of SDRs and remain participants in the SDR Department. A participant can opt out from allocations only if (a) its governor did not vote in favor of the allocation decision and (b) it formally informs the Fund of its opting out before the first allocation of SDRs under the decision.[216] A country might do this when it believes there is no global need for more SDRs, does not anticipate a need of its own for SDRs, and wishes to avoid being designated as a transferee to receive larger quantities of SDRs.[217] A member opting out of an allocation may be allowed by the Fund to opt back in later, but cannot receive allocations made in the interim.[218]

Termination of Participation, Cancellation of SDRs, and Liquidation of the SDR Department

Any participant in the Special Drawing Rights Department may terminate its participation at any time. Interest and charges are to be brought up to date. The Fund is required to redeem all SDRs held by the participant and provide in exchange the participant's own currency or a freely usable currency, and the participant is required to pay to the Fund SDRs and/or freely usable currencies equivalent to its net cumulative allocation of SDRs. The two obligations are offset—the participant has a net receipt of currency if, after interest and charges are brought up to date, it holds SDRs above net cumulative allocation, and it makes a net payment of currency if its holding of SDRs is below allocation.[219] A country can terminate participation in the Special Drawing Rights Department while remaining a member of the Fund.[220] One might expect a country to terminate participation if the SDR system appeared to be operating in a manner seriously adverse to its interests. This could happen if other participants fail to abide by the rules or if Fund decisions and policies relating to the SDR are not to its liking.

---

[215] See *Increases in Quotas of Members—Sixth General Review: Report of the Executive Directors to the Board of Governors* in IMF, *Annual Report, 1976*, pp. 103–11, especially paragraph 2 of the report at pp. 103–04. See generally Chapter 1, *supra*, pages 12–14.

[216] Article XVIII, section 2(e).

[217] The smaller the net cumulative allocation, the fewer SDRs the participant can be designated to accept before its holdings reach 300 percent of allocation.

[218] Article XVIII, section 2(e).

[219] Article XXIV and Schedule H. The procedure, which may involve transactions with other participants, results in the Fund cancelling SDRs equivalent to the terminating participant's net cumulative allocation. The settlement between the Fund and the terminating participant may take place in installments over several years.

[220] Article XXIV, section 1. A country that withdraws from membership in the IMF automatically terminates its participation in the Special Drawing Rights Department.

The IMF Articles provide for the possibility that the SDR system may be liquidated.[221] A decision to liquidate the Special Drawing Rights Department can be made only by the Board of Governors, but the vote required is a simple majority of the weighted votes cast.[222] Sir Joseph Gold in another context commented, "Countries give scrupulous attention to liquidation provisions even when they intend a scheme for the creation of a reserve asset to be permanent, because they regard rights in liquidation an important component in the economic and legal quality of the asset."[223]

The liquidation provisions drive home the point that special drawing rights are not to be understood as a permanent form of financing for balance-of-payments deficits. In the event of liquidation of the SDR Department, participants that have made a net use of SDRs will be required to pay freely usable currencies or other acceptable currencies to the Fund. The provisions, however, by providing for liquidation by installments over a period of five years or longer, safeguard the expectation that it is reasonable to make use of SDRs to finance balance-of-payments deficits over at least a five-year period.[224]

The operation of the liquidation provisions is not easily summarized. The effort to design rules for a situation in which relations may be severely strained among participants created complexity. The effect of the rules is as if, after interest and charges are brought up to date, participants that have made a net use of SDRs were required to acquire SDRs so that holdings match net cumulative allocations, and participants with holdings above allocations were to reduce their holdings, and then the SDRs were cancelled. While this is the theoretical concept, the rules are designed to minimize the need for transfers of SDRs among participants. They are intended to assure that the burden of any default is distributed in proportion to net cumulative allocations and does not fall more heavily on participants with large holdings of SDRs in relation to their allocations. The rules also deal with SDRs held by "other holders" that may or may not be Fund members. And, the rules are intended to function in a liquidation that will take place by installments.[225]

The liquidation provisions stand as the ultimate device for correcting misuse of the SDR system, whether by participants in debtor or creditor positions. The activation of the provisions would probably be an act of desperation, for a

---

[221] Article XXV and Schedule I.

[222] Article XXV(a). Although the matter is not free from doubt, a decision to liquidate the SDR Department should probably be understood as a decision pertaining solely to the SDR Department so that only governors of participants would participate in the vote. See Article XXI. See also Chapter 1, *supra*, page 33. A decision to liquidate the International Monetary Fund is automatically a decision to liquidate the SDR Department. Article XXV(a). See also Article XXVII, section 2; and Schedule K.

[223] Joseph Gold, "Developments in the International Monetary System, the International Monetary Fund, and International Monetary Law Since 1971," in Hague Academy of International Law, *Recueil des Cours,* vol. 174 (1982–I), p. 107 at p. 321. Sir Joseph was speaking about the European currency unit (ECU) discussed in Chapter 8.

[224] See Schedule I, paragraph 1.

[225] See generally Article XXV and Schedule I.

liquidation decision would halt all transactions and operations in SDRs except those specifically sanctioned by the liquidation provisions.[226] If a decision is made in the future to replace the SDR system with a different system, more or less ambitious than the present one, the procedure to be used might well involve the cancellation provisions discussed below or a special international agreement because of the time that would be consumed by liquidation in the "regular" way.

Without liquidating the system, SDRs can be reduced through the cancellation procedure of Article XVIII. Decisions to cancel under the authority of that article require the same special 85 percent majority as decisions to allocate SDRs and are made in accordance with the same procedure.[227] Cancellations are to be expressed as a percentage of net cumlative allocations and, thus, would be distributed among participants in the same proportion as allocations. Cancellations, if decided upon, are normally to be phased.[228]

Although the provisions for termination of participation may rarely be used and those for cancellation of all or part of previous SDR allocations and for liquidation of the Special Drawing Rights Department may never be invoked, they constitute incentives to keep the system operating in a manner that is fair to all participants.

Chapter Conclusion—Interim Appraisal of the Special Drawing Right

Statistical information is regularly published on transactions and operations in special drawing rights. The IMF's *Annual Report, International Financial Statistics,* and the IMF's quarterly financial statements list SDR allocations and holdings of each participant, summarize transactions and operations by participants and by the General Resources Account, and report other information.[229] Between the first allocation in January 1970 and the end of April 1983, transfers of SDRs totaled 57.5 billion.[230] The volume of transfers can be expected to increase significantly as the total amount allocated becomes larger and as velocity increases by greater use in both transactions and operations.

Any appraisal of the special drawing right must be cautious. SDRs are re-

---

[226] Article XXV(b).

[227] Article XVIII, section 4. See pages 213–217, *supra*. The 85 percent majority of the total weighted voting power of participants required to cancel SDRs under the procedure of Article XVIII is substantially higher than the simple majority of the weighted vote required to liquidate the SDR Department under Article XXV. Sir Joseph Gold has predicted that the Fund will never deliberately contract the quantity of SDRs. Gold, *Special Drawing Rights: Character and Use, supra* note 9, p. 14.

[228] Article XVIII, sections 1–3. Article XVIII, section 2(f), deals with participants that hold less than their share of the SDRs being cancelled.

[229] Tables in IMF, *Annual Report, 1980,* at pp. 124 and 129, provide information for the 10-year period January 1, 1970, through April 30, 1980.

[230] IMF, *Annual Report, 1983,* p. 127.

serve assets created by the judgment of governments. The judgment of 85 percent of the voting power of the Fund can be good or bad. Determining the optimal amount of SDRs to allocate over any future period will be difficult. The flow of SDRs from one holder to another in exchange for currencies never results in the extinction of SDRs, and thus they are unlike a credit which is automatically cancelled upon repayment. SDRs are a permanent addition to the stock of world reserves, and may be reduced only by a deliberate decision taken within the IMF to cancel all or a portion of them. In an early draft of this chapter the author wrote, ''One can expect that political pressures will normally be to expand and rarely to contract the supply of this form of international money. One can also expect pressures to relax the reconstitution requirement, a step that can be taken by a 70 percent majority of the total voting power.'' Not only have there been pressures, but they were yielded to. The reconstitution requirement, as noted earlier, was reduced to 15 percent effective January 1, 1979, and was abolished April 30, 1981.[231]

There is a risk that a substantial number of IMF members will spend their SDRs and maintain very low average daily balances.[232] One can imagine that these same countries will press for the allocation of additional SDRs which will be used in the same way. At some point when SDRs are concentrated in the hands of a few countries and those countries show a disposition not to support the creation of additional SDRs, the countries with low balances may lose interest in keeping the system working. This could pose serious problems for those participants with substantial SDR holdings. This remote but potentially very serious risk is, in the author's mind, of greater concern than the general structural bias of the SDR system toward postponement of balance-of-payments adjustment.[233]

The SDR system is dependent upon countries being transferors at one time and transferees at another and abiding by the rules. The payment of an interest rate on SDR holdings comparable to that available on short-term investments in widely used currencies can encourage countries, while they use SDRs, to maintain average holdings over time closer to the level of net allocations than to some lower level.[234] A return to a meaningful reconstitution requirement (on the order of 30 percent) would give greater assurance that countries be transferees as well as transferors and would provide additional incentive to participants to keep the system working because they will hold significant numbers of SDRs, the value and usefulness of which they will want to maintain. Balanced holdings of SDRs over time should encourage confidence in the asset.

---

[231] See pages 211–212, *supra*.

[232] See note 204, *supra*.

[233] A bias toward postponement of adjustment (or prevention of premature adjustment) is a normal consequence of increasing unconditional liquidity.

[234] Interest and charges are presently set at the market rate. As noted earlier, the Fund has authority to change the interest rate. See pages 193–194, *supra*.

Another matter that deserves long-term attention is the principle of valuation of the SDR.[235] It is presently valued in relation to a market basket of national currencies. The ability of the SDR to command real resources is thus dependent upon the purchasing power of the national currencies in terms of which it is valued. National monetary and fiscal policies directly affect the ultimate purchasing power of the SDR. Up to the present time the Fund's role in influencing decision-making in the more powerful member states has been relatively limited. We shall return to this matter in the final chapter of this book.[236] At that time we shall explore the implications of Article XXII:

GENERAL OBLIGATIONS OF PARTICIPANTS

In addition to the obligations assumed with respect to special drawing rights under other articles of this Agreement, each participant undertakes to collaborate with the Fund and with other participants in order to facilitate the effective functioning of the Special Drawing Rights Department and the proper use of special drawing rights in accordance with this Agreement and with the objective of making the special drawing right the principal reserve asset in the international monetary system.[237]

Margaret Garritsen de Vries, the Fund's historian, after surveying the negotiations that led to the creation of the special drawing right, was moved to comment on the persistence of the officials involved in pursuing the negotiations. Time and again they came together at the highest levels to try to resolve their differences.[238] Ultimately agreement was reached and implemented and later, if necessary, modified as experience was gained. The special drawing right, because of the shared commitment involved in creating and sustaining it, carries a special aura and engenders a hope that financial problems can be surmounted through multilateral collaboration.

---

[235] The Fund, as previously explained, has authority to change the principle and method of valuation. See pages 187–192, *supra*.

[236] At pages 630–638, *infra*.

[237] Recall also the general obligations of Article VIII, section 7.

[238] See *IMF History 1966–71, supra* note 7, vol. 1, p. 189.

Chapter 6: Drawing Rights in the IMF General Resources Account and Related IMF Accounts

Introductory Comments

The rights and obligations of member countries of the International Monetary Fund were briefly surveyed in Chapter 1. Among these is the right to make drawings in the General Resources Account.[1] As we noted in Chapter 1, each member pays into the General Resources Account a subscription equal to the amount of its quota at the time the country joins the Fund, and it pays in additional amounts when its quota is increased.[2] The member is required to pay part of its quota in reserve assets (special drawing rights or foreign currencies) and the remainder in its national currency.[3]

    The value of the currencies of members held in the General Resources Account is maintained in terms of the special drawing right. At the present time currencies are valued using the representative rate determined by the Fund between the particular currency and the composite of national currencies in terms of which the special drawing right is valued.[4] The Fund's holdings of a country's currency are adjusted under the maintenance-of-value provision on the oc-

---

[1] See pages 12–16, *supra.*

The financial accounts of the General Department are the General Resources Account, the Special Disbursement Account, and, if established, the Investment Account. All members have drawing rights in the General Resources Account unless the country has been declared ineligible to use the Fund's resources. The Special Disbursement Account receives the proceeds of gold sales to the extent that they exceed the carrying value of the gold on the Fund's books and also receives repayments of loans made by a Trust Fund. That account is described at page 296, *infra.* The Investment Account provides a means for the Fund, should it choose do so, to invest its general reserve or special reserve or the proceeds of gold sales above the carrying value.

[2] See pages 12–14 and 30–32, *supra.*

[3] Article III, sections 1 and 3. See Chapter 1, *supra,* pages 12–14. Normally, the Fund holds part of its currency holdings in the form of bank deposits maintained with the central banks of the issuing states. For the bulk of its currency holdings, the Fund obtains non-negotiable, non-interest-bearing securities issued by the national monetary authorities and payable at face value on demand. The Fund's practice with respect to its gold holdings is to designate specific national central banks as depositories to maintain custody of the gold for the account of the Fund. Article III, Section 4; Article XIII; and Rules E-1–E-3 and F-1, *By-Laws, Rules and Regulations* (40th issue, 1983).

[4] Article V, section 11(a). See pages 225–227, *infra.*

casion of the use of the currency in an operation or transaction between the Fund and another member and at such other times as the Fund may prescribe or the member requests. If the exchange value of the currency depreciates in relation to the SDR, additional currency must be paid by the member to the Fund. If the currency appreciates, the Fund returns a portion of the currency that reflects the appreciation.[5]

Members of the Fund, having contributed reserve assets and their national currencies into the General Resources Account, in turn have drawing rights in that pool of resources. A member also has certain rights should the Fund be liquidated or the member withdraw.

Technical Background

"Drawings" in the General Resources Account

Each IMF member designates a fiscal agency of its country which is the only agency authorized to make drawings from the IMF's General Resources Account.[6] Usually that agency is the state's official treasury, although it may instead be the country's central bank.

In the typical transaction in the General Resources Account, a member (with balance-of-payments need) purchases from the Fund currencies issued by one or more other members, or SDRs, and sells to the Fund in exchange an equivalent amount of its own currency.[7] The rights of a member to obtain national currencies or SDRs from the General Resources Account are called "drawing rights." The transactions are called "drawings" or "purchases." They are cast in the form of a purchase and sale with a repurchase obligation. In some respects they are like a loan with a deposit of collateral, but a significant difference is that the repurchase obligation cannot always be satisfied by returning to the Fund the same currency drawn. That is, the Fund may require the country at the time of the repurchase ("paying off the loan") to transfer to the Fund a currency that the Fund needs at that time. Also, if in the meantime another country has drawn currency of the first member from the Fund, that reduces the first member's repurchase obligation.

Most of this chapter is devoted to the rights of IMF members to make drawings in the General Resources Account and the Fund's policies related thereto. Particular attention will be given to the exercise of discretion, where it

---

[5] Article V, section 11(b). See E.B. Decision No. 5590 -(77/163)(December 5, 1977, effective April 1, 1978); IMF, *Annual Report, 1978*, p. 122; IMF, *Selected Decisions of the International Monetary Fund and Selected Documents* (10th issue; Washington, 1983) [hereinafter *Selected Decisions*], p. 112.

[6] Article V, section 1; and Rules G-1 and G-2, *By-Laws, Rules and Regulations* (40th issue, 1983).

[7] Article V, section 3.

is permitted, by the Fund. Before proceeding to these matters, the reader should understand how the Fund selects currencies to be sold to a country making a drawing, the exchange rates used, repurchase obligations, and charges. To these mundane, and sometimes important, details we now turn.

Particular Currencies Provided by the Fund

A country making a drawing in the General Resources Account is entitled to obtain a "freely usable currency" or a currency that can be exchanged for a freely usable currency.[8] A freely usable currency is "a member's currency that *the Fund determines* (i) is, in fact, widely used to make payments for international transactions, and (ii) is widely traded in the principal exchange markets." [emphasis added][9] At the present time the Fund has determined that five currencies are "freely usable" currencies. They are the United States dollar, Deutsche mark, French franc, Japanese yen, and United Kingdom pound sterling. The Fund has authority to add currencies to or delete them from the list.[10]

In only one type of case is the country making a drawing entitled to a particular currency: When a member intends to use the currency drawn to redeem balances of its own currency held and offered by another member, it is entitled to obtain the currency of that member.[11]

Aside from the case where a member is making a drawing in order to redeem its own currency held by another member, the Fund decides which currencies will be sold to countries making drawings.[12] For this purpose, it period-

---

[8] Article V, section 3(d) and (e).

[9] Article XXX(f).

[10] See discussion of the concept of "freely usable currency" in Chapter 5, *supra*, pages 197–200.

[11] Article V, section 3(d).

For most international transactions one freely usable currency is as good as another, since it can probably be exchanged for the currency desired. One reason for the special rule giving a right to a particular currency for redeeming balances is illustrated by this example: Suppose the U.S. Federal Reserve System has drawn heavily on a swap line with the Bundesbank and sold Deutsche mark in the market to prevent depreciation of the dollar. The Bundesbank as a consequence has accumulated a large holding of U.S. dollars which U.S. authorities are obligated to redeem. Suppose the United States wishes to draw mark from the IMF to redeem these dollar balances rather than sell dollars in the exchange markets for mark which would depress the dollar's rate. If the Fund provided U.K. sterling, the U.S. purpose in coming to the Fund would be frustrated, for at the present time sterling is usually not exchanged in large quantities in the markets directly for mark but rather by selling sterling for dollars and then selling dollars for mark, a transaction which could depress the dollar's rate in relation to the mark.

The provision also makes it possible for participants in the exchange rate arrangement of the European Monetary System (EMS) to obtain the particular partner's currency needed to settle the very-short-term credits financing EMS interventions. Market exchanges in which any other currency is traded for the currency needed could in some situations adversely affect exchange rate relationships among EMS currencies. See generally Chapter 8, *infra*, pages 327–332.

If the particular currency desired has been declared by the IMF to be "scarce" pursuant to Article VII, section 3, then the country making the drawing cannot demand it. The IMF has never yet formally declared a currency to be scarce.

[12] Article V, section 3(d).

ically draws up lists of currencies to be sold.[13] The Fund places at the top of its lists currencies held in the General Resources Account in amounts above 75 percent of quota that are issued by members in strong balance-of-payments and reserve positions. The particular currency to be provided when a drawing is made will be determined following consultation between the Managing Director and the country proposing a drawing. The Fund makes arrangements designed to ensure that all steps (including necessary exchanges) can be carried out on the same day or, if this is not practicable, as expeditiously as possible.[14]

Under the policies and procedures it adopts, the Fund may agree to provide special drawing rights held in the General Resources Account instead of currencies to a member making a purchase in that account.[15] The IMF includes SDRs in its operational budgets.[16]

If the General Resources Account's holdings of particular currencies are low, the account can obtain needed currencies through transactions in other currencies, transfers of special drawing rights, or sales of gold. The Fund also has the power, under Article VII, Section 1, to borrow currencies needed to replenish its holdings.[17]

Exchange Procedures and Exchange Rates Applicable to Drawings and Subsequent Exchanges

The General Resources Account's holdings of members' currencies are valued in terms of the special drawing right.[18] The basic rule when SDRs are transferred is that the transferor of SDRs "shall receive the same value whatever currencies might be provided and whichever participants provide those currencies."[19] All computations for transactions through the General Resources Account are made in accordance with this same principle.[20] Thus, if the transaction involves the exchange of one currency for another, the exchange rate used shall be such that the currency obtained has the same value when stated in terms of SDRs as the currency sold.[21]

---

[13] See, e.g., E.B. Decisions Nos. 6273, 6274, and 6275 -(79/158)(September 14, 1979); Decision No. 6352 -(79/183)(December 12, 1979); and Decisions Nos. 6772 and 6774 -(81/35)(March 5, 1981); *Selected Decisions* (10th issue, 1983), pp. 88–98. See also E.B. Decision No. 7397 -(83/70)(May 16, 1983); IMF, *Annual Report, 1983*, p. 145. A currency budget is adopted at quarterly intervals.

[14] See *Proposed Second Amendment to the Articles of Agreement of the International Monetary Fund: A Report by the Executive Directors to the Board of Governors* (1976), part 2, chapter D, section 11. This report, published in IMF, *Summary Proceedings, 1976—Supplement,* is hereinafter cited *Report on Second Amendment.* See also Rules O-4–O-8, *By-Laws, Rules and Regulations* (40th issue, 1983).

[15] Article V, section 3(f). See Chapter 5, *supra,* pages 205–209.

[16] See, e.g., E.B. Decisions Nos. 6275, 6772, and 7397, *supra* note 13.

[17] See page 283 et seq.

[18] Article V, section 11(a). See *Report on Second Amendment, supra* note 14, part 2, chapter H, section 4.

[19] Article XIX, section 7(a). See discussion of the concept of "same value" in Chapter 5, *supra,* pages 200–201.

[20] Article V, sections 10 and 11.

[21] Article V, section 3(e) (purchases); and Article V, section 7(j)(i) (repurchases).

All currencies held in the General Resources Account are, under present Fund rules, valued in terms of the SDR based on market exchange rates between the particular currency and the exchange value of the SDR.[22] Exchanges of one currency for another through the General Resources Account are effected at these exchange values with the SDR as the common denominator.[23]

If the Fund provides a currency that is not itself a "freely usable currency," the member issuing the currency is required to ensure that it can be exchanged at the time of purchase for a freely usable currency. The issuer has the right and obligation to make the exchange unless it and the country drawing the currency agree on another procedure.[24] The exchange rate between the currency initially provided and the freely usable currency obtained shall be the rate based on Article XIX, Section 7(a), and Fund regulations that assure that the member making the drawing receives the same value (in relation to special drawing rights) regardless of which currencies are purchased from the Fund. In other words, if the drawer purchases Kenyan shillings from the Fund, Kenyan authorities must be willing to exchange those shillings for the same quantity of a freely usable currency chosen by Kenya, say U.K. sterling, as the drawer could have purchased from the Fund had the Fund initially provided U.K. sterling.[25]

A country receiving one freely usable currency and desiring another is not entitled to demand an "official exchange;" it must make the exchange at its own exchange risk and in any manner it chooses that is consistent with the Fund Agreement—e.g., by a transaction in the exchange markets or by a transaction with a country holding the currency it desires.[26] There is an exception to this general statement: If the issuer of the freely usable currency to be sold requests, the drawing country must, at the time of its purchase, allow the issuer to make the exchange. In that case the rate of exchange shall be the rate that assures "same value" based on Article XIX, Section 7(a), and Fund regulations.[27] The

---

[22] Article V, sections 10 and 11; and Rule O-2, *By-Laws, Rules and Regulations* (40th issue, 1983). See also E.B. Decision No. 5590, *supra* note 5. Rule O-2 is quoted and its application is explained in Chapter 5, *supra*, pages 178–185.

[23] Rules O-2, O-4, and O-6; *By-Laws, Rules and Regulations* (40th issue, 1983).

Under the original Articles transactions through the General Account were computed on the basis of the par values of the currencies involved. See Chapter 3, *supra*, pages 115–117; and Joseph Gold, *Maintenance of the Gold Value of the Fund's Assets* (IMF Pamphlet Series no. 6; Washington, 1965).

[24] Article V, section 3(e)(i)–(iii). In accordance with Rule O-4, *supra* note 23, each issuer of a non-freely usable currency files with the Fund a statement on procedures for exchanging its currency for a freely usable currency. A sample statement appears in Joseph Gold, *Use, Conversion, and Exchange of Currency Under the Second Amendment of the Fund's Articles* (IMF Pamphlet Series no. 23; Washington, 1978), p. 117.

[25] Article V, section 3(e)(i); and Rules O-2 and O-4–O-8 of *By-Laws, Rules and Regulations* (40th issue, 1983).

[26] Article V, section 3(e)(iv); and *Report on Second Amendment, supra* note 14, part 2, chapter D, section 12.

[27] Article V, section 3(e)(iv). An example: Brazil, say, desires French francs but the currency provided by the Fund is Kenyan shillings. Kenya converts its shillings to U.K. pounds sterling, which is a freely usable currency. At that point any further exchange is to be arranged by Brazil at its own risk and at whatever ex-

issuer of a freely usable currency legally has the right to decide whether to require an official exchange each time its currency is drawn from the Fund when another currency is desired by the purchaser. The Fund, however, has tried to reach administrative understandings with issuers on general procedures.[28]

Beyond the specific obligations explained above, Section 3(e)(ii) of Article V imposes a general obligation on all members to collaborate to make the system work, so that by means of market transactions or official exchanges currency purchased from the Fund can at the time of purchase be exchanged for a desired freely usable currency issued by another member.[29] Normally the currency will be delivered in the form of bank balances at an official agency of the issuer.

Repurchase Obligations

Subject to certain qualifications, the Fund levies periodic charges on its General Resources Account holdings of a member's currency resulting from purchases in the credit tranches. Periodic charges are not assessed on the Fund's currency holdings resulting from reserve tranche drawings.[30] A member has a right at any time to repurchase the Fund's holdings of its currency that are subject to periodic charges.[31]

A basic principle is that the Fund's general resources are available only for short-term use. A country that has made a purchase is "expected normally," as its "balance of payments and reserve position improves," to repurchase the Fund's holdings of its currency that are subject to periodic charges. The repurchases should keep pace with the improvement and should not await total recovery from the problem for which the original purchase was made.[32] The expectation of repurchase is not a legal obligation and the word "normally" indicates there may be exceptional circumstances. "Balance of payments and

---

change rates it can obtain, unless the United Kingdom requests that it be allowed to arrange the exchange. In that event, the United Kingdom then must assure that Brazil obtains the same amount of French francs as Brazil would have received had the Fund originally provided francs. One reason for allowing the country of issue (here the United Kingdom) to make the exchange if it requests is that the sale by Brazil of sterling for francs on the exchange markets might lead to the depreciation of the sterling's exchange rate or unsettle the market.

In fact, the United Kingdom has requested that exchanges like that described, involving the pound sterling, be made through the Bank of England. See IMF, *User's Guide to the SDR: A Manual of Transactions and Operations in Special Drawing Rights* (Washington: IMF Treasurer's Department, 1982), p. 92.

[28] See Rule O-4, *By-Laws, Rules and Regulations* (40th issue, 1983); and summary of present procedures in *User's Guide, supra* note 27, p. 92. See also Gold, *Use, Conversion, and Exchange of Currency, supra* note 24, p. 71.

[29] See also *Report on Second Amendment, supra* note 14, part 2, chapter D, section 13; and Gold, *Use, Conversion, and Exchange of Currency, supra* note 24, pp. 68–77.

[30] See generally page 229, *infra.*

[31] Article V, section 7(a).

[32] Article V, section 7(b); and *Report on Second Amendment, supra* note 14, part 2, chapter E, section 2(ii).

reserve position'' is a combined criterion that can be satisfied if the improvement in one element compensates for a slower improvement in the other.[33] Nowhere in the Articles, however, is the phrase defined. The words are to be applied in the context of actual situations as they are presented. The Executive Board has adopted guidelines which, if complied with, give assurance to members that they are meeting the ''expectations.''[34] If the Fund is of the opinion that a member's position has improved and that it has not repurchased in accordance with the expectation, the Fund may after consultation with the member ''represent'' to the member that it should repurchase. At that point the country incurs an obligation to repurchase.[35]

Whether or not the country's position improves, it is legally required to repurchase, not later than five years from the date of a purchase, the Fund's holdings of its currency resulting from that purchase if they are subject to periodic charges.[36] The Fund has prescribed that repurchase shall be made in installments beginning three years, and ending five years, after the date of the purchase.[37] To the extent the Fund has sold the currency to other members in the meantime, the repurchase obligation is reduced. The Fund, by 85 percent of its total voting power, may uniformly for all members shorten or lengthen the maximum period for completing repurchase and the time when repurchase installments are to begin. By the same majority the Fund may prescribe different repurchase periods for purchases made under special policies.[38] The Fund has provided a longer repurchase period under the extended facility, enlarged access policy, supplementary financing facility, and oil facility.[39]

The Fund has authority in individual cases to postpone the date of an installment repurchase and, on a showing of exceptional hardship, to extend the final completion date.[40] If a member does not meet its repurchase obligations, the Fund, if certain stated conditions are met, has authority to sell the member's currency to the extent that it is subject to the repurchase obligation.[41]

When a member makes a repurchase, it is free (within certain limits) to in-

---

[33] *Report on Second Amendment, idem,* part 2, chapter E, section 2(ii).

[34] See E.B. Decision No. 6172 -(79/101)(June 28, 1979); IMF, *Annual Report, 1979,* p. 138; *Selected Decisions* (10th issue, 1983), p. 103. This decision supersedes E.B. Decision No. 5704 -(78/39)(March 22, 1978, effective April 1, 1978); IMF, *Annual Report, 1978,* p. 125; *Selected Decisions,* p. 101.

[35] Article V, section 7(b). See *Report on Second Amendment, supra* note 14, part 2, chapter E, section 2(ii).

[36] Article V, section 7(c). Members are not required or entitled to make repurchases with respect to reserve tranche drawings. See note 82, *infra,* and accompanying text.

[37] E.B. Decision No. 5703 -(78/39)(March 22, 1978, effective April 1, 1978), as amended by E.B. Decision No. 6862 -(81/81)(May 13, 1981); *Selected Decisions* (10th issue, 1983), p. 105.

[38] Article V, section 7(c) and (d).

[39] See pages 250 and 291–294, *infra.*

[40] Article V, section 7(g).

[41] Article V, section 7(h).

dicate to the Fund the previous drawing to which the repurchase is to be attributed. Where drawings were made at different times or under different Fund policies, this can be a very useful right.[42]

Currencies to be Used in Repurchases

Repurchases must be made with special drawing rights or with the currencies of other members specified by the Fund. A member cannot make the repurchase with the same currency originally drawn unless that currency is specified by the Fund. The Fund adopts policies and procedures on currencies to be used in repurchases that take into account the same criteria applied in selecting currencies to be used in purchases.[43] In a repurchase transaction the Fund cannot buy a currency that would raise its holdings to a level where periodic charges would be assessed its issuer under Article V, Section 8(b)(ii).

The Fund in specifying currencies for use in repurchase makes no distinction between members that have accepted the convertibility obligations of Article VIII, Sections 2, 3, and 4, and those that have not done so.[44] Where a currency specified by the Fund for use in effecting a repurchase is not itself a freely usable currency, and may indeed be subject to exchange restrictions, Fund rules establish procedures for the member to obtain it in exchange for a freely usable currency. The issuer of the specified currency is required to make the exchange if requested to do so at the time of the repurchase.[45]

Charges and Remuneration

A word should be said about interest rates. In Fund parlance the language is "charges" and "remuneration." Section 8 of Article V provides authority for assessing charges. The Fund levies a charge (like an interest charge) on a member on the average daily balances of that member's currency held by the General Resources Account in excess of 100 percent of quota. Reserve tranche drawings, thus, are not subject to periodic charges. The General Resources Account's holdings of a member's currency are subject to charges even if the holdings are not in excess of quota if they result from a country's purchases that are excluded in calculating that country's reserve tranche position.[46]

---

[42] E.B. Decision No. 6831 -(81/65)(April 22, 1981, effective May 1, 1981), as amended by E.B. Decision No. 7059 -(82/23)(February 22, 1982); *Selected Decisions* (10th issue, 1983), p. 108. See note 82, *infra*, where portions of the decision are quoted.

[43] Article V, section 7(i). See pages 224–225, *supra*.

[44] See *Report on Second Amendment, supra* note 14, part 2, chapter E, section 2(ix).

[45] Article V, section 7(j); and Rule O-9, *By-Laws, Rules and Regulations* (40th issue, 1983). See generally Gold, *Use, Conversion, and Exchange of Currency, supra* note 24, pp. 77–83.

[46] Article V, section 8(b)(i). See also pages 235–238, *infra*.

The Articles require the Fund to levy a service charge on drawings at the time they are made. The service charge may be lower for reserve tranche purchases than on other purchases. The Fund may levy a charge for stand-by or extended arrangements even if not activated. The Fund may also impose a charge if a repurchase is not made when required. The particular rates of these various charges, which may vary with time, tranche, and facility, are set and changed by decisions of 70 percent of the total voting power of the Fund.[47]

A member pays the charges assessed on its use of the General Resources Account in special drawing rights. In exceptional circumstances, or if it is not a participant in the Special Drawing Rights Department, it may be able to pay the charges in its own or another member's currency.[48]

The Fund pays "remuneration" (like interest) to a member on its net creditor position with the Fund.[49] The remuneration is paid on the amount by which a specified portion of the member's quota, which can be between 75 percent and 100 percent, exceeds the daily average balances of the member's currency held in the General Resources Account.[50] Rates within certain parameters (which are related to the interest rate of the SDR) are set and changed by decisions of 70 percent of the total voting power.[51] The Fund pays remuneration in special drawing rights or the country's own currency.

---

[47] Article V, section 8. The Executive Board sets the charges under a delegation of authority from the Board of Governors. By-Laws, sections 15 and 16; *By-Laws, Rules and Regulations* (40th issue, 1983). Charges are set forth in Rule I of the Fund's Rules and Regulations. Because the charges may vary, the IMF has adopted decisions for identifying the portions of the General Resources Account's holdings of a country's currency that are subject to the different charges. See, e.g., E.B. Decision No. 6834 -(81/65)(April 22, 1981, effective May 1, 1981), and E.B. Decision No. 6861 -(81/81)(May 13, 1981); IMF, *Annual Report, 1981*, pp. 163–67 and 171.

[48] Article V, section 8(e). See E.B. Decision No. 5702 -(78/39) G/S (March 22, 1978, effective April 1, 1978), as amended by E.B. Decision No. 7096 -(82/57) G/S (April 23, 1982); IMF, *Annual Report, 1982*, p. 132; *Selected Decisions* (10th issue, 1983), p. 110.

[49] Article V, section 9.

[50] Balances of the member's currency acquired by the Fund under certain decisions are excluded from the calculations. Article V, section 9; and *Report on Second Amendment, supra* note 14, part 2, chapter G, section 3.

[51] The basis for calculating remuneration is set forth in Rule I of the Fund's Rules and Regulations. The rate of remuneration cannot be more than the rate of interest on the SDR nor less than three-fourths of that rate. See Article V, section 9(a); and E. B. Decision No. 7603 -(84/3) (January 6, 1984) in IMF, *Annual Report, 1984*, p. 129. The determination of the SDR's interest rate is explained in Chapter 5, *supra*, pages 193–194.

Limits on the Volume of Drawings in the Credit Tranches

Under Article V, Section 3(b)(iii), a proposed drawing must not, in the absence of a formal "waiver" by the Fund, raise the Fund's holdings of the purchasing member's currency above 200 percent of its quota.[52] The *Report on the Second Amendment* states:

> This limit [the 200 percent limit] refers to the Fund's total holdings of a currency. That is to say, holdings obtained under a special policy are not deducted, so that a waiver is necessary for any proposed purchase, other than a reserve tranche purchase, that would increase the Fund's holdings in the General Resources Account above two hundred percent of quota.[53]

Thus, any drawing beyond the fourth credit tranche is not permitted unless a waiver is obtained under Section 4 of Article V. In October 1963 the United Arab Republic, by drawing U.S. $16,000,000, increased the Fund's holdings of Egyptian pounds to 215 percent of quota. This was the first time the 200 percent limit was exceeded. This resulted from use of the facility for compensatory financing of export fluctuations, and a waiver was granted.[54] As explained later in this chapter, the extended facility, compensatory financing facility, buffer stock financing facility, enlarged access policy, and some other policy decisions contemplate that waivers will be granted for purchases under those decisions that raise the Fund's holdings of the purchasing member's currency above 200 percent of quota.[55] It is no longer a rare phenomenon for a country's currency held in the General Resources Account to amount to more than 200 percent of quota.

---

[52] Prior to the Second Amendment, Article V also required a waiver whenever a purchase, other than a reserve tranche purchase (then called a gold tranche purchase), would cause the Fund's holdings to increase by more than 25 percent during a twelve-month period. Former Article V, section 3(a)(iii), *original* and *first*. The waiver of this limitation became routine. See J. Keith Horsefield and Margaret Garritsen de Vries, *The International Monetary Fund, 1945–1965: Twenty Years of International Monetary Cooperation* (3 vols.; Washington: IMF, 1969) [hereinafter *IMF History 1945–65*], vol. 2, pp. 403 and 530–32; and Margaret Garritsen de Vries, *The International Monetary Fund, 1966–1971: The System Under Stress* (2 vols.; Washington: IMF, 1976) [hereinafter *IMF History 1966–71*], vol. 1, p. 322. See also *Report on Second Amendment, supra* note 14, part 2, chapter D, section 8.

[53] *Report on Second Amendment, idem,* chapter D, section 8.

[54] *IMF History 1945–65, supra* note 52, vol. 2, p. 403.

[55] These facilities are treated at pages 248, 277, 282, and 291, *infra*.

In June 1980 the Fund approved a stand-by arrangement for Turkey in an amount that exceeded 400 percent of Turkey's quota. IMF, *Annual Report, 1981,* p. 86. This was prior to the adoption of the policy on enlarged access discussed at pages 291–292, *infra*.

Fund Policies on Access to the General Resources Account

Historical Note—Automaticity Versus Conditionality of Drawing Rights

The proper balance between, on the one hand, assuring members that they can draw on the Fund's general resources in time of need and, on the other hand, assuring the Fund that the member needs the resources (and that the member's policies to be supported by the use of those resources are appropriate) has presented a challenge since the Fund was first conceived. In the negotiations that preceded the 1944 Bretton Woods Conference, Lord Keynes had argued that "if countries are to be given sufficient confidence they must be able to rely in all normal circumstances on drawing a substantial part of their quota without policing or facing unforeseen obstacles."[56] United States experts believed that "discretion on the part of the Fund was essential if the Fund's resources were to be conserved for the purposes for which the Fund was established and if the Fund were to be influential in promoting what it considered to be appropriate financial policies."[57] The divergence of view was not resolved at Bretton Woods. Article V of the Fund's Articles of Agreement adopted at the Conference provided that a member "shall be entitled" to purchase the currency of another member from the Fund in exchange for its own currency if the member "represents" that the currency is "presently needed for making in that currency payments which are consistent with the provisions of this Agreement."[58] Article V also required that the member be "eligible" to make drawings, established certain objective limits on the size of drawings, and stipulated that the currency drawn not be held against forward exchange transactions.[59]

The Bretton Woods Agreements Act, authorizing the United States to become a member of the IMF, directed the governor representing the United States to obtain a formal interpretation by the Fund that the Fund's resources were to be used only to finance "temporary" balance-of-payments problems and were not to be used to finance the "reconstruction" of Europe's war-torn economies.[60] The IMF Executive Board following the first annual meeting gave such an interpretation in 1946:

> The Executive Directors of the International Monetary Fund interpret the Articles of Agreement to mean that authority to use the resources

---

[56] Letter from Lord Keynes to Professor Jacob Viner, October 17, 1943. Donald Moggridge (ed.), *The Collected Writings of John Maynard Keynes* (London: Macmillan and Cambridge University Press), vol. 25 (1980), p. 332 at p. 333.

[57] John Parke Young, "Developing Plans for an International Monetary Fund and a World Bank," *Department of State Bulletin,* vol. 23 (1950), p. 778 at p. 783.

[58] Article V, section 3(a)(i), *original.* For background see Sidney Dell, *On Being Grandmotherly: The Evolution of IMF Conditionality* (Essays in International Finance no. 144; Princeton: Princeton University International Finance Section, 1981), pp. 1–7.

[59] Article V, section 3(a)(ii)–(iv) and (b), *original.*

[60] Bretton Woods Agreements Act, section 13(a), *U.S. Statutes at Large,* vol. 59 (1945), p. 512 at p. 517.

of the Fund is *limited* to use in accordance with its purposes to give *temporary* assistance in financing balance of payments deficits on *current account* for *monetary stabilization operations.* [emphasis added][61]

The Executive Directors in 1947 adopted a landmark decision that clearly established the conditional character of drawing rights in the general account:

The word "represents" in Article V, Section 3(a)(i) [*original*], means "declares." The member is presumed to have fulfilled the condition mentioned in Article V, Section 3(a)(i), if it declares that the currency is presently needed for making payments in that currency which are consistent with the provisions of the Agreement. But the Fund may, for good reasons, challenge the correctness of this declaration, on the grounds that the currency is not "presently needed" or because the currency is not needed for payment "in that currency," or because the payments will not be "consistent with the provisions of this Agreement." If the Fund concludes that a particular declaration is not correct, the Fund may postpone or reject the request, or accept it subject to conditions.[62]

The 1947 decision, which continues to have force today, requires the Fund to assess a country's need for foreign exchange and the country's policies. It established the right of the Fund to reject a request for a drawing or to accept it subject to conditions. However, the decision, until clarified in 1952, led to a virtual paralysis in the financial operations of the IMF. The U.S. Executive Director in the 1948–51 period took the position that the Fund should not permit drawings unless the member's currency exchange rate was appropriate, the member was moving toward liberalization of exchange restrictions, and the member's balance-of-payments problems were of a temporary character. The criteria were rather stringently applied.[63]

A way out of the excessive stringency created by the 1946 and 1947 deci-

---

[61] Pursuant to E.B. Decision No. 71-2 (September 26, 1946); *IMF History 1945–65, supra* note 52, vol. 3, p. 245; *Selected Decisions* (10th issue, 1983), p. 18. This interpretation was buttressed by IMF Article XIV, section 1, *original,* which stated: "The Fund is not intended to provide facilities for relief or reconstruction or to deal with international indebtedness arising out of the war."

For background on Decision No. 71-2, see *IMF History 1945–65,* vol. 1, pp. 127 and 148–49; and Dell, *supra* note 58, pp. 7–9. The decision as it applied to the financing of capital movements was "clarified" in 1961. See note 97, *infra.*

[62] Adopted May 6, 1947; text in *IMF History 1945–65, supra* note 52, vol. 1, p. 189. Confirmed in 1948 as E.B. Decision No. 284-4 (March 10, 1948); *IMF History 1945–65,* vol. 3, p. 227. For background see *IMF History 1945–65,* vol. 1, pp. 187–89 and 217–26, and vol. 2, pp. 385–86 and 522–24.

[63] See *Foreign Relations of the United States,* 1949, vol. 1 (1976), pp. 729–51 at p. 746; and *IMF History 1945–65, supra* note 52, vol. 2, pp. 398–401.

sions, as they had been applied, was created by a 1952 decision of the Executive Directors. The decision invented the concept of the "gold tranche" (now "reserve tranche") —that a portion of a member's quota could be drawn without conditions and that drawings above that would be subject to policy conditions. It also stated the principle of conditionality (applicable to drawings outside the reserve tranche) in positive terms that gave confidence to members that they would be able to use the Fund's resources. It foreshadowed the stand-by arrangement. It clarified what the Fund would understand as "temporary" use of its resources.[64] Joseph Gold has described the 1952 decision as "the Mount Everest that towers over all other decisions on the use of the Fund's resources."[65]

The next big step in the continuing balance of automaticity versus conditionality was the creation of stand-by arrangements. Rather than wait until a request for a drawing had been received before determining if it would be met, a country could define its balance-of-payments problems and its policies, the IMF would review the situation and the country's policies, and the IMF would then commit itself to stand-by the country—to make the Fund's resources available for future requested drawings up to a stated amount for a stated period—in support of the country's program.[66]

By the end of the 1950s IMF decisions and practice had established that drawings of a portion of a member's quota (the "gold tranche," now "reserve tranche") was unconditional and that drawings in the credit tranches were conditional—to be evaluated on a case-by-case basis. It was generally assumed that the larger the drawing in relation to quota the more serious the country's situation must be and, thus, the more stringent the measures required to correct it.[67] Stand-by arrangements gave assurance to members entering into them that Fund resources would be available.

In 1963 when the Executive Board adopted its first decision on the compensatory financing of export fluctuations,[68] it recognized the principle that if a member's situation met certain objective criteria defined in particular Fund decisions of general application, the member could make drawings under those decisions in the credit tranches without additional conditions being applied.

---

[64] E.B. Decision No. 102 -(52/11) (February 13, 1952); *IMF History 1945–65, supra* note 52, vol. 3, p. 228; *Selected Decisions* (10th issue, 1983), p. 19.

For background on Decision No. 102, see *IMF History 1945–65*, vol. 1, pp. 321–26. The evolution of Fund policies is described in *IMF History 1945–65*, vol. 2, chapters 18 and 23. On U.S. policy change in 1950-1952 that emerged as support for Decision No. 102, see *Foreign Relations of the United States, 1950*, vol. 1 (1977), pp. 824–28; and *idem*, 1951, vol. 1(1979), pp. 1613–14 and 1626–40. See also Frank A. Southard, Jr., *The Evolution of the International Monetary Fund* (Essays in International Finance no. 135; Princeton: Princeton University International Finance Section, 1979), pp. 16–19.

[65] *IMF History 1945–65, supra* note 52, vol. 2, pp. 523–24.

[66] The first stand-by arrangement was the one approved for Belgium in June 1952. *IMF History 1945–65, idem*, vol. 1, pp. 328–30. See generally, *infra*, page 248 et seq.

[67] See text accompanying note 109, *infra*.

[68] E.B. Decision No. 1477 -(63/8)(February 27, 1963), *infra*, note 214.

The general decisions are described as creating special "facilities"—special sets of rules for drawings to meet particular problems such as export fluctuations, the financing of buffer stocks under commodity agreements, or oil import financing problems.[69]

The "gold tranche–reserve tranche" concept was codified in the First Amendment of the IMF Articles.[70] Some other aspects of the evolution of Fund practice in the balancing of automaticity/conditionality were codified in the Second Amendment.[71]

Practice continues to change and evolve. In recent years there has been a tendency to move increasingly toward policies of general application that can be directly applied to individual cases as compared to the development of policy conditions in the course of examining individual cases. That is, the tendency has been toward becoming more rule oriented.[72]

Drawings in the Reserve Tranche

To make a drawing in the General Resources Account, a member is required to make a representation of need under Article V, Section 3(b)(ii):

> The member represents that it has a need to make the purchase because of its balance of payments or its reserve position or developments in its reserves.

This representation is not subject to challenge by the Fund where the request is for a "reserve tranche" drawing.[73] The rationale is that, in order for each member to have some "elbow room" in conducting its international monetary affairs, a portion of the Fund's holdings of currencies and SDRs should be available to each member without any conditions. That portion is equivalent to the net economic contribution of the country to the General Resources Account—the reserve asset part of its quota subscription payment plus the net use made by others of its currency contribution. The concept of the reserve tranche was not expressed in the original Articles but evolved with practice. The idea was formally introduced into the Articles when they were first amended in 1969.[74]

"Reserve tranche purchase" is defined in Article XXX(c) of the present IMF Agreement:

---

[69] See page 277 et seq.

[70] Article V, section 3(a)(iii), *first.*

[71] Article V, section 3(a)–(c), *second.*

[72] See page 247, *infra.*

[73] Article V, section 3(c).

[74] The term used in the First Amendment was "gold tranche," derived from the portion of the quota paid in gold. Article V, section 3, and Article XIX(j), *first.* For background see note 64, *supra,* and accompanying text.

Reserve tranche purchase means a purchase by a member of special drawing rights or the currency of another member in exchange for its own currency which does not cause the Fund's holdings of the [purchasing] member's currency in the General Resources Account to exceed its quota, provided that for the purposes of this definition the Fund may exclude purchases and holdings under. . . .

The elipsed language permits the Fund by a simple majority of the weighted votes cast to exclude purchases by members (and corresponding holdings by the Fund of the countries' currencies) under the facility for compensatory financing of export fluctuations and the buffer stock financing facility when calculating each country's reserve tranche position. By an 85 percent majority of the total voting power, the Fund can exclude purchases under other policies (and corresponding Fund holdings of the countries' currencies) when calculating reserve tranche positions. After initially excluding drawings under the compensatory financing facility, buffer stock facility, and several other policies in making reserve tranche calculations, the Fund adopted a general decision effective May 1, 1981, to exclude all purchases under all policies relating to the credit tranches (including those under stand-by arrangements and extended arrangements), and corresponding currency holdings acquired by the Fund in those transactions, in making reserve tranche calculations.[75] Thus, a member is no longer, in any case, required to exhaust its reserve tranche drawing rights before making drawings in the credit tranches. Those rights are preserved when drawings are made under credit tranche policies. The member, of course, must pay charges on its currency acquired by the Fund in credit tranche purchases while no charges are assessed on currency acquired by the Fund that corresponds to a reserve tranche purchase.[76]

The reserve tranche is defined (disregarding the exclusions for the moment) as the excess of a member's quota over the Fund's holdings of that member's currency. Assuming no Fund transactions in the currency of a member (A) and that A originally paid 75 percent of its quota subscription in its own currency and 25 percent in SDRs, A's reserve tranche is 25 percent of quota. If the quota is SDR 100,000,000, the reserve tranche would be SDR 25,000,000. If, prior to a drawing by A, the Fund has sold currency issued by A equivalent to SDR 10,000,000 to another country (B), then A's reserve tranche position would be SDR 35,000,000. If, in addition, another member (C) had transferred A's currency equivalent to SDR 5,000,000 to the Fund in satisfaction of a repurchase obligation, the reserve tranche position of A would be SDR 30,000,000. If prior to the current requested drawing, A had made a reserve

[75] E.B. Decision No. 6830 -(81/65) (April 22, 1981, effective May 1, 1981); IMF, *Annual Report, 1981*, p. 162; *Selected Decisions* (10th issue, 1983), pp. 58 and 299.

[76] See note 82, *infra*, and accompanying text, and pages 229–230, *supra*.

tranche purchase of the currency of D equivalent to SDR 7,000,000 and in exchange sold its own currency to the Fund, A's reserve tranche position would then be SDR 23,000,000.

Now, as an example of an exclusion: Suppose that during the same period, A had purchased currency issued by B equivalent to SDR 50,000,000 under the Fund's facility for the compensatory financing of export fluctuations or under an extended arrangement and sold the General Resources Account its currency in exchange; then A's reserve tranche position would be either SDR 23,000,000 or exhausted, depending upon the Fund's decisions under Article XXX(c). If present exclusion policies are continued, A's reserve tranche position would be SDR 23,000,000 in that case.

When the Fund receives a request for a reserve tranche drawing involving the purchase of a currency, it must, no later than the close of the first business day following receipt of the request, instruct the appropriate depository to make the transfer.[77]

The proceeds of a reserve tranche drawing can be used for any purpose consistent with the IMF Agreement. Some uses of the proceeds of reserve tranche drawings are explicitly permitted that are normally not allowed uses of credit tranches, including the financing of large and sustained capital outflows.[78] Even if the IMF believes that the member's representation of need is improper or that it will use the funds in a manner that will violate the Articles, the requested drawing must be permitted to go forward so long as the member remains eligible to use the Fund's resources.[79] However, the Fund does have remedies.[80] The unconditional right to make reserve tranche drawings, stated in Article V, Section 3(c), is relied upon by a member when it includes its reserve tranche position in the Fund in official statements of monetary reserves.[81]

It is important to note that under the Second Amendment a member is neither obligated *nor permitted* to repurchase its currency sold to the General Resources Account in a reserve tranche purchase. Thus, following a reserve

---

[77] A request for a purchase under a stand-by or extended arrangement that is in effect is handled with the same speed as a reserve tranche request (unless borrowed resources are involved). The review of other requests for drawings may take somewhat longer. Rule G-4; *By-Laws, Rules and Regulations* (40th issue 1983).

[78] Article VI, section 2.

[79] Even if the member has been declared ineligible, which is a very unusual event, the Fund can grant a waiver pursuant to Article V, section 4, that permits the drawing.

[80] Pursuant to Article V, section 5, the Fund can, after allowing the transaction, present a report to the member in which the Fund indicates its view that the member's representation of need was not accurate or that the currencies or SDRs purchased from the Fund were used in a manner inconsistent with the IMF Agreement or the Fund's policies. If the member does not take corrective action, the Fund may thereafter limit the member's use of the General Resources Account. The procedure can lead to a formal declaration of ineligibility to use the Fund's general resources. See Chapter 1, *supra*, pages 40–41.

[81] See Chapter 3, *supra*, page 112.

tranche drawing, the country's position is restored only as other countries draw (or otherwise obtain) its currency from the Fund.[82]

Tranche Concept

The drawing capacity of a member is measured in terms of the member's quota in the Fund and the amount of currency of that member in relation to its quota which will be held by the Fund after the proposed drawing is made. For some purposes references are made to "credit tranches." The particular tranche is related to the amount of a member's currency held by the Fund in relation to the country's quota.

Assuming (a) that the member initially paid 25 percent of its quota in reserve assets (gold, special drawing rights, or currencies of other countries) and 75 percent in its own currency, (b) that no other member has purchased or sold the country's currency in transactions with the Fund, and (c) that the member first exhausts its reserve tranche rights before making drawings outside the reserve tranche, then the relationships between drawings by the country and the Fund's holdings of its currency are as follows:

---

[82] See text accompanying notes 30 and 46, *supra*. A member is obligated and permitted to repurchase from the General Resources Account only balances of its currency that are subject to charges. Currency acquired by the Fund in a reserve tranche purchase by a member is not subject to periodic charges. Article V, section 8(b). E.B. Decision No. 6831, as amended by Decision No. 7059, *supra* note 42, provides:

> 1. (a) Subject to paragraphs (b) and (c) below a member shall be free to attribute a reduction in the Fund's holdings of its currency (i) to any of its obligations to repurchase, and (ii) to enlarge its reserve tranche.
> (b) . . . .
> (c) An attribution to create a reserve tranche may only be made if the reduction results from the sale of the member's currency or from operational payments by the Fund in that currency and if the member's obligations to repurchase do not include an obligation relating to a purchase financed through borrowing under the GAB [General Arrangements to Borrow].
> 2. A reduction attributed to a reserve tranche position will not discharge an expectation of repurchase under the Guidelines for Early Repurchase.
> 3. If the member when asked does not make an attribution in accordance with 1 above, it will be deemed to be discharging the first maturing repurchase obligation.

See also E.B. Decision No. 7060 -(82/23)(February 22, 1982); IMF, *Annual Report, 1982*, p. 128; *Selected Decisions* (10th issue, 1983), p. 300.

Total currencies drawn	Size of IMF's holding of drawing member's currency after the drawings	Tranche exhausted
25% of quota	100% of quota	Reserve tranche
50% of quota	125% of quota	First credit
75% of quota	150% of quota	Second credit
100% of quota	175% of quota	Third credit
125% of quota	200% of quota	Fourth credit

Further drawings require a waiver by the IMF.

The drawing rights of a country (call it M) are affected by transactions of other members with the Fund in which M's currency is used. Suppose that other members have purchased M's currency from the Fund, so that the Fund's holding of M's currency has been reduced to 60 percent of quota. M would now have reserve tranche drawing rights equal to 40 percent of its quota.

Conversely, sales of M's currency to the Fund by other members (for example in the context of satisfying the repurchase obligations of those members) will cause the Fund's holding of M's currency to increase. The effect of these sales of M's currency to the Fund by other members is to reduce M's drawing rights. The Fund cannot, however, purchase from other members the currency of M if that raises the Fund's holdings of M's currency to a level at which M would be subjected to charges under Article V, Section 8(b)(ii).[83]

Drawings Outside the Reserve Tranche— Introductory Comments on Legal Requirements

Consideration of drawings outside the reserve tranche has two aspects: (1) does the request meet the threshold legal requirements stated in the Articles, and (2) does the proposed use of the Fund's resources and the terms for that use conform to the policies adopted by the Fund on the use of its resources? We shall first consider the threshold legal requirements.

A member desiring to purchase foreign currencies from the General Resources Account will in the case of drawings in the credit tranches, just as in the case of drawings in the reserve tranche, make a request that includes a representation, pursuant to Article V, Section 3(b)(ii), "that it has a need to make the purchase because of its balance of payments or its reserve position or develop-

---

[83] Article V, section 7(i).

ments in its reserves.'' This representation of need is subject to challenge. The proposed drawing must also satisfy additional conditions: The proposed use will be in accordance with the provisions of the Articles and the policies adopted under them, and the proposed purchase will not cause the Fund's holdings of the purchasing member's currency to exceed 200 percent of quota.[84]

The Fund cannot waive the requirement that the proposed use be in accordance with the Articles and Fund policies nor can it waive the "need" requirement. It can under Section 4 of Article V grant a waiver and approve a drawing by a country that has been declared ineligible to use the Fund's general resources and it can grant a waiver and approve a drawing that would cause the Fund's holdings of the purchasing member's currency to exceed 200 percent of quota. Granting these waivers is discretionary and if granted they can include terms, such as the pledge of collateral security, to safeguard the Fund's interests.[85]

When a request is received, the Fund (acting under Section 3(c) of Article V) examines the representation to determine whether the member has need for the Fund's resources and whether the use of the Fund's general resources will be in accordance with the provisions of the IMF Agreement and with the policies adopted by the Fund.[86] The conditional character of the right to make drawings beyond the reserve tranche was established in a 1947 decision of the Executive Directors (confirmed in 1948) that interpreted Article V, Section 3, in its earlier form. That decision requires the Fund to assess the country's need and the country's policies. It established the right of the Fund to reject an application for a drawing or to accept it subject to conditions.[87] The basic principle of conditionality of credit tranche drawings is retained in the present Articles.[88]

Concept of ''Need''

Commenting on the requirement of ''need,'' the *Report on the Second Amendment* states:

> Under the concept of need in [new] Article V, Section 3(b)(ii), a member will be able to purchase the currencies of other members from the Fund if its balance of payments position or its reserve position is unfavorable, or if there is an unfavorable development in its reserves, e.g., because of an impending discharge of liabilities, even though it does not have a deficit in its balance of payments according to accepted definitions of the balance of payments.[89]

---

[84] Article V, section 3(b)(i) and (iii).

[85] Article V, section 4. Waivers of the 200 percent limit have been frequent; pledges rare.

[86] See Article V, section 3(b)(i).

[87] See note 62, *supra*, and accompanying text.

[88] See also text accompanying note 103, *infra*.

[89] *Report on Second Amendment, supra* note 14, part 2, chapter D, section 7. The concept of ''need'' in Article XIX, section 3(a), relating to the use of special drawing rights has the same meaning.

All balance-of-payments needs are included in the concept of "need" whether they arise from current or capital transactions. However, the Fund can challenge for good cause a member's representation that it has need when the proposed drawing is not in the reserve tranche.[90]

Meaning of "in Accordance with . . . this Agreement"

The member's use of the Fund's general resources is to be "in accordance with the provisions of this Agreement. . . ."[91] The contemplated use of the currencies to be purchased must thus be consistent with the various provisions of the Articles and with the purposes of the Fund.[92]

It deserves emphasis that the IMF Articles do not require the Fund to specify particular uses that must be made of currencies and SDRs drawn from the General Resources Account. The Fund's normal practice is not to specify particular uses. The resources may normally be used for general undifferentiated balance-of-payments support so long as the uses are consistent with the IMF Articles. The currencies and SDRs may be used to replenish reserves that have been depleted.

It is, for example, consistent with the provisions of the Agreement and its purposes for a member to purchase foreign currency required by the government or its private residents (banks, firms, and individuals) to make payments or transfers for current international transactions, and Article XXX(d) defines "payments for current transactions" very broadly. It is also consistent with the Agreement and its purposes for a member to purchase foreign currency to sell on the exchange markets to maintain orderly exchange conditions, to maintain a pegged rate for its currency, or to manage a floating rate for its currency—so long as these actions are in accord with Article IV and other provisions of the IMF Agreement. The use of Fund resources to finance a maturing obligation under a currency swap arrangement is permitted,[93] as is use of the Fund's resources to finance forward exchange transactions.[94] Other uses may also be in accordance with the Articles.

Use of the Fund's resources in the credit tranches to finance a "large" or "sustained" outflow of capital is prohibited.[95] Outflows that are neither sus-

---

[90] See *Report on Second Amendment, supra* note 14, part 2, chapter D, section 7. When the representation of need is made in support of a reserve tranche drawing, it is not subject to challenge. See pages 235–238.

[91] Article V, section 3(b)(i). See also section 3(c).

[92] See E.B. Decision No. 287-3 (March 17, 1948); *IMF History 1945–65, supra* note 52, vol. 3, p. 228; *Selected Decisions* (10th issue, 1983), p. 18.

[93] This is an impending discharge of liabilities. See quotation on page 240, *supra*.

[94] Under former Article V, section 3(b), *original* and *first*, a member had to obtain the Fund's permission to acquire currency in the credit tranches to hold against forward exchange transactions.

[95] Article VI, section 1. Section 2 of Article VI permits the use of currency obtained in a reserve tranche purchase to finance capital transfers, even large and sustained ones.

tained nor large can be financed.[96] The Fund's resources in the credit tranches can be used for capital transactions of "reasonable amount" required for the expansion of exports or required in the "ordinary course" of trade, banking, or other business in countries without exchange controls as well as those having controls.[97] The Fund has in practice willingly provided resources to members even when their payments difficulties were attributable wholly or substantially to outflows of capital.[98]

Use of Fund drawings for payments consistent with the provisions of the Agreement may have the effect of releasing the member's other resources for other payments. A member is permitted by the Articles to use its own foreign exchange resources to finance a large and continuing outflow of capital while at the same time it uses currencies purchased from the Fund in the credit tranches for payments on current transactions. The member's actions must, however, be consistent with the purposes of the Fund.[99]

It appears that the IMF has never required a country to institute capital controls in order to make a drawing or obtain a stand-by arrangement.[100] The Fund does expect members to deal with the underlying conditions that cause undesired large outflows. In practice, the correction of conditions causing outflows is the primary focus of attention, and the complexities of Article VI are largely irrelevant. If a country fails to deal with the underlying conditions (e.g., a high inflation rate) that prompt a large and sustained outflow of capital, the Fund has authority (drawing on its powers under Article V, Section 3(a)) to decline to approve a proposed credit-tranche drawing on the ground that the country's actions are not in accord with Fund policies on the use of its resources. The Fund has assisted countries in formulating programs to stabilize financial conditions, improve debt structures, and restore confidence in their currencies;

[96] According to Fund practice a capital outflow is not "sustained" if the country's policies can be expected to arrest or reverse the flow within the period for which Fund assistance is provided. The word "large" has never been defined. Because it is difficult to determine how much of a balance-of-payments problem is attributable to net capital movements, the Fund has considerable flexibility in applying Article VI, section 1.

[97] Article VI, section 1(b)(i). E.B. Decision No. 1238 -(61/43) (July 28, 1961); *IMF History 1945-65, supra* note 52, vol. 3, p. 245; *Selected Decisions* (10th issue, 1983), p. 18, states that Fund resources can be used to finance capital transfers so long as the requirements of Article VI are met. The effect of E.B. Decision No. 1238 was to repeal through "clarification" a 1946 formal "interpretation" by the Executive Board that had determined (against the plain meaning of Article VI) that Fund resources could only be used to finance current account deficits. The 1946 interpretation is quoted in the text accompanying note 61, *supra*. See generally *IMF History 1945-65*, vol. 1, pp. 503-06, and vol. 2, pp. 415-16; and Gold, *International Capital Movements Under the Law of the International Monetary Fund* (IMF Pamphlet Series no. 21; Washington, 1977), pp. 23-27.

[98] Statement of Joseph Gold, then General Counsel of the IMF, in *International Capital Movements, idem,* p. 46.

[99] Article VI, section 1(b)(ii). See discussion of the stand-by arrangement for Venezuela in 1960; *IMF History 1945-65, supra* note 52, vol. 2, pp. 413-14.

[100] This statement is based on the author's inquiries supplementing Mr. Gold's statement in *International Capital Movements, supra* note 97, pp. 3 and 20.

and the Fund has made its financial resources available to support these programs.[101]

Drawings Outside the Reserve Tranche— Preliminary Comments on Fund Policies

As already noted, a proposed drawing outside the reserve tranche must be in accord with the Fund's policies on the use of its resources.[102] The Fund is required to have policies:

> The Fund shall adopt policies on the use of its general resources, including policies on stand-by or similar arrangements, and may adopt special policies for special balance of payments problems, that will assist members to solve their balance of payments problems in a manner consistent with the provisions of this Agreement and that will establish adequate safeguards for the temporary use of the general resources of the Fund.[103]

Authority to adopt policies resides in the Board of Governors and pursuant to its delegation is exercised by the Executive Board.[104] Specific policies are not prescribed, and the language quoted above would appear to permit the Fund to amend its policies from time to time. The policies are to facilitate the carrying out of all of the Fund's purposes, including:

> (v) To give confidence to members by making the general resources of the Fund temporarily available to them under adequate safeguards, thus providing them with opportunity to correct maladjustments in their balance of payments without resorting to measures destructive of national or international prosperity.
> (vi) In accordance with the above, to shorten the duration and lessen the degree of disequilibrium in the international balances of payments of members.[105]

A very general statement of the Fund's policies on drawings in the credit tranches was made in 1959 and continues to serve as a point of reference:

> The Fund's attitude to requests for transactions within the first credit tranche[106] . . . is a liberal one, provided that the member itself is also

---

[101] See Gold, *idem*, pp. 23–28 and 46–47.
[102] Article V, section 3(b)(i).
[103] Article V, section 3(a).
[104] See Chapter 1, *supra*, pages 28–30.
[105] Article I (v) and (vi).
[106] The tranche concept is explained at pages 238–239, *supra*.

making reasonable efforts to solve its problems. Requests for transactions beyond these limits require substantial justification. They are likely to be favorably received when the drawings or stand-bys are intended to support a sound program aimed at establishing or maintaining the enduring stability of the member's currency at a realistic rate of exchange.[107]

The "liberal" policy of the Fund on drawings in the first credit tranche is given legal embodiment in the rule that regular drawings can be made in that tranche without the need to obtain a stand-by arrangement or to fit within a specifically defined Fund policy. The IMF need only be satisfied that the country is making reasonable efforts to solve its problems and that use of the currencies purchased by the member will be in accordance with the Articles. Where a stand-by arrangement is used, there are no "performance criteria" that can interrupt the right to make drawings in the first credit tranche.[108] It is worth noting, however, that there have been occasions when countries have refrained from requesting drawings or stand-by arrangements, even ones limited to the first credit tranche, when the Fund staff expressed concern about governmental stability or found the financial and monetary policies of the country seriously deficient in relation to the problems faced.

While Pierre-Paul Schweitzer, when Managing Director, stated in 1966 that "the larger the amount required in relation to the member's quota, the more stringent the criteria which must be satisfied,"[109] this is not an accurate statement today. It is true that under virtually all Fund policies a relevant consideration is not the actual amount of resources to be drawn by a country but the relative size of the amount already drawn and to be drawn by the country *in relation to that country's quota size*. However, the idea of greater stringency of conditions in each successive credit tranche has too many exceptions to even be asserted as a generality. The conditions of an extended arrangement into the sixth credit tranche may not necessarily be more stringent than conditions of a stand-by arrangement into the third credit tranche. A number of Fund policies, such as those relating to the financing of export fluctuations and financing of buffer stocks, permit drawings with minimal reference to the outstanding or anticipated drawings under other policies.[110]

It can be said as a generality that drawings beyond the first credit tranche must (a) be made under special policies of the Fund in which criteria are care-

---

[107] IMF, *Annual Report, 1959*, p. 22. Similar statements appeared in *Annual Reports* for subsequent years.

[108] E.B. Decision No. 6056 -(79/38) (March 2, 1979), *infra* note 112, paragraph 6. "Performance criteria" are objective (and usually quantitative) tests or ceilings set out in a member's policy declarations that are treated by the Fund as appropriate criteria for judging the performance of the country's policies. Failure to meet performance criteria interrupts drawing rights above the first credit tranche under a stand-by arrangement. See pages 265–266 and 267–268, *infra*.

[109] *Finance and Development*, vol. 3 (1966), p. 102.

[110] The rules under these various policies are examined in subsequent sections of this chapter.

fully specified, usually in statistically measurable terms as in the compensatory financing facility, or (b) be made pursuant to stand-by arrangements or extended arrangements.[111] A country drawing upon a special facility must meet the requirements for use of the particular facility. The general test for approval of stand-by arrangements that provide for drawings beyond the first credit tranche is "substantial justification" that the country is pursuing a sound program. As explained in the next section, all stand-bys for drawings in the second and higher tranches include performance clauses.

In 1979 the Fund adopted a decision entitled "Use of Fund's General Resources and Stand-By Arrangements" and informally called "guidelines on conditionality."[112] The decision applies to stand-by and extended arrangements and to drawings in the credit tranches that are not made under decisions pertaining to "special facilities." Decisions defining special facilities are essentially special rules for access to the General Resources Account for particular problems such as compensatory financing of export fluctuations. The conditionality decision properly focuses primarily on the adequacy of the country's policies in relation to the problems it faces and only secondarily on the magnitude of the financial resources required:

> Members should be encouraged to adopt corrective measures, which could be supported by use of the Fund's general resources in accordance with the Fund's policies, at an early state of their balance of payments difficulties or as a precaution against the emergence of such difficulties. . . .
>
> In helping members to devise adjustment programs, the Fund will pay due regard to the domestic social and political objectives, the

---

[111] In rare cases, large direct drawings have been permitted in emergencies caused by earthquakes or other disasters. India was permitted in 1966 to make a drawing (without using a stand-by arrangement) into the third credit tranche for an emergency caused by a severe drought. Egypt in 1968 made a direct purchase beyond the first credit tranche when it faced severe problems as a result of the 1967 six-day war with Israel and the closure of the Suez Canal. The Dominican Republic in September 1979 made a direct purchase of SDR 23 million to cope with emergency conditions caused by a hurricane earlier that month. At the time the Dominican Republic had a quota of SDR 55 million and outstanding obligations to the Fund amounting to SDR 54 million. See *IMF History 1966–71, supra* note 52, vol. 1, pp. 318–19; Southard, *Evolution of the International Monetary Fund, supra* note 64, pp. 27–29; and *IMF Survey*, October 15, 1979, p. 331.

[112] E.B. Decision No. 6056 -(79/38) (March 2, 1979), IMF, *Annual Report, 1979*, p. 136; *Selected Decisions* (10th issue, 1983), p. 20. For a detailed commentary on the decision, see Joseph Gold, *Conditionality* (IMF Pamphlet Series no. 31; Washington, 1979), pp. 14–37. See also Manuel Guitián, *Fund Conditionality: Evolution of Principles and Practices* (IMF Pamphlet Series no. 38; Washington, 1981); Dell, *supra* note 58, pp. 10–33; and the papers collected in John Williamson (ed.), *IMF Conditionality* (Washington: Institute for International Economics, 1983).

The 1979 decision was adopted following a review of the Fund's policies on conditionality during which a number of developing countries criticized past policies. See IMF, *Summary Proceedings, 1978*, especially speeches by governors for Bangladesh, Cameroon, Guyana, India, Malta, Pakistan, Paraguay, Sri Lanka, Thailand, and Venezuela. See also the IMF Managing Director's address of May 8, 1978; *IMF Survey*, May 22, 1978, p. 145. The 1979 decision supersedes E.B. Decision No. 2603 -(68/132)(September 20, 1968); *IMF History 1966–71, supra* note 52, vol. 2, p. 197.

economic priorities, and the circumstances of members, including the causes of their balance of payments problems. . . .

The Managing Director will recommend that the Executive Board approve a member's request for the use of the Fund's general resources in the credit tranches when it is his judgment that the program is consistent with the Fund's provisions and policies and that it will be carried out.[113]

In order to assure similar treatment of countries in similar situations, the Executive Board has adopted decisions of general application on some serious and recurrent problems. Examples include a decision that limits use of Fund resources by countries with "payments arrears"[114] and a decision dealing with external debt management policies.[115]

A country that is in breach of the Articles is not precluded from obtaining a stand-by arrangement or extended arrangement or making a drawing in the credit tranches.[116] The IMF staff, however, usually consults with the member about the violations during negotiations preceding the request.[117] Even if a member country has been declared ineligible to use the Fund's resources because of certain acts in breach of the Articles, the Fund in its discretion can grant a waiver and approve the stand-by arrangement or drawing.[118] The Fund, however, must always be assured that the country to which resources are to be provided in the credit tranches is meeting the Fund's policy conditions established in accordance with the Articles.[119]

The Fund's resources are intended to assist members in dealing with balance-of-payments problems. The Fund's resources are provided for general support and not for particular projects. Although some Fund policies, such as the facility for compensatory financing of export fluctuations, are directed to the

---

[113] E.B. Decision No. 6056, *supra* note 112, paragraphs 1, 4, and 7.

[114] Payments arrears occur, for example, when foreigners who have shipped goods to nationals of a country encounter delays in obtaining payment because of excessive delays in the administrative processings of exchange applications or restrictions on the availability of funds. E.B. Decision No. 3153 -(70/95)(October 26, 1970); *IMF History 1966–71, supra* note 52, vol. 2, p. 214; *Selected Decisions* (10th issue, 1983), p. 243, applies to the first as well as higher credit tranches. See also Chapter 10, *infra*, pages 411–413.

[115] The debt decision provides that when the size and the rate of growth of external indebtedness is a relevant factor in the design of an adjustment program, a performance criterion relating to official and officially guaranteed foreign borrowing will be included in upper-credit-tranche arrangements. E.B. Decision No. 6230 -(79/140)(August 3, 1979); IMF, *Annual Report, 1980,* p. 138; *Selected* Decisions (10th issue, 1983), p. 23; and chairman's summary of Executive Board discussion, April 6, 1983, in IMF, *Annual Report, 1983,* p. 160. See also W. A. Beveridge and Margaret R. Kelly, "Fiscal Content of Financial Programs Supported by Stand-By Arrangements in the Upper Credit Tranches, 1969–78," *IMF Staff Papers,* vol. 27 (1980), p. 205.

[116] The Dominican Republic, for example, made drawings in the first credit tranche in March and April 1977 although it had unapproved exchange practices. See Chapter 10, *infra,* page 414.

[117] See note 190, *infra.* See Chapter 10, *infra,* pages 410–411 and 412–413 (Mexico).

[118] See page 240, *supra.*

[119] See pages 240 and 241, *supra.*

problems of developing countries, the Fund does not as a rule provide long-term support for development programs.[120] There are exceptions: The extended facility provides general balance-of-payments support for periods of four to ten years to countries making structural changes in their economies. The Special Disbursement Account, which contains assets separate from the General Resources Account, can be used for long-term assistance to IMF members with low per-capita incomes.[121]

The variety of Fund policies and their frequent amendment in recent years, indeed what might be called tinkering with them, make it difficult to ascertain overall guiding principles. The statements above are, at best, generalities that are subject to qualification. There has also been a tendency in recent years for the Fund to become more rule oriented—indeed more legalistic—than a lawyer might deem wise. One reason is concern in an organization of many members that members in similar situations be treated consistently. Another factor may be bureaucratic tendencies as the size of staff has increased over what it was fifteen or twenty years ago. A consequence has been increasing, and probably unnecessary, complexity. Member countries—even those with very able economic and legal personnel—find they must rely on the advice of Fund staff as to which of many different policies to use when they consider seeking financial assistance from the Fund. An effort is made in the following sections of this chapter to identify fundamental features of these various policies.

As we conclude this section, worth bearing in mind is a comment made in 1952 by Ivar Rooth, when Managing Director, that continues to have relevance today:

> I think it must be clear that access to the Fund should not be denied because a member is in difficulty. On the contrary, the task of the Fund is to help members that need temporary help, and requests should be expected from members that are in trouble in greater or lesser degree. The Fund's attitude toward the position of each member should turn on whether the problem to be met is of a temporary nature and whether the policies the member will pursue will be adequate to overcome the problem within such a period. The policies, above all, should determine the Fund's attitude.[122]

---

[120] The original IMF Articles stated: "The Fund is not intended to provide facilities for relief or reconstruction or deal with international indebtedness arising out of the war [World War II]." Former Article XIV, section 1, *original* and *first*. The language was deleted by the Second Amendment.

At the 1944 Bretton Woods Conference, India proposed that the purpose clauses in Article I include a reference to development of the economically underdeveloped countries, but this was opposed on the ground that this was a matter for the International Bank for Reconstruction and Development rather than the Fund. See Chapter 12, *infra*, pages 644–647.

[121] The Special Disbursement Account is treated, *infra*, at page 294.

[122] Quoted in E.B. Decision No. 102 -(52/11), *supra* note 64.

Stand-By and Extended Arrangements

Introductory Comments

Since drawing rights beyond the reserve tranche are conditional, procedures have been developed whereby a member can obtain assurances from the Fund that drawings will be permitted in the future when needed. Thus, a member can avoid the risk that only after a serious balance-of-payments problem has arisen it would learn that the Fund would not permit it to make a credit tranche drawing. The advance understandings between a member and the Fund are called "stand-by arrangements" or "extended arrangements."[123]

Stand-by arrangements were first introduced in 1952.[124] They soon became the principal means by which the Fund provided financial assistance to its members in the credit tranches. Article V, Section 3(a), specifically authorizes the Fund to adopt policies on the use of stand-by arrangements.[125] Article XXX(b) defines a stand-by arrangement as "a decision of the Fund by which a member is assured that it will be able to make purchases from the General Resources Account in accordance with the terms of the decision during a specified period and up to a specified amount." Stand-by arrangements until 1977 did not exceed one year in length, but now may permit drawings over a period of up to three years.[126]

In 1974 the Fund adopted a decision establishing what is called the Extended Fund Facility and introduced "extended arrangements."[127] Extended arrangements are a special class of "stand-by or similar arrangements" from

---

[123] The IMF's principal policy decision on stand-by arrangements is E.B. Decision No. 6056 -(79/38) (March 2, 1979), *supra* note 112, referred to as "guidelines on conditionality." The principal policy decision on extended arrangements is E.B. Decision No. 4377 -(74/114) (September 13, 1974), as amended by E.B. Decision No. 6339 -(79/179) (December 3, 1979) and E.B. Decision No. 6830 -(81/65) (April 22, 1981); *Selected Decisions* (10th issue, 1983), p. 27.

[124] The first stand-by arrangement was the one for Belgium approved in June 1952. The first stand-by arrangement decision of general application was approved later in 1952. E.B. Decision No. 155 -(52/57)(October 1, 1952); *IMF History 1945–65, supra* note 52, vol. 3, p. 230. For background see *IMF History 1945–65*, vol. 1, pp. 328–32.

[125] Prior to the Second Amendment of the IMF Agreement, the authority was implied.

[126] E.B. Decision No. 6056, *supra* note 112, paragraph 2. When stand-by arrangements were first introduced in 1952, they were limited to six months. Subsequently, one year became the normal length of a stand-by. One year also stood as the limit until January 1977, when a stand-by was approved for the United Kingdom for a two-year period. For background see three basic IMF stand-by arrangement decisions that preceded Decision No. 6056: E.B. Decision No. 155 -(52/57), *supra* note 124; E.B. Decision No. 270 -(53/95) (December 23, 1953), as amended by Decisions No. 876 -(59/15) (April 27, 1959) and No. 1151 -(61/6) (February 20, 1961) (*IMF History 1945–65, supra* note 52, vol. 3, pp. 230–34; *Selected Decisions* [10th issue, 1983], p. 46; and E.B. Decision No. 2603, *supra* note 112.

The Fund may approve a new stand-by arrangement to take effect for a country upon expiration of an earlier arrangement. Peru has benefited from successive stand-bys for over fifteen years and some other countries for over ten. See Joseph Gold, *The Stand-By Arrangements of the International Monetary Fund* (Washington: IMF, 1970), pp. 85–86; *IMF History 1966–71, supra* note 52, vol. 1, pp. 358–59; and IMF, *Annual Report, 1981*, p. 120.

[127] E.B. Decision No. 4377, *supra* note 123. Kenya in 1975 was the first country to obtain an extended arrangement.

the standpoint of Article V, Section 3(a), and Article XXX(b). The Extended Fund Facility is simply a special set of rules for this class of arrangements. The principal differences between extended arrangements and regular stand-by arrangements are that extended arrangements almost always run for the maximum period of three years, the arrangements are normally for larger amounts in relation to quota, the repurchase period is longer, and the schedule of charges may be less. The decision on extended arrangements explicitly states that, except as provided in that or subsequent related decisions, the policies and decisions of the Fund on stand-by arrangements also apply to extended arrangements.[128]

Extended arrangements are intended to make resources available to members, particularly developing members, for balance-of-payments support while they pursue economic programs dealing with structural maladjustments in production and trade. However, in accordance with the Extended Fund Facility decision, it is the structural nature of the problems facing the country and the magnitude and duration of assistance required, rather than the country's developing or industrial status, that determines whether it may qualify for an extended arrangement as compared to a regular stand-by arrangement.[129]

In order to obtain a stand-by or extended arrangement, a country must submit a program to correct its balance-of-payments problems. This program will be outlined in a letter of intent to the Fund as explained below. The letter will set forth the objectives and policies for the whole period of the arrangement and will include a detailed statement of policies for the first year. If the arrangement is for longer than one year, there will be an understanding that progress will be reviewed at the end of the first year and the country at that time will submit a detailed program for the second year, and so on.[130]

The Fund's decision approving each stand-by or extended arrangement will state the duration of the arrangement, the total amount of Fund resources available for purchase by the country, and the annual installments within the total. Purchases within each installment will be phased with "suitable" performance clauses related to implementation of the country's program for correction of its problems.

Drawings can be made under stand-by or extended arrangements, while preserving reserve tranche drawing rights for emergency.[131] Drawings under an extended arrangement may also preserve drawing rights in the first credit tranche.[132] A country's total outstanding purchases using the Fund's regular re-

---

[128] E.B. Decision No. 4377, as amended, *supra* note 123, paragraph 8.

[129] E.B. Decision No. 4377, as amended, *supra* note 123.

[130] E.B. Decision No. 6056, *supra* note 112, paragraphs 7–10 (stand-by arrangements); and E.B. Decision No. 4377, as amended, *supra* note 123, section 1 and section 2, paragraphs 1–3 (extended arrangements).

[131] E.B. Decision No. 6830, *supra* note 75, paragraph 1.

[132] E.B. Decision No. 4377, as amended, *supra* note 123, section 2, paragraph 4. "Regular" drawing rights in the first credit tranche are preserved if the extended arrangement is for the normal maximum of 140 percent of quota. If the amount is for less, "regular" drawing rights into the second credit tranche may be preserved.

sources are normally limited under a stand-by arrangement to 100 percent of quota or less,[133] and under an extended arrangement are limited to 140 percent of quota.[134] Stand-by or extended arrangements may provide for the use of resources borrowed by the Fund above these amounts.[135]

It is routine for the Fund to grant waivers of the 200 percent of quota limit on currency holdings in order to permit drawings of the magnitude permitted under extended arrangements.[136] The Fund may also grant waivers of the 200 percent limit for stand-by arrangements.[137]

The normal repurchase period under a stand-by arrangement is three to five years.[138] Under an extended arrangement, repurchases are to be completed within an outside period of four to ten years.[139] Repurchases are to be made earlier if the balance-of-payments situation of the country permits.

Stand-by and extended arrangements are reported in the IMF's *Annual Report* and, at the time each arrangement is approved, a note about the country's program is carried in *IMF Survey*.[140]

Documentary Form of Stand-By and Extended Arrangements

Each stand-by or extended arrangement is approved by a separate Executive Board decision. The decision is typically only two or three paragraphs long and states approval of an attached Fund document entitled, for example, "Extended Arrangement—India" or whatever country requested the arrangement. The decision will grant the appropriate waiver if purchases under the arrangement are to be allowed to raise the Fund's holdings of the purchasing member's currency above 200 percent of quota.[141] The attached document states the terms of the Fund's assistance.

Appended to the Fund's "stand-by arrangement" or "extended arrangement" document is a letter from the requesting country to the Fund. In many respects this is the most important paper. This "letter of intent" will be submitted to the Fund after negotiations with the Managing Director and with a

---

[133] Although E.B. Decision No. 6056, *supra* note 112, does not say so, stand-by arrangements normally do not exceed 100 percent of quota unless borrowed resources are used.

[134] E.B. Decision No. 4377, as amended, *supra* note 123, section 2, paragraph 4.

[135] See generally pages 283–293, *infra*, and especially pages 291–292 (policy on enlarged access to the Fund's resources).

[136] E.B. Decision No. 4377, as amended, *supra* note 123, section 2, paragraphs 3 and 4.

[137] See page 231, *supra*.

[138] See notes 36–38, *supra*, and accompanying text.

[139] E.B. Decision No. 4377, as amended, *supra* note 123, section 2, paragraph 5.

[140] As of April 30, 1983, a total of 521 stand-by arrangements had been approved by the Fund since 1952 for a total amount equivalent to SDR 45.0 billion. A total of 31 extended arrangements had been concluded for an amount equivalent to SDR 24.5 billion. IMF, *Annual Report, 1983*, p. 119 and 124.

[141] The Executive Board may at the same time adopt separate but related decisions approving particular exchange restrictions, approving coordinated drawings under special Fund facilities, and/or approving borrowings by the Fund should it need to supplement its resources in connection with providing the stand-by or extended arrangement.

Fund staff mission. The letter (which may be signed by the minister of finance and/or the governor of the central bank) describes the balance-of-payments problems facing the country and the policies that will be pursued by the country to solve its problems. Sometimes the country will append a detailed statement of its economic policies to the letter of intent.

Set forth below, as an illustrative case, are the IMF Executive Board decision of November 9, 1981, approving an extended arrangement for India, the IMF's extended arrangement document, the letter of intent submitted by the Finance Minister of India, and excerpts from the statement of economic policies appended to that letter. This extended arrangement for India was the largest stand-by or extended arrangement in absolute amount in the history of the Fund.[142]

IMF Executive Board Decision
Approving Extended Arrangement for India[143]

1. The Government of India has requested an extended arrangement for a period of three years from November 9, 1981 in an amount equivalent to SDR 5,000 million.

2. The Fund approves the extended arrangement [reproduced below] attached to EBS/81/198 (10-7-81).

3. The Fund waives the limitation in Article V, Section 3(b)(iii), of the Articles of Agreement.[144]

---

[142] The Fund does not publish its individualized stand-by or extended arrangement decisions and documents, nor does it publish the texts of letters of intent or statements of policies submitted by governments. A member may publish its own letter of intent, though most countries do not do so. In the case of the Indian arrangement, public debate and criticism were anticipated. N. Ram, a reporter for the Madras newspaper, *The Hindu*, obtained a set of the confidential documents and published them in that newspaper in order that the public debate would be an informed one.

Letters of intent supporting stand-by arrangements for the United Kingdom approved in January 1977, for Italy approved in April 1974 and April 1977, and extended arrangement for Mexico approved in December 1982 appear, respectively, in *Financial Times* (London), December 16, 1976, p. 9; Williamson, *IMF Conditionality, supra* note 112, pp. 466 and 468; and *Comercio Exterior* (Mexico City) (English edition), vol. 28, no. 11 (November 1982), p. 412. A memorandum supplementing the Mexican letter appears in *Proceso* (Mexico City), November 29, 1982, p. 23. The United Kingdom letter of December 1976 also appears in Leonard Lazar, *Transnational Economic and Monetary Law* (7 vols.; Dobbs Ferry: Oceana Publications, binder service, 1983 ed.), vol. 2, booklet 22, p. 1.7.036.

Letters of intent published up to 1970 are listed in Gold, *Stand-By Arrangements, supra* note 126, pp. 269–70. See *idem*, pp. 57–64, for illustrative documents for a stand-by arrangement circa 1970.

[143] Printed in *The Hindu* (Madras), November 11, 1981, p. 9. The decision was adopted by the IMF Executive Board on November 9, 1981. The executive director representing the United States abstained. The arrangement, to be financed in part with the Fund's ordinary resources (SDR 2,404.5 million) and in part with borrowed resources (SDR 2,595.5 million), was equivalent to 291 percent of India's quota. See *IMF Survey*, November 23, 1981, p. 365.

[144] See notes 135 and 136, *supra*, and accompanying text. See also page 231, *supra*.

Extended Arrangement - India[145]

Attached hereto is a letter, with annexed memorandum, dated September 28, 1981 from the Minister of Finance of India, requesting an extended arrangement and setting forth:

(a) the objectives and policies that the authorities of India intend to pursue for the period of this extended arrangement;

(b) the policies and measures that the authorities of India intend to pursue for the first year of this extended arrangement; and

(c) understandings of the authorities of India with the Fund regarding reviews that will be made of progress in realizing the objectives of the program and of the policies and measures that the authorities of India will pursue for the second and third years of this extended arrangement.

To support these objectives and policies the International Monetary Fund grants this extended arrangement in accordance with the following provisions:

1. For a period of three years from November 9, 1981, India will have the right to make purchases from the Fund in an amount equivalent to SDR 5,000 million, subject to Paragraphs 2, 3, 4, and 5 below, without further review by the Fund.

2. (a) Until June 30, 1982, purchases under this extended arrangement shall not, without the consent of the Fund, exceed the equivalent of SDR 900 million, provided that purchases shall not exceed the equivalent of SDR 300 million until January 15, 1982, and SDR 600 million until March 25, 1982.

(b) Until June 30, 1983, purchases under this extended arrangement shall not, without the consent of the Fund, exceed the equivalent of SDR 2,700 million.

(c) The right of India to make purchases during the period from July 1, 1982 to June 30, 1983, and from July 1, 1983 to the end of the extended arrangement shall be subject to such phasing as shall be determined.

3. Purchases under this extended arrangement shall be made from ordinary and borrowed resources in the ratio of one to one until purchases under this arrangement reach the equivalent of SDR 4,809 million, and then from borrowed resources, provided that any modification by the Fund of the

---

[145] Printed in *The Hindu* (Madras), November 11, 1981, p. 9. Paragraphs 6, 7, and 9 were not published in *The Hindu*. Minor corrections have been made to conform to the official document.

This document, while tailored to India's particular situation, in general follows a standard form. For the text of the form, see Attachment B to E.B. Decision No. 6838 -(81/70) (April 29, 1981); IMF, *Annual Report, 1981*, p. 156; *Selected Decisions* (10th issue, 1983), p. 48. This is the form used if the arrangement, as in the Indian case, provides both for the use of the General Resources Account's regular resources and for the use of borrowed resources. If only the Fund's regular resources are to be used, paragraph 3 is deleted and the language in paragraphs 7 and 9 is appropriately amended.

For the text of the form for a stand-by arrangement, see Attachment A to E.B. Decision No. 6838, *supra*.

proportions of ordinary and borrowed resources shall apply to amounts that may be purchased after the date of modification.

    4. India will not make purchases under this extended arrangement:[146]

(a) during the period through June 30, 1982 in which the data at the end of the preceding period indicate that

    (i) the ceiling on domestic credit of the banking system described in Paragraph 17 and the associated table of the annexed statement of economic policies, or

    (ii) the ceiling on net credit to the Government of the banking system described in Paragraph 17 and the associated table of the annexed statement of economic policies[147]

are not observed; or

(b) with respect to the period after March 24, 1982 if the reviews contemplated in Paragraph 5 of the attached letter have not been completed,[148] or if following these reviews, any new understandings reached in these reviews are not observed; or

(c) if India fails to observe the limits on authorizations of new official and officially-guaranteed foreign indebtedness described in Paragraph 21 of the attached memorandum;[149] or

(d) for the period from July 1, 1982 to June 30, 1983 and from July 1, 1983 through the end of the extended arrangement, if before June 30, 1982 and June 30, 1983, respectively, suitable performance clauses for these periods have not been established in consultation with the Fund, or if such clauses, having been established, are not observed; or

(e) throughout the duration of the extended arrangement, if India

    (i) imposes or intensifies restrictions on payments and transfers for current international transactions, or

    (ii) introduces multiple currency practices, or

    (iii) concludes bilateral payments agreements which are inconsistent with Article VIII, or

    (iv) imposes or intensifies import restrictions for balance of payments reasons.

When India is prevented from purchasing under this extended arrangement because of this Paragraph 4, purchases will be resumed only after consultation has taken place between the Fund and India and understandings

---

[146] This paragraph states what are called "performance criteria." Performance criteria will vary a great deal from one arrangement to another except for sub-paragraph (e) which uses language that is standard in stand-by and extended arrangements.

[147] Pages 260 and 263, *infra.*

[148] Page 256, *infra.* See also notes 158 and 174, *infra.*

[149] See page 262, *infra.*

have been reached regarding the circumstances in which such purchases can be resumed.

5. India's right to engage in the transactions covered by this arrangement can be suspended only with respect to requests received by the Fund after (a) a formal ineligibility, or (b) a decision of the Executive Board to suspend transactions, either generally or in order to consider a proposal, made by an Executive Director or the Managing Director, formally to suppress or to limit the eligibility of India. When notice of a decision of formal ineligibility or of a decision to consider a proposal is given pursuant to this Paragraph 5, purchases under this arrangement will be resumed only after consultation has taken place between the Fund and India and understandings have been reached regarding the circumstances in which such purchases can be resumed.

6. Purchases under this extended arrangement shall be made in the currencies of other members selected in accordance with the policies and procedures of the Fund, and may be made in SDRs if, on the request of India, the Fund agrees to provide them at the time of the purchase.

7. The value date of a purchase under this extended arrangement involving borrowed resources will be normally either the fifteenth day or the last day of the month, or the next business day if the selected day is not a business day. India will consult the Fund on the timing of purchases involving borrowed resources.

8. India shall pay a charge for this arrangement in accordance with the decisions of the Fund.[150]

9. (a) India shall repurchase the amount of its currency that results from a purchase under this extended arrangement in accordance with the provisions of the Articles of Agreement and decisions of the Fund, including those relating to repurchase as India's balance of payments and reserve position improves.

(b) Any reduction in India's currency held by the Fund shall reduce the amounts subject to repurchase under (a) above in accordance with the principles applied by the Fund for this purpose at the time of the reduction.[151]

(c) The value date of a repurchase in respect of a purchase financed with borrowed resources under this extended arrangement will be normally either the sixth day or the twenty-second day of the month, or the next busi-

---

[150] The member is required to pay a charge (currently 0.25 percent per year) in consideration of the commitment by the Fund to make currencies available on call. This charge is credited to the service charge when drawings are made and in some circumstances may be partially refunded. See Article V, section 8(a); and Rule I-8, *By-Laws, Rules and Regulations* (40th issue, 1983).

[151] A stand-by or extended arrangement is not a revolving credit arrangement. Under the IMF's present policies there are no augmentation rights under a stand-by or extended arrangement. That is, once a country has made a drawing under a stand-by, a subsequent repurchase does not augment its drawing rights so that it can draw that amount again under that stand-by. E.B. Decision No. 5706 -(78/39) (March 22, 1978); IMF, *Annual Report, 1978,* p. 129; *Selected Decisions* (10th issue, 1983), p. 57.

ness day if the selected day is not a business day, provided that repurchase will be completed not later than seven years from the date of purchase.

10. During the period of the extended arrangement, India shall remain in close consultation with the Fund. These consultations may include correspondence and visits of officials of the Fund to India or of representatives of India to the Fund. India shall provide the Fund, through reports at intervals or dates requested by the Fund, with such information as the Fund requests in connection with the progress of India in achieving the objectives and policies set forth in the attached letter and annexed memorandum.

11. In accordance with Paragraph 5 of the attached letter[152] India will consult the Fund on the adoption of any measures that may be appropriate at the initiative of the Government or whenever the Managing Director requests consultation because any of the criteria under Paragraph 4 above have not been observed or because he considers that consultation on the program is desirable. In addition, after the period of the arrangement and while India has outstanding purchases under this extended arrangement, the Government will consult with the Fund from time to time, at the initiative of the Government or at the request of the Managing Director, concerning India's balance of payments policies.

Letter of Intent
from the Finance Minister of India
to the Managing Director of the IMF[153]

September 28, 1981

Dear Mr. De Larosière,

1. The Government of India is currently implementing a set of policies designed to achieve a medium-term adjustment to the structural changes to which the economy has been subjected following, among other things, the sharp deterioration in terms of trade, and to higher oil prices. These policies are an integral part of the Sixth Plan (1980/81–1984/85).

2. After several years of strong economic performance marked by sustained growth in output, internal price stability and a healthier external payments situation, India's economic position suffered a serious setback in 1979/80. Severe drought resulted in a sharp reduction in domestic output, agricultural production fell substantially, and the deterioration extended to basic infrastructure and industry as well. The shortfall in supplies affected export performance at a time when the import bill rose sharply. Inflation re-

---

[152] Page 256, *infra.*
[153] Printed in *The Hindu* (Madras), October 16, 1981, p. 9.

emerged early in 1979 and the balance of payments deteriorated sharply in the second half of that year. Since 1980/81 the economy has been moving upward with recovery in agricultural production and improvement in infrastructure performance. Real GDP [gross domestic product] has risen strongly, and improved supplies and restrained financial policies have helped to bring about some subsidence in inflation. However, the balance of payments has weakened further to a deficit of SDR 1.6 billion as a result of a further deterioration in the terms of trade, reflecting mainly the full impact of the rise in prices of oil and related products, the earlier disruptions to domestic oil production, weak market demand and restricted access for our exports due to increased protectionism.

3. We expect that India's balance of payments position will be under pressure for several years to come. The details of the adjustment programme adopted by the Government of India are contained in the attached memorandum. In brief, the programme aims to resolve the medium-term balance of payments problems by measures to promote higher export growth and efficient import substitution, especially in the energy sector. It will take some time for these measures to show results and in the meantime, the balance of payments will continue to be in deficit. During the adjustment period, the programme provides for measures to increase domestic savings and for appropriate demand management.

4. In support of its programme, and in view of the present and prospective balance of payments need, the Government of India requests an extended arrangement for a period of three years for an amount equivalent to SDR 5 billion.

5. The Government of India believes that the policies to be followed in 1981/82, which are described in the attached memorandum, are adequate to achieve the objectives of its programme, but will take any further measures that may become appropriate for this purpose. The Government will consult with the Fund on the adoption of any appropriate measures, consistent with the national policies accepted by our Parliament, in accordance with policies of the Fund on such consultation. In particular, the Government will review with the Fund the progress made in implementing the programme, normally about midway through each year, as part of the ongoing dialogue with the Fund. With respect to the programme for the first year, the Government will, in conjunction with the next Article IV consultation discussions,[154] consult with the Fund before March 25, 1982 on the Government's measures, which are in line with its declared policies, and have a bearing on the programme and, in particular, on those relating to resource mobilisation and exports in view of paragraphs 13, 15 and 18 of the annexed memorandum and reach such

---

[154] IMF Article IV consultations are discussed in Chapters 11 and 12, *infra*.

understandings with the Fund as are necessary for the purposes of achieving the objectives of the programme.

Yours sincerely,

Sd/R. Venkataraman
Finance Minister

Statement of Economic Policies[155]
[Attachment to Letter of the Finance Minister of India,
dated September 28, 1981]

[The first several paragraphs of the statement describe India's current economic situation and elaborate the points in paragraphs 1 and 2 of the Finance Minister's letter.]

[Fund's Role; India's Adjustment Strategy]

4. The present balance of payments difficulties are expected to persist for several years before policies to strengthen the balance of payments have their full effect. It is in this context that Fund financing can play an important role. Balance of payments adjustment will be achieved through a range of measures which are being implemented and will be continued through the programme period. There is considerable scope to replace large imports of items where India is an efficient producer and to increase self-reliance in energy. . . . The Government of India also accords high priority to the objective of achieving a dynamic export performance. To this end, the Government has already taken a number of measures to promote exports. However, it will take time for these measures to bear fruit. Such measures to promote external adjustment, including efforts to overcome bottlenecks in industry and basic infrastructure, will require a sizable step-up in investment. Large investments will require higher domestic savings. . . . The containment of inflation is an important objective, and domestic financial policies will be oriented to achieve this and to strengthen the efficiency of resource allocation.

5. The adjustment strategy outlined in the preceding paragraph is a part of the Sixth Plan efforts. The plan (1980/81 through 1984/85) aims to achieve economic growth of 5.2 per cent per annum, or 3.3 per cent in per capita terms. . . . [T]o finance plan investments, domestic savings are projected to rise from 21.2 per cent of GDP in 1979/80 to 24.5 per cent of GDP in 1984/85, implying a marginal savings rate in excess of 33 per cent. A

---

[155] Printed in *The Hindu* (Madras), October 19, 1981, p. 8. Only selected excerpts are printed here, and some corrections have been made to conform to the official document. This document gives the flavor of the policies of a country that are reviewed during the negotiation of a stand-by or extended arrangement.

major effort will be made to increase public sector savings to finance 21 per cent of total plan investments over the plan period. Private savings are estimated to account for 73 per cent of the total. Foreign capital inflows, mainly on concessional terms, will finance the remaining 6 per cent. . . .

[Plan Investment]
    6. Total investment is estimated to be Rs. 1,587 billion during the five-year period through 1984–85. Compared with the Fifth Plan, there is a projected real increase in investment outlays of more than 80 per cent. The share of the public sector rises from 45 per cent to 53 per cent, reflecting the emphasis of the Plan on overcoming bottlenecks in the infrastructure. . . .

[Agricultural Development]
    7. The agricultural development strategy followed in the late 1960s will be maintained and strengthened. In addition, agricultural policy will aim at improving the balance of production, with a major emphasis on efforts to overcome domestic shortages in non-foodgrain production, including oilseeds, pulses, and sugarcane. This should help to reduce import needs and contain inflation while also creating and enlarging exportable surpluses in some commodities. . . .

[Public Sector Programme]
    8. The public sector programme will. . . . [The memorandum offers estimates of production of various commodities and also deals with aspects of management of public enterprises.]

[Private Sector Policies]
    9. Policies relating to private sector industry will aim at encouraging production, investment and economic efficiency. . . . [A] number of important policy initiatives have already been taken. Additional capacities created since 1975 are being regularised for a wide range of industries; existing arrangements providing for the automatic expansion of capacity have been extended to 19 additional industries; fully export-oriented units have been given additional concessions, and export capacity has been exempted from antimonopoly regulations and domestic licensing provisions; policies favouring small-scale industries are being implemented in a way which places a much increased emphasis on economic efficiency; and import of foreign technology needed by the economy is being permitted liberally.

[Energy]
    10. . . . . It is the Government's policy objective that domestic coal and electricity prices should reflect economic cost and generate internal resources for investment.
    11. . . . . Recently, it has been decided to step up the production of

oil, mainly from offshore sources, beyond the levels projected in the Sixth Plan. The Government has also invited foreign parties to tender for exploration and development in designated areas on a profit-sharing basis. . . . [I]n July 1981 the Government implemented a substantial upward adjustment in the price of domestically produced crude oil. The price of domestic crude is now on par with international prices. This latest price increase will raise a substantial volume of additional resources to finance plan expenditure. Oil pricing policy thus serves the dual objective of moderating growth of demand and contributing to non-inflationary financing of the public sector investment targets.

[Government Revenues; Subsidies]

12. The financing pattern of the Plan . . . places greater emphasis than in the past on non-tax resources. . . . Total tax revenues (including the States) have already reached about 20 per cent of national income and there is consequently only limited scope for the Central Government to increase tax rates. Nevertheless, new Central Government tax measures are expected to yield Rs 51 billion over the Plan period. . . . The Central Government also intends to contain, and wherever possible, reduce subsidies, even though this might entail price adjustment for important commodities. It is expected that measures to contain subsidies will yield resource savings totalling Rs 33 billion during the Plan period. . . . Pricing and administrative improvements to be implemented during the Plan period will aim to achieve a 10 per cent rate of return on investments in public enterprises, 2 percentage points above the previous norm.

[Price Reform]

13. An important objective during the programme period is to achieve a substantial increase in domestic resource mobilisation. . . . [The memorandum lists government-supplied commodities and items for which prices were already raised in 1980/81.] It is the Government's intention to ensure that this flexibility in pricing will continue. . . .

[Government Spending]

14. The underlying strategy with respect to Government spending is to curtail the growth of non-Plan expenditures in order to redirect resources toward the Plan. . . . Despite the ambitious Central plan . . . the Central Government budget for 1981/82 is stringent by historical standards. In current price terms, total expenditure is budgeted to increase by only 9 per cent, revenue disbursements by 12 per cent, and capital disbursements by 5 per cent over the revised estimates for 1980/81. To finance Central Government expenditures, budgetary receipts are projected to rise by 12 per cent. Of the increase, new tax measures are projected to constitute less than 2 percentage points in net terms. . . . This is because considerable direct tax relief has been allowed with the aim of promoting savings and stimulating investment.

However, the revenue loss from direct taxes will be more than compensated for by an increase in indirect taxes.

[Incentives for Private Sector Savings]

15. The achievement of the planned step-up in investment depends on the continued buoyancy of private sector savings. . . . [T]he Government intends to strengthen the activities of the financial institutions in rural areas, and widen the scope of attractive financial assets available to private savers. . . . The Government budget for 1980/81 also includes tax concessions designed to encourage private savings. Interest rate policy will be deployed flexibly keeping in mind these objectives and progress in reducing inflation. The authorities intend to review policy options to promote the desired growth in private savings.

[Monetary and Financial Policies]

16. The emphasis on monetary and financial policies in the recent past has been on containing inflationary pressures and restraining the rate of monetary expansion. . . . The principal objective of monetary policy over the programme period will be to promote relative stability in prices while supporting more rapid growth and supply-side policies. Despite the large volume of investment envisaged in infrastructure, it is intended to keep the Government's total recourse to bank credit within limits consistent with overall financial stability. . . . Interest rates on bank advances were further adjusted upward. . . . Interest rates charged by the term-lending institutions were stepped up substantially. . . . The liquidity of commercial banks will be contained by phased increases in the cash reserve ratio and the statutory liquidity ratio. . . . [The latter] will be raised from 34 per cent to 34.5 per cent by September 25, 1981 and again to 35 per cent effective October 31, 1981. These adjustments, when complete, are estimated to reduce loanable funds with the scheduled banks by about Rs 9 billion or 2 per cent of their demand and time liabilities as at end-March 1981.

[Ceilings on Net Credit to Government and on Total Domestic Credit]

17. . . . . Consistent with real growth of about 5 per cent which appears feasible if weather conditions are favourable . . ., the Government will aim to limit the growth of total liquidity to about 15.7 per cent in 1981/82. . . . Taking account of the projected balance of payments deficit, total domestic credit expansion is to be limited to 19.4 per cent. . . . [See annexed table on page 263] Corrective measures will be taken promptly if developments suggest that the ceilings may be exceeded.

[Export Promotion]

18. A critical objective of the programme is to increase the growth in exports. The Government has recently reviewed export promotion and de-

velopment policies and a number of new initiatives have already been taken. Export production has been freed from restrictions arising from industrial licensing. Exports will not be included in the calculation of capacity for purposes of industrial licensing or for purposes of the Monopolies and Restrictive Trade Practices Act. . . . The Government is currently considering . . . extending concessions to less than 100 per cent export-oriented units; expanding the coverage and simplifying procedures of the advance licensing (duty exemption) scheme for exporters; extending access of exporters to imports; liberalising access of exporters to foreign technology; improving procedures for fixing duty drawback rates and settling drawback claims; and the coordination of supply and demand policies to promote consistent exportable surpluses of agricultural commodities. . . . [T]he Government intends to take further significant measures to strengthen the export effort during the programme period.

[Import Liberalisation]
   19. Import restrictions were progressively relaxed in the late 1970s. This has greatly increased access of domestic producers to imports of raw materials and intermediate goods. Restrictions on imports of capital goods have also been eased. . . . Import policy for the period ahead will be guided by the need to ensure that import requirements and technology needs of a growing economy and a heavy investment programme are adequately and expeditiously met. . . . [I]t is our intention to carry forward the progress achieved over recent years toward liberalisation of imports of raw materials, intermediate and capital goods needed by the economy. It is our intention that the import policies for 1982/83 and 1983/84 will contain significant steps aimed at liberalising imports. . . . Specific measures contemplated include increasing the access to imports of restricted and banned items permitted under automatic import licenses as well as changes in the classification of items under the restricted, banned and open lists.

[Balance of Payments Financing Gap]
   20. Our export and import policies are guided by the objective of achieving external adjustment during the 1980s. . . . Projections for 1981/82 indicate that the deterioration in the current account will be arrested in that year. However, in the two subsequent years, the current account deficit would widen as non-oil imports are expected to expand strongly to support expanding investment and production. The current account deficit as a proportion of GDP would peak in 1983/84, at 2.2 per cent of GDP, it would decline markedly to 1.8 per cent in 1984/85 and gradually thereafter during the remainder of the decade. Taking into account official capital receipts, increased recourse to commercial credits and the possibility of private capital inflows, the balance of payments financing gap is projected to be SDR 6.4 billion during the 1981/82–1983/84 period.

[External Borrowing and External Debt]

21. Until very recently, India has resorted only modestly to external borrowing on commercial terms, and the bulk of its foreign debt arises from assistance channeled through the India Consortium and is predominantly on concessional terms. India's outstanding disbursed external debt currently amounts to about SDR 14 billion, equivalent to some 11 per cent of GDP. The external debt service ratio declined steadily during the 1970s and in 1980/81 debt service payments are estimated to be 8 per cent of current account receipts. . . . The ratio is projected to rise over the coming years, reflecting an expected increase in recourse to borrowing on commercial terms, and an expected hardening of the average terms of multilateral flows. Nevertheless, the debt servicing burden will remain manageable. In order to avoid an undue deterioration of the debt service profile, the Government intends to take a cautious approach to foreign borrowing on commercial terms. The Government is considering two large projects in the steel and electric power sectors. The two projects, which are still at the planning stage, would have a combined foreign exchange cost of about SDR 3 billion. A considerable portion of the external financing arrangements for these projects would be on non-concessional terms. . . . [W]hile it is expected that external borrowing commitments for both projects will be undertaken at some stage during the programme period, only a part of the loans would be disbursed by 1983/84. As an order of magnitude, these disbursements, which are excluded from balance of payments projections, would be expected to be about SDR 1 billion during the programme period. Bearing these borrowings in mind, during the first year of the extended arrangement the Government will limit the contracting or guaranteeing of other non-concessional loans with an original maturity of between one and twelve years to no more than SDR 1.4 billion. With this ceiling, new commitments of between one and five years will be limited to SDR 400 million.

[Exchange Rate Policy]

22. The rupee has been pegged to a basket of currencies of India's trading partners since September 1975, with the pound sterling as the intervention currency. The relationship between the rupee and the basket of currencies is maintained within margins of 5 per cent. This system has proved highly satisfactory. . . . The Government also recognises that exchange rate policy has an important bearing on export growth. During the programme period the Government intends to pursue a realistic policy in regard to exchange rates keeping in mind, inter alia, their objectives with regard to the overall balance of payments and export promotion.

Ceilings on Net Credit to Government
and Total Domestic Credit[156]
(in billions of rupees)

Item	Amount outstanding on March 27 1981	Ceiling amounts outstanding on		
		Nov. 27 1981	Feb. 26 1982	March 26 1982
(a) Net credit to government	258.06	294.29	304.64	309.81
(b) Total domestic credit	621.26	703.59	733.20	741.81

The IMF Executive Board approved the SDR 5 billion Indian extended arrangement on November 9, 1981. Under the IMF's decision Indian authorities were authorized to draw an amount equivalent to SDR 900 million during the first eight months provided that performance criteria, to be explained below, were being met. An additional SDR 1,800 million could be drawn in the period July 1, 1982–June 30, 1983, provided that performance clauses continued to be met (including establishment of performance clauses for this period). The remainder of the SDR 5 billion could subsequently be drawn provided performance criteria for the remainder of the arrangement would be established and observed.[157] The arrangement contemplated that before June 30, 1982, and again before June 30, 1983, the Fund would conduct reviews of the progress of the Indian economy.[158]

---

[156] Printed in *The Hindu* (Madras), October 16, 1981, p. 9. This table, annexed to the Statement of Economic Policies, relates to paragraph 17 of the statement.

[157] See paragraphs 1, 2, and 4 of the extended arrangement document, page 252–253 *supra*.

[158] See introduction to the extended arrangement document, page 252, and paragraph 5 of the letter of intent, page 256. The IMF announced in July 1982 that it had approved India's economic program for the second year of the arrangement and that, as of that time, all performance criteria had been observed. All performance criteria had also been observed at the time of the review in the summer of 1983. *IMF Survey,* July 19, 1982, p. 217; February 6, 1984, p. 33; and March 26, 1984, p. 81.

Procedures in the Negotiation of Stand-By and Extended Arrangements

Most countries seeking stand-by arrangements do so to obtain balance-of-payments support while they undertake programs to maintain or restore the domestic purchasing power of the country's currency, to increase export earnings, or to liberalize trade or payments restrictions. Stand-bys can also be used to provide temporary balance-of-payments support when no policy changes by the government are necessary, though this is less frequent.[159] Extended arrangements, which have features comparable to stand-bys, are available under the Extended Fund Facility for balance-of-payments support while countries undertake programs that involve significant changes in their economic structures.[160]

The preparatory steps leading to a stand-by or extended arrangement include a comprehensive review by the Fund of the member's economy and the country's policies that affect its internal and external financial position.[161] A Fund staff mission will visit the country, usually for a period of about two weeks but sometimes longer. The letter of intent will be submitted to the Fund following this review of the country's policies and negotiations with the Fund. As illustrated above, the letter will state the policies the country intends to pursue to correct its particular balance-of-payments problems.[162]

Depending on the problems facing the country, the letter will state the country's policies and target levels for exports, projected government tax reve-

---

[159] A stand-by arrangement may, for example, be used to supplement resources available under the Fund's facility for compensatory financing of export fluctuations in the case, say, of a country that suffers a severe drought. See pages 277–280, *infra.*

[160] See pages 248–250, *supra.*

[161] Article IV consultations, discussed in Chapters 11 and 12, also provide occasions on which the Fund may discuss adjustment programs that would enable the Fund to approve a stand-by or extended arrangement for a member. E.B. Decision No. 6056, *supra* note 112, paragraph 1.

[162] The procedures followed by the IMF in consultations with members are described in Chapter 12, *infra,* pages 571–580. See generally Andrew Crockett, "Issues in the Use of Fund Resources," *Finance and Development,* vol. 19, no. 2 (June 1982), p. 10.

The economic strategy and policies described in the Indian Finance Minister's letter and the accompanying statement of policies were discussed with two IMF staff missions which visited India in January and April 1981. There were further negotiations in Paris in June, London in July, and Washington, D.C., in August 1981. There was also close contact between the staffs of the IMF and the World Bank, and two Bank staff members participated in the Fund mission that went to India in April 1981. Tun Thin, Director of the Fund's Asian Department, participated in all of the discussions and was the principal negotiator for the IMF. Substantial excerpts from the IMF staff report, normally never published, appear in *The Hindu* (Madras), October 20, 1981, p. 7; and October 21, 1981, p. 7. See generally Catherine Gwin, "Financing India's Structural Adjustment: The Role of the Fund," in Williamson, *IMF Conditionality, supra* note 112, p. 511.

The negotiation of the stand-by arrangement for the United Kingdom, approved January 3, 1977, is vividly described in A.F. Ehrbar, "The IMF Lays Down the Law," *Fortune,* July 1977, p. 98 at pp. 106–10; and in F. Lisle Widman, *Making International Monetary Policy* (Washington: Georgetown University International Law Institute, 1982), pp. 166–70. *IMF History 1966–71, supra* note 52, vol. 1, pp. 320–69 and 431–46, comments on stand-by arrangements with both developed and developing countries during the period covered by the history.

nues and expenditures and size of budget deficits, ceilings on volume of bank credit in the economy, policies on wage rates and price inflation, exchange and trade restrictions, exchange rate policies, anticipated changes in the balance of payments, changes in monetary reserves, and the like. Each letter will not necessarily deal with all of these matters. The choice of policy instruments is affected by not only the problems the country faces but also by the level of its institutional development; in particular, the government's fiscal organization, the banking system, the labor market, and foreign trade and payments system.[163] There may be debate among officials and economists about which policies are appropriate and wise in the particular case.[164]

In the case of arrangements for drawings beyond the first credit tranche, the country's letter of intent must state the intended results of some of its policies in specific quantitative terms which will be used as "performance criteria."[165] The number and content of performance criteria may vary depending on the institutional arrangements of the member and the problems it faces. An effort is made to identify and use a few carefully selected macroeconomic variables that have objective characteristics, will be subject to measurement, and will be accurate indicators of whether the country's policies are achieving intended results.[166] "Performance criteria" also include statements of actions that will be taken to implement specific provisions of the IMF Articles or policies adopted under them.[167] More specificity in the definition of policies and their intended effects will be expected by the Fund in the case of arrangements covering the third or fourth credit tranches than the second.[168]

In the Indian extended arrangement, ceilings on domestic credit and on

---

[163] Most of the subjects listed in the text (with the exception of wage policies) are, in fact, mentioned in the Indian letter and accompanying statement set forth above. The formulation of programs supported by stand-by arrangements is treated in Crockett, "Issues in the Use of Fund Resources," *supra* note 162; and Omotunde E.G. Johnson, "Use of Fund Resources and Stand-By Arrangements," *Finance and Development*, vol. 14, no. 1 (March 1977), p. 19. See the country studies and other papers collected in Williamson, *IMF Conditionality, supra* note 112. See also *IMF History 1945–65, supra* note 52, vol. 2, pp. 472–75 and 492–510; and *IMF History 1966–71, supra* note 52, vol. 1, pp. 343–48 and 363–69.

[164] Legal parameters of the economic prescription are stated in the quotation from E.B. Decision No. 6056 on pages 245–246, *supra.*

[165] E.B. Decision No. 6056, *supra* note 112, paragraphs 6, 9, and 10. This decision supersedes E.B. Decision No. 2603, *supra* note 112, which first required use of performance criteria. For background see *IMF History 1966–71, supra* note 52, vol. 1, pp. 343–48.

If a letter of intent supporting a stand-by arrangement limited to the first credit tranche includes quantitative targets, these are not used as performance criteria which if not met would interrupt the right to make drawings under the arrangement.

[166] E.B. Decision No. 6056, *supra* note 112, paragraph 9. See also paragraph 10 which deals with the situation where it is not possible at the time a stand-by or extended arrangement is requested to state performance criteria for the entire period.

[167] E.B. Decision No. 6056, *idem,* paragraph 9. See paragraph 4(e) of the Extended Arrangement-India document at page 253, *supra.*

[168] A member may be expected to adopt some corrective measures before a stand-by arrangement is approved. See E.B. Decision No. 6056, *idem,* paragraph 7. Note the actions taken by India in 1981 that are mentioned in the statement of economic policies at pages 257–262, *supra.*

credit to the government were used as the principal performance criteria. Also limits on official and officially guaranteed foreign indebtedness were used as performance criteria. In both cases the Indian submissions stated the intentions and the Fund chose them as criteria.[169]

India's letter of intent and statement of economic policies also stated the government's intentions respecting other matters of concern to the Fund. The Indian statement of policies declared that "the Government intends to pursue a realistic policy in regard to exchange rates" and "recognises that exchange rate policy has an important bearing on export growth."[170] Exchange rate policies are often mentioned in letters of intent and figure in negotiations of stand-by arrangements. The Fund will want to avoid providing resources to finance balance-of-payments deficits that are likely to continue because of an overvalued exchange rate.

Import liberalization is almost always mentioned where countries have exchange or trade controls.[171] The extended arrangement document uses India's refraining from introducing or intensifying exchange restrictions as a performance criterion.[172] In other words, India would not take actions requiring Fund approval under Article VIII, Sections 2 and 3. In addition, the imposition or intensification of trade restrictions (for balance-of-payments reasons) would interrupt the right to make drawings.[173]

At the end of the letter of intent, India assumed a broad commitment to consult with the Fund on "any appropriate measures." It would consult with the Fund before March 25, 1982; it would review progress in the summers of 1982 and 1983. These statements are reinforced in the consultation clauses in the IMF's extended arrangement document.[174]

---

[169] See paragraph 4 of the IMF extended arrangement document, page 253, and the referenced statements in India's letter of intent and statement of policies. See note 115, *supra,* regarding an IMF general decision on external debt policies.

India's liberalized treatment of private investment described in paragraph 9 of the Statement of Policies, while no doubt welcomed by the IMF staff, was not made a performance criterion.

[170] See paragraph 22 of the statement of economic policies at page 262, *supra.*

[171] See paragraph 19 of India's statement of economic policies at page 261, *supra.*

[172] See paragraph 4(e) of the IMF's extended arrangement document at page 253, *supra.* This is a standard performance criterion in almost all stand-by and extended arrangements. See also note 190, *infra.*

[173] See paragraph 4(e)(iv) of the IMF's extended arrangement document at page 253, *supra.* Trade restrictions are treated in Chapter 10, *infra,* at pages 428–442.

[174] See paragraphs 10 and 11 of the IMF's extended arrangement document, page 255, and paragraph 5 of India's letter of intent, pages 256–257.

Stand-by and extended arrangements for periods in excess of one year contain review clauses. Review clauses are themselves performance criteria in the sense that drawings are interrupted if the Executive Board fails to complete its formal review or, following the review, fails to establish performance criteria for the next phase. See paragraph 4(b) and (d) of the IMF's document at page 253, *supra.* See also note 158, *supra.*

Legal Character of Stand-By and Extended Arrangements

The Executive Board, in response to the member's letter of intent and with the benefit of the recommendation of the Managing Director and the report of the staff mission, adopts a decision approving the stand-by or extended arrangement. Such an arrangement has a peculiar legal character. It is not treated as a contract or international agreement: A Fund decision states explicitly that "language having a contractual connotation will be avoided in stand-by arrangements and letters of intent."[175] Rather, the arrangement is treated as a unilateral statement of intention on the part of the member country to pursue stated policies and a unilateral decision of the Fund to provide a specified amount of resources of the General Resources Account upon call to support those policies. Since a stand-by or extended arrangement is not an "agreement," the executive branch in many countries has greater leeway to conclude such an arrangement than it would have if the arrangement were an international agreement that under the country's law required parliamentary approval.

The member is not under a legal obligation to pursue the policies stated in the letter of intent. Indeed, the failure of a country to achieve the results stated in its letter does not even permit the interruption of the right to purchase within the first credit tranche. This reflects the Fund's policy that drawings in the first credit tranche, although conditional, are not subject to significant restraints upon the state's freedom of action.[176]

Stand-by and extended arrangements permitting drawings beyond the first credit tranche are required to contain phasing and performance clauses that are applicable to purchases beyond the first credit tranche.[177] The Fund's document will provide for drawings under the stand-by or extended arrangement to be phased over time with specified performance criteria applicable to drawings in each advancing phase.[178] Observance of the performance criteria guarantees the member's right to make drawings under the arrangement. What happens if the member fails to achieve the performance criteria? These failures do not *ipso facto* make the country a law breaker. However, they create a new situation. The Fund has decided to make its resources available to support policies and intentions stated in the letter of intent. The criteria not being observed, the country's right to make further drawings under the arrangement is automati-

---

[175] E.B. Decision No. 6056, *supra* note 112, paragraph 3. E.B. Decision No. 2603, adopted in 1968, *supra* note 112, conclusions—paragraph 7, contained similar language. James E.S. Fawcett, General Counsel of the Fund 1955–1960, writing in 1965 (before the 1968 decision) characterized the stand-by arrangement as contractual. "The International Monetary Fund and International Law," *British Yearbook of International Law,* vol. 40 (1964) p. 32 at pp. 72 and 74. See generally Joseph Gold, *The Legal Character of the Fund's Stand-By Arrangements and Why It Matters* (IMF Pamphlet Series no. 35; Washington, 1980).

[176] See note 165, *supra.* The country may also request drawings under other policies not keyed to the stand-by or extended arrangement (such as the compensatory financing facility or buffer stock facility treated at pages 277–283, *infra*).

[177] E.B. Decision No. 6056, *supra* note 112, paragraph 6.

[178] See paragraphs 2 and 4 of the extended arrangement document at pages 252–253, *supra.*

cally interrupted without the need for any action by the Executive Board. This legal effect is accomplished by the language in the stand-by or extended arrangement document and the references made therein to performance criteria drawn from the country's letter.[179]

The Fund and the member have consultations (often involving a staff visit to the country) when performance criteria are not met. If the divergences are small and technical, a waiver may be recommended to the Executive Board and, if approved, drawing rights under the arrangement are restored. If the divergence is more substantial, there will be negotiations on new policies to establish momentum for adjustment.[180] If in these negotiations the country and the IMF reach new understandings on the policies the country intends to pursue, the Executive Board may amend the stand-by or extended arrangement to again make resources available. This is formally done either by making references in the Fund's document refer to a supplementary letter of intent attached to the document or by cancelling the outstanding arrangement and approving a new arrangement.[181] In the absence of action by the Executive Board, drawing rights under the arrangement remain interrupted.[182]

All stand-by and extended arrangements are required to include consultation clauses.[183] Note the sentence in the last paragraph of India's letter: "The Government will consult with the Fund on the adoption of any appropriate measures, consistent with the national policies accepted by our Parliament, in accordance with policies of the Fund on such consultation."[184] Consultation clauses, unlike statements of policy intentions, are understood to impose binding legal obligations.[185] The clauses set forth in the Extended Arrangement—India document are standard clauses which incorporate into the arrangement all of the Fund's policies on consultations applicable to stand-by and extended arrangements. Among these policies is the following requirement:

---

[179] See paragraphs 2, 4, 10, and 11 of the Extended Arrangement-India document at pages 252–255, *supra*. Under established procedures the member supplies data which show that it is observing the performance criteria. If it is not observing the criteria, both it and the Fund will know that. The IMF only rarely comments on the interruption of stand-bys, but the press more frequently. See, e.g., *Wall Street Journal*, April 19, 1982, p. 8 (interruptions affecting 15 countries); March 18, 1983, p. 32 (Chile); and July 6, 1983, p. 26, and July 20, 1983, p. 31 (Brazil). See also note 191 (Jamaica) and note 205 (Peru and Zaire).

[180] See final sentence of paragraph 4 of the Extended Arrangement-India document at page 253, *supra;* and Crockett, "Issues in the Use of Fund Resources," *supra* note 162, p. 15. See also *IMF Survey*, December 5, 1983, p. 373 (Brazil).

[181] Examples include Jamaica (cancellation of outstanding stand-by and approval of new extended arrangement, June 1978), Panama (new stand-by, March 1979), and Peru (new stand-by, September 1978). In each case the country had encountered difficulties in achieving the objectives of its earlier program. *IMF Survey*, June 19, 1978, p. 186; September 18, 1978, p. 283; April 9, 1979, p. 110; and December 15, 1980, pp. 378–82.

[182] See note 191 and text accompanying note 196 regarding Jamaica.

[183] See paragraphs 10 and 11 of the Extended Arrangement-India document, page 255, and paragraph 5 of India's letter of intent, pages 256–257.

[184] Paragraph 5 of India's letter at page 256, *supra*.

[185] Gold, *Stand-By Arrangements, supra* note 126, p. 68.

Appropriate consultation clauses will be incorporated in all stand-by arrangements. Such clauses will include provision for consultation from time to time during the whole period in which the member has outstanding purchases in the upper credit tranches [i.e., beyond first credit tranche]. This provision will apply whether the outstanding purchases were made under a stand-by arrangement or in other transactions in the upper credit tranches.[186]

The quoted provision contemplates that consultations will continue until the repurchases are effected, which may be five years or more in some cases. The consultations can relate to any aspect of the country's policies toward its balance-of-payments situation as it develops and not simply to the original program the stand-by or extended arrangement was granted to support.[187]

India's letter of intent also includes the clause: "The Government of India believes that the policies . . ., which are described in the attached memorandum, are adequate to achieve the objectives of its programme, but will take any further measures that may become appropriate for this purpose."[188] This sentence is also standard in letters of intent.[189] Through this clause and the other consultation clauses in the Fund's document and the letter of intent, a country obligates itself to consult with the Fund respecting further measures. The appropriate measures will be tied to the broad objectives of the member's program as stated in the letter of intent.

Further Comments on the Negotiation and Approval of Stand-By and Extended Arrangements

While the legal theory of stand-by and extended arrangements is that the member defines its policies and the Fund then decides whether or not to make its resources available, the reader should not take this to mean that the terms are not negotiated. Indeed, intensive negotiations may take place between the IMF staff and the country's authorities. The correction of domestic policies that adversely impact the country's external financial position come within the scope of these discussions. Exchange restrictions and exchange rate policies are reviewed.[190] There is very little, if anything, that affects the balance of payments

---

[186] E.B. Decision No. 6056, *supra* note 112, paragraph 5.

[187] Gold, *Stand-By Arrangements, supra* note 126, p. 74.

[188] Paragraph 5 of the letter of intent at page 256, *supra*.

[189] The United Kingdom's letter of intent, *supra* note 142, in support of a stand-by arrangement approved in 1977 used almost identical language.

[190] The Fund has authority to approve a stand-by or extended arrangement for a country which maintains exchange restrictions or exchange rate policies inconsistent with the Articles. If a country maintains exchange restrictions inconsistent with the Articles, performance criteria for arrangements in the second and higher credit tranches will always explicitly deal with them. There will be a general statement in all stand-by or extended arrangement documents relating to the introduction or intensification of exchange restrictions, multi-

that is beyond the purview of discussion. The IMF mission will press for the adoption of policies that can be predicted to correct the country's balance-of-payments problems, even if those policies happen to be unpopular domestically. Occasionally, discussions will break down when a country's officials are unwilling or unable to commit the country to policies that the IMF mission indicates will be necessary if the Executive Board is to approve the request.[191]

Also, economists may differ about the economic policies to be pursued. Marxist economists have often been especially critical of economic policies favored by the IMF.[192]

ple currency practices, or import restrictions. See paragraph 4(e) of the Extended Arrangement-India document at page 253, *supra.*

Often, as a prelude to IMF approval of a stand-by or extended arrangement, the country may withdraw unapproved exchange restrictions or indicate its intention to do so, or the Executive Board may review and approve the restrictions. Numerous stand-bys and extended arrangements have been approved to support currency stabilization programs that involved the liberalization of exchange restrictions. See Chapter 10, *infra,* page 427. See also Gold, *Stand-By Arrangements, supra* note 126, pp. 142–44.

[191] In the spring of 1976 Italy intended to request a stand-by arrangement equivalent to U.S. $530 million. When the IMF mission to Italy reached the conclusion that the government would be unable to reduce the government's budget deficit to an acceptable level to control inflation even with IMF financial assistance, negotiations were broken off. See *Corriere della Sera* (Milan), March 30, 1976, p. 1. Following renewed negotiations a stand-by for Italy was approved by the IMF on April 25, 1977; *IMF Survey,* May 2, 1977, p. 140. The Italian letter of intent is cited in note 142, *supra.* See also Luigi Spaventa, "Two Letters of Intent: External Crises and Stabilization Policy, Italy, 1973–77," in Williamson, *IMF Conditionality, supra* note 112, p. 441.

It has been reported that Brazil refused to request an arrangement with the IMF in 1980 because of conditions the IMF was likely to impose. The IMF, it was said, would have required changes in Brazil's import restrictions, exchange controls, subsidized domestic credit, and government finance. Everett G. Martin, "Brazil Seeks to Augment its Heavy Debt," *Wall Street Journal,* September 15, 1980, p. 37. See generally Edmar L. Bacha, "Vicissitudes of Recent Stabilization Attempts in Brazil and the IMF Alternative," in Williamson, *IMF Conditionality, supra,* p. 323.

The economic and social situation in Jamaica and the negotiations between the IMF and Jamaican authorities that led to approval of a stand-by arrangement in 1977, its interruption at the end of that year when performance criteria were not met, a new three-year extended arrangement at a level of 270 percent of quota approved in 1978, its subsequent interruption when performance criteria were not met, and abortive negotiations in the spring of 1980 seeking common ground for a new arrangement are detailed in G. Russell Kincaid, "Conditionality and the Use of Fund Resources: Jamaica," *Finance and Development,* vol. 18, no. 2 (June 1981), p. 18; and *IMF Survey,* December 15, 1980, pp. 378–82. See also Jennifer Sharpley, "Economic Management and IMF Conditionality in Jamaica," in Williamson, *IMF Conditionality, supra,* p. 233.

United States legislation requires the U.S. National Advisory Council on International Monetary and Financial Policies to report on the impact on "basic human needs" of national adjustment programs supported by IMF stand-by and extended arrangements. *United States Code,* title 22, section 286s. See also section 804 of Public Law 98–181, approved November 30, 1983, *United States Statutes at Large,* vol. 97, p. 1153 at pp. 1270–71.

[192] For criticism of IMF policies, see, e.g., Amiya Kumar Bagchi, "Conditionality and Its Implications," *Eastern Economist,* December 4, 1981, p. 1068; Virendra Agarwala, "Needed: Discipline from Within," *Eastern Economist,* October 30, 1981, p. 806; Cheryl Payer, *The Debt Trap: The IMF and the Third World* (New York: Monthly Review Press, 1974); Cheryl Payer, "The Bretton Woods Twins," *Counterspy,* September–November 1982, p. 37; and Walden Bello and Robin Broad, "Twenty Years of Intervention: The IMF and the Philippines," *Counterspy,* September–November 1982, p. 53. While the IMF has been criticized for being "too tough" in negotiating stand-by and extended arrangements, it has also been accused of not being tough enough. See Art Pine, "Disputed Terms: Critics Charge the IMF Eases its Rules Forcing Borrowers to Shape Up," *Wall Street Journal,* September 21, 1981, pp. 1 and 20. For more balanced views, see Corrado Pirzio-Biroli, "Making Sense of the IMF Conditionality Debate," *Journal of World Trade*

Political Dimension of Stand-By and Extended Arrangements

Political considerations often must be taken into account in financial discussions whether the country seeking assistance is small or large. For example, the final terms stated by United Kingdom authorities, in the letter of intent to the IMF[193] in support of a stand-by arrangement approved by the Fund in January 1977, had to take the domestic political situation into account. The domestic political situation placed limits on the actions the U.K. government could undertake.[194] This was even more clear in India's negotiations with the IMF leading to the extended arrangement, approved in November 1981, detailed earlier.[195]

At times the political conditions within a country prevent the country and the IMF from reaching an understanding on the conditions to be associated with a stand-by or extended arrangement. When it became apparent in the early fall of 1979 that Jamaica would not meet performance criteria under an extended arrangement, negotiations began and continued for a period of six months on economic policies the Fund could support. Disagreement on the magnitude and speed of adjustment measures, which were perceived by Jamaican authorities as affecting the domestic credibility of the government's previous socialist policies, led finally to a break-off in the negotiations.[196] Perspectives differ on how far an international institution should penetrate into the monetary, fiscal, and other economic policies of countries requiring its assistance.

Political considerations may also affect the attitudes of IMF executive directors considering requests for assistance. Since the IMF is a multilateral institution, there is sensitivity within the staff and within governments with which the IMF may be negotiating to any efforts of countries with large quotas to influence those negotiations. It is not, however, unusual for the U.S. Executive Director, for example, to have informal conversations with the Managing Director during the course of the IMF's negotiations with a third country in which U.S. views are informally made known.[197]

Law, vol. 17 (1983), p. 115; Bahram Nowzad, *The IMF and Its Critics* (Essays in International Finance no. 146; Princeton: Princeton University International Finance Section, 1981), pp. 7–22; and the papers collected in Williamson, *IMF Conditionality, supra* note 112.

[193] Note 142, *supra.*

[194] See Ehrbar, *supra* note 162.

[195] See the text of India's letter of intent and statement of policies, pages 255–263, *supra*. See also note 162, *supra*. Political and economic dimensions of the Indian–IMF arrangement are discussed from various points of view in articles in *The Hindu* (Madras), November 16, 1981, p. 9; November 24, 1981, pp. 1 and 11; December 3, 1981, pp. 1 and 9; and December 4, 1981, p. 9; in articles in the *Eastern Economist*, October 30, 1981, pp. 805–07; November 13, 1981, pp. 896–97; and December 4, 1981, pp. 1065–75; and in the parliamentary debates. See India (Republic) Parliament, House of the People (Lok Sabha), *Debates*, 7th series, 1981, vol. 21, columns 321–38 and 390–98.

[196] See note 191, *supra.*

[197] See *U.S. Foreign Economic Policy Issues: The United Kingdom, France, and West Germany—A Staff Report Prepared for the Subcommittee on Foreign Economic Policy of the Committee on Foreign Relations,* U.S. Senate, 95th Congress, 1st Session (1977), pp. 11–12; and *Oversight Hearings on U.S. International*

It has been reported to the author that the Executive Board has never formally declined to approve a stand-by or extended arrangement requested in a letter of intent formally transmitted to the Board. Countries have, however, refrained from submitting letters and on a few occasions have withdrawn them when the Executive Board deferred taking action to approve the arrangement. Even proposed stand-by arrangements limited to the first credit tranche have on occasion not been pursued because the Fund staff expressed concern about governmental stability or believed the financial and monetary policies of the country seriously deficient in relation to the problems faced.[198] Given the more stringent requirements for use of the second and higher credit tranches, negotiations have sometimes been discontinued after preliminary soundings with staff in Washington and in other cases after the staff mission has visited the country.[199] In practice members formally submit letters only after discussions with IMF staff indicate that the Managing Director and staff will recommend approval. Fund staff members involved in negotiations have understood the views of executive directors well enough so as not to judge that the Board would approve an arrangement that it would not. On some occasions the Board has approved stand-by arrangements after discussions that showed the Board was not happy with the terms that had been negotiated. These discussions have provided guidance to staff in negotiating subsequent arrangements with that country and others.[200]

Value of IMF Stand-By and Extended Arrangements to Other Creditors

Stand-by and extended arrangements, because they involve a statement of economic policy intentions with performance monitored by the IMF, have been important to other creditors. A stand-by or extended arrangement is seen as evidence of creditworthiness. On a few occasions the World Bank has conditioned

Monetary Policies: Hearings before the Subcommittee on International Trade, Investment and Monetary Policy of the Committee on Banking, Finance and Urban Affairs, U.S. House of Representatives, 97th Congress, 1st Session (1981), pp. 205–19. See also note 198, infra.

[198] While the IMF is concerned with government stability, it is required by Article XII, section 8, to avoid passing judgment on the political form of a government. It has approved stand-bys for Brazil, Chile, Indonesia, and the Philippines, for example, when those countries were governed by military dictatorships. See report of the U.S. Executive Director on the IMF's handling of a Nicaraguan request in 1978–79 in *Authorization for Treasury's International Affairs Functions: Hearing [on S.976] before the Subcommittee on International Finance of the Committee on Banking, Housing, and Urban Affairs*, U.S. Senate, 96th Congress, 1st Session (1979), pp. 49–51. See also Joseph Gold, "Political Considerations Are Prohibited by Articles of Agreement When the Fund Considers Requests for Use of Resources," *IMF Survey*, May 23, 1983, p. 146. The IMF in November 1982 approved a stand-by arrangement for South Africa despite a UN General Assembly resolution calling upon it not to do so. See Chapter 2, *supra*, page 50.

[199] See note 191, *supra*.

[200] See Alexandre Kafka, "The International Monetary Fund in Transition," *Virginia Journal of International Law*, vol. 13 (1972–73), pp. 135–57 and 539–52 at pp. 148–49; and Crockett, "Issues in the Use of Fund Resources," *supra* note 162, p. 14.

its lending on the conclusion by the borrower of a stand-by or extended arrangement with the IMF. When this has been the case, the condition was usually satisfied before the loan was approved by the Executive Directors of the Bank and, thus, no specific covenant appeared in the loan or guarantee agreement.[201] In the case of a loan agreement with Jamaica approved December 13, 1977, there was a specific provision tying the World Bank's disbursement to the ability of Jamaica to purchase stated amounts under stand-by arrangements with the IMF.[202]

Governmental creditors sometimes require a borrowing country to maintain a stand-by arrangement with the IMF. This is a frequent condition for rescheduling amortization payments due under loans previously extended. The stand-by arrangement gives confidence to the creditors that the debtor's policies will be adequate to permit payments of interest and principal as they become due and that it is pursuing appropriate policies.[203] In some instances funds are

---

[201] Letter dated January 26, 1978, from Georges R. Delaume, Legal Department of the International Bank for Reconstruction and Development, to the author.

In 1965 the IBRD declined to consider a request from Ceylon (now Sri Lanka) until it had concluded a stand-by arrangement with the IMF. After Brazil in 1959 failed to pursue a stabilization program worked out with the IMF the preceding year, the IBRD did not make further loans for several years. See Edward S. Mason and Robert E. Asher, *The World Bank Since Bretton Woods* (Washington: Brookings Institution, 1973), pp. 199, 440, 554, and 662–63.

[202] Loan Agreement (Program Loan) between Jamaica and the IBRD, Loan No. 1500 JM, dated December 16, 1977 (paragraph 2(b) and (c) of Schedule 1).

[203] The Bank of England's eligibility to draw on a BIS facility to finance the reduction of sterling balances in the period 1977–1978 (Chapter 3, *supra*, page 108, note 26) was conditional upon the United Kingdom continuing to be able to draw upon the stand-by arrangement the IMF had approved for it in January 1977 and upon the U.K. continuing to make reasonable efforts to achieve reductions in the sterling balances held by foreign authorities with the Bank of England. The Managing Director of the IMF was asked to assist in making a determination on this latter matter. See IMF, *Annual Report, 1977*, p. 70; and Joseph Gold, *Order in International Finance, the Promotion of IMF Stand-By Arrangements, and the Drafting of Private Loan Agreements* (IMF Pamphlet Series no. 39; Washington, 1982), pp. 6–7.

A loan agreement between the United States and Portugal for balance-of-payments support, signed at Lisbon March 1, 1978, in Article III included as a condition precedent to the first disbursement that Portugal provide to the U.S. Agency for International Development "a letter from the Managing Director of the International Monetary Fund (IMF) indicating that negotiations with the IMF regarding drawdown under the second IMF credit tranche for Portugal are proceeding in good faith." *United States Treaties and Other International Agreements*, vol. 30, part 2, p. 1761. See Gold, *supra*, p. 8.

See, as one of many examples of debt reschedulings tied to IMF stand-bys, the understanding on the external debt of Chile signed at Paris May 6, 1975, that accompanies the agreement between Chile and the United States signed July 3, 1975; *United States Treaties and Other International Agreements*, vol. 28, part 5, p. 5587 at p. 5601. In some cases where the IMF has not provided a stand-by, the Fund has nevertheless, at the request of the country, surveyed the implementation of its financial program and transmitted performance data to the creditors. See generally Eduard Brau, Richard C. Williams, et al., *Recent Multilateral Debt Restructurings with Official and Bank Creditors* (IMF Occasional Paper no. 25; Washington, 1983); Allen P.K. Keesee, "Legal Aspects of Multinational, Public Sector Debt Rescheduling," *International Business Lawyer*, vol. 8 (1980), p. 149; Christopher Prout, "Finance for Developing Countries," in Andrew Shonfield (ed.), *International Economic Relations of the Western World, 1959–1971* (2 vols.; London: Oxford University Press for Royal Institute of International Affairs, 1976), vol. 2, p. 360 at pp. 389–404; and John A. Boyd (ed.), *Digest of United States Practice in International Law, 1977* (Washington: U.S. Government Printing Office, 1979), pp. 784–85. See also Tim Anderson, "The Year of the Rescheduling," "Step by Step Through the Costa Rica Saga," and William Ollard and Anne Sington, "The Unique Club of Michel Camdessus," in *Euromoney*, August 1982, pp. 19, 33, and 54.

provided to central banks under short-term facilities with the understanding that they will be repaid with resources to be purchased from the IMF after a stand-by arrangement then under negotiation is approved.[204]

Commercial banks sometimes make loans to a government contingent upon the borrowing country concluding a stand-by or extended arrangement with the Fund.[205] The conclusion of an arrangement in the higher credit tranches gives confidence to creditors that the country's situation has been reviewed by respected experts and that the country has subjected itself to a discipline the IMF believes will correct the nation's balance-of-payments problems and safeguard the use of the IMF's own resources should the country draw on the stand-by. This does not, however, guarantee that the country will achieve the targets it has set.

Commercial banks may go further than simply requiring a government to have a stand-by or extended arrangement approved by the IMF. Loan agreements may condition disbursements on the country's adhering to performance criteria stated in the IMF stand-by arrangement (with specific reference to numbered paragraphs in the IMF's confidential stand-by arrangement document).[206] It has become fairly common for commercial bank loan agreements

[204] For example, in 1982 the Banco de Mexico received funds from other central banks, acting through the Bank for International Settlements, with this understanding. See Chapter 4, *supra*, pages 164–165.

[205] For example, Brazil's private and public creditors in 1982 and 1983 attached great importance to Brazil's negotiating and complying with an adjustment program supported by the IMF. Brazil's debt negotiations are examined from a legal perspective in Andreas F. Lowenfeld, *The International Monetary System* (2d ed.; New York: Matthew Bender, 1984), pp. 291–304.

The precedent of tying commercial bank loan agreements to IMF stand-by or extended arrangements was set in the Zaire case. As part of an agreement of Citibank and other commercial banks with Zaire concluded in November 1976 (which involved a new loan of U.S. $250 million by the commercial banks to Zaire and procedures for paying arrears on loans in default), Zaire was obligated to obtain a stand-by arrangement with the IMF into the third credit tranche but not to immediately draw upon it. The purpose was to have the IMF monitor Zaire's economic policies during the period of the stand-by as a means of assuring the private creditors that appropriate policies were being followed. Zaire did not carry out the expected policies. See *U.S. Loans to Zaire: Hearing Before the Subcommittee on International Finance of the Committee on Banking, Housing, and Urban Affairs,* U.S. Senate, 96th Congress, 1st Session (1979), pp. 19–23; *Wall Street Journal,* November 9, 1976, p. 8, January 7, 1977, p. 7, June 15, 1978, p. 4, September 14, 1981, p. 34, and February 22, 1983, p. 35; *New York Times,* November 13, 1979, p. A-2; and *IMF Survey,* May 2, 1977, p. 140, and September 3, 1979, p. 265.

See *IMF Survey,* July 23, 1979, p. 217, and *Wall Street Journal,* June 14, 1979, p. 18, and December 4, 1979, p. 36, respecting the importance of an IMF stand-by for Turkey to official and private creditors; and *Wall Street Journal,* May 22, 1978, p. 6, reporting the suspension of lending by U.S. commercial banks to Peru after it failed to achieve performance criteria stated in a letter of intent to the IMF.

See generally Charles Lipson, "The International Organization of Third World Debt," *International Organization,* vol. 35 (1981), p. 603 at pp. 617–26; Christopher G. Oechsli, "Procedural Guidelines for Renegotiating LDC Debt: An Analogy to Chapter 11 of the U.S. Bankruptcy Reform Act," *Virginia Journal of International Law,* vol. 21 (1981), p. 305 at pp. 326–28; Bahram Nowzad, Richard C. Williams, et al., *External Indebtedness of Developing Countries* (IMF Occasional Paper no. 3; Washington, 1981), pp. 21–40; and Brau and Williams, *Recent Multilateral Debt Restructurings, supra* note 203, pp. 20 and 26–27.

[206] See Gold, *Order in International Finance, supra* note 203, especially pp. 30–35 where clauses used in commercial bank loan agreements are discussed; and Joseph Gold, "Relations Between Banks' Loan Agreements and IMF Stand-By Arrangements," *International Financial Law Review,* September 1983, p. 28 at pp.

with a government, that make reference to performance criteria in a stand-by arrangement, to require the borrowing government to periodically provide the lenders with certificates by the IMF that the country is observing all applicable performance criteria under the stand-by arrangement and that its right to draw on the arrangement has not been interrupted. The IMF has established procedures under which the Managing Director on behalf of the Fund makes such certifications which are delivered to the member and passed by it to the commercial banks.[207]

Arthur F. Burns, then Chairman of the U.S. Federal Reserve Board, urged in a major speech in April 1977 that governmental and private lenders take their cue from the IMF and not loan to countries with substantial debts that have failed to work out effective stabilization programs with the IMF.[208] It appears that, as a matter of prudence as well as cooperativeness, both governmental and commercial lenders are advised to give weight to IMF appraisals of economic policies.

Stand-By and Extended Arrangements—Conclusion

As previously explained, the essence of a stand-by or extended arrangement is that the Fund's decision to make its resources available to a member during the period of the arrangement is not subject to further review by the Fund. However, a stand-by or extended arrangement decision will give the Fund certain carefully circumscribed "outs." We have already noted that a member country's failure to observe the performance criteria stated in its program interrupts the country's right to make further purchases under the arrangement, unless the purchases are in the first credit tranche. The member must consult the Fund and reach understandings on the terms for any further purchases.

The right of the country to make drawings under the stand-by or extended arrangement can otherwise be suspended by the Fund only if:

(1) the member has been declared ineligible to use the Fund's resources; or

(2) the Executive Board has decided to suspend the member's right to make drawings in order to consider a proposal to suppress or limit the eligibility of the member under Article V, Section 5; or

(3) the Executive Board because of an emergency has decided to suspend the right of all members to make drawings in the General Resources

---

32–34. See also *IMF Survey,* December 5, 1983, pp. 373 and 384 (Brazil). Performance criteria are discussed at pages 265–266 and 267–268, *supra.*

[207] See Gold, *Order in International Finance, supra* note 203, pp. 36–39. IMF Article V, section 2(b), is understood to authorize the Fund to perform these services.

[208] *Federal Reserve Bulletin,* vol. 63 (1977), p. 456 at p. 460.

Account. (The Board has never taken this action authorized by Article XXVII.)[209]

A member can terminate a stand-by or extended arrangement at any time prior to the date at which it would expire. Repurchase obligations and some consultation obligations may continue.

The stand-by technique can make resources of great magnitude available to the member—both the immense resources of the Fund itself and, often, resources from other public and private sources given confidence by the Fund's "seal of approval." The arrangement may calm the fears of commercial banks and others holding deposits in the country's currency. The statement by a member of performance criteria and of international and domestic policies to be pursued, together with consultation procedures, in the context of the country's letter of intent and the Fund's document, is a technique by which the Fund reviews national policies and has an input into the formulation of those policies. The reader should now understand why the stand-by arrangement has been characterized as "the IMF's most flexible device for combining the discipline which promotes balance of payments equilibrium with the assurance of support which permits a country to accomplish an orderly and gradual adjustment of its external accounts."[210]

---

[209] See paragraph 5 of the Extended Arrangement-India document at page 254, *supra*. This language is boiler-plate. The Fund has never in fact interrupted drawings under a stand-by arrangement for any of these reasons. No stand-bys were in effect in the French, Cuban, Czechoslovakian, and Kampuchean situations mentioned in Chapter 1, *supra*, pages 40–41.

[210] Statement of Robert V. Roosa in review of Joseph Gold, *The Stand-By Arrangements of the International Monetary Fund*, in *Law and Policy in International Business*, vol. 4 (1972), p. 171 at p. 172.

The Fund staff, to guide the continuing review of the Fund's policies, prepares studies of the programs supported by stand-by and extended arrangements, the observance of the programs, and the results achieved. See Thomas M. Reichmann and Richard T. Stillson, "Experience with Programs of Balance of Payments Adjustment: Stand-By Arrangements in the Higher Credit Tranches, 1963–72," *IMF Staff Papers*, vol. 25 (1978), p. 293; Thomas M. Reichmann, "The Fund's Conditional Assistance and the Problems of Adjustment, 1973–75," *Finance and Development*, vol. 15, no. 4 (December 1978), p. 38; Donal J. Donovan, "Macroeconomic Performance and Adjustment Under Fund-Supported Programs: The Experience of the Seventies," *IMF Staff Papers*, vol. 29 (1982), p. 171; and Paul Coulbois (ed.), *Le Système Monétaire International Face aux Déséquilibres* (Paris: Economica, 1982). For assessments by non-Fund personnel, see the country studies collected in Williamson, *IMF Conditionality*, *supra* note 112; Tony Killick (ed.), *Adjustment and Financing in the Developing World: The Role of the International Monetary Fund* (Washington: IMF, 1982); William R. Cline and Sidney Weintraub (ed.), *Economic Stabilization in Developing Countries* (Washington: Brookings Institution, 1981); Thomas A. Conners, *The Apparent Effects of IMF Stabilization Programs* (International Finance Discussion Paper no. 135; Washington: Federal Reserve System, 1979); and Sidney Dell and Roger Lawrence, *The Balance of Payments Adjustment Process in Developing Countries* (New York: Pergamon Press in cooperation with United Nations, 1980).

Special Facilities Using Regular Resources

Introduction

Although the pool of currencies in the General Resources Account is primarily intended to assist members in overcoming difficulties in the balance of payments taken as a whole, the Fund has in several decisions identified the specific character of some payments difficulties. Section 3(a) of Article V states that the Fund "may adopt special policies for special balance of payments problems. . . ." Fund decisions have created what are called "facilities" in the General Resources Account. At the present time these special facilities include: (1) Extended Fund Facility for use by members making structural changes in their economies (discussed earlier),[211] (2) Facility for the Compensatory Financing of Export Fluctuations, (3) Facility for Compensatory Financing of Cereal Import Cost Fluctuations, and (4) Buffer Stock Financing Facility for use in stabilizing prices of primary products. The General Arrangements to Borrow and the Policy on Enlarged Access, financed by Fund borrowings, make very substantial resources available to assist members. During 1974 and 1975 the Fund operated an Oil Import Financing Facility, and from 1979 to 1982 it operated a Supplementary Financing Facility. Each of these facilities is discussed below.

In the case of each of the special facilities now in operation, the Fund has adopted decisions to make the resources of the General Resources Account available to members facing particular balance-of-payments problems. In the case of several of the facilities, a member meeting the criteria for use of the facility can draw upon it and at the same time preserve for future use its general credit tranche as well as reserve tranche drawing rights.[212] The effect is to enable a member to make more substantial drawings than would otherwise be possible. In all cases the drawings take place through the General Resources Account. The Special Disbursement Account and the Trust Fund, which are operated separately from the General Resources Account, are addressed later in this chapter.

Facility for Compensatory Financing of Export Fluctuations

The decision on Compensatory Financing of Export Fluctuations sets forth policies on access to the General Resources Account for the purpose of financing export shortfalls.[213] A "shortfall" occurs when a country's exports fall short of

---

[211] At pages 248–250, *supra.*

[212] See text accompanying notes 75 and 110, *supra.*

[213] E.B. Decision No. 6224 -(79/135) (August 2, 1979); IMF, *Annual Report, 1980*, p. 136; *Selected Decisions* (10th issue, 1983), p. 61. For a detailed explanation of the application of the decision, see Louis M. Gorex, *Compensatory Financing Facility* (IMF Pamphlet Series no. 34; Washington, 1980). The access limit under the decision was modified by E.B. Decision No. 7602 -(84/3) (January 6, 1984); IMF, *Annual Report, 1984*, p. 138.

Decision No. 6224 supersedes E.B. Decision no. 4912 -(75/207) (December 24, 1975); IMF, *Annual Re-*

the projected level and thus yield less foreign exchange to the exporting country. The financing of balance-of-payments deficits arising out of export shortfalls, particularly of countries dependent upon earnings from the sale of primary products, has always been a legitimate basis for making drawings in the General Resources Account. The decision, however, establishes criteria which if met by the member permit very substantial drawings without performance criteria.

A proposal for compensatory financing of export fluctuations was made in 1953 by a group of experts appointed by the Secretary-General of the United Nations. In the decade that followed, several proposals were discussed within the United Nations, the Organization of American States, and the International Monetary Fund. The general decline of world market prices for primary products, which started in the second half of the 1950s, aggravated the balance-of-payments problems of developing countries and drew attention to the problem. The IMF facility was established in 1963.[214] Access to the facility was liberalized in 1966[215] and further liberalized in 1975 and 1979.[216]

The compensatory financing decision of 1979 states the Fund's latest policies on access to the General Resources Account to provide funds compensating for short-term declines in export earnings caused by drops in world prices or by crop failures or other causes beyond the control of the exporting state. A member can "expect" that its request for a drawing will be approved if:

(a) the shortfall is of a short-term character and is "largely attributable" to circumstances beyond the control of the member; and

(b) the member will cooperate with the Fund in an effort to find, where required, appropriate solutions for its balance-of-payments difficulties.

The decision is designed to give assurance of financing to members so they can plan on the basis of medium- and long-term economic trends without being overly influenced by short-term fluctuations in export earnings.

The methods for determining the existence of a shortfall and measuring its magnitude are defined by the decision. Basically, the country's export earnings during the latest twelve-month period for which statistical data are available are measured against the geometric average of the country's export earnings for the five-year period centered on the shortfall year. The earnings in the two future

---

port, 1976, p. 101, as amended by E.B. Decision No. 5348 -(77/33) (March 11, 1977). See notes 214 and 215, *infra*, for citations to earlier decisions.

[214] E.B. Decision No. 1477 -(63/8) (February 27, 1963); *IMF History 1945–65, supra* note 52, vol. 3, p. 238. For historical background see *IMF History 1945–65*, vol. 2, pp. 417–27, and vol. 3, pp. 442–57 and 469–96.

[215] E.B. Decision No. 2192 -(66/81) (September 20, 1966); *IMF History 1966–71, supra* note 52, vol. 2, p. 198. For background see *IMF History 1966—71*, vol. 1, chapter 14.

[216] See note 213, *supra*.

years in the five-year period are estimated using a judgmental forecast. The existence of a shortfall gives entitlement to make a drawing unless the Fund determines (a) that the decline in earnings is not short-term in character, (b) that the decline was caused by actions of the member itself, (c) that the member's balance-of-payments and reserve position notwithstanding the export shortfall is sufficiently strong that there is no "need" as required by Article V, Section 3(b)(ii), of the IMF Agreement, or (d) that the member will not cooperate with the Fund.

With respect to the "cooperation" clause of the decision, the Fund is guided by its previous dealings with the member as well as that member's stated desire to cooperate. It is not necessary for a country, even if it has already drawn substantial amounts from the Fund, to submit a letter of intent describing its policies in order to make a compensatory drawing, as would be required under the Fund's normal policies for drawings that raise the Fund's holdings of a currency above 100 percent of quota. A country's statement of intention to cooperate with the Fund is normally accepted, unless the Fund has reason to question it, where the total amount to be drawn under the facility does not exceed 50 percent of the member's quota. Where total outstanding drawings under the facility will exceed that amount, the burden falls on the member to "satisfy" the Fund that it "has been cooperating with the Fund" to find "appropriate solutions" for its balance-of-pyaments difficulties.[217]

Total outstanding drawings under the decision may amount to up to 83 percent of the member's quota (figure was 100 percent prior to January 1984). [218] The Fund is prepared to grant the necessary waivers of the 200-percent-of-quota basic limitation on General Resources Account purchases.[219] The first waiver under the compensatory financing facility of the 200 percent limit was for the United Arab Republic (1963) and in recent years many waivers have been granted.

In evaluating requests from a member to make "regular" drawings in the General Resources Account, the Fund applies its tranche policies as if the member had not made a drawing under the compensatory financing decision.[220] Drawings under the facility are said to "float" in the credit tranches. Thus, if a member had drawn 50 percent of quota under the compensatory financing facility, raising the Fund's holdings of its currency to 125 percent of quota, the Fund in handling a new request for an additional drawing of 25 percent of quota would treat this as a reserve tranche drawing or first credit tranche drawing, de-

---

[217] E.B. Decision No. 6224, *supra* note 213, paragraph 2(b) and 3. See discussion of the "cooperation" clause in speech of the Governor for Nicaragua in IMF, *Summary Proceedings, 1978,* p. 150 at pp. 152–53. See also Gorex, *supra* note 213, pp. 44–46. See also E.B. Decision No. 7528-(83/140)(September 14,1983); IMF, *Annual Report, 1984,* p. 137.

[218] E.B. Decision No. 6224, *supra* note 213, paragraph 3, as amended by E.B. Decision No. 7602, *supra* note 213.

[219] E.B. Decision No. 6224, *idem,* paragraph 9. See page 231, *supra.*

[220] See Article XXX(c)(i); and paragraph 9 of E.B. Decision No. 6224, *idem.*

pending on the country's choice. However, the preservation of reserve tranche drawing rights has a cost. All of the General Resources Account's holdings of a country's currency resulting from the country's compensatory drawings are subject to charges on average daily balances. Countries, as a consequence of this rule, are careful about how drawings and repurchases are classified to minimize charges and at the same time preserve reserve tranche and regular credit tranche drawing rights to the extent desired.[221]

It should also be noted that, while there is an 83-percent-of-quota ceiling on drawings under the compensatory financing facility for export fluctuations, this does not prevent a country with a need for, say, a drawing of 175 percent of quota to finance a serious temporary balance-of-payments deficit caused by a major crop failure from requesting a stand-by arrangement for the additional amount.

The presently operative Fund decision prescribes that a member repurchase the Fund's holdings of its currency resulting from a compensatory facility drawing in installments beginning three years and ending five years after the date of the drawing.[222] As a member effects repurchases it acquires the ability to make new drawings up to the 83 percent total, provided the shortfall recurs and the other conditions stated above obtain.[223]

In conclusion, it should be re-emphasized that the IMF's receipt of a request for a compensatory facility drawing does not trigger a searching review of the requesting country's economic policies. If the statistical criteria are met, the compensatory drawing will normally be allowed up to 50 percent of quota without further question and up to 83 percent if the Fund is satisfied that the member has cooperated with the Fund to solve its balance-of-payments problems. As a consequence, the facility has been used by some countries that would not have obtained regular stand-bys for equivalent amounts unless they undertook currency stabilization programs. The amounts available under this facility—equivalent to over three credit tranches—are substantial, and the facility receives much use during periods when commodity prices are in decline.[224]

---

[221] See Article V, section 8(b)(i); and Article XXX(c)(i).

[222] Article V, section 7(c) and (d); and E.B. Decision No. 5703, as amended, *supra* note 37. If the amount purchased from the Fund based on estimated data exceeds the actual export shortfall, the country may be requested to promptly repurchase the excess. See IMF, *Annual Report, 1980*, p. 80.

[223] E.B. Decision No. 6224, *supra* note 213, paragraph 8.

[224] Detailed tables covering drawings during the period 1963–1980 appear in Gorex, *supra* note 213, at pp. 3, 45, and 52–57. The IMF's *Annual Report* each year provides information on drawings during the fiscal year covered by the report.

The second Convention between the European Economic Community and African, Caribbean, and Pacific States, signed at Lomé October 31, 1979, entered into force January 1, 1981, in Articles 23–47 establishes the so-called STABEX system of compensatory financing of fluctuations in primary product exports. The Convention appears in *Official Journal of the European Communities*, no. L-347, December 22, 1980, p. 1; *International Legal Materials*, vol. 19 (1980), p. 327. See discussion in Gorex, *supra*, pp. 80–84. The Arab Monetary Fund also operates a compensatory financing facility.

Compensatory Financing of Cereal Import Cost Fluctuations

The objective of the IMF cereal import financing facility, established in 1981,[225] is to help members prevent cereal consumption levels from falling in the face of surges in import costs caused by factors largely beyond their control, such as a temporary decline in domestic production or a sharp rise in import prices. The assistance under this decision is integrated with that under the compensatory financing decision[226] and gives an option to members to treat cereal imports essentially as negative exports.[227] Compensatory drawings can be made in relation to an export shortfall, a cereal import excess, or the total of both. Drawings to finance cereal import excess costs can be made only to the extent that the excess is not offset by higher export earnings. In the same way, for countries opting into the cereal facility, compensatory financing of export shortfalls are offset by declines in cereal import costs.

The amount to be purchased from the Fund in relation to an import excess, or an export shortfall, cannot exceed 83 percent of quota (figure was 100 percent prior to January 1984). The total amount purchased for an export shortfall and cereal import excess cost together cannot exceed 105 percent of quota (figure was 125 percent prior to January 1984). As in the regular compensatory financing facility, 50 percent is normally available without challenge if the statistical tests are met; drawing of the remaining 55 percent is conditioned on the Fund being "satisfied" that the member "has been cooperating with the Fund" in an effort to find "appropriate solutions" for its balance-of-payments difficulties.[228]

Drawings under the cereals decision, like drawings under the regular compensatory financing decision, do not affect reserve tranche drawing rights, and the drawings float in the credit tranches in the same manner as drawings under the regular compensatory financing decision.[229]

---

[225] E.B. Decision No. 6860 -(81/81) (May 13, 1981); IMF, *Annual Report, 1981,* p. 169; *Selected Decisions* (10th issue, 1983), p. 65. For background see IMF, *Annual Report, 1981,* pp. 81 and 84–85; *IMF Survey,* June 8, 1981, p. 165; and C. Green and C. Kirkpatrick, "The IMF's Food Financing Facility," *Journal of World Trade Law,* vol. 16 (1982), p. 265. The access limits under the decision were modified by E.B. Decision no. 7602, *supra* note 213.

[226] E.B. Decision No. 6224, *supra* note 213, discussed at pages 277–280. A member making a drawing under the cereals decision must for the following three years make drawings for compensatory financing of export fluctuations under the terms of E.B. Decision No. 6860, instead of No. 6224.

[227] A cereal import excess is defined as the amount by which a country's cereal import costs are more than an arithmetic average of the country's cereal imports for a five-year period centered on the excess year.

[228] E.B. Decision No. 6860, *supra* note 225, paragraph 9. See discussion at page 279, *supra,* of comparable language in Decision No. 6224.

[229] E.B. Decision No. 6860, *supra* note 225, paragraph 11. See discussion at pages 279–280, *supra.*

Facility for Financing Commodity Buffer Stocks

Drawings can be made in the General Resources Account to finance international buffer stocks of primary products.[230] Under some international commodity agreements, producing countries hold back a portion of production as a buffer stock to stabilize prices and prevent their decline. The control of supply is designed to maintain "fair" prices; when supply in the judgment of the producers is too small, a portion of the buffer stock is sold to prevent prices from becoming so high that purchasers will shift to buying alternative products.

The IMF's buffer stock decision permits members to draw on the General Resources Account to finance their contributions to international buffer stocks. Purchases are limited to 45 percent of quota (figure was 50 percent prior to January 1984), and the country must have balance-of-payments need. The buffer stock decision indicates that the Fund is prepared to waive, where appropriate, the limit on purchases that raise the Fund's total holdings of a member's currency above 200 percent of quota. The basic buffer stock decision is supplemented by decisions dealing with particular commodity agreements. These decisions may carry special features.[231]

The Fund has decided that members preserve their reserve tranche rights when they draw on the buffer stock facility, which also means that all of the Fund's currency holdings acquired under buffer stock drawings are subject to charges on average daily balances.[232] The presently operative Fund decision requires that repurchases of the member's currency resulting from use of the buffer facility be made in installments beginning three years and ending five years after the purchase. If buffer stocks are sold at an earlier date and the currency proceeds distributed to the producing countries participating in the commodity agreement, the member must make repurchases at the time of the distribution and to the extent of the distribution.[233]

On October 1, 1980, following protracted negotiations for several years in the United Nations Conference on Trade and Development, the Agreement Establishing the Common Fund for Commodities was opened for signature.[234]

---

[230] E.B. Decision No. 2772 -(69/47) (June 25, 1969), as amended by Decision No. 4913 -(75/207) (December 24, 1975); IMF, *Annual Report, 1976*, p. 103; *Selected Decisions* (10th issue, 1983), p. 70. For historical background on the 1969 decision, see *IMF History 1966-71, supra* note 52, vol. 1, chapter 15, and vol. 2, pp. 201 and 227-50. The access limit in the buffer stock facility was modified by E.B. Decision no. 7602, *supra* note 213.

[231] See buffer stock facility decisions collected in *Selected Decisions* (10th issue, 1983), pp. 70-79.

[232] Article V, section 8(b)(i); Article XXX(c)(ii); and E.B. Decision No. 5591 -(77/163) (December 5, 1977) in IMF, *Annual Report, 1978*, p. 123; *Selected Decisions* (10th issue, 1983), p. 298.

[233] E.B. Decision No. 5703, as amended, *supra* note 37. Article V, section 7(d), of the IMF Agreement states the Fund's authority to adopt a different repurchase rule for a special facility than would otherwise be required under Article V, section 7(c).

[234] United Nations document no. TD/IPC/CF/Conf/24(1980); *International Legal Materials*, vol. 19 (1980), p. 896. The agreement was opened for signature at New York October 1, 1980. See generally Robin Trevor Tait and George N. Sfeir, "The Common Fund for Commodities," *George Washington Journal of International Law and Economics*, vol. 16 (1982), p. 483.

The agreement provides for use of a single fund to finance buffer stocks rather than financing each one separately. At the time this book went to press, the agreement was not yet in force. The relationship between the IMF's buffer stock facility and the Common Fund has not yet been defined in Fund decisions.[235]

Special Facilities Using Borrowed Resources

Introduction

The IMF has authority under Article VII, Section 1, to borrow currencies, but not SDRs, to "replenish" its holdings.[236] In some cases the lender to the

---

[235] A Preparatory Commission, created by the United Nations Negotiating Conference, has been preparing rules and regulations to be applied once the Agreement Establishing the Common Fund enters into force.

[236] The Executive Board has established self-imposed guidelines, which are subject to change, limiting the overall magnitude of borrowings by the Fund. E.B. Decision No. 7040 -(82/7) (January 13, 1982); IMF, *Annual Report, 1982*, p. 125; *Selected Decisions* (10th issue, 1983), p. 231; and E.B. Decision No. 7589 -(83/181)(December 23, 1983); IMF, *Annual Report, 1984*, p. 138.

Borrowing agreements under which the IMF has supplemented its resources include:

> General Arrangements to Borrow [from the Group of Ten]. E.B. Decision No. 1289 -(62/1) (January 5, 1962) and annexes, as amended and extended [hereinafter GAB]. The GAB were most recently amended by Decision No. 7337 -(83/37) (adopted February 24, 1983, effective December 26, 1983). The consolidated text appears in *Selected Decisions*, pp. 131–45, with related documents at pp. 128–31 and 146–47. See also note 261, *infra*.

> Association of Switzerland with the GAB. E.B. Decision No. 1712 -(64/29) (June 8, 1964), as extended by Decision No. 6524 -(80/88) (June 9, 1980), and exchange of letters of June 11, 1964. *Selected Decisions*, pp.148–52. Decision No. 7337, *supra*, authorizes the Swiss National Bank to be a participating institution in the GAB rather than an associate as previously.

> Borrowing agreement with Saudi Arabia in association with the GAB. E.B. Decision No. 7403 -(83/73) (May 20, 1983). IMF, *Annual Report, 1983*, p. 154.

> Borrowing agreement with the Saudi Arabian Monetary Agency. E.B. Decision No. 6843 -(81/75) (May 6, 1981) and related documents [hereinafter SAMA borrowing agreement]. *Selected Decisions*, pp. 173–203.

> Borrowing agreements with central banks pursuant to E.B. Decision No. 6864 -(81/81) (May 13, 1981) and related documents [hereinafter E.B. Decision No. 6864 borrowing agreements]. *Selected Decisions*, pp. 207–19.

> Borrowing agreement with the Bank for International Settlements. E.B. Decision No. 6863 -(81/81) (May 13, 1981) and annex, as amended [hereinafter BIS borrowing agreement]. *Selected Decisions*, pp. 204–07.

> Supplementary Financing Facility borrowing agreements. E.B. Decision 5509 -(77/127) (August 29, 1977) and related documents. *Selected Decisions*, pp. 162–72.

Fund does not condition the uses to which the Fund may put the borrowed currencies, although the Fund may earmark the currencies for particular uses if it chooses, such as for the Policy on Enlarged Access to the Fund's Resources to be discussed below.[237]

In some cases agreements under which the Fund borrows currencies may impose conditions on their use by the Fund. An example is the General Arrangements to Borrow pursuant to which the Fund is authorized to borrow currency under one set of conditions to provide assistance to a member of the Group of Ten and under another set of conditions to provide assistance to other members. [238] Lenders providing currencies to the Fund under borrowing agreements for the Enlarged Access Policy or for the earlier Supplementary Financing Facility[239] expected the Fund to use the currencies in accordance with the decisions establishing the particular facility or policy.

When the Fund uses borrowed resources to provide assistance to a member, its policies may be affected by (even if not formally conditioned by) its own need to later repay the borrowings, the interest rate it will have to pay, and in some cases special interests of the lenders.[240]

Note on IMF Borrowing Arrangements

Up to the present time the IMF has borrowed currencies, under the authority of Article VII, Section 1(i), only from official agencies. However, it has not limited its borrowings to members and their central banks. It has also borrowed from Switzerland, from the Swiss National Bank, and from the Bank for International Settlements. While the Fund has not borrowed from commercial banks, private firms, or individuals, it has in some cases issued bearer notes to

Oil Facility borrowing agreements. E.B. Decision No. 4242 -(74/67) (June 13, 1974), Decision No. 4635 -(75/47) (April 4, 1975), and related documents. *Selected Decisions*, pp. 219–31.

Borrowing agreements with the Swiss National Bank of 1976 and 1977. E.B. Decision No. 5288–(76/167) (December 22, 1976), Decision No. 5387 -(77/61) (April 25, 1977), and related documents. *Selected Decisions*, pp. 152–62.

Borrowing agreement with Italy of 1966. E.B. Decision No. 2151 -(66/66) (August 3, 1966). *IMF History 1966–71, supra* note 52, vol. 2, pp. 211–13. See also *idem*, vol. 1, pp. 376–77.

[237] Discussed at pages 291–292, *infra*.
[238] Discussed at pages 290–291, *infra*.
[239] Discussed at pages 291–293, *infra*.
[240] See, e.g., letter of the Managing Director of the IMF to the Governor of the Saudi Arabian Monetary Agency, dated May 6, 1981. IMF, *Annual Report, 1981*, p. 187; *Selected Decisions* (10th issue, 1983), p. 199.

A recent amendment to the General Arrangements to Borrow states: "Nothing in this Decision shall affect the authority of the Fund with respect to requests for the use of its resources by individual members, and access to these resources by members shall be determined by the Fund's policies and practices, and shall not depend on whether the Fund can borrow under this Decision." E.B. Decision No. 7337, *supra* note 236, paragraph 10. The statement makes sense as an affirmation of Fund jurisdiction. It should not be understood to imply that the Fund will provide assistance when it lacks resources to do so.

official lenders which could be transferred to private parties and which could ultimately be collected on by them. The Fund has studied the possibility of borrowing in the private market, as is done by the International Bank for Reconstruction and Development.

Features of Fund borrowing agreements that impact Fund policies on the use of its resources are discussed below in connection with particular facilities. Here some issues that cut across the various borrowing arrangements can be noted.

The Fund's borrowing agreements with national treasuries, central banks, and other official agencies are agreements governed by public international law. Unless the agreements provide otherwise, the Fund cannot unilaterally change the terms of the agreements or invoke an action of a Fund organ as an excuse for non-performance.[241] While the Fund is vested with authority to interpret its constitution (the Articles of Agreement), it does not have the right to unilaterally interpret a borrowing agreement.[242] While most borrowing agreements are silent or vague on dispute settlement, some have contained provisions for arbitration.[243] Agreements may contain provisions to protect the lender against subsequent mortgages or liens by others on the Fund's property.[244]

In recent years borrowing agreements have been denominated in the Fund's unit of account—the special drawing right (SDR).[245] Because the IMF Agreement gives the Fund authority to change the principle and method of valuing the SDR,[246] lenders have wished to protect themselves against a potential adverse change. Borrowing agreements may provide that if the Fund changes the principle or method of valuing the SDR, the lender has the option, to be exercised promptly, to require that the immediately preceding method be used to value obligations under the agreement. If the lender exercises that option, the IMF in return may be given the option to terminate the agreement and prematurely repay its obligations.[247]

---

[241] See Memorandum of the Director of the Legal Department of the International Monetary Fund entitled "Borrowing Agreements Between IMF and Its Members," paragraphs 1–5. The memorandum appears in IMF, *Annual Report, 1981*, at p. 187; *Selected Decisions* (10th issue, 1983), p. 199.

[242] *Idem,* paragraph 6. See GAB, *supra* note 236, paragraphs 20 and 22f. For background see Chapter 1, *supra,* pages 37–39.

[243] See, e.g., SAMA borrowing agreement, *supra* note 236, paragraph 18. Compare GAB, *supra* note 236, paragraph 20.

[244] SAMA borrowing agreement, *supra* note 236, paragraph 12.

[245] Borrowing agreements denominated in SDRs include: Oil Facility borrowing agreements, annex, paragraph 1; Supplementary Financing Facility borrowing agreements, annex, paragraph 1; SAMA borrowing agreement, attachment, paragraph 8; BIS borrowing agreement, annex, paragraph 3; and E.B. Decision No. 6864 borrowing agreements, introductory paragraph. Following a 1983 amendment to the GAB (paragraphs 2 and 3), borrowing agreements under the GAB are also denominated in SDRs. See note 236, *supra,* for citations.

[246] See Chapter 5, *supra,* pages 187–192.

[247] See, e.g., Supplementary Financing Facility borrowing agreements, annex, paragraph 7; SAMA borrowing agreement, attachment, paragraph 8; and BIS borrowing agreement, annex, paragraph 10. The GAB, *supra* note 236, does not include a comparable provision.

When the IMF changed the method of valuing the SDR effective July 1, 1978, and January 1, 1981, no

Lenders have often not been willing to leave the interest rate at the SDR interest rate as set by the Fund from time to time. While some earlier agreements set interest rates in specific figures,[248] recent agreements have instead spelled out in some detail rules and procedures for determining interest rates, which may differ from the interest rate for the SDR set by the Fund.[249]

Since the Fund is authorized by the Articles to borrow only currencies and cannot borrow SDRs, the agreements establish procedures for determining exchange rates between the SDR and the currencies to be borrowed or to be used in repayment. Normally the "equal value" provisions of Article XIX, Section 7(a), are used.[250]

Normally the lender loans the currency it issues to the Fund, although in some cases a country other than the United States may loan dollars (or potentially other currencies). The Fund cannot borrow Swiss francs, as Switzerland is not an IMF member. Normally the Fund is given the right to repay loans and to pay interest in the currency lent to it, in the currency of the present holder of the claim to repayment if the claim has been transferred, and with agreement of the claimant in SDRs, U.S. dollars, or another currency. The repayment provisions vary considerably from one borrowing agreement to another. The maturities also vary.[251]

It is standard form for the borrowing agreements with IMF members to include a clause permitting the lender to suspend its obligation to loan further currency and to require premature prompt repayment of amounts loaned by it if the country encounters balance-of-payments difficulties.[252] Subject to conditions which may vary from agreement to agreement, a lender may transfer a claim for repayment.[253]

Some recent borrowing agreements have contained provisions for the Fund to issue bearer notes to the lender if the lender so requests, but then the claim of the lender is cancelled *pro tanto*. A bearer note can be transferred to anyone, including a private party. A holder of a bearer note is not entitled to repayment prior to maturity. It can demand repayment only in the currency

---

lender requested that the former method of valuing the SDR be retained.

[248] See, e.g., Oil Facility borrowing agreements, annex, paragraph 4.

[249] See, e.g., SAMA borrowing agreement, attachment, annex A; BIS borrowing agreement, annex, paragraphs 7 and 8; and E.B. Decision No. 6864 borrowing agreements, paragraph 4.

Following a 1983 amendment, the GAB, paragraph 9, uses the interest rate on the SDR as the interest rate for Fund borrowings under the GAB, and it establishes a procedure for substituting a different rate. For the IMF's rules and procedures for setting the interest rate on the SDR, see Chapter 5, *supra,* pages 193–194.

[250] See, e.g., GAB, paragraph 12; SAMA borrowing agreement, attachment, paragraph 3; BIS borrowing agreement, annex, paragraphs 3–6; and E.B. Decision No. 6864 borrowing agreements, paragraph 6.

[251] See, e.g., GAB, paragraphs 9 and 11; SAMA borrowing agreement, attachment, paragraphs 3, 6, and 14; BIS borrowing agreement, annex, paragraphs 3 and 5; and E.B. Decision No. 6864 borrowing agreements, paragraphs 3 and 6.

[252] See Chapter 3, *supra,* pages 112–114.

[253] See Chapter 3, *supra,* page 114.

named in the note.[254] The notes normally state that they are governed by the laws of the country issuing the currency named in the note.[255] The Fund may waive its immunity from jurisdiction and execution of judgments so that courts of that country can entertain suits on the notes.[256]

The Fund has studied the possibility of borrowing directly in the private market as is done by the International Bank for Reconstruction and Development. Up to the present time it has not made any such borrowing. One consideration has been concern about disclosures the Fund might be expected to make in an offering prospectus. Another consideration has been concern about possible limitations on the Fund's freedom to determine policies on the use of the borrowed resources.[257]

General Arrangements to Borrow

When the major industrial countries of Western Europe accepted the convertibility obligations of Article VIII, Sections 2, 3, and 4, of the IMF Agreement effective February 1961,[258] it was apparent that thereafter they and the United States might on occasion require large quantities of foreign currencies for interventions in the exchange markets. How could they obtain foreign currencies in the substantial quantities they would need?

In 1962 bilateral currency swap arrangements were negotiated between the central banks of the major market-economy industrial countries and the U.S. Federal Reserve Bank of New York. These arrangements for short-term reciprocal credits were described earlier.[259] Parallel with the negotiation of the original swap arrangements, efforts were made to assure that foreign currencies would be made available from the IMF promptly and in large amounts, if necessary, for use in currency stabilization activities. The Executive Board adopted a decision that Fund resources could be used to finance capital transfers in accordance with Article VI.[260] That, however, left the problem whether the Fund would have adequate resources in quantitative terms, especially if the United States should make a substantial drawing. On January 5, 1962, the IMF Executive Board formally adopted its decision entitled "General Arrangements to Borrow." The General Arrangements to Borrow (GAB) have been renewed and modified from time to time.[261]

---

[254] SAMA borrowing agreement, attachment, paragraph 15 and annex B; and E.B. Decision No. 6864 borrowing agreements, paragraph 10 and annexes A, B, and C.

[255] Bearer notes denominated in U.S. dollars issued under the SAMA borrowing agreement and under E.B. Decision No. 6864 borrowing agreements are governed by the laws of the State of New York, U.S.A.

[256] Bearer notes issued under SAMA borrowing agreement and under E.B. Decision No. 6864, *idem*.

[257] See speech of the Governor of France in IMF, *Summary Proceedings, 1981*, p. 49 at p. 53.

[258] See Chapter 10, *infra*, page 403 (note 94).

[259] Chapter 4, *supra*, pages 135–166.

[260] See pages 241–242 and note 97, *supra*.

[261] The General Arrangements to Borrow [hereinafter GAB] were established by E.B. Decision No. 1289

The GAB assure the Fund that under agreed conditions the Fund can borrow currencies from the ten industrial countries that are parties to the GAB if the Fund's General Resources Account needs the currencies to supply a member of the group. The ten countries participating in the GAB are: United States, United Kingdom, Canada, France, Italy, Japan, Netherlands, Belgium, Federal Republic of Germany (through its central bank) and Sweden (through its central bank). They are called the "Group of Ten" or sometimes "G-10."[262] Following a 1983 amendment to the GAB, the Swiss National Bank is authorized to be a participating lender.[263]

Note that the benefits of the General Arrangements to Borrow, prior to a 1983 amendment, have been limited to the Group of Ten; that is, the purpose has been to assure that none of these ten members of the IMF would be denied access to the Fund's resources because the General Resources Account lacked necessary currencies. The other members of the Group of Ten are obligated to loan their currencies to the Fund to prevent such a denial. However, the IMF is still to apply its tranche policies to drawings or stand-by or extended arrangements requested by a member of the Group of Ten. Further, the other members of the Group of Ten are involved through the Fund's normal processes in the review of the member's request for access to Fund resources. At the time the Fund adopted the initial GAB decision it was frankly described as "a compromise between the ideology of the Fund as a global monetary institution and a newer ideology which sought solutions by closer cooperation between the main industrial countries."[264]

If a member of the Group of Ten contemplates a General Resources Account stand-by or drawing that may be of a magnitude that necessitates Fund borrowing from the other members of the Group of Ten, the member first consults the Managing Director of the Fund and then the other participants in the GAB. The Managing Director consults with the participants in the GAB to learn the amounts they are prepared to loan to the Fund in the particular case.[265]

-(62/1)(January 5, 1962) and have been subsequently extended and modified a number of times. Decisions amending the GAB are No. 1362 -(62/32) (July 9, 1962); No. 1415 -(62/47)(September 19, 1962); No. 4421 -(74/132)(October 23, 1974); No. 5792 -(78/79)(June 2, 1978); No. 6241 -(79/144)(August 24, 1979); and, most recently, No. 7337 -(83/37) (adopted February 24, 1983, effective December 26, 1983). The consolidated text appears in *Selected Decisions* (10th issue, 1983), pp. 131–45, with related documents at pp. 128–31 and 146–47. The original decision appears in *IMF History 1945–65, supra* note 52, vol. 3, p. 246.

The Fund's authority to borrow and the repayment provisions applicable to Fund borrowings under the General Arrangements to Borrow were treated at pages 112–114 and 283–286, *supra*.

[262] See Chapter 2, *supra*, pages 72–74.

[263] E.B. Decision No. 7337, *supra* note 261, paragraph 22.

[264] *IMF History 1945–65, supra* note 52, vol. 1, p. 514. See generally *idem*, pp. 507–16. Had the Fund not established these general arrangements to borrow, it is likely that the ten countries would have developed procedures for mutual assistance, supplementing their reciprocal currency arrangements, outside IMF institutions. See Erin E. Jacobsson, *A Life for Sound Money: Per Jacobsson, His Biography* (Oxford: Oxford University Press, 1979), pp. 358–85.

[265] Although the Fund, prior to a 1983 amendment, could borrow under the GAB only to supplement its resources for an exchange transaction or stand-by with one of the ten countries, the Fund's General Counsel

The IMF normally attempts to borrow from the participants (excluding the country benefiting from the borrowing) proportionately to their commitments under the GAB. However, the Fund will not borrow any currencies held in the General Resources Account above 75 percent of quota. Also, adjustments may be made where a participant's balance-of-payments position indicates that it would be unwise for that country to loan its currency at that time.[266] A "proposal for calls" is then formulated. This proposal does not become effective until approved by both the participants in the GAB and the IMF's Executive Board. If unanimous agreement cannot be reached among the participants, there is a provision for taking a binding weighted vote within the group.[267] After the proposal for future calls has been established, the Fund then acts to approve the drawing or the stand-by or extended arrangement for the member.[268] While the prospective drawer's votes can be cast in the IMF in its own cause to approve the stand-by arrangement for itself and to give IMF approval to the proposal for future calls under the GAB, the country is not permitted to vote in the poll of participants on the proposal for future calls.[269]

Switzerland has agreed in the past to lend Swiss francs directly to a member of the Group of Ten up to an amount agreed with the participant upon the proposal of the Managing Director of the Fund.[270] A procedure different from such a parallel operation has been used at least twice: The Swiss National Bank in December 1976 agreed to lend U.S. dollars directly to the Fund to augment the Fund's resources in connection with the stand-by arrangement for the United Kingdom approved in January 1977, and a similar loan agreement was concluded by the Swiss National Bank and the IMF in connection with the stand-by for Italy approved in April 1977.[271]

Following a 1983 amendment to the GAB, the Swiss National Bank is authorized to be a participating institution in the GAB. This means it can take part in the poll of participants on whether to loan to the Fund.[272] This also means it

---

long ago stated that "the Fund is not precluded from taking into account its prospective needs for other transactions in determining whether it needs to replenish its holdings." Joseph Gold, *Stand-By Arrangements, supra* note 126, p. 117. See notes 279–282, *infra,* and accompanying text.

[266] GAB, *supra* note 261, paragraph 7.

[267] GAB, paragraphs 6 and 7; and letter of the French Minister of Finance to the U.S. Secretary of the Treasury, December 15, 1961, in *Selected Decisions* (10th issue, 1983), p. 128.

[268] See GAB, paragraph 10. See also Gold, *Stand-By Arrangements, supra* note 126, pp. 115–17. On at least one occasion a stand-by was approved before the proposed calls under the GAB had been worked out. *IMF History 1945–65, supra* note 52, vol. 1, p. 568.

[269] Paragraph C of letter of the French Minister of Finance, *supra* note 267. See Chapter 1, *supra,* pages 32–35.

[270] Switzerland's undertakings are set forth in exchanges of letters with the Managing Director of the IMF accompanying E.B. Decision No. 1712, *supra* note 236. See also Joseph Gold, *Membership and Nonmembership in the International Monetary Fund* (Washington: IMF, 1974), pp. 457–61.

[271] See *IMF Survey,* January 10, 1977, p. 5; and IMF, *Annual Report, 1977,* p. 58, and *Annual Report, 1978,* p. 69. The texts of the IMF's borrowing agreements with the Swiss National Bank and related IMF decisions appear in *Selected Decisions* (10th issue, 1983), pp. 152–62. See note 236, *supra.*

[272] See note 267, *supra,* and accompanying text.

can rely on the creditworthiness of the Fund and not just the beneficiary country for repayment.[273]

The Fund pays interest on its borrowings,[274] and it may repay borrowings from members at its option with special drawing rights instead of currencies.[275] Under the GAB the Fund has an obligation to make repayments to the participants that have loaned their currencies when the beneficiary country to which the IMF sold currency effects a repurchase allocable to the borrowing. In any event, the IMF must repay the participants loaning currencies not later than five years or other date set in the particular borrowing agreement. Other features of the General Arrangements to Borrow were discussed earlier.[276]

The first occasion on which the General Arrangements to Borrow were activated was in November–December 1964 to meet drawings by the United Kingdom under a stand-by arrangement.[277] Subsequently the arrangements have been activated on several occasions.[278] Typically, the General Resources Account's own resources have been used together with the currencies borrowed from the GAB participants.

A 1983 amendment to the GAB made a number of changes, several of which have been mentioned above. The most important change is that the Fund is now able to make calls under the GAB to finance exchange transactions requested by IMF members that are not GAB participants (i.e. not members of the Group of Ten) if stated conditions are met. The funds borrowed by the IMF for this purpose are only available to finance transactions in the upper credit tranches or under stand-by or extended arrangements. The Managing Director may initiate the procedure for making calls if he "considers that the Fund faces an inadequacy of resources to meet actual and expected requests for financing that reflect the existence of an exceptional situation associated with balance of payments problems of members of a character or aggregate size that could threaten the stability of the international monetary system."[279] The participants

[273] See generally E.B. Decision No. 7337, *supra* note 261, paragraph 22. Switzerland, until it becomes a member of the IMF, will of course not be able to become a beneficiary of the funds loaned to the Fund under the GAB.

[274] GAB, *supra* note 261, paragraph 9.

[275] GAB, paragraph 11.

[276] See pages 112–114 and 283–286, *supra*.

[277] *IMF History 1945–65, supra* note 52, vol. 1, p. 569, and vol. 2, pp. 455–56.

[278] May 1965 for the United Kingdom, June 1968 for France, June 1968 for the United Kingdom, June 1969 for the United Kingdom, September 1969 for France, February 1970 for France, January 1977 for the United Kingdom, April 1977 for Italy, and November 1978 for the United States. The activation valued at SDR 777 million (U.S. $1 billion) in November 1978 for the United States involved IMF borrowings only from the Deutsche Bundesbank (mark equivalent to SDR 583 million) and Japan (yen equivalent to SDR 194 million) and the interest paid was "out of pocket" for the IMF because the U.S. drawing was in the reserve tranche. Total U.S. drawings, all in the reserve tranche and all in Deutsche mark and Japanese yen, amounted to the equivalent of U.S. $3 billion (about SDR 2.22 billion). See *IMF History 1966–71, supra* note 52, vol. 1, pp. 370–76; IMF, *Annual Report, 1977,* pp. 57–58; *Annual Report, 1978,* p. 69; and *IMF Survey,* November 6, 1978, pp. 337 and 347–49, and November 20, 1978, p. 361. See also Chapter 11, *infra,* page 533.

[279] E.B. Decision No. 7337, *supra* note 261, paragraph 21.

in the GAB will vote on the Managing Director's proposal in the same manner as if the beneficiary were a member of the GAB.[280] The criterion quoted above is, however, a more demanding one than applies when the beneficiary is a member of the Group of Ten. In the latter case, funds may be made available to finance any Fund transaction with the beneficiary, and the Fund's need to supplement its resources is defined in the terms "in order to forestall or cope with an impairment of the international monetary system."[281]

Following a 1983 amendment to the GAB, a total of SDR 17 billion in currencies is potentially available to the Fund under the GAB.[282]

Policy on Enlarged Access to the Fund's Resources

The IMF's Policy on Enlarged Access to the Fund's Resources permits the Fund to approve stand-by or extended arrangements for a member country that needs balance-of-payments financing in excess of the amount available to it in the four credit tranches or under the Extended Fund Facility. The policy was initially adopted to make it possible for members to draw larger amounts than would otherwise be possible until the larger quotas provided for in the Eighth General Review of Quotas would become effective, but has since been extended.[283] The policy has been financed with borrowed resources, and drawings are approved only to the extent of the available financing. The policy is operated through the General Resources Account and is administered in accordance with decisions of the Executive Board.[284]

The problem facing the country must require a relatively long period of adjustment. Use of the enlarged access policy requires the country to have a stand-by or extended arrangement in accordance with the IMF's policies, including policies on conditionality, phasing, and performance criteria. The country in a letter of intent is required to make a detailed statement of its economic and financial policies.[285]

Executive Board decisions establish principles for apportioning ordinary

---

[280] See notes 267–269 and accompanying text. See also note 240, *supra.*

[281] GAB, *supra* note 261, paragraph 6. The GAB was activated to finance a reserve tranche drawing by the United States in 1978. See note 278, *supra.*

[282] E.B. Decision No. 7337, *supra* note 261, annex.

[283] The basic decision is E.B. Decision No. 6783 -(81/40) (March 11, 1981); IMF, *Annual Report, 1981,* p. 153; *Selected Decisions* (10th issue, 1983), p. 40. That decision has been amended and supplemented by three Executive Board decisions adopted January 6, 1984: No. 7599 -(84/3) (period and annual review of the policy); No. 7600 -(84/3) (access limits); and No. 7601 -(84/3) (apportionment of ordinary and borrowed resources); IMF, *Annual Report, 1984,* pp. 130–35.

[284] To obtain currency to be used under the Policy on Enlarged Access, the IMF initially concluded borrowing agreements with the Saudi Arabian Monetary Agency, entered into force May 7, 1981, with the Bank for International Settlements, entered into force June 1, 1981, and with several central banks under E.B. Decision No. 6864. For citations see note 236, *supra.*

[285] E.B. Decision No. 6783, *supra* note 283, paragraphs 1–6 and 11. The extended arrangement for India, discussed at page 251 et seq., included funds under the enlarged access policy. See note 143, *supra.*

and borrowed resources. Borrowed resources under the Supplementary Financing Facility, if available, were normally to be used before borrowed resources under the Policy on Enlarged Access.[286] Drawings under the enlarged access policy do not affect the country's reserve tranche position. The IMF applies its credit tranche policies as if the Fund's holdings of the member's currency did not include holdings resulting from purchases under the enlarged access policy that involve borrowed resources. Charges are keyed to the Fund's borrowing costs.[287]

Supplementary Financing Facility

The Supplementary Financing Facility (sometimes called the "Witteveen Facility" after H. Johannes Witteveen, the IMF Managing Director who proposed it) became effective in February 1979.[288] The facility, financed with borrowed funds,[289] made it possible for the Fund to approve stand-by and extended arrangements larger in size and longer in term than the Fund's resources would otherwise have permitted.[290] In February 1982 the IMF made its final commitments of the borrowed funds. The facility is now in the process of being phased out as members that drew upon it make their repurchases and the Fund, in turn, repays its borrowings.

The IMF's *Annual Reports* for 1979–1982 describe the facility and the adjustment programs of members that were supported by it.[291] To obtain a stand-by or extended arrangement which included supplementary financing, the member had to submit a "detailed statement" of the economic and financial policies that it intended to follow.[292] IMF decisions established formulas for apportioning the Fund's regular resources and supplementary financing when stand-by or extended arrangements made use of supplementary financing.[293]

---

[286] See E.B. Decision No. 7601, *supra* note 283. See also E.B. Decision No. 6783, *supra* note 283, paragraphs 7–9, 13, and appendix; and E.B. Decisions Nos. 7047 and 7048, *infra* note 288.

[287] E.B. Decision No. 6783, *supra* note 283, paragraphs 10–14.

[288] The basic decision establishing the Supplementary Financing Facility and defining the applicable policies is E.B. Decision No. 5508 -(77/127) (August 29, 1977); IMF, *Annual Report, 1978*, p. 112; *Selected Decisions* (10th issue, 1983), p. 33. The facility became effective February 23, 1979. *IMF Survey*, March 5, 1979, p. 65. E.B. Decision No. 5508 was extended by E.B. Decision No. 6725 -(81/5)(January 9, 1981); IMF, *Annual Report, 1981*, p. 151; *Selected Decisions*, p. 40. See also E.B. Decisions Nos. 7047 and 7048 -(82/13)(February 5, 1982); IMF, *Annual Report, 1982*, pp. 126–27; *Selected Decisions*, pp. 58–61.

[289] E.B. Decision No. 5509, *supra* note 236, defined the terms under which the IMF borrowed currencies for the facility. For background see *IMF Survey*, March 5, 1979, p. 65; and IMF, *Annual Report, 1977*, pp. 24, 47, and 115. Some general aspects of the IMF's borrowing agreements are treated at pages 112–114 and 283–287, *supra*.

[290] E.B. Decision No. 5508, *supra* note 288, paragraph 5. The maximum period for repurchase was longer than arrangements that did not use borrowed funds. *Idem*, paragraph 7.

[291] See IMF, *Annual Report, 1979*, pp. 74–75 and 78; *1980*, pp. 79–80; *1981*, pp. 85–87 and 91; and *1982*, pp. 81–82. *IMF Survey*, 1979–82, carried summaries of members' programs.

[292] E.B. Decision No. 5508, *supra* note 288, paragraphs 2 and 4.

[293] *Idem*, paragraph 5.

Charges on the IMF's holdings of a drawing country's currency resulting from the use of supplementary financing were at rates slightly higher than those paid by the Fund on its borrowings.[294] To assist low-per-capita-income countries to meet the higher charges on use of the supplementary facility (caused by the use of borrowed resources in the facility), the Fund established a special subsidy account to subsidize those charges.[295]

Oil Facility

The Oil Facility was created by a decision of the Executive Board in June 1974.[296] The rules of access to the facility were revised in 1975.[297] The right of access to the facility expired in March 1976.[298] The facility was a temporary measure to assist IMF members to meet the immediate impact upon their balances of payments of increased costs of imports of petroleum and petroleum products caused by a dramatic increase in petroleum prices on the world market in the period 1973-75.[299] The Fund acted as a financial intermediary, borrowing from oil exporting and other countries and making the funds available to countries most severely affected. The total resources available under the credit arrangements determined the total that the Executive Board made available for drawings.

The charges on drawings under the facility were related to the interest costs incurred by the Fund.[300] Because of the relatively high charges, the Fund established a subsidy account to receive donations to be distributed to those members most adversely affected by oil price increases that drew upon the facility.[301]

The OECD Council on April 9, 1975, adopted the text of an Agreement Establishing a Financial Support Fund which had been negotiated under the auspices of that organization. The purpose of the agreement was to provide what was called a "safety net" to assure that OECD members would be able to finance oil imports at rising prices. The OECD Financial Support Fund, which

[294] Rule I-6, paragraph 3; *By-Laws, Rules and Regulations* (40th issue, 1983).

[295] See generally E.B. Decision No. 6683 -(80/185) G/TR (December 17, 1980); IMF, *Annual Report, 1981*, p. 147; *Selected Decisions* (10th issue, 1983), p. 321. See also IMF, *Annual Report, 1982*, pp. 93–95; and *IMF Survey*, August 16, 1982, p. 252.

[296] E.B. Decision No. 4241 -(74/67) (June 13, 1974) as amended; *Selected Decisions* (10th issue, 1983), pp. 80–85.

[297] E.B. Decision No. 4634 -(75/47)(April 4, 1975) as amended; *Selected Decisions* (10th issue, 1983), pp. 85–87.

[298] E.B. Decision No. 4986 -(76/47)(March 18, 1976); IMF, *Annual Report, 1976*, p. 98.

[299] During the period the facility was in operation a total of 55 countries drew currencies equivalent to SDR 6,902 million. See IMF, *Annual Report, 1976*, pp. 53–54, 82, and 87; and *Annual Report, 1977*, p. 54.

[300] Fund decisions relating to borrowings for the Oil Facility are cited in note 236. See also IMF, *Annual Report, 1976*, pp. 54 and 91.

[301] The operation of the subsidy account was quite complicated. See, e.g., IMF, *Annual Report, 1978*, pp. 75–76; *Annual Report, 1979*, pp. 84–86; and *IMF Survey*, June 21, 1982, p. 182.

never became effective, would have been entirely separate from any IMF facility.[302]

Special Disbursement Account and Trust Funds

Introduction

Up until now this chapter has focused on rules for drawings in the IMF's General Resources Account. The special "facilities" examined in the previous part of the chapter are simply special rules on access to that account. The Special Disbursement Account is also maintained within the General Department of the IMF but is entirely separate from the General Resources Account.[303] The IMF may also operate trust funds.[304]

Trust Fund Operated in Period 1976–1981

A political compromise struck in the negotiation of the Second Amendment to the IMF Articles required the IMF to sell 50 million ounces of gold.[305] Of this amount, 25 million ounces were to be sold at the carrying value (SDR 35 per ounce) to members in proportion to their quotas on August 31, 1975.[306] The other 25 million ounces were to be sold at market-related prices with the profit above the carrying value being exclusively dedicated to the benefit of developing countries. Part of this profit was to be remitted directly to each developing country—an amount that bore the same relation to the total profit on the sale of the 25 million ounces as the particular country's quota bore to total IMF quotas on August 31, 1975.[307] The balance of the profit (i.e., the total of the parts other members could have claimed if they had been developing countries) was to be set aside for the benefit of a smaller number of specified especially needy

---

[302] The currency to be loaned by the Financial Support Fund would have been obtained through borrowings by the OECD Fund on the collective undertaking of the participants or obtained in response to calls made upon the participants. The total of the quotas was set at SDR 20 billion. The U.S. Congress did not enact the necessary legislation for the United States to become bound, and the agreement did not enter into force among any countries. The text appears in *International Legal Materials*, vol. 14 (1975), p. 979; *European Yearbook*, vol. 23 (1975), p. 383.

[303] The Special Disbursement Account is defined in Article V, section 12(f).

[304] Article V, section 2(b), recognizes the IMF's authority to operate trust funds. For a discussion of legal principles applicable to the operation of trust funds at the international level and specific principles that have been applied by the IMF, see Joseph Gold, "Trust Funds in Interntional Law: The Contribution of the International Monetary Fund to a Code of Principles," *American Journal of International Law*, vol. 72 (1978), p. 856.

[305] Schedule B, paragraph 7. For background, see Chapter 3, *supra*, pages 119–123.

[306] Developing members as well as other members were entitled to purchase in proportion to their quotas on August 31, 1975, the 25 million ounces of gold sold at the carrying value in accordance with Schedule B, paragraph 7(a). These sales were completed in May 1980.

[307] Schedule B, paragraph 7(b). See also Section I, paragraph 2, of the trust instrument, *infra* note 309.

developing-country members.[308] The IMF in May 1976—after the Second Amendment had been approved by the Board of Governors for submission to member countries for their acceptance, but before it had entered into force— established a Trust Fund that subsequently sold the 25 million ounces that were to be sold at market-related prices and applied the proceeds as mandated by paragraph 7(b) of Schedule B.[309]

Among legal issues concerning use of the profits from gold sales by the Trust Fund were:

(1) Criteria for determining whether a member country was a developing country for purposes of receiving profit distributions in accordance with its quota proportion as of August 31, 1975.

(2) Criteria for determining whether a member country was an especially needy (low-income) developing country that would benefit from the profits retained by the Trust Fund after the above profit distributions.

(3) Terms for providing assistance to the especially needy (low-income) developing countries.

The first issue provoked some controversy when Singapore was not included on the list of countries entitled to profit distributions. The matter was finally settled through negotiation, with Singapore being included in the list.[310] With respect to the second issue, per-capita income data were used in preparing the list of especially needy countries.

With respect to the third issue, it was decided that, although Schedule B,

---

[308] *Idem.*

[309] The Trust Fund was operated independently of both the General Resources Account and the Special Disbursement Account. The Trust Fund was operated in accordance with E.B. Decision No. 5069 -(76/72)(May 5, 1976) and the Trust Instrument appended to that decision, as amended by various subsequent decisions. For the texts, see *Selected Decisions* (10th issue, 1983), pp. 302–20.

Since the IMF's General Account in which the gold had been held was not authorized (prior to the entry into force of the Second Amendment) to sell gold at a price above its carrying value, the following scheme was used. The General Account sold the 25 million ounces—to be sold in accordance with Schedule B, paragraph 7(b), of the Second Amendment—to certain members in exchange for currencies at the carrying value of SDR 35 per ounce under "non-contractual" gentlemen's agreements that the members would resell the gold to the Trust Fund at the same price, which was done. The Trust Fund then sold the gold at auction during the period June 1976–May 1980. Proceeds equal to the carrying value were remitted to the members that had sold the gold to the Trust Fund. Profits allocable to the quotas of developing countries were remitted directly to them. The balance was used by the Trust Fund for loans to developing countries as explained in the text. See IMF, *Annual Report, 1976*, pp. 54–56 and 60; *Annual Report, 1977*, pp. 58–60 and 66–67; and *Annual Report, 1978*, pp. 70–72 and 76–78. See also E.B. Decision No. 5709 -(78/41)TR (March 23, 1978); *Selected Decisions*, p. 314.

When the gold sales provided for by Schedule B, paragraph 7(b), were completed in May 1980, total profits to the Trust Fund amounted to U.S. $4.6 billion of which U.S. $1.3 billion was distributed to 104 developing countries and the balance was retained in the Trust Fund for assistance to a smaller number of especially needy developing countries on concessional terms. Several of the 104 developing countries contributed their distributions back to the Trust Fund, thus augmenting its resources for concessional lending. See IMF, *Annual Report, 1978*, p. 71; and *idem, 1981*, pp. 102–04.

[310] See IMF, *Annual Report, 1978*, p. 107.

paragraph 7(b), and the Trust Fund Instrument permitted assistance in the form of loans or grants, assistance would take the form of loans. Loans would be made to members with especially low per-capita incomes that had balance-of-payments need. Loans would be conditioned on satisfaction of a "reasonable effort" criterion, and once the Fund had found reasonable effort by the requesting country it would be precluded from reexamining the country's program for at least twelve months. Interest would be at a rate of 0.5 percent per annum and repayment was to be completed in 10 years.[311]

The final loan disbursement under the Trust Fund was made in March 1981. The Trust Fund was terminated as of April 30, 1981. The resources of the Trust Fund, including claims for repayment, were transferred to the Special Disbursement Account. Part of these resources assigned to the Special Disbursement Account were in turn transferred to the Subsidy Account of the Supplementary Financing Facility and the balance was retained by the Special Disbursement Account to be used for assistance to low-income developing countries.[312]

Special Disbursement Account

As explained earlier in this book, the IMF (acting by 85 percent of the total voting power) can sell additional amounts of gold beyond the 50 million ounces whose sale was required by the transitional provisions of Schedule B.[313] When gold acquired before the entry into force of the Second Amendment is sold on the basis of market prices, proceeds equivalent to the carrying value are placed in the General Resources Account and the profit is assigned to the Special Disbursement Account unless it is decided (again by 85 percent of the total voting power) to transfer the profit to the Investment Account.[314]

At a first reading the provisions respecting the use of the Special Disbursement Account's assets have a similar ring to paragraph 7(b) of Schedule B. Careful study indicates differences that endow the Special Disbursement Account with much greater flexibility. By a decision of 70 percent of the total voting power, all or part of the assets in the Special Disbursement Account can be transferred to the General Resources Account for immediate use in that ac-

---

[311] See Section II of the Trust Fund Instrument as amended, *supra* note 309. The operation of the Trust Fund is described in IMF, *Annual Report, 1977*, pp. 66–67; *1978*, pp. 76–78; *1979*, pp. 86–87; *1980*, pp. 85–89; and *1981*, pp. 102–04.

[312] See generally E.B. Decision No. 6704 -(80/185) TR (December 17, 1980); IMF, *Annual Report, 1981*, p. 146; *Selected Decisions* (10th issue, 1983), p. 318. See also IMF, *Annual Report, 1981*, p. 146 (note 14).

The Special Disbursement Account is discussed further below. The Subsidy Account of the Supplementary Financing Facility is mentioned at page 293.

[313] See Chapter 3, *supra*, pages 119–123. See generally IMF Article V, section 12.

[314] Article V, section 12(f) and (g). The Investment Account is mentioned in note 1, *supra*.

count's transactions and operations.[315] By the same majority, the Special Disbursement Account can be liquidated, in which case its assets are to be gradually transferred to the General Resources Account and put to immediate use.[316]

Acting by an 85 percent majority of the total voting power, the Fund can decide to allocate all or a portion of the Special Disbursement Account's assets for "operations and transactions that are not authorized by other provisions of this Agreement but are consistent with the purposes of the Fund."[317] Having pronounced those magic words, the Fund by the same majority can decide (although it is not required to do so) to make direct payments to developing countries of a portion of the amount allocated—the portion being determined by the ratio as of August 31, 1975, between each developing country's quota and the total of all quotas in the General Account.[318] The balance of the amount allocated may be used for assistance to developing countries on special (concessional) terms or presumably put to any other use consistent with the purposes of the Fund. Assistance can be provided on a conditional basis and in the form of loans or subsidies.[319] Assets of the account not otherwise put to use can be invested.[320]

Prior to the establishment of the Trust Fund, the IMF had not made a formal distinction between developing countries and other members.[321] The full consequences upon the organization of making such a distinction cannot now be assessed. An immediate problem when special benefits are given to certain countries and not to others is to develop appropriate criteria for the differ-

[315] Article V, section 12(f)(i). The currency transferred must be used immediately in the General Resources Account so as not to adversely affect the issuer's drawing rights in the General Resources Account or increase the level of charges (or reduce the level of remuneration) to the issuer. In accordance with Article III, section 2(b), quotas in the General Resources Account may be increased for members proportional to their quotas on August 31, 1975, and in a total amount not in excess of the amount transferred to the General Resources Account. See *Report on Second Amendment, supra* note 14, part 2, chapter I, sections 8(b)(i) and 13(b).

[316] Article V, section 12(j). Special rules apply if the entire IMF organization should be liquidated. See also *Report on Second Amendment, supra* note 14, part 2, chapter I, section 13(f).

[317] Article V, section 12(f)(ii).

[318] See generally Article V, sections 12(e) and 12(f)(iii); and *Report on Second Amendment, supra* note 14, part 2, chapter I, section 8(c). The IMF may permit a developing country to buy gold at the carrying value equal to its allocable share instead of taking sale–profit payments.

[319] The author uses the word "presumably" because the language of section 12(f)(ii) is very general. The language would appear to permit the Fund to use the funds for the benefit of other countries besides developing countries and for countries that joined the IMF after August 31, 1975. Further, the form of the assistance is not specified. The *Report on Second Amendment, supra* note 14, part 2, chapter I, section 8(b)(ii), mentions, as an example, subsidies for payment of charges levied in connection with use of the Fund's general resources.

[320] Article V, section 12(h). Compare Article XII, section 6(f) (iii) and (iv). Issuers of currencies held in the Special Disbursement Account are not under an obligation to maintain the value of those currencies in relation to the special drawing right unless they undertake to do so. See *Report on Second Amendment, supra* note 14, part 2, chapter I, section 13(a); and Article V, section 11, of the IMF Agreement.

[321] See Joseph Gold, "Uniformity as a Legal Principle of the Fund," in Joseph Gold, *Legal and Institutional Aspects of the International Monetary System: Selected Essays* (Washington: IMF, 1979), p. 469 and especially pp. 504–07.

entiation. The Fund encountered this problem in determining which countries were "developing" countries to receive the benefits of the Trust Fund.[322]

Note

Concluding comments on financing techniques appear at pages 374–376.

---

[322] The lists of countries that were eligible for loans appear as Annexes A and B to the Trust Fund Instrument, *supra* note 309. The annexes, printed in IMF *Annual Reports*, were revised from time to time. The composition of the lists and their amendment were negotiated with per-capita income taken into account as one criterion. The establishment of a particular per-capita income figure and its application to particular countries were subjects that resulted in some disputes.

Chapter 7: Regional Payments Systems and Credit Arrangements

Note

A variety of multilateral arrangements for balance-of-payments financing, operated separately from the International Monetary Fund, are in use at the present time, usually on a regional basis. Legal aspects of these arrangements are reviewed in this and the two following chapters.

We begin with the European Payments Union which functioned in the period 1950–1958. It is the historical prototype for regional systems for clearing payments that are in use today by developing countries. Legal aspects of current regional clearing arrangements are then surveyed. The Andean Reserve Fund and the Arab Monetary Fund, while not currently operating payments facilities, provide financing for countries in their areas that encounter balance-of-payments difficulties.[1] Monetary unions of French-speaking African states are considered at the end of the chapter.

Credit arrangements for balance-of-payments support operated under the auspices of the European Economic Community (EEC) are complex and involve the use of a unique currency unit, the European currency unit (ECU). Chapter 8 is devoted to the ECU and the EEC facilities for balance-of-payments financing.

The multilateral payments arrangement operated by the International Bank for Economic Cooperation (IBEC) serves the socialist states that belong to the Council for Mutual Economic Assistance (CMEA). This system also uses a unique unit, the transferable ruble, but, compared to the EEC system, is somewhat simpler in its legal structure. However, features of product and service pricing in socialist countries complicate understanding of the CMEA system. Payments and credit arrangements serving CMEA countries are treated in Chapter 9.

---

[1] A number of regional organizations, such as the African Development Bank, Asian Development Bank, and Inter-American Development Bank, provide financing for projects and programs as distinguished from general support of the balance of payments. This book does not examine their activities.

European Payments Union

Historical Background

In the era immediately after the devastation of World War II, the currencies of the countries that are today the major industrial countries of Western Europe were not convertible. Payments and trade restrictions were extensive. The first steps to promote international trade in the postwar period involved bilateral trade and payments agreements between pairs of countries.[2] These arrangements were supplemented by foreign aid, the aid coming primarily from the United States and Canada.

To support the United Kingdom's postwar reconstruction and an early return to sterling convertibility, the Anglo-American Financial Agreement was concluded in 1945.[3] Under the Agreement, the United States made a long-term loan of $3,750 million to the United Kingdom and this was supplemented by a $1,250 million loan from Canada. By July 15, 1947, convertibility of sterling was declared effective, in the sense that nonresidents obtaining current sterling balances could use them for settlement of current transactions with virtually any country in the world including the United States. However, in the weeks that immediately followed, the conversion of sterling into dollars occurred in such large volumes that on August 20, 1947, the convertibility of sterling had to be suspended.[4] It was against this background that discussions began of multilateral arrangements to facilitate intra-European payments while currencies would otherwise remain inconvertible.

An Agreement on Multilateral Monetary Compensation was concluded among Belgium, Luxembourg, the Netherlands, France, and Italy in November 1947,[5] and subsequently other agreements were concluded among European countries.[6] It was recognized that these were not a satisfactory solution. In December 1949 the U.S. Economic Co-operation Administration submitted a proposal to the Organisation for European Economic Co-operation (OEEC)[7] that

---

[2] The operation of bilateral payments agreements is explained in Chapter 9, *infra*, pages 358–360. For an example of such an agreement between two Western European countries, see Monetary Agreement between Belgium and the United Kingdom, signed November 14, 1947. *United Nations Treaty Series*, vol. 25, p. 269. The agreement is no longer in effect. See generally Bank for International Settlements, *18th Annual Report 1947/48*, pp. 142–53.

[3] United States–United Kingdom Financial Agreement, signed December 6, 1945, entered into force July 15, 1946. *U.S. Statutes at Large*, vol. 60, p. 1841; *United Nations Treaty Series*, vol. 126, p. 13. For subsequent amendments, see *United States Treaties and International Agreements*, vol. 8, p. 2443; *United Nations Treaty Series*, vol. 303, p. 332. See generally Richard N. Gardner, *Sterling-Dollar Diplomacy* (rev. ed.; New York: McGraw-Hill Book Co., 1969), pp. 188–254.

[4] See Gardner, *idem*, pp. 313–25; OEEC, *A Decade of Co-operation: Achievements and Perspectives, 9th Report of the O.E.E.C.* (Paris, 1958), pp. 75–81; and *Foreign Relations of the United States* (Washington: U.S. Government Printing Office), 1947, vol. 3 (1972), pp. 1–94.

[5] First Agreement on Multilateral Monetary Compensation, signed November 18, 1947. The text appears in BIS, *Documents and Statistics Relating to the Various Agreements Dealing with Intra-European Payments and Compensations, 1947–1950* (Basle, 1951), pp. 1–3.

[6] For the texts, see *idem*, pp. 4–19 and 37–57. See generally William Diebold, Jr., *Trade and Payments in Western Europe: A Study in Economic Cooperation, 1947–51* (New York: Harper & Brothers for Council on Foreign Relations, 1952), pp. 21–86.

[7] OEEC, *A Decade of Co-operation*, *supra* note 4, pp. 79–91. For general information on the OEEC, see Chapter 2, *supra*, pages 68–69.

became the basis for the Agreement for the Establishing of a European Payments Union, signed September 19, 1950.[8]

Description of the System

The European Payments Union (EPU), in operation from 1950 to 1958, was a multilateral payments arrangement among countries of Western Europe belonging to the OEEC. The EPU facilitated multilateral settlements at a time when the currencies of the participants were not readily convertible into the U.S. dollar or into gold. The EPU was similar in concept to a bilateral payments arrangement with the added feature that foreign currency earned by one country in transactions with another member could be used for payments to any other member of the group.[9]

Exchange restrictions channeled international payments through the central banks. Each central bank registered payments and receipts from other participating central banks. The residual balance of each country toward each one of its partners was communicated monthly to the Bank for International Settlements (BIS), which acted as Agent for the OEEC in operating the EPU. The BIS cancelled out the claims and debts accumulated during the month by each country with respect to all of its partners. Thus, each central bank was left with a single residual claim or debt running to the EPU.[10]

---

[8] For the text of the Agreement, signed September 19, 1950, effective retroactively to July 1, 1950, see *British and Foreign State Papers,* vol. 156 (1950), pp. 883–915. For the subsequent protocols, see *idem,* vol. 159 (1952), pp. 351–55 and 384–91; vol. 160 (1953), pp. 414–17; vol. 161 (1954), pp. 347–58; vol. 162 (1955–56), pp. 277–81, 284–94, and 746–50; and vol. 163 (1957–58), pp. 148–52, 716, and 722–27. The Agreement of 1950 and the first six protocols also appear in *European Yearbook,* vol. 2 (1954), p. 362.

The EPU was administered, under the authority of the OEEC Council, by a Managing Board of seven persons. The EPU was an organ of the OEEC and did not have legal personality apart from the OEEC.

[9] The EPU is treated from a legal perspective in Yves Biclet, "L'Union Européene des Paiements," *European Yearbook,* vol. 2 (1954), p. 151; Pierre Huet, "Aspects Juridiques de l'Union Européene de Paiements," *Journal du Droit International,* vol. 78 (1951), p. 770; and Walther Hug, "The Law of International Payments," in Hague Academy of International Law, *Recueil des Cours,* vol. 79 (1951-II), p. 511 at pp. 678–710.

For additional background, see the *Annual Reports* of the Managing Board of the EPU issued for 1950–1958 and the *Final Report* issued in 1959; the *Annual Reports* of the Bank for International Settlements for this same period; J. Keith Horsefield and Margaret Garritsen de Vries, *The International Monetary Fund, 1945–1965: Twenty Years of International Monetary Cooperation* (3 vols.; Washington: IMF, 1969) [hereinafter *IMF History 1945-65*], vol. 2, chapter 15; Raymond F. Mikesell, *Foreign Exchange in the Postwar World* (New York: Twentieth Century Fund, 1954), chapter 6; W. M. Scammell, *International Monetary Policy* (2d ed.; London: Macmillan, 1961), chapter 10; Robert Triffin, *Europe and the Money Muddle: From Bilateralism to Near-Convertibility, 1947–1956* (New Haven: Yale University Press, 1957), pp. 161–233; Marjorie M. Whiteman, *Digest of International Law* (Washington: U.S. Department of State), vol. 14 (1970), pp. 562–70; and Leland B. Yeager, *International Monetary Relations: Theory, History, and Policy* (2d ed.; New York: Harper & Row, 1976), pp. 411–24.

[10] See EPU Agreement, *supra* note 8, Articles 3–8.

The first draft of the 1947 Agreement on Multilateral Monetary Compensation, *supra* note 5, provided that the International Monetary Fund would be the clearing agent, but it was not represented at a critical meeting in Paris in October 1947. Under the agreement signed in November 1947, the BIS assumed responsibility as clearing agent. The BIS also served as agent under subsequent agreements. See *IMF History 1945-65, supra*

The residual claim or debt was settled with the EPU. The settlement was financed, in accordance with a formula, partly through credit and partly through transfers of gold, U.S. dollars, or other currency acceptable to the creditor countries. The settlement formula was modified several times by OEEC Council decisions.[11] The United States contributed a capital fund to the EPU to cushion possible defaults or delays of payment by debtors and to meet the asymmetry between the amount of gold and dollar payments to creditors and the amount of gold and dollar payments from debtors.

Consultations were held within the OEEC on problems created when some countries accumulated large creditor or debtor positions in the EPU. In addition to credits available under quotas stated in the agreement, special short-term credit facilities were created *ad hoc* in the EPU for countries in need of financial support while they undertook stabilization measures.

Appraisal

The European Payments Union permitted an expansion of trade at a time when gold and U.S. dollars were in short supply. By its nature, however, it was a discriminatory arrangement. The existence of the EPU created incentives for its members to export to the United States, thus earning dollars that could be used to finance imports from any area. And, the EPU arrangement encouraged its members, wishing to conserve dollar holdings, to import from EPU countries rather than the United States or Latin America. While there was some tension between the IMF and the EPU in the early 1950s,[12] the EPU proved to be a transitional arrangement on the road to convertibility for the participating countries. When the currencies of the more industrialized members of the OEEC became externally convertible in 1958, the EPU was terminated.[13]

---

note 9, vol. 1, pp. 212–23, and vol. 2, pp. 323–25. For internal U.S. documents on possible conflicts between the EPU and the IMF, see *Foreign Relations of the United States, 1950*, vol. 1 (1977), pp. 815–24, and *idem, 1950*, vol. 3 (1977), pp. 623–25 and 652–53.

[11] See EPU Agreement, *supra* note 8, Articles 9–17 and the accompanying tables. Article 11 and its accompanying tables were amended in successive protocols.

In the latter years of the Union the proportion of accounting deficits settled in gold or U.S. dollars (the dollar being convertible into gold at the time based on its par value) was increased and the use of credit reduced. In the early years rather elaborate formulas were used to deal with the dollar shortage at that time and to encourage balance-of-payments adjustment by EPU members. Within certain limits, settlement consisted merely of crediting or debiting each member's account. A debtor country, once a threshold was passed, had to pay an increasing portion of its debt to the EPU in gold or U.S. dollars and proportionally less credit was extended to it. After a creditor country's surplus crossed a threshold, it was entitled to receive a portion of the payments due it in gold or U.S. dollars until a limit was reached above which it was not entitled to demand these assets. See tables illustrating the rules in Scammell, *supra* note 9, pp. 292, 293, and 297.

[12] See *IMF History 1945–65, supra* note 9, vol. 2, chapter 15.

[13] The European Monetary Agreement (EMA), signed August 5, 1955, entered into force December 27, 1958, upon termination of the EPU. See documents in *European Yearbook*, vol. 3 (1955), pp. 212–55; and vol. 7 (1959), pp. 266–303. For the revised and consolidated text as of March 1962, see *European Yearbook*, vol. 9 (1961), pp. 174–241. See also amendments, *idem*, vol. 13 (1965), pp. 320–27; vol. 15 (1967), pp. 210–13; and vol. 16 (1968), pp. 286–89. See generally Alexander Elkin, "The European Monetary Agree-

Regional Payments Arrangements

While the European Payments Union (EPU) was terminated in 1958, other multilateral arrangements for clearing payments on a regional basis are in active use today in several parts of the world. Some of these payments unions have operated for many years,[14] while others have only recently begun operation.[15] Others have recently been proposed but have not yet commenced to function.[16]

A variety of clearing arrangements serve countries in Latin America, including the payments system of the Latin American Integration Association,[17]

---

ment: Its Structure and Working,'' *European Yearbook,* vol. 7 (1959), p. 148; M.R. Shuster, *The Public International Law of Money* (Oxford: Oxford University Press, 1973), pp. 260–65; and Yeager, *supra* note 9, pp. 423–24. The EMA provided a system for multilateral settlement of selected monthly balances among participating central banks together with a credit facility. Settlements were in gold or U.S. dollars. The EMA was terminated December 31, 1972. See BIS, *43d Annual Report 1972/73,* pp. 175–82.

[14] The agreement establishing the Central American Clearing House was signed in Tegucigalpa, Honduras, July 28, 1961, and the clearing house began operation in October 1961. The initial members were the central banks of El Salvador, Guatemala, and Honduras. The central bank of Nicaragua joined in 1962 and that of Costa Rica in 1963. This agreement was followed by the Agreement for the Establishment of the Central American Monetary Union, signed at San Salvador February 25, 1964; a revised Agreement Governing the Central American Clearing House, signed at San Salvador May 20, 1964; the Agreement Governing the Central American Monetary Stabilization Fund, signed at Washington, D.C., October 1, 1969; and the Central American Monetary Agreement, approved at San José, Costa Rica, August 24, 1974, entered into force October 25, 1974.

The Spanish text of the 1974 Central American Monetary Agreement, which superseded the earlier agreements, appears in *Revista de la Integración Centroamericana,* no. 14 (1975), p. 81; and in United Nations document no. TD/B/609/add. 1 (vol. I)(1976), p. 118. The Spanish texts of the 1964 and 1969 agreements appear in *Revista de la Integración Centroamericana,* no. 1 (1971), pp. 213, 218, and 224. English translations of the two 1964 agreements appear in Miguel S. Wionczek (ed.), *Economic Cooperation in Latin America, Africa, and Asia: A Handbook of Documents* (Cambridge, Massachusetts: MIT Press, 1969), pp. 324 and 334. See also notes 28 and 49, *infra.*

See generally J. G. del Valle, "Monetary Integration in Latin America," in Khair El-Din Haseeb and Samir Makdisi (ed.), *Arab Monetary Integration: Issues and Prerequisites* (London: Croom Helm, 1981), p. 205; Eduardo Lizano, *Cooperación Monetaria e Integración Económica en el Mercado Común Centroamericano* (Mexico City: Center of Latin American Monetary Studies, 1978); Mario Rietti, *Money and Banking in Latin America* (New York: Praeger Publishers, 1979), pp. 194–98; and Institute for Latin American Integration, *The Latin American Integration Process in 1981* (Buenos Aires: Institute for Latin American Integration; Washington: Inter-American Development Bank), pp. 148–50.

[15] The payments system of the Great Lakes Economic Community was established March 13, 1981. It serves Burundi, Rwanda, and Zaire. IMF, *Annual Report on Exchange Arrangements and Exchange Restrictions, 1982,* p. 39.

The Treaty for Establishment of the Preferential Trade Area for Eastern and Southern African States, signed at Lusaka December 21, 1981, contains detailed provisions for regional payments arrangements in Article 22 and Annex VI . The parties to the treaty are Comoros, Djibouti, Ethiopia, Kenya, Malawi, Mauritius, Somalia, Uganda, and Zambia. For the text of the treaty and the Protocol on Clearing and Payments Arrangements (Annex VI), see *International Legal Materials,* vol. 21 (1982), p. 479. For an in-depth discussion of the payments arrangements, see Shailendra J. Anjaria, Sena Eken, and John F. Laker, *Payments Arrangements and the Expansion of Trade in Eastern and Southern Africa* (IMF Occasional Paper no. 11; Washington, 1982). Implementing regulations were under negotiation when this book went to press.

[16] The members of the Arab Monetary Fund are considering the establishment of an arrangement for settlement of payments among the member countries. See Arab Monetary Fund, *Annual Report, 1981,* pp. 12–13; and *idem, 1982,* pp. 13–15 and 17–18. The Arab Monetary Fund is discussed, *infra,* page 311 et seq.

[17] The payments system of the Latin American Integration Association (ALADI) is currently based on the

the Central American Clearing House,[18] and the clearing facility of the Caribbean Common Market.[19] The West African Clearing House[20] serves the countries in Western Africa, the clearing arrangement of the Economic Community of Great Lakes States[21] serves the countries in Central Africa, and a new clearing arrangement serves the members of the Preferential Trade Area for Eastern and Southern African States.[22] The Asian Clearing Union[23] serves countries in

Convention on Reciprocal Payments and Credits, signed at Montego Bay, Jamaica, August 25, 1982. The Spanish texts of the Convention and implementing regulations appear in *Instrumentos Financieros Vigentes* (Montevideo: Asociación Latinoamericana de Integración, 1983), pp. A.1–B.26. The parties include the central banks of Argentina, Bolivia, Brazil, Chile, Colombia, Dominican Republic, Ecuador, Mexico, Paraguay, Peru, Uruguay, and Venezuela. See also note 49, *infra*, regarding the Santo Domingo Agreement among the same parties. Central banks of states that are not members of the ALADI may be permitted to adhere to the payments and credits system.

The 1982 Convention replaces the Agreement on Reciprocal Payments and Credits, signed at Mexico City September 22, 1965, to which the above-mentioned central banks previously were parties. For the Spanish texts of the 1965 agreement and rules, see United Nations document no. TD/B/609/add. 1 (vol. II) (1976), pp. 44 and 47.

The ALADI system involves the multilateral agreement coupled with bilateral agreements between each pair of countries (that tend to follow a standardized form) that specify eligible transactions, interim credit arrangements, and the like. Clearing is done in U.S. dollars through accounts for this purpose held by each bank with the U.S. Federal Reserve Bank of New York. The central bank of Peru acts as the system's agent. See generally *ALADI: Cooperación Financiera Monetaria* (Montevideo: ALADI, 1983); Valle, *supra* note 14, pp. 198–202; Wionczek, *Economic Cooperation, supra* note 14, pp. 347–53; Barry N. Siegel, "Payments Systems for the Latin American Free Trade Association," in Miguel S. Wionczek (ed.), *Latin American Economic Integration: Experiences and Prospects* (New York: Frederick A. Praeger, 1966), p. 239; *Latin American Integration Process in 1981, supra* note 14, pp. 49–56; and *idem, 1982*, pp. 56–63.

The treaty establishing the Latin American Integration Association, signed at Montevideo August 12, 1980, entered into force March 18, 1981, appears in *International Legal Materials*, vol. 20 (1981), p. 672. The ALADI succeeded the Latin American Free Trade Association.

[18] See note 14, *supra.*

[19] The Caribbean Community Multilateral Clearing Facility was established in March 1977 and began operation June 16, 1977. The members are the central banks of Barbados, Belize, Guyana, Jamaica, Trinidad and Tobago, and the East Caribbean Central Bank. The central bank of Trinidad and Tobago acts as agent. See *Latin American Integration Process in 1977, supra* note 14, pp. 213–15; and *idem, 1981*, pp. 185–86. See also note 28, *infra.*

The East Caribbean Central Bank issues the regional currency and is the common monetary authority for Antigua and Barbuda, Dominica, Grenada, Montserrat, St. Kitts-Nevis, St. Lucia, and St. Vincent and Grenadines. These states belong to the Organization of East Caribbean States established by the treaty signed at Basseterre June 18, 1981. *International Legal Materials*, vol. 20 (1981), p. 1166. See Charles Collyns, *Alternatives to the Central Bank in the Developing World* (IMF Occasional Paper no. 20; Washington, 1983), pp. 14–15.

[20] The agreement establishing the West African Clearing House was signed in Lagos, March 14, 1975, by representatives of the central banks of twelve countries: Benin, Gambia, Ghana, Ivory Coast, Liberia, Mali, Niger, Nigeria, Senegal, Sierra Leone, Togo, and Upper Volta. Guinea, Guinea-Bissau, and Mauritania subsequently joined the agreement. The French text appears in United Nations document no. TD/B/609/add. 1 (vol. III) (1976), p. 108. The clearing house began operations in Freetown, Sierra Leone, on July 1, 1976. See generally John B. McLenaghan, Saleh M. Nsouli, and Klaus-Walter Riechel, *Currency Convertibility in the Economic Community of West African States* (IMF Occasional Paper no. 13; Washington, 1982); and Eghosa Osagie, "West African Clearing House, West African Unit of Account, and Pressures for Monetary Integration," *Journal of Common Market Studies*, vol. 17 (1979), p. 227. See also note 28, *infra.*

[21] See note 15, *supra.*

[22] See note 15, *supra.*

[23] The members of the Asian Clearing Union are the central banks of Bangladesh, Burma, India, Iran, Nepal, Pakistan, and Sri Lanka. The union began operation in Tehran in November 1975. The Agreement

South Asia and the Near East, and another payments arrangement serves Turkey, Iran, and Pakistan.[24]

Virtually all of the members of the above arrangements are members of the International Monetary Fund. The arrangements must be operated in a manner that is consistent with the members' obligations under the IMF Agreement and, in particular, Articles VIII and XIV. Several of the regional arrangements include at least some members that have accepted IMF Article VIII, Sections 2, 3, and 4.[25] In the case of others, all of the members avail themselves of Article XIV, Section 2.[26] As explained in Chapter 10, while IMF members under the Article XIV regime may "adapt to changing circumstances" their restrictions on payments, the introduction of new restrictions (on payments or transfers for current international transactions) that are not "adaptations" requires IMF approval under Article VIII, Section 2(a), and sometimes also under Section 3.[27]

Regional payments facilities are often part of more comprehensive approaches to economic integration and development. The overall arrangements may involve free trade areas in which barriers to trade among member countries are to be reduced or eliminated. In some cases the overall arrangements take the form of customs unions in which the members, in addition to reducing barriers to trade among themselves, establish common tariffs and common trade policies against the rest of the world.[28] If the trade arrangements involve preferences or discrimination, there is a risk that the monetary institutions will also have discriminatory features.

Members of the IMF are required to obtain the approval of that organiza-

---

Establishing the Asian Clearing Union, opened for signature in Tokyo April 1973, and the Rules of the Union, adopted June 1976, appear in Michael Haas (ed.), *Basic Documents of Asian Regional Organizations* (Dobbs Ferry: Oceana Publications), vol. 6 (1979), pp. 174 and 194. For background see *idem*, p. 8.

[24] The three countries are parties to an agreement on multilateral payments arrangements, signed at Ankara April 25, 1967. The text appears in United Nations document no. TD/B/609/add. 1 (vol. V)(1976), p. 190.

[25] All of the members of the Central American Clearing House have accepted the obligations of IMF Article VIII. The Latin American Integration Association payments arrangement and the Caribbean Community clearing facility include both countries that have and countries that have not accepted the Article VIII regime. Djibouti, a member of the Eastern and Southern African States arrangement, has accepted Article VIII, although none of its partners has done so to date.

[26] None of the members of the Asian Clearing Union or the West African Clearing House has accepted the Article VIII regime. Turkey, Iran, and Pakistan also continue to rely on Article XIV.

[27] The application of Article VIII, sections 2, 3, and 4, is examined at page 389 et seq., and the application of Article XIV, section 2, at page 423 et seq.

[28] The states served by the payments arrangements of the Latin American Integration Association are parties to the treaty establishing that organization, which is cited in note 17, *supra*. The states served by the Central American Clearing House (except Honduras) are parties to the General Treaty for Central American Economic Integration, signed at Managua December 13, 1960, entered into force April 27, 1962. *United Nations Treaty Series,* vol. 455, p. 3. The states served by the Caribbean Community Multilateral Clearing Facility are parties to the Treaty Establishing the Caribbean Community, concluded at Chaguaramas July 4, 1973, entered into force August 1, 1973. *United Nations Treaty Series,* vol. 946, p. 17.

States served by the West African Clearing House are parties to the Treaty of the Economic Community of West African States, done at Lagos May 28, 1975; *International Legal Materials,* vol. 14 (1975), p. 1200. The payments arrangements of Eastern and Southern African States are provided for in the treaty establishing the preferential trade area, cited in note 15, *supra*.

tion, under Article VIII, Section 3, for the introduction of discriminatory currency arrangements involving current transactions, and the Fund's attitude is adverse to such arrangements. If a country permits its residents to make payments through a regional payments union to residents of agreement countries (and allows uncleared balances to build up in that facility), while it denies residents the right to make payments through normal channels to non-agreement countries, the discriminatory effect is clear. Often the discriminatory effect is more subtle, but still present. Whether a particular regional payments union is a discriminatory currency arrangement will usually depend on the rules relating to its use and the procedures of the participating monetary authorities for clearing residual balances.[29] It is possible for a regional clearing house to function effectively and not be a discriminatory currency arrangement, as exemplified by the Central American Clearing House.

Typically, a multilateral payments union is operated by central bank officials. An agent, which may be one of the participating central banks, is designated to handle the record-keeping and technical features of the operation.[30] A board, normally composed of the governors of the participating central banks, sets policies. In addition, there can be a senior policy-making body in which finance ministries are represented.[31]

The regional payments systems take as their basic model the European Payments Union in operation during the 1950s, discussed earlier in this chapter. In the light of that discussion, the mechanics of multilateral clearing need not be repeated.[32] Our discussion here centers on some of the policy choices that have to be made in the design and operation of a regional system.

A major issue is whether payments that are eligible for clearing through the union must be cleared in that manner or whether use of the union's facilities is optional.[33] If payments must be channeled through the official mechanism,

---

[29] See discussion of discriminatory currency arrangements in Chapter 10, *infra*, page 400. Regional payments unions have the same potential for discrimination against nonparticipants as do bilateral payments arrangements. The European Payments Union in its effects discriminated against imports from Latin America as compared to Europe. For the IMF's attitude toward the EPU, see *IMF History 1945-65, supra* note 9, vol. 2, pp. 325-31.

[30] For example, the central bank of Honduras acts as agent for the Central American Clearing House. The central bank of Peru and the U.S. Federal Reserve Bank of New York handle the accounts and technical operations of the Latin American Integration Association arrangement.

[31] See generally Anjaria, *supra* note 15, which is a rich source of information and insights.

[32] In some of the regional systems, instead of central banks dealing directly with each other on individual transactions on a bilateral basis and then periodically clearing balances on a multilateral basis as was the practice in the EPU (see page 301, *supra*), individual payments may be transmitted through the central facility. In the West African Clearing House system, the payor firm requests its commercial bank to make a payment, that bank in turn requests its central bank to make payment, that bank requests the payee's central bank to make payment (and informs the payee's central bank that an equivalent amount of West African units of account (WAUA) has been credited to that bank's account with the Clearing House). Then the payee's commercial bank's account with the central bank is credited, and finally the payee's account with its commercial bank is credited. See explanation and diagrams in McLenaghan, *supra* note 20, pp. 25-27. Long delays have been reported in completing some payments through the West African system. *Idem*, pp. 27-28 and 32-33.

[33] All of the Latin American arrangements are, in principle, voluntary. Both the private and public sectors

participating countries that are members of the International Monetary Fund may find their actions inconsistent with IMF Article VIII, Section 2(a). For example, if a country previously allowed commercial banks in its country to make payments for their customers via head offices of the bank or through foreign correspondents of the bank,[34] and now the country requires that payments be channeled through the clearing system, the channeling requirement, if it causes substantial delay or increases the cost of the payments, is a payments restriction inconsistent with Article VIII, Section 2(a), unless the IMF grants approval of it.[35] The IMF staff, when consulted about proposed regional clearing arrangements, has recommended that use of the system by commercial banks be voluntary. It has also argued that the potential competition from normal commercial bank payments procedures using correspondents will be an incentive to make the official system function efficiently.[36]

Whether payments are required, or permitted but not required, to be channeled through a payments system, the eligible payments must be defined. In the case of the Central American Clearing House, all payments with respect to current or capital transactions are permitted if ultimately to be settled in the national currency of a participating country.[37] The payments arrangements of the Latin American Integration Association leave it to each pair of countries to decide which classes of payments may be cleared under the arrangements.[38] Some systems exclude payments for capital transactions[39] or invisible transactions.[40] Some exclude payments that might put strains on the system because of their size, such as payments for petroleum imports.[41]

---

of the participating countries may use the official facilities or conventional commercial bank channels, unless the particular payor country has chosen to make channeling through the facility compulsory.

Pursuant to a decision of the Board of Directors of the Asian Clearing Union in February 1980, all eligible payments between members of the union must be channeled through the union. See IMF, *Annual Report on Exchange Arrangements and Exchange Restrictions, 1981*, p. 34.

[34] The conventional method used by commercial banks in making international payments is explained in Appendix A, *infra*, page 672 et seq.

[35] See Chapter 10, *infra*, page 389 et seq., for discussion of restrictions prohibited by IMF Article VIII, section 2(a).

[36] The IMF staff recommended, when the clearing system for Eastern and Southern African States was being designed, that the channeling of payments through the system should not be compulsory. The staff discounted the argument that costs to customers are excessive when commercial banks handle payments in the conventional manner. See Anjaria, *supra* note 15, p. 23.

Even with competition, a clearing system can work poorly. Payments through the West African Clearing House have been delayed as much as four or six months. It has been suggested that central banks should guarantee to commercial banks using the system that payment will be made immediately if documents are in good order. See McLenaghan, *supra* note 20, pp. 27 and 37.

[37] See table displaying the main features of presently operative regional clearing arrangements in Anjaria, *supra* note 15, pp. 48–49.

[38] See table cited in note 37.

[39] The Asian Clearing Union and the West African Clearing House, for example, limit clearing to payments for current transactions. Table, *idem*.

[40] The arrangement of Turkey, Iran, and Pakistan, *supra* note 24, excludes invisible payments as well as payments for capital transactions. Table cited in note 37, *supra*.

[41] The Asian Clearing Union and the Turkey-Iran-Pakistan arrangement exclude payments for petroleum. Table, *idem*.

All payments arrangements must resolve questions concerning the unit of account, currencies in which residual balances are to be settled, procedures for determining exchange rates, and exchange rate guarantees. These questions have been dealt with in a variety of ways.

Regarding the unit of account, some systems use the U.S. dollar, some the special drawing right (SDR), and some an artificial currency unit usually defined in terms of the U.S. dollar or the SDR.[42] Most participants in regional clearing arrangements are developing countries that peg the rates of their currencies to the U.S. dollar or the SDR. It is common to use those official rates for valuing currencies although, alternatively, market rates may be used.[43] If a system uses pegged rates, and a currency is devalued or revalued, the normal rule is that payments already in the system are cleared at the rates before the change.[44]

The U.S. dollar is the currency most frequently specified for settlement of residual balances.[45] The frequency with which balances are to be settled varies considerably from one system to another.[46] Most systems establish net credit or debit limits that cannot be exceeded at any time within the period between settlement dates.[47]

All of the systems involve some form of short-term extension of credit until the periodic settlement dates.[48] In addition, credit facilities are associated

[42] Table, *idem.*

[43] The Central American Clearing House conducts its clearings in the national currencies of the participating countries. It uses the official pegged exchange rates for this purpose, all of which are maintained against a common denominator, currently the U.S. dollar.

The use of pegged rates works well only if the peg is to a common denominator. The West African Clearing House appears to have encountered some difficulties in choosing and applying exchange rate rules. Some members peg the rates of their currencies against the French franc, others the U.S. dollar, others the U.K. pound sterling, others the SDR, and some use other methods. The unit of account used by the clearing house is the West African unit of account (WAUA), which is equivalent to one SDR. See McLenaghan, *supra* note 20, p. 24. See also Anjaria, *supra* note 15, p. 24.

The Latin American Integration Association arrangement operates on the basis of the U.S. dollar, with payments being expressed in that currency, and with periodic clearings in that currency through the U.S. Federal Reserve Bank of New York. The agent is thus not called upon to make exchange rate determinations.

The use of pegged exchange rates by developing countries is explained in Chapter 11, *infra,* pages 521–524.

[44] See Anjaria, *supra* note 15, p. 24.

What constitutes an exchange rate adjustment may not be easy to define. For a discussion of difficulties in the assignment of the burden of exchange risk in the West African Clearing House, see McLenaghan, *supra* note 20, pp. 24 and 33. The Latin American Integration Association avoids the problem by having all transactions take place in U.S. dollars.

[45] See Table cited in note 37, *supra.* Where the dollar is specified for settlement, the arrangement may in some cases permit participating central banks holding residual net credit and debit balances to agree to settlement in another currency.

[46] In the West African Clearing House, settlement of balances is every month. In the Central American Clearing House it is every six months.

[47] Where long time periods are used between dates for settling residual balances, limits will normally be placed on net debit and credit positions that can be maintained at any time. See Table cited in note 37, *supra.*

[48] Credit is normally extended by the creditor banks with interest at mutually agreed rates. In the Central

with some arrangements to finance, for a longer term, residual balances that would otherwise be payable at the periodic settlement dates.[49]

The primary purpose of regional payments arrangements is to minimize the use of monetary reserves for intra-regional settlements, and permit the participating central banks to maintain smaller working balances in foreign currencies. Questions have been raised about whether that economic purpose is in fact achieved in practice.[50] Economic appraisal of this matter is beyond the scope of this book. Economic considerations are, however, highly relevant to whether the establishment of regional payments systems should be encouraged or discouraged. If the arrangements involve any discriminatory features, the economic benefits would have to be very substantial to justify them. The International Monetary Fund's firm policy, where discriminatory arrangements require approval under IMF Article VIII, Section 3, is not to approve them.[51] A regional clearing system can probably operate in a manner that is not discriminatory and that does not involve restrictions on payments for current transactions. All of the parties to the Central American Clearing House and many of the parties to the Latin American Integration Association system have accepted Article VIII; and, as far as is known, the IMF has not determined that either of the systems has involved practices requiring approval under that article.

The European Payments Union was a step in a process leading to acceptance of IMF Article VIII, Sections 2, 3, and 4, by the participating countries. It is to be hoped that the regional arrangements discussed in this section will make it possible for the developing countries that continue to rely on Article XIV to

---

American Clearing House a member grants credit through the system to the other central banks as a group. In the arrangements of the Latin American Integration Association, the amount of credit and its terms are agreed bilaterally between each pair of countries.

[49] The central banks that are members of the Central American Clearing House on December 7, 1979, in San José, Costa Rica, signed an agreement to create the Fund to Finance Negative Balances in the Central American Clearing House, but, because of technical difficulties, this agreement has not been implemented. In its place the central banks in Resolutions No. AG–7/81 and No. AG–8/81 and Agreement No. AG–4/81, approved at San José May 28–29, 1981, established the Central American Common Market Fund to assist in financing negative balances in the Clearing House. The Fund is operated within the Central American Bank for Economic Integration. The central banks also benefit from the Central American Monetary Stabilization Fund provided for in the Central American Monetary Agreement, *supra* note 14. See Valle, *supra* note 14, pp. 212–14 and 219–20; Lizano, *supra* note 14, pp. 77–97; *Latin American Integration Process in 1980*, *supra* note 14, pp. 150–52; and *idem, 1981*, pp. 125–26 and 150.

The Financial Assistance Agreement of the Latin American Integration Association (called the "Santo Domingo Agreement"), signed September 26, 1969, provides for balance-of-payments financing to those countries that adhere to the agreement. The Santo Domingo financing system consists of contingent lines of credit agreed among the participants. The credit lines provide refinancing of net debtor positions under the Latin American Integration Association clearing system. Since November 1981, second and third mechanisms under the Santo Domingo Agreement can, if conditions are met, provide support for global balance-of-payments deficits and support in the event of natural catastrophes. The Spanish texts of the Santo Domingo Agreement, as amended, and implementing regulations appear in *Instrumentos Financieros Vigentes, supra* note 17, pp. C.1–E.3. See generally note 17, *supra*.

[50] See Anjaria, *supra* note 15, pp. 2–3 and 21–23.

[51] See Chapter 10, *infra*, page 400 et seq.

expedite the movement to Article VIII status and, at the least, not inhibit movement in that direction.

Although regional payments facilities are initially instituted with the primary objective of facilitating international payments and conserving monetary reserves, the operation of the facilities may lead monetary authorities to consider a wider range of concerns. The European Payments Union was a catalyst in the evolution of the process of multilateral surveillance of national economic policies. Balance-of-payments problems of individual members became known to all and then became a subject of multilateral consideration. Out of this evolved procedures for multilateral surveillance of national economic policies now carried out under the auspices of the Organisation for Economic Co-operation and Development, the European Economic Community, and other bodies.[52] Of all the regional arrangements discussed in this section, the Central American countries appear to have made the most progress in this direction.[53]

Regional Arrangements for Balance-of-Payments Financing

Regional Payments Arrangements

All of the regional payments systems discussed above involve interim financing between settlement dates. Several of the systems also include procedures for temporary financing of residual balances following the periodic settlements.[54] Financial arrangements associated with some of the payments systems are available for use in financing balance-of-payments deficits in excess of residual balances under the particular clearing system.[55]

Andean Reserve Fund

Bolivia, Colombia, Eucador, Peru, and Venezuela are members of the Andean Reserve Fund. This organization was established by the Treaty for the Creation of the Andean Reserve Fund, signed at Caracas November 12, 1976, entered into force June 8, 1978.[56] The organization consists of an Assembly (in which members are represented by their ministers of finance), a Board of Governors

---

[52] See Chapter 12, *infra*, pages 580–585 and 589–598.

[53] See Valle, *supra* note 14, pp. 217–23.

[54] See note 49, *supra*, regarding the Central American Monetary Stabilization Fund and the Financial Assistance Agreement of the Latin American Integration Association, as examples.

[55] Both financial mechanisms mentioned in note 54, *idem*, can now be drawn upon for purposes other than refinancing residual balances under the clearing systems.

[56] An English translation of the Treaty for the Creation of the Andean Reserve Fund appears in *International Legal Materials*, vol. 18 (1979), p. 1191. See generally Valle, *supra* note 14, pp. 212–23; and *Latin American Integration Process in 1981, supra* note 14, pp. 109–12.

(in which representation is by central bank governors), and an Executive President and staff.[57]

Unlike the organizations discussed in the section above, the Andean Reserve Fund does not operate a facility for clearing payments. It is a regional fund that makes loans to members, that have subscribed to its capital, for balance-of-payments support. The maximum size of a loan is limited by a formula that takes into account the country's balance-of-payments deficit, its capital subscription to the Fund, and its imports from other members of the Andean Group.[58]

In order to receive a loan, the beneficiary country must declare that "it possesses insufficient reserves," and this declaration must be certified by the Fund's Board of Directors. The country must accompany its application for a loan with a written report indicating the measures which have been adopted, and those which are to be adopted, to reestablish balance-of-payments equilibrium. This report must also indicate that the country is fulfilling its obligations under the Cartagena Agreement relating to intra-Andean Pact trade.[59] The loans require a commitment of the beneficiary country that if it adopts restrictive measures to deal with its balance-of-payments deficit, these restrictions, even if they comply with safeguard clauses, shall not affect imports from the subregion.[60]

Loans are granted for a term of one year and may be extended for up to a total period of three years. In order to apply for a new loan, the country must have satisfactorily fulfilled its debt service requirements with the Fund and a period of at least one year must elapse following the complete cancellation of the prior loan. Rates of interest are set by the Fund. The Fund may also make guarantees to aid central banks in borrowing from other sources.[61]

Arab Monetary Fund

The Articles of Agreement of the Arab Monetary Fund were signed at Rabat on April 27, 1976, and entered into force February 2, 1977.[62] The headquarters of the Fund are in Abu Dhabi, and the members are Algeria, Bahrain, Iraq, Jordan, Kuwait, Lebanon, Libya, Mauritania, Morocco, Oman, "Palestine," Qatar, Saudi Arabia, Somalia, Sudan, Syria, Tunisia, United Arab Emirates,

---

[57] See Treaty for the Creation of the Andean Reserve Fund, Articles 1–7 and 13–34.

[58] Article 9.

[59] Article 9(a).

[60] *Idem.*

[61] Articles 9 and 10.

[62] The author has used an English translation of the Articles of Agreement provided by the Arab Monetary Fund. The Fund issues an *Annual Report* in English. See generally Haseeb and Makdisi, *supra* note 14, which contains the proceedings of a conference on Arab monetary integration held in November 1980. See also Arab Monetary Fund, *The Arab Monetary Fund, 1977–1981: A Summary of Objectives and Activities* (Abu Dhabi, 1982).

Yemen Arab Republic, and People's Democratic Republic of Yemen.[63] The Arab Monetary Fund provides financial support for member countries that encounter balance-of-payments problems. Like the Andean Reserve Fund, it does not at present operate a facility for clearing payments. Also, it is not intended to be a developmental aid institution.

The structure of the Arab Monetary Fund is patterned after that of the IMF. There is a Board of Governors, a Board of Executive Directors, a Director-General/President, committees, and a professional staff.[64] Each member subscribes a portion of the Fund's capital and in turn has drawing rights.[65] A system of weighted voting power is used in decision-making, with votes based on capital subscriptions.[66] The Fund may supplement its resources by borrowing from member states and from Arab and foreign monetary and financial institutions and markets.[67]

Members of the Fund may obtain loans to finance overall balance-of-payments deficits. A member may obtain on request an "automatic" loan up to 75 percent of the borrowing country's paid-up subscription that has been paid in convertible currencies, the loan being repayable in installments within three years.[68] "Ordinary" and "extended" loans are in excess of the above limit. Ordinary loans may be in an amount up to 225 percent of the paid-up subscription. Extended loans may be in an amount up to 325 percent of the paid-up subscription. These loans are granted only in support of a program mutually agreed upon by the Arab Monetary Fund and the member. They are normally repayable within five or seven years. Whereas an automatic loan is unconditional and is normally disbursed in one installment, ordinary and extended loans are normally disbursed in accordance with a schedule and are subject to observance of performance criteria.[69] In addition, "compensatory loans" can be obtained by a member in overall balance-of-payments deficit where the deficit results from a decline in export receipts or from a large increase in the cost of importing agricultural products.[70] A short-term trade financing facility provides financing for intra-Arab trade.[71] A member's total borrowing under all facilities is not to exceed 400 percent of that part of its paid-up subscription made in convertible currencies.[72] The Articles of Agreement of the Fund and decisions

---

[63] Egypt was an original member, but its membership was suspended by Board of Governors Resolution No. 2 of 1979. It is anticipated that Egypt will be reinstated as an active member.

[64] Articles of Agreement, Articles 29–34.

[65] Articles 11–15.

[66] Articles 31 and 32.

[67] Articles 17 and 18.

[68] Article 22.

[69] Articles 19–22.

[70] Article 23.

[71] Decision of the Board of Executive Directors, July 1981. See Arab Monetary Fund, *Annual Report, 1981*, p. 9.

[72] See *Annual Report, 1981*, pp. 8–9.

taken by the Fund define eligibility to borrow, state the terms and conditions of loans, set overall limits on the Fund's lending, and establish interest rates.[73]

In addition to providing balance-of-payments financing, the Arab Monetary Fund has broader purposes, including the promotion of stable exchange rates among Arab currencies, the elimination of restrictions on current payments and trade among members, and the encouragement of Arab monetary cooperation in order to promote economic integration and the development of Arab capital markets.[74]

Monetary Unions in French-Speaking Africa— The C.F.A. Franc

Two groups of countries in Africa, formerly governed by France, have established monetary unions and share common central banks.[75] The Banque Centrale des Etats de l'Afrique de l'Ouest issues the currency for Benin, Ivory Coast, Mali, Niger, Senegal, Togo, and Upper Volta.[76] The bank is headquartered in Dakar, Senegal, and has branches in each member state. The Banque des Etats de l'Afrique Centrale issues the currency for Cameroon, Central Afri-

---

[73] Articles of Agreement, Articles 25–28.

[74] See Articles 4–9.

[75] There are other monetary unions besides those discussed here. Belgium and Luxembourg maintain an economic union, established in 1922. The Luxembourg franc is at par with the Belgian franc and is issued by the central bank of Belgium. Negotiations are currently in progress that may result in restructuring the economic union.

See note 19, *supra,* regarding the East Caribbean Central Bank.

[76] The Banque Centrale des Etats de l'Afrique de l'Ouest was originally created by the Traité Instituant une Union Monétaire Ouest Africaine, signed at Paris May 12, 1962. The bank functions today on the basis of four documents concluded in November and December 1973 that entered into force in 1975: Traité Constituant l'Union Monétaire Ouest Africaine, signed at Paris November 14, 1973; Statuts de la Banque Centrale des Etats de l'Afrique de l'Ouest, signed at Dakar December 4, 1973; Accord de Coopération entre la République Française et les Républiques Membres de l'Union Monétaire Ouest Africaine, signed at Dakar December 4, 1973; and Convention de Compte d'Opérations [between the bank and France], done at Dakar December 4, 1973. English translations of these four documents appear in Robert C. Effros (ed.), *Emerging Financial Centers: Legal and Institutional Framework* (Washington: IMF, 1982), pp. 434–66. The French texts of the documents (except the operations account agreement) appear in United Nations document no. TD/B/609/add. 1 (vol. IV)(1976), pp. 23, 30, and 34.

The previous treaty of May 12, 1962, and related documents appear in Michel Leduc, *Les Institutions Monétaires Africaines: Pays Francophones* (Paris: A. Pedone, 1965), pp. 213–40; and in Louis B. Sohn (ed.), *Basic Documents of African Regional Organizations* (4 vols.; Dobbs Ferry: Oceana Publications, 1971–1972), vol. 2, pp. 933–62. See also earlier bilateral agreements concluded by France with Dahomey (now Benin), Ivory Coast, Niger, and Upper Volta, signed at Paris April 24, 1961; Leduc, *supra,* pp. 202–08; *Journal du Droit International,* vol. 89 (1962), pp. 794–803.

The six states served by the Banque Centrale des Etats de l'Afrique de l'Ouest also belong to the Economic Community of West African States and participate in the West African Clearing House, *supra* notes 20 and 28.

Mali joined the Union Monétaire Ouest Africaine, in October 1983. Prior to that time it maintained a bilateral operations account arrangement with France based on an agreement of May 1977. Comoros has a bilateral operations account arrangement with France based on an agreement of July 1977.

can Republic, Chad, the Congo, and Gabon.[77] Its headquarters is in Yaoundé, Cameroon, and it likewise has branches in each of its member states. The currencies issued by the two central banks carry the same name—"*le franc de la Communauté Financière Africaine,*" generally known as the "C.F.A. franc." Each central bank keeps separate accounts for each member state that show both currency in circulation and the member state's share in the central bank's pool of external reserves.[78]

The member states of each of the two unions have agreed to allow free circulation of the currency issued by the shared central bank in their territories and not to restrict transfers of the currency within the territory of the union to which they belong. The member states of each union are required to maintain uniform rules on external exchange control. The interest rate structure and banking legislation are also harmonized. France has concluded agreements with each bank, and with the member states, which provide for the maintenance of convertibility between the French franc and the C.F.A. franc.[79] Each of the two African central banks holds portions of its union's monetary reserves with the French Treasury. At the present time transfers between a member state of one bank and a member of the other, as well as transfers with France, are unrestricted.[80]

---

[77] The Banque des Etats de l'Afrique Centrale is governed by the convention on monetary cooperation of the five Central African states, signed at Brazzaville November 22, 1972; the statutes of the bank annexed to that convention; the convention between France and the member states of the bank, signed at Brazzaville November 23, 1972; and an operations account agreement between the bank and France. The French texts of the documents (except the operations account agreement) appear in United Nations document no. TD/B/609/add. 1 (vol. IV)(1976), pp. 116, 120, and 124.

Prior to the conclusion of the above agreements, the bank (under the name "Banque Centrale des Etats de l'Afrique Equatoriale et du Cameroun") functioned on the basis of agreements on monetary, economic, and financial cooperation between France and the Central African Republic, the Congo, and Chad, signed at Brazzaville August 15, 1960; agreements between France and Gabon, signed August 17, 1960; and agreements between France and Cameroon, signed November 13, 1960. Texts of the principal agreements of France with the five states appear in Leduc, *supra* note 76, pp. 156–74; and the principal agreement with the first three states also appears in Sohn, *supra* note 76, vol. 2, pp. 780–86. The principal agreement between France and Cameroon together with an implementing agreement (not in Leduc and Sohn collections) appears in *United Nations Treaty Series*, vol. 741, pp. 159–95.

[78] CFA notes are marked following the serial number with a code letter for the particular country to enable separate accounts to be maintained. As mentioned in the text, the notes freely circulate among the countries of the union.

[79] See documents cited in notes 76 and 77, *supra*.

[80] Publications subsequent to the revised arrangements of 1972 and 1973 include: Robert A. Franks, "Financial System of Ivory Coast," in Effros, *supra* note 76, p. 423; Dominique Carreau, Patrick Juillard, and Thiébaut Flory, *Droit International Économique* (2d ed.; Paris: R. Pichon & R. Durand-Auzias, 1980), pp. 247–52; Geneviève Burdeau, "Le Statut Juridique des Franc C.F.A.," in Werner Flume et al. (ed.), *International Law and Economic Order: Essays in Honour of F.A. Mann* (Munich: Verlag C.H. Beck, 1977), p. 657; and "Chronique de Droit International Économique," *Annuaire Français de Droit International*, 1973, pp. 799–801, and *idem*, 1974, pp. 725–29. See also Samuel C. Nana-Sinkam, *Monetary Integration and Theory of Optimum Currency Areas in Africa* (The Hague: Mouton, 1978); and Collyns, *Alternatives to the Central Bank, supra* note 19, pp. 13–14.

Useful earlier writings, although not up to date, include Leduc, *supra* note 76; Shuster, *supra* note 13, pp. 240–46; Stephen A. Silard, "Money and Foreign Exchange," *International Encyclopedia of Comparative Law* (Tübingen: J.C.B. Mohr; The Hague: Mouton, 1975), vol. 17, chapter 20, sections 168–71; and works cited therein.

Chapter 8: The European Currency Unit
and the Credit Facilities of
the European Economic Community

Introductory Note

From a lawyer's point of view, the most interesting multilateral credit facilities for balance-of-payments support that are operated outside the International Monetary Fund are those of the European Economic Community.[1] These facilities are adapted to the needs of the member states of the EEC. Not only are the amounts of funds involved large, but the rules and technical features of the several arrangements merit study from a legal perspective.

The European currency unit (ECU), which is a unique monetary instrument used by the European Communities, is studied in the first part of this chapter. The second part of the chapter is devoted to balance-of-payments financing facilities of the European Economic Community. The final part considers possible future changes in the rules for the creation and use of ECUs, and the possible consolidation of balance-of-payments financing mechanisms.

The European Currency Unit (ECU)
Historical Note

During the period since its creation the European Communities have successively used several different units of account and during some periods of time have simultaneously used different units of account for different purposes. The European Communities initially used a unit of account defined in terms of gold and identical to the stated gold value of the 1944 U.S. dollar. This was called

---

[1] Background information on the European Economic Community and its monetary institutions is provided in Chapter 2, *supra,* page 76 et seq. References to the "Council" in this chapter are to the Council of Ministers of the European Communities and not to the European Council. References to the European Council will explicitly say "European Council."

the "European monetary unit of account" (EMUA).[2] In 1975 a new unique unit of account, called the "European unit of account" (EUA), was introduced. Its use was gradually expanded, and beginning in 1978 the budget of the European Economic Community was stated in EUAs.[3] A new unit, called the "European currency unit" (ECU), was introduced in 1979. While initially valued identically with the EUA, the ECU is a monetary asset and not simply a unit of account. The ECU is issued by the European Monetary Cooperation Fund (FECOM), as explained below, and serves as FECOM's unit of account, as denominator of the European Monetary System's exchange rate arrangement, and as a means of settlement under FECOM financing facilities.[4] The ECU is expected to serve as the unit of account of the European Monetary Fund when that institution is established.[5] The use of the ECU has steadily expanded and it has now replaced the EUA as the unit of account in all legal instruments of the European Communities.[6]

[2] See, e.g., Article 5 of the Statutes of the European Monetary Cooperation Fund (FECOM) prior to the adoption of the ECU as the FECOM's unit of account effective January 1, 1979. For citations see Chapter 2, *supra*, page 84 (note 193).

[3] The first uses of the EUA were as the unit of account in the Lomé Convention between the EEC and associated Caribbean, African, and Pacific states and as the unit of account of the European Investment Bank and the European Development Fund. This occurred in 1975. The EUA was adopted as the unit of account of the European Coal and Steel Community as of the beginning of 1976 and of the general budget of the European Communities as of the beginning of 1978. It was adopted for customs matters as of the beginning of 1979. See *9th General Report on the Activities of the European Communities in 1975,* points 71–72 and 177–78; *11th General Report 1977,* point 66; *12th General Report 1978,* point 67; and *13th General Report 1979,* point 54.

[4] See European Council Resolution of December 5, 1978, on the establishment of the European Monetary System, *Bulletin of the European Communities,* 1978, no. 12, p. 10; Council of Ministers Regulation No. 3180/78 of December 18, 1978, *Official Journal of the European Communities* [hereinafter *Official Journal*], no. L-379, December 30, 1978, p. 1; and Council of Ministers Regulation No. 3181/78 of December 18, 1978, *Official Journal,* no. L-379, December 30, 1978, p. 2. The three documents are reprinted in European Communities Monetary Committee, *Compendium of Community Monetary Texts* (Brussels-Luxembourg, 1979), pp. 40–43, 53–54, and 133–34. The legal character of the European Council resolution is considered in Chapter 2, *supra,* pages 80–81.

[5] European Council Resolution of December 5, 1978, *supra* note 4, Part A, paragraph 1.4; and Council of Ministers Regulation No. 3181/78, *supra* note 4, preamble. For background on the proposed European Monetary Fund, see Chapter 2, *supra,* pages 84–86.

[6] The ECU was first used by the European Monetary Cooperation Fund and the central banks participating in the European Monetary System's exchange rate and financing procedures. See documents cited in note 4, *supra.* Parallel with these uses, it was decided to state quotas in balance-of-payments financial assistance arrangements under EEC Treaty Article 108 in ECUs. See Council Decision No. 78/1041, *infra* note 105. In late 1980 and early 1981, a series of decisions were adopted that resulted in the ECU replacing the EUA in the general budget of the European Communities, in the operating budget of the European Coal and Steel Community, in the Lomé Convention between the EEC and associated Caribbean, African, and Pacific States, in the accounts of the European Investment Bank, and in all legal instruments of the European Economic Community and the European Atomic Energy Community. See *13th General Report on the Activities of the European Communities in 1979,* point 54; *14th General Report 1980,* points 81 and 85; *Bulletin of the European Communities,* 1980, no. 12, point 3.1.2; and Council Regulation No. 3308/80 of December 16, 1980, *Official Journal,* no. L-345, December 20, 1980, p. 1.

Valuation of the ECU

The value of the European currency unit (ECU) is presently defined in terms of a composite consisting of portions of national currencies. The value of the ECU is currently set as the sum of the following amounts of the currencies of EEC member states:[7]

Deutsche mark	0.828	Belgian franc,	3.66
U.K. pound sterling	0.0885	Luxembourg franc	0.140
French franc	1.15	Danish krone	0.217
Italian lira	109.0	Irish pound	0.00759
Netherlands guilder	0.286		

The equivalent of the ECU in any currency is equal to the sum of the equivalents of the above amounts in the particular currency. The value of the ECU in terms of each of the currencies of EEC states and other selected states is calculated for each working day on the basis of market exchange rates by the Commission of the European Communities and is published in the *Official Journal of the European Communities.*[8]

The valuation of the ECU in terms of a "basket" of currencies is similar in concept to the valuation of the IMF special drawing right (SDR). While the principle and method of valuing the SDR are subject to change by the International Monetary Fund, the composite used for valuing the ECU is controlled by the Council of Ministers of the European Communities. The present components of the ECU and their amounts were agreed in 1975, when the EUA (the predecessor of the ECU) was introduced. Criteria taken into account at that

---

[7] Council Regulation No. 3180/78, *supra* note 4, Article 1. The composition of the composite has not yet been changed since it was introduced. See note 16, *infra,* and accompanying text regarding the Greek drachma.

The composite used for valuing the ECU is identical with the composite used to value the EUA at the time the ECU was introduced. See Article 10 of European Communities Financial Regulation of December 21, 1977. *Official Journal,* no. L-356, December 31, 1977, p. 1; *Compendium of Community Monetary Texts* (1979), *supra* note 4, p. 132.

[8] The value of the ECU is calculated for each working day as follows: The central bank in each member state identifies the representative market exchange rate between its currency and the U.S. dollar in the country's exchange market as of 2:30 p.m. Brussels time. The rate is communicated to the Banque Nationale de Belgique, which in turn communicates the rates to the Commission. The Commission then calculates the value in dollars of each component of the ECU and adds them up to determine the dollar value of the ECU. The value of the ECU in terms of a particular EEC currency or any other currency is then obtained by multiplying the dollar value of the ECU by the market exchange rate between the dollar and the relevant currency.

The dollar has been chosen as the reference currency as giving the most representative rate in all financial centers. If an exchange market is closed, the EEC central banks agree on a representative exchange rate for the currency against the dollar, which is communicated to the Commission. At one time the Belgian franc was the reference currency for calculating the value of the EUA, but it was found that the franc market against other EEC currencies did not have as much depth as the dollar market. See Commission communication published in *Official Journal,* no. C-69, March 13, 1979, p. 4. Earlier superseded communications relating to calculations of the value of the former unit, the European unit of account (EUA), appear in *Official Journal,* no. C-21, January 30, 1976, p. 4; and no. C-225, September 22, 1978, p. 2.

time in establishing the currency weightings were gross national product, shares of intra-Community trade, and shares in the EEC system of short-term monetary support.[9] The basket was fixed as to total value so that retroactively on June 28, 1974, it had the same market value as one SDR when a basket valuation was first introduced for the SDR. Care was taken to maintain the same value at that point in time because the Communities' original unit of account was stated in terms of gold—the same amount of gold as the 1944 U.S. dollar and the SDR prior to the Second Amendment of the IMF's Articles of Agreement.

The definition of the ECU and the method of its valuation are not fixed for all time. In most cases where the unit is used, the Council of Ministers retains authority to change the definition and valuation method. Care has been taken, especially where the introduction of the ECU has required the use of a treaty instrument, to assure flexibility. The regulation making the ECU the unit of account of the European Monetary Cooperation Fund provides:

> The Council [Council of Ministers of the European Communities], acting unanimously on a proposal from the Commission after consulting the Monetary Committee and the Board of Governors of the Fund, shall determine the conditions under which the composition of the ECU may be changed.[10]

The Treaty Amending Certain Provisions of the Protocol on the Statute of the European Investment Bank provides:

> The Board of Governors [of the European Investment Bank], acting unanimously on a proposal from the Board of Directors, may alter the definition of the unit of account.
>
> . . . .
>
> Furthermore it [Board of Governors] may, acting unanimously on a proposal from the Board of Directors, alter the method of converting sums expressed in units of account into national currencies and vice versa.[11]

---

[9] The considerations favoring a unit with a basket valuation are spelled out in a report of the Monetary Committee of the European Communities of March 4, 1975, to the Council of Ministers and the Commission. The report also states reasons for valuing the Communities' unit of account by its own basket rather than use the SDR or an independent unit. The report appears as Annex I to the *17th Report on the Activities of the Monetary Committee; Official Journal*, no. C-132, June 14, 1976, p. 1 at p. 6. The valuation of the IMF special drawing right is explained in Chapter 5, *supra*, pages 176–194.

[10] Council Regulation No. 3180/78, *supra* note 4, Article 2.

[11] Amendments to Article 4(1) and Article 7(4) of the Protocol on the Statute of the European Investment Bank. The amending treaty, to which all member states of the EEC are parties, was signed July 10, 1975, and entered into force October 1, 1977. It appears in *Official Journal*, no. L-91, April 6, 1978, p. 1. The text of

The language respecting the European Investment Bank, quoted above, permits the Board of Governors to make changes in both the definition and method of valuing its unit of account. The authority was used when the Board replaced the EUA with the ECU as the Bank's unit of account.[12] The language quoted would even permit the Board to substitute the SDR for the ECU as the unit of account should it decide to do so. The language respecting the FECOM, quoted above, while less broadly drawn, probably permits the Council of Ministers, through changes in the "composition" of the ECU, to accomplish the same results. Further, the Council, having created the FECOM, retains broad powers to make changes in the unit of account in any event.[13]

The basic European Council resolution, although probably not legally binding,[14] specifies the following procedure for making changes in the composite used for valuing the ECU:

> The weights of currencies in the ECU will be re-examined and if necessary revised within six months of the entry into force of the system and thereafter every five years or, on request, if the weight of any currency has changed by 25%.
>
> Revisions have to be mutually accepted; they will, by themselves, not modify the external value of the ECU. They will be made in line with underlying economic criteria.[15]

---

the Statute following its amendment appears in Commerce Clearing House, *Common Market Reports* (Chicago: CCH looseleaf service), paragraph 4115.

[12] Board of Governors of the European Investment Bank decision of May 13, 1981, amending Article 4(1) of the Statute of the Bank effective January 1, 1981. *Official Journal,* no. L-311, October 30, 1981, p. 1.

[13] See FECOM Statutes, *supra* note 2, Article 5, final paragraph.

[14] See Chapter 2, *supra,* pages 80–81.

[15] European Council Resolution of December 5, 1978, *supra* note 4, Part A, paragraph 2.3. No changes in the currencies in the composite or their amounts had been made as of January 1, 1984. The relative weights of the currency components in the ECU basket on March 13, 1979, when the European Monetary System began were:

Deutsche mark	32.98%
French franc	19.83%
U.K. pound sterling	13.34%
Netherlands guilder	10.51%
Belgian-Luxembourg franc	9.63%
Italian lira	9.50%
Danish krone	3.06%
Irish pound	1.15%

See Directorate-General for Economic and Financial Affairs, "The European Monetary System," in *European Economy* (published by the Commission of the European Communities), no. 12 (July 1982), p. 71 (table 2). Issue no. 12 of *European Economy* will hereinafter be cited *Directorate-General Report.*

The way in which the weight of a currency in the ECU composite can change as a result of changes in exchange rates is illustrated, *idem,* p. 71. See also discussion of this point in regard to the IMF special drawing right in Chapter 5, *supra,* pages 188–189. The official change in the SDR composite in 1978 was no doubt in the minds of the drafters of the European Council resolution when they provided for possible revisions in the amounts of the currency components in the ECU basket.

Greece became a member of the European Communities effective January 1, 1981. The Act of Accession provides that after a transition period, which is not to extend beyond December 31, 1985, the Greek drachma is to be included in the composite used for valuing the ECU. At the time the drachma is added, the amounts of other currencies will be altered so that the external value of the ECU will be the same immediately before and immediately after the change of currency weights in the composite.[16] No formula has been spelled out for determining appropriate relative weights of currencies or the basis on which the amount of each currency in the composite will be revised. Presumably, the matter will be negotiated taking into account such "underlying economic criteria" as gross national product and shares of intra-Community trade.

Issuance of the ECU

The European currency unit (ECU) is both a unit of account and a monetary asset. Pending the creation of the European Monetary Fund, the European Monetary Cooperation Fund (FECOM) is the issuer of this monetary instrument. While there are no restrictions on the use of the ECU as a unit of account, the true ECU (monetary asset) can at present be used only in official settlements between monetary authorites of the member states of the EEC and in transactions between those authorities and the FECOM.

The Council of Ministers has authorized the FECOM to issue ECUs against "monetary reserves from the monetary authorities of the Member States."[17] While the Council's broad language authorizes the FECOM to issue ECUs against SDRs, foreign currencies held in reserves, and gold, the FECOM at the present time, as explained below, issues ECUs only against gold and U.S. dollars.

Each EEC central bank participating in the European Monetary System's exchange rate mechanism has undertaken to contribute 20 percent of its gold holdings and 20 percent of its gross U.S. dollar reserves to the FECOM.[18] In return, the FECOM credits the monetary authorities with ECUs equivalent to

---

[16] Act of Accession of Greece, Annex VIII, point III(3). *Official Journal*, no. L-291, November 19, 1979, p. 17 at p. 164. See also the declaration of Greece on monetary questions annexed to the Final Act. *Idem*, p. 190. As of January 1,1984, the Greek drachma was not yet included in the composite.

[17] Council Regulation No. 3181/78, *supra* note 4, Article 1. See also European Council Resolution of December 5, 1978, *supra* note 4, Part A, paragraphs 2 and 3.8.

[18] Agreement between the Central Banks of the Member States of the European Economic Community, dated March 13, 1979, laying down the operating procedures for the European Monetary System, Article 17.1. The agreement appears in *Compendium of Community Monetary Texts* (1979), *supra* note 4, p. 55; and in *European Economy*, no. 3 (July 1979), p. 102.

A somewhat similar arrangement for contributing national reserves to the FECOM was proposed, but not implemented, in 1973. See Commission proposal of June 28, 1973, for pooling reserves; opinion of Parliament of October 18, 1973; and Article 5 of Commission proposal of November 15, 1973, to amend the FECOM's statutes. *Bulletin of the European Communities*, 1973, supplement, nos. 5 and 12; and *Official Journal*, no. C-95, November 10, 1973, p. 27, and no. C-114, December 27, 1973, p. 41 at p. 42.

the gold and dollars contributed to it. EEC central banks that do not participate in the EMS exchange rate mechanism are permitted, but are not required, to similarly contribute 20 percent of their gold and dollar reserves in return for ECUs.[19]

The arrangement for contributing 20 percent of central bank reserves of gold and of U.S. dollars and in exchange receiving ECUs is provided for in the Agreement between the Central Banks of the Member States of the European Economic Community, dated March 13, 1979, laying down the operating procedures for the European Monetary System[20] and by a decision of the same date of the FECOM's Board of Governors.[21] The central bank agreement[22] and another FECOM decision of March 13[23] also establish the European Monetary System's exchange rate arrangement and confirm the obligations of participating central banks to maintain exchange rates within defined margins.[24] In the absence of the central bank agreement and the FECOM decisions, the ECU would simply be a unit of account and not a monetary instrument. In agreeing on the provisions of the central bank agreement, the banks appear to have relied primarily upon their powers under national and international law[25] rather than powers derived from the decisions or regulations of the Council of Ministers. The agreement should probably be understood as governed by public international law but creating Community law.[26] The FECOM decisions appear to derive their authority from powers granted by the Council of Ministers and by the central bank agreement. These actions implemented the European Council Resolution of December 5, 1978, on the European Monetary System.[27]

Unlike the IMF special drawing right (SDR), which is a form of fiat

[19] Agreement of EEC central banks on EMS operating procedures, *supra* note 18, Article 17.1; and FECOM Board of Governors Decision No. 12/79 (March 13, 1979), Article 2.1. The FECOM decision appears in *European Economy,* no. 3 (July 1979), p. 109.

The Bank of England, although not at present a participant in the EMS exchange rate mechanism, contributes gold and dollars in exchange for ECUs in the same manner as central banks of other EMS participants. The central bank of Greece at this time does not do so.

[20] Agreement of EEC central banks on EMS operating procedures, *supra* note 18, Articles 17–20.

[21] FECOM Decision No. 12/79, *supra* note 19, Articles 2–6.

[22] Agreement of EEC central banks on EMS operating procedures, *supra* note 18, Articles 1–5.

[23] FECOM Board of Governors Decision No. 13/79 (March 13, 1979), Article 1. The decision appears in *European Economy,* no. 3 (July 1979), p. 111.

[24] The exchange rate mechanism of the European Monetary System, which is designed to maintain stable rates among participating national currencies, is described and critiqued in Chapter 11, *infra,* page 536 et seq.

[25] The legal character of agreements between central banks is discussed in Chapter 4, *supra,* pages 157–164. See also Luca Radicati di Bròzolo, ''Some Legal Aspects of the European Monetary System,'' *Rivista di Diritto Internazionale,* vol. 63 (1980), p. 330 at pp. 335–44.

[26] Treaties between member states of the European Communities, while governed by public international law, may create or contribute to the regime of Community law. See Chapter 2, *supra,* pages 86–87.

[27] European Council Resolution of December 5, 1978, *supra* note 4, Part A, paragraph 3.8. See also Council of Ministers Regulation No. 3181/78, *supra* note 4, which authorizes the FECOM to issue ECUs and to engage in transactions in ECUs with monetary authorities of EEC member states. The legal status of the European Council resolution is examined in Chapter 2, *supra,* pages 80–81.

money created (allocated) by the International Monetary Fund,[28] the European currency unit is created through asset substitution. ECUs are issued by the European Monetary Cooperation Fund in exchange for gold and U.S. dollars of equivalent value. The ECU-issuance transaction takes the form of a three-month revolving swap. A "swap" is the simultaneous purchase and sale of a foreign currency (or other monetary asset) for different maturities.[29] The central bank receives ECUs from the FECOM in exchange for gold and dollars in a spot contract and simultaneously makes a forward contract with the FECOM to sell back the same amount of ECUs to the FECOM in three months at the same gold price and ECU-dollar exchange rate. At the beginning of each quarter the swap is renewed for an additional three-month period. At that time the necessary adjustments are made so that the renewed swap involves at least 20 percent of the central bank's gold and 20 percent of its dollar reserves on the basis of its gross reserve position recorded on the last working day of the quarter just concluded. Adjustments are also made to establish the renewed swap at new exchange rates.[30]

The exchange rates for each three-month swap, which are the same for both its spot and forward aspects, are established at the beginning of the period as follows:

—The ECU-dollar rate is the market rate two working days prior to the beginning of the swap period, the rate being determined by the Commission of the European Communities as explained in the previous section.

—The ECU-gold rate is the average of the prices, converted into ECUs, recorded daily at the two London fixings during the six months preceding the beginning of the swap period in question, but not exceeding the average price of the two fixings on the penultimate working day preceding the beginning of the swap period.[31]

The FECOM in certain circumstances may make supplementary issues of ECUs to individual EEC central banks against gold and dollar contributions in excess of the basic 20 percent-of-reserves contribution. As in the basic ECU-

---

[28] See Chapter 5, *supra*, pages 172–173 and 210–221.

[29] Swap arrangements between monetary authorities are treated in some detail in Chapter 4, *supra*, page 135 et seq.

[30] Agreement of EEC central bank on EMS operating procedures, *supra* note 18, Article 17; and FECOM Decision No. 12/79, *supra* note 19, Article 2. See "Le Système Monétaire Européen," *Bulletin de la Banque Nationale de Belgique*, vol. 54, part 2, nos. 1–2 (July–August 1979), p. 3 at pp. 27–29 and illustrations of adjustments that are made when swaps are renewed at pp. 40–41.

[31] Agreement of EEC central banks on EMS operating procedures, *supra* note 18, Article 17.4; and FECOM Decision No. 12/79, *supra* note 19, Article 2.4.

issuance transaction, the ratio of gold and dollars contributed is to be the same as the ratio of these two assets in the particular country's reserves. The supplementary transaction, like the basic ECU-issuance transaction, is in the form of a swap.[32]

Note that, under this swap system, the FECOM carries no exchange rate risk. The ECUs issued will be cancelled in exchange for the same assets against which they were created.

Right of Access to Assets Backing ECUs

While the 1978 European Council resolution speaks of the FECOM providing ECUs against the "deposit" of gold and U.S. dollars,[33] the word "deposit" is studiously avoided in the Council of Ministers regulation authorizing the FECOM to issue ECUs, in the central bank agreement (except in the preamble), and in the FECOM decision that together establish procedures for the issuance of ECUs. According to the legally operative language, the central banks make "contributions"[34] of gold and dollars to the FECOM, which the FECOM "receives,"[35] and "against such assets"[36] the FECOM "credits"[37] the banks with ECUs "corresponding to these contributions."[38] "Contribution" is not a word of art in the law of central banking. The term appears to have been selected in order to give the FECOM and the participating central banks maximum freedom in structuring the rules and procedures for the issuance of this unique monetary instrument.[39]

Contracts between the FECOM and the central banks establish the "arrangements for the delivery of the gold and dollars to the EMCF [FECOM] and for their management in so far as this is entrusted to the central banks."[40] The normal practice is for a central bank, contributing gold to the FECOM in an ECU-issuance swap transaction, to earmark the gold for the FECOM and for the FECOM's Agent (the BIS) to entrust the central bank with custody of it. The normal procedure for the contribution of dollars is for the contributing

---

[32] Agreement of EEC central banks on EMS operating procedures, *supra* note 18, Article 16.3; and FECOM Decision No. 12/79, *supra* note 19, Article 4.3. See text accompanying note 74, *infra*.

[33] European Council Resolution of December 5, 1978, *supra* note 4, Part A, paragraph 3.8. The legal character of the resolution is considered in Chapter 2, *supra*, pages 80–81.

[34] Agreement of EEC central banks on EMS operating procedures, *supra* note 18, Article 17; and FECOM Decision No. 12/79, *supra* note 19, Article 2.

[35] Council of Ministers Regulation No. 3181/78, *supra* note 4, Article 1.

[36] *Idem.*

[37] Agreement of EEC central banks on EMS operating procedures, *supra* note 18, Article 17.1; and FECOM Decision No. 12/79, *supra* note 19, Article 2.1.

[38] *Idem.*

[39] See Joseph Gold, *SDRs, Currencies, and Gold: Fourth Survey of New Legal Developments* (IMF Pamphlet Series no. 33; Washington, 1980), pp. 56–60. See also Radicati di Bròzolo, *supra* note 25, pp. 344–49.

[40] Agreement of EEC central banks on EMS operating procedures, *supra* note 18, Article 17.5; and FECOM Decision No. 12/79, *supra* note 19, Article 2.5. The language is identical.

central bank to send the FECOM's Agent a statement of the selected U.S. dollar assets which have been placed at the disposal of the FECOM, and at the same time the Agent entrusts the contributing central bank with the management of those assets on behalf of and for the account of the FECOM.[41]

While the FECOM appears to have the legal right to manage the gold and dollars contributed to it, its agreements with the central banks "entrust" the management of these assets to the individual central banks contributing them.[42] While the FECOM's authority to use the gold contributed to it is unclear (and in any event would require a unanimous decision of its Board of Governors), it is reasonably clear that a central bank cannot use the gold entrusted to it (e.g., pledge it to a third party) without first unwinding the ECU-issuance swap with the FECOM or obtaining the FECOM's permission for the use.[43]

The FECOM also entrusts the management of the dollar balances to the respective central bank contributing them. The credits in favor of the FECOM do not bear interest to the FECOM, and the dollars behind the credits can be invested by the EEC central bank for that bank's own profit and risk.[44] The central bank's management does not, however, include the right to sell the dollars to increase yield by investing in another currency.[45]

A central bank can unwind the swap with the FECOM on two-working-days' notice. Since the value date for currency exchange transactions in the market is normally two business days, this means that a central bank can sell gold and/or dollars in the market and, by giving notice on the same day to the FECOM of prematurity of a swap, can surrender ECUs for gold and dollars previously contributed to the FECOM which it then can use to fulfill its market contracts with third parties. It is understood that a central bank will request a premature partial or total unwinding of a swap only to the extent there is a fall in the dollar reserves of the central bank.[46]

The International Monetary Fund treats ECU holdings of central banks as monetary reserves. The gold and dollars contributed to the FECOM, and entrusted by the FECOM to the respective contributing central banks for manage-

---

[41] Letter dated November 11, 1983, to the author from A. Bascoul, Assistant Secretary General, Committee of Governors of the Central Banks of the Member States of the European Economic Community.

[42] See Bank for International Settlements, *49th Annual Report 1978/79*, pp. 146–47 and 172–74.

[43] This consequence flows logically from the phrase "against such assets," *supra* note 36.

[44] See "The European Monetary System: Structure and Operation," *Monthly Report of the Deutsche Bundesbank*, March 1979, p. 11 at p. 16.

[45] Letter of A. Bascoul dated November 11,1983, *supra* note 41. See also Gold, *SDRs, Currencies, and Gold: Fourth Survey, supra* note 39, p. 129 (note 154).

[46] Agreement of EEC central banks on EMS operating procedures, *supra* note 18, Articles 17.3 and 18.3; and FECOM Decision No. 12/79, *supra* note 19, Articles 2.3 and 3.3.

If, after unwinding its ECU swaps with the FECOM, a central bank holds ECU balances (e.g., ECU balances previously acquired in transfers from other central banks) that it needs to exchange for dollars to meet a decline in its dollar reserves, it is possible that it could acquire the needed dollars against ECUs from the FECOM (but the procedures for this exchange have not yet been established). See Article 18.3 of the central bank agreement and Article 3.3 of FECOM Decision No. 12/79.

ment, are shown in IMF statistics as owned by the FECOM and are not included in the reserves of the contributing countries.[47]

Utilization of ECUs

At the present time the only authorized holders of ECUs are the FECOM and EEC central banks.[48] Others, of course, can use the ECU as a unit of account although not as a monetary asset. The principal use of ECUs as a monetary asset is in transfers among EEC central banks and between EEC central banks and the FECOM in settlement of debts incurred under the very-short-term financing facility, treated below, which is related to the exchange market intervention mechanism of the European Monetary System.[49]

Other uses are also permitted. The EEC central banks are given a broad authorization to transfer ECUs to one another by agreement against U.S. dollars, EEC currencies, SDRs, or gold, without any limitation as to the type of transaction except that the sole purpose must not be to alter the composition of a central bank's reserves.[50] The exchange of ECUs for gold and dollars through the unwinding of an ECU-issuance swap transaction, as explained above, can be categorized as another use. A central bank, that holds an ECU balance after unwinding its swap transactions with the FECOM, may be able to transfer those ECUs to other central banks or, if procedures are established, transfer them to the FECOM to obtain dollars if it needs them to meet a decline in its dollar reserves.[51]

Interest

Central banks that make a net use of ECUs (hold less ECUs than they were issued by the FECOM) pay an interest charge; and banks that are net accumulators receive remuneration (interest). Interest is charged and paid monthly and is calculated on average daily balances. It is paid in ECUs. The interest rate is based on the official discount rates of the central banks issuing the currencies in the ECU valuation basket, weighted in accordance with the amount of each currency in the basket. The rate is calculated once a month on the basis of the dis-

---

[47] IMF, *International Financial Statistics*, vol. 37, no. 1 (January 1984), p. 7.

[48] Council Regulation No. 3181/78, *supra* note 4, in Article 2, states that the FECOM and "monetary authorities" (a term wide enough to include national treasuries) are empowered to use ECUs. The Agreement of central banks on EMS operating procedures, *supra* note 18, in Articles 16–18, and FECOM Decision No. 12/79, *supra* note 19, in Articles 2 and 3, provide for only the FECOM and EEC central banks to hold and transfer ECUs.

[49] Agreement of EEC central banks on EMS operating procedures, *supra* note 18, Articles 16 and 18; and FECOM Decision No. 12/79, *supra* note 19, Article 3. The very-short-term financing facility is examined at pages 327–332, *infra*.

[50] Agreement of EEC central banks on EMS operating procedures, *supra* note 18, Article 18.2 and 18.4; and FECOM Decision No. 12/79, *supra* note 19, Article 3.2 and 3.4.

[51] See note 46, *supra*, and accompanying text.

count rates ruling on the last working day of the month and applies during the following month.[52]

The ECU System in Transition

The central bank agreement providing for the creation of ECUs stated that the system of revolving swaps of gold and dollars for ECUs would be liquidated in March 1981 unless there was a unanimous decision by the EEC central banks to the contrary. The time period has been extended.[53] At the time of liquidation, if and when that may be, outstanding swaps under which ECUs were issued will be unwound and balances of FECOM-issued ECUs reduced to zero. As a prelude to liquidation, central banks that are net accumulators of ECUs will transfer ECUs to net users in exchange for gold, dollars, or other assets.[54] The expectation that the system may be liquidated imposes some restraint on a central bank's use of ECUs to deal with balance-of-payments deficits that are of a medium- or longer-term character.

It is expected that a new institution called the "European Monetary Fund" will be established in the future and that it will succeed the FECOM as the issuer of ECUs.[55] In any event, one can expect the rules under which the system functions to be changed from time to time. Some of the issues are addressed at the end of the chapter.[56]

Mechanisms of Balance-of-Payments Support in the European Economic Community

Introductory Comments

The European Economic Community has established a group of special mechanisms to provide financial assistance to members facing balance-of-payments problems. These are distinguished by the length of the term for which assistance is provided, the source of the funds, and the conditions attached to their use. The European Monetary Cooperation Fund (FECOM) administers two short-term credit facilities: (1) a very-short-term facility for financing exchange market interventions under the European Monetary System's exchange rate mechanism, and (2) a facility that provides short-term monetary support which

---

[52] Agreement of EEC central banks on EMS operating procedures, *supra* note 18, Articles 8 and 19; and FECOM Decision No. 12/79, *supra* note 19, Article 5.

[53] See *Directorate-General Report, supra* note 15, p. 70.

[54] Agreement of EEC central banks on EMS operating procedures, *supra* note 18, Article 20; and FECOM Decision No. 12/79, *supra* note 19, Article 6.

[55] European Council Resolution of December 5, 1978, *supra* note 4, Part A, paragraph 1.4; and Council of Ministers Decision No. 3181/78, *supra* note 4, preamble. See generally Chapter 2, *supra*, pages 84–86.

[56] At page 342 et seq.

is available to all EEC central banks whether or not their currencies participate in the EMS exchange rate mechanism. In addition to the FECOM facilities, medium-term financial assistance is available in the form of loans from member states at the Community's direction. Loans for balance-of-payments support are also made by the Community itself.[57]

There is presently under discussion the possibility of establishing a European Monetary Fund (EMF). If established, the EMF might take over responsibility for administering the medium-term financial assistance and Community loans. In contrast with the FECOM, it will probably be administered at its highest level by finance ministry rather than central bank officials. It is likely that the short-term facilities now administered by the FECOM will continue to be managed by the governors of the central banks either through the FECOM or other institutional arrangements. While the precise institutional form of the proposed EMF and the facilities it will operate are not now known, new credit facilities it comes to operate may simply modify and supplement rather than replace arrangements now in use. Even where they replace present arrangements, they are likely to draw upon legal and technical features of the arrangements described below.

Very-Short-Term Financing of EMS Interventions

The Agreement between the Central Banks of the Member States of the European Economic Community laying down the operating procedures for the European Monetary System establishes a very-short-term financing facility in support of market interventions under the EMS exchange rate mechanism.[58] This facility is heavily used.[59] All of the central banks of the EEC states (except the central bank of Greece) are parties to the agreement. However, parties to the agreement that do not participate in the EMS exchange rate mechanism (currently the Bank of England) cannot make drawings under the agreement. The

[57] The institutions of the European Economic Community, including the European Monetary Cooperation Fund and the proposed European Monetary Fund, are described in Chapter 2, *supra*, page 76 et seq.

[58] Agreement of EEC central banks of March 13, 1979, on EMS operating procedures, *supra* note 18, Articles 6–16.

The agreement terminated and replaced the EEC central bank agreement of April 10, 1972, as amended July 8, 1975, that provided financing for market interventions in the European exchange rate arrangement called the "snake" that preceded the EMS. The text of the April 10, 1972, agreement appears in European Communities, *Compendium of Community Monetary Texts* (Luxembourg, 1974), p. 60. The amendment of July 8, 1975, appears in European Communities, *Compendium of Community Monetary Texts–Supplement* (Luxembourg, 1976), p. 19. The operation of the 1972 agreement, as amended in 1975, is explained in detail in Richard W. Edwards, Jr., "The European Exchange Rate Arrangement Called the 'Snake'," *University of Toledo Law Review*, vol. 10 (1978), p. 47 at pp. 59–63.

[59] About 10.7 billion ECUs were transferred between EMS central banks in the period April 1, 1982, through March 31, 1983. Most of the transfers were made under the very-short-term facility. There were also voluntary transactions between central banks participating in the EMS and transfers representing payment of interest. BIS, *53d Annual Report 1982/83*, p. 177.

facility is not available to non-EEC central banks that may choose to associate their currencies with the EMS exchange rate system.[60]

The market intervention system of the EMS is described in Chapter 11 and the reader may wish to refer to that discussion.[61] The financing facility described here provides a guaranteed source of foreign currency to a participating central bank that must sell in the market a currency issued by one of its partner banks to buy its own currency at the fluctuation limit in order to maintain exchange rates within narrow margins. Guaranteed access to the currency is important because central banks participating in the EMS do not hold their partners' currencies in substantial amounts in their reserves except by mutual agreement.[62] If the Banque Nationale de Belgique sells mark in Brussels, it can obtain on demand the mark needed to fulfill its contracts through this EMS facility. Since an EMS participant is required to intervene in the market, without limit as to amount at the published intervention points, the amount of funds available to a central bank under this special-purpose, very-short-term credit facility is also without any limitation as to amount. Only currencies of EMS participants (not dollars) are available under the facility. The sole purpose for which funds are provided under this facility is to finance market interventions.[63]

The beneficiary central bank obtains the foreign currency through the European Monetary Cooperation Fund (FECOM). The Bank for International Settlements, as agent for the FECOM, handles the bookkeeping. The currency is provided in the form of bank balances by its issuer. The central bank providing the currency (the creditor) obtains a claim against the FECOM denominated in European currency units (ECUs), on the basis of the daily conversion rate between the creditor's currency and the ECU. The beneficiary incurs a liability, equal in amount, to the FECOM denominated in ECUs.[64]

Booking the amounts in ECUs means that each central bank bears the consequences of a change in the conversion rate of its currency against the ECU. This has important consequences when currencies in the EMS are devalued or revalued. If a creditor's currency is revalued, the debtor needs less of it to satisfy a pre-existing obligation. When a currency is devalued in the EMS, the practice of the EMS participants in agreeing on a new set of central rates is to

---

[60] Financing facilities that may be available to non-EEC states if they associate their currencies with the EMS are noted in Chapter 11, *infra*, page 550 (note 240).

[61] At page 536 et seq.

[62] Agreement of EEC central banks on EMS operating procedures, *supra* note 18, Article 15. See also Chapter 11, *infra*, page 549.

[63] Agreement of EEC central banks on EMS operating procedures, *supra* note 18, Article 6.

[64] *Idem*, Articles 6 and 7.

The creditor currency–ECU rate used for determining the ECU value of the transaction is the rate calculated by the Commission for the relevant business day on the basis of market exchange rates of the currencies in the ECU basket. The rate ruling on the day of the intervention is the one that is used. See generally pages 317–320, *supra*.

establish new central rates for all the participating currencies against the basket value of the ECU.[65] The revaluation of the other currencies mitigates the debtor's increased cost caused by the devaluation of its currency.

The beneficiary central bank has an obligation to liquidate the financing operation on the last working day preceding the sixteenth day of the second month following that in which the value date of the original intervention fell.[66] At the request of the beneficiary bank the liquidation date may, subject to certain conditions, be automatically extended for an additional three months. The automatic extension is limited to the amount of the central bank's debtor quota under the short-term monetary support arrangement of February 9, 1970, as amended.[67] Any debt exceeding this ceiling can be renewed with the agreement of the creditors in the FECOM.[68] Settlement can be deferred a further three months if the agreement of the creditors in the FECOM is obtained.[69] Special rules determine the priority of creditor claims against the FECOM and the offsetting of debts and claims, so that debtor settlements with the FECOM can be properly allocated among the creditors.[70]

The beneficiary bank liquidating its debt must first use for this purpose currencies of FECOM creditors if it holds any beyond working balances.[71] A debtor bank can, with the agreement of a creditor bank, sell the debtor's currency in the market for the creditor's currency during the period preceding settlement in order to use the currency obtained for repayment even though the debtor's currency was never at its EMS upper intervention limit. The Deutsche Bundesbank, when a creditor, appears to have encouraged its debtor partners to do this. Such actions have the effect of reducing the liquidity of German banks and other financial institutions, which can at times be desirable from the Bundesbank's point of view.[72]

The debtor bank has the right to settle all or part of the remaining debt in ECUs with the proviso that a creditor bank shall not be obliged to accept settlement by means of ECUs of an amount more than 50 percent of its claim which is being settled, although it can agree to do so.[73] If a debtor central bank no lon-

---

[65] See Chapter 11, *infra,* pages 544–546. The booking of liabilities and claims under the financing mechanism of the predecessor "snake" is explained in Edwards, *supra* note 58, p. 60.

[66] Agreement of EEC central banks on EMS operating procedures, *supra* note 18, Article 9. In accordance with market convention in the case of spot contracts, the value date is usually two business days after the exchange contract is made.

[67] Described at page 332, *infra.*

[68] Agreement of EEC central banks on EMS operating procedures, *supra* note 18, Articles 10 and 11.

[69] *Idem.*

[70] *Idem,* Articles 11–13.

[71] *Idem,* Articles 15 and 16.1.

[72] See *Report of the Deutsche Bundesbank for the Year 1976,* pp. 53–54. The referenced comment, although describing procedures prior to the EMS, continues to be applicable to the acquisition of creditor-country currencies for use in liquidating very-short-term financing of EMS interventions.

[73] Agreement of EEC central banks on EMS operating procedures, *supra* note 18, Article 16.1; and FECOM Decision No. 12/79, *supra* note 19, Article 4.1.

ger possesses ECUs and wishes to acquire some for use in a settlement, it is to apply in the first instance to central banks that hold net accumulations of ECUs or possibly to the FECOM. The assets it exchanges with another central bank for ECUs can be negotiated. If ECUs are acquired from the FECOM, the bank will contribute gold and U.S. dollars totaling the value of the ECUs received and in the ratio these two assets are held in the debtor bank's reserves.[74]

For that portion of the settlement not settled by the use of creditor currencies or ECUs, the debtor is to use SDR-denominated assets (i.e., SDR holdings plus reserve position in the IMF), as one category of assets, and U.S. dollars and other acceptable currencies, as a second category, in the same proportion that the one group of assets has to the other in the debtor country's monetary reserves. Gold holdings do not figure in these calculations. Within the two categories of assets, the debtor is free to choose the reserve elements that it will deliver, while the creditor is obliged to accept the assets chosen. The rules were devised to permit the debtor to have an unchanged reserve composition after settlement while protecting the creditors against an arbitrary composition of assets transferred in settlement. Settlement can be effected on different terms, including settlement in the currency issued by the beneficiary bank, if the central banks agree. Gold can be used in settlement if the parties agree on the valuation.[75]

Exchange rates for settlement transactions are based on the daily rates at the time of settlement between the ECU and the currencies or other assets involved in the settlement transaction.[76] Creditor banks receive remuneration (interest) and debtor banks pay an interest charge.[77]

A debtor's balance can be settled before its maturity only under the following conditions:

(a) at any time in the currency of a creditor of the FECOM; or

(b) at the monthly settlement date by transfer of reserve elements as described above.[78]

A central bank that uses the renewal facility of the very-short-term financing mechanism continuously for six months must submit to a consultation pro-

---

[74] Agreement of EEC central banks on EMS operating procedures, *supra* note 18, Articles 16–18; and FECOM Decision No. 12/79, *supra* note 19, Article 4.3. See text accompanying note 32, *supra.*

[75] Agreement of EEC central banks on EMS operating procedures, *supra* note 18, Article 16; and FECOM Decision No. 12/79, *supra* note 19, Article 4.

It was once thought that rules on assets to be used in settlements would encourage greater uniformity in the composition of monetary reserves of the several EEC states, but there is little evidence of such an effect. See generally Chapter 12, page 630 et seq., where the harmonization of reserve asset policies is discussed.

[76] Agreement of EEC central banks on EMS operating procedures, *supra* note 18, Article 16; and FECOM Decision No. 12/79, *supra* note 19, Article 4. For background on the determination of ECU exchange rates, see page 317 et seq.

[77] Agreement of EEC central banks on EMS operating procedures, *supra* note 18, Article 8. The debtor and creditor interest rates applicable to very-short-term financing operations are the same rates as for ECU net accumulation and net use positions. See note 52, *supra,* and accompanying text.

[78] Agreement of EEC central banks on EMS operating procedures, *supra* note 18, Article 14.

cedure in which the reasons for the persistent indebtedness are discussed. These consultations may suggest that the country's problems are of a longer-term nature that might better be handled through use of other EEC facilities discussed below.[79] Otherwise, use of the very-short-term financing mechanism does not involve a policy review, use of the funds for required EMS interventions being adequate justification.

The central bank whose currency has to be supported in the market is free to choose to not use the FECOM very-short-term facility and instead, for example, to sell foreign currency in its reserves, negotiate a direct purchase from the central bank issuing the currency to be sold with immediate settlement, or draw on its reserve position with the International Monetary Fund. The FECOM is then not involved in the transaction.

While central banks participating in the EMS exchange rate arrangement are required to intervene in the markets at the fluctuation limits,[80] they may choose to intervene when the divergence indicator threshold has been passed[81] or before either the divergence threshold or a fluctuation limit has been reached. A central bank engaging in such intra-marginal interventions may believe that stable rates can be maintained at less cost than if it waits until market rates hit the fluctuation limit and it is required to intervene in whatever amount necessary to hold rates within the limit. Intra-marginal interventions require the concurrence of the central bank that issues the currency to be sold or acquired.[82] Where a currency issued by an EMS participant is sold in intra-marginal interventions, the very-short-term facility, discussed in this section, is not available on demand for the financing of the sale, as it is for interventions at the fluctuation limits. While this may not be perfectly apparent from the text of the central bank agreement laying down operating procedures for the EMS,[83] the central banks have understood the agreement in this manner. It appears from its rules that the very-short-term facility can be used to finance intra-marginal interventions if the creditor central bank's agreement is obtained. In the first three years of the EMS operation, about 55 percent of total interventions were intra-marginal interventions, and it has been reported that none (or only a very small part) of the intra-marginal interventions were financed under the rules of the very-short-term facility discussed in this section.[84] By contrast, in the year ended March 31, 1982, there were ECU 8.5 billion in transactions under the facility to finance interventions at the fluctuation limits.[85]

---

[79] *Idem*, Article 10.

[80] See Chapter 11, *infra*, pages 539–540.

[81] See pages 540–541 and 542–544, *infra*.

[82] See generally pages 540–541, *infra*.

[83] See Agreement of EEC central banks on EMS operating procedures, *supra* note 18, Articles 6 and 15.

[84] Report of February 3, 1982, of the Alternates of the Monetary Committee of the European Communities, in *Directorate-General Report*, *supra* note 15, p. 79 at p. 83. See also *Report of the Deutsche Bundesbank for the Year 1979*, p. 59.

[85] BIS, *52d Annual Report 1981/82*, p. 181.

It has been suggested that the central bank agreement be amended to permit financing of intra-marginal interventions in EMS currencies through the very-short-term facility on demand if market rates pass certain previously agreed thresholds. If the central bank agreement is modified in this manner in the future, the amount of financing available would probably not be unlimited, as it is when interventions are made at the fluctuation limits.[86]

Short-Term Monetary Support

The system of short-term monetary support is governed by an agreement among EEC central banks of February 9, 1970, to which the central banks of Denmark, Ireland, and the United Kingdom acceded on January 8, 1973, which was amended March 12, 1974, December 13, 1977, and March 13, 1979, and to which the central bank of Greece acceded on January 1, 1981.[87] The system is available to all EEC central banks whether or not their currencies participate in the EMS exchange rate mechanism. Although administered by the European Monetary Cooperation Fund (FECOM), the policy decisions respecting the use of this facility are made by the Committee of Governors of the EEC central banks.[88]

Under the agreement each central bank of the EEC has undertaken to grant a line of credit to its partners up to a stated ceiling. The quotas are divided into debtor quotas, which determine the amount of support which each central bank may receive under terms laid down in the agreement, and creditor quotas, which determine the amount of support which each central bank undertakes to finance under the same terms.[89] These quotas may be supplemented by debtor or creditor rallonges as explained below.

A central bank that wishes to draw upon the facility informs the Chairman of the Committee of Governors of the EEC central banks that a need has arisen for short-term financing "in consequence of a temporary balance-of-payments

---

[86] See Commission proposal submitted to the Council of Ministers on March 15, 1982, in *Directorate-General Report, supra* note 15, p. 53 at p. 54. See also *Directorate-General Report,* pp. 49, 57, 83–84, and 90–91. Compare the views of the Deutsche Bundesbank, *Report of the Deutsche Bundesbank for the Year 1981,* pp. 78–81 at p. 80.

[87] The text of the agreement, hereinafter called "short-term support agreement," as amended March 13, 1979, appears in *Compendium of Community Monetary Texts* (1979), *supra* note 4, p. 62. The provisions of the agreement were adopted as FECOM regulations by FECOM Board of Governors Decision No. 13/79 of March 13, 1979, printed in *European Economy,* no. 3 (July 1979), p. 111. The amounts of debtor and creditor quotas were amended by the Act of Accession of Greece, Annex I, point VII(1). *Official Journal,* no. L-291, November 19, 1979, p. 17 at 95.

The text of the original agreement of February 9, 1970, appears in *Compendium of Community Monetary Texts* (1974), *supra* note 58, pp. 67–72. The instrument of accession of the central banks of Denmark, Ireland, and the United Kingdom, dated January 8, 1973, appears in *Compendium* (1974), *idem,* pp. 73–75.

[88] Short-term support agreement, *supra* note 87, Article I, section 4. See also Chapter 2, *supra,* pages 83–84.

[89] The quotas are set forth in Annex 1 to the short-term support agreement, *supra* note 87. Quotas are stated in terms of the ECU.

deficit which is due to unforeseen difficulties or to conjunctural divergences and which has emerged despite the coordination of economic policies."[90] The funds can be used to finance sales of foreign currencies against purchases of the country's own currency to maintain order in the exchange markets or for other purposes.

The central bank using the facility will indicate the amount of support desired and the particulars of any other sources of financing it might consider in order to overcome its difficulties. Assuming that the requesting bank has fulfilled repayment obligations on previous drawings and is not making continual use of the facility, the amount requested if within the quota limit can be granted. There are no formal statements of policy conditions to guide the consideration of requests except for the duration, which is three months and renewable twice for a total period of nine months.[91] The Committee of Governors (acting unanimously as it does in taking all decisions) may establish a "debtor rallonge" that permits a drawing in excess of quota. When assessing a request for a debtor rallonge the Governors are to take particular account of the balance-of-payments trend and foreign exchange reserve position of the state to which each central bank belongs, as well as facilities available under other international agreements.[92]

The procedure, assuming the request for a drawing is in order, is for the Chairman of the Committee of Governors, after consulting the central banks, to inform them and the Commission representative of the granting of the support, the amount, the currency to be delivered, the apportionment of the financing burden among the banks, and the timing of the provision of the funds.[93] The monetary support is normally financed by each participating central bank, other than the beneficiary, providing currency proportionate to its quota share and within the limit of its quota.[94] If a central bank which is to provide a currency informs the Chairman of the Governors Committee that its country is itself experiencing balance-of-payments difficulties or is suffering a disturbing decline in its foreign exchange reserves, the other creditor banks are to partially or totally refinance its contribution. Other adjustments can be made by unanimous decision of the Governors.[95]

---

[90] Short-term support agreement, *supra* note 87, Article III.

[91] *Idem,* Articles II, III, and VI. Unless the Governors decide otherwise, a beneficiary bank is not to make a request until a period has passed of its non-use of the facility at least equal in length to the period for which the previous support was utilized. Article VI, section 3.

[92] The Governors may, but are not required to, increase over and above its quota the amount of support a central bank may receive. The basic instrument places limits on the size of such a rollange. Short-term support agreement, *idem,* Articles II and III and Annex 1.

[93] Article IV.

[94] The Governors acting unanimously may establish a "creditor rallonge"—an increase over and above its quota which a central bank undertakes to finance. Articles II and IV.

[95] Article IV. If a creditor central bank later finds that its own country is encountering difficulties in its balance-of-payments or reserve position, it can apply to the Committee of Governors to obtain premature repayment or the transfer of its claim. Article V.

The beneficiary central bank receives currency balances through the Bank for International Settlements as agent for the FECOM or directly from its partner central banks in accordance with the Governors' decisions specifying the currencies to be provided and the amounts. A granting central bank cannot simply provide its own currency. It must provide its own currency or "other means of payment" (U.S. dollars, other currencies, or SDRs) as desired by the drawing central bank and agreed upon by the Governors Committee.[96] In the past the U.S. dollar has been the currency provided.

The accounting for drawings and repayments under this facility is made in the currency effectively provided to the beneficiary. The creditor is repaid in the same currency (or other means of payment) as the original drawing and no adjustment is made for changes in the exchange rate of that currency in relation to any other currency or the ECU that take place between the time of the drawing and the time of repayment. If the facility is used to refinance a drawing originally accounted for in ECUs under the very-short-term EMS financing arrangement, then the drawing and repayment would be accounted for in ECUs.[97]

The central bank drawing upon the facility has an obligation to effect repayment within three months. The beneficiary bank may obtain two three-month extensions raising the maximum duration to nine months. Interest is charged for the use of the facility, the interest being paid over to the creditors.[98]

The agreement setting up the facility provides:

> 1. The central banks agree that on each occasion when monetary support is granted the Committee of Governors shall undertake an examination of the monetary situation and of the monetary policy of the beneficiary country.
> 2. The Governors shall be regularly informed of the course of the Community procedures as regards coordination of short and medium-term economic policies.[99]

The procedure is designed to assure that the Governors are informed of the country's subsequent actions to correct its problems. At the same time it avoids a proliferation of procedures for economic and monetary policy reviews.

Use of this short-term facility by the Banca d'Italia is illustrative. In June 1973 the bank obtained approval for a credit line amounting to U.S. $1,885 million. No economic or monetary policy conditions were imposed on Italy,

---

[96] Article VI. The normal practice is for the creditor central banks to transfer to the BIS, as agent for the FECOM, balances of the currency (e.g., U.S. dollars) which the beneficiary is to receive, and the BIS then transfers the balances to the beneficiary central bank.

[97] See Article VI, section 4. The very-short-term financing facility is treated at pages 327–332, *supra.*

[98] The interest due is presently calculated from the return on investments with similar maturities in the currency delivered to the debtor central bank.

[99] Short-term support agreement, *supra* note 87, Article VII. The coordination of economic policy within the EEC is treated in Chapter 12, *infra,* page 589 et seq.

but its situation was looked into. Drawings were not in fact made by the Banca d'Italia until March 1974 when the full amount was drawn in U.S. dollars.[100] The repayment period was extended in June and again in September 1974. As the time came for repayment and Italy's balance-of-payments situation remained serious, the state requested the EEC's medium-term assistance described below. The Banca d'Italia also sought and obtained a credit line under the short-term facility in May 1976. This credit line was renewed on four occasions. Following a Community loan to Italy in May 1977, the Banca d'Italia in June 1977 relinquished this short-term monetary support which had been made available to it but never in fact used.[101] It should be noted that if a facility is made available but is not drawn upon within one month, and is not renewed, it is cancelled.[102]

Medium-Term Assistance under EEC Treaty Article 108

Medium-term financial assistance is available under decisions of the Council of Ministers of the European Communities pursuant to Article 108 of the EEC Treaty. This financial arrangement operates independently of the European Monetary Cooperation Fund. Decisions are made by finance ministers rather than by central bank governors. The machinery for medium-term financial assistance finds its genesis with the resolution adopted by the Council and the representatives of the governments of the member states on March 22, 1971, relating to the achievement by stages of economic and monetary union in the Community.[103] Since the 1971 program contemplated the achievement of balance-of-payments equilibrium primarily through multilateral coordination of economic policies rather than exchange rate changes, a means had to be provided for financing balance-of-payments deficits that would arise from time to time. Further, since the economic policy measures might in application take time to show their effects, medium- as compared to short-term financing would be necessary. Council Decision No. 71/143 of March 22, 1971, adopted the same day as the resolution looking toward monetary union, set up machinery for medium-term financial assistance.[104] The decision has been amended and extended a number of times,[105] and our discussion will center on the present ar-

---

[100] *16th Report on the Activities of the Monetary Committee*, points 19–22, in *Official Journal*, no. C-174, July 31, 1975, p. 1. The IMF approved a stand-by arrangement for Italy in April 1974 equivalent to SDR 1 billion. The Banca d'Italia also drew U.S. $2 billion under a bilateral currency facility with the Deutsche Bundesbank, pledging gold as collateral. Italy was thus able to obtain the financing that it needed at the time by drawing on several sources.

[101] *10th General Report on the Activities of the European Communities in 1976*, point 209; and *11th General Report 1977*, point 110. The Community loan is mentioned at pages 339–340, *infra*.

[102] Short-term support agreement, *supra* note 87, Article VI, section 2.

[103] See Chapters 2 and 12, pages 77 and 591.

[104] Council of Ministers Decision No. 71/143 of March 22, 1971; *Official Journal*, no. L-73, March 27, 1971, p. 15; *Official Journal—Special [English] Edition*, 1971(I), p. 177.

[105] Council Decision No. 71/143, *idem*, was amended and extended by the Act of Accession of Denmark,

rangement. The machinery is based on Articles 103 and 108 of the EEC Treaty, and is intended to avoid the necessity for countries in balance-of-payments difficulty to resort to the safeguards clauses of Article 108, subdivision 3, and Article 109, which permit derogations from Treaty obligations.[106]

Article 108, subdivision 2(c), of the Treaty of Rome provides that the Council, acting by a qualified majority, has authority to direct member states to grant limited credits, subject to their agreement, to a member that is in difficulties or threatened with difficulties because of an overall disequilibrium in the balance of payments or a shortage of a needed currency. The article provides in subdivisions 1 and 2 that the Council act following receipt of a recommendation for granting "mutual assistance" submitted by the Commission after the Commission has made a finding that the measures taken by the country, and those the Commission has recommended it take, are insufficient alone to promptly overcome the difficulties. Council Decision No. 71/143, as amended, settles in advance the ceilings and general terms on which credits are to be provided and, further, embodies a commitment of the member states to supply funds when subsequently directed to do so in accordance with that decision.[107]

A country contemplating a request for assistance first consults within the Monetary Committee with representatives of the Commission and representatives of the member states. A recommendation for medium-term assistance is then formulated by the Commission in consultation with the Monetary Committee. The recommendation is then submitted to the Council for adoption, by a qualified majority vote, as a decision or directive.[108] Each other member state, unless the Council grants an exemption, is obligated to grant its share of the credits decided upon. These credits are granted directly by the creditor states to the beneficiary state unless a different procedure is agreed upon. The credits are granted for two-to-five years, with the precise dates for repayment and rate of interest determined by the Council in each case.[109] The obligation to provide

Ireland, and the United Kingdom, Annex I, point VII(2); Act of Accession of Greece, Annex I, point VII(2); and Council Decisions No. 75/785 of December 18, 1975 (*Official Journal*, no. L-330, December 24, 1975, p. 50); No. 78/49 of December 19, 1977 (*O.J.*, no. L-14, January 18, 1978, p. 14); No. 78/1041 of December 21, 1978 (*O.J.*, no. L-379, December 30, 1978, p. 3); No. 80/1264 of December 15, 1980 (*O.J.*, no. L-375, December 31, 1980, p. 16); and No. 82/871 of December 17, 1982 (*O.J.*, no. L-368, December 28, 1982, p. 43).

The consolidated text, except for the subsequently revised commitment ceilings and expiration date, appears in *Compendium of Community Monetary Texts* (1979), *supra* note 4, p. 67. The revised commitment ceilings are set forth in Council Decision No. 80/1264, *supra*.

[106] See Chapter 2, pages 78–79, and Chapter 10, pages 473–477.

[107] Articles 1 and 4 of Decision No. 71/143 do not affect the rights granted member states in EEC Treaty Article 108, subdivision 2(c), to decline to agree to provide credits, but, in adopting the decision, the ministers as representatives of governments agreed to limitations on the exercise of those rights. See Hans Smit and Peter E. Herzog, *The Law of the European Economic Community: A Commentary on the EEC Treaty* (6 vols.; New York: Matthew Bender, binder service, 1983 ed.), part 3, p. 630.

[108] Articles 1 and 2 of Council Decision No. 71/143 as amended, *supra* note 105. For background on the organs and procedures of the European Communities, see Chapter 2, *supra*, page 79 et seq.

[109] Decision No. 71/143 as amended, *supra* note 105, Article 3.

funds under this facility falls on the national treasuries rather than the central banks of the EEC states. The commitment ceilings are currently expressed in ECUs.[110]

Claims and obligations arising from the implementation of this medium-term arrangement are expressed in ECUs. Where a national currency is provided, the amount will be determined on the basis of the daily conversion rate between that currency and the ECU at the time it is to be provided. The amount of a currency to be used to meet an interest payment or a repayment obligation is determined by the conversion rate between the currency used and the ECU at the due date of the particular operation.[111]

Normally no member state may draw more than 50 percent of the total credit ceilings. Use of the facility is conditional upon "undertakings aimed at restoring internal and external economic equilibrium." The Council, acting by a qualified majority vote on the basis of a recommendation of the Commission which shall have consulted the Monetary Committee, determines the undertakings the recipient must enter into. In making this determination the Council is to take into account the EEC guidelines on medium-term economic policy. Quantitative targets, together with a timetable for their achievement, may be set.[112] The general decision governing the facility, as amended, further provides:

> To ensure compliance with the conditions of economic policy, resources made available should, as far as possible, be paid in successive instalments, the release of each instalment being conditional on a review of the results obtained when compared with the targets set in the Decision granting the assistance.[113]

The Council by affirmative decision decides on the release of installments. If the conditions which brought about recourse to the facility subsequently change because, for example, the country obtains other financing or its balance-of-payments situation improves more rapidly than originally contemplated, the Council can call for advance repayment of the debt either in whole or in part.[114]

---

[110] The commitment ceilings currently total ECU 14,370 million. Annex to Decision No. 71/143 as amended by Council Decision No. 80/1264 of December 15, 1980, *supra* note 105.

[111] See Decision No. 71/143 as amended, *supra* note 105, Article 3, section 5. There is an exception. If credits advanced by member states under this facility are refinanced from outside the system, the debtor state is required to agree that the debt, originally denominated in ECUs, shall be replaced by a debt denominated in the currency used for the refinancing. If the rate of interest is altered in connection with the refinancing, the debtor country bears the additional cost unless the Council by an *ad hoc* decision makes some other arrangement for sharing the additional cost. Article 5, section 2.

See note 8, *supra,* and accompanying text regarding the determination of the conversion rate between the ECU and a national currency.

[112] Decision No. 71/143 as amended, *supra* note 105, Article 3. The formulation and use of economic policy guidelines in the European Economic Community are treated in Chapter 12, *infra,* page 589 et seq.

[113] Article 3, section 2.

[114] Article 3, sections 2 and 3.

Member states provide funds to the beneficiary in proportion to their quotas adjusted for all their claims outstanding.[115] Prior to an amendment effective in 1978, a member state that was to provide assistance could unilaterally exempt itself from that obligation if it maintained that difficulties existed or were foreseen in its own balance of payments.[116] Now it can be exempted only by an affirmative decision of the Council taken by a qualified majority vote.[117] A creditor state that has provided assistance can, at any time, by mutual agreement with another member state transfer its claim for interest and repayment to that state. Further, if a creditor subsequently encounters or is severely threatened with balance-of-payments difficulties, the Council is to arrange for "mobilization" of its claim through transfer of it to another member state, refinancing the claim from outside the system (e.g., by the provision of a Community loan to the debtor), or by early repayment by the debtor state.[118] Under an agreement between the EEC and the Bank for International Settlements, EEC creditor-country central banks can, on the basis of their claims, conclude stand-by credit arrangements with the BIS.[119]

The first and only use to date of this assistance mechanism was in December 1974 when the Council directed the member states pursuant to EEC Treaty Article 108, subdivision 2, to loan Italy a total of 1,159,200,000 units of account (U.S. $1,398,400,920).[120] Because the United Kingdom maintained that it was suffering balance-of-payments problems at the time, it was not directed to participate.[121] The funds provided by the other seven states amounted to ap-

---

[115] Article 3, section 4.

[116] Article 4 of the original Decision No. 71/143 of March 22, 1971, *supra* note 104. The United Kingdom exempted itself from providing medium-term assistance to Italy in 1974. See note 121, *infra*, and accompanying text.

[117] Article 4, section 1, of Decision No. 71/143 as amended by Decision No. 78/49 of December 19, 1977, *supra* note 105.

[118] Decision No. 71/143 as amended, *supra* note 105, Article 4, section 2.

[119] Agreement between the EEC and the Bank for International Settlements of October 30, 1978, appended to Council of Ministers Decision No. 78/897 of October 30, 1978; *Official Journal*, no. L-316, November 10, 1978, p. 21; *Compendium of Community Monetary Texts* (1979), *supra* note 4, p. 70.

[120] Council of Ministers Directive No. 74/637 of December 17, 1974, granting medium-term financial assistance to Italy. *Official Journal*, no. L-341, December 20, 1974, p. 51; *Compendium of Community Monetary Texts—Supplement* (1976), *supra* note 58, p. 26.

The directive required that assistance to Italy be provided in the form of U.S. dollars and fixed a single exchange rate between the U.S. dollar and the decision's unit of account to be used in connection with the provision of assistance and subsequent interest payments and repayments of principal. The effect was to make the dollar the effective denominator of all operations in connection with the assistance. See Article 4 of Directive No. 74/637. Today, the ECU would be used as the denominator. See notes 110 and 111, *supra*, and accompanying text.

For background on the Italian situation at the time this assistance was granted, see Smit and Herzog, *supra* note 107, part 3, pp. 620–22 and 631–32; and European Communities, *16th Report on the Activities of the Monetary Committee, Official Journal*, no. C-174, July 31, 1975, p. 1 at p. 11.

[121] The Bank of England continued to grant and renew short-term credits to the Banca d'Italia under the short-term support facility described at pages 334–335. The Banca d'Italia repaid the Bank of England's short-term credits in December 1976.

Today, the United Kingdom in a similar case could not unilaterally exempt itself from participation. The

proximately two-thirds of their total commitments under the facility at the time. The amounts were provided immediately the next day in the form of U.S. dollar balances. Repayment was completed in September 1978. The interest rate approximated the market rate at the time. The 1974 directive stated economic policy undertakings of Italy for the first 15 months in considerable detail. Some of the conditions, such as those relating to credit in the economy, government expenditure levels, and the deficit on treasury transactions, were stated in quantitative terms. After the Community itself made loans to Italy in 1976 and 1977, the economic policy conditions used for the medium-term assistance were the same as for the Community loans.[122]

European Community Loans

The problems encountered in the mid-1970s by EEC countries (particularly Italy) in financing oil imports at increasingly higher prices led Community officials, while leaving the medium-term facility in place, to explore financing techniques that would not be dependent on the resources of the treasuries and central banks of the member states, since the oil crisis was expected to cause deterioration in the balance-of-payments positions of most EEC countries. Regulation No. 397/75, adopted by the Council of Ministers in February 1975, authorized the Community itself to borrow funds directly from third countries, from public or private financial institutions, or on the capital markets, with the sole aim of relending them to one or more member states in balance-of-payments difficulties caused by increases in prices of petroleum products.[123] Another regulation, No. 398/75 adopted at the same time, established a procedure whereby the Council could require the member states to provide foreign exchange to the Community to enable it to make payments on its borrowings should the member to which it reloaned the funds happen to default.[124]

The first Community borrowings under Regulation No. 397/75 were in March and April 1976. A total equivalent to approximately U.S. $1.3 billion was borrowed through private placements and public issues and re-loaned to

Council would examine its balance-of-payments position and exempt it only if justified. See note 117, *supra,* and accompanying text.

[122] Council Directive No. 74/637, *supra* note 120, Articles 5–9; Council Directive No. 75/784 of December 18, 1975, *Official Journal,* no. L-330, December 24, 1975, p. 48; and Council Directive No. 77/360 of May 17, 1977, *O.J.*, no. L-132, May 27, 1977, p. 36.

Italy did not achieve all of the performance targets. As the revised mechanism now works, drawings are normally to be phased with each successive drawing keyed to the observance of policy commitments associated with the earlier ones. See page 337, *supra.*

[123] Council Regulation No. 397/75 of February 17, 1975; *Official Journal,* no. L-46, February 20, 1975, p. 1; *Compendium of Community Monetary Texts* (1979), *supra* note 4, p. 77. The broad enabling power granted by Article 235 of the EEC Treaty (quoted in Chapter 2 at page 80) is the authority for adoption of the regulation. See also the opinion of the Monetary Committee; *Compendium* (1979), p. 73.

[124] Council Regulation No. 398/75 of February 17, 1975; *Official Journal,* no. L-46, February 20, 1975, p. 3; *Compendium of Community Monetary Texts* (1979), *supra* note 4, p. 80.

Italy and Ireland.[125] Subsequently a part of this loan was refinanced, and in May 1977 a second loan was floated.[126] The Community's on-lending to Italy in 1976 and 1977, equivalent to approximately U.S. $1.5 billion, was accompanied by economic policy conditions including limits on government expenditures, the treasury deficit, the financing of this deficit by the monetary authorities, and the growth of total domestic lending.[127] The conditions on the loan to Ireland, equivalent to approximately U.S. $300 million, were keyed to control of government borrowing, the financing of government borrowing by non-monetary means, and control of private credit.[128]

Regulations Nos. 397/75 and 398/75 were replaced by Council Regulation No. 682/81 of March 16, 1981.[129] This regulation simplified the procedure for the Community to borrow funds from third countries, financial institutions, and the capital markets, and to re-lend those funds to member states in balance-of-payments difficulties directly or indirectly related to increases in prices of petroleum products. The new regulation eliminated the Council's authority to require member states to provide funds, if necessary, for the Community to meet its obligations under its borrowings.

The first use of Regulation No. 682/81 was in 1983 when the Council approved a Community loan equivalent to ECU 4 billion (about U.S. $3.7 billion) to France.[130] The Community borrowed the needed funds on the international capital markets.[131] The Council's decision approving the loan to France did not include any explicit policy conditions, but the "whereas" clauses recited key

---

[125] See Council Decision No. 76/322 of March 15, 1976; *Official Journal,* no. L-77, March 24, 1976, p. 12; *Compendium of Community Monetary Texts—Supplement* (1976), *supra* note 58, p. 38. See also Bank for International Settlements, *47th Annual Report 1976/77,* pp. 155–56.

[126] A portion of the borrowing in March and April 1976 was at a variable interest rate, and the Community subsequently refinanced that portion through public offerings and a private placement at fixed interest rates. A second loan for the benefit of Italy was floated by the EEC in May 1977 in the form of a Eurobond issue in two tranches totaling U.S. $500 million. See *Bulletin of the European Communities,* 1977, no. 3, point 2.1.5, and no. 5, point 2.1.2; and Council Decisions No. 76/771 of September 20, 1976, No. 77/232 of March 14, 1977, No. 77/361 of May 17, 1977, and No. 77/414 of June 14, 1977; *Official Journal,* no. L-265, September 29, 1976, p. 27; no. L-72, March 19, 1977, p. 25; no. L-132, May 27, 1977, p. 37; and no. L-149, June 17, 1977, p. 24. See also "The Community's Borrowing and Lending Operations: Recent Developments Affecting Certain Instruments," *European Economy,* no. 8 (March 1981), p. 101 at p. 107 (table 3).

[127] Council Decision No. 76/324 of March 15, 1976; *Official Journal,* no. L-77, March 24, 1976, p. 16; *Compendium of Community Monetary Texts—Supplement* (1976), *supra* note 58, p. 41.

[128] Council Decision No. 76/323 of March 15, 1976; *Official Journal,* no. L-77, March 24, 1976, p. 15; *Compendium of Community Monetary Texts—Supplement* (1976), *supra* note 58, p. 40.

[129] Council Regulation No. 682/81 of March 16, 1981; *Official Journal,* no. L-73, March 19, 1981, p. 1. See *22d Report on the Activities of the Monetary Committee, Official Journal,* no. C-124, May 25, 1981, p. 1 at pp. 11–16 and 18–19; and "The Community's Borrowing and Lending Operations," *supra* note 126, pp. 105–11.

[130] Council Decision No. 83/298 of May 16, 1983; *Official Journal,* no. L-153, June 11, 1983, p. 44.

[131] The EEC launched the borrowings in June 1983. The borrowings included bonds denominated in ECUs with fixed interest rates and notes denominated in U.S. dollars with a floating interest rate. European Communities press release of June 10, 1983.

elements of France's adjustment program which had been described to the Council.[132]

Regulation No. 682/81, as its predecessors, is limited to the financing of balance-of-payments problems related directly or indirectly to petroleum price increases. The limitation did not prevent the loan to France in 1983 at a time when world petroleum prices expressed in francs were rising but expressed in dollars were steady or declining. There is no legal impediment to the regulation being amended or supplemented to deal with balance-of-payments problems that have causes not even indirectly related to changes in petroleum prices. Indeed, the Community has loaned funds for purposes not explicitly related to the balance of payments, such as investment projects financed under the New Community Instrument.[133]

Other EEC Financing Procedures

In addition to the four procedures described above, all of which are designed to provide balance-of-payments support (very-short-term financing through the European Monetary Cooperation Fund in connection with EMS market interventions, short-term monetary support through the FECOM, medium-term support directly from member states under Article 108, and Community loans under Regulation No. 682/81), other forms of assistance that are not specifically directed to balance-of-payments problems are available in the Community. These include, for example, loans under the New Community Instrument, loans from the European Investment Bank and the European Regional Development Fund, and assistance from the European Social Fund.[134] Thus, members of the European Economic Community have a variety of sources of funds available to them through Community organs.

---

[132] "Whereas" clauses in Decision No. 83/298, *supra* note 130. The recitals, *inter alia,* included: Budget deficits would be held to 3 percent of gross domestic product in 1983 and 1984, the annual rate of growth of the money supply would be reduced to 9 percent for 1983, and limitations on foreign currency for tourist travel would be abolished by December 31, 1983. Compare the procedure for imposing conditions contemplated by the Monetary Committee when Regulation No. 682/81 was adopted; *22d Report on the Activities of the Monetary Committee, supra* note 129, p. 14. See also Chapter 10, *infra,* page 476 (note 452).

[133] Council Decision No. 78/870 of October 16, 1978, as amended by Decision No. 82/169 of March 15, 1982, and Decision No. 83/200 of April 19, 1983. *Official Journal,* no. L-298, October 25, 1978, p. 9; no. L-78, March 24, 1982, p. 19; and no. L-112, April 28, 1983, p. 26.

[134] See *CCH Common Market Reports, supra* note 11, paragraphs 3601.62, 3622.20, 4001–4025, and 4100–4115. See also "Borrowing and Lending Instruments in the Context of the Community's Financial Instruments," *European Economy,* no. 6 (July 1980), p. 75; and "The Community's Borrowing and Lending Operations," *supra* note 126, pp. 108–11.

Reflections

Legal Characteristics of the ECU

At the present time the European currency unit (ECU) is used as a monetary asset in EEC central bank transactions, and that use is primarily in the very-short-term financing mechanism, administered by the European Monetary Cooperation Fund (FECOM), that is related to the European Monetary System's exchange rate arrangement.[135] The ECU is also used as a unit of account in other financing procedures.[136] One can expect organs of the European Communities to take actions to further widen the use of the ECU as both a unit of account and monetary asset.[137]

The present system under which ECUs are issued through revolving swaps between EEC central banks and the FECOM was originally scheduled for liquidation in early 1981, but the date was postponed. It is expected that a new institution, the European Monetary Fund, will be established at a future time and that it will succeed the FECOM as the issuer of ECUs. Many of the rules respecting the issuance and use of ECUs will be reviewed and some may be changed.

A basic issue to be addressed is whether the ECU is to be a fully-backed monetary instrument. At the present time, for each ECU issued, an equivalent amount of gold and U.S. dollars has been contributed to the FECOM. A central bank has a right to exchange ECUs held by it, up to the amount issued to it by the FECOM, for an equivalent amount of gold and dollars.[138]

The ECU, as a backed monetary instrument, can be contrasted with the IMF special drawing right (SDR). The SDR is a form of fiat money. An IMF member holding SDRs has a right to exchange them for a freely usable currency. The practical exercise of that right is dependent upon the good faith of the participants in the SDR system to honor their legal commitments to accept SDRs and provide freely usable currency in exchange. So long as participants and holders of SDRs are confident that the asset is exchangeable in fact for freely usable currency, the SDR system can function smoothly.[139] While the IMF and its members hold substantial quantities of gold, there is no obligation on the IMF or its members to provide gold in exchange for SDRs. The FECOM has an obligation to provide gold in exchange for ECUs, but only in one situation—the unwinding of a swap transaction with a central bank that was issued ECUs—and then the central bank receives back only the amount of gold it contributed. Whether the ECU should continue to be a fully backed asset is an

---

[135] The very-short-term facility is treated at page 327 et seq.
[136] See, e.g., notes 6, 89, 110, 111, *supra,* and accompanying text.
[137] See pages 316 and 320–323, *supra.*
[138] See note 46, *supra,* and accompanying text.
[139] See Chapter 5, *supra,* pages 172–173 and 210–221.

open question. If the ECU does not remain a fully backed asset, there may be a need for a designation procedure similar to that used for the SDR.[140]

If it is decided to maintain the ECU as a backed asset, it will be necessary to decide whether to issue ECUs only against gold and U.S. dollars or to broaden or narrow the list of acceptable counterpart assets. The Council of Ministers regulation authorizing the FECOM to issue ECUs provides that they are to be issued against "monetary reserves from the monetary authorities of the Member States."[141] This language would permit the FECOM, if it should decide to do so, to issue ECUs against SDRs or currencies other than the dollar. In order for the FECOM to accept SDRs, it would, of course, have to be prescribed by the International Monetary Fund as an "other holder" of SDRs.[142]

At the present time ECUs can be held and used only by monetary authorities of EEC countries.[143] Should monetary authorities of other countries, and/or the IMF, be authorized to obtain and use ECUs in transactions with central banks of the EEC or with the FECOM? Should the FECOM be authorized to issue ECUs to monetary authorities outside the EEC that contribute to the FECOM gold, dollars, or other acceptable assets?[144] Should commercial banks and private firms be permitted to hold and use ECUs? They can now, of course, use the ECU as a unit of account but are not permitted to hold ECUs directly.[145] The reader will recall that only official entities are permitted to hold SDRs.[146]

At the present time the EEC central banks that are parties to the central bank agreement on operating procedures for the European Monetary System contribute 20 percent of their gold and U.S. dollar reserves and in turn are issued an equivalent amount of ECUs under a revolving swap arrangement with a three-month maturity.[147] The key variables that determine the number of ECUs issued are the price of gold, the exchange rate of the dollar against the ECU, and the total holdings of gold and dollars and their relative proportions. Neither the FECOM nor any other institution of the European Communities has control

---

[140] See Chapter 5, *supra*, pages 194–201. See also *Directorate-General Report, supra* note 15, pp. 60–61 and 86–87.

[141] Council Regulation No. 3181/78, *supra* note 4, Article 1.

[142] See Chapter 5, *supra*, pages 175–176.

[143] See page 320, *supra*.

[144] See Report by Alternates of the Monetary Committee of February 3, 1982, in *Directorate-General Report, supra* note 15, p. 79 at p. 84. See also *Directorate-General Report, idem*, pp. 122–24.

[145] See Commission communication to the Council of March 15, 1982, in *Directorate-General Report, idem*, p. 88 at p. 89; and Commission communication to the Council of May 24, 1983, in *European Economy*, no. 18 (November 1983), p. 185. See also *Directorate-General Report, supra*, pp. 50–51, 56, and 72–73; David F. Lomax, "International Moneys and Monetary Arrangements in Private Markets," in George M. von Furstenberg (ed.), *International Money and Credit: The Policy Roles* (Washington: IMF, 1983), p. 261; André L. Swings and Robert Triffin (ed.), *The Private Use of the ECU* (Brussels: Kredietbank, 1980); and Robert Triffin, "The European Monetary System and the Dollar in the Framework of the World Monetary System," in Banca Nazionale del Lavoro, *Quarterly Review*, no. 142 (September 1982), p. 245 at pp. 256–59.

[146] See Chapter 5, *supra*, pages 175–176.

[147] See pages 320–323, *supra*.

over any of these variables. Of all the variables, the price of gold has fluctuated the most widely and has caused wide swings in the volume of ECUs in existence from one three-month period to another. When the EMS began, 23 billion ECU were issued in March 1979. The total issued in April 1981 was almost 50 billion. The number fell to 42 billion at the beginning of 1982. The number created appears to have no particular relation to need.[148]

Should the total quantity of ECUs to be issued continue to be determined, as now, by a formula keyed to the size of national monetary reserves or should the quantity be deliberately managed by joint decisons?[149] If by joint decisions, who should prepare and who should make the decisions—Commission, central banks, finance ministers? Should ECUs be issued to central banks, as at present, or to national treasuries?

Should swap transactions continue to be used as the mechanism for issuing ECUs or should EEC countries contribute reserves to a common fund and give up some of their rights to return of those reserves? How should the contributed reserves be managed? Jean-Jacques Rey has pointed out:

> Practical considerations were clearly given overwhelming priority in designing the legal framework which supports the creation of ECUs. The process of asset substitution is carried far enough to be fully reflected in the accounting and settlement practices of central banks . . . but not so far as to be irreversible or to require major changes in the management of exchange reserves and in the administrative equipment of the E.M.C.F. [FECOM].[150]

Perhaps changes in the management of the contributed reserves should be considered. But, if the FECOM is to manage the reserves, it probably should bear a portion of the risk and reward resulting from that management.[151]

The present right of a central bank on two-working-days' notice to unwind the revolving swap under which it was issued ECUs by the FECOM makes it very attractive for a central bank to participate in the ECU system. At the same time, to the extent that a bank makes a net transfer of ECUs to another participant in the system, the bank loses a claim on gold and dollars. If the gold and dollars redeemable by a central bank for ECUs can be predicted to rise in value relative to the basket value of the ECU (which is determined by market values of EEC national currencies) financial incentives are created for a central bank to hold rather than use ECUs. The reverse situation would create opposite incen-

[148] See *Directorate-General Report, supra* note 15, p. 71 (table 3).

[149] For discussion of this issue, see *Directorate-General Report, idem,* pp. 42–45, 79–83, and 88–89.

[150] Jean-Jacques Rey, "The European Monetary System," *Common Market Law Review,* vol. 17 (1980), p. 7 at pp. 26–27. The management of the gold and dollars contributed to the FECOM under swap agreements at the present time is treated at pages 323–325, *supra.*

[151] See *Directorate-General Report, supra* note 15, pp. 62 and 108–13.

tives. What is the proper balance between incentives to hold and incentives to use this asset? The short-term character of the three-month swap arrangements under which ECUs are issued appears to encourage central banks to maintain holdings near equilibrium levels and to be cautious in their use of ECUs.[152]

At the present time interest is paid by a central bank only on net use of ECUs and earned only on net accumulations, using the amount of ECUs issued to the central bank as the benchmark. Under this system, each central bank is entrusted with the safekeeping of the gold and the investment of the dollars it contributes to the FECOM in ECU-issuance transactions and, in turn, that bank keeps the interest earned. An alternative system would provide for interest to be paid on all ECU balances and for the FECOM to manage the investment of the assets contributed to it and obtain the interest and the profits and losses on its investments.[153]

At the present time, central banks participating in the very-short-term financing facility are not required to accept ECUs in settlements in an amount exceeding 50 percent of the claim being settled.[154] Proposals have been made to abolish this limit, although to date the limit does not appear to have significantly impacted the use of ECUs.[155]

Finally, should the ECU, like the SDR, continue to be valued on the basis of a composite consisting of portions of national currencies? Inevitably, officials of countries holding such a composite asset will examine the components of the basket and may not like all that they see. Comments in Chapters 5 and 12 about the valuation and interest rate of the SDR may also have relevance to the ECU.[156] The European currency unit might at some point be freed from formal valuation in terms of any other monetary instruments. Robert Triffin has argued: "The ECU is—like the dollar—a reference currency and should *not* be defined by the currencies referring themselves to it. . . . The ECU should be merely an ECU, as the dollar is a dollar, and—according to Gertrude Stein—a rose is a rose, is a rose. . . ."[157]

The long list of questions above, which are prompted by reflection on the legal characteristics of the European currency unit, suggests that the legal features of this recently introduced monetary instrument need not be treated as frozen.

---

[152] See *Directorate-General Report, idem,* p. 46 (table 18).

[153] See *Directorate-General Report, idem,* pp. 108–13.

[154] See note 73, *supra,* and accompanying text.

[155] See *Directorate-General Report, supra* note 15, pp. 44, 53, 55–57, 60–61, and 101–03. Compare *Report of the Deutsche Bundesbank for the Year 1981,* p. 80. The reader will recall that a participant in the IMF's Special Drawing Rights Department is not required to accept SDRs that would raise its total holdings above 300 percent of net cumulative allocation.

[156] At pages 193, 221 and 630–638.

[157] Triffin, "The European Monetary System and the Dollar," *supra* note 145, p. 259. See Appendix A, *infra,* pages 664–665.

Credit Mechanisms

The credit facilities described earlier in this chapter are of a bewildering variety. Some are operated by the European Monetary Cooperation Fund while, for others, decisions on each extension of credit are made by the Council of Ministers. The very-short-term financing facility operated by the FECOM is used frequently and in large amounts. By contrast, the medium-term mechanism specifically provided for in Article 108 of the Treaty of Rome has been used only once, for the benefit of Italy in 1974. One can anticipate that at some time in the future there will be an effort to rationalize the disparate facilities.[158]

The use of all the facilities, except the very-short-term facility for financing EMS interventions, involves a review of the drawing country's economic policies. Use of the facility for financing EMS interventions requires a commitment to that narrow margins regime. The multilateral review of national economic policies in the European Economic Community is treated further in Chapter 12.[159]

---

[158] See *Directorate-General Report, supra* note 15, pp. 59–64, 114–20, and 126 (table).
[159] At page 589 et seq.

Chapter 9: The Transferable Ruble
and the Settlement and Credit Operations
of the International Bank for Economic
Cooperation

Introduction

The institutional structure and purposes of the International Bank for Economic Cooperation (IBEC), to which all members of the Council for Mutual Economic Assistance (CMEA) belong and which has its headquarters in Moscow, were described in Chapter 2.[1] The focus of this chapter is on the settlement of international transactions by the socialist countries generally and on the settlement and credit operations of the IBEC in particular. However, before proceeding to these matters, it is necessary to understand aspects of the economic organization of CMEA countries and the role of the price system in the international trade of these countries.

Economic Organization and Pricing in CMEA Countries

Economic Organization

Each member state of the Council for Mutual Economic Assistance has a centrally planned economy with state ownership of the principal means of production. Government authorities make decisions on the growth and structure of the economy, the sectors to be favored for development, the allocations of resources and labor, the production of goods, the distribution of goods, and the supply of services. These decisions are made both in the aggregate and down to the level of individual industrial plants. The degree to which discretion in decision-making is delegated varies from one CMEA country to another and from one economic sector to another within a country. The monetary system and ac-

---

[1] At pages 90–93, *supra*. See generally page 87 et seq. where the institutional structure of the CMEA is treated.

counting procedures are used to facilitate the carrying out of the national economic plan.[2]

A commentator has pointed out that "the relevant and operational difference between socialist and capitalist economies is not so much ownership of the means of production as the role assigned to the price system."[3] The focus of attention of central planners is on the optimal deployment of human and material resources in terms of the planners' judgment of the country's social objectives. Domestic prices of all manner of goods and services as well as salaries and wages for workers in the various industries and callings can be dictated by government and need not constrain central planners. World prices as they affect planning for exports and imports and industrial specialization will receive comment later.

To facilitate planning, and the monitoring of plan performance, a national monetary unit is used as a common denominator for cost accounting (khozraschet). In most CMEA countries the cost of labor and materials used by a firm and the social value of its output are assigned monetary values. Firms operate under approved budgets which include items not only for costs and receipts but also planned profits and taxes. The decisions of managers of firms are guided by the government plans and directions received, by the budgets under which the firms operate, and by prevailing prices in the economy to the extent that managers have discretion in the selection of suppliers and customers. In some cases managers may be given a measure of discretion in pricing the firm's product within a range established centrally. The manager's task is, first, to meet production goals and, second, to maximize profitability.[4] Adam Zwass,

---

[2] In capitalist countries, by comparison, the government (with some exceptions) does not plan and supervise the economic activities of individual enterprises. The government may have the capability, of course, to deliberately determine specific economic decisions in areas of government procurement, government-provided services, and to some extent with respect to regulated industries. It can influence decisions by taxation and subsidy policies. But, in capitalist countries, to a large extent, economic decisions are made privately in a decentralized manner on the basis of present and anticipated market prices and costs. The effective functioning of the price system, and the underlying monetary and banking system, is critical to a system of decentralized economic decision-making; and governmental policies may be directed to smooth functioning of these market mechanisms. In developed capitalist countries, and in many less developed countries as well, fiscal and monetary policy is used by governmental authorities to influence broad economic aggregates such as general levels of consumption, general levels of investment, levels of prices, and labor employment—policymakers being prevented in large measure from dictating the decisions of individual enterprises and persons.

[3] Comment of George Garvy in introduction to Adam Zwass, *Monetary Cooperation Between East and West* (trans. by Michel Vale; White Plains, N.Y.: International Arts and Sciences Press, 1975), p. xv.

[4] On the price system in Eastern European countries, see generally Alan Abouchar (ed.), *The Socialist Price Mechanism* (Durham: Duke University Press, 1977); Jozef M. van Brabant, *Socialist Economic Integration* (Cambridge: Cambridge University Press, 1980), pp. 55–98; J. Wilczynski, *Comparative Monetary Economics* (London: Macmillan, 1978), pp. 64–77; Adam Zwass, *Money, Banking and Credit in the Soviet Union and Eastern Europe* (trans. by Michel C. Vale; White Plains, N.Y.: M. E. Sharpe, 1979), pp. 24–56; and Mark Allen, "The Structure and Reform of the Exchange and Payments Systems of Some East European Countries," *IMF Staff Papers*, vol. 23 (1976), p. 718 at pp. 718–29.

In recent years Hungary has simplified its domestic price system and has sought to harmonize domestic

who has held official posts in Poland and in the CMEA Secretariat in Moscow, has commented:

> Even the planned economies have been unable to devise a better criterion than profit by which to measure the efficiency of production. In all the planned economies, whatever their specific form, profit is becoming a universal standard for assessing enterprise performance. Experience has shown that peak performance cannot be expected unless a reasonable portion of the profit is left to the enterprise and its management. However, profit can fulfill the function intended for it only if other factors are allowed some play, and one of the most important of these is prices, which must remain within striking range of the social value of the product.[5]

Each CMEA member has a state bank that issues the country's currency. Money is created primarily through the extension of credit by banking institutions in the form of deposit money with the banks to be used for payments effected by deposit transfers and in the form of cash for consumer trade. The socialist organizations and enterprises to which credit will be extended and the terms of that credit are marked out as part of the central planning process and implement decisions on production and trade. At the domestic level, the extension of credit by the banking system to an enterprise serves an accounting function. It is not, as in capitalist countries, an independently determined variable that affects economic performance.[6]

Banks in socialist countries play an important role in monitoring plan performance. All enterprises are obligated to keep deposits with government banks and to settle their business transactions through them. Credit to enterprises is extended by the banks. By handling payments, the banks monitor the movement of goods; through granting short-term credits they supervise inventories; they keep track of project costs and construction deadlines on investment proj-

---

wholesale prices and export prices. See László Rácz, "On the New Price System," *Közgazdasági Szemle*, vol. 27 (1980), no. 2, p. 129, trans. in *Eastern European Economics*, vol. 20, no. 1 (Fall 1981), p. 49; and Patrick de Fontenay et al., *Hungary: An Economic Survey* (IMF Occasional Paper no. 15; Washington, 1982), pp. 11–12.

For procedures followed in Bulgaria for setting prices, see Bulgaria Ministry of Finance, Regulation on the Procedure and Documents for Setting, Approving, and Registering Prices of Goods, Work, and Services. *Durzhaven Vestnik* (Sofia), November 2, 1982, p. 1046, trans. in Joint Publications Research Service, *East Europe Report: Economic and Industrial Affairs* (no. 2352), J.P.R.S. no. 82505 (December 21, 1982), p. 1.

[5] Zwass, *Monetary Cooperation, supra* note 3, p. 4. See also N. Duta, "Profits: An Essential Requirement of Economic Management," *Revista Economica* (Bucharest), January 5, 1979, no. 1, p. 7, trans. in Joint Publications Research Service, *Translations on Eastern Europe: Economic and Industrial Affairs (no. 1878)*, J.P.R.S. no. 73177 (April 6, 1979), p. 103.

[6] See generally Zwass, *Money, Banking and Credit, supra* note 4, pp. 78–154; and George Garvy, *Money, Financial Flows, and Credit in the Soviet Union* (Cambridge, Mass.: Ballinger Publishing Co., 1977), pp. 36–133 and 190–198.

ects; and they see that wage funds of enterprises are maintained at proper levels as they disburse wages and salaries.

Control of International Trade

In all CMEA countries, trade with nonresidents requires governmental approval whether the transactions are with residents of other CMEA member states or with other countries.[7] Approval may be granted or withheld for broad classes of transactions or be given on a case-by-case basis. To put it simply, at the present time (except for tourist and some other limited transactions) nonresidents do not have the right to enter a CMEA country and purchase desired goods at local prices. The prices for approved export transactions may be very different from internal prices. Also, residents do not have freedom to purchase goods and services from nonresidents.

Most enterprises in the Soviet Union do not handle their own foreign trade. Foreign trade is usually handled centrally through state foreign trade organizations linked to the Ministry of Foreign Trade. These trade organizations are specialized in terms of the goods and services with which they deal.[8] In other CMEA countries large firms and industrial associations are granted the right to carry out foreign trade transactions on their own behalf. Alternatively, they may trade through specialized government foreign trade enterprises working on commission. In either case the activities are subject to supervision by central government authorities.[9]

In a highly centralized planned economy, imports are not expected to compete with domestic products or to stimulate domestic output or efficiencies in those product lines. Imports are seen as simply supplementing the domestic production, as supplying desired items not otherwise available quite apart from price.

---

[7] One of the early actions of socialist officials upon coming to power in Russia was to declare foreign trade to be a state monopoly. Decree on Nationalization of Foreign Trade, *Izvestia*, April 23, 1918, p. 4; *Sobranie Uzakonenii i Rasporiazhenii Raboche-Krest'ianskogo Pravitel'stva Rossiiskoi Sovetskoi Federativnoi Sotsialisticheskoi Respubliki*, 1918, no. 33, item 432; trans. in William E. Butler, *Commercial, Business, and Trade Laws: The Soviet Union and Mongolia* (Dobbs Ferry: Oceana Publications, 1982), p. 1. See generally John B. Quigley, Jr., *The Soviet Foreign Trade Monopoly: Institutions and Laws* (Columbus: Ohio State University Press, 1974); and V. Pozdnyakov, "The Constitutional Principles of the State Monopoly of Soviet Foreign Trade," *Foreign Trade* (Moscow), 1978, no. 7, p. 11.

[8] See generally sources cited in note 7, *supra;* and Zwass, *Monetary Cooperation, supra* note 3, pp. 52–56. See also Dietrich André Loeber, *East-West Trade* (4 vols.; Dobbs Ferry: Oceana Publications, 1976), vol. 2, pp. 3–9, 41–56, and 80–101.

[9] See Zwass, *Monetary Cooperation, supra* note 3, pp. 77–85; and Loeber, *supra* note 8, vol. 2, pp. 18–40, 57–63, 73, and 102–53. See, e.g., Hungary Decree No. 1 of 1974 on foreign exchange management, trans. in Loeber, *idem*, vol. 4, p. 77.

Prices Used in International Trade

Prices used in trade between firms in CMEA countries and firms in capitalist countries are negotiated. They are influenced by supply and demand factors on the world market and can be described as market prices. They may diverge widely from internal prices in the CMEA country, which may have an economy that for planning purposes has been deliberately insulated from the outside world. Prices are normally quoted in a widely used convertible currency such as the U.S. dollar.

In the past most intra-CMEA trade has consisted of bartered transactions. While prices stated in terms of a currency served an accounting function, what was important in the end was that 60 wigets manufactured in country A were in fact exchanged for 40 gigets manufactured in country B. If the contract was properly performed, no money would permanently change hands.

In order to facilitate the transition of intra-CMEA trade from bilateral barter to increased use of multilateral transactions and to the exchange of goods for financial instruments, the International Bank for Economic Cooperation was formed, beginning operations in 1964. The Bank issues the "transferable ruble," which is a common denominator for intra-CMEA trade. It can properly be called the "IBEC ruble," to make clear that it is independent of the ruble of the Soviet Union.[10]

A process that properly assigns prices in intra-CMEA trade will become increasingly important as trade is multilateralized and monetized. Officials of CMEA countries have generally in the past been of the view that, in trade between themselves, world market prices were not satisfactory because their fluctuation added an element of uncertainty to long-term planning, since agreements among CMEA countries for exchange of goods often run for a period of five years. They have also been reluctant to use world prices that were viewed as biased by cyclical and other factors peculiar to capitalist markets. Internal prices in individual CMEA countries could not be used because those prices reflected individual national priorities and were not intended as a basis for international trade.

To date transferable ruble values have been assigned to trade transactions using prices in world markets, after certain critical adjustments, as the measure of the relative value of one good compared to another, where there is active world trade in the commodity. The procedure is that negotiators submit data on prices in world markets, especially in markets in which CMEA members might be inclined to buy Western goods. These world prices are carefully documented for the most recent five-year period. Average prices are calculated. These prices are then adjusted for transportation costs. They may also be adjusted for

---

[10] This monetary instrument is described, *infra,* page 360 et seq.

taxes and subsidies in effect in capitalist countries and other factors described as cyclical, seasonal, and speculative features of capitalist markets. In addition there may be adjustments for national costs of producing the goods in socialist countries. Since these adjustments involve the exercise of judgment, there is in practice an opportunity for bargaining among CMEA countries about correct prices. Inevitably to some degree, a country's representatives make judgments about what other CMEA members will be prepared to exchange for their exports and seek to assure that relative prices reflect those judgments. The agreed adjusted world prices are expressed in a widely used Western convertible currency (such as the U.S. dollar) and are then translated into transferable rubles (IBEC rubles) using a unitary and essentially arbitrary translation rate.[11] A formal consensus is then reached on the prices stated in transferable rubles. These common prices for intra-CMEA trade were formerly set at stable levels for the entire term of a five-year goods exchange plan. Since 1975 they have usually been set for one year at a time. While trade is supposed to take place at prices based on the CMEA prices, no country is required to trade any class of goods which it does not wish to trade. Further, there may be some deviation from these CMEA prices in bilateral trade arrangements with the agreement of the two parties involved. In conclusion, it is proper to say that to the present time the prices of goods in intra-CMEA trade are in some measure independent of both world prices and national internal prices in CMEA countries and, further, are not tied to national production costs in CMEA countries.[12]

The 1971 Comprehensive Program[13] authorized the use of adjusted world trade prices, explained above, in the negotiation of intra-CMEA trade agreements for the 1976–1980 period:

> CMEA member nations will, for the time being, base their reciprocal trade on the price-forming principles currently in force, i.e., prices will be set on the basis of world market prices, after adjustments to

[11] The accounting term "translation rate" is used here rather than "exchange rate," because we are primarily considering the translation of a price stated in one currency to a price stated in terms of another (rather than the exchange of one payment instrument for another).

[12] The price-forming procedure for intra-CMEA trade is explained in Béla Csikós-Nagy, *Socialist Price Theory and Price Policy* (trans. by Elek Helvey, István Véges, and Tamás Bácskai; Budapest: Akadémaii Kiadó, 1975), pp. 303–07; Herwig Haase, "The COMECON Foreign Trade Price System," *Osteuropa Wirtschaft*, 1975, no. 3, trans. in *Soviet and Eastern European Foreign Trade*, vol. 12, no. 2–3 (Summer-Fall 1976), p. 81; Edward A. Hewett, *Foreign Trade Prices in the Council for Mutual Economic Assistance* (London: Cambridge University Press, 1974), pp. 31–35 and 178; Kálmán Pécsi, *The Future of Socialist Economic Integration* (trans. by George Hajdu and Keith Crane; Armonk, N.Y.: M. E. Sharpe, 1981), pp. 96–107; and Wilcznyski, *Comparative Monetary Economics, supra* note 4, pp. 78–96. For a discussion of factors that affect the bargaining-out of intra-CMEA trade prices, see Oto Hlaváček, "Contract Prices in Trade Among CMEA Countries," *Zahraniční Obchod*, 1980, no. 1, p. 10, trans. in *Soviet and Eastern European Foreign Trade*, vol. 17, no. 1 (Spring 1981), p. 42 at pp. 47–48.

[13] Comprehensive Program for the Intensification and Improvement of Cooperation and the Development of Socialist Economic Integration of CMEA Member Countries, discussed in Chapter 2, *supra*, page 90. For citations to the Russian text and translations, see Chapter 2, *supra*, page 90 (note 224).

cleanse them of the harmful influences of the conjunctural[14] factors of
the capitalist market.[15]

This price-setting approach was confirmed for the 1976–80 plan period at
a meeting in January 1975 of the Executive Committee of the CMEA.[16] In 1980
the CMEA Executive Committee decided to continue the same price-setting approach
for the 1981–85 plan period.[17]

The price-forming procedure to be used in intra-CMEA trade subsequent
to 1985 is currently the subject of debate and study. Some scholars and officials
urge the retention of the present system. Others recommend the use of world
market prices that are more current than five-year averages and they recommend
that adjustments to those prices be smaller than in the past. Others favor a
price-forming procedure based on socialist value judgments independent of
world prices.[18] The Comprehensive Program contemplates that the relationship
between domestic wholesale prices and the foreign trade prices used in intra-
CMEA trade will be made more rational.[19] This entire subject is presently
being studied by the Meeting of Heads of Price Departments of CMEA Member
Countries.[20]

There are essentially two ways in which a link between domestic wholesale prices and intra-CMEA prices could be established. One is to continue to
use adjusted world prices and to bring national internal prices into harmony
with them. The other method is to harmonize national internal prices and to derive intra-CMEA prices from the harmonized prices. Under either method
countries will have to make changes in their internal price-forming systems and
reduce the diversity of practices in assigning added value at the various stages
of production and distribution.

The Comprehensive Program called for consideration in 1980 of a possi-

---

[14] The Russian term ("koniunkturnyi") is borrowed from the German term "konjunktur" (English
"conjunctural"). Economists use the term to refer to oscillations in economic activity. The fiscal and monetary policies used by capitalist countries to tune their economies and to control inflation, unemployment, and
business conditions are called "conjunctural policies."

[15] Comprehensive Program, *supra* note 13, chapter 2, section 6, subsection 28. The translation is by James
F. Allen, research assistant to the author.

[16] The CMEA Executive Committee, at its meeting in Moscow in January 1975, adopted recommendations on questions pertaining to contract prices for trade among CMEA countries for the period 1976–80. The
price-forming procedures were essentially as described in the text. See *Pravda* (Moscow), January 24, 1975,
p. 4; trans. in *Current Digest of the Soviet Press,* vol. 27, no. 4 (February 19, 1975), pp. 21–22. See also
Hlaváček, *supra* note 12; and Pécsi, *supra* note 12, pp. 96–107.

[17] See Pécsi, *supra* note 12, p. 101.

[18] See Pécsi, *idem,* pp. 107–16; and papers cited and discussed in Haase, *supra* note 12.

[19] Comprehensive Program, *supra* note 13, chapter 2, section 7, subsection 16.

[20] See Statute on the Meeting of Heads of Price Departments of CMEA Member Countries, confirmed October 17, 1974. The Russian text appears in P. A. Tokareva (ed.), *Mnogostoronnee Ekonomicheskoe
Sotrudnichestvo Sotsialisticheskikh Gosudarstv: Dokumenty [Multilateral Economic Cooperation of the Socialist Countries: Documents]* (Moscow: Iuridicheskaia Literatura, 1967, 1972, 1976, 1981), 1976 ed., p.
79; trans. in William E. Butler, *A Source Book on Socialist International Organizations* (Alphen aan den
Rijn: Sijthoff & Noordhoff, 1978), p. 241.

ble CMEA recommendation for the establishment of a unitary exchange rate for the national currency of each member country stated in terms of the transferable ruble as a common denominator.[21] It was contemplated that if unitary rates should be established, a country could change its particular unitary rate under agreed procedures to be worked out. No recommendation was published in 1980. The important point is that if a firm link were to be established between internal and foreign trade prices, the relative internal prices among goods within a CMEA country would in general vary proportionately with intra-CMEA trade prices, unlike the present situation where domestic prices stated in the national currency cannot always be translated into intra-CMEA trade prices at a uniform rate.[22]

A decision to proceed to establish unitary rates could have profound effects. It might permit central planning in CMEA countries to be subjected to a price discipline not previously known under socialism in some CMEA countries. In the short-term one could expect subsidy and tax instruments to be used to moderate the effects. In the longer term, a firm link between domestic prices and intra-CMEA trade prices, if established, would make it possible to open the economies to freer intra-CMEA trade and would facilitate the development of regional planning throughout the CMEA territory.

If the CMEA countries were to decide to closely link domestic prices to intra-CMEA prices and, further, to link intra-CEA prices to current world prices without significant adjustments, the resulting linkage of domestic prices to world prices could potentially lead to the rationalization of industry both within the CMEA territory and with the rest of the world. It is doubtful, however, that national central planning could be made sufficiently adaptable to function well in such a market environment.

As noted earlier, a key distinguishing factor between planned economies and market economies is the role assigned to the price system. In a centrally planned economy, pricing is an instrument of planning and economic control. There must, almost inevitably, be some buffering between domestic prices and the international market place. Most CMEA countries will probably see improved coordination of national planning and somewhat stronger CMEA cen-

---

[21] Comprehensive Program, *supra* note 13, chapter 2, section 7, subsections 16 and 17.

[22] It has been reported that the bookkeeping at the joint Polish-Hungarian Haldex enterprise (engaged in processing waste from coal mining) at one time required the use of more than 60 product-specific currency translation factors to maintain accounting records in both Polish and Hungarian currencies. Adam Zwass, "A Unified World Monetary System," *Europäische Rundschau*, 1975, no. 3, trans. in *Soviet and Eastern European Foreign Trade*, vol. 12, no. 2–3 (Summer-Fall 1976), p. 18 at p. 25. See also Vratislav Válek, "Price Setting within the Framework of Joint Enterprises of COMECON Member Nations," *Politická Ekonomie*, 1976, no. 7, trans. in *Eastern European Economics*, vol. 15, no. 4 (Summer 1977), p. 29.

Model Statutes on the Financing and Settling of Accounts of the International Economic Organizations of the Member States of CMEA, published in 1975, contemplate a simplified procedure of currency translation rates. The text in Russian appears in Council for Mutual Economic Assistance, *Basic Documents of the Council for Mutual Economic Assistance* (Supplement to 3d rev. ed.; Buffalo, N.Y.: William S. Hein & Co., 1979), document III.

tral institutions as the appropriate instruments for rationalizing the price system within the CMEA group. World prices may be allowed to put pressure on planning to a greater extent than now, but the full discipline of world prices will not be accepted in the domestic context.[23]

International Payments Practices

Transactions with Residents of Non-CMEA Countries— Settlement in Convertible Currencies

The currencies of all CMEA countries are subject to restrictions. The use that a nonresident is permitted to make of holdings of these currencies is very limited. The national paper currencies are used for tourist expenses and some other invisible transactions by nonresidents.[24] Trade between firms in CMEA states and firms resident in Western states is normally conducted through bank accounts denominated in Western convertible currencies, as will now be explained.[25]

While in some CMEA countries foreign trade payments are handled

---

[23] See generally Petr Spacek, "Convertibility in the System of CMEA Foreign Exchange Relations," *Finance a Úvěr*, 1980, no. 2, p. 27; trans. in *Soviet and Eastern European Foreign Trade*, vol. 17, no. 1 (Spring 1981), p. 63.

Hungary has gone furthest of the CMEA countries in rationalizing its exchange rate system. See Paul Marer, "Exchange Rates and Convertibility in Hungary's New Economic Mechanism," in *East European Economic Assessment: A Compendium of Papers,* Joint Economic Committee, U.S. Congress, 97th Congress, 1st Session (1981), part 1, p. 525; and Fontenay, *Hungary, supra* note 4.

[24] Westerners principally use CMEA paper currencies for tourist and business travel transactions. Special exchange rates are used for this purpose.

[25] In the absence of an agreement making a contrary stipulation, the practice is to use Western convertible currencies. Trade agreements may make this explicit. The Long Term Economic and Trade Agreement between Hungary and the United Kingdom signed at Budapest, March 21, 1972, states in Article 5:

> Payments for goods and services within the terms of this Agreement shall be effected in freely convertible currency, in accordance with the foreign exchange regulations in force in the respective territories of the Contracting Parties. (*United Nations Treaty Series* [hereinafter *UNTS*], vol. 868, p. 23.)

This clause, or a minor variation of it, is typically used in agreements of the Soviet Union and other Eastern European states with member countries of the International Monetary Fund, both countries that are industrialized and those that are developing, countries that have accepted IMF Article VIII and those that have not. See, e.g., the trade agreements of Bulgaria with Australia, signed December 5, 1974 (*UNTS,* vol. 975, p. 97), Poland with Singapore, signed April 7, 1975 (*UNTS,* vol. 972, p. 235), Poland with the United Kingdom, signed April 21, 1971 (*UNTS,* vol. 805, p. 51), Romania with the United Kingdom, signed June 15, 1972 (*UNTS,* vol. 864, p. 203), Romania with Zambia, signed May 14, 1970 (*UNTS,* vol. 931, p. 53), U.S.S.R. with Argentina, signed June 25, 1971 (*UNTS,* vol. 941, p. 5), U.S.S.R. with Bolivia, signed August 17, 1970 (*UNTS,* vol. 957, p. 361), U.S.S.R. with Federal Republic of Germany, signed July 5, 1972 (*UNTS,* vol. 941, p. 99), U.S.S.R. with Japan, signed May 22, 1981 (*Foreign Trade* [Moscow], 1981, no.

through a department of the state bank, a number of Eastern European countries operate separate foreign trade banks. These banks for foreign transactions, closely affiliated with the state banks, are organized under the laws of their own countries—e.g. Vneshtorgbank in the U.S.S.R., Bulgarska Vunshnoturgovska Banka in Bulgaria, Ceskoslovenska Obchodni Banka in Czechoslovakia, etc.[26] The foreign trade banks maintain correspondent relationships with commercial banks in Western Europe, the United States, and other countries, and hold deposit accounts with these Western banks. Western importers of socialist goods can make payments in Western convertible currencies to these accounts with Western banks for the credit of the socialist trade bank or trade organization. Socialist organizations can make outpayments to Westerners in convertible currencies from these accounts. The foreign trade banks, in addition to handling international payments, extend credit to socialist export and import organizations and to state enterprises that manufacture goods for export.[27]

The Soviet Union and several other CMEA states own commercial banks in Western countries chartered under the law of the countries in which they are located and operating under the banking law of the respective Western country. They hold deposits for their customers in the convertible currency of the state where located and also handle foreign exchange transactions for their customers. They also engage in Eurocurrency banking.[28] State agencies of CMEA members maintain accounts in these banks denominated in convertible currencies. These banks are authorized under the law where chartered to extend credit

---

11, p. 52), U.S.S.R. with Nigeria, signed October 29, 1971 (*UNTS*, vol. 941, p. 19), and U.S.S.R. with Sweden, signed April 7, 1976 (*Foreign Trade* [Moscow], 1977, no. 2, p. 54).

The agreement between the European Economic Community and Romania on trade in industrial products, signed at Bucharest July 28, 1980, entered into force January 1, 1981, provides in Article 11:

> The Contracting Parties shall agree that payments for transactions shall be made, in accordance with their respective laws and regulations, in any convertible currency agreed by the two Parties concerned in the transaction. (*Official Journal of the European Communities*, 1980, no. L-352, December 29, 1980, p. 5.)

[26] The capital of a foreign trade bank is typically held by the state bank and government ministries. Usually, a member of the board of the state bank is the head of the foreign trade bank and there are interlocking relationships of some personnel. See the table listing the state bank and foreign trade bank for each CMEA member in Giuseppe Schiavone, *The Institutions of Comecon* (New York: Holmes & Meier, 1981), pp. 134–35. For the statutes of the Bank for Foreign Trade of the U.S.S.R. (Vneshtorgbank), see *Foreign Trade* (Moscow), 1983, no. 4, p. 49.

[27] See generally Suzanne F. Porter, *East West Trade Financing* (Washington: U.S. Department of Commerce, 1976); and Garvy, *Money, Financial Flows, and Credit in the Soviet Union, supra* note 6, pp. 134–55.

[28] Commercial banks in the West controlled by the Soviet state bank and/or foreign trade bank include Moscow Narodny Bank in London with branches in Beirut and Singapore, Banque Commerciale pour l'Europe du Nord (Eurobank) in Paris, Wozchod Handelsbank in Zurich, Ost-West Handelsbank in Frankfurt, Donaubank in Vienna, East-West United Bank in Luxembourg, and Bank Russo-Iran in Tehran. Hungary owns the Hungarian International Bank in London. Bulgaria owns Litex Bank in Beirut. A number of CMEA state banks have branches in London and other cities in the West. Banks owned as joint ventures with Western commercial banks include Mittel-Europäische Handelsbank in Frankfurt (Poland), Anglo-Romania Bank in London (Romania), and Central European International Bank in Budapest (Hungary).

to their customers (including Eastern state agencies and Western businesses) in the convertible currencies of the countries in which they are sited and to extend credit denominated in other convertible currencies. They also deal with other banks in the West. Thus, authorized agencies of socialist countries, either through the correspondent relationships of their foreign trade banks with Western banks or through relationships with Eastern-owned Western banks, are able without difficulty to receive and make payments in convertible currencies, to buy and sell convertible currencies, and to participate in the Eurocurrency market. They can also engage in these activities through the International Bank for Economic Cooperation, to be described later.[29]

Socialist countries carefully budget their exchange earnings and negotiate needed credits. Typically, a socialist state prepares a separate foreign exchange budget for transactions in convertible currencies.[30] Planning of payments with capitalist countries must take into consideration not only the Eastern state's import needs and export plans but also price fluctuations in the West that affect its export earnings and import costs.

Not being members of the International Monetary Fund, the CMEA member states (except Hungary, Romania, and Vietnam) lack the assured procedures available to IMF members to obtain foreign exchange to carry them through periods when out-payments exceed in-payments. The CMEA countries, like others, do have reserves in the form of gold holdings and foreign exchange balances. These can be substantial or modest.[31] The desire to avoid committing reserves for current purchases has caused the state and foreign trade banks of the socialist states to become actively engaged in negotiating lines of credit with foreign commercial banks and with foreign government agencies.

---

[29] Some Western commercial banks have representative offices or branches in CMEA countries. These offices provide assistance in arranging payments in East-West trade. See Zwass, *Monetary Cooperation, supra* note 3, pp. 220–21; and Porter, *supra* note 27, pp. 18–20.

[30] See generally Jan Vit, "Methods Employed by COMECON Members in Drawing Up Their Balance of Payments," *Finance a Úvěr,* 1975, no. 9, trans. in *Soviet and Eastern European Foreign Trade,* vol. 12, no. 2–3 (Summer-Fall 1976), p. 66; and Milos Churánek, "Some Problems and Linkages in the Foreign-Currency Planning of External Economic Relations," *Finance a Úvěr,* 1975, no. 11, trans. in *Soviet and Eastern European Foreign Trade,* vol. 12, no. 2–3 (Summer-Fall 1976), p. 38.

Virtually all CMEA countries maintain, in some form, a foreign currency surrender requirement. This means that socialist organizations engaged in foreign trade are required to sell all foreign currency receipts to the country's foreign trade bank for the local domestic currency (unless specially authorized to retain a portion of the receipts). Payments to nonresidents require approval of the Ministry of Finance. To avoid case-by-case approvals, approvals may be granted for classes of transactions in accordance with economic plans. Paper notes in the local currency are not allowed to be transported in or out of the country except in small amounts for tourist expenditures. These restrictions are not in principle different from the stringent exchange restrictions maintained by a number of IMF members. Exchange controls receive comprehensive attention in Chapter 10 of this book.

[31] The Soviet Union is second only to South Africa in gold production. Its mines produce approximately 200 tons of gold annually.

Each CMEA country manages its gold and foreign exchange reserves independently. However, loans of foreign currencies have been made by CMEA countries to each other directly and through the International Bank for Economic Cooperation and the International Investment Bank to be described later.

The International Bank for Economic Cooperation, to be described below, also maintains credit lines with Western banks.[32]

In recent years CMEA countries have negotiated what are called "compensation agreements" with Western governments and businesses. Under these agreements loans are extended by Western governments or commercial banks to the CMEA country in convertible currency to pay for the purchase of goods and services in the West for installation in the East. Western firms or governments obligate themselves to purchase the output of the factories, mines, or gas fields for convertible currencies at world competitive prices, under a schedule that will likely assure repayment of the loans and a profit to the Eastern government.[33]

Transactions with Residents of Non-CMEA Countries— Bilateral Payments Agreements

Bilateral payments arrangements were widely used in the past. They continue to be used for effecting payments between CMEA members and some countries that have significant exchange restrictions. Under bilateral payments agreements, payments are made by crediting and debiting special accounts maintained by the central banks of the two countries with each other. Because payments between the two countries are rarely perfectly matched at any one time, the two banks agree to extend to each other a "swing credit." The accounts can be denominated in any agreed currency (the U.S. dollar often being used) without the necessity for the partners to actually own that currency. Selected examples of such agreements follow.

The Payments Agreement between Iran and the U.S.S.R., signed June 20, 1964,[34] provided that the Foreign Trade Bank of the U.S.S.R. "will open in the name of the Central Bank of Iran an account in American dollars under the designation 'Clearing Account of the Central Bank of Iran.' " The Central Bank of Iran opened an account in the name of the Foreign Trade Bank of the U.S.S.R. also denominated in U.S. dollars as a clearing account. The agreement provided that each bank extend to the other a credit of $2,000,000. Thus, the U.S. dollar was used as a unit of account in the bilateral clearing arrangement with-

---

[32] For additional information on banking practices of socialist countries, see Zwass, *Money, Banking and Credit, supra* note 4; Zwass, *Monetary Cooperation, supra* note 3; Garvy, *Money, Financial Flows, and Credit in the Soviet Union, supra* note 6; George Garvy, *Money, Banking, and Credit in Eastern Europe* (New York: Federal Reserve Bank of New York, 1966); and Iván Meznerics, *Law of Banking in East-West Trade* (trans. by Emil Böszörményi Nagy; Budapest: Akadémiai Kiadó; Leiden: A. W. Sijthoff; Dobbs Ferry: Oceana Publications, 1973).

[33] See symposium on counter-purchase contracts and collection of documents in *Droit et Pratique du Commerce International*, vol. 8 (1982), pp. 157–223 and 343–83; and another symposium on countertrade in *Journal of Comparative Business and Capital Market Law*, vol. 5 (1983), pp. 327-441. See also OECD, *East-West Trade: Recent Developments in Countertrade* (Paris, 1981).

[34] *Foreign Trade* (Moscow), 1964, no. 9, p. 41; *International Legal Materials*, vol. 4 (1965), p. 152.

out the necessity of any actual dollar deposits held with U.S. banks changing hands.

Bilateral payments agreements used by Romania, now an IMF member that continues its membership in the CMEA, provide further illustrations. Under the Trade and Payments Agreement between Romania and Guinea, signed December 1, 1966,[35] a government bank in each country opened a clearing account in the name of the other bank denominated in U.S. dollars. Each bank extended to the other a "technical credit" of $700,000. The Long-Term Payments Agreement between Romania and the United Arab Republic (Egypt), signed November 14, 1966,[36] was similar, except that accounts were denominated in U.K. sterling and each bank extended a "swing credit" of £ 2,000,000. The Long-Term Payments Agreement between Romania and Ghana signed November 23, 1966,[37] was similar except that the Cedi was the unit of account and the "swing credit" was 600,000 Cedis. Each of these bilateral clearing agreements contained clauses providing for adjustments in the event of changes in the exchange rate of the clearing currency.

Bilateral agreements may provide for settling imbalances from time to time in a convertible currency. In the absence of such an agreement, difficulties are presented if one of the two parties obtains credits in a non-convertible currency that it cannot advantageously use.[38] Ingenious schemes have been used to dispose of unwanted balances. At times these schemes have involved third countries with convertible currencies. In 1965, for example, Czechoslovakia transferred its credit balances with Guinea to the United Kingdom as partial payment for a ship purchased from the United Kingdom; the latter then used the funds to purchase ore in Guinea.[39]

Bilateral agreements by their nature create incentives for the parties to import from the bilateral partner rather than other countries, in order to avoid the necessity of using a convertible currency. Bilateral payments arrangements are

---

[35] *United Nations Treaty Series*, vol. 642, p. 89. The agreement was terminated in October 1976. Romania and Guinea now make settlements by transfer of deposits maintained with banks in countries issuing convertible currencies.

[36] *United Nations Treaty Series*, vol. 642, p. 141. The agreement was terminated in July 1976.

[37] *United Nations Treaty Series*, vol. 642, p. 79. A bilateral payments arrangement between Romania and Ghana continued in force at the time this book went to press.

[38] A clause that recognizes the difficulty, but does not solve it, is the following in the trade agreement between the U.S.S.R. and India, signed in New Delhi on December 10, 1980, which provides for payments through bilateral accounts in rupees:

> Any balance in the Rupee accounts of the Bank for Foreign Trade of the USSR or any debt of the Bank for Foreign Trade of the USSR in connection with the grant of technical credit will, upon expiry of this Agreement, be used during the ensuing 12 months for the purchase of Indian or Soviet goods as the case may be or shall be settled in such other ways as may be agreed upon between both Governments. (Article 7, section 6. Text in *Foreign Trade* (Moscow), 1981, no. 3, p. 51.)

[39] Garvy, *Money, Banking, and Credit in Eastern Europe, supra* note 32, pp. 99–100.

viewed by the IMF as discriminatory practices that require approval under IMF Article VIII, Section 3, when instituted by IMF members. In recent years the Fund has refused to approve the introduction of such arrangements between IMF members and between IMF members and nonmembers and has urged IMF members not to renew existing arrangements.[40] As a result, the number of bilateral agreements in effect between IMF members and socialist states has sharply declined. Instead, payments are made by the transfer of deposits maintained with banks in countries issuing convertible currencies.[41]

CMEA countries, as described below, use the multilateral payments system of the International Bank for Economic Cooperation (IBEC) for payments among themselves. All CMEA countries (including Hungary and Romania) continue to use bilateral payments arrangements for settlements with some socialist states that do not belong to the IBEC, such as Albania, People's Republic of China, Democratic People's Republic of Korea, and Laos.

Intra-CMEA Payments—The Clearing System of the International Bank for Economic Cooperation

The Agreement on Multilateral Payments in Transferable Rubles and on the Organization of the International Bank for Economic Cooperation (IBEC) and the Charter of the IBEC were signed October 22, 1963, and the bank began operations in 1964.[42] It has its seat in Moscow. All active CMEA members belong to

---

[40] See Chapter 10, *infra*, page 400. For a detailed discussion of the legal structure of bilateral payments agreements, see Athanasios D. Paroutsas, *Interstate Agreements on International Payments* (Athens: privately printed, 1970), pp. 18–100.

[41] Agreements for settlement in convertible currencies have on occasion included clauses intended to minimize the net use of convertible currencies. The Trade Agreement between Colombia and the U.S.S.R., signed June 3, 1968, includes an understanding that trade will be balanced so that neither party will be required to make a net use of foreign convertible currency. Article 8 provides:

> All payments between the U.S.S.R. and the Republic of Colombia shall be made in freely convertible currency in accordance with the laws, rules and regulations which are in force or will come into force subsequently in relation to currency control in each of the two countries.
>
> Both Contracting Parties shall take necessary measures so that trade between the two countries is carried out on a balanced basis.

Foreign Trade (Moscow), 1969, no. 8, supplement, p. 5; *International Legal Materials*, vol. 8 (1969), p. 1302. Since both the Soviet Union and Colombia have used exchange and trade controls, the application of the agreement could result in discriminatory practices like those associated with bilateral payments arrangements.

[42] The Agreement on Multilateral Payments in Transferable Rubles and on the Organization of the International Bank for Economic Cooperation, and the Charter of the International Bank for Economic Cooperation (IBEC), were amended December 18, 1970, and November 23, 1977. Unofficial translations of the Agreement on Multilateral Payments and the Charter of the IBEC following the 1977 amendments appear in Appendix D of this work at pages 777 and 782. See Chapter 2, *supra*, page 91 (note 227), for citations to the original texts and texts as amended in 1970 and 1977 in Russian and the original texts and texts as amended in 1970 in translation. For general background on the IBEC, see Chapter 2, *supra*, pages 90–93. See also Iurii

the bank. Membership is open to non-CMEA members.[43] All payments respecting intra-CMEA trade transactions denominated in transferable rubles are normally handled through the IBEC.[44]

The primary operation of the IBEC is the clearing of accounts among CMEA countries on a multilateral basis. One authorized bank of each member state maintains an account with the IBEC. Settlements are carried out through these accounts. The accounts are denominated in "transferable rubles," the CMEA collective currency. The clearing has been described as follows:

> At the end of each working day, the authorized bank in each country notifies the IBEC (by cable) of that day's export transactions with all other CMEA countries. The IBEC then credits the account of the authorized bank in the exporting country and debits the accounts of the authorized banks in the importing countries. Thus the authorized bank in each country, instead of acquiring separate bilateral claims on, or debts to, the authorized banks in other countries, acquires one net accounting surplus or deficit with the IBEC. A surplus on bilaterally agreed transactions with one member is thus offset by a deficit on bilaterally agreed transactions with another country, and to that extent the transferable rubles are actually transferable among member countries.[45]

The principal form of settlement in intra-CMEA trade is documentary collection with immediate payment and settlement by subsequent acceptance.[46] It works as follows: Upon dispatching goods to the foreign socialist buyer, the socialist selling organization presents the invoice to his own bank which (without

---

A. Konstantinov, *Den'gi v Sisteme Mezhdunarodnykh Ekonomicheskikh Otnoshenii Stran SEV [Money in the System of International Economic Relations of the CMEA Countries]* (Moscow: Finansy, 1978), pp. 141–42.

[43] Agreement on Multilateral Payments, Article XIII.

[44] Agreement on Multilateral Payments, Article I.

[45] Henryk Francuz, "The International Bank for Economic Cooperation," *IMF Staff Papers,* vol. 16 (1969), p. 489 at pp. 492–93. See Agreement on Multilateral Payments, Article V; and IBEC Charter, Articles 9–11. See also Jozef M. van Brabant, *East European Cooperation: The Role of Money and Finance* (New York: Praeger Publishers, 1977), p. 158; V. P. Komissarov, *Mezhdunarodnye Valiutno-Kreditnye Otnosheniia SSSR i Drugikh Sotsialisticheskikh Stran [International Currency and Credit Relations of the U.S.S.R. and Other Socialist Countries]* (Moscow: Mezhdunarodnye Otnosheniia, 1976), pp. 179–82; and Konstantinov, *Den'gi v Sisteme, supra* note 42, pp. 148–49.

[46] The immediate payment system is provided for in the CMEA's General Conditions for Delivery of Goods, Chapter XI. The Russian text as amended effective January 1, 1980, appears in Tokareva, *supra* note 20, 1981 ed., p. 319. A translation of the text prior to the most recent amendments appears in Butler, *Source Book, supra* note 20, p. 925; and a translation of the amendments effective in 1980 appears in *Review of Socialist Law,* vol. 6 (1980), p. 477.

For background see Thomas W. Hoya and John B. Quigley, Jr., "COMECON 1968 General Conditions for Delivery of Goods," *Ohio State Law Journal,* vol. 31 (1970), p. 1; Peter J. Katona, "The International Sale of Goods Among Member States of the Council for Mutual Economic Assistance," *Columbia Journal of Transnational Law,* vol. 9 (1970), p. 226; and Mikhail Rosenberg, "New Elements in the General Conditions Governing CMEA Deliveries," *Foreign Trade* (Moscow), 1980, no. 5, p. 36.

awaiting any special instructions from the buyer or its bank) immediately credits the seller's account in the equivalent amount of local currency. The seller's bank (a) transmits the documents directly to the buyer's bank and (b) the same day informs the IBEC of its claim against the buyer's bank. The IBEC, as explained above, credits the bank of the seller with the stated number of transferable rubles. The IBEC debits the transferable ruble account of the buyer's bank. That bank in turn debits the local currency account of the buyer and transmits the invoice to it for acceptance. The IBEC clearing system is also capable of handling other settlement techniques including letter-of-credit transactions familiar in the West.[47]

Note that under the IBEC clearing system, the bank in a CMEA country need never in an intra-CMEA trade transaction acquire or sell the national currency of another CMEA country. At the present time the exchange rate at which a national bank credits or debits the local currency account of its customer (which is a socialist government-owned organization) in connection with an intra-CMEA trade transaction denominated in transferable rubles is for that country's government to decide. The normal practice is for the country's bank to credit the local exporting organization with the amount of local currency equivalent to the transferable ruble value of the transaction at the government-set trade exchange rate with a further adjustment by application of what are called "coefficients." In some CMEA countries (e.g., Hungary, Poland, and Romania) the official trade exchange rate of the local currency against the transferable ruble is stated directly, while in other countries (e.g., Soviet Union) the trade exchange rate is derived by applying a multiplication factor to a parity rate originally stated in terms of gold. The trade exchange rate under either procedure may be changed from time to time.

Coefficients, which vary depending on the goods and services involved and whether the transaction is an import or an export, are designed to buffer the domestic price system from the international price system. The coefficients when applied to the basic trade exchange rate result in a highly complex multiple rate system (different final rates for different classes of transactions). The consequence intended is that the local seller of goods receives the local price for goods exported. The multiple rate practices make it possible to insulate the relative prices of one good compared to another domestically from different relative prices in intra-CMEA trade or in world markets.[48]

---

[47] Agreement on Multilateral Payments, Article V. See Meznerics, *supra* note 32, pp. 405–17.

[48] For a detailed discussion of trade exchange rates of Eastern European countries, coefficients used for adjustments in trade transactions, and exchange rates for non-trade payments, see Jozef M. van Brabant, "Eastern European Exchange Rates and Exchange Policies," *Yearbook of East-European Economics,* vol. 11 (1983), p. —.

Hungary has greatly simplified its exchange rate system for trade transactions, but other CMEA countries continue to make complex adjustments by application of coefficients as explained in the text. See, e.g., explanation of the exchange rate and price system in Romania in 1981; *IMF Survey,* September 7, 1981, p. 262. Regarding Hungary, see sources cited in note 23, *supra.* See generally Zwass, *Monetary Cooperation, supra*

The Comprehensive Program for Integration contemplated that in 1980 the CMEA would consider recommending that its members establish unitary exchange rates for these national banking operations and also agreed procedures for changing the unitary rates and assuring that the rates are economically justified, but a recommendation was not published at that time.[49]

Intra-CMEA Payments for Non-Trade Transactions

Payments in respect of non-trade transactions (e.g., tourist transactions, business travel, diplomatic services, educational expenses, family remittances, and many other invisible transactions)[50] can involve the actual use of national currencies by nonresidents. Unlike exchanges of goods between socialist organizations in one country and socialist organizations in another, these kinds of payments cannot be balanced. Intra-CMEA payments with respect to non-trade transactions are settled in accordance with an agreement signed at Prague in 1963,[51] an agreement signed at Bucharest in 1971,[52] and subsequent agreements and practices to which CMEA members and other socialist countries are parties. Special exchange rates are used for these payments.

The 1963 Prague agreement established a list of non-trade payments, which the 1971 agreement replaced with a longer and more detailed list.[53] The 1971 agreement also provides for the payments to be settled in transferable rubles through the IBEC.[54]

note 3, pp. 86–90; Brabant, *East European Cooperation, supra* note 45, pp. 245–99; and Loeber, *supra* note 8, vol. 2, pp. 215–28.

The system of crediting and debiting the accounts in the national currency of exporting and importing organizations when trade is settled in convertible currencies is similar to that described in the text. Currently most Eastern European countries set a trade exchange rate of the local currency against a basket containing small amounts of Western convertible currencies (the number of currencies in the basket varying from nine to thirteen). The rates against any one convertible currency thus fluctuate depending upon movements in the Western exchange markets. The coefficients used to buffer the domestic price system from the world price system may be different for trade conducted in convertible currencies compared to trade denominated in transferable rubles. See generally Brabant, "Eastern European Exchange Rates," *supra,* pp. —.

[49] Comprehensive Program for Integration, *supra* note 13, chapter 2, section 7, subsections 15–19. See also pages 353–355, *supra.*

[50] In intra-CMEA trade, the costs of freight and insurance related to goods transactions are treated as "trade" rather than "invisible" items. They are covered by agreements on payments in respect to trade transactions.

[51] Agreement on Accounts for Non-Trade Payments, done at Prague February 8, 1963, entered into force April 1, 1963; Russian text in Tokareva, *supra* note 20, 1967 ed., p. 294; trans. in Butler, *Source Book, supra* note 20, p. 1028.

[52] Agreement on a List of Non-Trade Payments and on a Coefficient for Conversion of Sums of Non-Trade Payments into Transferable Rubles, done at Bucharest July 28, 1971. A Polish translation from the original Russian text appears in Boguslaw W. Reutt (ed.), *Podstawowe Dokumenty RWPG i Organizacji Wyspecjalizowanych* (Warsaw: Ksiazka i Wiedza, 1972), p. 543. See also Iurii A. Konstantinov, "Currency and Financial Relations Between the CMEA Countries," *Foreign Trade* (Moscow), 1972, no. 10, p. 2 at p. 6.

[53] Prague Agreement, Article 1; and Bucharest Agreement, Article 1.

[54] Bucharest Agreement, Article 2.

Neither the 1963 agreement nor the 1971 agreement, by its terms, established a formula for determining the exchange rates to be used in making settlements.[55] It has been written that rates have been set on the basis of a purchasing-power formula. The purchasing power of each national currency would be measured in terms of an agreed market basket consisting of various kinds of foodstuffs, consumer durables, and services. Rates for each national currency would then be determined against the Soviet ruble as a common denominator. Finally, a uniform coefficient would be applied to translate the rates of the national currencies against the Soviet ruble into rates against the transferable ruble. In principle these rates were to be readjusted whenever there was a significant shift in relative consumer price levels.[56]

A purchasing-power-parity approach to determining exchange rates does not guarantee a balance between payments and receipts. As tourist receipts and expenditures have become more significant elements in the balances of payments of some CMEA countries, imbalances between payments and receipts have placed strains on exchange rates for tourist transactions. A further problem is that, while payments for non-trade transactions may be cleared through the facilities of the International Bank for Economic Cooperation,[57] a residual net credit balance in transferable rubles may be of limited usefulness.[58] In this environment the exchange rates for settling non-trade payments are negotiated from time to time. Since 1974 it has been permissible for tourist rates to differ by $\pm$ 10 percent from rates for other non-trade payments. Some of the rates used in recent years for tourist and non-trade payments have been set in bilateral negotiations between pairs of countries and as a consequence there may be broken cross-rates.[59]

---

[55] The Bucharest Agreement, Article 3, provides for the central or authorized banks of the parties to establish the exchange rate coefficients, and does not provide any guidance for making that decision.

[56] See generally Jerzy Wesolowski and Pawel Wyczanski, "Effectiveness of Currency Rates in CMEA Tourism," *Bank i Kredyt* (Warsaw), 1980, no. 1, p. 12; trans. in Joint Publications Research Service, *East Europe Report: Economic and Industrial Affairs (no. 2017)*, J.P.R.S. no. 75896 (June 17, 1980), p. 21. See also Komissarov, *supra* note 45, pp. 203–11; Brabant, *East European Cooperation, supra* note 45, pp. 264–78; Zwass, *Monetary Cooperation, supra* note 3, pp. 71–77; and Lawrence J. Brainard, "CMEA Financial System and Integration," in Paul Marer and John Michael Montias (ed.), *East European Integration and East-West Trade* (Bloomington: Indiana University Press, 1980), p. 121 at pp. 129–34.

[57] Agreement on Multilateral Payments, Article VIII. Prior to 1974 each IBEC member annually transferred its bilateral balance for invisible transactions with each other IBEC member to the IBEC and the accounts were then cleared multilaterally. Since the beginning of 1975 it has been legally possible to clear balances more frequently. Credit and debit balances remaining after the clearing may be transferred to accounts in transferable rubles.

[58] See pages 369–373, *infra.*

[59] Wesolowski and Wyczanski, *supra* note 56, pp. 23–24 and 28–29 (J.P.R.S. trans.); and Brabant, "Eastern European Exchange Rates," *supra* note 48, pp. —.

See, e.g., the rates for non-trade payments agreed upon by seven CMEA countries on December 28, 1974, displayed in the table in Komissarov, *supra* note 45, p. 210. Although the rates have subsequently been revised, the table illustrates the character of the system. Note the broken cross-rates when the Soviet ruble/Bulgarian lev, Soviet ruble/Hungarian forint, and lev/forint rates are compared. The use of bilaterally negotiated rates was authorized by the agreement on exchange rates for non-trade payments, signed Decem-

Intra-CMEA Trade with Payment in Convertible Currencies

A substantial amount of intra-CMEA trade, perhaps as much as ten percent of that trade, is denominated and settled in Western convertible currencies. The commodities involved are usually ones in demand in Western markets. Convertible currency accounts with the IBEC may be used for the settlement of this trade,[60] or accounts with banks in the West may be used. Because convertible currency balances can be readily used to finance imports from any country, trade agreements with convertible currency payment provisions need not be bilaterally balanced. Prices for goods and services can be bargained out (in the light of contemporary world prices) independently of the elaborate price-forming rules, explained earlier, normally applicable to intra-CMEA trade.[61]

Credit Operations of the International Bank for Economic Cooperation

To ensure that settlements between CMEA members through the facilities of the IBEC, described earlier, are executed without delay, the members of the IBEC have agreed that the bank may grant credit in transferable rubles to the authorized state banks and to international organizations established by CMEA members. The IBEC grants two types of credits in transferable rubles:[62]

> (1) Settlement (payment) credit, which is a short-term revolving credit with limits set by the Bank's Council. The amount drawn by an IBEC member on this credit line with the IBEC cannot at any time exceed two percent of the previous year's total intra-CMEA trade of that country. The purpose of this credit is to bridge short-term imbalances in payments and receipts and it is granted automatically. There is no repayment deadline for settlement credit, but usually it is repaid within 30 days. This revolving credit line is used each day as payments are cleared.
>
> (2) Fixed-term credit, which is provided for up to a year or, with ap-

---

ber 28, 1974, to which all CMEA countries except Romania, Cuba, and Vietnam are parties. See Komissarov, *supra,* pp. 209–10.

[60] See IBEC, *Annual Report, 1973.*

[61] See Pécsi, *The Future of Socialist Economic Integration, supra* note 12, pp. 122–48; Brainard, *supra* note 56, pp. 126–27; and S. Richter, "Hungary's Foreign Trade with CMEA Partners in Convertible Currency," *Acta Oeconomica,* 1980, nos. 3–4, reprinted in *Soviet and Eastern European Foreign Trade,* vol. 18, no. 1 (Spring 1982), p. 79.

[62] Agreement on Multilateral Payments, Article VI. Specification of these two types of credit followed amendment of the agreement, December 18, 1970. Originally there were six types of credit but available facts did not always permit differentiation as to which was the appropriate rule to use. The revised system is simpler and more flexible. See IBEC, *Annual Report, 1971;* and Komissarov, *supra* note 45, pp. 190–94.

IBEC also grants credit to international production organizations owned jointly by CMEA countries, using funds allocated by the interested countries. IBEC Charter, Articles 19, 23, and 24.

proval of the IBEC's Council, up to two or three years. Use of this credit requires the submission of an application showing need. The application may, for example, show that the country's payments problem results from costs associated with industrial specialization, industrial expansion, or seasonal fluctuations.

A debtor country repays credit advanced by the IBEC in transferable rubles by making deliveries of commodities or services to other CMEA countries with payment specified in transferable rubles. It is important to note that credit in transferable rubles granted by the IBEC is not a market mechanism that promotes the exports of one country by expanding the import possibilities of another; rather, it is a stopgap instrument used to maintain an uninterrupted flow of already agreed bilateral trade.[63]

In addition to handling the clearing of accounts in transferable rubles and extending credit in transferable rubles, the IBEC is an active financial intermediary dealing in Western convertible currencies. It borrows currencies from Western banks (often Eurocurrency deposits) and re-loans those currencies to its member banks. It also has authority to deal in non-convertible currencies and to engage in operations in gold.[64]

The IBEC is authorized to charge interest for the use of credits.[65] Its present practice is to provide settlement credits at a low interest rate. The interest charges on fixed-term credits provided in transferable rubles are higher than for settlement credits, but are usually lower than rates charged by the Bank on credits in Western convertible currencies.[66]

If, as a result of multilateral clearings through the IBEC, a member's account has a credit balance in excess of what the member bank wishes to keep as a working balance on current deposit, the excess may be transferred to a time deposit account paying a higher interest rate.[67] The IBEC also accepts deposits in convertible and non-convertible currencies and in gold.[68] Although the

---

[63] Zwass, *Money, Banking, and Credit, supra* note 4, pp. 164–67.

[64] Authority for these transactions is provided by the IBEC Charter, Articles 19–24.

[65] Agreement on Multilateral Payments, Article VI; and IBEC Charter, Article 21. Lower preferential interest rates are charged for fixed-term credit extended to countries whose exports have a pronounced seasonal character, such as Cuba, and to developing socialist countries, such as Vietnam.

[66] In 1982 the interest rate for settlement credit was 2 percent per annum unless total credits to the country exceeded one percent of the country's annual trade turnover, in which case the rate was 3 percent. The interest rate for term credit was kept within a range of 3–5 percent per annum. Cuba, Mongolia, and Vietnam were granted preferential rates within a range of 0.5–2.0 percent.

[67] The fact that a member holds a credit balance in transferable rubles does not give that member a right to demand desired goods from other CMEA members, unless those members are willing to sell. If an attractive purchase cannot be arranged, the member will leave the transferable rubles in a time deposit to earn interest. Interest on transferable ruble deposits is usually paid by the IBEC at rates lower than those prevailing in the West for convertible currency deposits. In 1982 the IBEC paid interest on deposits in transferable rubles at annual rates within a range of 1.5–4.0 percent depending on time length.

[68] IBEC Charter, Article 24.

IBEC pays interest on convertible currency deposits placed with it, it has been reported that IBEC members appear to prefer to hold convertible currency deposits with banks in the West rather than with the IBEC.[69]

To assist the IBEC in planning its operations, the state bank of each country annually, or more frequently, prepares payments plans and related credit plans. In these plans, payments by each country to all partners combined—trade payments, payments for services, credits, and all other payments—are in total matched against anticipated total receipts from the same group of countries. On the basis of plans submitted by its members, the IBEC formulates credit plans to assist its members and then opens credits in tranferable rubles in appropriate amounts in favor of the member banks.[70]

Central banks, commercial banks, and other organizations in non-CMEA countries are permitted to open and use accounts with the IBEC denominated in transferable rubles, convertible currencies, and other currencies. The terms and conditions are determined by decisions of the Bank's Council and agreements between the Bank and interested countries and institutions.[71] Efforts have been made to encourage non-CMEA central banks and commercial banks to operate in transferable rubles. Western exporters can, if they choose, accept payment through a bank correspondent of the IBEC, in transferable rubles for exports to CMEA countries. It has been recommended, however, that Western exporters do so only under agreements for balanced trade.[72] This is because the use of transferable rubles to obtain goods or a convertible currency is not a matter of right and normally should be negotiated in advance with the CMEA partner to the trade or service transaction.[73] Developing socialist countries that are not members of the CMEA have been encouraged to use transferable rubles, and

[69] Zwass, *Monetary Cooperation, supra* note 3, p. 240.

[70] IBEC Charter, Article 20. See also note 30, *supra*.

[71] Agreement on Multilateral Payments, Article IX; and IBEC Charter, Articles 9, 10, 14, 18, 19, and 24. The Bank's Council has adopted rules and procedures implementing the cited articles, which were amended November 23, 1977, to expand the Bank's authority.

In October 1977 the IBEC and the National Bank of Yugoslavia concluded an Agreement on Basic Principles of Cooperation and an Agreement on Banking Technical Procedure and Terms of Settlement in Transferable Rubles. See Konstantinov, *Den'gi v Sisteme, supra* note 42, pp. 201–02. The central banks of a number of socialist non-CMEA countries, the Bank of Finland, the African Development Bank, and many commercial banks maintain accounts with the IBEC.

[72] At one time IBEC procedures required nonmembers participating in transferable ruble settlements to do so only on a balanced basis. The revision of the procedures in 1976 changed this from a requirement to a recommendation. IBEC, *Procedure for Performance of Settlements in Transferable Roubles between Member Countries and Non-Member Countries of the IBEC* (Moscow, 1976), printed in Moscow Narodny Bank (London), *Press Bulletin*, no. 788 (December 8, 1976), p. 14. The earlier procedure appears in Loeber, *supra* note 8, vol. 4, p. 168. See generally essays by Jozef M. van Brabant, Zdislaw Fedorowicz, and Friedrich Levcik in Jean-Louis Guglielmi and Marie Lavigne (ed.), *Unités et Monnaies de Compte* (Paris: Economica, 1978); and Andrzej Bień and Grzegorz Nosiadek, "The Transferable Ruble and Cooperation between Member Countries of the IBEC and Third Countries," *Handel Zagraniczny*, 1979, no. 2, p. 19, trans. in *Soviet and Eastern European Foreign Trade*, vol. 16, no. 2 (Summer 1980), p. 26.

[73] See generally pages 369–373, *infra*.

aid to these countries from CMEA countries has been denominated in this instrument.[74] It should also be noted that two non-IBEC institutions can settle payments between themselves in transferable rubles if the IBEC consents.

The IBEC is authorized to extend credit in transferable rubles to nonmember banks to finance purchases from CMEA countries that are to be paid for in transferable rubles. The credit can be repaid either in transferable rubles obtained as a result of balancing sales of goods or services to CMEA countries or can be repaid in a Western convertible currency.[75] The IBEC is also authorized to extend credit to non-CMEA banks and institutions in convertible currencies and other currencies under terms and conditions set by the Bank's Council.[76]

In the most recent year for which information is available, 1983, mutual settlements among IBEC member countries that were accounted for in transferable rubles amounted to TR 180 billion (about U.S. $ 233 billion) of which 93–95 percent represented trade turnover. The volume of operations in convertible currencies has not been reported.[77]

At the present time there are relatively few occasions when transferable rubles are exchanged for U.S. dollars except in transactions intended to be reversed. The transferable ruble rate against the U.S. dollar is set monthly by the IBEC on the basis of a weighted basket consisting of small amounts of thirteen convertible currencies.[78] At January 1, 1984, the rate quoted by the IBEC was U.S. $ 1.00 = TR 0.7737.

[74] The central banks of Afghanistan, Angola, Ethiopia, Laos, Mozambique, and Yemen (Aden) and the African Development Bank maintain accounts with the IBEC and representatives of these banks often attend the IBEC's annual meeting. See also note 80, *infra,* and accompanying text relating to the Special Fund of the International Investment Bank.

The problem of converting transferable ruble balances into goods or into usable national currencies has limited the use made of this instrument even by socialist non-CMEA banks. See Kálmán Pécsi, "The CMEA Monetary System and Developing Countries," *Penzugyi Szemle* (Budapest), 1979, no. 12, p. 890; trans. in Joint Publications Research Service, *East Europe Report: Economic and Industrial Affairs (no. 1986),* J.P.R.S. no. 75258 (March 6, 1980), p. 1.

[75] Agreement on Multilateral Payments, Article II; and IBEC Charter, Article 19, paragraph 3. See IBEC, *Procedure for Performance of Settlements in Transferable Roubles between Member Countries and Non-Member Countries of the IBEC, supra* note 72. See also Moscow Narodny Bank (London), *Press Bulletin,* no. 805 (April 13, 1977), p. 14; and *IMF Survey,* June 6, 1977, p. 170.

If convertible currency is used to repay credit extended by the IBEC in transferable rubles, the exchange rate to be used is that set by the IBEC.

[76] Agreement on Multilateral Payments, Article II; and IBEC Charter, Article 24.

[77] Konstantin Nazarkin, "Twenty Years of the International Bank for Cooperation (IBEC)," *Foreign Trade* (Moscow), 1983, no. 12, p. 2 at p. 2. For other years, see IBEC, *Annual Report.*

[78] *See* Iurii A. Konstantinov, *"On the Function of the Transferable Ruble as a Measure of Value,"* *Finansy SSSR* (Moscow), 1981, no. 6, p. 67; trans. in Joint Publications Research Service, *USSR Report: International Economic Relations (no. 17),* J.P.R.S. no. 79221 (October 1981), p. 22 at pp. 32–33. See also Moscow Narodny Bank (London), *Press Bulletin,* no. 887 (February 14, 1979), p. 18.

Credit Operations of the International Investment Bank

The organization and purposes of the International Investment Bank (IIB) were explained in Chapter 2.[79] The IIB extends credit in transferable rubles and other currencies to finance industrial projects and other projects of CMEA countries, especially joint projects. It also extends credit, through its Special Fund,[80] for development projects in non-CMEA countries under which equipment is acquired in CMEA countries.

Credit is normally extended at medium-term (up to five years) or long-term (up to fifteen years). Loans are for projects rather than general balance-of-payments support. The operations of the IIB are in some respects comparable to those of the International Bank for Reconstruction and Development.

As in the case of transferable ruble credit granted by the IBEC, transferable ruble credit extended by the IIB is not a market mechanism to stimulate investment or trade. Every loan financing equipment for an investment must be preceded by a commitment of the seller to deliver goods to the buyer and a guarantee by the buyer of a reciprocal transfer of goods to the seller's country.[81]

Further Comments on the Transferable Ruble

The basic clearing operations of the IBEC, as we have noted, are conducted in "transferable rubles" of which the bank is the issuer.[82] The reader can translate "transferable rubles" to mean "IBEC rubles." They are readily transferable on the books of the IBEC from one authorized holder to another. Although each unit is assigned a gold value of 0.987412 gram[83]—which is the same gold value in which the ruble of the Soviet Union is styled—neither the IBEC nor the U.S.S.R. has up to now expressed its readiness to freely convert transferable rubles (TR) into Soviet rubles or vice versa. The holder of transferable rubles has the right to use them as a means of payment for goods previously contracted for in intra-CMEA trade,[84] but has no automatic right to purchase goods nor to

---

[79] At pages 93–94, *supra*. Major loans are described in the *Annual Report* of the Bank.

[80] Agreement Establishing within the International Investment Bank a Special Fund to Grant Credits for Economic and Technical Assistance to Developing Countries, done at Moscow April 11, 1973, entered into force April 11, 1973. The Russian text appears in *United Nations Treaty Series*, vol. 870, p. 237; and in Tokareva, *supra* note 20, 1976 ed., p. 176. Translations appear in *UNTS*, vol. 870, p. 242; and in Butler, *Source Book, supra* note 20, p. 347. See also International Investment Bank, *Annual Report, 1973*, pp. 15–16, and *idem, 1974*, p. 16. See generally Andrej Bień and Grzegorz Nosiadek, "The Special Fund of the International Investment Bank," *Handel Zagraniczny*, 1979, no. 3, p. 37, trans. in *Soviet and Eastern European Foreign Trade*, vol. 16, no. 2 (Summer 1980), p. 35.

An Agreement on Main Principles of Cooperation between Yugoslavia and the International Investment Bank, signed April 26, 1974, entered into force September 24, 1974, appears in Tokareva, *supra,* 1976 ed., p. 173; trans. in Butler, *supra,* p. 343.

[81] See Bień and Nosiadek, "Special Fund," *supra* note 80, pp. 42–43.

[82] Agreement on Multilateral Payments, Articles I, II, and V; and IBEC Charter, Articles 9, 10, and 14.

[83] Agreement on Multilateral Payments, Article I.

[84] Agreement on Multilateral Payments, Article I.

purchase national currencies or gold. Some countries that have accumulated credit balances in transferable rubles appear to have encountered difficulties in using them.[85] This has led countries (both CMEA members and nonmembers) to provide goods and services for transferable rubles only as part of a reciprocal exchange of goods and services.[86] An IBEC member, under present conditions, accumulates TR credits not because it wishes to save them to meet an unexpected need in the future or because it wishes to collect interest on this instrument, but because it has not received planned deliveries of goods at the specified time. It can buy nothing with the accumulated credits but what has previously been agreed upon and then only from the source specified in the plan, unless a new *ad hoc* agreement is worked out to deal with the particular TR balance.[87] Since the transferable ruble is convertible neither into national currency (of CMEA states or Western states) on demand nor into goods on demand, two credit balances (with equal TR values) may be settled on different terms[88] and in some cases the creditor may be left with nothing to do with TR balances but accumulate further interest on them.

There are a number of ways, through agreement of IBEC members, in which transferable ruble net credit balances could be made usable (both to CMEA resident and nonresident holders) in commercial transactions. The members of IBEC could enter into a general agreement under which each IBEC member would promise to deliver goods (or alternatively national currencies) on demand at defined prices to any country holding a net creditor position in the IBEC. The beneficiaries of such an agreement could initially be limited to holders of TR net credits above a stated threshold for longer than a minimal time, and the obligation to deliver goods (or currencies) could be placed on a defined class of debtors. The types of goods (or currencies) to be delivered could be specified in the agreement. The goods should be of a type in demand which the supplier, nevertheless, could provide without excessive disruption of national economic plans for production and export. Such an agreement would implement the provision of the Agreement on Multilateral Payments which commits each member country to "ensure the balancing of receipts and payments in transferable rubles with all other member countries of the Bank as a whole within the calendar year or other period agreed by the member countries of the

---

[85] See generally Ferenc Bartha, "Some Ideas on the Creation of a Multilateral Clearing System Among the COMECON Countries," *Külgazdaság*, 1975, no. 1, trans. in *Soviet and Eastern European Foreign Trade*, vol. 12, no. 1 (Spring 1976), p. 19. See also Brabant, *East European Cooperation, supra* note 45, pp. 88–98 and 108–16.

[86] It has been estimated that no more than 3 percent of intra-CMEA trade settled in transferable rubles is in multilateral form.

[87] See Petr Spacek, "Convertibility in the System of CMEA Foreign Exchange Relations," *Finance a Úvěr*, 1980, no. 2, p. 27, trans. in *Soviet and Eastern European Foreign Trade*, vol. 17, no. 1 (Spring 1981), p. 63 at p. 81; and Zwass, *Money, Banking, and Credit, supra* note 4, pp. 167 and 211 (note 15).

[88] It has been said that in some cases the transferable ruble prices set for transactions involving similar goods under bilateral agreements have varied by more than 20 percent. See generally Brabant, *East European Cooperation, supra* note 45, p. 113.

Bank.''[89] The limited convertibility of TR balances into goods on demand suggested here could probably be accommodated within national economic plans. Any wider guarantee of the convertibility of TR balances into goods might disrupt national planning.

An alternative or complementary approach would be an agreement that TR net credit balances could be converted into national currencies of CMEA members. The Comprehensive Program for Integration called for a recommendation to be agreed within the CMEA in 1980 on the establishment of ''mutual convertibility'' of national currencies and the use of unitary exchange rates.[90] This has not yet been done. And, it could be that all the drafters had in mind by ''mutual convertibility'' was that CMEA countries agree (a) that their domestic prices shall be translated into transferable ruble prices at unitary rates; (b) that their state banks shall debit and credit the local currency accounts of their local customers (primarily their own state enterprises) for transferable ruble payments and receipts at unitary rates; and (c) that, at the same time, each CMEA country can continue to prohibit the acquisition of local currency balances by banks or enterprises resident in other CMEA states since they have no need for local currency balances so long as payments in intra-CMEA trade can be made in transferable rubles through the facilities of the IBEC.[91] Obviously, this understanding of ''convertibility'' would do little or nothing to make TR credit balances more usable. On the other hand, if holders of TR balances were permitted to exchange those balances on demand for national currencies of other CMEA members, which could be used to buy desired goods and services, then TR net credit balances would be made more usable. It is worth noting that the IBEC has authority to enter into agreements for the conversion of transferable rubles into national currencies of CMEA countries or into currencies of Western states should it decide to do so.[92] The complex multiple rate systems of most CMEA countries would require simplification if TR balances and national currencies are to be made exchangeable, even for limited purposes, in the commercial area.

As previously explained, unitary exchange rates are supposed to be used for converting national currencies of CMEA countries into transferable rubles for certain noncommercial purposes, such as maintenance of diplomats.[93] The idea that nonresident banks and enterprises would be permitted to acquire and use substantial local currency balances for commercial purposes has met great resistance. As explained earlier, in CMEA countries the government's central

---

[89] Agreement on Multilateral Payments, Article I.

[90] Comprehensive Program, *supra* note 13, chapter II, section 7, subsections 15–19.

[91] The provisions in the Comprehensive Program appear intended primarily to lead to harmonization of internal with intra-CMEA trade prices to facilitate regional planning and industrial specialization. See pages 351–355, *supra*.

[92] Agreement on Multilateral Payments, Article IX; and IBEC Charter, Articles 14, 18, and 24. See note 96, *infra*, and accompanying text.

[93] See pages 363–364, *supra*.

plan determines production, the inputs into that process, and the allocation of the products manufactured. Money is not used to determine these decisions but rather functions as a means of accounting and of monitoring.[94] If nonresident firms were to be given general license to acquire local currency and to use that currency as they choose, the planning process could be frustrated.[95]

If transferable rubles are not to be endowed with the power to command goods or be convertible into national currencies of CMEA countries which would in turn be endowed with that power, the idea has been put forth that the transferable ruble could, nevertheless, be made convertible into Western convertible currencies—that is, given what might be called financial convertibility. In 1973, several CMEA countries took what they thought was a limited step in this direction, but it was frustrated.

In 1973 five central banks participating in the IBEC put into effect a Polish proposal that ten percent of a country's net debit balance on current account with the IBEC over a given limit (over 2 percent of the previous year's trade turnover) would be converted into Western convertible currencies or gold.[96] The idea was that over time the percentage of the net balance that was convertible might be increased.[97] This effort to introduce greater discipline into the settlement process by giving transferable ruble balances limited convertibility apparently did not in fact result in significant conversions of those balances into convertible currency. It appears that when IBEC members had net debits approaching the conversion threshold, their practice was to obtain fixed-term credit denominated in transferable rubles from the IBEC and to use the proceeds to reduce the current account (settlement) debit and thus avoid the conversion obligation. It appears that as a result of the experience, the arrangement calling for conversions into convertible currency was suspended.[98] Had the escape valve not been provided, the 1973 arrangement might have put pressures on CMEA countries to increasingly orient their economies to the world market. It is not surprising that Soviet writers have suggested that any arrangement permitting large volumes of transferable rubles to be converted into Western

---

[94] See pages 347–350, *supra*.

[95] See Spacek, "Convertibility," *supra* note 87, p. 85; and J. Wilczynski, "The Rouble Versus the Dollar," in Banca Nazionale del Lavoro, *Quarterly Review,* no. 135 (December 1980), p. 455 at p. 472.

[96] The arrangement made September 1, 1973, is discussed in Eugeniusz Drabowski, *Rubel Transferowy: Miedzynarodowa Waluta Krajów RWPG* (Warsaw: Państwowe Wydawnictwo Naukowe, 1974), pp. 104–05, 108, and 123; Wilczynski, "The Rouble Versus the Dollar," *supra* note 95, pp. 478–79; Brainard, *supra* note 56, pp. 135–36; and comment of Adam Zwass in Marer and Montias, *supra* note 56, p. 145. See also Stanislaw Raczkowski, "International Money of Socialist Countries," *Oeconomica Polona,* 1975, no. 3, p. 315 at p. 326. Only Czechoslovakia, the German Democratic Republic, Hungary, Poland, and the U.S.S.R. agreed to participate in the 1973 arrangement, which was developed in the CMEA's Permanent Commission on Financial and Monetary Questions.

[97] Compare the movement that occurred under the European Payments Union toward settling a larger portion of net balances with the EPU in dollars. Eventually the members of the EPU were prepared to make their own currencies convertible. See Chapter 7, *supra,* pages 300–302.

[98] See Brainard, *supra* note 56, pp. 135–36. See also Wilczynski, "The Rouble Versus the Dollar," *supra* note 95, p. 479. See pages 365–366, *supra,* regarding settlement credit and fixed-term credit.

convertible currencies would require economic and organizational changes that, from their perspective, would be unwise.[99]

Until CMEA countries are willing to give market forces greater sway in guiding economic decisions, it is unlikely that the transferable ruble or national CMEA currencies will be made convertible into Western currencies or, alternatively, will be endowed with significant powers to command goods produced in CMEA states.

[99] See, e.g., Konstantinov, *Den'gi v Sisteme, supra* note 42, pp. 189–201; and Konstantinov, ''On the Function of the Transferable Ruble,'' *supra* note 78.

Balance-of-Payments Financing: Concluding Note to Chapters 3–9

In the preceding chapters we examined in some detail the sources of foreign exchange available to monetary authorities for the financing of balance-of-payments transactions. Monetary authorities facing a need to use foreign currencies may, first of all, draw down their existing reserves. This may be the principal means used if reserves are large and the need for currency small or very temporary. The reserves used can be foreign currencies, special drawing rights (SDRs), reserve tranche drawing rights in the International Monetary Fund, gold, and other assets.

Authorities in many countries satisfy part of their foreign currency needs for balance-of-payments support through official borrowings from commercial banks, usually on a short-term basis. Funds may also be obtained through sale of bonds and borrowings from foreign governments. Bilateral payments agreements may be relied upon, mostly by nonmembers of the IMF. For a country that neither belongs to the International Monetary Fund nor participates in other multilateral arrangements that give access to significant amounts of foreign exchange, the foregoing are almost the exclusive methods.[1]

The member countries of the International Monetary Fund have substantial resources available to them through that organization. They are allocated special drawing rights (SDRs) and obtain reserve tranche drawing rights. They have credit tranche drawing rights in accordance with the IMF's general policies and its policies directed to particular problems (such as the compensatory financing of export fluctuations). If a country's balance-of-payments situation requires or might require financing on a large scale and the country is prepared to accept the necessary Fund discipline, it can request the Fund to approve a stand-by arrangement. If special conditions are met, a country may qualify for the larger amounts available under an extended arrangement. Most IMF members coordinate their use of Fund resources with their use of existing reserves and credits available from other sources. For many countries, the IMF is the principal official external source of foreign exchange for the financing of balance-of-payments deficits.

In recent years IMF stand-by and extended arrangements for individual

---

[1] Legal aspects of the payments practices of the People's Republic of China, prior to its becoming a member of the IMF, are described in the symposium, "Trade with China," *Law and Contemporary Problems,* vol. 38 (1973), p. 173 at pp. 217–21, 234–38, and 245–47. See also *China: A Reassessment of the Economy—A Compendium of Papers, Joint Economic Committee,* U.S. Congress, 94th Congress, 1st Session (1975), pp. 653–67; and *Chinese Economy Post-Mao: A Compendium of Papers, Joint Economic Committee,* U.S. Congress, 95th Congress, 2d Session (1978), vol. 1, pp. 719–20, 731–32, 749–50, 759–61, and 772–74.

countries have assumed sizes dramatically larger than in earlier years. Time periods have been extended and other terms liberalized. Assistance continues to be directed to general balance-of-payments support, but greater attention has been given to structural changes to correct payments problems over the longer-term than was true only a few years ago. The security of the IMF's assistance and the likelihood of repurchase by the beneficiary country do not as yet appear in doubt. Nevertheless, a degree of caution may be advised in the application of the Fund's more liberal policies.

Industrialized free-market economies with currencies that are essentially free of restrictions can encounter, sometimes for extended periods, huge payments financing needs that far exceed the resources available to them through the International Monetary Fund. These countries have designed procedures tailored to the specific problems they encounter. The reciprocal currency arrangements between the U.S. Federal Reserve System and other central banks are especially noteworthy. The financial mechanisms for balance-of-payments support in the European Economic Community can make available very large sums to EEC members. Some of these Federal Reserve and EEC facilities are used routinely. The socialist countries that belong to the Council for Mutual Economic Assistance participate in the multilateral payments and credit facilities of the International Bank for Economic Cooperation. Developing countries often are members of regional payments and credit arrangements in their parts of the world.

Authorities in a country often have a choice among sources for foreign exchange needed for balance-of-payments support. This is probably a good thing. It guards against the potential massive power that might otherwise be lodged in the International Monetary Fund or another organization. The competition stimulates invention of facilities to meet the needs as they appear. But there are also weaknesses. With a range of financing procedures open to them, national officials are tempted to use procedures that require the minimal policy adjustments so long as adequate reserves can be maintained. This can result in postponement of needed policy changes. Concerned about this problem, the IMF has encouraged members to adopt corrective measures, which could be supported by use of the Fund's general resources in accordance with the Fund's policies, at an early stage of their balance-of-payments difficulties.

The policies of different financial institutions do not always neatly mesh. But, maybe they should not be expected to do so, given our incomplete knowledge of what are and are not wise policies. Consultations of organizations with their members provide opportunities for the review of corrective measures by the examinee country and the effectiveness of the particular organization's rules and policies. Consultations under IMF Article IV are among the occasions in which the International Monetary Fund is able to discuss with members their adjustment programs, including corrective measures, whether financed by the Fund's resources or other sources. These consultations consider the magnitude, maturities, and cost of servicing all external debt. The consultations encompass the full range of a member's policies as they relate to balance-of-payments adjustment and can consider the interaction of domestic economic policies, exchange rate arrangements, policies respecting exchange controls, and the means used to finance balance-of-payments deficits. These consultations and the nature of the obligations of deficit and surplus countries in the adjustment process are examined in Chapter 12.

III
Code of Good Conduct

Introduction to Chapters 10–12

The following chapters deal with what may be called the "rules of good conduct" in international monetary affairs. Exchange controls, relating to current transactions and to capital movements, and the international legal regimes applicable to them are examined in Chapter 10. Exchange rate arrangements and the regimes applicable to them are treated in Chapter 11.

The most fundamental obligations of the international monetary order are to consult and to collaborate. In Chapter 12, drawing on ideas considered in previous chapters, we re-examine these obligations. We also consider the meaning of consultation and collaboration in contexts that were not studied earlier, including consultations on general economic policies, obligations in the balance-of-payments adjustment process, supervision of commercial bank prudential practices, management of monetary reserves, management of international liquidity, and assistance to developing countries. We conclude with reflections on the broad implications of consultation and collaboration duties in the monetary sphere.

Chapter 10: Exchange Controls

Introduction

After a few introductory comments, this chapter proceeds into a detailed examination of the more frequently used exchange controls, with examples from paradigm regimes. The heart of the chapter is a description and appraisal of efforts in multilateral forums to reduce exchange restrictions or lessen their impact. The first half of the chapter concerns currency controls relating to current international transactions, with principal attention being given to the role of the International Monetary Fund. The second half of the chapter deals with controls on capital movements and controls on current and capital transactions underlying monetary transfers. Here, in addition to the IMF, we shall consider the rules and practices of the General Agreement on Tariffs and Trade, the Organisation for Economic Co-operation and Development, and the European Economic Community. Often the same control measure falls within the jurisdiction of several organizations. Extraterritorial recognition of national exchange controls is considered at the very end of the chapter.

The subject of this chapter sometimes is put under the heading ''convertibility.'' There is, however, no single definition of the minimum characteristics a currency must possess to be called ''convertible.''[1] A widely used criterion is whether or not the state of issue has accepted the convertibility obligations of Sections 2, 3, and 4 of Article VIII of the IMF Agreement. However, a state accepting Article VIII obligations is permitted to circumscribe the convertibility of its currency in capital transactions. And, in some cases a state that has accepted the obligations of Article VIII may in fact have restrictions on current payments and transfers or engage in multiple exchange rate practices.

The concept of ''freely usable currency'' in the IMF's Articles of Agreement was treated in Chapter 5.[2] That term is used in applying particular articles

---

[1] Varieties of meanings, and lack of explicit meanings, given to the terms ''convertible currency'' and ''freely convertible currency'' in different legal instruments are explored in Joseph Gold, ''Convertible Currency Clauses Under Present International Monetary Arrangements,'' *Journal of International Law and Economics,* vol. 13 (1979), p. 241.

[2] At pages 197–200, *supra.*

for the Fund Agreement.[3] As explained in Chapter 5, a member-participant in the Special Drawing Rights Department that is designated by the Fund to provide currency in exchange for special drawing rights has an obligation to provide a freely usable currency.[4] As delineated in Chapter 6, each IMF member has an obligation to ensure that its currency, when drawn from the General Resources Account, is freely usable or can be exchanged for a freely usable currency.[5] The definition of "freely usable currency" says nothing about exchange controls.[6] The term has not yet been given wide application outside the IMF.

It may be helpful to define the conceptual extremes of the convertibility/non-convertibility spectrum. It is suggested that a paradigm of a freely convertible currency would have the following characteristics:

(1) The issuing state in no way restricts the right to hold the currency. Both residents and nonresidents are permitted to hold the currency with no restrictions on the amount of the currency held or the form in which it is held (coins, paper money, bank balances, notes).

(2) The issuing state in no way restricts the manner in which the currency can be exchanged by a holder of it for the currency of another state. The issuing state does not restrict the manner in which its currency can be acquired. That is, the currency can be bought and sold in private markets in the issuing state or in other states.

(3) The issuing state in no way restricts the currency for which its currency can be exchanged. It imposes no limits on the foreign currencies that a holder of its currency, whether a resident or a nonresident, may hold, buy, or sell.

(4) The issuing state does not restrict the uses that can be made of its currency by a nonresident holder. That is, a nonresident can use the currency for the same purposes for which a resident holder can lawfully use it.

Examples of actual exchange control regimes will be examined below. Before proceeding, we should note the typical purposes for which a country maintains exchange restrictions. A state may wish to control the magnitude and nationality of the claims that foreigners may have upon its economy. Since currency is a claim upon the economy of the issuing state, restrictions may be imposed on transfers of the currency from residents to nonresidents, tranfers be-

---

[3] The term "freely usable currency" appears in the following provisions: Article V, sections 3(e) and 7(j); Article XIX, section 4(a); Article XX, section 5; Article XXIV, sections 3, 5, and 6; Article XXX(f); Schedule G, paragraph 1(a)(iv); Schedule H, paragraphs 1 and 2; Schedule I, paragraph 1; and Schedule J, paragraphs 2 and 4. The IMF has used the term "freely usable currency" in some other legal instruments, such as agreements under which it has borrowed currencies.

[4] At pages 197–200, *supra*.

[5] At pages 225–227, *supra*.

[6] Article XXX(f).

tween nonresidents, and uses of the currency by nonresident holders. The state may also wish to control the use of foreign currencies held by its residents. It may, for example, centralize foreign currency holdings and establish priorities for the use of those currencies in relation to its development plans and governmental objectives. Exchange controls are used as one among a variety of methods to deal with balance-of-payments problems.

A comprehensive system of exchange controls takes the place, entirely or partly, of an ordinary market for foreign exchange. A paradigm of a comprehensive system of exchange controls would have the following characteristics:

(1) Residents are not permitted to transfer the state's currency to nonresidents except with the state's permission and this permission, in a paradigm regime, is granted on a case-by-case basis. Nonresident holders of the state's currency are not permitted to transfer their holdings to other nonresidents except with permission.

(2) Nonresident holders of the state's currency are not permitted to transfer their holdings to residents except in approved transactions. A nonresident holding the state's currency may be "blocked" from using the currency even for purchase of goods and services in the issuing state. The uses that a nonresident holder may lawfully make of the currency are circumscribed by regulations.

(3) Residents are not permitted to hold foreign currencies except with the state's permission and this permission, in a paradigm regime, is granted on a case-by-case basis. A resident acquiring foreign currency (for example, in an export transaction) is required to sell that currency to a government agency, licensed dealer, or the central bank. Foreign currency must be purchased through such an agency, licensed dealer, or central bank. Government policies determine the availability of foreign currencies for particular uses.

The United States dollar, the Deutsche mark, and the United Kingdom pound sterling are examples, at the time this book goes to press, that approach the paradigm of a freely convertible currency. The currencies of some developing countries and socialist countries come close to matching the paradigm of a currency under comprehensive exchange controls. The nature and magnitude of restrictions in most countries place their currencies somewhere between the two extremes.

Countries with comprehensive exchange controls typically have enacted laws that are broad in coverage, with delegation of authority to the ministry of finance, central bank, or other body to issue regulations to implement the control policy. These regulations in turn may vary in their degree of restrictiveness or permissiveness, depending on the current policy objectives. The laws may provide for sanctions in the form of fines and/or imprisonment for violations. The government will have a right to recapture foreign exchange unlawfully obtained or withheld. Compliance with exchange controls is, however, primarily achieved through supervision of the country's commercial banks. The transactions of large governmental and private corporations may also be closely monitored.[7] Compliance may be assisted by other countries' extraterritorial recognition of the exchange restrictions, a topic treated at the end of this chapter.

Examples of Exchange Control Regimes

Note

The exchange restrictions of members of the International Monetary Fund are summarized annually in the Fund's *Annual Report on Exchange Arrangements and Exchange Restrictions*. The report includes country-by-country summaries of exchange control systems as currently in operation, together with chronologies of changes in exchange controls during the preceding year. Each summary has been reviewed by the authorities of the member country concerned. The report also presents comparative tables and general comments on the incidence of exchange controls throughout the world.[8] New and amended laws and regulations concerning foreign exchange are reported in *Forex Service.*[9] Two books that describe exchange control regimes in some detail are Jozef Swidrowski, *Exchange and Trade Controls,*[10] and Gilbert P. Verbit, *International Monetary Reform and the Developing Countries: The Rule of Law Problem.*[11] The National Bureau of Economic Research has made studies of exchange controls and trade controls, and their effects upon development, in ten countries.[12]

---

[7] See generally Jozef Swidrowski, "Controls on External Economic Transactions," *University of Toledo Law Review,* vol. 12 (1981), p. 183.

[8] Unless otherwise indicated, the author has used the 1983 issue of the IMF's *Annual Report on Exchange Arrangements and Exchange Restrictions.* Prior to 1979 the title of this publication was *Annual Report on Exchange Restrictions.* The reports have been issued annually since 1950. The first report, 1950, in addition to country surveys, at pp. 3–37 described the general techniques of currency restriction in use at the time the series was begun. See also Raymond F. Mikesell, *Foreign Exchange in the Postwar World* (New York: Twentieth Century Fund, 1954).

[9] Published by International Reports, Inc., New York.

[10] Epping, Essex: Gower Press, 1975.

[11] New York: Columbia University Press, 1975. This book is devoted almost entirely to an analysis of exchange control regimes.

[12] The studies, financed by a grant from the U.S. Agency for International Development, were published under the title *Foreign Trade Regimes and Economic Development: [country]* (New York: National Bureau of Economic Research), and include the following volumes: vol. 1, Turkey (1974), by Anne O. Krueger; vol. 2, Ghana (1974), by J. Clark Leith; vol. 3, Israel (1975), by Michael Michaely; vol. 4, Egypt (1975), by Bent Hansen and Karim Nashashibi; vol. 5, The Philippines (1975), by Robert E. Baldwin; vol. 6, India (1975), by Jagdish N. Bhagwati and T. N. Srinivasan; vol. 7, South Korea (1975), by Charles R. Frank, Jr., Kwang Suk Kim, and Larry E. Westphal; vol. 8, Chile (1976), by Jere R. Behrman; and vol. 9, Colombia (1976), by Carlos F. Díaz-Alejandro. In addition there are two summary volumes: vol. 10, *Foreign Trade Regimes and Economic Development: Liberalization Attempts and Consequences* (1978), by Anne O. Krueger; and vol. 11, *Foreign Trade Regimes and Economic Development: Anatomy and Consequences of Exchange Control Regimes* (1978), by Jagdish N. Bhagwati. A paper on Brazil was prepared but not published; see Fishlow, *infra* note 27.

Controls on the Holding, Use, and Transfer of the Issuing-State's Currency

A currency holding, as already noted, represents a claim upon the economy of the issuing state, and an issuing state may wish to control the nationality and magnitude of those claims. A state may fear that if its residents are allowed freedom to transfer the domestic currency to foreigners in payment for imports or in other international transactions, or to sell the currency for foreign currency in private markets, the result would be increased imports, capital flight (transfer of savings abroad), and a depreciation of that nation's currency in relation to foreign currencies.

A number of countries have laws and regulations designed to control the transfer of the national currency from residents to nonresidents. These countries and others may also restrict what a nonresident can do with the local currency even when lawfully obtained. These restrictions are summarized in the IMF's *Annual Report on Exchange Arrangements and Exchange Restrictions* under the heading "nonresident accounts."[13]

In some countries the approval of the state's exchange control authorities is required for a nonresident to open an account with a local bank.[14] Separate nonresident accounts may be prescribed, with different rules on the permitted uses of the funds, depending on whether the funds entering the account were convertible currencies transferred by the nonresident holder from abroad, payments by residents to the nonresident authorized in convertible currencies, payments by residents to the nonresident authorized in the local currency, or payments by residents to the nonresident made without exchange control approval.[15] The last account may be a "blocked account," which usually means that the funds cannot be transferred abroad or used in the country to buy goods or services for export.[16] These restrictions implement national policies designed to control the size of foreign-currency liabilities toward nonresidents. Further, some restrictions (such as those on the use of blocked accounts) can control the claims, even for goods and services, that foreigners may make upon a domestic economy.

The national regulations dealing with the payment or transfer of currencies

---

[13] The London-based exporter in an example in Appendix A of this book, page 673, maintains an account with a New York bank. American importers can make payments by crediting that dollar account. The United States does not restrict the use or transfer of these funds, but other countries in a similar case might do so.

[14] See, e.g., Bangladesh in IMF, *Annual Report on Exchange Arrangements and Exchange Restrictions, 1983*, pp. 87–88.

[15] Egypt prior to an exchange reform in 1976 had one of the most elaborate systems of nonresident accounts. See IMF, *27th Annual Report on Exchange Restrictions, 1976*, p. 161.

[16] Sometimes the use of blocked funds even for goods or services to be consumed in the country is limited. See generally Swidrowski, *Exchange and Trade Controls, supra* note 10, pp. 103–06, 113–14, and 153–55.

from a resident to a nonresident or from one nonresident holder to another often require that all exchange transactions involving the currency take place through banks supervised by the central bank or other institutions approved by the government. Thus, both the magnitude of exchange transactions involving the currency and the exchange rates at which the transactions take place can be controlled by the government. Further, if a state prohibits its residents from transferring its currency to nonresidents and, as shall be seen in the next section, prohibits its residents from holding foreign currencies or transferring foreign currencies to nonresidents, except in accordance with government permission, the state is in a position by means of currency restrictions to control imports of goods and purchase of services from foreigners by its residents.

Controls on the Holding, Use, and Transfer of Foreign Currencies

One of the purposes of exchange controls is to centralize foreign-currency holdings and to marshall those holdings for use in accordance with government plans and policies. Many countries require their residents to sell any acquired foreign exchange to the government, the central bank, or an authorized dealer without delay. Such a law or regulation is said to establish a "surrender requirement." A surrender requirement is a basic feature of currency control systems. Without such a rule it may be easy for residents to frustrate a control plan. Over one hundred IMF members require the surrender of foreign currencies received in export sales.[17] Many of these countries also require that foreign currencies received in non-trade transactions be surrendered or accounted for. The central bank may prescribe the exchange rate for surrender transactions.

To assure that foreign-currency surrender regulations are complied with, the usual practice is for the regulations to require all or most exporters to register their exports, specifying value, destination, and means of payment. Goods are not allowed to be exported through customs without a registration statement or export license.[18]

---

[17] IMF, *Annual Report on Exchange Arrangements and Exchange Restrictions, 1983*, pp. 524–29. Typical are the requirement of India, *idem*, p. 250, and the requirement of the United Kingdom prior to an exchange reform in 1979. *Idem, 1979*, pp. 425–26. Every IMF member that maintains restrictions on current payments maintains a foreign-currency surrender requirement except Yugoslavia, and in that country exports are handled primarily through state agencies subject to government supervision. Countries with a surrender requirement may permit a resident exporter, with the approval and supervision of exchange authorities, to maintain an account with a foreign bank into which customers make payments and from which it makes payments.

[18] The Monetary Board in Colombia, in order to prevent Colombian exporters from unlawfully declaring and surrendering substantially less foreign exchange than they receive, sets minimum surrender prices for coffee, bananas, and some other products. The exporter is required to surrender export proceeds in a quantity not less than the minimum surrender price. Some other countries have similar practices. See, e.g., IMF, *Annual Report on Exchange Arrangements and Exchange Restrictions, 1983*, pp. 66 (Argentina), 114 (Brazil), 146–47 (Colombia), and 372 (Paraguay). If the minimum export prices are unrealistically high, they can in-

Countries with a foreign-currency surrender requirement sometimes also establish "retention quotas." That is, exporters from the state are allowed to keep and not surrender a portion of certain foreign currencies received. In some cases this may simply avoid the administrative costs associated with collecting exchange and then providing it back to the firm for approved expenditures. In other cases, the retention quota may work as an incentive to exporters to demand payment in one of the quota currencies, as the firm may dispose of foreign currency out of its retention quota account for imports of its choice. The firm may find it difficult otherwise to obtain that foreign currency for use in paying for imports that may not have a high governmental priority. In some countries an exporter, obtaining foreign currencies of which he is allowed to retain a part, may be able to sell "his share" in private markets at premium prices.[19]

A state, in addition to maintaining a surrender requirement, may require its residents when exporting to accept payment in only certain designated foreign currencies. This is called a currency "prescription" requirement. One of the purposes of such a requirement is to assure that exports yield currencies that can best be used to further the state's development plans and governmental objectives.[20]

A consequence of a surrender requirement is that, if an importer wishes to make a payment in a foreign currency, he is required to obtain that currency from a governmental agency or authorized bank. If, as a corollary, permission is required for the payment of the country's own currency to a nonresident, the country through currency controls is able to control imports and other international transactions of its residents.

Determining the Use of Foreign Exchange

A country that has a foreign-currency surrender requirement, and that prohibits residents from transferring the local currency to nonresidents without permission, must establish a mechanism and criteria for granting permission for pay-

---

hibit exports. See Krueger, *Foreign Trade Regimes and Economic Development: Turkey, supra* note 12, pp. 188–90.

[19] Pakistan's "export bonus-voucher scheme" for sales of non-traditional items in the period 1959–1972 is illustrative. See Verbit, *supra* note 11, pp. 176–81; Nurul Islam, *Foreign Trade and Economic Controls in Development: The Case of United Pakistan* (New Haven: Yale University Press, 1981), pp. 121–36; and Andreas S. Gerakis, "Pakistan's Export Bonus Scheme," *Finance and Development*, vol. 11, no. 2 (June 1974), p. 10. See also Baldwin, *Foreign Trade Regimes and Economic Development: The Philippines, supra* note 12, pp. 76–78.

[20] About one hundred member countries of the IMF had currency prescription requirements as of December 1982. IMF, *Annual Report on Exchange Arrangements and Exchange Restrictions, 1983*, pp. 524–29. Although somewhat simplified from an earlier time, India continues to tailor its prescription requirements to the economic circumstances of the countries to which it exports. Compare *idem*, pp. 246–47; and *29th Annual Report on Exchange Restrictions, 1978*, pp. 197–98.

ments to nonresidents and for providing necessary foreign currencies for approved payments. It may decide to permit its residents to make payments to nonresidents for any lawful transaction or at least for any lawful current transaction. However, if demands for foreign currency exceed funds available and the country is reluctant to take steps to obtain the needed funds,[21] then it must establish rules and procedures to ration foreign-currency holdings.

Governments, particularly in developing countries, have sought to assure that foreign-exchange resources are used in support of governmentally determined priorities for development. First priority is usually given to imports by governmental agencies. Next in priority are imports of capital goods needed for industrial development and essential foodstuffs. Imports of goods competing with those available locally and imports of luxury goods are usually given the lowest priorities. The criteria for the allocation of foreign exchange may be embodied in brief official statements or in elaborate plans. Many countries with exchange controls regularly prepare an exchange budget and forecast of foreign-currency·receipts.[22]

The administrative mechanisms used for distributing foreign exchange vary widely. Many countries require residents needing foreign currencies to file an application for the exchange with a designated agency which may be the central bank, a licensed commercial bank, or a government trade agency. For some transactions, foreign exchange will be granted routinely on the basis of "general licenses," "declarations," or "free lists," which permit within certain limits designated foreign payments, as for instance, for specified imports, for foreign travel, or for family remittances abroad. For other transactions the applications are appraised individually, and granted in the form of a license, on the basis of the priority to be accorded the transaction. Whether the application will be granted or denied, or placed on a waiting list, will depend on the judgment of administrative officials applying criteria like those stated in the previous paragraph. If the criteria are objectively defined and easily applied, the decisions are essentially clerical ones. If the criteria used by the country do not lend themselves to objective application, control administrators may be called upon to exercise discretion in passing upon applications for foreign exchange.

The actual application of the criteria to the particular case thus may be a function of the criteria themselves, their ease of application, and the abilities and qualities of the administrators applying them. To simplify the process, in some countries an established importer may be assured a certain volume of foreign exchange based upon his use of foreign exchange in a previous base pe-

---

[21] To obtain additional foreign exchange, a country might purchase or borrow currencies, alter exchange rates or take other policy measures to increase export earnings, or take other steps.

[22] See Verbit, *supra* note 11, pp. 129–62.

riod.[23] Normally, if the transaction is approved, the foreign currency will be provided at the official rate of exchange.

Countries with exchange control regimes may permit some residents to maintain "resident foreign accounts" denominated in the national currency or in foreign currencies with the country's banks or with banks abroad. Usually the holders of these accounts are companies making frequent international settlements (e.g., banks, insurance companies, airlines, shipping companies, oil companies). They must regularly report their currency holdings to exchange authorities and may be required to sell "excess" foreign-currency holdings to the central bank or other authority.[24]

In a system that rations foreign exchange, firms that receive licenses are able to import at a lower cost in local currency than would be possible if there were no exchange control and the local currency's exchange value were lower.[25] Individuals and firms unable to obtain exchange lawfully may be tempted to purchase foreign currencies in the "black market." Importers may be tempted to arrange for over-invoicing in order to obtain additional foreign exchange for use in transactions that would not be approved.[26]

A few countries have experimented with the use of auctions as a technique to distribute foreign exchange on the basis of demand, Brazil in the period 1953–1957 being the most innovative.[27] Without necessarily using an auction technique, a number of countries have provided foreign currencies to resident-payors at different exchange rates depending upon the priority assigned to the purpose of the payment. This is called a "multiple currency practice." About 30 IMF members as of December 1982 engaged in multiple currency practices with respect to trade transactions. Thirty-six maintained different exchange rates for some or all capital transactions or for invisible transactions as compared to trade transactions.[28]

---

[23] Gilbert P. Verbit has studied the various procedures in use and the extent to which they are subject to bribery and corruption. See *International Monetary Reform and the Developing Countries, supra* note 11, especially pp. 19–44 and 229–33.

[24] See note 17, *supra.*

[25] It has been suggested that favored industries under exchange control tend to increase their imports faster than their output. Industries denied licenses may stagnate. See Leith, *Foreign Trade Regimes and Economic Development: Ghana, supra* note 12, pp. 96–105.

[26] In an over-invoicing scheme, the importer arranges with the foreign exporter to invoice the goods at an excessive amount. The foreign exchange is obtained on the basis of the fraudulent invoice. The exporter on receipt of the funds first applies them to the actual amount due and the balance is deposited for the benefit of the importer. An over-invoicing scheme was involved in *United City Merchants (Investments) Ltd. v. Royal Bank of Canada,* discussed in notes 489, 490, and 508, *infra,* and accompanying text.

[27] See Alexandre Kafka, "The Brazilian Exchange Auction System," *Review of Economics and Statistics,* vol. 38 (1956), p. 308; and Albert Fishlow, *Foreign Trade Regimes and Economic Development: Brazil* (conference paper; New York: National Bureau of Economic Research, 1975), pp. 21–28.

[28] IMF, *Annual Report on Exchange Arrangements and Exchange Restrictions, 1983,* pp. 524–29. The multiple buying and selling rates used in Colombia have been sufficiently complicated that they were set out in tabular form in *28th Annual Report on Exchange Restrictions, 1977,* pp. 128 and 132. Stephen A. Silard, a member of the IMF's Legal Department, gives examples of multiple rate practices in "Money and Foreign Exchange," *International Encyclopedia of Comparative Law* (Tübingen: J.C.B. Mohr; The Hague: Mouton,

Some countries engage in "discriminatory currency practices."[29] That is, they permit their residents to transfer the local currency to payees of one foreign nationality but not to payees of another. Or, they provide foreign currencies on preferential terms for payments to residents of favored countries.[30] Discrimination is a natural effect of bilateral payments agreements, such as those discussed in Chapters 4 and 9.[31] The associated regulations usually encourage exporters and importers to buy from and sell to the bilateral partners rather than the international market in order that the bilateral accounts be kept balanced.[32]

In addition to the currency controls discussed so far in this chapter, countries may also use what are called "passive controls." That is, they maintain reporting requirements for the purpose of obtaining data and statistics.

As an alternative to exchange controls or as a supplement to them, states may directly control the volume of imports, and thus the demand for foreign exchange for import payments, by tariff policies or quantitative restrictions on imported goods. These techniques will be examined later in this chapter. The control of capital movements by exchange controls and other techniques also receives separate treatment later in this chapter. Discussion will now turn to efforts within international organizations to regulate the use of exchange restrictions.

The Regime of Article VIII of the IMF Agreement

Note

The legal regime created by Article VIII of the IMF Agreement was outlined in Chapter 1.[33] Only 59 members of the International Monetary Fund had formally accepted the obligations of Sections 2, 3, and 4 of Article VIII, as of January 1, 1984.[34] However, these states include the larger free-market industrialized countries of the world as well as many other countries. All five of the

---

1975), vol. 17, chapter 20, sections 60–67. See pages 410–411, *infra,* regarding Mexico's "preferential rate" and "ordinary rate" system instituted in 1982.

[29] For a survey of various discriminatory practices, see Swidrowski, "Controls on External Economic Transactions," *supra* note 7, pp. 200–203.

[30] Broken cross-rates evidence both discriminatory practices and multiple rate practices. See text accompanying notes 67 and 70, *infra.*

[31] At pages 135 and 358–360, *supra.*

[32] The number of operative bilateral payments agreements between IMF members and the number of bilateral agreements maintained between Fund members and nonmembers (principally socialist state-trading countries) are reported in the introduction each year to the IMF's *Annual Report on Exchange Arrangements and Exchange Restrictions.* At the present time a few members account for the bulk of the agreements.

[33] At pages 19–21, *supra.*

[34] The members that have accepted Article VIII, sections 2, 3, and 4, are listed each year in IMF, *Annual Report,* and in IMF, *Annual Report on Exchange Arrangements and Exchange Restrictions.*

countries whose currencies presently constitute the SDR "market basket" accept the obligations of Article VIII.[35]

Those IMF members under the transitional regime of Article XIV, applicable to all members that have not yet accepted Article VIII, Sections 2, 3, and 4, are committed to the goal of eventual acceptance of Article VIII. It must also be emphasized that the obligations of Article VIII apply to the introduction of new exchange restrictions, multiple currency practices, and discriminatory currency arrangements by those countries under the Article XIV regime as well as those that have accepted Article VIII. That is, an Article XIV country may not lawfully, without the Fund's approval, introduce new measures inconsistent with Article VIII.[36]

We shall first sketch the obligations of Sections 2(a) and 3 of Article VIII. We shall then examine the Fund's practice in approving and refusing to approve measures that in the absence of approval violate those sections. Finally, we shall consider the obligations of Section 4.

Obligations of Section 2(a)

Overview. Section 2(a) of Article VIII is directed at payments and transfers in settlement of current international transactions. It does not prohibit restrictions on international capital movements nor on transactions that underly monetary payments and transfers. It provides:

> Subject to the provisions of Article VII, Section 3(b) [relating to "scarce" currencies] and Article XIV, Section 2 [transitional regime to be discussed below], no member shall, without the approval of the Fund, impose restrictions on the making of payments and transfers for current international transactions.[37]

Payments by Residents to Nonresidents. Section 2(a) imposes an internationally mandated obligation on member countries toward their own resi-

---

[35] See Chapter 5, *supra*, pages 178–185. Previously, when the basket included sixteen currencies, the issuers of two of them (Iran and Spain) had not accepted the obligations of Article VIII, sections 2, 3, and 4.

[36] Article VIII, section 1; and Article XIV, section 2.

[37] John Maynard Keynes shortly after the Bretton Woods Conference sought to have Article VIII, section 2(a), amended to narrow the scope of the obligation. See Lord Keynes' letter to Harry Dexter White of October 6, 1944, in Donald Moggridge (ed.), *The Collected Writings of John Maynard Keynes* (London: Macmillan and Cambridge University Press), vol. 26 (1980), p. 142 at p. 145. He was not successful. The understanding of section 2(a) that prevailed is stated in a note of Dennis H. Robertson of August 29, 1944, and a letter of Henry Morgenthau, Jr. to Sir John Anderson of June 8, 1945. *Idem.* pp. 126–27 and 183–84. See also Joseph Gold, *The Multilateral System of Payments: Keynes, Convertibility, and the International Monetary Fund's Articles of Agreement* (IMF Occasional Paper no. 6; Washington, 1981).

dents. They must permit their residents purchasing goods or services from non-residents, or engaging in other current international transactions with IMF members, to acquire and use the needed currencies to make payments in settlement of those transactions. The purpose of the rule is to ensure that currency restrictions in the purchaser's (payor's) state do not prevent or delay receipt of payment by the foreign seller or creditor (payee).

Does Section 2(a) require a member country to permit its residents to use the payor-country's own currency to settle current international transactions if that currency is demanded by the foreign payee? Prohibitions on taking domestic banknotes (national paper currency) out of a country are consistent with Section 2(a) so long as the banking system can be used for making payments. Further, it appears that a payor-country can require that a currency other than its own (say, U.S. dollars) normally be used for payments through the banking system to nonresidents, provided this currency is acceptable to the payee and its use does not increase the payor's cost. But if the payor country's currency is demanded by the payee, it must be provided.

The country must not delay, limit, or prevent any of its residents from obtaining a foreign currency issued by an IMF member that the resident needs for making payments to nonresidents in settlement of current international transactions.[38] In many countries subscribing to Article VIII a resident-payor can purchase foreign currencies needed for current payments from commercial banks. In other countries the payor may be required to purchase the currency from a central monetary authority. The key element is that the payor be able to obtain the currency needed in the amount required for the current payments without delay. Also, the authorities are not to impose charges, such as taxes, on currency payments or transfers that have the effect of inhibiting or increasing the costs of payments.[39]

---

[38] E.B. Decision No. 3153 -(70/95)(October 26, 1970); in Margaret Garritsen de Vries, *The International Monetary Fund, 1966–1971: The System Under Stress* (2 vols.; Washington: IMF, 1976) [hereinafter *IMF History 1966–71*], vol. 2, p. 214; and in *Selected Decisions of the International Monetary Fund and Selected Documents* (10th issue; Washington: IMF, 1983) [hereinafter *Selected Decisions*], p. 243. See Joseph Gold, *The Fund's Concepts of Convertibility* (IMF Pamphlet Series no. 14; Washington, 1971), p. 7.

[39] A memorandum attached to E.B. Decision No. 5712, implementing the Second Amendment to the IMF Articles, states that members are expected to inform the Fund of all actions involving exchange taxes and subsidies and adds, "Indeed, under Article VIII, Section 3, members will continue to be required to request prior Fund approval of any multiple currency practices that may be involved in such actions." E.B. Decision No. 5712 -(78/41(March 23, 1978); IMF, *Annual Report, 1978*, p. 126; *Selected Decisions* (10th issue, 1983), p. 8. See also paragraph II(C) of the memorandum appended to E.B. Decision No. 237-2 (December 18, 1947), which early recognized Fund jurisdiction over exchange taxes. That decision appears in J. Keith Horsefield and Margaret Garritsen de Vries, *The International Monetary Fund, 1945–1965: Twenty Years of International Monetary Cooperation* (3 vols.; Washington: IMF, 1969) [hereinafter *IMF History 1945–65*], vol. 3, p. 261; *Selected Decisions* p. 247. See also note 66, *infra*, and accompanying text.

In the period October 1976–February 1977, Italy imposed a surtax *(sovrattassa)* as a special levy on foreign currency purchases. Such a tax can be lawfully imposed only with the approval of the IMF, and the IMF did not approve the tax. An exchange tax that together with other governmental action does not of itself cause spreads between buying and selling rates of currencies to be more than 2 percent does not currently require special IMF approval. See text accompanying notes 66 and 153–157, *infra*.

A surrender requirement, which requires a resident-*payee* to surrender to the central authority or authorized dealers any foreign currency received in settlement of international transactions, is not a "restriction" within the meaning of Section 2(a). So long as resident-*payors* can obtain promptly, from the central authority or from banks, the foreign currency needed in order to make payments to nonresidents, a surrender requirement is consistent with Section 2(a).[40] Where retention quotas are used with a surrender requirement, a result can be multiple currency practices that violate Section 3 of Article VIII.[41] Multiple currency practices also result if different exchange rates are used depending on the types of transactions in which the foreign currency is received.

Section 2(a) obligations are imposed on the state of the payor, not the state of the payee. The obligation is to avoid restrictions on the *making* of payments and not on their *receipt*. A member, consistent with Section 2(a), may thus prescribe that its residents shall accept payments only in specified currencies and this list of prescribed currencies need not include the member's own currency. Such a prescription requirement is consistent with a multilateral system of payments because all other countries, in accordance with Section 2(a), are to permit their resident-payors to obtain and use the currency prescribed.[42] However, a prescription requirement may in certain cases be a "discrimatory currency arrangement" or a "multiple currency practice" offending Section 3 of Article VIII.[43]

Use and Transfer of Balances by Nonresidents.

Section 2(a) imposes an obligation on member countries toward nonresidents. Nonresidents that have

[40] As of December 1982, about three-fifths of the IMF members that accepted Article VIII required the surrender of export proceeds. IMF, *Annual Report on Exchange Arrangements and Exchange Restrictions, 1983*, pp. 524–29.

[41] The IMF has given attention to retention quotas (described at page 386) since the early 1950s. See Stephen A. Silard, "The Impact of the International Monetary Fund on International Trade," *Journal of World Trade Law*, vol. 2 (1968), p. 121 at pp. 144–46; and *IMF History 1945–65, supra* note 39, vol. 2, pp. 263–66 and 293–95. Some countries have apparently avoided IMF scrutiny by using only "trade" regulations rather than currency retention quotas. New Zealand had an elaborate "replacement import license" scheme in the period 1967–1980. See IMF, *Annual Report on Exchange Arrangements and Exchange Restrictions, 1979*, pp. 296–97.

[42] See Joseph Gold, *Use, Conversion, and Exchange of Currency Under the Second Amendment of the Fund's Articles* (IMF Pamphlet Series no. 23; Washington, 1978), p. 6; and Gold, *Fund's Concepts of Convertibility, supra* note 38, p. 9. As of December 1982, 23 IMF members that accepted the obligations of Article VIII maintained currency prescription requirements. IMF, *Annual Report on Exchange Arrangements and Exchange Restrictions, 1983*, pp. 524–29.

[43] See James E.S. Fawcett, "The International Monetary Fund and International Law," *British Yearbook of International Law*, vol. 40 (1964), p. 32 at p. 45. Mr. Fawcett was General Counsel of the IMF 1955–1960.

Egypt at one time required that payments for exports of raw cotton to convertible currency countries be received only in Swiss francs, Deutsche mark, or other currency acceptable to the Exchange Control Administration; IMF, *27th Annual Report on Exchange Restrictions, 1976*, p. 160. This was not a discriminatory practice or a multiple rate arrangement so long as those currencies were readily available in the exchange markets.

recently acquired balances of the country's currency as a result of current international transactions must be permitted to transfer those balances.[44] The state of issue cannot, by currency regulations, restrict the nonresident's choice to sell or transfer the currency to nationals or government agencies in its own state, in other member states, or in the issuing state so long as the transfers do not represent capital movements.[45] This rule makes it possible for nonresident payees to use the proceeds of current transactions in one country to engage in current transactions in other countries. As Joseph Gold has said, "By not restricting transfers, members avoid an impediment to the freedom of parties to buy and sell in markets of their choice and contribute to 'a multilateral system of payments in respect of current transactions between members.' "[46]

Types of Restrictions Prohibited by Section 2(a).

To run afoul of Section 2(a) the restriction must be a "currency" restriction. According to a frequently cited Fund decision, "The guiding principle in ascertaining whether a measure is a restriction on payments and transfers for current transactions under Article VIII, Section 2, is whether it involves a direct governmental limitation on the availability or use of exchange as such."[47] A measure that is a currency restriction comes within Fund jurisdiction under Section 2(a) even if it has a non-balance-of-payments motivation.[48]

A measure that is articulated in the form of a quantitative limitation on imports has the effect of limiting the quantity of payments to nonresidents, but it is not a payments restriction. A country that limits the importation of particular commodities, or requires that exporters and importers insure all risks of loss with local insurance companies, does not breach Section 2(a). Restrictions that are formulated as trade restrictions *do not* become payments restrictions within the meaning of Section 2(a) because they are imposed for the purpose of conserving foreign exchange.

---

[44] Section 2(a) has been understood in Fund practice to permit a country to restrict the transfer of balances recently acquired as a result of current transactions from subsequent use in capital transactions. Also, if the currency was not "recently acquired" (to be judged by usual business practices, for example, in repatriation of profits) or was acquired in a capital transaction, its transfer for current as well as capital transactions can be restricted. James G. Evans, Jr., "Current and Capital Transactions: How the Fund Defines Them," *Finance and Development*, vol. 5, no. 3 (September 1968), p. 30 at p. 32. The obligation toward foreign monetary authorities stated in section 4(a) of Article VIII is broader. See pages 421–422, *infra*.

[45] The nonresident's own state may, of course, require that the currency be surrendered to its monetary authorities. The state of issue in compliance with section 2(a) must permit that transfer.

[46] Gold, *Fund's Concepts of Convertibility, supra* note 38, p. 9. The inner quotation is from Article I(iv) of the IMF Agreement.

[47] E.B. Decision No. 1034 -(60/27)(June 1, 1960), paragraph 1; *IMF History 1945–65, supra* note 39, vol. 3, p. 260; *Selected Decisions* (10th issue, 1983), p. 241.

[48] E.B. Decision No. 1034, *idem,* paragraph 2; and E.B. Decision No. 144 -(52/51), *infra* note 159. The Fund also has jurisdiction, under section 3 of IMF Article VIII, over multiple currency practices and discriminatory currency arrangements regardless of whether they have a balance-of-payments motivation. E.B. Decision No. 1034, *supra;* and E.B. Decision No. 6790, *infra* note 64, paragraph 4.

Further, the IMF has taken the position that a general law that prohibits banks from providing exchange to finance forbidden imports does not violate Section 2(a). If a country, for example, has a trade restriction forbidding the import of automobiles or cinema films and includes in its exchange controls a provision prohibiting the use of foreign exchange for prohibited imports, that is not an exchange restriction prohibited by Section 2(a).[49]

If a country's authorities condition the validation of a new foreign-owned investment in the country upon a specific commitment of the owners to reinvest profits rather than distribute dividends, this is a transaction control outside the scope of Section 2(a). On the other hand, a law that establishes a class of companies (in which it is lawful for nationals and foreigners to invest) that are forbidden to transfer dividends to nonresidents would violate Section 2(a).[50]

"Restrictions" are only those measures that interfere with payments and transfers for current transactions. A member may maintain controls to obtain statistical data or to segregate capital transactions from current ones. These "passive" controls so long as they not inhibit, delay, or prevent payments or transfers in respect of current transactions are consistent with Article VIII.[51]

What is Capital, What is Current?   Section 2(a) is directed only to payments and transfers for current international transactions. The Fund Articles explicitly permit the regulation of international capital movements. Section 3 of Article VI provides:

> Members may exercise such controls as are necessary to regulate international capital movements, but no member may exercise these controls in a manner which will restrict payments for current transactions or which will unduly delay transfers of funds in settlement of commitments. . . .

---

[49] See Joseph Gold, *The Fund Agreement in the Courts* (2 vols.; Washington: IMF, vol. 1, 1962; vol. 2, 1982), vol. 2, pp. 190–97 especially pp. 194–96. The case discussed by Sir Joseph involved a service contract between a Japanese motion picture corporation and a French resident which under Japanese law required government approval.

A question that remains in some doubt is the effect of laws vesting exchange control authorities with discretion to approve or disapprove the underlying transaction. If they deny approval, is that act an exchange restriction masquerading as a transaction control or can the "two hats" worn by the authorities be separated?

[50] See text accompanying note 57, *infra*, respecting controls in Japan. See also note 51.

[51] An example of a passive control is the requirement, at one time imposed by Japan, that the transfer abroad of dividends of yen 3.6 million or more required the filing of an auditor's certificate. Also a dividend transfer from a company more than 30 percent owned by nonresidents required such a certificate. Japanese authorities examined the certificate to assure that the proposed transfer accorded with terms of the original approval of the investment. Such a control is in accord with Article VIII so long as the procedure does not result in undue delay for bona fide transfers. See text accompanying note 57, *infra;* and Price Waterhouse & Co., *Doing Business in Japan* (New York, 1975), p. 10.

Regulations issued under the U.S. Currency and Foreign Transactions Reporting Act require banks, financial institutions, and corporations to regularly report their foreign currency transactions. *United States Code,* title 31, sections 1051–1143; and *Code of Federal Regulations,* title 31, part 128.

How are capital movements to be distinguished from current payments and transfers? Article XXX(d)[52] provides the following definition of payments for current transactions:

Payments for current transactions means payments which are not for the purpose of transferring capital, and includes, without limitation:
(1) all payments due in connection with foreign trade, other current business, including services, and normal short-term banking and credit facilities;
(2) payments due as interest on loans and as net income from other investments;
(3) payments of moderate amount for amortization of loans or for depreciation of direct investments; and
(4) moderate remittances for family living expenses.

The Fund may, after consultation with the members concerned, determine whether certain specific transactions are to be considered current transactions or capital transactions.

The definition does not precisely track the use of the words "current" and "capital" by economists or cost accountants. It was adopted to obtain certain policy objectives and extends to all payments which in pursuance of these objectives are to be given preferential treatment.[53] The phrase "payments for current transactions" encompasses all payments due in connection with foreign trade, with current business, and in connection with services. It includes all payments due in connection with "normal short-term banking and credit facilities."[54] Payments of interest on loans, net income from investments, and moderate amounts for amortization of loans and depreciation of direct investments are brought within the definition.[55] The application of the definition in Article XXX(d) is illustrated by the following example:[56]

A company, planning to expand its operations, purchases new machinery

---

[52] Formerly Article XIX(i), *original* and *first*. The language is the same.

[53] Rainer Geiger, "Legal Aspects of Convertibility," *Georgia Journal of International and Comparative Law*, vol. 4 (1974), p. 74 at p. 78.

[54] The drafting history and Fund practice make clear that "short-term" means "within one year," and "normal facility" means "the customary practice in the particular trade or business for which the facility is being made available." If in the particular line of business the normal facility is 180 days, that would appear to be the criterion. The banking and credit facilities covered are those necessary to keep trade moving and to sustain current business operations, not those related to direct investment and other capital movements. See Evans, *supra* note 44, p. 35.

[55] Economists for some purposes treat amortization and depreciation as "capital" items; the IMF Articles treat them as "current." There is a qualifying phrase, that the payments be "of moderate amount." The regularity of these payments and the problems caused by their interruption justify their treatment as current payments for purposes of exchange regulation.

The staff of the Fund has taken the position that the first consideration in measuring depreciation is the local experience as to the "useful lifespan" of any item of plant or equipment. Evans, *supra* note 44, p. 34.

[56] This example, although somewhat modified, was suggested by Evans, *idem,* p. 30.

from abroad. Since this machinery is unfamiliar, the company decides to have the installation done by a foreign firm. For accounting or tax purposes the costs of the machinery and its installation may be treated as "capital" expenditures. An exchange controller, applying the IMF Agreement, would view the payments made for the machinery and its installation as payments for "current" transactions. If the purchase of the machinery and the cost of its installation were financed through a normal short-term credit extended by a bank in the exporter's country or other IMF member country, the company's payment liquidating the loan would also be a payment for a current transaction.

Suppose the purchase of the machinery was financed by a ten-year loan extended by a bank in the exporter's country. Exchange regulations relating to capital movements in the purchaser's country or in the bank's country could, consistent with the Fund Agreement, prohibit the loan from being made. However, if the loan is lawfully made, the exchange control regulations of the purchaser's country must permit the company to pay the interest on the loan and "reasonable amounts" for amortization of the principal as these payments become due—these payments being treated by the Fund Agreement as "current."

While the Fund's definition of current payments is very broad, a country can sometimes accomplish the substance of a restriction on current payments by means of a capital control. When Japan assumed Article VIII status in 1964, it had to terminate its system that channeled investment from abroad into "yen base companies" that by law were forbidden to transfer dividends abroad. In its place Japan put new controls on the entry of capital—entry being conditioned upon the investor making commitments respecting arrangements with joint venture partners, royalty calculations, and *reinvestment of profits*—that as capital controls did not offend Article VIII.[57]

Obligations of Section 3

Multiple Exchange Rates. Different exchange rates for different classes of transactions can have essentially the same effects as taxes and subsidies upon trade in the goods or services affected. Multiple rate systems have been used to limit the amount of foreign exchange provided by authorities for import of low-priority items. Multiple rates have also been used to raise revenue where monetary authorities maintained a significant spread between buying and selling rates. According to the IMF's research, multiple rate systems can be expected to distort economies and are difficult to administer.[58] Further, their use nor-

---

[57] See Robert S. Ozaki, *The Control of Imports and Foreign Capital in Japan* (New York: Praeger Publishers, 1972), pp. 50, 83, and 104; and Dan Fenno Henderson, *Foreign Enterprise in Japan: Laws and Policies* (Chapel Hill: University of North Carolina Press, 1973), pp. 269–72. See also note 51, *supra.* The controls were subsequently liberalized. See notes 398–403, *infra,* and accompanying text.

[58] See notes 27, 28, 41, and 43, *supra,* and accompanying text for examples of multiple currency practices. See generally Swidrowski, *Exchange and Trade Controls, supra* note 10, pp. 70–84. W. John R.

mally does not promote a stable system of exchange rates, a specific concern articulated in Article XIV, Section 2, as well as in Section 1 of Article IV.

The introduction of multiple rates that raise the cost of currency for any class of current transactions, unless the IMF approves, violates Article VIII, Section 2(a).[59] Section 3 of Article VIII, complementing Section 2(a), specifically prohibits multiple currency practices (multiple exchange rates). Section 3, in its present form, makes clear that multiple currency practices, whether within or outside margins under Article IV or prescribed by or under Schedule C, except as authorized by the Articles or approved by the Fund, are prohibited. A member's freedom to choose exchange arrangements under Article IV does not authorize the imposition of multiple currency practices or changes in those practices that violate Article VIII, Section 3.[60] Further, all multiple rate systems are subject (as exchange rate systems) to the notification, consultation, and surveillance provisions of Article IV and its implementing decisions.[61]

An early decision of the Fund established that multiple currency practices affecting current transactions can be introduced or *adapted to new conditions* only with the approval of the Fund under Article VIII, Section 3, even if the country relies upon the transitional regime of Article XIV.[62] The rule still applies.[63]

The Executive Board in 1979 confirmed as policy that, under the Second Amendment, only multiple currency practices resulting from official action come within the Fund's approval jurisdiction under Article VIII, Section 3.[64] Official actors include the government and any of its fiscal agencies (treasury, central bank, stabilization fund, and similar agency). Diverse exchange rates that result solely from the interplay of market forces do not require the Fund's approval. The Executive Board in 1981 adopted a decision[65] that sets forth criteria for identifying multiple currency practices that require Fund approval under Article VIII, Section 3:

    (a) Action by a government or its fiscal agencies that of itself gives rise to a spread of more than 2 percent between buying and selling rates for

Woodley, "Multiple Currency Practices," *Finance and Development,* vol. 3, no. 2 (June 1966), p. 113, examines the economic effects of multiple rates. Fishlow, *supra* note 27, appraises the tax and subsidy effects of multiple rate systems that have been used in Brazil.

[59] See pages 390–391, *supra.*

[60] Sir Joseph Gold recently stated that the contrary view "has never been suggested." Joseph Gold, *SDRs, Currencies, and Gold: Sixth Survey of New Legal Developments* (IMF Pamphlet Series no. 40; Washington, 1983), p. 18.

[61] See Chapter 11, *infra,* pages 527–530 and 558–568.

[62] E.B. Decision No. 237-2 (December 18, 1947), *supra* note 39, paragraph II(B)(5).

[63] See Gold, *Sixth Survey, supra* note 60, pp. 18–19.

[64] IMF, *Annual Report on Exchange Arrangements and Exchange Restrictions, 1980,* p. 17. This policy was reaffirmed in E.B. Decision No. 6790 -(81/43)(March 20, 1981); IMF, *Annual Report, 1981,* p. 163; *Selected Decisions* (10th issue, 1983), p. 257. For background on the adoption of Decision No. 6790, see IMF, *Annual Report on Exchange Arrangements and Exchange Restrictions, 1981,* pp. 22–25; and *IMF Survey,* July 6, 1981, pp. 197 and 204–09. See generally Gold, *Sixth Survey, supra* note 60, pp. 17–35.

[65] E.B. Decision No. 6790, *supra* note 64.

spot exchange transactions between the member's currency and any other member's currency,[66] or

(b) Action by a government or its fiscal agencies which results in midpoint spot exchange rates of other members' currencies against its own currency in a relationship which differs by more than 1 percent from the midpoint spot exchange rates for these currencies in their principal markets (i.e. broken cross-rates).[67]

In the case of spreads ("a" above), Fund approval is required for such a scheme to be introduced and for any significant changes in it. The Fund will normally grant approval for a temporary period provided it is satisfied that the measure is temporary, the member is endeavoring to correct its balance-of-payments problems, the measure does not discriminate among IMF members, and the measure does not give the country an unfair competitive advantage over other members.[68]

If the scheme ("a" above) is a "complex multiple rate system"—that is, sets up different classes of current transactions with different buying rates or different selling rates for one class of transactions compared to another—the Fund will not approve the practice unless the country is "making reasonable progress toward simplification and ultimate elimination" of the system.[69]

In the case of broken cross-rates ("b" above), if the differentials of more than 1 percent persist for more than one week, the practice is subject to approval under Article VIII, Section 3. The Fund is "very reluctant" to grant approval for the maintenance of broken cross-rates, because they usually discriminate among IMF members or foster instability.[70]

Some practices that do not obviously display themselves in the exchange markets may, nevertheless, be multiple currency practices. A currency retention scheme usually results in a practice requiring approval under Section 3 of Article VIII.[71]

Any IMF approval of a multiple currency practice is always on a temporary basis and subject to further review.[72]

---

[66] *Idem*, paragraph 1(a). When governments or their fiscal agencies decree buying and selling rates with spreads of more than 2 percent, that is a multiple currency practice. On the other hand, where commercial banks are allowed to set rates and a spread exceeds 2 percent (say, amounts to 4.5 percent), a multiple currency practice is involved only if official action (say, an exchange tax) is of itself responsible for more than 2 percent of that spread.

[67] E.B. Decision No. 6790, *supra* note 64, paragraph 1(b).

[68] *Idem*, paragraph 2. See also E.B. Decision No. 1034, *supra* note 47, paragraph 2.

[69] E.B. Decision No. 6790, *supra* note 64, paragraph 3. This paragraph reaffirms the policies stated in E.B. Decision No. 649 -(57/33)(June 26, 1957); *IMF History 1945–65, supra* note 39, vol. 3, p. 265; *Selected Decisions* (10th issue, 1983), p. 255. For background see *IMF History 1945–65*, vol. 1, p. 408, and vol. 2, p. 145.

[70] E.B. Decision No. 6790, *supra* note 64, paragraphs 1(b) and 2.

[71] See E.B. Decision No. 201 -(53/29)(May 4, 1953); *IMF History 1945–65, supra* note 39, vol. 3, p. 258; *Selected Decisions* (10th issue, 1983), p. 237. See also Gold, *Sixth Survey, supra* note 60, p. 35. Retention quotas are explained in the text accompanying note 19, *supra*.

[72] See text accompanying note 86, *infra*. See also IMF, *Annual Report on Exchange Arrangements and Exchange Restrictions, 1983*, p. 40.

Whether Section 3 of Article VIII applies only to multiple currency practices that relate to payments and transfers for current transactions or also applies to rates applicable to capital transactions is an unresolved issue. This issue and related matters concerning the application of the IMF Articles to two-tier exchange markets, where exchange transactions related to capital movements take place at a different rate from the one applicable to current transactions, are treated in Chapter 11.[73]

When multiple currency practices operate as a subsidy to exports, they may be met by countervailing duties where the countries are parties to the General Agreement on Tariffs and Trade.[74]

When monetary assets are nationalized it is not always easy to tell whether or not multiple currency practices and/or restrictions on payments prohibited by Article VIII, Sections 2(a) and 3, are involved. Many residents of the United States in 1982 held certificates of deposit issued by Mexican commercial banks denominated in U.S. dollars and payable in Mexico. In regulations effective August 13, 1982, Mexican authorities decreed "pesofication" of these certificates—the obligations to be paid in pesos at a rate of 70 pesos to the dollar.[75] Because this rate was different from other exchange rates between the peso and the dollar (the lawful free rate then exceeded 105 pesos to the dollar), a question arose whether the Mexican action required IMF approval as a multiple currency practice. Mexican authorities argued that the commercial banks were never obligated to pay in U.S. dollars and the dollar was simply used for valuation purposes. They argued that the government's action was not an exchange rate practice (since, by their argument, the exchanges of U.S. dollars for pesos were made when the accounts were opened) or a restriction on international payments (since the nonresidents could convert the pesos received into dollars, admittedly at a different rate, and transfer them out of the country). The IMF's legal staff, at least initially, accepted the argument.[76] The Mexican argument that "pesofication" at a special rate was not an exchange measure, and thus did not require IMF approval under Article VIII, sections 2(a) and 3, is probably unsound. The matter is in litigation.[77]

---

[73] At pages 551–554, *infra*. The reader is advised to first read the discussion of capital controls at pages 449–477 of this chapter.

[74] See interpretative notes in General Agreement on Tariffs and Trade, Annex 1, Ad Article VI, paragraphs 2 and 3, note 2; and Ad Article VIII, paragraph 1. The notes appear in GATT, *Basic Instruments and Selected Documents* (Geneva: GATT), vol. 4 (1969), pp. 64–65; reprinted in John H. Jackson, *World Trade and the Law of GATT* (Indianapolis: Bobbs-Merrill Co., 1969), pp. 868–69. See also Professor Jackson's comments, *idem*, pp. 401–38 and 455; and Gold, *Sixth Survey, supra* note 60, pp. 34–35.

[75] *El Nacional*, August 13, 1982; and *Diario Oficial*, August 13, 18, and 25, 1982, and September 1, 1982 (Article 3 of exchange control decree). See also Stephen Zamora, "Peso-Dollar Economics and the Imposition of Foreign Exchange Controls in Mexico," *American Journal of Comparative Law*, vol. 32 (1984), p. 99 at pp. 105–06.

[76] Letter dated May 3, 1983, from George P. Nicoletopoulos, Director, Legal Department of the IMF, to Preston Brown, Curtis Mallet-Prevost Colt & Mosle, Washington, D.C.

[77] *Frankel v. Banco Nacional de Mexico*, Case No. 82-Civil-6457, United States District Court for the Southern District of New York; and *Callejo v. Bancomer, S.A.*, Cases Nos. CA-3-82-1604-D and CA-3-82-1605-D, United States District Court for the Northern District of Texas.

Discriminatory Currency Arrangements; Bilateral Payments Agreements. Section 3 of Article VIII prohibits discriminatory currency arrangements. While such arrangements can take a variety of forms, [78] bilateral payments arrangements are among the chief offenders. These arrangements have in recent years been used primarily by socialist countries to shepherd their holdings of convertible currencies. Operations under bilateral arrangements were examined in Chapters 4 and 9.[79] National regulations of countries that are parties to bilateral agreements usually encourage importers and exporters to buy from and sell to bilateral partners rather than from the international market in order that the bilateral accounts be kept in balance.

All discriminatory currency arrangements, including bilateral payments agreements with members or nonmembers, maintained by Article VIII countries require the IMF's approval. The Fund's policy is not to approve the renewal of these agreements. Among all Article VIII countries, only Ecuador, Mexico, and Finland presently maintain any operative bilateral arrangements with members and only Costa Rica, Ecuador, Finland, and Peru maintain any operative bilateral arrangements with nonmembers. The People's Republic of China and a number of other countries under the Article XIV transitional regime maintain a significant number of bilateral payments arrangements. [80]

Most bilateral payments agreements are for a stated number of years (typically five or ten years) and provide for renewal by mutual consent. It appears that a renewal is normally treated by the IMF as an "adaptation" of a restrictive practice that is legally permitted a member that relies upon Article XIV, Section 2. The Fund, nevertheless, presses for the termination of these arrangements because of their discriminatory effects. A Fund decision adopted in 1955, and still in force, "urges the full collaboration of all its members to reduce and to eliminate as rapidly as practicable reliance on bilateralism."[81] The IMF's *Annual Report on Exchange Arrangements and Exchange Restrictions* always discusses those bilateral arrangements still in operation.

---

[78] See notes 29–32 and 43, *supra,* and accompanying text.

[79] At pages 135 and 358–360.

[80] See IMF, *Annual Report on Exchange Arrangements and Exchange Restrictions, 1983,* pp. 44–46 and 524–29. As of December 31, 1982, there were 62 operative bilateral payments agreements between pairs of IMF members.

[81] E.B. Decision No. 433 -(55/42)(June 22, 1955); *IMF History 1945–65, supra* note 39, vol. 3, p. 258; *Selected Decisions* (10th issue, 1983), p. 236. See also E.B. Decision No. 201 -(53/29), *supra* note 71; and E.B. Decision No. 955 -(59/45)(October 23, 1959); *IMF History 1945–65,* vol. 3, p. 260; *Selected Decisions,* p. 240.

Bilateral payments arrangements, and the Fund's attitude toward them, are discussed in *IMF History 1945–65,* vol. 2, pp. 280–83; Silard, "Impact of the International Monetary Fund," *supra* note 41, pp. 140–44; Swidrowski, *Exchange and Trade Controls, supra* note 10, pp. 54–60; and Jozef Swidrowski, "Bilateralism in Payments and Trade," *Finance and Development,* vol. 5, no. 3 (September 1968), p. 18. See also IMF, *Annual Report on Exchange Arrangements and Exchange Restrictions, 1983,* pp. 44–46.

The Fund's Practices in Granting and Withholding Approvals Under Sections 2(a) and 3

Introductory Comment.   If a member that has accepted the obligations of Article VIII, Sections 2, 3, and 4, believes that it must impose restrictions, multiple currency practices, or discriminatory arrangements prohibited by Section 2(a) and/or Section 3, it can request the approval of the Fund. If the Fund approves, the action is then consistent with obligations of those sections. Members that are under the transitional regime of Article XIV must obtain the Fund's approval for "new" restrictions.[82]

The request for approval is to be in writing and state the reasons for the request.[83] An early Fund decision states that members have a duty to consult with the Fund and obtain its approval before introducing a multiple currency practice or making a significant change in their exchange systems.[84] While this sometimes occurs, often the measure inconsistent with Section 2(a) and/or Section 3 is introduced, and approval is requested afterwards. The decision to approve, approve subject to conditions, or to decline to approve, is normally made by the Executive Board. The Board is directed to decide the request expeditiously.[85] Normally the Board's decision is made by consensus; but, if a formal vote is taken, action requires a simple majority of the weighted votes cast. Approvals are normally not retroactive. Approvals usually have an expiration date which is normally not beyond the time of the next regular Article IV consultation with the country (usually no longer than a year).[86]

The failure to obtain approval from the Fund can have important consequences. It is a violation of the Articles subject to the sanctions applicable to violations generally.[87] The maintenance of unapproved restrictions and practices in breach of the Articles may be taken into account by the Fund in determining whether a proposed drawing in the General Resources Account is in accord with the Fund's policies.[88] The introduction or intensification of such

---

[82] See pages 423–425, *infra.*

[83] Rule H-4; *By-Laws, Rules and Regulations* (40th issue, 1983).

[84] E.B. Decision No. 237-2 (December 18, 1947); *supra* note 39, paragraphs I(A)(i) and II(B)(5). See also quotation from E.B. Decision No. 5712 in note 39, *supra.*

Sir Joseph Gold, writing in 1983, stated: "The Fund has always understood the necessity for approval to mean approval before a practice is instituted." Gold, *Sixth Survey, supra* note 60, p. 18.

[85] Rule H-5; *By-Laws, Rules and Regulations* (40th issue, 1983).

[86] See, e.g., E.B. Decision No. 6790, *supra* note 64, paragraph 5.

[87] See Chapter 1, *supra,* pages 39–42. One of the factors leading to the withdrawal of Cuba from the IMF in 1964 was its failure to provide information required by the Fund in order to determine whether or not to approve currency restrictions. Joseph Gold, *Membership and Nonmembership in the International Monetary Fund* (Washington: IMF, 1974), pp. 342–44; and *IMF History 1945–65, supra* note 39, vol. 1, pp. 548–50.

[88] See Chapter 6, *supra,* page 246. See also, *infra,* pages 410–411 and 412–413.

measures usually interrupts drawings under stand-by and extended arrangements.[89] There is no obligation upon members to give extraterritorial recognition to unapproved restrictions maintained by IMF members in violation of the Articles of Agreement.[90]

The Fund does not approve a country's law or regulation as such. Its approval is required only for restrictions and practices inconsistent with Sections 2(a) and 3 that are caused by application of the law or regulation. Many countries that have accepted Article VIII have laws authorizing exchange restrictions, but if the laws are not implemented there is no need for Fund approval. Also, if requests for foreign exchange must be submitted to the central bank, a trade agency, or other body that by law has discretion to determine whether or not exchange shall be provided, there is no restriction requiring Fund approval so long as all bona fide requests for exchange for payments and transfers respecting current transactions are in fact promptly granted.[91]

It should also be said at the outset of this discussion that, with certain exceptions, restrictions imposed only against the territory of a nonmember of the Fund do not require approval under Article VIII.[92] It should also be noted that the currency convertibility provisions of IMF Article VIII may be reinforced in other international agreements. Thus, a country imposing restrictions may have to get approval not only from the IMF but also from the parties to other instruments.[93]

Fund Policies.   The Fund's attitude toward restrictions imposed for balance-of-payments purposes is stated in an often-cited decision of June 1, 1960:

> If members, for balance of payments reasons, propose to maintain or introduce measures which require approval under Article VIII, the Fund will grant approval only where it is satisfied that the measures

---

[89] See page 253 for the language in paragraph 4(e) of the 1981 extended arrangement for India, which is typical.

[90] See pages 477–484, *infra.*

[91] In Italy effective May 6, 1974, the supervision over the allocation of foreign exchange for family remittances, gifts, and medical expenses was tightened. Approval authority delegated to commercial banks for these items was reduced from 1 million lire for each remitter during a period of three months to 35,000 lire a transfer. Since remittances of reasonable additional amounts for family or medical expenses or gifts were permitted by the Italian Exchange Office in all bona fide cases, the Fund's approval was not required. Letter dated March 2, 1976, from F. Palamenghi-Crispi, Executive Director of the IMF (Italy), to the author; and IMF, *26th Annual Report on Exchange Restrictions, 1975,* p. 263. See pages 406–407, *infra,* respecting travel restrictions introduced by Italy in May 1974 that required IMF approval.

[92] See pages 420–421, *infra.*

[93] For example, Article 106 of the Treaty Establishing the European Economic Community provides that each member state authorize the transfer of funds relating to movements of goods, services, and capital, to the extent that such movements have been liberalized pursuant to the Treaty. Member states facing serious balance-of-payments problems may derogate from these obligations only with the authorization of the Commission granted under Article 108, subdivision 3, unless there is a "sudden crisis" in which case Article 109 applies. See discussion of the application of these provisions at pages 446–448 and 473–477, *infra.*

are *necessary* and that their use will be *temporary* while the member is seeking to eliminate the need for them. [emphasis added][94]

The application of this statement and of more specific policies articulated in other decisions will be discussed below.

The Fund has jurisdiction under Article VIII, Sections 2(a) and 3, over all currency restrictions respecting current transactions, multiple currency practices, and discriminatory currency arrangements including those introduced and maintained for reasons unrelated to the balance of payments.[95] The Fund "believes that the use of exchange systems for nonbalance of payments reasons should be avoided to the greatest possible extent."[96] It is, however, prepared to grant temporary approval provided the measures do not materially impede the member's balance-of-payments adjustment, do not harm the interests of other members, and do not discriminate among members.[97]

The tables at the end of each *Annual Report on Exchange Arrangements and Exchange Restrictions* list IMF member-countries that have restrictions on payments in respect of current transactions with other member-countries. These are currency restrictions in the form of quantitative limits or undue delay other than restrictions imposed for security reasons. Except for the security reason exception, the definition is intended to have the same meaning as "restrictions on the making of payments and transfers for current international transactions" as used in Section 2(a) of Article VIII. The tables also display information on multiple currency practices and bilateral payments arrangements. The particular practices can be identified through a careful reading of the country summaries and chronologies.

Usually each year at least a few countries that have accepted the obligations of Article VIII are listed in the tables as having restrictions on current payments or transfers or multiple currency practices. Some of these practices may have been approved by the Fund, while others may be unapproved. A number

---

[94] E.B. Decision No. 1034, *supra* note 47, paragraph 2. The decision was adopted at a time when a number of European countries were considering a coordinated move from Article XIV to Article VIII status. The decision clarified the rights and obligations that members would have upon assuming the obligations of Article VIII. Belgium, France, Federal Republic of Germany, Ireland, Italy, Luxembourg, the Netherlands, Sweden, and the United Kingdom accepted Article VIII, sections 2, 3, and 4, effective February 15, 1961. Peru also accepted Article VIII effective February 15, 1961, and Saudi Arabia as of March 22, 1961. The Fund's experience in working over the preceding decade for the withdrawal of restrictions by these countries is set forth in *IMF History 1945–65, supra* note 39, vol. 2, chapters 6 and 10–16. The drafting of Decision No. 1034 is described in *IMF History 1945–65,* vol. 1, pp. 477–82. See also Alfred E. Eckes, Jr., *A Search for Solvency* (Austin: University of Texas Press, 1975), chapter 8; Erin E. Jacobsson, *A Life for Sound Money: Per Jacobsson, His Biography* (Oxford: Oxford University Press, 1979), pp. 303–10; and Committee on the Working of the Monetary System (Radcliffe Committee), *Report* (Cmnd. 827; London: Her Majesty's Stationery Office, 1959).

[95] See note 48, *supra,* and accompanying text.

[96] E.B. Decision No. 1034, *supra* note 47, paragraph 2.

[97] *Idem;* and E.B. Decision No. 6790, *supra* note 64, paragraph 4. See also discussion of security restrictions at pages 415–420, *infra.*

of Article XIV countries, subsequent to becoming Fund members, have also imposed new restrictions that were subject to approval under Article VIII. These practices can be identified by studying the country summaries in the *Annual Report on Exchange Arrangements and Exchange Restrictions* and comparing the summaries with those of previous years. Again, some may be approved and others unapproved. The Fund sometimes publicly announces its approval of restrictions, but often does not. The Fund does respond to inquiries about whether particular restrictions have or have not been approved.[98]

Restrictions in Effect Upon Acceptance of Article VIII.   In a number of cases in the past when countries moved from Article XIV to Article VIII status, they have retained restrictions on some current payments. The Executive Board in February 1961 approved on a "temporary basis" the continuance of certain restrictions by Belgium, France, Luxembourg, and the Netherlands at the time they accepted the obligations of Article VIII. The restrictions were "not extensive" and most were subsequently eliminated.[99]

When Japan assumed Article VIII status in April 1964 the Fund gave temporary approval to two restrictions respecting the settlement of current transactions. The Japanese requirement that its residents make payments to residents of the Republic of Korea only through the mechanism of a bilateral payments agreement ended when that agreement was terminated in March 1966. The second approved restriction, relating to the provision of exchange for foreign travel, was eliminated in April 1969.[100]

It appears that in recent years countries have been encouraged to eliminate all restrictions before formally assuming the obligations of Article VIII, Sections 2, 3, and 4. To the best of the author's knowledge, since 1970 no country at the time it assumed Article VIII status has maintained any currency restrictions or multiple currency practices (other than ones related to security) that required Fund approval.[101]

---

[98] E.B. Decision No. 446-4 (June 10, 1949); *IMF History 1945–65, supra* note 39, vol. 3, p. 256; *Selected Decisions* (10th issue, 1983), p. 233.

[99] *IMF History 1945–65, supra* note 39, vol. 1, pp. 481–82, and vol. 2, pp. 289–90. The Netherlands, for example, had restrictions on the transfer of funds abroad to nonresidents on account of inheritances and legacies. These restrictions were abolished in October 1961. IMF, *13th Annual Report on Exchange Restrictions, 1962,* p. 248. The Netherlands also placed limits on the amount of currency that a resident could take abroad while traveling. Since the latter limitations were reasonable and were waived if there was bona fide need for more, it appears that the Fund's approval of these controls was not required. The Belgium-Luxembourg Economic Union retains with important modifications a dual exchange market, basically one for current and one for capital transactions, introduced before the two countries accepted the obligations of Article VIII. See Chapter 11, *infra,* page 553 (note 248).

[100] IMF, *15th Annual Report on Exchange Restrictions, 1964,* pp. 275–82; *16th Report 1965,* pp. 305–11; *17th Report 1966,* pp. 316–22; *18th Report 1967,* pp. 353–59; *20th Report 1969,* p. 538; and *21st Report 1970,* pp. 3 and 281.

[101] After it accepted the obligations of Article VIII in August 1962, Austria continued to maintain some restrictions on payments to residents of IMF member states. These restrictions were terminated following the expiration of the payments agreement with the German Democratic Republic (a nonmember) in January

Limitations on Travel Allowances. A number of countries, after assuming Article VIII status, have at various times imposed currency restrictions affecting foreign travel. Of all invisible transactions, transactions made by residents while traveling abroad are among the most difficult to control without regulating the quantity of currency that can be taken abroad. Restrictions on the amount of exchange to be used by a resident for travel have often been adopted not simply to control travel expenditures but mainly to prevent circumventions of controls on capital movements (e.g., the resident while abroad purchases an investment security for cash). As noted above, the Fund approved Japan's currency restrictions on travel expenditures in effect until 1969. Only a few out of many other examples can be cited here.

The United Kingdom maintained restrictions on travel allowances for residents from April 1966 until January 1970.[102] These restrictions were approved by the Executive Board in a series of decisions, the last of which was in October 1969.[103]

France restricted allowances for foreign travel by residents in the period May 1968–December 1971. Their introduction was triggered by widespread strikes throughout France in May 1968 that led to large sales of francs in the exchange markets. French authorities imposed comprehensive restraints on capital movements complemented by restrictions on allowances for foreign travel by French residents. The controls were terminated in September. Faced with a fresh wave of currency speculation which led to the closing of European exchange markets on November 20, French authorities on November 24 reintroduced controls primarily directed to capital movements but accompanied by restrictions that tightly limited the amount of currency French residents could use for foreign travel and controls on payments for some other invisibles.[104] French authorities requested Executive Board approval under Article VIII of the restrictions on current payments and transfers, the capital controls not re-

1974. IMF, *25th Annual Report on Exchange Restrictions, 1974,* pp. 43–47. The Fund today, if faced with a similar case and the prospect of an 11½-year wait for the lapse of a preferential bilateral agreement, would informally recommend to the country that it take steps to negotiate the early termination of the agreement and not to accept Article VIII status until the agreement had been terminated.

[102] A limit of foreign exchange equivalent to £250 per person per year was originally imposed on travel expenses abroad by U.K. residents. Effective November 1, 1966, the basic allowance was reduced to £50 (then about U.S. $140) per year. Special allotments were made for business travel, travel by officials, travel for health, and in some other cases. The regulations are set forth in Bank of England, *Notice to Banks and Travel Agents, E.C. (General) 12,* 8th Issue, (April 7, 1966) through 14th Issue (November 28, 1969). The actions were taken under the authority of the Exchange Control Act, 1947, sections 34 and 37.

[103] Letter dated February 3, 1976, from B.L. Morris, Bank of England (Exchange Control), to the author.

[104] For background on the crisis, see *IMF History 1966–71, supra* note 38, vol. 1, pp. 352–57 and 449–56. The travel restrictions prohibited French residents touring abroad from taking with them more than 200 francs (then about U.S. $40) in French currency and the equivalent of 500 francs in foreign currencies. For business travel the maximum allowance was the equivalent of 2,000 francs in foreign currencies. Higher amounts required authorization from the Banque de France. Persons going outside France for less than 24 hours were not permitted to take more than 50 francs in French currency. *Journal Officiel de la République Française: Lois et Décrets,* November 25, 1968, p. 11081 at p. 11085.

quiring Fund approval. The Executive Board on December 4, 1968, granted approval on a temporary basis of those restrictions on payments and transfers respecting current transactions. The approval of the IMF in December 1968 on a "temporary" basis was understood to mean a few months only. The approval was renewed in March 1969, December 1969, and December 1970. Consultations between the IMF and France over a three-year period about removal of the restrictions receive comment in Chapter 12.[105] The restrictions were terminated in December 1971.[106] France did not again introduce travel restrictions requiring IMF approval until the spring of 1983.[107]

On May 6, 1974, Italy imposed restrictions on foreign exchange available to residents for tourist and business travel that required IMF approval. Italy had travel allowance limits in effect before that date, but, because reasonable amounts were available upon application, IMF approval was not required.[108] Under the regulations effective May 6 the basic allowance was set at Lire 500,000 (then about U.S. $800) per person per year plus the travel fare. Applications for additional amounts for travel abroad for business, study, and health reasons had to be screened by the Italian Exchange Office and were granted within five or six days provided the authorities were satisfied the request was bona fide. For tourism, applications for exchange in excess of the basic allowance were no longer considered.[109] IMF approval was thus required. The Italian authorities stated to the IMF that the restrictions were introduced on a temporary basis for balance-of-payments purposes and that they would endeavor to remove the restrictions progressively as and when the balance-of-payments position improved. The Executive Board on August 16, 1974, approved the restrictions and subsequently renewed its approval.[110]

In February 1976 a modification in the form in which residents could take funds out of Italy was made to inhibit capital flight through spurious "travel" expenditures. Limits were placed on the amount of travelers checks and Italian and foreign banknotes that the traveler could take aborad, with the authorized balance to be taken in the form of letters of credit, foreign payment orders, or nontransferable checks drawn on foreign banks—all requiring personal presen-

---

[105] At page 605 (note 166), *infra.*

[106] The French controls also involved derogations from obligations under the OECD's Codes of Liberalisation of Current Invisible Operations and of Capital Movements and obligations as a member of the European Economic Community. See pages 463 and 474, *infra.*

[107] Restrictions on foreign exchange for tourist travel were introduced March 28, 1983. *Journal Officiel de la République Française: Lois et Décrets,* March 29, 1983, pp. 956–57; and April 9, 1983, p. 1106. The IMF on June 3, 1983, approved the restrictions on travel payments for the period to the end of 1983. Letter dated November 18, 1983, from George P. Nicoletopoulos, Director, Legal Department of the IMF, to the author. See note 452, *infra,* concerning action of the European Economic Community.

[108] Letter of F. Palamenghi-Crispi, *supra* note 91.

[109] See IMF, *26th Annual Report on Exchange Restrictions, 1975,* pp. 261 and 263.

[110] Letter of F. Palamenghi-Crispi, *supra* note 91. See also note 91, *supra,* regarding practices that did not require approval.

tation to the foreign bank. These modifications were approved by the IMF.[111] Later, beginning in October 1977 the basic allowance was raised and amounts above the basic limit were approved by exchange authorities if reasonable.[112]

Other Article VIII countries that have used travel restrictions at one time or another include Argentina, Costa Rica, Dominican Republic, El Salvador, Guatemala, Guyana, Jamaica, Mexico, the Netherlands, and Peru, and there may be others. These restrictions have also been extensively used by Article XIV countries. If the limit is a reasonable one in the light of the country's problems, the Fund has approved it. The Fund has sometimes refused to approve what it judged to be unreasonable travel allowance restrictions.[113]

Multiple Exchange Rate Practices and Restrictions on Current Payments Resulting from Such Practices.

As explained earlier, multiple exchange rate practices, unless approved by the Fund, violate Section 3 of Article VIII.[114] Multiple rate systems to the extent that they increase the cost of exchange for some current transactions, by routing them to higher rates, are restrictions within the meaning of Section 2(a) on payments and transfers respecting current international transactions. As a consequence, multiple rate systems usually require the Fund's approval under both Sections 2(a) and 3.[115]

In March 1981 the Fund adopted a decision redefining multiple currency practices. That decision, which also outlines the Fund's policies on granting and withholding approval of these practices, was treated earlier.[116]

Recent examples of multiple currency practices by Article VIII countries resulting in currency restrictions that have drawn the Fund's attention include those of Argentina, the Dominican Republic, and Mexico. Argentina's practices in the 1970s were approved in the period before they were terminated in 1977.[117] The Fund did not approve the Dominican Republic's multiple currency practices resulting from an officially tolerated black market during the late 1970s.[118] Mexico's multiple currency practices introduced in 1982 are treated below.[119]

Fund approval jurisdiction over "two-tier" markets, in which exchanges

---

[111] Letter of F. Palamenghi-Crispi, *supra* note 91; and letter dated August 11, 1977, from Lamberto Dini, Executive Director of the IMF (Italy), to the author. The practices are described in IMF, *28th Annual Report on Exchange Restrictions, 1977,* pp. 255 and 258.

[112] IMF, *29th Annual Report on Exchange Restrictions, 1978,* pp. 227 and 229.

[113] See text accompanying note 152, *infra,* regarding the Dominican Republic.

[114] See pages 396–399, *supra.*

[115] See E.B. Decision No. 237-2, *supra* note 39.

[116] E.B. Decision No. 6790, *supra* note 64, discussed at pages 397–398, *supra.*

[117] Argentina during 1976 and 1977 took a series of steps to bring together the rates in its dual exchange market and then unified its market. See IMF, *28th Annual Report on Exchange Restrictions, 1977,* pp. 13 and 40–44; and *29th Report 1978,* pp. 14 and 39.

[118] See text accompanying note 152, *infra.*

[119] At pages 410–411, *infra.* See also page 399, *supra.*

for current transactions take place at one rate and exchanges for capital transactions take place at a different rate, receives further attention in Chapter 11.[120]

The Fund on a few occasions has approved, on a temporary basis, restrictions on current payments or multiple exchange rates instituted pending acceptance within the General Agreement on Tariffs and Trade of the member's proposal of a new customs tariff. This has been done mostly for countries holding Article XIV status.

Emergencies.   When countries have faced severe economic problems and the loss of substantial reserves, the Fund has sometimes approved for a temporary period draconian measures affecting a broad range of transactions. Such approvals by the Fund are extraordinary and can be expected only in emergencies. Only a small number of cases have involved Article VIII countries, the following ones being illustrative.

The Dominican Republic in January 1961 made all imports subject to prior approval of the Export-Import Coordinating Committee. This requirement was imposed to restore foreign exchange reserves. The IMF gave approval to the associated payments restrictions on a "temporary basis." The requirement was terminated in 1963 and a year later a "prompt payment system" was introduced for current transactions.[121] This is the only case the author has identified where a comprehensive scheme of import payment licensing by an Article VIII country has been approved.

Costa Rica accepted Article VIII effective February 1965 only to reinstitute restrictions in January 1967 as part of an economic emergency program. Foreign exchange at the official rate was made available only for a limited list of imports. Residents could lawfully obtain foreign exchange for other imports in the free market, but the rates were higher. The Fund, acting under Sections 2(a) and 3, gave temporary approval to the restrictions. Costa Rica unified its exchange rate structure in December 1969 and abolished its exchange restrictions at that time.[122]

Italy has in recent years faced almost perennial balance-of-payments problems, and has frequently resorted to restrictive measures to deal with them. We had occasion earlier to consider travel allowance limitations.[123] Another technique favored by Italian authorities has been import deposit requirements. Italian authorities used this technique in May 1976 as an emergency measure after they had been unable to negotiate a stand-by arrangement with the IMF[124] and

---

[120] At pages 551–554, *infra.*

[121] IMF, *13th Annual Report on Exchange Restrictions, 1962*, pp. 3–4 and 103–05; *15th Report 1964*, pp. 147–49; and *16th Report 1965*, p. 173.

[122] IMF, *18th Annual Report on Exchange Restrictions, 1967*, pp. 6 and 169–70; and *21st Report 1970*, pp. 3 and 129–30.

[123] See pages 406–407, *supra.*

[124] See Chapter 6, *supra,* page 270 (note 191).

the lira's exchange rate had declined about 25 percent in a three-month period. Whenever foreign currency was purchased by a resident or when lire were credited to a foreign account, a deposit had to be lodged with Banca d'Italia. The non-interest-bearing deposit, equal to 50 percent of the amount of the transaction, would be held for 90 days. The requirement applied to a wide range of transactions including about all imports except wheat (to keep bread prices from rising).[125] The effect of the measure was to require importers and users of foreign services to tie up a portion of their working capital or borrowed funds, thus increasing their costs and discouraging the transactions. It also rapidly drained liquidity from the credit system.

The Italian measure required IMF approval under Article VIII, Section 2(a), because it was a restriction on payments and not just the underlying transactions.[126] The action also required approval under Section 3 because it was a multiple currency practice, since the cost of foreign exchange was proportionately higher for payments to which the requirement applied than for those payments excluded from the requirement. The IMF granted approval of the application of the deposit requirement and of the multiple currency practice involved and, subsequently, approved the gradual phasing out of the deposit requirement until it was terminated April 15, 1977.[127] The Italian measure was also authorized by the Commission of the European Communities under EEC Treaty Article 108(3) during the period it was in effect,[128] and was examined within the General Agreement on Tariffs and Trade.[129]

Italy in May 1981 again introduced a deposit requirement. Italian residents purchasing foreign currencies for a wide range of imports were required to lodge a non-interest-bearing deposit (up to 30 percent) for 90 days.[130] The requirement was clearly both a payments restriction and a multiple rate practice that required IMF approval under Article VIII, Sections 2(a) and 3. Consultations were held between Italian authorities and the Fund. Approval was not granted until July and then only for the period to September 30. A further approval was given in October 1981, which was done only after Italian authorities committed themselves to a specific timetable for phasing out the requirement.[131] The deposit requirement was eliminated in February 1982. The Italian

---

[125] See *Gazzetta Ufficiale della Repubblica Italiana*, no. 119, May 6, 1976; and IMF, *28th Annual Report on Exchange Restrictions, 1977*, pp. 258–60.

[126] Letter of Lamberto Dini, *supra* note 111. Import deposit requirements that do not take the form of currency restrictions are treated at pages 437–439, *infra*.

[127] Letter of Lamberto Dini, *supra* note 111.

[128] See note 449, *infra*.

[129] The Italian measures were examined in a GATT working party which concluded that "the measures, although monetary in form, affected all external transactions, *inter alia* trade, but were not more restrictive than an application of measures to safeguard the balance of payments expressly provided for in the General Agreement." GATT, *Basic Instruments and Selected Documents*, 24th supplement (1978), p. 129 at p. 134.

[130] See IMF, *Annual Report on Exchange Arrangements and Exchange Restrictions, 1982*, pp. 251–52.

[131] Letter dated August 5, 1982, from Giovanni Lovato, Executive Director of the IMF (Italy), to the author; and letter of June 1982 from C. David Finch, Director, Exchange and Trade Relations Department of

measure, like the import deposit scheme in 1976–77, was also examined within the European Economic Community[132] and within the GATT.[133]

The IMF's policy is not to approve restrictions or multiple currency practices, even in an emergency, if the particular measures are not reasonable actions. The IMF's response to Mexico's multiple exchange rate systems introduced in 1982 and Mexico's arrears problems beginning that year illustrate the Fund's contemporary policy. As is well known, Mexico's balance-of-payments problems reached an emergency state by the summer of 1982. Markets for Mexico's principal exports, especially petroleum, had contracted. The servicing of public and private external debt required almost 40 percent of foreign exchange earnings. Foreign commercial banks resisted requests that they extend further credit. The situation was aggravated by large public sector expenditures and by capital flight motivated by fears in the private sector about governmental policies. Beginning in August, Mexican authorities instituted a series of rigorous measures including the introduction of a multiple exchange rate system intended to discourage imports and to shepherd foreign exchange for priority uses. However, some of the early measures were counterproductive.

During the period September 1 to December 19, 1982, Mexico operated a two-tier exchange system with two official rates. A "preferential rate" of 50 pesos to the U.S. dollar applied to payments to nonresidents of interest and principal on public sector debt, "productive" private debt, and "essential" imports. For other payments the official rate (called the "ordinary rate") was 70 pesos to the dollar.[134] However, many residents that qualified for the preferential rate were unable to obtain dollars. There were virtually no dollars for sale at the 70 peso rate, because almost all foreign exchange acquired abroad by the private sector was kept abroad and not exchanged for pesos. As a consequence Mexican residents could not lawfully obtain foreign currency for needed imports, reasonable foreign travel, and other uses. The black market rate was al-

the IMF, to the editors of *Law and Policy in International Business,* cited in Deborah L. Guider, "1981 Italian Deposit Requirement: Proper Remedy Under the Treaty of Rome, GATT, or IMF Agreement?" *Law and Policy in International Business,* vol. 14 (1982), p. 927 at pp. 949–50.

[132] See note 450, *infra.*

[133] The IMF's representative told GATT's Committee on Balance-of-Payments Restrictions that the Fund considered that the maintenance of the exchange measure for a limited period, while regrettable, would give time for alternative policies on public sector finance (judged to be Italy's principal problem) to take hold. Letter of Giovanni Lovato, *supra* note 131. Guider, *supra* note 131, discusses the GATT's consideration of the Italian measure.

[134] *Diario Oficial,* September 1 and 14, 1982. The more important Mexican documents are reprinted in the monthly publication of Banco Nacional de Comercio Exterior, *Comercio Exterior,* in Spanish and English editions. See also IMF, *Annual Report on Exchange Arrangements and Exchange Restrictions, 1983,* pp. 321 and 323–25.

In the period August 5–31, 1982, Mexico had a preferential rate and a floating rate, similar to the two-tier system after December 20, 1982, except that the preferential rate was set unrealistically at 50 pesos to the dollar. *El Nacional,* August 6, 1982; and *Diario Oficial,* August 18, 1982. The IMF did not approve this short-lived arrangement.

most double the ordinary rate. The IMF did not approve this two-tier exchange system or the restrictions on payments caused thereby.

Following prolonged consultations between the IMF and outgoing and incoming Mexican officials, effective December 20, 1982, the preferential rate was set at a more realistic rate of 95 pesos to the dollar accompanied by a formula for inflation adjustment. The fixed ordinary rate was replaced by a floating rate determined by the market.[135] Thus, Mexican residents could lawfully obtain foreign exchange if they were prepared to pay the market price. The IMF on December 23, 1982, approved the new multiple currency practice for a temporary period.[136] The IMF at the same time also approved Mexico's restrictions in the form of payments arrears, discussed in the next section,[137] and approved an SDR 3.4 billion extended financial arrangement for Mexico.[138]

Payments Arrears.   The Fund has taken a "hard line" against one type of restriction—payments arrears.[139] Payments arrears arise from governmentally imposed delays in making foreign currency available for payments and transfers recognized as legitimate under a country's exchange control system. Delays can be caused by administrative inefficiencies or by a shortage of foreign exchange. If the problem is an administrative one, Fund technical assistance is available to design a better system. If the problem is a shortage of foreign exchange, the country, if it is pursuing appropriate policies, would have access to the Fund's general resources to prevent the arrears from occurring.

The Fund made comprehensive reviews of payments arrears in 1970, in 1980, and in 1983. In 1970, it stated a number of conclusions which hold true today:

> Undue delays in the availability or use of exchange for current international transactions that result from a governmental limitation give rise to payments arrears and are payments restrictions under Article VIII, Section 2(a), and Article XIV, Section 2. The limitation

---

[135] *Diario Oficial*, December 13, 1982. See generally Zamora, "Peso-Dollar Economics," *supra* note 75, especially pp. 113–27; Fernando A. Vazquez-Pando, *El Control de Cambios en Mexico* (Mexico: Distribuidora Themis, 1982); Sam Y. Cross, "Treasury and Federal Reserve Foreign Exchange Operations," in Federal Reserve Bank of New York, *Quarterly Review*, vol. 8, no. 1 (Spring 1983), p. 55 at pp. 76–77; and IMF, *Annual Report on Exchange Arrangements and Exchange Restrictions, 1983*, pp. 324–25 (Mexico).

[136] Letter dated December 29, 1982, from George P. Nicoletopoulos, Director, Legal Department of the IMF, to John J. Hannaway, Sage Gray Todd & Sims, New York. See also notes 75–77, *supra*, and accompanying text regarding a related matter.

[137] At pages 412–413, *infra*.

[138] See notes 145 and 148, *infra*.

[139] The delays encountered in the processing of license applications in Colombia in 1964 and 1965 are vividly described in Díaz-Alejandro, *Foreign Trade Regimes and Economic Development: Colombia, supra* note 12, pp. 196–97.

may be formalized, as for instance compulsory waiting periods for exchange, or informal or ad hoc.

. . . payments arrears arising from informal or ad hoc measures do particular harm to a country's international financial relationships because of the uncertainty they generate. This uncertainty . . . has pronounced adverse effects on the creditworthiness of the debtor country which may extend beyond the period of the existence of the restrictions.[140]

The Fund's 1980 review clarified the distinction between governmental actions that cause undue delay in the making of payments or transfers and defaults by governments in their own financial obligations to nonresidents caused by governmental budget problems. Only the former is a "restriction" within the meaning of Article VIII, Section 2(a), and then only if the payments or transfers are for current international transactions.[141] It is Fund policy to require a member to present a satisfactory program for reduction and/or elimination of the arrears before the Fund grants approval. An approval, if granted, will be for a temporary period and carry a fixed terminal date.[142] If the Fund provides financial assistance in the context of a stabilization program, the member country will be expected to take steps to reduce and eventually eliminate payments arrears, including arrears arising from governmental default and arrears relating to capital transactions, as well as arrears in payments and transfers relating to current transactions.[143]

The application of the Fund's policy is illustrated by the case of Mexico. Beginning in August 1982, arrears on Mexican public and private sector debt to nonresidents multipled rapidly. Mexican residents could not lawfully obtain the foreign currency (primarily U.S. dollars) required to service their debts, and even the public sector lacked the foreign currency needed to meet its obligations.[144] Months of consultations passed before Mexican authorities submitted a program satisfactory to the IMF to deal with the problem. In a memorandum

---

[140] E.B. Decision No. 3153 -(70/95)(October 26, 1970), *supra* note 38. For background on the adoption of the decision, see *IMF History 1966–71*, *supra* note 38, vol. 1, pp. 591–93.

[141] IMF, *Annual Report on Exchange Arrangements and Exchange Restrictions, 1981*, p. 21; and *idem, 1983*, p. 37.

[142] E.B. Decision No. 3153, *supra* note 38, conclusions—paragraph 3; and summaries of Fund policy in IMF, *Annual Report on Exchange Arrangements and Exchange Restrictions, 1981*, p. 21; and *idem, 1983*, p. 38.

Only a few Article VIII countries, all in Latin America, have incurred serious payments arrears subsequent to the 1970 decision. The number of Article XIV countries that have incurred arrears is large. The problem is usually mentioned each year in the introduction to the IMF's *Annual Report on Exchange Arrangements and Exchange Restrictions*.

[143] IMF, *Annual Report on Exchange Arrangements and Exchange Restrictions, 1981*, p. 21. See also Chapter 6, *supra*, page 246 with respect to the Fund's policies on the use of its general resources by countries with payments arrears.

[144] See pages 410–411, *supra*. See also Chapter 12, *infra*, pages 619–620.

to the IMF supplementing their letter of intent of November 10, 1982, requesting an extended financial arrangement, Mexican authorities stated their intentions: (a) to establish a system of counterpart deposits in pesos to be converted in an orderly manner into U.S. dollars for debt payments, (b) to reduce arrears by at least U.S. $600 million during 1983 and completely eliminate them as soon as possible, (c) to review in May 1983 progress in reducing arrears and to consult further with the IMF before January 1984, (d) to negotiate with Mexico's creditors a restructuring of the maturities of external debt, and (e) to consider modifying the exchange rate system to better achieve equilibrium in external transactions.[145] Effective December 20, 1982, some of the steps above were put in place. The exchange rate system was modified as discussed previously.[146] Mexican debtors could now lawfully obtain foreign currency to service their debts. With respect to debt incurred by the public and private sectors before December 20, 1982, a counterpart deposit system was implemented. Management of debt service was taken over by the Banco de Mexico upon the debtors' making deposits with the bank in pesos. The obligations to the nonresidents would not be immediately paid, but the arrears would be reduced in an orderly manner.[147] With the assurances of the Mexican authorities and part of the program in place, the IMF on December 23, 1982, approved an SDR 3.4 billion extended arrangement for Mexico and approved for a temporary period Mexico's multiple currency practices and restrictions in the form of payments arrears.[148]

Other Approvals.   The IMF in 1968 approved the limitation on the use and convertibility of U.K. sterling that resulted from agreements of sterling holders with the United Kingdom to maintain a "minimum sterling proportion" in their reserves as a *quid pro quo* for an exchange value guarantee.[149]

Scarce Currencies.   A member is authorized, under Article VII, Section 3(b), to temporarily impose restrictions in consultation with the Fund on the use of a foreign currency formally declared by the Fund to be a "scarce" currency. Section 3(a) of Article VII defines scarcity as occurring when "it becomes evident to the Fund that the demand for a member's currency seriously threatens

---

[145] The text appears in *Proceso* (Mexico City), November 29, 1982, p. 23. The letter of intent (without the supplementary memorandum) appears in *Comercio Exterior* (Mexico City)(English edition), vol. 28, no. 11 (November 1982), p. 412.

[146] At pages 410–411, *supra*.

[147] *Diario Oficial*, December 13, 1982. The counterpart deposit system was modified in April and May 1983, apparently in response to suggestions of the IMF staff. See *Wall Street Journal*, May 24, 1983, p. 40. See generally Zamora, "Peso-Dollar Economics," *supra* note 75, especially pp. 134–41.

[148] Letter dated December 29, 1982, of George P. Nicoletopoulos to John J. Hannaway, *supra* note 136. See also *IMF Survey*, January 10, 1983, p. 1; and sources cited in note 145, *supra*.

[149] Unpublished Executive Board decision of November 18, 1968. See *IMF History 1966–71*, *supra* note 38, vol. 1, pp. 441–42. For background see Chapter 3, *supra*, pages 104–107 (and note 15).

the Fund's ability to supply that currency." The Fund, however, has never made a formal declaration that a particular currency was "scarce."[150]

Unapproved Restrictions. In some cases currency restrictions, discriminatory arrangements, and multiple currency practices inconsistent with Sections 2(a) or 3 may go months or even years without receiving IMF approval. In a few of these cases the Fund may not know of the particular currency practices. More typically, the Fund, knowing of the practices, chooses not to approve them. After the country submits a program and timetable for elimination of the offending restrictions and practices, the Fund may approve them for a temporary period. A few examples follow.

The Dominican Republic has imposed controls off and on again. As mentioned earlier, emergency controls were imposed with IMF approval in 1961 and terminated in 1963.[151] In 1967 the Dominican Republic imposed new restrictions on payments for invisibles (including tourist travel and insurance premiums), again receiving Fund approval for a temporary period. In 1972 the Dominican Republic intensified its restrictions on payments for current transactions, this time without obtaining the approval of the IMF. As a consequence of the official payments restrictions, a black market developed in foreign exchange for use in transactions (such as tourism) where official exchange was not available. Different rates between official and black markets are viewed by the IMF as multiple currency practices requiring approval only when the government acknowledges and tolerates black market transactions. The Dominican Republic tolerated this black market.[152] The multiple currency practices and other Dominican Republic restrictions on current payments were maintained for several years without IMF approval and thus were maintained in violation of Article VIII.

While an Italian deposit requirement, discussed earlier,[153] was in effect (May 1976–April 1977), Italian authorities imposed an additional measure on October 4, 1976—a ten percent surtax *(sovrattassa)* on all purchases of foreign exchange for current transactions. This action was adopted as an emergency measure. The tax was removed effective October 18, but was reintroduced at a rate of seven percent on October 25, 1976, with a number of exemptions.[154]

---

[150] See Joseph Gold, "Symmetry as a Legal Objective of the International Monetary System," *New York University Journal of International Law and Politics,* vol. 12 (1980), p. 423 at pp. 465–68; and Joseph Gold, " 'Pressures' and Reform of the International Monetary System," in Joseph Gold, *Legal and Institutional Aspects of the International Monetary System: Selected Essays* (Washington: IMF, 1979), p. 182 at pp. 207–12.

[151] See text accompanying note 121, *supra.*

[152] See IMF, *Annual Report on Exchange Arrangements and Exchange Restrictions, 1981,* p. 137. See also *28th Annual Report on Exchange Restrictions, 1977,* pp. 10 and 154; and *29th Report 1978,* pp. 9 and 130.

[153] At pages 408–409, *supra.*

[154] See IMF, *28th Annual Report on Exchange Restrictions, 1977,* p. 260.

The IMF did not approve the restrictions on current payments and transfers and the multiple currency practices involved in the measures of October 4 and October 25.[155] They were, thus, imposed and maintained in violation of the IMF Agreement. Italy did not obtain the approval of the Commission of the European Communities either, but invoked EEC Treaty Article 109 to justify its derogation from its obligations under that treaty.[156] The tax was scaled down and ceased to be applied on February 18, 1977. The end of the deposit requirement discussed earlier and the removal of this tax appear to have been essential to Italy's obtaining a stand-by arrangement with the IMF. In a letter of intent to the IMF in April 1977 Italian authorities stated their intention, *inter alia,* not to adopt new measures that would split exchange rates, restrict payments respecting current transactions, or restrict imports for balance-of-payments reasons.[157]

Mexican multiple exchange rate practices introduced in the early fall of 1982 and accumulating arrears on external debt during 1982 went unapproved for months. As detailed above, the IMF granted its approval only after modifications were made in the exchange rate system and an acceptable plan was submitted for reducing the arrears.[158]

National Security Restrictions.   In 1952 the Executive Board of the IMF adopted an important decision on currency restrictions imposed solely for reasons of national or international security.[159] Decision No. 144 -(52/51) recognizes Fund jurisdiction over all currency restrictions on current transactions including those adopted for reasons unrelated to the balance of payments. The first sentence states: "Art. VIII, Sec. 2(a), in conformity with its language, applies to all restrictions on current payments and transfers, irrespective of their motivation and the circumstances in which they are imposed." Later in the

---

[155] Letter dated August 11, 1977, of Lamberto Dini, *supra* note 111.

[156] *10th General Report on the Activities of the European Communities in 1976,* point 211; and *Bulletin of the European Communities,* 1976, no. 10, point 2204. EEC Treaty Article 109 is treated at pages 473–477, *infra.*

[157] Letter of Lamberto Dini, *supra* note 111. The IMF on April 25, 1977, approved an SDR 450 million stand-by arrangement for Italy. The Italian letter of intent to the IMF appears in John Williamson (ed.), *IMF Conditionality* (Washington: Institute for International Economics, 1983), p. 468. See also Luigi Spaventa, "Two Letters of Intent: External Crises and Stabilization Policy, Italy, 1973–77," in Williamson, *supra,* p. 441.

[158] See pages 410–411 and 412–413, *supra.* See also page 399 respecting Mexico's "pesofication" of certain bank accounts held by nonresidents, an action that the IMF did not approve under Article VIII, sections 2(a) or 3.

[159] E.B. Decision No. 144 -(52/51)(August 14, 1952); *IMF History 1945-65, supra* note 39, vol. 3, p. 257; *Selected Decisions* (10th issue, 1983), p. 235. The stimuli for the decision were U.S. currency restrictions adopted in 1950 and Cuban restrictions adopted in 1951 on payments and transfers involving residents of the portion of China controlled by the People's Republic of China. The IMF treated the actions as restrictions on payments to a member ("China") represented in the IMF at the time by the Republic of China. Following the adoption of Decision No. 144, the U.S. and Cuban restrictions were approved. See *IMF History 1945-65,* vol. 1, pp. 275–76, and vol. 2, pp. 259–60 and 588–91; Gold, *Fund Agreement in the Courts, supra* note 49, vol. 2, pp. 365–67 and 416–18; and Gold, *Membership and Nonmembership, supra* note 87, p. 279.

same paragraph the decision states: "The Fund does not . . . provide a suitable forum for discussion of the political and military considerations leading to actions [for the preservation of national security]."[160]

The desire to enable members to stay in compliance with Fund law (maintain no unapproved restrictions) led to the decision's establishing a simplified procedure for granting approval without passing on the merits of political-military disputes between members. The procedure is as follows: A member imposing a restriction for security reasons is required to notify the Fund promptly. If the Executive Board believes that security reasons do not justify the restriction, it must inform the member of its objection within 30 days of receiving the notification. A proposal for such an objection, if called to a vote, must obtain a majority of the weighted votes cast for adoption. If the Board does not object formally, after 30 days have elapsed the restriction is treated as approved retroactively to the date of notification. Further, unlike approvals of restrictions adopted for economic reasons, which normally carry a time limit and require affirmative IMF action for renewal, approvals of security restrictions normally do not carry a time limit, but the Fund reserves the right to revoke or amend them.

Since its adoption, Decision No. 144 has been invoked in a variety of international situations.[161] Restrictions on payments and transfers for current transactions involving Rhodesia prior to its obtaining independence as Zimbabwe in December 1979,[162] adopted by IMF members pursuant to United Nations Security Council resolutions,[163] were approved employing the procedure of Decision No. 144.[164] The procedure established by the decision was used to approve restrictions imposed in November 1979 and intensified in April 1980 by the United States against Iran during the diplomatic hostages crisis,[165]

---

[160] See Article I; and Article XII, section 8.

[161] The restrictions on payments and transfers imposed in 1956 by Egypt, the United Kingdom, and the United States in connection with the liquidation of the Suez Canal Company and action against the Canal were not approved under Decision No. 144 because they were not formally notified to the IMF. Fawcett, "International Monetary Fund and International Law," *supra* note 43, p. 65. The restrictions are described in IMF, *8th Annual Report on Exchange Restrictions, 1957*, pp. 117, 287, and 337.

[162] The Fund treated Rhodesia as a dependent territory of the United Kingdom, not as a nonmember, until its independence in December 1979. Zimbabwe joined the Fund in 1980.

[163] UN Security Council Resolutions No. 221 (April 9, 1966), No. 232 (December 16, 1966), and No. 253 (May 29, 1968).

[164] Gold, *Membership and Nonmembership, supra* note 87, pp. 277–78; and *IMF History 1945–65, supra* note 39, vol. 2, p. 260. See also James E.S. Fawcett, "Trade and Finance in International Law," in Hague Academy of International Law, *Recueil des Cours*, vol. 123 (1968-I), p. 219 at pp. 306–07; IMF, *20th Annual Report on Exchange Restrictions, 1969*, p. 3; and IMF, *Annual Report on Exchange Arrangements and Exchange Restrictions, 1980*, p. 9. Techniques used by firms and bankers to avoid exchange restrictions respecting Rhodesia are noted in Harry R. Strack, *Sanctions: The Case of Rhodesia* (Syracuse, N.Y.: Syracuse University Press, 1978), pp. 110–11.

[165] After American diplomatic and consular personnel in Iran were taken hostage in that country and Iranian authorities stated their intention to make massive transfers of dollar deposits, the U.S. Treasury on November 14, 1979, promulgated the Iranian Assets Control Regulations. The regulations used both transaction

restrictions imposed in April 1982 by the United Kingdom against Argentina during the Falkland Islands (Islas Malvinas) conflict,[166] and restrictions imposed by Argentina against the United Kingdom in the same conflict.[167]

The Fund has not definitively resolved the question whether measures directed against nonresidents generally (not just the adversary) for purposes of conserving foreign exchange during a military conflict are "solely" related to security as required for application of Decision No. 144.[168] During the Falkland Islands conflict in 1982, Argentina, in addition to measures directed against U.K. residents,[169] suspended the transfer of profits, dividends, royalties, and repatriation of capital by foreign investors generally and substituted payment in the form of "external bonds of the Argentine Republic."[170] The

and currency controls and covered both current transactions and capital movements. The regulations were directed against the government of Iran, the central bank, and official entities.

The U.S. executive director of the IMF informed the Executive Board of the regulations the day they were adopted (November 14). However, the regulations were not formally notified to the Board until November 29. In the meantime, in response to concerns about the scope of U.S. jurisdiction voiced by officials of other governments and the IMF and by lawyers for commercial banks, the regulations had been amended to exclude accounts with overseas branches of U.S. commercial banks that were denominated in currencies other than the U.S. dollar. However, accounts with overseas branches of U.S. banks payable in dollars were still covered by the regulations. Although the executive director representing Iran objected to approval, the Board took no action and, thus, the currency restrictions on current payments caused by the regulations became approved on December 29, 1979, retroactive to November 29.

Effective April 7 and 17, 1980, the regulations were amended to cover, with certain exceptions, any person in Iran and not just governmental entities. The amendments intensifying the regulations were formally notified to the Executive Board on April 28, and the Board did not object within the 30-day period. The fact that the regulations by April had clearly assumed the character of economic sanctions did not lead the Fund to object to them.

For further explanations and citations to the regulations, see Richard W. Edwards, Jr., "Extraterritorial Application of the U.S. Iranian Assets Control Regulations," *American Journal of International Law*, vol. 75 (1981), p. 870 at pp. 870–76; letter dated January 9, 1981, from George P. Nicoletopoulos, Director, Legal Department of the IMF, to the author, reproduced *idem*, pp. 900–02; and Gold, *Fund Agreement in the Courts, supra* note 49, vol. 2, pp. 360–427 at pp. 360–69. See also IMF, *Summary Proceedings, 1980*, pp. 180–82. Litigation involving the regulations is discussed at page 479 and note 467 et seq.

[166] The U.K. regulations appear in *Control of Gold, Securities, Payments and Credits (Argentine Republic) Directions 1982, Statutory Instrument No. 512* (April 3, 1982). The U.K. regulations, unlike the U.S. regulations against Iran, did not attempt to reach the accounts of Argentine government agencies or residents with overseas branches of U.K. commercial banks even if payable in sterling. See *Bank of England Notice of April 13, 1982 (Emergency Laws [Re-enactments and Repeals] Act 1964: Argentine Republic)*, paragraph 7.

The United Kingdom notified the IMF of the restrictions on April 5, 1982. The notice was circulated immediately to the members of the Executive Board. The Fund did not object to the United Kingdom's restrictions. Thus, after 30 days, they became approved retroactively to April 5. Letter dated August 5, 1982, from Christopher T. Taylor, Alternate Executive Director of the IMF (U.K.), to the author. The restrictions were lifted September 14, 1982.

[167] Argentine central bank communications Nos. 4615, 4618, 4619, 4623, and 4625 of April 5, 1982, suspended sales of foreign exchange for benefit of U.K. residents, suspended rights of U.K. residents to use or transfer Argentine or foreign currency held in Argentina, suspended payments of debts to U.K. residents, and suspended transactions in U.K. diplomatic and consular accounts. An IMF staff paper analyzed the effects of these measures as falling within the scope of Decision No. 144. The Executive Board did not object to them. They were lifted September 14, 1982.

[168] The word "solely" appears three times in E.B. Decision No. 144, *supra* note 159.

[169] See note 167, *supra*.

[170] Argentine Decrees Nos. 786 and 787 of April 20, 1982; *Boletín Oficial*, April 23, 1982. The two de-

IMF Executive Director for Argentina transmitted the decrees embodying the regulations to the Managing Director in April 1982. When the Executive Board made no formal objection to the restrictions, the Argentine director assumed they were approved pursuant to the procedure established by Decision No. 144.[171] The IMF staff, however, apparently viewed the measures as outside the scope of Decision No. 144. In the absence of affirmative approval by the Board, the staff saw the restrictions on current payments as violating Article VIII, Section 2(a).[172]

In the studies and discussions that led to the adoption of Decision No. 144 in 1952, no mention was made of the effect that approved restrictions would have under Section 2(b) of Article VIII.[173] It is now reasonably well settled that IMF-approved security restrictions come within the scope of Section 2(b).[174] One of the consequences is that a third country may find that an IMF approval (granted in circumstances where the Fund intended to avoid deciding the merits of a dispute between members) requires it to enforce an exchange restriction imposed by one IMF member against another. The problem was presented in sharp relief after the IMF approved U.S. currency restrictions directed against Iran. Iran's central bank, Bank Markazi Iran, sued the Paris and London branches of U.S. commercial banks for withdrawal or transfer of Eurodollar deposits booked with the branches. One of the commercial banks' defenses was that IMF Article VIII, Section 2(b), required the French and English courts to recognize the U.S. Treasury's Iranian Assets Control Regulations as barring enforcement of the deposit contracts, since the U.S. restrictions had been approved by the IMF.[175]

Much thought has been given to the best way out of this problem. One approach would be to take narrow views of such key terms as "exchange control regulations," "exchange contracts," and "involve the currency" in Section 2(b), but that would also limit the application of Section 2(b) in cases where security issues were not present. Another possibility would be for the Fund to fashion a special sort of "approval" for security restrictions under Section 2(a) that would deny the country imposing them the benefits of Section 2(b), but it is difficult to see how that could be done without amending Article VIII. The author's position is that, while the Fund should continue to maintain jurisdiction

---

crees continued in force after restrictions specifically directed against U.K. residents, *supra* note 167, were terminated in September 1982.

[171] Letter dated August 13, 1982, from Juan Carlos Iarezza, Executive Director of the IMF (Argentina), to the author.

[172] Decrees Nos. 786 and 787 were transmitted to the Managing Director on April 29, 1982. It appears that the staff did not present the Executive Board with a paper analyzing the effects of the decrees as it did in the case of other Argentine actions. See note 167, *supra.*

[173] Gold, *Fund Agreement in the Courts, supra* note 49, vol. 2, p. 417.

[174] See pages 480–481, *infra.* The last part of this chapter, beginning at page 477, is devoted to the application of Article VIII, section 2(b).

[175] See discussion at page 479 and note 467 et seq.

over all restrictions on payments and transfers for current transactions, it should recognize that it is sometimes best to leave restrictions unapproved.

The IMF in its relationship agreement with the United Nations and in a 1951 resolution of its Board of Governors recognizes the special role of the UN Security Council (and the General Assembly when it acts under the Uniting for Peace Resolution).[176] While the IMF, as noted at the outset of this section, lacks the authority to appraise the merits of security measures, the Security Council is vested with that authority. When the Security Council calls for currency restrictions, as it did in the case of Rhodesia, the IMF should approve members' restrictions under Section 2(a). A procedure in which the Fund would act affirmatively in such a case is probably preferable to a nonobjection procedure. The approved restrictions would be entitled to extraterritorial application under Section 2(b) to the same extent as any other approved restrictions.

Where the Security Council does not call for a restriction, the IMF should continue to require that the restriction be notified, but the Fund should not treat its failure to object as the equivalent of approval under Section 2(a). Courts in third countries would be free, in accordance with their laws and treaties, to enforce or refrain from enforcing contracts that are contrary to the unapproved restrictions.[177] The Fund can adapt its policies on the use of its general resources to deal with the phenomenon of unapproved security restrictions. Members have in many cases been permitted to make drawings outside the reserve tranche even though they had unapproved restrictions.[178] Members with unapproved restrictions are entitled by the IMF Agreement to use special drawing rights and to make drawings in the reserve tranche of the General Resources Account.

In some cases restrictions imposed for security reasons can have valid balance-of-payments justifications. In such cases the Fund should approve the restrictions applying economic criteria. The U.S. action against Iran on November 14, 1979, might have been justified for an initial short period on economic grounds alone. Action by the U.S. authorities may well have been necessary to prevent withdrawals or transfers, that Iranian officials said they intended to make, from disrupting the international banking system. Transfers on the order of U.S. $6 billion or more (possibly in a single day) were certain to cause strains on the inter-bank transfer system, even if all they involved were movements of dollar balances booked with banks with U.S. ties to dollar-denominated balances booked with banks of other nationalities.[179] Had the Ira-

---

[176] See Chapter 2, *supra,* pages 48–50.

[177] See Edwards, "Extraterritorial Application," *supra* note 165, pp. 876–81 and 898–900.

[178] See Chapter 6, *supra,* page 246.

[179] For a review, with the benefit of hindsight, of how such transfers could have been handled, see *Iran: The Financial Aspects of the Hostage Settlement Agreement; Staff Report Prepared for the Committee on Banking, Finance, and Urban Affairs,* U.S. House of Representatives, 97th Congress, 1st Session (Committee Print, 1981), pp. 3–5, 12–14, and 43.

nians contemplated massive sales of dollars for other currencies, and the early morning reports from Tehran were unclear,[180] the potential was present for a panic in the exchange markets. To many outsiders the Iranian government, with its strong religious orientation, was capable of suicidal acts, including acts that might rapidly depreciate the value but increase the usability of its monetary reserves. One must not discount the importance of the psychological element in market stability. When expectations of exchange market participants are upset, disorder and disruption can quickly follow.[181]

Concluding Comment on Approvals. In all of the cases examined above (except security restrictions), the IMF's approvals, if granted, were intended to be temporary. In many cases the currency practices were ended in a year or less. Often approved restrictions affected only a small range of current transactions (such as travel restrictions complementing capital controls). In a few cases, such as Costa Rica (1967), Dominican Republic (1961), Italy (1976 and 1981), and Mexico (1982),[182] restrictions with broad impacts, imposed in emergencies by Article VIII countries, have been approved for temporary periods.

Countries that maintain measures that are approved by the Fund under Sections 2(a) or 3 of Article VIII are required to consult with the Fund about the continuance of the measures.[183] The consultation process in its many aspects is examined in Chapter 12 of this book.[184]

Transactions with Nonmembers. Members of the IMF retain the right to impose restrictions on exchange transactions with residents of countries that are not members of the Fund "unless the Fund finds that such restrictions prejudice the interests of members and are contrary to the purposes of the Fund."[185] Members are required to inform the Fund of restrictions they impose on exchange transactions with nonmembers, but normally need not request Fund approval.[186] A member of the Fund that is prejudiced by exchange restrictions im-

---

[180] See dispatch from Tehran datelined November 14 in *New York Times,* November 15, 1979, pp. A-1 and A-16.

[181] See Appendix A, *infra,* pages 686–687.

[182] The cases are discussed at pages 408–411, *supra.*

[183] E.B. Decision No. 1034, *supra* note 47, paragraph 3. Countries under the Article XIV regime are required by that article to consult annually with the Fund.

[184] The procedures followed in IMF consultations are treated, *infra,* at page 571 et seq.

[185] Article XI, section 2.

[186] Restrictions imposed by the United States in December 1950 on the making of payments or transfers to North Korea and in May 1964 on payments and transfers to North Vietnam (both nonmembers) did not require Fund approval. Gold, *Membership and Nonmembership, supra* note 87, pp. 51 and 279.

Fund Rule M-6, *By-Laws, Rules and Regulations* (40th issue, 1983), states that IMF members should not institute restrictions on exchange transactions with nonmembers that have concluded special exchange agreements under the GATT unless the restrictions "(a) if instituted on transactions with other members, or persons in their territories, would be authorized under the Articles, or (b) have been approved in advance by the Fund." Only four special exchange agreements have been concluded and none is in effect today. Gold, *Membership and Nonmembership,* p. 436.

posed by another member on transactions with a nonmember, and believes the restrictions are contrary to the purposes of the Fund, may bring the matter to the Fund's attention.[187]

Obligations of Section 4

International transactions are facilitated if payees in international transactions are willing to accept payments in the payor's currency. Section 4 of Article VIII is designed to give confidence to nonresident payees that they can convert into other currencies the currency of a member that has accepted the obligations of Article VIII. The procedure contemplated by Section 4 is that the payee sells to the authorities of its country the foreign currency it acquires in a current transaction. Those authorities then present the currency balance to the state of issue (e.g., payor's country) for conversion. Section 4 establishes the obligation on the part of the payor's state to convert the balances of its currency obtained by the payee's authorities as a result of current transactions, provided the conversion is requested promptly. A state is also required to convert balances of its currency held by another member, even balances that have been held for some time, if the latter country requests the conversion in order for it or its residents to make payments for current transactions.[188]

The state called upon to purchase its own currency has the option to provide to the state making the request either the currency of the requesting state or special drawing rights.[189] The exchange rates applicable to these transactions are the "representative rates" ascertained in accordance with procedures agreed with the Fund.[190]

The obligation to convert foreign-held balances is subject to a number of important qualifications. The reader should study the text of Section 4 (which is in Appendix B to this volume). It should also be noted that the obligation runs only between central monetary authorities (the treasuries or central banks of the member countries). The idea is that a central monetary authority requesting conversion will, for example, have acquired the foreign balances from its residents who recently were payees or transferees in current transactions.

While it was thought when the Articles were originally negotiated in 1944 that the conversion of foreign-held balances would take place through the Fund,

---

[187] Rules M-3 - M-5, *By-Laws, Rules and Regulations* (40th issue, 1983). See Gold, *Membership and Nonmembership, supra* note 87, pp. 446–51; and Gold, *Fund Agreement in the Courts, supra* note 49, vol. 2, pp. 458–61.

[188] If, however, the balances represent capital movements, the convertibility of which is restricted by controls consistent with Article VI, section 3, then the state of issue can refuse to convert the balances. Article VIII, section 4(b)(i).

[189] A state purchasing its own currency for special drawing rights must have the agreement of the country presenting the balances if the latter's holdings of SDRs would be raised above 300 percent of net cumulative allocation. Article VIII, section 4(a); and Article XIX, section 4.

[190] See Chapters 5 and 6, *supra,* pages 184–185, 200–201 and 225–226.

the mechanisms typically used today are outside the Fund. The clearing systems of the Central American Clearing House, the Asian Clearing Union, and other regional clearing associations perform this function for their members.[191] The clearing of claims in widely traded currencies takes place through the market, in direct dealings of treasuries and central banks, and through the agency of the Bank for International Settlements. Currency can also be redeemed by its issuer by agreement in exchange for special drawing rights.

Holdings of foreign currencies that are judged in excess of needs are in practice often sold on the market. There is no obligation on an issuing country to provide for conversion of its currency through a Section 4 mechanism if the exchange markets (with freedom of transfers pursuant to Section 2(a)) provide an effective mechanism for foreign monetary authorities to readily convert holdings of its currency. The *Report on the Second Amendment* states, in what is intended to be a definitive interpretation, that "no obligation will be applied for a member [under Section 4 of Article VIII] so long as exchange markets for the currency held normally serve this [conversion] function."[192] In fact, Section 4 has been formally invoked only very rarely.

Concluding Comments on Article VIII

Article VIII embodies the basic scheme for assuring convertibility of currencies as envisioned by the drafters of the IMF's Articles. We have delved into Sections 2(a) and 4 in order to understand both the obligations that flow from those sections and their limits. We have commented on discriminatory currency arrangements and multiple currency practices that are prohibited by Section 3. Later in this chapter we shall look at efforts to expand convertibility obligations beyond the requirements of Article VIII. Section 5 dealing with the supply of information was discussed in Chapter 1.[193]

A final point needs to be made: The Fund has seen Article VIII status as "a goal which involved the *elimination* of restrictions on current payments, of multiple exchange rates, and of other practices."[194] The Executive Board has not wanted members to formally accept the obligations of Sections 2, 3, and 4 of Article VIII and at the same time or thereafter to request Fund approval of significant restrictions. The Board has, rather, preferred that a member delay

---

[191] Several of these payments arrangements are described in Chapter 7.

[192] See IMF, *Proposed Second Amendment to the Articles of Agreement of the International Monetary Fund: A Report by the Executive Directors to the Board of Governors* (1976), part 2, chapter C, section 18. See also sections 15–17. The report is printed in IMF, *Summary Proceedings, 1976 — Supplement.* It is cited hereinafter *Report on Second Amendment.*

The IMF's General Counsel, Joseph Gold, commented *in extenso* on the cited sections of the *Report on Second Amendment* in *Use, Conversion, and Exchange of Currency, supra* note 42, pp. 22–32. See also Gold, *Multilateral System of Payments, supra* note 37, pp. 20–27.

[193] At page 21, *supra.*

[194] *IMF History 1945-65, supra* note 39, vol. 2, p. 285.

formally accepting Article VIII obligations until it is prepared to abide by them, without exceptions, into the foreseeable future.[195]

The Regime of Article XIV of the IMF Agreement

Provisions of Article XIV

The International Monetary Fund has not required liberalization of exchange restrictions as a precondition for membership in the organization.[196] A majority of the members have not yet accepted the obligations of Article VIII, Sections 2, 3, and 4, and instead rely upon the "transitional arrangements" of Article XIV, Section 2. A member availing itself of that section is permitted to "maintain and adapt to changing circumstances" the restrictions on payments and transfers for current international transactions that were in effect on the date on which it became a member.[197]

Pursuant to Section 1 of Article XIV, each member upon joining the Fund notifies the Fund whether it avails itself of the transitional arrangements of Article XIV, Section 2, or accepts the obligations of Article VIII, Sections 2, 3, and 4. A member initially availing itself of Article XIV, Section 2, that later decides to accept the obligations of Article VIII notifies the Fund of this acceptance. However, this formal change in status may be slow in coming, for once a member has accepted the obligations of Article VIII it is not permitted to return to the transitional regime of Article XIV.[198] A number of countries, although formally relying upon Article XIV, in fact comply with all of the currency convertibility provisions of Article VIII.[199]

Unlike members under the Article VIII regime that must have Fund approval for measures inconsistent with that article (approvals that are temporary and subject to review), an Article XIV country does not need approvals to continue its practices that are inconsistent with Article VIII, Sections 2, 3, and 4. Further, a member availing itself of Article XIV, Section 2, has the right to "adapt" its restrictions to changing circumstances without the need for Fund approval. But, Article XIV does not permit a member to introduce new restrictions (or reintroduce restrictions that have been withdrawn). The introduction of a new restriction by an Article XIV country requires approval under Article

---

[195] E.B. Decision No. 1034, *supra* note 47, paragraph 2.

[196] See Gold, *Membership and Nonmembership, supra* note 87, pp. 197–98.

[197] Prior to the Second Amendment, section 2 of Article XIV spoke of a "post-war transitional period" in which the section was operative, but the Fund never announced the end of that period. The present language of Article XIV makes it clear that the transition is to be related to the member's circumstances.

[198] A member under the Article VIII regime, with the Fund's approval as explained earlier in this chapter, may impose measures that would otherwise violate Article VIII.

[199] Venezuela, for example, was in *de facto* compliance with Article VIII for several years before it formally accepted its obligations in July 1976.

VIII. In distinguishing an "introduction" from an "adaptation," the novelty, practical effect, and role of the measures in the restrictive system as a whole are considered.[200] However, even the adaptation of a multiple currency practice requires Fund approval.[201] It is difficult to judge as a practical matter whether it is easier for an Article XIV country to obtain a needed approval under Article VIII for a new restriction (not an adaptation) than a similarly situated country that has accepted Article VIII. The Fund in its formal policies has not drawn a distinction.[202] A country by accepting Article VIII does, however, create certain expectations in other countries about the convertibility of its currency that would be frustrated if Article VIII countries could easily obtain approvals for restrictive practices.[203]

A member availing itself of Article XIV is expected to withdraw restrictions when they are no longer necessary to protect its balance of payments:

> Members shall . . . have continuous regard in their foreign exchange policies to the purposes of the Fund. . . . In particular, members shall withdraw restrictions maintained under this Section as soon as they are satisfied that they will be able, in the absence of such restrictions, to settle their balance of payments in a manner which will not unduly encumber their access to the general resources of the Fund.[204]

While decisions to withdraw restrictions, and the timing of those decisions, are to be made by the individual country, Section 3 of Article XIV requires members availing themselves of "transitional arrangements" to consult with the Fund each year about the "further retention" of any currency restrictions inconsistent with Article VIII, Sections 2, 3, and 4. The consultation obligations are central to the regime of Article XIV. The consultations required by that article are "comprehended" by the broad-ranging periodic consultations under Article IV, discussed in Chapter 12, so as to avoid a multiplicity of overlapping meetings.[205] The consultation process under Article IV embraces all aspects of the member's economic and financial position and not just exchange restrictions, multiple currency practices, and discriminatory currency arrangements. The consultations may result in recommendations by the Fund for the removal or modification of restrictions. The Executive Board's conclusions at the end of Article IV–Article XIV consultations, for example, may "suggest re-examination" of particular restrictions or "urge action" to deal with various problems. The Board will neither "approve" nor "object" to par-

---

[200] Gold, *Use, Conversion, and Exchange of Currency, supra* note 42, p. 9.
[201] See notes 62 and 63, *supra,* and accompanying text.
[202] See, e.g., E.B. Decision No. 1034, *supra,* note 47.
[203] See text accompanying notes 194 and 195, *supra.*
[204] Article XIV, section 2.
[205] See Chapter 12, *infra,* page 571 et seq.

ticular restrictions if they are lawfully maintained under Article XIV. A decision will be adopted at the end of an Article IV consultation to explicitly approve "new" restrictions (including renewals of earlier approvals) if the restrictions require Fund approval under Article VIII, and the Executive Board deems them justified.[206]

The Fund can "in exceptional circumstances" make "representations" to a member that conditions are favorable for the withdrawal of a particular restriction or the general abandonment of restrictions inconsistent with Articles I, IV, VIII, or others. Formal representations, if made, are more than advisory. If the member continues to maintain the restrictions notwithstanding the representations of the Fund, the member may be declared ineligible to use the general resources of the IMF.[207] The Fund, however, has never made such a formal representation under Article XIV.

The Fund's Approach to the Withdrawal of Article XIV Restrictions

The IMF directed its attention during the 1950s to the dismantling of exchange controls and multiple-rate systems in Western Europe. It may be difficult for some readers to comprehend that the currencies of the Western European democracies (including the U.K. pound sterling, French franc, Deutsche mark, and Netherlands guilder, as well as others) were not readily convertible from the time of the Second World War until the late 1950s. The Organisation for European Economic Co-operation played an important role, parallel with the Fund, in coordinating national actions that eventually led major European countries to shift from Article XIV to Article VIII status in 1961.[208]

While some developed countries continue to rely upon Article XIV, Section 2, today most Article XIV countries are developing countries. The standard of living of people in these countries often is low, the internal economy is weak, and export earnings are inadequate in relation to import demand. These countries use a variety of techniques, often in conjunction, to stimulate exports and to shepherd the foreign exchange obtained: export subsidies, import restrictions, domestic price controls, as well as currency over-valuation, multiple exchange rates, and payments restrictions.

Authorities in countries that maintain restrictions usually believe restrictions to be necessary to force deployment of domestic resources and to avoid dependence on external finance.[209] By contrast, a substantial body of research

---

[206] See Chapter 12, *infra*, page 575.

[207] Article XIV, section 3; and Article XXVI, section 2(a). The Fund has power to determine what is meant by "in exceptional circumstances." E.B. Decision No. 117-1 (January 6, 1947); *IMF History 1945-65, supra* note 39, vol. 3, p. 269; *Selected Decisions* (10th issue, 1983), p. 267.

[208] See sources cited in note 94, *supra*.

[209] See generally Cheryl Payer, *The Debt Trap: The IMF and the Third World* (New York: Monthly Review Press, 1974).

generally concludes that distorted economies and hampered development are the normal consequences of multiple exchange rates and payments restrictions.[210] However, the choice for many countries is between market systems that are in fact highly imperfect and systems of central control. The choice requires study of the effects of the systems and appraisal in terms of social values on which persons may disagree. Research can be helpful in projecting the economic and other effects of particular control regimes.[211] The IMF has provided technical assistance to members desiring to improve the administration of controls or to adapt them to changing circumstances.[212]

Regular Article IV-Article XIV consultations invariably identify restrictions and practices inconsistent with Article VIII and consider whether they could be withdrawn without damage to the country's economy and balance of payments. The Fund has been successful in persuading its members not to renew bilateral payments agreements.[213] Dismantling of multiple-rate systems has been a major focus of Fund attention. The Fund usually has not urged the immediate discontinuance of multiple-rate systems that have been in existence for a long time, because members might simply introduce hastily devised tax and subsidy substitutes. Instead, the Fund has chosen to work with members to reduce domestic inflation, to make comprehensive reforms of fiscal systems, and to work out changes in customs schedules. Emphasis has been placed first on simplifying the exchange rate systems (e.g., by reducing the number of rates) and then finally on unification of the rates.[214]

Many Article XIV countries use foreign exchange licensing systems that are incompatible with Article VIII, Section 2(a). The IMF has had a reasonably consistent alternative approach that it has recommended to developing countries when they have found their foreign-currency holdings inadequate to service external debts and pay for essential imports. The approach involves (1) lowering the exchange value of the country's currency to stimulate exports and discourage imports, (2) adopting domestic anti-inflation programs to stabilize the domestic purchasing power of the currency, and (3) simplifying exchange restrictions to facilitate their administration and to remove their tax and subsidy effects. The consequences of this approach have been debated and studied.[215]

---

[210] See J. Marcus Fleming, "Mercantilism and Free Trade Today," summarized in *IMF Survey*, May 3, 1976, p. 132 at p. 135; and sources cited in note 211, *infra*.

[211] See studies by the National Bureau of Economic Research, *supra* note 12; and papers collected in Williamson, *IMF Conditionality*, *supra* note 157. See also Verbit, *supra* note 11.

[212] See generally Swidrowski, *Exchange and Trade Controls*, *supra* note 10.

[213] Egypt and Romania are among countries that in recent years reduced their reliance on bilateral agreements.

[214] See generally *IMF History 1945–65*, *supra* note 39, vol. 2, pp. 122–46, and chronological table of national actions at pp. 147–51. As of December 31, 1982, about one-fourth of the members under the Article XIV regime maintained multiple exchange rates applicable to imports or exports. IMF, *Annual Report on Exchange Arrangements and Exchange Restrictions, 1983*, pp. 524–29.

[215] The studies and papers cited in notes 209–212, *supra*, assess the effects of these programs. See also sources cited in Chapter 6, *supra*, page 276 (note 210).

Modifications in exchange control practices have often been key elements in persuading the Fund to approve drawings requested by members. Numerous press releases of the Fund have reported that stand-by or extended arrangements were approved to support currency stabilization programs that included simplification or termination of payments restrictions or multiple currency practices. Fund resources would be used by the country to tide it over the immediate period following relaxation of restrictions when the heavy, pent-up demand for foreign exchange would be unleashed.[216]

The Fund's attitude favoring liberalization of restrictions has caused some countries to refrain from requesting stand-by arrangements in the higher credit tranches. Although India has in gross terms been the largest user of IMF resources among developing countries, it did not until 1981 conclude a stand-by or extended arrangement to draw into its third or higher credit tranches. It feared (perhaps incorrectly) that the IMF would expect a full-scale currency stabilization program with significant liberalization of the exchange licensing system.[217] In 1981 India concluded an extended arrangement with the IMF. At the time India had begun a modest, but not full-scale, liberalization of its system.[218]

With respect to one form of payments restriction, the IMF has explicitly adopted a general decision tying use of its resources to correction of the problem. A Fund decision states that failure of a country to have a viable program to eliminate payments arrears (undue delay in settling current transactions) is evidence that it is not making "reasonable efforts" to deal with its international financial situation.[219] This means that, unless the country undertakes corrective action, it will not be permitted to make a regular drawing even in the first credit tranche.[220]

---

[216] See, e.g., IMF press releases collected in Joseph Gold, *The Stand-By Arrangements of the International Monetary Fund* (Washington: IMF, 1970), pp. 257–67. A few of many examples include financial arrangements for Argentina (1976 and 1977), Egypt (1977), Equatorial Guinea (1980), Romania (1981), Sri Lanka (1977), and Turkey (1980 and 1983). See also pages 410–411 and 412–413, *supra*, regarding the extended arrangement for Mexico approved in 1982.

Uruguay had continuous, repeated stand-by arrangements with the IMF all through the 1970s. By the end of April 1980 Uruguay had eliminated the last exchange restrictions subject to IMF approval, and in May 1980 it accepted the obligations of IMF Article VIII, sections 2, 3, and 4. *IMF Survey*, May 19, 1980, p. 155. See "The International Monetary Fund: Its Code of Good Behavior and the Uruguayan Stabilization Program of 1968," *Virginia Journal of International Law*, vol. 10 (1969–70), p. 359 (written from a legal perspective in the early stages of the program).

[217] Payer, *supra* note 209, p. 182. In 1966 India made a direct drawing into the third credit tranche in an emergency without being required to conclude a stand-by arrangement. See Chapter 6, *supra*, page 245 (note 111). India also made drawings in the compensatory financing facility and other facilities that did not require negotiation of a stand-by or extended arrangement.

[218] The documents of the 1981 extended arrangement for India are reproduced in Chapter 6, *supra*, page 250 et seq. See generally Catherine Gwin, "Financing India's Structural Adjustment: The Role of the Fund," in Williamson, *IMF Conditionality*, *supra* note 157, p. 511.

[219] E.B. Decision No. 3153, *supra* note 38, quoted in part at pages 411–412.

[220] See Chapter 6, *supra*, pages 243–247.

A country under Article XIV will usually liberalize its exchange restrictions by stages. A first step often is the gradual reduction in the number of bilateral payments arrangements, with transactions instead settled in a foreign convertible currency. A major step is taken when the country grants general permission for nonresidents that obtain the country's currency in current international transactions to transfer that currency freely to other nonresidents. Alternatively, or in conjunction with such general permission, the country may establish procedures whereby its monetary authorities will buy the local currency from nonresident holders and provide a foreign convertible currency in exchange (usually U.S. dollars, French francs, or U.K. sterling). This establishment of "external convertibility" may be done by the country while continuing to prohibit its residents from transferring the local currency to nonresidents except upon governmental approval granted only for settlement of transactions having priority in the country's economic plans.

Relaxing restrictions so that residents may, without the need for governmental approval, transfer the local currency to nonresidents in settlement of current transactions marks a further move toward *de facto* compliance with Article VIII. A country making this modification may maintain extensive reporting requirements to assure that the settlements are for "current" and not "capital" transactions and for the purpose of obtaining statistics for planning purposes.

The provision of foreign currencies without limit to residents for use by them in settling current transactions marks a further move toward compliance with Article VIII, particularly if the foreign currencies are provided at a single exchange rate. The foreign currencies may be provided either by governmental authorities or through a free market mechanism. Eventually the country may bring itself into compliance with all of the requirements of Article VIII, Sections 2, 3, and 4.

Exchange Restrictions and Trade Restrictions

General Comment

Countries faced with balance-of-payments problems may use a variety of regulatory techniques that are not, in form, currency exchange controls or exchange rate adjustments. Because the trade account is often its largest balance-of-payments item, a country may concentrate its efforts on controlling trade. A country that determines, for example, that the importation of automobiles shall receive a low priority for the use of foreign exchange may implement this policy through a foreign exchange licensing system or it may, alternatively, adopt a trade restriction placing a quantitative limit on the number or total value of automobiles that can be imported. The effect will be the same—automobiles will not be imported and foreign exchange will be conserved.

Restrictions that are cast in the form of exchange controls are, as we have seen, under the jurisdiction of the IMF. We shall now consider restrictions cast in the form of trade controls although used for balance-of-payments reasons. Trade measures that have been used with some frequency include quantitative restrictions (import quotas), increased tariffs (often through the use of tariff surcharges), and import deposit requirements. These receive attention below. Internal taxes and subsidies and export taxes and subsidies have also been used but are not discussed here.[221]

The General Agreement on Tariffs and Trade explicitly contemplates that for countries that belong to both the IMF and the GATT, the IMF will regulate currency exchange matters and the GATT will not intrude upon the Fund's exercise of jurisdiction.[222] We have seen that the Fund, when determining whether a restriction is a currency restriction, looks primarily at the technique used rather than the purpose or effect.[223] The legal staff of the IMF in 1960 advised the Executive Board that the Fund does not have ''approval jurisdiction'' under Article VIII over nondiscriminatory import restrictions even when imposed for balance-of-payments reasons. However, where a member imposes discriminatory import restrictions for balance-of-payments reasons, ''the currency considerations are so clear that the restrictions partake of exchange as well as trade, and fall under the parallel jurisdiction of the Fund and the GATT.''[224] In the sections that follow we shall examine the role of the GATT with respect to trade controls for balance-of-payments purposes and the interaction of the GATT with the IMF. We shall then later look again at the IMF's policies.

GATT Treatment of Trade Restrictions Maintained for Balance-of-Payments Reasons

Import Quotas.   Article XI of the General Agreement on Tariffs and Trade[225] contains a general prohibition (subject to some exceptions) on the use of import quotas and import licensing. The Agreement on Import Licensing Procedures, concluded under the auspices of the GATT, contains additional provisions requiring the simplification of licensing procedures and fairness in their administration. It further provides that foreign exchange necessary to pay

---

[221] See Frieder Roessler, ''Selective Balance-of-Payments Adjustment Measures Affecting Trade: The Roles of the GATT and the IMF,'' *Journal of World Trade Law,* vol. 9 (1975), p. 622 at pp. 622–33; and OECD, *Trade Measures and Adjustment of the Balance of Payments* (Paris, 1971), pp. 51–65.

[222] The General Agreement on Tariffs and Trade is described in Chapter 2, *supra,* page 63 et seq.

[223] See pages 393–394, *supra.*

[224] *IMF History 1945–65, supra* note 39, vol. 2, p. 287.

[225] For citation to the GATT Agreement, see Chapter 2, *supra,* page 63 (note 103).

for licensed imports shall be made available to license holders on the same basis as to importers of goods not requiring import licenses.[226]

Article XII and Section B of Article XVIII of the GATT General Agreement set forth an exception to the ban on import quotas of special interest to us: A member is permitted to introduce or maintain quantitative restrictions to safeguard its balance of payments. These are restrictions that prohibit the importation of particular classes of merchandise or that limit the quantity or value of such goods that can be imported. These are the only provisions that authorize deviations from general GATT obligations specifically because of balance-of-payments need. Paragraph 2(a) of Article XII states that import restrictions imposed by a contracting party under that article may not exceed those necessary:

(i) to forestall the imminent threat of, or to stop, a serious decline in its monetary reserves, or

(ii) in the case of a contracting party with very low monetary reserves, to achieve a reasonable rate of increase in its reserves.[227]

The language in paragraph 9 of Article XVIII, relating to developing countries, is identical except that the word "imminent" is eliminated from clause (i) and the words "very low" are replaced by "inadequate" in clause (ii).[228]

When trade restrictions are imposed under Articles XII or XVIII, consultations with the GATT are required:

Any contracting party applying new restrictions or raising the general level of its existing restrictions by a substantial intensification of the measures applied under this Article shall immediately after instituting or intensifying such restrictions (or, in circumstances in which prior consultation is practicable, before doing so) consult with the CONTRACTING PARTIES as to the nature of its balance of payments difficulties, alternative corrective measures which may be available, and the possible effect of the restrictions on the economies of other contracting parties.[229]

These consultations are followed by annual consultations in the case of developed countries (consultations every two years in the case of developing

---

[226] Agreement on Import Licensing Procedures, opened for signature at Geneva, April 12, 1979, entered into force January 1, 1980. See especially Article I, paragraph 9, of the agreement. The text appears in GATT, *Basic Instruments and Selected Documents,* 26th supplement (1980), p. 154.

[227] Articles XII–XV and Section B of Article XVIII of the GATT Agreement resulted from negotiations that are described in Jackson, *World Trade and the Law of GATT, supra* note 74, chapters 18, 25, and 26. See also Christian Vincke, "Trade Restrictions for Balance of Payments Reasons and the GATT: Quotas v. Surcharges," *Harvard Journal of International Law,* vol. 13 (1972), p. 289 at pp. 297–305.

[228] *Idem.*

[229] Article XII, paragraph 4(a). Article XVIII, paragraph 12(a), is virtually identical.

countries) so long as the restrictions are maintained.[230] The consultations examine the trade effects of the restrictions and whether the balance-of-payments position of the country justifies the trade restrictions. Unlike the IMF which places heavy reliance on staff and a full-time executive board, GATT consultations are usually conducted by the Committee on Balance of Payments Restrictions composed of representatives of member states assisted by the GATT staff.[231]

The GATT agreement requires the CONTRACTING PARTIES to "accept" the determination of the IMF as to *what* constitutes a "serious decline" in a country's monetary reserves or "very low" or "inadequate" monetary reserves.[232] These are key criteria in the application of GATT Articles XII and XVIII.[233] The CONTRACTING PARTIES are also required to accept the IMF's determination of "whether action by a contracting party in exchange matters is in accordance with the Articles of Agreement [of the IMF]."[234] IMF representatives attend meetings of the relevant GATT committees and working parties and submit the Fund's findings and determinations.[235] The IMF determines the seriousness of the balance-of-payments problem not merely in statistical terms or in the abstract by applying a verbal label (like "very low monetary reserves") but, most importantly, in relation to the general level of restrictions being imposed by the country. The Fund's communications thus address the basis on which a GATT decision under Article XII or Section B of Article XVIII is to be based.[236] However, any ultimate decisions on the lawful-

[230] Article XII, paragraph 4(b); Article XVIII, paragraph 12(b). There are also procedures for review of restrictions on complaint by a contracting party. Article XII, paragraph 4(d); Article XVIII, paragraph 12(d). If there is widespread use of restrictions by developed countries, under Article XII there is a special procedure for extraordinary consultations involving both countries in balance-of-payments deficit and countries in surplus. Article XII, paragraph 5.

[231] GATT procedures for consultations on new or intensified restrictions, approved November 16, 1960, appear in GATT, *Basic Instruments and Selected Documents*, 9th supplement (1961), p. 18. Procedures for periodic consultations with countries maintaining restrictions, approved April 28, 1970, amended December 19, 1972, appear *idem*, 18th supplement (1972), p. 48, and 20th supplement (1974), p. 47. See also *idem*, 24th supplement (1978), p. 60. The Declaration on Trade Measures Taken for Balance-of-Payments Purposes, adopted November 28, 1979, clarified procedures; *idem*, 26th supplement (1980), p. 205.

[232] Article XV, paragraph 2.

[233] See text accompanying notes 227 and 228, *supra*.

[234] Article XV, paragraph 2.

[235] While the GATT Agreement requires that organization to consult with the IMF on the currency implications of trade measures, the IMF is not obligated by its Articles of Agreement to consult the GATT on the trade implications of currency measures that it approves for countries that belong to both organizations. However, Article X of the IMF Agreement states that the Fund "shall cooperate" with "public international organizations having specialized responsibilities in related fields." Procedures for consultations between the GATT and the IMF were first spelled out in a 1948 exchange of letters. IMF, *Annual Report, 1949,* pp. 75–78. See also GATT, *Basic Instruments and Selected Documents*, vol. I (1952), pp. 120–23. Current procedures are discussed in GATT, *Basic Instruments and Selected Documents*, 24th supplement (1978), p. 58 at pp. 59–60.

[236] In the case of "intensification" consultations under GATT Article XII, paragraph 4(a), and Article XVIII, paragraph 12(a), the Fund typically presents its views, if it is of the opinion that the level of restric-

ness of the import restrictions in terms of the GATT Agreement are for the GATT CONTRACTING PARTIES to make.

GATT consultations have been described as "blunt" and "hard-hitting," often inducing a party to modify its restrictions or to terminate them sooner than it otherwise would have done.[237] For the most part, GATT members that have relaxed currency restrictions in accordance with the Fund Articles have not substituted trade restrictions in their place.[238] While developing countries have imposed quantitative restrictions for payments reasons, no major industrialized country has in recent years imposed temporary quotas on the basis of GATT Article XII.[239]

Tariff Surcharges. A "tariff surcharge" is a temporary addition of a uniform specific or *ad valorem* tariff charge on all imports or a substantial portion of them. A surcharge is administratively simple for national authorities to apply and can be put into effect quickly. An import surcharge, by increasing the cost of imported goods to domestic purchasers, has effects on the import account similar to a currency devaluation or depreciation, but without directly affecting the prices at which other international transactions take place.[240] Tariff surcharges, although in form a trade control technique, are sufficiently akin to exchange restrictions that the IMF includes information about them in its *Annual Report on Exchange Arrangements and Exchange Restrictions*. Both developed

---

tions is not excessive in relation to the balance-of-payments and reserve developments, in language like the following:

> The general level of restrictions of [country] which are under reference does not go beyond the extent necessary at the present time to [stop a serious decline in its monetary reserves] [achieve a reasonable rate of increase in its reserves].

At the regular annual or biennial consultations under GATT Article XII, paragraph 4(b), and Article XVIII, paragraph 12(b), the IMF's statements have varied according to the circumstances. For background see *IMF History 1945–65, supra* note 39, vol. 2, pp. 335–46; and Roessler, "Selective Balance-of-Payments Adjustment Measures," *supra* note 221, pp. 645–48.

[237] An example is the GATT Council decision of October 1973 that adopted a report of a working group which, following a consultation with Spain, concluded that the then-existing Spanish import restrictions could no longer be justified under the balance-of-payments provisions of GATT Articles XII and XVIII. The Council recommended that Spain intensify its efforts to liberalize its import policies. See GATT, *GATT Activities in 1973* (Geneva, 1974), pp. 55–56.

[238] See *Trade Measures and Adjustment of the Balance of Payments, supra* note 221, pp. 19–26; *IMF History 1945–65, supra* note 39, vol. 2, p. 346; and Gerard Curzon, *Multilateral Commercial Diplomacy* (New York: Frederick A. Praeger, 1965), pp. 144–65.

[239] France in the period July 1968-January 1969 imposed quotas on a large number of products but did not assert a balance-of-payments justification under GATT Article XII. See Gerard and Victoria Curzon, "The Management of Trade Relations in the GATT," in Andrew Shonfield (ed.) *International Economic Relations of the Western World 1959–1971* (2 vols.; London: Oxford University Press for Royal Institute of International Affairs, 1976), vol. 1, p. 141 at pp. 219–22. A table listing GATT balance-of-payments consultations in 1978–1982 appears in S. J. Anjaria et al., *Developments in International Trade Policy* (IMF Occasional Paper no.16; Washington, 1982), p. 121.

[240] The economic effects of tariff surcharges are analyzed in *Trade Measures and Adjustment of the Balance of Payments, supra* note 221, pp. 33–42.

and developing countries have made use of this technique. At the present time, over one-third of the IMF's members impose an import surcharge.[241]

A tariff surcharge, to the extent that it raises the incidence of customs charges beyond the maximum rates bound under Article II of the General Agreement on Tariffs and Trade is incompatible with the Agreement. While the GATT Agreement permits quantitative trade restrictions for balance-of-payments reasons, there is no explicit authority to increase tariffs because of balance-of-payments need. GATT Article II's prohibition of tariff increases, like other provisions of the GATT Agreement, can be waived under the procedure of Article XXV, paragraph 5.[242] In most cases no waiver is granted and consultations, looking toward removal of the surcharge, are held with the country. In some cases the GATT has granted a formal waiver for surcharges.

Uruguay, for example, was granted a waiver by the GATT in 1961 which has been successively extended. By the time of the GATT consultation in 1974, the Uruguayan surcharge appeared to have lost its temporary character. A question was asked whether Uruguay's frequent adjustment of its exchange rate on the basis of the difference between domestic price changes and foreign price changes made a tariff surcharge unnecessary. Questions were also asked about the complexity of Uruguay's highly regulated import and export regime. In the end the GATT waiver for the surcharge was extended.[243] In general the GATT has been liberal in granting waivers for tariff surcharges imposed by developing countries. A GATT staff member has advanced two reasons for this: (a) the developing country usually has bound tariffs on only a small number of items so the surcharge affects only a few items to which GATT Article II applies, and (b) the individual country's share of world trade is generally so small that the restrictive measures excite little opposition.[244]

The GATT has never granted a waiver for an import surcharge imposed by a developed country. In 1954 France placed a surcharge on certain imports. In response to a complaint filed by Italy with the GATT, French authorities explained that the import tax was intended to serve as a temporary and transitional device to facilitate removal of quantitative import restrictions that had been imposed pursuant to GATT Article XII. The CONTRACTING PARTIES concluded that, whatever the motivation of the tax, it increased the incidence of

---

[241] See tables at the end of the IMF's *Annual Report on Exchange Arrangements and Exchange Restrictions.*

[242] See Chapter 2, *supra,* page 66. While requests for waivers are normally to be submitted 30 days in advance, requests for waivers to permit tariff surcharges are almost always submitted after they are imposed in order to prevent traders from taking advantage of an advance announcement. Roessler, "Selective Balance-of-Payments Adjustment Measures," *supra* note 221, p. 630.

[243] GATT, *Basic Instruments and Selected Documents,* 21st supplement (1975), p. 29 (GATT decision of November 19, 1974) and p. 129 (report of Committee on Balance-of-Payments Restrictions). The waiver was subsequently extended again and again. GATT, *Basic Instruments and Selected Documents,* 23d supplement (1977), pp. 11–12 and 93–98; and 29th supplement (1983), pp. 27–28.

[244] Roessler, "Selective Balance-of-Payments Adjustment Measures," *supra* note 221, pp. 630–31. See also Vincke, *supra* note 227, pp. 306–07.

duties beyond the rates bound under Article II and that the situation justified resort by affected countries to the compensation and retaliation provisions of Article XXIII. France removed the surcharge in August 1957, replacing it with a system of import levies and export subsidies which was removed when the franc was devalued in 1958.[245]

The United Kingdom introduced a tariff surcharge in October 1964 (initially at 15 percent and later reduced to 10 percent).[246] The British argued that the surcharge should be deemed compatible with the GATT Agreement because, in compliance with its GATT commitments, the United Kingdom had over a period of years dismantled quotas and thus lacked the administrative machinery to put a quota system quickly into effect in a payments crisis. The GATT working party, however, refused to state that the U.K. surcharge was consistent with its GATT obligations, but no action was taken to formally determine the legal issue. The United Kingdom removed the surcharge at the end of November 1966.[247]

The United States imposed a temporary tariff surcharge on imports (generally ten percent *ad valorem*) from August 15, 1971, to December 20, 1971.[248] The United States imposed the surcharge at the time it announced that it was suspending the convertibility of the dollar into gold or other reserve assets on the basis of par values. The tariff surcharge and the suspension of convertibility on the basis of par values were intended to force a realignment of exchange rates.[249] The United States argued that its surcharge should not be challenged, since surcharges were less damaging to international trade than quantitative restrictions which it could have applied under GATT Article XII. The United States did not, however, request a waiver.

In the GATT consultations the IMF stated its determination that ''in the

[245] See *Executive Branch GATT Studies: Compilation of 1973 Studies Prepared by the Executive Branch*, Committee on Finance, U.S. Senate, 93d Congress, 2d Session (committee print, 1974), p. 116; and *Trade Measures and Adjustment of the Balance of Payments*, supra note 221, pp. 37–40. See also GATT, *Basic Instruments and Selected Documents*, 3d supplement (1955), p. 26; 4th supplement (1955), p. 20; 5th supplement (1956), p. 27; and 7th supplement (1957), p. 68.

[246] Finance (No. 2) Act 1964. *Public General Acts and Measures*, Elizabeth II, 1964, part II, chapter 92, section 3 (December 17, 1964).

[247] See GATT, *Basic Instruments and Selected Documents*, 15th supplement (1968), p. 113; Curzon, ''Management of Trade Relations in the GATT,'' supra note 239, pp. 217–19; and *Trade Measures and Adjustment of the Balance of Payments*, supra note 221, pp. 41–42.

The U.K. surcharge was a violation of the Convention Establishing the European Free Trade Association to which the United Kingdom was also a party. Consultations in that organization were more penetrating than in the GATT and are credited with getting the United Kingdom to lower the surcharge to 10 percent and to later eliminate it entirely notwithstanding that its balance-of-payments position was still unsatisfactory. See European Free Trade Association, *Building EFTA* (rev. ed.; Geneva: EFTA, 1968), pp. 27–28; Curzon, *supra*, pp. 217–19; and Robert Middleton, *Negotiating on Non-Tariff Distortions of Trade: The EFTA Precedents* (London: Macmillan for Trade Policy Research Centre, 1975), pp. 107–08.

[248] Presidential Proclamation No. 4074 (August 15, 1971) entitled ''Imposition of Supplemental Duty for Balance of Payments Purposes,'' *Federal Register*, vol. 36 (1971), p. 15,724; and U.S. Treasury Department Additional Duty Orders.

[249] See Chapter 11, *infra*, pages 496–498.

absence of other appropriate action and in the present circumstances, the import surcharge can be regarded as being within the bounds of what is necessary to stop a serious deterioration in the United States balance-of-payments position." The IMF representative informed the GATT working party that the IMF at the time (September 1971) had no alternative measures to suggest.[250] The GATT working party, to use the words of its report, "took note" of the findings of the IMF and "recognized" that the United States found itself in a serious balance-of-payments situation that required urgent action. However, the members of the working party (the United States dissenting) "considered that the surcharge, as a trade restrictive measure, was inappropriate given the nature of the United States balance-of-payments situation and the undue burden of adjustment placed upon the import account" and was "not compatible" with the GATT Agreement.[251]

While in this particular case it does not appear that the working party disagreed with the IMF's assessment of the seriousness of the balance-of-payments problem of the United States, it is worth pointing out that paragraph 2 of GATT Article XV requires the GATT to accept and not merely take note of the IMF's determination on this point.[252] Whether, having accepted the IMF's appraisal of the seriousness of the payments problem, the surcharge (as a trade measure) or some other measure was the appropriate remedy was of course a proper subject for GATT determination. The phrase in the report quoted above, "the surcharge, as a trade restrictive measure," recognized that if the surcharge were understood to be a currency exchange measure, the GATT would not have jurisdiction over it.

Although authorities abroad continued to make condemnatory speeches and diplomatic representations, there were no significant retaliatory trade measures to the U.S. action. When the Smithsonian agreement on new exchange rates among the Group of Ten was reached in December 1971, the United States announced the end of the surcharge.[253]

In the case of a Danish surcharge in effect from October 1971 to April 1973, the GATT working party again noted that a surcharge is not compatible with the provisions of the General Agreement. The membership was divided on whether the surcharge was nevertheless an appropriate measure in the Danish case.[254]

The GATT Secretariat in 1965 prepared a paper that outlined reasons in

---

[250] GATT Working Party Report on United States Temporary Import Surcharge (September 1971), paragraph 8; GATT, *Basic Instruments and Selected Documents*, 18th supplement (1972), p. 212 at p. 214.

[251] GATT Working Party Report, *idem*, at pp. 222–23.

[252] GATT Article XV, paragraph 2, requiring GATT acceptance of IMF determinations, applies not just to cases arising under paragraph 2(a) of Article XII or paragraph 9 of Article XVIII (quota cases) but to all cases "involving the criteria" set forth in those paragraphs.

[253] See Chapter 11, *infra*, page 498 (note 39).

[254] See GATT, *Basic Instruments and Selected Documents*, 19th supplement (1973), p. 120. See Middleton, *supra* note 247, pp. 109–10, regarding EFTA review of the Danish surcharge.

terms of trade policy for preferring the use of tariff surcharges to quantitative restrictions.[255] In trade negotiations during the 1970s, the United States took the position that, if any trade controls are to be permitted on balance-of-payments grounds, they should be in the form of tariff surcharges or across-the-board taxes which are less trade-diverting than quotas and less likely to discriminate among domestic importers and among foreign suppliers.[256] Following extended negotiations, the GATT CONTRACTING PARTIES in November 1979 adopted by consensus a Declaration on Trade Measures Taken for Balance-of-Payments Purposes.[257] In order to avoid inconsistency with the General Agreement and because some parties believed that the legalization of surcharges would stimulate more extensive use of them, the declaration does not explicitly mention import surcharges. The declaration states that all restrictive import measures taken for balance-of-payments purposes are to be promptly notified to the GATT at the time of their introduction or intensification. The declaration makes clear that GATT consultation procedures applicable to quantitative restrictions for balance-of-payments purposes also apply to surcharges and all other import trade restrictions taken for balance-of-payments reasons.[258]

The 1979 declaration states criteria for the selection among alternative trade measures when trade restrictions are used for balance-of-payments purposes. The country shall "give preference to the measure which has the least disruptive effect on trade." The simultaneous application of more than one type of trade measure for payments purposes should be avoided. A developed country applying a trade restrictive measure shall take into account the export interests of less developed contracting parties. Whenever practicable the party introducing a restrictive measure shall publicly announce a time schedule for its removal. The negotiating history of the declaration demonstrates that the CONTRACTING PARTIES through the declaration have indicated that they prefer the use of a surcharge to the use of quotas, as the lesser of the evils, where a surcharge better satisfies the above criteria, notwithstanding that the surcharge is *per se* illegal under the General Agreement.[259]

---

[255] GATT document COM.TD/F/W.3 (1965), pp. 1–2, quoted in John H. Jackson, *Legal Problems of International Economic Relations: Cases, Materials, and Text on National and International Regulation of Transnational Economic Relations* (St. Paul: West Publishing Co., 1977), p. 902; and in Jackson, *World Trade and the Law of GATT, supra* note 74, pp. 712–13.

[256] See *Executive Branch GATT Studies, supra* note 245, pp. 118–20. See also *GATT Plus—A Proposal for Trade Reform* (New York: Praeger Publishers for the Atlantic Council of the United States, 1976), pp. 31–35; and *Long-Term International Monetary Reform: A Proposal for an Improved International Adjustment Process* (Washington: American Society of International Law, 1972), p. 24.

[257] Declaration on Trade Measures Taken for Balance-of-Payments Purposes, adopted November 28, 1979, *supra* note 231.

[258] Paragraphs 3 and 4 of the Declaration, *idem.*

[259] See Frieder Roessler, "The GATT Declaration on Trade Measures Taken for Balance-of-Payments Purposes: A Commentary," *Case Western Reserve Journal of International Law,* vol. 12 (1980), p. 383.

Import Deposit Requirements. An import deposit requirement imposes upon an importer an obligation to place money on deposit with a government agency equal to a stated portion of the value of the imported goods, or in some cases, in excess of the value.[260] The money normally does not earn interest during the period of deposit. The exact form of the requirement may vary. Deposits may be collected in advance or at the time of importation, may be held for long or short periods, and may be applicable to different classes of imports. The importer, required to place money on deposit, is forced to tie up its own or borrowed funds. The economic effect is to reduce the working capital of the importer or increase the cost of the import by the amount of interest payable on borrowed funds. It also quickly drains liquidity from the banking system.

If an import deposit requirement by its terms relates to payments or settlements in connection with trade transactions, the IMF has approval jurisdiction over it under IMF Article VIII, Section 2(a). That was the case with deposit requirements maintained by Italy in the period May 1976 to April 1977 and in the period May 1981 to February 1982.[261] The IMF has viewed import deposit requirements as trade and not payments restrictions if the deposit requirement is strictly related to the import transaction and not to the settlement on its account. If so characterized, the restriction is not subject to IMF approval jurisdiction under IMF Article VIII, Section 2(a). Import deposit requirements, whether characterized as trade or payments restrictions, are reported in the IMF's *Annual Report on Exchange Arrangements and Exchange Restrictions.*[262]

Because a deposit does not take the form of a payment to the government but, instead, an indirect burden in the form of interest cost or the tying up of working capital, there was until recently some uncertainty whether a deposit requirement is barred by GATT Article II's prohibition of "charges of any kind imposed on or in connection with importation" in excess of the bound tariff rate. This question was resolved in October 1978 when the CONTRACTING PARTIES adopted a GATT conciliation panel's determination that interest charges and costs associated with security deposits for imports come within the scope of Article II.[263]

The GATT's 1979 Declaration on Trade Measures Taken for Balance-of-Payments Purposes, although it does not explicitly mention import deposit requirements, applies to them in the same way that it applies to tariff sur-

---

[260] See Eugene A. Birnbaum and Moeen A. Qureshi, "Advance Deposit Requirements for Imports," *IMF Staff Papers*, vol. 8 (1960), p. 115; *Trade Measures and Adjustment of the Balance of Payments*, *supra* note 221, pp. 43–50; and David W. Heleniak, "The United Kingdom's Import Deposit Scheme," *Journal of World Trade Law*, vol. 3 (1969), p. 584.

[261] See pages 408–410, *supra*. See notes 129 and 133 regarding the GATT's consideration of these cases.

[262] At the present time about twenty IMF members require advance import deposits.

[263] See paragraphs 4.6 and 4.15 of the report of the panel, adopted October 18, 1978, that examined the complaint of the United States against the European Economic Community relating to security deposits for imports of processed fruits and vegetables into the EEC area. GATT, *Basic Instruments and Selected Documents*, 25th supplement (1979), p. 68 at pp. 97 and 103.

charges.[264] The GATT's responses to deposit schemes of the United Kingdom (1968–70) and of Italy (1974–75, 1976–77 and 1981–82) illustrate that the primary legal issues are whether, in the particular case, restrictive trade measures of any type are justified by the country's balance-of-payments situation and, if so, whether the import deposit scheme employed is less restrictive than other trade measures that would be equally effective in dealing with the balance of payments. Even if the answers to both of these questions are in the affirmative, pressure will nevertheless be placed on the party to remove the deposit requirement.

The United Kingdom made use of an import deposit scheme in the period November 1968–December 1970.[265] Deposits, initially at 50 percent of each import's value, were collected at the time of import, and held for 180 days, on about one-third of the U.K.'s imports. The British argued in a GATT working party that the requirement, instituted for balance-of-payments reasons, was in accordance with Article XII of the General Agreement. While the working party did not accept the British argument that the control was authorized by the GATT Agreement, it concluded that the measure was no more restrictive than quotas the United Kingdom could have applied under Article XII. Modification and withdrawal of the system was urged, but no formal action was taken to challenge it.[266]

Italy in May 1974 decreed an import deposit scheme.[267] The Italian importer or foreign exporter was required to place funds amounting to 50 percent of the value of the goods (25 percent for beef and certain cattle) in a non-interest-bearing account with Banca d'Italia for six months. The measure, adopted for balance-of-payments reasons, was designed primarily to reduce consumer goods imports and did not apply to raw materials, energy products, and capital equipment.[268] The representative of the European Economic Community stated to the GATT working party that the Community had authorized Italy to impose the deposit requirement, given its balance-of-payments difficulties. The Community representative argued that the measure should not be challenged by the GATT because it was no more restrictive than the quantitative re-

---

[264] See notes 257 and 258, *supra,* and accompanying text.

[265] Customs (Import Deposits) Act 1968. *Public General Acts and Measures,* Elizabeth II, 1968, part II, chapter 74 (December 5, 1968).

[266] See GATT, *Basic Instruments and Selected Documents,* 17th supplement (1970), pp. 144–51, 18th supplement (1972), pp. 210–12; Helenick, *supra* note 260; and *Trade Measures and Adjustment of the Balance of Payments, supra* note 221, pp. 47–49. See Middleton, *supra* note 247, pp. 108–09, regarding EFTA review of the U.K. deposit requirement.

[267] Ministerial Decree of May 2, 1974; *Gazzetta Ufficiale della Repubblica Italiana,* no. 115 of May 4, 1974, supplement – part 1, pp. 1–23.

[268] For background see the symposium, "Italy and Its Partners: A Case Study in International Crisis Management," *International Affairs* (London), vol. 51, no. 1 (1975), p. 1; and Hans Smit and Peter E. Herzog, *The Law of the European Economic Community: A Commentary on the EEC Treaty* (6 vols.; New York: Matthew Bender, binder service, 1983 ed.), part 3, pp. 620–22.

strictions specifically provided for in Article XII of the GATT Agreement.[269] The IMF supplied a comprehensive background document and its representative informed the GATT working party at its September 1974 meeting of the "finding of the International Monetary Fund that the imposition of the import deposit requirement was warranted on a temporary basis, given the exceptionally serious balance-of-payments problems, including a large deficit on non-oil transactions. . . ." The IMF representative also informed the working party that the Italian Government had informed the Fund of its intention to terminate the requirement by early 1975.[270] Some members of the working party were concerned that the Italian measure, which had seriously hurt the trade of their countries, might lead to a chain reaction of protective trade measures, given the problems most countries were having at the time in financing oil imports.[271] Without prejudice to the rights of contracting parties to seek compensation for the trade damage, the working party concluded that "the Italian import deposit scheme was not more restrictive than measures that an application of the provisions of Article XII of the GATT permits."[272]

The IMF in the Italian case played a greater role than its formal relationship with the GATT might suggest. While the Fund viewed the deposit requirement as a restriction on trade and not a currency control, Italy, in a letter of intent in support of a stand-by arrangement approved by the IMF in April 1974, had stated that it would not introduce new trade restrictions. Since the import deposit scheme introduced a few weeks later was a new restriction, the Fund consulted with Italian officials. In those consultations Italian authorities committed themselves to terminate the deposit requirement by the end of March 1975, which they did.[273]

GATT Members that Are Not IMF Members. Under paragraph 6 of Article XV of the GATT Agreement, members of the GATT that do not belong to the IMF are required to conclude a special exchange agreement with the GATT. The Fund collaborated with the GATT in preparing a "model" of such a special exchange agreement. The model agreement was used in a few cases but in no case is it in force today.[274]

Each of the present members of the GATT that is not a member of the

---

[269] Report of GATT Working Party adopted October 21, 1974, in GATT, *Basic Instruments and Selected Documents,* 21st supplement (1975), p. 121 at pp. 121–22. See page 475, *infra,* regarding the EEC's action in this case.

[270] *Idem,* pp. 122, 123, and 125.

[271] *Idem,* p. 124.

[272] *Idem,* p. 125.

[273] Letter of F. Palamenghi-Crispi, IMF Executive Director (Italy), to the author dated March 2, 1976. The Italian letter of intent to the IMF appears in Williamson, *IMF Conditionality, supra* note 157, p. 466. See also Spaventa, *supra* note 157.

[274] See Gold, *Membership and Nonmembership, supra* note 87, pp. 426–45 and 536–45, where the text of the model agreement is set forth. See also GATT, *Basic Instruments and Selected Documents,* vol. 2 (1952), pp. 115–38.

IMF, instead of signing a special exchange agreement with the GATT, has given formal assurances to the GATT that it will act in exchange matters "in a manner fully consistent with the principles" of the model exchange agreement. The GATT has accepted these statements, recorded in a protocol of accession and GATT decision, as satisfying the substance of the requirement of GATT Article XV, paragraph 6. In addition, accession protocols contain specific provisions on consultation in exchange matters.[275] At the present time Cuba, Czechoslovakia, Poland, and Switzerland belong to the GATT but not to the IMF.

IMF Actions Concerning Trade Controls

As previously explained, the Executive Board of the International Monetary Fund, consistent with a staff legal opinion of 1960, has not exercised "approval jurisdiction" over nondiscriminatory trade controls, and has left approval to the GATT.[276] Mexico,[277] Venezuela, Iran, Saudi Arabia, and about thirty other countries are members of the IMF but not of the GATT. The legal staff of the Fund has considered whether the words "restrictions on the making of payments and transfers for current international transactions" in Section 2(a) of Article VIII of the IMF Agreement might be given a more extensive meaning when applied to IMF members that have not adhered to the GATT Agreement on the theory that the drafters of the Fund Agreement had assumed that IMF members would also belong to the GATT. The Fund decided that Section 2(a) should not be applied differently to different IMF members.[278]

Since 1974 the Fund has, however, sought to exercise somewhat greater authority over trade restrictions of all IMF members than it had exercised previously. This change in approach was prompted by concern with trade measures countries were contemplating to deal with payments problems created by the rapid rise in world petroleum prices. An Executive Board decision in January 1974 called upon IMF members to collaborate with the Fund to avoid the escalation of restrictions on trade as well as on payments.[279] The Fund in a deci-

---

[275] See Gold, *Membership and Nonmembership, supra* note 87, pp. 438–43. See also Jackson, *World Trade and the Law of GATT, supra* note 74, pp. 486–91.

The withdrawal of Czechoslovakia from the IMF presented the GATT with the question: How could it be assured that Czechoslovakia would comply with Article XV of the GATT Agreement and not frustrate the intent of the GATT by currency exchange actions? When Czechoslovakia refused to sign a special exchange agreement, the GATT CONTRACTING PARTIES in a decision of March 5, 1955, accepted its assurance that used the language quoted in the text. Subsequent decisions and protocols respecting non-IMF members have tracked this formula. GATT, *Basic Instruments and Selected Documents,* 3d supplement (1955), p. 43.

[276] See text accompanying notes 223 and 224, *supra.*

[277] A protocol for Mexico's accession to the GATT was negotiated in 1979, but Mexico decided not to accept it. See Dale Story, "Trade Politics in the Third World: A Case Study of the Mexican GATT Decision," *International Organization,* vol. 36 (1982), p. 767.

[278] Gold, *Membership and Nonmembership, supra* note 87, p. 445.

[279] E.B. Decision No. 4134 -(74/4) (January 23, 1974); quoted in full in Chapter 11, *infra,* page 510.

sion of June 1974 invited IMF members to join in a voluntary declaration that they would not introduce or intensify trade or other current-account measures for balance-of-payments purposes without a prior finding by the Fund that there is a balance-of-payments justification for them.[280] The declaration provided that it would become effective among subscribing members when members holding 65 percent of the voting power in the Fund accepted it. It did not receive this measure of acceptance and and never entered into effect. A number of countries refused to subscribe on the ground that the Fund was exceeding its jurisdiction.

The Committee on Reform of the International Monetary System and Related Issues (the ''related issues'' referring to trade) in 1974 recommended that the IMF Articles be amended to provide that no IMF member accepting a new clause to be inserted in Article VIII would, without the Fund's prior finding of justification, introduce restrictions on merchandise trade or services for balance-of-payments reasons.[281] The IMF Executive Board considered two drafts of a possible amendment, but no such change was included in the Second Amendment to the IMF Articles.[282]

The IMF has for many years included trade controls within the scope of its periodic consultations with its members.[283] A decision implementing Article IV, following the Second Amendment, states that ''the introduction, substantial intensification, or prolonged maintenance, for balance of payments purposes, of restrictions on, or incentives for, current transactions or payments'' may indicate the need for discussion by the Fund with the member.[284] The decision is understood to apply to restrictions on the transactions themselves as well as their currency aspects.[285] The decision does not recognize IMF approval jurisdiction over trade controls but does recognize consultation jurisdiction.[286]

The IMF has considered it appropriate to consider the trade measures of a

[280] See declaration and letter to members appended to E. B. Decision No. 4254 -(74/75)(June 26, 1974); IMF, *Annual Report, 1974*, p. 126; *Selected Decisions* (10th issue, 1983), p. 259. See also Joseph Gold, ''Recent International Decisions to Prevent Restrictions on Trade and Payments,'' *Journal of World Trade Law*, vol. 9 (1975), p. 63.

[281] IMF Committee on Reform of the International Monetary System and Related Issues (Committee of Twenty), *International Monetary Reform: Documents of the Committee of Twenty* (Washington, 1974), pp. 20, 22, and 23 (Outline of Reform, June 14, 1974, paragraphs 36 and 41, and Appendix).

[282] The reasons for objection to the merger of approval jurisdiction over trade and currency in the IMF are not entirely clear. Among reasons that have been suggested are that different ministries may be involved domestically, weighted voting power prevails in the IMF, and fear that the IMF would come to exercise authority over trade controls maintained for other than balance-of-payments reasons. The negotiations are described in Gold, *Use, Conversion, and Exchange of Currency, supra* note 42, pp. 6–7.

[283] See Silard, ''Impact of the International Monetary Fund on International Trade,'' *supra* note 41, pp. 146–48.

[284] E.B. Decision No. 5392 -(77/63)(April 29, 1977), subpart Principles of Fund Surveillance Over Exchange Rate Policies, paragraph 2 (iii)(a); IMF, *Annual Report, 1977*, p. 107; *Selected Decisions* (10th issue, 1983), p. 10.

[285] Gold, *Use, Conversion, and Exchange of Currency, supra* note 42, pp. 14–15.

[286] IMF consultation practice is treated in Chapter 12, *infra,* page 571 et seq.

country when evaluating a request for use of Fund resources. The 1974 decision establishing the facility for financing oil imports stated that IMF members requesting purchases through the facility were ''expected to represent'' that they would refrain from imposing new, or intensifying existing, restrictions on ''current international transactions'' (which included trade measures) without prior consultation with the Fund.[287] Letters of intent supporting stand-by and extended arrangements for the use of the Fund's general resources indicate the country's intentions respecting trade restrictions.[288] Stand-by and extended arrangements today regularly include a performance clause on trade restrictions. The Fund's standard forms for stand-by and extended arrangement documents now explicitly provide that drawing rights are interrupted if the member ''imposes or intensifies import restrictions for balance of payments reasons.''[289]

The full extent of the Fund's jurisdiction over trade restrictions is as yet unresolved. While the meaning of ''restriction'' in Article VIII, Section 2(a), has been interpreted narrowly for ''approval jurisdiction,''[290] it is, as we have seen, not the only applicable provision in the IMF Agreement. Consultations under Article IV comprehend trade restrictions. Acting on the authority of Article V, Section 3(a), the Fund has established policies on the use of the General Resources Account that require members to consult on trade measures, and the Fund conditions drawings under stand-by and extended arrangements on the member's refraining from imposing or intensifying import restrictions for balance-of-payments reasons. One of the purposes of the Fund is ''to facilitate the expansion and balanced growth of international trade.''[291] Certainly the jurisdictions of the IMF and the GATT are not mutually exclusive. As noted, there has been effective cooperation between the Fund and the GATT and deference by each organization to the other in the exercise of its jurisdiction. Deference by the Fund to the GATT does not, however, logically entail lack of Fund jurisdictional competence.

---

[287] Paragraph 5(c) of E.B. Decision No. 4241 -(74/67)(June 13, 1974); IMF, *Annual Report, 1974*, p. 122; *Selected Decisions* (10th issue, 1983), p. 80. The facility for financing oil imports is discussed in Chapter 6, *supra*, pages 293–294.

[288] See discussion of Italian stand-by arrangement in text accompanying note 273, *supra*.

[289] See paragraph 4(e) of the 1981 Extended Arrangement-India document and paragraphs 18 and 19 of India's statement of economic policies; Chapter 6, *supra*, pages 253 and 260–261. Paragraph 4(e) is a standard formulation used in stand-by and extended arrangement documents. To get a sense of IMF interest in trade control liberalization, see the discussion of India's export and import policies in the IMF staff report, excerpts from which are published in *The Hindu* (Madras), October 21, 1981, p. 7.

Letters of intent in support of stand-by arrangements, even before 1974, often stated that the member would not request further drawings if it introduced trade restrictions. See Silard, ''Impact of the International Monetary Fund on International Trade,'' *supra* note 41, pp. 146–48.

[290] See pages 393–394 and 402, *supra*.

[291] Article I(ii).

Invisible Transactions

Note

The Articles of Agreement of the International Monetary Fund in Section 2(a) of Article VIII, discussed extensively earlier, bar restrictions (unless approved by the IMF) on payments and transfers for current international transactions. "Current international transactions" as used in Section 2(a) includes the so-called current "invisible" transactions—insurance charges, warehousing charges, shipping, business and tourist travel, family remittances, services, salaries, wages, royalties, dividends, interest, and other non-capital transactions. As noted previously, Section 2(a) is intended to assure that currency restrictions do not frustrate the consummation of otherwise lawful transactions; it does not require that the underlying transactions be permitted.[292] Although the General Agreement on Tariffs and Trade deals with some aspects of taxes and shipping, its primary concern is tariffs, quantitative restrictions, and other barriers to trade in goods. The members of the Organisation for Economic Co-operation and Development and the European Economic Community have assumed additional obligations.

Liberalization of Invisible Transactions in the OECD

The Organisation for Economic Co-operation and Development (OECD)[293] in 1961 adopted a Code of Liberalisation of Current Invisible Operations.[294] The Code has subsequently been amended by OECD Council decisions.[295] The approach of the Code is a comprehensive one. It applies to restrictions on payments and transfers respecting items covered by the Code. It also applies to non-monetary restrictions imposed on the underlying transactions.[296]

    All members of the OECD have adhered to the Code. The first sentence in Article 1 states: "Members *shall eliminate* between one another, in accordance

---

[292] See pages 390–396 and 402, *supra.*

[293] The OECD is described in Chapter 2, *supra,* page 68 et seq.

[294] Some provisions relating to invisibles were incorporated as early as 1951 into a Code of Liberalisation adopted by the Organisation for European Economic Co-operation, which was the predecessor of the OECD. This Code was amended a number of times to expand the list of invisible operations covered. The 1955 text appears in *European Yearbook,* vol. 3 (1955), p. 255. This Code, with amendments, was adopted by the OECD Council as the OECD Code of Liberalisation of Current Invisible Operations on December 12, 1961. OECD document no. C(61)95, in *European Yearbook,* vol. 10 (1962), p. 331.

[295] The Code of Liberalisation of Current Invisible Operations has been amended a number of times, the annexes quite frequently, by decisions of the OECD Council. The author has used the April 1980 edition of the Code, published by the OECD. The OECD's Committee on Capital Movements and Invisible Transactions is presently considering revisions to further up-date the Code.

[296] Various types of barriers to invisible transactions are described in Brian Griffiths, *Invisible Barriers to Invisible Trade* (London: Macmillan, 1975).

with the provisions of Article 2, restrictions on current invisible transactions and transfers, hereinafter called 'current invisible operations.' " [emphasis added][297] The Code goes on to explicitly provide: "Members shall grant any authorisation required for a current invisible operation specified in an item set out in Annex A to this Code."[298] The current invisible operations that are liberalized are listed in detail in Annex A (summarized in the footnote).[299] The members have also declared that they "shall endeavour" to extend the measures of liberalization to all members of the International Monetary Fund.[300]

Because members were not prepared to immediately end restrictions on all transactions listed in Annex A of the Code, and because the list in Annex A would be expanded and made even more comprehensive over time, the Code uses an elaborate reservation procedure. Members are permitted to lodge reservations when an item is added to Annex A or its definition is extended or when the item first begins to apply to that member.[301] Annex B to the Code lists the reservations of each member, item by item. Thus, it is relatively easy for a user of the Code to determine the reservations of each member country.[302] The Code

---

[297] Greece, Portugal, Spain, and Turkey have adhered to the Code, but have not yet accepted the obligations of IMF Article VIII, sections 2, 3, and 4.

[298] Article 2(a). See also Article 6 relating to payments and transfers.

[299] A summary of the operations listed in Annex A follows. It should be noted that in many cases the item's description has been expanded or qualified in the actual language of the Annex:

Business and industry: Repair and assembly; finishing; processing under contract; technical assistance; construction and maintenance of buildings, roads, etc.; author's royalties; salaries and wages of nonresidents; overhead expenses of subsidiary companies.

Foreign trade: Business travel; commission and brokerage; differences, margins, and deposits in normal commodity transactions; charges for documentation; warehousing and customs clearance; transit charges; customs duties and fees.

Transport: Road transport; air transport; inland waterway freights; maritime transport; repairs.

Insurance: Social security; life insurance; insurance relating to goods in international trade; other insurance; reinsurance; insurance business operations abroad.

Films: Export, import, distribution, and use of films and recordings.

Income from capital: Dividends, interest, profits, rent.

Private travel and immigrants' remittances: Tourism; educational, health, and family travel; immigrants' remittances.

Personal income and expenditures: Pensions, maintenance payments, repair of private property abroad.

Public income and expenditure: Taxes; government expenditure; consular receipts; transport, postal, and telephone service payments and receipts.

Other: Advertising; court expenses; damages; fines; organizational membership expenses; services of doctors, lawyers, accountants, engineers, and other professionals; registration of patents and trademarks; refunds on cancellation of contracts; refunds of uncalled-for payments.

[300] Article 1(d).

[301] Article 2. As an alternative to item-by-item reservations, a member can, "if its economic and financial situation justifies such a course," enter a general derogation to all of its obligations when it first adheres to the Code. At the present time only Turkey relies on this provision, which is in Article 7(a); OECD document no. C(62)21(final). In 1977 Greece terminated its reliance on Article 7(a) and filed specific reservations to various items in Annex A. See OECD Council decision of July 22, 1977; OECD Document no. C(77)19(final), in *European Yearbook*, vol. 25(1977), p. 237.

[302] As of April 1980, there were relatively few reservations to the Code, many reservations formerly in effect having been withdrawn. Most reservations now relate to just a few items: inland waterway freights, road transport, life insurance, some other forms of insurance, and films and recordings.

establishes procedures for the periodic review of reservations (at least every eighteen months) with the view toward their withdrawal.[303] This review is conducted by the Committee on Capital Movements and Invisible Transactions.[304] Some countries are more liberal than would appear from the Code, but are reluctant to withdraw reservations since their margin of freedom to reintroduce restrictions would be limited. The OECD Secretariat makes an effort to have the reservations withdrawn when the restrictions are no longer in effect.

In addition to the limited right to lodge reservations, a member may "temporarily suspend" its liberalization (i.e., impose restrictions on payments or underlying transactions) if its overall balance of payments, including the state of its monetary reserves, develops adversely at a rate and in circumstances which it considers serious.[305] It may withdraw measures of liberalization that result in "serious economic disturbance."[306] These derogations are to be notified "forthwith,"[307] and the Code provides procedures for the organization to review these actions.[308] The Code also permits a state to take "action which it considers necessary" to maintain public order, morals, health, and safety, to honor international peace and security obligations, and to protect its essential security interests.[309]

The Code embodies a principle of nondiscrimination: "A Member shall not discriminate as between other Members in authorising current invisible operations which are listed in Annex A and which are subject to any degree of liberalisation."[310] Further, any member lodging a reservation to items in Annex A or invoking the derogation provisions nevertheless benefits from the measures of liberalization taken by the other members.[311]

The experience with the OECD Code of Liberalisation of Current Invisible Operations shows the value of explicitly dealing with the liberalization of underlying transactions at the same time that monetary restrictions are removed.[312]

---

[303] Articles 11–17.

[304] Articles 18–21. See also text accompanying note 404, *infra*.

[305] Derogation clause of Article 7(c). In recent years there have been relatively few derogations pursuant to Article 7(c). Examples include Portugal's invocation of the derogation clause in 1976 and its subsequent reliance upon it, and Italy's invocation of the clause when it imposed various restrictions during the 1970s. See, e.g., OECD Council resolution of July 25, 1980, concerning Italian currency restrictions on foreign travel; OECD document no. C(80)133, in OECD, *Acts of the Organisation,* 1980, p. 491. The comparable clause in the Code of Liberalisation of Capital Movements has been invoked more frequently. See note 390, *infra*.

[306] Article 7(b).

[307] Article 13(a).

[308] Articles 13–20.

[309] Article 3.

[310] Article 9.

[311] Article 8. The obligations of Article VIII, sections 2, 3, and 4, of the IMF Agreement also are operative without reciprocal concessions. A country that has accepted IMF Article VIII cannot refuse to honor its Article VIII obligations with other members availing themselves of Article XIV's transitional regime.

[312] An analysis of the volume of international invisible transactions and their composition (travel, transportation, services, investment income, government services, and other invisibles) of OECD countries during

Liberalization of Invisible Transactions in the European Economic Community

For states that are members of the European Economic Community, their obligations under the OECD Invisibles Code are reinforced by provisions of the Treaty of Rome. Article 106 of the Treaty Establishing the European Economic Community[313] provides:

> 1. Each Member State undertakes to authorise, in the currency of the Member State in which the creditor or the beneficiary resides, any payments connected with the movement of goods, services or capital, and any transfers of capital and earnings, to the extent that the movement of goods, services, capital and persons between Member States has been liberalised pursuant to this Treaty.
>
> The Member States declare their readiness to undertake the liberalisation of payments beyond the extent provided in the preceding subparagraph, in so far as their economic situation in general and the state of their balance of payments in particular so permit.
>
> 2. In so far as movements of goods, services, and capital are limited only by restrictions on payments connected therewith, these restrictions shall be progressively abolished by applying, *mutatis mutandis*, the provisions of the Chapters relating to the abolition of quantitative restrictions, to the liberalisation of services and to the free movement of capital.
>
> 3. Member States undertake not to introduce between themselves any new restrictions on transfers connected with the invisible transactions listed in Annex III to this Treaty.[314]
>
> The progressive abolition of existing restrictions shall be effected in accordance with the provisions of Articles 63 to 65, in so far as such abolition is not governed by the provisions contained in paragraphs 1 and 2 or by the Chapter relating to the free movement of capital.[315]

the period 1960–1969 appears in Eduardo Merigo and Stephen Potter, "OECD Invisibles in the 1960's," *OECD Economic Outlook*, July 1970, p. 3.

[313] The European Economic Community is described in Chapter 2, *supra*, page 76 et seq. All members of the EEC also belong to the OECD.

[314] The list of invisible transactions in Annex III of the EEC Treaty was copied almost verbatim from the list annexed to the OEEC's Code of Liberalisation [of Invisible Operations] as it stood in 1957. See note 294, *supra*.

[315] Council Directive No. 63/340 of May 31, 1963 (concerning currency payments and transfers where underlying service transactions are not restricted); and Council Directive No. 63/474 of July 30, 1963 (concerning liberalization of currency transfers unrelated to movements of goods, services, capital, or persons) implement Article 106. *Official Journal of the European Communities* [hereinafter *Official Journal*], no. 86,

4. If need be, Member States shall consult each other on the measures to be taken to enable the payments and transfers mentioned in this Article to be effected; such measures shall not prejudice the attainment of the objectives set out in this Chapter.

Subdivisions 1 and 2 of Article 106 are designed to assure that currency restrictions do not prevent or inhibit the consummation of transactions liberalized by the EEC Treaty. The Court of Justice of the European Communities has held that when restrictions on movements of goods were liberalized under Article 30, restrictions on payments for those goods (including restrictions on advance payments) were liberalized by Article 106.[316] Subdivisions 1 and 2 as well as subdivision 3 of Article 106 are applicable to invisible transactions as well as other transactions.

The Court of Justice ruled *In Re Guerrino Casati* that Italian regulations restricting the re-export from Italy of paper currency imported into Italy for a commercial purchase that was not completed did not run afoul of Article 106, but a reason given by the Court was that the normal method of effecting such a purchase was through use of bank accounts which was permitted by Italian authorities.[317]

The Court of Justice subsequently, in the *Luisi* and *Carbone* cases decided in 1984, held that Article 106 required Italy to permit the transfer by its residents of reasonable amounts of paper currency in normal tourist transactions where cash is the customary means of payment. The Court ruled that the member states of the EEC cannot place limits on the amount of currency that may be paid or transferred to residents of other EEC states in tourism, business travel, educational study, or medical services transactions (e.g., Italy's Lire 500,000

June 10, 1963, p. 1609, and no. 125, August 17, 1963, p. 2240; *Official Journal—Special [English] Edition,* 1963–1964, pp. 31 and 45.

The Act of Accession of Greece to the European Economic Community, Articles 38 and 116, requires Greece to progressively ease its import deposit requirements with liberalization to be completed by December 31, 1983. Articles 49-56 of the Act of Accession deal with invisible transactions (including monetary transfers relating to tourism) as well as capital movements. *Official Journal,* no. L-291, November 19, 1979, p. 17.

[316] *Commission v. Italian Republic,* Case No. 95/81, decided June 9, 1982. Court of Justice of the European Communities, *Reports of Cases Before the Court* [hereinafter *European Court Reports*], 1982, part 6, p. 2187; Commerce Clearing House, *Common Market Reports* (Chicago: CCH looseleaf service) [hereinafter *CCH Common Market Reports*], paragraph 8846. See also notes 319, 438, and 439, *infra.*

[317] *In Re Guerrino Casati,* Case No. 203/80, decided November 11, 1981. *European Court Reports, supra* note 316, 1981, part 8, p. 2595; *CCH Common Market Reports, supra* note 316, paragraph 8779. See Jean-Victor Louis, "Free Movement of Capital in the Community: The Casati Judgment," *Common Market Law Review,* vol. 19 (1982), p. 443; Carlo Mastellone, "Sul Principio Comunitario della Libera Circolazione dei Capitali," *Rivista di Diritto Internazionale,* vol. 65 (1982), p. 851; and Michael Peterson, "Capital Movements and Payments Under the EEC Treaty After Casati," *European Law Review,* vol. 7 (1982), p. 167.

limit for travel) unless additional amounts are authorized on the establishment of the bona fide character of the transactions.[318]

A further implication of the rulings in the *Luisi* and *Carbone* cases is that Article 106, in addition to creating obligations that are enforceable by other member states and by Community organs, creates some obligations that are directly applicable in the sense that individuals and firms are entitled to invoke the article in national tribunals when authorities seek to enforce regulations that violate those obligations.[319]

Article 106 is a basis upon which British courts initially rested decisions to give judgments in foreign currencies and not just the sterling equivalent.[320]

Liberalization of payments for invisible transactions, and the liberalization of the underlying transactions themselves, has been implemented through EEC Treaty Articles 59–66 (relating to services) and Articles 67–73 (relating to capital) as well as actions of member states and Community organs applying Article 106.[321]

The balance-of-payments safeguard clauses in Articles 108 and 109 of the EEC Treaty are applicable to the obligations of Article 106 as well as other articles liberalizing transactions and payments. These safeguard clauses are examined later in this chapter.[322]

---

[318] *Graziana Luisi v. Italian Ministry of the Treasury* and *Giuseppe Carbone v. Italian Ministry of the Treasury*, Cases Nos. 286/82 and 26/83, decided January 31, 1984, by the Court of Justice of the European Communities. *European Court Reports, supra* note 316, 1984, p.—; *CCH Common Market Reports, supra* note 316, paragraph 14,038.

[319] The Italian court that referred the questions in the *Luisi* and *Carbone* cases to the Court of Justice did not raise the question of direct applicability of Article 106. However, the parties argued the point and the rulings of the Court of Justice, appear to assume that Article 106 is directly applicable.

In earlier cases, decided in 1982, the Court of Justice avoided making a ruling on the direct applicability of Article 106. The Court in the 1982 cases ruled that an Italian requirement of a 5 percent security deposit to be placed in escrow when goods to be imported are paid for in advance, the deposit to be returned after the importation, was a measure having an effect equivalent to a quantitative restriction on imports and, as such, violated Article 30 of the Treaty of Rome unless imposed in accordance with Articles 108 and 109 of the Treaty. By treating the cases under Article 30, which it had previously held to be directly applicable, the Court postponed deciding whether Article 106 is directly invocable. *Orlandi Italo e Figlio et al. v. Italian Ministry of Foreign Trade*, Cases Nos. 206, 207, 209, and 210/80, decided June 9, 1982. *European Court Reports, supra* note 316, 1982, part 6, p. 2147; *CCH Common Market Reports, supra* note 316, paragraph 8847. The cases were companions to *Commission v. Italian Republic*, Case No. 95/81 (a case with no private parties) discussed in text accompanying note 316, *supra*, in which the Court applied Article 106 as well as Article 30.

[320] The United Kingdom Court of Appeal, applying Article 106, held that a German firm suing a British resident in the U.K. courts is entitled to obtain a judgment expressed in Deutsche mark (rather than only in sterling) for breach of a commercial contract that specified payment in mark. *Schorsch Meier G.m.b.H. v. Hennin*, reported in *Law Reports—Queen's Bench Division*, 1975, p. 416. See also the Commission's reply in the European Parliament to written question No. 705/74 relating to this case. *Official Journal*, no. C-170, July 28, 1975, p. 9. Subsequently the House of Lords, in a case where Article 106 was inapplicable, held that British courts can give judgments in foreign currencies. *Miliangos v. George Frank (Textiles) Ltd.*, decided November 5, 1975; *Law Reports—Appeal Cases*, 1976, p. 443.

[321] See generally *CCH Common Market Reports, supra* note 316, paragraphs 1501–1752 and 3701–3705; and Smit and Herzog, *supra* note 268, part 2, pp. 649–747, and part 3, pp. 599–605. EEC rules applicable to capital movements are explained, *infra*, page 465 et seq.

[322] At pages 473–477, *infra*.

Examples of Controls on Capital Movements

Note

When "current transactions" were defined earlier in this chapter, they were contrasted with capital movements.[323] Capital movements take a variety of forms. The monetary movements associated with direct investment, portfolio investment, long-term loans, short-term loans, transfers of bank deposits not related to trade or invisible transactions, purchases of life insurance policies, and transfers of personal savings by emigrants are all capital movements.

Various types of national controls on capital movements are identified below, looking first at controls on outward monetary movements and later at controls on inward movements. No attempt is made at this point to appraise whether the controls are consistent with international obligations. International obligations are analyzed later.[324] That is where efforts in multilateral forums to free capital movements from restrictions are surveyed.

National Controls on Outward Monetary Movements Associated with Capital Transactions

Capital controls, whether administered by central banks or ministries of finance, industry, or internal revenue, can be used for balance-of-payments reasons or have other motivations. Controls may be used to assure that locally owned capital is invested locally. Such a policy may be viewed as furthering the development of local resources and the employment of local labor. Efforts may be made to prevent residents from transferring their savings out of the country in the face of a local currency's decline in purchasing power, changes in political conditions, or other factors. Controls may be used to avoid the foreign exchange costs of defending an exchange rate or to avoid taking the domestic policy measures that would otherwise be necessary to stem an outflow of funds. Controls may also be used as temporary measures to allow time for more fundamental domestic policy changes to show their effects.

The United States, the Federal Republic of Germany, and the United Kingdom presently have no controls on outward monetary movements in capital transactions except for security reasons. Many countries make extensive use of capital controls. The techniques are here surveyed with footnote citations to a few of a potential multitude of examples.

Some countries control the repatriation of the proceeds received by nonresident investors upon the liquidation or sale of local direct investments (i.e., investments carrying some share in the control of the enterprise).[325]

---

[323] See pages 394–396, *supra.*
[324] Beginning at page 455, *infra.*
[325] See, e.g., the laws of India and Morocco summarized in IMF, *Annual Report on Exchange Arrangements and Exchange Restrictions, 1983,* pp. 251 and 331.

Direct investments abroad by residents are often controlled through requirements for prior governmental approval or the use of other techniques. Decisions on the granting of approval may be heavily influenced by balance-of-payments considerations. Exchange controls may be used to assure compliance with these policies.[326] Devices may be used that alter the sources from which investment abroad is financed or that increase the cost.[327]

A country may place controls on the purchase by its residents of investment securities issued abroad—stocks, bonds, certificates of deposit, and the like.[328] Prior to an exchange reform in 1979, the purchase by British residents of marketable foreign-currency securities was channeled to an insulated market where a premium obtained.[329] Restrictions may be placed on the acquisition of land or other immovable property abroad.[330]

---

[326] See, e.g., the rules and procedures applied by British authorities prior to an exchange reform in 1979 which are summarized in IMF, *Annual Report on Exchange Arrangements and Exchange Restrictions, 1979,* pp. 422 and 426–29.

[327] See, e.g., the former British practices, *idem.* During the period 1968–1974 United States controls on foreign direct investment encouraged U.S. companies to borrow abroad to finance investment abroad. The Foreign Direct Investment Regulations were adopted effective January 1, 1968, were frequently amended, and were terminated June 30, 1974. *Code of Federal Regulations,* title 15, part 1000, as it existed from 1968 to 1974. See Dominique G. Carreau, "The U.S. Balance of Payments Programs," *Journal of World Trade Law,* vol. 2 (1968), p. 601; John R. Garson and Jeffrey G. Miller, "The Foreign Direct Investment Regulations," *Boston College Industrial and Commercial Law Review,* vol. 11 (1970), p. 143; and Robert A. Anthony, "U.S. Capital Controls to Assist the Balance of Payments," in Walter Sterling Surrey and Don Wallace, Jr. (ed.), *A Lawyer's Guide to International Business Transactions* (2d ed.; Philadelphia: American Law Institute, 1980), part 4, p. 71.

[328] See, e.g., India's practice of requiring approval for these transactions and normally not giving it. IMF, *Annual Report on Exchange Arrangements and Exchange Restrictions, 1983,* p. 252. See generally OECD, *Controls on International Capital Movements: Experience with Controls on International Portfolio Operations in Shares and Bonds* (Paris, 1980).

The United States at one time imposed an "interest equalization tax" on purchases by residents of stocks, bonds, and other investment securities issued abroad when the purchase was made from a nonresident. The measure was in form a tax on underlying transactions in securities rather than an exchange control or multiple currency practice. It was instituted in 1964, renewed several times, reduced to 0 percent in 1974, and repealed in 1976. *United States Code* (1970 ed.), title 26, sections 4911–4931. The original act appears in *United States Statutes at Large,* vol. 78 (1964), p. 809. See Dominique G. Carreau, "The Interest Equalization Tax," *Journal of World Trade Law,* vol. 2 (1968), p. 47, especially pp. 81–83; "The Interest Equalization Tax," *Stanford Law Review,* vol. 17 (1965), p. 710; and Anthony, *supra* note 327.

[329] Prior to the abolition of exchange controls in 1979, U.K. residents purchasing marketable foreign-currency securities or residential property abroad were required to use "investment currency." Investment currency, also called "security sterling," was currency that represented the proceeds from sales by U.K. residents to foreigners of marketable foreign-currency securities or of personal residential property situated abroad. Instead of being required to surrender all of the foreign exchange obtained to the regular market, the seller was permitted to sell a portion of the proceeds in a separate "investment currency" market where a premium normally accrued to the seller (at times in excess of 40 percent). For the U.K. resident buying a foreign-currency security, the effect of the system was to increase his cost. See IMF, *Annual Report on Exchange Arrangements and Exchange Restrictions, 1979,* pp. 422 and 427; and Bank of England, *A Guide to United Kingdom Exchange Control* (London, 1973), pp. 17, 24–26, and 28. "The Investment Currency Market," *Bank of England Quarterly Bulletin,* vol. 16, no. 3 (September 1976), p. 314, provides a good description of the market. Two-tier exchange markets, of which the investment currency market is an example, are mentioned again at page 457 and the IMF's attitude toward them is studied in Chapter 11, *infra,* pages 551–554.

[330] Prior to an exchange reform in 1979, U.K. residents' purchase of foreign residential property was subject to exchange restrictions. See sources cited in note 329, *supra.*

Along with controls on foreign investment by residents and restrictions on the purchase of foreign securities, a country may limit the right of residents to loan money to nonresidents.[331]

Countries may control gifts made to relatives abroad and payment of inheritances to persons outside the country.[332]

Measures to prevent circumvention of capital controls include requiring approval of monetary authorities for a resident (bank, individual, or firm) to hold currency balances abroad, and placing limitations on the size and use made of approved holdings.[333] Restrictions may be imposed on business and tourist travel expenditures to prevent residents from engaging in unlawful capital transactions while abroad.[334] Prior approval may be required for the transportation of currency, stock and bond certificates and other evidence of investments, gold, and even jewelry or precious stones out of the country.[335] These regulations, and those applicable to loans and investment securities, can control transfers that are essentially permanent and also transfers made in the expectation of short-term profits.

National Controls on Inward Monetary Movements Associated with Capital Transactions

Capital controls affecting inward monetary movements, whether in the form of exchange controls or controls on underlying transactions, may have monetary policy motivations. Conversely, exchange controls may be used to implement policies toward foreigners and their economic activities that are not primarily motivated by balance-of-payments considerations, the exchange controls being used as a method to regulate underlying investment transactions. The motiva-

---

[331] See generally Silard, "Money and Foreign Exchange," *supra*, note 28, section 79. An example: Prior to the abolition of exchange controls in 1979, nonresident firms and individuals wishing to raise capital in the United Kingdom had to obtain permission from the Treasury. U.K. residents needed permission even to lend to U.K. companies if they were controlled by nonresidents. U.K. banks were prohibited from lending sterling to nonresidents to finance trade between foreign countries. Special rules then applied to residents of the European Economic Community. IMF, *Annual Report on Exchange Arrangements and Exchange Restrictions, 1979*, pp. 428–29.

In the period February 1965–January 1974 the U.S. Federal Reserve System administered a Voluntary Foreign Credit Restraint Program. U.S. banks and non-bank financial institutions were subject to extensive reporting requirements and were expected to restrain the volume of credit extended to nonresidents and to limit their investments abroad. Export financing was excepted from the guidelines. See *Federal Reserve Bulletin*, vol. 51 (1965), pp. 371–76; and vol. 54 (1968), pp. 63–71 and 257–65.

[332] Romania, for example, controls the payment of inheritances to nonresidents. IMF, *Annual Report on Exchange Arrangements and Exchange Restrictions, 1983*, p. 392. The reader will recall that moderate remittances for family living expenses are current payments by the IMF's definition. See page 395, *supra*.

[333] See pages 384–389, *supra*.

[334] See pages 405–407, *supra*.

[335] See, e.g., India, Foreign Exchange Regulation Act 1973, sections 13 and 19. See also pages 385–386 and 392, *supra*, regarding controls to assure that proceeds from exports are surrendered.

tions for controls that a country may place on the entry of foreign direct investment are often complex.

In many countries restrictions on the entry of foreign investment are intended to protect from foreign control or competition those local industries judged basic to the nation's economy or social foundations. The legislation and regulations may also be attuned to balance-of-payments considerations.[336] The authorities may wish to prevent the assumption of continuing obligations to pay interest and dividends to foreigners on their investments in the country.[337] Authorities may also wish to avoid outpayments associated with the possible future liquidation by nonresidents of their local direct or portfolio investments. Many countries have adopted policies to prevent or screen inward capital movements at the outset in order to avoid the subsequent problems of dealing with these outward movements. Foreign investments that will result in export growth (and foreign exchange earnings) are often welcomed.[338]

Controls may be placed on long- and short-term borrowing by residents from nonresidents.[339] Restrictions may limit the acquisition of domestic investment securities by nonresidents.[340] The acqusition of land by nonresidents may be subjected to control.

[336] Most countries bar investment by nonresidents in at least some businesses and industries. The use of investment screening procedures is fairly common. Canada, for example, reviews proposed investments by foreigners and takes balance-of-payments considerations along with other factors into account in making decisions. Transaction and not currency controls are used to implement its policies. See H. Heward Strikeman and R. Fraser Elliott (ed.), *Doing Business in Canada* (2 vols.; New York: Matthew Bender, binder service, 1980 ed.), section 3.04. Some countries use screening procedures to assure that local capital is not used to finance investments by nonresidents. India screens investments by foreigners and has implemented its policies through a combination of transaction and currency controls. Joint ventures with Indian partners that will cause a long-term improvement in India's foreign exchange position have been favored. IMF, *Annual Report on Exchange Arrangements and Exchange Restrictions, 1983*, pp. 250–51. Some countries with centrally planned economies (Romania being an example) bar foreign investment in most businesses and industries. *Idem*, p. 392. See generally International Centre for Settlement of Investment Disputes (ed.), *Investment Laws of the World* (binder service; Dobbs Ferry: Oceana Publications); and OECD, *International Investment and Multinational Enterprises: Investment Incentives and Disincentives and the International Investment Process* (Paris, 1983).

[337] Payments of interest and dividends, it will be recalled, are to be free from restrictions under Article VIII, section 2(a), of the IMF Agreement. The normal amortization of a loan and depreciation of a direct investment are also current payments. See pages 394–396, *supra*.

[338] See note 336, *supra*.

[339] For example, borrowing by French residents from nonresidents must receive authorization from the Ministry of Economy and Finance unless the borrowing falls within one of a number of enumerated exceptions. See IMF, *Annual Report on Exchange Arrangements and Exchange Restrictions, 1983*, pp. 201–202. See generally Silard, "Money and Foreign Exchange," *supra* note 28, section 78.

[340] Switzerland in the period February 1978 to January 1979 prohibited banks, brokers, and securities dealers from selling (or acting as go-betweens) in the sale of Swiss corporate securities to nonresidents. IMF, *Annual Report on Exchange Arrangements and Exchange Restrictions, 1979*, pp. 389–90; and *CCH Common Market Reports, supra* note 316, paragraph 31,009 (1978). See also note 345, *infra*, for another example. See generally OECD, *Experience with Controls on International Portfolio Operations in Shares and Bonds, supra* note 328.

National Controls on Monetary Movements Associated with Short-Term Capital Transactions

The national money and capital markets of the world have become more closely linked as a result of the growth of international transactions, the increase in number and size of corporations operating transnationally, the improved correspondent relationships among banks, the establishment of numerous foreign branches by large commercial banks, and the growth of Eurocurrency markets.

There are substantial capital flows among banks and corporations as they respond to capital demands or anticipate profits to be made by the purchase or sale of different currencies. The profit opportunities may arise for banks from transactions accommodating their customers who must buy or sell foreign currencies in their trade and investment transactions.[341] Corporations may operate in the market to hedge against anticipated payments or receipts to be made in foreign currencies and to maintain working balances.[342] Differentials in interest rates available on short-term investments in one country compared to another and predicted changes in currency exchange rates influence the decisions of investors (which can include individuals, companies, banks, and also governments) on the deployment of their reserve funds. They may also borrow in one currency that is then exchanged for another which is invested to take advantage of interest-rate differentials, or anticipated changes in exchange rates, or to be available to meet future demands. Short-term capital movements of substantial size, unless countered, can impact domestic interest rates and domestic monetary policies, as well as put pressure on exchange rates.

Authorities use a variety of monetary instruments to control or modulate short-term capital flows.[343] Capital controls described earlier may be used, especially controls respecting borrowings by residents from nonresidents and vice versa, dealings in portfolio securities and money market instruments, and uses of nonresident bank accounts.[344] Two-tier exchange markets may be used.[345]

---

[341] If a country has a surplus in the current account of its balance of payments, this usually means that nonresidents will have a net need for its currency to settle trade and other current transactions. One often sees large movements of short-term capital in advance of or immediately after the release of official reports on trade flows.

[342] See generally Appendix A, *infra*, pages 672–679.

[343] See generally Rodney H. Mills, Jr., "The Regulation of Short-Term Capital Movements in Major Industrial Countries," in Alexander K. Swoboda (ed.), *Capital Movements and Their Control* (Leiden: A.W. Sijthoff, 1976), p. 180; and OECD, *Controls on International Capital Movements: The Experience with Controls on International Financial Credits, Loans and Deposits* (Paris, 1982).

[344] See pages 449–452, especially notes 329, 331, and 340. In the period March 1972 - September 1974, German authorities imposed a requirement (called the *"bardepot"*) that funds equivalent to a stated portion of certain borrowings by residents from nonresidents (including certain deposit liabilities of German banks to nonresidents) be deposited with the Bundesbank, the deposit ranging as high as 50 percent. See IMF, *24th Annual Report on Exchange Restrictions, 1973*, pp. 194–98; and *26th Report 1975*, pp. 199–200.

[345] In the period September 1971–February 1974, nonresidents could acquire guilder bonds listed on the securities exchange in the Netherlands only with the proceeds from the sale of such bonds by nonresidents to residents. The system was designed to prevent net new investment by nonresidents in officially-listed guilder

Some official measures may be specially tailored to short-term capital movements. For example, approval of the Bundesbank (central bank of the Federal Republic of Germany) has been required for sales to nonresidents of domestic money-market paper and fixed-interest securities of German issuers with less than four years remaining to maturity. Such approval has at various times not been granted.[346] At various times German and Dutch commercial banks have not been permitted to pay interest on balances held for nonresidents.[347] Swiss banks have in the past been required to charge "commission" (negative interest) on nonresident-owned deposits.[348] Other countries (in the opposite situation from Germany, the Netherlands, and Switerland) have permitted their banks to pay interest at higher rates on balances held for nonresidents than those of residents. Many countries limit the net foreign-currency holdings of resident banks. Other official measures, that are not exchange controls, may be adopted to influence short-term capital movements or to neutralize the domestic and international monetary effects of them. These actions include policies affecting the general level of interest rates prevailing in the country, bank reserve requirements, open market operations affecting the money supply, and exchange market interventions.

A substantial volume of short-term capital movements takes place in the Eurocurrency markets, where currencies may often be borrowed at interest rates lower than available in the country of issue and, after the borrowed currency is exchanged, the currency obtained may be invested in Eurocurrency instruments that yield higher interest than investments in the country of issue of that currency. Central banks have maintained surveillance over Eurocurrency markets but have not made significant coordinated efforts to control them.[349]

The reader should now have at least a rough sense of the variety of techniques used to control capital movements and the factors motivating those controls. Attention will now turn to efforts in multilateral forums to place limits on the range of choice open to national governments—efforts to liberalize controls and also efforts to force the imposition of controls in some situations.

---

bonds. What was called the "O-guilder" which could be used to purchase the bonds went to a small premium. See IMF, *23d Annual Report on Exchange Restrictions, 1972*, pp. 308 and 311; *25th Report 1974*, p. 313; and *26th Report 1975*, p. 345. The system had similarities to the U.K. investment currency market described in note 329, *supra*, except that it was designed to discourage inward monetary movements while the U.K. system was intended to prevent outward movements. The IMF's jurisdiction over two-tier exchange markets is examined in Chapter 11, *infra*, pages 551–554.

[346] Compare IMF, *Annual Report on Exchange Arrangements and Exchange Restrictions, 1979*, p. 172, with *idem, 1981*, p. 175.

[347] See IMF, *24th Annual Report on Exchange Restrictions, 1973*, pp. 345 and 348; and *26th Report 1975*, pp. 198 and 199.

[348] See, e.g., IMF, *Annual Report on Exchange Arrangements and Exchange Restrictions, 1979*, p. 390. This requirement was suspended December 1, 1979. See *idem, 1980*, p. 388; and *idem, 1981*, p. 399.

[349] Eurocurrency markets are described in Appendix A, *infra*, pages 679–682. Surveillance of Eurocurrency markets is treated in Chapter 12, *infra*, pages 619–630.

International Regimes Applicable to Capital Movements

The IMF and Capital Controls

Primary objectives of the original drafters of the Articles of Agreement of the International Monetary Fund were growth of world trade and elimination of restrictions on payments for current transactions.[350] Freedom of capital movements was not a principle of the original Articles. The original negotiators thought that members should have the legal right to impose capital controls without the need for consultation or approval by the Fund.[351] Indeed, by Article VI the Fund was given, and continues to retain, authority to request a member to adopt capital controls to prevent Fund resources, drawn from the General Resources Account, from financing a large or sustained capital outflow.[352] The Fund has, however, never requested a country to initiate capital controls.[353]

Representatives of some countries in the IMF's Committee on Reform (Committee of Twenty) in negotiations in the 1973–74 period indicated that they favored an amendment to the Articles that would give the Fund power to require a member to adopt capital controls, particularly with respect to short-term movements, whether or not it was making use of Fund resources. Other representatives favored an enlarged Fund role in the liberalization of capital movements. A proposal was not recommended by the Committee. Instead, the Committee on Reform in its final report placed emphasis upon consultation among countries when faced with disequilibrating capital flows. A variety of

---

[350] Article VIII, section 2(a), of the IMF Agreement, as noted earlier, is concerned with assuring that currency controls do not restrict the making of payments and transfers in respect to current international transactions. We have observed that "current" is defined broadly and includes some transactions that economists might classify as "capital." See pages 394–396, *supra.*

[351] The prevalent attitudes of the 1940s are reflected in a U.S. Treasury statement on the eve of the Bretton Woods Conference in 1944 that "gold and foreign exchange resources of a country should be reserved primarily for the settlement of international balances on current account." Lord Keynes commented in 1943: "There is no country which can, in future, safely allow the flight of funds for political reasons or to evade domestic taxation or in anticipation of the owner turning refugee. Equally, there is no country that can safely receive fugitive funds, which constitute an unwanted import of capital, yet cannot safely be used for fixed investment. For these reasons it is widely held that the control of capital movements, both inward and outward, should be a permanent feature of the post-war system." Quotations from U.S. Treasury statement of June 10, 1944, and John Maynard Keynes, "Proposals for an International Clearing Union" (April 1943), in *IMF History 1945–65, supra* note 39, vol. 3, p. 136 at p. 176, and p. 19 at p. 31.

A year earlier, Lord Keynes wrote to Roy F. Harrod: "Freedom of capital movements is an essential part of the old *laissez-faire* system. . . . It assumes . . . that if the rate of interest which promotes full employment in Great Britain is lower than the appropriate rate in Australia, there is no reason why this should not be allowed to lead to a situation in which the whole of British savings are invested in Australia, subject only to different estimations of risk, until the equilibrium rate in Australia has been brought down to the British rate. In my view the whole management of the domestic economy depends upon being free to have the appropriate rate of interest without reference to the rates prevailing elsewhere in the world. Capital control is a corollary to this." *Collected Writings of John Maynard Keynes, supra* note 37, vol. 25 (1980), p. 146 at p. 149.

[352] Article VI, Section 1(a). See Chapter 6, *supra,* pages 241–243.

[353] Statements made to the author by a member of the Legal Department of the IMF.

means for dealing with undesired capital flows were mentioned, controls being only one. Concern was expressed that controls over capital transactions not be used to maintain inappropriate exchange rates or to avoid other appropriate adjustment action.[354]

The Second Amendment to the Articles that became effective April 1, 1978, includes the statement in Article IV that an essential purpose of the international monetary system is to provide a framework that facilitates the exchange of capital among countries.[355] This clause appears to favor freedom for capital movements. A decision implementing the Second Amendment states that "the introduction or substantial modification for balance of payments purposes of restrictions on, or incentives for, the inflow or outflow of capital" is a development that may indicate the need for discussion by the Fund with the member.[356] The Second Amendment, however, did not alter the language of Article VI, Section 3, which provides:

> Members may exercise such controls *as are necessary* to regulate international capital movements, but no member may exercise these controls in a manner which will restrict payments for current transactions or which will unduly delay transfers of funds in settlement of commitments. . . . [emphasis added][357]

An Executive Board decision, adopted in 1956, provides:

> Subject to the provisions of Article VI, Section 3 concerning payments for current transactions and undue delay in transfers of funds in settlement of commitments:
>
> (a) Members are free to adopt a policy of regulating capital movements for any reason, due regard being paid to the general purposes of the Fund and without prejudice to the provisions of Article VI, Section 1.
>
> (b) They may, for that purpose, exercise such controls as are necessary, including making such arrangements as may be rea-

---

[354] See *International Monetary Reform: Documents of the Committee of Twenty, supra* note 281, pp. 12–13 (Outline of Reform, June 14, 1974, paragraphs 15–17) and pp. 78–94 (Report of Technical Group on Disequilibrating Capital Flows). See also Robert Solomon, *The International Monetary System, 1945–1981* (New York: Harper & Row, 1982), p. 251.

[355] Article IV, section 1.

[356] E.B. Decision No. 5392, *supra* note 284, subpart Principles of Fund Surveillance Over Exchange Rate Policies, paragraph 2(iii)(b). The decision is analyzed in Chapter 11. See especially pages 558–559, *infra.* See also Gold, *Use, Conversion and Exchange of Currency, supra* note 42, pp. 14–15.

[357] "Settlement of commitments" as used here has been understood to refer only to settlement of commitments in respect to current international transactions as defined by the Fund. Also, Article VI, section 3, has been understood to permit members to prevent the proceeds of current transactions from being used for capital transactions. Evans, *supra* note 44, p. 31. See also Joseph Gold, *International Capital Movements Under the Law of the International Monetary Fund* (IMF Pamphlet Series no. 21; Washington, 1977), p. 55 (note 22).

sonably needed with other countries, without approval of the Fund.[358]

The right to exercise controls applies to both long-term and short-term movements of capital. The decision quoted above has been understood to permit members to use discriminatory currency arrangements to control capital movements so long as the controls are consistent with the purposes of the Fund and do not inhibit current payments. The legitimacy of discriminatory capital controls under the IMF Articles has made it lawful for liberalization to be pursued among groups of countries such as those belonging to the OECD or the European Economic Community without the necessity of generalizing benefits to others.[359] The wisdom of the 1956 decision's broad exemption of discriminatory capital controls from Fund approval jurisdiction has been questioned. The IMF's Committee on Reform (Committee of Twenty) expressed the view that capital controls should be applied without discrimination unless in favor of members of an economic union or countries with close financial ties, or in favor of developing countries.[360]

The 1956 decision quoted above makes clear that the exercise of capital controls does not require the approval of the Fund. Controls exercised by a member to regulate capital movements must, however, not restrict payments for current international transactions or unduly delay transfers in settlement of commitments.[361] The 1956 decision does not exempt multiple currency practices from Fund approval jurisdiction—that issue remains unresolved. The issue has not been faced squarely, because the use of two-tier exchange markets, in which current and capital transactions take place at different exchange rates, have in the past required Fund approval because in their actual operation some transactions the Fund regarded as "current" were routed to the capital market or were delayed.[362] Members under Article VIII, Section 5, and Rule L-3 are required to inform the Fund "in detail" of all measures to regulate international capital movements and changes made in those measures.[363]

---

[358] E.B. Decision No. 541 -(56/39)(July 25, 1956); *IMF History 1945–65, supra* note 39, vol. 3, p. 246; *Selected Decisions* (10th issue, 1983), p. 116. The deliberations of the Executive Board and the Committee on Interpretation prior to adoption of the decisions are described in *IMF History 1945–65,* vol. 1, pp. 403–04, and vol. 2, pp. 481–82. See also Chapter 11, *infra,* page 551 (note 243).

[359] See Gold, *International Capital Movements, supra* note 357, p. 16; and Gold, *Fund's Concepts of Convertibility, supra* note 38, p. 7.

[360] *International Monetary Reform: Documents of the Committee of Twenty, supra* note 281, pp. 12–13 (Outline of Reform, June 14, 1974, paragraphs 15–16).

[361] Article VI, section 3, quoted on page 456. If the IMF is of the opinion that a member is restricting current payments or delaying transfers, it is to consult with the member. If the Fund thereafter remains of the opinion that the capital controls are not exercised consistent with the Articles, it is required to submit a written report to the member and request the member to modify the controls. IMF Rule L-4 as amended April 1, 1978; *By-Laws, Rules and Regulations* (40th issue, 1983).

[362] See Chapter 11, *infra,* pages 551–554.

[363] See IMF Rule L-3 as amended April 1, 1978; *By-Laws, Rules and Regulations* (40th issue, 1983).

The language of the 1956 decision, which appears to go beyond the terms of Article VI, Section 3, must be read in harmony with the Second Amendment to the Articles. A country's exercise of capital controls must be consistent with its obligations under Article IV. Capital controls that are used to manipulate exchange rates in order to gain an unfair competitive advantage or to prevent balance-of-payments adjustment (by other IMF members as well as by the country initiating the control), as examples, violate Article IV, Section 1. The harmonization of the rights of Article VI, Section 3, with the obligations of Article IV can be achieved by recognizing that controls that are inconsistent with the obligations of Article IV are not "necessary." Broad-ranging consultations under Article IV can cover all types of capital controls and the wisdom of their relaxation or elimination.[364] As previously noted, the IMF's "principles of surveillance" recognize that restrictions on capital transfers may be among developments that indicate a need for discussions between the Fund and the member.[365]

There is nothing to prevent agreements from being reached under the auspices of the IMF that supplement the Articles and explicitly provide for liberalization of capital movements.[366] And, the IMF can continue, as it has done in the past, to make its financial resources available to countries relaxing capital controls.[367]

Liberalization of Capital Controls

Lord Keynes suggested that wise policies should seek to distinguish long-term loans by creditor countries to debtor countries to develop resources or maintain equilibrium, which he deemed desirable, from speculative flights of capital from deficit countries or "floating funds" moving from one country to another in response to short-term changes in interest rates, which he viewed as undesirable.[368] However, experience since major currencies became convertible twenty-five years ago has shown the difficulty of determining whether capital movements at a particular time are based upon speculative considerations or business judgments about fundamental changes. There is also lack of unanimity today among economists on whether capital movements motivated by speculative considerations are "bad."[369] More fundamentally, it has been suggested

---

[364] IMF consultations are treated in Chapter 11 at pages 558–568 and in Chapter 12 beginning at page 571.

[365] See text accompanying note 356, *supra*.

[366] The Joint Ministerial Committee of the Boards of Governors of the IBRD and the IMF on the Transfer of Real Resources to Developing Countries (see Chapter 2, page 48) and its Working Group on Access to Capital Markets have given thought to a general program of liberalization to which countries with capital markets can subscribe. See IMF, *Summary Proceedings, 1976*, pp. 263–73.

[367] See Chapter 6, *supra*, pages 241–243.

[368] See Keynes, "Proposals for an International Clearing Union," *supra* note 351, p. 32.

[369] See, e.g., *How Well are Fluctuating Exchange Rates Working? Hearings before the Subcommittee on International Economics of the Joint Economic Committee*, U.S. Congress, 93d Congress, 1st Session (1973); and *International Monetary Reform and Exchange Rate Management: Hearings before the Subcommittee on International Trade, Investment and Monetary Policy of the Committee on Banking, Currency and*

that in some cases it may be more important for a country experiencing capital flight to attempt to reverse an unfavorable trade balance or to improve the investment climate, which may have stimulated the capital flight, than to attempt to shut off the capital movement through direct controls. A panel of the American Society of International Law had this to say:

> The Bretton Woods drafters substantially overestimated the degree to which it was possible to segregate capital flows from trade flows and thus the degree to which it would be possible to regulate or control the former without impeding the latter. There was a tendency to underestimate the economic benefits of freedom of international capital movements relative to freedom of trade. On both economic welfare and administrative grounds, the presumption contained in the present Fund Articles of Agreement [prior to the Second Amendment] in favor of acting on capital rather than on trade flows when attempting to maintain exchange parity in times of balance-of-payments difficulties is not appropriate.[370]

Because of the low priority given to freedom of capital movements by the drafters of the IMF's Articles, international efforts to develop rules to liberalize capital movements shifted to other forums. Bilateral agreements between states may include provisions dealing with capital movements. Many friendship and commerce treaties contain provisions relating to national treatment of foreign investments, the repatriation of investment capital, and related matters. Bilateral treaties, in addition to including clauses assuring national and most-favored-nation treatment, may impose specific obligations respecting freedom of capital movements and associated monetary transfers.[371]

Housing, House of Representatives, and the Subcommittee on International Economics of the Joint Economic Committee, U.S. Congress, 94th Congress, 1st Session (1975).

[370] *Long-Term International Monetary Reform, supra* note 256, pp. 33–34. Countries are, of course, not foreclosed from acting on trade flows when facing a balance-of-payments problem. The GATT Agreement, as we noted earlier in this chapter, permits the use of trade controls in the face of balance-of-payments difficulties. See pages 428–440, *supra*. The use of exchange controls affecting payments and transfers respecting current transactions requires specific Fund approval. See pages 389–428, *supra*.

[371] See, e.g., Treaty Concerning the Reciprocal Encouragement and Protection of Investments between Egypt and the United States, signed September 29, 1982. *International Legal Materials,* vol. 21 (1982), p. 927. Article V of the treaty and paragraph 6 of the protocol specify monetary movements, including capital movements, that are to be freely allowed.

See, as another example, the Convention of Establishment between France and the United States, signed November 25, 1959, entered into force December 21, 1960. *U.S. Treaties and Other International Agreements,* vol. 11, p. 2398; *United Nations Treaty Series,* vol. 401, p. 75. Article X of the Convention provides for most-favored-nation treatment with respect to exchange controls, limits the use of exchange restrictions to those needed to prevent monetary reserves from falling to a very low level or to effect a moderate increase in very low monetary reserves, and places limits on controls imposed on movements of investment capital.

See generally the treaties listed and discussed in F.A. Mann, *The Legal Aspect of Money* (4th ed.; Oxford: Oxford University Press, 1982), pp. 522–30; the list of bilateral investment treaties in *International Legal Materials,* vol. 21 (1982), pp. 1208–09; and Patrick J. Broderick, "Foreign Exchange Controls: A Survey of

Among multilateral forums, the work of the OECD and the European Communities is particularly noteworthy. We shall now examine the legal obligations that members of those organizations have assumed.[372]

Liberalization of Capital Movements in the OECD

The Organisation for Economic Co-operation and Development (OECD)[373] in 1961 adopted a Code of Liberalisation of Capital Movements.[374] The Code has subsequently been amended by the OECD Council on a number of occasions.[375] All twenty-four OECD members with the exception of Canada adhere to the Code.

The members of the OECD share the general view that the free movement of capital under conditions of free trade, monetary stability, and adequate representation of both private and social costs in the price structure, helps to promote economic efficiency and growth. The Capital Code, like the Code of Liberalisation of Current Invisible Operations,[376] contains a general undertaking to abolish restrictions covered by the Code, but it is not as firmly stated as in the Invisibles Code. The first sentence in Article 1 of the Capital Code states: "Members shall progressively abolish between one another, in accordance with the provisions of Article 2, restrictions on movements of capital to the extent necessary for effective economic co-operation." Note the adverb "progressively" and the added qualification "to the extent necessary for effective economic co-operation."[377] Adherents also declare, as in the Invisibles Code, that

the Legal Protection Available to the American Investor," *Notre Dame Lawyer,* vol. 49 (1974), p. 589 at pp. 605–07 and the list of treaties at p. 610.

[372] Liberalization of capital movements has also received attention in other multilateral organizations. For example, the Treaty Establishing the Caribbean Community, concluded at Chaguaramas July 4, 1973, entered into force August 1, 1973, in Article 43 of the Annex on the Caribbean Common Market provides for freedom of payments on current account and, subject to important qualifications, freedom of payments on capital account. *United Nations Treaty Series,* vol. 946, p. 17. The Treaty Establishing the Latin American Integration Association, signed at Montevideo August 12, 1980, entered into force March 18, 1981, in Article 48 grants most-favored-nation treatment for investments. *International Legal Materials,* vol. 20 (1981), p. 672.

[373] The OECD is described in Chapter 2, *supra,* page 68 et seq.

[374] In 1955 the Council of the Organisation for European Economic Co-operation, the predecessor of the OECD, adopted a recommendation concerning liberalization of capital movements; OEEC document no. C(55)59 (final). This was followed by another Council decision in 1957; OEEC document no. C(57)226 (final). The OEEC Council adopted a Code of Liberalisation of Capital Movements on December 4, 1959; OEEC document no. C(59)244(final), in *European Yearbook,* vol. 7(1959), p. 239. That Code, with amendments, was adopted by the OECD Council as the OECD Code of Liberalisation of Capital Movements on December 12, 1961; OECD document no. C(61)96, in *European Yearbook,* vol. 10 (1962), p. 437.

[375] The Code of Liberalisation of Capital Movements has been amended a number of times, the annexes quite frequently, by decisions of the OECD Council. The author has used the March 1982 edition of the Code, published by the OECD.

[376] Discussed, *supra,* page 443 et seq.

[377] Compare the first sentence of Article 1 of the Invisibles Code, quoted in the text accompanying note 297, *supra.*

they "shall endeavour" to extend the measures of liberalization to all members of the International Monetary Fund.[378]

The OECD's Capital Movements Code lists various types of capital movements and provides a procedure for the withdrawal of controls on them. As in the case of the Invisibles Code, the approach of the Capital Code is comprehensive. Article 2(a) provides: ". . . Members shall grant any authorisation required for the conclusion or execution of transactions and for transfers specified in an item set out in List A or List B of Annex A to this Code." This provision means that, in the absence of a reservation or derogation, a member is obligated to ensure both that monetary controls do not interfere with any listed capital movement and that other governmental restrictions of a non-monetary character do not frustrate the transaction.[379] The Capital Code, like the Invisibles Code, contains general provisions authorizing "passive" controls—controls designed to gather information or to assure that transactions requiring approval are as represented by applicants.[380]

The Code contains two lists of capital transactions to be liberalized. List A in Annex A deals with direct investment, purchase and sale of investment securities, and a large number of other transactions.[381] List B in Annex A includes various types of capital movements not included in List A, including medium-term and long-term credits granted by resident financial institutions to nonresidents for purposes other than financing trade or service transactions. List B also includes medium-and long-term debts incurred by resident financial institutions to nonresidents for purposes other than financing trade or service transactions. It also includes a number of other items.

Some capital operations have not been placed on either List A or List B. At the present time short-term debts (less than one year) of resident financial institutions to nonresidents not linked to an underlying trade or service transaction are not listed. Some operations of accounts with banks and other credit institu-

---

[378] Article 1(d).

[379] Article 2. See also Article 6 relating to payments and transfers.

Revenue measures, with some exceptions, are not restrictions to which either the Capital Code or the Invisibles Code applies unless they are "frustrations" within the meaning of Article 16 of either Code, according to an OECD interpretative understanding of December 12, 1961. This appears to be the legal basis for the U.S. decision not to invoke safeguard clauses of the Code when it introduced its "interest equalization tax" in 1964 (note 328, *supra*). Apparently no member country of the OECD requested the Council to examine the compatibility of the U.S. measure with the Code. See Carreau, "Interest Equalization Tax," *supra* note 328, pp. 83–84.

The Committee on Capital Movements and Invisible Transactions is considering proposals to amend the Codes to deal more effectively with fiscal measures.

[380] Article 5.

[381] The items in List A of Annex A are grouped under the following headings: direct investment, liquidation of direct investment, admission of securities to capital markets, buying and selling of securities, buying and selling of collective investment securities, operations in real estate, credits directly linked with international commercial transactions, personal capital movements, capital transfers under life insurance contracts, sureties and guarantees, physical movement of securities and documents of title, use and transfer of nonresident-owned blocked funds.

tions are not listed. Money market securities (such as treasury bills and notes) also are not included. Thus, there was no liberalization obligation with respect to them.[382]

Although not so identified, the capital movements in List B can frequently be large and sudden and, in some situations, destabilizing. While the movements in List A can also be large, they are normally related to underlying investment, trade, or service transactions with a tie to the country. Thus, the Code draws a distinction between two types of capital movements—those in List A and those in List B—and, in addition, does not cover or liberalize other capital movements.

This division and the corresponding reservation procedure deserves note. Since items on List B may be particularly sensitive, members are given the right to lodge reservations at any time.[383] This right has the effect of encouraging members to delay lodging reservations to List B until they judge such action to be clearly necessary and to withdraw the reservations as soon as their need passes, since the country has the right to make them again later. On the other hand, the right to make reservations to items on List A is limited. A reservation to an item on List A can be made only when the item is added to that list or its definition extended or when the obligation to liberalize the item first begins to apply to the member.[384] The reason is that OECD members want to know at the outset the reservations that may be lodged to those items and to take steps where possible to encourage their early withdrawal. Reservations to Lists A and B must be nondiscriminatory as between other members.[385] Reservations to Lists A and B are reviewed within the OECD's Committee on Capital Movements and Invisible Transactions at least every eighteen months, with a view to "making suitable proposals designed to assist Members to withdraw their reservations."[386] So long as a country making reservations complies with the required notification and review procedures, it benefits from all of the liberalization measures of other members.[387]

In addition to specific reservations, the Capital Code, like the Invisibles Code, provides for general derogations under certain circumstances. Thus, if its economic and financial situation justifies such a course, a country need not take the whole of the liberalization measures prescribed,[388] and it may withdraw

---

[382] The United States, Canada, Federal Republic of Germany, Belgium-Luxembourg, and Switzerland have normally allowed individuals and non-financial firms to conduct money market operations. In many other countries only banking institutions, within specified limits, and government authorities can purchase and sell short-term securities unrelated to commercial transactions.

[383] Article 2(b)(iv). The reservations of each adherent are published in Annex B.

[384] Article 2(b). The reservations are published in Annex B.

[385] Article 9.

[386] Articles 11 and 12. Reservations to List B are initially reviewed within six months of notification. For an example of review of Capital Code reservations within the Committee on Capital Movements and Invisible Transactions, see *Activities of OECD in 1976* (Paris: OECD), p. 25.

[387] Article 8.

[388] Article 7(a). At the present time only Iceland and Turkey rely on this provision, both having invoked it

measures of liberalization that result in serious economic and financial disturbance.[389] A member may temporarily suspend liberalization if its balance of
payments develops adversely.[390] There is a public order and security clause.[391]
Special provisions deal with derogations by developing countries.[392] Derogations are to be notified "forthwith,"[393] and are subject to a review procedure.[394] In all cases a country derogating must avoid any discrimination as between one OECD member and another.[395] It will continue to benefit from the
liberalization of other OECD members.[396]

A study of the reservations that are presently in effect indicates that a large
number of the reservations center on a few types of transactions. With respect
to direct investment, a number of countries restrict investment in certain
enterprises—e.g., broadcasting—to nationals. By far the largest number of reservations relate to transactions in investment securities.[397]

The withdrawal of reservations by Japan provides an interesting case
study. Prior to joining the OECD, Japan in July 1963 signed a memorandum of

---

in 1962; OECD document no. C(62)21 (final). In 1980 Greece terminated its reliance on Article 7(a) and
filed specific reservations to various items in Lists A and B. See OECD Council decision of October 28,
1980; OECD document no. C(80)89(final), in *European Yearbook,* vol. 28 (1980), p. 203. Once reliance on
Article 7(a) has been terminated, it cannot be reinvoked.

[389] Article 7(b). France invoked this derogation clause in 1968 when in a currency crisis it took the capital
measures, described in the text accompanying note 442, *infra,* to halt an outflow of funds. This clause has
also been invoked by countries in balance-of-payments surplus. It was invoked by Austria, Federal Republic
of Germany, Japan, and Switzerland in 1972, when they imposed restrictions on inflows of nonresident long-
term capital. Japan and Switzerland invoked Article 7(b) in 1978 to restrict what they regarded as
destabilizing capital inflows. By 1980 all four countries had terminated their invocations of Article 7(b).
Other countries have invoked Article 7(b) from time to time. See e.g., *Activities of OECD in 1972,* p. 21;
idem, 1977, p. 26; *1978,* p. 28; *1979,* pp. 30–31; and *1980,* p. 26.

[390] Article 7(c). Greece during the 1960s relied both on the general derogation clause of Article 7(a) to
delay further liberalization and on the balance-of-payments derogation of Article 7(c) to temporarily suspend
some liberalization measures already taken. In 1969 Greece terminated its reliance on Article 7(c) but continued to invoke Article 7(a); OECD documents no. C(64)95(final) and no. C/M(69)5(final). In 1980 Greece
terminated its reliance on Article 7(a) as well. See note 388, *supra.*

Article 7(c) has been invoked fairly frequently in recent years by countries facing balance-of-payments difficulties, including Australia in 1977, Denmark in 1979, France in 1981, and Italy on several occasions. See,
e.g., *Activities of OECD in 1977,* p. 26; *idem, 1979,* pp. 30–31; and *1981,* p. 26.

[391] Article 3.

[392] Article 14.

[393] Article 13(a).

[394] Articles 13–19.

[395] Article 7(e).

[396] Article 8. To retain this benefit a country invoking Article 7 must comply with the Code's notification
and review procedures.

[397] The Federal Republic of Germany has no reservations to either List A or List B. The United States'
only reservation relates to direct investment by nonresidents in certain industries in the United States in which
alien ownership is restricted. In many OECD countries direct investment, both incoming or outgoing, is completely or almost completely free of restrictions. The ability of nonresidents to buy and sell investment securities and the ability of residents to buy and sell foreign investment securities is also, by and large, free of restrictions except in the case of new issues in many OECD countries. Compare reservations in 1972 discussed
in Donald C. Templeton, "Liberalization of Investments in the OECD: Portfolio Investments and Securities
Markets," *Journal of World Trade Law,* vol. 6 (1972), p. 425.

understanding with that organization that it would adhere to the Code of Liberalisation of Current Invisible Operations and to the Code of Liberalisation of Capital Movements. Japan listed nineteen reservations to the Codes.[398]

While there is no direct legal obligation to withdraw a reservation, there is, as previously noted, a procedure for periodic review of reservations within the OECD. The OECD Secretariat prepared a hard-hitting report on Japan's capital controls which was considered by the Committee for Invisible Transactions in 1967.[399] In response to pressure from members of the OECD, Japan embarked on a program to liberalize its controls. The program was carefully structured and some observers viewed it as unreasonably slow. Dan Fenno Henderson said that the actions of Japanese authorities were largely taken to comply with international standards rather than because of felt needs at home.[400] Both inward and outward capital movements were liberalized, although direct investments in Japan remained complex undertakings for foreigners. When Japan experienced extraordinarily large capital inflows in 1972 and the yen was subject to strong upward pressure, Japan in October 1972 had recourse to the derogation procedure of the Capital Code and temporarily restricted the purchase of all Japanese securities by nonresidents. These measures were withdrawn in November 1973.[401] Subsequently Japan liberalized its foreign exchange control and foreign investment laws and in 1979 amended and merged them into a liberalized single Foreign Exchange and Foreign Trade Control Law that became effective December 1, 1980.[402] As of March 1982, Japan's only reservations to the OECD Capital Code related to the acquisition of land for commercial purposes and direct investments in a few listed fields. In December 1983 Japan informed the OECD of its intention to withdraw its reservation on purchase of land by nonresidents. Japan's reservations to the Invisibles Code are limited to insurance.[403]

The OECD's Committee on Capital Movements and Invisible Transactions, as previously explained, reviews the application of the Capital Code and

---

[398] OECD document no. C(63)112, Annex B, in *European Yearbook,* vol. 12 (1964), p. 167.

[399] OECD, *Liberalisation of International Capital Movements: Japan* (Paris, 1968).

[400] Henderson, *supra* note 57, p. 237.

[401] See generally Henderson, *supra* note 57, chapters 6 and 7; Ozaki, *supra* note 57, chapters 7 and 8 and documents at pp. 223–44; Allan R. Pearl, "Liberalization of Capital in Japan," *Harvard Journal of International Law,* vol. 13 (1972), pp. 59–87 and 245–70; and "Liberalisation of Capital Movements by Japan," *OECD Observer,* no. 69 (April 1974), p. 32.

[402] The new law involved a change from a system of general prohibition of transactions unless expressly authorized (i.e., a positive list) to one under which, in principle, transactions involving nonresidents with prior notification to the authorities can be freely made unless expressly restricted (i.e., a negative list). The law contains a clause permitting imposition of controls in the event of emergency, which is defined to include a drastic depreciation of the yen or a sharp deterioration in the balance of payments. Masashige Ohba, "Recent Changes in the Foreign Exchange Control Law and the Law Concerning Foreign Investment in Japan," *International Contract Law & Finance Review Yearbook,* 1980, p. 162; IMF, *Annual Report on Exchange Arrangements and Exchange Restrictions, 1981,* pp. 240–43; and *IMF Survey,* October 27, 1980, p. 341.

[403] Capital Code, Annex B; Invisibles Code, Annex B.

the Invisibles Code. The Committee is composed of twelve persons chosen by reason of their knowledge and not as national representatives. Decisions require a majority of seven of the twelve members, contrary to the practice of unanimity in other OECD organs.[404] The Committee makes proposals for amendments in the Codes and reviews reservations and derogations to the Codes. In earlier years most of the Committee's attention was given to efforts to end reservations and derogations to the Invisibles Code. In recent years, greater attention has been given to the review of reservations and derogations to the Capital Code. The Committee has given special attention to the authorization procedures, policies, and practices regarding foreign direct investment, both inward and outward. Practices studied have included official national practices that are not embodied in formal instruments. The Committee has sought to ensure that such practices that are inconsistent with the Capital or Invisibles Codes are identified.[405]

The members of the OECD have also adopted a Declaration on International Investment and Multinational Enterprises.[406] The declaration established follow-up procedures for review of incentives and disincentives for international investment.

The work of the OECD has drawn attention to the importance of capital movements. The organization has made and published studies of the capital markets in a number of countries.[407] The pragmatic approach adopted in the OECD's Capital Code and its other actions has encouraged the member states to see freedom of capital movements as desirable and has assisted them to remove monetary and non-monetary barriers to capital transfers.

Capital Controls in the European Economic Community

Note. We have already seen that members of the European Economic Community have, under the EEC Treaty, assumed obligations concerning payments for current transactions that reinforce their obligations under the IMF Agreement and the OECD Invisibles Code.[408] Each EEC state also subscribes to the

---

[404] Partly because of the Committee's nonrepresentative character, it sometimes refers issues (after discussion) to the Committee on Payments and sometimes meets in common sessions with the Committee on Investment and Multinational Enterprises (both of which include the full OECD membership).

[405] See OECD, *International Direct Investment: Policies, Procedures and Practices in OECD Member Countries, 1979* (Paris, 1980).

[406] The declaration was adopted June 21, 1976, and was revised in 1979. For the revised text, see OECD, *International Investment and Multinational Enterprises: Revised Edition, 1979* (Paris, 1980). For papers considered during the revision process, see OECD, *International Investment and Multinational Enterprises—Review of the 1976 Declaration and Decisions* (Paris, 1979). See also "OECD Instruments on Multinational Enterprises and International Investment: Taking Stock of the Situation," *OECD Observer,* no. 117 (July 1982), p. 21.

[407] See, e.g., the OECD publications cited in notes 328, 336, 343, 399, 405, and 406, *supra.*

[408] See pages 446–448, *supra.* A general description of the European Economic Community appears in Chapter 2, *supra,* page 76 et seq.

OECD Code of Liberalisation of Capital Movements discussed in the previous section. Here we examine the application of the EEC Treaty to capital controls.

Liberalization Rules.   The starting point of our discussion is Article 106 of the Treaty Establishing the European Economic Community. That article, set forth earlier,[409] places limitations on the use of exchange controls. As applied to capital movements, the provisions of Article 106 mean, at the very least, that exchange controls are not to be allowed to frustrate transactions liberalized by the Treaty. Articles 67–73 deal specifically with the liberalization of capital transactions. Paragraph 1 of Article 67 is a key provision:

> During the transitional period[410] and to the extent necessary to ensure the proper functioning of the common market, Member States shall progressively abolish between themselves all restrictions on the movement of capital belonging to persons resident in Member States and any discrimination based on the nationality or on the place of residence of the parties or on the place where such capital is invested.

A second paragraph of Article 67 makes clear that current payments connected with movements of capital between member states, such as interest and profits, shall be freed of all restrictions. This obligation does not appear to go any further than Article VIII, Section 2(a), of the IMF Agreement, which all the member states except Greece have accepted.

Article 68 supplements Article 67: A member state's domestic rules governing the capital markets and credit system must be applied in a nondiscriminatory manner to capital movements liberalized by Article 67. Also, members shall ''be as liberal as possible'' in granting any exchange authorizations as are still necessary.

Article 69 authorizes the Council to issue the ''necessary directives'' for the implementation of Article 67. Article 71, complementing Article 67, provides in part: ''Member States shall endeavour to avoid introducing within the Community any new exchange restrictions on the movement of capital and current payments connected with such movements, and shall endeavour not to make existing rules more restrictive.'' To the extent that directives issued by

---

[409] At pages 446–447, *supra.*

[410] The transitional period has now passed for all member states except Greece. Articles 120–126 of the Act Concerning the Conditions of Accession and the Adjustments to the Treaties resulting from the entry of Denmark, Ireland, and the United Kingdom into the European Economic Community provided a grace period, which has now passed, for the three countries to liberalize certain capital transactions. The Commission authorized a further deferral for some capital movements. See note 441, *infra.*

Articles 49–56 of the Act of Accession of Greece provided a grace period for Greece's liberalization of certain direct investment, real estate, and other capital movements. *Official Journal of the European Communities*, no. L-291, November 19, 1979, p. 17.

the Council of Ministers under Articles 67 and 69 require the elimination of restrictions, the "stand-still" is mandatory.[411] It is also mandatory, pursuant to Article 106, as to invisible transactions listed in Annex III of the Treaty of Rome.[412]

There has been debate about the meaning of Article 67's qualifying phrase, "to the extent necessary to ensure the proper functioning of the common market."[413] The implication and reality are that Article 67 does not require the removal of all restrictions. The Treaty of Rome was drafted in the mid-1950s, when the original six members were just beginning to liberalize restrictions on payments. It is thus not surprising that the provisions of the Treaty as they relate to capital movements are cautious and somewhat vague. The Court of Justice of the European Communities in *In Re Guerrino Casati,* decided in 1981, stated that the "to the extent necessary" phrase in Article 67 continues in effect, although the Treaty's transitional period is over. The Court stated that the scope of the phrase "varies in time and depends on an assessment of the requirements of the Common Market and on an appraisal of both the advantages and risks which liberalization might entail for the latter. . . ." The Court went on to say: "Such an assessment is, first and foremost, a matter for the Council, in accordance with the procedure provided for by Article 69 [which authorizes issuance of Council directives to implement Article 67]."[414]

The pace of liberalization of capital movements under Articles 67–73 is set by the member states and by directives of the Council of Ministers. The Court of Justice in the *Casati* case ruled that, even though the transitional period has passed, Article 67, paragraph 1,[415] cannot be directly invoked by individuals and firms against governments that have not abolished restrictions on movements of capital where the restriction in question has not been liberalized by a Council directive. The Court also held that the provision of Article 71 that member states "shall endeavour to avoid introducing within the Community any new exchange restrictions on the movement of capital" cannot be directly invoked by individuals and firms, at least where the transaction is not otherwise liberalized by the EEC Treaty or Council directives.[416]

While Article 67 has not been fully implemented, it has been partially implemented by Council directives adopted in 1960 and 1962, referred to collectively as the "Capital Directive."[417] No further directives of broad application

---

[411] This obvious point is reinforced by dicta in the opinion of the Court of Justice of the European Communities in *In Re Guerrino Casati,* cited in note 317, *supra.* See articles by Louis, Mastellone, and Peterson, *supra* note 317.

[412] See pages 446–448, *supra.*

[413] See C.W.M. van Ballegooijen, "Free Movement of Capital in the European Economic Community," *Legal Issues of European Integration,* 1976, no. 2, p. 1 at pp. 5–7 and 11.

[414] *In Re Guerrino Casati,* cited in note 317, *supra. European Court Reports,* at p. 2614.

[415] Quoted in full in text accompanying note 410, *supra.*

[416] *In Re Guerrino Casati,* cited in note 317. See also articles cited in note 317, *supra.*

[417] Council Directive of May 11, 1960, entitled "First Directive for the Implementation of Article 67 of

have yet been adopted.[418] The Commission in a communication to the Council in April 1983 recommended new initiatives.[419]

The Capital Directive divides capital transactions into four categories (Lists A, B, C, and D annexed to the directive) with distinct liberalization requirements for each category. The directive, as generally understood, deals with only currency controls. With respect to List A, the Capital Directive states that member states shall "grant all foreign exchange authorisations required for the conclusion or performance of transactions or for transfers between residents of Member States in respect of the capital movements set out in List A of Annex I of this Directive."[420] List A includes direct investments, liquidation of direct investments, investments in real estate, personal capital movements (such as gifts, inheritances, and immigrant transfers), short- and medium-term credits linked to commercial and service transactions in which a resident participates, transfers in performance of insurance contracts, royalties for intellectual property, transfers required for the provision of services, and some other transactions.[421] Liberalization of the underlying transactions is accomplished through application of other articles of the EEC Treaty and could be supplemented by the issuance of additional directives implementing Article 67 should the Council decide to do so. Since often the principal form of regulation of some List A transactions has been by means of exchange controls, liberalizing those controls has resulted in completely freeing many transactions.

the Treaty"; and Council Directive No. 63/21 of December 18, 1962, called the "Second Directive." The latter directive amended and supplemented the first directive. The Act of Accession of Denmark, Ireland, and the United Kingdom in Annex I, point VII(3), made technical amendments to make clear that for an acceding state the relevant date for the stand-still provision is the date of accession. The First Directive as amended by the Second Directive and the Act of Accession is hereinafter cited "Capital Directive." The Act of Accession of Greece did not amend the directive.

The consolidated text appears in European Communities Monetary Committee, *Compendium of Community Monetary Texts* (Brussels-Luxembourg, 1979), p. 101. The two directives originally appeared in *Official Journal of the European Communities* [hereinafter *Official Journal*], no. 43, July 12, 1960, p. 921, and *idem*, no. 9, January 22, 1963, p. 62; *Official Journal—Special [English] Edition, 1959–1962*, p. 49, *idem*, 1963–1964, p. 5, and *Corrigenda to Special Edition, 1952–1972*, p. 3.

[418] Council Directives No. 77/780 of December 12, 1977, and No. 83/350 of June 13, 1983, deal with coordination of national banking laws. *Official Journal*, no. L-322, December 17, 1977, p. 30; and no. L-193, July 18, 1983, p. 18. The Council has also issued directives on the listing of securities on stock exchanges. See note 427, *infra*. See also notes 434 and 435, *infra*, on monetary policy instruments.

The Court of Justice of the European Communities has held that Belgium and Italy failed to fulfill obligations under Council Directive No. 77/780. *Commission v. Italian Republic*, Case No. 300/81, and *Commision v. Kingdom of Belgium*, Case No. 301/81, decided March 1, 1983. *European Court Reports, supra* note 316, 1983, part 3, pp. 449 and 467; *CCH Common Market Reports, supra* note 316, paragraphs 8944 and 8945.

[419] For the text see European Communities Commission document no. COM(83)207 final (April 20, 1983); printed in *European Economy* (published by the Commission of the European Communities), no. 18 (November 1983), p. 177; Agence Internationale d'Information pour la Presse (Brussels), *Europe — Documents*, no. 1251/52 (April 25, 1983).

[420] Capital Directive, Article 1.

[421] The United Kingdom, for a period, was permitted to defer complete liberalization of direct investments by U.K. residents in other EEC states and certain capital movements of a personal nature. See note 441, *infra*. See note 410, *supra*, concerning Greece.

While the Capital Directive's required liberalization of List A transactions is concerned with "foreign exchange authorisations," the concept is interpreted broadly. Prior to February 1971, France required that direct investments by French residents in other EEC states, as well as in countries outside the EEC, be screened by the Ministry of Economy and Finance and that investments in France by residents of other EEC states, as well as of third countries, also be screened. While a procedure involving individual authorization of List A transactions is permitted by the Capital Directive, the French authorities postponed granting authorizations for some activities. The Commission instituted a case against France in the Court of Justice of the Communities and withdrew the case when France modified its practices to assure that requests covered by the Capital Directive were granted promptly. What is interesting is that the financial controls operated by the Ministry of Economy and Finance, although used for the purpose of supporting the franc, were not technically exchange controls. The Commission, nevertheless, believed that they came within the scope of Article 1 of the Capital Directive, and French authorities modified the controls to avoid a test.[422]

In addition to requiring that all foreign exchange authorizations required for List A transactions be granted, the Capital Directive requires that either the state enable these transactions to take place at the same exchange rates applicable to current transactions or, if separate foreign exchange markets are maintained for capital transfers, the exchange rates "must not show any appreciable and lasting differences" from the rates relating to current transactions.[423]

List B deals with investment securities traded on stock exchanges. Here, the obligation of member states is to "grant general permission" "for the conclusion or performance of transactions and for transfers between residents of Member States in respect of the capital movements."[424] The latter language tracks that of the OECD Capital Code. One might expect the same language in the two instruments to mean the same thing and, thus, for the EEC liberalization to extend both to currency controls and to controls on underlying investment security transactions, as is done in the OECD Code.[425] However, it appears that the EEC Capital Directive is generally understood to deal with only currency controls.

The requirement to "grant general permission" for List B transactions means that the state is not to require individual authorizations that can result in administrative delays. In addition to barring restrictions on List B transactions,

---

[422] Court of Justice of the European Communities, *Commission v. French Republic,* Case No. 66/69, instituted November 10, 1969, and withdrawn March 25, 1971. *Official Journal,* no. C-156, December 18, 1969, p. 12; and no. C-41, April 29, 1971, p. 5. See also *Bulletin of the European Communities,* 1971, no. 5, point 147.

[423] Capital Directive, Article 1.

[424] Capital Directive, Article 2 and List B.

[425] Compare Article 2(a) of the OECD Code of Liberalisation of Capital Movements, quoted in text accompanying note 379, *supra.*

the directive provides that if payments related to the transactions are channeled to an exchange market separate from that for current transactions, the member "shall endeavour to ensure" (a weaker obligation than in the case of List A) that the exchange rates "do not show appreciable and lasting differences" from the rates relating to current transactions.[426] In the case of securities listed on stock exchanges, the Capital Directive is supplemented by several additional directives.[427]

A third class of transactions (List C) includes purchase and sale of new issues of investment securities and securities not traded on the stock exchanges, medium- and long-term loans and credits not related to commercial transactions or provision of services, medium- and long-term loans and credits related to commercial or service transactions in which no resident of the state is a participant, and long-term credits including those linked to commercial or service transactions in which a resident participates. In these cases a member is to grant all foreign exchange authorizations required *unless* "such free movement of capital might form an obstacle to the achievement of the economic policy objectives of a Member State." In that case it may, but is not required to, maintain or reintroduce restrictions on the capital movement. Any restrictions are to be imposed in consultation with the Commission, which is to examine the problem necessitating the restrictions and may recommend withdrawal of the restrictions.[428]

Finally, a fourth class of capital movements (List D) can be subjected to restrictions. Here, there is no liberalization obligation at all in the view of the Council's Capital Directive. This class includes short-term capital movements that can be, but by no means always are, associated with speculative activities. The only obligation is to report to the Commission any changes in rules governing these capital movements.[429] The Monetary Committee is supposed to examine these controls at least once a year.

---

[426] Capital Directive, Article 2. Compliance with the directive required the United Kingdom to modify its investment currency market (note 329, *supra*). The Commission authorized the United Kingdom to delay that liberalization, but the liberalization has now been achieved. The Commission authorized Denmark and Ireland to delay liberalization of portfolio investment transactions. See note 441, *infra*.

[427] The following Council directives concern the listing of securities on stock exchanges: Directives No. 79/279 of March 5, 1979; No. 80/390 of March 17, 1980; No. 82/121 of February 15, 1982; and No. 82/148 of March 3, 1982. *Official Journal*, no. L-66, March 16, 1979, p. 21; no. L-100, April 17, 1980, p. 1; no. L-48, February 20, 1982, p. 26; and no. L-62, March 5, 1982, p. 22.

[428] Capital Directive, Article 3.
Council Directive No. 72/156 of March 21, 1972, in the interest of controlling disruptive capital movements, permits a limited derogation from the obligations of Article 3 in order to allow controls on medium- and long-term loans and credits not related to commercial transactions or the provision of services. Directive No. 72/156 is summarized in the text accompanying note 434, *infra*.

[429] Article 7 of the Capital Directive indicates that the stand-still provision of Article 6 of the Directive does not apply to the capital movements set forth in List D, which include short-term investments in treasury bills and money market instruments, deposit accounts with banks and other credit institutions, short-term credits relating to underlying transactions in which no resident participates, short-term loans and credits that do not relate to commercial transactions or provision of services, certain guarantees and surety arrangements, personal loans, and the transportation of gold and paper notes.

Article 5 of the Capital Directive permits the member states to maintain passive controls to assure that transactions are treated within the proper categories. Members are called upon to simplify their authorization procedures and formalities.

The stand-still provision of Article 6 states that the member states "shall endeavour," as to capital movements liberalized by the directives, not to introduce exchange restrictions going beyond those in force on May 11, 1960 (January 1, 1973, in the case of Denmark, Ireland, and the United Kingdom; January 1, 1981, in the case of Greece). The rule is primarily of significance for transactions set out in List C, but it also applies to Lists A and B. To enable the Commission to satisfy itself that there is compliance with the directives, Article 7 requires the member states to provide the Commission with information.

The EEC system is directed primarily to liberalization between member states. Nevertheless, implementation of the Capital Directive has, in general, resulted in freeing transactions not only among Community countries but also with non-Community countries.[430] Article 70 of the EEC Treaty authorizes the Council acting unanimously to issue directives for coordination of members' exchange control policies concerning capital movements between EEC countries and third countries, the enunciated goal being "the highest possible degree of liberalisation."[431] Agreements between the European Economic Community and third states have contained special provisions dealing with payments and capital movements between the parties.[432]

---

[430] The OECD Capital Code, to which all EEC member states subscribe, requires liberalization of transactions set out in the OECD Code's Annex A (Lists A and B) to be on a nondiscriminatory basis with respect to OECD members that adhere to the Code. "Other measures of liberalisation" can be adopted to benefit partners in a customs union without being generalized to all OECD members that adhere to the Code. OECD Code of Liberalisation of Capital Movements, *supra* note 375, Articles 9 and 10. The provisions have been interpreted to allow an EEC state that maintains a reservation to the OECD Code to liberalize toward its EEC partners transactions that are covered by the reservation without generalizing the liberalization to other parties to the OECD Code.

Liberalization in the EEC has in some cases resulted in discrimination against non-EEC OECD members. For example, residents of EEC countries have in some cases been able to borrow funds in France when residents of non-EEC countries have been prohibited from doing so. Residents of EEC countries have in some cases made loans to French residents that if made by residents of other countries would not have been permitted.

Article 70(2) of the EEC Treaty authorizes a member state, subject to several conditions, to take protective measures if the liberalization of capital movements within the Community is utilized to evade that state's restrictions concerning capital movements to or from third countries.

[431] Council Directive No. 72/156 of March 21, 1972, *infra* note 434, was adopted on the basis of Articles 70 and 103.

[432] See Articles 156–159 of the second Convention between the European Economic Community and African, Caribbean, and Pacific States, signed at Lomé October 31, 1979, entered into force January 1, 1981. The Convention appears in *Official Journal*, no. L-347, December 22, 1980, p. 1; *International Legal Materials*, vol. 19 (1980), p. 327. A catalogue of economic agreements between the EEC and third parties appears in *CCH Common Market Reports, supra* note 316, paragraphs 3861–3875.

Monetary Policy Instruments. Capital movements in List D of the Capital Directive[433] are not subject to any required liberalization. Indeed, the Community can take coordinated action to impose controls. However, to take effective coordinated action, the member states need monetary instruments that complement each other. A Council Directive requires that member states take all necessary steps to ensure that the monetary authorities have available the following instruments and are able, where necessary, to put them into operation immediately without further enabling measures:

- Regulation of loans and credits which are not related to commercial transactions or to provision of services and are granted by nonresidents to residents;
- Rules governing investment on the money market and payment of interest on deposits held by nonresidents;
- Regulation of the net external position of credit institutions; and
- Rules setting minimum reserve ratios, in particular for the holdings of nonresidents.[434]

The instruments listed above can be used to regulate foreign participation in domestic money markets and to neutralize the effects of international capital movements on domestic liquidity.

Another Council directive requires member states to vest their monetary authorities with authority to use the following techniques for regulating domestic liquidity and credit:

- Imposition or modification of reserve ratios applying to the liabilities of monetary institutions;
- Imposition or modification of reserve ratios applying to the credit granted by monetary institutions;
- Recourse to an open market policy with wide scope for action, including the use, as necessary, of short-, medium- and long-term securities;
- Modification of the rediscount ceilings with the central bank; and
- Modification of the various intervention rates practiced by the monetary authorities.[435]

[433] See note 429, *supra,* and accompanying text.

[434] Article 1 of Council Directive No. 72/156 of March 21, 1972, on regulating international capital flows and neutralizing their undesirable effects on domestic liquidity. *Official Journal,* no. L-91, April 18, 1972, p. 13; *Official Journal—Special [English] Edition,* 1972(I), p. 296; *Compendium of Community Monetary Texts* (1979), *supra* note 417, p. 116. The directive was adopted on the basis of the authority of EEC Treaty Article 70, relating to coordination of exchange policies in respect of capital movements between EEC states and third countries, and Article 103, relating to conjunctural policy coordination. The immediate impetus for the directive was the need to protect the newly instituted "snake" arrangement of narrow margins among EEC currencies (Chapter 11, page 537, note 179) and the currency rates agreed in the December 1971 Smithsonian meeting (Chapter 11, pages 498–499 and note 40) against pressures caused by large capital movements.

[435] Article 9 of Council Directive No. 74/121 of February 18, 1974, on Stability, Growth, and Full Employment; *Official Journal,* no. L-63, March 5, 1974, p. 19; *Compendium of Community Monetary Texts* (1979), *supra* note 417, p. 95. This directive is discussed in Chapter 12, *infra,* pages 593–598.

The directive also requires member states to vest their monetary authorities, as far as possible, with the instruments and powers to enable them to implement the following measures:

- Modification of the borrowing and lending interest rates paid or charged by public credit agencies;
- Imposition or modification of conditions for consumer credit, hire-purchase sales, and mortgage credit; and
- Quantitative or qualitative credit control.[436]

Taken together the two directives are intended to establish the national machinery necessary for coordinated application of a variety of techniques for controlling domestic liquidity and speculative movements of international capital. With some exceptions, the central banks of the EEC countries possess the capacity to use the instruments listed in the two directives, but their approaches to monetary control still vary.[437] The economic wisdom of applying particular measures is beyond the scope of this book. The best choice in the particular case among controlling short-term capital flows, neutralizing their monetary effects, or making other adjustments is often not self-evident.

Safeguard Provisions. Articles 108 and 109 of the EEC Treaty permit the imposition of protective measures when a country suffers or is seriously threatened with balance-of-payments difficulties. Permitted derogations are not limited to any particular class of obligations and encompass obligations under the capital movements provisions as well as other provisions of the Treaty.[438] Article 73, limited to capital controls, permits their reintroduction when movements of capital lead to "disturbances" of the capital market. Article 73 provides:

1. If movements of capital lead to disturbances in the functioning of the capital market in any Member State, the Commission shall, after consulting the Monetary Committee, authorise that State to take protective measures in the field of capital movements, the conditions and details of which the Commission shall determine.

The Council may, acting by a qualified majority, revoke this authorisation or amend the conditions or details thereof.

2. A Member State which is in difficulties may, however, on grounds of secrecy or urgency, take the measures mentioned above, where this proves necessary, on its own initiative. The Commission

---

[436] Article 9 of Council Directive No. 74/121, *idem.*

[437] See Chapter 12, *infra,* pages 597–598. See also OECD, *Experience with Controls on International Financial Credits, Loans and Deposits, supra* note 343.

[438] The Court of Justice of the European Communities has held that Article 104 of the EEC Treaty (quoted in Chapter 12, *infra,* page 590) does not provide derogation rights independent of Articles 108 and 109. *Commission v. Italian Republic,* Case No. 95/81, discussed in text accompanying note 316, *supra.*

and the other Member States shall be informed of such measures by the date of their entry into force at the latest. In this event the Commission may, after consulting the Monetary Committee, decide that the State concerned shall amend or abolish the measures.

Because Article 73 does not require a balance-of-payments justification, but is limited to the field of capital movements, questions can arise as to whether a particular measure is a capital control. The Court of Justice of the European Communities has held that a security deposit required by Italy in connection with advance payments for imports of goods was not a capital control for purposes of Article 73.[439]

Protective measures under Articles 108 and 109 are not limited by field, but a prerequisite is that the country be in difficulties or be seriously threatened with difficulties in its balance of payments. If the authorization of the Commission is obtained, a state can take protective measures under Article 108(3) that derogate from its Treaty obligations. The Commission determines the permitted measures, their conditions, and details. While the authorized measures need not have a monetary character, in several cases the measures have taken that form. Examples follow.

The Act of Accession under which Denmark, Ireland, and the United Kingdom joined the European Economic Community permitted the three countries to defer until January 1975, and in some cases until January 1978, the liberalization of certain capital movements required by the Capital Directive.[440] The Commission, acting under Article 108(3) of the Treaty of Rome, later permitted the three countries to further delay liberalization of certain portfolio investments, and the United Kingdom was allowed to defer total liberalization of direct investments by U.K. residents in other EEC states.[441]

France during a currency crisis in the fall of 1968 received the Commission's authorization under Article 108(3) to impose exchange controls over French resident capital outflows to EEC countries and to third countries for direct investments, real estate investments, acquisition of investment securities, and a variety of other transactions, as well as currency restrictions affecting travel.[442]

---

[439] *Commission v. Italian Republic*, Case No. 95/81, *idem.*

[440] See note 410, *supra.*

[441] Commission decisions of July 23, 1975, June 28, 1977, and December 22, 1977; *Official Journal*, no. L-211, August 9, 1975, p. 29; no. L-179, July 19, 1977, p. 30; and no. L-45, February 2, 1978, pp. 28, 29, and 30. See also no. C-292, December 20, 1975, pp. 16–17; and no. C-99, May 3, 1976, pp. 21–22. The United Kingdom by October 1979 had virtually abolished its capital controls. See IMF, *Annual Report on Exchange Arrangements and Exchange Restrictions, 1979*, p. 430, and *idem, 1980*, pp. 421–22. Denmark substantially liberalized its capital controls effective May 1, 1983. See CCH *Common Market Reports, supra* note 316, *Euromarket News*, issue no. 745, report no. 473 (April 27, 1983), p. 7.

[442] Commission Decision No. 68/406 of December 4, 1968; *Official Journal*, no. L-295, December 7, 1968, p. 10. See the Commission's earlier Decision No. 68/301 of July 23, 1968; *O.J.*, no. L-178, July 25, 1968, p.15. See also notes 451 and 453, *infra*. The IMF approved those features of the French controls insti-

Italy in May 1974 imposed an import deposit scheme to protect its balance of payments.[443] The requirement applied not only to imports of goods, but also to payments associated with investments by Italian residents in other EEC states and to certain payments for services. The Commission recommended that the Council direct member states to grant financial assistance to Italy pursuant to Article 108(2) to avoid the need for Italy to take such drastic measures. When the Council did not adopt the recommended directive, the Commission acting under Article 108(3) authorized Italy to impose the deposit requirement.[444] Subsequently, in December 1974, the Council did direct member states to extend credits to Italy.[445] Later Italy terminated its deposit scheme as to imports of goods and services. The Commission continued to authorize the application of the deposit scheme to investments abroad by Italian residents.[446]

As illustrated by the Italian case, the Council may under Article 108(2) grant "mutual assistance" to avoid the necessity for protective measures. Mutual assistance can, as in the Italian case, take the form of financial assistance. Mutual assistance can also take the form of a concerted position by the EEC states in the IMF or the GATT. The position of the EEC states in favor of IMF approval of French travel allowance restrictions in 1968[447] and the support given in the GATT to Italy's deposit scheme in 1974[448] are examples.

The import deposit scheme introduced by Italy in May 1976 was authorized by the Commission under Article 108(3),[449] as was the deposit scheme imposed in May 1981.[450]

---

tuted in November 1968 that required Fund approval. See notes 104–106, *supra*, and accompanying text. For additional background, see Pierre Jasinski, "The Control of Capital Movements in France," *Journal of World Trade Law*, vol. 3 (1969), p. 209.

[443] The measure was discussed earlier at pages 438–439, *supra*.

[444] Commission Decision No. 74/287 of May 8, 1974; *Official Journal*, no. L-152, June 8, 1974, p. 18 (with amendments at *O.J.*, no. L-198, July 20, 1974, p. 37, and *O.J.*, no. L-223, August 13, 1974, p. 11). For further background, see *Bulletin of the European Communities*, 1974, no. 5, points 1101 and 1107; and Smit and Herzog, *supra* note 268, part 3, pp. 620–22.

[445] See Chapter 8, *supra*, pages 338–339.

[446] Commission Decision No. 75/355 of May 26, 1975; *Official Journal*, no. L-158, June 20, 1975, p. 25. Some of the protective measures applicable to investments abroad continued in place at the time this book went to press.

[447] See pages 405–406, *supra*.

[448] See pages 438–439, *supra*.

[449] For background and information on the IMF's actions, see text accompanying notes 123–129, *supra*. The Commission authorized the Italian action in Decision No. 76/446 of May 5, 1976, and subsequently extended its authorization. *Official Journal*, no. L-120, May 7, 1976, p. 30; no. L-196, July 22, 1976, p. 20; and no. L-268, October 1, 1976, p. 59. See also *10th General Report on the Activities of the European Communities in 1976*, points 114, 210, and 211; and *Bulletin of the European Communities*, 1976, no. 5, points 2203–05.

[450] The Italian deposit requirement introduced in May 1981 applied to purchases of foreign currency for a wide range of imports. See text accompanying notes 130–132, *supra*, for IMF actions. To justify its action under the EEC Treaty, Italy initially invoked Article 109 (discussed in text accompanying note 452). The Monetary Committee examined the Italian measure in June 1981, and the Commission in a decision in July made economic policy recommendations to Italy and stated that the deposit requirement should be terminated by October 1, 1981. In a decision in September the Commission, acting under Article 108(3), authorized Italy

A question has been raised about how long a temporary derogation under Article 108(3) of the EEC Treaty can be maintained. The answer is as long as the Commission continues to approve it. In some cases the authorizations, although subject to review and termination by the Commission, have not included a specific termination date.[451]

An EEC member state that faces a "sudden crisis" in its balance of payments may, under Article 109, if the Council does not grant mutual assistance, take protective measures temporarily derogating from Treaty obligations without the necessity for Commission authorization. The measures are to be only those strictly necessary and must cause the least possible disturbance in the common market.[452] The Court of Justice has held that the state must inform the Commission and other member states of its actions, and that they are taken under Article 109, no later than the day they enter into force.[453] The Council, after

to maintain the requirement until March 1, 1982, with provisos that certain products be excluded and that the rates be reduced. Italy, in compliance, terminated the scheme in February 1982. In the meantime the Monetary Committee in December 1981 in consultation with Italian authorities agreed on a procedure to monitor developments in Italy. Commission Recommendation of July 1, 1981, *Official Journal*, no. L-189, July 11, 1981, p. 60; and Commission Decision of September 23, 1981, *Official Journal*, no. L-296, October 15, 1981, p. 50. See also *Official Journal*, no. C-182, July 19, 1982, p. 114; *Bulletin of the European Communities*, 1981, no. 6, points 2.1.1 and 2.1.2; no. 9, point 2.1.5; and no. 12, point 2.1.7; *idem*, 1982, no. 1, point 2.1.3; and Guider, *supra* note 131, pp. 932–41.

[451] See *Official Journal*, no. C-38, April 21, 1971, p. 3, reporting a question raised in the European Parliament about some French "safeguards" in the form of exchange restrictions on capital movements authorized by the Commission in 1968 that were still in effect in April 1971. See also *Official Journal*, no. C-259, October 4, 1982, p. 26, reporting a Commission representative's statement that a derogation granted France in 1968 permitted it to reintroduce controls in 1982 on the purchase by French residents of moveable property abroad. Italy continues to rely on the Commission's authorization of protective measures applicable to investment abroad, *supra* note 446, granted in 1975. See also *Official Journal*, no. C-333, December 21, 1981, p. 10.

[452] Italy invoked Article 109 to justify the imposition of a special tax on purchases of foreign exchange during the period October 4, 1976, to February 18, 1977. See text accompanying notes 154–157, *supra*. Italy invoked Article 109 when it introduced a deposit requirement for foreign currency purchases on May 29, 1981. Later the Commission approved the measure under Article 108(3). See notes 130, 131, and 450, *supra*, and accompanying text.

France relied on Article 109 when it imposed restrictions on foreign exchange for tourist travel in March 1983. In connection with an EEC balance-of-payments loan approved by the Council in May 1983 (Chapter 8, *supra*, pages 340–341), France comitted itself to abolish the restrictions by the end of 1983. The Council's decision approving the loan recited: "Whereas, without prejudice to the question of their compatibility with Community rules, the restrictions on the allocation of foreign currency for tourist purposes decided upon on 28 March 1983 will be abolished by 31 December 1983 at the latest in accordance with the programme presented by the French authorities." Council Decision No. 83/298 of May 16, 1983; *Official Journal*, no. L-153, June 11, 1983, p. 44.

[453] The case centered around the Banque de France's practice of granting a lower, more favorable rediscount rate for credits financing exports from France to other Community countries than for domestic transactions. The practice was justified by France as a protective measure to safeguard its balance of payments. Commission decisions of July 1968 temporarily approved the practice under Article 108 and set deadlines for narrowing the rate differential which operated as a subsidy for French exports.

France did not narrow the rate differential as the Commission required in the fall of 1968. Rather, it claimed that there was a new "sudden crisis" which justified its action in keeping French goods competitive in other Community countries. The Court ruled (a) that France could not rely on Article 109 because it had not notified its action in the fall (and its reliance upon Article 109) to the Commission with sufficient prompt-

receiving an opinion from the Commission and consulting the Monetary Committee, may (acting by a qualified majority) require the member to amend, suspend, or terminate the protective measures it has taken.[454]

Extraterritorial Recognition of National Exchange Controls

Overview

Section 2(b) of Article VIII of the IMF Agreement provides:

> Exchange contracts which involve the currency of any member and which are contrary to the exchange control regulations of that member maintained or imposed consistently with this Agreement shall be unenforceable in the territories of any member. In addition, members may, by mutual accord, cooperate in measures for the purpose of making the exchange control regulations of either member more effective, provided that such measures and regulations are consistent with this Agreement.[455]

Section 2(b) was not written with the clarity one finds in other articles of the IMF Agreement, and its particular location in the text is somewhat puzzling. While one of its purposes was to force courts to recognize a *force majeure* defense where it might not have been recognized under traditional conflict-of-laws principles,[456] it is unwise to ascribe a single purpose to this subsection. In considering the application of Section 2(b), one must take into account its wording; its context within the IMF Agreement; its negotiating history;[457] its formal interpretation by the Fund;[458] other IMF actions respecting the subsection;[459] the extensive practice under it, including the many national court deci-

---

ness, and (b) that France breached its EEC Treaty obligations under Article 108 when it acted contrary to the Commission's decisions. *Commission v. French Republic,* Cases Nos. 6 and 11/69, decided December 10, 1969; *European Court Reports, supra* note 316, 1969, p. 523; *CCH Common Market Reports, supra* note 316, paragraph 8105. See Smit and Herzog, *supra* note 268, part 3, pp. 618–20, for background.

[454] Article 109, paragraph 3.

[455] The text has remained the same since the Articles of Agreement first entered into force in 1945.

[456] See Andreas F. Lowenfeld, *The International Monetary System* (1st ed.; New York: Matthew Bender, 1977), pp. 228–29; and Elias Krispis, "Money in Private International Law," in Hague Academy of International Law, *Recueil des Cours,* vol. 120 (1967-I), p. 191 at pp. 277–86.

[457] See *Proceedings and Documents of the United Nations Monetary and Financial Conference, Bretton Woods, New Hampshire, July 1–22, 1944* (2 vols.; Washington: U.S. Government Printing Office, 1948), vol. 1, pp. 54–55, 217, 230, 287–88, 334, 341, 502, 543, 575–76, 599, 605, 628, 671, 780, and 808; Gold, *Fund Agreement in the Courts, supra* note 49, vol. 2, pp. 429–38; and Krispis, *supra* note 456, pp. 286–88.

[458] See note 462, *infra,* and accompanying text.

[459] Statements by IMF officials in response to inquiries of national courts, lawyers, and scholars are examples. See note 481, *infra.*

sions in its 40-year history;[460] and the rich scholarly commentary arguing its scope and analyzing decisions applying it.[461]

A formal interpretation by the IMF adopted in 1949, which has been followed in most of the litigated cases, established the following principles:[462]

(1) Section 2(b) binds all IMF members including those that rely upon the Article XIV "transitional" regime.

(2) Section 2(b) is binding upon the judicial and administrative authorities of member states.[463] They shall not decree specific performance of an exchange contract or award damages for its nonperformance if the contract involves the currency of any member and is contrary to exchange control regulations of that member maintained or imposed consistently with the Fund Agreement.

(3) An exchange contract that is unenforceable under Section 2(b) cannot be enforced on the basis that the exchange control regulations of the state of issue of a currency involved are contrary to the public policy (ordre public) of the forum.

(4) An exchange contract that is unenforceable under Section 2(b) cannot be enforced on the basis that the exchange control regulations of the state of issue of a currency involved are not applicable under the private international law (choice-of-law principles) of the forum.

The duty of the forum under Section 2(b) is to refrain from enforcing a contract that is contrary to the exchange control regulations of an IMF member and that otherwise meets the criteria of Section 2(b). The effect of Section 2(b) is to make the contract "unenforceable," and a national court or administrative agency is not required to treat it as void. A contract that, when made, was contrary to the exchange control regulations of an IMF member whose currency is

---

[460] For over 30 years Sir Joseph Gold has written extensively on section 2(b) and on court decisions construing that and other provisions of the IMF Agreement in articles under the title "The Fund Agreement in the Courts" which have appeared in *International Monetary Fund Staff Papers*. The first seven articles are reprinted in Gold, *Fund Agreement in the Courts, supra* note 49, vol. 1 (1962), and the next ten articles, together with several related essays, are collected in *idem*, vol. 2 (1982). Part XVIII appears in *IMF Staff Papers*, vol. 29 (1982), p. 647.

[461] See, e.g., Gold, *Fund Agreement in the Courts, supra* note 49, vols. 1 and 2; Mann, *Legal Aspect of Money, supra* note 371, pp. 372–400; Edwards, "Extraterritorial Application," *supra* note 165; François Gianviti, "Réflexions sur l'Article VIII, Section 2(b) des Status du Fonds Monétaire International" (parts 1 and 2), *Revue Critique de Droit International Privé*, vol. 62 (1973), pp. 471 and 629; François Gianviti, "Le Blocage des Avoirs Officiels Iraniens par les Etats-Unis (Executive Order du 14 novembre 1979)," *Revue Critique de Droit International Privé*, vol. 69 (1980), p. 279; Silard, "Money and Foreign Exchange," *supra* note 28, sections 86–93; and John S. Williams, "Extraterritorial Enforcement of Exchange Control Regulations Under the International Monetary Fund Agreement," *Virginia Journal of International Law*, vol. 15 (1975), p. 319.

[462] E.B. Decision No. 446-4 (June 10, 1949), *supra* note 98. The decision was adopted as a formal interpretation made under old Article XVIII, *original* (now Article XXIX, *second*).

[463] By accepting the Fund Agreement members have undertaken to make the rule of section 2(b) part of their national law. If a court of a member country decides a case contrary to the requirements of section 2(b) of Article VIII, the country breaches its treaty obligations. Article XXXI, section 2(a); and E.B. Decision No. 446-4, *supra* note 98.

involved may be enforced if the regulation has been repealed when enforcement is sought. Similarly, a contract enforceable when made may subsequently become unenforceable if contrary to regulations adopted later.[464]

The Fund interpretation cited above speaks only of a member country's obligation to refrain from enforcing affected contracts in its courts and administrative agencies. Is a country required to take positive action (for example, by adopting regulations binding on commercial banks) to ensure that affected contracts are not performed? Members of the Fund's legal staff have expressed the view that there is no such obligation and this is supported by the negotiating history respecting Section 2(b).[465] Also, Section 2(b) does not require IMF members to permit suits to be brought in their courts on tort or quasi-contract theories of restitution to recover damages caused by the actual performance of a contract that, had it not been performed, was unenforceable under Section 2(b).[466]

Only a few of the more important issues in the application of Section 2(b), that arise with some regularity, are touched on below. Because the Fund has not formally adopted decisions on these issues, they all are to some degree controversial.

(a) What is the scope of the term "exchange control regulations"?
(b) What meaning is to be given to "maintained or imposed consistently with this agreement"?
(c) What is the scope of the term "exchange contracts"?
(d) What meaning is to be given to "involve the currency"?[467]

---

[464] Memorandum of the Solicitor General of the United States urging the U.S. Supreme Court to deny certiorari in *Pan American Life Insurance Co. v. Lorido*, reprinted in *International Legal Materials*, vol. 3 (1964), p. 721 at pp. 724–25, excerpt quoted in Gold, *Fund Agreement in the Courts*, supra note 49, vol. 2, p. 88. The writ of certiorari was denied. *United States Reports*, vol. 379, p. 871 (decided 1964). This position is also supported by the judgment of the Federal Supreme Court (Bundesgerichtshof) of the Federal Republic of Germany of February 17, 1971, summarized in *Neue Juristische Wochenschrift*, vol. 24 (1971), p. 983, discussed in Gold, *supra*, vol. 2, at pp. 149–51. See also Edwards, "Extraterritorial Application," *supra* note 165, p. 883 (note 54).

[465] A proposal that member countries be obligated to give active assistance to a member in the positive enforcement of its exchange control regulations was considered at the 1944 Bretton Woods Conference but was not adopted. See *Proceedings and Documents, supra* note 457, vol. 1, pp. 334, 341, 502, 543, 575–76, 605, 628, and 780.

[466] While section 2(b) does not require that such suits be allowed, a country can permit them if it chooses. The New York Court of Appeals held a foreign commercial bank was entitled to damages for fraud and deceit and to rescission of an exchange contract in *Banco Frances e Brasileiro, S.A. v. John Doe; New York Reports (2d Series)*, vol. 36, p. 592 (decided 1975). However, a Brazilian government bank was denied recovery of the proceeds of a coffee shipment that had not been surrendered in accordance with Brazilian law. *Banco do Brasil, S.A. v. A.C. Israel Commodity Co.; New York Reports (2d Series)*, vol. 12, p. 371 (decided 1963). For the application of English extradition law to a fugitive charged with violating Ghana's exchange control regulations, see *Regina v. Governor of Pentonville Prison, Ex Parte Khubchandani; Criminal Appeal Reports*, vol. 71 (1980), p. 241 (decision of Queen's Bench Divisional Court, 1980).

[467] All of these issues arose in litigation in the courts of France and the United Kingdom in 1979–81 concerning the extraterritorial application of the Iranian Assets Control Regulations promulgated by the U.S. Treasury following the seizure of American diplomatic and consular personnel in Tehran in November 1979. The regulations by their terms blocked transfers of bank deposits denominated in U.S. dollars held by Iran's

Scope of the Term "Exchange Control Regulations"

Judicial decisions support the view that the term "exchangé control regulations" in Section 2(b) includes all regulations that take the form of direct controls on international payments or transfers.[468] The term encompasses all "restrictions on the making of payments and transfers for current international transactions" as the latter term is applied in Fund practice under Article VIII, Section 2(a), and Article XIV, Section 2.[469] "Exchange control regulations" in Section 2(b) has also been understood to include all monetary controls imposed on capital movements.[470]

The decided cases support the view that it is the form and not the purpose of the measure that determines whether it is an "exchange control regulation" within the meaning of Section 2(b).[471] On this view, any law or regulation, regardless of by what governmental agency administered, is an exchange control regulation if it regulates monetary payments or transfers. Controls on underlying transactions (e.g., regulations on entry into certain types of service contracts) are not currency control regulations under Section 2(b) even if administered by exchange authorities, but the prohibition of payments connected with an unapproved contract does come within Section 2(b).[472] Sir Joseph Gold has argued that a control comes within the scope of Section 2(b) when it directly regulates international monetary payments or transfers even if it was adopted for reasons other than the protection of the balance of payments, such as protecting national security or increasing tax revenues.[473]

The matter, however, is not completely free from doubt. F.A. Mann and

central bank, Bank Markazi Iran, with the overseas branches of U.S. commercial banks. The cases never went to final judgment and became inactive following agreements and orders settling disputes between the United States and Iran. These cases are referred to hereinafter as the *Bank Markazi Iran* cases. For detailed discussions of the litigation, see Edwards, "Extraterritorial Application," *supra* note 165; Gianviti, "Le Blocage," *supra* note 461; and Gold, *Fund Agreement in the Courts, supra* note 49, vol. 2, pp. 360–427. Sir Joseph comments on the writings of virtually every legal scholar who wrote on the subject.

[468] See Gold, *Fund Agreement in the Courts, idem,* vol. 2, pp. 116–20, 194–96, 208–10, and 295–97.

[469] This position is supported by the decided cases and is also the position taken by the Legal Department of the IMF. See letter of George P. Nicoletopoulos, Director, Legal Department of the IMF, to the author dated January 9, 1981, printed in Edwards, "Extraterritorial Application," *supra* note 165, p. 900. The position is repeated in a letter of Mr. Nicoletopoulos to Professor Cynthia C. Lichtenstein, Boston College Law School, dated March 2, 1981.

[470] The cases applying section 2(b) uniformly hold that the provision applies to exchange controls on capital movements as well as exchange restrictions respecting current transactions. See Gold, *Fund Agreement in the Courts, supra* note 49, vol. 2, pp. 79–87, 208–10, and 276–77.

[471] Recall that it is the form and not the purpose of a measure that determines whether it is a "restriction" under Article VIII, section 2(a). See pages 393–394, *supra.* The Fund does not exercise approval jurisdiction under section 2(a) over trade restrictions that do not take the form of currency restrictions even when they are adopted for balance-of-payments reasons. See pages 428–429 and 440–442, *supra.*

[472] See Gold, *Fund Agreement in the Courts, supra* note 49, vol. 2, p. 195. See also note 49, *supra.*

[473] See Gold, *Fund Agreement in the Courts, idem,* vol. 2, pp. 294–99, where a decision of the Federal Supreme Court of the Federal Republic of Germany of March 8, 1979, is discussed.

Elias Krispis have argued that the form test for what is a "restriction" under Section 2(a) need not be carried over to Section 2(b). In their view, one should look to the purpose of a control to determine if it is an "exchange control regulation." They have argued that a control intended to put political pressure on a foreign government rather than to protect the balance of payments of the country imposing the control is not an "exchange control regulation."[474]

The Legal Department of the IMF has consistently taken the position that all exchange restrictions (including security restrictions) approved under Section 2(a) are clearly "exchange control regulations . . . imposed consistently with this Agreement" under Section 2(b).[475] To the author's knowledge, there are no court decisions to the contrary.[476]

Meaning to be Given to "Maintained or Imposed Consistently with this Agreement"

Only contracts that are contrary to exchange control regulations "maintained or imposed consistently with this [IMF] Agreement" come within the scope of Section 2(b) of Article VIII. There are two basic questions: (a) who determines consistency? and (b) what criteria are to be applied in determining consistency?

While one author has appeared to suggest that a court can independently determine whether a country's controls are maintained or imposed "consistently" with the IMF Agreement,[477] this is not correct. The drafters of the Articles of Agreement did not want tribunals outside the IMF structure to pass judgment on whether a member's conduct was in conformance with the Articles. Article XXIX provides that any question of interpretation of the provisions of the Articles arising between IMF members must be submitted to the Fund for decision.[478] The weight of authority holds that IMF interpretative decisions

---

[474] Mann, *Legal Aspect of Money, supra,* note 371, p. 393; and Krispis, *supra* note 456, p. 293.

Both authors cite Arthur Nussbaum as authority for the idea that security restrictions are not "exchange control regulations" within the meaning of section 2(b). However, what Mr. Nussbaum suggested was that security restrictions are outside the scope of *section 2(a)*—the provision requiring IMF approval of restrictions. Arthur Nussbaum, *Money in the Law, National and International* (rev. ed.; Brooklyn: Foundation Press, 1950), pp. 455–57. Moreover, Mr. Nussbaum's comments were made before E.B. Decision No. 144 of 1952, *supra* note 159, that recognized IMF approval jurisdiction under section 2(a) over security restrictions affecting current payments and transfers. Messrs. Mann and Krispis do not appear to have considered how the IMF's 1952 decision might affect the treatment of security restrictions under section 2(b).

[475] See notes 469 and 473, *supra,* and note 481, *infra.*

[476] Most authors who discussed the Iranian assets litigation in Paris and London, *supra* note 467, concluded that the U.S. regulations were "exchange control regulations" within the meaning of section 2(b). See Edwards, "Extraterritorial Application," *supra* note 165, p. 885; and Gold, *Fund Agreement in the Courts, supra* note 49, vol. 2, pp. 408–13.

[477] John S. Williams, "Foreign Exchange Control Regulation and the New York Court of Appeals: *J. Zeevi & Sons, Ltd. v. Grindlays Bank (Uganda) Ltd.,*" *Cornell International Law Journal,* vol. 9 (1976), p. 239 at pp. 247–48.

[478] See Chapter 1, *supra,* pages 37–39.

must be followed by national courts.[479] The Executive Board's 1949 decision formally interpreting Article VIII, Section 2(b), states that "the Fund is prepared to advise whether particular exchange control regulations are maintained or imposed consistently with the Fund Agreement."[480] The author believes that by this statement the Fund has reserved to itself final authority to determine whether a member's exchange controls are or are not consistent with the IMF Agreement. If a judge makes an independent determination, he commits an error. The Fund follows the policy of responding to inquiries from businessmen and lawyers, as well as from governmental officials, about whether specific exchange control regulations of members are consistent with the Articles of Agreement.[481] A Judge in a court proceeding should request a determination of "consistency" from the Fund. The Fund, in response to the national court's request, should state its conclusion about the consistency of the member's practices with the Articles of Agreement and should, in addition, explain the basis of its determination. (For example, if the Fund determines that a member's action is not an exchange measure and, for that reason, does not require IMF approval under Article VIII, Sections 2(a) or 3, that should be stated, so that the court will know that Section 2(b) is inapplicable.) The court should treat itself as bound by the Fund's determination, unless there is good reason to believe that the Fund was not fully informed of the member's currency practices or that there were irregularities in the process by which the Fund made its determination.[482]

Now let us turn to the criteria the Fund should apply in making its determinations of "consistency" or lack thereof. As explained earlier in this chapter, IMF members are permitted, pursuant to Article VI, Section 3, to exercise such controls as are necessary to regulate international capital movements. Such controls do not require approval under Article VIII, Section 2(a), except to the extent that they restrict payments for current transactions or unduly delay transfers of funds in settlement of commitments.[483] Members that rely on Article XIV are not required to obtain the Fund's approval for restrictions on payments and transfers for current international transactions that have been maintained con-

---

[479] See Chapter 1, *supra,* page 37 (note 165).

[480] E.B. Decision No. 446-4, *supra* note 98.

[481] See, e.g., IMF statements quoted in Gold, *Fund Agreement in the Courts, supra* note 49, vol. 2, pp. 45, 118-20, 191, and 196. The letter of George P. Nicoletopoulos to the author, dated January 9, 1981, *supra* note 469, stated that the U.S. Treasury's Iranian Assets Control Regulations "constitute exchange control regulations maintained consistently with the Fund's Articles in the sense of Article VIII, Section 2(b)."

The IMF, in response to an inquiry from the attorney for one of the parties in a case before the Iran-United States Claims Tribunal at the Hague, stated that the Fund had not approved under Article VIII any exchange measures imposed or reimposed by Iran since 1974. Letter dated November 18, 1983, of George P. Nicoletopoulos, Director, Legal Department of the IMF, to the author.

[482] Issues discussed in this paragraph are currently being debated in the American Law Institute. See *Restatement of the Law: Foreign Relations Law of the United States (Revised)* (Tentative Draft no. 5; Philadelphia: American Law Institute, 1984), section 852 and comments and reporters' notes thereon.

[483] See pages 455-458, *supra.*

tinuously since they joined the Fund. Other restrictions on payments and transfers for current international transactions do require the Fund's approval under Article VIII, Sections 2(a) or 3.[484]

There should be no question that measures that require Fund approval under Article VIII, Sections 2(a) or 3, that have been granted that approval, and that are operated in accordance with that approval, are imposed consistently with the Agreement. In granting approval and stating the terms of the approval, the Fund can be expected to consider, and normally does consider, the ramifications of the national measure in relation to the Articles of Agreement seen as a whole, including the purposes set forth in Article I and in Article IV, Section 1. The Executive Board should be made aware, if it is not always aware, that an approval under Section 2(a) or Section 3 may have a present or future impact pursuant to Section 2(b) on litigation in other countries. It should also be aware of the impact of a denial of approval, which means that under Section 2(b) the control is not imposed consistently with the IMF Agreement.

The more troubling problem concerns exchange control regulations, such as capital controls, that do not require approval under Sections 2(a) or 3. Statements by Sir Joseph Gold and by other members of the IMF's Legal Department have stated or implied that such regulations are in all cases consistent with the Agreement.[485] To the extent, however, that the Fund has no jurisdiction over a control, the wisdom of a rule requiring extraterritorial recognition of the control by other IMF members is put in some doubt. The author continues to hold the view that the Fund should not automatically treat such a control as consistent with the Articles. The Fund should in each case—at least where a request is formally made by a judge who must decide an actual case being litigated—make a contemporary assessment of the country's measure in relation to the Articles of Agreement, taking into account both the specific provisions of the IMF Agreement and the purposes stated in Article I and Article IV, Section 1.[486] There is no formal interpretation or general decision of the Fund that bars the procedure recommended here. In a decision concerning a similar phrase in Arti-

---

[484] See pages 389–428, *supra*. Article VII, section 3(b), could provide, in any case in the future to which it is applied, an alternative source of authority for limitations on exchange operations. It has never been invoked.

[485] Joseph Gold, as General Counsel of the IMF, distributed a statement to U.S. courts hearing the Cuban insurance cases that said, "To the extent any controls are confined to capital transfers, they are maintained or imposed consistently with the Fund's Articles of Agreement." The statement is quoted in *Blanco v. Pan American Life Ins. Co.; Federal Supplement*, vol. 221, p. 219 at pp. 224–25 (decided in 1963 by U.S. District Court for Southern District of Florida). See also Gold, *Fund Agreement in the Courts*, *supra* note 49, vol. 2, pp. 79–87, 195–96, and 209–10.

[486] The view was first argued by the author in Edwards, "Extraterritorial Application," *supra* note 165, p. 896. Sir Joseph Gold has pointed out that the Fund has considered freedom to control capital transfers as "something like a fundamental privilege of members." Gold, *Fund Agreement in the Courts*, *supra* note 49, vol. 2, pp. 413–14. The Second Amendment, however, while leaving Article VI, section 3, as it was, introduced language concerning capital movements in Article IV, section 1. Surveillance and consultation under Article IV encompass capital controls. See pages 456–458, *supra*.

cle V, relating to the use of the IMF's financial resources, the Executive Board has stated: "The phrase 'consistent with the provisions of this Agreement' in Article V, Section 3, means consistent both with the provisions of the Fund Agreement other than Article I and with the purposes of the Fund contained in Article I."[487] Considering issues of "consistency" under Article VIII, Section 2(b), in relation to the purposes stated in the Articles as well as specific provisions would be consistent with the increased importance placed by the Second Amendment on obligations of collaboration overarching more narrowly drafted stipulations.[488]

Scope of the Term "Exchange Contracts"

In the absence of an interpretation by the International Monetary Fund of the term "exchange contracts" in Section 2(b), national courts are free within reason to make interpretations of their own. The law in the United Kingdom is set forth in the House of Lords opinion in *United City Merchants (Investments) Ltd. v. Royal Bank of Canada.*[489] There, Lord Diplock, speaking for a unanimous court in 1982, stated:

> My Lords, I accept as correct the narrow interpretation that was placed upon the expression "exchange contracts" in this provision of the Bretton Woods Agreement by the Court of Appeal in *Wilson, Smithett & Cope Ltd. v. Terruzzi* [1976] Q.B. 683. It is confined to contracts to exchange the currency of one country for the currency of another; it does not include contracts entered into in connection with sales of goods which require the conversion by the buyer of one currency into another in order to enable him to pay the purchase price. As was said by Lord Denning M.R. in his judgment in the *Terruzzi* case at p. 714, the court in considering the application of the provision should look at the substance of the contracts and not at the form. It should not enforce a contract that is a mere "monetary transaction in disguise."[490]

---

[487] E.B. Decision No. 287-3 (March 17, 1948); *IMF History 1945–65, supra* note 39, vol. 3, p. 228; *Selected Decisions* (10th issue, 1983), p. 18.

[488] In the author's view, Article VIII, section 2(b), provides authority for the Fund to make determinations of consistency, and independent authority need not be sought in other articles such as Article XIV, section 3. Compare Gold, *Fund Agreement in the Courts, supra* note 49, vol. 2, p. 414.

[489] Decision of May 20, 1982. *Law Reports—Appeal Cases,* 1983, vol. 1, p. 168.

[490] *Idem,* at p. 188.

The British sellers' original quotation for fibre-glass manufacturing equipment to be installed in Peru was half the figure that ultimately became the invoice price for purposes of a documentary letter of credit. The buyers, who were desirous of converting Peruvian currency into U.S. dollars available to them in the United States (a transaction which was contrary to Peruvian exchange control regulations), persuaded the sellers to invoice the equipment to them at double the real sale price in U.S. dollars and to agree that they would, after

The courts in the United States, like the British courts, have tended to take a narrow view of the meaning of "exchange contracts" in Section 2(b).[491] Some courts in other countries have given a wider reading to "exchange contracts" in Section 2(b). They have been encouraged to do so by Sir Joseph Gold, F.A. Mann, Elias Krispis, and others. Sir Joseph has urged that "exchange contracts" should be understood to mean all contracts that provide for international payments or transfers, whether in foreign or domestic currency. This approach attaches the maximum scope to the word "exchange" so as to encompass all contracts that involve movements across "the exchanges," as that term is used by some economists.[492] Dr. Mann has argued that any contract that affects the exchange resources of a member of the International Monetary Fund is an "exchange contract."[493] Elias Krispis has gone even further. He has suggested that the word "exchange" in the term "exchange contracts" was retained by accident when the provision that became Section 2(b) of Article VIII was moved from its original location in Article IV during the drafting process at Bretton Woods. The term, he believes, should be read simply as "contracts."[494]

The District Court (Tribunal d'Arrondissement) of Luxembourg, Civil Division, held in 1956 that a contract for the sale of merchandise was an "exchange contract" within the meaning of Section 2(b).[495] The Federal Supreme Court (Bundesgerichtshof) of the Federal Republic of Germany in 1962 decided

---

drawing upon the documentary credit, remit one-half of the amount so drawn to the dollar account in Miami, Florida, of an American corporation controlled by the Peruvian buyers. The House of Lords held that the letter of credit contract between the Canadian confirming bank and the sellers was enforceable for the original quotation for the equipment but as to the balance was an "exchange contract in disguise" (with the sellers acting as trustees for the buyers) and was unenforceable. For discussion of the case prior to the House of Lords decision, see Gold, *Fund Agreement in the Courts, supra* note 49, vol. 2, pp. 299–303 and 331–53.

[491] The New York Court of Appeals in *Banco Frances e Brasileiro, S.A. v. John Doe* held that transactions in which Brazilian cruzeiros were exchanged for traveler's checks in U. S. dollars based on fraudulent applications submitted to the Brazilian bank were exchange contracts and that rescission of the transactions was a proper remedy. *New York Reports (2d Series),* vol. 36, p. 592 (decided 1975). However, the New York Court of Appeals in *J. Zeevi and Sons, Ltd. v. Grindlays Bank (Uganda) Ltd.* held that a letter of credit issued by a Ugandan bank and providing for payment in U.S. dollars to an Israeli partnership was not an "exchange contract" within the meaning of Article VIII, section 2(b). *New York Reports (2d Series),* vol. 37, p. 220 at pp. 228–29 (decided 1975), certiorari denied *United States Reports,* vol. 423, p. 866 (decided 1975). A United States District Court has held that an international loan agreement that provided for payments in U.S. dollars was not an exchange contract. *Libra Bank Ltd. v. Banco Nacional de Costa Rica; Federal Supplement,* vol. 570, p. 870 (decided by U.S. District Court for Southern District of New York, 1983). The *Banco Frances* and *Zeevi* cases are discussed in Gold, *Fund Agreement in the Courts, supra* note 49, vol. 2, pp. 197–202 and 219–21.

[492] Gold, *Fund Agreement in the Courts, idem,* vol. 2, pp. 214 and 217; and letter of Sir Joseph Gold to the author dated April 6, 1981.

[493] Mann, *Legal Aspect of Money, supra* note 371, pp. 384–91.

[494] Krispis, *supra* note 456, pp. 286–90. See also Williams, "Extraterritorial Enforcement," *supra* note 461, pp. 332–44.

[495] *Société "Filature et Tissage X. Jourdain" c. Epoux. Heynen-Bintner,* decision of February 1, 1956; *Pasicrisie Luxembourgeoise,* vol. 17 (1957–1959), p. 35; *International Law Reports,* vol. 22 (1958), p. 727; discussed in Gold, *Fund Agreement in the Courts, supra* note 49, vol. 1, pp. 94–96.

that a commission contract relating to the refining of maize was an "exchange contract."[496] The Court of Appeal (Cour d'Appel) of Paris in its 1961 decision in *Moojen v. Von Reichert*[497] held that an agreement between a Netherlands resident and a German resident for transfer of shares in a French company was an "exchange contract." The same court in 1970 in *Daiei Motion Picture Co. v. Zavicha*[498] held that a contract between a Japanese motion picture company and its French representative was an "exchange contract." Whether deposit contracts denominated in U.S. dollars between the central bank of Iran and the Paris and London branches of U.S. commercial banks were "exchange contracts" was an issue in Iranian assets litigation in 1979–81.[499]

Meaning to be Given to "Involve the Currency"

The IMF has not interpreted, and only a few court decisions have explicitly interpreted, the phrase "involve the currency" in Article VIII, Section 2(b). Most scholars who have considered the matter have argued for a criterion based on economic considerations: If the exchange resources of a country are affected by the contract, that country's currency is an "involved" currency. F.A. Mann, one of the first to state this position, wrote:

> It is not so much the denomination of a debt in a particular currency that matters, but the prejudicial effect which a transaction may have upon a member's financial position and which, by international cooperation, the members [of the IMF] have attempted to preclude. . . . There is no reason why in a document of this kind, "currency" should not be construed in the broad sense of economics rather than in a strictly legal sense.[500]

---

[496] Decision of April 9, 1962 (not officially reported). Noted with excerpts in *Aussenwirtschaftsdienst des Betriebs-Beraters*, 1962, p. 146; translated in Lowenfeld, *supra* note 456, p. 233; discussed in Gold, *Fund Agreement in the Courts, supra* note 49, vol. 2, pp. 18–21.

[497] Decision of June 20, 1961, Cour d'Appel, Paris (1st Chamber); *Journal du Droit International,* vol. 89 (1962), p. 718 (with translation); *Revue Critique de Droit International Privé,* vol. 51 (1962), p. 67 (with note by Yvon Loussouarn at p. 72). Discussed in Gold, *Fund Agreement in the Courts, supra* note 49, vol. 1, pp. 143–53; and in Joseph Gold and Philine R. Lachman, "The Articles of Agreement of the International Monetary Fund and the Exchange Control Regulations of Member States (A Note on the *Moojen* Decision)," *Journal du Droit International,* vol. 89 (1962), p. 666.

[498] Decision of May 14, 1970, Cour d'Appel, Paris (4th Chamber), appeal rejected March 7, 1972, Cour de Cassation (civil, commercial); *Juris-Classer Périodique,* 1971, part 2, p. 16,751; *Revue Critique de Droit International Privé,* vol. 63 (1974), p. 486 (with note by Jean-Pierre Eck at p. 492). Discussed in Gold, *Fund Agreement in the Courts, supra* note 49, vol. 2, pp. 190–97.

[499] See, e.g., Edwards, "Extraterritorial Application," *supra* note 165, pp. 888–89; and Gold, *Fund Agreement in the Courts, supra* note 49, vol. 2, pp. 393–95.

[500] F.A. Mann, "Der Internationale Währungsfonds und das Internationale Privatrecht," *Juristenzeitung* (Tübingen), vol. 8 (1953), p. 442 at p. 444, translated and quoted with approval in Gold, *Fund Agreement in the Courts, supra* note 49, vol. 1, pp. 92–93. See also Mann, *Legal Aspect of Money, supra* note 371, pp. 391–92. While Dr. Mann in the quotation mentions a "prejudicial effect" on a country's financial position as the rationale for the interpretation, Sir Joseph Gold and others who prefer the "effect on exchange resources"

Under this definition, the assets and liabilities of a resident of a country are attributed to the country itself. The transfer of any asset from a resident to a nonresident affects the resources of both countries of residency. Sir Joseph Gold has stated that he supports an economically oriented interpretation. In his view, the basic test for determining whether a particular country's currency is "involved" in the transfer of an asset to or from a nonresident is "whether the contract is entered into by a resident of that member [country] or deals with assets situated within the member's territory."[501] John S. Williams, François Gianviti, and other scholars have accepted the interpretation recommended by Dr. Mann and Sir Joseph.[502]

Among cases cited in support of this definition are the decisions by the Court of Appeal of Paris in *Moojen*[503] *and Zavicha.*[504] The Court of Appeal in *Moojen* refused to enforce a Dutch resident's assignment of shares in a French corporation to a German resident with payment in French francs. The court gave as one of the reasons for its decision that the contract violated Dutch exchange control regulations. The Court of Appeal in *Zavicha* in dicta assumed that a contract between a Japanese motion picture company and its French representative providing that he would be paid in French francs for work in France involved the currency of Japan.[505]

The New York courts have rejected the "effect on exchange resources" criterion in favor of a narrower reading of "involve the currency." The New York Court of Appeals in the *Zeevi* case in 1975 said that it "frowned on an interpretation of said provision [Article VIII, Section 2(b)] of the Bretton Woods Agreement which 'sweeps in all contracts affecting any member's exchange resources as doing considerable violence to the text of the section.'"[506]

When the Second Amendment to the IMF Articles was being negotiated, John S. Williams as an interested scholar recommended that the first sentence of Section 2(b) be amended to read (bracketed words to be deleted; italicized words to be added): "[Exchange] contracts which [involve the currency] *affect the exchange resources* of any member and which are contrary to the exchange control regulations of that member maintained or imposed consistently with this Agreement shall be unenforceable in the territories of any member."[507] U.S.

---

criterion do not require prejudicial effects. The effects may be negative or positive. Letter of Sir Joseph Gold to the author, dated April 6, 1981.

[501] Gold, *Fund Agreement in the Courts, supra* note 49, vol. 2, pp. 70 and 76. See also *idem,* pp. 263–64 and 281–82.

[502] Williams, "Extraterritorial Enforcement," *supra* note 461, pp. 345–51; and Gianviti, "Le Blocage," *supra* note 461, pp. 283–86.

[503] See text and sources cited at note 497, *supra.*

[504] See text and sources cited at note 498, *supra.*

[505] Although the court denied the French representative-plaintiff relief on a contractual theory because of Article VIII, section 2(b), it granted relief on a tort theory.

[506] *New York Reports (2d Series),* vol. 37, at p. 229. See note 491, *supra.* The court quoted from its 1963 opinion in *Banco do Brasil, S.A. v. A.C. Israel Commodity Co.,* cited and discussed in note 466, *supra.*

[507] Williams, "Extraterritorial Enforcement," *supra* note 461, p. 395.

officials were approached with this proposal and declined to support it. Changes in Section 2(b) were of less importance to them than other changes in the Articles of Agreement. Also, U.S. policy at the time favored freedom for international transactions and liberalization of exchange controls.

The author is one of the few persons who recommend a broad reading of "exchange contracts" to encompass all contracts, but a restrictive reading of "involve the currency." The following criterion is recommended: A currency is involved if the contract (a) contains an express or implied term providing for that currency to be the currency of payment, or (b) the payment or transfer of that currency is *in fact* necessary to the performance of the contract.[508] To give an example: A contract between an Italian speculator and a British metals broker providing for payment in sterling would be enforceable in England by the British broker (notwithstanding Italian regulations prohibiting such dealings) to the extent that the Italian resident has assets in England that could be applied to satisfy his obligation. If it were necessary in fact for the Italian to exchange lire for sterling to meet his obligation, the contract would to that extent involve the currency of Italy.[509]

The understanding of "involves the currency" recommended here adheres more closely to the text of Section 2(b) than the "exchange resources" criterion. It is also believed to be closer to the expectations of bankers and others

---

[508] This view of the scope of "involve the currency" is consistent with the results of most of the decided cases, if not with their stated rationales. The *United City Merchants* case involved Peruvian currency, although that currency was not named in the sales contract or letter of credit, because the British seller was on notice that the Peruvian importer would use the fraudulent invoice in a scheme to exchange Peruvian sols for U.S. dollars. The case is discussed in notes 489 and 490, *supra*, and accompanying text. Although the court in *Moojen*, note 497, gave as one of its reasons for denying enforcement of the contract that the Dutch party had violated Dutch exchange control regulations, the French court's decision can be fully explained by the failure of the Netherlands resident to obtain the necessary *French* approval for the transaction. *Journal du Droit International*, vol. 89, at pp. 726–27; *Revue Critique de Droit International Privé*, vol. 51, at p. 72. See also Gold and Lachman, *supra* note 497, pp. 680–83.

The German Federal Supreme Court (Bundesgerichtshof) has repeatedly stated that "effect on exchange resources" is the criterion of whether a country's currency is "involved." However, the Supreme Court in a 1976 decision pointed out that in each case where the Court had applied IMF Article VIII, section 2(b), to deny enforcement of a contract, the case involved assets sited in the prohibition country or a claim against a resident of the prohibition country. The Court was of the opinion that even if the defendant is a resident of the prohibition country, section 2(b) does not apply if the claim can be satisfied from the defendant's assets outside the prohibition country. The practice of the German courts appears consistent with the position recommended here. Decision of December 21, 1976 (not officially reported). Noted in *Wertpapier-Mitteilungen: Zeitschrift für Wirtschafts und Bankrecht*, vol. 31 (1977), p. 332, discussed in Gold, *Fund Agreement in the Courts*, *supra* note 49, vol. 2, pp. 272–77.

[509] Compare the facts in *Wilson, Smithett & Cope Ltd. v. Terruzzi*, cited and quoted in Lord Diplock's statement in *United City Merchants*, *supra*, page 484. The Supreme Court of Italy refused to enforce the British judgment against Terruzzi in Italy. Decision of the Corte Suprema di Cassazione of July 2, 1981. *Rivista di Diritto Iternazionale Privato e Processuale*, vol. 18 (1982), p. 107. For the intermediate appellate court decision, see *idem*, vol. 15 (1979), p. 271.

The position advocated in the text is also consistent with the majority opinion and dissent (which took different views of the facts) in the New York Court of Appeals 1982 decision in *Weston Banking Corp. v. Turkiye Garanti Bankasi; New York Reports (2d Series)*, vol. 57, p. 315 at pp. 325–26 and 332.

engaging in international transactions, while still providing a significant measure of respect to foreign exchange control regulations.

With regard to the first prong of the recommended test, whether a contract contains an express or implied term providing for payment in a particular currency, or only names a currency for purposes of denominating value, is a question regarding the interpretation of the particular contract. As to the second prong of the test, whether it is necessary in fact to use a particular currency in order to perform the contract is to be determined on the facts of each case. Customary banking and clearing practices are relevant in considering what is in fact necessary but are not necessarily decisive.

Whether deposit contracts denominated in U.S. dollars of government central banks with overseas branches of U.S. commercial banks (Eurodollar deposit contracts)[510] involve the currency of the United States was an issue much debated in the context of the *Bank Markazi Iran* cases in 1979–81.[511] On the one hand, it was argued that Eurodollar deposits are not a subcategory of U.S. dollars but an independent category. It was pointed out in support of this view that the deposit contracts, although denominated in U.S. dollars for purposes of valuation, were instruments of the commercial banks' own creation, were not subject to monetary regulation of U.S. authorities with respect to reserves and interest rates, and did not require the banks to make payments in the United States.[512]

On the other hand, it was argued that, under customary banking practice, transfers from the Eurodollar accounts were made through the New York Clearing House Interbank Payment System (CHIPS), that Bank Markazi Iran knew of this practice and had concurred in it, and as a practical matter it was not possible to transfer large deposits except through use of the New York clearing system or otherwise through accounts sited in the United States.[513] Under the second prong of the test recommended by the author, whether the use of accounts sited in the United States would be necessary for transfer of the large Eurodollar deposits would be determinative of whether the U.S. dollar was "involved" within the meaning of Section 2(b). The cases never went to judgment.[514]

Conclusion

It is well to bear in mind that all of the purposes of the IMF Agreement should be taken into account when Article VIII, Section 2(b), is interpreted and ap-

---

[510] See explanation of Eurocurrency deposits in Appendix A of this book at pages 679–682.

[511] See note 467, *supra,* and accompanying text.

[512] See Edwards, "Extraterritorial Application," *supra* note 165, pp. 879–80 and 892–93, where the allegations and arguments are explained. See also Gianviti, "Le Blocage," *supra* note 461, p. 287.

[513] See Edwards, "Extraterritorial Application," *supra* note 165, pp. 877–79 and 893.

[514] The courts in both France and the United Kingdom attached great importance to the factual allegations regarding clearing arrangements. *Idem,* pp. 876–81 and 889–96. The clearing arrangements are explained in the sources cited in Appendix A, *infra,* page 682 (note 55).

plied. An essential purpose of the international monetary system is to provide a framework that facilitates the exchange of goods, services, and capital.[515] Section 2(b), which requires respect for other countries' exchange controls, should be seen as a reasonable derogation from the basic principle that contracts are to be enforced in accordance with the expectations of the parties to them. The principle of mutual respect of other countries' laws that underlies Section 2(b) requires that the duty of a country to recognize another country's currency controls be balanced by a duty of the latter to act reasonably in the use of controls. The Fund's jurisdiction over controls of its members provides the best rationale for requiring recognition of those controls. That jurisdiction should be thoughtfully exercised. A decision by a country that its currency shall be free from restrictions also deserves respect by other countries. The language of Section 2(b) is not all-encompassing. The section has important, but limited, applications. Where difficulties in the application of Section 2(b) arise, the Fund's assistance can be sought.[516]

Chapter Conclusion

It is perhaps unfortunate that the persons involved in negotiating the Second Amendment of the Articles of Agreement of the International Monetary Fund made no concentrated effort to deal with exchange controls. Apparently they believed that Articles VI, VIII, and XIV have worked reasonably well. The Second Amendment simply brings the texts into accord with past practice. The only significant changes are the recognition in Article IV, Section 1, that the international monetary system should facilitate capital movements and the express provisions in that article concerning consultation and collaboration.

Procedures and rules for the multilateral liberalization of capital movements have been developed and applied within the Organisation for Economic Co-operation and Development and the European Economic Community. The terms of Article IV of the IMF Agreement should dispel any claim that the International Monetary Fund lacks jurisdiction to foster collaboration to liberalize capital movements. The IMF's authority to prescribe specific rules respecting the liberalization of capital controls, however, is limited by Article VI.

The internationally agreed legal rules applicable to exchange controls have been surveyed in this chapter. The consultation procedures used by international organizations, in the review of exchange controls and with respect to other matters, receive further attention in Chapter 12.

---

[515] Article IV, section 1.

[516] E.B. Decision No. 446-4, *supra* note 98, explicitly states that the Fund will lend its assistance to members in connection with problems that arise under section 2(b) or under the interpretation given in that decision.

Chapter 11: Exchange Rate Regime

Introduction

The legal regime applicable to exchange rate determination was briefly outlined in Chapter 1.[1] A detailed examination was postponed until this point in order that the reader first understand exchange controls, the composition and use of monetary reserves, the means available to national authorities to finance balance-of-payments deficits, and the legal rules surrounding the special drawing right.[2]

Our discussion will proceed as follows. Legal aspects of the operation of the Bretton Woods exchange rate system in the period 1945–71 and the collapse of that system in 1971–73 will be briefly reviewed. Historical highlights in the negotiation of present Article IV and Schedule C will be recounted. Then we shall turn to an exegesis of the provisions of Article IV. Various types of exchange rate arrangements will be treated from a legal perspective. This will be followed by an examination of the par value system that would be introduced by Schedule C should that schedule ever be applied. Our attention will then turn to surveillance procedures and collaboration obligations. The chapter concludes with some general observations.

Collapse of the Bretton Woods System

The original Articles of Agreement of the International Monetary Fund, agreed at Bretton Woods in 1944, established a system of exchange rates based on par values.[3] Each IMF member was required to state a par value of its currency in

---

[1] See pages 18–19, *supra.* The texts of Article IV and Schedule C appear in Appendix B of this volume at pages 697–699 and 748–749.

[2] An earlier version of portions of this chapter was published under the title "The Currency Exchange Rate Provisions of the Proposed Amended Articles of Agreement of the International Monetary Fund," *American Journal of International Law,* vol. 70 (1976), p. 722.

[3] The original text of Article IV appears in J. Keith Horsefield and Margaret Garritsen de Vries, *The International Monetary Fund, 1945–1965: Twenty Years of International Monetary Cooperation* (3 vols.; Washington: IMF, 1969) [hereinafter cited *IMF History 1945–65*], vol. 3, pp. 189–91. The text of Article IV

terms of gold or the U.S. dollar of the gold weight and fineness in effect in 1944.[4] From the time the original Articles entered into force until August 15, 1971, the U.S. authorities declared their readiness to buy and sell gold in transactions with foreign monetary authorities, on their demand, at prices based on $35 an ounce.[5] The U.S. dollar at the time the Bretton Woods Agreement was negotiated was the most widely used currency in international transactions and was subject to fewer restrictions than any other major currency.

Each IMF member was required to assure that spot transactions taking place in its territory involving the exchange of its currency for a foreign currency took place at rates at or close to the parity relationships of the currencies involved.[6]

The par value of a currency could, with the concurrence of the Fund, be changed to correct a fundamental disequilibrium in a state's balance of payments.[7] "Fundamental disequilibrium" was not defined in the Articles, but the practice of the Fund gave the words meaning.[8] Changes in the par value of a

following amendments to sections 7 and 8 effective July 28, 1969, appears in Margaret Garritsen de Vries, *The International Monetary Fund, 1966–1971: The System Under Stress* (2 vols.; Washington: IMF, 1976) [hereinafter *IMF History 1966–71*], vol. 2, pp. 99–101. See generally Joseph Gold, "Legal Structure of Par Value System Before Second Amendment," in Joseph Gold, *Legal and Institutional Aspects of the International Monetary System: Selected Essays* (Washington: IMF, 1979) [hereinafter *Selected Essays*], p. 520; Joseph Gold, "Developments in the International Monetary System, the International Monetary Fund, and International Monetary Law Since 1971," in Hague Academy of International Law, *Recueil des Cours*, vol. 174 (1982–I) [hereinafter "Hague Lectures"], p. 107 at pp. 174–92; Kenneth W. Dam, *The Rules of the Game: Reform and Evolution in the International Monetary System* (Chicago: University of Chicago Press, 1982), pp. 88–98, 128–33, and 175–92; IMF, "The Role of Exchange Rates in the Adjustment of International Payments: A Report by the Executive Directors" (1970), reprinted in *IMF History 1966–71*, vol. 2, p. 273; and Stephen A. Silard, "Money and Foreign Exchange," *International Encyclopedia of Comparative Law* (Tübingen: J.C.B. Mohr; The Hague: Mouton, 1975), vol. 17, chapter 20, sections 101–22.

All par values were officially abrogated when the Second Amendment to the IMF Articles of Agreement entered into force April 1, 1978.

[4] Old Article IV, section 1, *original* and *first*.

[5] See Chapter 3, *supra*, pages 115–119 and note 61. See also Gold, "Hague Lectures," *supra* note 3, pp. 180–85.

[6] Old Article IV, sections 3 and 4(b), *original* and *first*, provided that the maximum and minimum rates for exchange transactions between currencies of IMF members taking place within their territories should in the case of spot transactions not differ from parity by more than ±1 percent. An Executive Board decision stated that the Fund would not object to exchange rates which were within 2 percent of parity for spot transactions between a member's currency and the currencies of other members when the rates resulted from maintenance of margins of no more than 1 percent from parity for a convertible currency. E.B. Decision No. 904 -(59/32)(July 24, 1959); *IMF History 1945–65, supra* note 3, vol. 3, p. 226. See Gold, "Legal Structure of Par Value System," *supra* note 3, pp. 542–56.

The U.S. readiness to buy and sell gold at the request of foreign monetary authorities on the basis of the par value of the dollar, and within margins prescribed by the IMF, was deemed to satisfy the maintenance of parity obligation. The United States thus was not required to buy and sell foreign currencies in the market. Old Article IV, section 4(b), *original* and *first*.

[7] Section 5(a) of old Article IV, *original* and *first*, provided: "A member shall not propose a change in the par value of its currency except to correct a fundamental disequilibrium." The remainder of Section 5 established procedures whereby the Fund would concur in or object to the change.

[8] See IMF, "Role of Exchange Rates in the Adjustment of International Payments," *supra* note 3, pp.

currency were expected to be infrequent. If a member could correct a disequilibrium by techniques other than a change in exchange rates, the other measures if consistent with the Articles were generally to be preferred. The Fund encouraged members to adopt stabilization programs involving, for example, controls of government budget deficits, price and wage inflation, and the size of the domestic money supply.[9]

The system sketched above was not uniformly adhered to. A significant number of IMF members, mostly developing countries, never established par values for their currencies. Some countries did not consistently maintain market exchange rates within prescribed margins.[10] This lack of conformity, when engaged in by developing countries and smaller industrial countries, did not place severe strains on the par value system as a whole because the impact of the actions was not wide. However, strains on the parity relationships among currencies of the larger industrial countries ultimately led to the collapse of the Bretton Woods par value system. Inevitably we paint with a broad brush in the historical summary that follows, and many matters are not touched.[11]

The Fund in September 1949 concurred in a devaluation of a group of European currencies, most devaluations being by 30.5 percent. The first phase of European reconstruction after World War II financed by the Marshall Plan was then drawing to a close. The importation into Europe of American-made capital goods at the lowest cost in foreign exchange was no longer the critical feature in trade relations. In 1949 there was a need to open export markets for the manufactures of a reconstructed European industry. The devaluations were carefully orchestrated within the Organisation for European Economic Co-operation (OEEC) and the IMF.[12]

France made an unauthorized change in par value in 1948. Canada floated its currency for an extended period during the 1950s; that is, it let rates be determined by market forces without substantial governmental intervention in the market. Some other countries floated their currencies for brief periods before establishing new par values. These countries were the exception. Most major countries adhered to their Article IV obligations, and few strains were placed on the par value system until the 1960s.[13]

When the United Kingdom pound sterling, the French franc, the Deutsche

---

307-11 and 322-27; Gold, "Legal Structure of Par Value System," *supra* note 3, pp. 524-41; and Gold, "Hague Lectures," *supra* note 3, pp. 190-92.

[9] See IMF, "Role of Exchange Rates," *supra* note 3, p. 309.

[10] *Idem*, p. 292.

[11] See, e.g., the chronology of events, including the more important par value changes, in the period 1966-71, in *IMF History 1966-71, supra* note 3, pp. xviii-xxii.

[12] See *IMF History 1945-65, supra* note 3, vol. 1, pp. 234-42, and vol. 2, pp. 96-100; *Foreign Relations of the United States* (Washington: U.S. Government Printing Office), 1949, vol. 4 (1975), pp. 377-421 and 781-852; and Frank A. Southard, Jr., *The Evolution of the International Monetary Fund* (Essays in International Finance no. 135; Princeton: Princeton University International Finance Section, 1979), pp. 25-26.

[13] See Joseph Gold, "Unauthorized Changes of Par Value and Fluctuating Exchange Rates in the Bretton Woods System," *American Journal of International Law,* vol. 65 (1971), p. 113.

mark, and other major currencies became convertible, and restrictions on capital movements were reduced,[14] strains began to develop in the par value system. During the 1960s a number of widely used currencies were devalued or revalued. The Deutsche mark and Netherlands guilder were revalued upward by their governments in 1961. The U.K. pound sterling was devalued in 1967. The French franc was devalued and the Deutsche mark revalued in 1969. A number of changes in par values were made for other currencies. The magnitude and timing of some of these changes were significantly affected by political as well as economic considerations.[15]

The 1967 devaluation of the pound sterling, long anticipated but ultimately engineered in a crisis atmosphere, evidenced the strains that had developed in the Bretton Woods system of stable exchange rates. As early as 1964 it had become clear that the United Kingdom faced serious balance-of-payments problems. Credits were obtained from abroad and internal policy changes were made in the hope that devaluation could be avoided. The techniques chosen were not adequate to turn the tide. A payments crisis occurred in the fall of 1967. Efforts were made by some of Britain's Group of Ten partners to arrange a package of credits to head off a decision to devalue. In the end U.K. authorities saw no viable alternative to devaluation, and a devaluation amounting to 14.3 percent was announced November 18, 1967.[16] Many countries at the time held sterling in their reserves, and the devaluation demonstrated the risks of holders relying on the stability of par values.[17]

As the 1960s progressed, because of the costs of the war in Vietnam, an ambitious social program directed to problems of poverty in the United States, changes in the world economy, and other causes, the U.S. balance-of-payments position deteriorated.[18] A variety of techniques were used by U.S. authorities

---

[14] The following European countries accepted the convertibility obligations of sections 2, 3, and 4 of Article VIII of the IMF Agreement effective February 15, 1961: Belgium, France, Federal Republic of Germany, Ireland, Italy, Luxembourg, the Netherlands, Sweden, and the United Kingdom. Japan and a number of other countries subsequently accepted the obligations of Article VIII. During the 1960s members of the Organisation for Economic Co-operation and Development (OECD) and other countries also reduced restrictions on capital movements. See Chapter 10, *supra*, pages 402–403 and 460–465.

[15] See sources cited in note 16, *infra*.

[16] Although a definitive decision to devalue sterling was not communicated to other governments until the weekend of its announcement, the possibility and likelihood of a devaluation, and its magnitude, were discussed with other governments and within the Bank for International Settlements the preceding weekend. The seriousness of Britain's problems was well known and had been the subject of consultations over a long period.

The sterling devaluation and other par value changes are studied from a lawyer's perspective in Andreas F. Lowenfeld, *The International Monetary System* (1st ed.; New York: Matthew Bender, 1977), pp. 45–124. See also *IMF History 1945–65, supra* note 3, vol. 2, chapters 3–9; *IMF History 1966–71, supra* note 3, vol. 1, chapters 21–24; Dam, *supra* note 3, pp. 179–85; and Southard, *supra* note 12, pp. 29–36.

[17] See discussion of sterling guarantees in Chapter 3, *supra*, pages 104–107.

[18] See generally Robert Solomon, *The International Monetary System, 1945–1981* (New York: Harper & Row, 1982), chapters 3–11. See also *IMF History 1966–71, supra* note 3, vol. 1, chapters 24 and 25; Charles A. Coombs, *The Arena of International Finance* (New York: John Wiley & Sons, 1976), chapters 8–11; and Susan Strange, "International Monetary Relations," in Andrew Shonfield (ed.), *International Economic Re-*

and their colleagues abroad to counter downward pressure on the dollar in the exchange markets. These included introduction of a two-tier gold market,[19] interventions in exchange markets financed by drawings on currency swap arrangements between central banks,[20] and controls on capital movements including the U.S. interest equalization tax and controls on the financing of foreign investment by U.S. residents.[21]

A series of dramatic events began in the spring of 1971. In April the Council of Ministers of the European Communities debated whether the members of the EEC should take a united stand favoring a higher official price for gold, which was understood to mean a devaluation of the dollar. News of the debate leaked out.[22] In May, in response to heavy buying of Deutsche mark and Netherlands guilders, the issuing authorities allowed the two currencies to float upward in the exchange markets. That is, the monetary authorities of the two countries allowed exchange rates for their currencies to be determined by supply and demand; the authorities did not intervene in the markets to maintain stable rates for their currencies as then required by the IMF Articles.[23] Following these actions the Council of the European Communities on May 9, 1971, adopted a resolution which in substance decided that the Federal Republic of Germany, the Netherlands, and Belgium should not raise the par values of their currencies and that instead the United States should be forced to devalue.[24]

In a lengthy meeting on May 17 between the Managing Director of the IMF, Pierre-Paul Schweitzer, and the U.S. Secretary of the Treasury, John B. Connally, Mr. Schweitzer urged with diplomatic circumlocution that the United States should consider a devaluation of the dollar. Mr. Connally rebuffed the suggestion and, thereafter until August 15, declined to meet with Mr. Schweitzer.[25] There were negotiations in the summer about the possible

---

lations of the Western World 1959–71 (2 vols.; London: Oxford University Press for Royal Institute of International Affairs, 1976), vol. 2, chapters 9 and 11.

[19] See Chapter 3, *supra,* pages 117–118.

[20] See Chapter 4, *supra,* page 135 et seq.

[21] See Chapter 10, *supra,* pages 450–451 (notes 327, 328, and 331).

[22] *Washington Post,* April 28, 1971, p. A-19. For information on previous contingency planning in the United States, see John S. Odell, *U.S. International Monetary Policy: Markets, Power, and Ideas as Sources of Change* (Princeton: Princeton University Press, 1982), pp. 250–51; and Joseph Gold, "Strengthening the Soft International Law of Exchange Arrangements," *American Journal of International Law,* vol. 77 (1983), p. 443 at pp. 448–49.

[23] See *IMF History 1966–71, supra* note 3, vol. 1, pp. 519–26; Southard, *supra* note 12, p. 37; and "Anatomy of an International Monetary Crisis," in Federal Reserve Bank of Chicago, *Business Conditions,* May 1971, p. 12. Belgium-Luxembourg allowed rates in their separate market for certain capital transactions to move upward. Switzerland and Austria promptly raised the par values of their currencies by 7.07 percent and 5.05 percent respectively. See also Chapter 1, *supra,* page 41–42.

[24] Council of Ministers Resolution of May 9, 1971, on the monetary situation; *Official Journal of the European Communities,* no. C-58, May 10, 1971, p. 1; reprinted in European Communities, *Compendium of Community Monetary Texts* (Luxembourg, 1974), p. 55. See also Richard Norton-Taylor, "Currency Crisis Strains Solidarity," *European Community,* no. 146 (June 1971), p. 12; and Solomon, *supra* note 18, pp. 178–80.

[25] The other persons present were Frank A. Southard, Jr. (Deputy Managing Director of the IMF),

revaluation of the Deutsche mark, but the mark was not revalued.[26] While the refusal of senior U.S. officials to consider a devaluation can be ascribed in part to obstinacy, there was genuine concern that, if the United States did devalue, other countries would follow it down. The net result would be a higher price for gold, but the U.S. payments situation would not be improved. There was also concern that a devaluation of the currency at the center of the par value system would ultimately destabilize the system as a whole.[27]

A congressional report issued August 6, 1971, after reviewing the U.S. balance-of-payments position, stated that "the United States may have no choice but to take unilateral action to go off gold and establish new dollar parities."[28] This looked like a tip straight from the horse's mouth. The outflow of dollars in the first half of August reached enormous proportions, and the activities in the exchange markets drew daily headlines in the newspapers. In the second week of August the British ambassador appeared at the U.S. Treasury Department to ask that the United Kingdom's official dollar holdings, amounting to some $3 billion, be converted into gold (or be given a gold value guarantee); the U.S. Secretary of the Treasury deferred an answer.[29] President Richard M. Nixon and Secretary Connally were convinced that it was no longer possible to promise to convert the dollar into gold at the fixed price and at the same time prevent that promise from being fully tested. The President called a high-level meeting of his advisors on August 13.[30]

On August 15 in a dramatic radio and television broadcast the President announced a series of economic decisions. The United States would "suspend temporarily the convertibility of the dollar into gold or other reserve assets."

Jacques J. Polak (Economic Counselor of the IMF), and Paul A. Volcker (U.S. Under Secretary of the Treasury). See the account of the meeting in Southard, *supra* note 12, pp. 37–38.

It is widely believed, although never officially confirmed, that efforts of Mr. Schweitzer during 1970 and 1971 to persuade the U.S. authorities to devalue the dollar led the United States to oppose his reappointment as Managing Director. He was not reappointed when his term came up for renewal in 1973. See Solomon, *supra* note 18, pp. 176–77, 189–90, and 225.

[26] See *Minutes of Federal Open Market Committee* (described in Chapter 4, page 137, note 31), 1971, pp. 716–20 and 726.

[27] See Dam, *supra* note 3, pp. 188–89.

[28] *Action Now to Strengthen the U.S. Dollar: Report of the Subcommittee on International Exchange and Payments of the Joint Economic Committee*, U.S. Congress, 92d Congress, 1st Session (1971), pp. 13–14.

[29] See Richard M. Nixon, *R.N.: The Memoirs of Richard Nixon* (New York: Grosset & Dunlap, 1978), p. 518; and William Safire, *Before the Fall: An Inside View of the Pre-Watergate White House* (Garden City: Doubleday & Co., 1975), pp. 512 and 514.

The Federal Reserve System on August 13 entered into a swap transaction with the Bank of England that had the effect of providing the Bank of England with an exchange guarantee against a devaluation of the U.S. dollar for 750 million of U.S. dollars acquired by the Bank of England subsequent to August 1, although the British authorities wanted a guarantee for a larger portion of their dollar holdings. During the first two weeks of August the Federal Reserve also entered into large swap transactions to guarantee portions of dollar balances acquired by other central banks in their market interventions. See Chapter 4, *supra*, pages 160–161 (and sources there cited) and generally page 135 et seq.

[30] See Nixon, *supra* note 29, pp. 518–20; Safire, *supra* note 29, pp. 509–28; and Odell, *supra* note 22, pp. 251–71.

Further, as explained by the Secretary of the Treasury, the United States would not buy or sell foreign currencies in the exchange markets for the purpose of maintaining official parities between the dollar and other currencies.[31] The United States also imposed an import tariff surcharge.[32] And, domestic stabilization measures, including a wage–price freeze and a cutback in government spending, were announced. The decision of the United States to suspend the dollar's convertibility into gold was not vented with foreign officials or with the Managing Director of the IMF before it was finalized.[33]

Subsequent to the U.S. announcement, a number of countries stated that they would not necessarily maintain exchange rates within the required 1 percent of parity. Not only did rates between some widely traded currencies and the dollar float, but the movements in the market were often different for one currency compared to another, with the result that floating cross-rates developed.[34]

The United States was not legally obligated under the IMF Agreement, strictly construed, to freely buy and sell gold in exchange for dollars, and its rescission of that practice was not a breach of the verbal terms of the Agreement. However, other countries had relied on the U.S. practice which had come to be seen as a fundamental principle of the Bretton Woods system. Regardless of the legality or illegality of "closing the gold window," if the United States did not in fact freely buy and sell gold on demand of foreign monetary authorities, then it was obligated, like any other IMF member, to intervene in the exchange markets to maintain rates within the required margins of the parity relationships. By failing to do that, it placed itself in violation of Article IV as it then stood. Other

[31] President's Radio and Television Address to the Nation Outlining a New Economic Policy for the United States, August 15, 1971, in *Weekly Compilation of Presidential Documents*, vol. 7 (1971), p. 1168 at p. 1170; and press conference of John B. Connally, U.S. Secretary of the Treasury, August 15, 1971, in *New York Times*, August 17, 1971, p. 16.

The story of the events surrounding President Nixon's announcement and the negotiations in the fall of 1971 that culminated in the Smithsonian agreement of December 1971 is told, with some variations in the telling, in *IMF History 1966–71, supra* note 3, vol. 1, chapters 24–27; Solomon, *supra* note 18, chapters 11 and 12; Coombs, *supra* note 18, chapter 12; Odell, *supra* note 22, chapter 4; Lowenfeld, *supra* note 16, pp. 124–68; Southard, *supra* note 12, pp. 39–42; Dam, *supra* note 3, pp. 189–92; and *Minutes of Federal Open Market Committee, supra* note 26, 1971, pp. 802–39, 924–31, 1018–30, 1092–1121, 1185–99, and 1277–80.

[32] See Chapter 10, *supra*, pages 434–435.

[33] See Southard, *supra* note 12, pp. 38–39.

[34] The exchange markets in Western Europe, except for that in Zurich, were closed the full week of August 16. The market in Tokyo remained open and the Bank of Japan continued to buy dollars (taking in about $2.5 billion) to maintain yen–dollar rates within prescribed margins. When the markets reopened on August 23, Austria, Belgium, Denmark, Italy, Japan, the United Kingdom, and a number of other countries announced that they would not necessarily maintain exchange dealings within 1 percent of parity. The Netherlands and the Federal Republic of Germany announced that their currencies, floating since May, would continue to float. Canada continued to float its currency. France introduced a system of dual exchange markets in which capital and current transactions were separated. Many countries, particularly developing countries, continued to conduct exchange transactions on the basis of official parities. *International Financial News Survey*, vol. 23 (1971), pp. 261–62 and 269–70; and *IMF History 1966–71, supra* note 3, vol. 1, pp. 541–43.

countries that did not intervene to maintain rates were also in violation of the article.[35] The United States in its August 1971 communication to the IMF did state that it would "continue to collaborate with the Fund to promote exchange stability, to maintain orderly exchange arrangements with other members, and to avoid competitive exchange alterations."[36] The Fund's formal response was to note in diplomatic language that the United States was not fulfilling its maintenance-of-parity obligation and that the Managing Director would take appropriate initiatives toward achievement of a "viable structure of exchange rates."[37] Negotiations during the fall looking toward new parities took place primarily within the Group of Ten and not the IMF.[38]

In December 1971, at a meeting at the Smithsonian Institution in Washington, agreement was reached in the Group of Ten on the realignment of the exchange rates for the participants' currencies. The realignment would be accomplished by a devaluation of the dollar by 7.89 percent in relation to gold. Italy and Sweden agreed to establish central rates for their currencies that represented a 1 percent reduction in their values in relation to gold. The par values of the French franc and British pound sterling would remain unchanged. Belgium, the Federal Republic of Germany, Japan, and the Netherlands agreed to establish central rates that represented upward adjustments in the values of their currencies in relation to gold. Canada would continue to float its dollar.[39] As a consequence of the realignment of exchange rates among the Group of Ten, other countries made changes in the official rates for their currencies. No country (including the United States) committed itself to convert its currency into gold at the new rate.

Because the change in the par value of the dollar entailed delay pending congressional action, it was agreed that central rates would be used temporarily by those countries that would later be making par value changes, in order that the agreed exchange rates could be put into immediate effect. A "central rate" was a stable rate (stated in terms of gold, the special drawing right, or a foreign currency) on the basis of which rates for exchange transactions would be mai-

---

[35] See Gold, "Legal Structure of Par Value System," *supra* note 3, pp. 547–49 and 556–57. See also Joseph Gold, *Use, Conversion, and Exchange of Currency Under the Second Amendment of the Fund's Articles* (IMF Pamphlet Series no. 23; Washington, 1978), pp. 38–43; and Gold, "Hague Lectures," *supra* note 3, pp. 180–85.

[36] The quoted phrase from the letter of the U.S. Secretary of the Treasury to the IMF Managing Director tracks old Article IV, section 4(a), *original* and *first*, set out and discussed at page 508, *infra*. Part of the letter appears in *IMF History 1966–71, supra* note 3, vol. 1, p. 533.

[37] See *IMF History 1966–71, idem*, vol. 1, pp. 527–34, especially pp. 533–34.

[38] See sources cited in note 31, *supra*.

[39] See Communiqué of the Ministerial Meeting of the Group of Ten issued December 18, 1971, in *International Financial News Survey*, vol. 23 (1971), p. 417; *Senate Report No. 92-678 on S. 3160 [Modification in Par Value of the Dollar]*, 92d Congress, 2d Session (1972), p. 4; and *IMF History 1966–71, supra* note 3, vol. 1, pp. 553–56. The United States also terminated the import tariff surcharge it had imposed (Chapter 10, *supra*, pages 434–435).

tained pending par value changes. The Executive Board of the IMF gave effect to the understandings worked out in the Group of Ten.[40]

The realignment of exchange rates in December 1971 did not fully correct the balance-of-payments problems of the United States and it aggravated the payments position of the United Kingdom. In June 1972, when the pound came under pressure in the exchange markets, the British authorities announced that sterling would float "as a temporary measure."[41] In January 1973 Italy, troubled by downward pressure on the lira in the exchange markets, abandoned efforts to maintain a stable rate for capital transactions. Downward pressure then developed on the U.S. dollar. Following rapid consultations, the United States in February 1973 announced its intention to devalue the dollar a second time.[42] Despite the U.S. announcement, massive transactions continued to take place in the exchange markets in anticipation of further changes in exchange rates. Following intense consultations the European Economic Community and the Group of Ten jointly announced on March 16 that the central banks of their countries would withdraw from the role of buying and selling currencies in the markets in order to maintain stable rates with the dollar.[43] This marked the collapse of the Bretton Woods par value system.

The United Kingdom, Canada, and Japan pursued policies of floating their

---

[40] See generally *IMF History 1966–71, supra* note 3, vol. 1, pp. 553–66; and Dam, *supra* note 3, pp. 189–92. E.B. Decision No. 3463 -(71/126) of December 18, 1971 (*IMF History 1966–71*, vol. 2, p. 195) stated that IMF members using central rates and/or the wider margins of fluctuation described in that decision (up to 2¼ percent from parity or from the central rate in relation to the intervention currency) would be "deemed" to be in compliance with the collaboration obligation stated in section 4(a) of old Article IV which is set out on page 508. Under the decision, the spread between market rates for two currencies pegged to the dollar could be as wide as 4½ percent if one were 2¼ percent below its central rate with the dollar and the other 2¼ percent above. *IMF Circular No. 11: The Calculation of Par Values and Operational Rates* (Washington: IMF, 1972) explained technical points in the calculation of par values and central rates.

[41] See *Minutes of Federal Open Market Committee, supra* note 26, 1972, pp. 599–605, 608, 661–62, and 670–75; House of Commons, *Parliamentary Debates [Hansard]*, 5th series, vol. 839 (1972), columns 877–87 and 1700–814; and IMF Press Release No. 928 #8 (June 30, 1972). The pound in the period since that announcement has never returned to a fixed rate.

[42] The U.S. announcement of its intention to devalue the dollar a second time appears in *IMF Survey*, February 26, 1973, p. 56. See Odell, *supra* note 22, pp. 292–327.

[43] See Press Communiqué of the EEC Council of Finance Ministers, March 12, 1973, and Press Communiqué of the Ministerial Meeting of the Group of Ten and the European Economic Community, March 16, 1973, in *IMF Survey*, March 26, 1973, p. 88; and the statement of the Managing Director of the IMF, *idem*, p. 82.

On March 9, 1973, the EEC Finance Ministers had informed the United States that if their countries were to continue to maintain stable exchange rates with the dollar they would expect the following commitments from the U.S.: (a) the U.S. authorities would also intervene in the exchange markets to maintain stable rates or would restore the convertibility of the dollar into gold, (b) the U.S. Treasury would issue long-term bonds with an exchange-value guarantee to foreign official holders of dollar balances, (c) the U.S. authorities would control the outflow of capital from the United States, and (d) the U.S. authorities would take steps to cause U.S. commercial banks to increase interest rates on dollar deposits. These proposals were not accepted by the United States.

See generally Solomon, *supra* note 18, chapter 13; Coombs, *supra* note 18, pp. 223–31; Dam, *supra* note 3, pp. 192–94; Odell, *supra* note 22, pp. 292–327; and Bank for International Settlements, *43d Annual Report 1972/73*, pp. 20–26.

currencies against the dollar and independent of each other. The group of European states participating in the ''snake'' arrangement maintained relatively stable rates among their own currencies, by use of mutual intervention arrangements, while floating their currencies against the dollar.[44] While the March 16 communiqué, signaling the end of the Bretton Woods system, announced an agreement in principle that ''official intervention in exchange markets may be useful at appropriate times to facilitate the maintenance of orderly conditions,''[45] conditions in the exchange markets in fact became progressively disorderly. By July exchange trading was ''grinding to a standstill,'' especially in forward markets. Commercial banks became reluctant to make quotations and, when they did so, the spread between bid and asked prices was often unbelievably wide. Central bankers in a meeting in Basle, Switzerland, in July 1973 agreed on procedures for managing the float of those currencies floating against the dollar so as to restore order in the exchange markets.[46] Subsequent to July 1973 the central banks of the United Kingdom and Japan, while continuing to float their currencies against the dollar, intervened more actively in the market to maintain order and to affect rate movements. The European countries participating in the ''snake'' arrangement managed the joint float of their currencies against the dollar.

Other countries dependent on foreign trade, or with less diversified production structures, after the collapse of the Bretton Woods system, generally adopted policies that pegged the exchange value of their currencies to that of one of the larger trading nations. In some cases subsequent to June 1974, the value of a currency was pegged to a composite of currencies, for example, by valuing it in relation to the special drawing right.[47]

In the years immediately following the collapse of the Bretton Woods system, there were large movements in exchange rates, sometimes over long periods, sometimes over short periods. As would be expected in a market system, trends often fed on themselves, became overextended, and then reversed direction. While many economists had previously argued for a market system to determine exchange rates,[48] the actual experience intensified the debate between

---

[44] The ''snake'' arrangement is described in note 179, *infra*.

[45] Press communiqué of March 16, 1973, *supra* note 43.

[46] See Alfred Hayes, *Emerging Arrangements in International Payments—Public and Private* (Washington: Per Jacobsson Foundation, 1975), pp. 3–4; and Coombs, *supra* note 18, pp. 230–39; Solomon, *supra* note 18, pp. 336–39; and *Minutes of Federal Open Market Committee, supra* note 26, 1973, pp. 708–23.

The terms of reciprocal currency arrangements between the U.S. Federal Reserve System and other central banks were reviewed at the July 1973 Basle meeting. Modifications were made to adapt them for use in financing market interventions in a regime of managed floating. See Chapter 4, *supra*, page 139 (note 40) and pages 145–146.

[47] See IMF, *Annual Report, 1975*, pp. 23–33. In June 1974 the IMF decided to define the exchange value of the SDR in terms of a basket consisting of small amounts of sixteen currencies. Previously the exchange rate of the dollar had determined the exchange value of the SDR. See generally Chapter 5, *supra*, pages 176–185.

[48] See, e.g., the papers collected in George N. Halm (ed.), *Approaches to Greater Flexibility of Exchange*

those who favored governmentally determined stable rates and those who favored fluctuating rates.

The cost of international transactions increased as banks and businesses found it necessary to increase expenditures for staff and services to predict movements in exchange rates and design corporate strategies to maximize the benefits of predicted changes or at least to minimize potential losses. During this period the spreads between bid and asked quotations for currency exchanges widened over what they had been previously under a stable-rate system.

Weighed against the disadvantages of the floating-rate system was a recognition that governments almost certainly would not have been able to maintain stable rates in 1973 and the years immediately thereafter. There was a war in the Middle East in 1973 and a dramatic increase in petroleum prices in 1974 and 1975.[49] Most countries faced problems of labor unemployment and price inflation. The relative rates of domestic money expansion, wage increases, and price inflation diverged dramatically between one country and another.

No country following a policy of floating after March 1973 pursued that policy without qualification. The float was always "managed" in the sense that central banks tried to maintain some control over rate movements.[50] In its "cleanest" form this management involved a willingness to buy or sell currencies to narrow the spread between bid and asked quotations without attempting to influence the direction of rate movements. In other cases the management took the form of resisting movements in rates or defending particular rates. The policies might or might not be publicly announced; and changes in rates to be defended were made with or without public announcement. Basic differences among the exchange rate policies of IMF members prevailed throughout the period.

Rates: The Burgenstock Papers (Princeton: Princeton University Press, 1970). See also Dam, *supra* note 3, pp. 194–210.

[49] The increase in petroleum prices from about $2.75 a barrel to $10 and then more has been described as causing "the largest single mutation in payments patterns that the modern world economy has ever experienced, short of war." Khodadad Farmanfarmaian et al., "How Can the World Afford OPEC Oil?" *Foreign Affairs*, vol. 53 (1974–75), p. 201 at p. 205.

[50] The management of floating rates in the period March 1973 to April 1978, when the Second Amendment entered into force, is described in the quarterly reports entitled "Treasury and Federal Reserve Foreign Exchange Operations" published in the *Federal Reserve Bulletin* and the Federal Reserve Bank of New York's *Monthly Review*, succeeded in 1976 by the *Quarterly Review*. See also H. Fournier and J. E. Wadsworth (ed.), *Floating Exchange Rates—The Lessons of Recent Experience* (Leyden: A. W. Sijthoff, 1976), chapters 8 and 10; and Jacques R. Artus, "Exchange Rate Stability and Managed Floating: The Experience of the Federal Republic of Germany," *IMF Staff Papers*, vol. 23 (1976), p. 312.

Negotiation of Present IMF Article IV

Following the first devaluation of the U.S. dollar, announced in December 1971 and formally effected in May 1972, it was clear that changes in the role of the dollar and, more importantly, changes in the world economy since the end of World War II called for the reexamination of the Articles of Agreement of the International Monetary Fund. In July 1972 the Board of Governors established a special Committee on Reform of the International Monetary System and Related Issues, and formal negotiations looking toward amendment of the Articles got under way.[51]

The polar positions in the negotiation of the new Article IV were assumed by France and the United States. French officials were generally of the view that a system of stable exchange rates maintained on the basis of a common denominator was to be preferred. The common denominator should be a reserve asset like the special drawing right, the value, issue, and use of which are determined by concerted decisions of the member countries of the IMF. Gold should be treated as a monetary asset without an official price, with central banks free to buy and sell it at prices derived from the market. French officials were of the view that a system of stable exchange rates would assist the development of international trade, would be beneficial to developing countries, and would encourage domestic and international economic discipline. Generalized floating of currencies was viewed as "a dangerous phenomenon that disturbs the world economic order."[52]

By 1974, if not before, U.S. authorities had formulated an official position that called for the unequivocal right of IMF members to float their currencies without the requirement of special authorization. U.S. officials, after the experience with floating rates in 1973, did not want to be under an obligation to maintain fixed rates between the U.S. dollar and any other currency or group of currencies or to maintain exchange rates based on parities established with gold

---

[51] Board of Governors Resolution No. 27-10, effective July 26, 1972, in IMF, *Summary Proceedings, 1972,* p. 353. The organization and work of the Committee on Reform (which came to be called "Committee of Twenty") are described in Solomon, *supra* note 18, pp. 224 and 235–66; and Gold, "Hague Lectures," *supra* note 3, pp. 193–205. See also Chapter 1, *supra,* pages 9–10.

[52] The quotation is from the speech of Jean-Pierre Fourcade, French Minister of Economy and Finance, to the Board of Governors of the IMF in September 1975. IMF, *Summary Proceedings, 1975,* p. 92 at p. 96.

France, throughout the negotiation of the new Article IV, favored a par value system and gave much thought to the "numeraire" of the future system. See IMF, *Summary Proceedings, 1973,* p. 71 at pp. 74–76, and *idem, 1974,* p. 90 at pp. 96–99. Mr. Fourcade in his September 1975 speech, *supra,* declared: "We favor the creation of a new trading and reserve unit whose value, issue, and use will be determined by concerted decisions of the member countries of the Fund. We agree that the special drawing right should be the center of the new order." He stated that France did not urge a return to the gold standard system. France's primary concern was to achieve a return to stable exchange rates, which could take place by stages, but it was essential not to mistake the objective. Floating carried the risk of partitioning the world into rival, protected zones. IMF, *Summary Proceedings, 1975,* pp. 95–101.

or any commodity. The United States desired a system of legal provisions that would permit it to determine the exchange arrangements for the dollar. In particular, provisions were desired that would permit the United States to rely primarily on private markets rather than actions of government officials to determine exchange rates. In addition it wanted to reserve the right to intervene to maintain orderly market conditions. The announcement of this U.S. position occurred late in the negotiation of the new Article IV.[53]

Without ever evaluating the experience after 1971 in depth, the IMF's Committee on Reform of the International Monetary System (the so-called Committee of Twenty) early seized upon a verbal formula that the reformed

---

[53] The policy options from a conceptual point of view that were open to the United States are explored in C. Fred Bergsten, *The Dilemmas of the Dollar: The Economics and Politics of United States International Monetary Policy* (New York: New York University Press, 1975), especially pp. 491–559.

The U.S. official position shifted during the negotiation of the new Article IV. A paper circulated in November 1972 accepted the principle of a common denominator system. The principal concern of the paper was to assure that obligations to adjust an exchange rate would be symmetrical—that is, that states in balance-of-payments surplus would have an obligation to raise the par values of their currencies and would be subject to pressures at least as effective as pressures on states in balance-of-payments deficit to maintain economic discipline or to devalue their currencies. *Economic Report of the President, Transmitted to the Congress January 1973* (Washington: U.S. Government Printing Office, 1973), pp. 123–31 and 160–74. See also IMF, *Summary Proceedings, 1972*, p. 34 at p. 38. For background see Solomon, *supra* note 18, pp. 224–28 and 238–44. The proposal is treated in Chapter 12, *infra*, at pages 617–619. According to Kenneth W. Dam, Secretary of the Treasury George P. Shultz used the November 1972 paper to create a hidden agenda for consideration, both in international forums and internally within the U.S. government, of the merits of a floating rate system. Dam, *supra* note 3, pp. 223–24.

After the introduction of widespread floating in March 1973, U.S. officials gave greater attention to the treatment of floating rates in the exchange system then being negotiated, but still (at least in public statements) assumed that the new exchange arrangements would be based upon par values. See testimony of Paul A. Volcker, Under Secretary of the Treasury for Monetary Affairs, in *How Well Are Fluctuating Exchange Rates Working? Hearings before the Subcommittee on International Economics of the Joint Economic Committee*, U.S. Congress, 93d Congress, 1st Session (1973), and the testimony of Mr. Volcker and Arthur F. Burns, Chairman of the Federal Reserve Board, in *International Monetary Reform: Hearings before the Subcommittee on International Finance of the House Committee on Banking and Currency and the Subcommittee on International Economics of the Joint Economic Committee*, U.S. Congress, 93d Congress, 1st Session (November/December 1973). Both officials continued to expect a return to stable exchange rates. See also speech of Secretary Shultz to the IMF Annual Meeting in September 1973. IMF, *Summary Proceedings, 1973*, p. 53 at p. 54.

Pressure for a change in the U.S. official position was brought to bear by Representative Henry S. Reuss and other members of Congress. In a report in January 1974, the Subcommittee on International Economics of the Joint Economic Committee recommended:

In the drafting of an agreement to reform the international monetary system, the U.S. monetary authorities should insist that each IMF member retain the option of letting its currency float in exchange markets without the need to obtain any advance authorization from Fund authorities.

The report also recommended that for the "forseeable future" the dollar should continue to float in exchange markets. *Making Floating Part of a Reformed Monetary System: Report of the Subcommittee on International Economics of the Joint Economic Committee*, U.S. Congress, 93d Congress, 1st Session (1974), pp. 3 and 10. See also the letter of August 16, 1974, from Mr. Reuss to Secretary of the Treasury William E. Simon, in *President Ford's Economic Proposals: Hearings before the Joint Economic Committee*, U.S. Congress, 93d Congress, 2d Session (1974), p. 31, and Mr. Simon's reply at p. 38. The position favoring an unequivocal right to float was adopted by U.S. officials in the IMF negotiations.

system should be based on "stable but adjustable par values" with recognition that in "particular situations" floating rates might be permitted.[54] This same language was carried over into the final report of the Committee of June 1974, but with the qualification that it might be "some time" before it would be possible to reintroduce a par value system. The report suggested guidelines for the management of floating rates.[55] The Executive Board adopted guidelines, but they were not well observed.[56]

As time passed and more experience was gained with floating rates, particularly the ability of the floating system to adapt rates to changes in underlying economic conditions brought on by the increase in oil prices, officials of some countries in addition to the United States came to have second thoughts about reintroducing a system of stable exchange rates. They too were of the view that a system of managed floating under international surveillance should be legitimized in the amended IMF Articles.[57]

In the spring of 1975 the IMF Executive Board considered drafts of a new Article IV. The United States opposed any obligation, legal or moral, to establish par values then or in the future. It supported a draft which (1) would oblige each member to foster exchange stability, to maintain orderly exchange arrangements, and to pursue cooperative policies; and (2) would assure that each member, in meeting these basic obligations, would have freedom to choose the exchange arrangements which it judged best suited to its needs and circumstances. Each member would have an obligation to provide the IMF with information so that the country's policies could be assessed and each member would

---

[54] Communiqué of March 27, 1973, in IMF Committee on Reform of the International Monetary System and Related Issues (Committee of Twenty), *International Monetary Reform: Documents of the Committee of Twenty* (Washington: IMF, 1974), p. 214 at p. 215. That communiqué was drafted in the immediate aftermath of the events summarized at pages 499–500 and before the significance of those events was generally appreciated. The statement that the Committee never discussed the exchange rate system in any depth was made by Tom de Vries, Alternate Executive Director of the IMF (Netherlands), in his article, "Jamaica, or the Non-Reform of the International Monetary System," *Foreign Affairs,* vol. 54 (1976), p. 577 at p. 585.

[55] *International Monetary Reform: Documents of the Committee of Twenty, supra* note 54, pp. 3–48, especially pp. 4, 8, 11, 12, and 33–37. Under an illustrative example in the report, a country would have to seek approval of the IMF's Executive Board in order to adopt a floating rate. The report spelled out illustrative criteria to be taken into account by the Board in determining whether or not to grant approval.

[56] E.B. Decision No. 4232 -(74/67)(June 13, 1974); IMF, *Annual Report, 1974,* p. 112, entitled "Guidelines for the Management of Floating Exchange Rates." The guidelines assumed that floating rates would be temporary and that "target areas" for exchange rates were desirable. The decision is no longer in effect. It was superseded by Decision No. 5392 -(77/63)(April 29, 1977), *infra* note 69, which is referred to as the "surveillance decision."

During the period the guidelines decision was in force, a number of countries that floated their currencies did not manage the float in accordance with the guidelines and avoided making commitments to do so. The United Kingdom, for example, in a letter of December 18, 1975, in support of a stand-by arrangement with the IMF made no explicit reference to the decision in describing the government's "flexible exchange rate policy."

[57] See the Per Jacobsson Foundation lecture favoring managed floating given by Conrad J. Oort, Treasurer-General of the Netherlands, *Steps to International Monetary Order: The Exchange Rate Regime of the Future* (Washington: Per Jacobsson Foundation, 1974), summarized in *IMF Survey,* November 4, 1974, p. 342.

be obligated to consult on its economic situation and the international implications of its policies.[58]

France and many other states favored a system of stable exchange rates. The principal disputed points were the definition of the objective of the exchange system and the rules for bringing a par value system into place including procedures for initial adherence and subsequent obedience. France wanted the new Article IV to state: "The ultimate objective is a system based on stable but adjustable par values." It and a number of other countries wanted authority for the Fund to introduce the par value system by a simple majority of the voting power.[59]

In June 1975 the negotiators came close to reaching agreement only to find that the words chosen were misunderstood. It has been reported that the French finance minister, Jean-Pierre Fourcade, left a dinner meeting of the IMF's Interim Committee of the Board of Governors,[60] in Paris in June 1975 believing that he had reached agreement with his U.S. counterparts that the new Article IV would be based on "a system of stable exchange rates." The transcript that became available the next morning spoke instead of "a stable system of exchange rates." The negotiations on Article IV were broken off.[61]

The failure to reach agreement on Article IV caused many governments to be concerned that the dispute between the United States and France on the exchange rate regime might prevent completion of the amendment package. Pressure was put on French and U.S. representatives to "resolve their differences," the implication being that whatever was acceptable to both France and the United States would be accepted by the others.

Subsequently, after renewed negotiations, at a conference of the heads of state and government of France, Federal Republic of Germany, Italy, Japan, the United Kingdom, and the United States at the Château de Rambouillet, the United States and France announced on November 17, 1975, that they had

---

[58] Statement by William E. Simon, U.S. Secretary of the Treasury, in *International Monetary Reform and Exchange Rate Management: Hearings before the Subcommittee on International Trade, Investment and Monetary Policy of the House Committee on Banking, Currency and Housing and the Subcommittee on International Economics of the Joint Economic Committee,* U.S. Congress, 94th Congress, 1st Session (1975), pp. 128–200, at p. 130.

[59] The drafts of Article IV considered during 1975 have not yet been published by the IMF. Portions of drafts, including alternative language, appear in Annex II of European Communities, *17th Report on the Activities of the Monetary Committee,* in *Official Journal of the European Communities,* no. C-132, June 14, 1976, p. 1 at p. 11 (quoted language on p. 12). Sir Joseph Gold quotes late drafts in "Strengthening the Soft International Law of Exchange Arrangements," *supra* note 22, pp. 452–55. See also discussion in Gold, "Hague Lectures," *supra* note 3, pp. 206–10.

The French, United States, and IMF staff drafts of Article IV will be published in Margaret Garritsen de Vries, *The International Monetary Fund, 1972–1978: International Monetary Cooperation on Trial* (3 vols.; Washington: IMF, scheduled for publication in 1985).

[60] See Chapter 1, *supra,* pages 9–10.

[61] De Vries, "Jamaica," *supra* note 54, pp. 588–89. See note 73, *infra,* respecting the meaning of the phrase "stable system of exchange rates."

reached agreement on a new Article IV.[62] The new article in effect adopted the U.S. and French positions, somewhat modified, as alternatives: The U.S. position (IMF members allowed to choose their own exchange rate arrangements) would be in effect at the outset; provision would be made for possible future adoption of a par value system along the lines France desired. However, initiation of a par value system would require an 85 percent majority of the Fund's total voting power and members would have considerable freedom of choice respecting participation in the system. Although the parties claimed that the language of their "compromise" was so finely balanced that not a single word could be altered, Joseph Gold, then General Counsel of the Fund, with the consent of the parties made some changes in the text.[63] The draft article was then presented to the Ministers of the Group of Ten at a meeting in Paris in mid-December. Later that month it was presented to the Executive Board of the IMF which considered the article at only a few formal sessions and agreed to it with some modifications on December 23, 1975. The Board submitted it to the Interim Committee of the Board of Governors on the International Monetary System at its meeting in Kingston, Jamaica, in January 1976. It was incorporated into the Second Amendment to the Articles of Agreement of the IMF and is now in force.[64]

The new Article IV (even after its redrafting with the assistance of Mr. Gold) reads somewhat more like a press communiqué than a formal statement of legal obligations. Mr. Gold's contemporary observation deserves quotation:

> I think it was the Grand Cham, Samuel Johnson himself, who once said of a particular activity that the wonder was not that it was performed well but that it was performed at all. The same remark may be made about the draft of Article IV.[65]

IMF officials were initially cautious in giving explanations of the new article.[66] They realized that what they said might prejudice compromises struck in the negotiations. The IMF's *Report on the Second Amendment* devoted only five pages to explanation of the new Article IV: Two pages were devoted to Sections 1, 2, and 3 (which are the "guts" of Article IV) and three pages were devoted to Section 4 and Schedule C relating to a par value system. The report,

[62] *Weekly Compilation of Presidential Documents,* vol. 11 (1975), pp. 1292–1300. See Solomon, *supra* note 18, pp. 268–74, for commentary on the negotiations.

[63] The successive drafts are quoted and explained in Gold, "Strengthening the Soft International Law of Exchange Arrangements," *supra* note 22, pp. 452–55.

[64] See Chapter 1, *supra,* pages 9–10.

[65] Letter of Joseph Gold to the author dated February 6, 1976. The reference is to *Boswell's Life of Johnson* (George Birkbeck Hill ed., revised by Lawrence Fitzroy Powell; London: Oxford University Press, 1934), vol. 1, p. 463.

[66] See the transcript of the press conference of H. Johannes Witteveen, Managing Director, April 2, 1976, excerpted in *IMF Survey,* April 19, 1976, pp. 116–21.

with few exceptions, did little more than draw attention to the language of the article.[67] A journal article by the author of this book, published when acceptance of the Second Amendment was under consideration by governments, commented on a range of issues to be addressed.[68] An implementing decision of the IMF, adopted in April 1977, provided early insight into how the article would be implied.[69]

Exegesis of IMF Article IV

Purpose Clause

Present IMF Article IV, entitled "Obligations Regarding Exchange Arrangements," together with Schedule C, entitled "Par Values," was intended by its drafters as a complete agreement on the exchange rate regime. It even has its own purpose clause. The first sentence of Article IV states that "the essential purpose" of the international monetary system is to provide a "framework" that "facilitates" the "exchange" of "goods, services, and capital"[70] among countries and "sustains sound economic growth." It continues that "a principal objective" is the "continuing development" of the *"orderly underlying conditions"* [emphasis added] that are necessary for "financial and economic stability."

The significance of the purpose clause cannot be overstated. Officials of both the U.S. and French Governments who negotiated the present Article IV placed much emphasis on their approach to the question of exchange arrangements which gives primacy to the achievement of orderly underlying condi-

---

[67] See part 2, chapter C, of *Proposed Second Amendment to the Articles of Agreement of the International Monetary Fund: A Report by the Executive Directors to the Board of Governors* (April 1976), reprinted as IMF, *Summary Proceedings, 1976—Supplement* [hereinafter *Report on Second Amendment*]. The report clarified the phrase "with due regard to its circumstances." See page 512, *infra*. The report repeated a point publicly emphasized by U.S. officials and which is in the text: If a par value system is introduced in accordance with Schedule C, a member retains the right to choose its own exchange arrangements which need not be based on par values. See pages 555–556, *infra*.

[68] Edwards, "Currency Exchange Rate Provisions," *supra* note 2.

[69] E.B. Decision No. 5392 -(77/63)(April 29, 1977, effective April 1, 1978); in IMF, *Annual Report, 1977*, p. 107; and in IMF, *Selected Decisions of the International Monetary Fund and Selected Documents* (10th issue; Washington, 1983) [hereinafter *Selected Decisions*], p. 10. This important decision, which became effective when the Second Amendment to the IMF Articles of Agreement entered into force, is discussed at a number of points later in this chapter. It is called the "surveillance decision" and is discussed in John H. Young, "Surveillance Over Exchange Rate Policies," *Finance and Development*, vol. 14, no. 3 (September 1977), p. 17. The decision is supplemented by E.B. Decision No. 6026, *infra* note 270, and Decisions Nos. 7088 and 7374, *infra* note 135.

[70] While the purpose clauses in Article I of the IMF Agreement make no reference to capital movements and Article VI authorizes restrictions on capital movements, the preambular language of present Article IV states that an "essential purpose" of the international monetary system is to provide a framework that facilitates exchanges of capital.

tions. Jacques J. Polak, when Economic Counsellor of the Fund, put it this way:

> They [the French and U.S. negotiators] reached the view that exchange rate stability should be pursued not primarily by intervention or exchange control, but by aiming at a stable domestic system. This is the message conveyed by Section 1 of the new Article IV. I heard it expressed, during some of the meetings, in terms of various layers. The most fundamental layer would be something like social and political conditions—if they are stable, then one is more likely to have stable economic conditions. Stable economic conditions provide a good basis for stable financial and monetary conditions, and these in turn create the likelihood of stability in the top layer, namely, exchange rate conditions.[71]

The concern with basic economic and financial conditions finds expression in the obligations stated in Section 1—obligations which we shall now examine.

Obligations of Section 1

Duty to Collaborate. Following the purpose clause, Section 1 states several general obligations. The first of these is:

> [E]ach member undertakes to collaborate with the Fund and other members to assure orderly exchange arrangements and to promote a stable system of exchange rates.

In the critical period following August 1971, when the United States suspended the convertibility of the dollar into gold and refused to maintain stable rates between the dollar and other currencies, it came to be seen that the most important obligation in the former Article IV was Section 4(a):

> Each member undertakes to collaborate with the Fund to promote exchange stability, to maintain orderly exchange arrangements with other members, and to avoid competitive exchange alterations.[72]

---

[71] Jacques J. Polak, "The Fund After Jamaica," *Finance and Development,* vol. 13, no. 2 (June 1976), p. 7 at p. 8. See also Gold, "Strengthening," *supra* note 22, pp. 452–54.

[72] When the United States by letter of August 15, 1971, informed the Fund that the United States no longer freely bought and sold gold in settlement of international transactions, the U.S. authorities explicitly recognized the obligations of old section 4(a) and stated that the United States would continue to comply with that

The substance of old Section 4(a) has been carried over into the phrase quoted from the new article. However, some changes in language were deliberate. It appears that the United States wanted to avoid an obligation to "promote exchange stability" which might be interpreted by some to mean stable exchange rates; the United States was willing to accept only an obligation to promote system stability. Also, the importance of assuring orderly exchange arrangements is put in first place.[73] A comparison of the language of the new Article IV, Section 1, with old Section 4(a) at first sight also suggests that while it may still be a purpose of the Fund to avoid competitive exchange depreciation (Article I), the legal obligation of members is to avoid manipulating exchange rates to gain an "unfair" competitive advantage. A careful analysis may reveal that the two concepts are not as different as they may seem.

The general obligation, to collaborate to assure orderly exchange arrangements and to promote a stable system of exchange rates, is followed by four somewhat more specific obligations:

In particular, each member shall:
(i)   endeavor to direct its economic and financial policies toward the objective of fostering orderly economic growth with reasonable price stability, with due regard to its circumstances;
(ii) seek to promote stability by fostering orderly underlying economic and financial conditions and a monetary system that does not tend to produce erratic disruptions;
(iii) avoid manipulating exchange rates or the international monetary system in order to prevent effective balance of payments adjustment or to gain an unfair competitive advantage over other members; and
(iv) follow exchange policies compatible with the undertakings under this Section.

The reader should note the words "endeavor to direct," "seek to promote," "avoid," and "follow." The first two phrases appear to be directed

---

provision. *International Financial News Survey*, vol. 23 (1971), p. 261. IMF Board of Governors Resolution No. 26-9 of October 1, 1971, adopted in an effort to maintain order in the aftermath of the U.S. announcement used the language of section 4(a). IMF, *Summary Proceedings, 1971*, p. 331.

A variety of decisions of the Executive Board during the period 1971-1976 made reference to former section 4(a), *original* and *first*, e.g.: E.B. Decision No. 3463 (1971) on central rates and wider margins of fluctuation, *supra* note 40; E.B. Decision No. 4232 (1974) relating to floating exchange rates, *supra* note 56; and E.B. Decision No. 4134 (1974) on consultations on members' policies, *infra* note 75. See also Joseph Gold, "Duty to Collaborate with the Fund and Development of Monetary Law," in *Selected Essays, supra* note 3, p. 390; and Mr. Gold's comments in *IMF History 1945-65, supra* note 3, vol. 2, pp. 573-75.

[73] It could be argued that during 1973-1975, when world oil prices increased dramatically, exchange system stability was maintained and orderly exchange arrangements continued, even though exchange rates changed very significantly. The rates in the floating system of the time adapted themselves to changes in the underlying conditions brought about by higher oil prices.

more to a state's general intentions than to its specific actions. The commanding words "avoid" and "follow" have greater force. Because of the IMF's consultation and review procedures, all of the language is more than simply an affirmation. It lends itself to use by the Executive Board and other organs in their communication with members. The language can, for example, be drawn to the attention of a member with a request to that member to appraise its policies. The provisions serve as a point of reference in consultations with members. It will not in every case be easy to determine whether a member country is or is not in compliance with these obligations that are stated in general terms, but it should not be necessary, except on rare occasions, to make a firm determination. The obligations of Section 1 apply to all members at all times no matter what their exchange arrangements may be.[74]

One of the roots of concepts in Section 1 is a January 1974 decision of the IMF Executive Board. The decision quoted below was adopted during the oil import finance crisis and at a time when widely used currencies were floating.

Consultations on Members' Policies in Present Circumstances

1. The Committee on Reform of the International Monetary System and Related Issues on January 18, 1974 reviewed important recent developments and agreed that, in the present difficult circumstances, all members, in managing their international payments, must avoid the adoption of policies which would merely aggravate the problems of other members. Accordingly, the Committee stressed the importance of avoiding competitive depreciation and the escalation of restrictions on trade and payments; and emphasized the importance of pursuing policies that would sustain appropriate levels of economic activity and employment, while minimizing inflation. It was also recognized that recent developments would create serious payments difficulties for many developing countries. The Committee agreed that there should be the closest international cooperation and consultation in pursuit of these objectives.

2. The Executive Directors call on all members to collaborate with the Fund in accordance with [old] Article IV, Section 4(a), with a view to attaining these objectives. The consultations of the Fund on the policies that members are following in present circumstances will be conducted with a view to the attainment of these objectives.[75]

---

[74] *Report on Second Amendment, supra* note 67, part 2, chapter C, section 3. See also Gold, "Strengthening," *supra* note 22, pp. 452–56.

[75] E.B. Decision No. 4134 -(74/4)(January 23, 1974); IMF, *Annual Report, 1974*, p. 108; *Selected Decisions* (10th issue, 1983), p. 246.

This decision figured in subsequent consultations with members.[76] What was originally a call for more intensive consultations in critical circumstances has been reformulated as a statement of binding obligations at all times in the new Section 1. The new language is more explicit, flows directly from the treaty, and imposes greater obligations.

Obligations to Endeavor to Foster Orderly Economic Growth and to Foster Orderly Underlying Economic and Financial Conditions.

Subsections (i) and (ii) of Section 1 state that each member of the International Monetary Fund shall: "(i) endeavor to direct its economic and financial policies toward the objective of fostering orderly economic growth with reasonable price stability, with due regard to its circumstances;" and "(ii) seek to promote stability by fostering orderly underlying economic and financial conditions and a monetary system that does not tend to produce erratic disruptions." Internal as well as external policies are brought within the Fund's jurisdiction. Reasonable price stability at both the domestic and international level is now an agreed objective of economic policy. The language reflects concern with economic growth, order, and stability, and the particular circumstances of each country.

The public statements of U.S. and French officials and inquiries made by the author indicate that the U.S. and French officials involved in the drafting of Article IV did not in their preparatory work nor during the negotiations develop concrete examples of conduct that would be treated as violating subsections (i) and (ii). Inquiries of the author suggest that the Fund did not during the negotiations work out concrete applications to be given to the language of these subsections.[77]

The phrases have parallels in other international instruments. In Article 2 of the Convention on the Organisation for Economic Co-operation and Development the member states of that organization agree that they will "pursue policies designed to achieve economic growth and internal and external financial stability and to avoid developments which might endanger their economies or those of other countries."[78]

Article 2 of the Treaty Establishing the European Economic Community states that one of the tasks of the Community is "to promote throughout the Community a harmonious development of economic activities, a continuous and balanced expansion, an increase in stability, an accelerated raising of the standard of living. . . ."[79] Article 6 obligates member states to "coordinate

---

[76] See, e.g., the reference to the decision in paragraph 23 of the United Kingdom's letter of December 15, 1976, in support of a stand-by arrangement approved by the IMF January 3, 1977. The text appears in *Financial Times* (London), December 16, 1976, p. 9.

[77] The IMF Executive Board's *Report on Second Amendment, supra* note 67, did not mention any concrete applications to be given to the words of subsections (i) and (ii). Neither did the Managing Director of the Fund in his press briefing of April 2, 1976, *supra* note 66.

[78] See Chapter 2, *supra*, pages 68–70. The Convention is cited on page 68 (note 138).

[79] See Chapter 2, *supra*, page 76 (and note 171).

their respective economic policies to the extent necessary to attain the objectives of this Treaty.''

Article 103 of the EEC Treaty states that member states ''shall regard their conjunctural policies as a matter of common concern.'' Article 104 provides: ''Each Member State shall pursue the economic policy needed to ensure the equilibrium of its overall balance of payments and to maintain confidence in its currency, while taking care to ensure a high level of employment and a stable level of prices.''

The members of OECD and EEC have within those institutions sought to harmonize economic policies and develop joint programs of action.[80] It appears that neither the OECD nor the EEC has ever made a formal determination that a member state has breached its broad economic policy obligations quoted above. The IMF, similarly, in the years since the Second Amendment entered into force has not formally determined that any member has breached subsections (i) and (ii) of Section 1 of Article IV. One might predict that only IMF members that pursue policies at wide deviance from policies pursued by others are ever likely to find their general conduct formally challenged as violative of subsections (i) and (ii). And, such a country may seek refuge in the phrase ''with due regard to its circumstances.'' The *Report on the Second Amendment* states:

> The phrase ''with due regard to its circumstances'' does not represent a dilution of members' general obligations under the Articles of Agreement, but refers to the differing economic needs and circumstances of members and the nature of the problems they face and the priorities they choose in the pursuit of their objectives consistently with the Articles of Agreement.[81]

While it can be predicted that the general conduct of a member will rarely if ever be formally challenged as ''unlawful,'' its general conduct is subject to review. Out of the practical application given to subsections (i) and (ii) in individual situations, a ''common law'' can develop about particular policies a country in this circumstance or that circumstance is expected, perhaps even required, to follow.

Practical Application of the Obligations of Subsections (i) and (ii).

It is submitted that sound policies in the application of subsections (i) and (ii) are most likely to be distilled from experience in handling individual problems.

---

[80] See Chapter 12, *infra*, pages 580–585 and 589–598.

[81] *Report on Second Amendment, supra* note 67, part 2, chapter C, section 2. The phrase ''with due regard to its circumstances'' was added to the U.S.-French draft of Article IV when it was considered by the IMF Executive Board in December 1975. The fact that this language was added would suggest that IMF members were of the view that subsection (i) of section 1 does impose significant obligations. See also Gold, ''Hague Lectures,'' *supra* note 3, pp. 218–19.

Practical application is given to the economic policy commitments when the Fund reviews a member's, a group of members', or all members' economic policies on a regular basis and as particular problems arise; when the Fund considers making financial resources available to a member; and when the Fund provides technical assistance. Authority for Fund initiatives can be found in Section 3 of Article IV which provides that the Fund "shall oversee the compliance of each member with its obligations under Section 1." That authority is supplemented by the provision of Section 1 which obliges members to "collaborate" with the Fund to "promote a stable system of exchange rates."[82]

With the entry into force of the Second Amendment, the Fund began the practice of holding regular consultations, in principle annually, with each member under Article IV.[83] This represented a further evolution of a major feature of the Fund's work for many years—the practice of regularly holding consultations with its members. Each regular Article IV consultation begins with the preparation by the IMF staff of a detailed report on the country's economic situation and policies, proceeds with a visit by an IMF mission to the country to discuss the country's policies with high officials, and concludes with a discussion in the IMF Executive Board of the staff's consultation report. The procedures and subject matter are explained more fully in Chapter 12.[84] What deserves emphasis here is that the consultations are comprehensive reviews of the member's monetary and financial situation and policies. Domestic as well as international policies are discussed.

A concluding phase of each regular consultation under Article IV is a statement of "conclusions" by the Executive Board.[85] The conclusions, or "summing up" by the Managing Director of the views stated in the Executive Board, deal with the country's domestic and international economic policies which come within the scope of Article IV, Section 1 (including subsections (i) and (ii)). An example is set forth in Chapter 12.[86] The language chosen normally avoids the aura of formal determination of compliance or noncompliance.

Fund consultations are not the only settings in which subsections (i) and (ii) are applied. The Fund's practice under stand-by and extended arrangements provides guidance to the meaning of subsections (i) and (ii), particularly for countries in deficit. Under stand-by and extended arrangements for the use of the Fund's general resources, the Fund has required members to state the domestic and international financial and economic policies they intend to pursue

---

[82] In particular situations other provisions of the Articles may also provide authority for oversight or initiatives by the Fund. See Chapter 12, *infra,* pages 633–634. See also Joseph Gold, " 'Pressures' and Reform of the International Monetary System," in *Selected Essays, supra* note 3, p. 182.

[83] E.B. Decision No. 5392, *supra* note 69, subpart Procedures for Surveillance.

[84] At page 571 et seq.

[85] The legal character of a "conclusion" is examined in Chapter 12, *infra,* pages 575–578.

[86] See pages 575–577, *infra.*

during the period the financial arrangement is outstanding. As observed earlier, the policies stated by governments in letters of intent seeking stand-by or extended arrangements typically deal with government budgets, financing of budget deficits, wage and price policies, control of domestic credit, exchange restrictions, import restrictions, and other matters.[87] These are precisely the kinds of policies with which subsections (i) and (ii) are concerned.

Does this mean that members of the IMF in deficit situations are required by subsections (i) and (ii) to pursue domestic economic and financial policies as constrictive of their freedom of action as they would be expected to pursue in order to obtain approval of a stand-by or extended arrangement in a higher credit tranche? The answer is neither simply "yes" nor "no." The policies required will depend upon the circumstances. If a country's financial situation requires it to seek external assistance on a large scale to finance balance-of-payments deficits, whether that assistance is sought from the Fund or from other institutions, the country has an obligation under Article IV to pursue policies designed to correct, within a reasonable period of time which will vary with the circumstances of the country, any underlying conditions that account for its financial problems. If the financial problems are small in scale or of a very short-term nature, the particular policies would of course be different.

In some cases countries have not pursued requests for stand-by or extended arrangements when it became clear that the Fund would expect the country to pursue stabilization policies that the country was not at that time prepared to implement. Do subsections (i) and (ii) place upon the country an independent obligation to pursue such economic and financial policies? One thing should be clear: To the extent that these are the *only* wise policies for a country in that financial situation, pursuit of those policies is required by Article IV. To the extent, however, that the policies expected by the Fund would be justified only because of the Fund's position as a creditor, such policies may not be required by Article IV. The articulation of performance criteria of the detailed type found in some letters of intent supporting stand-by or extended arrangements is probably not required. Such performance criteria (which may include carefully drawn statistical projections of budget deficits, trade flows, and the like) are designed so that the Fund can measure the progress being made by the country at subsequent points in time.[88]

The economic policies, including domestic policies, pursued by surplus countries may contribute to the problems faced by other IMF members. The economic policy obligations of Article IV apply to countries in surplus as well as to those in deficit. Again, the appropriate policies will vary with the country's economic objectives and its circumstances, including its relationships to other countries and their situations. The key factor, about which there should be

---

[87] See generally Chapter 6, *supra*, pages 248–276.
[88] See Chapter 6, *supra*, pages 265–266 and 267–268.

no question, is that every member of the IMF must be prepared to enter into a discussion of its economic and financial policies with the IMF, to define its policies with reasonable specificity, and to evaluate with the Fund whether and to what extent the policies are in fact fostering the desired conditions. It should also be recognized that the general language of subsections (i) and (ii) provides room for experimentation and variation of policies even among countries in similar circumstances.

While the IMF has for years been concerned with domestic as well as international policies of countries, Article IV provides a firm legal basis for the IMF to review, comment upon, and influence domestic policies. Previously the concern was justified on economic grounds related to the international effects of the policies. The Fund now does not have to give an economic justification for its concern because Article IV assumes the relationship proven and gives it a *de jure* basis. Thus, the Managing Director was clearly correct when he said that "a member which persists in inflating rapidly or in growing at a rate far below that of its potential output may not be fulfilling its obligations under Article IV, even though it may not appear to be contributing to exchange market disturbances in some overt way."[89] Subsections (i) and (ii) of Section 1 require the pursuit of policies that foster orderly underlying economic and financial conditions, orderly economic growth, reasonable price stability, and a monetary system that does not produce erratic disruptions. The policies are to be pursued even if economic evidence should happen to show that their nonpursuit would have no adverse effects on exchange rate arrangements.

General Obligations with Respect to Exchange Policies. Subsection (iii) of Section 1 states an obligation that is somewhat more specific than the general policy obligations discussed so far. It provides that each member shall

> avoid manipulating exchange rates or the international monetary system in order to prevent effective balance of payments adjustment or to gain an unfair competitive advantage over other members. . . .

It is important to point out that subsection (iii) is only one sentence in Article IV. It is possible for a country to be in compliance with subsection (iii) and yet to be in violation of other provisions of Article IV.

The word "manipulate" means to manage or influence by exercise of one's abilities or skills. It need not automatically carry a pejorative connotation. Whether manipulation is good or bad depends on the circumstances, objectives, and effects. The expectation of officials and most scholars, at the time the Second Amendment entered into force, was that in the future, as in the past, ex-

---

[89] Speech of Jacques de Larosière, Managing Director of the IMF, of November 14, 1978, on consultation practice under Article IV; *IMF Survey,* November 20, 1978, p. 357 at p. 359.

change rates of most currencies would be managed. The degree of management would vary from country to country.

National treasuries and central banks find it necessary to participate in exchange markets given the international activities of their countries. Their actions do influence rates. Further, exchange rate changes have an important impact on a country's economic situation. Despite protestations to the contrary, the U.S. government cannot ignore what happens in the stock markets. Nor can it continuously ignore what happens in the currency exchange markets.[90] One can expect government agencies to take actions that influence stock and bond prices through such means as adjustment of margin requirements and changes in interest rate policies, as well as changes in taxation policies, government spending, and the like. Actions by the Federal Reserve System respecting interest rate policies and reserve requirements, as well as direct intervention in the exchange markets, influence currency exchange rates. The way in which the U.S. Treasury handles the sale of a bond issue can influence exchange rates. Other countries also "manipulate" exchange rates, in the neutral nonpejorative sense used here, by a variety of actions including intervention in the markets.

Any deliberate change in an exchange rate is a manipulation. Governmental authorities that maintain a rate that in the absence of the central bank's intervention would be substantially different also manipulate the rate or the exchange system; this action is "manipulation" whether the state floats or uses a fixed rate. Manipulation occurs when policies are changed respecting market intervention. Changes in domestic policies known to affect the exchange rate can "manipulate" the rate.[91]

---

[90] See, e.g., text accompanying note 156, *infra*.

[91] The following examples, mentioned in a contemporary article of the author, were known to officials and members of national parliaments at the time acceptance of the Second Amendment was under consideration:

U.K. Actions in 1975–76. The U.K. pound sterling closed slightly above $2.00 at the end of November 1975. This was a record low at the time. The *Wall Street Journal,* December 1, 1975, at p. 7, said: "British monetary authorities, however, have made it clear that they won't jeopardize their efforts to pull Britain out of its economic slump by resisting the pound's basic decline."

The previous week on November 28, 1975, the Bank of England had reduced its interest rate on loans to commercial banks. That action had the purpose of stimulating domestic demand. It was apparent that the bank's action and official attitudes toward the decline in the pound's rate would in fact encourage a further depreciation of sterling.

By May of 1976 the pound had declined below $1.80. When the pound touched a new low of $1.777 on May 21, the Bank of England raised the minimum lending rate to financial institutions. The *Wall Street Journal,* May 24, 1976, at p. 7, reported that the Bank of England raised the rate to prevent the pound from declining further even though the interest rate change would raise the cost of domestic borrowing for capital investment, which was not an effect desired by U.K. authorities.

Italian Action in 1976. On February 25, 1976, Italian authorities announced that as of March 1 the Banca d'Italia, which had previously allowed the lira to float downward, would intervene in the markets to support the lira. The return to a "controlled" float was accompanied by domestic measures to reduce bank liquidity. This was done by increasing the discount rate and increasing minimum reserves. Exchange controls were tightened.

The "Guidelines for the Management of Floating Exchange Rates," adopted in June 1974 and terminated when the Second Amendment entered into force, attempted to define "action to influence an exchange rate" for purposes of that decision. It used a purpose test related to the balance of payments.[92] The Fund's surveillance decision presently in force does not define "manipulation." However, its list of developments that might indicate a need for discussions includes only actions specifically directed to the exchange rate, the behavior of the exchange rate, or actions that have a balance-of-payments purpose.[93]

This author has previously suggested,[94] and continues to believe, that the "likely results" test is better than a purpose test for determining "manipulation." Indeed, the known or predictable effects of an action, rather than the particular technique used or the ostensive purpose of the action or inaction, should be the principal test of "manipulation" in applying subsection (iii).

Recognizing that manipulation will take place, that the Fund has jurisdiction to oversee all forms of manipulation, and that manipulation is not necessarily bad, we turn to what is proscribed.

Manipulation that prevents effective balance-of-payments adjustment must be avoided. An example is the maintenance of the external value of a currency at so high a level that the rate creates balance-of-payments difficulties for the issuing country. Actions that prevent effective balance-of-payments adjustment by other states as well as actions that prevent effective adjustment by the manipulator also run afoul of subsection (iii). If a country accumulates monetary reserves at what would appear to be an excessive rate or, alternatively, if its reserves decline rapidly, an inquiry should be made as to whether the situation and policies of the country are impeding balance-of-payments adjustment by that country or other countries. William E. Simon, when U.S. Secretary of the Treasury, in explaining subsection (iii) stated:

> [A] surplus country which refused to allow its currency to appreciate and accumulated excessive reserves would be preventing effective balance-of-payments adjustment.[95]

All of the above actions—both "allowing" a currency rate to decline and taking different actions that halted or retarded a decline—involved "manipulation" of an exchange rate as that word is used in subsection (iii) of new Article IV, section 1. See Edwards, "Currency Exchange Rate Provisions," *supra* note 2, pp. 743–45.

[92] E.B. Decision No. 4232, *supra* note 56. It specifically said: "Monetary or interest rate policies adopted for demand management purposes or other policies adopted for purposes other than balance of payments purposes would not be regarded as action to influence the exchange rate."

[93] E.B. Decision No. 5392, *supra* note 69, subpart Principles of Fund Surveillance Over Exchange Rate Policies. The list is quoted in the text accompanying note 267, *infra*.

Decision No. 5392 does not contain any language similar to that quoted in note 92, *supra*.

[94] Edwards, "Currency Exchange Rate Provisions," *supra* note 2, p. 744.

[95] *Hearings on H.R. 13955 [To Provide for Amendment of the Bretton Woods Agreements Act] before the*

Manipulation is also proscribed if it is used in order to gain an unfair competitive advantage over other IMF members. The negotiators probably thought primarily of actions to depreciate the exchange rate of a currency, or to maintain a rate against forces pressing for its appreciation, in order to facilitate exports of goods. The language is not limited to trade, and the same principle would properly apply to any manipulation of an exchange rate known or expected to create an unfair competitive advantage in any class of economic transactions—trade in goods, services and invisible transactions, and movements of capital. Competitive appreciation of a currency as a means of combating inflation may have results as serious as competitive depreciation intended to increase a country's share of exports, and also comes within the scope of subsection (iii).

The more difficult question is determining what is an "unfair" competitive advantage. It is suggested that such a determination should be made by reference to the economic and financial circumstances of the countries involved. Balance-of-payments data may provide assistance in making the judgment, but need not be conclusive. A paradigm case of a breach of subsection (iii) can be identified: A country in a strong reserve position with a substantial surplus in its goods and services account deliberately depreciates its currency to gain a larger share of export markets. The country's competitors are in a situation where they cannot reduce prices without bringing on domestic recessions. These countries are themselves then forced to depreciate their currencies in order to maintain their shares in the export markets.

A country running a current account deficit also can create an unfair competitive advantage. This happens, for example, when, as a consequence of its devaluation or depreciation of its currency, other states would be justified in responding by depreciating their currencies to counter or eliminate the export advantage of the "initiator." This matter was explicitly mentioned in the hearings in the United States Congress on the Second Amendment.[96] The IMF Execu-

---

Subcommittee on International Trade, Investment and Monetary Policy of the Committee on Banking, Currency and Housing, U.S. House of Representatives, 94th Congress, 2d Session (1976), p. 6 at p. 10.

C. Fred Bergsten, speaking before the same subcommittee on June 3, 1976, stated with respect to Japan's practices in the spring of 1976:

> Japan is likely to run the largest trade surplus in its history this year, yet has been buying dollars massively for the past five months to keep the exchange rate of the yen from rising significantly and thus hurting its competitive position. . . .
> When countries intervene in the exchange market to check a strengthening of their currencies, as the Japanese are now doing so heavily, they increase their reserves. Thus reserve increases, like reserve declines, are an indicator that countries *may* be following inappropriate exchange rate or internal economic policies. [emphasis added] (*Idem,* p. 97 at pp. 104–05.)

---

[96] C. Fred Bergsten, testifying in hearings on the Second Amendment, commented on the actions of the British and Italian authorities in allowing the rates for their currencies to decline as far as they did in the spring of 1976 (recall note 91):

tive Board confirmed this understanding of Article IV, Section 1(iii), in consultations with Sweden in the fall of 1982. There was a clear general consensus in the Board that Sweden's sharp devaluation of the krona by 16 percent on October 8, 1982, was a manipulation of exchange rates to gain an unfair competitive advantage and was prohibited by Section 1(iii).[97]

Also consider "competitive appreciation." A country adopts high-interest-rate policies that attract savings from abroad and engender expectations of continuing exchange rate appreciation. Countries that had been pursuing sound economic and monetary programs find themselves forced to implement high-interest-rate policies or to impose capital controls if they are to stem the outflow of savings. There may be a variety of other cases of "unfair" advantage as well.

Subsection (iv) of Section 1 states that each IMF member shall follow exchange policies "compatible" with its other undertakings under Section 1. In some respects this provision is unnecessary; its inclusion drives home the point that all exchange policies are subject to the general obligations of Section 1.

Principles for Guidance of Members (Section 3(b)). Under Section 3(b) of Article IV, the Fund is directed to adopt "specific principles for the guidance of all members" with respect to exchange rate policies. The principles can be adopted by a simple majority of the weighted votes cast. It is clear from the language in Section 3 that the Fund cannot, under the guise of adopting such principles, expand the legal obligations of Sections 1 and 2. Any guidelines must be compatible with the right of members under Section 2 to choose their own exchange arrangements. The principles must respect the domestic social and political policies of members. They have to take into account differences between countries in which the central banks tightly regulate exchange transactions as compared to those countries that have active private markets.

Shortly after the text of Article IV was finalized, U.S. officials stated:

> In developing specific principles, the Fund will need to proceed cautiously. Such principles must have very broad acceptance by Fund

---

The British and Italian depreciations almost certainly exceed the amounts justified by their underlying competitive positions, enhancing their trade balances, and there is strong evidence that Britain deliberately pushed its rate down to achieve just such an advantage. History suggests that other countries will not be slow to emulate these moves when the effects begin to pinch, although the French have exercised admirable restraint so far. Such moves violate the obligation of countries, contained in Section 1(iii) of Article IV of the proposed Amendments to "avoid manipulating exchange rates or the international monetary system in order to prevent effective balance-of-payments adjustment or to gain an unfair competitive advantage over other members."

Hearings, supra note 95, p. 104. The factual situations would, of course, have to be explored more fully before drawing a conclusion in a particular case.

[97] The Swedish devaluation and IMF consultations with Sweden are discussed in Chapter 12, *infra,* page 606.

members. Their development cannot be forced, but they can be expected to emerge over time in the light of general and specific consultations with members.[98]

Principles for guidance can be adopted and amended by a simple majority of the weighted votes cast. The Fund has so far adopted three principles under Section 3 for guidance of members' exchange rate policies:

A. A member shall avoid manipulating exchange rates or the international monetary system in order to prevent effective balance of payments adjustment or to gain an unfair competitive advantage over other members.
B. A member should intervene in the exchange market if necessary to counter disorderly conditions which may be characterized inter alia by disruptive short-term movements in the exchange value of its currency.
C. Members should take into account in their intervention policies the interests of other members, including those of the countries in whose currencies they intervene.[99]

The first principle is simply a repetition of Section 1(iii) of Article IV. It uses the word "shall" which is used in that article. The other two principles are not directly derived from Section 1 and deliberately use the word "should," to avoid the firm legal demand of "shall." While the second and third principles are not in themselves legally binding, it can be argued that a member that does not comply with them has a collaboration obligation to explain how its conduct is nevertheless consistent with Section 1.

The three principles above are not understood to be a comprehensive list. They may be amended or supplemented.[100] The decision listing the principles above also identifies certain symptoms that a country's policies may not be in accord with its Section 1 obligations. These are discussed below in connection with Fund surveillance over exchange rate policies.[101]

---

[98] Statement of William E. Simon, Secretary of the Treasury, in *Hearings on H.R. 13955, supra* note 95, p. 11; and statements of Edwin H. Yeo III, Under Secretary of the Treasury for Monetary Affairs, in *Hearings on S. 3454 [International Monetary Fund Amendments] before the Committee on Foreign Relations,* U.S. Senate, 94th Congress, 2d Session (1976), p. 4 at p. 15, and in *Hearing on H.R. 13955 [Amendments of the Bretton Woods Agreements Act] before the Subcommittee on International Finance of the Committee on Banking, Housing and Urban Affairs,* U.S. Senate, 94th Congress, 2d Session (1976), p. 131 at p. 137. See also Mr. Simon's speech in IMF, *Summary Proceedings, 1976,* p. 87 at pp. 94–96.

[99] E.B. Decision No. 5392, *supra* note 69, subpart Principles for the Guidance of Members' Exchange Rate Policies.

[100] E.B. Decision No. 5392, *idem,* subpart General Principles. See Gold, "Hague Lectures," *supra* note 3, p. 221.

[101] At pages 558–559, *infra.*

What is the legal character of guiding principles adopted by the Fund under Section 3? Sir Joseph Gold recently commented:

> If the Fund were to find that a member was not observing a principle, the finding would not be equivalent automatically to a decision that the member was failing to perform its obligations. The member's behaviour, whether in the form of acts or omissions, could be a violation, but before this conclusion could be reached the Fund would have to find that the member was neglecting an obligation imposed by the Articles. The further finding would be necessary because a specific principle of guidance is not equivalent in law to an obligation. The function of the word "guidance" is to avoid the suggestion of obligation. This analysis does not apply to Principle A because it does repeat an obligation imposed by the Articles.[102]

There is another way of looking at the matter, not inconsistent with what Sir Joseph has said, that emphasizes the positive legal functions played by the adoption of principles. The principles may play an interpretative as compared to a legislative role. They indicate the Fund's understanding of conduct expected of a country that follows exchange rate policies compatible with its Section 1 undertakings. Under Article XXIX the Executive Board and Board of Governors are given the power to render a formal interpretation of any provision of the Articles of Agreement. Many decisions of the Executive Board operate as less formal interpretations of the Articles. Thus, by adopting "principles for guidance" the Fund can give specific applications to general obligations stated in Section 1. The "principles" provide criteria for assessing whether or not a member's exchange rate policies and actions are consistent with its obligations under Article IV. Sir Joseph Gold has recently suggested that the Fund adopt additional or amended principles and state them with greater precision. He has also pointed out that the Fund has the power to adopt authoritative interpretations of the several subsections of Article IV, Section 1.[103]

Obligations of Section 2

Choice of Exchange Rate Arrangements. An IMF member is free to choose the exchange arrangements for its currency so long as those arrangements are consistent with the purposes of the Fund and with its obligations under Section 1. The member has an obligation to inform the Fund of the arrange-

---

[102] Gold, "Hague Lectures," *supra* note 3, p. 221.
[103] Gold, "Strengthening," *supra* note 22, p. 483. On the Fund's power of interpretation, see generally Chapter 1, *supra*, pages 37–39.

ments it chooses and of any changes that it makes. This is the substance of the obligations imposed by Section 2 of Article IV.[104]

Since the obligations of Section 1 are contextual, the particular actions required of a state to fulfill its Section 1 obligations may vary over time with developments in its economy and the world economy. Circumstances may change. In the historical context of January 1, 1976,[105] exchange arrangements compatible with Section 1 obligations could include:

(i)   The maintenance of the exchange value of a currency in terms of the special drawing right. (The exchange value of a currency is not to be maintained in terms of gold.)

(ii)   The maintenance of the exchange value of a currency in terms of the currency of another IMF member or a composite of such currencies.

(iii) Cooperative arrangements whereby a group of countries maintain stable rates among their currencies while allowing them to float against other currencies.

(iv)   Other exchange arrangements including the floating of currencies with rates determined by market forces.

Pegging Against the SDR.   In the initial notification process after the Second Amendment entered into effect, fifteen IMF members indicated that they maintained the exchange values of their currencies in relation to the special drawing right: Bahrain, Burma, Guinea, Iran, Jordan, Kenya, Malawi, Mauritius, Sao Tomé and Principe, Tanzania, Uganda, United Arab Emirates, Vietnam, Zaire, and Zambia. There have subsequently been changes in the list.[106] The SDR's exchange value is presently determined by a composite of portions of five different currencies.[107]

A disadvantage of pegging to any composite is that the determination of whether the exchange rate of the pegging currency is deviating from the composite by more than, say, $2\frac{1}{4}$ percent involves a complex set of calculations. Where the peg is to the SDR, the effect of market interventions to maintain the stated rate may not be precisely known until the next day when the IMF's computations of the value of the SDR in terms of major currencies are made and communicated. This may be only an inconvenience for a developing country with a tightly controlled exchange market but could be a serious problem in active sophisticated markets of exchange. Where exchange markets are well de-

---

[104] Each member was required to notify the IMF of its exchange arrangements within 30 days after the Second Amendment became effective. Members are to notify the Fund promptly of any changes. See pages 527–530.

[105] Article IV, section 2, uses this reference date because it was not possible to describe in simple terms the international monetary system at the time Article IV was negotiated.

[106] See IMF, *Annual Report, 1978*, pp. 90–93, reporting exchange rate arrangements as of June 30, 1978. Compare IMF, *Annual Report, 1983*, pp. 65–66 and 114–17, reporting exchange rate arrangements as of June 30, 1983.

[107] See Chapter 5, *supra*, pages 178–185.

veloped, pegging to a composite may entail decisions on which of several foreign currencies to use for market intervention to maintain pegged rates.

Where a currency is pegged to the SDR, the country retains the right to change the official rate, to change to an exchange arrangement that substitutes a different denominator, or to introduce a floating rate. Rates may be changed on the basis of a formula or when officials judge a change to be appropriate.

Pegging Against Another Currency. The right of an IMF member to maintain a stable or fixed rate between its currency and that of another IMF member is stated by implication in Section 2(b)(i). That section permits a member to set an exchange rate for its currency in terms of the special drawing right or "another denominator" (other than gold) selected by the member. In Schedule C outlining a particular generalized par-value system there is a provision that rates under that system could be set in terms of the special drawing right or other common denominator which is not gold or a currency. The failure to exclude a currency from being "another denominator" in Section 2(b)(i) was deliberate. The U.S. Secretary of the Treasury and the Under Secretary for Monetary Affairs both stated explicitly that Section 2 authorizes "pegging to another currency."[108] At the time the new Article IV was negotiated over 75 countries used such an exchange arrangement.[109]

A country unilaterally maintaining a fixed rate between its currency and another currency must, of course, comply with its obligations under Section 1 as those affect the choice of the currency pegged against, the choice of the rate, and the means used to maintain it. If the country issuing the currency pegged against wishes a different rate or a floating rate with the pegging currency, there must be consultations between the countries and efforts to work out cooperative arrangements.

At the present time more IMF members maintain stable rates between their currencies and the currency of one other IMF member than use any other technique. The technique is simple. The currency pegged against is usually a convertible currency widely used in international trade. In the initial notification process after the Second Amendment entered into effect, 64 members stated that they used this type of exchange arrangement: 42 countries maintained a fixed rate with the U.S. dollar, 14 with the French franc, 5 with the U.K. pound sterling, and 3 with other currencies.[110] Most of these countries are developing countries. In some countries the rate is maintained by governmental purchases and sales of foreign currencies intended to control fluctuations in an otherwise free market. In many countries exchange transactions can lawfully take place

---

[108] Statement of William E. Simon in *Hearings on H.R. 13955, supra* note 95, p. 9; and statement of Edwin H. Yeo III in *Hearings on S. 3454, supra* note 98, p. 15.

[109] IMF, *Annual Report, 1975,* pp. 23–24.

[110] See note 106, *supra.* An additional five countries in 1978 pegged their currencies to a single foreign currency but under a formula that permitted frequent changes in the rate. See pages 525–526, *infra.*

only through authorized banks, and the government or its central bank decrees the rates to be used in these transactions. The ability of governments and national central banks to supply foreign currencies to the "market" at official rates is facilitated in many countries by exchange controls that (a) limit the transactions for which residents are permitted to obtain foreign currencies to make payments abroad, and (b) require resident exporters to surrender foreign currencies obtained to central authorities.[111]

Pegging has the advantage of administrative simplicity, since it often involves no more than the continuation of a long existing practice in the foreign exchange market. It also avoids the process of continuous decision-making that would be necessary under a system of managed floating. In addition, it ensures that trade denominated in the currency pegged against, frequently the currency of the major trading partner, will be conducted at a stable exchange rate. Whenever a number of countries peg against the same currency, there is the further consequence of stable cross-rates between these currencies. Pegging does subject a currency's rate in relation to other floating currencies to determination by factors affecting the rate between its partner's currency and the other floating currency, factors not necessarily related to its own external adjustment needs.[112] However, a country pegging its currency retains the right to alter the rate, if necessary, between its own currency and the currency pegged against.[113] This, of course, must be done in a manner that is consistent with Section 1 obligations.

A number of countries peg against specially selected composites of currencies designed to model that country's trading relationships. This is similar to pegging against the SDR, except that the composite is different. In the initial notification process after the Second Amendment entered into force, 17 IMF members were identified as pegging the rates of their currencies against their own specially selected "weighted baskets."[114]

Joint Floats. The principal experience with joint floats referred to in Article IV, Section 2(b)(ii), has been in the European Monetary System and in the European narrow margins arrangement that preceded it. The exchange rate mechanism of the EMS is discussed in a separate section below.[115]

---

[111] Exchange restrictions are treated in Chapter 10 of this book.

[112] Although in 1978 some 79 IMF members maintained a stable rate between their currencies and another currency or the SDR, and another 17 maintained a stable rate against a specially selected composite of currencies, the IMF estimated that less than one-fifth of world trade moved across pegged exchange rates. IMF, *Annual Report, 1978*, p. 38.

[113] In the three years 1974 through 1976, of the 73 IMF members that continuously maintained a unitary peg to another currency (or to the SDR), 19 of them made one or more changes in their intervention points. IMF, *Annual Report, 1977*, p. 27. For changes in the first two years after the Second Amendment entered into force, see IMF, *Annual Report, 1980*, pp. 54–60.

[114] See note 106, *supra*.

[115] At page 536 et seq.

Other Exchange Arrangements. The open-ended language "other exchange arrangements of a member's choice" in Article IV, Section 2(b)(iii), was intended to accommodate countries that wished to allow their currencies to float. The United States, as we saw earlier, was particularly insistent during the negotiation of the new Article IV on the right to use a floating rate. The volume of exchange transactions between the dollar and other currencies is so great that U.S. authorities have not been willing to commit the financial resources that could be required to maintain stable rates between the dollar and other widely traded currencies, at least in the context of present conditions.[116] The U.S. Policy, which is consistent with the resources available to it, its policies favoring maximum freedom for private transactions, and its policies favoring reliance on market forces to determine prices, is to counter disorderly conditions when they appear in the exchange markets in the United States and, sometimes, to resist trends in rates that in the judgment of U.S. authorities have grossly overshot themselves. The United States does not have a policy to maintain any particular rate.[117]

Currencies that have continuously floated independently from the time of the collapse of the Bretton Woods exchange rate system in March 1973 until the present time include the U.S. dollar, Canadian dollar, Japanese yen, U.K. pound sterling, and a number of other currencies. The policies that guide the management of floating rates by the authorities vary among the countries. Because these currencies are actively traded in large amounts, official market interventions to influence rates, and not merely counter disorderly conditions, can be very expensive. For example, U.S. authorities in just two months, at the end of 1978, made a net use of foreign currencies equivalent to over $6.6 billion to reverse a downward trend of the dollar's rate.[118] Japanese reserves fell by some $12.5 billion in the course of 1979 while the authorities moderated the yen's fall as the dollar rose.[119] Legal issues respecting the management of floating rates are treated further below.[120]

Several countries, most being in Latin America, peg the rates of their currencies to another currency but under a procedure in which the peg is adjusted at relatively frequent intervals on the basis of selected indicators, such as differen-

---

[116] According to an April 1977 survey by the Federal Reserve Bank of New York, 44 U.S. banking institutions sampled had a gross turnover—the sum of all foreign currency sales and purchases—of more than $100 billion that month (an average in excess of $5 billion per business day). See Roger M. Kubarych, *Foreign Exchange Markets in the United States* (1st ed.; New York: Federal Reserve Bank of New York, 1978), p. 5.

[117] See discussion of United States market intervention policies at pages 532–535 and 546–548, *infra.*

[118] See notes 156 and 158, *infra.* Beryl W. Sprinkel, Under Secretary of the Treasury for Monetary Affairs, has stated: "Activist intervention policy [by the United States] is doomed to fail, because exchange markets are sufficiently large, efficient, and well-informed to make short work of any official attempts to hold exchange rates [of the dollar] at levels not justified by market forces." Speech at Institut Auguste Comte, Paris, France, September 11, 1981. Treasury Department press release, p. 5.

[119] Victor Argy, *Exchange-Rate Management in Theory and Practice* (Princeton Studies in International Finance no. 50; Princeton: Princeton University International Finance Section, 1982), p. 52.

[120] At pages 531–535 and 546–548, *infra.*

tial rates of inflation.[121] The IMF describes these countries as using "other exchange arrangements" rather than maintaining the values of their currencies in terms of another currency or other denominator.[122]

Some countries officially peg the rates of their currencies to another currency but with margins of fluctuation so wide (e.g., in excess of ± 5 percent) that the countries cannot be described as maintaining the value of their currencies in terms of the currency "pegged" against. These countries are also described by the IMF as using "other exchange arrangements." In addition, a number of countries, such as Afghanistan and Nigeria, do not fit neatly into any of the classes previously discussed. At the time this book is written the authorities in these countries do not maintain stable rates nor do the countries have well-developed free markets for exchange.[123] Finally, the language of Section 2(b)(iii) would appear to permit the introduction of new types of exchange arrangements as the international monetary system evolves.

Limitations on Freedom of Choice. An exchange rate "in its very nature is a two-ended thing."[124] While it is one of the most important prices in the economy of a country, it is a relationship with foreign economies and they with it. If every country were to unilaterally choose its exchange rate arrangements, at least one country (the "nth" country) would find its choice foreclosed. Given the interconnections of international monetary relations, no country can choose an exchange rate arrangement for its currency without to some degree impinging on the freedom of others to choose arrangements for themselves.[125] The choice of exchange rate arrangements is under IMF surveillance and should be made in consultation with affected countries.

In the former Bretton Woods system, it was the unwritten but firm rule of law that monetary authorities would not buy or sell another country's currency in the exchange markets for the purpose of affecting rates without the request, authorization, or permission of the monetary authorities of that country. The United States, whose currency was at the center of the system, tolerated official interventions in the market against the dollar by countries maintaining ex-

---

[121] The use of indicators is described in *IMF Survey*, February 2, 1976, pp. 36–37. Brazil, Chile, Colombia, Peru, Portugal, and Uruguay have used this method. See generally John Williamson (ed.), *Exchange Rate Rules: The Theory, Performance and Prospects of the Crawling Peg* (New York: St. Martin's Press, 1981).

[122] See note 106, *supra*.

[123] See note 106, *supra*.

[124] Statement of Louis Rasminsky (Canada) in presenting the Report of Commission I containing the Articles of Agreement of the International Monetary Fund to the Executive Plenary Session of the Bretton Woods Conference, July 20, 1944. *Proceedings and Documents of the United Nations Monetary and Financial Conference, Bretton Woods, New Hampshire, July 1–22, 1944* (2 vols.; Washington: U.S. Government Printing Office, 1948), vol. 1, p. 864 at p. 867.

[125] See Peter B. Kenen, "Techniques to Control International Reserves," in Robert A. Mundell and Jacques J. Polak (ed.), *The New International Monetary System* (New York: Columbia University Press, 1977), p. 202 at p. 208.

change rates on the basis of par values established with the concurrence of the IMF.[126] In the present IMF regime, where countries are not required to obtain the formal concurrence of the IMF with their exchange rate arrangements, the United States cannot be expected to simply acquiesce in the choices made by other countries of exchange rate arrangements between their currencies and the dollar. The IMF's surveillance decision that became effective April 1, 1978, implementing the new IMF Article IV, states as a principle: "Members should take into account in their intervention policies the interests of other members, including those of the countries in whose currencies they intervene."[127] While the word "should" was used in place of "shall" to avoid a sense of clearly defined legal obligation, the statement articulates a widely shared view of the proper conduct of market interventions. "Take into account" was deliberately chosen to convey a stronger tone than "bear in mind."[128] The principle applies whether a country uses a floating rate, a fixed rate, or some other arrangement.

Where exchange rate arrangements involve the use of the U.S. dollar in interventions to maintain or influence rates, the policies should be developed and implemented in consultation with U.S. authorities.[129] Where currencies of other countries are used, their issuers should be consulted and mutually satisfactory arrangements worked out. The Fund through its powers to call for consultation and collaboration can assist members in dealing with the problems involved. These problems include the selection of the currency for intervention, the movement of the intervention currency's rate in a direction not desired by its issuer, and mutually offsetting interventions. Surveillance of exchange rate arrangements by the Fund is important to assure that the necessary consultations take place and that the exchange rate arrangements chosen and applied by each IMF member take into account the interests of affected countries.

Notifications to the IMF. IMF members were required to formally notify the Fund by May 1, 1978, of their exchange rate arrangements. The Fund took the initiative to contact each member and drafted a description of the member's arrangements. The description was reviewed, corrected, and supplemented by the member.[130] The pressure to complete the initial notifications process within

---

[126] See Silard, "Money and Foreign Exchange," *supra* note 3, section 68. The reader may also recall the discussion in Chapter 3, page 108, of this book about the deference due a country's request that its currency not be held above working balances.

[127] Principle C of E.B. Decision No. 5392, quoted at page 520, *supra*.

[128] See Young, *supra* note 69, p. 18. "Bear in mind" was the phrase used in Guideline 6 of E.B. Decision No. 4232, *supra* note 56.

[129] The United States at the present time appears to accept the use of managed floating rates between actively traded currencies and the U.S. dollar so long as it is consulted by countries that seek to manage rates, and they bear the costs and risks of dollar balances that they may obtain as a result of their own interventions.

[130] Article IV, section 2; E.B. Decision No. 5712 -(78/41)(March 23, 1978), in IMF, *Annual Report, 1978*, p. 126, *Selected Decisions* (10th issue, 1983), p. 8; and E.B. Decision No. 5392, *supra* note 69, subpart Procedures for Surveillance, section I.

a short time period may have resulted in less specificity in descriptions of some arrangements than Section 2 of Article IV should be understood to require.

The idea of Section 2 is that each member has the freedom to choose its exchange rate arrangements, but, balanced against this right, is the obligation to inform the Fund of the choice and to conform actions to the notified arrangements. One of the values of a notification procedure is to force national authorities to articulate their choices to an international institution. If a notification fails to state the operationally important criteria, it is not possible to determine if a member's actions are in accord with the notification or whether the arrangement is consistent with Section 1. Such a notification is an abuse of the right granted under Section 2 to choose exchange arrangements. The fact that the Fund can learn what a country's authorities are in fact doing in the exchange markets is not a satisfactory substitute for the Fund's right to be formally notified of the country's arrangements.

If, for example, a country's arrangement is to float its currency, it is submitted that it has an obligation to state the operationally significant criteria that guide the actions of its monetary authorities in participating or intervening in the market. In April 1978 the United States notified the Fund that ". . . exchange rates are determined on the basis of demand and supply conditions in the exchange markets. However, the [U.S.] authorities will intervene when necessary to counter disorderly conditions in the exchange markets."[131] The definition of "disorderly conditions" was left open.[132] In the period since that notice was filed, U.S. authorities have given the phrase significantly different interpretations.[133] The author has the impression that participants in the European Monetary System did not in their notifications to the IMF in 1979 describe in much detail the criteria for the management of the floating rates between their currencies and the U.S. dollar or when and when not the dollar would be used in interventions to maintain intra-EMS rates within the agreed narrow margins. Yet these are critical issues in the operation of the system.[134] The Managing Director of the IMF has emphasized the Fund's need for comprehensive information on the intervention policies of countries with flexible exchange rate regimes as well as the policies of countries with pegged arrangements.[135]

There is no requirement of Fund approval for changes in exchange rate arrangements provided that multiple currency practices or other restrictions are not involved.[136] Thus, a country using a pegged rate is not required to obtain

---

[131] *Economic Report of the President, Transmitted to the Congress February 1982* (Washington: U.S. Government Printing Office, 1982), p. 190.

[132] *Idem.*

[133] See pages 532–535, *infra.*

[134] See pages 539–541 and 546–548, *infra.*

[135] Attachment to E.B. Decision No. 7088 -(82/44)(April 9, 1982); IMF, *Annual Report, 1982,* p. 128 at p. 132. See also attachment to E.B. Decision No. 7374 -(83/55) (March 28, 1983); IMF, *Annual Report, 1983,* p.142 at pp. 144–45.

[136] See note 138, *infra.*

the Fund's concurrence either for a change in the rate or for a change from one type of exchange rate system to another (e.g., a change from a pegged to a floating rate). The change must, however, be consistent with the country's Article IV, Section 1, obligations; and the country must formally notify the Fund of the change. While not necessarily required to do so, members are encouraged to discuss with the Managing Director changes that they are contemplating in their exchange arrangements before the decisions to make the changes are adopted.[137]

The Fund has stated general criteria for identifying changes that require formal notification. A change from one type of arrangement to another type (e.g., a change from a pegged rate to a floating rate) requires notification. Significant changes within an arrangement that has already been notified are also to be notified. Where a country uses a pegged rate, a change in the rate requires notification. Where the peg is to a composite of currencies, a change in the weighting of currencies within the composite requires notification unless the change results from application of a formula already communicated to the Fund. If the Fund was previously told that a currency's exchange rate would be changed in accordance with certain indicators, the Fund is to be informed when rate changes deviate from the indicator formula. Where flexible exchange rate arrangements are used (any arrangement that is different from a stable pegged rate), the member is to notify the Fund whenever a public statement about a change in policy is issued. The member is also to notify the Fund of every "significant decision" even if no public statement about it is issued.[138] The general rule is that notification is to be made within three days of the change in arrangements.[139] If the Managing Director considers that a significant change has occurred in any member's exchange policy (including intervention arrangements), he is to consult with the member to obtain information on the background of developments and, if he considers it appropriate, seek formal notification of the change from the member.[140] Notifications are circulated to the Executive Board and, whenever they report a significant change, the staff is to prepare a report for the Board that describes the context of the policy change and gives the staff's assessment.[141]

The obligation to notify the Fund of exchange arrangements (Section 2) is supplemented by the obligation to provide the Fund with the information necessary for it to exercise firm surveillance over the exchange rate policies of mem-

[137] E.B. Decision No. 5392, *supra* note 69, subpart Procedures for Surveillance.

[138] E.B. Decision No. 5712, *supra* note 130. The decision also states that the introduction of, or changes in, multiple currency practices and exchange taxes and subsidies are to be notified. These practices require Fund approval as well as notification by the country. See Chapter 10, *supra,* page 389 et seq. See also the discussion of two-tier markets at pages 551–554, *infra.*

[139] Attachment to E.B. Decision No. 7088, *supra* note 135, p. 132.

[140] E.B. Decision No. 5712, *supra* note 130.

[141] *Idem.* See also attachment to E.B. Decision No. 7374, *supra* note 135, pp. 144–45.

bers (Section 3). What is the nature of the distinction between "exchange arrangements" which a member is free to choose but must notify the Fund (Section 2) and "exchange rate policies" over which the Fund exercises firm surveillance (Section 3)? If the two terms are not allowed to overlap and "arrangements" is given a narrow reading, the obligation to notify the Fund of chosen exchange arrangements is trivialized and, of equal importance, the right to choose arrangements is trivialized. On the other hand, a narrow reading of "policies" would limit the scope of the Fund's surveillance jurisdiction. It is probably best to understand "exchange rate policies" as a broad inclusive term, and policies on the structure of a member's exchange rate system ("exchange arrangements") as a subclass of exchange rate policies. With respect to this subclass, a member has freedom of choice provided the obligations of Section 1 of Article IV are observed. The interpretative approach recommended recognizes both the Fund's broad surveillance jurisdiction and a meaningful right of members to choose exchange arrangements. The broad reading of the word "policies" is consistent with the general use of the word in public life and academic writing.[142]

Additional Requirements of the IMF Articles

Although Article IV does not specifically say so, the exchange arrangements of a member must meet the other requirements stated in the Articles of Agreement, including but not limited to:

(i)   The unitary exchange rate and nondiscrimination provisions of Article VIII, Section 3, and Article XIV. Spreads—the difference between buying and selling rates for a currency at any one time—must be held within the range required by Article VIII, Section 3.[143]

(ii) The currency convertibility obligations of Article VIII, Sections 2, 3, and 4, and Article XIV.[144]

(iii) The currency "usability" provisions of Article V, Sections 3(e) and 7(j). (Members must also fulfill the maintenance of value provisions of Article V, Section 11.)[145]

(iv) The provisions of Article XIX, Section 7, applicable to exchange rates in transactions involving special drawing rights and transactions involving the General Resources Account.[146]

---

[142] This understanding of "policies" is fully consistent with the use of the term in E.B. Decision No. 5712, *supra*, note 130, relating to notifications under Article IV, section 2. Compare Gold, "Hague Lectures," *supra* notes 3, p. 220.

[143] See Chapter 10, *supra*, pages 396–399.

[144] See Chapter 10, *supra*, page 389 et seq.

[145] See Chapters 5 and 6, *supra*, pages 197–200 and 225–227.

[146] See Chapters 5 and 6, *supra*, pages 200–201 and 225–227.

Section 5 of Article IV establishes a rebuttable presumption that a country's currency policies also apply to all its territories and to any separate currencies in use in those territories in respect to which the member has accepted the Articles of Agreement. This presumption can be overcome by a declaration to the contrary by the member or by the Fund.

Comments on Specific Exchange Arrangements

Management of a Floating Exchange Rate Arrangement

A country with a floating rate exchange arrangement has considerable freedom in choosing how it wishes to "manage" the float, but has a duty to inform the Fund of its policies and to adhere to them. All members floating have a Section 1 obligation to maintain orderly exchange arrangements. There is, of course, no obligation to maintain a particular rate or to maintain rates within a particular zone unless the country has chosen such a policy. But there is an obligation to intervene when necessary to counter disorderly conditions.[147] Disruptive short-term rate movements may indicate disorderly conditions. Other indications are wide spreads between "bid" and "asked" quotations and the reluctance of commercial banks to make quotations.[148]

A country with a floating rate is not presently required to deal with rate movements related to different business cycle stages in different countries. It can let private actions in the market adjust these disparities and accept the fact that there may be significant rate movements. Alternatively, it can have a policy to "look over the valley" and intervene to smooth out the rate movements. Such a policy may lead to considerable official activity in the market.[149]

If a country with a floating rate intervenes in the market one would expect that intervention, to the extent that it occurs, would be "against trend." It should not act to further depress the value of its currency when it is falling or to enhance its value when rising. There is no duty under Section 1 of Article IV to

---

[147] See principle B of the surveillance decision, E.B. Decision No. 5392, quoted on page 520, *supra*. It is interesting to note that Guideline 1 of the June 1974 IMF "Guidelines for Management of Floating Exchange Rates," E.B. Decision No. 4232, *supra* note 56, contemplated interventions from day to day and week to week to moderate disruptive rate fluctuations. That decision is no longer in force. Principle B of Decision No. 5392 does not require such active intervention, although a country can adopt such a policy. It calls only for intervention to counter "disorderly conditions."

[148] See Roger Kubarych's description of one-sided markets in Appendix A, *infra*, page 686. See also Charles A. Coombs' description of market conditions in early July 1973, a clear case of disorderly conditions. *The Arena of International Finance, supra* note 18, pp. 231–32. It should be noted that sharp changes in exchange rates are often the result of changed expectations regarding underlying economic and social conditions. Intervention can to some degree help to keep the rate movement from becoming disorderly.

[149] The problem is discussed in Solomon, *supra* note 18, pp. 323–27; and Raymond F. Mikesell and Henry N. Goldstein, *Rules for a Floating-Rate Regime* (Essays in International Finance no. 109; Princeton: Princeton University International Finance Section, 1975), pp. 7–10.

have a policy to resist trends in the market; there is a duty not to act aggressively to accelerate a trend.[150]

An exception is the case where a country has adopted a policy to move an exchange rate in a particular direction.[151] A policy of this sort would require very close consultation with the Fund. It is suggested that such a decision should be taken collaboratively with other members that will be affected by the deliberate change of the rate. There should be a review of the circumstances of the members and a projection of the effects of the change on balance-of-payments and reserve positions of those countries affected. The consistency of the policy with the Section 1 obligations of all those affected would require careful assessment. Decisions on pegging exchange rates and changes in pegged rates should similarly be made collaboratively.

Finally, it should also be pointed out that at the present time there is no obligation on a country to redeem balances of its currency purchased by another country in market interventions unless an agreement has been made to redeem the balances.[152] As we shall see later, the participants in the European Monetary System's exchange rate arrangement have made such an agreement. In the absence of an agreement, each country intervenes at its own risk.

United States Policy Shifts

The United States formally notified the Fund in April 1978 that ". . . exchange rates are determined on the basis of demand and supply conditions in the exchange markets. However, the [U.S.] authorities will intervene when necessary to counter disorderly conditions in the exchange markets."[153] While this

---

[150] These concepts were expressed in Guideline 2 of old E.B. Decision No. 4232, *supra* note 56.

The effort to halt or even slow a trend may require a considerable commitment of resources. The timing of official interventions and market participants' understanding of the official actions, as well as fundamental economic conditions, may significantly affect the impact of official interventions on the market. See text accompanying notes 118 and 119, *supra*. See generally Appendix A, *infra*, pages 686–688.

[151] Guidelines 3 and 4 of old E.B. Decision No. 4232, *idem*, used the concept of a "target zone." The assumption was that fixed exchange rates were desirable and the establishment of a target zone might be an intermediate step between floating and the establishment of a fixed or stable rate. The present Article IV does not contain a bias toward fixed rates. This is indeed one of the principal differences between the 1974 guidelines and the principles adopted by the Fund under section 3 of present Article IV. See note 56, *supra*.

The "target zone" concept is discussed in Wilfred Ethier and Arthur I. Bloomfield, *Managing the Managed Float* (Essays in International Finance no. 112; Princeton: Princeton University International Finance Section, 1975).

[152] The issuer satisfies its IMF Article VIII convertibility obligations so long as the holder is permitted to sell the currency in the market, even though the holder may not wish to do so. See discussion of Article VIII, section 4, in Chapter 10, *supra*, pages 421–422.

[153] See note 131, *supra*, and accompanying text.

The notice to the Fund was transmitted by the U.S. Department of the Treasury, the Secretary of the Treasury being the chief financial officer of the United States. The Federal Reserve System's Open Market Committee (FOMC) is a legally independent body, but in practice gives great weight to Treasury views in establishing Federal Reserve intervention policies. There is close coordination of Treasury and Federal Reserve exchange market operations. The Federal Reserve Bank of New York acts as agent for both the Federal Restatement has remained the constant official statement of U.S. exchange arrangements,[154] official understanding of the meaning of the last quoted sentence has gone through at least two, and probably three, metamorphoses since the Second Amendment of the IMF Articles entered into force.

At the time the notification was filed, the principal criteria used by U.S. authorities to gauge order or disorder in the markets were the width of spreads between bid and asked quotations and the sharpness of movements in rates within one day and between one day and the next. Official actions often took the form of offers that narrowed the spread between bid and asked quotations without an attempt to move rates in one direction or another.[155]

On November 1, 1978, following a persistent decline of the dollar, the Treasury and Federal Reserve announced a dramatic change of policy:

> Recent movement in the dollar exchange rate has exceeded any decline related to fundamental factors, is hampering progress toward price stability, and is damaging the climate for investment and growth. The time has come to call a halt to this development. . . . In addition to domestic measures being taken by the Federal Reserve, the United States will, in cooperation with the governments and central banks of Germany and Japan, and the Swiss National Bank, intervene in a forceful and coordinated manner in the amounts required to correct the situation.[156]

serve System and the Treasury in managing market interventions. See FOMC Foreign Currency Directive set forth in Chapter 4, *supra*, page 136 (note 27).

[154] *Economic Report of the President, 1982, supra* note 131, p. 190.

The U.S. Federal Open Market Committee's Foreign Currency Directive provides: "[Federal Reserve] System operations in foreign currencies shall generally be directed at countering disorderly market conditions, provided that market exchange rates for the U.S. dollar reflect actions and behavior consistent with the IMF Article IV, Section 1." Board of Governors of the Federal Reserve System, *68th Annual Report, 1982* (Washington, 1983), p. 84.

[155] This summary is based on conversations with officials of the Federal Reserve Board and Federal Reserve Bank of New York in the spring of 1978. See Richard K. Abrams, "Federal Reserve Intervention Policy," in Federal Reserve Bank of Kansas City, *Economic Review,* March 1979, p. 15. Recall illustrations of Federal Reserve intervention in Deutsche mark in Chapter 4, *supra,* pages 148–151.

[156] U.S. Treasury and Federal Reserve System press releases of November 1, 1978. See Alan R. Holmes and Scott E. Pardee, "Treasury and Federal Reserve Foreign Exchange Operations," in Federal Reserve Bank of New York, *Quarterly Review,* vol. 3, no. 4 (Winter 1978–79), p. 63 at p. 65; and *IMF Survey,* November 6, 1978, pp. 337 and 347–49. See also Solomon, *supra* note 18, pp. 348–54; F. Lisle Widman, *Making International Monetary Policy* (Washington: Georgetown University International Law Institute, 1982), pp. 175–85; and Herman Nickel, "The Inside Story of the Dollar Rescue," *Fortune,* vol. 98, no. 11 (December 4, 1978), p. 40.

To build a "war chest" to finance the more active intervention policy, U.S. authorities judged it necessary to draw the equivalent of $3 billion in Deutsche mark and Japanese yen on the U.S. reserve tranche position with the IMF, to use U.S. holdings of SDRs equivalent to $2 billion, to issue Treasury securities denominated in foreign currencies, and to sharply increase the size of reciprocal currency arrangements with the central banks of Germany, Japan, and Switzerland. The total of the foreign currencies made available to U.S. authorities by these actions was equivalent to about $30 billion. Steps were also taken to increase interest rates in the

The new policy, applauded at the time by officials of other countries,[157] was intended to achieve a change in the direction of rate movements.[158] The policy suggested that, when rates significantly diverged from what officials believed they should be, market participants might expect official intervention.[159] U.S. authorities intervened not only in New York but also in markets in other countries using foreign central banks as agents. Operating through U.S. commercial banks with foreign branches, the Federal Reserve intervened in Hong Kong, Singapore, and other markets where the time differential was significant.[160] After the dollar subsequently rose, the Federal Reserve and Treasury became net buyers of foreign currencies.[161]

Shortly after the Administration of Ronald Reagan came to office in 1981, intervention policy went through a second metamorphosis. The dollar was continuing to rise in the markets and officials appear to have welcomed that trend as an aid in controlling domestic inflation. It was announced that authorities would no longer attempt to influence the direction of rate movements. Officials would be even more hesitant about interventions than in the pre-November 1978 period. The new test was not disorder, but "severe disorder."[162] The authorities did intervene on March 30, 1981—the day President Reagan was shot in an assassination attempt.[163] No further interventions took place until June 1982.

The "severe disorder" test was modified after the meeting of heads of state and government of Canada, France, Federal Republic of Germany, Italy,

United States and to increase required reserves of U.S. banks for certain liabilities. Legal aspects of reciprocal currency arrangements, reserve tranche drawings, and activations of the General Arrangements to Borrow are treated in this book at pages 135, 235, and 287.

[157] See note 270, *infra,* respecting IMF consultations concerning the November 1978 actions.

[158] In the two months following the announcement, U.S. authorities sold foreign currencies in the exchange markets equivalent to over $6.6 billion. See Alan R. Holmes and Scott E. Pardee, "Treasury and Federal Reserve Foreign Exchange Operations," in Federal Reserve Bank of New York, *Quarterly Review,* vol. 4, no. 1 (Spring 1979), p. 67 at pp. 68–70.

[159] Anthony M. Solomon, Under Secretary of the Treasury for Monetary Affairs, in May 1979 stated: "In circumstances in which rate movements are clearly exceeding changes warranted by underlying factors, intervention—undertaken within the context of appropriate basic policies and in cooperation with other countries—will be used to restore market stability." *Authorization for Treasury's International Affairs Functions: Hearing before the Subcommittee on International Finance of the Committee on Banking, Housing, and Urban Affairs,* U.S. Senate, 96th Congress, 1st Session (1979), p. 8.

[160] See Alan R. Holmes and Scott E. Pardee, "Treasury and Federal Reserve Foreign Exchange Operations," in Federal Reserve Bank of New York, *Quarterly Review,* vol. 4, no. 1 (Spring 1979), p. 67 at p. 72; and Pardee, *idem,* vol. 5, no. 1 (Spring 1980), p. 36 at p. 43.

[161] When the Administration of Jimmy Carter left office in January 1981, U.S. authorities had net holdings of foreign currencies amounting to about $5 billion after making allowance for currency swap obligations and other foreign currency liabilities. Statement of Beryl W. Sprinkel, Under Secretary of the Treasury for Monetary Affairs, in *International Economic Policy: Hearing before the Joint Economic Committee,* U.S. Congress, 97th Congress, 1st Session (1981), p. 2 at p. 12.

[162] *Economic Report of the President, 1982, supra* note 131, p. 173. See also testimony of Beryl W. Sprinkel, *supra* note 161, pp. 4–6.

[163] Scott E. Pardee, "Treasury and Federal Reserve Foreign Exchange Operations," in Federal Reserve Bank of New York, *Quarterly Review,* vol. 6, no. 2 (Summer 1981), p. 76 at p. 77.

United Kingdom, and United States at Versailles in June 1982. A joint statement issued at the conclusion of that meeting stated:

> We are ready, if necessary, to use intervention in exchange markets to counter disorderly conditions, as provided for under Article IV of the IMF Articles of Agreement.[164]

On June 14, 1982, the U.S. authorities intervened for the first time in almost fifteen months.[165] Thereafter U.S. authorities have intervened occasionally in a manner reminiscent of the 1975–early 1978 period, but have not done so frequently.[166]

Other countries with floating currency rates have also had to develop intervention policies. Their policies, like those of the United States, have not always been fully articulated or consistently applied.[167]

Questions can be raised about whether abrupt changes in policy in the management of floating rates, whether by the United States or other countries, are consistent with the obligation of IMF Article IV, Section 1, to promote a stable system of exchange rates. In any event, they are manipulations,[168] the good and bad effects of which call for assessment.[169] Also, what is meant by "disorderly conditions" still remains a subject of dispute. The coincidence of the term in IMF guiding principle B,[170] the U.S. 1978 notification to the Fund,[171] and the Versailles communiqué[172] probably reflects acoustic agreement. The U.S. authorities and their counterparts utter the same words but do not mean the same thing.[173]

---

[164] Paragraph 5 of the Joint Statement on International Monetary Undertakings, issued at Versailles, June 6, 1982. *Weekly Compilation of Presidential Documents*, vol. 18 (1982), p. 756 at p. 758; *IMF Survey*, June 21, 1982, p. 189. See Gold, "Hague Lectures," *supra* note 3, pp. 229–31.

[165] A realignment of central rates of currencies in the European Monetary System became effective June 14, 1982. See note 210, *infra*. Not only were rates between EMS currencies and the dollar unsettled when the market opened, but rates with the Japanese yen were also in disorder. See Donald T. Regan, "The Versailles Summit and the World Economy," *Wall Street Journal*, June 15, 1982, p. 26; and Sam Y. Cross, "Treasury and Federal Reserve Foreign Exchange Operations," in Federal Reserve Bank of New York, *Quarterly Review*, vol. 7, no. 3 (Autumn 1982), p. 53 at pp. 55, 60, and 65.

[166] The Federal Reserve Bank of New York has also intervened fairly frequently in the New York market as agent of foreign central banks on their instructions and at their risk.

[167] See discussion at pages 546–548, *infra*, of the management of floating rates between the dollar and the currencies participating in the European Monetary System. See generally Argy, *Exchange-Rate Management*, *supra* note 119; and Otmar Emminger, *Exchange Rate Policy Reconsidered* (Occasional Paper no. 10; New York: Group of Thirty, 1982).

[168] See notes 91–94, *supra*, and accompanying text.

[169] See notes 95–97, *supra*, and accompanying text.

[170] Note 99, *supra*, and accompanying text.

[171] Note 131, *supra*, and accompanying text.

[172] Note 164, *supra*, and accompanying text.

[173] See, e.g., Solomon, *supra* note 18, chapters 18 and 19; and Emminger, *Exchange Rate Policy Reconsidered*, *supra* note 167.

For discussions of policy reasons favoring and opposing official intervention in a floating system, see Philippe Jurgensen et al., *Report of the Working Group on Exchange Market Intervention* (Washington: U.S.

European Monetary System Exchange Rate Arrangement

Description. Among the exchange rate arrangements IMF members may choose, in the context of prevailing conditions, are ''cooperative arrangements by which members maintain the value of their currencies in relation to the value of the currency or currencies of other members.''[174] This is the procedure chosen by the member states of the European Economic Community that participate in the European Monetary System (EMS).[175] The EMS is a complex system involving an exchange rate arrangement, related financing mechanisms, and consultation procedures. The basic European Council resolution introducing the EMS states: ''The EMS is and will remain fully compatible with the relevant articles of the IMF Agreement.''[176] Thus, all documents relating to the EMS must be interpreted in a manner that is consistent with the IMF Articles.

The European Monetary System is intended to be a durable and effective scheme for close monetary cooperation leading to a zone of monetary stability in Europe. Stabilization of exchange rates among EEC currencies is seen as important to economic integration and a necessary step to an ultimate goal of economic and monetary union.[177] All the member states of the EEC, except the United Kingdom and Greece, participate in the EMS exchange rate arrange-

---

Department of the Treasury, March 1983); Michael Mussa, *The Role of Official Intervention* (Occasional Paper no. 6; New York: Group of Thirty, 1981); and Argy, *Exchange Rate Management, supra* note 119. Many other works could be cited. The *Report of the Working Group on Exchange Market Intervention* was commissioned by the June 1982 Versailles Summit Conference and was prepared by officials of the finance ministries and central banks of Canada, France, Federal Republic of Germany, Italy, Japan, United Kingdom, and United States and officials of the European Economic Community. See also U.S. Treasury and Federal Reserve System staff studies that are cited and summarized in *Federal Reserve Bulletin,* vol. 69 (1983), pp. 830–37.

[174] IMF Article IV, section 2(b)(ii).

[175] The institutional structure of the European Economic Community is explained in Chapter 2, *supra,* page 76 et seq.

[176] Part A, paragraph 5.3, of European Council Resolution of December 5, 1978, on the establishment of the European Monetary System; *Bulletin of the European Communities,* 1978, no. 12, p. 10. The resolution is reprinted in European Communities Monetary Committee, *Compendium of Community Monetary Texts* (Brussels–Luxembourg, 1979), p. 40. The legal character of the resolution is considered in Chapter 2, *supra,* pages 80–81.

[177] European Council Resolution of December 5, 1978, *supra* note 176, Part A, paragraph 1. See also the conclusions of the Presidency of the European Council of July 7, 1978; *Bulletin of the European Communities,* 1978, no. 6, p. 17 at pp. 17–18 and 20–21.

The development of plans for the EMS is summarized in *20th Report on the Activities of the Monetary Committee,* in *Official Journal of the European Communities,* no. C-240, September 25, 1979, p. 1, at paragraphs 3–13 and Annex I; and Niels Thygesen, ''The Emerging European Monetary System: Precursors, First Steps, and Policy Options,'' in Robert Triffin (ed.), *EMS: The Emerging European Monetary System* (Brussels: Banque Nationale de Belgique, 1979), p. 87 at pp. 103–120, and comments on Mr. Thygesen's paper at pp. 138–39 and 144–45. See also Solomon, *supra* note 18, pp. 293–97.

ment and these two countries have indicated that they may join at a later time.[178] The EMS, which began operation March 13, 1979, replaced an earlier European exchange rate arrangement called the ''snake.''[179]

The European currency unit (ECU), described in Chapter 8,[180] is the denominator (numeraire) for the EMS exchange rate mechanism. Each participating country, in agreement with the other participants, sets an official central rate for its currency in terms of the ECU. On the basis of these official central rates with the ECU, official cross-rates between each pair of currencies are calculated. The resulting matrix of official currency equivalencies can be called a parity grid.[181] The maximum deviations from bilateral parity grid rates permitted in the spot market over time are defined by intervention points that are $2\frac{1}{4}$ percent above and $2\frac{1}{4}$ percent below each bilateral parity grid rate.[182] Mem-

---

[178] While the U.K. pound sterling is included in the ''basket'' by which the European currency unit (ECU) is measured, the Greek drachma, as of January 1, 1984, was not. The drachma is to be included by December 31, 1985, at the latest. See Chapter 8, *supra,* page 320.

[179] The ''snake'' exchange rate arrangement was instituted in March 1972—a year before the final collapse of the Bretton Woods system. When begun, the snake involved maintaining narrow margins of rate fluctuation around pegged rates among EEC currencies while maintaining fixed, but wider, margins of fluctuation against the U.S. dollar in accordance with the IMF's wider margins decision, E.B. Decision No. 3463, *supra* note 40. This was the so-called snake-in-the-tunnel arrangement. If the exchange rates between each snake currency and the U.S. dollar were charted over time and the charts overlaid each other, the image of a snake would appear: the exchange rates among the snake currencies would fluctuate within a narrow band (the snake's body) which would never exceed $2\frac{1}{4}$ percent in width, while the body would squirm up and down in relation to the dollar within a $4\frac{1}{2}$ percent band. With the advent of floating rates for actively traded currencies in March 1973, the arrangement was modified so that narrow margins continued to be maintained among participating currencies but no defined margins (no ''tunnel'') would be maintained with the U.S. dollar.

The snake arrangement had a checkered history. The only currencies participating in the snake at the time it was superseded by the EMS in March 1979 were the Deutsche mark, Netherlands guilder, Belgium–Luxembourg franc, and Danish krone. At various times France, Italy, the United Kingdom, Norway, and Sweden participated in, or associated their currencies with, the snake arrangement. For a legal and technical analysis of the snake and a detailed chronology, see Richard W. Edwards, Jr., ''The European Exchange Rate Arrangement Called the 'Snake,' '' *University of Toledo Law Review,* vol. 10 (1978), p. 47. See also Directorate-General for Economic and Financial Affairs, ''The European Monetary System,'' *European Economy* (published by the Commission of the European Communities), no. 12 (July 1982), p. 7 [hereinafter *Directorate-General Report*], at pp. 67–69.

[180] At pages 315–326 and 342–345.

[181] European Council Resolution of December 5, 1978, *supra* note 176, Part A, paragraphs 2 and 3; and Agreement between the Central Banks of the Member States of the European Economic Community, dated March 13, 1979, laying down the operating procedures for the European Monetary System, Articles 1 and 2. The central bank agreement appears in *European Economy, supra* note 179, no. 3 (July 1979), p. 102; and in *Compendium of Community Monetary Texts* (1979), *supra* note 176, p. 55. The legal character of this agreement is considered in Chapter 8, *supra,* page 321. See also Article 1 of Decision No. 12/79 (March 13, 1979) of the Board of Governors of the European Monetary Cooperation Fund; *European Economy,* no. 3 (July 1979), p. 109.

[182] The exact margins are -2.2247 percent and $+2.2753$ percent so that the upper intervention point, say of the Deutsche mark in Brussels, is the exact arithmetical inverse of the lower intervention point of the Belgian franc in Frankfurt. $97.7753 : 100 = 100: 102.2753$.

A country (such as Belgium) that has a two-tier system of exchange markets (in which currency exchanges for some capital transactions take place at rates different from those for current transactions) is only committed to keep the rates in the regulated market (market for current transactions) within the defined margins. This was also the understanding in the previous snake arrangement. See Edwards, ''European Exchange Rate Arrangement,'' *supra* note 179, p. 50.

ber states of the EEC whose currencies were not in the snake at the time of its replacement by the EMS in March 1979 were permitted to temporarily establish fluctuation margins of $\pm$ 6 percent, but are expected to reduce the margins as economic conditions permit; Italy was the only EMS participant to choose this option.[183] Each central bank publishes the intervention points for its currency against each other EMS currency, calculated as explained above.[184] The market is thus informed that, barring official changes in central rates, spot rates will be kept within the stated bounds. Maintenance of rates within the stated bilateral limits is a formal legal obligation of the monetary authorities in each country participating in the EMS, and official intervention in the markets at the fluctuation limits is compulsory.[185]

An interesting result is logically compelled by the mathematics of the system: Forgetting the Italian lira for a moment, so long as each EMS participant intervenes as required to keep market rates involving its currency within $\pm$ $2\frac{1}{4}$ percent of its parity grid rate with each other currency, the band of fluctuation separating the strongest and weakest currencies will never at any one time exceed $2\frac{1}{4}$ percent.[186] Where the $2\frac{1}{4}$ percent band falls in the $4\frac{1}{2}$ percent potential range seen from the standpoint of any one currency can vary over time. The management of the EMS requires constant monitoring of the market by the central banks.[187]

Legal issues involved in the establishment and operation of the EMS include:

— Defining the terms of obligations to intervene in the market to contain rate fluctuations within the agreed narrow range, the countries upon which those obligations fall, and the currencies to be used.
— Establishing procedures to assure that underlying economic and monetary policies of the participating countries are consistent with the

[183] European Council Resolution of December 5, 1978, *supra* note 176, Part A, paragraph 3.1.

[184] For a table displaying the official central rates of each currency against the ECU and the bilateral central rates and intervention limits of each pair of currencies when the EMS began March 13, 1979, see "The European Monetary System: Its Structure and Operation, " *Monthly Report of the Deutsche Bundesbank,* March 1979, p. 11 at p. 14. For comparable tables showing central rates and intervention limits following the rate changes effective March 21, 1983, see *IMF Survey,* April 4, 1983, p. 103. See also note 211, *infra,* and accompanying text.

[185] European Council Resolution of December 5, 1978, *supra* note 176, Part A, paragraph 3.4; and Agreement of EEC central banks on EMS operating procedures, *supra* note 181, Article 2.

[186] This can be illustrated by a simple example. Assume that the official EMS rates for currencies A, B, and C are 100 A = 100 B = 100 C. Intervention points on all exchanges are 97.7753 and 102.2753. Further, suppose that A is a strong currency and C a weak currency so that rates diverge toward the margins in the market.

It is not possible for 100 B to at the same time buy 98 A and 102 C, because that would mean that 100 A could then buy 104 C which would exceed the A–C intervention limit. If the A–B, A–C, and B–C intervention limits are all maintained, the band of fluctuation cannot in logic exceed $2\frac{1}{4}$ percent.

[187] Some commercial banks use computers to identify rates that are approaching the intervention limits with signals to their traders to anticipate central bank intervention.

agreed official central rates and that central rates are changed when they impede balance-of-payments adjustment for any of the participating countries.

— Determining responsibilities and coordinating policies in managing the rates between EMS currencies and the U.S. dollar (and other actively traded currencies).

— Arranging financing for market interventions and establishing rules on how profits and losses from market interventions are to be shared.

Intra-EMS Intervention Obligations. The basic rule is that a central bank must buy or sell its currency for its partner's currency on the exchange markets, without limit as to amount, at the agreed and published exchange limits. These intervention points, as explained above, are (except with respect to the Italian lira) $2\frac{1}{4}$ percent above and $2\frac{1}{4}$ percent below the official parity grid rates. The interventions of the central banks issuing the two currencies are supposed to take place simultaneously. That is, if the Deutsche mark is at the top of the EMS band and the Belgian franc is on the floor, with the spot rate for exchanges of the currencies deviating from parity by the full $2\frac{1}{4}$ percent, the Deutsche Bundesbank is to intervene in Frankfurt buying Belgian francs in exchange for mark and the Banque Nationale de Belgique is to buy francs in the Brussels market in exchange for mark.[188] Interventions at the limits normally in fact occur at both places. The interventions may not always be simultaneous because it may take a certain, though limited, time for arbitrage to work through from one market to another. The interventions in Frankfurt may be larger than those in Brussels, or vice versa, depending on the requirements of the markets.

The European Council resolution establishing the EMS, which is probably not legally binding, states: "Intervention in *participating currencies* is compulsory when the intervention points defined by the fluctuation margins are reached." [emphasis added] [189] With respect to interventions generally, the resolution states that they will "in principle" be made in participating currencies.[190] The central bank agreement implementing the EMS, an agreement that is legally binding, does not require that interventions, even at the compulsory intervention points, be effected in participating currencies. Speaking of interventions generally, it states, like the European Council resolution, that they shall "in principle" be effected in currencies of the participating central

---

[188] See European Council Resolution of December 5, 1978, *supra* note 176, Part A, paragraph 3.4; and Agreement of EEC central banks on EMS operating procedures, *supra* note 181, Article 2. Technical aspects of the compulsory market interventions are similar to the practices under the earlier snake arrangement. Those practices are described in "The European System of Narrower Exchange Rate Margins," *Monthly Report of the Deutsche Bundesbank,* vol. 28, no. 1 (January 1976), p. 22.

[189] European Council Resolution of December 5, 1978, *supra* note 176, Part A, paragraph 3.4. See Chapter 2, *supra,* pages 80–81, regarding the resolution's legal character.

[190] *Idem,* paragraph 3.3.

banks.[191] It appears that the normal practice, when a bilateral compulsory intervention point is reached, is for the authorities of the two countries to each intervene in the EMS partner's currency as contemplated by the European Council resolution and illustrated in the example above.[192]

The authorities in most EMS countries (Germany being the principal exception) appear to believe that it is easier, and less costly in foreign exchange, to maintain a position within the EMS band than to accept the full range of fluctuation. As a result, there is a great deal of intervention before compulsory intervention limits are reached. These interventions, if conducted in EMS currencies, have up to now required case-by-case concurrence of the authorities issuing the currencies involved. This concurrence is required whether the partner's currency is bought or sold and, if sold, whether the currency employed is taken from the central bank seller's own holdings or comes from other sources.[193] By contrast, the U.S. authorities have not required concurrence on a case-by-case basis for the use of dollars to maintain intra-EMS rates whether the interventions are at the fluctuation limits or intra-marginal. As a consequence, the larger share of intra-marginal interventions intended to maintain EMS rates have been made in U.S. dollars. The dollar is also convenient as EMS countries hold substantial amounts of that currency in their reserves.

Where a "threshold of divergence" has been passed between the market rate of an EMS currency and the basket value of the ECU, even though a compulsory bilateral intervention point has not been reached, the issuer may engage in "diversified intervention." Diversified intervention consists of buying or selling several EMS currencies in the market in exchange for the issuer's currency in order to bring the rate between that currency and the basket value of the ECU closer to the official central rate.[194] The operation of the "divergence indicator" is explained below.[195]

Unlike compulsory interventions at the fluctuation limits in the EMS partner's currency (that do not require concurrence of the issuer), diversified interventions, like other intra-marginal interventions in EMS currencies, require the concurrence of the issuers of the EMS currencies used (unless, for the particular

---

[191] Agreement of EEC central banks on EMS operating procedures, *supra* note 181, Article 2.2.

[192] Scott E. Pardee, "Treasury and Federal Reserve Foreign Exchange Operations," in Federal Reserve Bank of New York, *Quarterly Review*, vol. 5, no. 1 (Spring 1980), p. 36 at p. 37.

Originally under the predecessor snake, the U.S. dollar was only to be used to affect rates between the snake currencies and the dollar, but it was later used to also maintain intra-snake rates. Thus, in the example above, instead of using its partner's currency, the Belgian central bank might simply buy francs in exchange for U.S. dollars and the Bundesbank might sell mark for dollars in the market. See Edwards, "European Exchange Rate Arrangement," *supra* note 179, at p. 57; "European System," *supra* note 188; and Joanne Salop, "Dollar Intervention Within the Snake," *IMF Staff Papers*, vol. 24 (1977), p. 64.

[193] See Agreement of EEC central banks on EMS operating procedures, *supra* note 181, Article 2.2; and "European System," *supra* note 188, p. 25. See also Deutsche Bundesbank, *Report of the Deutsche Bundesbank for the Year 1981*, p. 80.

[194] European Council Resolution of December 5, 1978, *supra* note 176, Part A, paragraph 3.6.

[195] At page 542, *infra*.

currency, the compulsory intervention limit has also been reached).[196] It was expected at the outset of the EMS,[197] and has turned out to be the case, that the U.S. dollar is the principal currency, but not the only currency, used in "diversified interventions." As noted earlier, dollars are held in reserves and can be used in market interventions without the necessity of obtaining the special concurrence of U.S. authorities.

In order to facilitate the greater use of EMS currencies in intra-marginal interventions, the Commission of the European Communities has proposed that the authorities give broad advance authorizations for the use of their currencies in diversified interventions when the divergence indicator crosses a predetermined threshold and for use in intra-marginal interventions generally, in accordance with stated criteria.[198]

Adjustment of Official Rates and the Pursuit of Appropriate Underlying Policies.   Article 107 of the EEC Treaty requires member states to treat their policies respecting exchange rates as matters of "common concern." A 1974 Council of Ministers decision states: "Any Member State intending *de jure* or *de facto*, to change, discontinue or re-establish the parity, central rate or intervention points of its currency shall initiate a prior consultation."[199] Difficulties were encountered, however, during the period the snake was in operation in giving practical application to the 1974 decision. Changes in the official central rates, that served as reference points for measuring intervention limits in the snake, were not always made promptly or in the magnitude necessary in the light of changes in the balance of payments. While agreed changes in central rates involved both devaluations of some currencies and upward revaluations of others, the revaluations of the Deutsche mark and other currencies that proved to be "strong" were not always as large as their partners desired. The changes in official central rates were made after consultations among the national authorities issuing the snake currencies, but those consultations did not always involve other EEC states or the EC Commission.[200]

---

[196] See note 193, *supra,* and accompanying text.

[197] See "European Monetary System Has as Objectives Greater Economic Stability, Policy Convergence," *IMF Survey,* March 19, 1979, p. 97 at p. 98.

[198] See Commission proposal to the Council of Ministers of March 15, 1982, in *Directorate-General Report, supra* note 179, p. 53 at p. 54. See also *Directorate-General Report,* pp. 49 and 56. Compare Deutsche Bundesbank, *Report of the Deutsche Bundesbank for the Year 1981,* p. 80.

[199] Article 7 of Council Decision No. 74/120 of February 18, 1974, on the attainment of a high degree of convergence of the economic policies of the Member States of the EEC. *Official Journal of the European Communities,* no. L-63, March 5, 1974, p. 16; *Compendium of Community Monetary Texts* (1979), *supra* note 176, p. 90.

[200] During the period the snake was in operation, the Deutsche mark was revalued in March 1973, June 1973, October 1976, and October 1978. The official central rates of other snake currencies were devalued or

The European Council resolution establishing the EMS provides:

> Adjustments of central rates will be subject to mutual agreement by a common procedure which will comprise all countries participating in the exchange rate mechanism and the Commission. There will be reciprocal consultation in the Community framework about important decisions concerning exchange rate policy between countries participating and any country not participating in the system.[201]

The European Monetary System includes a tool, the "divergence indicator," which was not a part of the snake. The divergence indicator measures a currency's deviation from the constellation of parity-grid rates by comparing the currency's market exchange rate against the ECU basket value[202] with the currency's official central rate against the ECU as numeraire of the EMS parity grid. Where the deviation exceeds 75 percent of the maximum possible deviation, the currency's market rate is said to have crossed a "divergence threshold." This is an objective indicator that pinpoints the currency putting a strain on the system. While at the bilateral intervention points there is a simultaneous intervention obligation on the authorities issuing both the weaker and stronger currencies, the divergence indicator when it flashes identifies the issuer of the one currency (strong or weak) that has a special responsibility for taking corrective action, which may take any of a variety of forms.

The concept can best be understood if it is assumed for the moment that all currencies that figure in the ECU basket valuation participate in the EMS. The maximum possible upward divergence of, say, the French franc market rate from its central rate would occur if the franc were simultaneously at its bilateral upper intervention points against all other EMS currencies. Assuming that were the case, the basket value of the ECU in terms of the French franc is computed by adding up the French franc value of each currency component in the basket including the French franc component. The resulting figure is the French franc

revalued on a considerable number of occasions. See Edwards, "European Exchange Rate Arrangement," *supra* note 179, pp. 69–72.

In March 1976 when the Deutsche mark was at the top of the snake and the French franc at the bottom, French officials proposed that the franc be devalued by 3 percent and that Germany revalue the mark by an equivalent percentage. When German authorities indicated they would only revalue by 2 percent, France withdrew from.the snake. See Agence Internationale d'Information pour la Presse (Brussels), *Europe,* no. 1941, March 15–16, 1976, pp. 4–6. In August 1977 at a time when the German mark was at the top of the snake and the Swedish krona at the bottom with Sweden selling foreign currencies to keep rates within the $2\frac{1}{4}$ percent limit, Sweden proposed to devalue the krona by 10 percent. When German officials indicated opposition to the proposed Swedish action, Sweden withdrew from the snake and pegged its currency against a specially selected trade-weighted basket of currencies at a rate effectively 10 percent below the previous rate. See Sveriges Riksbank, *Annual Report,* 1977, pp. 62–75; and *Wall Street Journal,* August 29, 1977, p. 6, and August 30, 1977, p. 4.

[201] European Council Resolution of December 5, 1978, *supra* note 176, Part A, paragraph 3.2.

[202] The basket value of the ECU is explained in Chapter 8, *supra,* pages 317–320.

rate against the ECU basket at the point of maximum possible upward divergence from the central rate. Now, conversely, assume that the French franc is simultaneously at its bilateral lower intervention points against all other EMS currencies. Assuming that were the case, the basket value of the ECU in terms of the French franc is computed by adding up the French franc value of each currency component in the basket including the French franc component. The resulting figure is the franc rate against the ECU basket at the point of maximum possible downward divergence. If the market rate of the French franc against the basket value of the ECU crosses a point that is 75 percent of the way from the central rate to an upper or lower maximum possible divergence rate, the currency's rate is said to have crossed a "threshold of divergence."[203]

Adjustments are made in the indicator system to take account of rate movements of the U.K. pound sterling which is included in the ECU basket valuation but is not currently a participating currency in the EMS. Refinements are also made in handling rates of the Italian lira so that the wider band of fluctuation permitted the lira does not distort the divergence indicator.[204]

In some cases the divergence indicator may flash before a currency reaches its bilateral intervention limit with any other EMS currency and in other cases only after this has happened. Calculations of each EMS currency's market rate against the ECU basket in relation to the currency's divergence threshold are made as often as necessary and at least daily.[205] When a currency's rate crosses the threshold of divergence, this flashes a presumption that the authorities concerned should correct this situation by "adequate measures." According to the

---

[203] The principle described in the text is expressed crudely in a mathematical formula which defines the divergence threshold in terms of a percentage deviation from the central rate:

0.75 x 2.25 [or 6.00 for lira] x (1 minus proportionate weight of the currency in ECU composite)

The adjustment for the weight of the currency in the ECU basket is necessary because a portion of the currency is included in the basket and a currency cannot change its rate against itself. This is consistent with the explanation in the text where the French franc component of the ECU is included in the calculation of the franc–ECU market rate at the point of maximum possible divergence. See "European Monetary System Has as Objectives Greater Economic Stability, Policy Convergence," *supra* note 197, p. 98; and Jacques van Ypersele de Strihou, "Operating Principles and Procedures of the European Monetary System," in Philip H. Trezise (ed.), *The European Monetary System: Its Promise and Prospects* (Washington: Brookings Institution, 1979), p. 5 at pp. 14–15.

Regarding technical aspects of the parity grid and the divergence indicator, see generally "Intervention Arrangements in the European Monetary System," *Bank of England Quarterly Bulletin*, vol. 19 (1979), p. 190; "Le Système Monétaire Européen," *Bulletin de la Banque Nationale de Belgique*, vol. 54, part 2, nos. 1–2 (July–August 1979), p. 3 at pp. 18–22 and 37–39; Jean-Jacques Rey, "Some Comments on the Merits and Limits of the Indicator of Divergence of the European Monetary System," *Revue de la Banque* (Brussels), 1982, no. 1, p. 3; and Joanne Salop, "The Divergence Indicator: A Technical Note," *IMF Staff Papers*, vol. 28 (1981), p. 682.

[204] The Agreement of EEC central banks on EMS operating procedures, *supra* note 181, contains a formal description in Article 3.1. See also European Council Resolution of December 5, 1978, *supra* note 176, Part A, paragraph 3.5.

[205] Agreement of EEC central banks on EMS operating procedures, *supra* note 181, Article 6.

European Council's EMS resolution, these measures can include, but are not limited to, the following:[206]

> *Diversified intervention.* Rather than wait until the currency's rate hits the bilateral limit with another EMS currency and intervention in that currency must be undertaken, diversified intervention can be undertaken before the compulsory limit is reached. Where EMS currencies are used, the interventions will be undertaken with agreement of the monetary authorities involved. "Diversified intervention" is also understood to include intervention in third currencies such as the U.S. dollar.
>
> *Measures of domestic monetary policy.* Changes in interest rates and other domestic monetary policy adjustments that impact movements of funds from one currency to another and hence exchange rates may be considered.
>
> *Changes in central rates.* It is assumed that changes in central rates will adapt rates to fundamental changes in underlying economic relationships and will not be made frequently.
>
> *Other measures of economic policy.* The Council of Ministers and other bodies have recognized that long-term exchange rate stability depends upon convergence of the economic policies of EMS participants.

It should be emphasized that the divergence indicator is a trigger for policy coordination. A country is not under a legal obligation to take immediate action when the indicator flashes for its currency. If the country does not take any of the measures listed above, it has a legal obligation of consultation. It must give the reasons for its failure to act to the other authorities, especially in the "concertation between central banks." In some cases the consultations may not lead to any official actions at the domestic or international level except the decision to wait until bilateral intervention points are hit and then to intervene to halt further rate movements. Additional consultations, if judged necessary, are to take place in appropriate Community bodies, including the Council of Ministers.[207]

The initial EMS official central rates were based on market rates in March 1979 when the EMS began operation. There are no specific rules for determining the timing or magnitude of changes in central rates except that the divergence indicator may suggest the need for changes in those rates or for other policy adjustments. Changes in central rates require the mutual agreement of EMS participants.[208] Officials have stated an assumption that changes must be infre-

---

[206] European Council Resolution of December 5, 1978, *supra* note 176, Part A, paragraph 3.6, as elaborated in "European Monetary System Has as Objectives Greater Economic Stability," *supra* note 197, p. 98, and in *20th Report of Monetary Committee, supra* note 177, Annex I, paragraphs 12–16.

[207] European Council Resolution of December 5, 1978, *supra* note 176, Part A, paragraph 3.6.

[208] See paragraph 3.2 of Part A of European Council Resolution of December 5, 1978, quoted on page 542, *supra*. See also *20th Report of Monetary Committee, supra* note 177, Annex I, paragraphs 9–11.

quent, small, and "reflect only objective trends." If rate changes are too frequent the EMS will not promote the rate stability desired by the participants.[209]

In the first five years of the EMS there were seven changes in official central rates among EMS currencies. They are displayed in the table below.

Realignments in Central Rates[210]

(Percentage Change Against the Group of Currencies Whose Bilateral Parities Were Not Changed)

	Dates of realignments						
	24 Sept. 1979	30 Nov. 1979	22 March 1981	5 Oct. 1981	22 Feb. 1982	14 June 1982	21 March 1983
Belgium-Luxembourg franc	—	—	—	—	−8.5	—	+1.5
Danish krone	−2.9	−4.8	—	—	−3.	—	+2.5
Deutsche mark	+2.	—	—	+5.5	—	+4.25	+5.5
French franc	—	—	—	−3.	—	−5.75	−2.5
Irish pound	—	—	—	—	—	—	−3.5
Italian lira	—	—	−6.	−3.	—	−2.75	−2.5
Netherlands guilder	—	—	—	+5.5	—	+4.25	+3.5

Whenever an EMS currency is devalued or revalued (value raised), new official central rates against the ECU must be established for all the currencies, and bilateral central rates and intervention limits are recalculated for each pair of currencies.[211]

---

[209] See speech by François-Xavier Ortoli of February 14, 1979, summarized in Commerce Clearing House, *Common Market Reports* (Chicago: CCH looseleaf service), paragraph 10,117 at p. 10,395. See also discussion in Thygesen, "Emerging European Monetary System," *supra* note 177, at pp. 97–99 and 111–22.

[210] Data obtained from table in Horst Ungerer, with Owen Evans and Peter Nyberg, *The European Monetary System: The Experience, 1979–82* (IMF Occasional Paper no. 19; Washington, 1983), p. 25 (table 3).

In all but two cases (the rate changes effective Friday, November 30, 1979, and Monday, March 21, 1983), the changes were announced over a weekend and became effective before markets opened on Monday. In the case of the rate changes effective March 21, 1983, agreement was not reached over the weekend, rates were allowed to float at the opening of the markets on Monday, and later that day the changes were announced.

[211] For comprehensive tables displaying all central rates against the ECU and all bilateral central rates at the beginning of the EMS and after each valuation change through the change effective March 21, 1983, see Ungerer, *supra* note 210, pp. 24 and 25 (tables 2 and 4). See also note 184, *supra*, and accompanying text.

The configuration of rates against the ECU, and changes in that configuration, has practical consequences where pre-existing financial obligations are expressed in ECUs and central banks bear the risk of changes in the values of their currencies against the ECU. See Chapter 8, *supra*, pages 328–329.

While the U.K. pound sterling does not participate in the EMS exchange rate mechanism, the "notional" central rate of sterling against the ECU and the central rates of EMS currencies against the ECU were adjusted May 17, 1983, without altering the bilateral central rates among EMS currencies. The change, while

The first adjustment in official rates in September 1979 was preceded by extensive consultation among finance ministry and central bank officials of the countries participating in the EMS rate system. Commission officials were involved and the Monetary Committee was also consulted.[212] This pattern of consultation, with some procedures expedited, has continued with each of the later adjustments.[213] As previously noted, changes in central rates are negotiated and require the mutual agreement of EMS participants. The negotiations can become tense and difficult. The ultimate agreement may be coupled with commitments regarding underlying economic policies by the countries making the parity changes.[214]

The basic decision whether to resist rate movements in the market or accomodate central rates to them remains a matter for judgment although some guidance may be provided by the divergence indicator. Some commentators, reviewing the frequency of official central rate changes, have described the EMS as a "crawling peg" arrangement rather than a system of stable exchange rates. There have been calls for more effective economic policy coordination to avoid the necessity for central rate changes.[215] Legal considerations in the choice of alternative policy instruments for dealing with balance-of-payments deficit or surplus situations are examined in Chapter 12.[216]

Management of EMS Float Against the U.S. Dollar.   As noted in the earlier discussion of the "nth" country problem, an exchange rate is a two-ended thing. The authorities of the EMS countries do not have the right by themselves to determine how the rates between EMS currencies and other currencies (such as the U.S. dollar) are to be managed. Intervention policies must take into account the interests of countries whose currencies are used in the in-

---

not affecting bilateral intervention rates, affected the operation of the divergence indicator. See *Bulletin of the European Communities,* 1983, no. 5, point 2.1.8.

[212] See *Europe, supra* note 200, no. 2754 (September 24–25, 1979), pp. 4–5. See also *Wall Street Journal,* September 24, 1979, p. 6, and September 25, 1979, p. 4.

[213] See *Directorate-General Report, supra* note 179, pp. 35–37; and *Bulletin of the European Communities,* 1983, no. 3, points 1.2.1–1.2.4.

[214] A table showing economic policy measures in connection with central rate realignments appears in Ungerer, *supra* note 210, p. 27 (table 6). See also *Bulletin of the European Communities,* 1983, no. 3, point 1.2.3.

The monetary authorities of EEC states issuing currencies that do not participate in the EMS exchange rate system do not have a right to directly take part in the negotiations. However, they do take part in the Monetary Committee's consideration of the proposed rate changes. See generally *Directorate-General Report, supra* note 179, pp. 35–37.

[215] See generally the papers collected in the symposium, "The European Monetary System: The First Two Years," in Banca Nazionale del Lavoro, *Quarterly Review,* no. 138 (September 1981), pp. 261–370; and papers collected in Jean-Paul Abraham and Michel Vanden Abeele (ed.), *European Monetary System and International Monetary Reform* (Brussels: Editions de l'Université de Bruxelles, 1981).

[216] At pages 608–619. See also pages 589–598.

terventions.[217] The European Council's EMS resolution, recognizing this, explicitly states: "The durability of EMS and its international implications require coordination of exchange rate policies *vis-à-vis* third countries and, as far as possible, a concertation with the monetary authorities of those countries."[218]

In accordance with a working understanding between U.S. monetary authorities and the issuers of actively traded EMS currencies, the market rates between the dollar and these currencies are presently allowed to float in response to market forces with official interventions taking place to maintain orderly trading conditions and to counter what are judged to be excessive movements in the rates.[219] Thus, one of the challenges for the central banks participating in the EMS is to maintain the agreed rate relationships among their currencies and at the same time maintain orderly trading conditions in the joint float of their currencies against the U.S. dollar (which in accordance with market practice is a vehicle currency in exchanges between EMS currencies[220]). The U.K. pound sterling, Swiss franc, Japanese yen, and Canadian dollar also float in relation to the EMS currencies.

Of all the markets between EMS currencies and third currencies, the U.S. dollar–Deutsche mark market has the largest volume. This results from the size of the German economy, the relative strength of its currency, freedom from exchange controls, and the willingness of nonresidents to hold large balances in mark. Thus, attention has focused on the management of the dollar–mark rate. From time to time the Deutsche Bundesbank has engaged in very substantial dollar–mark interventions in Frankfurt and, through the agency of the Federal Reserve Bank of New York, may intervene in the New York market. The Bundesbank is also involved in decisions by the U.S. Treasury and the Federal Reserve System to intervene in mark in New York and at one time shared in the profits and losses from the Treasury and Federal Reserve's market interventions conducted in Deutsche mark.[221]

Sometimes movements into or out of the dollar are accompanied by the weakening or strengthening of all EMS currencies. Other times a change in the dollar–mark rate may place internal strains on the EMS. For example, Belgian authorities attributed the weakening of the Belgian franc in the EMS in November 1979 to Germany's purchase of mark financed by the sale of dollars from its reserves.[222] It is also important to avoid interventions at cross purposes. When

---

[217] See pages 526–527, *supra.*

[218] European Council Resolution of December 5, 1978, *supra* note 176, Part A, paragraph 5.1.

[219] See pages 526–527 and 532–535, *supra.*

[220] While there can be direct exchanges between, say, Deutsche mark and Irish pounds, there are greater volumes of transactions, and thus more market depth, in exchanges of mark for dollars and dollars for Irish pounds.

[221] See Chapter 4, *supra,* pages 143–151.

[222] See N. Thygesen, "Are Monetary Policies and Performances Converging?" in Banca Nazionale del Lavoro, *Quarterly Review,* no. 138 (September 1981), p. 297 at pp. 316–18; and Alexander J. Swoboda,

the Bundesbank sells dollars to resist a decline in the mark in relation to the dollar, central banks in a "strong" position should acquire mark balances, not dollars, to maintain intra-EMS rates.[223]

While the sale of one Community currency for another to maintain intra-EMS margins is supposed to be automatic when the intervention points are reached, the exchange of a Community currency for dollars to influence rates is in principle subject to prior consultations among the EMS participants. Operating understandings appear to have been developed; and, if the actions are within those general understandings, subsequent notification is sufficient.[224]

Consultation sessions involving the exchange of information are held several times a day through a telephone network among all EEC central banks (whether they are EMS participants or not). Telephone conversations between some of these banks and issuers of other currencies, including authorities in the United States, Canada, Japan, Switzerland, Sweden, and Norway also take place at least daily. They share information on the tone of their markets, official interventions that have taken place or are planned, and other matters.

One often hears calls in the EEC for a "common policy" of the EMS vis-à-vis the dollar.[225] These calls may reflect problems in achieving economic convergence within the European Economic Community as much as problems relating to the United States. As long as there is no procedure for sharing among EMS participants the costs, burdens, and internal consequences of dollar interventions, it will be difficult to develop a common policy on the management of the exchange rates between the dollar and currencies participating in the EMS.

Introduction to Symposium "The European Monetary Fund: Internal Planning and External Relations," in Banca Nazionale del Lavoro, *Quarterly Review*, no. 134 (September 1980), p. 307 at pp. 314-15.

[223] See R.S. Masera, "The First Two Years of the EMS: The Exchange-Rate Experience," in Banca Nazionale del Lavoro, *Quarterly Review*, no. 138 (September 1981), p. 271 at p. 279.

[224] The Agreement of EEC central banks on EMS operating procedures, *supra* note 181, states in Article 2.2 that interventions in the foreign exchange market in non-EEC currencies "shall be conducted in accordance with the relevant guidelines that were adopted by the Committee of Governors [of EEC Central Banks] in its Report of 9th December 1975 or that may be adopted in the future, or shall be subject to concertation among all the participating central banks." See also "European System," *supra* note 188, p. 25.

[225] See, e.g., Commission Communication to the Council of Ministers of March 15, 1982, in *Directorate-General Report, supra* note 179, p. 88 at pp. 90-91.

Thought continues to be given to the idea of establishing a target zone, subject to continuing management and adjustment, between the ECU and the U.S. dollar or between the Deutsche mark and the dollar. The idea is not new. During the period France was a participant in the "snake," French officials argued that a float by the snake against the dollar, with intervention only to counter disorderly conditions, was not viable over the long term. See *Europe, supra* note 200, no. 1787, July 11, 1975, pp. 9-10; and no. 1941, March 15-16, 1976, pp. 4-6.

Financing of Interventions. The participants in the EMS have arranged large-scale financing facilities to support market interventions that may be required under the EMS. The availability of these facilities to authorities issuing EMS currencies is also intended to convince other actors in the exchange market of the determination of the authorities to honor their EMS obligations. The facilities are described in Chapter 8 and it is necessary here to make only a few supplementary comments.[226]

In accordance with an understanding made several years ago and reaffirmed in 1979, EEC central banks hold their partners' currencies only in amounts necessary for working balances and do not hold substantial amounts of EEC currencies in their reserves except by mutual agreement. Under present procedures, the Committee of Governors of the EEC Central Banks lays down limits on working balances. These limits may be exceeded only with the consent of the central bank issuing the currency.[227] Thus, if the Banque Nationale de Belgique must sell Deutsche mark in Brussels it needs an assured supply of mark.[228] An agreement of the EEC central banks of March 13, 1979, guarantees that the bank issuing the currency needed, in this case the Deutsche Bundesbank, will make the currency available to its partner bank through the European Monetary Cooperation Fund (FECOM). The amount available is in theory without any limitation so long as the funds are used to finance official interventions at the fluctuation limits to maintain rates within EMS margins.[229] If the Belgian central bank sells U.S. dollars to acquire Belgian francs in the market, it can draw the dollars from its reserves; exchange special drawing rights (SDRs),[230] European currency units (ECUs),[231] or other assets held in its reserves for dollars; or in appropriate cases draw dollars from certain EEC financing facilities,[232] from the International Monetary Fund,[233] from the U.S. Federal Reserve System under a reciprocal currency arrangement,[234] or from other sources.

The Deutsche Bundesbank has a choice with respect to the francs it ac-

---

[226] See page 326 et seq.

[227] Agreement of EEC central banks on EMS operating procedures, *supra* note 181, Article 15. The agreement also requires that a central bank liquidating a drawing under the very-short-term financing facility first use any holdings it may have of currencies issued by EMS creditor countries. See Chapter 8, *supra,* page 329.

[228] See intervention example at page 539, *supra.*

[229] Agreement of EEC central banks on EMS operating procedures, *supra* note 181, Articles 6–16. The operation of this very-short-term financing facility is explained in Chapter 8, *supra,* pages 327–332.

[230] See generally Chapter 5, *supra.*

[231] See Chapter 8, *supra,* pages 315–326 and 342–345.

[232] Dollars are not available under the very-short-term financing facility operated by the FECOM, but are available under the FECOM short-term monetary support facility and other EEC arrangements. See generally Chapter 8, *supra,* page 326 et seq.

[233] See generally Chapter 6, *supra.*

[234] See Chapter 4, *supra,* page 135 et seq.

quires in exchange for mark in its compulsory interventions in our example.[235] If it chooses to hold the francs, it bears the profit or loss from any subsequent sale. It has the right, however, at the time it purchases the Belgian currency in Frankfurt to require the Belgian central bank to purchase the newly acquired francs from it, for the same value date, on terms that yield the same result as if the Belgian central bank had itself acquired the francs in exchange for mark in its own market. This is the course the Bundesbank normally follows. The Banque Nationale de Belgique can finance its acquisition of the franc balance from the Bundesbank through the European Monetary Cooperation Fund.

In the case of intra-marginal interventions in EMS currencies, the very-short-term facility of the FECOM is not available on demand but requires the special agreement of the creditor. With the concurrence of the creditor central bank (Deutsche Bundesbank in our example), the Belgian central bank could sell mark in the Brussels market and finance the sale, again if the Bundesbank agrees, under the rules of the FECOM very-short-term financing facility.[236] It appears that normally the Bundesbank or other EMS creditor bank would provide its currency to its partner bank in a direct exchange for dollars or ECUs rather than under the very-short-term facility.[237] Sales of dollars in intra-marginal interventions can be financed in a variety of ways.[238]

An alternative procedure, which to the author's knowledge has not been discussed, is for the European Monetary Cooperation Fund or its successor to intervene in the exchange markets at its own risk to maintain exchange rates within the agreed limits. Amendments to instruments governing the EMS and the FECOM would be required to authorize the FECOM (or a new European Monetary Fund) to buy and sell Community currencies and actively traded third currencies in the market for rate stabilization purposes.

The European Council resolution providing for the EMS invites European countries that are not members of the EEC, but have close economic and financial ties with it, to participate in the EMS exchange rate and intervention mechanism; but participation in the credit procedures is not contemplated.[239] Supplementary bilateral or multilateral facilities could be arranged.[240]

---

[235] See intervention example at page 539, *supra.*

[236] See Chapter 8, *supra,* pages 331–332. See also Deutsche Bundesbank, *Report of the Deutsche Bundesbank for the Year 1979,* p. 59.

[237] *Report of the Deutsche Bundesbank for the Year 1979,* p. 59.

[238] See notes 230–34, *supra,* and accompanying text.

[239] European Council Resolution of December 5, 1978, *supra* note 176, Part A, paragraph 5.2.

[240] When Norway and Sweden participated in the snake exchange rate arrangement they did not benefit from credit facilities operated by the FECOM. Instead, each of the other snake central banks maintained bilateral reciprocal currency arrangements with the central banks of Norway and Sweden. Each central bank agreed to provide its own currency with subsequent settlements in U.S. dollars. "European System," *supra* note 188, p. 28. The Nordic Swap Agreement, effective February 1, 1976, was also used by Norway and Sweden. See Chapter 4, *supra,* page 157 (note 95).

Concluding Comment on the EMS. While the foregoing discussion has focused on legal and technical features of the EMS, the ultimate success of the system will probably depend on the strength of the political commitment of the participants. A good start has been made because, at its beginning, the EMS has had that commitment.

The relative responsibilities of surplus and deficit countries in the adjustment process remain to be worked out, although the "divergence indicator" provides some guidance. Perhaps the most important aspect of the EMS is the pressure it creates for deliberate convergence of economic policies. The participants recognize that only through harmonization of their economic policies can the necessary underlying stability be created to maintain a system of stable exchange rates.[241] In a world of closely integrated financial markets, success in achieving intra-EMS stability may depend in large measure on coordination of EEC policies with policies of the United States and other countries outside the EEC. Inevitably there is an interface of the regional and the international institutions.

Two-Tier Exchange Markets

Article VIII, Section 3, of the IMF Agreement provides that no member shall maintain multiple currency practices, whether within or outside margins under Article IV or prescribed by or under Schedule C, unless authorized by the IMF Agreement or approved by the Fund. It is universally recognized that exchange arrangements that result in different exchange rates for different classes of current transactions require Fund approval under Article VIII, Sections 2 and 3, unless the arrangements are maintained on the basis of Article XIV.[242] Whether approval under Section 3 of Article VIII is required for systems in which a unitary rate applies to all current transactions and a different rate applies to some or all capital transactions has never been formally resolved within the IMF.

When the IMF Executive Board in 1956 adopted E.B. Decision No. 541 -(56/39) that interpreted Article VI to permit capital controls that discriminate between one country and another, the discussions in the Board and the Committee on Interpretation show that the question of whether multiple exchange rates could be used to control capital movements was explicitly reserved.[243] A dis-

---

[241] See, e.g., Ortoli speech, *supra* note 209.

[242] See Chapter 10, *supra,* pages 396–399.

[243] The Executive Board approved the following statement when it adopted Decision No. 541 -(56/39)(July 25, 1956):

> The Committee has not fully examined the question whether multiple currency practices solely designed to control capital movements would require the prior approval of the Fund under Arti-

tinction was thus recognized between controls that bar capital movements and those that raise or lower the cost of transactions via different exchange rates. In 1961 when a number of major countries were preparing to move from Article XIV to Article VIII status, the IMF staff and the U.S. Executive Director, Frank A. Southard, expressed the view that every multiple rate system requires Fund approval under Article VIII, Section 3 (unless maintained on the basis of Article XIV) whether or not any current transactions are subjected to different rates.[244] That position is supported by the broad language used in the text of Section 3 of Article VIII. Those who argue that there is no requirement for Fund approval of multiple rates that apply only to capital transactions point to Article VI, Section 3, which permits countries to control capital movements. Section 3 of Article VI, however, does not make any explicit reference to exchange rates or multiple currency practices and there is no need to imply that such practices come within the exemption carved out by that section.

In fact, it appears that every exchange system up to the present time that has applied different rates to some or all capital transactions has delayed, or routed to the capital category, at least some transactions which are "current" by the IMF's definition.[245] Thus, it has always been necessary for the Fund to review the multiple currency practice. In approving dual exchange markets in which capital and current transactions were separated, the Fund in 1961 conceived a verbal formula under which it gave such approval as was "necessary."[246] The use of the formula to approve the dual market in France in the period 1971–1974 is illustrative. The Fund granted approval "to the extent necessary." Thus, the rate for current transactions was approved. The language permitted those who believed rates applicable to capital transactions required approval to say they had been approved and those who believed the practices were outside Fund jurisdiction to say the Fund had not exercised jurisdiction with regard to them.[247]

cle VIII, Section 3. The question is of a somewhat complex nature as it involves the relationship between Article VIII, Section 3, and the provisions of the Fund Agreement with regard to rates. However, it was the opinion of the Committee that, in the experience of the Fund, the application of differential rates to capital movements in the form of either a fixed rate or a free market generally embraced some current transactions and that in these cases at least members must seek prior approval of the Fund.

Gold, "Hague Lectures," *supra* note 3, pp. 172 and 344–45. See *IMF History 1945–65, supra* note 3, vol. 1, pp. 403–04 and 482, and vol. 2, pp. 548–49. E. B. Decision No. 541 -(56/39) appears in *IMF History 1945–65*, vol. 3, p. 246; *Selected Decisions* (10th issue, 1983), p. 116. Article VI, section 3, and Decision No. 541 are also discussed in Chapter 10, *supra*, pages 455–458.

[244] See *IMF History 1945–65, supra* note 3, vol. 1, pp. 481–82, and vol. 2, pp. 548–49.

[245] See Chapter 10, *supra*, pages 394–396, where the definition of "current" is explained.

[246] See *IMF History 1945–65, supra* note 3, vol. 1, pp. 481–82, and vol. 2, pp. 548–49.

[247] The French two-tier market was in effect August 21, 1971, to March 21, 1974. Foreign exchange for use in settling current transactions was bought and sold in the "official market" with the government's Exchange Stabilization Fund actively intervening to maintain rates within a narrow range. Capital transactions took place in a separate market called the "financial franc market" where rates were allowed to fluctuate in response to market forces. While an effort was made to separate current and capital transactions in accordance

The verbal formula disguised an important point. Should the Fund's review of a country's multiple rate system center on its effects on current transactions only or should it consider the beneficial and adverse effects on the full spectrum of transactions? The author would urge the latter course. In several recent cases, the Fund has approved dual markets without using the phrase "to the extent necessary."[248] It is to be hoped that these latter precedents and further review of the issues will lead the Executive Board to explicitly accept a wide view of Fund jurisdiction under Article VIII, Section 3, over multiple rate systems.

Even if it should be decided that multiple rate systems applicable only to capital transactions do not require IMF approval under Article VIII, Section 3, that would not mean that countries have complete freedom in their use. It should be clear that the exchange rate system in all its aspects must also meet the obligations of Article IV. In countries with two-tier systems, the authorities have an obligation under Article IV, Section 1, to counter disorder in the capital market as well as in the regular market. They may intervene to affect rates in the capital market but only in accordance with arrangements notified to the IMF under Article IV, Section 2.

---

with the IMF's definitions, some current transactions were delayed or routed to the capital category. The IMF approved the dual market during the period of its operation, with some brief gaps, using the "to the extent necessary" formula. Letter of Joseph Gold, General Counsel of the IMF, to the author dated November 3, 1975. The dual market is described in IMF, *25th Annual Report on Exchange Restrictions, 1974* p. 160.

[248] Since 1955 the Belgium–Luxembourg Economic Union has used a dual exchange market system that routes a range of capital transactions (and some current transactions) to a separate "free" market. Prior to May 1971, however, the rates in the official and free markets did not differ substantially and those in the free market could never be at a premium. In May 1971 new measures were introduced to make the separation of the two markets more effective by eliminating the option between the two markets which until then existed for inward capital flows. Since that time the rate on the free market could be at a discount or premium *vis-à-vis* the official market. In whatever direction, the spread has in fact remained fairly low. The IMF approved the dual market in each consultation between 1971 and 1981. The "to the extent necessary" formula has not been used. Letter of John V. Surr, Senior Counsellor, Legal Department of the IMF, to the author, dated March 6, 1978. The market is described in Silard, "Money and Foreign Exchange," *supra* note 3, section 65; and IMF, *29th Annual Report on Exchange Restrictions, 1978*, pp. 61–65.

The Netherlands "O-guilder" market in use in the period 1971–1974 (described in Chapter 10, page 453, note 345) is another example of a dual market that segregated a class of capital transactions and affected some current transactions. This market was approved by the Fund from the March 2, 1973, consultation with the Netherlands until termination of the market in 1974. Again, the "to the extent necessary" formula was not used. Letter of John V. Surr, *idem.*

In the period January 22, 1973, to March 22, 1974, Italy maintained a dual exchange market in which capital and current transactions took place at different rates. The exchange measures involved in the dual market in Italy were approved by the IMF on October 19, 1973. The words "to the extent necessary" did not appear in that decision. Letter of F. Palamenghi-Crispi, Executive Director of the IMF (Italy), to the author dated March 2, 1976. The dual market was abolished after a stand-by arrangement equivalent to SDR 1 billion was negotiated with the IMF. Approval of the stand-by was announced by the Fund on April 10, 1974. The market is described in IMF, *25th Annual Report on Exchange Restrictions, 1974*, pp. 238–39.

An early difference of views on Fund jurisdiction over British multiple currency practices is reported in *IMF History 1945–65, supra* note 3, vol. 1, p. 405. It appears that the IMF in the latter years of the United Kingdom investment currency market (described in Chapter 10, page 450, note 329; now abolished) did not take any formal action with respect to it.

Typically, the operations channeled to the capital market are adjusted from time to time in an effort to achieve the supply and demand balance that authorities believe desirable in the capital market. A dual market with different rates for capital transactions is obviously a manipulation of exchange rates; and if the exchange rate system seen as a whole can be expected to result in an unfair competitive advantage, or to retard rather than assist balance-of-payments adjustment, the dual market runs afoul of Article IV, Section 1. The fundamental character of Article IV, as well as the importance attached to that article by high officials involved in the negotiation of the Second Amendment, argues for it being given primacy over Article VI, Section 3, in case of conflict. One way to avoid a conflict of provisions is to recognize that controls which are inconsistent with the obligations of Article IV are not "necessary."

It is worth noting that the dual markets introduced by France, Italy, and the Netherlands in the early 1970s have been abolished and the rates for current and capital transactions unified. Reliance by industrialized countries on two-tier markets to deal with "disruptive" capital flows appears to have declined.

General Exchange Arrangements

Section 2(c) of the Article IV authorizes the Fund, acting by an 85 percent majority of its total weighted voting power, to establish general exchange arrangements. The establishment of such arrangements would be intended to result in greater uniformity in exchange practices. For example, the Fund could provide for a system of pegging of exchange rates to the special drawing right and for limited margins of fluctuation.

If the Fund should adopt a decision pursuant to Section 4 to apply Schedule C, a par value system would be established with par values based on the special drawing right or another common denominator other than gold or a currency (depending on the Fund's decision). Members would define the values of their currencies in terms of this common denominator. Particular procedures for changing par values are set forth in Schedule C.

For Schedule C to apply, the Fund (acting under Section 4 of Article IV) must first take a decision by an 85 percent majority of its total voting power that international economic conditions permit the introduction of a widespread system of exchange arrangements based on "stable but adjustable par values." The Fund is not under any circumstances required to take that decision.

Without using the talismanic words quoted, the Fund can adopt decisions by the same 85 percent majority, acting under Section 2(c), to "make provision for general exchange arrangements." The words "make provision" in Section 2(c) of Article IV mean that the Fund can work out the details of an exchange rate system and need not limit itself to generally worded formulations. General exchange arrangements can be established, modified, and terminated by an 85 percent majority. By acting pursuant to Section 2(c) to provide for general exchange arrangements, rather than under Section 4 to apply a par value system, the Fund has much greater flexibility. It can adopt a system similar in substance to Schedule C or an entirely different system. It can change the system in the light of changes in the world economy.

While the report of the Executive Directors states that the Fund can under Section 2(c) "recommend" general exchange arrangements,[249] the section does not use that word. It is clear, however, that a member is not obligated under that section to conform its exchange practices to the general arrangements. It may at any time choose different arrangements so long as they are consistent with the purposes of the Fund[250] and with the member's obligations under Section 1. It would be appropriate for the Fund to request, pursuant to Section 3, that a member taking such a course consult with the Fund about its exchange rate policies. During that consultation an opinion could be expressed as to whether the member's exchange policies fulfill the obligations of Section 1, including the obligations to collaborate to promote a stable system of exchange rates.

Par Value System of Schedule C

The procedures for the Fund to adopt a decision, should it wish to do so, to apply Schedule C were outlined in the preceding section and receive further attention at the end of this section. The Fund is not under any circumstances required to make such a decision. The author believes that the use of Section 2(c) provides a wiser and more flexible approach to achieving uniformity in exchange arrangements. Nevertheless, the reader should be familiar with some of the features of a par value system conceived in Schedule C.[251]

If the Fund should decide by an 85 percent of its total voting power to apply Schedule C, its decision will also define the common denominator in which currency values are to be stated. This can be the special drawing right or any other denominator other than gold or a currency. There is no provision for changing the common denominator once it has been chosen.[252]

A decision having been made to apply Schedule C and the common denominator designated, each member will then propose a par value of its currency in terms of the common denominator.[253] The Fund is to concur in or object to the proposed value which will not take effect for purposes of the IMF

---

[249] *Report on Second Amendment, supra* note 67, part 2, chapter C, section 4.

[250] "Purposes of the Fund" refers to Article I and also, it is submitted, to the "recognizing" clause at the beginning of Article IV.

[251] For an elaborate treatment of the par value system conceived in Schedule C, see Gold, "Hague Lectures," *supra* note 3, pp. 245–62.

[252] See Schedule C, paragraph 1. If the special drawing right is chosen as the common denominator, its principle and method of valuation can be changed in accordance with Article XV, section 2. See Chapter 5, *supra*, pages 187–192.

[253] Schedule C, paragraph 2.

Agreement if the Fund objects to it. The Fund can object on economic grounds but not because of social or political policies of the member.[254] A member may decline to establish a par value for its currency and, instead, choose its own exchange arrangements provided that they are consistent with the purposes of the Fund and are adequate to fulfill the member's obligations under Section 1 of Article IV. A member that takes this course must consult with the Fund pursuant to paragraph 3 of Schedule C.[255]

A member, once it has established a par value, is required to maintain exchange rates for its currency on the basis of it. The maximum and minimum rates for spot exchange transactions taking place within its territories between its currency and the currency of other members maintaining par values shall be maintained within 4½ percent on either side of parity.[256] By an 85 percent majority of the total voting power, the Fund can adopt narrower or wider margins. Members can maintain narrower margins than provided in Fund decisions should they wish to do so.[257] The Fund exercises approval jurisdiction over multiple rates maintained by a member even if all the rates fall within the prescribed margins.[258]

A member may propose a change in the par value of its currency only in order to correct, or prevent the emergence of, a "fundamental disequilibrium." The change will take place only if the Fund concurs in it. It must concur if it is satisfied that the change is necessary. The Fund is not to object to a change because of domestic social or political policies of a member. It can object on the basis that the country is not pursuing appropriate economic policies. While the Fund can discourage the maintenance of an unrealistic par value, it cannot compel a member to change the par value of its currency.[259] "Fundamental disequilibrium" is the same term used in the original Articles and, as in the original Articles, is not defined.[260] While under former Article IV a country

---

[254] Schedule C, paragraph 4.

[255] The right to choose other exchange arrangements is explicitly recognized in paragraph 3 of Schedule C. U.S. officials in testimony before congressional committees emphasized this right that members retain upon the introduction of a par value system. See statement of William E. Simon in *Hearings on H.R. 13955, supra* note 95, p. 12; and statement of Edwin H. Yeo III in *Hearings on S3454, supra* note 98, p. 16.

[256] No margin is prescribed for transactions in the forward market. Flexibility is, thus, allowed for official intervention in the forward market. Forward intervention can influence leads and lags—e.g., create disincentives for importers to delay payments to weak currency countries in the expectation that payments can be made later at less cost in terms of the importer's currency.

[257] Schedule C, paragraph 5. See also *Report on Second Amendment, supra* note 67, part 2, chapter C, section 8.

[258] Article VIII, section 3. Spreads—the difference between buying and selling rates of a currency in the market at any one time—must be held within the range required by Article VIII, section 3. See Chapter 10, *supra*, pages 396–399. See generally with respect to multiple rate practices pages 396–399, 407–408, 410–411, 530, and 551–554. See also *Report on Second Amendment, supra* note 67, part 2, chapter C, section 8.

[259] Schedule C, paragraphs 6 and 7. See also *Report on Second Amendment, supra* note 67, part 2, chapter C, sections 9 and 10. Paragraph 11 of Schedule C of the IMF Agreement establishes a procedure whereby, if the SDR is the common denominator, uniform proportionate changes in all par values can be made.

[260] Old Article IV, section 5(a), *original* and *first*. See note 7, *supra*. W.M. Scammell, *International Monetary Policy: Bretton Woods and After* (London: Macmillan, 1975), pp. 71–74, has suggested that an equilib-

could propose a change in par value only to "correct" a fundamental disequilibrium,[261] present Schedule C, paragraph 6, adds "or prevent the emergence of."

Should a member wish to terminate a par value for its currency (once it has been established) and choose other exchange arrangements, it must do so in accordance with paragraphs 8 and 9 of Schedule C. The Fund can object to a termination of a par value, but only by a decision supported by an 85 percent majority of the total voting power. In contrast, the Fund does not have authority to object to a member's withdrawing from general exchange arrangements established under Section 2(c) of Article IV.[262]

Under the former Bretton Woods par value system, changes in par values tended to be traumatic events. Changes were often postponed. It was also difficult to assess the proper magnitude of proposed changes in par values. The burden of adjustment fell primarily on countries in balance-of-payments deficit.[263] The new Schedule C does not explicitly address any of these problems. However, Section 4 of Article IV makes clear that these and other issues are to be addressed before a decision is taken to apply Schedule C. In addition to requiring an 85 percent weighted majority vote of the total voting power for Schedule C to be applied, Section 4 lists other prerequisites for introduction of the Schedule C system of stable but adjustable par values. There must be "arrangements under which both members in surplus and members in deficit in their balances of payments take prompt, effective, and symmetrical action to achieve adjustment." There must also be adequate sources of liquidity to finance temporary imbalances without the need to alter par values, procedures for treating imbalances, and acceptable arrangements for market intervention to maintain exchange rates on the basis of par values. Since Schedule C does not itself deal with any of these matters, it is submitted that such arrangements must be established in advance and thoroughly tested, perhaps using the authority to provide for general exchange arrangements under Section 2(c), before any decision is made to apply Schedule C.[264]

---

rium exchange rate is one that over a period of, say, three years together with other appropriate policies results in no net change in a country's monetary reserves.

[261] Old Article IV, section 5(a), *original* and *first*.

[262] See *Report on Second Amendment, supra* note 67, part 2, chapter C, sections 4, 11, and 12.

If the Fund makes a formal finding that a member does not maintain rates for a substantial volume of exchange transactions within the margins prescribed under paragraph 5 of Schedule C, the par value of the country's currency shall cease to exist for purposes of the IMF Agreement, Schedule C, paragraphs 8, 9, and 10.

[263] See note 8, *supra,* and the materials cited therein.

[264] It has been precisely with such issues, assuring symmetry in balance-of-payments adjustment being but one example, that there has been the greatest controversy. The United States in a paper circulated to the IMF's Committee on Reform (Committee of Twenty) in November 1972 proposed that a system of objective indicators related to changes in countries' monetary reserves be used to trigger decisions to adjust par values. See Chapter 12, *infra,* pages 617–619.

Surveillance, Consultation, and Collaboration

Surveillance

Section 3(a) of Article IV provides:

> The Fund shall oversee the international monetary system in order to ensure its effective operation, and shall oversee the compliance of each member with its obligations under Section 1 of this Article.

This section provides authority for the Fund to conduct consultations with all members concerning their domestic and international policies within the scope of Section 1, whether or not directly related to exchange rates. As noted earlier, efforts to make *formal* determinations of compliance or lack of it with important Section 1 obligations may well be avoided. The Fund's goal must be to assure compliance, and this can best be accomplished through consultation, collaboration, and efforts to give practical application in the particular historical circumstances to the general obligations of Article IV.[265]

The Fund's surveillance powers as they relate to exchange rate policies are stated with force in Section 3(b):

> [T]he Fund shall exercise firm surveillance over the exchange rate policies of members, and shall adopt specific principles for the guidance of all members with respect to those policies. Each member shall provide the Fund with the information necessary for such surveillance, and, when requested by the Fund, shall consult with it on the member's exchange rate policies. . . .

In addition to the three "principles" quoted earlier that the Fund has adopted to guide members' exchange rate policies,[266] the Fund has identified the following developments as among those which "might indicate the need for discussion with a member":[267]

(i) protracted large-scale intervention in one direction in the exchange market;

---

[265] See pages 512–515, *supra.* Consultations on domestic and international policies within the IMF are treated in Chapter 12, *infra,* page 571 et seq.

[266] See page 520, *supra.*

[267] E.B. Decision No. 5392, *supra* note 69, subpart Principles of Fund Surveillance Over Exchange Rate Policies, paragraph 2.

(ii) an unsustainable level of official or quasi-official borrowing, or excessive and prolonged short-term official or quasi-official lending, for balance of payments purposes;

(iii) (a) the introduction, substantial intensification, or prolonged maintenance, for balance of payments purposes, of restrictions on, or incentives for, current transactions or payments, or

   (b) the introduction or substantial modification for balance of payments purposes of restrictions on, or incentives for, the inflow or outflow of capital;[268]

(iv) the pursuit, for balance of payments purposes, of monetary and other domestic financial policies that provide abnormal encouragement or discouragement to capital flows; and

(v) behavior of the exchange rate that appears to be unrelated to underlying economic and financial conditions including factors affecting competitiveness and long-term capital movements.

The developments listed above are only symptoms that something may be amiss. Several of these symptoms are stated with a balance-of-payments qualification. It is submitted that it should be enough to trigger discussions under Section 3(b) that the developments are intended to have effects on the balance of payments or, if done for other reasons, can be expected to have effects on the balance of payments.

The last item on the list above is something of a catch-all. It goes directly to the issue of the appropriateness of the exchange rate. It has been said to be invocable both because of movements in an exchange rate and also because of lack of movement when movement would be expected.[269] The existence of item (v) is somewhat less subject to direct cognizance than the others.

The Executive Board adopted a supplemental decision on surveillance procedure that is very simple and cuts through much of the complexity of the five categories quoted above. The decision states in part:

Whenever the Managing Director considers that a modification in a member's exchange arrangements or exchange rate policies or the behavior of the exchange rate of its currency may be important or may have important effects on other members, whatever the member's exchange arrangements may be, he shall initiate informally and confidentially a discussion with the member. . . . If he considers after

---

[268] Note that the decision refers to restrictions or incentives related to underlying transactions as well as their payments aspects. Note also that capital movements as well as current transactions are included.

[269] Young, *supra* note 69, p. 18.

this prior discussion that the matter is of importance, he shall initiate
and conduct an ad hoc consultation with the member. . . .[270]

This decision gives the Managing Director broad authority to initiate consultations when there is a change in an exchange rate but not of arrangements and when there is a change in underlying circumstances with no change in rate, as well as in other situations. The Managing Director can initiate consultations with a country when it makes a change in policy that appears to be sound as well as a change in policy that would appear to be questionable.

Consultation Procedures

Pursuant to the Executive Board's surveillance decision the periodic consultations under Article IV comprehend the regular consultations under Articles VIII and XIV, thus avoiding the need to schedule separate consultations. These regular consultations are, in principle, to take place with each member annually. The consultations, as they relate to Article IV, include consideration of the member's observance of its obligations under Section 1 of Article IV and its observance of the principles adopted by the Fund under Section 3(b) for guidance of members' exchange rate policies.[271]

While the surveillance decision does not explicitly implement the full scope of responsibilities under Section 3(a) of Article IV, it recognizes that "there is a close relationship between domestic and international economic policies."[272] The Fund has in fact given considerable attention to domestic policies in its regular consultations under Article IV.[273] The surveillance decision is fairly explicit in stating factors to be taken into account in appraising a member's exchange rate policies:

> The Fund's appraisal of a member's exchange rate policies shall be based on an evaluation of the developments in the member's balance of payments against the background of its reserve position and its external indebtedness. This appraisal shall be made within the framework of a comprehensive analysis of the general economic situation

[270] E.B. Decision No. 6026 -(79/13)(January 22, 1979); IMF, *Annual Report, 1979*, p. 136; *Selected Decisions* (10th issue, 1983), p. 15. Following the November 1, 1978, announcement of the United States, *supra* note 156, the IMF held consultations with the United States that culminated in Executive Board discussion of the U.S. program on December 13, 1978, and the Board's expression of support fot the U.S. action. The usefulness of that consultation led to the adoption of Decision No. 6026 which simplifies procedures for initiating ad hoc consultations. See statement of the U.S. Secretary of the Treasury to the Joint Economic Committee of the U.S. Congress in *The Dollar Rescue Operations and Their Domestic Implications: Hearings before the Subcommittee on International Economics of the Joint Economic Committee,* U.S. Congress, 95th Congress, 2nd Session (1978), p. 8 at pp. 14 and 19.

[271] E.B. Decision No. 5392, *supra* note 69, subpart Procedures for Surveillance, section II.

[272] E.B. Decision No. 5392, *idem,* subpart General Principles.

[273] See Chapter 12, *infra,* pages 575–577.

and economic policy strategy of the member, and shall recognize that domestic as well as external policies can contribute to timely adjustment of the balance of payments. The appraisal shall take into account the extent to which the policies of the member, including its exchange rate policies, serve the objectives of the continuing development of the orderly underlying conditions that are necessary for financial stability, the promotion of sustained sound economic growth, and reasonable levels of employment.[274]

For most market-economy countries in which international trade and financial activity represents a substantial part of total transactions, the country's exchange rate is a very important price that influences both the financial world (asset values and rates of return) and the "real" world (production, employment, and trade). No country can be truly indifferent to the exchange rate of its currency. It is virtually inevitable that the appropriateness of the exchange rate maintained by a country using a pegged arrangement will be discussed in an Article IV consultation, and especially when a rate has been maintained despite fundamental changes in the competitiveness of the country's economy. It has been reported that a perennial topic of Article IV consultations, where floating currencies are involved, is whether exchange rate movements are conforming to shifts in "basic determinants" of exchange rates or whether they are responding "unjustifiably and uncontrollably" to "evanescent or perverse influences." Another topic is overshooting or too wide swings in the basic movements of rates.[275] Differences in views of appropriate market intervention policies are aired. Staff papers include consideration of the exchange rate setting and the appropriateness of the exchange rate regime.[276]

The factors listed earlier[277] are pointers or symptoms that a member may not be fulfilling its Section 1 obligations as they relate to its exchange arrangements. They do not create an irrebuttable presumption that a member is in breach of its obligations. For example, a country would be permitted to show that its decision to defend its current pegged exchange rate, which on the surface appears to overvalue its currency in the face of a deterioration in the country's balance-of-payments position, is sound when seen in the context of a pro-

---

[274] E.B. Decision No. 5392, *supra* note 69, subpart Principles of Fund Surveillance Over Exchange Rate Policies, paragraph 3.

[275] William C. Hood, "Surveillance Over Exchange Rates," *Finance and Development*, vol. 19, no. 1 (March 1982), p. 9 at p. 11. See also Solomon, *supra* note 18, pp. 342–44, 358–61, and 368–71.

A former U.S. Secretary of the Treasury stated: "Fund surveillance of members' policies should not be aimed at trying to calculate a zone, or target, or right rate for individual currencies. . . . Such an approach is, in my view, inconsistent with the new Article IV. . . ." Statement of William E. Simon in *Hearings on H.R. 13955, supra* note 95, p. 11. See also statement of Edwin H. Yeo III in *Hearings on S. 3454, supra* note 98, at p. 15.

[276] Attachment to E.B. Decision No. 7088, *supra* note 135, p. 131. See also attachment to E.B. Decision No. 7374, *supra* note 135.

[277] At pages 558–559, *supra*.

gram to control domestic inflation and to encourage local firms to be more cost efficient. The country's exports are expected to again become competitive in world markets without the need for exchange rate depreciation.[278] A Fund staff member has also pointed out that balance-of-payments positions must be examined in a world context. If, for example, some oil exporting countries have large current account surpluses, one would expect counterbalancing deficits elsewhere in the world. One could not expect the deficits to be reduced without also expecting and planning for the surpluses to correspondingly decline.[279]

The surveillance decision provides that the Executive Board "shall reach conclusions" in each regular consultation under Article IV. The Board is to reach its conclusions no later than three months after the termination of discussions between the member and the staff.[280] The procedure followed in stating "conclusions" and their legal character are subjects treated in Chapter 12.[281] It can be expected that the language used in stating conclusions will normally avoid making broad judgments on the compatibility of the country's exchange rate policies seen as a whole with its obligations under Section 1 of Article IV. The conclusions may well be more explicit on narrower issues.[282]

Procedures have been established for discussions between members and the Fund in the interval between regular Article IV consultations. These discussions may be initiated by the Managing Director, applying the criteria quoted in the previous section from the surveillance decision and the supplemental decision on surveillance procedure. The initial step is for the Managing Director to raise the matter informally and confidentially with authorities of the member. If he considers that there is a question about the observance of the principles stated in the surveillance decision or, even if there is no question of compliance, that the matter is important or may have important effects, the Managing Director is to initiate a more formal consultation. As soon as circumstances permit, the Managing Director is to report to the Executive Board or advise the Executive Directors informally of the consultation. Formal discussion in the Executive Board may take place, as was done in the U.S. and Swedish cases,[283] if this appears desirable.[284]

The regular consultations with each member, and the special discussions just mentioned, are informed by and in turn provide insights for the periodic

---

[278] This example develops a comment of Young, *supra* note 69, p. 19.

[279] See Young, *idem,* p. 18.

[280] E.B. Decision No. 5392, *supra* note 69, subpart Procedures for Surveillance, section II.

[281] At pages 575–578.

[282] See Chapter 12, *infra,* page 606. The illustrative conclusion of an actual Article IV consultation, quoted at page 576, *inter alia,* makes the general statement, "Taking into account the recent deterioration in the external current account and in the overall balance of payments, it was important, in the view of Directors, that the exchange rate remain competitive. . . ."

[283] See notes 97 and 270, *supra.*

[284] E.B. Decision No. 5392, *supra* note 69, subpart Procedures for Surveillance, section V; and E.B. Decision No. 6026, *supra* note 270.

wide-ranging discussions of the Executive Board that take place under the agenda heading "World Economic Outlook." These discussions deal with the international adjustment process and review broad developments in exchange rates. Consultation procedures are described more fully in Chapter 12.[285]

Use of Econometric Models

Robert Solomon has expressed a frustration encountered by officials:

> With respect to the determination of exchange rates, it is easy enough to identify the variables at work: differences in price performance and in interest rates, movements of current-account balances, and the expectations about future exchange rates engendered by these variables. What is difficult to know is how important each of these factors is in influencing exchange rates.[286]

While it is always possible to identify further analytical work to be done by economists, progress has been made. The appraisal of the interrelationships of exchange rates and other economic policies and of the economic effects of exchange rate movements and changes in economic policy is facilitated by the use of econometric models. An econometric model consists of a group of mathematical equations. Some of the equations state definitions. Other equations state hypotheses of the economist. Statistical or empirical data where known are substituted for letters, and the equations solved. Through testing and modification the predictive power of the model is improved. An advantage of using an econometric model is that a number of variables with complex interrelationships can be handled simultaneously. Another advantage is that construction of the model requires the economist to be explicit about his or her assumptions, definitions, and theories. The model's predictive power is, of course, dependent upon the assumptions built into it and the quality of the data. The model can be refined as assumptions are refined. The tool permits experience in the form of empirical data to inform theory. The staffs of the IMF, government agencies, and commercial banks, as well as academic economists, have devoted considerable resources to the development of economic models. Econometric models have been developed that attempt to relate policies on exchange rate arrangements, international trade and investment policies, domestic fiscal policies, and domestic monetary policies.[287]

---

[285] At page 571 et seq.

[286] Solomon, *supra* note 18, p. 358.

[287] See generally Jean L. Waelbroeck (ed.), *The Models of Project LINK* (Amsterdam: North Holland Pub. Co., 1976); R. J. Ball (ed.), *The International Linkage of National Economic Models* (Amsterdam: North Holland Pub. Co., 1973); Albert Ando, Richard Herring, and Richard Marston (ed.), *International Aspects of Stabilization Policies* (Conference Series no. 12; Boston: Federal Reserve Bank of Boston, 1974),

In studying changes in exchange rates, economists take special note of what is called the "effective exchange rate" which is an economic calculation differing from the rate quoted in the market. This is the weighted average rate against the currencies of the country's major trading partners.[288] In sophisticated analyses the calculation takes into account the policy adjustments that accompany changes in nominal or market exchange rates including exchange controls, trade controls, domestic credit changes, and the like. In some cases the determination of effective exchange rate changes may require a product-by-product examination of the effects.[289]

Historical studies of the economic effects over time of previous policy changes may also be helpful in appraising contemporary economic policies.[290]

Information Flow

The Fund obtains information daily on exchange rates in various markets. This information is obtained in order to calculate the exchange value of the special drawing right in relation to different currencies. Under the authority of Section 5 of Article VIII, the Fund also periodically obtains information from its members on the composition of monetary reserves, balance-of-payments data, and other economic information.

Our previous discussion of "manipulation" suggested that all countries manage exchange rates, at least to some degree. In order for the Fund to maintain a watchful eye over how exchange rates are being managed and with what effects, it needs a continuous flow of information about the uses being made of all the various monetary instruments that affect exchange rates or cause important changes in the financial conditions that underly them. "Firm surveillance" in Section 3(b) of Article IV means more than infirm surveillance or mere observation. The Fund's decision on notification of changes in exchange rate policies[291] takes a too-gingerly approach to the Fund's information needs. That de-

---

especially papers at pp. 147, 201, and 285; and Jacques R. Artus and Anne Kenny McGuirk, "A Revised Version of the Multilateral Exchange Rate Model," *IMF Staff Papers*, vol. 28 (1981), p. 275. See also Chapter 12, *infra*, page 595 (note 118).

[288] For discussion of the concept of "effective exchange rate" and various approaches to its measurement, see the Annual Report of the Council of Economic Advisers in *Economic Report of the President, Transmitted to the Congress February 1974* (Washington: Government Printing Office, 1974), pp. 220–26; and Rudolf R. Rhomberg, "Indices of Effective Exchange Rates," *IMF Staff Papers*, vol. 23 (1976), p. 88.

[289] See generally Artus and McGuirk, "Multilateral Exchange Rate Model," *supra* note 287. See also the economic analyses of exchange rate changes in the series of studies issued under the title *Foreign Trade Regimes and Economic Development* cited in Chapter 10, *supra*, page 383 (note 12). Differences between nominal and real changes in exchange rates are displayed in the table in IMF, *Annual Report, 1981*, p. 50.

[290] See, e.g., two studies made some years after the event of the longer-term effects of the 1967 devaluation of the U.K. pound sterling. D.C. Hague, W.E.F. Oakeshott, and A.A. Strain, *Devaluation and Pricing Decisions* (London: Allen & Unwin, 1974); and Jacques R. Artus, "The 1967 Devaluation of the Pound Sterling," *IMF Staff Papers*, vol. 22 (1975), p. 595.

[291] E.B. Decision No. 5712, *supra* note 130, discussed in text accompanying note 138.

cision should be amended or supplemented to make clear that each member should provide the following information on a regular basis:

(i)   The volume of exchange transactions reported by banks in that country categorized by the foreign currencies involved.

(ii) The fluctuations in exchange rates during the period.

(iii) Actions by monetary authorities during the period including but not limited to:

(a) Participation in exchange transactions, including information on the volume of each currency bought and sold, the dates of the transactions, and the exchange rates.[292]

(b) Important changes during the period in arrangements available to finance international transactions whether or not actually used, such as amendments in the amount of currencies available under swap arrangements or in the terms of the arrangements[293] and loans obtained by government agencies during the period.

(c) Changes in interest rates, bank reserve requirements, exchange control regulations, and other monetary control measures during the period.[294]

In the case of currencies that are widely used to make payments for international transactions or are actively traded in the exchange markets, some of this information may be regularly required on a frequent schedule. In cases where exchange markets appear unsettled, it may also be necessary to obtain information more frequently and to supplement this information with other inquiries.

Scope of Consultations

The Fund's consultations since the Second Amendment entered into force have drawn on the authority of both Section 3(a) and 3(b) of Article IV and on Arti-

---

[292] The Federal Reserve Bank of New York every three months issues a report on U.S. Treasury and Federal Reserve System actions in the exchange markets. These narrative and statistical reports are published under the title "Treasury and Federal Reserve Foreign Exchange Operations" in the *Federal Reserve Bulletin* and the Federal Reserve Bank of New York's *Quarterly Review*. It is appropriate that the IMF require all members to provide this kind of information, only on a more frequent basis.

[293] Examples of such arrangements are the reciprocal currency arrangements maintained by the U.S. Federal Reserve System with foreign central banks explained in Chapter 4, *supra,* page 135 et seq., and the financing facilities available to members of the European Economic Community described in Chapter 8, *supra,* page 326 et seq.

[294] The author understands that in the past the Fund has encountered difficulties in obtaining some of the information listed in these paragraphs. The Fund has clear authority under Article IV to obtain this information. In some countries this information is known to central banks but not readily available in finance ministries. See Thomas D. Willett, "Alternative Approaches to International Surveillance of Exchange-Rate Policies," in Federal Reserve Bank of Boston, *Managed Exchange-Rate Flexibility: The Recent Experience* (Conference Series no. 20; Boston: Federal Reserve Bank of Boston, 1978), p. 148 at p. 171.

cles VIII and XIV, and thus comprehend all obligations under Articles IV, VIII, and XIV. The surveillance decision will be reviewed at least every two years.[295] It could be that experience will show that members can tolerate a higher degree of "firm surveillance" and "oversight" than they initially thought when the decision was adopted in April 1977. It is, of course, important that the discussions and consultations involve national officials holding decision-making responsibilities in their governments and not merely persons whose jobs are to defend the decisions of "higher-ups."

It has been informally reported that the consultations in the Organisation for Economic Co-operation and Development have in the past been more comprehensive than those in the Fund. One of the lessons of the OECD experience is the usefulness of examining the policies of all members or groups of members in terms of their interrelationships. The economic integration of the European Economic Community has required the harmonization of domestic policies. Monetary matters are reviewed within the Monetary Committee and the Committee of Central Bank Governors. The European Community's experience points to the importance of involving the governors of central banks, as well as finance ministers, in the policy consultations. Up to the present time the central bank governors of the developed countries have used the Bank for International Settlements in Basle, rather than the Fund, as their principal forum for discussion and coordination of policies. The procedures used in consultations within the IMF and within these other organizations receive further attention in Chapter 12 of this book.

Summary

We have surveyed the structure of Article IV and have attempted to gain an understanding of the purpose of that article and the obligations of its various components. Let us now examine how the provisions fit together. In dealing with a problem in the exchange markets, the following questions are illustrative of those that can arise:

> (i) Are the specific actions taken by members in the exchange markets (say, a central bank's selling its own currency and buying foreign currencies against an upward trend in the exchange rate of its currency) consistent with the exchange rate policies that the countries described to the Fund under Section 2? A stable system of exchange rates is based on the expectation that countries will follow the exchange policies they communicate to the Fund. Actions that deviate from policies articulated to the Fund require notification. If changes are made for reasons that are not apparent, they require explanation.

---

[295] E. B. Decision No. 5392, *supra* note 69, paragraph 2. The scope of consultations as presently conducted by the Fund is described further in Chapter 12, *infra,* page 571 et seq.

(ii) Are the countries' actions consistent with their exchange policy obligations under Section 1, subsections (iii) and (iv)? Are exchange markets orderly? Do the members' actions result in an unfair competitive advantage? Are the actions preventing balance-of-payments adjustment by that country or other countries? Answers to these questions require not only information, but also an analysis of the economic and financial situations of the countries involved.

(iii) Are the countries fulfilling their general obligations under Section 1, subsections (i) and (ii)? Take the following example: A country that has adopted a policy of floating allows its currency to depreciate in the exchange markets. The action is consistent with its exchange policy communicated to the Fund. The action does not give the country an unfair competitive advantage because in the particular case the exchange depreciation appears simply to compensate for a rapid inflation in domestic prices. While the country may not be in violation of Section 2 or subsections (iii) and (iv) of Section 1, its failure to endeavor to maintain reasonably stable domestic prices could be considered to be a failure to observe the requirements of subsection (i) of Section 1. Experts may be of the view that had a reasonably stable system of prices been maintained, the exchange rate would not have depreciated. Thus, surveillance of the exchange markets may lead to an inquiry into basic economic and financial policies.

(iv) Even if countries are in compliance with their obligations under subsections (i) to (iv) of Section 1 and under Sections 2 and 3, there is a further duty. If exchange markets are likely to remain unsettled or if there is an emerging problem with respect to the stability of the system, the duty to collaborate stated in Section 1 may in some circumstances include the obligation to reconsider economic policies and exchange policies and, in collaboration with other members and paying due regard to the IMF's advice, to make changes in those policies as necessary in order that a stable system of currency exchange and orderly exchange markets are maintained.

Throughout the above discussion we have spoken of countries in the plural. An exchange rate is, as previously pointed out, a two-ended thing.[296] While it may be possible in some situations to focus on the actions and policies of one country as the "black sheep," in most cases it is necessary to examine the actions and policies of all the relevant participants. The system effects of actions of countries on both sides of transactions must be seen.

What can all this mean in practice? From its study of information obtained or its observation of the markets in exercise of its surveillance function, the Fund may identify existing or potential problems. It may seek additional information and it may request countries involved to consult with the Fund. These

[296] See page 526, *supra.*

consultations may occur among government officials and with the Managing Director and staff of the Fund, within the Executive Board of the Fund, within the Interim Committee (or Council if created), and even within the Board of Governors itself. The Fund may request countries to give their appraisals of the problems and the Fund may communicate its views. Questions may be raised whether the actions of members are consistent with the policies previously communicated to the Fund. Questions may also be raised about whether the policies of the various countries are adequate to deal with the problems. The Fund may press for the harmonization of policies and the Fund and its members may formulate joint programs of action. This short scenario is not simply an ideal. It is what the obligations of Article IV entail.

Chapter Conclusion

Rather than adopt an elaborate set of specific rules narrowly defining approved and prohibited practices in the management of exchange rates, Article IV of the IMF Articles of Agreement in its present form takes a different approach. Particular attention is given to purposes and effects. Obligations are defined in general terms. Attention is directed to fundamental economic policies and to the underlying economic and financial conditions of the member countries. Much use is made of enabling clauses giving the Fund power to obtain information, to raise questions, to articulate guidelines, to give practical application to general clauses, and, if a broad measure of agreement can be obtained (85 percent of the total voting power), to establish general exchange arrangements and adapt them to changing circumstances.

Article IV reserves to each member the right to choose the exchange arrangements for its currency so long as it acts in a responsible manner, fulfills its general obligations respecting the management of its economy in its interconnections with those of other states, and collaborates with the Fund and other members to accomplish the purpose of the article.

Because of the powers reserved to states, the use of general language in the article, and the necessity in any case for a full exploration of the economic and historical context before attempting to give answers to questions that will arise in the future, the Fund faces a major challenge in building a body of practice on the application of the words of Article IV. The Fund's surveillance decisions and practice in the past six years represent a good beginning in this effort.

Chapter 12: Consultation and Collaboration

Introductory Note

Undertakings to consult and to collaborate permeate the entire system of international monetary law. This final chapter reexamines these obligations. The first part surveys periodic consultations on national economic policies. The second part, drawing on discussions in earlier chapters, comments on the practices of consultation and collaboration in connection with the use of financial facilities, exchange controls, and the management of exchange rates. The third part examines obligations in the balance-of-payments adjustment process, supervision of commercial bank lending, collaboration on reserve asset policies, management of international liquidity, and assistance to developing countries. The fourth part formulates an obligation placed by general international law on all countries to consult and to collaborate in international monetary matters. The book concludes with a few general reflections.

All of the monetary organizations studied in this book are intended to facilitate consultation and collaboration. The first purpose of the International Monetary Fund is to "promote international monetary cooperation through a permanent institution which provides the machinery for consultation and collaboration on international monetary problems."[1] A purpose of the Bank for International Settlements is to "promote the co-operation of central banks."[2] The members of the Organisation for Economic Co-operation and Development have agreed to "consult together on a continuing basis" and to "co-operate closely and where appropriate take co-ordinated action."[3] The Charter of the Council for Mutual Economic Assistance states that a purpose of this socialist organization is to promote "the further deepening and improvement of cooperation."[4] Within these and other organizations countries have agreed to share in-

---

[1] Articles of Agreement of the International Monetary Fund, Article I(i).

[2] Statutes of the Bank for International Settlements, Article 3. For background on the organization, see Chapter 2, *supra,* page 52 et seq.

[3] Convention on the Organisation for Economic Co-operation and Development, Article 3. For background on the organization, see Chapter 2, *supra,* page 68 et seq.

[4] Charter of the Council for Mutual Economic Assistance, Article I. For background on the organization, see Chapter 2, *supra,* page 87 et seq.

formation, to consult with one another, and to collaborate in solving economic problems.

Information Sharing

Effective international monetary cooperation is dependent upon reliable systems of information exchange. The Articles of Agreement of the IMF give that organization extensive powers to gather data. The Fund may require information in its role of monitoring the operation of the international monetary system and on particular problems that it observes.[5] The Treaty Establishing the European Economic Community grants that organization broad powers to collect information.[6] Information relating to monetary policy, conjunctural policy, and general economic policy is shared under the EEC's "convergence" and "stability" directives discussed later in this chapter.[7] The members of the OECD have agreed to "keep each other informed and furnish the Organisation with the information necessary for the accomplishment of its tasks."[8] The Group of Ten share information on their financing of balance-of-payments surpluses and deficits and on Eurocurrency placements.[9] Other examples could be cited.

After the President of the United States on August 15, 1971, without prior consultation, announced that the convertibility of the dollar into gold was being suspended, foreign central banks for a period stopped providing information to U.S. authorities on their actions in the exchange markets. This break in communication was of grave concern at the time to officials of the U.S. Federal Reserve System.[10] This experience indicates that the sharing of information, although it takes place regularly, should not be taken for granted.

Consultation and Collaboration—Nuances in Meaning

When a country consults with international organizations or other countries, an opportunity is provided for these "outsiders," who are often directly affected, to comment upon the country's policies. Consultation includes:

(i) provision of information;
(ii) willingness to explain policies and their intended effects;
(iii) willingness to engage in a mutual assessment of policies and their effects; and

---

[5] See IMF Article VIII, section 5; and Article IV, sections 2 and 3.

[6] See, e.g., Articles 72, 73, 109, and 213 of the Treaty Establishing the European Economic Community. For background on the Community, see Chapter 2, *supra,* page 76 et seq.

[7] See pages 589–598, *infra.*

[8] Convention on the Organisation for Economic Co-operation and Development, Article 3.

[9] See pages 583 and 629–630, *infra.*

[10] *Minutes of the Federal Open Market Committee* (described in Chapter 4, *supra,* page 137, note 31), 1971, pp. 948–49. For background see Chapter 11, *supra,* pages 495–498.

(iv) willingness to receive advice from others, but without a duty to follow it.

Consultation, in addition to permitting outsiders to comment on a country's policies, may permit those outsiders to adjust their own actions to minimize adverse effects to them from a country's policy changes.

The duty to collaborate encompasses a broader range of obligations than the duty to consult. Collaboration involves the elements of consultation described above. In addition, it involves mutual assistance, the harmonization of policies, and joint action. The duty to collaborate involves more than a willingness to negotiate. Literally, it means to labor together to solve problems.

Consultation Procedures—Periodic Consultations on Economic Policy

Note

Consultations in some sense take place whenever officials, whether holding high- or low-level responsibilities, communicate. The focus in the sections below is on formalized consultation procedures used in the periodic review of national economic policies as one example of a multifaceted process. These consultations are of interest because they bring within their scope not only international policies but also domestic economic policies about which countries have traditionally sought to preserve the widest freedom of action.

International Monetary Fund

The basic premise of IMF Article IV, relating to exchange rates, is that exchange stability is to be achieved through underlying economic policies.[11] A decision implementing Article IV requires the International Monetary Fund to periodically hold formal consultations with each member on its economic policies.[12] The consultation system under Article IV represents a further evolution of the Fund's procedure, begun over thirty years ago under Article XIV, of engaging in consultations with members maintaining exchange restrictions.[13] As early as the 1950s the Fund's management recognized that "the need for ex-

---

[11] See Chapter 11, *supra,* pages 507–515.

[12] Subpart Procedures for Surveillance, section II, of E.B. Decision No. 5392 -(77/63)(adopted April 29, 1977, effective April 1, 1978); in IMF, *Annual Report, 1977,* p. 107; and in IMF, *Selected Decisions of the International Monetary Fund and Selected Documents* (10th issue; Washington, 1983)[hereinafter *Selected Decisions*], p. 10. The decision is called the "surveillance decision" and is also discussed in Chapter 11, *supra,* pages 507, 520, and 558.

[13] Article XIV, section 3 (which replaced former Article XIV section 4, *original* and *first*) states, *inter alia:* "Any member retaining any restrictions inconsistent with Article VIII, Sections 2, 3, or 4 shall consult the Fund annually as to their further retention." See Chapter 10, *supra,* pages 423–425.

change restrictions in a country cannot be assessed without a study of the whole complex of financial and monetary developments, including such aspects of national policy as the budget, credit policy, development plans, and even prices and wages, as they affect the country itself and its international relations."[14] Stephen A. Silard, a member of the Fund's Legal Department, stated the legal justification:

> [E]xchange policies in effect subsume a wide range of economic policies as well; and . . . if the exchange policies foreseen by the Fund Agreement are to be fully achieved, a significant number and variety of economic policies outside of the exchange field must be appropriately aligned with that objective.[15]

Following a decision adopted in 1960, consultations have regularly been held with countries that have accepted the convertibility obligations of Article VIII.[16] These consultations have been as broad-ranging as those under Article XIV, but there has been a formal difference. While consultations under Article XIV are concluded with a decision of the Executive Board, consultations under Article VIII only result in decisions if the country's measures require approval under that article.[17]

Article IV, *second,* discussed in detail in Chapter 11, is now the principal source of the Fund's authority for regular consultations with all members. Article IV provides a legal foundation for Fund oversight over all of a country's domestic and external economic and financial policies within the scope of Section 1 of that article, whether or not economic evidence would indicate that the policies affect exchange stability.[18] The broad terms of reference stated in the Fund's principal decision on surveillance were quoted in the previous chapter.[19] There is little, if anything, outside the potential scope of an Article IV

---

[14] Speech of Per Jacobsson, IMF Managing Director, to the UN Economic and Social Council, April 16, 1958, printed in Per Jacobsson, *International Monetary Problems, 1957–1963: Selected Speeches* (Washington: IMF, 1964), p. 35 at p. 36.

[15] Stephen A. Silard, "The Impact of the International Monetary Fund on International Trade," *Journal of World Trade Law,* vol. 2 (1968), p. 121 at p. 128.

[16] Paragraph 3 of E.B. Decision No. 1034 -(60/27) (June 1, 1960); in J. Keith Horsefield and Margaret Garritsen de Vries, *The International Monetary Fund, 1945–1965: Twenty Years of International Monetary Cooperation* (3 vols.; Washington: IMF, 1969) [hereinafter *IMF History 1945–65*], vol. 3, p. 260; and in *Selected Decisions* (10th issue, 1983), p. 241. See also Erin E. Jacobsson, *A Life for Sound Money: Per Jacobsson, His Biography* (Oxford: Oxford University Press, 1979), pp. 307–10.

[17] See generally Joseph Gold, "Certain Aspects of the Law and Practice of the International Monetary Fund," in Stephen M. Schwebel (ed.), *The Effectiveness of International Decisions* (Dobbs Ferry: Oceana Publications; Leyden: A.W. Sijthoff, 1971), p. 71 at pp. 90–94.

[18] Article IV, sections 1 and 3. See Chapter 11, *supra,* page 515.

[19] E.B. Decision No. 5392, *supra* note 12, subpart Principles of Fund Surveillance Over Exchange Rate Policies, paragraph 3, quoted in full in Chapter 11, *supra,* pages 560–561.

consultation so long as the basic constitutional system of the country is respected.[20]

The Fund has so far adopted five general decisions on consultations under Article IV. The first, the decision mentioned above, establishes the procedures for regular and special consultations and states criteria for appraisal of members' policies.[21] The second facilitates the holding of special consultations.[22] The third, fourth, and fifth clarify the earlier decisions and summarize experience.[23] Regular consultations under Article IV bring within their scope ("comprehend") the periodic consultations under Articles VIII and XIV.[24] This avoids a proliferation of consultations and also avoids the need to finely delineate which policies can be reviewed in consultations under one article compared to another. The Fund's recent goal has been to hold a regular consultation with every member at least every two years, while maintaining an annual consultation cycle with countries that have Fund-supported programs or economies that have substantial impacts on other countries.[25]

A regular consultation begins, where sufficient data and information are available at the Fund, with the preparation by the IMF staff of a background paper entitled "Recent Economic Developments." The paper describes the country's general economic and financial situation and recent developments. The existing system of exchange rate arrangements and exchange controls and changes made since the previous consultation are described; restrictions and currency practices that require Fund approval under Article VIII are noted. Reviews of trends in production, wages and prices, consumption and savings, money and credit, and the budget–fiscal situation are nearly always included.

---

[20] Changes in the fundamental structure of the economic organization of a member are beyond the authority of the IMF to censor. Article XII, section 8. Principles for guidance on exchange rate policies adopted by the IMF under Article IV, section 3, must respect the domestic social and political policies of members. Andreas F. Lowenfeld has given an example. The Fund can in consultations with a country express its view that the country should not run a budget deficit of more than, say, 50 million crowns. Whether this is to be accomplished through cuts in farmers' subsidies, veterans' benefits, educational programs, or military spending, by raising taxes, or by other means is largely for the country to decide. Andreas F. Lowenfeld, *The International Monetary System* (1st ed.; New York: Matthew Bender, 1977), p. 186. There are, however, limits to Fund deference. Legally sanctioned racially discriminatory employment practices that result in inefficient use of human resources have been discussed and criticized in the IMF's Executive Board. See Jonathan Kwitny, "Going Along: How IMF Overcame Political Issues to Vote a Loan to South Africa," *Wall Street Journal*, May 5, 1983, p. 1 at p. 26. See generally Joseph Gold, "Political Considerations Are Prohibited by Articles of Agreement When the Fund Considers Requests for Use of Resources," *IMF Survey*, May 23, 1983, p. 146; and Joseph Gold, *The Rule of Law in the International Monetary Fund* (IMF Pamphlet Series no. 32; Washington, 1980), pp. 60–68.

[21] E.B. Decision No. 5392, *supra* note 12.

[22] E.B. Decision No. 6026 -(79/13)(January 22, 1979); IMF, *Annual Report, 1979*, p. 136; *Selected Decisions* (10th issue 1983), p. 15. The decision is quoted and discussed in Chapter 11, *supra*, pages 559–560.

[23] E.B. Decision No. 7088 -(82/44)(April 9, 1982); IMF, *Annual Report, 1982*, p. 129; E.B. Decision No. 7374 -(83/55) (March 28, 1983); IMF, *Annual Report, 1983*, p. 142; and E.B. Decision No. 7646 -(84/40) (March 12, 1984); IMF, *Annual Report, 1984*, p. 124. The texts in the *Annual Report* include attachments.

[24] E.B. Decision No. 5392, *supra* note 12, subpart Procedures for Surveillance, section II.

[25] See section entitled "Frequency of Article IV Consultations" in attachment to E.B. Decision No. 7374, *supra* note 23. See also IMF, *Annual Report, 1983*, pp. 62–65.

The volume and composition of exports and imports, capital movements, foreign debt, and foreign aid are described as well as other factors affecting the balance of payments in the short run and long run. The staff also drafts a confidential briefing paper that outlines the preliminary policy positions the mission proposes to take. This paper is reviewed by the Fund's management with particular attention given to sensitive policy issues.[26]

The second phase of the consultation is the formal visit by Fund officials to the country. The mission usually consists of four or five professionals and a secretary. It is headed by a senior Fund official, normally from the area department involved. The Fund mission spends from a few days to three weeks in the country. It meets with senior officials at both the policy and technical levels of the ministry of finance and the central bank. If the administration of exchange restrictions is handled by another body, it meets with its officials. The mission may also meet with staff of other ministries such as agriculture, industry, trade, planning, and the like. Occasionally the head of government may directly participate in the consultations. The effect of holding consultations in the country concerned is that staff members make regular visits to member countries and engage in intensive discussions in the field. It also means that more persons holding responsible positions in the "examinee" country can be directly involved in the consultations than if they were held in Washington. Legal obligations of the member are always noted in a consultation discussion, and a Fund staff member has stated that "the discussion focuses on the member's compliance with its obligations under Article IV."[27] The statement should not be taken too literally, as the focus of the discussion is usually not on legal obligations as such but rather the economic problems of the country and its policies seen in relation to Article IV. Consultations normally avoid the overtone of a country being on trial.

A Fund decision states that the Executive Board "shall reach conclusions" not later than three months after the termination of discussions between the member and the staff (which is normally taken to mean the end of the staff's visit to the country).[28] In preparation for the discussion in the Executive Board, the staff revises the Recent Economic Developments paper in the light of observations made and information subsequently obtained. A separate paper, informally called the "staff report," is prepared which describes the policy discussions held in the country. It analyzes and critiques the country's economic position, policies, and prospects in terms that are intended to be

---

[26] The role of the IMF executive director representing the examinee country is a delicate one during the preparatory stage for a consultation. See the section "Consultation and Surveillance Procedures" in attachment to E.B. Decision No. 7088, *supra* note 23. See also Rule N-16(c); *By-Laws, Rules and Regulations* (40th issue, 1983).

[27] Eduard Brau, "The Consultation Process of the Fund," *Finance and Development*, vol. 18, no. 4 (December 1981), p. 13 at p. 15.

[28] E.B. Decision No. 5392, *supra* note 12, subpart Procedures for Surveillance, section II.

nonjudgmental. This report, normally not over twenty pages in length, concludes with a "staff appraisal" in which judgments are expressed.[29] The staff will also make recommendations for Executive Board action where the consultation involves a country availing itself of Article XIV or exchange restrictions or multiple currency practices require approval under Article VIII. After the staff report is prepared, the executive directors are normally allowed four weeks to study the report and consult with their constituencies before the report is formally discussed in the Executive Board.

The discussions in the Executive Board in Washington permit directors to ask questions of staff members who visited the country, to comment on the situation and policies of the country, and to voice complaints of their constituents about the examinee's policies. The head of the IMF mission will be present and the executive director representing the examinee country usually makes a statement. The discussion in the Executive Board is an important part of the consultation process, is not perfunctory, and may often last two hours or more. At the end the Managing Director states a "summing up" in the form of "conclusions." The statement may be approved by the Board without modification, or changes may be made on the basis of proposals of the executive director representing the examinee country or by other executive directors. The procedure within the Board is one of consensus-seeking, although formal votes on amendments to a draft statement and adoption of it can be taken if requested.

For the purpose of appraising policies of countries under Article IV, no legal distinction is made between countries that have accepted the obligations of Article VIII, Sections 2, 3, and 4, and those that avail themselves of Article XIV, Section 2. The "conclusions" may include comments on exchange restrictions. Where exchange restrictions, multiple currency practices, or discriminatory arrangements are inconsistent with Article VIII, the Executive Board incorporates paragraphs recording its actions in the "conclusions" or adopts a separate decision on these matters, for example, granting a temporary approval under Aticle VIII.[30] The Board's "conclusions" and any separate decisions are transmitted to the country through its executive director. The documents are not published by the Fund, but the examinee may publish them if it wishes to do so.[31] Aspects of the consultation process as it relates to the obligations of Article IV were previously discussed,[32] and only a few additional points about the process need to be made.

Set forth below is the statement of conclusions (omitting the name of the country) following an actual Article IV consultation in 1981:

---

[29] See section "Reporting on Consultations" in attachment to E.B. Decision No. 7088, *supra* note 23.

[30] See Chapter 10, *supra,* pages 401–420 and 423–425.

[31] It is rare for an examinee to publish the "conclusions." Belgium released a summary in October 1982. See note 33, *infra.*

[32] See Chapter 11, *supra,* pages 558–568.

Executive Directors have congratulated the [country's] authorities on the success of their stabilization efforts, which in the past two years have led to a marked improvement in the balance of payments and to a lowering of the underlying rate of inflation, while allowing a level of economic growth higher than the average for [similarly placed] countries. This remarkable success was seen as largely reflecting the adoption of exchange rate and interest rate policies directed at improving competitiveness and restoring the relative attractiveness of domestic financial assets. The moderation of wage increases and a strong increase in the private savings ratio were seen as important and successful contributing forces.

The Directors were gratified that the stabilization effort has laid the basis for a more sustained rate of growth, and they encouraged the authorities in their efforts to promote a further recovery of investment. Taking into account the recent deterioration in the external current account and in the overall balance of payments, it was important, in the view of Directors, that the exchange rate remain competitive and that interest rates be maintained at levels adequate to attract continued inflows of workers remittances and foreign capital and to mobilize an increasing volume of domestic savings.

Many Directors observed that the situation of public finances, including the unsustainably high public sector deficit as a ratio of GNP, continued to be a cause of concern. They welcomed the efforts currently being made by the authorities to bring about a more equitable distribution of the tax burden, to reduce tax evasion, and to improve productivity in the public enterprise sector. They also stressed the importance of tightening controls over expenditures, especially by the social security system, and the local authorities, and of pursuing appropriate pricing policies, particularly in the public enterprise sector and in the energy field, in order to contain the growth of subsidies. Furthermore, they emphasized the importance of increasing the nonmonetary financing of the budget deficit.

Most Executive Directors felt that the authorities' goal of reducing inflation would require a somewhat tighter stance of financial policies. In this respect, concern was expressed about the rapid growth of domestic bank credit in recent months, which was regarded as excessive, and Directors welcomed the authorities' intentions to keep under close scrutiny policies in this area.

Directors expressed satisfaction with the recent measures to liberalize the trade and payments system and the hope that further steps in that direction would be taken.

Finally, Executive Directors expressed their gratification concerning the very positive and fruitful relationship between [country] and the Fund and their confidence that this collaboration will continue to strengthen in view of the medium-term aspects of [country's] economic strategy.[33]

The wide range of the discussion is impressive. The following subjects were explicitly treated: balance-of-payments position over several years and the current situation, inflation, economic growth, labor policy, savings and investment policies, attraction of foreign capital and workers' remittances, exchange rate policies, interest rate policies, domestic credit policies, public sector finance (including government expenditures and taxes, financing of budget deficits, productivity of public sector enterprises and related pricing policies and subsidies), trade liberalization, and payments liberalization.

The statement quoted above avoided making any formal determination that the country was or was not in compliance with the obligations of Article IV, Section 1(i) and (ii) or even Section 1(iii) and (iv). The statement also eschewed the use of imperative language. The conclusions did not state a position of the Executive Board as such; rather, it said "directors," "most directors," "many directors." Note the verbs used to convey appraisals of the examinee's policies: "expressed satisfaction," "welcomed," "continued to be a cause of concern." Policy prescriptions were offered, but the tone was muted. The statement said "many" directors "stressed" the importance of tightening controls over government expenditures and of pursuing appropriate public-sector pricing policies. "Most" directors "felt" that reducing inflation would "require a somewhat tighter stance of financial policies," and they regarded the growth of domestic bank credit as "excessive." There is considerable potential for nuance of language in consultation conclusions, and in appropriate cases the language can be strong and specific.

What is the legal character of "conclusions"? Joseph Gold wrote in 1978: "[A]lthough they may be less formal or less precise, or more in the nature of views, than other decisions, and although they may be adopted according to a different procedure, they have the same legal quality as those formulations adopted by the Executive Board that are acknowledged to be decisions." He suggested that in time "conclusions" may be recognized as equivalent in all respects to decisions.[34] Sir Joseph later modified his view because in practice "conclusions," as illustrated above, have normally not stated a collective view of the Executive Board as a Fund organ, but rather have been compendia of

[33] Reproduced from Brau, *supra* note 27, p. 16. In October 1982 Belgium released a summary of its consultation with the IMF. *Financial Times* (London), October 23, 1982, p. 2.

For an illustrative decision concluding an Article XIV consultation circa 1967, see Gold, "Certain Aspects of the Law and Practice of the International Monetary Fund," *supra* note 17, p. 99. Selected extracts from consultation decisions in the 1960s and early 1970s appear in Joseph Gold, " '. . . To Contribute Thereby To . . . Development . . .': Aspects of the Relations of the International Monetary Fund with its Developing Members," *Columbia Journal of Transnational Law*, vol. 10 (1971), p. 267 at pp. 298–301.

[34] Joseph Gold, *Use, Conversion, and Exchange of Currency Under the Second Amendment of the Fund's Articles* (IMF Pamphlet Series no. 23; Washington, 1978), pp. 13–14.

views expressed by directors. He has recommended that the Board adopt decisions and not just summing-ups of discussion.[35]

Sir Joseph's recommendation should be implemented. Summarizing the various views expressed by directors, as now, could be retained to avoid descending to a least common denominator. But, the conclusions should conclude in expressions of the collective view of the Executive Board as the responsible Fund organ. In that form, they would have greater force. They would be more consonant with the Fund's obligation to "oversee the compliance of each member with its obligations under Section 1 [of Article IV]."[36] Such conclusions (decisions) would constitute what international lawyers call "judgments of peers" and, in appropriate cases, would facilitate the sanction of "mobilization of shame" (especially if the decision became public).[37] It appears that, in a consultation with Sweden in the fall of 1982, the Board did express, or came close to expressing, a collective judgment that the member had breached Article IV, Section 1(iii).[38]

While the consultation reports are primarily for the use of the Fund and its members, copies of the Recent Economic Developments papers with the consent of the examinees are regularly supplied to other organizations to which the examinees are members including the International Bank for Reconstruction and Development, United Nations Conference on Trade and Development, General Agreement on Tariffs and Trade, Organisation for Economic Cooperation and Development, European Communities, and other organizations. The secretariats of some of these organizations also receive the staff reports and the "conclusions."

General comments have been made which indicate that the Managing Director and staff believe the Fund's consultation process to be worthwhile but not completely satisfactory.[39] A country's annual consultation with the Fund provides it with informed outside advice. Where a country can undertake its own economic analyses, the opportunity to discuss these with international officials still is valuable. Countries often use the preparation for IMF consultations as a time when the country's policies are given a careful internal review. Fund advice, even in those cases where no changes in policy are suggested, can help

---

[35] Joseph Gold, "Strengthening the Soft International Law of Exchange Arrangements," *American Journal of International Law*, vol. 77 (1983), p. 443 at pp. 464–65 and 483.

[36] Article IV, section 3(a).

[37] See Schwebel, *supra* note 17, pp. 434–35, 442, 447–56, and 496–97. See generally Roger Fisher, *Improving Compliance with International Law* (Charlottesville: University Press of Virginia, 1981), pp. 129–32 and 270–72.

[38] See notes 171–73, *infra*, and accompanying text.

[39] See, e.g., attachments to E.B. Decisions No. 7088 and No. 7374, *supra* note 23; Joseph Gold, "Strengthening," *supra* note 35; and the earlier comments of Joseph Gold in *IMF History 1945–65*, *supra* note 16, vol. 2, pp. 557–58, and in Schwebel, *supra* note 17, pp. 90–94 and 467–70.

Preparing and conducting annual consultations take about one-half of the time of the staff in the IMF's area departments. About one-fifth of the time of the Executive Board is directly devoted to regular individual consultations with member countries. Brau, *supra* note 27, pp. 13–14.

authorities to persevere with sound policies. The process can help to identify and address emerging payments problems at an early stage. For the Fund, the annual consultation process is the primary means of keeping informed of each member's economic and financial situation. It also provides an information base that permits the IMF to act quickly if exchange rate problems later arise or a country requests a General Resources Account drawing. The information from an annual consultation, for example, can at a later time be used in fixing performance criteria to be employed in a stand-by arrangement.[40] The consultation process makes it possible for the Executive Board to maintain multilateral surveillance over members, give advice for adjustments in member policies, and gain knowledge to guide the formulation of general policies of the Fund. And, most importantly, it provides a mechanism, even if a limited one, for the Fund to exercise its responsibilities to ensure the effective operation of the international monetary system, coordination of national policies, and compliance by members with their legal obligations.

In addition to the regular consultations, previously described, there are more frequent consultations with members "whose exchange rate policies have a major impact on the international monetary system."[41] In addition, the Managing Director has authority to initiate consultations with any member on exchange rate policies in the period between regular consultations where he believes the country's policies may not be in accord with the exchange rate principles adopted by the Fund or if the matter is of importance.[42]

When exchange restrictions requiring Fund approval are introduced, there are consultations at that time.[43] Consultations are also held in connection with stand-by arrangements and other Fund policies on the use of its resources.[44] And, of course, the Fund at all times has the right to communicate its views informally to any member on any matter arising under the Articles of Agreement.[45]

The regular consultations with each member, and the special discussions mentioned above, are informed by and in turn provide insight for the wide-

---

[40] E.B. Decision No. 6056 -(79/38)(March 2, 1979), which sets forth guidelines for Fund financial assistance, states in paragraph 1: "The Article IV consultations are among the occasions on which the Fund would be able to discuss with members adjustment programs, including corrective measures, that would enable the Fund to approve a stand-by arrangement." The decision, discussed in detail in Chapter 6, appears in IMF, *Annual Report, 1979*, p. 136; *Selected Decisions* (10th issue, 1983), p. 20. See also section "Combining Consultations and Use of Fund Resources Missions" in attachment to E.B. Decision No. 7088, *supra* note 23.

[41] E.B. Decision No. 5392, *supra* note 12, subpart Procedures for Surveillance. See also E.B. Decision No. 4076 -(73/101)(October 31, 1973) in IMF, *Annual Report, 1974*, p. 102.

[42] E.B. Decision No. 5392, *supra* note 12, subpart Procedures for Surveillance, section V; and E.B. Decision No. 6026, *supra* note 22.

[43] See Chapter 10, *supra*, page 401.

[44] See Chapter 6, *supra*, page 248 et seq. and 277 et seq. When a stand-by or extended arrangement is being negotiaged, a Fund mission, comparable to that in a regular consultation under Article IV, usually visits the country for two or three weeks.

[45] Article XII, section 8. See generally Chapter 1, *supra*, pages 39–42.

ranging discussions of the Executive Board held several times a year under the agenda heading "World Economic Outlook."[46] These discussions deal with the international adjustment process and review broad developments in exchange rates and other matters of concern. An effort is made in these discussions and in deliberations in the Interim Committee of the Board of Governors to develop broad understandings on coordinated strategies on such matters as achieving noninflationary growth and balance-of-payments adjustment. Multinational analyses and forecasting are used in staff papers for these discussions. Special consultations with individual countries or groups of countries may be held in preparation for the discussions.[47] Whether collaboration under IMF Article IV will in the future go as far as the formulation of domestic economic policy guidelines comparable to those used in the European Economic Community, described later in this chapter,[48] remains to be seen.

The basic decision under which the Fund presently engages in surveillance and conducts consultations respecting matters within the scope of Article IV is to be re-examined at least every two years. The intention is to adapt the Fund's practice to the needs of international adjustment as those needs are identified.[49]

Organisation for Economic Co-operation and Development

The OECD's involvement with coordination of economic policy[50] had its origin in the work of its predecessor, the OEEC, which pioneered multilateral efforts to coordinate national economic policies. The U.S. Economic Cooperation Act of 1948, which established the Marshall Plan program of aid for European recovery, made assistance "contingent upon continuous effort of the participating countries to accomplish a joint recovery program . . . and the establishment of a continuing organization for this purpose."[51] The Organisation for European Economic Co-operation was established for this purpose[52] and early initiated an annual country review procedure to assure wise use of Marshall Plan aid. Participants in those review sessions were sensitized to the close link between domestic policies and balance-of-payments problems.[53] The

---

[46] Each year the IMF issues a publication in its Occasional Papers series entitled *World Economic Outlook: A Survey by the Staff of the International Monetary Fund.* These staff surveys analyze data and identify issues for discussion by the Executive Board and Interim Committee. The surveys include information and projections respecting individual countries and groups of countries as well as general assessments.

[47] E.B. Decision No. 5392, *supra* note 12, subpart Procedures for Surveillance, section III.

[48] At pages 589–598.

[49] E.B. Decision No. 5392, *supra* note 12, paragraph 2, and subpart Procedures for Surveillance, section VI.

[50] The purpose and structure of the OECD are described in Chapter 2, *supra,* page 68 et seq.

[51] Economic Cooperation Act of 1948, section 115(b); *United States Statutes at Large,* vol. 62, part 1, p. 137 at pp. 150–51.

[52] Convention for European Economic Co-operation, Article 1. See Chapter 2, *supra,* page 68 (note 137).

[53] See generally Henry G. Aubrey, *Atlantic Economic Cooperation: The Case of the OECD* (New York: Frederick A. Praeger, 1967), pp. 38–39 and 107–09. See also Lincoln Gordon, "The Organization for European Economic Cooperation," *International Organization,* vol. 10 (1956), p. 1.

present consultation practice in the OECD represents an evolution and development of this experience.

While OECD Council meetings today deal with coordination of economic policy as well as other matters,[54] the intensive work takes place in committees. There is both a comprehensive annual review of the economic problems and prospects of each member country within the Economic and Development Review Committee and a system of more frequent consultations within the Economic Policy Committee and its working parties.

In preparation for the annual examinations in the Economic and Development Review Committee, the OECD Secretariat prepares an economic survey of each country. The EDRC's consultation with each member normally takes place at the OECD's headquarters in Paris. High officials of the country whose policies are under examination are usually in attendance. Other OECD members are normally represented by members of permanent delegations but may be represented by higher officials. Representatives from the IMF, BIS, and EEC are also present. For the examination of each country, a panel of representatives of other member governments is designated to conduct the examination. The Secretariat's paper is discussed and the panel asks questions.[55] The "examinee" has the right to refuse to reply, but in fact this is rarely done and then usually for security reasons.

It has been reported that the country reviews in the EDRC, with some exceptions, are quite gentle. Participants are hesitant to ask questions that would appear to interfere in the examinee's domestic affairs.[56] The *Economic Survey* of the individual OECD country that results from the EDRC's discussions is published.[57] While the original staff document may be hard-hitting, the published revision may be softened to represent a shared view of all members. The country under review can assure that the published version is consistent with its position and policies and is not an independent conflicting appraisal.[58]

The EDRC's procedure can be contrasted with annual consultations as presently conducted within the International Monetary Fund. The OECD's staff is much smaller than the IMF's and it plays a more subdued role in the consultation process. The reader will recall that a central feature of each IMF regular consultation is a visit by a staff team to the examinee country and consultations there with high-level officials. These national officials normally do

---

[54] See F. Lisle Widman, *Making International Monetary Policy* (Washington: Georgetown University International Law Institute, 1982), pp. 91–97.

[55] See Hugo J. Hahn and Albrecht Weber, *Die OECD: Organisation für Wirtschaftliche Zusammenarbeit und Entwicklung* (Baden-Baden: Nomos Verlagsgesellschaft, 1976), pp. 280–84.

[56] See generally Michael Henderson, "The OECD as an instrument of National Policy," *International Journal*, vol. 36 (1981), p. 793 at pp. 797–800.

[57] The surveys are published under the title *Economic Survey of [Country]*.

[58] See discussion of the changes insisted upon by France before publication of the *Economic Survey of France* in 1983; *Wall Street Journal*, April 14, 1983, p. 32. See also Henderson, *supra* note 56, pp. 798–99.

not, however, participate directly in the subsequent discussion in the IMF Executive Board. At that point the examinee country is usually represented only by its IMF executive director and alternate (who may not be of its nationality[59]) and other countries voice their views through their executive directors.[60] In the OECD the examinees are represented in the Paris review by relatively high national officials who have policy-making responsibilities in their governments. While OECD staff members also visit the examinee countries, the consultations in the field are not as extensive as those of the IMF.

More important than the annual EDRC consultations described above are the economic policy discussions that take place in the OECD's Economic Policy Committee and its working parties. This Committee meets several times a year to review broad economic problems of concern to the OECD membership as a whole. The Chairman of the President's Council of Economic Advisors usually heads the U.S. delegation to meetings of the Committee, and other countries are represented by equally high-level officials. Representatives of the IMF, BIS, and EEC also regularly attend the Committee's meetings. To assist the Committee and its working parties, as well as the EDRC, the OECD Secretariat prepares twice a year short-term forecasts for demand, output, prices, and the balance of payments. These forecasts are elaborated in detail for the major countries and in more summary form for the others. The forecasts are intended to be integrated and internationally consistent.[61]

The Economic Policy Committee attempts to formulate desired economic policies at both the domestic and international levels and to orchestrate the timing of their implementation. The emphasis is primarily on a matrix of macroeconomic policies. Specific problems may be discussed such as means for avoiding competitive increases in interest rates, the implications of tax cut proposals, and the financing of petroleum imports without resort to trade restrictions. Persistent, less tractable problems of inflation, unemployment, and the slowness of economic growth have recently been on the agenda. Discussions may penetrate deeply into domestic policies. Collaboration is sought to ease problems and to avoid "exporting" them from one country to another. A goal is that the several members' policies be coordinated and consistent with one another. The atmosphere in the Committee's meetings has been described as "polite frankness,"[62] but on occasion has been contentious when one or two countries have been charged with creating economic problems for other countries.[63]

---

[59] An IMF member that does not appoint an executive director in accordance with Article XII, section 3(b)(i), is permitted to send a representative without vote to the meeting at which its consultation is concluded. By-Laws, section 19; *By-Laws, Rules and Regulations* (40th issue, 1983).

[60] Even if the IMF Board of Governors should decide to form a Council (see Chapter 1, pages 26–28), the Executive Board will probably continue to be the organ that conducts the regular annual consultations with members.

[61] The forecasts are published in modified form in July and December in the *OECD Economic Outlook*.

[62] Henderson, *supra* note 56, p. 794.

[63] The economic policies of the Federal Republic of Germany were challenged in the Economic Policy

Working parties of the Economic Policy Committee consider particular types of problems and prepare materials for the Committee. Working Party No. 3, concerned with policies for the promotion of better international payments equilibrium, is of particular interest.[64] It was formed in 1961 as a forum in which a limited group of countries (the Group of Ten plus Switzerland) could engage in frequent reviews of trends in world trade, monetary and fiscal policies, and balance-of-payments problems.[65] Representatives of other OECD member states are not permitted to attend, even as observers. The working party meets frequently, often as many as four or five times a year. Each member of the Group of Ten and Switzerland usually sends two representatives (normally a deputy of the finance minister and the governor or deputy governor of its central bank) plus advisers. The U.S. delegation is normally led by the Under Secretary of the Treasury for Monetary Affairs (who carries higher rank than the U.S. Executive Director of the IMF). Representatives of the BIS, IMF, and EEC attend the meetings. Deliberations are confidential.

Working Party No. 3 regularly considers the short-term balance-of-payments positions of the G-10 countries and Switzerland. Participants share information on the means used to finance balance-of-payments deficits and surpluses, and for this purpose provide information to the BIS which assembles and distributes it on a confidential basis to the members of the working party.[66] The working party also discusses the participants' medium-term balance-of-payments aims with respect both to their current and capital accounts. The stated aims are examined for mutual consistency and for their trade and payments implications. The working party also considers the external effects of domestic monetary policies. It reviews the working of the exchange rate system and official intervention in the exchange markets.[67] In their role as deputies of finance ministers, members of the working party act as the Deputies of the Group of Ten and Switzerland.

While the work of Working Party No. 3 focuses almost exclusively on international monetary problems, Working Party No. 1 considers a broader range of economic issues. It considers such subjects as determinants of investment, wage and labor market rigidities, budget financing and domestic monetary control, and macro-economic consequences of public sector deficits.[68]

Committee's meeting in November 1977 when other countries believed German policies should have been more growth oriented. See Henderson, *idem*, pp. 795–97.

[64] See Chapter 2, *supra*, page 71. See generally Widman, *supra* note 54, pp. 79–90.

[65] See *Statement by Ministers of the Group of Ten and Annex Prepared by their Deputies, Issued August 10, 1964* (London: Her Majesty's Stationery Office, 1964), annex, paragraphs 8–10 and 35–37.

[66] See paragraph 37 of the annex to the *Statement by Ministers of the Group of Ten, idem*; and Bank for International Settlements, *The Bank for International Settlements and the Basle Meetings* (Basle: BIS, 1980) [hereinafter *BIS 1930–80*], pp. 61–63.

[67] See, e.g., *Activities of OECD in 1978*, pp. 18–19; *idem, 1980*, pp. 17 and 18; *idem, 1981*, pp. 17–18; and *idem, 1982*, pp. 19–20.

[68] See, e.g., *Activities of OECD in 1980*, pp. 16–17; *idem, 1981*, pp. 16–17; and *idem, 1982*, pp. 18–19.

Economic policy positions worked out in the OECD's Economic Policy Committee are often reflected in communiqués of OECD meetings at the higher Ministerial Level. For example, in June 1978 the OECD Council at the Ministerial Level adopted a "programme of concerted action" that had been worked out by the EPC. Concerned with unemployment, slower than expected growth, and inflation, the program encouraged certain countries to apply demand stimulation:

> Belgium, Canada, France, Germany, Italy, Japan, Switzerland and the United Kingdom should ensure, by appropriate measures as necessary, that the expansion of their domestic demand is significantly greater than in 1977. . . . The Netherlands should consolidate the effects of the boost in domestic demand which was achieved last year. . . . Such action should not undermine anti-inflationary policies.
>
> All other Member countries, which are not currently in a position to take explicit action to expand domestic demand beyond what is now in prospect, should concentrate primarily on reducing inflation and improving their balance-of-payments position. . . . It is particularly important that the recent acceleration of inflation in the United States should be reversed.[69]

We shall later consider the general obligations of countries in the balance-of-payments adjustment process.[70] Here it is important to emphasize that the OECD's law in practice is that OECD members will consult in depth on their economic policies, but this practice is accompanied by the understanding that no country is legally obligated to change its policies except to the extent it accepts an obligation to do so or has an independent obligation to do so. Each representative participating in the Council can veto the policy prescription directed to his country.[71]

While a program like that quoted above is not legally binding, the governments joining in such a communiqué have a good faith obligation to give great weight to the statement when they modify and apply their policies. This is so even though the policies may be bad ones. If each country is subsequently completely free to decide whether the coordinated policies are good or bad and to choose whether or not to pursue them, the trust and expectations that must underlie joint efforts in uncertain economic environments will be lacking. Thus, once a program has been jointly adopted and problems arise in its implementation, representatives should meet to consider those problems, make changes

---

[69] Communiqué issued by meeting of the OECD Council at the Ministerial Level, June 1978, paragraph 11; *Activities of OECD in 1978*, p. 97 at pp. 98–99. See also *idem*, pp. 17–18.

[70] At page 608 et seq.

[71] See Chapter 2, *supra*, pages 69–70.

that are mutually acceptable, and then implement the policies in accord with agreed expectations. The above example is a good one because, in retrospect, the agreed policies for demand stimulation may have been unwise. But, economic policy coordination will be an unworkable sham if each country considers itself free to determine whether the already agreed matrix of policies is a wise configuration and to change its own policies at will. At the same time, efforts to give the force of law to such statements would probably result in discontinuance of the present process of policy harmonization in the OECD. Good faith deference to agreed policies falls somewhere between independent action and formal legal commitment.

The members of the OECD are committed to policies favoring full employment, a satisfactory rate of growth, and reasonable price stability, as well as liberalization of trade, other current operations, and capital movements. They are also committed to orderly exchange arrangements and balance-of-payments adjustment. The simultaneous achievement of these objectives is far from easy.[72]

Bank for International Settlements

There is a long tradition of consultations among governors of central banks.[73] The Bank for International Settlements (BIS) has served as a forum for central bank consultations since its establishment in 1930.[74] It has assumed an especially significant role during the last twenty years. Activities of the BIS have been mentioned throughout this book, and our attention here centers on economic policy consultations.

The Board of Directors of the BIS normally meets in the morning of the second Tuesday of each month except August and October.[75] There was a long tradition of using the weekend before this brief formal meeting (which was formerly held on Monday) for confidential consultations among central bank governors and other high central bank officials, but now these consultations, except in emergencies, usually take place on Monday and Tuesday. For these consultations the governors or deputies of the eight central banks represented on the

[72] See generally Miriam Camps and Catherine Gwin, *Collective Management: The Reform of Global Economic Organizations* (New York: McGraw-Hill Book Co. for Council on Foreign Relations, 1981); and Miriam Camps, *"First World" Relationships: The Role of the OECD* (Paris: Atlantic Institute for International Affairs; New York: Council on Foreign Relations, 1975).

[73] See Jean-Jacques Rey, "Le Développement de la Coopération entre Banques Centrales dans les Relations Monétaires Internationales," in Centre d'Études Européenes de Waterloo, *Les Relations Financières Internationales: Facteurs de Solidarités ou de Rivalités* (Brussels: Bruylant, 1979), p. 139; and statement of Henri Guisan in *Aspects du Droit International Économique* (Colloque d'Orléans de la Société Française pour le Droit International, May 1971; Paris: A. Pedone, 1972), pp. 128–35.

[74] The organization and activities of the Bank for International Settlements are described in Chapter 2, *supra*, page 52 et seq.

[75] No meeting is held in August because it is a vacation time. No meeting is held in October because the IMF's Annual Meeting is held in late September.

BIS Board of Directors are joined by representatives of the central banks of the United States,[76] Canada, and Japan—thus constituting the Group of Ten and Switzerland. The General Manager and Economic Counsellor of the BIS are also in attendance.[77]

The main attraction of the periodic meetings in Basle is the opportunity to exchange information on their respective countries' problems and on the international monetary situation. A number of informal meetings, free from publicity, are arranged, some being bilateral and others multilateral. Representatives and experts of international organizations and central banks other than the Group of Ten may attend some of the meetings. There are usually several lunches and dinners attended by different groups of participants. Perhaps the most important meeting is a dinner of governors with a "tour d'horizon" discussion. The conversation ranges through the international situation, internal and external monetary policies of the participating banks, and emerging problems that deserve attention by central bankers. By tradition the discussion is carefully structured. Statements made are addressed directly to points of concern and are not lengthy. A governor can frankly voice his concern about policies being pursued by other central banks represented by governors in attendance. The discussions provide an opportunity for a central bank contemplating a policy change to test reaction to it. Those listening will indicate the expected reactions in their own countries. They may, also, out of previous experience in the use of similar policies, suggest reactions the change might stir in the proposer's own country. Frequently governors share in confidence information on internal differences within their own governments which might not be shared in other forums such as OECD Working Party No. 3 or IMF consultations.

The central bankers are usually not accompanied by legal advisers, and normally no effort is made to fashion formal agreements among those present at the sessions. One participant has said: "No agreements were ever signed nor memoranda of understanding ever initialed. The word of each official was sufficient."[78] "Gentlemen's understandings" may be reached on such matters as actions that will be taken domestically (e.g., expansion or contraction of money supply), actions to be taken in the exchange markets, and the provision of credit

---

[76] The persons normally making up the U.S. Federal Reserve System's "delegation" are a member of the Board of Governors, a senior member of the Washington staff, the President of the Federal Reserve Bank of New York, and the officer of the New York Bank in charge of foreign currency operations. The Chairman of the System's Board of Governors normally attends meetings two or three times a year.

[77] On occasion the Managing Director of the IMF or his personal representative may be invited to attend a meeting, but normally neither the Managing Director nor any other representative of the IMF attends the Basle meetings. The IMF's Managing Director is usually briefed about each session, and there are frequent contacts between the IMF's Managing Director and his representatives and the President, General Manager, and staff of the BIS.

[78] Charles A. Coombs, *The Arena of International Finance* (New York: John Wiley & Sons, 1976), p. 26. Mr. Coombs regularly attended the sessions, as a representative of the Federal Reserve Bank of New York, from their inception in 1961 until his retirement in 1975. The format of Basle meetings during that period is described at pp. 24–29.

to countries in difficulty.[79] Because the meetings occur regularly they are not surrounded by a sense of crisis or great expectations. Normally there are no press releases or press briefings after these meetings. On occasion the President of the BIS may make an agreed announcement to the press.[80] Others in attendance usually try to maintain the confidential character of the discussions, although newspaper reporters may pry for information. The meeting of the Federal Open Market Committee of the U.S. Federal Reserve System following a Basle session always includes a rather complete oral report on the discussions by persons who had been in attendance, but at the present time no record is kept that is available to the public.[81] The *Annual Reports* of the BIS do not provide information on the subject matter or tenor of the monthly discussions in Basle.

While the press loves secrecy—particularly when reporters are able to break through it[82]—it is easy to assume that central bank governors, when they convene in Basle or at other places, have greater practical control of economic events than they do in fact. The responsibilities of central banks include (a) issuing the national currency and serving as banker for the government, (b) management of the volume of domestic credit and its allocation and the level and structure of interest rates, (c) management of the exchange rate and administration of exchange controls, and (d) maintenance of confidence in the banking system. While the powers possessed by central banks are important, they are limited. Parliaments, heads of government, and government ministers make decisions on taxes and expenditures, labor legislation, social security, regulation of business activities, and other economic matters. Central bankers often can only lament and accommodate policies they believe unwise.

Central bankers do have some advantages. Because of long tenure in office, expert staffs, and the technical character of their actions, they are often in a more secure position than other officials to withstand short-term politcal pressures. The frequent sessions in Basle can build tight personal bonds among governors. Henry H. Schloss has commented: "The personal contacts, the regular exchange of views as a matter of routine—not requiring communiqués and 'results'—have permitted a degree of collaboration and personal contact which would otherwise have been almost impossible to attain."[83] The sessions in Basle can strengthen the resolve of governors to pursue policies they personally believe wise in the face of pressure for temporary expedients to stimulate economic activity. Perhaps as much as any other official, a central bank governor can be expected to appreciate the importance of maintaining public confidence

---

[79] The central bank support to the Bank of England in 1968 and in 1977 are examples. See Chapter 3, pages 106 and 108 (notes 17 and 26).

[80] See quotations accompanying notes 252 and 277, *infra*, for examples.

[81] See Chapter 4, *supra*, page 137 (note 31), regarding the *Minutes of Federal Open Market Committee*. Minutes of these reports on Basle sessions have not been kept subsequent to March 1976.

[82] See, e.g., Paul Lewis, "When High Priests of Finance Meet," *New York Times,* June 12, 1977, p. F-3.

[83] Henry H. Schloss, "The Bank for International Settlements," in New York University Graduate School of Business Administration, Institute of Finance, *The Bulletin,* nos. 65–66 (September 1970), p. 1 at p. 36.

in the monetary instrument (the national currency) and its issuer. Because the psychological element is important to monetary confidence, the Basle meetings make it possible for governors to know each other well and to come to place confidence in each other.

In addition to meetings of central bank governors of the Group of Ten and Switzerland, the BIS serves as a forum for other consultations on economic policy. Since 1976 governors of central banks represented on the Board of Directors of the BIS and the Bank's senior managers have held meetings (usually twice a year) with governors of central banks of Eastern European countries.[84]

There are a variety of meetings on technical topics related to economic policy. Economists from the central banks of the Group of Ten, Switzerland, and some other countries meet in Basle to exchange views on economic analysis. Senior central bank officials (below the rank of governor) responsible for domestic monetary policies meet from time to time under the auspices of the BIS.[85] The Eurocurrency Standing Committee and the Committee on Banking Regulations and Supervisory Practices meet in Basle.[86]

There are daily multilateral telephone conversations (usually four a day) at the level of foreign exchange department officers among the central banks of the EEC countries, Norway, Sweden, Switzerland, and the United States. BIS officers participate in these conversations. The central banks of Canada and Japan are associated with the information network. Consultations can easily be raised to higher levels if need arises.

A Footnote—Understandings Among Central Bank Governors.   The author has previously argued that the Bank for International Settlements and national central banks have the capacity to conclude agreements governed by public international law as well as by national laws.[87] A question can be raised whether oral understandings reached among central bank governors at Basle meetings are only gentlemen's agreements implicating the personal integrity of the individuals or whether at least some of the understandings also carry legal commitments of the central banks the governors represent.

While the International Court of Justice has recognized that legal effects can be attributed to oral statements made by representatives of a state,[88] the author would urge caution in attributing a legally binding character to oral understandings reached during a meeting of central bank governors in Basle. Much,

---

[84] See *BIS 1930–80, supra* note 66, p. 60.

[85] *Idem,* pp. 58–59.

[86] See pages 620–624 and 628–630, *infra.*

[87] See Chapter 2, *supra,* pages 60–63, and Chapter 4, pages 157–164.

[88] See *Nuclear Tests Case (Australia v. France),* judgment of December 20, 1974, in International Court of Justice, *Reports of Judgments, Advisory Opinions and Orders [I.C.J. Reports],* 1974, p. 253 at pp. 267–268; and *Legal Status of Eastern Greenland (Denmark v. Norway),* judgment of April 5, 1933, in Permanent Court of International Justice, *Series A/B (Judgments, Orders and Advisory Opinions),* no. 53, 1933, p. 1.

of course, will depend on the subject matter of the understanding and the circumstances. Other considerations that should come into play in attempting to answer the question in a particular case include the intentions of the participants; their expectations in the event of nonperformance by one of their counterparts; authority of the governors to make binding commitments under their national laws, bank charters, and regulations;[89] the extent to which central bank governors generally are perceived in practice to have authority; the formalities associated with the conclusion of the agreements; the degree and reasonableness of reliance; and the extent of resulting damage.

The difficulty of applying these criteria, the lack of a reliable record of oral communications, and the fact that governors are normally not accompanied by their lawyers when they attend Basle meetings are factors that should place a heavy burden on any bank that would subsequently argue that a particular oral statement was legally binding in a case where the statement was not promptly confirmed by a writing. Where there is a desire to bind the banks, telex messages or other written instruments confirming and elaborating the understandings can be exchanged before the governors leave Basle or when they return home.[90] Where circumstances prevent the use of written instruments, language can be chosen for oral communications that leaves no doubt that legally binding obligations have been assumed.[91]

European Economic Community

The system of domestic economic policy guidelines for harmonizing economic and monetary policies in the European Economic Community will be examined in some detail.[92] It is the most intensive multilateral effort to date to harmonize national economic policies. Our starting point is Article 2 of the Treaty Establishing the European Economic Community. It states that one of the tasks of the

[89] Documents bearing on the delegation of authority through the Federal Open Market Committee of the U.S. Federal Reserve System are cited in Chapter 4, *supra,* page 136 (note 27).

[90] The sterling guarantee arrangements negotiated in Basle in 1968 were subsequently embodied in formal instruments. The arrangements respecting sterling balances negotiated in Basle in December 1976 and January 1977 which involved an agreement of central banks to extend a $3 billion line of credit to the Bank of England through the BIS were also confirmed by telex messages or other written instruments. The reactivation of the currency swap network following meetings in Basle in July 1973 was followed by exchanges of telex messages defining the commitments. See Chapter 3, *supra,* pages 104–108, and Chapter 4, page 139 et seq.

[91] In some situations an oral understanding must be legally binding even though not promptly confirmed in writing. When a general strike in France in May 1968 disrupted post, telex, and cable communications, Federal Reserve officials in New York continued to accept and act upon telephoned instructions from the Banque de France. Lawyers in the New York Bank heaved a sigh of relief when two weeks later the daughter of the governor of the Banque de France personally delivered written confirmations. See Coombs, *Arena of International Finance, supra* note 78, pp. 176–77. It is submitted that, given the circumstances, if no confirmations had been sent, the Banque de France would have been legally bound by the oral instructions it gave.

[92] A general description of the European Economic Community and its activities in the monetary field appears in Chapter 2, *supra,* page 76 et seq.

organization is to "promote throughout the Community a harmonious development of economic activities, a continuous and balanced expansion, an increase
in stability, an accelerated raising of the standard of living. . . ."[93] The pursuit of economic policies consistent with this objective is made an obligation of
member states by Article 104:

> Each Member State shall pursue the economic policy needed to en-
> sure the equilibrium of its overall balance of payments and to main-
> tain confidence in its currency, while taking care to ensure a high
> level of employment and a stable level of prices.

Article 6 obligates member states to "coordinate their respective economic policies to the extent necessary to attain the objectives of this Treaty."
This coordination obligation is reinforced by Article 105 which in paragraph 1
provides: "Member States shall coordinate their economic policies. They shall
for this purpose provide for cooperation between their appropriate administrative departments and between their central banks." Article 145 provides:

> To ensure that the objectives set out in this Treaty are attained, the
> Council shall, in accordance with the provisions of this Treaty:
> — ensure coordination of the general economic policies of the Mem-
>   ber States;
> — have power to take decisions.[94]

While Article 145, quoted above, gives the Council authority to deal with
general economic policy, Article 103 contains somewhat more specific provisions, and an independent source of authority, for dealing with the coordination
of conjunctural policy—a subspecie of economic policy.[95] Its first three paragraphs provide:

> 1. Member States shall regard their conjunctural policies as a
> matter of common concern. They shall consult each other and the
> Commission on the measures to be taken in the light of the prevailing
> circumstances.
> 2. Without prejudice to any other procedures provided for in

---

[93] See Chapter 2, *supra,* page 76 (note 171), respecting the text of the treaty.

[94] At the time the Treaty of Rome was signed in 1957 the Committee of Heads of Delegations issued an
authentic interpretation that Article 145's reference to economic policies is to be understood in the widest
possible sense and includes economic policy, monetary policy, social policy, and the like. The declaration is
quoted in Hans Peter Ipsen, *Europäisches Gemeinschaftsrecht* (Tübingen: J.C.B. Mohr, 1972), p. 777. See
also Hans Smit and Peter E. Herzog, *The Law of the European Economic Community: A Commentary on the
EEC Treaty* (6 vols.; New York: Matthew Bender, binder service, 1983 ed.), part 5, p. 95.

[95] Economists' use of the term "conjunctural policy" is explained in Chapter 9, *supra,* page 353 (note 14).

this Treaty, the Council may, acting unanimously on a proposal from the Commission, decide upon the measures appropriate to the situation.

3. Acting by a qualified majority on a proposal from the Commission, the Council shall, where required, issue any directives needed to give effect to the measures decided upon under paragraph 2.[96]

Until 1971 Council actions under Article 103 were cast in the form of "recommendations."[97] In March of that year the Council and representatives of member states by unanimous agreement resolved to unify by stages the monetary system applicable throughout the Community.[98] Since that time the Council has adopted a number of decisions and directives under Article 103 and under the combined authority of Articles 103 and 145.[99] While efforts to achieve the grandiose plan of March 1971 faltered,[100] a political commitment to even-

---

[96] While paragraph 3 provides for directives to be adopted by a qualified majority, unanimity has been the normal practice. See pages 595–596, *infra.* See also Chapter 2, page 79 (note 181). The negotiating history of Article 103 is summarized in Smit and Herzog, *supra* note 94, part 3, pp. 566–67.

[97] See generally Smit and Herzog, *idem*, part 3, pp. 564–65.

[98] In October 1970 a study group under the chairmanship of Pierre Werner (Prime Minister and Minister of Finance of Luxembourg) issued a report on "the realisation by stages of economic and monetary union in the Community." *Bulletin of the European Communities*, 1970, supplement, no. 11.

The Council of Ministers and representatives of the governments of the member states in March 1971 set economic and monetary union as an objective to be achieved not later than December 31, 1980. A single monetary area with a common central banking system was the goal. See Resolution of the Council and the Representatives of Governments of March 22, 1971, on the achievement by stages of economic and monetary union; *Official Journal of the European Communities* [hereinafter *Official Journal*], no. C-28, March 27, 1971, p. 1; *Official Journal—Special [English] Edition*, 2d series, vol. 9, p. 40; reprinted in European Communities Monetary Committee, *Compendium of Community Monetary Texts* (Brussels-Luxembourg, 1979), p. 25. A resolution adopted by the Council and governmental representatives a year later, on March 21, 1972, dealt with the application of the 1971 resolution. *Official Journal*, no. C-38, April 18, 1972, p. 3; *Special [English] Edition*, 2d series, vol. 9, p. 65; *Compendium* (1979), p. 30. These resolutions were adopted by the ministers in their capacity as members of the Council and in their capacity as representatives of member states because the program outlined in the resolutions went beyond the terms of the Treaty of Rome. While the 1971 and 1972 resolutions created no binding legal obligations on the Community or member states, they represented important political commitments.

The plan for monetary union, because of its comprehensive scope and novelty, excited much scholarly interest. See, e.g., Hans J. Dörsch, Jean-Victor Louis, and Marc Michiels, *L'Union Économique et Monétaire, 1970-1973* (Brussels: Editions de l'Université de Bruxelles, 1977); Giovanni Magnifico, *European Monetary Unification* (London: Macmillan; New York: John Wiley & Sons, 1973); and Lawrence B. Krause and Walter S. Salant (ed.), *European Monetary Unification and Its Meaning for the United States* (Washington: Brookings Institution, 1973). Loukas Tsoukalis, *The Politics and Economics of European Monetary Integration* (London: George Allen & Unwin, 1977), has a historical study of the period 1957–1976.

[99] For a list of directives adopted under Article 103, see Smit and Herzog, *supra* note 94, part 3, pp. 564–65. See generally H.H. Maas, "The Powers of the European Community and the Achievement of the Economic and Monetary Union," *Common Market Law Review*, vol. 9 (1972), p. 2; Michael H. Ryan, "The Treaty of Rome and Monetary Policy in the European Community," *Ottawa Law Review*, vol. 10 (1978), p. 535; and D.C. Kruse, *Monetary Integration in Western Europe: EMU, EMS and Beyond* (London: Butterworths, 1980), pp. 177–99. The legal effect of a "directive" is explained in Chapter 2, *supra*, page 86.

[100] Lack of progress toward monetary union was appraised in a report issued in 1975 by an EEC study

tual achievement of monetary union was reaffirmed by the heads of governments of the EEC states at a meeting in Bremen in July 1978.[101] The European Council in December 1978 adopted a resolution on the establishment of the European Monetary System (EMS).[102] The EMS, consisting of a unique currency unit (the European currency unit - ECU),[103] an exchange rate arrangement,[104] and financial facilities,[105] began operation in March 1979. The European Council resolution on the establishment of the EMS states that "the most important concern should be to enhance the convergence of economic policies towards greater stability," and at the same time the resolution recognizes that convergence "will not be easy to achieve."[106]

Jacques van Ypersele de Strihou, one of the principal architects of the European Monetary System's exchange rate arrangement, observed in 1979:

> To be successful, the EMS, first of all, will have to be accompanied by policies designed to achieve a greater convergence of the economies of member states. The EMS cannot be durable and effective unless it is backed by complementary policies.[107]

The principal decision on the coordination of economic policies, adopted by the Council of Ministers in February 1974, is entitled "the attainment of a high degree of convergence of the economic policies of the Member States."

group chaired by Robert Marjolin; text in Commission, *Report of the Study Group "Economic and Monetary Union 1980"* (document II/675/3/74-E final; Brussels, March 8, 1975). A report that sought to define elements of a European Union, and not simply a monetary union, was submitted to the European Council by Leo Tindemans in December 1975; text in *Bulletin of the European Communities,* 1976, supplement no. 1.

[101] See annex to the speaking note of the President of the European Council of July 7, 1978. *Compendium of Community Monetary Texts* (1979), *supra* note 98, p. 39; Agence Internationale d'Information pour la Presse (Brussels), *Europe—Documents,* no. 1013, July 10-11, 1978.

[102] European Council Resolution of December 5, 1978, on the establishment of the European Monetary System; *Bulletin of the European Communities,* 1978, no. 12, p. 10; *Compendium of Community Monetary Texts* (1979), *supra* note 98, p. 40. See discussion of the legal character of the resolution and implementing acts in Chapter 2, *supra,* pages 80–81. For a historical study of the negotiations, see Peter Ludlow, *The Making of the European Monetary System* (London: Butterworths, 1982).

[103] See Chapter 8, *supra,* pages 315–326 and 342–345.

[104] See Chapter 11, *supra,* pages 536–551.

[105] See Chapter 8, *supra,* pages 326–332.

[106] European Council Resolution of December 5, 1978, *supra* note 102, Part B, paragraphs 1 and 2.

[107] Jacques van Ypersele de Strihou, "Operating Principles and Procedures of the European Monetary System," in Philip H. Trezise (ed.), *The European Monetary System: Its Promise and Prospects* (Washington: Brookings Institution, 1979), p. 5 at p. 8. See also *20th Report on the Activities of the Monetary Committee; Official Journal,* no. C-240, September 25, 1979, p. 1 at annex I, paragraph 3.

For discussions of the potential and actual conflict between exchange rate policies and domestic economic policies in the countries participating in the European Monetary System's exchange rate arrangement, see Report of the Working Party on Harmonization of Monetary Policy Instuments in *23d Report on the Activities of the Monetary Committee* (Brussels–Luxembourg: European Communities, 1982), annex IV. See also Directorate-General for Economic and Financial Affairs, "The European Monetary System," *European Economy* (published by the Commission of the European Communities), no. 12 (July 1982), p. 7 [hereinafter *Directorate-General Report*], pp. 13–34, 54, 89–90, and 93–95.

This decision, as amended, is hereinafter called the "Convergence Decision."[108] Under Article 4 of the decision, the Council, acting on a proposal of the Commission and after consulting the Parliament and the Economic and Social Committee, is required, during the fourth quarter of each year, to adopt an annual report on the economic situation in the Community and to set economic policy guidelines to be followed by each member state in the following year.[109]

In addition to annual economic policy guidelines, the Convergence Decision calls for a medium-term economic policy program to be adopted at least every five years "to facilitate and guide structural changes—sectoral, regional and social—and to ensure the convergence of overall economic policies."[110] At two-and-a-half year intervals the Council is to examine a report on the situation and socio-economic developments in the regions of the Community.[111]

The Commission's draft of the annual economic policy guidelines for the following calendar year is normally submitted to the Council in the fall; and the Council, after review and amendment, adopts the guidelines, usually in December.[112] The Council adopts the guidelines each year and makes amendments to them using the legal form of a Council "decision" which it addresses to the member states. A Council "directive" (called the "Stability Directive")

---

[108] Council Decision No. 74/120 of February 18, 1974; *Official Journal*, no. L-63, March 5, 1974, p. 16. The decision was adopted under the combined authority of Articles 103 and 145. The decision was amended by Council Decision No. 75/787 of December 18, 1975; *Official Journal*, no. L-330, December 24, 1975, p. 52; and Council Decision No. 79/136 of February 6, 1979; *Official Journal*, no. L-35, February 9, 1979, p. 8. The amended text appears in *Compendium of Community Monetary Texts* (1979), *supra* note 98, p. 90.

[109] The annual report and economic policy guidelines as adopted by the Council are published in the *Official Journal*. The Commission's proposal, together with background analyses, is normally printed in the November issue of *European Economy* (prior to November 1978, *Economic Situation in the Community*). The opinions of the Parliament and the Economic and Social Committee are printed in the *Official Journal*.

[110] Convergence Decision, *supra* note 108, Article 6.
The Council and representatives of the governments of the member states in Decision No. 77-294 of March 14, 1977, adopted a medium-term economic program for the period 1976–1980; *Official Journal*, no. L-101, April 25, 1977, p. 1. The program contemplated, for the Community as a whole, a minimum annual economic growth rate of 4.5–5 percent, a reduction in the inflation rate to 4–5 percent by 1980, an improvement of the labor market, and a reduction in external disequilibria. In retrospect it appears the goals were set unrealistically and the means chosen inadequate.
The Council and the representatives of the governments of the member states, in Decision No. 82/534 of July 28, 1982, adopted a medium-term economic program for the period 1981–1985; *Official Journal*, no. L-236, August 11, 1982, p. 10. The text adopted was brief and general and included no quantitative targets. The draft submitted by the Commission with supporting documents appears in *European Economy*, no. 9 (July 1981), p. 5.

[111] Article 4a of Convergence Decision, *supra* note 108. Article 4a was added February 6, 1979, shortly before the European Monetary System's exchange rate mechanism was activated. Ireland and Italy were particularly concerned that their commitment to a system of stable exchange rates be balanced by a Community commitment to assistance in dealing with regional disparities in economic achievement.

[112] See Article 4 of the Convergence Decision as amended, *supra* note 108.
The economic policy guidelines for 1979 appear in *Official Journal* [hereinafter *O.J.*], no. L-8, January 12, 1979, p. 16; for 1980 in *O.J.*, no. L-17, January 23, 1980, p. 20; for 1981 in *O.J.*, no. L-375, December 31, 1980, p. 17, and no. L-211, July 31, 1981, p. 58; for 1982 in *O.J.*, no. L-385, December 31, 1981, p. 1, and no. L-78, March 24, 1982, p. 22; for 1983 in *O.J.*, no. L-386, December 31, 1982, p. 1; and for 1984 in *O.J.*, no. L-378, December 31, 1983, p. 1.

adopted at the same time as the 1974 Convergence Decision states that member states "shall implement" their short-term and medium-term economic policies "in accordance with the guidelines" adopted by the Council under the Convergence Decision.[113] Thus, member states are legally obligated under the Treaty of Rome to conform their policies to the guidelines but are given some freedom as to the means chosen for this purpose.[114] The Council has "invited" the central bank governors, meeting within the Committee of Governors of the Central Banks, to collectively establish guidelines for each central bank (dealing with such subjects as trends of bank liquidity, terms for supply of credit, and levels of interest rates) having regard to the economic policy guidelines laid down by the Council.[115]

There has now been about ten years of experience in implementing the 1974 Convergence Decision. During this period the guidelines have been confined to a few carefully worded paragraphs directed to the situation in each country. They tend to be more descriptive than prescriptive and it takes a skilled eye to discern specific obligations. The following excerpts from the guidelines for Italy for 1983 give the flavor:

> Italy has made progress toward adjusting its economy to external constraints. . . .
>
> Progress to date is not, however, sufficient to justify anything more than a limited expansion in domestic demand, and in particular consumption, in the short term. . . .
>
> An important set of financial decisions was taken at the end of July 1982. . . . It is foreseen that the overall effect of these measures, combined with others still to be specified, should be to reduce the Treasury's net borrowing requirement from about 15% of the gross domestic product in 1982 to about 12% in 1983. Such an effort is indispensable to ensure that total domestic credit does not expand beyond reasonable limits, and that the liquidity ratio declines without imposing excessively high interest rates on the private sector.
>
> It is now up to the two sides of industry, during the present round of negotiations for renewal of working conditions, to commit themselves to voluntary restraints on the nominal trend of incomes. . . . As a first step towards gradual disinflation, a target rate

[113] Article 1 of Council Directive No. 74/121 of February 18, 1974, on stability, growth, and full employment; *Official Journal*, no. L-63, March 5, 1974, p. 19; *Compendium of Community Monetary Texts* (1979), *supra* note 98, p. 95.

[114] The legal character of directives is explained in Chapter 2, *supra*, page 86.

[115] Council Decision No. 71/142 of March 22, 1971, on strengthening cooperation between central banks. *Official Journal*, no. L-173, March 27, 1971, p. 14; *Special [English] Edition*, 1971(I), p. 176; *Compendium of Community Monetary Texts* (1979), *supra* note 98, p. 89.

for the rise in prices and unit labour costs of at most 13% should be set, for 1983, some four points lower than in 1982.[116]

The policies set forth in guidelines each year differ from country to country. The guidelines for the Netherlands for 1976, 1977, and 1978 called for stimulation of demand. The guidelines in 1978 used this language:

> The Netherlands appear to be well placed to give a stronger impetus to demand. . . . Accordingly, economic policy should do more within the framework of joint action in a certain number of Member States, to stimulate activity in 1978. Since, however, it is important to avoid a situation in which the rise in public expenditure assumes a permanent character, the action of the authorities should be reversible. Moreover, since the possibility of expanding private investment seems limited in the short term, it will be necessary to encourage private consumption. [The guidelines then discussed a reduction in social security contributions and measures to reduce unemployment.] These measures as a whole will cause the Government net borrowing requirement to rise from Fl 7,500 million in 1977 to Fl 13,000 million in 1978 (4.6% of gross domestic product).[117]

The policies of the member states should complement each other. Guidelines for a country with a balance-of-payments deficit and a depreciating currency may call for restrictive measures designed to contain cost and price inflation while guidelines for a surplus country may call for it to reflate its economy and stimulate imports. Agreement on a matrix of economic policies to be pursued by ten countries for an area like the EEC may require some countries to pursue policies that are less favorable to them than to others in order to benefit the Community as a whole. Serious participation in a program of economic policy coordination requires this to be recognized and accepted.[118] To a large extent, however, the guidelines simply state policies that a government has in fact already chosen to pursue. Indeed, given the practice of adopting the guidelines

---

[116] Council Decision No. 82/950 of December 17, 1982, adopting the annual report on the economic situation in the Community and laying down economic policy guidelines for 1983. *Official Journal,* no. L-386, December 31, 1982, p. 1 at pp. 18–19 (annex, part II).

[117] Council Decision No. 77/778 of November 21, 1977, adopting the annual report on the economic situation in the Community and laying down the economic policy guidelines for 1978. *Official Journal,* no. L-323, December 19, 1977, p. 1 at p. 11 (annex, point 3.17).

[118] See Jean Waelbroeck and A. Dramais, "DESMOS: A Model for the Coordination of Economic Policies in the EEC Countries," in Albert Ando, Richard Herring, and Richard Marston (ed.), *International Aspects of Stabilization Policies* (Conference Series no. 12; Boston: Federal Reserve Bank of Boston, 1974), p. 285 at pp. 314–21. See also Commission of the European Communities, "Annual Economic Review 1983–84," *European Economy,* no. 18 (November 1983), p. 45 at pp. 152–63.

by unanimity, a country can prevent the adoption of guidelines it does not desire.

As already seen, the statements tend to be general. The Commission has recommended that guidelines for monetary policy—particularly money supply growth—be stated in quantitative terms.[119] In the guidelines for 1983, projections of monetary expansion or price inflation were made for some countries but not all. Similarly the guidelines projected the rate of growth in gross domestic product for some but not all countries. The only target or ceiling formulated in statistical terms for every country was the size of the net government borrowing requirement in 1983 stated as a percentage of the gross domestic product.[120] Achieving agreement on a credible percentage figure for each country obviously required negotiation. The increased use of quantitative measures for all members is likely to generate pressures for effective negotiations as compared to "guiding" a country along its already chosen path.

Member states are obligated to submit the EEC economic policy guidelines to their national parliaments.[121] The intention is that the guidelines should be taken into account in the formulation of national budgets and be considered in national parliamentary debates on economic policy.

The economic policy guidelines adopted under the Convergence Decision are reviewed periodically by the Council and may be revised in the course of the year.[122] A Coordinating Group on Economic Policy, consisting of a representative of each member state and a representative of the Commission, is attached to the Council and is a forum for continuous consultations on economic policy and implementation of the guidelines. It meets at least once every month. The chairmen of the Economic Policy Committee, Monetary Committee, and Committee of Governors of the Central Banks meet with the Coordinating Group.[123] The Economic Policy Committee, Monetary Committee, and Governors Committee also meet separately. It is not unusual for the Council in the course of a year to hold eight meetings at the ministerial level on the economic situation.

If problems arise during the year, the Commission, pursuant to the Convergence Decision, may address a recommendation to a member state.[124] In July 1981, for example, the Commission addressed a recommendation to Belgium to hold its budget deficit to a stated level, to control government expenditures, to reduce the government net-borrowing requirement to a stated

---

[119] *Economic Situation in the Community,* 1977, no. 3, p. 6 (point 3.6).

[120] See Council Decision No. 82/950, *supra* note 116, pp. 13–21 (annex, part II). See quotation from guidelines for Italy at page 594, *supra.*

[121] Article 5 of Convergence Decision as amended, *supra* note 108.

[122] Convergence Decision, *idem,* Articles 2–4. The guidelines are normally reviewed and adjusted in March.

[123] Convergence Decision, *idem,* Article 9.

[124] Convergence Decision, *idem,* Article 11.

level, and to maintain a tight monetary policy.[125] A month later the Belgian government informed the Commission that it had taken the recommendation into account in drawing up the budget for 1982.[126]

The divergence indicator in the European Monetary System's exchange rate arrangement is intended to trigger consultations—not only on exchange rate policies, but on broader economic policies as well. It is intended to identify the particular country (or countries) that is presumptively under a burden to modify or, at least, explain its policies.[127] It appears that the most frequent response of a country whose currency crosses the divergence threshold has been to modify interest rate policies to make its currency more, or less, attractive to holders. Faced with the choice of major changes in economic policies or changes in official exchange rates, it appears that EMS participants have usually chosen the latter. Often changes in central rates are accompanied by understandings about changes in economic policies.[128]

The procedures under Articles 108 and 109 for derogating from the EEC Treaty's obligations because of balance-of-payments problems, discussed earlier in this book,[129] can in appropriate cases be used to justify departures from economic policy guidelines. Normally, however, a country whose policies depart from the guidelines has not been required to invoke Articles 108 or 109.

Economic policies can only be effectively applied if the countries have the instruments necessary to implement the agreed policies. The Stability Directive requires member states to adopt the necessary legislation to enable their "competent authorities" to accelerate or slow down government spending, to control indebtedness of governmental agencies, to modify direct or indirect taxes, and to take other actions.[130] The directive contains a detailed list of monetary policy instruments and powers that member states are required to confer on their monetary authorities.[131] However, until there is greater agreement among the mone-

---

[125] Commission Recommendation No. 81/629 of July 22, 1981; *Official Journal*, no. L-228, August 13, 1981, p. 29. See also *Bulletin of the European Communities*, 1981, no. 7/8, points 2.1.4 - 2.1.7.

[126] *15th General Report on the Activities of the European Communities in 1981*, point 112.

[127] See Chapter 11, *supra*, pages 541–544.

[128] A table showing economic policy measures in connection with each of the seven central rate realignments in the EMS through March 1983 appears in Horst Ungerer, with Owen Evans and Peter Nyberg, *The European Monetary System: The Experience, 1979–82* (IMF Occasional Paper no. 19; Washington, 1983), p. 27 (table 6). See also *Bulletin of the European Communities*, 1983, no. 3, point 1.2.3.

France in 1981 and 1982 placed greater importance on measures to reduce unemployment than to control inflation as compared to its EMS partners. A consequence was the necessity for sharp adjustments in exchange rates in June 1982 and March 1983. See Ungerer, *supra*, pp. 4–13; and *Directorate-General Report, supra* note 107, pp. 23–24. A table displaying central rate changes in the EMS appears in Chapter 11, *supra*, page 545.

[129] See Chapter 10, *supra* pages 473–477.

[130] Stability Directive, *supra* note 113, Articles 5 and 7.

[131] Stability Directive, *idem*, Article 9. See also Council Directive No. 72/156 of March 21, 1972; *Official Journal*, no. L-91, April 18, 1972, p. 13. The two directives, as they relate to monetary control instruments, are discussed in Chapter 10, *supra*, pages 472–473.

tary authorities in the EEC on the primary criteria for guiding monetary policy, applying harmonized instruments will remain difficult.[132]

The authorities of nation states, even states that are members of a regional economic community with the shared objectives of the EEC, find the coordination of national economic policies to be a very delicate matter. These policies are often at the center of political debates in the member countries. And, there are deeply rooted disparities in the economic and social structures of the ten countries. National officials tend to reserve the ultimate right to interpret and evaluate the effects of their own actions or inactions.[133] Nevertheless, more progress has been made in the EEC than in other multilateral organizations.

Summit Conferences

Periodic "summit" conferences on economic issues began at Rambouillet, France, in November 1975. These meetings, normally held once a year, bring together the heads of government of the United States, Canada, France, Federal Republic of Germany, Italy, Japan, and United Kingdom and the president of the Commission of the European Communities. While the meetings are surrounded by a great deal of ceremony and culminate formally only in a brief communiqué, the preparatory and follow-up consultations at the ministerial and deputy ministerial levels may be intensive.[134]

Summary Note on Consultation Procedures

The Versailles Summit Conference communiqué of June 1982 stated:

> 1. We accept a joint responsibility to work for greater stability of the world monetary system. We recognize that this rests primarily on convergence of policies designed to achieve lower inflation, higher employment, and renewed economic growth; and thus to maintain the internal and external values of our currencies. We are determined to discharge this obligation in close collaboration with all interested countries and monetary institutions.
>
> 2. We attach major importance to the role of the IMF as a mon-

---

[132] See annexes I and II of the *21st Report on the Activities of the Monetary Committee, Official Journal,* no. C-166, July 7, 1980, p. 1; annex IV of the *22d Report* (1981), *Official Journal,* no. C-124, May 25, 1981, p. 1; and annex IV of the *23d Report* (1982), *supra* note 107.

[133] See Niels Thygesen, "International Coordination of Monetary Policies—with Special Reference to the European Community," in John E. Wadsworth and François Léonard de Juvigny (ed.), *New Approaches in Monetary Policy* (Alphen aan den Rijn: Sijthoff & Noordhoff, 1979), p. 205 at pp. 208–10.

[134] See Widman, *supra* note 54, pp. 66, 68–72, 76–79, and 270–71.

etary authority and we will give it our full support in its efforts to foster stability.[135]

While national officials may make unilateral or joint statements like that above, translating those statements into effective action is another matter. A former president of the Federal Reserve Bank of New York colorfully remarked:

> Summit meetings and meetings of finance ministers from Rangoon to Rambouillet, and pronouncements of the IMF, have exhorted the nations to coordinate their domestic economic policies with their international economic responsibilities. The overall result has been a surplus of communiqués and not much concrete action.[136]

In modern parliamentary democracies, and in countries with other types of governments as well, national economic policies are major national issues, and governments assume office and fall on their promises and performance. While national officials know that their countries' situations are impacted by actions abroad, and their own policies impact others, they are simply not prepared to go very far in delegating decision-making authority in the economic sphere. Unless the benefits are specific and tangible—like large-scale financial assistance—there is reluctance to submit to internationally agreed economic programs. Consultation and a measure of coordination is about all one can expect in the immediate future. While procedures and institutions cannot guarantee that the substance of policies will be wise, they can facilitate effective communication and deliberation.

Of all the organizations studied, consultations in the European Economic Community are the most penetrating. This should not be surprising in view of the comprehensive scope of the Treaty of Rome, the limited number of countries involved, and their shared democratic values. The economic policy consultations in the Community are conducted at a high level involving both finance ministers and their deputies and central bank governors within a matrix of committees with overlapping memberships. Consultations at the deputy level take place at least once a month and at the ministerial level several times a year.

Working Party No. 3 of the OECD, consisting of the Group of Ten plus Switzerland, is a relatively homogenous grouping when compared to the OECD

---

[135] Paragraphs 1 and 2 of joint statement on monetary undertakings, issued at Versailles, June 6, 1982; *Weekly Compilation of Presidential Documents,* vol. 18 (1982), p. 756 at p. 758; *IMF Survey,* June 21, 1982, p. 189. See also the annex entitled "Strengthening Economic Cooperation for Growth and Stability" to the Williamsburg Summit Conference Declaration on Economic Recovery, issued May 30, 1983; *Weekly Compilation of Presidential Documents,* vol. 19 (1983), p. 806 at p. 808; *IMF Survey,* June 13, 1983, p. 171.

[136] Speech of Allan Sproul in 1977, in Lawrence S. Ritter (ed.), *Selected Papers of Allan Sproul* (New York: Federal Reserve Bank of New York, 1980), p. 232.

membership as a whole or to the broader-based IMF. All the countries have market-based economies and a democratic tradition of government. Working Party No. 3 meets at the deputy level four or five times a year. Central bank governors of the Group of Ten and Switzerland meet regularly in Basle. One of the reasons senior officials travel to OECD and BIS meetings so frequently is the opportunity for contact with their counterparts. The wide range of subjects considered in the OECD and the BIS, and the minimal role given formal procedures, encourages the use of these forums for discussions of sensitive matters upon which national authorities are not yet ready to make formal commitments. Consultations can take place before national actions are undertaken to assure adequate knowledge of their consequences and to test the expected reactions of other countries.

The IMF has a membership of some 146 countries representing both market-based and planned economies, at various stages of development, and with different governmental structures. The Executive Board has found it possible to engage in consultations that bridge these differences. One of the factors making this possible is that executive directors, although elected or appointed by governments, meet in continuous session and carry no heavy operating responsibilities in the countries that elect or appoint them. The regular economic policy consultations are primarily bilateral, between the IMF and the country under review, although recently greater attention has been given to the interface of policies pursued by groups of countries. The Interim Committee of the Board of Governors has served as a forum for consultation among high national officials. However, the Committee usually meets only two or three times a year and its deliberations to date have not probed deeply into the domestic economic policies of IMF member countries to anything like the degree of IMF regular consultations under the supervision of the Executive Board. Of course, changes in practice may evolve. The Interim Committee and the Council, if established, might develop procedures under IMF auspices for more penetrating economic policy consultations among high national officials. The Council, if established, is unlikely to assume responsibility for regular consultations because of the time demands, although, perhaps, conclusions of consultations with the economically most powerful countries could take place in the Council.

A few generalizations may be advanced about the manner in which concepts of legal obligation enter into economic policy consultation. In all the organizations the primary focus of economic policy consultations is usually on the economic wisdom of a course of action already taken or proposed rather than on legal questions. The participants typically have a background in economics, banking, or finance and combine this background with a political awareness that comes from holding high office. Normally legal counsel in national governments do not play prominent roles in economic policy consultations under the auspices of the IMF, OECD, BIS, or EEC. If a central bank governor brought his lawyer to a "tour d'horizon" discussion in Basle, this would probably create a stir. The services of lawyers on the staffs of the IMF and the European Communities' Commission have frequently been called upon, but the role of the in-house lawyer appears to be less prominent, although important, in the other organizations.

Legal concepts are more prominent in economic policy consultations in the IMF and the EEC compared to the OECD and the BIS. The periodic consultations under IMF Articles IV, VIII, and XIV consider the conformance of national actions with obligations under those articles, and "conclusions" and decisions are adopted. The system of consultation in the EEC involves the periodic promulgation of economic policy guidelines to which members are directed to conform their policies. The guidelines have, at least to some degree, a legally binding character.

Advantages flow from the use of legal concepts. They encourage careful definition of policy intentions. If legal consequences flow from non-achievement of policy commitments, those commitments are more likely to reflect economic realities than overly optimistic hopes. And, officials are more likely to choose means that will accomplish the objectives. Further, the statement of policy objectives in specific terms makes it possible to engage in an objective review of performance as compared to a situation where policies are stated in general terms using hortatory language. But, in the end, one must recognize that the success of consultations usually depends most heavily on the personal commitments of high level participants and the staffs that back them up.

While it is easy to bemoan the lack of international leverage over national domestic economic policies, Ralph C. Bryant was certainly correct when he said: "Defending one's policies in a critical forum of other policymakers involves some de facto surrender of the freedom to implement national policy independently of other nations' preferences."[137]

Consultation and Collaboration Duties that Accompany Other Rights and Obligations

Note

Obligations to consult and to collaborate often accompany and complement other rights and obligations. Drawing on discussions in earlier chapters, we shall review a few examples below. Consultations facilitate the application of rules in a proper manner, and they provide a method to fill in lacunae in the application of the rules. In some cases consultations are required to take place and normally do take place prior to action. In other cases consultations are supposed

---

[137] Ralph C. Bryant, *Money and Monetary Policy in Interdependent Nations* (Washington: Brookings Institution, 1980), p. 478.

to take place prior to action, but often only take place afterwards. In still other cases an obligation to consult arises after action is taken.

Consultation and Collaboration in Connection with the Use of Financial Facilities

In the case of the International Monetary Fund, consultations are required to and do take place prior to the Fund's approval of a drawing or a stand-by or extended arrangement, unless only a reserve tranche drawing is contemplated, to determine that the proposed purchase or financial arrangement is consistent with the Articles of Agreement and the policies of the Fund.[138] The Fund's authority to condition access to its general resources gives it leverage to insist that the country collaborate with the Fund to solve its balance-of-payments problems and not simply draw resources to postpone addressing the difficulties. Consultation obligations accompany the use of special facilities, like the compensatory financing facility, as well as use of resources under decisions of more general application.[139]

Consultations during the process of formulating a stand-by or extended arrangement may penetrate more deeply into domestic and international economic policies than regular consultations discussed earlier in this chapter. The shared goal is a program adequate to deal with the country's problems. The determination of objective performance criteria requires study of the country's situation, its policies, and also its statistical practices.

The development of a program to be supported by a stand-by or extended arrangement often takes several months of intensive work whether the country is industrialized or developing. Negotiations for a stand-by arrangement for Italy were broken off in early 1976, but, after renewed efforts, an arrangement was approved in the spring of 1977.[140] The design of the United Kingdom's program for which a stand-by was approved in early 1977 involved difficult decisions for officials of that country.[141] A Fund mission visited India in May of 1981, but the extended arrangement was not approved until November.[142] Mexico's consultations with the IMF looking toward financial assistance began in earnest in August of 1982, but the extended arrangement was not approved until December.[143] The delays were not because of choice but because the problems of the countries were serious ones that required careful assessments and

---

[138] See Chapter 6, *supra*, pages 239–240.

[139] See Chapter 6, *supra*, pages 248 et seq. and 277 et seq.

[140] See Chapter 6, *supra*, page 270 (note 191).

[141] Chapter 6, *supra*, page 264 (note 162).

[142] *Idem.* See generally page 246 et seq.

[143] See Chapter 10, *supra*, pages 410–411 and 412–413. See also speech of the Managing Director at the 1982 IMF annual meeting. IMF, *Summary Proceedings, 1982*, p. 13 at p. 23.

projections, and involved difficult policy choices for the authorities. The design of a stand-by or extended arrangement is a collaborative action *par excellence.*

Consultations continue after financial assistance has been provided by the Fund. The performance of the country is monitored. Is the country's performance conforming to expectations stated in the stand-by documents? Have unforeseen problems arisen? Is the country's position improving at a rate that will permit it to make early repurchases of its currency?[144]

The arrangements under which the European Economic Community's institutions provide assistance to members in balance-of-payments difficulty incorporate provisions for consultations.[145] Consultations take place in connection with drawings under reciprocal currency arrangements such as those maintained by the U.S. Federal Reserve System.[146] Sometimes balance-of-payments financing involves collaboration among organizations. The bridging financings provided by central banks through the Bank for International Settlements to Mexico and Brazil in 1982 and 1983, while negotiations continued with the IMF, are examples.[147]

Obligations to consult also fall on organizations. The International Monetary Fund consults a member through its executive director before placing the country's currency high on the list of currencies to be sold by the General Resources Account to countries making drawings in that account.[148] The IMF consults a member-participant—again through its executive director—before placing the participant high on its list of potential designees for transactions in special drawing rights.[149] While the Fund is vested with authority to adopt the regulations that define the procedure for determining exchange rates between each member's currency and the SDR, it is required to consult the member prior to adopting the decision on how the representative rate is determined.[150]

The creation and refinement of financial facilities are collaborative acts. The formulation and reformulation of IMF policies on regular drawings and the establishment of special facilities within the General Resources Account are examples.[151] Arrangements worked out in Basle for the support of central banks, such as the support given to the Bank of England in June 1976 and the arrangements for financing draw-downs of sterling balances agreed in January 1977, are collaborative acts.[152] When France was in crisis in the summer of 1968, the General Arrangements to Borrow were activated to assist the IMF in meeting a

---

[144] See Chapter 6, *supra,* pages 268–269.
[145] See Chapter 8, *supra,* page 326 et seq.
[146] See Chapter 4, *supra,* page 135 et seq.
[147] See Chapter 2, *supra,* page 58 (note 72), and Chapter 4, pages 164–165.
[148] See Chapter 6, *supra,* pages 224–225.
[149] See Chapter 5, *supra,* pages 210–211.
[150] See Chapter 5, *supra,* pages 184–185.
[151] See Chapter 6, *supra,* pages 232–235.
[152] See Chapter 3, *supra,* pages 107–108, and Chapter 4, pages 165–166.

drawing by France.[153] In addition, the U.S. Federal Reserve organized a line of credit for France of about U.S. $1.3 billion, with about half coming from the United States and half from the central banks of the EEC and the BIS. President Lyndon B. Johnson wrote in his memoirs, ''DeGaulle and his government had been most uncooperative in the previous monetary difficulties [of the U.K. and the U.S.]. Nonetheless in July we led the way with other nations in arranging a $1.3 billion stand-by credit for France. The international monetary system is not a field for pettiness or retribution.''[154]

Consultation and Collaboration Respecting Exchange Controls

The imposition by an IMF member of restrictions on payments or transfers respecting current transactions requires Fund approval under Article VIII. Multiple exchange rate practices and discriminatory currency arrangements also require approval under that article. The process of obtaining approval involves consultation with the Fund.[155] Annual consultations always review exchange restrictions that are inconsistent with Article VIII whether maintained by countries that have accepted Article VIII, Sections 2, 3, and 4, or that avail themselves of Article XIV.[156]

The OECD Code of Liberalisation of Current Invisible Operations and the Code of Liberalisation of Capital Movements are collaborative arrangements for the liberalization of these transactions. Each code includes provisions for periodic joint reviews of the necessity for any restrictions.[157] Decisions of the European Economic Community allowing restrictions pursuant to the derogation clauses of Articles 108 and 109 of the Treaty of Rome have included consultation clauses.[158] The use of trade restrictions for balance-of-payments reasons is subject to a consultation obligation as well as other obligations for parties to the General Agreement on Tariffs and Trade. The GATT Secretariat and committees also consult with the IMF in these cases.[159]

While consultations are normally supposed to precede the imposition of exchange measures requiring approval of the IMF,[160] the EEC,[161] or the

---

[153] The 1968 GAB activation also assisted the IMF in meeting a drawing by the United Kingdom. See Chapter 6, *supra*, page 290 (note 278).

[154] Lyndon B. Johnson, *The Vantage Point: Perspectives on the Presidency, 1963–1969* (New York: Holt, Rinehart & Winston, 1971), pp. 319–20. See also Coombs, *Arena of International Finance, supra* note 78, pp. 180–81.

[155] See generally Chapter 10, *supra*, page 401 et seq.

[156] See page 575, *supra*.

[157] See Chapter 10, *supra*, pages 443 and 460.

[158] See Chapter 10, *supra*, pages 473–477.

[159] See Chapter 10, *supra*, pages 429–440.

[160] See Chapter 10, *supra*, page 401.

[161] See Chapter 10, *supra*, pages 473–477.

GATT,[162] and are to be notified "forthwith" in the case of the OECD,[163] it is common for measures to be imposed and approval to be sought afterwards. At the present time the law in practice is post act consultation. One of the positive consequences of post act consultation is that the organizations are under less pressure to grant the approvals that are sought. Mexican restrictions imposed in August 1982 were not approved by the IMF until December and only after they had been modified.[164] The IMF delayed approving an Italian import deposit requirement in 1981 until Italian authorities set a timetable for its termination. The EEC also insisted on a timetable for termination.[165] While a practice of prior consultation might head off a nation's action or make it more palatable from the outset, consultations after the fact are not without effects.

There has over the years been a reduction of exchange restrictions. While it has been a slow process, what needs to be noted is the persistence of the IMF and other institutions, in annual and other consultations, in urging countries to liberalize their exchange systems.[166]

Consultation and Collaboration in the Management of Exchange Rates

Sir Joseph Gold has characterized the law of exchange rate arrangements as "soft."[167] Under IMF Article IV a great deal of freedom is reserved to national authorities. The obligations of collaboration are stated in very general terms in Section 1 of that article.[168] Highly specific obligations relate principally to notification and consultation. Fund decisions do not at the present time require prior notification of changes in exchange rate arrangements. Subsequent notification is required and consultations can take place immediately on the heels of the national action.[169] While post act consultation may have only minimal ef-

---

[162] See Chapter 10, *supra,* page 430.

[163] OECD Code of Liberalisation of Current Invisible Operations, Articles 7 and 13; and OECD Code of Liberalisation of Capital Movements, Articles 7 and 13. For citations see Chapter 10, *supra,* pages 443 and 460 (notes 295 and 375).

[164] See Chapter 10, *supra,* pages 410–411 and 412–413.

[165] See Chapter 10, *supra,* pages 409–410.

[166] An example of the IMF's persistence is the way it handled the currency restrictions affecting travel introduced by France in November 1968. The IMF gave its approval on a temporary basis, initially to March 1969, and later to the end of 1969. In view of France's continuing balance-of-payments problems, the Fund in December 1969 extended the approval for an additional year. France eased the restrictions somewhat during 1970. In December 1970 the IMF, while continuing to press for complete withdrawal of the restrictions, approved those that remained for another year subject to review during the regular consultation with France under Article VIII in the spring of 1971. In March and August 1971 France further relaxed the restrictions and in December 1971 abolished them. See Chapter 10, *supra,* pages 405–406. See also Margaret Garritsen de Vries, *The International Monetary Fund, 1966–1971: The System Under Stress* (2 vols.; Washington: IMF, 1976), vol. 1, pp. 356–57.

[167] Gold, "Strengthening the Soft International Law of Exchange Arrangements," *supra* note 35.

[168] See Chapter 11, *supra,* pages 507–519.

[169] See Chapter 11, *supra,* pages 527–530.

fects in the particular case, the consultations can clarify the meaning to be ascribed to the general language of Article IV, Section 1. Sir Joseph's comment is pertinent: "If obligations [stated in the IMF Articles and general decisions] cannot be formulated in language that will make breach obvious when it occurs, effectiveness will depend on the explicit expression of censorious judgments by peers whenever censure is justified."[170]

To take an example: On Wednesday, October 6, 1982, Finland announced a devaluation of its markka by 4 percent. On Friday, October 8, the new government of Sweden, led by Prime Minister Olaf Palme, on taking office announced a 16 percent devaluation of the krona, which followed a 10 percent devaluation of the Swedish currency a year earlier.[171] Officials in other countries were alarmed by the October 8 announcement and viewed the Swedish devaluation as excessive and competitive in character. The Managing Director of the IMF promptly initiated consultations with the Swedish authorities and within a week the IMF Executive Board considered the matter in detail. Although the Board did not adopt a formal decision, the executive directors clearly expressed a consensus that the Swedish devaluation was inconsistent with Article IV, Section 1(iii), which prohibits manipulation of exchange rates to gain an unfair competitive advantage. The Managing Director was asked to urge the Swedish authorities to reconsider their action. There was also concern that the Swedish action not trigger a string of devaluations.[172]

Although it is difficult to prove cause and effect, the IMF consultation in the Swedish case, though post act, appears to have had practical consequences even though Sweden did not rescind its action. The consultation clarified the obligations of Article IV. Aside from an adjustment by Finland,[173] IMF members refrained from devaluing in response to Sweden's action. What Sweden had done was now recognized as a "no-no." Subsequently there has been no deep devaluation by an industrialized country in circumstances comparable to those of Sweden in the fall of 1982.

Where a country's problems are recognized by the IMF or other bodies before national officials are ready to take action, multilateral consultations can help lead to corrective actions and shape the content of those measures. The announcement by the United States of November 1, 1978, of forceful intervention in the exchange markets to retard the further decline of the dollar (in relation to the Deutsche mark, Swiss franc, and Japanese yen) was preceded by consultations in the IMF and other bodies over an extended period in which the United

---

[170] Gold, "Strengthening," *supra* note 35, p. 465.

[171] See Sveriges Riksbank, *Quarterly Review*, 1982, no. 4, pp. 5–19; *Wall Street Journal*, October 11, 1982, p. 27; and *Financial Times* (London), October 11, 1982, p. 1. The devaluation was in relation to a trade-weighted basket of currencies in terms of which the market value of the krona was maintained.

[172] See *Wall Street Journal*, October 18, 1982, p. 39; and Agence Internationale d'Information pour la Presse (Brussels), *Europe*, no. 3469 (October 20, 1982), p. 12. See also IMF, *Annual Report, 1983*, pp. 65 and 104. For background on IMF Article IV, section 1(iii), see Chapter 11, *supra*, pages 515–519.

[173] Finland devalued its currency by a further 6 percent before markets opened on October 11, 1982.

States had been encouraged to take the kind of actions it then announced. The November 1 actions included a number of elements that the United States had been requested to consider in March 1973 at the time of the collapse of the Bretton Woods system and had not accepted: active intervention in the exchange markets, offering securities denominated in foreign currencies to foreign holders of dollar balances, and steps to increase interest rates in the United States.[174] The German, Swiss, and Japanese central banks, collaborating with the United States, agreed to dramatic increases in the amounts available to the Federal Reserve under reciprocal currency arrangements. They would also share in the profits and losses to be realized from the Federal Reserve's interventions financed by those facilities.[175] The United States actions included a drawing on its reserve tranche position with the IMF financed in part by activation of the General Arrangements to Borrow (another collaborative arrangement) in order that the United States have currencies needed for market interventions.[176] The U.S. policies announced November 1, 1978, were discussed in detail at an IMF Executive Board meeting on December 13, and the Board expressed support.[177]

While IMF decisions at the present time only require subsequent notification of changes in exchange rate arrangements, there is nothing to prevent the Fund from adopting decisions calling for prior notification so long as the right of members to choose their exchange arrangements consistent with Article IV is retained.[178]

Participants in the exchange rate arrangements of the European Economic Community's European Monetary System have agreed that central rates in that system will only be changed by mutual agreement, which obviously requires consultation prior to action. The devaluation or revaluation of any EMS currency involves the establishment of new central rates for all the currencies.[179] When an exchange rate hits a bilateral intervention limit, both issuers (not just one) have intervention obligations.[180]

Consultation and Collaboration Duties in the Absence of Defined Obligations

Note

While in the previous section we discussed duties to consult and collaborate that overarch or complement specific rights and duties in the monetary sphere, in

---

[174] Compare notes 43 and 156 in Chapter 11, *supra,* pages 499 and 533.
[175] See Chapter 4, *supra,* pages 143–146.
[176] See Chapter 6, *supra,* page 290 (note 278).
[177] See Chapter 11, *supra,* page 560 (note 270).
[178] See Chapter 11, *supra,* pages 527–530.
[179] See Chapter 11, *supra,* pages 541–546.
[180] See Chapter 11, *supra,* page 539.

this section we turn to important subjects on which few specific rules have been formulated. When it is not possible to formulate rights and duties in specific language and, at the same time, complete freedom of national action is not to be tolerated, drafters of treaties and other instruments insert provisions of a general character calling for consultation and collaboration.[181] The provisions also serve, to use Dominique Carreau's phrase, as "reservoirs of competence" for the international organizations involved.[182]

Many scholars and officials were disappointed that the Second Amendment to the IMF's Articles of Agreement did not incorporate comprehensive sets of rules dealing with the choice of policy instruments for balance-of-payments adjustment, regulation of international activities of commercial banks, harmonization of reserve asset policies, control of international liquidity, and assistance to developing countries.[183] The difficulty of devising treaty rules for these problems that are both wise and workable probably made the ultimate outcome a fortunate one, at least until a stronger consensus emerges. The duty to consult and to collaborate is thus the principal obligation. In some cases even this duty is not clearly stated. What legal duties or principles of good conduct are associated with these tough problems? We shall here suggest a few implications.

Choice of Policy Instruments for Correcting a Payments Deficit

A country facing a balance-of-payments deficit that appears temporary, for example one caused by an export shortfall, may simply finance the deficit until its payments position improves.[184] In cases where a deficit is likely to persist, the economic situation will press the country to take corrective measures sooner or later. But, in the individual case there is often debate about what corrective actions should be taken and what actions can be postponed.

Interestingly, there is no explicit statement in the IMF Articles of a general affirmative obligation of each member to maintain balance-of-payments equilibrium, even on average over a long period of time. The whole agreement,

---

[181] For a survey and analysis of consultation clauses in bilateral and multilateral treaties, see Judo Umarto Kusumowidagdo, *Consultation Clauses as Means of Providing for Treaty Observance: A Study in the Law of Treaties* (Stockholm: Almquist & Wiksell International, 1981). See generally Frederic L. Kirgis, Jr. *Prior Consultation in International Law* (Charlottesville: University Press of Virginia, 1983).

[182] Dominique Carreau, *Le Système Monétaire International: Aspects Juridiques* (Paris: Armand Colin, 1972), p. 62.

[183] See, e.g., John Williamson, *The Failure of World Monetary Reform, 1971–74* (Sunbury-on-Thames: Thomas Nelson & Sons, 1977); Tom de Vries, "Jamaica, or the Non-Reform of the International Monetary System," *Foreign Affairs,* vol. 54 (1976), p. 577; Tom de Vries, "Amending the Fund's Charter: Reform or Patchwork?" in Banca Nationale del Lavoro, *Quarterly Review,* no. 118 (September 1976), p. 272; and comments of Robert Triffin in Edward M. Bernstein et al., *Reflections on Jamaica* (Essays in International Finance no. 115; Princeton: Princeton University International Finance Section, 1976), pp. 45–53.

[184] See, e.g., Chapter 6, *supra,* pages 277–280 (IMF compensatory financing facility).

however, is laced with provisions designed to promote balance-of-payments adjustment. Article IV, which deals with exchange rate policies and other economic policies, has this purpose. IMF members are forbidden to manipulate exchange rates or the international monetary system in order to prevent effective balance-of-payments adjustment by them or by others.[185] Article V authorizes the Fund to condition access to its general resources outside the reserve tranche upon the pursuit of policies to solve the drawing country's balance-of-payments problems.[186] The IMF, acting by a special majority under Article XII, can publicly censor a member through issuing a report on its "monetary or economic conditions and developments which directly tend to produce a serious disequilibrium in the international balance of payments of members."[187] Such a report, however, has never been published. In some other organizations the maintenance of payments equilibrium is made an explicit obligation of all members, but the statements are usually very general.[188]

No multilateral organization, to the author's knowledge, has adopted a systematic approach to the achievement of balance-of-payments equilibria by its members over either the medium-term (3–5 years) or a longer term (6–20 years). What we have instead are:

(a) Systems of consultations and arrangements for economic and monetary policy coordination (discussed earlier in this chapter).

(b) Systems of rules and guidelines, including consultation procedures, applicable to exchange rate arrangements (discussed in Chapter 11).

(c) Systems of consultation and conditionality associated with the use of some forms of balance-of-payments financing available to countries in deficit (discussed in Chapters 4–9).

(d) Special rules and procedures that deal with particular types of corrective actions that countries in deficit are tempted to employ that may adversely impact other states and the international system: exchange controls, trade restrictions of various types, and controls on invisible transactions and capital movements (discussed in Chapter 10).

The rules and procedures, drawing their authority from different sources, are not always neatly coordinated in application. The lack of systemization is partly compensated by the comprehensiveness of the consultation processes.

Can any general statements be made about the order of preferred use of the various policy instruments by a country in deficit, assuming that it complies with the specific legal requirements applicable to the employment of each measure? This question was considered by a study panel of the American Society of International Law some years ago. The panel decided that it could not *a priori* rule out the use of any particular kind of adjustment measure as contrary to the

---

[185] Article IV, section 1(iii). See Chapter 11, *supra,* pages 515–519.

[186] See Chapter 6, *supra,* pages 243–247.

[187] Article XII, section 8.

[188] See, e.g., Article 104 of the EEC Treaty, quoted at page 590, *supra.*

proper functioning of the international monetary system. The panel was of the view that trade quotas, tariff surcharges, and exchange restrictions, as examples, should be permissible as adjustment devices if approved by the appropriate international bodies. The panel was unable to identify adjustment techniques, other than internal policy measures, that were so much more desirable than others that they were entitled to be employed without the necessity of immediate international review.[189]

The accumulated experience of the IMF and EEC in working with countries facing severe deficits provides some guidance on the choice of policy instruments. Per Jacobsson once said, "In discussing monetary problems it is always necessary to consider the impact of domestic policies on the balance of payments."[190] If domestic policies are unwise there are practical limits to the extent to which international policies, no matter their form, can compensate for the deficiencies. Section 1 of IMF Article IV is a point of reference in appraising domestic policies. In general, if external payments problems can be corrected through internal policy adjustments without adverse effects, that procedure is to be favored over the use of external controls.[191] Techniques that least distort the allocation of human, material, and financial resources through the price system should be preferred.[192] As a general principle, when two alternative national economic policies are available, the policy predicted to have the least harmful international effects should be chosen.[193] Measures that liberalize rather than restrict international transactions are to be favored. To the extent that measures chosen restrict freedom in international transactions, they should be conceived as temporary and be capable of dismantlement after they have served their purpose. Exchange rate changes are an appropriate method of balance-of-payments adjustment, as recognized in IMF Article IV. Indeed, needed exchange rate changes should not be postponed.[194] But, exchange rate changes should be used in conjunction with, and not as a substitute for, the pursuit of economic and financial policies consistent with Article IV, Section 1. These

---

[189] Panel on International Monetary Policy, *Long-Term International Monetary Reform: A Proposal for an Improved Adjustment Process* (Washington: American Society of International Law, 1972), p. 24.

[190] Per Jacobsson, *The Market Economy in the World of Today* (Philadelphia: American Philosophical Society, 1961), p. 28.

[191] See generally the OECD paper, *The Balance of Payments Adjustment Process* (Paris: OECD, 1966).

[192] An OECD study group has recommended that when a government intervenes in national or international market processes, its acts should be "transparent" so insiders and outsiders can assess their consequences. OECD, *Positive Adjustment Policies—Managing Structural Change* (Paris, 1983), p. 21 (paragraph 69).

[193] This principle is not always easy to apply. The United States in 1980–83 pursued a tight monetary policy and a relaxed budgetary policy. Consequences were high interest rates, international capital movements into dollar-denominated assets, and appreciation of the dollar's exchange rate in relation to virtually all other currencies. Other countries found themselves forced to pursue policies resulting in higher interest rates than they desired. It is far from clear, however, that a more relaxed monetary policy and tighter fiscal policy would have been as effective in reducing price inflation in the United States.

[194] See IMF, *Annual Report, 1981*, pp. 55 and 59.

comments summarize what appear to be shared official attitudes, but are not intended to state an integrated firm set of rules.

In the individual case the consultation process should reveal relevant considerations. The choice should be influenced by an appraisal of the nature of the country's problems, judgments about the economic effectiveness of applying the particular measure or combination of measures compared to other alternative policies to correct the problems; identification of associated desirable and undesirable economic consequences of employing the measures; political considerations both domestic and international; legal considerations including need for approvals if any, legal justification of the chosen action, and future problems for the international monetary system if the contemplated action creates a precedent; and, finally, the extent to which other countries take actions that lessen the need for the deficit country to carry the full burden of adjustment.

Symmetrical Adjustment—Obligations of Surplus Countries

The idea that it is desirable for countries in surplus as well as those in deficit to take actions to promote balance-of-payments adjustment is generally accepted. The IMF Agreement, for example, makes no explicit distinction between the obligations of members in surplus and those in deficit. No one has seriously challenged the statement in a 1966 OECD report that an important object of international consultation is to "ensure that both surplus and deficit countries take appropriate action to restore international balance and that such measures are adequate and compatible with the interests of other countries."[195] There is little doubt that payments difficulties of deficit countries are often caused, or aggravated, by actions of surplus countries.

Evidence of a legal principle that surplus countries share responsibility with deficit countries to make exchange rate changes or adopt other measures for balance-of-payments adjustment can be found in state practice. The Group of Ten in the Smithsonian agreement of December 18, 1971, which was intended to improve payments equilibrium, agreed on currency devaluations by the United States, Italy, and Sweden and revaluations by the Federal Republic of Germany, Japan, Netherlands, and Belgium.[196] Under the agreement concluded by the U.S. Federal Reserve and the Swiss National Bank in October 1976 for repayment of outstanding pre-August 1971 currency swap drawings by the Reserve, the Swiss bank agreed to a procedure under which it shared in the loss incurred by the Federal Reserve as a result of the rise in the value of the Swiss franc in relation to the dollar.[197] The surplus countries participating in the exchange rate arrangements of the European Monetary System have from time

---

[195] *Balance of Payments Adjustment Process, supra* note 191, p. 25 (paragraph 61).
[196] See Chapter 11, *supra*, page 498 (note 39).
[197] See Chapter 4, *supra*, pages 157–164.

to time revalued their currencies so that the full burden of adjustment would not fall on the deficit countries.[198] While in some situations it may be possible to identify a particular country that bears primary responsibility for taking adjustment action,[199] the examples cited above evidence the concept that adjustment is a mutual responsibility.

Article IV, Section 4, of the IMF Agreement provides that "arrangements under which both members in surplus and members in deficit in their balances of payments take prompt, effective, and symmetrical action to achieve adjustment" are to be taken into account if the Fund makes a decision to institute a system of currency par values in accordance with Schedule C. While the section does not explicitly say that a system of symmetrical adjustment is a precondition to the application of Schedule C, that is a reasonable inference. The sentence is also a recognition that the Fund Agreement itself has not established all of the features of a system of symmetrical adjustment. Under the par value system of Schedule C, should it be applied, a regime of relatively stable exchange rates is contemplated. Market rates are to be maintained within defined margins of parity relationships. Changes in currency par values are to be made with the concurrence of the IMF.[200] Procedures for effective balance-of-payments adjustment that do not rely heavily on exchange rate changes are essential to the proper functioning of such a par value regime. Such procedures are also necessary in a regime of floating exchange rates if wide movements in exchange rates are to be avoided.

Surplus countries, since they do not require external financing, are not subjected to the discipline associated with IMF stand-by arrangements, European Economic Community balance-of-payments loans, or similar arrangements. They are, nevertheless, like deficit countries, legally committed to the growth and stability obligations of IMF Article IV, Section 1. The policies of surplus countries are reviewed in the periodic consultations on economic policy discussed earlier in this chapter. When deficit countries take actions or propose to take actions derogating from commitments (e.g., instituting exchange or trade controls) because they claim surplus countries are not taking appropriate actions to assist in correcting a payments maladjustment, the policies of surplus countries may figure in the consultations.

There are many actions a surplus country can take to improve payments

---

[198] See Chapter 11, *supra,* pages 544–546. Revaluations by creditor countries in the EMS mitigate the cost to the debtors of settling outstanding obligations denominated in European currency units (ECUs). See Chapter 8, pages 328–329.

[199] A member of the IMF's Legal Department has suggested that the burden of adjustment weighs most heavily on a country whose initiation of adjustment action would remove the pressure for adjustment from the largest number of economically important countries. Stephen A. Silard, "Money and Foreign Exchange," *International Encyclopedia of Comparative Law* (Tübingen: J.C.B.Mohr; The Hague: Mouton, 1975), vol. 17, chapter 20, section 195. See also IMF, *Reform of the International Monetary System: Report by the Executive Directors* (Washington, 1972), pp. 16–17.

[200] See Chapter 11, *supra,* pages 555–557.

equilibria besides providing financing to deficit countries. These include reducing subsidies to exports, improving access for imports to its markets by lowering tariffs and liberalizing import controls, liberalizing currency exchange restrictions, controlling inward capital movements, permitting the exchange rate of its currency to appreciate in the market or establishing a new higher rate, and adopting domestic policy actions such as easing credit conditions or reducing taxes or increasing government spending that spur demand for goods and services (including imports) within its economy. We have previously examined the rules and procedures applicable to most of these actions. The choice of techniques is largely for the surplus country to decide so long as its actions are consonant with its international undertakings. If the choice can be made with the explicit concurrence of the other countries affected, that is desirable, but this does not appear to be required by the IMF Agreement, EEC Treaty, or GATT Agreement.

To the extent that restrictive actions of a surplus country deny access to its markets while its exporters exploit the markets of deficit countries, principles of fairness call for it to reduce its restrictions. To the extent that a surplus country pursues a liberal policy with respect to trade, exchange, and capital movements, the burden of balance-of-payments adjustment may weigh on it less heavily. This assumes that the country does not maintain the exchange rate for its currency at an inappropriate level. A country has an obligation under IMF Article IV, Section 1(iii), discussed at length in the previous chapter, to "avoid manipulating exchange rates or the international monetary system in order to prevent effective balance of payments adjustment or to gain an unfair competitive advantage over other members. . . ."[201] This formulation was deliberately chosen to encompass actions by countries in surplus as well as those in deficit.

What is the proper role in the balance-of-payments adjustment process of a surplus country that earns its foreign exchange from exporting a nonrenewable resource if the country has a limited capacity to absorb imports? During the 1970s some oil exporting countries ran exceptionally high current account surpluses by historical standards, and their monetary reserves dramatically increased.[202] Concern for safety, maintenance of value, return, and political power led these surplus countries to place the bulk of the accumulated funds in highly liquid financial instruments, a large portion in the Eurocurrency markets.[203] The IMF's surveillance decision properly draws a distinction between

---

[201] See Chapter 11, *supra,* pages 515–519.

[202] The cumulative 1974–81 cash surplus of all members of the Organization of Petroleum Exporting Countries was about $433 billion as reported to the IMF. Some 72 percent of this total was accounted for by Saudi Arabia, Kuwait, Qatar, and United Arab Emirates. Some 85 percent of the assets accumulated belonged to governments or public sector agencies. Jahangir Amuzegar, *Oil Exporters' Economic Development in an Interdependent World* (IMF Occasional Paper no. 18; Washington, 1983), pp. 68–69.

[203] See Amuzegar, *idem,* pp. 68–71.

short-term lending by a surplus country, which may indicate a need for consultations, and longer-term lending or investment of funds that are not immediately needed for imports of goods or services.[204] It is submitted that countries with large reserve holdings in excess of short- or intermediate-term needs have a collaboration obligation, for the stability of the international monetary system, to place excess holdings in forms that cannot be transformed immediately into monetary demands on national economies (assuming relatively safe and attractive investment instruments are available).[205]

Another issue is: Does an industrialized country in surplus, whose external and internal policies are otherwise in compliance with international commitments, have an obligation to adopt internal financial and monetary measures to stimulate demand in its economy, thus increasing its imports and consequently improving the export earnings of its trading partners? The question is not academic. Calls for precisely this type of action have been made upon surplus countries in the OECD and the EEC.[206] Lord Keynes recognized the issue long ago:

> Some countries are likely to be more successful than others in preserving stability of internal prices and efficiency wages—and it is the off-setting of that inequality of success which will provide an international organisation with its worst headaches.[207]

Is there ever a legal obligation for a surplus country to "reflate" its economy, to take actions to stimulate domestic demand even though the consequence is some domestic inflation (the reduction of the purchasing power of the national currency measured in terms of domestic goods and services)? The question is posed in this manner because increasing demand is almost always inflationary to some degree.

If a country has voluntarily and explicitly made a commitment to stimulate domestic demand, it would appear to be bound. Economic policy decisions adopted by the Council of the European Communities under the "convergence" and "stability" directives[208] have in the past set guidelines for economic policy in the Federal Republic of Germany and the Netherlands that

---

[204] E.B. Decision No. 5392, *supra* note 12, subpart Principles of Fund Surveillance Over Exchange Rate Policies, paragraph 2 (ii).

[205] The obligation advocated here goes beyond that recommended in IMF Committee on Reform of the International Monetary System and Related Issues (Committee of Twenty), *International Monetary Reform: Documents of the Committee of Twenty* (Washington: IMF, 1974), p. 141 at pp. 151–52 (Report of Technical Group on Adjustment, paragraphs 46–50).

[206] See quotations at pages 584 and 595, *supra,* from the 1978 OECD concerted action programme and EEC guidelines for the Netherlands.

[207] John Maynard Keynes, "The Objective of International Price Stability," *Economic Journal*, vol. 53 (1943), p. 185 at p. 187; reprinted in Donald Moggridge (ed.), *The Collected Writings of John Maynard Keynes* (London: Macmillan and Cambridge University Press), vol. 26 (1980), p. 30 at p. 33.

[208] Notes 108 and 113, *supra.*

called for "reflating" the economies and stimulating demand.[209] The guidelines were in fact negotiated with the Dutch and German authorities and were accepted and voted for by them.

Whether the Treaty of Rome authorizes the Council by a special majority to impose a duty to "reflate" on a member state that votes against the Council's action is far from clear. One would think that the obligations of a surplus country under EEC Treaty Article 104, to assure equilibrium in its overall balance of payments, could be fulfilled by means other than stimulating domestic demand. However, if, within the EEC, trade barriers have been reduced as far as they can be and exchange controls are liberalized, that essentially leaves changes in exchange rates and modifications in domestic policies as the techniques available by which a surplus country can change the balance of trade and other transactions. While exchange rates in the EMS system can be changed by mutual agreement, the objective is to stabilize exchange rates in the context of eventually achieving monetary union. The shared commitment to monetary union may thus entail pursuit of domestic economic policies necessary to ensure the equilibrium of each country's overall balance of payments. EEC Treaty Article 104 assumes that appropriate economic policies can be pursued while maintaining a stable level of prices and is silent on the relative burdens on surplus and deficit countries.[210] An argument could be made that the stimulation of domestic demand is a "measure" for coordinating economic policies that under paragraph 2 of Article 103 requires a unanimous decision in principle on its appropriateness and cannot simply be imposed by a qualified majority under paragraph 3.[211]

If implementation of an EEC decision calling for demand stimulus would go so far as to seriously weaken confidence in the future purchasing power of a currency, the decision would be inconsistent with EEC Treaty Article 104. Further, the states of the EEC have obligations as IMF members under IMF Article IV, Section 1, to maintain reasonable price stability.

Let us turn to the International Monetary Fund. Are there ever circumstances in which the IMF Agreement or general international law imposes a legal obligation on a surplus country to take domestic policy actions known to be inflationary, even only moderately inflationary, in the absence of an explicit acceptance of such a commitment? This is a matter on which there has been very little legal writing. It is submitted that a review of state practice and official discussions indicates that there is no such obligation at the present time and there is little evidence that such an obligation is emerging.

First, no hint of such an obligation can be found in the language of the IMF Articles. Second, performance of such an obligation, were it to be im-

---

[209] See page 595, *supra*.
[210] EEC Treaty Article 104 is quoted at page 590, *supra*.
[211] These paragraphs of EEC Treaty Article 103 are quoted at pages 590–591, *supra*.

posed, could undermine confidence in the long-term purchasing power of the currency and, concomitantly, confidence in the national issuing authority. The effective functioning of a money depends upon confidence in its purchasing power. If authorities of a surplus country adopt policies that cause the purchasing power of the currency to decline, they can do so if the action is otherwise consistent with the obligations of Section 1 of Article IV including the obligation to maintain "reasonable" price stability. There is no legal obligation imposed on IMF members to attempt such a delicate maneuver.

The issue of whether a surplus country ever has a duty to deliberately adjust its domestic price level upward was addressed by Working Party No. 3 of the OECD Economy Policy Committee in a 1966 report. The answer given was "no." The Working Party agreed that, with respect to demand management, the respective responsibilities of surplus and deficit countries depend primarily on the domestic situation in each country. Where imbalances develop because domestic demand is too high or too low, the responsibility for action rests on the countries whose own demand is inappropriate. It went on to say that in cases where imbalances arise from divergent price trends in different countries, the respective responsibilities of surplus and deficit countries may vary. It said, "Countries in surplus positions because of their competitive strength cannot realistically be called on deliberately to adjust their [domestic] price levels upwards." However, if that does not naturally occur, the report said that the country should allow the exchange rate of its currency to appreciate.[212]

The issue was raised again in the work of the OECD study group, under the chairmanship of Paul McCracken, that in 1977 issued the report, *Towards Full Employment and Price Stability*.[213] The report spoke of what the expert group believed desirable policy; it did not attempt to define legal obligations. The report proposed that policymakers regularly make judgments on the need to stimulate or restrain demand in the world economy as a whole.[214] With respect to demand expansion, the report stated: "[C]ountries which should take the lead in expanding demand are those with high unemployment, low inflation, favourable balances of payments, large reserves and good credit-worthiness."[215]

Professor Ryutaro Komiya of the University of Tokyo, a member of the study group, commenting on the foregoing passage, said that surplus countries should not be urged to take expansionary measures for the purpose of improving the balance-of-payments performance of other countries unless this can be done without spurring inflation.[216] Professor Herbert Giersch, a former mem-

---

[212] *The Balance of Payments Adjustment Process, supra* note 191, pp. 20 and 25–26 (paragraphs 46 and 61–64).

[213] Paul McCracken et al., *Towards Full Employment and Price Stability* (Paris: OECD, 1977).

[214] *Idem*, p.30 (in summary) and p. 236 (paragraph 444).

[215] *Idem*, p. 30 (in summary) and p. 236 (paragraph 444).

[216] *Idem*, p. 249 at pp. 252–54. See also Professor Komiya's article, "Is International Co-ordination of

ber of the German Council of Economic Advisers and a member of the study group, argued that the average inflation of a group of countries (such as the Group of Ten) should not be considered a norm.[217] The dissenters were of the view that countries that had been successful in controlling inflation should not be called upon to reduce the domestic purchasing power of their currencies in order to stimulate imports from countries suffering inflation and unemployment.

To sum up the state of the law, it is submitted that Lord Lionel C. Robbins' statement is correct: "[I]nternational good conduct does not impose any obligation to import other people's inflation."[218] But, to say that countries, absent their agreement such as found when the Council of the European Communities unanimously adopts an economic policy directive, have no legal obligation to spur domestic demand does not mean that they have no obligation to reduce their payments surpluses. All we have said is that stimulating domestic demand is not the technique they are required to choose. It is, however, a technique that may be used with, or as an alternative to, exchange rate changes or other policy adjustments. In the absence of other meaningful actions, exchange rate appreciation must be allowed.[219]

Some scholars and officials have proposed formal mechanisms to pressure surplus countries to take actions to reduce their surpluses.[220] In 1972 a study panel of the American Society of International Law proposed a reserve indicator system that would trigger consultations and result in the application of pressures on both surplus and deficit countries to adjust their balances of payments.[221] A similar proposal was formally submitted by the U.S. government to the IMF's Committee on Reform (Committee of Twenty) later that year.[222] The latter paper was discussed extensively in the C-20's Technical Group on Adjustment.[223] The core idea was that base levels would be established for re-

National Economic Policies Necessary?'' in Peter Oppenheimer (ed.), *Issues in International Economics* (Stocksfield, England: Oriel Press, 1980), p. 16 at p. 19.

[217] *Towards Full Employment and Price Stability, supra* note 213, p. 247 at p. 248.

[218] Statement at conference in Frankfurt in 1977, in Randall Hinshaw (ed.), *Domestic Goals and Financial Interdependence: The Frankfurt Dialogue* (New York: Marcel Dekker, 1980), p. 22.

[219] Jacques J. Polak, *Coordination of National Economic Policies* (New York: Group of Thirty, 1981), pp. 9–19, writing from an economist's perspective, has pointed out practical difficulties of coordinating demand policies on a multinational basis.

[220] The scarce currency provisions of IMF Article VII, sections 2–5, incorporate pressures, but they have never been invoked.

[221] *Long-Term International Monetary Reform, supra* note 189.

[222] *Economic Report of the President, Transmitted to the Congress January 1973* (Washington: U.S. Government Printing Office, 1973), pp. 123–31 and 160–74. See also Robert Solomon, *The International Monetary System, 1945–1981* (New York: Harper & Row, 1982), pp. 224–28 and 238–44.

[223] *International Monetary Reform: Documents of the Committee of Twenty, supra* note 205, pp. 7–18, 23–30, 51–77, and 141–61 (Outline of Reform, paragraphs 4–10 and annexes 1 and 2; and reports of technical groups on ''indicators'' and ''adjustment''). See also the paper submitted by the EEC states to the C-20 in *14th Report on the Activities of the [EEC] Monetary Committee; Official Journal of the European Communities*, no. C-94, November 9, 1973, p. 1 at p. 18 (annex IV).

serves of each IMF member. A disproportionate change in a country's reserves in either direction from a norm would be used as an objective indicator to trigger consultations on the need of the country to adjust its balance of payments. Pressures would be applied if adjustment did not occur. In the case of surplus countries these pressures could include charges on reserve accumulations, required deposit of excess reserves with negative interest charges, withholding of future allocations of special drawing rights, publication of a report, and authorization to other countries to impose discriminatory exchange controls. While the system also included pressures on deficit countries to maintain the system's apparent symmetry, it was recognized that those countries would in any event be under pressure from the need to finance their deficits.

In the discussions in the Committee of Twenty and its technical group on adjustment in the period 1972–1974, various problems with the proposed system were identified. How would reserves be defined, base levels determined, and changes measured? Should the mechanism involve more than consultations? If the system was to include pressures, should their application be automatic, presumptive, or discretionary? Should legal obligations to adjust be formulated with pressures used as sanctions or should the pressures be seen as part of an adjustment mechanism divorced from concepts of legal obligation?[224] Although a system of objective reserve indicators was recommended by the Committee of Twenty,[225] the concept was not embodied in the amended IMF Articles.

Substantial changes in reserves may evidence policy developments that will prompt the IMF's Managing Director to initiate consultations with the member under the surveillance decision.[226] The U.S. Secretary of the Treasury in 1979 made a modest proposal for something more:

> Another possibility would be to provide that any nation with an exceptionally large payments imbalance—deficit or surplus—must submit for IMF review an analysis showing how it proposes to deal with that imbalance. Now, only those countries borrowing from the Fund have their adjustment programs subjected to such IMF scrutiny. Greater symmetry is needed.[227]

---

[224] See Joseph Gold, " 'Pressures' and Reform of the International Monetary System," in Joseph Gold, *Legal and Institutional Aspects of the International Monetary System: Selected Essays* (Washington: IMF, 1979), p. 182.

[225] *International Monetary Reform: Documents of the Committee of Twenty, supra* note 205, p. 9 (Outline of Reform, June 14, 1974, paragraph 4(b)).

[226] E.B. Decision No. 5392, *supra* note 12, subpart Principles of Fund Surveillance Over Exchange Rate Policies and subpart Procedures for Surveillance. See Chapter 11, *supra*, pages 558–559.

[227] *IMF, Summary Proceedings, 1979*, p. 113 at p. 116. The proposal was repeated at the 1980 annual meeting. See generally Joseph Gold, "Symmetry as a Legal Objective of the International Monetary System," *New York University Journal of International Law and Politics*, vol. 12 (1980), p. 423, especially pp. 473–77.

While this specific proposal has not been implemented, staff reports for recent Article IV consultations with surplus countries, including those with substantial voting power, "show that the formulation of policy recommendations has tended to be more candid and more precise than in the past."[228]

Whether some system of objectively allocating burdens of balance-of-payments adjustment between surplus and deficit countries will be adopted in the future remains to be seen. To some extent the "divergence indicator" in the European Monetary System's exchange rate arrangements performs this function.[229] While in the contemporary setting there is a considerable amount of room for give and take negotiation, and exercise of discretion, the practice of states as seen at the outset of this section evidences the legal principle that surplus countries share responsibility with deficit countries for balance-of-payments adjustment.

Regulation of International Activities of Commercial Banks

Background. The most striking element in the growth of total outstanding debt of developing countries during the 1970s and early 1980s was the rapid increase in debt by both the private and public sectors to foreign commercial banks.[230] By 1982 annual total external debt service obligations of Mexico, Brazil, and Argentina amounted respectively to 37 percent, 45 percent, and 44 percent of exports of goods and services, and other countries also faced serious problems.[231] The loans extended by commercial banks of various nationalities were typically denominated in U.S. dollars and often were made through branches or subsidiaries of the banks in territories other than the parent's home office.[232] The loans were financed by deposits, often very short-term, solicited by the banks from throughout the world. In a weak world economy the stage was set for a banking crisis. The crisis of 1982 was avoided (or postponed) by the provision of financial assistance by central banks and the International Monetary Fund to the governments and central banks of the debtor countries

---

[228] Section "General Remarks" in attachment to E.B. Decision No. 7088, *supra* note 23.

[229] See Chapter 11, *supra,* pages 542–544.

[230] See discussion in Chapter 4, *supra,* pages 129–133, of commercial bank lending to governments for balance-of-payments support. That lending is, of course, only a part of commercial bank international lending.

[231] Pedro-Pablo Kuczynski, "Latin American Debt," *Foreign Affairs,* vol. 61 (1982–83), p. 344 at p. 347. See generally G.G. Johnson with Richard K. Abrams, *Aspects of the International Banking Safety Net* (IMF Occasional Paper no. 17; Washington, 1983), pp. 6–9; Eduard Brau, Richard C. Williams, et al., *Recent Multilateral Debt Restructurings with Official and Bank Creditors* (IMF Occasional Paper no.25; Washington, 1983); William R. Cline, *International Debt and the Stability of the World Economy* (Washington: Institute for International Economics, 1983); and Bahram Nowzad, Richard C. Williams, et al., *External Indebtedness of Developing Countries* (IMF Occasional Paper no. 3; Washington, 1981), pp. 8–11 and 30–40.

[232] See explanation of Eurocurrency credits in Appendix A, *infra,* pages 679–682.

and by commercial banks agreeing to extend maturities of substantial parts of the debts due them.[233]

Our discussion here centers on three topics related to international activities of commercial banks: (1) assuring that commercial banks follow prudential practices and that central banks are able to provide liquidity in the event of default by a major borrower, substantial withdrawals of funds from banks, or other problems; (2) assuring that large-scale commercial bank lending to governments and central banks does not inhibit balance-of-payments adjustment; and (3) assuring that extension of credit in the Eurocurrency markets does not unduly interfere with the conduct of domestic monetary policies. Primary attention will be given to consultation and collaboration of monetary authorities in these matters.

Supervision of Prudential Practices.   The collapse or feared collapse of a large commercial bank in which banks and institutions in other countries hold substantial deposits, or have contracts awaiting performance, has the potential to set off a chain reaction:

> The collapse of an important bank within the international banking system can lead to a loss of confidence in banks related or perceived to be related, in banks actually weaker or perceived by the market to be so, and in the markets themselves. A loss of confidence in banks can lead to their exclusion from Eurocurrency and foreign exchange markets or to discriminatory treatment in the form of higher rates in those markets. Because of the interrelationship of banks, a loss of confidence in and market reaction to one bank or group of banks can create a chain reaction which spreads to other banks. A loss of confidence in the international interbank markets can lead to a withdrawal of funds generally and a slowdown or even a paralysis of activity.[234]

Following the failure of Bankhaus I.D. Herstatt[235] in Germany and the Franklin National Bank[236] in the United States in 1974, central bank governors

---

[233] The value of IMF stand-by and extended arrangements to governmental and commercial bank creditors when debts are rescheduled is treated in Chapter 6, *supra,* pages 272–275. The ability of some important debtor countries to service their debts, even on a rescheduled basis, will likely require stabilization policies in the debtor countries, increased world demand for the products of the debtor countries, price inflation in the United States (reducing the real value of the dollar-denominated debt), and a large measure of luck. See generally John Williamson (ed.), *Prospects for Adjustment in Argentina, Brazil, and Mexico: Responding to the Debt Crisis* (Washington: Institute for International Economics, 1983).

[234] Joan Edelman Spero, *The Failure of the Franklin National Bank: Challenge to the International Banking System* (New York: Columbia University Press, 1980), p. 102. See also Geoffrey L. Bell, John G. Heimann, et al., *Risks in International Bank Lending* (New York: Group of Thirty, 1982), pp. 16–21.

[235] See Joseph D. Becker, "International Insolvency: The Case of Herstatt," *American Bar Association Journal,* vol. 62 (1976), p. 1290.

[236] See Spero, *supra* note 234.

recognized the necessity for better supervision of commercial banks with substantial international operations. In December 1974 a Committee on Banking Regulations and Supervisory Practices (hereinafter Basle Committee) was established with secretariat support provided by the Bank for International Settlements. It brings together officials of central banks and other bank supervisory agencies of the Group of Ten, Luxembourg, and Switzerland. The Committee has operated on the assumption that supervision by national authorities can be made adequate and effective and there is no need for a supranational authority.[237]

The Basle Committee in September 1975 agreed on a "concordat" that delineated responsibilities for supervising branches, subsidiaries, and joint venture banks located outside the territory of the parent bank.[238] In May 1983 the Basle Committee agreed on a new statement, entitled "Principles for the Supervision of Banks' Foreign Establishments,"[239] which replaced the 1975 concordat. Like the concordat, it is a statement of principles and not a legally binding agreement.[240] Basic premises of the statement are: (a) branches, subsidiaries,

[237] See *Minutes of Federal Open Market Committee, supra* note 81, 1974, pp. 1358–59; and George Blunden, "International Co-operation in Banking Supervision," *Bank of England Quarterly Bulletin*, vol. 17 (1977), p. 325 at p. 327. For general reports on the Committee's work, see Blunden, *idem;* Spero, *supra* note 234, pp. 159–66; Johnson, *Banking Safety Net, supra* note 231, pp. 16–17 and 24–30; W. Peter Cooke, "The International Banking Scene: A Supervisory Perspective," *Bank of England Quarterly Bulletin*, vol. 23 (1983), p. 61; W. Peter Cooke, "Developments in Co-operation Among Banking Supervisory Authorities," and oral discussion, *Journal of Comparative Corporate Law and Securities Regulation*, vol. 3 (1981), pp. 244–62, reprinted (without discussion) in *Bank of England Quarterly Bulletin*, vol. 21 (1981), p. 238; and Christopher W. McMahon, "Central Bankers as Regulators and Lenders of Last Resort in an International Context: A View from the United Kingdom," in Federal Reserve Bank of Boston, *Key Issues in International Banking* (Conference Series no. 18; Boston: Federal Reserve Bank of Boston, 1977), p. 102.

[238] The concordat, dated September 1975, was released in March 1981 and appears in Richard C. Williams et al., *International Capital Markets: Recent Developments and Short-Term Prospects, 1981* (IMF Occasional Paper no. 7; Washington, 1981), p. 29. The principles stated therein were generally accepted by bank supervisors from some 80 countries who met in London in July 1979. Cooke, "Developments," *supra* note 237, pp. 255–57.

[239] The text of the "Principles," released in early June 1983, appears in *IMF Survey*, July 11, 1983, p. 201 at p. 202; and in *International Legal Materials*, vol. 22 (1983), p. 900.

[240] In the case of the European Economic Community, legally binding directives issued by the Council of Ministers institutionalize cooperation among supervisory authorities of the member states in an Advisory Committee which is supported by the "Groupe de Contact." The directives mandate collaboration of supervisory authorities in monitoring the liquidity and solvency of banks and other credit institutions with activities in two or more member states and mandate the use of consolidated supervision. Council of Ministers Directives No. 77/780 of December 12, 1977; and No. 83/350 of June 13, 1983. *Official Journal of the European Communities*, no. L-322, December 17, 1977, p. 30; and no. L-193, July 18, 1983, p. 18. See Paolo Clarotti, "The Harmonization of Legislation Relating to Credit Institutions," *Common Market Law Review*, vol. 19(1982), p. 245; or Paolo Clarotti, "La Coordination des Législations Bancaires," *Revue du Marché Commun*, no. 254 (1982), p. 68. The Court of Justice of the European Communities has held that Belgium and Italy failed to fulfill certain obligations (not relating to supervision) under Council Directive No. 77/780. *Commission v. Italian Republic*, Case No. 300/81, and *Commission v. Kingdom of Belgium*, Case No. 301/81, decided March 1, 1983; Court of Justice of the European Communities, *Reports of Cases Before the Court [European Court Reports]*, 1983, part 3, pp. 449 and 467; Commerce Clearing House, *Common Market Reports* (Chicago: CCH looseleaf service) paragraphs 8944 and 8945.

In addition to the Basle Committee and the EEC's Groupe de Contact, there are the Offshore Supervisors Group and the Commission of Latin American and Caribbean Banking Supervisors and Regulatory Bodies.

and joint ventures should not escape supervision; (b) supervisors cannot fully satisfy themselves about the soundness of a bank unless they can examine the totality of its world-wide business on a consolidated basis; (c) supervision should not be frustrated by the existence of holding companies and nonbanking companies within banking groups; and (d) responsibilities of host and parent authorities are both complementary and overlapping.

The statement of principles emphasizes the importance of supervision on the basis of consolidated accounts:

> The principle of consolidated supervision is that parent banks and parent supervisory authorities monitor the risk exposure—including a perspective of concentrations of risk and of the quality of assets—of the banks or banking groups for which they are responsible, as well as the adequacy of their capital, on the basis of the totality of their business wherever conducted. This principle does not imply any lessening of host authorities' responsibilities for supervising foreign bank establishments that operate in their territories. . . .[241]

Omitting refinements, primary supervisory responsibilities are basically allocated as follows:

(a) Supervision of foreign exchange operations and positions of a foreign establishment (branch, subsidiary, or joint venture) is the joint responsibility of host and parent authorities. Particular importance is attached to a parent bank's having a system for monitoring the banking group's overall foreign exchange exposure and the authorities in the parent's territory monitoring the system.[242]

(b) Primary responsibility for supervision of liquidity (system and procedures to assure that obligations can be met as they fall due) of a foreign establishment (branch, subsidiary, or joint venture) rests with the local authorities. This responsibility includes supervising compliance with local regulations and practices and the functioning of domestic money markets. If the local authority has difficulty in supervising liquidity in foreign currencies, it is expected to inform the parent authorities and together they are to make appropriate arrangements. In the case of a branch, liquidity is frequently controlled by the parent, and the parent's control system should be supervised by the authorities in the parent's territory.[243]

(c) Primary responsibility for supervising a branch's solvency rests with

---

[241] Principles, *supra* note 239, section III.
[242] Principles, *idem*, section IV(3).
[243] Principles, *idem*, section IV(2).

the parent authorities since, according to the statement, solvency of a branch is "indistinguishable from that of the parent bank as a whole."[244] Supervision of the solvency of a subsidiary is the joint responsibility of host and parent authorities. Supervision of the solvency of a joint venture is normally the primary responsibility of host authorities.[245]

(d) In supervising liquidity and solvency, parent authorities should take into account any standby or other facilities granted by the parent to the foreign establishment as well as any other commitments of the parent bank, for example through comfort letters.[246]

The statement of principles recognizes the importance of consultation and prompt transmission of information by one supervisory authority to another:

> [H]ost authorities should ensure that parent authorities are informed immediately of any serious problems which arise in a parent bank's foreign establishment. Similarly, parent authorities should inform host authorities when problems arise in a parent bank which are likely to affect the parent bank's foreign establishment.[247]

While many factors bear upon solvency and liquidity (including capital adequacy, quality of loans, maturity transformation risk, foreign currency exposure, general management, and unlawful activity),[248] the ultimate risk in lending is that the borrower may not repay its debt. In international lending the risk is compounded by the possibility that the servicing of all loans by private and public debtors in a particular country may be affected by the country's balance-

---

[244] Principles, *idem*, section IV(1). The Principles state that "dotation de capital" requirements imposed by host authorities do not negate the quoted phrase. See generally Patrick Heininger, "Liability of U.S. Banks for Deposits Placed in their Foreign Branches," *Law and Policy in International Business*, vol. 11 (1979), p. 903. For choice of law purposes in depositor–bank contract disputes, branches and home offices may be distinguished. See Richard W. Edwards, Jr., "Extraterritorial Application of the U.S. Iranian Assets Control Regulations," *American Journal of International Law*, vol. 75 (1981), p. 870 at pp. 876–81.

[245] Principles, *supra* note 239, section IV(1).

[246] Principles, *idem*, section IV(1) and (2). The Bank of England has obtained formal acknowledgements from foreign commercial parent banks of their "moral responsibility" to come to the aid of their subsidiaries and joint venture banks in London. See Spero, *supra* note 234, pp. 156–58.

[247] Principles, *supra* note 239, section III.

[248] See generally Richard Dale, *Bank Supervision Around the World* (New York: Group of Thirty, 1982); Johnson, *Banking Safety Net*, *supra* note 231, pp. 10–19; and Williams, *International Capital Markets, 1981*, *supra* note 238, pp. 12–16; Neal L. Peterson, "Supervising Multinational Banking Organizations: Responsibilities of the Host Country," oral discussion, and documents, *Journal of Comparative Corporate Law and Securities Regulation*, vol. 3 (1981), pp. 225–37; Alain Hirsch, "Responsibilities of the Home Country," and oral discussion, *idem*, pp. 238–43; Cooke, "Developments," *supra* note 237; Betsy Buttrill White, "Foreign Banking in the United States: A Regulatory and Supervisory Perspective," in Federal Reserve Bank of New York, *Quarterly Review*, vol. 7, no. 2 (Summer 1982), p. 48; and Cynthia C. Lichtenstein, "U.S. Banks and the Eurocurrency Markets: The Regulatory Structure," *Banking Law Journal*, vol. 99 (1982), p. 484 at pp. 508–11. See also Appendix A, *infra*, page 681 (note 50).

of-payments problems. Restrictions imposed by Argentina and Mexico in 1982 that interrupted payments to nonresidents are striking examples.[249] These problems brought into prominence the importance of appraising country exposure and transfer risk and guarding against it.[250] Cooperative efforts have been mounted to improve the quality of information available for evaluation.[251]

Lender of Last Resort. The governors of the central banks of the Group of Ten and Switzerland in a communiqué issued by the Bank for International Settlements in 1974 stated:

> The governors . . . had an exchange of views on the problem of the lender of last resort in the Euromarkets. They recognized that it would not be practical to lay down in advance detailed rules and procedures for the provision of temporary liquidity. But they were satisfied that means are available for that purpose and will be used if and when necessary.[252]

The application of the statement, as compared to its emotive message, is far from clear. The Principles for the Supervision of Banks' Foreign Establishments, discussed earlier, are directed to supervision and not to lender-of-last-

---

[249] See Chapter 10, *supra*, pages 410–411, 412–413, and 417–418.

[250] U.S. bank examiners currently place individual countries in categories defined by degree of risk as determined by an Interagency Country Exposure Review Committee. The U.S. system is described in an appendix to the statement of Paul A. Volcker, Chairman of the Board of Governors of the Federal Reserve System, in *International Debt: Hearings on Proposals for Legislation to Increase the Resources of the International Monetary Fund before the Subcommittee on International Finance and Monetary Policy of the Committee on Banking, Housing, and Urban Affairs*, U.S. Senate, 98th Congress, 1st Session (1983), p. 240 at pp. 323–28. See also Ingo Walter, "Country Risk and International Bank Lending," *University of Illinois Law Review*, 1982, p. 71. For comments on country exposure analysis in other countries, see Dale, *supra* note 248.

The U.S. Domestic Housing and International Recovery and Financial Stability Act of 1983, in section 905, directs Federal regulatory agencies to require commercial banks under their jurisdiction to maintain special reserves where the quality of the bank's assets has been impaired by the failure of foreign public or private borrowers to make full interest payments or other conditions are not met. Public Law 98–181, approved November 30, 1983, *United States Statutes at Large*, vol. 97, p. 1153 at pp. 1278–79. See generally sections 901–913 of the act. See also *Senate Report No. 98–122* and *House of Representatives Reports No. 98–175* and *No. 98–177*, 98th Congress, 1st Session (1983).

[251] The U.S. Domestic Housing and International Recovery and Financial Stability Act of 1983 requires the U.S. Secretary of the Treasury to instruct the U.S. Executive Director of the IMF to propose that the Fund obtain and publish data on international credit extended by commercial banks and other institutions to private and public borrowers. See note 268, *infra*, and accompanying text. The recent establishment of the Institute of International Finance (Chapter 4, pages 132–133) by a group of commercial banks is also intended to alleviate the information problem.

[252] Bank for International Settlements communiqué of September 10, 1974; *Minutes of Federal Open Market Committee, supra* note 81, 1974, p. 1055. See generally *Minutes, idem,* 1974, pp. 1005–11; *New York Times*, September 11, 1974, p. 64; and Johnson, *Banking Safety Net, supra* note 231, pp. 20–23 and 31–35.

resort responsibilities. While, for example, U.S. authorities have broad powers to supervise branches of foreign banks in the United States, the U.S. Federal Reserve System is permitted to provide lender-of-last-resort facilities to those branches only if they are subject to the System's reserve requirements under Regulation D.[253] There are cases where authorities in other countries have disclaimed responsibility even to assist banking organizations formally incorporated and doing business on their territories on the ground that responsibility lay with authorities in the territory of the parent.[254] In a number of developing countries that are active banking centers for Eurocurrency operations, the authorities appear to in fact lack the financial resources to cope with a major banking crisis, quite apart from issues of legal power to act.

The U.S. Federal Reserve System has demonstrated that it will provide lender-of-last-resort assistance to parent banks in the United States, against appropriate collateral, to enable them to provide liquidity to foreign branches.[255] It has not, however, committed itself to do the same thing where the foreign entity is a separately incorporated subsidiary or joint venture. It hardly needs saying that a central bank in the territory of a parent should not be expected to provide funds to the parent for use in supporting a subsidiary or joint venture abroad when the parent's authorities are not permitted by the host authorities to obtain the necessary information or to effectively supervise the activities of the foreign subsidiary or joint venture.[256]

In considering lender-of-last-resort issues, one must bear in mind the distinction between illiquidity and insolvency. Central banks generally have authority under their governing national laws to provide funds in the event of a liquidity crisis. National laws and practices vary widely on the protection

---

[253] *United States Code*, title 12, section 3102(b); and *Code of Federal Regulations*, title 12, section 201.1 (Regulation A).

[254] Both Israeli and British authorities initially denied responsibility to assist the London subsidiary (separately incorporated) of the Israel-British Bank of Tel Aviv which failed in July 1974, partly as a result of fraud in the parent bank and partly as a result of difficulties experienced after the failure of Bankhaus I.D. Herstatt. Israeli authorities eventually accepted responsibility, but only after the Bank of England made a contribution of £3 million as a "magnanimous gesture." Spero, *supra* note 234, pp. 156–57.

Luxembourg authorities in 1982 refused to accept the role of lender of last resort to Banco Ambrosiano Holding of Luxembourg, a subsidiary 65 percent controlled by the Italian Banco Ambrosiano. Johnson, *Banking Safety Net, supra* note 231, p. 35. See also Dale, *supra* note 248, pp. 16–17 and 47.

[255] The Federal Reserve provided funds to Franklin National Bank in 1974 to meet demands at its London branch. Spero, *supra* note 234, pp. 126–30 and 147–49. See also Edward J. Frydl, "The Debate Over Regulating the Eurocurrency Markets," in Federal Reserve Bank of New York, *Quarterly Review*, vol. 4, no. 4 (Winter 1979–80), p. 11 at p. 17.

[256] See Jack Guttentag and Richard Herring, *The Lender-of-Last-Resort Function in an International Context* (Essays in International Finance no. 151; Princeton: Princeton University International Finance Section, 1983), p. 13.

granted depositors in the event of insolvency.[257] Some countries lack depositor insurance schemes.[258]

Because large depositors can expect only limited protection in the event of insolvency of a bank with which they deal, their main concern is that if they deal with sound banks the authorities will provide needed liquidity in event of a crisis. In the international context this requires that the appropriate central bank(s) to act be identified. It also requires that the central bank(s) be able to distinguish illiquidity from insolvency as the authorities may only be permitted to provide assistance in the former case.[259] It is troubling that in a recent survey of commercial bankers about 60 percent expressed the view that in an emergency central banks do not in fact have the ability to make the distinction.[260] The implication is that central banks to forestall a crisis may need to maintain the liquidity of banks that are in fact, but have not yet been determined to be, insolvent. The alternative is to allow the crisis to build through denial of needed assistance to banks that are basically sound. One cannot quickly dismiss Charles P. Kindleberger's comment:

> The lender-of-last-resort principle presupposes a closed group, fully understanding one another, where action is taken rapidly, and the consequences sorted out more leisurely later on. . . . There is a question today, as in the past, whether the cohesion needed for the role to be properly discharged is available in sufficient abundance.[261]

The International Monetary Fund cannot provide liquidity directly to commercial banks. However, the IMF can provide assistance, in accordance with its policies, to fiscal agencies of the governments in the debtor countries (as it did for Mexico, Brazil, and Argentina in 1982 and 1983) or to fiscal agencies of the countries where the commercial banks in difficulty are located.

---

[257] See Johnson, *Banking Safety Net, supra* note 231, pp. 20–21; and Dale, *Bank Supervision, supra* note 248, pp. 14–16. Federal Deposit Insurance Corporation insurance in the United States only protects accounts up to $100,000 and certain accounts are excluded. See *United States Code,* title 12, sections 1813(l)(5), 1813(s), and 3104.

[258] When Bankhaus I.D. Herstatt failed in 1974, the Federal Republic of Germany did not have a broad scheme of deposit insurance. Foreign banks with spot exchange contracts half performed at the time of the collapse suffered losses of 14 percent or more. Other creditors suffered even larger losses. See Becker, *supra* note 235, pp. 1294–95; and Spero, *supra* note 234, pp. 110–12.

[259] For the current regulations of the U.S. Federal Reserve System, see *Code of Federal Regulations,* title 12, part 201.

[260] Robert Pringle and M.S. Mendelsohn, *How Bankers See the World Financial Market* (New York: Group of Thirty, 1982), pp. 22–23 and 41–42. The survey involved 111 commercial and investment bankers (55 in Europe, 29 in North America, and the remainder in other areas).

[261] Charles P. Kindleberger, "Central Banks as Regulators and Lenders of Last Resort: Discussion," *Key Issues in International Banking, supra* note 237, p. 111 at p. 113. See also Bell, *Risks in International Bank Lending, supra* note 234, pp. 23–27; and Guttentag and Herring, *supra* note 256, pp. 20–25.

Commercial Bank Activities and Balance-of-Payments Adjustment. During the decade of the 1970s, commercial banks became the main providers of international financial resources to governments as well as private entities in several large developing countries.[262] The Executive Board of the International Monetary Fund, recognizing a potential problem, in its 1977 *Annual Report* wrote:

> Access to private sources of balance of payments finance may . . . in some cases permit countries to postpone the adoption of adequate domestic stabilization measures. This can exacerbate the problem of correcting payments imbalances, and can lead to adjustments that are politically and socially disruptive when the introduction of stabilization measures becomes unavoidable.[263]

Adjustment problems caused by commercial banks lending freely and then abruptly cutting back, which was a serious concern in 1982 and 1983,[264] were also anticipated earlier.[265]

Governments that have borrowed from commercial banks have sometimes done so to avoid or postpone undertaking stabilization programs that the IMF would have expected under stand-by or extended arrangements.[266] At the same time it must be recognized that official assistance has not been adequate by itself to satisfy genuine, prudent balance-of-payments financing needs. The task is to strike a proper balance. Excesses in borrowing by the private sector from foreign banks can also cause problems. The servicing of private sector external debt places strains on the balance of payments in the same manner as the servicing of public debt.

The magnitude and structure of external debt (both public and private) is reviewed in consultations under IMF Article IV. Normally, warning flags can be raised before debt service obligations become unmanageable. The procedures are consultative and the authorities are not required to implement the particular advice that is offered.[267] Proposals have been made that would apply additional pressures through publicity. A recent act of the United States Congress requires the U.S. Secretary of the Treasury to instruct the U.S. Executive Director of the IMF to propose that the Fund adopt the following policy:

---

[262] See Charles Lipson,"The International Organization of Third World Debt," *International Organization*, vol. 35 (1981), p. 603; and sources cited in note 231, *supra*.

[263] IMF, *Annual Report, 1977*, p. 41.

[264] See Chapter 4, *supra*, page 131 (note 13). See also "A Tale of Three Nations: The Latin American Rescue," *National Journal*, March 19, 1983, p. 600.

[265] See Richard C. Williams, *International Capital Markets: Recent Developments and Short-Term Prospects [1980]* (IMF Occasional Paper no. 1; Washington, 1980), p. 13.

[266] See, e.g., reference to Brazil's policies in 1980 in Chapter 6, *supra*, page 270 (note 191).

[267] See the Chairman's summary of the IMF Executive Board's discussion on April 6, 1983, in IMF, *Annual Report, 1983*, p. 160.

(1) In its consultations with a member government on its economic policies pursuant to article IV of the Articles of Agreement of the Fund, the Fund should—

(A) intensify its examination of the trend and volume of external indebtedness of private and public borrowers in the member country and comment, as appropriate, in its report to the Executive Board from the viewpoint of the contribution of such borrowings to the economic stability of the borrower; and

(B) consider to what extent and in what form these comments might be made available to the international banking community and the public.

(2) As part of any Fund-approved stabilization program, the Fund should give consideration to placing limits on public sector external short- and long-term borrowing.

(3) As a part of its annual report, and at such times as it may consider desirable, the Fund should publish its evaluation of the trend and volume of international lending as it affects the economic situation of lenders, borrowers, and the smooth functioning of the international monetary system.[268]

When countries obtain stand-by or extended arrangements from the Fund, it is common for a performance criterion to limit public sector debt.[269] The Fund, to the author's knowledge, has never requested a member to impose capital controls that would prohibit private firms from borrowing abroad. When the Fund provides a stand-by to a country in the context of the rescheduling of debts to foreign governments and/or commercial banks, the Fund may have some influence on the terms of the rescheduled debts.[270]

Commercial Bank Eurocurrency Activities and Domestic Monetary Policies. While national authorities, as explained previously, exercise supervision over Eurocurrency banking for prudential purposes, Eurocurrency markets have in large measure operated free of monetary policy controls—reserve requirements, credit controls, and the like.[271] Economists have modeled and

---

[268] Section 809 of the Domestic Housing and International Recovery and Financial Stability Act of 1983, Public Law 98–181, approved November 30, 1983, *United States Statutes at Large,* vol. 97, p. 1153 at p. 1274. The act also contemplates that the U.S. Executive Director of the IMF will propose that the Fund collect and disseminate information on the international extension of credit by banks and nonbanks to private and public entities (including all governmental entities, instrumentalities, and central banks of member countries). See generally sections 802, 806, 807, and 809 of the act. The provisions will be incorporated into *United States Code,* title 22, section 286 et seq.

[269] See Chapter 6, *supra,* pages 253 and 262 for provisions of the 1981 extended arrangement for India. See also page 246 (note 115).

[270] See generally Chapter 6, *supra,* pages 272–275.

[271] See Appendix A, *infra,* pages 679–682.

debated the impact that credit creation in the relatively free Eurocurrency markets has on domestic monetary policies, control of inflation, and exchange market stability.[272] An interrelationship of the U.S. domestic economy and the Eurodollar market is apparent, even if the mechanism of transmission is not precisely defined.

With banks from over 85 countries participating in Eurocurrency markets and given the economic insignificance of the territorial locations of offices in which accounts are booked, regulation of the markets for monetary policy purposes would require cooperation of monetary authorities of many countries or effective control of transactions at the points where they are cleared. A proposal for imposition of a modest reserve on Eurocurrency deposits was seriously considered by the United States Congress in 1979.[273] At the time, it was argued in opposition that the proposal would only "penalize" the competitive position of U.S. banks unless the reserve requirement was imposed in a uniform manner by at least the authorities of the Group of Ten and Switzerland.[274] Many countries do not use reserve requirements as an instrument of monetary control and displayed skepticism about the proposal.[275]

The central bank governors of the Group of Ten and Switzerland in April 1980 issued a communiqué stating that the governors and their Standing Committee on Euromarkets would "monitor" international banking developments with a view to assessing their significance for the world economy and for the domestic economies of individual countries.[276] The communiqué concluded:

> The Governors note that differences in competitive conditions between domestic and international banking that arise out of official regulations and policies stimulate growth of [Eurocurrency] international bank lending in general; and that transactions channeled

---

[272] See, e.g., Benjamin J. Cohen with Fabio Basagni, *Banks and the Balance of Payments: Private Lending in the International Adjustment Process* (Montclair, N.J.: Allanheld, Osmun & Co., 1981); John Hewson and Eisuke Sakakibara, *The Eurocurrency Markets and their Implications* (Lexington: D.C. Heath, 1975); and Alexander K. Swoboda, *Credit Creation in the Euromarket: Alternative Theories and Implications for Control* (New York: Group of Thirty, 1980) and bibliography therein. See also Ira O. Scott, Jr., "The Euro-Dollar Market and Its Public Policy Implications," *Materials Prepared for the Joint Economic Committee* (Paper no. 12), U.S. Congress, 91st Congress, 2d Session, (1970).

[273] See *Eurocurrency Market Control Act of 1979: Hearings [on H.R. 3962] before the Subcommittee on Domestic Monetary Policy and the Subcommittee on International Trade, Investment and Monetary Policy of the Committee on Banking, Finance, and Urban Affairs,* U.S. House of Representatives, 96th Congress, 1st Session (1979). See also Frydl, "Debate Over Regulating the Eurocurrency Markets," *supra* note 255.

[274] *Hearings on H.R. 3962, supra* note 273, pp. 18, 26–27, and 83–84. For discussion of problems parent authorities or host authorities would encounter in imposing reserve requirements without support from other countries, see Kenneth W. Dam, *The Rules of the Game: Reform and Evolution in the International Monetary System* (Chicago: University of Chicago Press, 1982), pp. 323–25.

[275] See *Hearings on H.R. 3962, supra* note 273, p. 232; and *18th Report of the [EEC] Monetary Committee,* in *Official Journal of the European Communities,* no. C-195, August 15, 1977, p. 1 at pp. 22–24. See also sources cited in note 132, *supra.*

[276] Bank for International Settlements communiqué of April 14, 1980; *IMF Survey,* April 21, 1980, p. 113.

through the Eurocurrency market can pose problems for the effectiveness of domestic monetary policy in those countries where such differences are particularly significant. The Governors will continue efforts already being made to reduce differences of competitive conditions, fully recognizing the difficulties arising from differences in the national structure and traditions of banking systems.[277]

Publication of the communiqué ended serious official discussion of joint efforts to control Eurocurrency banking in the interest of domestic macroeconomic policies. One understanding, however, remains in place. The governors of the central banks of the G-10 and Switzerland in 1971 adopted the "attitude" that they would not increase placements of their own official reserves in the Eurocurrency markets, and that attitude was reaffirmed in 1978.[278]

Harmonization of Reserve Asset Policies

Multiple Reserve Asset System.   The legal characteristics of the various components of national monetary reserves were considered earlier.[279] National policies on the composition of reserves diverge widely. Some countries, such as France, the Netherlands, Switzerland, and the United States, have traditionally held a large part of their monetary reserves in gold.[280] For some other countries gold is only a small part of reserves. While most countries hold a substantial portion of their reserves in the form of foreign currencies, the United States does not. While some countries maintain their foreign currency reserve holdings with the official issuing authorities, others hold substantial parts of their holdings in Eurocurrency placements. The relative weight of IMF special drawing rights and reserve tranche drawing rights in relation to total reserves varies significantly from one country to another. Some developing countries hold almost all of their reserves in the form of SDRs and reserve position in the IMF; others hold almost none of their reserves in this form.[281]

Recent studies suggest that national policies are not simply the result of historical accident. Today central banks manage their reserves more actively than in the past for purposes of safety, maintenance of value and yield, the cur-

---

[277] *Idem*, p. 118. For background see *IMF Survey*, September 3, 1979, p. 269.

[278] See Chapter 3, *supra*, page 109 (note 30).

[279] These matters are treated in Chapter 3 and also in Chapter 5 (SDR) and Chapter 8 (ECU).

[280] The United States, as the issuer of the currency most widely used in international transactions, normally does not find it necessary to hold foreign currencies above working balances. It holds its reserves primarily in the form of gold, special drawing rights, and reserve position in the IMF. It finances payments deficits primarily through expansion of dollar liabilities. It maintains extensive reciprocal currency arrangements with foreign central banks. See Chapter 4, *supra*, page 148.

[281] Data on these matters are presented in the IMF's monthly publication *International Financial Statistics*.

rency structure of external indebtedness, exchange market intervention needs, and protection against political risks.[282] The untidy nature of the pattern of divergent practices and the potential instability of large portfolio shifts from one asset to another have generated proposals for harmonization of national policies on the composition of reserves.

The central banks of the European Economic Community have an understanding that they will not hold their partners' currencies above working balances except by agreement.[283] A feature of the EEC's European Monetary System is the substitution of European currency units (ECUs) for an agreed portion (currently 20 percent) of gold and U.S. dollar holdings.[284] Aside from this modest regional accomplishment, harmonization has not proceeded very far. In the mid-1960s Working Party No. 3 of the OECD's Economic Policy Committee considered a proposal that the Group of Ten countries harmonize their ratios of gold holdings to other reserve assets. The proposal was not agreed.[285] In 1971 the Group of Ten reached an understanding to limit official placements of reserves in Eurocurrency deposits. The formal understanding was, after only a short time, replaced with a less formal commitment which, in its weaker form, was reaffirmed in 1978.[286] In 1975 the Group of Ten reached an understanding not to increase their total gold holdings. The commitment was allowed to lapse in February 1978.[287] Johannes Witteveen, when IMF Managing Director, suggested in a 1975 speech that countries agree to hold a certain minimum portion of their reserves in SDRs,[288] but the idea was not picked up, and indeed, the reconstitution requirement was later abrogated.[289]

The IMF's Committee on Reform (Committee of Twenty) in its 1974 report conceived a reformed system in which international liquidity would be centrally managed.[290] Special drawing rights, over which the IMF has the power of allocation and cancellation, would be the principal reserve asset in the international monetary system.[291] The role of gold would be reduced.[292] The levels of official liabilities to foreign authorities in national currencies would be agreed between the issuing authorities and the Fund and between the holders and the

---

[282] *How Central Banks Manage Their Reserves* (New York: Group of Thirty, 1982). See also H. Robert Heller and Malcolm Knight, *Reserve Currency Preferences of Central Banks* (Essays in International Finance no. 131; Princeton: Princeton University International Finance Section, 1978); and Courtney Blackman, *Managing Foreign Exchange Reserves in Small Developing Countries* (New York: Group of Thirty, 1982).

[283] See Chapters 8 and 11, *supra*, page 328 (note 62) and page 549.

[284] See Chapter 8, *supra*, pages 320–325.

[285] See Chapter 3, *supra*, page 117 (note 64).

[286] See Chapter 3, *supra*, page 109 (note 30).

[287] See Chapter 3, *supra*, pages 122 and 125 (notes 91 and 105).

[288] See *IMF Survey*, October 28, 1975, p. 315.

[289] See Chapter 5, *supra*, pages 211–212.

[290] *International Monetary Reform: Documents of the Committee of Twenty*, *supra* note 205, pp. 8 and 13–14 (Outline of Reform, June 14, 1974, paragraphs 2(d), 18, and 19).

[291] *Idem*, pp. 8 and 15–17 (Outline, paragraphs 2(d) and 24–28).

[292] *Idem*, pp. 8 and 16–17 (Outline, paragraphs 2(d) and 28).

Fund.[293] Countries would not add to their official Eurocurrency holdings except within limits agreed with the Fund.[294] While some of the proposals, including those relating to gold, were implemented, the scheme as a whole was not adopted.

Why has it been so difficult to reach workable understandings on the harmonization of reserve asset policies? Quite apart from economic reasons for allowing management for value maintenance and yield, legal and political considerations argue for retention of a multiple reserve system. The IMF Articles and decisions define the rules under which the SDR system operates. By way of contrast, national laws and practices define the parameters within which national currencies can be used, and national currencies are the medium in which international trade, service, and capital transactions are conducted. Only a few currencies are in fact held in large amounts in monetary reserves. The U.S. dollar became the world's most widely used currency and a major component of monetary reserves as a result of many factors including the size, strength, and diversity of the U.S. economy, relative freedom from exchange controls, a rich supply of instruments of varying maturities for investment, and other factors. It would be difficult to design an artificial unit with all of the positive qualities.

Monetary authorities must consider whether use of an asset may be blocked in an emergency. An important factor in the initial development of Eurocurrency markets was concern of Eastern European governments to maintain dollar-denominated assets outside the normal jurisdictional reach of U.S. restrictions imposed for security reasons. The more diverse the portfolio, the more likely that substantial assets can be marshalled in event of emergency. A country pursuing political or military policies at variance from those approved by the international community might in the future find, despite the silence of the IMF Agreement, that its use of SDRs is blocked by IMF decisions taken in accordance with a United Nations Security Council decision dealing with a threat to or breach of the peace.[295] Even if a country plans to pursue policies generally approved by the international community, it may have lingering doubts about how the SDR system would work in the event of a major confrontation between members of the IMF commanding substantial voting power. By way of contrast, the physical properties of gold permit it to be readily transferred in large value quantities even when legal rules prohibit its use. A friend, who was in intelligence work in World War II, continues to wear a large gold ring and heavy gold watch whose instant purchasing power he had learned to appreciate.

Some oil exporting states were initially hesitant to participate in the Special Drawing Rights Department. They may have been concerned that the dis-

---

[293] *Idem,* pp. 9, 13–15, 37–42, and 162–82. (Outline, paragraphs 4(b) and 18–23; Annex 5 to Outline; and Report of Technical Group on Global Liquidity and Consolidation).

[294] *Idem,* p. 15 (Outline, paragraph 23). See Chapter 3, *supra,* pages 108–109.

[295] See discussion of IMF-United Nations relationship agreement in Chapter 2, *supra,* pages 48–50.

proportionate share of SDRs to be transferred to them by deficit countries would subject them to political pressures for adjustment. They may also have been concerned about the value and usability of the asset many years hence. Some Middle Eastern states place a large part of their reserves in Eurocurrency placements, not only because they are prepared to bear an economic risk for a larger interest return, but to avoid political problems that might be associated with their holding extraordinarily large dollar deposits directly with the Federal Reserve.[296]

The legal, economic, and political considerations, and the balance between short- and long-term perspectives, will weigh differently depending on the country's situation. It is submitted that any successful multilateral effort to harmonize reserve asset policies must first probe the reasons for the divergent policies and attitudes. One should not expect attitudes on this sensitive subject, nurtured by historical experience, to quickly change.

While the 1974 grand plan of the IMF's Committee on Reform mentioned at the outset of this section was not adopted, in part for the reasons explained above, one piece of the plan that entered the IMF's Articles deserves further comment. The Second Amendment added the following language as Section 7 of Article VIII:

> Each member undertakes to collaborate with the Fund and with other members in order to ensure that the policies of the member with respect to reserve assets shall be consistent with the objectives of promoting better international surveillance of international liquidity and making the special drawing right the principal reserve asset in the international monetary system.[297]

Article VIII, Section 7, quoted above, and its corollary in Article XXII are supplemented by a provision in Schedule G applicable to participants in the Special Drawing Rights Department: "Participants shall also pay due regard to the desirability of pursuing over time a balanced relationship between their holdings of special drawing rights and their other reserves."[298] Joseph Gold wrote many years ago that this latter provision "sags with many . . . uncertainties," and he pointed out the difficulty of converting it into a precise operating rule.[299] While one must be careful to avoid attributing too much specific legal force to the undertakings to "collaborate" and to pay "due regard" quoted above, it would be an equal or greater error to read these provisions as

---

[296] See Amuzegar, *supra* note 202, p. 69.

[297] See Chapter 3, *supra*, page 122, respecting alternate texts of section 7 that were considered. See also Gold, *Use, Conversion, and Exchange of Currency, supra* note 34, p. 104.

[298] Schedule G, paragraph 1(b).

[299] Joseph Gold, "The Composition of a Country's Reserves in International Law," *Journal of World Trade Law*, vol. 5 (1971), p. 477 at p. 498. See also discussion in Chapter 5, *supra*, pages 211–212.

mouthing mere platitudes. While the Executive Board's *Report on the Second Amendment* shied away from construing the meaning of Section 7 of Article VIII, it said that the addition of that sentence was one of the most important changes in the Articles.[300]

The provision holds the door open to future discussions of proposals like those considered by the Committee of Twenty that contemplate a systematic restructuring of the roles played by national currencies in the international system. It provides a touchstone for consultations and collaboration on more modest efforts to deal with actual or potential instabilities caused by portfolio shifts from one reserve asset to another in today's multiple reserve system.

Official changes in reserve asset portfolios can in market-type exchange markets lead to changes in exchange rates. While such a portfolio shift, if known to affect an exchange rate, may be properly viewed as a manipulation of exchange rates, it does not necessarily prevent effective balance-of-payments adjustment or gain an unfair advantage, although it may do so.[301] Portfolio shifts for the purpose of improving return, enhancing safety, or guarding against political risk should probably be permitted, even encouraged, rather than discouraged so long as they are not conducted in such magnitude and speed as to inflict harm on the exchange and payments system.[302] Over the longer term stability is probably enhanced by competition among reserve assets for attractiveness to holders. There are ways in which portfolio changes can be executed with minimum destabilizing effects, and those methods should be encouraged.

Suppose a state wishes to reduce its holdings of gold and increase its holdings of other assets. It can, with the agreement of the IMF, sell gold to it. The Articles grant the Fund authority to accept payments from a member in gold instead of SDRs or currency, on the basis of prices in the market, in any operation or transaction under the IMF Agreement. Such a purchase of gold by the Fund would, however, require an implementing decision by an 85 percent majority of the total voting power.[303] Alternatively, the state can sell its gold on the market, preferably in installments, as the IMF and the United States have done.

Suppose a country wishes to reduce the size of a foreign currency holding in its reserves. The country may within limits be able to sell the currency to the IMF's General Resources Account for its own currency in a "repurchase" transaction[304] or exchange the foreign currency for special drawing rights if the currency the Fund is to acquire is held below the level at which charges are as-

---

[300] *Proposed Second Amendment to the Articles of Agreement of the International Monetary Fund: A Report by the Executive Directors to the Board of Governors* (April 1976), reprinted as IMF, *Summary Proceedings, 1976—Supplement* [hereinafter *Report on Second Amendment*], part 2, chapter I, section 1; and part 2, chapter Q, section 2.

[301] See discussion of Article IV, section 1 (iii), in Chapter 11, *supra*, pages 515–519.

[302] See text accompanying note 380, *infra*.

[303] Article V, section 12(b) and (d).

[304] See Chapter 6, *supra*, pages 227–229.

sessed its issuer by the Fund and the issuer concurs.[305] It may enter into a voluntary transaction with another participant or other holder of SDRs in which it transfers the currency in exchange for SDRs.[306] It may negotiate an exchange of the currency for its own or another currency with another monetary authority. The simplest method of all is to sell the currency on the market for its own or another currency if that can be accomplished, as pointed out above, without manipulating exchange rates in a manner violating Article IV.

The discussion above suggests that countries that seriously wish to gradually reduce the size of the foreign currency component or the gold component of their reserves can probably do so. Technical means can almost certainly be found to accommodate this desire so long as new obligations are not placed on the issuers of currencies being phased out of reserves and the recipients of the new assets (say SDRs) do not expect them to have all of the positive attributes of the gold or currencies sold.[307]

Making the SDR the "Principal Reserve Asset."

Article VIII, Section 7, quoted above,[308] is binding on all IMF members whether or not they are participants in the Special Drawing Rights Department. It states an obligation to collaborate in making the SDR the principal reserve asset in the international monetary system. The term "principal reserve asset" does not carry a precise meaning. Relevant criteria of "principalness" include:

(a) The extent to which the SDR rather than another monetary asset is used as the unit of account in international organizations and in international agreements.

(b) The number of countries holding significant amounts of SDRs in their reserves compared to the number holding gold, the number holding dollars, the number holding sterling, etc.

(c) The total size of SDR holdings and SDR-denominated assets measured against the total size of gold holdings, dollar holdings, sterling holdings, etc.

(d) The volume of transfers of SDRs among monetary authorities compared to the volume of transfers of other monetary assets among them.

(e) The willingness of countries that are in balance-of-payments surplus to choose to augment their reserves in SDRs when given a choice among reserve assets.

The SDR has been adopted as a unit of account in a growing list of interna-

---

[305] See Chapter 5, *supra,* pages 207–209.
[306] See Chapter 5, *supra,* pages 201–203.
[307] Proposals for a substitution account in which the IMF would receive U.S. dollars and issue SDR-denominated assets in exchange are examined at pages 638–642, *infra.*
[308] At page 633, *supra.*

tional organizations and multilateral treaties.[309] Some governments and public agencies have borrowed in the markets with the SDR being the denominator of value.[310] The SDR's use as a denominator of value in private transactions has increased in recent years, but that type of use is still modest.[311] SDR-denominated private obligations are subject to such rules as the creditor and debtor may agree upon and are not constrained by the rules governing the use of true SDRs allocated by the IMF.[312]

The SDR's use as a unit of account is only one measure of "principalness." If the asset is to truly become the principal asset, this will probably develop from confidence gained in its use and appreciation of qualities that make it attractive to hold and to use. The simplicity of transfer, the uniformity and ease with which the IMF Articles and decisions are applied, and the extent to which short-term political considerations are not allowed to intrude upon management of the system will be important factors.

Most central bankers in a 1982 survey expected the SDR's reserve role to

---

[309] See Joseph Gold, *Floating Currencies, SDRs, and Gold: Further Legal Developments* (IMF Pamphlet Series no. 22; Washington, 1977), pp. 24–49; Gold, *SDRs, Gold, and Currencies: Third Survey of New Legal Developments* (IMF Pamphlet Series no. 26; Washington, 1979), pp. 19–28; Gold, *SDRs, Currencies, and Gold: Fourth Survey of New Legal Developments* (IMF Pamphlet Series no. 33; Washington, 1980), pp. 20–39; Gold, *SDRs, Currencies, and Gold: Fifth Survey of New Legal Developments* (IMF Pamphlet Series no. 36; Washington, 1981), pp. 26–43; and Gold, *SDRs, Currencies, and Gold: Sixth Survey of New Legal Developments* (IMF Pamphlet Series no. 40; Washington, 1983), pp. 1–7. See also Joseph Gold, "Development of the SDR as Reserve Asset, Unit of Account, and Denominator: A Survey," *George Washington Journal of International Law and Economics*, vol. 16 (1981), p. 1; and Stephen A. Silard, "Carriage of the SDR by Sea: The Unit of Account of the Hamburg Rules," *Journal of Maritime Law and Commerce*, vol. 10 (1978), p. 13. For a list of international organizations and international agreements in which the SDR is the unit of account, see *International Legal Materials*, vol. 22 (1983), pp. 209–13.

The Union of Soviet Socialist Republics in January 1982 stated that it was prepared to accept the SDR as the unit of account in multilateral conventions without reference to an alternative monetary unit, even though it is not a member of the IMF; but it later backed down from that statement. Gold, *Sixth Survey*, pp. 8–10. The unit of account of the International Bank for Reconstruction and Development is discussed in Chapter 2, *supra*, page 45.

[310] See Gold, *SDRs, Currencies, and Gold: Fourth Survey, supra* note 309, pp. 41–43; Gold, "Development of the SDR," *supra* note 309, pp. 12 and 42; and Dorothy Meadow Sobol, "The SDR in Private International Finance," in Federal Reserve Bank of New York, *Quarterly Review*, vol. 6, no. 4 (Winter 1981–82), p. 29 at p. 36.

[311] See Sobol, *idem;* Gold, *SDRs, Gold, and Currencies: Third Survey, supra* note 309, pp. 28–30; Gold, *Fourth Survey, supra* note 309, pp. 39–43; Gold, "Development of the SDR," *supra* note 309; Joseph Gold, "The Fund Agreement in the Courts—XVIII," *IMF Staff Papers*, vol. 29 (1982), p. 647; and Orren Merren, "The SDR as a Unit of Account in Private Transactions," *International Lawyer*, vol. 16 (1982), p. 503. See press release of Morgan Guaranty Trust Company of March 13, 1981, announcing acceptance of demand deposits denominated in SDRs, printed in Gold, "Development of the SDR," *supra*, p. 64; and specimen certificate of deposit of First National Bank of Chicago for deposits denominated in SDRs, *idem*, p. 63. The European currency unit (ECU) can be used as a unit of account in private transactions in a similar manner to the SDR. See Chapter 8, *supra*, page 343 (note 145).

[312] See Sobol, *supra* note 310, pp. 37–41; and Lawrence de V. Wragg, "Commercial Transactions in SDRs—Some Documentation Considerations," *Business Law Review* (London), vol. 2 (1981), p. 315. Proposals have been made for official participation in clearing arrangements for SDR-denominated claims. See Warren L. Coats, Jr., "The SDR as a Means of Payment," *IMF Staff Papers*, vol. 29 (1982), p. 422.

remain modest. This view was shared by central bank officials in both industrial and developing countries. Respondents noted that the SDR is not transferable to the private sector and cannot be used for direct intervention in the currency markets. They pointed out that the SDR is not used where anonymity must be maintained. The lack of a range of investment instruments of varying maturities denominated in SDRs was also mentioned.[313] These matters could be changed by Fund decisions or amendments to the Articles should there be a shared desire to make the changes.[314]

The purchasing power and interest rate of the SDR are particularly important and sensitive matters.[315] The principle and method of valuing the SDR can be changed by decisions within the Fund taken by qualified majorities. At the present time the SDR's exchange value is determined by reference to a "market basket" composed of portions of five national currencies. The currencies and their weighting are to be changed every five years in accordance with a formula, but can potentially be changed in the meantime if the required majorities are obtained.[316] The SDR by its composite valuation permits monetary authorities to hold a reserve unit the value of which is determined by a group of currencies, some of which they might not be able to hold directly in their reserves in large quantities.[317]

The purchasing power of the SDR in terms of goods and services is dependent upon the purchasing power of the currencies in the SDR "basket." The IMF and its members, thus, have an interest in the domestic purchasing power of those national currencies being maintained. This must be of particular concern to participants in the SDR Department that hold SDRs above cumulative net allocations. Collaboration among the countries issuing the basket's currencies to maintain the economic value of the SDR is of concern to all members of the Fund. It is submitted that the IMF's surveillance of these countries' economic policies should be more continuous and intensive than for other members. The IMF's Managing Director has in fact recognized the value of the Fund holding discussions with officials of the five countries (United States, Federal Republic of Germany, United Kingdom, Japan, and France) as a

---

[313] *How Central Banks Manage Their Reserves, supra* note 282, pp. 19–20.

[314] For a radical proposal to restructure the IMF, see Jacques J. Polak, *Thoughts on an International Monetary System Based Fully on the SDR* (IMF Pamphlet Series no. 28; Washington, 1979). See the papers on the future of the SDR, presented at a conference in Washington, D.C., in March 1983, that are collected in George M. von Furstenberg (ed.), *International Money and Credit: The Policy Roles* (Washington: IMF, 1983). See also William McChesney Martin, *Toward a World Central Bank?* (Washington: Per Jacobsson Foundation, 1970). Compare Richard N. Cooper, "Prolegomena to the Choice of an International Monetary System," *International Organization*, vol. 29 (1975), p. 63 at pp. 91–97

[315] See Chapter 5, *supra*, pages 176–194.

[316] See Chapter 5, *supra*, pages 187–192.

[317] Monetary authorities generally understand that they should not, if the issuer objects, hold a currency in reserves above the level of working balances. See Chapter 3, *supra*, pages 107–108.

group.[318] Sir Geoffrey Howe, the IMF governor for the United Kingdom, commented at the 1981 IMF annual meeting:

> The SDR cannot be a strong unit and a worthwhile asset unless those responsible for its component currencies ensure that those currencies retain their value. If, however, they indeed do that to the best of their ability, then there should be a developing obligation on central monetary institutions to consider holding SDRs, or SDR-denominated assets, and to avoid, as far as they can, destabilizing movements between major currencies.[319]

One can anticipate that over time thought will be given to ways in which the purchasing power of the SDR may be stabilized in terms of real goods and services. If that goal can be accomplished, the role of the SDR as a general standard of international value will be further enhanced.[320]

A Footnote—Proposal for a Substitution Account to be Operated by the IMF. The establishment of a "substitution account" figured actively in the deliberations of the IMF's Committee on Reform (Committee of Twenty), the Interim Committee of the Board of Governors, and the Executive Board during the 1970s.[321] The idea was that national monetary authorities would transfer substantial amounts of reserve holdings of U.S. dollars to a special account, to be administered by the International Monetary Fund, and receive in exchange an international monetary asset valued in terms of the special drawing right (SDR). The purpose of such a substitution would be to reduce the amount of dollars in monetary reserves, increase the amount of SDR-denominated assets in re-

---

[318] See section "General Remarks" in attachment to E.B. Decision No. 7088, *supra* note 23. See also Widman, *supra* note 54, pp. 66 and 68–72. Paragraph 3 of the joint statement on monetary undertakings issued at the Versailles Summit Conference in June 1982, *supra* note 135, stated: "We are ready to strengthen our cooperation with the IMF in its work of surveillance; and to develop this on a multilateral basis taking into account particularly the currencies constituting the SDR."

[319] IMF, *Summary Proceedings, 1981,* p. 81 at p. 87.

[320] See generally Stephen A. Silard, "The General Standard of International Value in Public International Law," in American Society of International Law, *Proceedings of the 73d Annual Meeting, 1979,* p. 15 at pp. 22–24; George M. von Furstenberg, "Price Deflators for Special Drawing Rights Over the Past Decade," *Review of Public Data Use,* vol. 9 (1981), p. 1; Robert C. Effros, "Unit of Account for International Conventions is Considered by UN Commission on Trade Law," *IMF Survey,* February 8, 1982, p. 40; Gold, *SDRs, Currencies, and Gold: Fifth Survey, supra* note 309, pp. 37–40; and Gold, *Sixth Survey, supra* note 309, pp. 10–11. See also Report of the United Nations Commission on International Trade Law on the work of its 15th session; *Official Records of the General Assembly;* 37th session, supplement no. 17 (document no. A/37/17)(1982), pp. 13–17, reprinted in Gold, *Sixth Survey,* pp. 97–99 (indexed SDR in liability conventions); and earlier working papers, UN documents no. A/CN.9/WG.IV/WP.27 (1981) and no. A/CN.9/200 (1981).

[321] For a summary of similar proposals advanced at earlier times, see Joseph Gold, "Substitution in the International Monetary System," *Case Western Reserve Journal of International Law,* vol. 12 (1980), p. 265 at pp. 265–87.

serves, and presumably improve the stability of international monetary relations.

The initial thrust for a substitution account came from European officials who wished to see the United States settle its balance-of-payments deficits by asset transfers rather than expansion of dollar liabilities. While other countries financed their balance-of-payments deficits primarily by transfers of reserve assets and borrowings in foreign currencies, the United States had financed its deficits primarily by issuing its own currency and, thus, increasing the dollar holdings of nonresidents. When the United States was in surplus, the result was not an increase in U.S. reserve holdings but rather a decrease in its reserve liabilities—i.e., nonresident holdings of U.S. dollars. Proposals were advanced that would require all IMF members (including the United States) to use international financial assets (not nationally created ones) to finance their deficits.[322] Complementing these proposals were proposals under which monetary authorities could reduce their dollar balances by exchanging them for SDR-denominated claims. The exchanges would be on a voluntary basis and the IMF would administer the mechanism.[323] The substitution account proposal stood on its own feet and was not dependent upon compulsory asset settlement. The Executive Board considered the following draft article, but it was not embodied in the Second Amendment:

Substitution of Special Drawing Rights for [Gold] [Other Reserve Assets]

In order to promote the gradual reduction of the role of [gold] [gold and reserve currencies] in the international monetary system and to make the special drawing right the principal reserve asset in the system, the Board of Governors may decide, by an eighty-five percent majority of the total voting power,

(i)   to establish a Substitution Account in the General Account and to issue special drawing rights in exchange for [gold][other reserve assets] transferred to the Substitution Account,

(ii) to prescribe the terms and conditions for the substitution, and

(iii) to make any modifications to this Agreement that may be necessary or appropriate for this purpose, provided that

---

[322] See *International Monetary Reform: Documents of the Committee of Twenty, supra* note 205, p. 14 (Outline of Reform, June 14, 1974, paragraphs 20 and 22), pp. 37–42 (annexes 5–7), and pp. 112–36 and 162–79 (technical papers). See also Gold, *Use, Conversion, and Exchange of Currency, supra* note 34, pp. 99–110 and sources there cited; and Williamson, *Failure of World Monetary Reform, supra* note 183, pp. 151–58.

[323] See sources cited in note 322, *supra;* and Gold, "Substitution," *supra* note 321, pp. 287–95. See also Solomon, *supra* note 222, pp. 244–46; and Dam, *supra* note 274, pp. 235–39.

(a) special drawing rights issued under this Article shall not differ from those allocated under Article XXII, and

(b) the assets of the Substitution Account shall be held separately from the other resources in the General Account.[324]

There was renewed consideration of a substitution account, in no way tied
to compulsory asset settlement, in the period 1978–1980.[325] One of the principal purposes of the account, as discussed at that time, would be to permit IMF
members and perhaps other countries (e.g., Switzerland) to reduce the dollar
component of their reserves without disturbing the exchange markets. The increase in SDR-denominated claims would enhance the role of the SDR, and
also the IMF, in international monetary affairs.[326] As envisaged in the latter negotiations the substitution account would be operated as a trust by the IMF,
drawing on the authority of Article V, Section 2(b). That section, which permits the IMF to perform services for members, does not grant as broad an enabling power as the draft article quoted above. Section 2(b) provides that, when
that section is used, no obligations are to be imposed on any member without its
consent and financial services performed by the Fund "shall not be on the account of the Fund."[327]

The proposed substitution account, as in earlier proposals, would accept
U.S. dollars from monetary authorities and issue SDR-denominated claims in
exchange. The claims would have many of the properties of SDRs, but would
not be identical.[328] Unlike the creation of SDRs which adds to the sum of international reserves,[329] the new claims would not result in an increase in international reserves because dollar holdings would be immobilized. While SDRs
have no backing but the promises of participants in the Special Drawing Rights
Departments to accept them and provide freely usable currency in exchange in
accordance with the Articles of Agreement and decisions of the Fund,[330] the
new SDR-denominated claims would be backed by dollars held by the substitution account. It was generally assumed that the interest rate on the new asset

---

[324] Quoted in Gold, "Substitution," *supra* note 321, p. 299; and in Gold, *Use, Conversion, and Exchange of Currency, supra* note 34, pp. 105–06. For commentary see Gold, "Substitution," pp. 295–302.

[325] See generally Gold, "Substitution," *supra* note 321, pp. 313–26; Solomon, *supra* note 222, pp. 285–93; and Dam, *supra* note 274, pp. 313–14.

[326] See IMF, *Annual Report, 1979,* p. 56; the Managing Director's statement at the 1979 annual meeting in IMF, *Summary Proceedings, 1979,* p. 14 at p. 24; and paragraph 7 of the Communiqué of the Interim Committee of October 1, 1979, in *Summary Proceedings, 1979,* p. 323 at p. 326.

[327] See *Report on Second Amendment, supra* note 300, part 2, chapter D, section 2. Amendment of the IMF's Articles of Agreement or a separate international agreement were also options. See generally Gold, "Substitution," *supra* note 321, p. 314.

[328] The IMF's General Resources Account, for example, could not accept the SDR-denominated claims in discharge of obligations that members are obligated to discharge in SDRs. For a comparison of the proposed claims and true SDRs, see Gold, "Substitution," *supra* note 321, pp. 319–20.

[329] See Chapter 5, *supra,* pages 213–217.

[330] See Chapter 5, *supra,* pages 172–173.

would be competitive with market rates, but should not undermine the attractiveness of holding the true SDR. The funds to pay interest would come from the investment of dollars held by the substitution account in special obligations of the United States Treasury.[331]

It appears that during 1979 and early 1980 general agreement was reached that participation would be voluntary,[332] that the account would accept only U.S. dollars and not other currencies or gold, and that the arrangement would involve a one-time exchange of dollars for the new assets rather than a procedure for periodic exchanges of dollars for the new claims. Negotiations also progressed on arrangements to assure transferability and liquidity of the claims. The claims would be transferable to commercial banks as well as official entities. A designation procedure, in some respects comparable to that operated by the IMF's Special Drawing Rights Department,[333] would be available to official holders of the new SDR-denominated claims. An ultimate right, in case of need and subject to circumscribed conditions, to surrender the claims to the substitution account for U.S. dollars would be reserved.[334]

The ostensible stumbling block to agreement was allocation of profits and losses. The United States was unwilling to guarantee a substitution account against losses from interest rate differences or losses from the dollar's possible depreciation. There were differences of views on the size of a potential loss, but one economist's study suggested that it could be very large.[335] Arrangements between the United States and the other participants for sharing profits and losses were considered by negotiators, but no formulas were agreed.[336] U.S.

---

[331] See Gold, "Substitution," *supra* note 321, pp. 313–26; H. Johannes Witteveen, Peter B. Kenen, et al., *Towards a Less Unstable International Monetary System: Reserve Assets and a Substitution Account* (New York: Group of Thirty, 1980); Dorothy Meadows Sobol, "A Substitution Account: Precedents and Issues," in Federal Reserve Bank of New York, *Quarterly Review*, vol. 4, no. 2 (Summer 1979), p. 40; and Stefano Micossi and Fabrizio Saccomanni, "The Substitution Account: The Problem, the Technique and the Politics," in Banca Nazionale del Lavoro, *Quarterly Review*, no. 137 (June 1981), p. 171. The position of the member states of the European Economic Community in April 1980 is stated in the opinion of the Community's Monetary Committee in annex III of the *22d Report on Activities of the Monetary Committee*, in *Official Journal of the European Communities*, no. C-124, May 25, 1981, p. 1 at pp. 20–21.

[332] Developing countries wished to preserve their freedom to determine the composition of their reserves and to invest their dollar holdings in the Eurocurrency markets for maximum return. Developing countries were also concerned that the lending capacity of the Eurocurrency markets, in which they were borrowing heavily, not be reduced.

[333] Transfer of true SDRs by designation is explained in Chapter 5, *supra*, pages 194–201.

[334] See Gold, "Substitution," *supra* note 321, pp. 318–22; and Micossi and Saccomanni, *supra* note 331, pp. 177–78. See also Walter O. Habermeier, "Substitution Account Plan Sought," *IMF Survey*, February 4, 1980, p. 33; and transcript of press conference of the Chairman of the Interim Committee and the Managing Director of April 25, 1980, *IMF Survey*, May 5, 1980, p. 133.

[335] Peter B. Kenen, "The Analytics of a Substitution Account," in Banca Nazionale del Lavoro, *Quarterly Review*, no. 139 (December 1981), p. 403; reprinted in *Reprints in International Finance*, no. 21 (Princeton: Princeton University International Finance Section, 1981).

[336] See transcript issued by U.S. Department of the Treasury of the press briefing of Anthony M. Solomon, Under Secretary of the Treasury for Monetary Affairs, September 24, 1979; and opinion of the European Communities Monetary Committee, *supra* note 331. See also Robert Solomon, *International Monetary Sys-*

Treasury officials apparently held the view that congressional action would be required for the United States to agree to an exchange guarantee or loss-sharing arrangement.[337] The idea of using a portion of the IMF's gold holdings to back the account was opposed by developing countries.[338] Following a meeting of the Interim Committee in Hamburg in April 1980, negotiation of a substitution account was put on a "back burner."[339]

The European Economic Community's system for issuing European currency units (ECUs) involves a substitution of these assets for gold and U.S. dollars "contributed" to the European Monetary Cooperation Fund. The profit and loss risk on the contributed gold and dollars is borne by the central bank contributing them.[340]

Creation and Control of International Liquidity

We now turn to collaboration in the creation and control of monetary reserves and their distribution among countries. While the IMF does not have control of the total size of the gold and currency components of world reserves, it does have control over the allocation (and cancellation) of SDRs. It also has control over the size and distribution of quotas in the General Resources Account.

Procedures and criteria for adopting a decision to allocate SDRs and the economic factors to be taken into account received attention earlier.[341] Similar issues arise when enlargement of quotas in the General Resources Account is considered.[342] Is there a need for additional liquidity? To what extent should additional liquidity be conditional versus unconditional in form?[343] SDRs and reserve tranche drawing rights in the General Resources Account are forms of unconditional liquidity. Conditional liquidity, by contrast, is not automatically available and usually includes repayment (repurchase) obligations. The deter-

---

tem, supra note 222, pp. 290–92; Widman, *supra* note 54, pp. 157–61; Dam, *supra* note 274, pp. 313–14; and Micossi and Saccomanni, *supra* note 331, pp. 178–81.

[337] Robert Solomon, *International Monetary System, supra* note 222, p. 292.

[338] Paragraph 11 of the communiqué of the Intergovernmental Group of Twenty-Four on International Monetary Affairs, issued at Hamburg, April 24, 1980, in *IMF Survey,* May 5, 1980, p. 136 at p. 137. Under one of Professor Kenen's simulations, the Fund's gold holdings would have been exhausted had a substitution account been instituted in 1964. "Analytics," *supra* note 335.

[339] See paragraph 6 of the communiqué of the Interim Committee issued at Hamburg, April 25, 1980, in IMF, *Annual Report, 1980,* p. 154 at pp. 156–57. See also Jacques J. Polak, "Hope for Substitution Account May Lie in a Simpler Scheme, Embodied in IMF," *IMF Survey,* October 27, 1980, p. 337.

[340] See Chapter 8, *supra,* pages 320–325.

[341] See Chapter 5, *supra,* pages 213–217.

[342] See Chapter 1, *supra,* pages 12–14.

[343] See generally Andrew D. Crockett, "Control Over International Reserves," *IMF Staff Papers,* vol. 25 (1978), p. 1; Gottfried Haberler, "How Important is Control Over International Reserves?" and discussion, in Robert A. Mundell and Jacques J. Polak (ed.), *The New International Monetary System* (New York: Columbia University Press, 1977), pp. 111–82; and Robert Solomon's and Peter B. Kenen's articles under the title of "Techniques to Control International Reserves," and discussion, *idem,* pp. 185–236. See also Report of Technical Group on Global Liquidity and Consolidation, in *International Monetary Reform: Documents of the Committee of Twenty, supra* note 205, p. 162.

mination of optimal levels of unconditional and of conditional liquidity is by no means an easy process and political as well as economic judgments come into play. The distribution of SDR allocations among participants is in accordance with their relative quota sizes in the General Resources Account.[344] Those quotas are set in a bargained-out process and are reviewed at least every five years.[345] Lacking control of the currency component of reserves, a difficult problem for the IMF is estimating in advance what portions of an allocation of SDRs or an increase in quotas will simply be added to world reserves, will in fact cause reserves to grow by a multiple (through extension of credit based on them), or will result in a contraction of the currency component of gross reserves with SDRs being substituted for a portion of previously borrowed resources.

Although the IMF does not have direct control of the gold and currency components of total world reserves, or credit mechanisms operated outside the Fund, it does have broad surveillance powers. These powers can be found in Article IV, Section 3; Article VIII, Section 7; and Article XXII, as well as in other provisions of the IMF Agreement.[346]

The appropriate size of deliberately created world reserves (like SDRs and the IMF reserve tranche) is intimately related to balance-of-payments adjustment practices. The more promptly that adjustment takes place, the less financing necessary. In recent years larger deficits have been tolerated for longer periods than in former times. IMF stand-by and extended arrangements often run for three years and the repurchase period under extended arrangements is now ten years.[347] Officials will testify that it is often much easier to reach agreement in bilateral negotiations or in a multilateral forum to expand financial resources than it is to agree to a joint program to end a payments imbalance. Notwithstanding their support for the large quota increase approved by the IMF Board of Governors in 1983, industrialized countries are showing signs of impatience with the incessant demands of developing countries for further increases in quotas and continuous allocations of SDRs. Sir Joseph Gold commented informally at a conference:

> Another reason for reluctance on their [industrialized countries] part might be the unrelenting pressure of developing countries to reduce the Fund's conditionality, with no apparent level at which the process would stop, together with pressure by these members to increase their relative voting power.[348]

---

[344] See Chapter 5, *supra*, pages 213–217.

[345] See Chapter 1, *supra*, pages 12–14.

[346] See previous discussions in this chapter at pages 571, 608, 619, and 630.

[347] See Chapter 6, *supra*, pages 248–250.

[348] Gary Clyde Hufbauer (ed.), *The International Framework for Money and Banking in the 1980s* (Washington: Georgetown University International Law Institute, 1981), p. 178. See also Richard W. Edwards, Jr.,

Policies on exchange rate arrangements may affect official needs for finance. The maintenance of stable exchange rates may call for access to greater resources than the use of floating rates with intervention limited to countering disorderly conditions. However, even carrying out the latter policy, given the volume of transactions in the exchange markets, can require amounts of currencies that in earlier times would have seemed astronomical.[349] Large actual reserve holdings for this purpose may, however, not be essential. Ready availability, even if repayment maturities are short-term, may be satisfactory.[350]

Only the IMF Board of Governors has authority to increase quotas and to allocate SDRs, the decisions requiring 85 percent of the total weighted voting power.[351] Increases in a country's own quota also require its consent and in many countries this requires special action by a parliamentary body.[352] A country is required to accept its share of an SDR allocation unless it voted against the allocation resolution and declined to accept its share.[353] Most countries permit their IMF governors to vote for SDR allocations without the need for special actions by their parliaments, but prior consultation with legislative leaders is required in the United States.[354]

Thoughts have been expressed that eventually the International Monetary Fund might be transformed into a supranational central bank. It would issue SDRs much as national central banks issue national currencies. It would have more comprehensive and penetrating regulatory authority over national monetary authorities than it does now and perhaps have direct regulatory authority over commercial banks as well.[355]

Economic Growth in Poorer Countries

While a purpose of the International Monetary Fund is to contribute to "the development of the productive resources of all members,"[356] no explicit special

---

"Responses of the International Monetary Fund and the World Bank to the Call for a 'New International Economic Order': Separating Substance from Rhetoric," *St. Louis University Public Law Forum,* vol. 3A (1984), p. 89.

[349] See Chapter 11, *supra,* pages 533–534 (notes 156 and 158).

[350] See Chapter 4 *supra,* page 135 et seq., and Chapter 8, page 326 et seq.

[351] See Chapters 1 and 5, *supra,* pages 12–14 and 213–217.

[352] Article III, section 2(d). For U.S. law, see Bretton Woods Agreements Act, *United States Code,* title 22, section 286c.

[353] Article XVIII, section 2(e).

[354] *United States Code,* title 22, section 286q(6)(b), added by section 803 of Public Law 98–181, approved November 30, 1983; *United States Statutes at Large,* vol. 97, p. 1153 at p. 1270.

[355] See sources cited in note 314, *supra.*

[356] Article I(ii). The Indian delegation at the 1944 Bretton Woods Conference proposed that the IMF Agreement include as a purpose "to assist in the fuller utilization of the resources of economically underdeveloped countries." The proposal was not accepted and the final language of Article I(ii) made no distinction between developed and underdeveloped members. *Proceedings and Documents of the United Nations Monetary and Financial Conference, Bretton Woods, New Hampshire, July 1–22, 1944* (2 vols.; Washington: U.S. Government Printing Office, 1948), vol. 1, pp. 22–23, 130–31, 184, 234, and 335–36; and vol. 2, pp.

duty to assist developing countries is stated. Nevertheless, this author takes it for granted that there is a duty on states, as well as individuals, primarily moral in character, to assist fellow human beings living in poverty in other countries to improve their situations.[357] It is appropriate that monetary instruments as well as other techniques be used for this purpose. While, as noted, the purpose clause of the IMF's Articles of Agreement does not refer to the special situation of developing countries, the Second Amendment in three places mentions them.[358] The Boards of Governors of the IMF and the World Bank have a joint ministerial committee on the transfer of real resources to developing countries.[359] The Intergovernmental Committee of Twenty-Four gives particular attention to monetary techniques for channeling resources to developing countries.[360]

Money is instrumental in character. Except in the case of a commodity currency, it is not a good or service itself. It is a claim on goods, services, and other assets in the economy of the issuer or, in the case of the special drawing right, is a claim on such a claim. The fact that goods and services can be exchanged for money, and do not have to be bartered, encourages production because it expands the available range of goods, services, and other assets that can be obtained for that production and the time period in which they can be purchased and consumed. The extension of credit permits a buyer to obtain goods, services, and other assets now and pay for them later. The monetary instrument can be manipulated by governments and their banks to encourage or discourage production, trade, or consumption. It is not easy to determine the best rules for creation, distribution, and use of money and to properly balance the rights of creditors and debtors. Above all, for a monetary system to work well, confidence must be maintained in the monetary claim and its issuer. These fundamentals apply to the international monetary system as well as domestic systems. The greater the confidence in the international monetary system, the more increased the freedom for the IMF to use and, to some measure, manipulate the system for development needs.

Spokesmen for developing countries have proposed schemes that would structure international monetary rules in favor of consumption without cost (or

---

1180–82, 1185–86, and 1213–14. For a full explanation, see Gold, " 'To Contribute Thereby,' " *supra* note 33, pp. 267–76.

[357] See Charter of Economic Rights and Duties of States, especially Articles 6–11. UN General Assembly Resolution No. 3281, Session XXIX, adopted December 12, 1974. See also Chapter 2, *supra*, pages 74–76, and sources there cited.

[358] Schedule D, paragraph 2(a), relating to a Council; and Article V, section 12(f), and Schedule B, paragraph 7(b), relating to gold sales. On the Council see Chapter 1, *supra*, pages 26–28. On gold sale profits, see Chapter 6, pages 294–298. See also discussion in Chapter 11, *supra*, page 512 (note 81), of Article IV, section 1(i). See generally Joseph Gold, "Uniformity as a Legal Principle of the Fund," in Gold, *Selected Essays, supra* note 224, p. 469.

[359] See Chapter 2, *supra*, pages 47–48.

[360] See Chapter 2, *supra*, pages 74–76.

at lower cost) in their countries.[361] The proposal to "link" allocations of special drawing rights to development needs, the idea being that a large portion of these claims would then be permanently transferred for real resources, is an example. Concern was expressed earlier in this book about potential consequences of a program of this type.[362]

While the IMF has avoided making formal distinctions between members based on their degrees of development,[363] a number of actions have been taken that especially benefit developing countries. A portion of the profits of gold sales by the IMF has been set aside for the benefit of developing countries.[364] Subsidy accounts have been used with the oil import financing facility and the supplementary financing facility.[365] SDRs can be used in donations.[366] Rules for access to the General Resources Account have been fashioned with the needs of developing countries in mind.[367] Perhaps the most important decisions to be made in the immediate future relate to the amount of SDRs to be allocated from time to time, the interest rate payable on their use, and the terms of access and costs for use of the general resources of the Fund. These decisions must strike a balance between the interests of creditor and debtor countries.[368] An important feature of the IMF is that most countries, developing and industrialized, at one time or another have found it necessary to draw on the Fund's general resources or to use SDRs allocated by the Fund. Countries are sometimes creditors and other times debtors. It should not be assumed that a country is forever assigned to one class.

The periodic revision of quotas in the IMF—which determine subscriptions in the General Resources Account, drawing rights in that account, shares in allocations of SDRs, and voting power—provides a procedure for adjusting relative powers and responsibilities of developing and industrialized countries. Quotas, while in large measure based on economic power in the world economy, are established in a bargained-out process.[369] They can be set to reflect to some extent, not only the world as it is, but the world as the members would like it to be. However, for the Fund to be effective in the world economy, quota relationships cannot diverge too far from real world economic relationships at the particular time. Developing countries have an interest in assuring that industrialized countries have enough power in the Fund, and the agendas have

---

[361] *Idem.*

[362] See Chapter 5, *supra*, pages 216 and 220.

[363] See Gold, "Uniformity," *supra* note 358.

[364] See Chapter 6, *supra*, pages 294–298.

[365] See Chapter 6, *supra*, pages 292–294.

[366] See Chapter 5, *supra*, pages 203–205.

[367] See, e.g., Chapter 6, pages 248–250 (extended facility), pages 277–281 (compensatory financing facility), and pages 282–283 (buffer stock facility).

[368] See generally Edwards, "Responses of the International Monetary Fund and the World Bank to the Call for a 'New International Economic Order,' " *supra* note 348.

[369] See Chapter 1, *supra*, pages 12–14. See also pages 642–644, *supra*.

enough of interest to them, to in fact guarantee their long-term commitments to the organization. A well-functioning international monetary organization supported by the broad and deeply held confidence of its members must be a paramount concern for developing as for all other IMF members. If developing countries press too hard for special benefits, industrialized countries may move important monetary issues to other forums.

Obligations of General International Law

Note

The reader of this volume is well aware by now of the important roles played by international organizations in the monetary field. The legal principles that have been studied often found their source in international agreements or in decisions and practices of international organizations. International agreements bind the parties to the instrument; they do not as such bind nonmembers without their consent, although they may affect the freedom of action of non-signatories.[370] For example, Article XI of the IMF Agreement obligates every IMF member "not to cooperate with a non-member or with persons in a non-member's territories in practices which would be contrary to the provisions of this Agreement or the purposes of the Fund."[371]

What obligations in the monetary area does general international law impose on nations of the world independent of commitments in international agreements? It is submitted that there are at least two obligations of a fundamental character. First, there is an obligation on all countries not to deliberately disrupt the international monetary and banking system. Second, there is an obligation to consult and collaborate with other countries in meeting transnational monetary problems that arise from the country's actions in the monetary sphere.

Obligation Not to Deliberately Disrupt the International Monetary and Banking System

Before the International Monetary Fund was formed there was very little international law, whether customary or treaty law, dealing with monetary matters. In the absence of a treaty, the regulation and use of monetary instruments were seen as matters exclusively for domestic regulation. The Permanent Court of International Justice in 1929 declared, "It is indeed a generally accepted princi-

---

[370] Vienna Convention on the Law of Treaties, Articles 34–38. For citation see Chapter 2, *supra*, page 64 (note 111).

[371] The application of IMF Article XI to exchange restrictions is treated in Chapter 10, *supra*, pages 420–421. See generally Joseph Gold, *Membership and Nonmembership in the International Monetary Fund* (Washington: IMF, 1974), chapters 20–23.

ple that a State is entitled to regulate its own currency.''[372] The Court implied that the application of this principle was not subject to significant restraints. The use of exchange restrictions and monetary manipulation by Germany and other countries prior to and during World War II made the necessity of international regulation apparent, but it appears that no consensus had emerged by the end of the war that any of these actions violated customary international law.[373] Harry Dexter White, writing in 1942, described the situation as "each country for itself and the devil take the weakest.''[374] It was the establishment of the International Monetary Fund and the subsequent work of that organization and other institutions studied in this book that led to the formulation and application of legal rules and principles that proscribe and prescribe the conduct of states in the monetary field.

General rules of international law—rules that are independent of treaty commitments—change and emerge with historical experience and practice. That is, today general international law may proscribe conduct that in 1929 or 1942 or even 1970 or 1975 was viewed as lawful.[375] It is submitted that today all states of the world have a legal obligation to refrain from deliberately disrupting the world's monetary and banking system or deliberately frustrating decisions taken by the membership of the International Monetary Fund in good faith for the development of the international monetary system.

For the vast majority of the countries of the world, countries that are members of the IMF, this general fundamental obligation of customary law is a necessary corollary to the specific treaty commitments accepted through membership in the IMF. Indeed, it can be said to flow from the customary law concept of *pacta sunt servanda*—that treaties are to be performed in good faith.

This principle proscribing deliberate disruption of the world monetary and banking system also applies to countries that are not members of the IMF. The reason for such a principle is its necessity for the effective functioning of monetary order upon which the economic well-being of peoples depend. The international monetary and banking system is a fragile system dependent upon the mutual confidence of the participants. Countries holding large currency balances with foreign banks can disrupt the operation of the system if they deliberately manipulate these balances to create apprehension and undermine confi-

---

[372] *Case Concerning the Payment of Various Serbian Loans Issued in France* (France v. Kingdom of the Serbs, Croats and Slovenes), judgment of July 12, 1929; Permanent Court of International Justice, *Series A (Judgments)*, 1929, nos. 20/21, p. 1 at p. 44.

[373] Ragnar Nurkse, *International Currency Experience: Lessons of the Inter-War Period* (Geneva: League of Nations; Princeton: Princeton University Press, 1944), pp. 210–29.

[374] Harry Dexter White, "Preliminary Draft Proposal for a United Nations Stabilization Fund and a Bank for Reconstruction and Development of the United and Associated Nations (April 1942)," in *IMF History 1945-65, supra* note 16, vol. 3, p. 37 at p. 40.

[375] See Michael Akehurst, "Custom as a Source of International Law," *British Yearbook of International Law*, vol. 47 (1974–1975), p. 1 at pp. 42–52. See generally Anthony A. D'Amato, *The Concept of Custom in International Law* (Ithaca: Cornell University Press, 1971).

dence in various currencies and their issuers. The international monetary system can also be disrupted by interference with communications. It can also be disrupted by a state that deliberately takes actions that will sharply and quickly alter the values and purchasing power of the currencies of other countries.

A skeptic may ask, ''Is there any evidence of the rule in state practice?'' First, the Articles of Agreement of the IMF seen as a whole are evidence of the rule. Anthony A. D'Amato has pointed out that classic writers on international law frequently derived customary rules from treaty commitments.[376] Other scholars have also noted that a treaty may serve as evidence of a rule of general applicability.[377]

Second, practice both by members and nonmembers of the IMF appears to confirm the rule. The general absence of deliberately disruptive actions is evidence of the legal principle. Those countries that are not members of the IMF have not claimed the freedom to deliberately disrupt the international monetary and banking system nor have they in recent years engaged in such acts. Third, the few cases in recent years in which the rule pleaded for here was breached, or arguably was breached, caused serious problems for the international system and demonstrate the necessity of the rule.

It could be argued that the actions taken, without adequate prior consultation, by the United States on August 15, 1971, to suspend its commitment to the exchange-rate-stability obligations of IMF Article IV, as it then stood, violated the principle pleaded for here. While the U.S. action did not have as its purpose the deliberate disruption of the monetary system, it was obviously predictable that it would have that effect. It was the disruptive aspect of the U.S. action as much as the formal violation of former Article IV that made the U.S. action so difficult for the Fund and for other countries to deal with at the time.[378]

The actions of oil-exporting countries in sharply raising the price of oil in the 1973–1974 period can also be cited as an example of disruptive conduct. Again, the case may not be clear, for the purpose of the actions was not to disrupt the monetary system but to obtain a higher price for the natural resource. Yet, the action could be predicted to have a severely disruptive effect by sharply altering the flow of monetary assets—drastically and quickly increasing the flow of monetary reserves into the treasuries of the exporting states—with an inadequate period of time permitted to other states to adjust to the change.[379] With the benefits of hindsight, it can be seen that the conduct because of its ob-

---

[376] Anthony A. D'Amato, ''The Concept of Human Rights in International Law,'' *Columbia Law Review,* vol. 82(1982), p. 1110 at pp. 1129–47. See also D'Amato, *Concept of Custom, supra* note 375, pp. 138–40.

[377] See, e.g., Ibrahim F. I. Shihata, ''The Treaty as a Law-Declaring and Custom-Making Instrument,'' *Revue Egyptienne de Droit International,* vol. 22 (1966), p. 51 at p. 90. Professor Kirgis, *supra* note 181, relies heavily on practice under treaties in his study. See also notes 389–394, *infra,* and accompanying text.

[378] For background, see Chapter 11, *supra,* pages 495–498.

[379] See Chapter 11, *supra,* page 501 (note 49). See also Chapter 6, pages 293–294.

vious disruptive character was in breach of a fundamental international norm, which should now be recognized, that proscribes deliberate disruption of the world's monetary system.

In the morning of November 14, 1979, during the crisis created by the seizure of United States diplomatic and consular personnel in Iran, Iranian authorities announced their intention to withdraw all deposits with American banks. To prevent the disruption that this would cause, the United States blocked transfers in accounts with U.S. banks and their foreign branches. Had the Iranians not been prevented from acting, their rapid acts might well have caused serious malfunctions in the banking system. Iran's intended acts, had they had that effect, would have violated an international norm.[380]

The author is not alone in urging recognition of the norm. Marjorie M. Whiteman, author of the respected *Digest of International Law,* has argued that a fundamental rule of general international law prohibits economic warfare with the purpose of upsetting (a) the world's banking systems, (b) the world's currencies, (c) the world's supply of energy, or (d) the world's food supply. Indeed, she has argued that this rule is so fundamental and compelling that no derogation, even by treaty, is permitted from it.[381]

It is also submitted that countries that are not members of the International Monetary Fund have an obligation to refrain from actions that deliberately frustrate decisions taken within the Fund for the development of the world's monetary system. The IMF's terms of membership are not especially onerous. It is not an exclusive club. While no country is required to join the IMF, those countries that choose not to participate in the IMF have an obligation to respect the right of others to do so. They have an obligation to refrain from deliberately frustrating the work of the organization.

Affirmative Duties to Consult and Collaborate in International Monetary Matters

Throughout this book we have studied obligations to consult and to collaborate in international monetary matters. Sometimes these obligations have been given very precise meanings—such as the obligations of a designee in a special drawing rights transaction.[382] Often we have worked with highly general language like that in Section 1 of IMF Article IV and in constituent instruments of other organizations. But, this general language, too, has been given meaning

---

[380] It is difficult to judge "what might have been." The amounts involved were large. The psychological impact on the markets should not be discounted. For background, see Chapter 10, *supra,* pages 419–420.

[381] Marjorie M. Whiteman, "*Jus Cogens* in International Law, With a Projected List," *Georgia Journal of International and Comparative Law,* vol. 7 (1977), p. 609 at p. 626. Miss Whiteman is author of *Digest of International Law* (15 vols.; Washington: U.S. Government Printing Office, 1963–1973).

[382] See Chapter 5, *supra,* page 194 et seq.

through the promulgation of principles, decisions of organizations, and the conduct of persons holding responsibilities in their governments.

F.A. Mann, writing in 1959, said that it was "open to some doubt" whether duties to consult and to collaborate expressed in international agreements in the monetary sphere create legally enforceable obligations. He said, "International law, of course, requires that a duty of consultation should be fulfilled *bona fide* and reasonably. Yet the duty of consultation has, almost by definition, in law a purely nominal character. . . ."[383] Dr. Mann was careful to limit his query to the issue of legal enforceability and did not deny that obligations to consult and to collaborate have a legal character.[384]

Dr. Mann appears to have been influenced by the generality of the concepts. He seemed more comfortable discussing the details of the par value system of exchange rates which was then in effect or matters relating to exchange restrictions. But detailed specificity is not a necessary feature of legal obligation. It is enough if the general statement of obligation can guide conduct and can be applied in the context of situations that actually arise.[385] Hersch Lauterpacht, in one of his typically insightful comments, wrote in a report on the law of treaties to the UN International Law Commission:

> Undoubtedly, the legal rights and obligations do not extend further than is warranted by the terms of the treaty. The fact that the instrument is a treaty does not imply an intention of the parties to endow it with the fullest possible measure of effectiveness. They may intend its effectiveness to be drastically limited. But, subject to that consideration which must be evidenced by the terms of the treaty and any other available evidence, the guiding assumption is that the instrument creates legal rights and obligations. Any measure of discretion and freedom of appreciation [sic: "application"?], however wide, which it leaves to the parties must be exercised in accordance with the legal principle of good faith.[386]

---

[383] See F.A. Mann, "Money in Public International Law," in Hague Academy of International Law, *Recueil des Cours,* vol. 96 (1959-I), p. 1 at pp. 40 and 43.

[384] *Idem,* pp. 40–44. See also F.A. Mann, *The Legal Aspect of Money* (4th ed.; Oxford: Oxford University Press, 1982), pp. 513–14.

[385] Domestic legal systems frequently apply general legal concepts. A large part of the law of torts involves the application of a duty to exercise "reasonable care." The concept of "abuse of right" has been applied in many different types of situations by continental legal systems.

[386] *Yearbook of the International Law Commission,* 1954, vol. 2, p. 123 at p. 125; United Nations document no. A/CN. 4/SER.A/1954/add.1. The International Court of Justice has held that a consultation obligation is a legal obligation to be performed in good faith. *Interpretation of the Agreement of 25 March 1951 between the WHO and Egypt,* advisory opinion of December 20, 1980; International Court of Justice, *Reports of Judgments, Advisory Opinions and Orders,* 1980, p. 73, especially pp. 94, 96, and 97. The Court stated that a duty of consultation arose from the circumstances of the relationship of the parties in the case and was not dependent upon a particular treaty provision. Judge Shigeru Oda, who was somewhat more explicit, in his separate opinion reasoned that an obligation of consultation arose from the circumstances of the case independent of the treaty in question. *Idem,* p. 131 at p. 154. See generally Kirgis, *supra* note 181;

We saw in Chapters 4 and 6 how the duty to consult which is stated in reciprocal currency agreements and in IMF stand-by arrangements is given application in practice. Indeed, the consultation clauses in a letter of intent supporting an IMF stand-by or extended arrangement create binding legal obligations while the economic policies stated in the letter are not legally obligatory.[387]

Another obvious point needs to be made. Concern with legal obligations need not be at the forefront of the minds of officials. When persons act in good faith and seek to pursue wise policies, their actions are likely to be consistent with their legal obligations. But, if the degree of collaboration that some believe necessary is not forthcoming, a careful effort can be made to give application to the legal obligation of collaboration stated in a treaty commitment. The discussion earlier in this chapter of the duties of surplus countries in the balance-of-payments adjustment process illustrates how legal obligations can be identified and clarified.[388]

It is submitted that the duty to consult in international monetary matters is not simply a treaty-based obligation but arises from general international law. A norm that is initially contractual in origin may become binding as a rule of general international law even for countries that have never, and do not, become parties to the agreement. Rules that emerge in this manner gain independent recognition because they are necessary to the functioning of international society as it has developed and/or because they have been generally accepted through widespread practice. This principle respecting the emergence of general rules of international law was articulated by the International Court of Justice in the *North Sea Continental Shelf Cases*[389] and is recognized in Article 38 of the Vienna Convention on the Law of Treaties.[390]

For a widespread practice of states to evolve into a rule of general international law, at some time in the evolutionary process a sense of legal obligation *(opinio juris)* must emerge. But, that sense of obligation need not be explicitly displayed. Richard R. Baxter stated:

> The hard fact is that States more often than not do not refer to or exhibit any sense of legal obligation in their own conduct . . . . There

Kusumowidagdo, *supra* note 181; and Stepehn L. Kass, "Obligatory Negotiations in International Law," *Canadian Yearbook of International Law,* vol. 3 (1965), p. 36.

[387] See Chapter 6, *supra*, pages 267–269.

[388] See pages 611–617, *supra*.

[389] *North Sea Continental Shelf Cases (Federal Republic of Germany/Denmark; Federal Republic of Germany/Netherlands);* judgment of February 20, 1969; International Court of Justice, *Reports of Judgments, Advisory Opinions and Orders,* 1969, p. 3 at pp. 41–45. See also dissenting opinion of Judge Kotaro Tanaka, p. 172 at pp. 175–79.

[390] Article 38 of the Vienna Convention on the Law of Treaties, *supra* note 370, states: "Nothing in articles 34 to 37 [relating to the non-binding effects of treaties on third parties] precludes a rule set forth in a treaty from becoming binding upon a third State as a customary rule of international law, recognized as such."

is much to commend the view that *opinio juris* is presumptively present unless evidence can be adduced that a State was acting from other than a sense of legal obligation.[391]

The practice of consultation on international monetary matters within international organizations and in other bilateral and multilateral settings is evidence of an evolving sense of responsibility. Austin Robinson once commented, "What was Bretton Woods about if it was not the creation of a world in which countries did not close their eyes to the repercussions of their actions on others?"[392] The embodiment of the consultation principle in many different legal instruments suggests that the duty to consult in monetary matters affecting other countries is a duty imposed by general international law, the particular instruments extending and structuring that obligation.[393] A cooperative world order requires that all countries be willing to consult with each other when the policies pursued by one cause adverse effects on the economies of others. This general obligation may not be as demanding as the consultation obligations flowing from the IMF Agreement or other treaties, but it exists at least in rudimentary form independent of that Agreement. It is submitted that those countries outside the IMF have a duty to consult with those within and vice versa. The manner in which the duty is to be discharged may vary, and consultation contemporaneous with or subsequent to action in many cases may meet legal obligations.[394]

Let us now turn to collaboration. Robert W. Russell has commented, "The most striking feature of recent international monetary relations is that part of the time the game resembles a classic power confrontation, but another part of the time it resembles a cooperative venture to improve the general welfare."[395] One who reads histories of monetary events of the past forty years is impressed by the efforts of officials to work together to develop shared solutions to common problems. We have seen many examples of collaboration within international institutions to deal with balance-of-payments problems, ex-

---

[391] Richard R. Baxter, "Treaties and Custom," in Hague Academy of International Law, *Recueil des Cours,* vol. 129 (1970-I), p. 25 at pp. 68–69.

[392] Austin Robinson, "A Personal View," in Milo Keynes (ed.), *Essays on John Maynard Keynes* (Cambridge: Cambridge University Press, 1975), p. 9 at p. 19.

[393] Judo Umarto Kusumowidagdo, following a study of treaties and state practice, concluded that a rule of customary international law has emerged, not dependent upon treaties, that requires consultation in matters of common economic interests and concerns of states. Kusumowidagdo, *supra* note 181, pp. 305–07.

Some decisions of courts in the United States have recognized that cooperation is required among countries in monetary matters even though no specific treaty rule makes cooperation in the circumstances mandatory. See Joseph Gold, *The Rule of Law in the International Monetary Fund* (IMF Pamphlet Series no. 32; Washington, 1980), pp. 8–9 and cases cited in note 25 therein.

[394] See pages 601–647, *supra.* Frederic L. Kirgis was correct in concluding that at the present time no *general* duty of *prior* consultation binds states in the monetary sphere. Kirgis, *supra* note 181, pp. 356–58 and 375.

[395] Robert W. Russell, "Transnational Interaction in the International Monetary System, 1960–1972," *International Organization,* vol. 27 (1973), p. 431 at p. 432.

change restrictions, and other matters. We have had occasion to remark about the persistence of officials who negotiated the arrangements leading to creation of the special drawing right. Time and again they came together at high levels to resolve their differences.[396] The negotiation of the Second Amendment to the IMF Agreement involved intensive effort over a four-year period.[397] The establishment of the European Monetary System involved a major effort to bridge differing positions of EEC member states.[398]

In addition to cooperation within international institutions, bilateral cooperation has been important. The U.S. Treasury and Federal Reserve market intervention arrangements with the Deutsche Bundesbank were during the period 1973–80 an intensive collaboration having the character of a joint venture.[399] In times of crisis the importance of cooperation has been evident. The day President John F. Kennedy was assassinated the Federal Reserve System sold foreign currencies it did not own to steady the exchange markets, without even having time to consult the issuers of the currencies sold, confident that the support of the foreign institutions would be immediately forthcoming.[400] While examples of noncooperation can also be cited, the cooperative actions are indeed impressive.

One is tempted to assert an obligation, going beyond consultation, to affirmatively collaborate in solving international monetary problems. While there is evidence in state practice to support such an assertion, one cannot say that general international law required the persistent and intensive efforts that have at times occurred. While affirmative collaboration, in the absence of a treaty commitment, may not be a firm legal duty, it is a principle of good conduct that should guide state actions. In any event, the practice of states clearly evidences a general obligation of a weaker sort. It is submitted that general international law, independent of specific treaty commitments, requires all countries to consult with other countries on the important international implications of their monetary policies, at least to consult with those countries that are adversely affected and at least to do so after the fact if not before. Because the effects of monetary policies are rarely simply bilateral, effective consultation usually requires the use of multilateral forums. If there is no existing forum involving the actor and affected parties that is jointly viewed by them as appropriate, there is an obligation to consider modifying existing institutions or the establishment of new ones in order that meaningful consultations can take place.

One of the obligations associated with the fundamental duty to collaborate (whether perceived in moral or legal terms) is to work to adapt existing institutions and to create new institutions to meet needs as they emerge. There is no

---

[396] See Chapter 5, *supra*, pages 169–171 and 221.
[397] See Chapters 1 and 11, *supra*, pages 8–11 and 502–507.
[398] See pages 591–592, *supra*.
[399] See Chapter 4, *supra*, pages 143–151.
[400] See Coombs, *Arena of International Finance*, *supra* note 78, chapter 6.

perfect institutional system to be put into place and then left to operate automatically. The international monetary system is in transition and will be into the foreseeable future. Members of organizations have an obligation to participate in the process of institutional adaptation.

Conclusion
Plurality of Institutions

In the course of this book we have studied the work of a number of international organizations. It is appropriate here to make a few very general remarks.

The International Monetary Fund is the dominant multilateral organization concerned with monetary affairs. It has a large membership drawn from all parts of the world and representing a wide spectrum of economic philosophies. It has a highly respected staff. It has substantial financial resources and a broad range of legal powers. But, although dominant, it is not the only organizaton in the system. The work of the Organisation for Economic Co-operation and Development and the European Economic Community penetrate somewhat more deeply into national life of developed countries. The International Bank for Economic Cooperation is the chosen instrument for monetary cooperation among the socialist states of Eastern Europe. The Bank for International Settlements stands, in some sense, in juxtaposition to the IMF. It is by tradition the principal forum for consultations among central bank governors of the industrialized countries. It also carries operational responsibilities, holding deposits for central banks and acting as agent for them. The membership of the BIS, which presently includes more countries from Eastern Europe than are in the IMF, opens up the possibility for the Bank to facilitate greater cooperation between East and West. There are also important bilateral relationships between national monetary authorities.

The existence of a variety of forums for consultation and decision-making makes it possible for skilled officials to channel emerging problems into organizations that can deal with them effectively. The OECD is particularly suited for discussions among industrialized countries of emerging problems on which they are not yet ready to take agreed positions or make binding commitments. The IMF is a better choice when a wider range of viewpoints should be shared. By tradition the IMF leans toward greater precision in the definition of rights and obligations than is the case in the OECD. The use of one organization to block cooperative action that would otherwise bear fruit in another organization appears not to have happened with any frequency. Overall, the pluralism of institutions is probably a good thing permitting cooperation among national authorities to be carried considerably further than might be the case if only the IMF were in the field. The existence of the several organizations breeds a certain amount of healthy competition and assures that at least one forum is in fact available for consideration of most any serious problem.

It is essential that communication be maintained among the organizations and among the participating countries. Secretariat personnel and representatives of one organization may observe or participate in the work of others. Some of the same national officials also attend meetings held within different organizations. In a few cases the same central bank official may participate in the Committee of Governors of Central Banks of the EEC, the Monetary Committee of the EEC, the BIS, the OECD's Working Party No. 3, and the IMF Interim Committee. In other cases a country's representation may vary from one institution to another.[401] Developing countries are effectively represented only in the IMF and in United Nations bodies. Per Jacobsson long ago saw the central role of the IMF:

> [T]here is *no other institution than the Fund* that can deal with the *internal* problems of the non-industrial countries. . . . Remember that the industrial countries have a position of power in the Fund—if the other countries were not able even to talk about the problems of the industrial countries, they might not accept for long the present arrangements.[402]

Economic structures and social values differ from one country to another. Some organizations, such as the IMF, encompass a wide range of countries. In the cases of the Group of Ten and the EEC the differences are narrower. There must constantly be an adjustment in the trade-off between shared decision-making and tolerance of policy differences among countries. A careful balance was struck in the language of IMF Article IV, Section 1, but the meaning to be given to that language must not be frozen. Rather, the application of the language should be allowed to evolve with time. While international collaboration has so far proved difficult in the areas of harmonization of national reserve asset policies, the sharing of balance-of-payments adjustment burdens, and the gearing together of domestic policies bearing upon such matters as economic growth, unemployment, and levels of prices and wages, there is increasing tolerance of inquiries into these national policies that affect international relationships.

Throughout the book we have seen the need for a system of institutions, rules, and practices that are flexible enough to meet changing needs, that encourage wise decision-making, that are structured to assure compliance with commitments once they are made, and that encourage the development of

---

[401] See Russell, *supra* note 395; and Susan Strange, "IMF: Money Managers," in Robert W. Cox and Harold K. Jacobson (ed.), *The Anatomy of Influence* (New Haven: Yale University Press, 1973), p. 263.

[402] Erin E. Jacobsson, *A Life for Sound Money: Per Jacobsson, His Biography, supra* note 16, p. 380.

mutual confidence among the persons in national governments and international organizations who carry responsibilities for operations and decisions. International monetary relations for the most part are "a clear example of a mixed-motive, nonzero-sum game."[403] Institutions must be designed to assure a net gain and that the gain is fairly shared.

Concluding Reflections

We have traversed some 650 pages. For purposes of organization the material covered in this book has been broken down into topics and segregated into chapters. The reader should be aware, from the many cross-references and frequent overlaps between discussions in one chapter and another, that we have been studying a system whose various components must be understood in terms of their functions and relationships. This last chapter, while not itself a summary of the earlier chapters, has sought to highlight the consultation and collaboration feature upon which the legal structure of international monetary relations is dependent. Indeed, the fundamental obligations of international monetary law are to consult and collaborate.

Some readers may believe that the author was looking at the world through rose-colored glasses when he put the word "collaboration" in the title of this book. Some would see both the methods and achievements of collaboration in monetary affairs to date to be quite limited. The dictionary indicates that the meaning of "collaboration" is similar to "cooperation," but "collaboration" emphasizes the aspects of will, of work, of "labor" which indeed is part of the word. There is no question that the further development of collaboration in international monetary affairs will require labor.

Some years from now a second edition of this book may be necessary if it is to serve as a description of the then-contemporary world monetary structure. But the force of future events, not now clearly predictable, may cause radical transformations. If radical change should occur, an entirely new book and new title may be necessary. In that event the present volume may be read in the future by persons who wish to gain an understanding for comparative purposes of what the legal and organizational structure of international monetary relations was in the mid 1980s. Development through evolutionary process is probably more likely. That process should be aided by a better understanding of the contemporary system and the commitments associated with it.

---

[403] Benjamin J. Cohen, *Organizing the World's Money: The Political Economy of International Monetary Relations* (New York: Basic Books, 1977), p. 50.

Suggestions for Further Reading

In the research for this book, primary reliance has been placed on official documents, writings by persons with official responsibilities, and information gained from personal inquiries. Primary sources are cited throughout the book, and the reader should be able to readily locate the official publications and documents.

Detailed footnote references are provided to a very large secondary literature, including books, articles, and other materials. Greater efforts have been made to identify writings on institutional, operational, and legal aspects of international monetary relations as compared to writings that primarily develop economic theory. Only selected citations are given to economic writings on exchange rate arrangements as this literature is extraordinarily voluminous.

The reader must exercise caution in the use of secondary materials written prior to the entry into force of the Second Amendment to the Articles of Agreement of the International Monetary Fund, effective April 1, 1978. The changes in the IMF Agreement had effects on other organizations as well as on the Fund itself.

Listed below are a few monographs of broad scope that are of enduring value. They merit reading in their entirety.

Charles A. Coombs, *The Arena of International Finance* (New York: John Wiley & Sons, 1976).

Kenneth W. Dam, *The Rules of the Game: Reform and Evolution in the International Monetary System* (Chicago: University of Chicago Press, 1982).

Margaret Garritsen de Vries, *The International Monetary Fund, 1966–1971: The System Under Stress* (2 vols.; Washington: International Monetary Fund, 1976).

Margaret Garritsen de Vries, *The International Monetary Fund, 1972–1978: International Monetary Cooperation on Trial* (3 vols.; Washington: International Monetary Fund, forthcoming in 1985).

Joseph Gold, "Developments in the International Monetary System, the International Monetary Fund, and International Monetary Law

Since 1971," in Hague Academy of International Law, *Recueil des Cours,* vol. 174 (1982–I), p. 107.

Joseph Gold, *Legal and Institutional Aspects of the International Monetary System: Selected Essays* (Washington: International Monetary Fund, 1979).

Joseph Gold, *The Rule of Law in the International Monetary Fund* (IMF Pamphlet Series no. 32; Washington, 1980).

J. Keith Horsefield and Margaret Garritsen de Vries, *The International Monetary Fund, 1945–1965: Twenty Years of International Monetary Cooperation* (3 vols.; Washington: International Monetary Fund, 1969).

Erin E. Jacobsson, *A Life for Sound Money: Per Jacobsson, His Biography* (Oxford: Oxford University Press, 1979).

Andreas F. Lowenfeld, *The International Monetary System* (1st ed.; New York: Matthew Bender, 1977). (The second edition is forthcoming in 1984.)

F. A. Mann, *The Legal Aspect of Money* (4th ed.; Oxford: Oxford University Press, 1982).

Stephen A. Silard, "Money and Foreign Exchange," *International Encyclopedia of Comparative Law* (Tübingen: J.C.B. Mohr; The Hague: Mouton, 1975), vol. 17, chapter 20.

Robert Solomon, *The International Monetary System, 1945–1981* (New York: Harper & Row, 1982).

Since this book, given the detailed footnotes, has the character of a bibliographical essay, no separate listing of items cited is provided. A separate list would have required that this book be published in two volumes. Condensed bibliographies can be found in Dam, *supra,* pp. 345–63; Gold, "Developments in the International Monetary System," *supra,* pp. 115–20 and 362–65; and Silard, *supra,* pp. 151–53.

Appendices

Appendix A

Briefing on Money, Banks, and Exchange Rates

Note

This appendix reviews monetary and banking concepts that figure in discussions throughout the book. It is designed especially for the lawyer reader who may not have formally studied international economics.

Money in National Economies

Short Lesson in Money

Basic to an understanding of the international monetary system is an understanding of money in a national economy—what it is, how it is created, how it is used, how its use can be controlled. Many of the coursebooks used in universities in a basic economics course or in an intermediate level course in money and banking trace the development of money.[1] When goods and services are exchanged by barter, money is not required. However, parties to a barter transaction may in their negotiations find it convenient to make reference to a third good which is used as a standard of value. The Indians of the Northern Plains of the United States in the nineteenth century used "one horse" and "one buffalo robe" as their standards of value in bartering all varieties of goods and services. Several colonial governments in what is now the United States published "standards of trade" in the eighteenth century with prices listed in terms of dressed beaver skins or what was called "made beaver."[2]

The use of commodity currency and coinage marks the first stage of formal monetary development. Particular goods (which are usually small, valued in the society, and easily transferred) are used as a medium of exchange as well as a standard of value. That is, the commodity is regularly used as a means of payment. A shell bead called "wampum" was used by Indians of the North-

---

[1] See, e.g., Paul A. Samuelson, *Economics* (11th ed.; New York: McGraw-Hill Book Co., 1980), pp. 260–65 and 277–82.

The functions that money serves are surveyed in Roy F. Harrod, *Money* (London: Macmillan, 1969), pp. 3–65; and Colin D. Campbell and Rosemary G. Campbell, *An Introduction to Money and Banking* (5th ed.; Chicago: Dryden Press, 1983), pp. 17–29.

[2] See Charles E. Hanson, Jr., "Trade Notes and Tokens," *Museum of the Fur Trade Quarterly* (Chadron, Nebraska), vol. 4, no. 1 (Spring 1968), p. 1.

east United States. Gold was used in Europe.[3] Governments would melt and press gold and other metals into uniform sizes to facilitate their use as media of exchange and as standards of value.

The next stage and a very important one is the development of banking. The Hudson's Bay Company, which functioned as both bank and general store in many remote parts of North America, issued trade tokens in exchange for animal furs, craft items, and other goods. The brass trade tokens, redeemable in merchandise of the company, were denominated in "made beaver": one beaver, half-beaver, quarter-beaver, etc.[4] These tokens were widely traded. They functioned as a standard of value, medium of exchange, and also as a store of purchasing power. Two half-beaver tokens would purchase goods equivalent to a beaver skin whether the tokens were presented immediately upon receipt or at a future time.

The Bank of Amsterdam, a famous early bank in Holland, was established in 1609 to hold and transfer gold and precious metals on instructions of its merchant customers so that the merchant himself need not carry sacks of coins with him on his business travels or himself assay the metallic content of the coins. The bank maintained books showing the holdings of its depositors.[5] When the Bank of England was founded under a royal charter in 1694,[6] it was authorized to issue paper notes that acknowledged the obligation of the bank to provide a defined quantity of gold of a particular fineness upon presentation of the paper. The paper notes in turn could be traded. In the eighteenth century in England, in addition to Bank of England notes, notes issued by a number of private banks (owned by individuals or partners) were also in circulation.[7]

The expansion of the money supply through loans extended by a bank to its depositors marks a further stage in the development of monetary instruments. From experience, banks knew that all the gold on deposit would not be claimed at once. A bank could loan a portion of the gold it held to its customers and receive interest payments in compensation for the use. The loan could simply take the form of crediting the customer's account with the right to obtain a stated amount of gold (which the bank continued to hold), with the customer giving the bank a promissory note in exchange. The customer in turn could transfer the credit by writing a check on his account. A check is an order by the drawer-depositor to the bank directing it to debit its account and to credit the drawee's account with the right to redeem a stated amount of money (in our example gold).

The next step, which marks a fundamental change, is when the defined relationship between

---

[3] Paul Einzig, *Primitive Money in its Ethnological, Historical and Economic Aspects* (2d ed.; London: Pergamon Press, 1966), describes commodity currencies used in different parts of the world at various times in human history.

[4] Hanson, *supra* note 2.

[5] John Kenneth Galbraith, *Money, Whence It Came, Where It Went* (Boston: Houghton Mifflin Co., 1975), p. 15; and Adam Smith, *Wealth of Nations* (R. H. Campbell, A. S. Skinner, and W. B. Todd, ed.; 2 vols.; Oxford: Oxford University Press, 1976), vol. 1, pp. 479–88 (book IV, chapter 3).

[6] The Bank of England is a "central bank." It is a bank for the government treasury and a bank for commercial banks. It accepts deposits from these "customers" and extends credit to them. Notes issued by the bank are recognized as the nation's currency. The Bank of England was initially founded to loan money to William III. See Andreas M. Andréadès, *History of the Bank of England, 1640–1903* (4th ed., trans. by Christabel Meredith; London: Cass & Co., 1966), p. 44. The functions performed by the U.S. Federal Reserve System, the central bank in the United States, are reviewed later in this chapter.

[7] Harrod, *supra* note 1, p. 25.

Until 1933 the U.S. Federal Reserve Banks issued notes (U.S. paper money) redeemable in gold by any holder. The Federal Reserve Banks continue to hold gold but no longer issue notes for public circulation that are redeemable in gold. The U.S. Treasury issued one-dollar notes redeemable in silver until June 1968. Until August 15, 1971, the U.S. Treasury stood ready to convert U.S. dollars held by foreign monetary authorities into gold at prices based on $35 an ounce. See Chapter 3, *supra*, pages 115–119 and Chapter 11, pages 491–501.

intangible money (tokens, paper money, and bank deposits) and the tangible commodity is broken. The currency, instead of being redeemable in terms of a commodity referent (such as an ounce of gold, a beaver pelt, or a silver fox), is officially valued only in an arbitrary unit styled by the issuer ("dollar," "rupee," "peso," "mark," "franc").[8]

Today, all United States money and the currencies of most other countries of the world cannot be surrendered to the government treasury or bank of issue for a stated amount of gold or other commodity. They are monies because the issuing authorities decree that they are monies, and because people are willing to accept them in exchange for their labor, goods, or other assets. There are essentially two ways in which these "managed" currencies may be issued. One method is simply by sovereign decree to churn the printing press and to distribute the paper produced to soldiers in the armed forces in payment of their salaries and to others who supply goods and services to the government. The government states its willingness to accept this money from any holder in payment of taxes and other governmental charges. Assuming that this "fiat" money is created in relatively small increments, its usability for paying taxes and other governmental charges leads to the acceptance of this money by persons in the society as a standard of value and means of payment in all kinds of economic transactions.[9] The purchasing power of a given unit of fiat money is affected by the total quantity in circulation and by the purchasing-power standard acknowledged by the government when it uses the money to pay for goods and services sold to the government. The effective use of the money as a store of purchasing power is dependent upon the predictions of the holders about the currency's future purchasing power.

Another way in which a managed currency is issued, and the primary method used by United States authorities and monetary authorities in many other countries, is through the assumption of debt. In its simplest form the U.S. Treasury issues a government bond (a promissory note) which is sold in the market; a Federal Reserve Bank (the central bank in the United States) buys the bond. The Federal Reserve credits the seller's deposit account with the bank. By law the bank is permitted to create money on the basis of the Treasury's promissory note that it receives without the need for further collateral.[10] The expansion of the money supply through deposit creation supported by promissory notes will be discussed further later in this chapter.

When there is no defined commodity referent in terms of which a currency is valued, it becomes possible for governments to manage their monetary systems in ways that might otherwise not be possible. Various techniques, some rather primitive and some highly sophisticated, have been put to use by governments to manage money supplies, interest rates, and price levels.

The reader should have grasped from this survey some of the forms money may take (commodities, coins, paper money, bank deposits) and also the essential functions money serves:

> *Standard of value.* Prices of goods, wages of workers, debts, and taxes are usually stated in terms of the monetary unit of the society. Even when items are bartered between two antique dealers the dollar will be used as the standard for communicating measures of value. *Medium of exchange.* Whatever instrument functions as money must, to be money, be widely used in the relevant society in payment for goods and services. A nation state

---

[8] See note 7, *supra.* In some monetary systems the break occurred late in time. In 1946 the Hudson's Bay Company still issued a commodity token—in this case equivalent to one arctic fox. Hanson, *supra* note 2, p. 2.

[9] The American Revolution was financed by the issuance of fiat currency. Galbraith, *supra* note 5, pp. 58–67. The currencies of a number of countries are issued today in essentially the manner described here.

[10] *United States Code,* title 12, section 412.

U.S. currency is also issued on the basis of reserves of IMF special drawing rights and of governmental holdings of gold. See page 669, *infra.*

through legislation may declare a particular commodity or currency to be "legal tender" in the society. That is, the state will accept the currency in payment of taxes and charges, and citizens are required by law to accept the currency in payment of debts, whether public or private. However, the economic utility of a money (whether a trade token or a national currency) ultimately depends on the willingness of persons to accept and use it.

Store of purchasing power. Money can be used not only upon immediate receipt as a means of payment, but it can be held and used later. Thus someone may accept money in exchange for his goods or services today not with the intention of immediately buying something but so that at a later time he can buy clothing, or take a vacation, or pay for a child's tuition in college.

Standard and means of deferred payment. This use of money becomes important when credit is extended. Debts are typically stated in terms of money and paid in money. A particular money's effective performance of this function is dependent upon the other three functions listed above.

Money is a tool that facilitates economic transactions. Its usefulness is directly related to how well it performs its functions as a medium of exchange, standard of value, and store of purchasing power. This in turn in fact depends on the confidence people have that a particular money will perform these functions well. That confidence is not simply a psychological matter; it is ultimately dependent upon confidence being deserved. Whether confidence in a currency is deserved, while influenced by wars, crises, and other events, is to a very large degree dependent upon the wisdom of the monetary, economic, and social policies of governments.

At a number of points in this book we discuss "currency stabilization programs." These are domestic programs, sometimes taken at the urging of the International Monetary Fund, to maintain or to restore confidence in a currency. When in Chapter 3 we discuss "reserve currencies," it must be borne in mind that a currency can function effectively as a "reserve" only if its holders believe it to be a dependable store of purchasing power. The special drawing right, discussed in Chapters 1, 5, and 12, is a monetary reserve asset created by decisions taken within the International Monetary Fund. We give attention to rules for defining its purchasing power and to the collaboration required to protect its value.

F.A. Mann in his treatise, *The Legal Aspect of Money,* concludes his discussion of the legal definition of money with the statement that "according to its intrinsic nature money represents purchasing power."[11] The purchasing power of a managed currency is, as we have emphasized, dependent upon the good judgment of the governmental manager. Limitation in the supply of a money is a necessary condition if it is to have value. Persons who argue today in favor of a defined value relationship between money and a commodity (such as a scarce metal) do not do so because of a belief that money can have no purchasing power absent such a defined link, but because such a link would limit the ability of issuing governments to expand the money supply.[12] To the extent that governments act prudently there is no need for such a defined link; indeed, such a link can inhibit efforts to control the expansion or contraction of the money supply. The task of managing the supply of money within an economy is to maintain a volume of money which, together with other policies in the context of the circumstances of that country, results in price lev-

[11] F. A. Mann, *The Legal Aspect of Money* (4th ed.; Oxford: Oxford University Press, 1982), p. 28.

[12] It should be noted that even if an automatic link were maintained, there could be a decline in the power of the monetary unit to purchase other goods. The gold and silver that flowed into Europe following the Spanish conquest of South America led to price inflation and wage increases in Spain and other countries of Europe during the sixteenth century. Galbraith, *supra* note 5, pp. 10–14.

els, wage levels, and interest rates most appropriate to economic growth in real terms (people healthier, better housed, better fed, and better educated) and the desired levels of social, political, and financial stability.

Economists, bankers, and government officials continue to debate in almost every country of the world what price trends, wage trends, and interest rates are most desirable in that country at the particular time and what level of monetary expansion or contraction can best contribute to the desired conditions. Without taking a position on the precise means to be used, the Articles of Agreement of the International Monetary Fund obligate each member country of that organization to "endeavor to direct its [domestic and international] economic and financial policies toward the objective of fostering orderly economic growth with reasonable price stability, with due regard to its circumstances." The Articles also state an obligation to "seek to promote stability by fostering orderly underlying economic and financial conditions and a monetary system that does not tend to produce erratic disruptions."[13]

Definition of "Currency"

Money, as we have seen, can take the form of demand deposits (or other checkable deposits) in a bank, as well as the forms of coins and paper notes. Today in the United States and other highly developed countries, demand deposits and other checkable deposits form the largest part of the basic money supply. A demand deposit is an entry in a ledger account on a bank's books surrounded with certain legal rights.

Economists distinguish types of bank accounts and other financial instruments in terms of their use for payments purposes versus investment purposes and their degree of liquidity.[14] The growth of checkable interest-bearing accounts offered by banks, savings associations, and brokers has, in the United States, blurred the distinction between accounts held primarily for payments purposes and accounts held primarily for investment purposes. The Bank for International Settlements commented in its *Annual Report* in 1982: "In some countries changes in the financial system made it more difficult in practice even to identify groups of assets which corresponded to plausible theoretical concepts of money."[15]

The use of the word "currency" in this book is more expansive than the layman's typical use of the word. The reader should be aware of the distinction between the monetary issue of a country as a general concept (U.S. dollar, British pound sterling, French franc) and the various specific forms that the monetary issue may take in the context of payment transactions (coins, paper money, bank balances, bankers acceptances,[16] short-term government obligations). The

---

[13] Article IV, section 1(i) and (ii). The meaning of the quoted language is discussed in Chapter 11.

[14] In the United States in December 1983, Federal Reserve paper notes and Treasury-issued coins in circulation totaled $149 billion. Demand deposits (excluding government deposits) held at commercial banks in the United States totaled $251 billion, and other checkable deposits $135 billion. For some purposes money supply is also defined to include time deposits and money market accounts with banks and brokers. In addition there is "near money"—short-term U.S. government obligations, commercial paper, and bankers acceptances held by individuals and businesses excluding financial institutions. See tables entitled "money stock measures and components" published monthly in the *Federal Reserve Bulletin*. For a helpful discussion, although somewhat dated, of the components of the money supply in the United States and their measurement, see Henry C. Wallich and Warren T. Trepata, "The Redefinition of the Official Monetary Aggregates," *Case Western Reserve Journal of International Law*, vol. 12 (1980), p. 405.

[15] Bank for International Settlements, *52d Annual Report 1981/82*, p. 84.

[16] A bankers acceptance is an instrument frequently used for making payments in international transac-

author has adopted the monetary issue concept. The term "currency" as used in this book is to be understood broadly and encompasses coins, paper money, bank balances, and other payment instruments. In most contexts the primary reference is to bank balances. In some contexts government bonds and notes, even though not widely used as a means of payment, are considered "currency."[17]

U.S. Federal Reserve System

Most countries of the world have a central bank that issues the country's currency and regulates commercial banking activities. In the United States the central banking function is performed by the Federal Reserve System.[18] The Federal Reserve System has three levels of organization. At the base of the system are the member commercial banks, which are all the local national banks in the United States and many state banks that have chosen to join the system. These commercial banks own and maintain deposits with the Federal Reserve Bank in their district—the middle layer in the system. Above the twelve district Federal Reserve Banks is the Board of Governors of the Federal Reserve System. The Board of Governors consists of seven members appointed by the President of the United States with the advice and consent of the Senate. The Board is not subject to Presidential direction and Governors serve for long terms.

Membership in the Federal Reserve System involves both rights and obligations for the local bank. Rights: (1) ability to borrow from the Federal Reserve when necessary; (2) the use of Federal Reserve facilities for clearing checks and transferring funds; (3) the right to acquire Federal Reserve notes at any time by drawing a check against balances held by that bank with the Federal Reserve; (4) the receipt of information and advice provided by the System; and (5) a share in the ownership and control of the Federal Reserve Bank in its district. Obligations: (1) maintenance of a reserve deposit with the Federal Reserve in an amount prescribed by the Board of Governors; (2) compliance with laws and regulations concerning bank operations; and (3) subjection to examination and general supervision by Federal Reserve authorities.

Federal Reserve notes are the most important component of U.S. paper money. This is the

---

tions. An example is a draft payable to an exporter or his order that has been acknowledged by the bank on which it is drawn. See Continental Bank, *Commercial Letters of Credit* (Chicago, 1976), pp. 32 and 42.

[17] The Articles of Agreement of the International Monetary Fund prior to the Second Amendment effective April 1, 1978, contained a definition of "currency" for the purposes of that agreement. Article XIX(d), *original* and *first*. The Articles of Agreement now contain no definition of "currency." The meaning of the word is now a matter for interpretation in the particular context of its use in each provision where it appears. The concept of "freely usable currency" is used for certain purposes in the present Articles. See Chapter 10, *supra*, pages 380–381.

[18] The organization of the Federal Reserve System is set forth at *United States Code*, title 12, sections 221 et seq. For descriptions of the Federal Reserve System and its operations, see *The Federal Reserve System—Purposes and Functions* (6th ed.; Washington: Board of Governors of the Federal Reserve System, 1974); and Ralph A. Young, *Instruments of Monetary Policy in the United States: The Role of the Federal Reserve System* (Washington: IMF, 1973). See also Commerce Clearing House, *Federal Banking Law Reporter* (Chicago: CCH looseleaf service), paragraphs 1,101–1,314; 19,101–21,501; 28,111–39,825; and 56,001–57,467.

The functions performed by central banks in other countries are surveyed in Stephen A. Silard, "Money and Foreign Exchange," *International Encyclopedia of Comparative Law* (Tübingen: J.B.C. Mohr; The Hague: Mouton, 1975), vol. 17, chapter 20, sections 8–17. For more detailed information see Hans Aufricht (ed.), *Central Banking Legislation: A Collection of Central Bank, Monetary and Banking Laws* (2 vols.; Washington: IMF, 1961, 1967); Robert C. Effros (ed.), *Emerging Financial Centers: Legal and Institutional Framework* (Washington: IMF, 1982); Hans Aufricht, *Comparative Survey of Central Bank Law* (London: Stevens; New York: Praeger, 1965); and M.H. de Kock, *Central Banking* (4th ed.; London: Crosby Lockwood Staples, 1974).

only form of paper money currently being issued for public circulation.[19] Each of the twelve Federal Reserve Banks is authorized by law to issue Federal Reserve notes—the paper currency an American citizen typically carries in his wallet. Federal Reserve notes are printed by the Bureau of Printing and Engraving of the United States Treasury and delivered to the individual Federal Reserve Banks. To issue $1 million in Federal Reserve notes, the particular Federal Reserve Bank is required by statute to set aside as collateral $1 million in gold certificates, IMF special drawing rights, government securities (bills, notes, bonds), or specified types of short-term debt obligations issued by financial institutions and corporations.[20] Most frequently, U.S. government bills, notes, and bonds are used as collateral. The apparent conception of the law is that each new dollar note, upon entering circulation, assuming a relatively small steady flow, will have the same purchasing power as dollars already in circulation.

Federal Reserve notes are placed into circulation as follows: A member bank, e.g., First National Bank of Hometown, writes a check against its account with the Federal Reserve Bank payable to that bank and receives in exchange paper notes issued by the bank. An individual or corporate customer then writes a check against his account with First National Bank payable to First National and takes the paper notes informally called "cash."

Creation of Money Through Bank Credit

If an individual loans money to another person directly, he parts with the use of the funds for a period of time in return for the receipt of interest from the borrower.[21] However, when a commercial bank uses funds that a customer deposits with it, the customer continues to have a right to withdraw or transfer those funds.[22] Thus, while a loan by one individual to another does not increase the money supply, although it may increase its turnover (velocity), the extension of credit by a bank increases the money supply.

Assume that the banking authorities require a commercial bank to maintain reserves (primarily in the form of a deposit with the Federal Reserve Bank of its district) equal to at least 10 percent of current demand deposits (checking accounts) in the bank. A bank that holds $50 million in customer deposits will, thus, keep $5 million in reserve for those deposits with the Federal Reserve Bank in its district. Funds above that amount can serve as reserves for new deposit liabilities or be otherwise invested. When the bank makes a loan, it accepts a promissory note (an asset for the bank) from its customer and in exchange credits the customer's account with the amount of the loan (the credit in favor of the customer being a deposit liability of the bank). When the bank credits its customer's account on its books, the bank creates money. The bank does not have to transfer funds from its reserves or any other source to make the credit, so long as the bank's total reserves equal or exceed ten percent of total deposit liabilities.[23] That amount is judged ade-

---

[19] For other forms of paper money issued in the United States during the last two hundred years, see Walter W. Haines, *Money, Prices and Policy* (2d ed.; New York: McGraw-Hill Book Co., 1966), chapters 3, 6, 7, and 11.

[20] *United States Code*, title 12, section 412. Prior to the enactment of Public Law 90-269, approved March 18, 1968 (*United States Statutes at Large*, vol. 82, p. 50), at least one-fourth of the collateral had to be gold.

[21] For the borrower, the interest rate is the cost of borrowing money. It is a function of supply and demand for money and influenced by governmental policies.

[22] A commercial bank is obligated to permit withdrawal of a demand deposit (checking account) on demand. Commercial banks and other financial institutions can require advance notice (e.g., 30 days' notice) before permitting a withdrawal from a time deposit (sometimes called a savings account).

[23] The multiplying power of bank reserves and the process of deposit expansion are explained in *Federal Reserve System, supra* note 18, pp. 25-47; and Samuelson, *supra* note 1, pp. 282-91.

quate by the authorities, in our example, to provide the necessary liquidity for net withdrawals that may take place.

If a substantial number of holders of deposits sought to collect at once and a significant portion of the bank's loans outstanding were not yet due or were uncollectable, the banking system would at that point be under severe strain. This latter factor is considered by the Board of Governors of the Federal Reserve System in setting reserve requirements in relation to different classes of deposits. But within the viable range, the primary concern of the Federal Reserve when it makes changes in reserve requirements is the control of the size of the money supply.[24]

Management of the Money Supply

In the United States money is created primarily through the extension of credit by the banking system. There are several different types of actions that the Federal Reserve System can take that affect the size of money volume in the economy.

Changes in bank reserve requirements can affect the size of total deposits with the banks. As reserve requirements are increased, the amount of deposits created by loan should decrease. (A 12 percent reserve requirement means $1000 in reserves can support deposits totaling $8,333; 20 percent, only $5,000). Changes in reserve requirements are made by the Board of Governors of the System.[25] Changes in the past have been relatively infrequent.

"Open market" transactions of the Federal Reserve System directly affect the size of money volume. When the Federal Reserve System buys a U.S. Treasury bond in the open market, its action causes an increase in the money supply as follows: The check written to the order of the seller by the Federal Reserve Bank entitles the seller (or his endorsee) to a deposit with the Federal Reserve, the bond acquired by the Federal Reserve serving as the asset balancing that deposit-liability of the Federal Reserve.[26] The seller endorses the check to the commercial bank with which he does business in exchange for a credit to his demand account. At that point the money supply has been increased (the seller has substituted a payment instrument for an investment instrument).[27] But this is not the end of the story. The commercial bank accepting the check obtains a deposit in the amount of the check with a Federal Reserve Bank, that deposit being a reserve on the basis of which the commercial bank can expand deposits several times over through loans as described in the previous section.

When the Federal Reserve sells on the open market government bonds that it has held, the money supply is contracted. Both the demand deposits of the purchaser and reserves of his commercial bank are reduced. This causes the commercial bank to shrink its deposit liabilities. Decisions on whether the Federal Reserve System during a particular time period will be a net buyer or seller of government securities in the market are made by the Open Market Committee of the System which acts on behalf of the several Federal Reserve Banks.[28]

---

[24] The Board of Governors of the Federal Reserve System is authorized by *United States Code,* title 12, sections 461, 601, 611, and 3105, to set reserve requirements. Federal Reserve System Regulation D, which is amended from time to time, sets the specific required reserves within the statutory range; *Code of Federal Regulations,* title 12, part 204. The policies implemented by the Board of Governors when it changes reserve requirements are discussed in Young, *supra* note 18, pp. 123–46 and 165–89.

[25] See note 24, *idem.*

[26] See text accompanying note 10, *supra.*

[27] See note 14, *supra,* and accompanying text.

[28] See generally Paul Meek, *U.S. Monetary Policy and Financial Markets* (New York: Federal Reserve Bank of New York, 1982), chapters 2, 5, 6, and 7.

Interest rates are a function of the supply of and demand for credit. The relationship between interest rates and credit volume is an interactive one. In addition to the monetary control techniques mentioned above which have an impact on interest rates, the Federal Reserve System controls certain interest rates directly. Federal Reserve Banks set the "discount rate" at which they are prepared to buy bankers acceptances not yet matured and other money market paper from the member banks. The Federal Reserve Banks also set the interest rates on loans of reserves they are prepared to make to member banks that must increase reserves to meet required levels.[29]

In addition to the techniques mentioned above, which are also used in other countries, another technique of monetary control is widely used by authorities abroad. This is the direct control of credit. The effects of changes in the quantity and terms of credit can be felt with less time lag than other techniques. Direct controls on credit do not require highly developed capital markets, although some countries that use direct controls have well developed markets.[30]

The techniques outlined above, which alter interest rates and money volume, are used to achieve more fundamental goals including desired levels of prices, levels of employment, and the relationship of consumption and savings. The primary objective of monetary policy must, however, be the maintenance of confidence in the monetary instrument, which means protection of its purchasing power. If confidence is lost the instrument cannot be used effectively to achieve the other goals.

Fiscal policy as well as monetary policy is used to promote the above objectives. Fiscal policy relates to the management of government income and expenditures and the management of the size and character of the national debt. It relates to decisions on spending and taxes, and whether, for example, the national debt should be financed through the issuance of short-term or long-term bonds. Effective governmental planning involves the use of both fiscal and monetary policies. The financing of government budget deficits, for example, impacts money supply. If the financing comes from sales of bonds to individuals and corporations, government spending may be substituted for private spending for consumption and investment. On the other hand, sales to the banking system of government bonds issued to finance a deficit may cause the money supply to increase and put inflationary pressure on prices and wages. International institutions give attention to national monetary and fiscal policies because those policies have international implications.

---

[29] The techniques discussed in this section and other techniques for controlling money volume are treated in *Federal Reserve System, supra* note 18; Young, *supra* note 18; and Ralph C. Bryant, *Controlling Money: The Federal Reserve and its Critics* (Washington: Brookings Institution, 1983).

[30] For information on techniques of monetary control used in European and other countries, see OECD, *The Role of Monetary Policy in Demand Management: The Experience of Six Major Countries* (Paris, 1975); *21st Report on the Activities of the [EEC] Monetary Committee,* in *Official Journal of the European Communities,* no. C-166, July 7, 1980, p. 1 at pp. 6–39; and Paul Meek (ed.), *Central Bank Views on Monetary Targeting* (New York: Federal Reserve Bank of New York, 1983). See also Silard, *supra* note 18, sections 18–22; and *Activities by Various Central Banks to Promote Economic and Social Programs; Staff Report, Committee on Banking and Currency,* U.S. House of Representatives, 91st Congress, 2d Session (1970).

Typical Foreign Currency Transactions

Overview

In the world in which we live, individual nations maintain a large measure of control over their monetary policies. While a few countries share common currencies, the general practice is that each country has its own currency. The price at which one currency is traded for another is called an "exchange rate." The *Wall Street Journal* includes a table each day listing the selling prices quoted by New York banks the previous business day for making bank transfers abroad in the listed foreign currencies. These are the rates quoted by banks to their customers for small transactions, and might be called the retail rates. The rates for larger transactions will usually be more attractive to the customer. The newspaper also usually carries a news article on developments in foreign exchange trading among commercial banks. The rates mentioned here are the rates in the inter-bank (wholesale) market.

Examples of transactions that may require an individual or corporation to obtain foreign currency balances include:

(1) Travel abroad by tourists, businessmen, or emigrants, necessitating the expenditure of foreign currency.
(2) Imports of goods from abroad against payment in the foreign exporter's currency.
(3) Costs of construction or manufacturing abroad to be paid in foreign currency.
(4) Purchase of securities against payment in foreign currency.
(5) Service of debts and dividend payments to be made in foreign currency.

Examples of transactions by an individual or corporation that result in the acquisition of foreign currency balances that it may wish to sell for its national currency include:

(1) Foreign currency balances unspent by tourists or businessmen returning from abroad or immigrants entering from abroad.
(2) Export of goods against payment in foreign currencies.
(3) Sale of securities against payment in foreign currencies.
(4) Receipts of interest, dividends, royalties, and principal in foreign currencies.

Foreign exchange transactions require that someone be willing to sell one currency and buy another. That "someone" may be a local bank, a large bank actively engaged in international transactions, a government central bank, or an international organization.

Acquisition and Use of Foreign Paper Money

A U.S. resident desiring to take a vacation in Canada may purchase from his local bank a small amount of Canadian paper notes. He can acquire additional Canadian money in Canada by endorsing "traveler's checks" payable in U.S. dollars or by writing a check drawn upon his U.S. bank. The Canadian individuals or banks who take these checks obtain rights to deposits of U.S. dollars in U.S. banks. The American tourist can also acquire Canadian funds in exchange for U.S. Federal Reserve notes.

At this point in the discussion several things need to be noted. The United States government permits U.S. citizens to write checks against their bank accounts in the U.S. payable to foreign nationals outside the United States. Some countries forbid their nationals to make such transfers. Also, the United States government permits U.S. citizens to transport U.S. paper money from inside to outside the United States. Some countries require that their paper money stay within that country's territory. Canadian law permits Canadian residents to accept U.S. Federal Reserve notes and checks drawn on U.S. banks. Finally, U.S. residents are fortunate that Canadian banks and most Canadian merchants will accept U.S. paper money and checks drawn in U.S. dollars on U.S. banks; the Canadian bank or merchant thus assumes the burden to use the dollars or to exchange them for Canadian funds.

Import of Goods Against Payment in the Importer's Currency

If a U.S. merchant wishes to buy goods from an exporter in London, he can send an ordinary check payable in U.S. dollars drawn on his local bank account to a New York bank, designated by the exporter, for deposit to that firm's account. This method of payment is very simple for the U.S. merchant.

A U. K. exporter's willingness to accept payment in dollars will depend upon whether there are items it wishes to buy in the United States and how soon, whether it can and wishes to invest the dollars, or whether it can readily exchange the dollars it obtains for pounds sterling or for another currency that it needs. Generally, exporters will only maintain accounts in foreign countries where they do sufficient business to justify assuming the burden of currency conversion. This method of payment is also dependent upon national law permitting the exporter to maintain a foreign currency account with a foreign bank and to receive payments for exports through that account.

Import of Goods Against Payment in the Exporter's Currency

Suppose that a resident of the United States, following correspondence with a British antique dealer, wishes to purchase an antique desk. Suppose that the British seller insists that payment be made in pounds sterling. In this case, if the purchaser's local bank has a sterling account with, say, Barclays Bank in London, the local bank will draw a draft by which it directs Barclays to pay £2000 to the order of the British antique dealer and to debit its account with Barclay by £2000. In simple terms, this is a check payable to the antique dealer and drawn upon the local bank's sterling account with Barclays Bank. The cost to the buyer will be based on the exchange rate for bank transfers plus a service charge. In this case, the U.S. buyer transfers dollars he owns to his local bank in return for that bank transferring sterling it owns to the British seller of the desk.[31]

Opening a Bank Account in a Foreign Country in that Country's Currency

Suppose a U.S. student plans to spend a year in the Netherlands. He does not wish to carry large amounts of U.S. or Netherlands paper money or persuade Dutch merchants to accept checks drawn in U.S. dollars on U.S. banks. He wishes to open a guilder deposit account with a Dutch bank. He will then be able to give Dutch merchants guilder checks written on his Dutch bank account. He could also obtain Netherlands paper money by writing a check on his Dutch bank account. How is a foreign account like this established?

A customer in this type of situation may go to, say, the First National Bank of Hometown

---

[31] If the buyer wishes to be sure that the desk is shipped before the British seller is paid and the British seller wishes to be assured that he will be paid if he ships the desk, a letter of credit may be used. See Andreas F. Lowenfeld, *International Private Trade* (2d ed.; New York: Matthew Bender, 1981), pp. 125–83. For general information on the financing of exports and imports, see Morgan Guaranty Trust Company of New York, *The Financing of Exports and Imports: A Guide to Procedures* (New York, 1980); or Continental Bank, *Commercial Letters of Credit, supra* note 16.

and say, "I want to open an account in an Amsterdam bank denominated in guilders in the amount of 10,000 guilders." The bank officer, after checking exchange rates and allowing a profit to the bank, says, "If you write our bank a check for $3,450, we shall arrange for an account in your favor in the amount of 10,000 guilders to be opened at the Algemene Bank Nederland in Amsterdam."

How does the First National Bank of Hometown handle the mechanics of this transaction? In the simplest of cases, the First National Bank may already hold a deposit account with Algemene Bank Nederland in guilders. If so, the Hometown bank may simply instruct Algemene Bank to debit Hometown's account and open an account for the student in the amount of 10,000 guilders.

Suppose that the requested transaction is larger or that the First National Bank of Hometown does not hold a deposit with Algemene Bank Nederland; but the two banks are "correspondents," that is, they have established arrangements to deal with each other and have agreed codes for verifying transactions and means of verifying signatures of bank officers. In that case, First National might contact the New York office of Algemene Bank by telephone to learn the rates at which that bank is willing to buy dollars and sell guilders. If the rate is mutually satisfactory, the transaction will proceed. Assume the exchange rate agreed upon by the two banks is 2.9240 (i.e., U.S. $0.3420 per guilder). The telephone agreement will be followed by a computer-coded message through SWIFT.[32] Two days after the deal was struck, in accordance with banking convention, First National will open a credit in favor of Algemene Bank Nederland on its books in the amount of $3,420 and Algemene Bank will credit the student with 10,000 guilders. In this example, First National Bank will keep $30 for its expenses and profit on the transaction.

As in the previous examples, the foreigner (Algemene Bank) is only willing to undertake this transaction if it can use the U.S. dollars or can conveniently exchange them for its own currency or another national currency that it can use. Algemene Bank will probably not leave idle the $3,420 credited to it on the books of First National Bank. It will probably transfer those funds to another U.S. bank and then sell the funds for guilders in another transaction, or pay off a loan it has undertaken, or invest in a short-term, interest-bearing security.

In the example above, First National Bank of Hometown obtained a quotation from Algemene Bank and, being satisfied on the rate, proceeded with the transaction. However, if the transaction is large, the First National Bank would usually contact several banks (U.S. and foreign) or brokers in New York and in Europe. It would be prepared to deal with any of a number of banks that hold guilder deposits in Netherlands banks, and will be interested in the best rate. Suppose the customer needs 10,000,000 guilders. And, suppose Morgan Guaranty Trust Co. quotes the best rate (2.9300) but its deposits are with Nederlandsche Middenstandsbank. In that event First National Bank of Hometown will credit Morgan Guaranty with $3,412,969 (2.9300/1 × 10,000,000). Morgan Guaranty will instruct Middenstandsbank to transfer 10,000,000 guilders to Algemene Bank Nederland for the credit of First National Bank of Hometown; First National will then instruct Algemene to transfer the credit to the account of Charles Customer. The transaction looks like this:

---

[32] For many years, virtually all foreign exchange transactions of significant size were settled through cabled instructions. Now North American and European banks write payment instructions in a standardized format and transmit the instructions through a computer-based system of the Society for Worldwide Interbank Financial Telecommunications (SWIFT). See Herbert F. Lingl, "Risk Allocation in International Interbank Electronic Fund Transfers: CHIPS & SWIFT," *Harvard International Law Journal*, vol. 22 (1981), p. 621; and Ezra U. Byler and James C. Baker, "S.W.I.F.T.: A Fast Method to Facilitate International Financial Transactions," *Journal of World Trade Law*, vol. 17 (1983), p. 458.

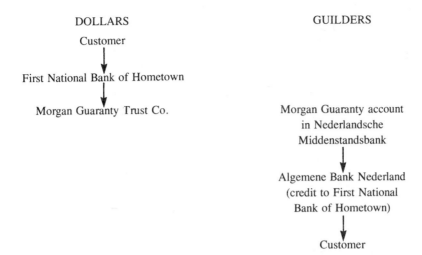

DOLLARS

Customer

↓

First National Bank of Hometown

↓

Morgan Guaranty Trust Co.

GUILDERS

Morgan Guaranty account
in Nederlandsche
Middenstandsbank

↓

Algemene Bank Nederland
(credit to First National
Bank of Hometown)

↓

Customer

All of these transactions involve bookkeeping entries with no physical paper money changing hands. The customer at the beginning had a bank account with First National Bank of Hometown. That is, the books of First National showed a credit entry in favor of Customer. When the customer wrote a check payable to First National, that credit was transferred to First National itself. First National then entered a credit of $3,412,969 from itself to Morgan Guaranty.

At the beginning, Morgan Guaranty had a credit of 1,000,000 guilders or more in its favor running from Middenstandsbank. It instructs Middenstandsbank to transfer a credit of 10,000,000 guilders to Algemene Bank. Then Algemene Bank becomes the owner of a credit running from Middenstandsbank to it, and Algemene enters a credit running from it to First National Bank. Upon First National's instructions the latter credit is transferred to run from Algemene to First National's customer.

Other Transactions

The currency exchange aspect of payment of a debt in a foreign currency, payment for goods, or payment for an investment security is essentially the same as in the examples above. There may be national legal restrictions on exchange transactions that bar transactions in certain categories or that structure the payments technique used. In some cases special permission may have to be obtained from exchange control authorities. Many Americans are not familiar with exchange restrictions. Chapter 10 is devoted to this subject.

Importance of the Banking System to International Transactions

At least one bank, and typically many more, of virtually all countries in the world maintains a bank account in U.S. dollars in a bank in New York City. Thus, if a U.S. exporter wants payment in U.S. dollars, the foreign importer can arrange for the transfer of U.S. dollars held by that foreign country bank with a bank in New York to be transferred to the credit of the U.S. exporter at a bank of the exporter's choice.[33]

A U.S. importer, who is required by a foreign seller to pay for goods in the seller's currency, can arrange to credit the dollar account maintained in a New York bank by a bank of the seller's country in return for that bank crediting the seller's account, say, in Italy with lire. In the case of an exporter in one country (say India) selling to an importer in another (say Colombia) when it happens that no Indian bank maintains accounts in Colombia and vice versa, the transaction can be handled through New York. For example, the Colombian importer's bank debits the importer's peso account and transfers dollars it holds in a New York bank to the exporter's bank. The Indian exporter's bank in turn credits the Indian seller's rupee account.

Roles Played by Banks in Transactions Previously Discussed

Typically banks themselves set the exchange rates for small transactions with customers. The bank will debit the customer's dollar account in an amount equivalent to the foreign currency provided, making allowance for the bank's profit. Or, when a foreign currency is received from a customer, it will credit the customer's account with dollars equivalent to the foreign currency, making allowance for a profit. The bank normally acts as a principal in these transactions. On larger transactions, the bank will quote, usually by telephone, specific rates to the customer for that transaction. Again, the bank acts as a principal. It quotes a rate intended to assure that the bank can "cover" the transaction at a profit.[34] A customer may instruct its bank to buy or sell "at best" in respect of currencies which do not have a good market. In this case, the bank will enter the market and gradually buy or sell the currency over a period of hours, with the customer paying or receiving the average rate after adjustment for the bank's profit.[35]

To accommodate trading requirements, banks maintain "working balances" in the form of foreign currency deposits held with correspondent banks abroad. The amount of foreign exchange held by a commercial bank, and the countries of issue of the currencies, will be related to the size and frequency of transactions with customers and its willingness or lack of willingness to hold foreign currencies. However, as in the United States, demand deposits in foreign banks usually earn no interest or very low interest. Thus, a bank will normally wish to maintain its foreign "working balances" as low as possible. If it wishes to hold a foreign currency above amounts

[33] If no bank in a particular country maintains a dollar account in New York, a bank of that country will almost certainly maintain a sterling account in London or a franc account in Paris. Thus, through exchange transactions in sterling or francs and then transactions between the sterling or francs and dollars, it will be possible for the foreign purchaser to arrange for payments to the American exporter to be made in dollars in the United States, unless exchange restrictions make the payment unlawful. What is essential is that there be a network of deposit accounts and lines of credit so that no country is so isolated that none of its banks hold deposit accounts in banks of other countries.

While the network of banking offices is much smaller than the network of correspondent accounts of banks worldwide, it is very substantial. At the end of 1981, some 600 banks, from about 85 countries, had offices in countries outside the legal domicile of the headquarters.

[34] When a bank buys or sells a foreign currency, an exposure called an "open position" is created. Until this position can be covered by buying or selling an equivalent amount of the same currency, the bank is exposed to the risk that exchange rates may move to create a loss. A "long position" is created when the bank buys more currency than is sold, and a "short position" when more currency is sold than bought. See Roger M. Kubarych, *Foreign Exchange Markets in the United States* (rev. ed.; New York: Federal Reserve Bank of New York, 1983), p. 23.

[35] Kubarych, *idem*, p. 33.

necessary for immediate needs, it may hold time deposits or purchase short-term foreign government bonds denominated in the foreign currency.

The transactions that customers bring to their banks are not entirely predictable. A commercial bank may accumulate deposits in foreign banks beyond what it judges appropriate working balances, which it wishes to sell as a principal. Or the bank may have a client for whom it acts as agent who wishes to sell foreign currency balances. The bank may wish to purchase foreign currencies to rebuild its own working balances in foreign countries or, acting as agent, may wish to purchase foreign currency for a client. A bank's working balances held in foreign banks may not cover, and are not necessarily intended to cover, all the spot transactions (exchange transactions executed with delivery immediately or within two business days) over an extended period of time or even over a single day. Thus, the bank may frequently in the course of a single day both buy and sell substantial amounts of foreign currencies. How does a bank deal in the foreign exchange market?

Further Points on How Foreign Exchange is Bought and Sold Among Banks

While a foreign exchange transaction in its simplest form is a trade of bank balances—one in currency A in country A and the other in currency B in country B—the mechanisms by which banks obtain quotations and enter into transactions in the inter-bank market are somewhat complex. The inter-bank wholesale foreign exchange market is immense. In an average day U.S. banks may engage in $20 billion or more in gross foreign exchange transactions.

Over half of the wholesale foreign exchange transactions by U.S. banks are arranged through foreign exchange brokers. Banks use brokers in order to maintain anonymity when seeking to buy or sell a currency and also to reduce the number of telephone calls they make before consummating a transaction. A bank will indicate to a broker bids or offers for specific foreign currency amounts at specified exchange rates. Banks may call the broker and the broker may call banks for quotations. The broker collects these bids and offers from its client banks and communicates back to the banks the highest exchange rate bid and the lowest exchange rate offered for the currency, along with the amounts of the currency bid and offered. Once the broker has arranged a deal, he discloses the counter-party and the contract is made directly between the two banks. For each transaction the broker arranges, he receives a commission which is paid one-half by the buying and one-half by the selling bank.[36]

Somewhat less than half of the wholesale foreign exchange transactions by U.S. banks involve direct dealings between banks without the use of brokers. In direct dealing in the New York market one bank typically telephones another to ask for what is called a "two-way price," which consists of an exchange rate at which the responding bank is prepared to buy, say, Deutsche mark against dollars and a different rate at which the responding bank will sell mark. The difference between the bid and offer quotations is known as the "spread." The spread reflects the respondent bank's assessment of the risk involved in doing business at that time and accepting potential adverse exchange rate movements before an offsetting transaction can be made. Generally, the greater the perceived risk the wider the spread.[37] The calling bank normally does not reveal in asking for the two-way price whether it wishes to buy or sell mark. If the bank's intentions are

[36] See Kubarych, *supra* note 34, pp. 12–15. The broker's commission varies depending upon the currency traded, but in general amounts to about $25 per $1 million. The amounts of currencies traded in a day through brokers amount to very large totals. While the broker's role was formerly only for dealings with New York and London banks, New York brokers now take bids and offers from around the world.

[37] See Kubarych, *idem*, pp. 12–13.

known or if the respondent bank guesses its intentions from market trends, the respondent is likely to shade its quotations accordingly. Banks respond to the requests from other banks for "two-way quotations" because they are in the business of trading currencies and wish to make a market. They know that at other times they will be initiating such calls. A bank can, however, unless forbidden by law, decline to respond to an invitation from another bank to quote rates. The degree of discretion banks have in quoting rates will depend upon the laws of their countries and the actions of the official monetary authorities.

Backing up the trading between commercial banks, including trading of currency balances between commercial banks in different countries, are the relations of the commercial banks and their national central banks. In most countries a state central bank will buy foreign currencies from the commercial banks of that country. In some countries commercial banks are required by law to sell foreign currency balances they obtain to their central bank. Conversely, central banks may sell foreign currency balances (held with banks abroad) to commercial banks. These transactions can occur directly between commercial banks and central banks or they can occur as the result of "open market" transactions by central banks. The Federal Reserve Bank of New York, for example, can instruct the Chase Manhattan Bank or another bank to buy or sell currencies for its account without Chase disclosing for whom it is acting just as it would not disclose the name of a corporate customer. In the United States the Federal Reserve System buys and sells foreign currencies in the market—thus supplying foreign currency to the market or withdrawing currency from the market—when necessary to counter disorderly conditions but without attempting to maintain a particular rate. In other countries the monetary authorities may intervene in the market not only to counter disorderly conditions but to influence rates or to assure that a particular rate range is maintained.[38]

A central bank, holding a foreign currency in excess of its needs, may sell the currency in an open market transaction or may clear it bilaterally with the central bank of the issuing state. Regional clearing arrangements, such as the arrangements of the Asian Clearing Union, are used in some cases. Sometimes there is no immediate way, because of exchange controls or the effects a large sale would have on the market, for a central bank to dispose of excess holdings of a currency.

Central monetary authorities may need to acquire foreign currencies to provide to their residents for making payments abroad, to sell in the exchange markets to counter disorderly conditions or maintain rates with their own currency, to redeem balances of their own currency held by foreign monetary authorities, or to restore reserve levels. Procedures by which monetary authorities can acquire foreign currencies are treated in Chapters 3–9.

Spot, Forward, and Swap Transactions

Up to this point in the discussion we have for simplicity assumed that the parties involved—individuals, corporations, banks—wished to buy or sell foreign exchange immediately. Such purchases and sales are called "spot" transactions which, by convention, are usually settled two business days after the transaction is originated. However, a merchant may sell goods with payment due in, say, 90 days. There are many situations in which an individual, company, or bank will know that it will acquire foreign currency on a future date or will need to use foreign currency

---

[38] While supplying foreign currency to the exchange market in its country and buying foreign currency from the exchange market are usually a central bank's most important foreign exchange operations, a central bank may also handle foreign currency payments and receipts for the government and public sector enterprises.

on a future date. It may wish to take action in advance of the settlement date to protect itself against an adverse change in exchange rates. However, it may not wish to acquire a non-interest-bearing deposit account in a foreign currency which it will simply hold for, say, 90 days and then transfer to the foreign vendor from whom it is, say, purchasing machinery.

Banks can enter into "forward" exchange contracts with their customers. Forward exchange contracts are bank-created instruments in which the bank promises to accept or deliver foreign currency at a future date at a stated price. The maturity of a forward exchange contract can be a few days, months, or even years. The exchange rate is fixed at the time the transaction is agreed, but until the maturity date no accounts are debited or credited. Banks or their larger customers can also purchase or sell foreign government obligations maturing on or near the appropriate dates. The use of the bank instruments or government obligations makes it possible to earn interest in the meantime.

A company that is to receive a foreign currency payment in the future can protect itself against an unfavorable change in exchange rates by purchasing a forward contract to sell that currency at a future date at a specified rate. Another technique is for the company to borrow foreign funds which are promptly converted to its own country's currency; later, the foreign currency payment upon receipt is used to pay off the foreign currency loan.[39]

Banks among themselves infrequently engage in simple forward exchange trading. For future maturities they, and sometimes corporations, instead trade on the basis of what is called a "swap." This involves the simultaneous purchase and sale of the same amount of a currency to the same counterparty for different maturities at specified rates. That is, a bank buys a currency and agrees to sell it back at a specified future date. A swap transaction allows each party to use a needed currency for a specified period of time in exchange for a currency not needed for that time. For example, a bank may foresee heavy buying of Deutsche mark in the next three months. Having a small supply of mark and an excess amount of Italian lire, the bank will seek a swap with a bank in the opposite position. The swap allows both banks to utilize needed currency for a period of time without fear of changing exchange rates in the interim. Similarly, it offers a useful investment possibility for temporarily idle currency balances.[40]

Eurocurrencies

Normally, a deposit account is denominated in the currency of the nation state where the deposit is maintained and is a claim on that state's economy. Foreign commercial banks and branches of U.S. banks situated in foreign countries also maintain on their books deposit accounts for customers (which can include other banks) denominated in U.S. dollars. The mechanism by which this occurs is as follows:

Suppose a corporation owns a deposit account denominated in U.S. dollars with a U.S. bank in the United States. It makes a time deposit with a European bank, transferring a claim on its New York account. Conventional practice in this situation, as described earlier, would be for the European bank to assume ownership of the deposit held in New York and for the European bank to credit the corporation with equivalent currency of that bank's state, say, Belgian francs. How-

---

[39] The practices of commercial firms in the management of their foreign currency positions are analyzed in Raj Aggarwal, *Financial Policies for the Multinational Company: The Management of Foreign Exchange* (New York: Praeger Publishers, 1976); and in David K. Eiteman and Arthur I. Stonehill, *Multinational Business Finance* (3d ed.; Reading, Massachusetts: Addison-Wesley Publishing Co., 1982).

[40] See Kubarych, *supra* note 34, pp. 10–12. For further information on foreign exchange trading by commercial banks, see generally Kubarych, *supra;* and Raymond G. F. Coninx, *Foreign Exchange Dealer's Handbook* (New York: Pick Publishing Co., 1982).

ever, instead of doing this, the European bank (upon assuming ownership of the deposit with the New York bank) credits its customer with a time deposit in the European bank denominated in U.S. dollars. The effect of the transaction is that while there has been a change of ownership of a deposit in the United States, the total remaining constant, an additional deposit denominated in dollars has been created outside the United States. To take the next step, the European bank can make a dollar-denominated loan to another customer receiving a promissory note carrying interest and payable in U.S. dollars. This loan is accomplished by the European bank crediting its new customer's account in its book in an amount denominated in U.S. dollars. That customer can in turn transfer the dollar-denominated funds to another bank.

Eurodollar banking received its impetus in the early 1960s when states in Eastern Europe desired to hold dollar-denominated deposits for use in commercial transactions but wished to hold them outside the United States to reduce the effective risk that U.S. authorities might "freeze" the accounts under foreign asset control regulations.[41] Rather than carry the deposits in their own names with U.S. banks, they were carried with banks in Europe, which in turn held deposits with U.S. banks. The growth of Eurodollar banking received further stimulus from U.S. corporations that found it necessary to borrow abroad rather than in the United States to finance foreign investments during the period 1965 to 1974 when the U.S. government and Federal Reserve System placed restraints on monetary transfers to nonresidents in capital transactions.[42] Accounts denominated in U.S. dollars maintained at banks outside the United States are called "Eurodollar" accounts whether the bank where they are booked is in Europe, the Caribbean, the Middle East, or the Far East. Similarly, banks outside the Netherlands may maintain accounts for customers and make loans denominated in guilders; these accounts are called "Euroguilder" accounts.[43]

In order to permit U.S. banks to participate in the Eurocurrency markets, including the Eurodollar market, without the necessity of booking accounts in branches in foreign countries, U.S. banks (and foreign banks) have been permitted since December 1981 to establish "international banking facilities" (IBFs) at their offices in the United States.[44] These facilities, which are

[41] See *Code of Federal Regulations,* title 31, chapter V, part 500. The regulations are presently applied to only a few countries.

[42] See Chapter 10, *supra,* page 450 (note 327) and 451 (note 331).

[43] The following books by economists and bankers provide overviews of the Eurocurrency markets: F. John Mathis (ed.), *Offshore Lending by U.S. Commercial Banks* (2d ed.; Washington, D.C.: Bankers Association for Foreign Trade; Philadelphia: Robert Morris Associates, 1981); R.B. Johnston, *The Economics of the Euro-Market: History, Theory and Policy* (New York: St. Martin's Press, 1982); Paul Einzig and Brian Scott Quinn, *The Euro-Dollar System* (6th ed.; London: Macmillan, 1977); John Hewson and Eisuke Sakakibara, *The Eurocurrency Markets and Their Implications* (Lexington, Massachusetts: D.C. Heath, 1975); Jane Sneddon Little, *Euro-Dollars: The Money-Market Gypsies* (New York: Harper & Row, 1975); and Geoffrey Bell, *The Euro-Dollar Market and the International Financial System* (New York and Toronto: John Wiley & Sons, 1973).

For legal analyses see Cynthia C. Lichtenstein, "U.S. Banks and the Eurocurrency Markets: The Regulatory Structure," *Banking Law Journal,* vol. 99 (1982), p. 484; John E. Hoffman, Jr., and Ian H. Giddy, "Lessons from the Iranian Experience: National Currencies as International Money," and oral discussion, *Journal of Comparative Corporate Law and Securities Regulation,* vol. 3 (1981), pp. 271–86; F.A. Mann, "Zahlungsprobleme bei Fremdwährungsschulden," *Annuaire Suisse de Droit International,* vol. 36 (1980), p. 93; Henry Harfield, "International Money Management: The Eurodollar," *Banking Law Journal,* vol. 89 (1972), p. 579; Robert C. Effros, "The Whys and Wherefores of Eurodollars," *Business Lawyer,* vol. 23 (1968), p. 629; and Joseph Dach, "Legal Nature of the Euro-Dollar," *American Journal of Comparative Law,* vol. 13 (1964), p. 30.

[44] *Code of Federal Regulations,* title 12, sections 204.8 and 217.1(1). See generally Lichtenstein, *supra* note 43; and Beth M. Farber, "International Banking Facilities: Defining a Greater U.S. Presence in the Eurodollar Market," *Law and Policy in International Business,* vol. 13 (1981), p. 997.

to some degree insulated from the U.S. domestic economy, are under a less stringent regulatory regime than "regular" U.S. banking offices. In the light of the establishment of IBFs, the critical criterion of a Eurocurrency deposit is no longer its physical location outside the territory of the country issuing the currency in which the claim is denominated. "Eurocurrency" is now probably best defined as a monetary claim that is not a direct demand on the domestic economy of the country issuing the currency in which the claim is denominated.

United States banks are not required by the Federal Reserve System to maintain reserves or observe interest rate ceilings with respect to deposit liabilities of their branches abroad so long as the depositors are entitled under the deposit contracts to demand payment only at an office located outside the United States,[45] nor are they required to maintain reserves or observe interest rate ceilings with respect to deposit liabilities of IBFs if stated conditions are met.[46] The foreign branches and the IBFs are, however, subject to supervision by U.S. authorities for prudential practices.[47] "Regular" U.S. banks are required to maintain reserves (being phased in at three percent) with respect to positive net balances due by those offices to the foreign branches or IBFs.[48] United States branches (other than IBFs) of foreign banks, with certain exceptions, are required to maintain reserves and observe interest rate ceilings established by the Federal Reserve in the same manner as other U.S. banks.[49] The regulations in other countries vary. Often banking offices conducting Eurocurrency activities are relieved of requirements imposed for purposes of monetary control or protection of local depositors. Offshore banking centers in some developing countries have very liberal regimes.[50]

The Eurocurrency markets have two main components. Bank dealings with corporations, investors, and governments constitute one component, with banks bidding both to attract deposits and to make loans. The other component is the inter-bank market in which banks bid for deposits of other banks, or place funds with them, to manage the balance between the maturities of their assets and liabilities. The mainstay of the markets is the non-negotiable fixed-term time deposit. There are also negotiable Eurodollar certificates of deposit. While delivery and custody of the certificates are normally in London, payment is made in New York clearing house funds.

The Eurocurrency markets have grown through effective financial intermediation. They provide funds to borrowers (usually commercial banks, large corporations, central banks, and governments) at interest rates that are lower than otherwise available. They usually pay interest to depositors at higher rates than available in the country of issue of the currency used. This is made possible by the efficiency of banking operations, the absence of reserve requirements, and the absence of legal limits on the interest rates that can be paid to depositors. Conditions that permit

---

[45] *Code of Federal Regulations*, title 12, sections 204.1(c)(5) and 217.0(d). Deposits payable to U.S. residents in amounts under $100,000 are not treated as "payable only at an office located outside the United States" regardless of the deposit contract terms. Sections 204.2(t) and 217.1(k). See generally Lichtenstein, *supra* note 43.

[46] *Code of Federal Regulations*, title 12, sections 204.8, 217.1(a), (b), and (1), and 217.7(a). See Lichtenstein, *supra* note 43.

[47] See Chapter 12, *supra*, page 619 et seq.

[48] *Code of Federal Regulations*, title 12, sections 204.2(h), 204.3, 204.4, and 204.9.

[49] *Code of Federal Regulations*, title 12, sections 204.1(c)(2) and 217.0(c).

[50] For summaries and texts of banking laws, see Effros, *Emerging Financial Centers, supra* note 18; OECD, *Regulations Affecting International Banking Operations, 1981-I*, and *idem, 1981-II* (Paris: OECD, 1981, 1982); Jane Welch (ed.), *The Regulation of Banks in the Member States of the EEC* (2d ed.; The Hague: Martinus Nijhoff; London: Graham & Trotman, 1981); and Stanley Crossick and Margie Lindsay, *European Banking Law: An Analysis of Community and Member State Legislation* (London: Financial Times Business Information, 1983).

Eurocurrency markets to work effectively include: (a) international interest-rate differences which reflect differences in money-market regulations and business conditions, (b) sufficient freedom from exchange controls to give borrowers and lenders access to the markets, (c) some stretching of maturity transformation,[51] (d) confidence of borrowers and lenders in the underlying currencies (dollar, guilder, mark, etc.), and (e) confidence of depositors in the banks in which Eurocurrency deposits are held and confidence by the banks in their borrowers. A large portion of the transactions is inter-bank. Banks deposit excess funds in the market and often borrow in the market to meet their liquidity needs. Some governments hold substantial portions of their monetary reserves in Eurocurrency deposits.[52]

The Bank for International Settlements, in its *Annual Report,* regularly publishes data on the external liabilities in Eurocurrencies of commercial banks in the major Eurocurrency banking centers. A special committee of central bank officials, with staff support from the Bank, reviews developments in the Eurocurrency markets and serves as a forum for sharing information. The International Monetary Fund in the future may also regularly publish data on external liabilities and assets of commercial banks.[53]

An immense literature appeared in the 1970s on the economic character of Eurocurrency bank deposit liabilities and related assets and the domestic monetary effects of Eurocurrency transactions.[54] It is important to note that, under current customary banking practice, the transfer by a commercial bank (whether U.S. or foreign) of a large Eurocurrency claim denominated in dollars involves use of the computerized Clearing House International Payments System (CHIPS) in New York. Net positions in the system are settled, the same day as the clearing, by transfers on accounts at the Federal Reserve Bank of New York. Thus, net positions are settled in regular dollar claims on the U.S. economy.[55]

Scholars and officials have been concerned about how to deal with liquidity or solvency crises involving banks engaged in large-scale Eurocurrency operations. Suppose, for example, that a group of loans made in Eurodollars to several developing countries or other large borrowers are not repaid and the liquidities of the lending banks are seriously threatened. What governments or central banks, if any, would bear responsibility to act? This question and questions concerning macroeconomic aspects of commercial bank activities conducted in Eurocurrencies are explored in Chapter 12.[56]

Exchange Rates

Varieties of Exchange Arrangements

There are several basic methods by which currencies can be exchanged and the rates of exchange (prices of currencies) determined. Among these are:

   (1) The authorities might require that any exchange of the local currency for a foreign cur-

---

   [51] Maturity transformation is the practice of banks in borrowing at short-term and lending at long-term at a somewhat higher interest rate.

   [52] See Chapter 3, *supra,* pages 102–110, and Chapter 12, *infra,* pages 630–635.

   [53] See Chapter 12, *supra,* pages 627–630.

   [54] See Chapter 12, *supra,* page 629 (note 272).

   [55] See Hoffman and Giddy, *supra* note 43; Lingl, *supra* note 32; and Mann, "Zahlungsprobleme," *supra* note 43.

   [56] At page 619 et seq.

rency be made at an official agency or authorized bank and at an exchange rate set by the authorities.

(2) The authorities might permit exchanges of the local currency for foreign currencies to take place in the market with the rates of exchange determined by supply and demand without official intervention to affect those rates.

(3) The authorities might permit exchanges to take place in the market as described in (2) above, but the central banks or other authorities of the countries whose currencies are exchanged, by their willingness to buy or sell currencies in the market, deliberately affect the rates of exchange.

Each of the three systems outlined above is in use today. Many developing countries and socialist countries apply the first system. Current United States practice is generally in line with the second system. The policy of the U.S. Treasury and the Federal Reserve System is to intervene in the market only when that is necessary to counter disorderly conditions. Most countries with currencies that are widely used for payments in international transactions and actively traded in the exchange markets follow the third system. In some cases the policy pursued in the third example is to maintain rates within a defined zone—a ''pegged'' rate. In other cases action is taken to moderate rate movements without attempting to contain fluctuation within any particular rate range. This is called ''managed floating.''[57]

The relative values of currencies can be expected to change with respect to each other over time. Exchange rates may be affected by the pressures of supply and demand for the currency resulting from trade and investment transactions. For example, an exchange rate may be affected by seasonal variations in a country's imports and exports. The relative values of one currency vis-à-vis another over time will be affected by the strength of the economies of the several countries, rates of inflation, and estimates of the future purchasing power of the different currencies.

A comment on vocabulary may be helpful. The word ''devaluation'' refers to a decrease in the official value of a currency in relation to a stated common denominator. ''Depreciation'' refers to a decrease in a currency's value in relation to other currencies in the exchange markets. ''Revaluation'' refers to an official increase in value in relation to a stated denominator and ''appreciation'' to an increase in market exchange rates.

Exchange Rates and Trade Flows

The appraisal of a country's export position affects official attitudes toward the exchange rate of the country's currency. If a country's officials perceive a need to increase foreign currency receipts, one of the first questions usually examined is how the volume of exports can be increased. To make its goods and services more competitive in world markets, the country's authorities may (assuming foreign demand is elastic as to price[58]) take actions to set a lower exchange rate for its currency or allow the exchange rate of its currency to depreciate in the exchange markets.

If the exchange rate for a country's currency is devalued or depreciates, the prices in the local currency paid by residents for foreign goods become higher. Again, if demand is elastic with price, fewer foreign goods will be imported. Total imports calculated in terms of foreign currency will decline. Imports when calculated in terms of the local currency may also decline. The effect is to conserve reserves.

---

[57] Policies in the management of floating rate and pegged exchange rate systems are treated in Chapter 11.

[58] Elasticities are measures of the extent to which demand decreases as prices increase and vice versa and the extent to which supply increases as prices increase and vice versa.

However, changes in domestic wages and prices may moderate the trade effects of a change in an exchange rate. If as the exchange rate for a country's currency declines, domestic wages and prices rise, one may find that the local prices of foreign goods when compared to the local prices of domestic goods are as cheap as earlier. If as a result of inflation, the prices of domestic products increase, foreigners may find that the new prices when converted into their currencies are little different than before the change in exchange rates. There is an extensive economic literature on the points discussed in the last few paragraphs.[59]

As an alternative to changing an exchange rate, a country may try other schemes to lower the prices in foreign markets of goods that it sells or make it more difficult for foreigners to sell in its market. These schemes may be implemented through trade controls, taxes and subsidies, or exchange controls.

An increase in foreign currency receipts may be achieved by means other than changes in the country's export-import position. The receipt of foreign aid, the use of credit facilities, or investment from abroad, may, for example, provide foreign currencies. Exchange controls may be used to limit payments to nonresidents.

Theories of Exchange Rate Determination

Various theories have been advanced to explain movements in exchange rates or to suggest how "optimal" exchange rates should be determined. A system of "pegged" exchange rates (governmentally fixed rates subject to change only by official decision) requires procedures whereby governments can determine "correct" rates. In a market-oriented system of "floating" rates, governments, businessmen, and bankers may turn to theories to assist in predicting future rates. Two theories receive comment here—the purchasing-power-parity theory and the financial asset theory.

The "purchasing-power-parity theory" (PPP) is designed to explain how rates are determined over time in completely free markets or how rates might be objectively determined in a fixed rate regime. In its simplest form, the PPP theory asserts that the rate of exchange should become stabilized at a point that best equalizes the prices of goods and services in the countries whose currencies are involved. The rationale of the theory is that the value of a currency is determined fundamentally by the amount of goods and services that a unit of the currency can buy in the country of issue. The reader will recall the discussion at the outset of this chapter of money as purchasing power. The primary functions of rates of exchange, according to the theory, are to equalize the purchasing power of national currencies.

The basic assumption, subject to statistical adjustments, is that like goods and services are of equal value to residents of the two countries or groups of countries whose currencies are being compared. An effort is made to determine the internal purchasing power of each currency in relation to all goods and services in each country (its gross domestic product). The stable exchange rate is postulated as the one that equalizes the domestic purchasing power of the two currencies. Absolute PPP derives an exchange rate from the ratio of two countries' price levels. Relative PPP starts from a base period exchange rate and derives present or future equilibrium rates from the relative differences between changes in price indices in the two countries. Relative PPP can be used to predict future exchange rates in a floating system or to guide government officials in

---

[59] The appraisal of economic effects of exchange rate changes is treated briefly in Chapter 11, *supra*, pages 558–568.

changing pegged exchange rates in situations where two countries or groups of countries experience different rates of inflation.[60]

The theory has been criticized. Capital investment and foreign aid involve foreign currencies, but the theory does not attempt to equalize them. Nor does the theory take account of income differentials that may affect spending patterns and preferences. The ratio of the price level of non-traded to that of traded commodities is not equal across countries nor does the ratio remain uniform in a country over time. Finally, as to goods that do enter international trade, the relationship between the prices of those goods and exchange rates is a complex one. To claim that price levels should determine exchange rates assumes that price levels are fixed by other economic factors. Actually, the prices of goods that can be exported or are subject to competition from foreign imports may be significantly affected by rates of exchange. Studies of European prices and rates of exchange during inflationary periods indicate that internal price levels are frequently determined by rates of exchange, and not the other way around.[61]

The factors that limit the use of the purchasing-power-parity theory should not be taken as eliminating its usefulness. Merchandise trade is probably the largest category of international transactions that calls for current foreign exchange payments, and there is a tendency for the prices of goods that move in international trade to respond to competitive economic forces. The theory suggests a useful technique for evaluating the exchange rate between currencies of countries undergoing radically different rates of domestic price inflation.[62]

An advantage of the theory is its simplicity. A small number of calculations from readily available statistics for industrial countries may indicate the direction of exchange rate change. The theory can be applied and tested empirically. It may be possible through long-range statistical observation to introduce factors or weights to account for the more important disparities in economic preferences between residents in one country and those in another and to make other adjustments to overcome problems of the theory noted above.[63]

Another theory of exchange rate determination views national currencies like other financial assets. Under this theory exchange rates move in a predictable manner in response to changes in the relative financial risks and rewards of holding and using the particular currency compared to other financial instruments. The International Monetary Fund in its 1978 *Annual Report* embraced this theory to explain rate movements in well-developed capital markets:

> For countries with well-developed money and capital markets, conditions in the financial markets are probably more important than those in the goods markets for determining short-run exchange rate movements. Indeed, the foreign exchange market can be thought of as an asset market, and the exchange rate between two currencies regarded as a relative asset price that moves with changes in the relative supply and demand for assets denominated in those currencies. As with other assets, current

[60] See the 1947 paper, "Exchange Rates and the International Monetary Fund," reprinted in Lloyd A. Metzler, *Collected Papers* (Cambridge: Harvard University Press, 1973), p. 112.

[61] See Lawrence H. Officer, "The Purchasing-Power-Parity Theory of Exchange Rates: A Review Article," *IMF Staff Papers*, vol. 23 (1976), p. 1 at p. 17.

[62] The IMF has observed that floating exchange rates have, in general, moved to compensate for differences in the domestic purchasing power of currencies. See IMF, *Annual Report, 1978*, pp. 24 and 40–41.

[63] The reader who wishes to learn more about the purchasing power parity theory of exchange rates will find the article by Lawrence H. Officer, *supra* note 61, a good place to start. See also Peter B. Kenen and Clare Pack, *Exchange Rates, Domestic Prices, and the Adjustment Process* (New York: Group of Thirty, 1980); and "Purchasing Power Parity: A Symposium," *Journal of International Economics*, vol. 8 (1978), p. 157.

rates of return, risk factors, and expected future rates of return will be important in determining the current price, and when the factors affecting these returns and risks fluctuate substantially, so too will the current price, that is, the exchange rate. In other words, periods of rapidly shifting interest rate differentials, sudden imposition or relaxation of capital and exchange controls, and changing exchange rate expectations are apt to be periods of large short-term exchange rate variability, even when relative prices [of goods] move only slowly.

The influence of exchange rate expectations or, more correctly, changes in exchange rate expectations are perhaps worthy of special note because of the many factors influencing these expectations, and because the factors themselves are subject to frequent change, especially in an environment of high inflation and irregular economic growth. . . . [T]hey include, inter alia, monetary and fiscal policies, relative cyclical positions, current account and trade account imbalances, inflation differentials and relative competitive positions, political uncertainties, official intervention in the exchange market, and, of course, the change in the exchange rate itself.[64]

A problem with the asset theory is the difficulty of using it to predict rate movements in the cases that matter. Why will an event or official statement sometimes result in rates going up, in other cases be blamed for rates going down, or in other cases appear to have no effect at all? Market movements are not always rational. Consider Roger M. Kubarych's comment about exchange market dynamics in actively traded currencies:

At any time for a given currency, there may be a rough balance of expectations among market participants, not only residents of the U.S. and Germany if it is the German mark, but all holders or potential holders of dollars and marks wherever they may be located. That means at the current exchange rate buyers and sellers exert an offsetting influence, and the exchange rate remains reasonably steady. But then something may happen to change expectations. The stimulus could be anything. New statistics suggest an unanticipated development in a country's economy. A governmental official says something which gives the impression that some aspect of economic policy is about to be or has been changed. A rumor about a particularly large order to buy or sell a currency circulates in the market. A civil disturbance erupts in some country.

The result is that the balance of expectations within the market is upset. Professional traders in the commercial banks try to guess the reaction of other market participants and adjust their positions accordingly by bidding for or offering the currency in question. If the exchange rate moves enough to attract the attention of companies and individuals with foreign currency commitments, they may seek to change the pattern of their purchases and sales. As more of them expect the currency to rise, commercial purchases of foreign exchange are speeded up and sales are delayed. As more expect the currency to fall, purchases are delayed and sales are speeded up. These shifts in what are called commercial leads and lags can magnify any movement in an exchange rate.

[64] IMF, *Annual Report, 1978,* p. 37. See generally Polly Reynolds Allen and Peter B. Kenen, *Asset Markets, Exchange Rates, and Economic Integration* (Cambridge: Cambridge University Press, 1980); and Kenen and Pack, *supra* note 63. Papers on the asset theory of exchange rate determination are collected in Jan Herin, Assar Lindbeck, and Johan Myhrman (ed.), *Flexible Exchange Rates and Stabilization Policy* (Boulder: Westview Press, 1977); and in Jacob A. Frenkel and Harry G. Johnson (ed.), *The Economics of Exchange Rates: Selected Studies* (Reading, Massachusetts: Addison-Wesley Publishing Co., 1978).

The dynamics of subsequent exchange rate changes depend upon market reactions to the factor that stimulated the initial rate movement and to the speed and sharpness of the rate change. Often, when some traders believe the movement has gone too far, they will step in and provide a counterweight to further bids or offers of the currency. Their purchases or sales of currency would tend to slow or reverse the rate movement.

But, occasionally, the movement develops momentum. Sometimes, the new factor which triggered the initial rate movement may have a powerful effect on expectations. Or a string of good (or bad) news may follow. Traders and bank customers may then assess the outlook for the currency, conclude that a major readjustment in the rate is appropriate, and accordingly keep buying or selling the currency.

Frequently, the market reassessment is not so carefully drawn, and the response to a sharp exchange rate change is more of a knee-jerk reaction. An individual trader's thinking may go something like this: "The factor that initially moved the rate wasn't so important by itself, but yet the rate moved sharply. Maybe somebody else knows something I don't know. Maybe not. In any case the very sharpness of the rate change opens up the risk that this currency could move a long way before things settle down. So I'll hop on the bandwagon now before it gets too late."

In any of these cases, trading can become one-sided—for a few minutes, hours, or longer. In certain cases, trading settles only after central banks intervene to provide the counterweight that may not be forthcoming from the market itself. . . .

Central bank intervention in the exchange market to buy or sell its currency has two kinds of effect. Intervention has an ordinary supply and demand effect. In this respect, a central bank purchase or sale of domestic currency has the same impact on the exchange rate as a purchase or sale by any other market participant.

In addition, central bank intervention, or the absence of central bank intervention, may have a continuing influence on market expectations. Through the size, timing, and visibility of their operations, monetary authorities provide indirect information about official attitudes toward current exchange market conditions. Do the authorities feel conditions are disorderly? Do they feel exchange rates are fluctuating too volatilely? Do they feel movements in exchange rates have become exaggerated and may have undesirable effects on the economy? Market participants may interpret the clues to official attitudes in different ways. But they rarely ignore them altogether when forming their own decisions on whether to buy or sell a currency. . . .

Action to influence exchange rates and market conditions is not limited to direct intervention, that is, market purchases or sales of foreign currency for domestic currency. Nor is that necessarily the most important. On a daily basis, domestic money market conditions and interest rates exert a major influence on the exchange market through their effects on short-term capital flows. A central bank which, for instance, is intervening to moderate the decline of its currency may decide to reinforce its exchange market intervention by temporarily tightening domestic monetary conditions and raising interest rates. Frequently, such complementary domestic operations are decisive in stabilizing an unsettled exchange market.

Those operations in turn raise broader questions of domestic economic management. The authorities of a country may seek to achieve a variety of basic economic goals through a mix of monetary and fiscal policies. They also may have interest rate, exchange rate, or other market objectives. Achieving all at the same time may be difficult, if not impossible. In the end, exchange rates are manifestations of a country's overall economic performance and policies.[65]

Article IV of the Articles of Agreement of the International Monetary Fund deals with exchange rate arrangements. That article grants each member country freedom to choose the exchange arrangements for its currency so long as the country meets certain policy obligations and collaborates with the Fund and other members to maintain a stable system of exchange rates and orderly exchange arrangements. Regardless of the exchange arrangements used, a country is obligated not to manipulate rates to prevent "effective balance of payments adjustment."[66]

Underlying much of the work of the IMF is a belief that the study of balance-of-payments data may provide guidance in appraising the appropriateness of a given exchange rate over a period of time. Because at various points in this book references are made to the balance-of-payments positions of countries, the reader should understand the basic concepts involved.

Balance-of-Payments Concepts

The Articles of Agreement of the International Monetary Fund at a number of points refer to a country's balance-of-payments and reserve position.[67] The reader should have some understanding of balance-of-payments tables and how they are prepared because of the important role they play in the appraisal of a country's position. A balance-of-payments table is a statistical tabulation that summarizes a country's international economic transactions. A typical table displays total transactions—public and private—between a given country and the rest of the world during a particular year. Tables can, alternatively, be prepared that cover only transactions with one other country, or a group of countries, or international organizations; and the time period can be shorter or longer than a year. All IMF members are required to prepare and submit these statements in accordance with a prescribed format. The IMF collates, edits, and publishes them in *Balance of Payments Statistics.*[68]

A balance-of-payments table is part of a larger system of national accounts.[69] One does not learn from it the total foreign direct investment in the economy, or total monetary reserve holdings, or other cumulative information. One does not learn the vigor and strength of the economy domestically, its gross national product, or domestic income. It is solely a statement of international economic transactions. The classification scheme is designed to provide an analytic summary of the economic transactions in the period covered that generated receipts from nonresidents or necessitated payments to nonresidents. The transactions are organized to the best of the compi-

---

[65] Kubarych, *supra* note 34, pp. 43–45.

[66] Article IV, section 1(iii).

[67] References to the balance of payments appear in Article I; Article IV, sections 1 and 4; Article V, sections 3 and 7; Article VIII, section 5; Article XII, section 8; Article XIV, section 2; Article XVIII, section 1; Article XIX, sections 3 and 5; Schedule C, paragraphs 6 and 7; and Schedule D, paragraph 2.

[68] *Balance of Payments Statistics* is issued in pamphlet form during the year and, once complete, the annual bound volume is published. The bound volume includes more statistical detail than the pamphlets, and the tables are accompanied by extensive notes.

Balance-of-payments tables for the United States are published in the IMF's *Balance of Payments Statistics.* The United States also separately publishes its balance-of-payments tables, in a somewhat different format, under the title "U.S. International Transactions" in the U.S. Department of Commerce's publication *Survey of Current Business.*

[69] See generally, Poul Host-Madsen, *Macroeconomic Accounts: An Overview* (IMF Pamphlet Series no. 29; Washington, 1979).

ler's ability according to their purpose. If the data are reliable and well organized, a balance-of-payments table can present in a reasonably clear manner how a national economy is interacting with the rest of the world, maybe demonstrating (or suggesting) certain strengths and weaknesses of various sectors of that economy relative to the country's stated international economic goals.

Conceptually every international economic transaction involves the exchange of goods, services, long-term capital, money, or something else *for* goods, services, long-term capital, money, or something else. In order to display both the outflow and inflow aspects of every transaction, a double-entry system of bookkeeping is used in which outflows are recorded as credits and inflows as debits. To aid study and analysis the flows of goods, services, long-term capital, and money are subdivided into additional categories. The IMF asks members to use a system of standard components that consists of over 80 categories.[70] The fineness of the screen depends on the available data-gathering and statistical techniques and the uses to be made of the data. For example, if exports of fish are a significant source of foreign exchange earnings, fish exports may be separated from other merchandise exports. Categories may be added or deleted as analytical needs change. Data assembled in accordance with the IMF's somewhat elaborate standard presentation are regrouped and consolidated for purposes of comparison with other countries in an analytic presentation. The accompanying table, entitled "Aggregated Presentation," displays the categories.

In the IMF's aggregated presentation the movements of non-monetary tangible and intangible assets are at the top of the table. Thus, merchandise and invisibles (services including insurance, shipping, and tourist travel) are in Group A. Changes in long-term investment positions are displayed in Group B. The movements of monetary assets are displayed in the lower part of the tables. Flows of monetary assets to and from the resident official sector, resident commercial banks, and other residents are separately categorized. This, again, is done to aid analysis.[71]

There is no omniscient bookkeeper that records every transaction, but the concept is that transactions are recorded as follows: Barter transactions are displayed by debit and credit entries in the merchandise and service grouping at the top of the table. Exports of goods against payment in the resident-exporter's currency result in credits divided between the merchandise and services categories at the top of the table and a debit in one of the categories covering deposit money movements between residents and nonresidents that is lower down in the table. Transactions in which one monetary asset is exchanged for another result in entries in the appropriate lines in the capital sections of the table with the debit and credit entries appearing on the same or different lines depending on the classification of the assets transferred. The counter-entry to the inflow of money (short-term capital) in a long-term investment transaction initiated by a nonresident is the outflow of an investment interest (long-term capital) to it. Special counterpart categories are invented for transactions that do not involve exchanges so that the double-entry bookkeeping system can be maintained. A money gift received by a resident or a grant received by the government is recorded as an inflow of short-term capital or reserves and an outflow of a "thank you," the transaction being labelled an unrequited transfer. An allocation of SDRs by the IMF to the country results in an increase in SDRs in the reserves group in the table with the counterpart "thank you" to the IMF recorded in counterpart items. Purchases and sales of gold by the monetary authorities are reflected in changes in reserves with the value of the asset sold or received in exchange assigned to its appropriate category. Since the compilers also want to report the increase or decrease in the course of the period in the value of gold already held in reserves and not exchanged, this is done by recording an increase in value as a debit in reserves-gold and an equal credit entry in counterpart items. The finer points in choosing the appropriate category for a par-

[70] See IMF, *Balance of Payments Manual* (4th ed.; Washington, 1977), chapter 8.
[71] See *Balance of Payments Manual, idem,* chapters 2 and 7.

Aggregated Presentation[72]
(All figures are usually shown as net debits or
credits unless otherwise indicated.)

A. Current Account (excluding Group F)
   Merchandise: exports f.o.b. [credit]
   Merchandise: imports f.o.b. [debit]
   Other goods, services, and income: credit
   Other goods, services, and income: debit
   Private unrequited transfers
   Official unrequited transfers

B. Direct Investment and Other Long-Term Capital
   (excluding Groups F through H)
   Direct investment [also includes short-term components
      of direct investment]
   Portfolio investment
   Other long-term capital
      Resident official sector
      Deposit money banks
      Other sectors

C. Other Short-Term Capital (excluding Groups F through H)
   Resident official sector
   Deposit money banks [net change in the short-term
      deposit asset-liability position of resident
      commercial banks with nonresidents]
   Other sectors [net change in the short-term asset-liability
      position of resident private non-bank entities with
      nonresidents, including net change in resident corporation
      short-term deposits with nonresident banks]

D. Net Errors and Omissions

E. Counterpart Items
   Monetization/demonetization of gold
   Allocation/cancellation of SDRs
   Valuation changes in reserves

F. Exceptional Financing

G. Liabilities Constituting Foreign Authorities' Reserves

H. Reserves [total change]
   Monetary gold
   SDRs
   Reserve position in the IMF
   Foreign exchange assets
   Other claims
   Use of IMF credit

---

[72] This is the presentation used in the IMF's *Balance of Payments Statistics* since the beginning of 1979.

ticular inflow or outflow are treated in the IMF's *Balance of Payments Manual* which is used by persons responsible for compiling the tables.[73]

Because there is no omniscient bookkeeper that records every transaction, data must be gathered from different sources. The figures on some lines of the tables are much more reliable than figures on other lines.[74] Since the concept of double-entry accounting is that the total credits should equal the total debits, every table includes an item for "net errors and omissions" to force it into final balance. The errors are probably much greater than the figure would suggest because all the errors are probably not in one direction. Because short-term capital movements can be large and because obtaining reliable data on them can be difficult, the IMF puts the net errors and omissions in its aggregated presentation immediately following the short-term capital section of the table.

Serious questions can be raised about the reliability of balance-of-payments data. On a global basis IMF statistics showed current account deficits exceeding current account surpluses by $89 billion in 1982. Since this is a net figure, current account balances of individual country groups could, in principle, be wrong by even larger amounts than the overall asymmetry might suggest. The IMF's staff has candidly admitted that the prospects for correcting the statistical deficiencies underlying the asymmetry in the global current account are not bright.[75]

Principles and conventions have been developed for determining whether an individual or entity is a resident or nonresident, the valuation of transactions, whether a transaction falls within or without the reporting period, and the conversion of data from foreign currencies or the national currency to the SDR (which is the unit of account in the tables published by the IMF). The IMF's *Balance of Payments Manual* gives detailed explanations of definitions and conventions to be followed in preparing the tables.[76] The residence classification is particularly important and the de-

---

[73] See IMF, *Balance of Payments Manual, supra* note 70, chapters 8–21.

[74] Some data are gathered and presented in gross terms and other data are collected and presented in net terms. The practice is to report total exports and total imports rather than simply a net figure. A number of other flows may be reported gross. Monetary flows, however, are usually reported net. The quality of the data varies. The data on changes in official reserves (Group H) are usually highly reliable as are the data on long-term and short-term capital flows to and from the country's official monetary institutions. The entries for flows to and from the government can be expected to be based on reliable sources. The data on "deposit money banks" usually are obtained by comparing resident commercial banks' deposit claims on foreign banks at the beginning and end of the period and noting the net change and comparing resident banks' deposit liabilities to nonresidents at the beginning and end of the period and noting the net change. The data on deposit liabilities contain a degree of error because the banks may not have been able to identify all the nonresidents that hold accounts with them.

The figures in a balance-of-payments table for short-term capital movements to and from non-bank residents (corporations and individuals) are often highly unreliable—particularly in countries that do not have tight exchange controls. The authorities simply will not know all the residents that have accounts with banks abroad or other short-term claims on nonresidents, let alone the size of the claims. The item may be based on the application of a multiplication factor to a sample. Some of the problems in data reliability for short-term capital flows also apply to long-term flows.

Information on imports is usually obtained from customs authorities. The information may not always include the prices actually paid by importers, but must in some countries be estimated using the customs valuation as a base. The IMF classification requires that the price of the goods be reported on one line and the transportation and insurance on other lines (as services), which may require estimates in breaking down totals that themselves may be estimates. The national compiler of a balance-of-payments table may obtain data on exports from trade returns. In countries with no duties on exports and few export controls, customs officers may give little attention to the valuation of exports. Export data may have to be obtained by sampling the experience of export industries.

[75] See IMF, *World Economic Outlook* (IMF Occasional Paper no. 21; Washington, 1983), pp. 161–67.

[76] See IMF, *Balance of Payments Manual, supra* note 70, chapters 3–6.

sire for a uniform rule leads to a certain amount of arbitrariness. The present definition makes territoriality the critical consideration. An enterprise engaged in production in the country is regarded as a resident even if it is owned by a foreigner. Transactions between the firm and other residents of the country are not to be reflected in the balance of payments at all. Transactions between that firm and the parent corporation abroad are treated as transactions between a resident and a nonresident.[77]

A few general comments may help the reader understand the terminology used by economists in appraising a country's position on the basis of balance-of-payments tables. If a country's merchandise and services exports (credits) exceed imports we say that it is running a "surplus" in those accounts because they must be generating a net inflow of monetary payments or other assets reflected elsewhere in the table. If the country's merchandise and service imports exceed exports we say it is running a "deficit" in those accounts. In the framework of the IMF's aggregated presentation, the total of Groups A and B is sometimes called the "basic balance" of transactions on current and long-term capital accounts. Again, if the net figure is a credit the country is said to be in surplus in those accounts because the monetary movements summarized in the remaining groups will show a net inflow. The basic balance plus Group C covers the so-called "autonomous transactions," that is, transactions undertaken for their own sake. The three groups together are sometimes referred to as the "overall balance." In saying this it must be recognized that parts of the net flow of funds to and from commercial banks recorded in Group C may be accommodating other transactions rather than truly being undertaken for their own sake. Group H, of course, records changes in the country's official reserve position. If the total net figure above that group is a credit, then reserves will show as a debit (an increase). If not, they will show as a credit (a decrease).

In order to make a preliminary judgment on a country's balance-of-payments and reserve position, one needs as a minimum a current balance-of-payments table, tables spanning a period of years, and a statement of the country's monetary reserve holdings. The latter is published in *International Financial Statistics,* a monthly publication of the IMF. If an examination of the balance-of-payments tables shows that credits have exceeded debits for several years in the merchandise and services accounts and that official reserves have shown net debits for several years, this means the country has run a "surplus" in its merchandise and service accounts and in its overall balance (assuming no exceptional financing). If the net figures are in relative terms large and, further, if total reserve holdings are large relative to the volume of transactions of the country when compared to other countries, this is a *prima facie* situation for describing the country as in a "strong" balance-of-payments and reserve position. If the opposite were true, the country would be described as in a "weak" position.

It must be emphasized, however, that in the individual case further study of data in the tables and other materials outside them may reveal that the first impression is not accurate. We must not forget that virtually all of the lines of a balance-of-payments table are affected by the country's general level of economic development and its government's policies respecting prices, wages, credit, export incentives, and the like. The table must be examined bearing in mind the policies in effect at the time.[78] Poul Host-Madsen has suggested a policy-oriented definition of "balance-of-

---

[77] *Idem,* chapter 3, paragraphs 63–67.

[78] See generally *Balance of Payments Manual, idem,* chapter 7; Poul Host-Madsen, *Balance of Payments: Its Meaning and Uses* (IMF Pamphlet Series no. 9; Washington: IMF, 1967); Host-Madsen, *Macroeconomic Accounts, supra* note 69, pp. 35–97; and Fred Hirsch, *Money International* (Garden City: Doubleday & Co., 1969), chapter 3 (entitled "Balance of Which Payments?").

payments deficit'': ''A balance of payments *deficit* may be defined as a negative balance of certain transactions drawn within the balance of payments as a whole, which, if large and persistent, will sooner or later cause trouble for the monetary authorities.''[79]

Changes in a country's balance-of-payments situation or its holdings of monetary reserve assets may be relevant to the appraisal of the country's compliance with its obligations concerning the management of its economy, its exchange rate arrangements, and its use of financial resources drawn from international organizations. Changes in a country's position reflected in balance-of-payments and monetary reserves data may suggest the desirability of changes in internal or external monetary and financial policies. Throughout the book we are concerned with the international policy implications of a country's balance-of-payments and reserve position.

[79] Host-Madsen, *Macroeconomic Accounts,* supra note 69, p. 44.

Appendix B

Articles of Agreement of the
International Monetary Fund[1]

The Governments on whose behalf the present Agreement is signed agree as follows:

Introductory Article

(i) The International Monetary Fund is established and shall operate in accordance with the provisions of this Agreement as originally adopted and subsequently amended.

(ii) To enable the Fund to conduct its operations and transactions, the Fund shall maintain a General Department and a Special Drawing Rights Department. Membership in the Fund shall give the right to participation in the Special Drawing Rights Department.

(iii) Operations and transactions authorized by this Agreement shall be conducted through the General Department, consisting in accordance with the provisions of this Agreement of the General Resources Account, the Special Disbursement Account, and the Investment Account; except that operations and transactions involving special drawing rights shall be conducted through the Special Drawing Rights Department.

Article I

Purposes

The purposes of the International Monetary Fund are:

(i) To promote international monetary cooperation through a permanent institution which provides the machinery for consultation and collaboration on international monetary problems.

(ii) To facilitate the expansion and balanced growth of international trade, and to contribute thereby to the promotion and maintenance of high levels of employment and real income and to the development of the productive resources of all members as primary objectives of economic policy.

---

[1] Reproduced from *United States Treaties and Other International Agreements,* vol. 29, p. 2204. This is the text of the Articles of Agreement following the Second Amendment approved by the Board of Governors of the International Monetary Fund at Washington April 30, 1976, entered into force April 1, 1978.

For citations to the original Articles of Agreement adopted at Bretton Woods July 22, 1944, opened for signature at Washington December 27, 1945, entered into force December 27, 1945, and the First Amendment approved by the Board of Governors May 31, 1968, entered into force July 28, 1979, see Chapter 1, *supra* (notes 14 and 15).

(iii) To promote exchange stability, to maintain orderly exchange arrangements among members, and to avoid competitive exchange depreciation.

(iv) To assist in the establishment of a multilateral system of payments in respect of current transactions between members and in the elimination of foreign exchange restrictions which hamper the growth of world trade.

(v) To give confidence to members by making the general resources of the Fund temporarily available to them under adequate safeguards, thus providing them with opportunity to correct maladjustments in their balance of payments without resorting to measures destructive of national or international prosperity.

(vi) In accordance with the above, to shorten the duration and lessen the degree of disequilibrium in the international balances of payments of members.

The Fund shall be guided in all its policies and decisions by the purposes set forth in this Article.

Article II
Membership

Section 1. *Original members*

The original members of the Fund shall be those of the countries represented at the United Nations Monetary and Financial Conference whose governments accept membership before December 31, 1945.

Section 2. *Other members*

Membership shall be open to other countries at such times and in accordance with such terms as may be prescribed by the Board of Governors. These terms, including the terms for subscriptions, shall be based on principles consistent with those applied to other countries that are already members.

Article III
Quotas and Subscriptions

Section 1. *Quotas and payment of subscriptions*

Each member shall be assigned a quota expressed in special drawing rights. The quotas of the members represented at the United Nations Monetary and Financial Conference which accept membership before December 31, 1945 shall be those set forth in Schedule A. The quotas of other members shall be determined by the Board of Governors. The subscription of each member shall be equal to its quota and shall be paid in full to the Fund at the appropriate depository.

Section 2. *Adjustment of quotas*

(*a*) The Board of Governors shall at intervals of not more than five years conduct a general review, and if it deems it appropriate propose an adjustment, of the quotas of the members. It may also, if it thinks fit, consider at any other time the adjustment of any particular quota at the request of the member concerned.

(*b*) The Fund may at any time propose an increase in the quotas of those members of the Fund that were members on August 31, 1975 in proportion to their quotas on that date in a cumulative amount not in excess of amounts transferred under Article V, Section 12(*f*), (*i*), and (*j*) from the Special Disbursement Account to the General Resources Account.

(*c*) An eighty-five percent majority of the total voting power shall be required for any change in quotas.

(*d*) The quota of a member shall not be changed until the member has consented and until payment has been made unless payment is deemed to have been made in accordance with Section 3 (*b*) of this Article.

Section 3. *Payments when quotas are changed*

(*a*) Each member which consents to an increase in its quota under Section 2 (*a*) of this Article shall, within a period determined by the Fund, pay to the Fund twenty-five percent of the increase in special drawing rights, but the Board of Governors may prescribe that this payment may be made, on the same basis for all members, in whole or in part in the currencies of other members specified, with their concurrence, by the Fund, or in the member's own currency. A non-participant shall pay in the currencies of other members specified by the Fund, with their concurrence, a proportion of the increase corresponding to the proportion to be paid in special drawing rights by participants. The balance of the increase shall be paid by the member in its own currency. The Fund's holdings of a member's currency shall not be increased above the level at which they would be subject to charges under Article V, Section 8 (*b*) (ii), as a result of payments by other members under this provision.

(*b*) Each member which consents to an increase in its quota under Section 2 (*b*) of this Article shall be deemed to have paid to the Fund an amount of subscription equal to such increase.

(*c*) If a member consents to a reduction in its quota, the Fund shall, within sixty days, pay to the member an amount equal to the reduction. The payment shall be made in the member's currency and in such amount of special drawing rights or the currencies of other members specified, with their concurrence, by the Fund as is necessary to prevent the reduction of the Fund's holdings of the currency below the new quota, provided that in exceptional circumstances the Fund may reduce its holdings of the currency below the new quota by payment to the member in its own currency.

(*d*) A seventy percent majority of the total voting power shall be required for any decision under (*a*) above, except for the determination of a period and the specification of currencies under that provision.

Section 4. *Substitution of securities for currency*

The Fund shall accept from any member, in place of any part of the member's currency in the General Resources Account which in the judgment of the Fund is not needed for its operations and transactions, notes or similar obligations issued by the member or the depository designated by the member under Article XIII, Section 2, which shall be non-negotiable, non-interest bearing and payable at their face value on demand by crediting the account of the Fund in the designated depository. This Section shall apply not only to currency subscribed by members but also to any currency otherwise due to, or acquired by, the Fund and to be placed in the General Resources Account.

Article IV

Obligations Regarding Exchange Arrangements

Section 1. *General obligations of members*

Recognizing that the essential purpose of the international monetary system is to provide a framework that facilitates the exchange of goods, services, and capital among countries, and that sustains sound economic growth, and that a principal objective is the continuing development of the orderly underlying conditions that are necessary for financial and economic stability, each member undertakes to collaborate with the Fund and other members to assure orderly exchange arrangements and to promote a stable system of exchange rates. In particular, each member shall:

(i) endeavor to direct its economic and financial policies toward the objective of fostering orderly economic growth with reasonable price stability, with due regard to its circumstances;

(ii) seek to promote stability by fostering orderly underlying economic and financial conditions and a monetary system that does not tend to produce erratic disruptions;

(iii) avoid manipulating exchange rates or the international monetary system in order to prevent effective balance of payments adjustment or to gain an unfair competitive advantage over other members; and

(iv) follow exchange policies compatible with the undertakings under this Section.

Section 2. *General exchange arrangements*

(*a*) Each member shall notify the Fund, within thirty days after the date of the second amendment of this Agreement, of the exchange arrangements it intends to apply in fulfillment of its obligations under Section 1 of this Article, and shall notify the Fund promptly of any changes in its exchange arrangements.

(*b*) Under an international monetary system of the kind prevailing on January 1, 1976, exchange arrangements may include (i) the maintenance by a member of a value for its currency in terms of the special drawing right or another denominator, other than gold, selected by the member, or (ii) cooperative arrangements by which members maintain the value of their currencies in relation to the value of the currency or currencies of other members, or (iii) other exchange arrangements of a member's choice.

(*c*) To accord with the development of the international monetary system, the Fund, by an eighty-five percent majority of the total voting power, may make provision for general exchange arrangements without limiting the right of members to have exchange arrangements of their choice consistent with the purposes of the Fund and the obligations under Section 1 of this Article.

Section 3. *Surveillance over exchange arrangements*

(*a*) The Fund shall oversee the international monetary system in order to ensure its effective operation, and shall oversee the compliance of each member with its obligations under Section 1 of this Article.

(*b*) In order to fulfill its functions under (*a*) above, the Fund shall exercise firm surveillance over the exchange rate policies of members, and shall adopt specific principles for the guidance of all members with respect to those policies. Each member shall provide the Fund with the information necessary for such surveillance, and, when requested by the Fund, shall consult with it on the member's exchange rate policies. The principles adopted by the Fund shall be consistent with cooperative arrangements by which members maintain the value of their currencies in relation to the value of the currency or currencies of other members, as well as with other exchange arrangements of a member's choice consistent with the purposes of the Fund and Section 1 of this Article. These principles shall respect the domestic social and political policies of members, and in applying these principles the Fund shall pay due regard to the circumstances of members.

Section 4. *Par values*

The Fund may determine, by an eighty-five percent majority of the total voting power, that international economic conditions permit the introduction of a widespread system of exchange arrangements based on stable but adjustable par values. The Fund shall make the determination on the basis of the underlying stability of the world economy, and for this purpose shall take into account price movements and rates of expansion in the economies of members. The determination shall be made in light of the evolution of the international monetary system, with particular reference to sources of liquidity, and, in order to ensure the effective operation of a system of par values, to arrangements under which both members in surplus and members in deficit in their balances of payments take prompt, effective, and symmetrical action to achieve adjustment, as well as to arrangements for intervention and the treatment of imbalances. Upon making such determination, the Fund shall notify members that the provisions of Schedule C apply.

Section 5. *Separate currencies within a member's territories*

(*a*) Action by a member with respect to its currency under this Article shall be deemed to apply to the separate currencies of all territories in respect of which the member has accepted this Agreement under Article XXXI, Section 2 (*g*) unless the member declares that its action relates either to the metropolitan currency alone, or only to one or more specified separate currencies, or to the metropolitan currency and one or more specified separate currencies.

(*b*) Action by the Fund under this Article shall be deemed to relate to all currencies of a member referred to in (*a*) above unless the Fund declares otherwise.

Article V

Operations and Transactions of the Fund

Section 1. *Agencies dealing with the Fund*

Each member shall deal with the Fund only through its Treasury, central bank, stabilization fund, or other similar fiscal agency, and the Fund shall deal only with or through the same agencies.

Section 2. *Limitation on the Fund's operations and transactions*

(*a*) Except as otherwise provided in this Agreement, transactions on the account of the Fund shall be limited to transactions for the purpose of supplying a member, on the initiative of such member, with special drawing rights or the currencies of other members from the general resources of the Fund, which shall be held in the General Resources Account, in exchange for the currency of the member desiring to make the purchase.

(*b*) If requested, the Fund may decide to perform financial and technical services, including the administration of resources contributed by members, that are consistent with the purposes of the Fund. Operations involved in the performance of such financial services shall not be on the account of the Fund. Services under this subsection shall not impose any obligation on a member without its consent.

Section 3. *Conditions governing use of the Fund's general resources*

(*a*) The Fund shall adopt policies on the use of its general resources, including policies on stand-by or similar arrangements, and may adopt special policies for special balance of payments problems, that will assist members to solve their balance of payments problems in a manner consistent with the provisions of this Agreement and that will establish adequate safeguards for the temporary use of the general resources of the Fund.

(*b*) A member shall be entitled to purchase the currencies of other members from the Fund in exchange for an equivalent amount of its own currency subject to the following conditions:

(i) the member's use of the general resources of the Fund would be in accordance with the provisions of this Agreement and the policies adopted under them;

(ii) the member represents that it has a need to make the purchase because of its balance of payments or its reserve position or developments in its reserves;

(iii) the proposed purchase would be a reserve tranche purchase, or would not cause the Fund's holdings of the purchasing member's currency to exceed two hundred percent of its quota;

(iv) the Fund has not previously declared under Section 5 of this Article, Article VI, Section 1, or Article XXVI, Section 2 (*a*) that the member desiring to purchase is ineligible to use the general resources of the Fund.

(*c*) The Fund shall examine a request for a purchase to determine whether the proposed purchase would be consistent with the provisions of this Agreement and the policies adopted under them, provided that requests for reserve tranche purchases shall not be subject to challenge.

(*d*) The Fund shall adopt policies and procedures on the selection of currencies to be sold that take into account, in consultation with members, the balance of payments and reserve position of members and developments in the exchange markets, as well as the desirability of promoting over time balanced positions in the Fund, provided that if a member represents that it is proposing to purchase the currency of another member because the purchasing member wishes to obtain an equivalent amount of its own currency offered by the other member, it shall be entitled to purchase the currency of the other member unless the Fund has given notice under Article VII, Section 3 that its holdings of the currency have become scarce.

(*e*) (i) Each member shall ensure that balances of its currency purchased from the Fund are balances of a freely usable currency or can be exchanged at the time of purchase for a freely usable currency of its choice at an exchange rate between the two currencies equivalent to the exchange rate between them on the basis of Article XIX, Section 7 (*a*).

(ii) Each member whose currency is purchased from the Fund or is obtained in exchange for currency purchased from the Fund shall collaborate with the Fund and other members to enable such balances of its currency to be exchanged, at the time of purchase, for the freely usable currencies of other members.

(iii) An exchange under (i) above of a currency that is not freely usable shall be made by the member whose currency is purchased unless that member and the purchasing member agree on another procedure.

(iv) A member purchasing from the Fund the freely usable currency of another member and wishing to exchange it at the time of purchase for another freely usable currency shall make the exchange with the other member if requested by that member. The exchange shall be made for a freely usable currency selected by the other member at the rate of exchange referred to in (i) above.

(*f*) Under policies and procedures which it shall adopt, the Fund may agree to provide a participant making a purchase in accordance with this Section with special drawing rights instead of the currencies of other members.

Section 4. *Waiver of conditions*

The Fund may in its discretion, and on terms which safeguard its interests, waive any of the conditions prescribed in Section 3 (*b*) (iii) and (iv) of this Article, especially in the case of members with a record of avoiding large or continuous use of the Fund's general resources. In making a waiver it shall take into consideration periodic or exceptional requirements of the member requesting the waiver. The Fund shall also take into consideration a member's willingness to pledge as collateral security acceptable assets having a value sufficient in the opinion of the Fund to protect its interests and may require as a condition of waiver the pledge of such collateral security.

Section 5. *Ineligibility to use the Fund's general resources*

Whenever the Fund is of the opinion that any member is using the general resources of the Fund in a manner contrary to the purposes of the Fund, it shall present to the member a report setting forth the views of the Fund and prescribing a suitable time for reply. After presenting such a report to a member, the Fund may limit the use of its general resources by the member. If no reply to the report is received from the member within the prescribed time, or if the reply received is unsatisfactory, the Fund may continue to limit the member's use of the general resources of the Fund or may, after giving reasonable notice to the member, declare it ineligible to use the general resources of the Fund.

Section 6. *Other purchases and sales of special drawing rights by the Fund*

(*a*) The Fund may accept special drawing rights offered by a participant in exchange for an equivalent amount of the currencies of other members.

(*b*) The Fund may provide a participant, at its request, with special drawing rights for an equivalent amount of the currencies of other members. The Fund's holdings of a member's currency shall not be increased as a result of these transactions above the level at which the holdings would be subject to charges under Section 8 (*b*) (ii) of this Article.

(*c*) The currencies provided or accepted by the Fund under this Section shall be selected in accordance with policies that take into account the principles of Section 3 (*d*) or 7 (*i*) of this Article. The Fund may enter into transactions under this Section only if a member whose currency is provided or accepted by the Fund concurs in that use of its currency.

Section 7. *Repurchase by a member of its currency held by the Fund*

(*a*) A member shall be entitled to repurchase at any time the Fund's holdings of its currency that are subject to charges under Section 8 (*b*) of this Article.

(*b*) A member that has made a purchase under Section 3 of this Article will be expected normally, as its balance of payments and reserve position improves, to repurchase the Fund's holdings of its currency that result from the purchase and are subject to charges under Section 8 (*b*) of this Article. A member shall repurchase these holdings if, in accordance with policies on repurchase that the Fund shall adopt and after consultation with the member, the Fund represents to the member that it should repurchase because of an improvement in its balance of payments and reserve position.

(*c*) A member that has made a purchase under Section 3 of this Article shall repurchase the Fund's holdings of its currency that result from the purchase and are subject to charges under Section 8 (*b*) of this Article not later than five years after the date on which the purchase was made. The Fund may prescribe that repurchase shall be made by a member in installments during the period beginning three years and ending five years after the date of a purchase. The Fund, by an eighty-five percent majority of the total voting power, may change the periods for repurchase under this subsection, and any period so adopted shall apply to all members.

(*d*) The Fund, by an eighty-five percent majority of the total voting power, may adopt periods other than those that apply in accordance with (*c*) above, which shall be the same for all members, for the repurchase of holdings of currency acquired by the Fund pursuant to a special policy on the use of its general resources.

(*e*) A member shall repurchase, in accordance with policies that the Fund shall adopt by a seventy percent majority of the total voting power, the Fund's holdings of its currency that are not acquired as a result of purchases and are subject to charges under Section 8 (*b*) (ii) of this Article.

(*f*) A decision prescribing that under a policy on the use of the general resources of the Fund the period for repurchase under (*c*) or (*d*) above shall be shorter than the one in effect under the policy shall apply only to holdings acquired by the Fund subsequent to the effective date of the decision.

(*g*) The Fund, on the request of a member, may postpone the date of discharge of a repurchase obligation, but not beyond the maximum period under (*c*) or (*d*) above or under policies adopted by the Fund under (*e*) above, unless the Fund determines, by a seventy percent majority of the total voting power, that a longer period for repurchase which is consistent with the temporary use of the general resources of the Fund is justified because discharge on the due date would result in exceptional hardship for the member.

(*h*) The Fund's policies under Section 3 (*d*) of this Article may be supplemented by policies under which the Fund may decide after consultation with a member to sell under Section 3 (*b*) of this Article its holdings of the member's currency that have not been repurchased in accordance with this Section 7, without prejudice to any action that the Fund may be authorized to take under any other provision of this Agreement.

(*i*) All repurchases under this Section shall be made with special drawing rights or with the currencies of other members specified by the Fund. The Fund shall adopt policies and procedures with regard to the currencies to be used by members in making repurchases that take into account the principles in Section 3 (*d*) of this Article. The Fund's holdings of a member's currency that is used in repurchase shall not be increased by the repurchase above the level at which they would be subject to charges under Section 8(*b*)(ii) of this Article.

(*j*)   (i) If a member's currency specified by the Fund under (*i*) above is not a freely usable currency, the member shall ensure that the repurchasing member can obtain it at the time of the repurchase in exchange for a freely usable currency selected by the member whose currency has been specified. An exchange of currency under this provision shall take place at an exchange rate between the two currencies equivalent to the exchange rate between them on the basis of Article XIX, Section 7 (*a*).

   (ii) Each member whose currency is specified by the Fund for repurchase shall collaborate with the Fund and other members to enable repurchasing members, at the time of the repurchase, to obtain the specified currency in exchange for the freely usable currencies of other members.

   (iii) An exchange under (*j*) (i) above shall be made with the member whose currency is specified unless that member and the repurchasing member agree on another procedure.

   (iv) If a repurchasing member wishes to obtain, at the time of the repurchase, the freely usable currency of another member specified by the Fund under (*i*) above, it shall, if requested by the other member, obtain the currency from the other member in exchange for a freely usable currency at the rate of exchange referred to in (*j*) (i) above. The Fund may adopt regulations on the freely usable currency to be provided in an exchange.

Section 8. *Charges*

  (*a*) (i) The Fund shall levy a service charge on the purchase by a member of special drawing rights or the currency of another member held in the General Resources Account in exchange for its own currency, provided that the Fund may levy a lower service charge on reserve tranche purchases than on other purchases. The service charge on reserve tranche purchases shall not exceed one-half of one percent.

   (ii) The Fund may levy a charge for stand-by or similar arrangements. The Fund may decide that the charge for an arrangement shall be offset against the service charge levied under (i) above on purchases under the arrangement.

(*b*) The Fund shall levy charges on its average daily balances of a member's currency held in the General Resources Account to the extent that they

   (i) have been acquired under a policy that has been the subject of an exclusion under Article XXX(*c*), or

   (ii) exceed the amount of the member's quota after excluding any balances referred to in (i) above.

The rates of charge normally shall rise at intervals during the period in which balances are held.

(*c*) If a member fails to make a repurchase required under Section 7 of this Article, the Fund, after consultation with the member on the reduction of the Fund's holdings of its currency, may impose such charges as the Fund deems appropriate on its holdings of the member's currency that should have been repurchased.

(*d*) A seventy percent majority of the total voting power shall be required for the determination of the rates of charge under (*a*) and (*b*) above, which shall be uniform for all members, and under (*c*) above.

(*e*) A member shall pay all charges in special drawing rights, provided that in exceptional circumstances the Fund may permit a member to pay charges in the currencies of other members specified by the Fund, after consultation with them, or in its own currency. The Fund's holdings of a member's currency shall not be increased as a result of payments by other members under this provision above the level at which they would be subject to charges under (*b*)(ii) above.

Section 9. *Remuneration*

(*a*) The Fund shall pay remuneration on the amount by which the percentage of quota prescribed under (*b*) or (*c*) below exceeds the Fund's average daily balances of a member's currency held in the General Resources Account other than balances acquired under a policy that has been the subject of an exclusion under Article XXX (*c*). The rate of remuneration, which shall be determined by the Fund by a seventy percent majority of the total voting power, shall be the same for all members and shall be not more than, nor less than four-fifths of, the rate of interest under Article XX, Section 3. In establishing the rate of remuneration, the Fund shall take into account the rates of charge under Article V, Section 8 (*b*).

(*b*) The percentage of quota applying for the purposes of (*a*) above shall be:

    (i) for each member that became a member before the second amendment of this Agreement, a percentage of quota corresponding to seventy-five percent of its quota on the date of the second amendment of this Agreement, and for each member that became a member after the date of the second amendment of this Agreement, a percentage of quota calculated by dividing the total of the amounts corresponding to the percentages of quota that apply to the other members on the date on which the member became a member by the total of the quotas of the other members on the same date; plus

    (ii) the amounts it has paid to the Fund in currency or special drawing rights under Article III, Section 3 (*a*) since the date applicable under (*b*)(i) above; and minus

    (iii) the amounts it has received from the Fund in currency or special drawing rights under Article III, Section 3 (*c*) since the date applicable under (*b*)(i) above.

(*c*) The Fund, by a seventy percent majority of the total voting power, may raise the latest percentage of quota applying for the purposes of (*a*) above to each member to:

(i) a percentage, not in excess of one hundred percent, that shall be determined for each member on the basis of the same criteria for all members, or

(ii) one hundred percent for all members.

(*d*) Remuneration shall be paid in special drawing rights, provided that either the Fund or the member may decide that the payment to the member shall be made in its own currency.

Section 10. *Computations*

(*a*) The value of the Fund's assets held in the accounts of the General Department shall be expressed in terms of the special drawing right.

(*b*) All computations relating to currencies of members for the purpose of applying the provisions of this Agreement, except Article IV and Schedule C, shall be at the rates at which the Fund accounts for these currencies in accordance with Section 11 of this Article.

(*c*) Computations for the determination of amounts of currency in relation to quota for the purpose of applying the provisions of this Agreement shall not include currency held in the Special Disbursement Account or in the Investment Account.

Section 11. *Maintenance of value*

(*a*) The value of the currencies of members held in the General Resources Account shall be maintained in terms of the special drawing right in accordance with exchange rates under Article XIX, Section 7 (*a*).

(*b*) An adjustment in the Fund's holdings of a member's currency pursuant to this Section shall be made on the occasion of the use of that currency in an operation or transaction between the Fund and another member and at such other times as the Fund may decide or the member may request. Payments to or by the Fund in respect of an adjustment shall be made within a reasonable time, as determined by the Fund, after the date of adjustment, and at any other time requested by the member.

Section 12. *Other operations and transactions*

(*a*) The Fund shall be guided in all its policies and decisions under this Section by the objectives set forth in Article VIII, Section 7 and by the objective of avoiding the management of the price, or the establishment of a fixed price, in the gold market.

(*b*) Decisions of the Fund to engage in operations or transactions under (*c*), (*d*), and (*e*) below shall be made by an eighty-five percent majority of the total voting power.

(*c*) The Fund may sell gold for the currency of any member after consulting the member for whose currency the gold is sold, provided that

the Fund's holdings of a member's currency held in the General
Resources Account shall not be increased by the sale above the level at
which they would be subject to charges under Section 8 (*b*) (ii) of this
Article without the concurrence of the member, and provided that, at the
request of the member, the Fund at the time of sale shall exchange for the
currency of another member such part of the currency received as would
prevent such an increase. The exchange of a currency for the currency of
another member shall be made after consultation with that member, and
shall not increase the Fund's holdings of that member's currency above
the level at which they would be subject to charges under Section 8 (*b*) (ii)
of this Article. The Fund shall adopt policies and procedures with regard
to exchanges that take into account the principles applied under Section
7(*i*) of this Article. Sales under this provision to a member shall be at a
price agreed for each transaction on the basis of prices in the market.

(*d*) The Fund may accept payments from a member in gold instead of
special drawing rights or currency in any operations or transactions
under this Agreement. Payments to the Fund under this provision shall
be at a price agreed for each operation or transaction on the basis of
prices in the market.

(*e*) The Fund may sell gold held by it on the date of the second
amendment of this Agreement to those members that were members on
August 31, 1975 and that agree to buy it, in proportion to their quotas on
that date. If the Fund intends to sell gold under (*c*) above for the purpose
of (*f*) (ii) below, it may sell to each developing member that agrees to buy
it that portion of the gold which, if sold under (*c*) above, would have
produced the excess that could have been distributed to it under (*f*) (iii)
below. The gold that would be sold under this provision to a member that
has been declared ineligible to use the general resources of the Fund
under Section 5 of this Article shall be sold to it when the ineligibility
ceases, unless the Fund decides to make the sale sooner. The sale of gold
to a member under this subsection (*e*) shall be made in exchange for its
currency and at a price equivalent at the time of sale to one special
drawing right per 0.888 671 gram of fine gold.

(*f*) Whenever under (*c*) above the Fund sells gold held by it on the date
of the second amendment of this Agreement, an amount of the proceeds
equivalent at the time of sale to one special drawing right per 0.888 671
gram of fine gold shall be placed in the General Resources Account and,
except as the Fund may decide otherwise under (*g*) below, any excess
shall be held in the Special Disbursement Account. The assets held in the
Special Disbursement Account shall be held separately from the other
accounts of the General Department, and may be used at any time:

    (i) to make transfers to the General Resources Account for
        immediate use in operations and transactions authorized by

provisions of this Agreement other than this Section;

(ii) for operations and transactions that are not authorized by other provisions of this Agreement but are consistent with the purposes of the Fund. Under this subsection (*f*) (ii) balance of payments assistance may be made available on special terms to developing members in difficult circumstances, and for this purpose the Fund shall take into account the level of per capita income;

(iii) for distribution to those developing members that were members on August 31, 1975, in proportion to their quotas on that date, of such part of the assets that the Fund decides to use for the purposes of (ii) above as corresponds to the proportion of the quotas of these members on the date of distribution to the total of the quotas of all members on the same date, provided that the distribution under this provision to a member that has been declared ineligible to use the general resources of the Fund under Section 5 of this Article shall be made when the ineligibility ceases, unless the Fund decides to make the distribution sooner.

Decisions to use assets pursuant to (i) above shall be taken by a seventy percent majority of the total voting power, and decisions pursuant to (ii) and (iii) above shall be taken by an eighty-five percent majority of the total voting power.

(*g*) The Fund may decide, by an eighty-five percent majority of the total voting power, to transfer a part of the excess referred to in (*f*) above to the Investment Account for use pursuant to the provisions of Article XII, Section 6 (*f*).

(*h*) Pending uses specified under (*f*) above, the Fund may invest a member's currency held in the Special Disbursement Account in marketable obligations of that member or in marketable obligations of international financial organizations. The income of investment and interest received under (*f*) (ii) above shall be placed in the Special Disbursement Account. No investment shall be made without the concurrence of the member whose currency is used to make the investment. The Fund shall invest only in obligations denominated in special drawing rights or in the currency used for investment.

(*i*) The General Resources Account shall be reimbursed from time to time in respect of the expenses of administration of the Special Disbursement Account paid from the General Resources Account by transfers from the Special Disbursement Account on the basis of a reasonable estimate of such expenses.

(*j*) The Special Disbursement Account shall be terminated in the event of the liquidation of the Fund and may be terminated prior to liquidation of the Fund by a seventy percent majority of the total voting power. Upon termination of the account because of the liquidation of the Fund, any assets in this account shall be distributed in accordance with the provisions of Schedule K. Upon termination prior to liquidation of the Fund, any assets in this account shall be transferred to the General Resources Account for immediate use in operations and transactions. The Fund, by a seventy percent majority of the total voting power, shall adopt rules and regulations for the administration of the Special Disbursement Account.

Article VI

Capital Transfers

Section 1. *Use of the Fund's general resources for capital transfers*

(*a*) A member may not use the Fund's general resources to meet a large or sustained outflow of capital except as provided in Section 2 of this Article, and the Fund may request a member to exercise controls to prevent such use of the general resources of the Fund. If, after receiving such a request, a member fails to exercise appropriate controls, the Fund may declare the member ineligible to use the general resources of the Fund.

(*b*) Nothing in this Section shall be deemed:
  (i) to prevent the use of the general resources of the Fund for capital transactions of reasonable amount required for the expansion of exports or in the ordinary course of trade, banking, or other business; or
  (ii) to affect capital movements which are met out of a member's own resources, but members undertake that such capital movements will be in accordance with the purposes of the Fund.

Section 2. *Special provisions for capital transfers*

A member shall be entitled to make reserve tranche purchases to meet capital transfers.

Section 3. *Controls of capital transfers*

Members may exercise such controls as are necessary to regulate international capital movements, but no member may exercise these controls in a manner which will restrict payments for current transactions or which will unduly delay transfers of funds in settlement of commitments, except as provided in Article VII, Section 3(*b*) and in Article XIV, Section 2.

Article VII

Replenishment and Scarce Currencies

Section 1. *Measures to replenish the Fund's holdings of currencies*

The Fund may, if it deems such action appropriate to replenish its holdings of any member's currency in the General Resources Account needed in connection with its transactions, take either or both of the following steps:

    (i) propose to the member that, on terms and conditions agreed between the Fund and the member, the latter lend its currency to the Fund or that, with the concurrence of the member, the Fund borrow such currency from some other source either within or outside the territories of the member, but no member shall be under any obligation to make such loans to the Fund or to concur in the borrowing of its currency by the Fund from any other source;

    (ii) require the member, if it is a participant, to sell its currency to the Fund for special drawing rights held in the General Resources Account, subject to Article XIX, Section 4. In replenishing with special drawing rights, the Fund shall pay due regard to the principles of designation under Article XIX, Section 5.

Section 2. *General scarcity of currency*

If the Fund finds that a general scarcity of a particular currency is developing, the Fund may so inform members and may issue a report setting forth the causes of the scarcity and containing recommendations designed to bring it to an end. A representative of the member whose currency is involved shall participate in the preparation of the report.

Section 3. *Scarcity of the Fund's holdings*

(*a*) If it becomes evident to the Fund that the demand for a member's currency seriously threatens the Fund's ability to supply that currency, the Fund, whether or not it has issued a report under Section 2 of this Article, shall formally declare such currency scarce and shall thenceforth apportion its existing and accruing supply of the scarce currency with due regard to the relative needs of members, the general international economic situation, and any other pertinent considerations. The Fund shall also issue a report concerning its action.

(*b*) A formal declaration under (*a*) above shall operate as an authorization to any member, after consultation with the Fund, temporarily to impose limitations on the freedom of exchange operations in the scarce currency. Subject to the provisions of Article IV and Schedule C, the member shall have complete jurisdiction in determining the nature of such limitations, but they shall be no more restrictive than is necessary to limit the demand for the scarce currency to the supply held by, or accruing to, the member in question, and they shall be relaxed and removed as rapidly as conditions permit.

(*c*) The authorization under (*b*) above shall expire whenever the Fund formally declares the currency in question to be no longer scarce.

Section 4. *Administration of restrictions*

Any member imposing restrictions in respect of the currency of any other member pursuant to the provisions of Section 3 (*b*) of this Article shall give sympathetic consideration to any representations by the other member regarding the administration of such restrictions.

Section 5. *Effect of other international agreements on restrictions*

Members agree not to invoke the obligations of any engagements entered into with other members prior to this Agreement in such a manner as will prevent the operation of the provisions of this Article.

Article VIII

General Obligations of Members

Section 1. *Introduction*

In addition to the obligations assumed under other articles of this Agreement, each member undertakes the obligations set out in this Article.

Section 2. *Avoidance of restrictions on current payments*

(*a*) Subject to the provisions of Article VII, Section 3(*b*) and Article XIV, Section 2, no member shall, without the approval of the Fund, impose restrictions on the making of payments and transfers for current international transactions.

(*b*) Exchange contracts which involve the currency of any member and which are contrary to the exchange control regulations of that member maintained or imposed consistently with this Agreement shall be unenforceable in the territories of any member. In addition, members may, by mutual accord, cooperate in measures for the purpose of making the exchange control regulations of either member more effective, provided that such measures and regulations are consistent with this Agreement.

Section 3. *Avoidance of discriminatory currency practices*

No member shall engage in, or permit any of its fiscal agencies referred to in Article V, Section 1 to engage in, any discriminatory currency arrangements or multiple currency practices, whether within or outside margins under Article IV or prescribed by or under Schedule C, except as authorized under this Agreement or approved by the Fund. If such arrangements and practices are engaged in at the date when this Agreement enters into force, the member concerned shall consult with the Fund as to their progressive removal unless they are maintained or imposed under Article XIV, Section 2, in which case the provisions of Section 3 of that Article shall apply.

Section 4. *Convertibility of foreign-held balances*

(*a*) Each member shall buy balances of its currency held by another member if the latter, in requesting the purchase, represents:

(i) that the balances to be bought have been recently acquired as a result of current transactions; or

(ii) that their conversion is needed for making payments for current transactions.

The buying member shall have the option to pay either in special drawing rights, subject to Article XIX, Section 4, or in the currency of the member making the request.

(*b*) The obligation in (*a*) above shall not apply when:

(i) the convertibility of the balances has been restricted consistently with Section 2 of this Article or Article VI, Section 3;

(ii) the balances have accumulated as a result of transactions effected before the removal by a member of restrictions maintained or imposed under Article XIV, Section 2;

(iii) the balances have been acquired contrary to the exchange regulations of the member which is asked to buy them;

(iv) the currency of the member requesting the purchase has been declared scarce under Article VII, Section 3(*a*); or

(v) the member requested to make the purchase is for any reason not entitled to buy currencies of other members from the Fund for its own currency.

Section 5. *Furnishing of information*

(*a*) The Fund may require members to furnish it with such information as it deems necessary for its activities, including, as the minimum necessary for the effective discharge of the Fund's duties, national data on the following matters:

(i) official holdings at home and abroad of (1) gold, (2) foreign exchange;

    (ii) holdings at home and abroad by banking and financial agencies, other than official agencies, of (1) gold, (2) foreign exchange;

  (iii) production of gold;

  (iv) gold exports and imports according to countries of destination and origin;

   (v) total exports and imports of merchandise, in terms of local currency values, according to countries of destination and origin;

  (vi) international balance of payments, including (1) trade in goods and services, (2) gold transactions, (3) known capital transactions, and (4) other items;

 (vii) international investment position, i.e., investments within the territories of the member owned abroad and investments abroad owned by persons in its territories so far as it is possible to furnish this information;

(viii) national income;

  (ix) price indices, i.e., indices of commodity prices in wholesale and retail markets and of export and import prices;

   (x) buying and selling rates for foreign currencies;

  (xi) exchange controls, i.e., a comprehensive statement of exchange controls in effect at the time of assuming membership in the Fund and details of subsequent changes as they occur; and

 (xii) where official clearing arrangements exist, details of amounts awaiting clearance in respect of commercial and financial transactions, and of the length of time during which such arrears have been outstanding.

(*b*) In requesting information the Fund shall take into consideration the varying ability of members to furnish the data requested. Members shall be under no obligation to furnish information in such detail that the affairs of individuals or corporations are disclosed. Members undertake, however, to furnish the desired information in as detailed and accurate a manner as is practicable and, so far as possible, to avoid mere estimates.

(*c*) The Fund may arrange to obtain further information by agreement with members. It shall act as a centre for the collection and exchange of information on monetary and financial problems, thus facilitating the preparation of studies designed to assist members in developing policies which further the purposes of the Fund.

Section 6. *Consultation between members regarding existing international agreements*

Where under this Agreement a member is authorized in the special or temporary circumstances specified in the Agreement to maintain or establish restrictions on exchange transactions, and there are other engagements between members entered into prior to this Agreement which conflict with the application of such restrictions, the parties to such engagements shall consult with one another with a view to making such mutually acceptable adjustments as may be necessary. The provisions of this Article shall be without prejudice to the operation of Article VII, Section 5.

Section 7. *Obligation to collaborate regarding policies on reserve assets*

Each member undertakes to collaborate with the Fund and with other members in order to ensure that the policies of the member with respect to reserve assets shall be consistent with the objectives of promoting better international surveillance of international liquidity and making the special drawing right the principal reserve asset in the international monetary system.

Article IX

Status, Immunities, and Privileges

Section 1. *Purposes of Article*

To enable the Fund to fulfill the functions with which it is entrusted, the status, immunities, and privileges set forth in this Article shall be accorded to the Fund in the territories of each member.

Section 2. *Status of the Fund*

The Fund shall possess full juridical personality, and in particular, the capacity:
  (i) to contract;
  (ii) to acquire and dispose of immovable and movable property; and
  (iii) to institute legal proceedings.

Section 3. *Immunity from judicial process*

The Fund, its property and its assets, wherever located and by whomsoever held, shall enjoy immunity from every form of judicial process except to the extent that it expressly waives its immunity for the purpose of any proceedings or by the terms of any contract.

Section 4. *Immunity from other action*

Property and assets of the Fund, wherever located and by whomsoever held, shall be immune from search, requisition, confiscation, expropriation, or any other form of seizure by executive or legislative action.

Section 5. *Immunity of archives*

The archives of the Fund shall be inviolable.

Section 6. *Freedom of assets from restrictions*

To the extent necessary to carry out the activities provided for in this Agreement, all property and assets of the Fund shall be free from restrictions, regulations, controls, and moratoria of any nature.

Section 7. *Privilege for communications*

The official communications of the Fund shall be accorded by members the same treatment as the official communications of other members.

Section 8. *Immunities and privileges of officers and employees*

All Governors, Executive Directors, Alternates, members of committees, representatives appointed under Article XII, Section 3 (*j*), advisors of any of the foregoing persons, officers, and employees of the Fund:

> (i) shall be immune from legal process with respect to acts performed by them in their official capacity except when the Fund waives this immunity;
>
> (ii) not being local nationals, shall be granted the same immunities from immigration restrictions, alien registration requirements, and national service obligations and the same facilities as regards exchange restrictions as are accorded by members to the representatives, officials, and employees of comparable rank of other members; and
>
> (iii) shall be granted the same treatment in respect of traveling facilities as is accorded by members to representatives, officials, and employees of comparable rank of other members.

Section 9. *Immunities from taxation*

(*a*) The Fund, its assets, property, income, and its operations and transactions authorized by this Agreement shall be immune from all taxation and from all customs duties. The Fund shall also be immune from liability for the collection or payment of any tax or duty.

(*b*) No tax shall be levied on or in respect of salaries and emoluments paid by the Fund to Executive Directors, Alternates, officers, or employees of the Fund who are not local citizens, local subjects, or other local nationals.

(*c*) No taxation of any kind shall be levied on any obligation or security issued by the Fund, including any dividend or interest thereon, by whomsoever held:

> (i) which discriminates against such obligation or security solely because of its origin; or
>
> (ii) if the sole jurisdictional basis for such taxation is the place or currency in which it is issued, made payable or paid, or the

location of any office or place of business maintained by the Fund.

Section 10. *Application of Article*

Each member shall take such action as is necessary in its own territories for the purpose of making effective in terms of its own law the principles set forth in this Article and shall inform the Fund of the detailed action which it has taken.

Article X

Relations with Other International Organizations

The Fund shall cooperate within the terms of this Agreement with any general international organization and with public international organizations having specialized responsibilities in related fields. Any arrangements for such cooperation which would involve a modification of any provision of this Agreement may be effected only after amendment to this Agreement under Article XXVIII.

Article XI

Relations with Non-Member Countries

Section 1. *Undertakings regarding relations with non-member countries*

Each member undertakes:
  (i) not to engage in, nor to permit any of its fiscal agencies referred to in Article V, Section 1 to engage in, any transactions with a non-member or with persons in a non-member's territories which would be contrary to the provisions of this Agreement or the purposes of the Fund;
  (ii) not to cooperate with a non-member or with persons in a non-member's territories in practices which would be contrary to the provisions of this Agreement or the purposes of the Fund; and
  (iii) to cooperate with the Fund with a view to the application in its territories of appropriate measures to prevent transactions with non-members or with persons in their territories which would be contrary to the provisions of this Agreement or the purposes of the Fund.

Section 2. *Restrictions on transactions with non-member countries*

Nothing in this Agreement shall affect the right of any member to impose restrictions on exchange transactions with non-members or with persons in their territories unless the Fund finds that such restrictions prejudice the interests of members and are contrary to the purposes of the Fund.

Article XII

Organization and Management

Section 1. *Structure of the Fund*

The Fund shall have a Board of Governors, an Executive Board, a Managing Director, and a staff, and a Council if the Board of Governors decides, by an eighty-five percent majority of the total voting power, that the provisions of Schedule D shall be applied.

Section 2. *Board of Governors*

(*a*) All powers under this Agreement not conferred directly on the Board of Governors, the Executive Board, or the Managing Director shall be vested in the Board of Governors. The Board of Governors shall consist of one Governor and one Alternate appointed by each member in such manner as it may determine. Each Governor and each Alternate shall serve until a new appointment is made. No Alternate may vote except in the absence of his principal. The Board of Governors shall select one of the Governors as chairman.

(*b*) The Board of Governors may delegate to the Executive Board authority to exercise any powers of the Board of Governors, except the powers conferred directly by this Agreement on the Board of Governors.

(*c*) The Board of Governors shall hold such meetings as may be provided for by the Board of Governors or called by the Executive Board. Meetings of the Board of Governors shall be called whenever requested by fifteen members or by members having one-quarter of the total voting power.

(*d*) A quorum for any meeting of the Board of Governors shall be a majority of the Governors having not less than two-thirds of the total voting power.

(*e*) Each Governor shall be entitled to cast the number of votes allotted under Section 5 of this Article to the member appointing him.

(*f*) The Board of Governors may by regulation establish a procedure whereby the Executive Board, when it deems such action to be in the best interests of the Fund, may obtain a vote of the Governors on a specific question without calling a meeting of the Board of Governors.

(*g*) The Board of Governors, and the Executive Board to the extent authorized, may adopt such rules and regulations as may be necessary or appropriate to conduct the business of the Fund.

(*h*) Governors and Alternates shall serve as such without compensation from the Fund, but the Fund may pay them reasonable expenses incurred in attending meetings.

(*i*) The Board of Governors shall determine the remuneration to be paid to the Executive Directors and their Alternates and the salary and terms of the contract of service of the Managing Director.

(*j*) The Board of Governors and the Executive Board may appoint such committees as they deem advisable. Membership of committees need not be limited to Governors or Executive Directors or their Alternates.

Section 3. *Executive Board*

(*a*) The Executive Board shall be responsible for conducting the business of the Fund, and for this purpose shall exercise all the powers delegated to it by the Board of Governors.

(*b*) The Executive Board shall consist of Executive Directors with the Managing Director as chairman. Of the Executive Directors:
  (i) five shall be appointed by the five members having the largest quotas; and
  (ii) fifteen shall be elected by the other members.

For the purpose of each regular election of Executive Directors, the Board of Governors, by an eighty-five percent majority of the total voting power, may increase or decrease the number of Executive Directors in (ii) above. The number of Executive Directors in (ii) above shall be reduced by one or two, as the case may be, if Executive Directors are appointed under (*c*) below, unless the Board of Governors decides, by an eighty-five percent majority of the total voting power, that this reduction would hinder the effective discharge of the functions of the Executive Board or of Executive Directors or would threaten to upset a desirable balance in the Executive Board.

(*c*) If, at the second regular election of Executive Directors and thereafter, the members entitled to appoint Executive Directors under (*b*)(i) above do not include the two members, the holdings of whose currencies by the Fund in the General Resources Account have been, on the average over the preceding two years, reduced below their quotas by the largest absolute amounts in terms of the special drawing right, either one or both of such members, as the case may be, may appoint an Executive Director.

(*d*) Elections of elective Executive Directors shall be conducted at intervals of two years in accordance with the provisions of Schedule E, supplemented by such regulations as the Fund deems appropriate. For each regular election of Executive Directors, the Board of Governors may issue regulations making changes in the proportion of votes required to elect Executive Directors under the provisions of Schedule E.

(*e*) Each Executive Director shall appoint an Alternate with full power to act for him when he is not present. When the Executive Directors appointing them are present, Alternates may participate in meetings but may not vote.

(*f*) Executive Directors shall continue in office until their successors are appointed or elected. If the office of an elected Executive Director becomes vacant more than ninety days before the end of his term, another Executive Director shall be elected for the remainder of the term by the members that elected the former Executive Director. A majority of the votes cast shall be required for election. While the office remains vacant, the Alternate of the former Executive Director shall exercise his powers, except that of appointing an Alternate.

(*g*) The Executive Board shall function in continuous session at the principal office of the Fund and shall meet as often as the business of the Fund may require.

(*h*) A quorum for any meeting of the Executive Board shall be a majority of the Executive Directors having not less than one-half of the total voting power.

(*i*)   (i) Each appointed Executive Director shall be entitled to cast the number of votes allotted under Section 5 of this Article to the member appointing him.

     (ii) If the votes allotted to a member that appoints an Executive Director under (*c*) above were cast by an Executive Director together with the votes allotted to other members as a result of the last regular election of Executive Directors, the member may agree with each of the other members that the number of votes allotted to it shall be cast by the appointed Executive Director. A member making such an agreement shall not participate in the election of Executive Directors.

     (iii) Each elected Executive Director shall be entitled to cast the number of votes which counted towards his election.

(iv) When the provisions of Section 5 (*b*) of this Article are applicable, the votes which an Executive Director would otherwise be entitled to cast shall be increased or decreased correspondingly. All the votes which an Executive Director is entitled to cast shall be cast as a unit.

(*j*) The Board of Governors shall adopt regulations under which a member not entitled to appoint an Executive Director under (*b*) above may send a representative to attend any meeting of the Executive Board when a request made by, or a matter particularly affecting, that member is under consideration.

Section 4. *Managing Director and staff*

(*a*) The Executive Board shall select a Managing Director who shall not be a Governor or an Executive Director. The Managing Director shall be chairman of the Executive Board, but shall have no vote except a deciding vote in case of an equal division. He may participate in meetings of the Board of Governors, but shall not vote at such meetings. The Managing Director shall cease to hold office when the Executive Board so decides.

(*b*) The Managing Director shall be chief of the operating staff of the Fund and shall conduct, under the direction of the Executive Board, the ordinary business of the Fund. Subject to the general control of the Executive Board, he shall be responsible for the organization, appointment, and dismissal of the staff of the Fund.

(*c*) The Managing Director and the staff of the Fund, in the discharge of their functions, shall owe their duty entirely to the Fund and to no other authority. Each member of the Fund shall respect the international character of this duty and shall refrain from all attempts to influence any of the staff in the discharge of these functions.

(*d*) In appointing the staff the Managing Director shall, subject to the paramount importance of securing the highest standards of efficiency and of technical competence, pay due regard to the importance of recruiting personnel on as wide a geographical basis as possible.

Section 5. *Voting*

(*a*) Each member shall have two hundred fifty votes plus one additional vote for each part of its quota equivalent to one hundred thousand special drawing rights.

(*b*) Whenever voting is required under Article V, Section 4 or 5, each member shall have the number of votes to which it is entitled under (*a*) above adjusted

(i) by the addition of one vote for the equivalent of each four hundred thousand special drawing rights of net sales of its currency from the general resources of the Fund up to the date when the vote is taken, or

(ii) by the subtraction of one vote for the equivalent of each four hundred thousand special drawing rights of its net purchases under Article V, Section 3 (*b*) and (*f*) up to the date when the vote is taken,

provided that neither net purchases nor net sales shall be deemed at any time to exceed an amount equal to the quota of the member involved.

(*c*) Except as otherwise specifically provided, all decisions of the Fund shall be made by a majority of the votes cast.

Section 6. *Reserves, distribution of net income, and investment*

(*a*) The Fund shall determine annually what part of its net income shall be placed to general reserve or special reserve, and what part, if any, shall be distributed.

(*b*) The Fund may use the special reserve for any purpose for which it may use the general reserve, except distribution.

(*c*) If any distribution is made of the net income of any year, it shall be made to all members in proportion to their quotas.

(*d*) The Fund, by a seventy percent majority of the total voting power, may decide at any time to distribute any part of the general reserve. Any such distribution shall be made to all members in proportion to their quotas.

(*e*) Payments under (*c*) and (*d*) above shall be made in special drawing rights, provided that either the Fund or the member may decide that the payment to the member shall be made in its own currency.

(*f*) (i) The Fund may establish an Investment Account for the purposes of this subsection (*f*). The assets of the Investment Account shall be held separately from the other accounts of the General Department.

(ii) The Fund may decide to transfer to the Investment Account a part of the proceeds of the sale of gold in accordance with Article V, Section 12 (*g*) and, by a seventy percent majority of the total voting power, may decide to transfer to the Investment Account, for immediate investment, currencies held in the General Resources Account. The amount of these transfers shall not exceed the total amount of the general reserve and the special reserve at the time of the decision.

(iii) The Fund may invest a member's currency held in the Investment Account in marketable obligations of that member or in marketable obligations of international financial organizations. No investment shall be made without the concurrence of the member whose currency is used to make the investment. The Fund shall invest only in obligations denominated in special drawing rights or in the currency used for investment.

(iv) The income of investment may be invested in accordance with the provisions of this subsection (*f*). Income not invested shall be held in the Investment Account or may be used for meeting the expenses of conducting the business of the Fund.

(v) The Fund may use a member's currency held in the Investment Account to obtain the currencies needed to meet the expenses of conducting the business of the Fund.

(vi) The Investment Account shall be terminated in the event of liquidation of the Fund and may be terminated, or the amount of the investment may be reduced, prior to liquidation of the Fund by a seventy percent majority of the total voting power. The Fund, by a seventy percent majority of the total voting power, shall adopt rules and regulations regarding administration of the Investment Account, which shall be consistent with (vii), (viii), and (ix) below.

(vii) Upon termination of the Investment Account because of liquidation of the Fund, any assets in this account shall be distributed in accordance with the provisions of Schedule K, provided that a portion of these assets corresponding to the proportion of the assets transferred to this account under Article V, Section 12 (*g*) to the total of the assets transferred to this account shall be deemed to be assets held in the Special Disbursement Account and shall be distributed in accordance with Schedule K, paragraph 2(*a*)(ii).

(viii) Upon termination of the Investment Account prior to liquidation of the Fund, a portion of the assets held in this account corresponding to the proportion of the assets transferred to this account under Article V, Section 12 (*g*) to the total of the assets transferred to the account shall be transferred to the Special Disbursement Account if it has not been terminated, and the balance of the assets held in the Investment Account shall be transferred to the General Resources Account for immediate use in operations and transactions.

(ix) On a reduction of the amount of the investment by the Fund, a portion of the reduction corresponding to the proportion of the assets transferred to the Investment Account under Article V, Section 12 (*g*) to the total of the assets transferred to this account shall be transferred to the Special Disbursement Account if it has not been terminated, and the balance of the reduction shall be transferred to the General Resources Account for immediate use in operations and transactions.

Section 7. *Publication of reports*

(a) The Fund shall publish an annual report containing an audited statement of its accounts, and shall issue, at intervals of three months or less, a summary statement of its operations and transactions and its holdings of special drawing rights, gold, and currencies of members.

(b) The Fund may publish such other reports as it deems desirable for carrying out its purposes.

Section 8. *Communication of views to members*

The Fund shall at all times have the right to communicate its views informally to any member on any matter arising under this Agreement. The Fund may, by a seventy percent majority of the total voting power, decide to publish a report made to a member regarding its monetary or economic conditions and developments which directly tend to produce a serious disequilibrium in the international balance of payments of members. If the member is not entitled to appoint an Executive Director, it shall be entitled to representation in accordance with Section 3 (j) of this Article. The Fund shall not publish a report involving changes in the fundamental structure of the economic organization of members.

Article XIII

Offices and Depositories

Section 1. *Location of offices*

The principal office of the Fund shall be located in the territory of the member having the largest quota, and agencies or branch offices may be established in the territories of other members.

Section 2. *Depositories*

(a) Each member shall designate its central bank as a depository for all the Fund's holdings of its currency, or if it has no central bank it shall designate such other institution as may be acceptable to the Fund.

(b) The Fund may hold other assets, including gold, in the depositories designated by the five members having the largest quotas and in such other designated depositories as the Fund may select. Initially, at least one-half of the holdings of the Fund shall be held in the depository designated by the member in whose territories the Fund has its principal office and at least forty percent shall be held in the depositories designated by the remaining four members referred to above. However, all transfers of gold by the Fund shall be made with due regard to the costs of transport and anticipated requirements of the Fund. In an emergency the Executive Board may transfer all or any part of the Fund's gold holdings to any place where they can be adequately protected.

Section 3. *Guarantee of the Fund's assets*

Each member guarantees all assets of the Fund against loss resulting from failure or default on the part of the depository designated by it.

Article XIV

Transitional Arrangements

Section 1. *Notification to the Fund*

Each member shall notify the Fund whether it intends to avail itself of the transitional arrangements in Section 2 of this Article, or whether it is prepared to accept the obligations of Article VIII, Sections 2, 3, and 4. A member availing itself of the transitional arrangements shall notify the Fund as soon thereafter as it is prepared to accept these obligations.

Section 2. *Exchange restrictions*

A member that has notified the Fund that it intends to avail itself of transitional arrangements under this provision may, notwithstanding the provisions of any other articles of this Agreement, maintain and adapt to changing circumstances the restrictions on payments and transfers for current international transactions that were in effect on the date on which it became a member. Members shall, however, have continuous regard in their foreign exchange policies to the purposes of the Fund, and, as soon as conditions permit, they shall take all possible measures to develop such commercial and financial arrangements with other members as will facilitate international payments and the promotion of a stable system of exchange rates. In particular, members shall withdraw restrictions maintained under this Section as soon as they are satisfied that they will be able, in the absence of such restrictions, to settle their balance of payments in a manner which will not unduly encumber their access to the general resources of the Fund.

Section 3. *Action of the Fund relating to restrictions*

The Fund shall make annual reports on the restrictions in force under Section 2 of this Article. Any member retaining any restrictions inconsistent with Article VIII, Sections 2, 3, or 4 shall consult the Fund annually as to their further retention. The Fund may, if it deems such action necessary in exceptional circumstances, make representations to any member that conditions are favorable for the withdrawal of any particular restriction, or for the general abandonment of restrictions, inconsistent with the provisions of any other articles of this Agreement. The member shall be given a suitable time to reply to such representations. If the Fund finds that the member persists in maintaining restrictions which are inconsistent with the purposes of the Fund, the member shall be subject to Article XXVI, Section 2 (*a*).

Article XV

Special Drawing Rights

Section 1. *Authority to allocate special drawing rights*

To meet the need, as and when it arises, for a supplement to existing reserve assets, the Fund is authorized to allocate special drawing rights to members that are participants in the Special Drawing Rights Department.

Section 2. *Valuation of the special drawing right*

The method of valuation of the special drawing right shall be determined by the Fund by a seventy percent majority of the total voting power, provided, however, that an eighty-five percent majority of the total voting power shall be required for a change in the principle of valuation or a fundamental change in the application of the principle in effect.

Article XVI

General Department and Special Drawing Rights Department

Section 1. *Separation of operations and transactions*

All operations and transactions involving special drawing rights shall be conducted through the Special Drawing Rights Department. All other operations and transactions on the account of the Fund authorized by or under this Agreement shall be conducted through the General Department. Operations and transactions pursuant to Article XVII, Section 2 shall be conducted through the General Department as well as the Special Drawing Rights Department.

Section 2. *Separation of assets and property*

All assets and property of the Fund, except resources administered under Article V, Section 2 (*b*), shall be held in the General Department, provided that assets and property acquired under Article XX, Section 2 and Articles XXIV and XXV and Schedules H and I shall be held in the

Special Drawing Rights Department. Any assets or property held in one Department shall not be available to discharge or meet the liabilities, obligations, or losses of the Fund incurred in the conduct of the operations and transactions of the other Department, except that the expenses of conducting the business of the Special Drawing Rights Department shall be paid by the Fund from the General Department which shall be reimbursed in special drawing rights from time to time by assessments under Article XX, Section 4 made on the basis of a reasonable estimate of such expenses.

Section 3. *Recording and information*

All changes in holdings of special drawing rights shall take effect only when recorded by the Fund in the Special Drawing Rights Department. Participants shall notify the Fund of the provisions of this Agreement under which special drawing rights are used. The Fund may require participants to furnish it with such other information as it deems necessary for its functions.

Article XVII

Participants and Other Holders of Special Drawing Rights

Section 1. *Participants*

Each member of the Fund that deposits with the Fund an instrument setting forth that it undertakes all the obligations of a participant in the Special Drawing Rights Department in accordance with its law and that it has taken all steps necessary to enable it to carry out all of these obligations shall become a participant in the Special Drawing Rights Department as of the date the instrument is deposited, except that no member shall become a participant before the provisions of this Agreement pertaining exclusively to the Special Drawing Rights Department have entered into force and instruments have been deposited under this Section by members that have at least seventy-five percent of the total of quotas.

Section 2. *Fund as a holder*

The Fund may hold special drawing rights in the General Resources Account and may accept and use them in operations and transactions conducted through the General Resources Account with participants in accordance with the provisions of this Agreement or with prescribed holders in accordance with the terms and conditions prescribed under Section 3 of this Article.

Section 3. *Other holders*

The Fund may prescribe:
  (i) as holders, non-members, members that are non-participants, institutions that perform functions of a central bank for more than one member, and other official entities;
 (ii) the terms and conditions on which prescribed holders may be permitted to hold special drawing rights and may accept and use them in operations and transactions with participants and other prescribed holders; and
(iii) the terms and conditions on which participants and the Fund through the General Resources Account may enter into operations and transactions in special drawing rights with prescribed holders.

An eighty-five percent majority of the total voting power shall be required for prescriptions under (i) above. The terms and conditions prescribed by the Fund shall be consistent with the provisions of this Agreement and the effective functioning of the Special Drawing Rights Department.

Article XVIII

Allocation and Cancellation of Special Drawing Rights

Section 1. *Principles and considerations governing allocation and cancellation*

(*a*) In all its decisions with respect to the allocation and cancellation of special drawing rights the Fund shall seek to meet the long-term global need, as and when it arises, to supplement existing reserve assets in such manner as will promote the attainment of its purposes and will avoid economic stagnation and deflation as well as excess demand and inflation in the world.

(*b*) The first decision to allocate special drawing rights shall take into account, as special considerations, a collective judgment that there is a global need to supplement reserves, and the attainment of a better balance of payments equilibrium, as well as the likelihood of a better working of the adjustment process in the future.

Section 2. *Allocation and cancellation*

(*a*) Decisions of the Fund to allocate or cancel special drawing rights shall be made for basic periods which shall run consecutively and shall be five years in duration. The first basic period shall begin on the date of the first decision to allocate special drawing rights or such later date as may be specified in that decision. Any allocations or cancellations shall take place at yearly intervals.

(*b*) The rates at which allocations are to be made shall be expressed as percentages of quotas on the date of each decision to allocate. The rates at which special drawing rights are to be cancelled shall be expressed as percentages of net cumulative allocations of special drawing rights on the date of each decision to cancel. The percentages shall be the same for all participants.

(*c*) In its decision for any basic period the Fund may provide, notwithstanding (*a*) and (*b*) above, that:

> (i) the duration of the basic period shall be other than five years; or
>
> (ii) the allocations or cancellations shall take place at other than yearly intervals; or
>
> (iii) the basis for allocations or cancellations shall be the quotas or net cumulative allocations on dates other than the dates of decisions to allocate or cancel.

(*d*) A member that becomes a participant after a basic period starts shall receive allocations beginning with the next basic period in which allocations are made after it becomes a participant unless the Fund decides that the new participant shall start to receive allocations beginning with the next allocation after it becomes a participant. If the Fund decides that a member that becomes a participant during a basic period shall receive allocations during the remainder of that basic period and the participant was not a member on the dates established under (*b*) or (*c*) above, the Fund shall determine the basis on which these allocations to the participant shall be made.

(*e*) A participant shall receive allocations of special drawing rights made pursuant to any decision to allocate unless:

> (i) the Governor for the participant did not vote in favor of the decision; and
>
> (ii) the participant has notified the Fund in writing prior to the first allocation of special drawing rights under that decision that it does not wish special drawing rights to be allocated to it under the decision. On the request of a participant, the Fund may decide to terminate the effect of the notice with respect to allocations of special drawing rights subsequent to the termination.

(*f*) If on the effective date of any cancellation the amount of special drawing rights held by a participant is less than its share of the special drawing rights that are to be cancelled, the participant shall eliminate its negative balance as promptly as its gross reserve position permits and shall remain in consultation with the Fund for this purpose. Special drawing rights acquired by the participant after the effective date of the cancellation shall be applied against its negative balance and cancelled.

Section 3. *Unexpected major developments*

The Fund may change the rates or intervals of allocation or cancellation during the rest of a basic period or change the length of a basic period or start a new basic period, if at any time the Fund finds it desirable to do so because of unexpected major developments.

Section 4. *Decisions on allocations and cancellations*

(*a*) Decisions under Section 2(*a*), (*b*), and (*c*) or Section 3 of this Article shall be made by the Board of Governors on the basis of proposals of the Managing Director concurred in by the Executive Board.

(*b*) Before making any proposal, the Managing Director, after having satisfied himself that it will be consistent with the provisions of Section 1(*a*) of this Article, shall conduct such consultations as will enable him to ascertain that there is broad support among participants for the proposal. In addition, before making a proposal for the first allocation, the Managing Director shall satisfy himself that the provisions of Section 1(*b*) of this Article have been met and that there is broad support among participants to begin allocations; he shall make a proposal for the first allocation as soon after the establishment of the Special Drawing Rights Department as he is so satisfied.

(*c*) The Managing Director shall make proposals:
  (i) not later than six months before the end of each basic period;
  (ii) if no decision has been taken with respect to allocation or cancellation for a basic period, whenever he is satisfied that the provisions of (*b*) above have been met;
  (iii) when, in accordance with Section 3 of this Article, he considers that it would be desirable to change the rate or intervals of allocation or cancellation or change the length of a basic period or start a new basic period; or
  (iv) within six months of a request by the Board of Governors or the Executive Board;

provided that, if under (i), (iii), or (iv) above the Managing Director ascertains that there is no proposal which he considers to be consistent with the provisions of Section 1 of this Article that has broad support among participants in accordance with (*b*) above, he shall report to the Board of Governors and to the Executive Board.

(*d*) An eighty-five percent majority of the total voting power shall be required for decisions under Section 2 (*a*), (*b*), and (*c*) or Section 3 of this Article except for decisions under Section 3 with respect to a decrease in the rates of allocation.

Article XIX

Operations and Transactions in Special Drawing Rights

Section 1. *Use of special drawing rights*

Special drawing rights may be used in the operations and transactions authorized by or under this Agreement.

Section 2. *Operations and transactions between participants*

(*a*) A participart shall be entitled to use its special drawing rights to obtain an equivalent amount of currency from a participant designated under Section 5 of this Article.

(*b*) A participant, in agreement with another participant, may use its special drawing rights to obtain an equivalent amount of currency from the other participant.

(*c*) The Fund, by a seventy percent majority of the total voting power, may prescribe operations in which a participant is authorized to engage in agreement with another participant on such terms and conditions as the Fund deems appropriate. The terms and conditions shall be consistent with the effective functioning of the Special Drawing Rights Department and the proper use of special drawing rights in accordance with this Agreement.

(*d*) The Fund may make representations to a participant that enters into any operation or transaction under (*b*) or (*c*) above that in the judgment of the Fund may be prejudicial to the process of designation according to the principles of Section 5 of this Article or is otherwise inconsistent with Article XXII. A participant that persists in entering into such operations or transactions shall be subject to Article XXIII, Section 2(*b*).

Section 3. *Requirement of need*

(*a*) In transactions under Section 2(*a*) of this Article, except as otherwise provided in (*c*) below, a participant will be expected to use its special drawing rights only if it has a need because of its balance of payments or its reserve position or developments in its reserves, and not for the sole purpose of changing the composition of its reserves.

(*b*) The use of special drawing rights shall not be subject to challenge on the basis of the expectation in (*a*) above, but the Fund may make representations to a participant that fails to fulfill this expectation. A participant that persists in failing to fulfill this expectation shall be subject to Article XXIII, Section 2 (*b*).

(*c*) The Fund may waive the expectation in (*a*) above in any transactions in which a participant uses special drawing rights to obtain an equivalent amount of currency from a participant designated under Section 5 of this Article that would promote reconstitution by the other participant under Section 6 (*a*) of this Article; prevent or reduce a negative balance of the other participant; or offset the effect of a failure by the other participant to fulfill the expectation in (*a*) above.

Section 4. *Obligation to provide currency*

(*a*) A participant designated by the Fund under Section 5 of this Article shall provide on demand a freely usable currency to a participant using special drawing rights under Section 2 (*a*) of this Article. A participant's obligation to provide currency shall not extend beyond the point at which its holdings of special drawing rights in excess of its net cumulative allocation are equal to twice its net cumulative allocation or such higher limit as may be agreed between a participant and the Fund.

(*b*) A participant may provide currency in excess of the obligatory limit or any agreed higher limit.

Section 5. *Designation of participants to provide currency*

(*a*) The Fund shall ensure that a participant will be able to use its special drawing rights by designating participants to provide currency for specified amounts of special drawing rights for the purposes of Sections 2 (*a*) and 4 of this Article. Designations shall be made in accordance with the following general principles supplemented by such other principles as the Fund may adopt from time to time:

    (i) A participant shall be subject to designation if its balance of payments and gross reserve position is sufficiently strong, but this will not preclude the possibility that a participant with a strong reserve position will be designated even though it has a moderate balance of payments deficit. Participants shall be designated in such manner as will promote over time a balanced distribution of holdings of special drawing rights among them.

(ii) Participants shall be subject to designation in order to promote reconstitution under Section 6(*a*) of this Article, to reduce negative balances in holdings of special drawing rights, or to offset the effect of failures to fulfill the expectation in Section 3(*a*) of this Article.

(iii) In designating participants the Fund normally shall give priority to those that need to acquire special drawing rights to meet the objectives of designation under (ii) above.

(*b*) In order to promote over time a balanced distribution of holdings of special drawing rights under (*a*)(i) above, the Fund shall apply the rules for designation in Schedule F or such rules as may be adopted under (*c*) below.

(*c*) The rules for designation may be reviewed at any time and new rules shall be adopted if necessary. Unless new rules are adopted, the rules in force at the time of the review shall continue to apply.

Section 6. *Reconstitution*

(*a*) Participants that use their special drawing rights shall reconstitute their holdings of them in accordance with the rules for reconstitution in Schedule G or such rules as may be adopted under (*b*) below.

(*b*) The rules for reconstitution may be reviewed at any time and new rules shall be adopted if necessary. Unless new rules are adopted or a decision is made to abrogate rules for reconstitution, the rules in force at the time of review shall continue to apply. A seventy percent majority of the total voting power shall be required for decisions to adopt, modify, or abrogate the rules for reconstitution.

Section 7. *Exchange rates*

(*a*) Except as otherwise provided in (*b*) below, the exchange rates for transactions between participants under Section 2(*a*) and (*b*) of this Article shall be such that participants using special drawing rights shall receive the same value whatever currencies might be provided and whichever participants provide those currencies, and the Fund shall adopt regulations to give effect to this principle.

(*b*) The Fund, by an eighty-five percent majority of the total voting power, may adopt policies under which in exceptional circumstances the Fund, by a seventy percent majority of the total voting power, may authorize participants entering into transactions under Section 2(*b*) of this Article to agree on exchange rates other than those applicable under (*a*) above.

(*c*) The Fund shall consult a participant on the procedure for determining rates of exchange for its currency.

(*d*) For the purpose of this provision the term participant includes a terminating participant.

Article XX

Special Drawing Rights Department
Interest and Charges

Section 1. *Interest*

Interest at the same rate for all holders shall be paid by the Fund to each holder on the amount of its holdings of special drawing rights. The Fund shall pay the amount due to each holder whether or not sufficient charges are received to meet the payment of interest.

Section 2. *Charges*

Charges at the same rate for all participants shall be paid to the Fund by each participant on the amount of its net cumulative allocation of special drawing rights plus any negative balance of the participant or unpaid charges.

Section 3. *Rate of interest and charges*

The Fund shall determine the rate of interest by a seventy percent majority of the total voting power. The rate of charges shall be equal to the rate of interest.

Section 4. *Assessments*

When it is decided under Article XVI, Section 2 that reimbursement shall be made, the Fund shall levy assessments for this purpose at the same rate for all participants on their net cumulative allocations.

Section 5. *Payment of interest, charges, and assessments*

Interest, charges, and assessments shall be paid in special drawing rights. A participant that needs special drawing rights to pay any charge or assessment shall be obligated and entitled to obtain them, for currency acceptable to the Fund, in a transaction with the Fund conducted through the General Resources Account. If sufficient special drawing rights cannot be obtained in this way, the participant shall be obligated and entitled to obtain them with a freely usable currency from a participant which the Fund shall specify. Special drawing rights acquired by a participant after the date for payment shall be applied against its unpaid charges and cancelled.

Article XXI

Administration of the General Department and the Special Drawing Rights Department

(*a*) The General Department and the Special Drawing Rights Department shall be administered in accordance with the provisions of Article XII, subject to the following provisions:

(i) For meetings of or decisions by the Board of Governors on matters pertaining exclusively to the Special Drawing Rights Department only requests by, or the presence and the votes of, Governors appointed by members that are participants shall be counted for the purpose of calling meetings and determining whether a quorum exists or whether a decision is made by the required majority.

(ii) For decisions by the Executive Board on matters pertaining exclusively to the Special Drawing Rights Department only Executive Directors appointed or elected by at least one member that is a participant shall be entitled to vote. Each of these Executive Directors shall be entitled to cast the number of votes allotted to the member which is a participant that appointed him or to the members that are participants whose votes counted towards his election. Only the presence of Executive Directors appointed or elected by members that are participants and the votes allotted to members that are participants shall be counted for the purpose of determining whether a quorum exists or whether a decision is made by the required majority. For the purposes of this provision, an agreement under Article XII, Section 3 (*i*) (ii) by a member that is a participant shall entitle an appointed Executive Director to vote and cast the number of votes allotted to the member.

(iii) Questions of the general administration of the Fund, including reimbursement under Article XVI, Section 2, and any question whether a matter pertains to both Departments or exclusively to the Special Drawing Rights Department shall be decided as if they pertained exclusively to the General Department. Decisions with respect to the method of valuation of the special drawing right, the acceptance and holding of special drawing rights in the General Resources Account of the General Department and the use of them, and other decisions affecting the operations and transactions conducted through both the General Resources Account of the General Department and the Special Drawing Rights Department shall be made by the majorities required for decisions on matters pertaining exclusively to each Department. A decision on a matter pertaining to the Special Drawing Rights Department shall so indicate.

(*b*) In addition to the privileges and immunities that are accorded under Article IX of this Agreement, no tax of any kind shall be levied on special drawing rights or on operations or transactions in special drawing rights.

(*c*) A question of interpretation of the provisions of this Agreement on matters pertaining exclusively to the Special Drawing Rights Department shall be submitted to the Executive Board pursuant to Article XXIX (*a*) only on the request of a participant. In any case where the Executive Board has given a decision on a question of interpretation pertaining exclusively to the Special Drawing Rights Department only a participant may require that the question be referred to the Board of Governors under Article XXIX (*b*). The Board of Governors shall decide whether a Governor appointed by a member that is not a participant shall be entitled to vote in the Committee on Interpretation on questions pertaining exclusively to the Special Drawing Rights Department.

(*d*) Whenever a disagreement arises between the Fund and a participant that has terminated its participation in the Special Drawing Rights Department or between the Fund and any participant during the liquidation of the Special Drawing Rights Department with respect to any matter arising exclusively from participation in the Special Drawing Rights Department, the disagreement shall be submitted to arbitration in accordance with the procedures in Article XXIX (*c*).

Article XXII

General Obligations of Participants

In addition to the obligations assumed with respect to special drawing rights under other articles of this Agreement, each participant undertakes to collaborate with the Fund and with other participants in order to facilitate the effective functioning of the Special Drawing Rights Department and the proper use of special drawing rights in accordance with this Agreement and with the objective of making the special drawing right the principal reserve asset in the international monetary system.

Article XXIII

Suspension of Operations and Transactions in Special Drawing Rights

Section 1. *Emergency provisions*

In the event of an emergency or the development of unforeseen circumstances threatening the activities of the Fund with respect to the Special Drawing Rights Department, the Executive Board, by an eighty-five percent majority of the total voting power, may suspend for a period of not more than one year the operation of any of the provisions relating to operations and transactions in special drawing rights, and the provisions of Article XXVII, Section 1(b), (c), and (d) shall then apply.

Section 2. *Failure to fulfill obligations*

(a) If the Fund finds that a participant has failed to fulfill its obligations under Article XIX, Section 4, the right of the participant to use its special drawing rights shall be suspended unless the Fund otherwise decides.

(b) If the Fund finds that a participant has failed to fulfill any other obligation with respect to special drawing rights, the Fund may suspend the right of the participant to use special drawing rights it acquires after the suspension.

(c) Regulations shall be adopted to ensure that before action is taken against any participant under (a) or (b) above, the participant shall be informed immediately of the complaint against it and given an adequate opportunity for stating its case, both orally and in writing. Whenever the participant is thus informed of a complaint relating to (a) above, it shall not use special drawing rights pending the disposition of the complaint.

(d) Suspension under (a) or (b) above or limitation under (c) above shall not affect a participant's obligation to provide currency in accordance with Article XIX, Section 4.

(e) The Fund may at any time terminate a suspension under (a) or (b) above, provided that a suspension imposed on a participant under (b) above for failure to fulfill the obligations under Article XIX, Section 6(a) shall not be terminated until one hundred eighty days after the end of the first calendar quarter during which the participant complies with the rules for reconstitution.

(f) The right of a participant to use its special drawing rights shall not be suspended because it has become ineligible to use the Fund's general resources under Article V, Section 5, Article VI, Section 1, or Article XXVI, Section 2(a). Article XXVI, Section 2 shall not apply because a participant has failed to fulfill any obligations with respect to special drawing rights.

Article XXIV

Termination of Participation

Section 1. *Right to terminate participation*

(a) Any participant may terminate its participation in the Special Drawing Rights Department at any time by transmitting a notice in writing to the Fund at its principal office. Termination shall become effective on the date the notice is received.

(b) A participant that withdraws from membership in the Fund shall be deemed to have simultaneously terminated its participation in the Special Drawing Rights Department.

Section 2. *Settlement on termination*

(a) When a participant terminates its participation in the Special Drawing Rights Department, all operations and transactions by the terminating participant in special drawing rights shall cease except as otherwise permitted under an agreement made pursuant to (c) below in order to facilitate a settlement or as provided in Sections 3, 5, and 6 of this Article or in Schedule H. Interest and charges that accrued to the date of termination and assessments levied before that date but not paid shall be paid in special drawing rights.

(b) The Fund shall be obligated to redeem all special drawing rights held by the terminating participant, and the terminating participant shall be obligated to pay to the Fund an amount equal to its net cumulative allocation and any other amounts that may be due and payable because of its participation in the Special Drawing Rights Department. These obligations shall be set off against each other and the amount of special drawing rights held by the terminating participant that is used in the setoff to extinguish its obligation to the Fund shall be cancelled.

(c) A settlement shall be made with reasonable despatch by agreement between the terminating participant and the Fund with respect to any obligation of the terminating participant or the Fund after the setoff in (b) above. If agreement on a settlement is not reached promptly the provisions of Schedule H shall apply.

Section 3. *Interest and charges*

After the date of termination the Fund shall pay interest on any outstanding balance of special drawing rights held by a terminating participant and the terminating participant shall pay charges on any outstanding obligation owed to the Fund at the times and rates precribed under Article XX. Payment shall be made in special drawing rights. A terminating participant shall be entitled to obtain special drawing rights with a freely usable currency to pay charges or assessments in a transaction with a participant specified by the Fund or by agreement from any other holder, or to dispose of special drawing rights received as interest in a transaction with any participant designated under Article XIX, Section 5 or by agreement with any other holder.

Section 4. *Settlement of obligation to the Fund*

Currency received by the Fund from a terminating participant shall be used by the Fund to redeem special drawing rights held by participants in proportion to the amount by which each participant's holdings of special drawing rights exceed its net cumulative allocation at the time the currency is received by the Fund. Special drawing rights so redeemed and special drawing rights obtained by a terminating participant under the provisions of this Agreement to meet any installment due under an agreement on settlement or under Schedule H and set off against that installment shall be cancelled.

Section 5. *Settlement of obligation to a terminating participant*

Whenever the Fund is required to redeem special drawing rights held by a terminating participant, redemption shall be made with currency provided by participants specified by the Fund. These participants shall be specified in accordance with the principles in Article XIX, Section 5. Each specified participant shall provide at its option the currency of the terminating participant or a freely usable currency to the Fund and shall receive an equivalent amount of special drawing rights. However, a terminating participant may use its special drawing rights to obtain its own currency, a freely usable currency, or any other asset from any holder, if the Fund so permits.

Section 6. *General Resources Account transactions*

In order to facilitate settlement with a terminating participant, the Fund may decide that a terminating participant shall:

(i) use any special drawing rights held by it after the setoff in Section 2 (*b*) of this Article, when they are to be redeemed, in a transaction with the Fund conducted through the General Resources Account to obtain its own currency or a freely usable currency at the option of the Fund; or

(ii) obtain special drawing rights in a transaction with the Fund conducted through the General Resources Account for a currency acceptable to the Fund to meet any charges or installment due under an agreement or the provisions of Schedule H.

Article XXV

Liquidation of the Special Drawing Rights Department

(*a*) The Special Drawing Rights Department may not be liquidated except by decision of the Board of Governors. In an emergency, if the Executive Board decides that liquidation of the Special Drawing Rights Department may be necessary, it may temporarily suspend allocations or cancellations and all operations and transactions in special drawing rights pending decision by the Board of Governors. A decision by the Board of Governors to liquidate the Fund shall be a decision to liquidate both the General Department and the Special Drawing Rights Department.

(*b*) If the Board of Governors decides to liquidate the Special Drawing Rights Department, all allocations or cancellations and all operations and transactions in special drawing rights and the activities of the Fund with respect to the Special Drawing Rights Department shall cease except those incidental to the orderly discharge of the obligations of participants and of the Fund with respect to special drawing rights, and all obligations of the Fund and of participants under this Agreement with respect to special drawing rights shall cease except those set out in this Article, Article XX, Article XXI(*d*), Article XXIV, Article XXIX(*c*), and Schedule H, or any agreement reached under Article XXIV subject to paragraph 4 of Schedule H, and Schedule I.

(*c*) Upon liquidation of the Special Drawing Rights Department, interest and charges that accrued to the date of liquidation and assessments levied before that date but not paid shall be paid in special drawing rights. The Fund shall be obligated to redeem all special drawing rights held by holders, and each participant shall be obligated to pay the Fund an amount equal to its net cumulative allocation of special drawing rights and such other amounts as may be due and payable because of its participation in the Special Drawing Rights Department.

(*d*) Liquidation of the Special Drawing Rights Department shall be administered in accordance with the provisions of Schedule I.

Article XXVI

Withdrawal from Membership

Section 1. *Right of members to withdraw*

Any member may withdraw from the Fund at any time by transmitting a notice in writing to the Fund at its principal office. Withdrawal shall become effective on the date such notice is received.

Section 2. *Compulsory withdrawal*

(*a*) If a member fails to fulfill any of its obligations under this Agreement, the Fund may declare the member ineligible to use the general resources of the Fund. Nothing in this Section shall be deemed to limit the provisions of Article V, Section 5 or Article VI, Section 1.

(*b*) If, after the expiration of a reasonable period the member persists in its failure to fulfill any of its obligations under this Agreement, that member may be required to withdraw from membership in the Fund by a decision of the Board of Governors carried by a majority of the Governors having eighty-five percent of the total voting power.

(*c*) Regulations shall be adopted to ensure that before action is taken against any member under (*a*) or (*b*) above, the member shall be informed in reasonable time of the complaint against it and given an adequate opportunity for stating its case, both orally and in writing.

Section 3. *Settlement of accounts with members withdrawing*

When a member withdraws from the Fund, normal operations and transactions of the Fund in its currency shall cease and settlement of all accounts between it and the Fund shall be made with reasonable despatch by agreement between it and the Fund. If agreement is not reached promptly, the provisions of Schedule J shall apply to the settlement of accounts.

Article XXVII

Emergency Provisions

Section 1. *Temporary suspension*

(*a*) In the event of an emergency or the development of unforeseen circumstances threatening the activities of the Fund, the Executive Board, by an eighty-five percent majority of the total voting power, may suspend for a period of not more than one year the operation of any of the following provisions:

(i) Article V, Sections 2, 3, 7, 8(*a*)(i) and (*e*);

(ii) Article VI, Section 2;

(iii) Article XI, Section 1;

(iv) Schedule C, paragraph 5.

(*b*) A suspension of the operation of a provision under (*a*) above may not be extended beyond one year except by the Board of Governors which, by an eighty-five percent majority of the total voting power, may extend a suspension for an additional period of not more than two years if it finds that the emergency or unforeseen circumstances referred to in (*a*) above continue to exist.

(*c*) The Executive Board may, by a majority of the total voting power, terminate such suspension at any time.

(*d*) The Fund may adopt rules with respect to the subject matter of a provision during the period in which its operation is suspended.

Section 2. *Liquidation of the Fund*

(*a*) The Fund may not be liquidated except by decision of the Board of Governors. In an emergency, if the Executive Board decides that liquidation of the Fund may be necessary, it may temporarily suspend all operations and transactions, pending decision by the Board of Governors.

(*b*) If the Board of Governors decides to liquidate the Fund, the Fund shall forthwith cease to engage in any activities except those incidental to the orderly collection and liquidation of its assets and the settlement of its liabilities, and all obligations of members under this Agreement shall cease except those set out in this Article, in Article XXIX (*c*), in Schedule J, paragraph 7, and in Schedule K.

(*c*) Liquidation shall be administered in accordance with the provisions of Schedule K.

Article XXVIII

Amendments

(*a*) Any proposal to introduce modifications in this Agreement, whether emanating from a member, a Governor, or the Executive Board, shall be communicated to the chairman of the Board of Governors who shall bring the proposal before the Board of Governors. If the proposed amendment is approved by the Board of Governors, the Fund shall, by circular letter or telegram, ask all members whether they accept the proposed amendment. When three-fifths of the members, having eighty-five percent of the total voting power, have accepted the proposed amendment, the Fund shall certify the fact by a formal communication addressed to all members.

(*b*) Notwithstanding (*a*) above, acceptance by all members is required in the case of any amendment modifying:

> (i) the right to withdraw from the Fund (Article XXVI, Section 1);
> (ii) the provision that no change in a member's quota shall be made without its consent (Article III, Section 2(*d*)); and
> (iii) the provision that no change may be made in the par value of a member's currency except on the proposal of that member (Schedule C, paragraph 6).

(*c*) Amendments shall enter into force for all members three months after the date of the formal communication unless a shorter period is specified in the circular letter or telegram.

Article XXIX

Interpretation

(*a*) Any question of interpretation of the provisions of this Agreement arising between any member and the Fund or between any members of the Fund shall be submitted to the Executive Board for its decision. If the question particularly affects any member not entitled to appoint an Executive Director, it shall be entitled to representation in accordance with Article XII, Section 3(*j*).

(*b*) In any case where the Executive Board has given a decision under (*a*) above, any member may require, within three months from the date of the decision, that the question be referred to the Board of Governors, whose decision shall be final. Any question referred to the Board of Governors shall be considered by a Committee on Interpretation of the Board of Governors. Each Committee member shall have one vote. The Board of Governors shall establish the membership, procedures, and voting majorities of the Committee. A decision of the Committee shall be the decision of the Board of Governors unless the Board of Governors, by an eighty-five percent majority of the total voting power, decides otherwise. Pending the result of the reference to the Board of Governors the Fund may, so far as it deems necessary, act on the basis of the decision of the Executive Board.

(*c*) Whenever a disagreement arises between the Fund and a member which has withdrawn, or between the Fund and any member during liquidation of the Fund, such disagreement shall be submitted to arbitration by a tribunal of three arbitrators, one appointed by the Fund, another by the member or withdrawing member, and an umpire who, unless the parties otherwise agree, shall be appointed by the President of the International Court of Justice or such other authority as may have been prescribed by regulation adopted by the Fund. The umpire shall have full power to settle all questions of procedure in any case where the parties are in disagreement with respect thereto.

Article XXX

Explanation of Terms

In interpreting the provisions of this Agreement the Fund and its members shall be guided by the following provisions:

(*a*) The Fund's holdings of a member's currency in the General Resources Account shall include any securities accepted by the Fund under Article III, Section 4.

(*b*) Stand-by arrangement means a decision of the Fund by which a member is assured that it will be able to make purchases from the General Resources Account in accordance with the terms of the decision during a specified period and up to a specified amount.

(*c*) Reserve tranche purchase means a purchase by a member of special drawing rights or the currency of another member in exchange for its own currency which does not cause the Fund's holdings of the member's currency in the General Resources Account to exceed its quota, provided that for the purposes of this definition the Fund may exclude purchases and holdings under:

    (i) policies on the use of its general resources for compensatory financing of export fluctuations;

    (ii) policies on the use of its general resources in connection with the financing of contributions to international buffer stocks of primary products; and

    (iii) other policies on the use of its general resources in respect of which the Fund decides, by an eighty-five percent majority of the total voting power, that an exclusion shall be made.

(*d*) Payments for current transactions means payments which are not for the purpose of transferring capital, and includes, without limitation:

    (1) all payments due in connection with foreign trade, other current business, including services, and normal short-term banking and credit facilities;

    (2) payments due as interest on loans and as net income from other investments;

    (3) payments of moderate amount for amortization of loans or for depreciation of direct investments; and

    (4) moderate remittances for family living expenses.

The Fund may, after consultation with the members concerned, determine whether certain specific transactions are to be considered current transactions or capital transactions.

(*e*) Net cumulative allocation of special drawing rights means the total amount of special drawing rights allocated to a participant less its share of special drawing rights that have been cancelled under Article XVIII, Section 2 (*a*).

(*f*) A freely usable currency means a member's currency that the Fund determines (i) is, in fact, widely used to make payments for international transactions, and (ii) is widely traded in the principal exchange markets.

(*g*) Members that were members on August 31, 1975 shall be deemed to include a member that accepted membership after that date pursuant to a resolution of the Board of Governors adopted before that date.

(*h*) Transactions of the Fund means exchanges of monetary assets by the Fund for other monetary assets. Operations of the Fund means other uses or receipts of monetary assets by the Fund.

(*i*) Transactions in special drawing rights means exchanges of special drawing rights for other monetary assets. Operations in special drawing rights means other uses of special drawing rights.

Article XXXI

Final Provisions

Section 1. *Entry into force*

This Agreement shall enter into force when it has been signed on behalf of governments having sixty-five percent of the total of the quotas set forth in Schedule A and when the instruments referred to in Section 2 (*a*) of this Article have been deposited on their behalf, but in no event shall this Agreement enter into force before May 1, 1945.

Section 2. *Signature*

(*a*) Each government on whose behalf this Agreement is signed shall deposit with the Government of the United States of America an instrument setting forth that it has accepted this Agreement in accordance with its law and has taken all steps necessary to enable it to carry out all of its obligations under this Agreement.

(*b*) Each country shall become a member of the Fund as from the date of the deposit on its behalf of the instrument referred to in (*a*) above, except that no country shall become a member before this Agreement enters into force under Section 1 of this Article.

(*c*) The Government of the United States of America shall inform the governments of all countries whose names are set forth in Schedule A, and the governments of all countries whose membership is approved in accordance with Article II, Section 2, of all signatures of this Agreement and of the deposit of all instruments referred to in (*a*) above.

(*d*) At the time this Agreement is signed on its behalf, each government shall transmit to the Government of the United States of America one-hundredth of one percent of its total subscription in gold or United States dollars for the purpose of meeting administrative expenses of the

Fund. The Government of the United States of America shall hold such funds in a special deposit account and shall transmit them to the Board of Governors of the Fund when the initial meeting has been called. If this Agreement has not come into force by December 31, 1945, the Government of the United States of America shall return such funds to the governments that transmitted them.

(*e*) This Agreement shall remain open for signature at Washington on behalf of the governments of the countries whose names are set forth in Schedule A until December 31, 1945.

(*f*) After December 31, 1945, this Agreement shall be open for signature on behalf of the government of any country whose membership has been approved in accordance with Article II, Section 2.

(*g*) By their signature of this Agreement, all governments accept it both on their own behalf and in respect of all their colonies, overseas territories, all territories under their protection, suzerainty, or authority, and all territories in respect of which they exercise a mandate.

(*h*) Subsection (*d*) above shall come into force with regard to each signatory government as from the date of its signature.

[The signature and depositary clause reproduced below followed the text of Article XX in the original Articles of Agreement]

Done at Washington, in a single copy which shall remain deposited in the archives of the Government of the United States of America, which shall transmit certified copies to all governments whose names are set forth in Schedule A and to all governments whose membership is approved in accordance with Article II, Section 2.

Schedule A

Quotas

(In millions of United States dollars)

Australia	200	Iran	25
Belgium	225	Iraq	8
Bolivia	10	Liberia	.5
Brazil	150	Luxembourg	10
Canada	300	Mexico	90
Chile	50	Netherlands	275
China	550	New Zealand	50
Colombia	50	Nicaragua	2
Costa Rica	5	Norway	50
Cuba	50	Panama	.5
Czechoslovakia	125	Paraguay	2
Denmark*	*	Peru	25
Dominican Republic	5	Philippine	

Ecuador	5	Commonwealth	15
Egypt	45	Poland	125
El Salvador	2.5	Union of South Africa	100
Ethiopia	6	Union of Soviet Socialist	
France	450	Republic	1200
Greece	40	United Kingdom	1300
Guatemala	5	United States	2750
Haiti	5	Uruguay	15
Honduras	2.5	Venezuela	15
Iceland	1	Yugoslavia	60
India	400		

*The quota of Denmark shall be determined by the Fund after the Danish Government has declared its readiness to sign this Agreement but before signature takes place.

Schedule B

Transitional Provisions with Respect to Repurchase, Payment of Additional Subscriptions, Gold, and Certain Operational Matters

1. Repurchase obligations that have accrued pursuant to Article V, Section 7(b) before the date of the second amendment of this Agreement and that remain undischarged at that date shall be discharged not later than the date or dates at which the obligations had to be discharged in accordance with the provisions of this Agreement before the second amendment.

2. A member shall discharge with special drawing rights any obligation to pay gold to the Fund in repurchase or as a subscription that is outstanding at the date of the second amendment of this Agreement, but the Fund may prescribe that these payments may be made in whole or in part in the currencies of other members specified by the Fund. A non-participant shall discharge an obligation that must be paid in special drawing rights pursuant to this provision with the currencies of other members specified by the Fund.

3. For the purposes of 2 above 0.888 671 gram of fine gold shall be equivalent to one special drawing right, and the amount of currency payable under 2 above shall be determined on that basis and on the basis of the value of the currency in terms of the special drawing right at the date of discharge.

4. A member's currency held by the Fund in excess of seventy-five percent of the member's quota at the date of the second amendment of

this Agreement and not subject to repurchase under 1 above shall be repurchased in accordance with the following rules:

 (i) Holdings that resulted from a purchase shall be repurchased in accordance with the policy on the use of the Fund's general resources under which the purchase was made.

 (ii) Other holdings shall be repurchased not later than four years after the date of the second amendment of this Agreement.

5. Repurchases under 1 above that are not subject to 2 above, repurchases under 4 above, and any specification of currencies under 2 above shall be in accordance with Article V, Section 7(*i*).

6. All rules and regulations, rates, procedures, and decisions in effect at the date of the second amendment of this Agreement shall remain in effect until they are changed in accordance with the provisions of this Agreement.

7. To the extent that arrangements equivalent in effect to (*a*) and (*b*) below have not been completed before the date of the second amendment of this Agreement, the Fund shall

 (*a*) sell up to 25 million ounces of fine gold held by it on August 31, 1975 to those members that were members on that date and that agree to buy it, in proportion to their quotas on that date. The sale to a member under this subparagraph (*a*) shall be made in exchange for its currency and at a price equivalent at the time of sale to one special drawing right per 0.888 671 gram of fine gold, and

 (*b*) sell up to 25 million ounces of fine gold held by it on August 31, 1975 for the benefit of developing members that were members on that date, provided, however, that the part of any profits or surplus value of the gold that corresponds to the proportion of such a member's quota on August 31, 1975 to the total of the quotas of all members on that date shall be transferred directly to each such member. The requirements under Article V, Section 12 (*c*) that the Fund consult a member, obtain a member's concurrence, or exchange a member's currency for the currencies of other members in certain circumstances shall apply with respect to currency received by the Fund as a result of sales of gold under this provision, other than sales to a member in return for its own currency, and placed in the General Resources Account.

Upon the sale of gold under this paragraph 7, an amount of the proceeds in the currencies received equivalent at the time of sale to one special drawing right per 0.888 671 gram of fine gold shall be placed in the General Resources Account and other assets held by the Fund under arrangements pursuant to (*b*) above shall be held separately from the general resources of the Fund. Assets that remain subject to disposition by the Fund upon termination of arrangements pursuant to (*b*) above shall be transferred to the Special Disbursement Account.

Schedule C

Par Values

1. The Fund shall notify members that par values may be established for the purposes of this Agreement, in accordance with Article IV, Sections 1, 3, 4, and 5 and this Schedule, in terms of the special drawing right, or in terms of such other common denominator as is prescribed by the Fund. The common denominator shall not be gold or a currency.

2. A member that intends to establish a par value for its currency shall propose a par value to the Fund within a reasonable time after notice is given under 1 above.

3. Any member that does not intend to establish a par value for its currency under 1 above shall consult with the Fund and ensure that its exchange arrangements are consistent with the purposes of the Fund and are adequate to fulfill its obligations under Article IV, Section 1.

4. The Fund shall concur in or object to a proposed par value within a reasonable period after receipt of the proposal. A proposed par value shall not take effect for the purposes of this Agreement if the Fund objects to it, and the member shall be subject to 3 above. The Fund shall not object because of the domestic social or political policies of the member proposing the par value.

5. Each member that has a par value for its currency undertakes to apply appropriate measures consistent with this Agreement in order to ensure that the maximum and the minimum rates for spot exchange transactions taking place within its territories between its currency and the currencies of other members maintaining par values shall not differ from parity by more than four and one-half percent or by such other margin or margins as the Fund may adopt by an eighty-five percent majority of the total voting power.

6. A member shall not propose a change in the par value of its currency except to correct, or prevent the emergence of, a fundamental

disequilibrium. A change may be made only on the proposal of the member and only after consultation with the Fund.

7. When a change is proposed, the Fund shall concur in or object to the proposed par value within a reasonable period after receipt of the proposal. The Fund shall concur if it is satisfied that the change is necessary to correct, or prevent the emergence of, a fundamental disequilibrium. The Fund shall not object because of the domestic social or political policies of the member proposing the change. A proposed change in par value shall not take effect for the purposes of this Agreement if the Fund objects to it. If a member changes the par value of its currency despite the objection of the Fund, the member shall be subject to Article XXVI, Section 2. Maintenance of an unrealistic par value by a member shall be discouraged by the Fund.

8. The par value of a member's currency established under this Agreement shall cease to exist for the purposes of this Agreement if the member informs the Fund that it intends to terminate the par value. The Fund may object to the termination of a par value by a decision taken by an eighty-five percent majority of the total voting power. If a member terminates a par value for its currency despite the objection of the Fund, the member shall be subject to Article XXVI, Section 2. A par value established under this Agreement shall cease to exist for the purposes of this Agreement if the member terminates the par value despite the objection of the Fund, or if the Fund finds that the member does not maintain rates for a substantial volume of exchange transactions in accordance with 5 above, provided that the Fund may not make such finding unless it has consulted the member and given it sixty days notice of the Fund's intention to consider whether to make a finding.

9. If the par value of the currency of a member has ceased to exist under 8 above, the member shall consult with the Fund and ensure that its exchange arrangements are consistent with the purposes of the Fund and are adequate to fulfill its obligations under Article IV, Section 1.

10. A member for whose currency the par value has ceased to exist under 8 above may, at any time, propose a new par value for its currency.

11. Notwithstanding 6 above, the Fund, by a seventy percent majority of the total voting power, may make uniform proportionate changes in all par values if the special drawing right is the common denominator and the changes will not affect the value of the special drawing right. The par value of a member's currency shall, however, not be changed under this provision if, within seven days after the Fund's action, the member informs the Fund that it does not wish the par value of its currency to be changed by such action.

Schedule D

Council

1. (*a*) Each member that appoints an Executive Director and each group of members that has the number of votes allotted to them cast by an elected Executive Director shall appoint to the Council one Councillor, who shall be a Governor, Minister in the government of a member, or person of comparable rank, and may appoint not more than seven Associates. The Board of Governors may change, by an eighty-five percent majority of the total voting power, the number of Associates who may be appointed. A Councillor or Associate shall serve until a new appointment is made or until the next regular election of Executive Directors, whichever shall occur sooner.

   (*b*) Executive Directors, or in their absence their Alternates, and Associates shall be entitled to attend meetings of the Council, unless the Council decides to hold a restricted session. Each member and each group of members that appoints a Councillor shall appoint an Alternate who shall be entitled to attend a meeting of the Council when the Councillor is not present, and shall have full power to act for the Councillor.

2. (*a*) The Council shall supervise the management and adaptation of the international monetary system, including the continuing operation of the adjustment process and developments in global liquidity, and in this connection shall review developments in the transfer of real resources to developing countries.

   (*b*) The Council shall consider proposals pursuant to Article XXVIII(*a*) to amend the Articles of Agreement.

3. (*a*) The Board of Governors may delegate to the Council authority to exercise any powers of the Board of Governors except the powers conferred directly by this Agreement on the Board of Governors.

   (*b*) Each Councillor shall be entitled to cast the number of votes alloted under Article XII, Section 5 to the member or group of members appointing him. A Councillor appointed by a group of members may cast separately the votes allotted to each member in the group. If the number of votes allotted to a member cannot be cast by an Executive Director, the member may make arrangements with a Councillor for casting the number of votes allotted to the member.

(*c*) The Council shall not take any action pursuant to powers delegated by the Board of Governors that is inconsistent with any action taken by the Board of Governors and the Executive Board shall not take any action pursuant to powers delegated by the Board of Governors that is inconsistent with any action taken by either the Board of Governors or the Council.

4. The Council shall select a Councillor as chairman, shall adopt regulations as may be necessary or appropriate to perform its functions, and shall determine any aspect of its procedure. The Council shall hold such meetings as may be provided for by the Council or called by the Executive Board.

5. (*a*) The Council shall have powers corresponding to those of the Executive Board under the following provisions: Article XII, Section 2(*c*), (*f*), (*g*), and (*j*); Article XVIII, Section 4(*a*) and Section 4(*c*)(iv); Article XXIII, Section 1; and Article XXVII, Section 1(*a*).

(*b*) For decisions by the Council on matters pertaining exclusively to the Special Drawing Rights Department only Councillors appointed by a member that is a participant or a group of members at least one member of which is a participant shall be entitled to vote. Each of these Councillors shall be entitled to cast the number of votes allotted to the member which is a participant that appointed him or to the members that are participants in the group of members that appointed him, and may cast the votes allotted to a participant with which arrangements have been made pursuant to the last sentence of 3(*b*) above.

(*c*) The Council may by regulation establish a procedure whereby the Executive Board may obtain a vote of the Councillors on a specific question without a meeting of the Council when in the judgment of the Executive Board an action must be taken by the Council which should not be postponed until the next meeting of the Council and which does not warrant the calling of a special meeting.

(*d*) Article IX, Section 8 shall apply to Councillors, their Alternates, and Associates, and to any other person entitled to attend a meeting of the Council.

(*e*) For the purposes of (*b*) and 3(*b*) above, an agreement under Article XII, Section 3(*i*)(ii) by a member, or by a member that is a participant, shall entitle a Councillor to vote and cast the number of votes allotted to the member.

6. The first sentence of Article XII, Section 2 (*a*) shall be deemed to include a reference to the Council.

Schedule E

Election of Executive Directors

1. The election of the elective Executive Directors shall be by ballot of the Governors eligible to vote.

2. In balloting for the Executive Directors to be elected, each of the Governors eligible to vote shall cast for one person all of the votes to which he is entitled under Article XII, Section 5(*a*). The fifteen persons receiving the greatest number of votes shall be Executive Directors, provided that no person who received less than four percent of the total number of votes that can be cast (eligible votes) shall be considered elected.

3. When fifteen persons are not elected in the first ballot, a second ballot shall be held in which there shall vote only (*a*) those Governors who voted in the first ballot for a person not elected, and (*b*) those Governors whose votes for a person elected are deemed under 4 below to have raised the votes cast for that person above nine percent of the eligible votes. If in the second ballot there are more candidates than the number of Executive Directors to be elected, the person who received the lowest number of votes in the first ballot shall be ineligible for election.

4. In determining whether the votes cast by a Governor are to be deemed to have raised the total of any person above nine percent of the eligible votes the nine percent shall be deemed to include, first, the votes of the Governor casting the largest number of votes for such person, then the votes of the Governor casting the next largest number, and so on until nine percent is reached.

5. Any Governor part of whose votes must be counted in order to raise the total of any person above four percent shall be considered as casting all of his votes for such person even if the total votes for such person thereby exceed nine percent.

6. If, after the second ballot, fifteen persons have not been elected, further ballots shall be held on the same principles until fifteen persons have been elected, provided that after fourteen persons are elected, the fifteenth may be elected by a simple majority of the remaining votes and shall be deemed to have been elected by all such votes.

Schedule F

Designation

During the first basic period the rules for designation shall be as follows:

(*a*) Participants subject to designation under Article XIX, Section 5(*a*)(i) shall be designated for such amounts as will promote over time equality in the ratios of the participants' holdings of special drawing rights in excess of their net cumulative allocations to their official holdings of gold and foreign exchange.

(*b*) The formula to give effect to (*a*) above shall be such that participants subject to designation shall be designated:

(i) in proportion to their official holdings of gold and foreign exchange when the ratios described in (*a*) above are equal; and

(ii) in such manner as gradually to reduce the difference between the ratios described in (*a*) above that are low and the ratios that are high.

Schedule G

Reconstitution

1. During the first basic period the rules for reconstitution shall be as follows:

(*a*) (i) A participant shall so use and reconstitute its holdings of special drawing rights that, five years after the first allocation and at the end of each calendar quarter thereafter, the average of its total daily holdings of special drawing rights over the most recent five-year period will be not less than thirty percent of the average of its daily net cumulative allocation of special drawing rights over the same period.

(ii) Two years after the first allocation and at the end of each calendar month thereafter the Fund shall make calculations for each participant so as to ascertain whether and to what extent the participant would need to acquire special drawing rights between the date of the calculation and the end of any five-year period in order to comply with the requirement in (*a*)(i) above. The Fund shall adopt regulations with respect to the bases on which these calculations shall be made and with respect to the timing of the designation of participants under Article XIX, Section 5(*a*)(ii), in order to assist them to comply with the requirement in (*a*)(i) above.

(iii) The Fund shall give special notice to a participant when the calculations under (*a*)(ii) above indicate that it is unlikely that the participant will be able to comply with the requirement in (*a*)(i) above unless it ceases to use special drawing rights for the rest of the period for which the calculation was made under (*a*)(ii) above.

(iv) A participant that needs to acquire special drawing rights to fulfill this obligation shall be obligated and entitled to obtain them, for currency acceptable to the Fund, in a transaction with the Fund conducted through the General Resources Account. If sufficient special drawing rights to fulfill this obligation cannot be obtained in this way, the participant shall be obligated and entitled to obtain them with a freely usable currency from a participant which the Fund shall specify.

(*b*) Participants shall also pay due regard to the desirability of pursuing over time a balanced relationship between their holdings of special drawing rights and their other reserves.

2. If a participant fails to comply with the rules for reconstitution, the Fund shall determine whether or not the circumstances justify suspension under Article XXIII, Section 2(*b*).

Schedule H

Termination of Participation

1. If the obligation remaining after the setoff under Article XXIV, Section 2(*b*) is to the terminating participant and agreement on settlement between the Fund and the terminating participant is not reached within six months of the date of termination, the Fund shall redeem this balance of special drawing rights in equal half-yearly installments within a maximum of five years of the date of termination. The Fund shall redeem this balance as it may determine, either (*a*) by the payment to the terminating participant of the amounts provided by the remaining participants to the Fund in accordance with Article XXIV, Section 5, or (*b*) by permitting the terminating participant to use its special drawing rights to obtain its own currency or a freely usable currency from a participant specified by the Fund, the General Resources Account, or any other holder.

2. If the obligation remaining after the setoff under Article XXIV,

Section 2(*b*) is to the Fund and agreement on settlement is not reached within six months of the date of termination, the terminating participant shall discharge this obligation in equal half-yearly installments within three years of the date of termination or within such longer period as may be fixed by the Fund. The terminating participant shall discharge this obligation, as the Fund may determine, either (*a*) by the payment to the Fund of a freely usable currency, or (*b*) by obtaining special drawing rights, in accordance with Article XXIV, Section 6, from the General Resources Account or in agreement with a participant specified by the Fund or from any other holder, and the setoff of these special drawing rights against the installment due.

3. Installments under either 1 or 2 above shall fall due six months after the date of termination and at intervals of six months thereafter.

4. In the event of the Special Drawing Rights Department going into liquidation under Article XXV within six months of the date a participant terminates its participation, the settlement between the Fund and that government shall be made in accordance with Article XXV and Schedule I.

Schedule I

Administration of Liquidation of the Special Drawing Rights Department

1. In the event of liquidation of the Special Drawing Rights Department, participants shall discharge their obligations to the Fund in ten half-yearly installments, or in such longer period as the Fund may decide is needed, in a freely usable currency and the currencies of participants holding special drawing rights to be redeemed in any installment to the extent of such redemption, as determined by the Fund. The first half-yearly payment shall be made six months after the decision to liquidate the Special Drawing Rights Department.

2. If it is decided to liquidate the Fund within six months of the date of the decision to liquidate the Special Drawing Rights Department, the liquidation of the Special Drawing Rights Department shall not proceed until special drawing rights held in the General Resources Account have been distributed in accordance with the following rule:

> After the distributions made under 2(*a*) and (*b*) of Schedule K, the Fund shall apportion its special drawing rights held in the General Resources Account among all members that are participants in proportion to the amounts due to each participant after the distribution under 2(*b*). To determine the amount due to each

member for the purpose of apportioning the remainder of its holdings of each currency under 2(*d*) of Schedule K, the Fund shall deduct the distribution of special drawing rights made under this rule.

3. With the amounts received under 1 above, the Fund shall redeem special drawing rights held by holders in the following manner and order:

(*a*) Special drawing rights held by governments that have terminated their participation more than six months before the date the Board of Governors decides to liquidate the Special Drawing Rights Department shall be redeemed in accordance with the terms of any agreement under Article XXIV or Schedule H.

(*b*) Special drawing rights held by holders that are not participants shall be redeemed before those held by participants, and shall be redeemed in proportion to the amount held by each holder.

(*c*) The Fund shall determine the proportion of special drawing rights held by each participant in relation to its net cumulative allocation. The Fund shall first redeem special drawing rights from the participants with the highest proportion until this proportion is reduced to that of the second highest proportion; the Fund shall then redeem the special drawing rights held by these participants in accordance with their net cumulative allocations until the proportions are reduced to that of the third highest proportion; and this process shall be continued until the amount available for redemption is exhausted.

4. Any amount that a participant will be entitled to receive in redemption under 3 above shall be set off against any amount to be paid under 1 above.

5. During liquidation the Fund shall pay interest on the amount of special drawing rights held by holders, and each participant shall pay charges on the net cumulative allocation of special drawing rights to it less the amount of any payments made in accordance with 1 above. The rates of interest and charges and the time of payment shall be determined by the Fund. Payments of interest and charges shall be made in special drawing rights to the extent possible. A participant that does not hold sufficient special drawing rights to meet any charges shall make the payment with a currency specified by the Fund. Special drawing rights received as charges in amounts needed for administrative expenses shall not be used for the payment of interest, but shall be transferred to the Fund and shall be redeemed first and with the currencies used by the Fund to meet its expenses.

6. While a participant is in default with respect to any payment required by 1 or 5 above, no amounts shall be paid to it in accordance with 3 or 5 above.

7. If after the final payments have been made to participants each participant not in default does not hold special drawing rights in the same proportion to its net cumulative allocation, those participants holding a lower proportion shall purchase from those holding a higher proportion such amounts in accordance with arrangements made by the Fund as will make the proportion of their holdings of special drawing rights the same. Each participant in default shall pay to the Fund its own currency in an amount equal to its default. The Fund shall apportion this currency and any residual claims among participants in proportion to the amount of special drawing rights held by each and these special drawing rights shall be cancelled. The Fund shall then close the books of the Special Drawing Rights Department and all of the Fund's liabilities arising from the allocations of special drawing rights and the administration of the Special Drawing Rights Department shall cease.

8. Each participant whose currency is distributed to other participants under this Schedule guarantees the unrestricted use of such currency at all times for the purchase of goods or for payments of sums due to it or to persons in its territories. Each participant so obligated agrees to compensate other participants for any loss resulting from the difference between the value at which the Fund distributed its currency under this Schedule and the value realized by such participants on disposal of its currency.

Schedule J

Settlement of Accounts with Members Withdrawing

1. The settlement of accounts with respect to the General Resources Account shall be made according to 1 to 6 of this Schedule. The Fund shall be obligated to pay to a member withdrawing an amount equal to its quota, plus any other amounts due to it from the Fund, less any amounts due to the Fund, including charges accruing after the date of its withdrawal; but no payment shall be made until six months after the date of withdrawal. Payments shall be made in the currency of the withdrawing member, and for this purpose the Fund may transfer to the General Resources Account holdings of the member's currency in the Special Disbursement Account or in the Investment Account in exchange for an equivalent amount of the currencies of other members in the General Resources Account selected by the Fund with their concurrence.

2. If the Fund's holdings of the currency of the withdrawing member are not sufficient to pay the net amount due from the Fund, the balance shall be paid in a freely usable currency, or in such other manner as may

be agreed. If the Fund and the withdrawing member do not reach agreement within six months of the date of withdrawal, the currency in question held by the Fund shall be paid forthwith to the withdrawing member. Any balance due shall be paid in ten half-yearly installments during the ensuing five years. Each such installment shall be paid, at the option of the Fund, either in the currency of the withdrawing member acquired after its withdrawal or in a freely usable currency.

3. If the Fund fails to meet any installment which is due in accordance with the preceding paragraphs, the withdrawing member shall be entitled to require the Fund to pay the installment in any currency held by the Fund with the exception of any currency which has been declared scarce under Article VII, Section 3.

4. If the Fund's holdings of the currency of a withdrawing member exceed the amount due to it, and if agreement on the method of settling accounts is not reached within six months of the date of withdrawal, the former member shall be obligated to redeem such excess currency in a freely usable currency. Redemption shall be made at the rates at which the Fund would sell such currencies at the time of withdrawal from the Fund. The withdrawing member shall complete redemption within five years of the date of withdrawal, or within such longer period as may be fixed by the Fund, but shall not be required to redeem in any half-yearly period more than one-tenth of the Fund's excess holdings of its currency at the date of withdrawal plus further acquisitions of the currency during such half-yearly period. If the withdrawing member does not fulfill this obligation, the Fund may in an orderly manner liquidate in any market the amount of currency which should have been redeemed.

5. Any member desiring to obtain the currency of a member which has withdrawn shall acquire it by purchase from the Fund, to the extent that such member has access to the general resources of the Fund and that such currency is available under 4 above.

6. The withdrawing member guarantees the unrestricted use at all times of the currency disposed of under 4 and 5 above for the purchase of goods or for payment of sums due to it or to persons within its territories. It shall compensate the Fund for any loss resulting from the difference between the value of its currency in terms of the special drawing right on the date of withdrawal and the value realized in terms of the special drawing right by the Fund on disposal under 4 and 5 above.

7. If the withdrawing member is indebted to the Fund as the result of transactions conducted through the Special Disbursement Account under Article V, Section 12 (f) (ii), the indebtedness shall be discharged in accordance with the terms of the indebtedness.

8. If the Fund holds the withdrawing member's currency in the Special Disbursement Account or in the Investment Account, the Fund may in an

orderly manner exchange in any market for the currencies of members the amount of the currency of the withdrawing member remaining in each account after use under 1 above, and the proceeds of the exchange of the amount in each account shall be kept in that account. Paragraph 5 above and the first sentence of 6 above shall apply to the withdrawing member's currency.

9. If the Fund holds obligations of the withdrawing member in the Special Disbursement Account pursuant to Article V, Section 12(*h*), or in the Investment Account, the Fund may hold them until the date of maturity or dispose of them sooner. Paragraph 8 above shall apply to the proceeds of such disinvestment.

10. In the event of the Fund going into liquidation under Article XXVII, Section 2 within six months of the date on which the member withdraws, the accounts between the Fund and that government shall be settled in accordance with Article XXVII, Section 2 and Schedule K.

Schedule K

Administration of Liquidation

1. In the event of liquidation the liabilities of the Fund other than the repayment of subscriptions shall have priority in the distribution of the assets of the Fund. In meeting each such liability the Fund shall use its assets in the following order:

> (*a*) the currency in which the liability is payable;
>
> (*b*) gold;
>
> (*c*) all other currencies in proportion, so far as may be practicable, to the quotas of the members.

2. After the discharge of the Fund's liabilities in accordance with 1 above, the balance of the Fund's assets shall be distributed and apportioned as follows:

> (*a*) (i) The Fund shall calculate the value of gold held on August 31, 1975 that it continues to hold on the date of the decision to liquidate. The calculation shall be made in accordance with 9 below and also on the basis of one special drawing right per 0.888 671 gram of fine gold on the date of liquidation. Gold equivalent to the excess of the former value over the latter shall be distributed to those members that were members on August 31, 1975 in proportion to their quotas on that date.
>
> (ii) The Fund shall distribute any assets held in the Special

Disbursement Account on the date of the decision to liquidate to those members that were members on August 31, 1975 in proportion to their quotas on that date. Each type of asset shall be distributed proportionately to members.

(*b*) The Fund shall distribute its remaining holdings of gold among the members whose currencies are held by the Fund in amounts less than their quotas in the proportions, but not in excess of, the amounts by which their quotas exceed the Fund's holdings of their currencies.

(*c*) The Fund shall distribute to each member one-half the Fund's holdings of its currency but such distribution shall not exceed fifty percent of its quota.

(*d*) The Fund shall apportion the remainder of its holdings of gold and each currency
   (i) among all members in proportion to, but not in excess of, the amounts due to each member after the distributions under (*b*) and (*c*) above, provided that distribution under 2(*a*) above shall not be taken into account for determining the amounts due, and
   (ii) any excess holdings of gold and currency among all the members in proportion to their quotas.

3. Each member shall redeem the holdings of its currency apportioned to other members under 2(*d*) above, and shall agree with the Fund within three months after a decision to liquidate upon an orderly procedure for such redemption.

4. If a member has not reached agreement with the Fund within the three-month period referred to in 3 above, the Fund shall use the currencies of other members apportioned to that member under 2(*d*) above to redeem the currency of that member apportioned to other members. Each currency apportioned to a member which has not reached agreement shall be used, so far as possible, to redeem its currency apportioned to the members which have made agreements with the Fund under 3 above.

5. If a member has reached agreement with the Fund in accordance with 3 above, the Fund shall use the currencies of other members apportioned to that member under 2(*d*) above to redeem the currency of that member apportioned to other members which have made agreements with the Fund under 3 above. Each amount so redeemed shall be redeemed in the currency of the member to which it was apportioned.

6. After carrying out the steps in the preceding paragraphs, the Fund shall pay to each member the remaining currencies held for its account.

7. Each member whose currency has been distributed to other members under 6 above shall redeem such currency in the currency of the member requesting redemption, or in such other manner as may be agreed between them. If the members involved do not otherwise agree, the member obligated to redeem shall complete redemption within five years of the date of distribution, but shall not be required to redeem in any half-yearly period more than one-tenth of the amount distributed to each other member. If the member does not fulfill this obligation, the amount of currency which should have been redeemed may be liquidated in an orderly manner in any market.

8. Each member whose currency has been distributed to other members under 6 above guarantees the unrestricted use of such currency at all times for the purchase of goods or for payment of sums due to it or to persons in its territories. Each member so obligated agrees to compensate other members for any loss resulting from the difference between the value of its currency in terms of the special drawing right on the date of the decision to liquidate the Fund and the value in terms of the special drawing right realized by such members on disposal of its currency.

9. The Fund shall determine the value of gold under this Schedule on the basis of prices in the market.

10. For the purposes of this Schedule, quotas shall be deemed to have been increased to the full extent to which they could have been increased in accordance with Article III, Section 2(b) of this Agreement.

Appendix C

Bank for International Settlements

Convention
respecting the Bank for International Settlements

The duly authorised representatives of the Governments of Germany, of Belgium, of France, of the United Kingdom of Great Britain and Northern Ireland, of Italy and of Japan of the one part

And the duly authorised representatives of the Government of the Swiss Confederation of the other part

Assembled at the Hague Conference in the month of January, 1930, have agreed on the following:

Article 1. Switzerland undertakes to grant to the Bank for International Settlements, without delay, the following Constituent Charter having force of law: not to abrogate this Charter, not to amend or add to it, and not to sanction amendments to the Statutes of the Bank referred to in Paragraph 4 of the Charter otherwise than in agreement with the other signatory Governments.

Art. 2. Any dispute between the Swiss Government and any one of the other signatory Governments relating to the interpretation or application of the present Convention shall be submitted to the Arbitral Tribunal provided for by the Hague Agreement of January, 1930. The Swiss Government may appoint a member who shall sit on the occasion of such disputes, the President having a casting vote. In having recourse to this Tribunal the Parties may always agree between themselves to submit their dispute to the President or to one of the members of the Tribunal chosen to act as sole arbiter.

Art. 3. The present Convention is entered into for a period of 15 years. It is entered into on the part of Switzerland under reserve of ratification and shall be put into force as soon as it shall have been ratified by the Government of the Swiss Confederation.

The instrument of ratification shall be deposited with the Ministry of Foreign Affairs at Paris. Upon the entry into force of the Convention, the Swiss Government will initiate the necessary constitutional procedure in order that the assent of the Swiss people may be obtained for the maintenance in force during the whole of the Bank's existence of the provisions of the present Convention. As soon as these measures have become fully effective the Swiss Government will notify the other signatory Governments and these provisions shall become valid during the Bank's existence.*

---

* On 10th June, 1930 the Convention was prolonged for the existence of the Bank. According to an announcement made by the Swiss Government on 26th December, 1952, Japan renounced all rights, titles and interests acquired under the Convention.

Constituent Charter
of the Bank for International Settlements

Whereas the Powers signatory to the Hague Agreement of January, 1930, have adopted a Plan which contemplates the founding by the central banks of Belgium, France, Germany, Great Britain, Italy and Japan and by a financial institution of the United States of America of an International Bank to be called the Bank for International Settlements;

And whereas the said central banks and a banking group including Messrs. J. P. Morgan & Company of New York, the First National Bank of New York, New York, and the First National Bank of Chicago, Chicago, have undertaken to found the said Bank and have guaranteed or arranged for the guarantee of the subscription of its authorised capital amounting to five hundred million Swiss francs equal to 145,161,290.32 grammes fine gold, divided into 200,000 shares;

And whereas the Swiss Federal Government has entered into a treaty with the Governments of Germany, Belgium, France, Great Britain, Italy and Japan whereby the said Federal Government has agreed to grant the present Constituent Charter of the Bank for International Settlements and not to repeal, amend or supplement the said Charter and not to sanction amendments to the Statutes of the Bank referred to in Paragraph 4 of the present Charter except in agreement with the said Powers;

1. The Bank for International Settlements (hereinafter called the Bank) is hereby incorporated.

2. Its constitution, operations and activities are defined and governed by the annexed Statutes which are hereby sanctioned.

3. Amendment of Articles of the said Statutes other than those enumerated in Paragraph 4 hereof may be made and shall be put into force as provided in Article 57 of the said Statutes and not otherwise.

4. Articles 2, 3, 8, 14, 19, 24, 27, 44, 51, 54, 57 and 58 of the said Statutes shall not be amended except subject to the following conditions: the amendment must be adopted by a two-thirds majority of the Board, approved by a majority of the General Meeting and sanctioned by a law supplementing the present Charter.

5. The said Statutes and any amendments which may be made thereto in accordance with Paragraphs 3 or 4 hereof respectively shall be valid and operative notwithstanding any inconsistency therewith in the provisions of any present or future Swiss law.

6. The Bank shall be exempt and immune from all taxation included in the following categories:

(a) stamp, registration and other duties on all deeds or other documents relating to the incorporation or liquidation of the Bank;

(b) stamp and registration duties on any first issue of its shares by the Bank to a central bank, financial institution, banking group or underwriter at or before the time of incorporation or in pursuance of Articles 5, 6, 8 or 9 of the Statutes;

(c) all taxes on the Bank's capital, reserves or profits, whether distributed or not, and whether assessed on the profits of the Bank before distribution or imposed at the time of distribution under the form of a coupon tax payable or deductible by the Bank. This provision is without prejudice to the State's right to tax the residents of Switzerland other than the Bank as it thinks fit;

(d) all taxes upon any agreements which the Bank may make in connection with the issue of loans for mobilising the German annuities and upon the bonds of such loans issued on a foreign market;

(e) all taxes on the remunerations and salaries paid by the Bank to members of its administration or its employees of non-Swiss nationality.

7. All funds deposited with the Bank by any Government in pursuance of the Plan adopted by the Hague Agreement of January, 1930, shall be exempt and immune from taxation whether by way of deduction by the Bank on behalf of the authority imposing the same or otherwise.

8. The foregoing exemptions and immunities shall apply to present and future taxation by whatsoever name it may be described, and whether imposed by the Confederation, or by the cantonal, communal or other public authorities.

9. Moreover, without prejudice to the exemptions specified above, there may not be levied on the Bank, its operation or its personnel any taxation other than that of a general character and to which other banking establishments established at Basle or in Switzerland, their operations and their personnel, are not subjected *de facto* and *de jure*.

10. The Bank, its property and assets and all deposits and other funds entrusted to it shall be immune in time of peace and in time of war from any measure such as expropriation, requisition, seizure, confiscation, prohibition or restriction of gold or currency export or import, and any other similar measures.

11. Any dispute between the Swiss Government and the Bank as to the interpretation or application of the present Charter shall be referred to the Arbitral Tribunal provided for by the Hague Agreement of January, 1930.

The Swiss Government shall appoint a member to sit on the occasion of such dispute, the President having a casting vote.

In having recourse to the said Tribunal the Parties may nevertheless agree to submit their dispute to the President or to a member of the Tribunal chosen to act as sole arbiter.

Done at The Hague, the 20th January, 1930.*

---

* Text amended on account of the renumbering of the Articles of the Statutes and sanctioned on 10th December, 1969 in accordance with the conditions laid down in Article 1 of the Convention respecting the Bank for International Settlements.

Statutes
of the Bank for International Settlements*

Chapter I

Name, Seat and Objects

Article 1. There is constituted under the name of the Bank for International Settlements (hereinafter referred to as the Bank) a Company limited by shares.

Art. 2. The registered office of the Bank shall be situated at Basle, Switzerland.

Art. 3. The objects of the Bank are: to promote the co-operation of central banks and to provide additional facilities for international financial operations; and to act as trustee or agent in regard to international financial settlements entrusted to it under agreements with the parties concerned.

Chapter II

Capital

Art. 4. (1) The authorised capital of the Bank shall be one thousand five hundred million gold francs, equivalent to 435,483,870.96 grammes fine gold.

(2) It shall be divided into 600,000 shares of equal gold nominal value. A first tranche of 200,000 shares has already been issued; the other two tranches, of 200,000 shares each, shall be issued on the terms and conditions laid down in Articles 5 and 6.

(3) The nominal value of each share and the amount remaining to be paid up shall be stated on the face of the share certificates.

Art. 5. (1) The subscription of the whole of the second tranche of 200,000 shares has been guaranteed by a group of central banks. Notwithstanding the provisions of Article 8, each shareholder shall be entitled to subscribe for one share in respect of each share registered in his name in the Bank's books at the time when the shares are offered for subscription. The Board of Directors of the Bank (hereinafter referred to as the Board) shall set the time-limit for subscription.

(2) The central banks or financial institutions of countries in which the shares of the first tranche were subscribed shall, notwithstanding the provisions of Article 14, exercise the rights of voting and of representation at the General Meeting that pertain to shares issued under the present

---

* Amendments to the original text of the Statutes of 20th January 1930 were adopted by Extraordinary General Meetings held on 3rd May 1937, 12th June 1950, 9th October 1961, 9th June 1969, 10th June 1974 and 8th July 1975. The amendments adopted in 1969 and 1975 were sanctioned in accordance with the conditions laid down in Article 1 of the Convention respecting the Bank for International Settlements.

Article and shall be competent to authorise the transfer of these shares in accordance with the terms and conditions laid down in Article 12.

Art. 6. The Board, upon a decision taken by a two-thirds majority, may, when it considers it advisable, issue on one or more occasions a third tranche of 200,000 shares and distribute them in accordance with the provisions of Article 8. Shares thus issued may be subscribed or acquired only by central banks or financial institutions appointed by the Board in accordance with the terms and conditions laid down in Article 14.

Art. 7. (1) Twenty-five per cent. only of the value of each share shall be paid up at the time of subscription. The balance may be called up at a later date or dates at the discretion of the Board. Three months' notice shall be given of any such calls.

(2) If a shareholder fails to pay any call on a share on the day appointed for payment thereof the Board may, after giving reasonable notice to such shareholder, forfeit the share in respect of which the call remains unpaid. A forfeited share may be sold on such terms and in such manner as the Board may think fit, and the Board may execute a transfer in favour of the person or corporation to whom the share is sold. The proceeds of sale may be received by the Bank, which will pay to the defaulting shareholder any part of the net proceeds over and above the amount of the call due and unpaid.

Art. 8. (1) The capital of the Bank may be increased or reduced on the proposal of the Board acting by a two-thirds majority and adopted by a two-thirds majority of the General Meeting.

(2) In the event of an increase in the authorised capital of the Bank and of a further issue of shares, the distribution among countries shall be decided by a two-thirds majority of the Board. The central banks of Belgium, England, France, Germany, Italy and the United States of America, or some other financial institution of the last-named country acceptable to the foregoing central banks, shall be entitled to subscribe or arrange for the subscription in equal proportions of at least fifty-five per cent. of such additional shares.

(3) In extending invitations to subscribe for the amount of the increase in capital not taken up by the banks referred to in clause (2), consideration shall be given by the Board to the desirability of associating with the Bank the largest possible number of central banks that make a substantial contribution to international monetary co-operation and to the Bank's activities.

Art. 9. Shares subscribed in pursuance of Article 8 by the banks referred to in clause (2) of that Article may be placed at the Bank's disposal at any time for the purposes of cancellation and the issue of an equivalent number of shares. The necessary measures shall be taken by the Board by a two-thirds majority.

Art. 10. No shares shall be issued below par.

Art. 11. The liability of shareholders is limited to the nominal value of their shares.

Art. 12. The shares shall be registered and transferable in the books of the Bank.

The Bank shall be entitled without assigning any reason to decline to accept any person or corporation as the transferee of a share. It shall not transfer shares without the prior consent of the central bank, or the institution acting in lieu of a central bank, by or through whom the shares in question were issued.

Art. 13. The shares shall carry equal rights to participate in the profits of the Bank and in any distribution of assets under Articles 51, 52 and 53 of the Statutes.

Art. 14. The ownership of shares of the Bank carries no right of voting or representation at the General Meeting. The right of representation and of voting, in proportion to the number of shares subscribed in each country, may be exercised by the central bank of that country or by its nominee. Should the central bank of any country not desire to exercise these rights, they may be exercised by a financial institution of widely recognised standing and of the same nationality, appointed by the Board, and not objected to by the central bank of the country in question. In cases where there is no central bank, these rights may be exercised, if the Board thinks fit, by an appropriate financial institution of the country in question appointed by the Board.

Art. 15. Any subscribing institution or banking group may issue or cause to be issued to the public the shares for which it has subscribed.

Art. 16. Any subscribing institution or banking group may issue to the public certificates against shares of the Bank owned by it. The form, details and terms of issue of such certificates shall be determined by the bank issuing them, in agreement with the Board.

Art. 17. The receipt or ownership of shares of the Bank or of certificates issued in accordance with Article 16 implies acceptance of the Statutes of the Bank and a statement to that effect shall be embodied in the text of such shares and certificates.

Art. 18. The registration of the name of a holder of shares in the books of the Bank establishes the title to ownership of the shares so registered.

Chapter III

Powers of the Bank

Art. 19. The operations of the Bank shall be in conformity with the monetary policy of the central banks of the countries concerned.

Before any financial operation is carried out by or on behalf of the Bank on a given market or in a given currency, the Board shall afford to the central bank or central banks directly concerned an opportunity to dissent. In the event of disapproval being expressed within such reasonable time as the Board shall specify, the proposed operation shall not take place. A central bank may make its concurrence subject to conditions and may limit its assent to a specific operation, or enter into a general arrangement permitting the Bank to carry on its operations within such limits as to time, character and amount as may be specified. This Article shall not be read as requiring the assent of any central bank to the withdrawal from its market of funds to the introduction of which no objection had been raised by it, in the absence of stipulations to the contrary by the central bank concerned at the time the original operation was carried out.

Any Governor of a central bank, or his alternate or any other Director specially authorised by the central bank of the country of which he is a national to act on its behalf in this matter, shall, if he is present at the meeting of the Board and does not vote against any such proposed operation, be deemed to have given the valid assent of the central bank in question.

If the representative of the central bank in question is absent or if a central bank is not directly represented on the Board, steps shall be taken to afford the central bank or banks concerned an opportunity to express dissent.

Art. 20. The operations of the Bank for its own account shall only be carried out in currencies which in the opinion of the Board satisfy the practical requirements of the gold or gold exchange standard.

Art. 21. The Board shall determine the nature of the operations to be undertaken by the Bank.

The Bank may in particular:

(a) buy and sell gold coin or bullion for its own account or for the account of central banks;

(b) hold gold for its own account under earmark in central banks;

(c) accept the custody of gold for the account of central banks;

(d) make advances to or borrow from central banks against gold, bills of exchange and other short-term obligations of prime liquidity or other approved securities;

(e) discount, rediscount, purchase or sell with or without its endorsement bills of exchange, cheques and other short-term obligations of prime liquidity, including Treasury bills and other such government short-term securities as are currently marketable;

(f) buy and sell exchange for its own account or for the account of central banks;

(g) buy and sell negotiable securities other than shares for its own account or for the account of central banks;

(h) discount for central banks bills taken from their portfolio and rediscount with central banks bills taken from its own portfolio;

(i) open and maintain current or deposit accounts with central banks;

(j) accept:
  (i) deposits from central banks on current or deposit account;
  (ii) deposits in connection with trustee agreements that may be made between the Bank and Governments in connection with international settlements;
  (iii) such other deposits as in the opinion of the Board come within the scope of the Bank's functions.

The Bank may also:

(k) act as agent or correspondent of any central bank;

(l) arrange with any central bank for the latter to act as its agent or correspondent. If a central bank is unable or unwilling to act in this capacity, the Bank may make other arrangements, provided that the central bank concerned does not object. If in such circumstances it should be deemed advisable that the Bank should establish its own agency, the sanction of a two-thirds majority of the Board will be required;

(m) enter into agreements to act as trustee or agent in connection with international settlements, provided that such agreements shall not encroach on the obligations of the Bank towards third parties; and carry out the various operations laid down therein.

Art. 22. Any of the operations which the Bank is authorised to carry out with central banks under the preceding Article may be carried out with banks, bankers, corporations or individuals of any country provided that the central bank of that country does not object.

Art. 23. The Bank may enter into special agreements with central banks to facilitate the settlement of international transactions between them.

For this purpose it may arrange with central banks to have gold earmarked for their account and transferable on their order, to open accounts through which central banks can transfer their assets from one currency to another and to take such other measures as the Board may think advisable within the limits of the powers granted by these Statutes. The principles and rules governing such accounts shall be fixed by the Board.

Art. 24. The Bank may not:
(a) issue notes payable at sight to bearer;
(b) "accept" bills of exchange;
(c) make advances to Governments;
(d) open current accounts in the name of Governments;
(e) acquire a predominant interest in any business concern;
(f) except so far as is necessary for the conduct of its own business, remain the owner of real property for any longer period than is required in order to realise to proper advantage such real property as may come into the possession of the Bank in satisfaction of claims due to it.

Art. 25. The Bank shall be administered with particular regard to maintaining its liquidity, and for this purpose shall retain assets appropriate to the maturity and character of its liabilities. Its short-term liquid assets may include bank-notes, cheques payable on sight drawn on first-class banks, claims in course of collection, deposits at sight or at short notice in first-class banks, and prime bills of exchange of not more than ninety days' usance, of a kind usually accepted for rediscount by central banks.

The proportion of the Bank's assets held in any given currency shall be determined by the Board with due regard to the liabilities of the Bank.

Chapter IV

Management

Art. 26. The administration of the Bank shall be vested in the Board.

Art. 27. The Board shall be composed as follows:
(1) The Governors for the time being of the central banks of Belgium, France, Germany, Great Britain, Italy and the United States of America (hereinafter referred to as *ex-officio* Directors).

Any *ex-officio* Director may appoint one person as his alternate who shall be entitled to attend and exercise the powers of a Director at meetings of the Board if the Governor himself is unable to be present.

(2) Six persons representative of finance, industry or commerce, appointed one each by the Governors of the central banks mentioned in clause (1), and being of the same nationality as the Governor who appoints him.

If for any reason the Governor of any of the six institutions above mentioned is unable or unwilling to serve as Director, or to make an appointment under the preceding paragraph, the Governors of the other institutions referred to or a majority of them may invite to become members of the Board two nationals of the country of the Governor in question, not objected to by the central bank of that country.

Directors appointed as aforesaid, other than *ex-officio* Directors, shall hold office for three years but shall be eligible for reappointment.

(3) Not more than nine persons to be elected by the Board by a two-thirds majority from among the Governors of the central banks of countries in which shares have been subscribed but of which the central bank does not delegate *ex-officio* Directors to the Board.

The Directors so elected shall remain in office for three years but may be re-elected.

Art. 28. In the event of a vacancy occurring on the Board for any reason other than the termination of a period of office in accordance with the preceding Article, the vacancy shall be filled in accordance with the procedure by which the member to be replaced was selected. In the case of Directors other than *ex-officio* Directors, the new Director shall hold office for the unexpired period only of his predecessor's term of office. He shall, however, be eligible for re-election at the expiration of that term.

Art. 29. Directors must be ordinarily resident in Europe or in a position to attend regularly at meetings of the Board.

Art. 30. No person shall be appointed or hold office as a Director who is a member or an official of a Government unless he is the Governor of a central bank and no person shall be so appointed or hold office who is a member of a legislative body unless he is the Governor or a former Governor of a central bank.

Art. 31. Meetings of the Board shall be held not less than ten times a year. At least four of these shall be held at the registered office of the Bank.

Art. 32. A member of the Board who is not present in person at a meeting of Directors may give a proxy to any other member authorising him to vote at that meeting on his behalf.

Art. 33. Unless otherwise provided by the Statutes, decisions of the Board shall be taken by a simple majority of those present or represented by proxy. In the case of an equality of votes, the Chairman shall have a second or casting vote.

The Board shall not be competent to act unless a quorum of Directors is present. This quorum shall be laid down in a regulation adopted by a two-thirds majority of the Board.

Art. 34. The members of the Board may receive, in addition to out-of-pocket expenses, a fee for attendance at meetings and/or a remuneration, the amounts of which will be fixed by the Board, subject to the approval of the General Meeting.

Art. 35. The proceedings of the Board shall be summarised in minutes which shall be signed by the Chairman.

Copies of or extracts from these minutes for the purpose of production in a court of justice must be certified by the General Manager of the Bank.

A record of decisions taken at each meeting shall be sent within eight days of the meeting to every member.

Art. 36. The Board shall represent the Bank in its dealings with third parties and shall have the exclusive right of entering into engagements on behalf of the Bank. It may, however, delegate this right to the Chairman of the Board, to another member or other members of the Board, to the President of the Bank or to a member or members of the permanent staff of the Bank, provided that it defines the powers of each person to whom it delegates this right.

Art. 37. The Bank shall be legally committed *vis-à-vis* third parties either by the signature of the President of the Bank, or by the signatures of two members of the Board or of two members of the staff of the Bank who have been duly authorised by the Board to sign on its behalf.

Art. 38. The Board shall elect from among its members a Chairman and one or more Vice-Chairmen, one of whom shall preside at meetings of the Board in the absence of the Chairman.

The Board shall elect a President of the Bank. If the President of the Bank is not Chairman of the Board nor a member thereof, he shall nevertheless be entitled to attend all meetings of the Board, to speak, to make proposals to the Board and, if he so desires, to have his opinions specially recorded in the minutes.

The appointments referred to in this Article shall be made for a maximum of three years and may be renewed.

The President of the Bank will carry out the policy decided upon by the Board and will control the administration of the Bank.

He shall not hold any other office which, in the judgment of the Board, might interfere with his duties as President.

Art. 39. At the meeting at which the Board elects its Chairman, the Chair shall be taken by the oldest member of the Board present.

Art. 40. A General Manager and an Assistant General Manager shall be appointed by the Board on the proposal of the Chairman of the Board. The General Manager will be responsible to the President of the Bank for the operations of the Bank and will be the chief of its operating staff.

The Heads of Departments and any other officers of similar rank shall be appointed by the Board on recommendations made by the President of the Bank after consultation with the General Manager.

The remainder of the staff shall be appointed by the General Manager with the approval of the President of the Bank.

Art. 41. The departmental organisation of the Bank shall be determined by the Board.

Art. 42. The Board may, if it thinks fit, appoint from among its members an Executive Committee to assist the President of the Bank in the administration of the Bank.

The President of the Bank shall be a member of this Committee.

Art. 43. The Board may appoint Advisory Committees chosen wholly or partly from persons not concerned in the Bank's management.

Chapter V

General Meeting

Art. 44. General Meetings of the Bank may be attended by nominees of the central banks or other financial institutions referred to in Article 14.

Voting rights shall be in proportion to the number of shares subscribed in the country of each institution represented at the meeting.

The Chair shall be taken at General Meetings by the Chairman of the Board or in his absence by a Vice-Chairman.

At least three weeks' notice of General Meetings shall be given to those entitled to be represented.

Subject to the provisions of these Statutes, the General Meeting shall decide upon its own procedure.

Art. 45. Within three months after the end of each financial year of the Bank, an Annual General Meeting shall be held upon such date as the Board may decide.

The meeting shall take place at the registered office of the Bank.

Voting by proxy will be permitted in such manner as the Board may have provided in advance by regulation.

Art. 46. The Annual General Meeting shall be invited:
(a) to approve the Annual Report, the Balance Sheet upon the Report of the Auditors, and the Profit and Loss Account, and any proposed changes in the remuneration, fees or allowances of the members of the Board;
(b) to make appropriations to reserve and to special funds, and to consider the declaration of a dividend and its amount;
(c) to elect the Auditors for the ensuing year and to fix their remuneration; and
(d) to discharge the Board from all personal responsibility in respect of the past financial year.

Art. 47. Extraordinary General Meetings shall be summoned to decide upon any proposals of the Board:
(a) to amend the Statutes;
(b) to increase or decrease the capital of the Bank;
(c) to liquidate the Bank.

Chapter VI

Accounts and Profits

Art. 48. The financial year of the Bank will begin on 1st April and end on 31st March. The first financial period will end on 31st March, 1931.

Art. 49. The Bank shall publish an Annual Report, and at least once a month a Statement of Account in such form as the Board may prescribe.

The Board shall cause to be prepared a Profit and Loss Account and Balance Sheet of the Bank for each financial year in time for submission to the Annual General Meeting.

Art. 50. The Accounts and Balance Sheet shall be audited by independent auditors. The Auditors shall have full power to examine all books and accounts of the Bank and to require full information as to all its transactions. The Auditors shall report to the Board and to the General Meeting and shall state in their Report:

(a) whether they have obtained all the information and explanations they have required; and

(b) whether, in their opinion, the Balance Sheet and the Profit and Loss Account dealt with in the Report are properly drawn up so as to exhibit a true and fair view of the state of the Bank's affairs according to the best of their information and the explanations given to them, and as shown by the books of the Bank.

Art. 51. The yearly net profits of the Bank shall be applied as follows:

(1) Five per cent. of such net profits, or such proportion of five per cent. as may be required for the purpose, shall be paid to a reserve fund called the Legal Reserve Fund until that Fund reaches an amount equal in value to ten per cent. of the amount of the paid-up capital of the Bank for the time being.

(2) Thereafter the net profits shall be applied in or towards payment of the dividend which is declared by the General Meeting on the proposal of the Board. The portion of the net profits so applied shall take into account the amount (if any) which the Board decides to draw from the Special Dividend Reserve Fund of the Bank pursuant to Article 52.

(3) After making provision for the foregoing, one-half of the yearly net profits then remaining shall be paid into the General Reserve Fund of the Bank until it equals the paid-up capital. Thereafter forty per cent. shall be so applied until the General Reserve Fund equals twice the paid-up capital; thirty per cent. until it equals three times the paid-up capital; twenty per cent. until it equals four times the paid-up capital; ten per cent. until it equals five times the paid-up capital; and from that point onward, five per cent.

In case the General Reserve Fund, by reason of losses or by reason of an increase in the paid-up capital, falls below the amounts provided for above after having once attained them, the appropriate proportion of the yearly net profits shall again be applied until the position is restored.

(4) The disposal of the remainder of the net profits shall be determined by the General Meeting on the proposal of the Board, provided that a

portion of such remainder may be allotted to the shareholders by way of a transfer to the Special Dividend Reserve Fund.

Art. 52. Reserve Funds. The General Reserve Fund shall be available for meeting any losses incurred by the Bank. In case it is not adequate for this purpose, recourse may be had to the Legal Reserve Fund provided for in clause (1) of Article 51.

The Special Dividend Reserve Fund shall be available, in case of need, for paying the whole or any part of the dividend declared pursuant to clause (2) of Article 51.

These reserve funds, in the event of liquidation, and after the discharge of the liabilities of the Bank and the costs of liquidation, shall be divided among the shareholders.

Chapter VII

General Provisions

Art. 53. The Bank may not be liquidated except by a three-fourths majority of the General Meeting.

Art. 54. (1) If any dispute shall arise between the Bank, on the one side, and any central bank, financial institution, or other bank referred to in the present Statutes, on the other side, or between the Bank and its shareholders, with regard to the interpretation or application of the Statutes of the Bank, the same shall be referred for final decision to the Tribunal provided for by the Hague Agreement of January, 1930.

(2) In the absence of agreement as to the terms of submission either party to a dispute under this Article may refer the same to the Tribunal, which shall have power to decide all questions (including the question of its own jurisdiction) even in default of appearance by the other party.

(3) Before giving a final decision and without prejudice to the questions at issue, the President of the Tribunal, or, if he is unable to act in any case, a member of the Tribunal to be designated by him forthwith, may, on the request of the first party applying therefor, order any appropriate provisional measures in order to safeguard the respective rights of the parties.

(4) The provisions of this Article shall not prejudice the right of the parties to a dispute to refer the same by common consent to the President or a member of the Tribunal as sole arbitrator.

Art. 55. In all cases not covered by the preceding Article, or by some other provision for arbitration, the Bank may proceed or be proceeded against in any court of competent jurisdiction.

The assets of the Bank may be subject to measures of compulsory execution for enforcing monetary claims. On the other hand, all deposits entrusted to the Bank, all claims against the Bank and the shares issued by the Bank shall, without the prior agreement of the Bank, be immune from seizure or other measures of compulsory execution and sequestration, particularly of attachment within the meaning of Swiss law.

Art. 56. For the purposes of these Statutes:
(a) central bank means the bank in any country to which has been

entrusted the duty of regulating the volume of currency and credit in that country; or, where a banking system has been so entrusted, the bank forming part of such system which is situated and operating in the principal financial market of that country;

(b) the Governor of a central bank means the person who, subject to the control of his Board or other competent authority, has the direction of the policy and administration of the bank;

(c) a two-thirds majority of the Board means not less than two-thirds of the votes (whether given in person or by proxy) of the whole directorate.

Art. 57. Amendments of any Articles of these Statutes other than those enumerated in Article 58 may be proposed by a two-thirds majority of the Board to the General Meeting and if adopted by a majority of the General Meeting shall come into force, provided that such amendments are not inconsistent with the provisions of the Articles enumerated in Article 58.

Art. 58. Articles 2, 3, 8, 14, 19, 24, 27, 44, 51, 54, 57 and 58 cannot be amended except subject to the following conditions: the amendment must be adopted by a two-thirds majority of the Board, approved by a majority of the General Meeting and sanctioned by a law supplementing the Charter of the Bank.

Appendix D

Agreement on Multilateral Payments in Transferable Rubles and on the Organization of the International Bank for Economic Cooperation and the Charter of the International Bank for Economic Cooperation

Translator's Note[1]

On October 22, 1963, eight member countries of the Council for Mutual Economic Assistance concluded an agreement to facilitate the settlement of accounts on a multilateral basis in a clearing unit designated as the transferable ruble and, for this purpose, to found the International Bank for Economic Cooperation. The Agreement entered into force provisionally on January 1, 1964, and formally on May 18, 1964. The Agreement and the Charter of the Bank are reproduced here with the changes introduced by the Protocols of December 18, 1970, and November 23, 1977. Cuba acceded to the Agreement and became a member of the Bank on January 23, 1974, and Vietnam on May 27, 1977.

The charter capital of the Bank was increased with membership of Cuba (4,410,000 transferable rubles) and Vietnam (852,000 transferable rubles) to the present total of 305,262,000 transferable rubles.

The Russian texts of the Agreement on Multilateral Payments and the Charter of the Bank appear in P. A. Tokareva (ed.), *Mnogostoronnee Ekonomicheskoe Sotrudnichestvo Sotsialist-icheskikh Gosudarstv: Dokumenty [Multilateral Economic Cooperation of the Socialist Countries: Documents]* (Moscow: Iuridicheskaia Literatura, 1981 ed.), pp. 128 and 135.

W.E.B.

---

[1] Translation © 1983 by William Elliott Butler. Reproduced with permission.

Agreement on Multilateral Payments in Transferable Rubles and on the Organization of the International Bank for Economic Cooperation

The governments of the People's Republic of Bulgaria, the Hungarian People's Republic, the German Democratic Republic, the Mongolian People's Republic, the Polish People's Republic, the Socialist Republic of Romania, the Union of Soviet Socialist Republics, and the Czechoslovak Socialist Republic,[2]

being guided by the interests of developing and deepening the international socialist division of labor and the further expansion and strengthening of trade and economic links, and for the purposes of improving the system of payments and of strengthening the influence of currency and finance on the fulfillment of mutual obligations,

have agreed on the following:

Article I

Payments stipulated by bilateral and multilateral agreements and particular contracts concerning mutual deliveries of goods, and also agreements on other payments between the Contracting Parties will be carried out from 1 January 1964 in transferable rubles.

The gold content of the transferable ruble shall amount to 0.987412 gram of pure gold.

Each member country of the Bank which has funds in accounts in transferable rubles may freely dispose of those funds.

Each member country of the Bank when concluding trade agreements will ensure the balancing of receipts and payments in transferable rubles with all other member countries of the Bank as a whole within the calendar year or other period agreed by the member countries of the Bank. In so doing the creation or utilization of possible reserves in transferable rubles, and also credit operations, will be taken into account.

Each member country of the Bank will ensure the timely and complete fulfillment of its payment obligations in transferable rubles to other member countries of the Bank and to the International Bank for Economic Cooperation.

Article II

The International Bank for Economic Cooperation, with headquarters in Moscow, shall be founded for the purpose of furthering the economic cooperation and the development of the national economy of the Contracting Parties, and also expanding cooperation between these Parties and other countries.

The Contracting Parties shall be the founder members of the Bank.

There shall be entrusted to the Bank:

(a) the implementation of multilateral accounts in transferable rubles;

(b) the provision of credit for foreign trade and other operations of member countries of the Bank;

(c) the attraction and custody of free funds in transferable rubles;

(d) the attraction of gold and of freely convertible and other currency from member countries of the Bank and from other countries, and also the implementation of other operations with gold and with freely convertible and other currency.

---

[2] See Translator's Note, *supra* page 776.

The Bank Council shall study the possibility of implementation by the Bank of operations for the exchange of transferable rubles for gold and freely convertible currency;

(e) the performance of other banking operations corresponding to the purposes and tasks of the Bank which arise out of its Charter.

In addition to the functions enumerated above, the Bank may make provision of credit from its own and from attracted funds for international economic organizations, banks, and other organizations created by member countries of the Bank, and also the banks of other countries in accordance with the principles and basic conditions established by the Bank Council.

The Bank may from resources allocated by interested countries finance international economic and other organizations created by member countries of the Bank.

The activity of the Bank shall be regulated by the present Agreement, by the Bank Charter, which shall be an integral part of this Agreement, and also by instructions and rules promulgated by the Bank within the limits of its competence.

Article III

The charter capital of the International Bank for Economic Cooperation shall be set at the sum of 300 million transferable rubles.[3] By decision of the Bank Council, a part of this charter capital may be in gold and freely convertible currency. The share contributions (quotas) of the Contracting Parties to this capital shall be established on the basis of the volume of exports in their mutual trade and shall comprise the following:

People's Republic of Bulgaria	17 million rubles
Hungarian People's Republic	21 million rubles
German Democratic Republic	55 million rubles
Mongolian People's Republic	3 million rubles
Polish People's Republic	27 million rubles
Socialist Republic of Romania	16 million rubles
Union of Soviet Socialist Republics	116 million rubles
Czechoslovak Socialist Republic	45 million rubles

The contributions to the charter capital of the Bank in transferable rubles will be provided from the excess of goods deliveries over imports above the balanced deliveries of goods of Contracting Parties in sums equal to the amounts of their quotas. If a country so desires, it may also make contributions to the charter capital of the Bank (in transferable rubles) in freely convertible currency or gold.

Contributions will be made by each Contracting Party in the first year in the amount of 20 percent of its quota, and subsequently according to decisions of the Bank Council.

The sum of the charter capital of the Bank may be increased with the consent of the member countries of the Bank upon the proposal of the Bank Council.

The sum of the charter capital of the Bank shall be increased upon the admission of a new country to Bank membership in the amount of its share contribution (quota) to such capital. The sum, method, and terms for the contribution shall be determined by the Bank Council by agreement with this country.

The Bank shall have reserve capital, the term, amount, purposes, and procedure for the formation of which shall be determined by the Bank Council.

The Bank may have its own special funds created by decision of the Bank Council.

---

[3] See Translator's Note, *supra* page 776.

In accordance with agreements concluded between interested countries and the Bank, special funds may be created in the Bank at the expense of the resources of these countries.

Article IV

The activity of the International Bank for Economic Cooperation shall be implemented on the basis of complete equality and of respect for the sovereignty of the member countries of the Bank.

The member countries of the Bank shall enjoy equal rights in the consideration and solution of problems connected with the activity of the Bank.

Article V

Payments between the member countries of the Bank will be made in transferable rubles through the International Bank for Economic Cooperation with the participation of the banks of member countries of the Bank. The following basic principles shall be established for the system of multilateral accounts:

(a) payments shall be made through accounts in transferable rubles of banks of member countries of the Bank, which are to be opened at the International Bank for Economic Cooperation or by agreement with it at the banks of member countries. In so doing, the bank of the exporting country shall send the appropriate goods-disposition and the payment documents direct to the bank of the importing country. The banks of the countries shall report information daily to the International Bank for Economic Cooperation in the established form, indicating respectively the totals of claims (proceeds) or the total of payments for the benefit of the exporting bank;

(b) payments shall be made within the limits of the funds available in the accounts of each bank in transferable rubles, in which shall be entered all receipts for the benefit of the bank-account holder, including the totals of credits received;

(c) the bank of the member country of the Bank in whose name the account was opened shall have authority over the funds in accounts in transferable rubles;

(d) the funds proper and the loan funds of banks of member countries of the Bank in transferable rubles shall be differentiated, for which purpose separate accounts shall be opened for these banks in which the funds belonging to the banks shall be kept and separate loan (credit) accounts [shall be opened] in which the indebtedness for credits received by such banks in the International Bank for Economic Cooperation shall be taken into account;

(e) collection with subsequent acceptance (collection with immediate payment) shall be established as the preferential form of payments. Other forms of payment (collection with preliminary acceptance, letters of credit, bank transfers, and others) may also be used by mutual agreement between the banks of member countries of the Bank;

(f) interest shall be paid by the International Bank for Economic Cooperation on cash funds in accounts and on deposit, differentiated according to the period for which they are held.

By decision of the Bank Council, interest on current accounts may not be paid.

Article VI

The Bank may grant the following credits in transferable rubles:

(a) payment credit, to cover the requirements of authorized banks for funds during the short-term excess of payments over receipts. This credit is revolving in character. It shall be granted immediately as necessary, within the limit established by the Bank Council. No time shall be established for clearance of the credit. Credit indebtedness may be carried over to the following year; (b) fixed-term credit, to cover the requirements of authorized banks for funds for more prolonged periods. The credit shall be granted for measures in the specialization and cooperation of production, for expansion of trade turnover, for evening out the balance of payments, seasonal needs, and so on. The Bank shall grant this credit on the basis of justified applications from authorized banks for set periods of up to one year, and for up to two or three years in individual instances by decision of the Bank Council.

Interest shall be recovered for the use of credits. The interest rates for credits in transferable rubles shall be established by the Bank Council on the basis of the necessity for stimulating the economic utilization of cash funds and ensuring the profitability of the Bank.

Countries whose exports have a pronounced seasonal character shall be granted fixed-term credit for seasonal needs in the procedure established by the Bank Council on preferential terms (as regards interest rates).

Article VII

In exercising the functions entrusted to it with respect to payments and credit, the International Bank for Economic Cooperation will further in every possible way the fulfillment by member countries of the Bank of obligations for mutual goods deliveries and the strengthening of plan and payment discipline in payments between them.

In connection with this, the Bank shall be authorized to:

(a) limit or completely terminate the granting of credits to the banks of those member countries of the Bank which violate their obligations for payment to the Bank or other member countries of the Bank. The limitation and termination of credit shall be for the periods established by the Bank Council;

(b) inform the appropriate agencies, or when necessary the governments of member countries of the Bank, on the basis of the data at its disposal about violations of obligations for payments for goods delivered to them.

In effecting payments and credits in transferable rubles, the Bank will maintain records of the fulfillment of obligations of member countries of the Bank for their payments.

Article VIII

Payments in respect of nontrade operations to be effectuated at internal retail prices and tariffs for services will be made in national currencies through separate accounts in the banks of member countries of the Bank on the basis of the agreements in force between those countries concerning accounts for nontrade payments. These accounts may be supplemented from accounts in transferable rubles with conversion according to the coefficient and the exchange rate with the additions (or discounts) for nontrade payments established by said agreements on payments for nontrade payments. Funds from the accounts for nontrade payments also may be transferred to accounts in transferable rubles, using the above-mentioned ratio and exchange rate.

Article IX

The International Bank for Economic Cooperation may effectuate accounts in transferable rubles with countries which are not members of the Bank. The procedure and conditions for payments shall be determined by the Bank Council by arrangement with the interested countries.

Article X

The participation of countries in the International Bank for Economic Cooperation and the activities of that Bank may not serve as an obstacle to the development of direct financial and other business links by member countries of the Bank, both *inter se* and with other countries.

Article XI

The International Bank for Economic Cooperation shall be a juridical person. The Bank shall enjoy the legal capacity necessary to fulfill its functions and attain its purposes in accordance with the provisions of the present Agreement and the Charter of the Bank.

As an international organization, the Bank may conclude international agreements.

The Bank, and also the representatives of countries in the Bank Council and the officials of the Bank, shall enjoy on the territory of each member country of the Bank the privileges and immunities that are necessary for the fulfillment of the functions and the achievement of the purposes provided for by the present Agreement and by the Bank Charter. The aforementioned privileges and immunities shall be defined by the Bank Charter.

The Bank may open on the territory of the headquarters country, and likewise on the territory of other countries, its departments, agencies, and representations. Relations between the Bank and the headquarters country of the Bank or its departments, agencies, and representations shall be determined by the respective agreements.

Article XII

The Contracting Parties will make the changes which arise out of the present Agreement to the bilateral agreements in force between them which establish payments by clearing accounts, or conclude new agreements which provide for payments in transferable rubles.

After the signing of the present Agreement, the Contracting Parties shall announce the denunciation of the Agreement on Multilateral Clearing of 20 June 1957, in accordance with Article 15 of that Agreement.

The indebtedness of the Contracting Parties which existed on 1 January 1964 on bilateral clearing accounts will be taken into account when concluding trade agreements for 1964 and settled within the framework of those agreements in transferable rubles in the procedure agreed between the interested Parties.

Article XIII

Other countries may accede to the present Agreement and become members of the Bank. For this purpose a country shall submit to the Bank Council an official application indicating that it shares the aims and principles of Bank activity and assumes the obligations which arise out of the present Agreement and the Bank Charter.

Admission to membership of the Bank shall be by decision of the Bank Council.

A duly certified copy of the decision of the Bank Council concerning the admission of a new country to membership of the Bank shall be sent to this country and the depository of the present Agreement. The date of receipt by the depository of the said document together with the document (or application) concerning the accession of the country shall be considered to be that of accession to the Agreement and admission to membership of the Bank, of which the depository shall notify the member countries of the Bank and the Bank.

Article XIV

The present Agreement shall be subject to ratification and shall enter into force from the date on which the last of the Contracting Parties transmits its instrument of ratification to the depositary of this Agreement.

However, the Agreement will be put into effect temporarily from 1 January 1964, only if it does not enter into force on that date under the first paragraph of the present Article.

Article XV

The present Agreement may be changed only with the agreement of all member countries of the Bank.

Each country may withdraw from participation in the present Agreement and from membership in the Bank on giving not less than six months' notice thereof to the Bank Council. In the course of the said period, relations between the Bank and the appropriate country as to their mutual obligations should be settled. The Council shall officially notify the depositary of the present Agreement about the withdrawal of a country from participation in the present Agreement and of its departure from the Bank.

The present Agreement shall cease to have effect if not less than two-thirds of the member countries of the Bank declare their withdrawal from participation in the Agreement and from membership in the Bank, observing the provisions of the second paragraph of the present Article.

Article XVI

The present Agreement will be transmitted for safe keeping to the Secretariat of the Council of Mutual Economic Assistance, which will fulfill the functions of depositary of this Agreement.

Done at Moscow, 22 October 1963, in one copy in the Russian language. Certified copies of the present Agreement will be circulated by the depositary to all Contracting Parties.

CHARTER OF THE INTERNATIONAL BANK
FOR ECONOMIC COOPERATION

The International Bank for Economic Cooperation was founded by an agreement between the governments of the People's Republic of Bulgaria, the Hungarian People's Republic, the German Democratic Republic, the Mongolian People's Republic, the Polish People's Republic, the Socialist Republic of Romania, the Union of Soviet Socialist Republics, and the Czechoslovak Socialist Republic for the purposes of furthering the economic cooperation and developing the national economies of member countries of the Bank and expanding their trade and economic links with other countries.

I. General Provisions

Article 1

The International Bank for Economic Cooperation, hereinafter "the Bank", shall organize and implement payments, credit, financial, and other banking operations.

Article 2

1. The Bank shall be a juridical person, to be called "The International Bank for Economic Cooperation".
2. The Bank shall be empowered to:
(a) conclude agreements, and also perform any transactions within the limits of its competence;
(b) acquire, lease, and alienate property;
(c) sue and be sued in court or arbitration;
(d) open departments and agencies and have its own representatives on the territory of the country of its headquarters, and also on the territory of other countries;
(e) promulgate instructions and rules on questions relegated to its competence;
(f) perform other acts directed toward the fulfillment of the tasks entrusted to the Bank by the present Charter.
3. The Bank shall bear liability for its own obligations within the limits of the property belonging to it. The Bank shall not bear liability for the obligations of member countries of the Bank, just as the member countries of the Bank shall not be liable for the obligations of the Bank.
4. The Bank shall have a seal with the inscription "International Bank for Economic Cooperation". Departments and agencies of the Bank shall have a seal with the same inscription, with the addition of the name of the department or agency.

The location of the Bank shall be the city of Moscow, USSR.

Article 3

The Bank shall guarantee secrecy regarding the operations, accounts, and deposits of its clients and correspondents.

All officials and employees of the Bank shall be obliged to maintain secrecy regarding the operations, accounts, and deposits of the Bank, its clients, and correspondents.

II. Capital and Funds of the Bank

Article 4

The Bank shall have charter capital and reserve capital. The Bank also may have special funds.

Article 5

The charter capital of the Bank shall amount to 300 million transferable rubles and shall be formed by contributions in transferable rubles. By decision of the Bank Council, a part of this charter capital may be in gold and freely convertible currency.

A member country of the Bank shall have the right to make its contribution to the charter capital of the Bank (in transferable rubles) also in freely convertible currency or in gold.

The contributions to the charter capital shall be made in the procedure and at the times established by the Bank Council.

The charter capital of the Bank shall serve as security for its obligations and shall be utilized for the purposes provided for by the Bank Charter.

The sum of the charter capital of the Bank may be increased in accordance with the provisions of Article III of the Agreement.

The contributions of a country shall be subject to return if the country withdraws from the Bank. In these circumstances the sum of the indebtedness of that country to the Bank shall be withheld from the sum of the contribution.

If the Bank terminates its activity, the contributions and other available assets of the Bank shall, after satisfaction of the demands of creditors in respect of its obligations, be subject to return to the countries which are members of the Bank and to distribution among them, deducting sums to cover indebtedness during the mutual settlement of the claims of member countries of the Bank.

Article 6

A country which has made its contribution to the charter capital of the Bank shall be issued a certificate, which shall be confirmation and proof of the contribution made by that country.

Article 7

The Bank shall have a reserve capital, the term, amount, purposes, and procedure for the formation of which shall be determined by the Bank Council.

Article 8

The Bank may have its own special funds. The purposes, amount, terms, and conditions for the creation and utilization of these funds shall be determined by the Bank Council.

Special funds also may be created in the Bank from the resources of interested countries. The purposes, amounts, and procedure for the creation and utilization of these funds shall be determined by agreements between the interested countries and the Bank.

III. Operations of the Bank

Payment Operations of the Bank

Article 9

The Bank shall organize and implement multilateral payments in transferable rubles for trade and other operations.

Payments shall be made through the accounts in transferable rubles of banks of member countries, hereinafter authorized banks, to be opened in the International Bank for Economic Cooperation or in other authorized banks by agreement with it.

Payments shall be made within the limits of the funds available to each authorized bank in the accounts in transferable rubles.

Article 10

The Bank may open accounts in transferable rubles for international economic organizations, banks, and other organizations created by member countries of the Bank, and likewise for banks and organizations of other countries, and effectuate payments for these accounts in the procedure established by the Bank.

Article 11

The Bank shall receive and invest funds in transferable rubles and other currency on the basis of the principles established by the Bank Council. The Bank also shall perform other banking operations.

The performance of operations and the opening, conduct, and closure of accounts at the Bank shall be on the basis of the principles established by the Bank Council.

The owners of accounts who have funds in accounts of the Bank in transferable rubles and in other currencies may freely dispose of these funds.

Article 12

Interest at rates established by the Bank Council shall be calculated and paid on funds in transferable rubles kept in accounts at the International Bank for Economic Cooperation.

Article 13

The Bank may carry out payment operations connected with the financing of capital investments and credit for enterprises and other installations being jointly built, reconstructed, and operated by interested countries.

Article 14

The Bank also may implement payments in transferable rubles with countries which are not members of the Bank. The procedure and conditions for such payments in transferable rubles shall be determined by the Bank Council by arrangement with the interested countries.

Article 15

The Bank may issue checks in transferable rubles and other currencies and conduct operations with these checks and with the checks of other banks. Other payment documents may be issued by decision of the Bank Council.

Article 16

The Bank may issue guarantees for the cash obligations of the banks of member countries, other juridical persons, and also natural persons.

Article 17

The Bank may cooperate or participate in organizations whose activity accords with the tasks of the Bank.

Article 18

The Bank shall conclude agreements with other banks and with international organizations on the procedure for payments and the management of accounts opened at the Bank, and also shall conclude correspondent and other contracts.

Credit Operations of the Bank

Article 19

The Bank shall grant credits to authorized banks. Credit shall be for specific purposes and on conditions of return of the credit within stipulated periods.

The purposes for which credits shall be granted, and the procedure for their issue, security, and cancellation, shall be determined by the Bank Council.

The Bank also may grant credits to international economic organizations, banks, and other organizations created by member countries of the Bank, and likewise to banks of other countries in accordance with the principles and basic conditions established by the Bank Council.

Article 20

The Bank shall draw up credit plans for the implementation of credit operations.

The credit plans of the Bank shall be drawn up on the basis of credit applications from authorized banks, which shall proceed in this connection from data on plans for the development of the national economy and foreign trade, and also from trade agreements and contracts. The credit procurement orders of international economic organizations, banks, and other organizations created by member countries of the Bank, and likewise the credit procurement orders of banks of other countries, shall be incorporated in the Bank credit plans. In drawing up the credit plans the Bank also shall utilize its own data and payments. The credit plans shall be confirmed by the Bank Council. When the authorized bank of a country requests credits in excess of the sums provided by the credit plan, the Bank shall consider this request, having regard to data provided by the authorized bank on the course of fulfillment by the country of trade agreements and to other materials necessary for this purpose.

Article 21

Debtors shall pay interest in the amount established by the Bank Council for credits obtained at the Bank.

Article 22

A credit granted by the Bank shall be repaid when the term for payment ensues in the procedure established by the Bank Council.

Article 23

The Bank may finance, from resources allocated by interested countries, international economic and other organizations created by member countries of the Bank.

Article 24

The Bank may grant and receive credits and loans in freely convertible and other currencies on the basis of agreements concluded with banks and other organizations and institutions of member countries of the Bank and non-member countries and conduct deposit, arbitrage, bill of exchange, guarantee, payment, and other operations accepted in international banking practice in these currencies, and also operations with gold.

IV. Administration of the Bank

Article 25

The Bank Council and the Bank Board shall be the organs of administration of the Bank.

The Bank Council

Article 26

The Bank Council shall be the highest organ of administration, implementing general direction of the activity of the Bank.

The Bank Council shall consist of representatives of all member countries of the Bank, each member country of the Bank having one vote irrespective of the amount of its contribution to the capital of the Bank.

The members of the Bank Council shall be appointed by the governments of the member countries of the Bank.

The Bank Council shall assemble for sessions as necessary, but at least twice a year.

The representatives of each member country of the Bank shall preside in turn at sessions of the Council.

Article 27

Decisions by the Bank Council shall be adopted unanimously.

The rules of procedure of the Council shall be established by the Council itself.

Article 28

The Bank Council shall consider and decide questions of principle determining the policy and direction of work of the Bank:

(a) determine the general orientation of Bank activity in establishing business links and cooperation with the banks of member countries, with the banks of other countries, with financial, banking, and other international economic organizations, and also cooperation with or participation in organizations whose activity is in accordance with the tasks of the Bank;

(b) confirm the credit and other plans of the Bank, the annual report, the balance sheet, and the distribution of Bank profits, upon proposals from the Bank Board; determine the principles for planning of credits and resources, and also for performing credit and other banking operations; establish the amounts of interest rates for credits, deposits, and current and other accounts in transferable rubles, the structure and personnel establishment of the Bank, and the estimated costs of Bank administration and management;

(c) create special Bank funds;

(d) appoint the Chairman and members of the Bank Board;

(e) appoint the Bank Audit Commission, hear its reports, and adopt decisions regarding them;

(f) authorize the opening and closing of departments, agencies, and representations of the Bank;

(g) hear reports from the Bank Board on its activity and adopt decisions regarding them;

(h) adopt decisions on the admission of new members of the Bank;

(i) confirm the Rules on Working Conditions for Bank Employees;

(j) implement other functions arising out of the present Charter which prove to be necessary for the achievement of the purposes and tasks of the Bank.

The Bank Board

Article 29

The Bank Board shall be the executive organ and shall implement the direct management of the operative activity of the Bank within the limits of the powers granted to it by the present Charter and in accordance with decisions of the Bank Council.

The Board shall be responsible to the Bank Council and accountable to it.

The Board shall consist of a Chairman and Board members appointed from citizens of all member countries of the Bank for a term of up to five years. The number of Board members shall be determined by the Bank Council.

In the event of temporary absence of the Chairman of the Board, his duties shall be entrusted to one of the Board members by decision of the Board.

In the execution of their official duties, the Chairman and members of the Board shall act as international officials, independent of the organizations and officials of the countries of which they are citizens.

Article 30

The Bank Board, in the person of its Chairman or other officials of the Bank authorized by the Board, shall act as representative in all questions and matters of the Bank before officials, state and international organizations, and other juridical persons, and shall bring claims and suits in court and in arbitration proceedings on behalf of the Bank.

The Bank Board may empower officials of the Bank to act on its behalf on the basis of a special power of attorney.

The obligations and powers of attorney of the Bank shall be valid with two signatures; that of the Chairman and that of a member of the Board, and in the absence of the Chairman with the signatures of two members of the Bank Board, one of whom must be the Board member who is acting as Chairman of the Board, or of other officials of the Bank authorized for this purpose by the Bank Board.

Article 31

The Bank Board shall consider basic questions in the operative activity of the Bank, in particular:

(a) questions whose solution or confirmation has been referred by virtue of the present Charter to the competence of the Bank Council, and shall prepare the appropriate materials and proposals for consideration by the Bank Council;

(b) on the establishment of a procedure for the signing of financial and account documents and correspondence on behalf of the Bank, a procedure for the signing and issue of powers of attorney on behalf of departments and agencies of the Bank, the forms of financial and account documents used in relations between the Bank and its clients, interest rates for credits, deposits, and current and other accounts in accordance with decisions of the Bank Council, the rates of commission payable for the fulfillment of commissions from its clients and correspondents, the procedure and conditions for the issue of guarantees by the Bank, and also the conditions of acceptance for discounting and the guaranteeing of bills of exchange and other monetary obligations;

(c) on the control of the activity of administrations and sections of the Bank, its departments, agencies, and representations;

(d) questions of utilization of Bank property and assets.

There shall also be referred to the competence of the Board:

the drawing up of credit plans for the Bank and their submission for confirmation by the Bank Council;

the confirmation of instructions on the procedure for performing credit and other banking operations on the basis of the principles established by the Bank Council;

the establishment of business links with financial, banking, and other international economic organizations in accordance with decisions of the Council on the general direction of Bank activities in this domain, subsequently informing the Bank Council on this matter;

the establishment of personnel numbers and amounts of wages for service and technical personnel within the limits of the wage fund confirmed by the Bank Council for these purposes.

The Bank Board shall have the right, within the limits of its competence, to put forward proposals for discussion by the Bank Council.

The Board working procedure shall be established by the Board itself.

Decisions adopted by the Bank Board shall be formalized by protocols. Orders, instructions, or rules may be published in execution of the decisions of the Board; these shall be signed by the Chairman of the Board or by one of the Board members with his authority.

Article 32

The Chairman of the Board shall direct the activity of the Bank Board and shall implement measures to ensure the fulfillment of the tasks entrusted to the Bank by the present Charter.

The Chairman of the Board shall:

(a) dispose of all property and funds of the Bank in accordance with the present Charter and with decisions of the Bank Council;

(b) act as representative on behalf of the Bank;

(c) promulgate orders and make decisions on operative questions of the activity of the Bank;

(d) sign obligations and powers of attorney on behalf of the Bank in accordance with Article 30 of the present Charter;

(e) appoint and dismiss employees of the Bank, with the exception of directors who are members of the Bank Board, and also establish salaries and reward members of staff who have distinguished themselves in accordance with the personnel establishment and estimated costs of Bank administration and management confirmed by the Council;

(f) fulfill other functions arising out of the present Charter and the decisions of the Bank Council.

V. Organization of the Bank

Article 33

The Bank shall have administrations, sections, departments, agencies, and representations, to be formed in accordance with the structure of the Bank confirmed by the Bank Council.

The Bank personnel shall be composed of citizens of member countries of the Bank in accordance with the Rules on Working Conditions for Bank Employees.

Employees of the Bank shall be granted privileges and immunities under Article 40 of the present Charter for the purposes of independent fulfillment of their duties.

VI. Audit of Bank Activity

Article 34

The audit of the Bank activity, including the verification of the annual report of the Bank Board, cash, and property, the audit of records, accounting and business correspondence of the Bank, its departments and agencies, shall be conducted by the Audit Commission appointed by the Bank Council for a period of two years and consisting of the Chairman of the Audit Commission and five members.

The Chairman and members of the Audit Commission may not hold any other official positions in the Bank.

The organization and procedure of audits shall be established by the Bank Council.

Article 35

The Bank Board shall put at the disposal of the Audit Commission all the necessary materials for the conduct of the audits.

The reports of the Audit Commission shall be submitted to the Bank Council.

VII. Procedure for Consideration of Disputes

Article 36

Claims against the Bank may be submitted within two years from the moment the right to sue arose.

Article 37

Disputes of the Bank with its clientele should be considered in an arbitration tribunal, to be selected from among those already operating or to be newly formed by agreement of the parties.

In the absence of such agreement, the resolution of the dispute shall be sent for consideration to the arbitration tribunal attached to the Chamber of Commerce in the country where the Bank has its headquarters.

VIII. Privileges and Immunities of the Bank and its Officials

Article 38

1. The property of the Bank, its assets and documents, irrespective of their location, and also the operations of the Bank, shall enjoy immunity from any form of administrative and judicial interference, with the exception of instances in which the Bank itself waives the immunity. The premises of the Bank, and also of its departments, agencies, and representations on the territory of any member country of the Bank, shall be inviolate.

2. On the territory of member countries of the Bank, the Bank shall:

(a) be exempt from all direct taxes and charges, both state and local. This provision shall not be applied in relation to payments for the provision of municipal and other services;

(b) be exempt from customs charges and restrictions in the importing and exporting of articles destined for official use;

(c) enjoy on the territory of each member country of the Bank all the concessions in relation to priority, tariffs, and rates for communication by post, telegraph, and telephone which are enjoyed in that country by diplomatic missions.

Article 39

1. The following privileges and immunities shall be granted on the territory of each member country of the Bank to the representatives of countries in the Bank Council in executing their official duties:

(a) immunity from personal arrest or detention, and also from the jurisdiction of judicial institutions in relation to all acts which may be performed by them in their capacity as representatives;

(b) inviolability of all papers and documents;

(c) the same customs privileges in relation to their personal luggage as are granted to personnel of corresponding rank of diplomatic missions in that country;

(d) exemption from personal duties and from direct taxes and charges in relation to the cash sums paid to the representatives by the country which appointed them.

2. The privileges and immunities provided for by the present Article shall be granted to the persons mentioned in it exclusively in the interests of their official duties. Each member country of the Bank shall have the right and shall be obliged to waive the immunity of its representative in all instances in which, in the opinion of that country, the immunity obstructs the effectuation of justice and the waiver of immunity will not prejudice the purposes for which it was granted.

3. The provisions of point 1 of the present Article shall not apply to mutual relations between a representative and the agencies of the country of which he is a citizen.

Article 40

1. The Bank Council shall, at the recommendation of the Bank Board, determine the categories of Bank officials to which the provisions of the present Article shall apply. The surnames of such officials shall be communicated periodically by the Chairman of the Board to the competent agencies of member countries of the Bank.

2. In executing their official duties on the territory of each member country of the Bank, the officials of the Bank shall:

(a) not be subject to judicial or administrative responsibility for any acts which might be performed by them in their official capacity;

(b) be exempt from personal duties and from direct taxes and charges in relation to the wages paid to them by the Bank. This provision shall not apply to officials of the Bank who are citizens of the country where the Bank has its headquarters, departments, agencies, and representations;

(c) have the right to the same customs privileges in relation to their personal luggage as are granted to personnel of diplomatic missions in that country of corresponding rank.

3. The privileges and immunities provided for by the present Article shall be granted to officials of the Bank exclusively in the interests of their official duties.

The Chairman of the Bank Board shall have the right and duty to waive the immunity of officials of the Bank in all instances in which, in his opinion, the immunity obstructs the effectuation of justice and the waiver of immunity will not damage the purposes for which it was granted. The right of waiver of immunity in relation to the Chairman and members of the Bank Board appertains to the Bank Council.

IX. Accounting

Article 41

The operational year of the Bank shall be reckoned from 1 January to 31 December inclusive.

The annual balance sheets shall be published by the Board in the procedure established by the Bank Council.

X. Distribution of Profit

Article 42

After confirmation of the annual report, the profit of the Bank shall be distributed by decision of the Bank Council, and may be used to supplement the reserve capital and for other purposes.

XI. Procedure for Admission of New Bank Members and Withdrawal from the Bank

Article 43

The procedure for admission of new Bank members and withdrawal from the Bank shall be determined by Articles XIII and XV of the Agreement.

XII. Concluding Provisions

Procedure for Changing the Charter

Article 44

Each member country of the Bank may put forward a proposal to change the present Charter. Changes of the Bank Charter shall be made with the consent of all member countries of the Bank.

Termination of Bank Activity

Article 45

The activity of the Bank may be terminated in accordance with the provisions of the third paragraph of Article XV of the Agreement. The times and procedure for the termination of Bank activity and for the liquidation of its affairs shall be determined by the member countries of the Bank.

INDEX

Index